CATALOGUE OF BOOKS

ADDED TO THE

LIBRARY OF CONGRESS

DURING

THE YEAR 1871.

WASHINGTON:
GOVERNMENT PRINTING OFFICE.
1872.

LIST OF ABBREVIATIONS EMPLOYED.

anon. Anonymous.
b. l. Black letter.
col. Colored.
ed. Edition.
eng. Engraved.
facs. Facsimile.
fol. Folio. 4°. Quarto. 8°. Octavo. 12°. Duodecimo, etc.
incl. Including.
l. Leaves.
n. d. No date.
n. p. No place of publication.
numb. Numbered.
obl. Oblong.
p. Page.
phot. Photograph.
pl. Plates.
p. l. Preliminary leaves.
pp. Pages.
pseudon. Pseudonymous.
sm. Small.
sq. Square.
t. Tome.
tab. Tables.
unp. Unpaged.
v. Volume or volumes.

The books are described as folio, quarto, octavo, duodecimo, etc., according to the apparent size of the volume, and not according to the printer's designations derived from the fold of the sheets.

In the alphabetical arrangement, the prefix *Mc*, *M'*, or *Mac*, is treated uniformly as a component part of the word, as if spelled *Mac*. Thus, *McLeod* or *M'Leod* precedes *Maclure*. In like manner, the prefixes *New*, *La*, *Du*, etc., are treated as component parts of the words to which they belong. Thus *New England* follows *Newell* instead of preceding it, as it would do if the prefix *New* were treated as a separate word.

It is one of the aims of the present catalogue to furnish with the titles a sufficiently full collation of each work. Thus it is made a part of the description to give the number of pages, in the case of all works not exceeding two volumes, together with the number of maps and plates, if any, and the name of the publisher. The information thus conveyed will, it is believed, be found of practical value to readers, as conveying at a glance some idea of the extent of each work, while the addition of publishers' names is useful as supplying a guide to the identification of editions. In the case of books printed without date, the actual or approximate date is usually supplied in brackets.

Brackets in any part of a title indicate that the words included in them are not found in the title, but are inserted.

The titles of most modern books are given with approximate fullness, but it is to be understood that long titles are uniformly abridged, the more significant words of the title only being inserted.

The letter S, affixed to any title, denotes that the work belongs to the library of the Smithsonian Institution, now deposited in the Library of Congress.

CATALOGUE.

A. (C.) Jerubbaal: or, a vindication of the sober testimony against sinful complyance, from the exceptions of mr. [John] Tombs, in answer to his Theodulia. Wherein the unlawfulness of hearing the present conform ing ministers is more largely discussed and proved. [*anon.*] 489 pp. sm. 4°. *London*, 1668.

A. (D. D.) *See* **Dreux du Radier** (Jean François).

A. (F. S.) Great success. *See* **Flint** (S. A.)

A. (H.) Partheneia sacra. *See* **Hawkins** (Henry).

A. (J.) The ocean harp. *See* **Agg** (John).

A. (J.) Princely excellency: or, regal glory. Being an exact account of the most glorious actions of that most potent prince, William the third, late king of England. By J. A. [*anon.*] 6 p. l. 168 pp. 1 portrait. 18°. *London, W. Spiller*, 1702.

A. (J. M.) Noticia de los procedimientos en la reposicion de la sagrada imagen renovada del sr. de santa Teresa, y afectos de un pecador à sus pies. Por J. M. A. [*anon.*] 31 pp. 18°. *Mexico, R. Rafael*, 1846.

A. (L.) Histoire des Wahabis. *See* **Corancez** (L. A. O. de).

A. (R. P.) Sister Ruth's stories for the young: or evenings with John Woolman. By R. P. A. [*anon.*] 121 pp. 1 pl. 18°. *Philadelphia, T. E. Chapman*, 1865.

A. (S. A.) *See* **Allibone** (Samuel Austin).

Aa (A. Jan van der). Nieuw biografiesch, anthologiesch en kritiesch woordenboek van nederlandsche dichters, uitmakende tevens een verfolg op Witsen Geysbeeks. Nieuwe uitgave van J. A. Alberdingk Thijm. 3 v. 8°. *Amsterdam, C. L. van Langenhuysen*, 1864.

Aanmerkingen van eenen reiziger over Hollande, [etc.] *See* **Remarques** d'un voyageur sur la Hollande, [etc.]

Abailard *or* **Abélard** (Pierre). Petri Abælardi opera hactenus seorsim edita, nunc primum in unum collegit, textum ad fidem librorum editorum scriptorumque recensuit, notas, argumenta, indices adjecit Victor Cousin, adjuvantibus C. Jourdain et E. Despois. 2 v. 2 p. l. vi, 731 pp. 1 l; 2 p. l. 830 pp. 1 l. 4°. *Parisiis, A. Durand*, 1849–59.

CONTENTS.

v. 1. Magistri Petri Abælardi et Heloissæ conjugis ejus epistolæ, p. 1.
Andreæ Quercetani turonensis notæ ad historiam calamitatum Petri Abælardi, p. 38
Petri Abælardi et Heloissæ epistolæ, p. 72.
Heloissæ paraclitensis problemata cum mag. Petri Abælardi solutionibus, p. 237.
Carmina, p. 295.
Sermones per annum legendi, p. 349.
Expositio orationis dominicæ, p. 596.
Expositio symboli quod dicitur apostolorum, p. 603.
Expositio fidei in symbolum Athanasii, p. 615.
Epistola ad divum Bernardum claraevallensem abbatem, p. 618.
Expositio in hexameron, p. 625.
Epistola et fidei confessio ad Heloissam, p. 680.
De Dionysio areopagita epistola, p. 681.
Contra quemdam canonicum regularem, p. 686.
Invectiva in quemdam ignarum dialectices, p. 695,
Appendix, p. 701.

v. 2. Introductio ad theologiam, p. 1.
Commentariorum super s. Pauli epistolam ad Romanos libri v, p. 152.
Theologia christiana, p. 357.
Excerpta ex epitome theologiæ christianæ, p. 567.
Ethica seu liber dictus: scito teipsum, p. 593.
Dialogus inter philosophum, judaeum et christianum, p. 643.
Apologia seu confessio fidei, p. 719.
Expositio super psalterium, p. 723.
Expositio super epistolas Pauli. In epistolam ad Romanos, p. 725.
In libro incerto, p. 727.
Ex apologia, p. 730.
Tractatus de intellectibus, p. 733.
Glosulæ super Porphyrium, p. 756.
Appendix, p. 763.

Abati (Francesco, *pseudon.*) *See* **Reade** (W. Winwood).

Abauzit (Firmin). Miscellanies of the late ingenious and celebrated M. [Firmin] Abauzit, on historical, theological, and critical subjects. Translated from the french by E[dward] Harwood, d. d. 2 p. l. xxiv, 376 pp. 12°. *London, T. Becket*, 1774.

Abbadie (Jacques). A sovereign antidote against arian poyson: or, the divinity of our blessed saviour asserted and plainly prov'd. In full answer to dr. Clarke, mr. Whiston, mr. Emlyn and the rest of their adherents. 4 p. l. 423 pp. 8°. *London, J. Booth*, 1719.

Abbey (Henry). Ballads of good deeds, and other verses. 129 pp. 16°. *New York, D. Appleton & co.* 1872.

——— Stories in verse. 128 pp. 16°. *New York, A. D. F. Randolph & co.* 1869.

Abbey (Henry L.) May dreams. 143 pp. 12°. *New York, Abbey & Abbot*, 1862.

Abbey (*Rev.* Richard). An inquiry into the ecclesiastical constitution, the origin and character of the church of Christ, and the gospel ministry. In four parts. Edited by Thomas O. Summers, d. d. 432 pp. 12°. *Nashville (Tenn.) methodist episcopal church south*, 1856.

Abbot (Ezra). The literature of the doctrine of a future life: or, a catalogue of works relating to the nature, origin, and destiny of the soul. The titles classified, and arranged chronologically, with notes, and indexes of authors and subjects. Compiled (originally) as an appendix to the "History of the doctrine of a future life," by William R. Alger. 1 p. l. pp. 679-914. 8°. *New York, W. J. Widdleton*, 1871.

Abbot (*Rev.* Hull). The duty of God's people to pray for the peace of Jerusalem. A sermon on occasion of the rebellion in Scotland; preach'd at Charlestown, Jan. 12, 1745-6. 26 pp. 8°. *Boston, Rogers & Fowle*, 1746.

Abbot, Downing & co. manufacturers of coaches and wagons. [Illustrations]. Charts A-C. 3 parts in 1 v. 18°. *Boston, Hooper, Lewis & co.* [1871].

Abbott (Edward). The baby's things: a story in verse for christmas eve. 53 pp. 5 pl. 12°. *New York, A. D. F. Randolph & co.* [1871].

Abbott (Henry, *m. d.*) Catalogue of a collection of Egyptian antiquities, now exhibiting at the Stuyvesant institute, New York. 72 pp. 8°. *New York, proprietor*, 1854.

Abbott (*Rev.* Jacob). The August stories. v. 1-3. 16°. *New York, Dodd & Mead*, 1871-72.

CONTENTS.

v. 1. August and Elvie. 388 pp. 2 pl.
v. 2. Hunter and Tom. 383 pp. 2 pl.
v. 3. The schooner Mary Ann. 348 pp. 3 pl.

——— Gentle measures in the management and training of the young. 330 pp. 12 pl. 12°. *New York, Harper & brothers*, 1872.

——— History of Genghis Khan. 335 pp. 16°. *New York, Harper & brothers*, 1860.

——— History of Margaret of Anjou, queen of Henry vi. of England. 316 pp. 16°. *New York, Harper & brothers*, 1861.

——— History of Peter the great, emperor of Russia. Eng. title. 368 pp. 1 portrait. 16°. *New York, Harper & brothers*, 1860.

——— The little learner. Learning to think. Consisting of easy and entertaining lessons, designed to assist in the first unfolding of the reflective and reasoning powers of children. 192 pp. sq. 16°. *New York, Harper & brothers*, 1856.

——— The little philosopher. With a copious introduction, explaining fully the method of using the book. 172 pp. 18°. *Boston, Hickling, Swan, & Brown*, [1855].

——— Science for the young; or, the fundamental principles of modern philosophy explained and illustrated in conversations and experiments, and in narratives of travel and adventure by young persons in pursuit of knowledge. 3 v. 12°. *New York, Harper & brothers*, 1872.

CONTENTS.

v. 1. Heat. 306 pp. 21 pl.
v. 2. Light. 313 pp. 16 pl.
v. 3. Water and land. 330 pp. 24 pl.

Abbott (James, *of Queen's college, Cambridge*). A history of the roman and english hierarchies; with an examination of the assumptions, abuses, and intolerance of episcopacy; proving the necessity of a reformed english church. 2 p. l. xxxii, 356 pp. 8°. *London, Simpkin & Marshall*, 1831.

Abbott (*Rev.* John Sebastian Cabot). The history of the empire of Russia: containing an account of all the most interesting events in that vast monarchy, from its earliest origin in the remote ages of barbarism to the present day. 546 pp. 2 pl. 8°. *Boston, B. B. Russell*, 1872.

——— History of Frederick the second, called Frederick the great. 584 pp. 1 pl. 8°. *New York, Harper & brothers*, 1871.

——— History of Josephine. With engrav-

Abbott (*Rev.* J. S. C.)—continued. ings. Engraved title. 4 p. l. 328 pp. 1 portrait. 6 pl. 16°. *New York, Harper & brothers,* [1851].

——— History of Louis xiv. 410 pp. 20 pl. 16°. *New York, Harper & brothers,* 1871.

——— History of Louis Philippe, king of the french. 405 pp. 16°. *New York, Harper & brothers,* 1871.

——— Italy and the war for italian independence: including a biographical sketch of pope Pius ix. 638 pp. 5 pl. 12°. *Boston, B. B. Russell,* 1871.

——— The path of peace: or a practical guide to duty and happiness. viii, 13–192 pp. 1 pl. 16°. *Boston, Crocker & Brewster,* 1836.

——— Practical christianity. A treatise specially designed for young men. 302 pp. 16°. *New York, Harper & brothers,* 1862.

——— Prussia and the franco-prussian war. Containing a brief narrative of the origin of the kingdom, its past history, and a detailed account of the causes and results of the late war with Austria; with an account of the origin of the present war with France, and of the extraordinary campaign into the heart of the empire. Including biographical sketches of king William and count von Bismarck. 311 pp. 2 pl. 4 maps. 12°. *Boston, B. B. Russell,* 1871.

——— The same. Preussen und der französisch-preussische krieg. Aus dem englischen übersetzt von dr. F. Stähli. 312 pp. 6 maps, 2 pl. 12°. *Boston, B. B. Russell,* 1871.

——— The school-boy; or, a guide for youth to truth and duty. 180 pp. 1 pl. 18°. *Boston, Crocker & Brewster,* 1839.

——— The school-girl; or, the principles of christian duty familiarly enforced. 180 pp. 1 pl. 18°. *Boston, Crocker & Brewster,* 1840.

Abbott (Lyman). Laicus; or, the experiences of a layman in a country-parish. 358 pp. 16°. *New York, Dodd & Mead,* 1872.

A, b, c (The) of animals. By aunt Lutie. [*pseudon.*] 14 l. [col. pl.] 8°. *New York, R. Shugg & co.* [1871].

Abcedario (L') pittorico. *See* **Orlandi** (Pellegrino Antonio).

Abdalla *of Beyza.* *See* **Nasir-ed-din** Abu Said Abdallah ben Omar el-Beidhawí.

Abd-el-Kerim (Ben Akebut Mahmood, *Khojeh*). The memoirs of Khojeh Abdulkurreem. Including the history of Hindostan, from a. d. 1739 to 1749; with an account of the european settlements in Bengal and on the coast of Coromandel. Translated from the original persian by Francis Gladwin. xi, 219 pp. 8°. *Calcutta, W. Mackay,* 1788.

Abdulkurreem (*Khojeh*). *See* **Abd-el-Kerim**

Abeel (*Rev.* David). Journal of a residence in China, and the neighboring countries, from 1829 to 1833. 398 pp. 12°. *New York, Leavitt, Lord & co.* 1834.

Abeille (L') américaine. Journal historique et littéraire. [Weekly]. April, 1815, to Jan. 1818. v. 1–5. 8°. *Philadelphia, A. J. Blocquerst,* 1815–17.

[MARKOE pamphlets, v. 53 and 54].

Abel (F. A.) On recent investigations and applications of explosive agents. A lecture delivered to the members of the British association at Edinburgh, August, 1871. 35 pp. 2 pl. 8°. *Washington, government printing office,* 1871.

Abel (Thomas). Subtensial plain trigonometry, wrought with a sliding-rule, with Gunter's lines: and also arithmetically. And this method apply'd to navigation, and surveying. To which is added, i. Mensuration of mason's work. ii. A solution of rota, or Aristotle's wheel. iii. A brief discourse upon gravity. 2 p. l. 86 pp. 7 pl. 18°. *Philadelphia, A. Steuart,* 1761.

Abel Remusat. *See* **Remusat.**

Abélard. *See* **Abailard.**

Abelous (L.) Gustavus Adolphus; the hero of the reformation. From the french, by mrs. C. A. Lacroix. 193 pp. incl. 5 pl. 16°. *New York, Carlton & Lanahan,* [1871].

Abenteuer eines maurers zur warnung für geweihete und profane. [*anon.*] 2 p. l. 100 pp. 8°. *Berlin & Libau, Lagarde & Friedrich,* 1788.

Aborigines protection society. Extracts from the papers and proceedings of the aborigines protection society. Nos. i. and ii. May and June, 1839. 64 pp. 8°. *London, W. B. Arnold & co.* 1839.

——— Report on the Indians of Upper Canada. By a sub-committee. 52 pp. 8°. *London, W. B. Arnold & co.* 1839.

——— Second annual report, presented at the meeting in Exeter hall, May 21st, 1839. With a list of officers, subscribers, benefactors, and honorary members. 32 pp. 8°. *London, P. White & Son,* 1839.

Abraham (*Rev.* Charles John). The unity of history; or outlines of lectures on ancient and modern history, considered on the principles of the church of England. xvi, 176 pp. 1 l. 8°. *Eton, E. P. Williams*, 1846.

Abrégé de la vie des peintres, dont les tableaux composent la galerie electorale de Dresde. Avec le détail de tous les tableaux de cette collection et éclaircissemens historiques sur ces chefs-d'œuvres de la peinture. [*anon.*] 9 p. l. 468 pp. 1 pl. 16°. *Dresde, frères Walther*, 1782.

Abrégé de l'histoire romaine à l'usage des élèves de l'ancienne école royale militaire. [*anon.*] Nouv. [12e ?] éd. 1 p. l. 226 pp. 16°. *Avallon, Comynet*, 1830.

Abridged (An) history of the United States of America. For the use of schools. Intended as a sequel to Hildreth's view of the United States. [*anon.*] xii, 248 pp. 12°. *Boston, Carter, Hendee & Babcock*, 1831.

Abudacnus *or* **Abu-dh-Dhakn** (Joseph). Historia Jacobitarum, seu Coptorum in Ægypto, Libya, Nubia, Æthiopia tota, & Cypri insulæ parte habitantium. Opera. Cum annotationibus Johannis Nicolai. Vulgavit nunc primum s. Havercampus. 4 p. l. 206 pp. 5 l. 8°. *Lugduni Batavorum, apud J. Haserbrœk*, 1740.

Abulfeda (Ismael). Αμπουλφεδα Ισμαηλ βασιλεως Απαμειας εκ των γεωγραφικων πινακων περιγραφη Χορασμιας, Μαουαραλναχρης ήτοι των περαν του ποταμου 'Ωξου τοπων, Αραβιας, Αιγυπτου, Περσιδος, ἐτι δε της Περσικης και Ερυθρας θαλασσης, μεταφρασθεισα εκ της Αραβικης διαλεκτου υπο Δημητριου Αλεξανδριδου. 292 pp. 8°. *εν Βιεννη της Αυστριας*, A. Σχμιδιος, 1807.

[*With* ΣΥΛΛΟΓΗΣ των εν επιτομη παλαι γεωγραφηθεντων.
Note.—Printed in arabic and greek on opposite pages].

Abu'l Ghazi, *bahader*. The genealogical history of the Tatars. Translated from the tatar manuscript. Containing the antiquities of the Moguls and Tatars from Adam, according to the account of the mohammedan Tatars. A curious description of all the tribes into which the turkish nation is divided: the life of Zingiz khân the great, [etc.] With a complete history of the Uzbek khâns of Khowârazm, [1494–1663]. Illustrated. With notes. The whole made english [from the french of Bentinck]. 1 v. in 2. 2 p. l. xliii, 792 pp. 2 maps. 8°. *London, J. & J. Knapton*, [*etc.*] 1729–30.

Abu-'l-Kasim (Mahmud ben Omar Ez-Zamakhshari). Anthologia sententiarum arabicarum. Cum scholiis Zamachsjarii. Edidit, vertit, et illustravit Henricus Albertus Schultens. [Arab. et lat.] 10 p. l. 172 pp. 4°. *Lugduni Batavorum, apud J. Le Mair*, 1772.

Abu Mohammed al Kasim ben Alí al Harirí al Basrí. Six assemblies; or ingenious conversations of learned men among the Arabians, upon a great variety of useful and entertaining subjects; formerly published by the celebrated Schultens, in arabic and latin, with large notes and observations. The whole now translated into english, with improvements. By Leonard Chappelow. 2 p. l. viii, 134 pp. 8°. *Cambridge (Eng.) J. Archdeacon, for Merrill*, 1767.

Abú Músá Jábir ben Hayyan et-Tarsusé. La somme de la perfection, ou l'abrégé du magistère parfait de Geber. 12°. [*Paris, A. Cailleau*, 1741].

[*In* SALMON (William). Bibliothèque des philosophes chimiques. 1741. pp. 85–384, 20 l.]

Abu Taleb (*khan meerza*). The travels of mirza Aboo Talib khan, in the persian language. Abridged by David Macfarlane. 2d ed. 70 l. 12°. *Calcutta, the baptist mission press*, 1836.

Academia cæsarea naturæ curiosorum. Miscellanea curiosa; sive ephemeridum medico-physicarum decuriæ i et ii, 1670–1689. 18 v. in 15. 4°. *Francoforti*, 1684–90.

Academical contributions of original and translated poetry. [By junior members of the university of Cambridge, Eng. *anon.*] viii, 111 pp. 8°. *Cambridge (Eng.) B. Flower*, 1795.

Academy (The). A monthly record of literature, learning, science, and art. Oct. 9, 1869, to Dec. 15, 1871. v. 1–2. 4°. *London, J. Murray*, 1869–71.

Accolti (Benedetto, *cardinale*). Epigrammata. 16°. *Florentiæ, apvd Ivntas*, 1562.

[*In* CARMINA qvinqve Hetrvscorvm poetarvm, pp. 129–136].

Account (An) of a visit lately made to the people called quakers, in Philadelphia, by Papoonahoal, an Indian chief, and several other Indians, chiefly of the Minisink tribe. With the substance of their conferences on that occasion. [*anon.*] 21 pp. 18°. *London, S. Clark*, 1761.

Account (An) of the french settlements in North America, shewing the towns, ports, etc. of Canada, claimed by the french king. By a gentleman. [*anon.*] 26 pp. 8°. *Boston, Rogers & Fowle*, 1746.

Account (An) of the present state of Nova Scotia: in two letters to a noble lord, etc. [*anon.*] 31 pp. 12°. *London*, 1756.

Accum (Frederick) *and* **Parkes** (Samuel). Manuel de chimie amusante, ou nouvelles récréations chimiques. Traduit de l'anglais, par J. Riffault. 3e éd. Revue soigneusement sur le texte anglais, augmentée de plusieurs expériences nouvelles, etc. Par A. D. Vergnaud. 1 p. l. 321 pp. 1 pl. 18°. *Paris, Roret*, 1829.

Accurate (An) description and history of the cathedral and metropolitan church of St. Peter, York, from its first foundation to the present year. 2d ed. with additions. [*anon.*] 2 v. xi, 126 pp. 13 pl; 3 p. l. 274 pp. 16°. *York, A. Ward*, 1783.

Achard (Louis Amédée Eugène). Parisiennes et provinciales. 2 p. l. 315 pp. 1 l. 12°. *Paris, M. Lévy frères*, 1856.

CONTENTS.

La chambre rouge, pp. 1-89.
Ursule voisin, pp. 90-183.
L'école buissonnière, pp. 184-252.
Les trois amoureux de Jeannette, pp. 253-274.
Les lilas blancs, pp. 275-315.

Achilles Tatius. Ερωτικων βιβλια η. De Clitophontis et Leucippes amoribus libri viii. Græce et latine [interprete Cruceio]. xx, 363 pp. 8°. *Biponti*, 1792.

[Mitscherlich (C. W.) Scriptores erotici græci, v. 1].

——— The same. Achille Tazio degli amori di Leucippe e Clitofonte libri viii, ridotti in italiano da f. Angelo Coccio. 2 v. in 1. 3 p. l. 166 pp; 164 pp. 18°. *Crisopoli, dalla tipografia della società lett.* 1803.

Acht tage in München. Eine kurzgefasste beschreibung der in dieser hauptstadt befindlichen sehenswürdigkeiten; als unentbehrliches handbuch für jeden fremden. Mit xylographischen vignetten. [*anon.*] 2 l. 120 pp. 1 plan. 18°. *München, Georg Franz*, 1834.

Ackermann (Peter Fourier). Archæologia biblica breviter exposita. iv, 522 pp. 1 l. 8°. *Viennæ, F. Volke*, 1826.

Acosta (Jérome, *pseudon.*) *See* **Simon** (Richard).

Acta Mechemeti i. saracenorum principis. Auszführlicher bericht, von ankünfft, zunehmen, gesatzen, regirung vnd jämerlichem absterben Mechemeti i. Genealogia seiner successorn, bisz auff den jetzregirenden Mechmetem iii. Auss vielen autoribus fleissig zusammen getragen. ii. Propheceyung. Keysers

Acta Mechemeti i.—continued.
Seueri vñ Leonis, sampt etlichen anderen weissagungen, vom undergang dess türkischen regiments. Von neuwem an tag geben, [etc.] 4 p. l. 102 pp. 1 l. 4°. [*Frankfurt*], *H. D. und H. I. von Bry*, 1597.

Actes (Les) des apôtres. [Journal royaliste publié pendant la révolution française. Par Jean Gabriel Peltier et autres]. v. 1-5. no. 1-146, 1789-90. 8°. *Paris, l'an de la liberté* 0, [1789-90].

[*Note.*—Eleven volumes of this journal (1789-92), in 311 numbers, were issued. Much information respecting it is given by Quérard, in his Dictionnaire des ouvrages polyonymes et anonymes].

Actor (The); or, a treatise on the art of playing. A new work, adapted to the present state of the theatres. [etc. *anon.*] 284 pp. 10 l. 12°. *London, R. Griffiths*, 1755.

Actuarius (Joannes). *See* **Joannes** *actuarius, i. e. medicus.*

Adair (D. L.) Progressive bee culture, or apine instincts and labors defined, illustrated and systematized, upon a new theory. 24 pp. 8°. *Cincinnati, author*, 1872.

Adam *of Merioneth.* Adami murimuthensis chronicon, sive historia sui temporis; cui subjicitur ejusdem chronici continuatio. E codice reginensi nunc primum edidit Antonius Hallius. 8°. *Oxonii, e theatro sheldoniano*, 1721.

[*In* Trivet (Nicholas). Annalium continuatio, pp. 31-152].

Adam (Alexander, *ll. d.*) A summary of geography and history, both ancient and modern; with an abridgment of the fabulous history or mythology of the Greeks. To which is prefixed, an historical account of the progress and improvements of astronomy and geography: also a brief account of the principles of the newtonian philosophy, [etc.] 5th ed. corrected. xii, 858 pp. 13 maps, 1 pl. 8°. *London, T. Cadell & W. Davies*, [*etc.*] 1816.

Adam (Melchior). Dignorum laude virorum, quos musa vetat mori, immortalitas, seu vitæ theologorum, jure-consultorum, & politicorum, medicorum, atque philosophorum, maximam partem germanorum, nonnullam quoque exterorum. Ed. 3a. 10 p. l. 1306 pp. fol. *Francofurti ad Mœnum, apud J. M. à Sande*, 1705.

Adam (*Rev.* M. T.) The millenium; being a series of discourses illustrative of its nature, the means by which it will be introduced, and the time of its commencement. xii, 224 pp. 12°. *New York, R. Carter*, 1837.

Adams (Catharine A. Van Buren). Music: an apotheosis: and other poems. 66 pp. 1 portrait. sm. 4°. *New York,* 1871.

Adams (Charles, *d. d.*) The poet preacher: a brief memorial of Charles Wesley, the eminent preacher and poet. 234 pp. 16°. *New York, Carlton & Porter,* 1859.

Adams (Charles Francis). The struggle for neutrality in America: an address delivered before the New York historical society, at their sixty-sixth anniversary, December 13, 1870. 2 p. l. 52 pp. 8°. *New York, C. Scribner & co.* 1871.

——— *and* **Adams** (John Quincy). The life of John Adams. 684 pp. 8°. *Boston, Little, Brown & co.* 1856.

[*In* ADAMS (John, *2d president of the United States*). Works. 1856, v. 1].

——— ——— The same. Begun by J. Q. Adams. Completed by C. F. Adams. Revised and corrected. 2 v. 498 pp; 416 pp. 16°. *Philadelphia, J. B. Lippincott & co.* 1871.

Adams (Daniel). The understanding reader: or, knowledge before oratory. Being a new selection of lessons, suited to the understandings and the capacities of youth, and designed for their improvement, 1. In reading. 2. In the definition of words. 3. In spelling, particularly, compound and derivative words. 3d ed. 224 pp. 16°. *Leominster, Mass. S. Wilder, for the author,* 1805.

Adams (*Rev.* Eliphalet). A sermon preached at Windham, July 12th, 1721, on a day of thanksgiving for the late remarkable success of the gospel among them. 1 p.l. vi, 40 pp. 18°. *New London, T. Green,* 1721.

Adams (Francis). The elementary education act, 1870 (33 & 34 Vict. c. 75); with analysis, index, and appendix. xv, 132 pp. 8°. *London, Simpkin, Marshall & co.* 1870.

——— Addenda to the analysis of the elementary education act, 1870. 14 pp. 8°. [*London,* 1870].

Adams (F. Colburn). Justice in the bye-ways. A tale of life. 438 pp. 12°. *New York, Livermore & Rudd,* 1856.

Adams (*Rev.* Henry W.) The book of Job in poetry; or, a song in the night. 380 pp. 18 pl. 1 portrait. 8°. *New York, author,* 1864.

Adams (*Rev.* James). The pronunciation of the english language vindicated from imputed anomaly & caprice: in two parts. With an appendix, on the dialects of human

Adams (*Rev.* James)—continued.
speech in all countries, and an analytical discussion and vindication of the dialect of Scotland. 164 pp. 8°. *Edinburgh, for the author by J. Moir,* 1799.

Adams (John, *d. d., b.* 1662, *vice-chancellor of Cambridge university*). An essay concerning self-murther. Wherein it is endeavour'd to prove, that it is unlawful according to natural principles. With some considerations upon what is pretended from the said principles, by the author of a treatise, intituled, Biathanatos, and others. 8 p. l. 320 pp. 8°. *London, T. Bennet,* 1700.

Adams (John Greenleaf). The christian's triumph: including happy death scenes, illustrative of the power of the gospel. Drawn from facts. 216 pp. 18°. *Boston, A. Tompkins,* 1840.

——— Practical hints to believers in the gospel of universal grace and salvation. 1 p. l. 272 pp. 12°. *Boston, T. Whittemore,* 1840.

Adams (John Jay). The charter oak, and other poems. 60 pp. 12°. *New York, S. Colman,* 1839.

Adams (John Quincy, *6th president of the U. S.*) Dermot Mac Morrogh, or the conquest of Ireland; an historical tale of the twelfth century. In four cantos. 108 pp. 8°. *Boston, Carter, Hendee & co.* 1832.

——— The same.

[MOORE pamphlets, v. 141].

——— The same.

[MISCELLANEOUS pamphlets, v. 287].

——— Life of John Adams. *See* **Adams** (Charles Francis).

Adams (John Quincy, *a freedman*). Narrative of the life of John Quincy Adams, when in slavery, and now as a freedman. 64 pp. 32°. *Harrisburg (Pa.) Sieg,* 1872.

Adams (J. S. *colonist*). The Florida colonist, or settler's guide. Answers to the question "Where in Florida shall we locate?" 2d ed. enlarged. 1 p. l. 86 pp. 1 map. 8°. *Jacksonville (Florida) Union job printing rooms,* 1871.

Adams (*Mrs.* J. S.) Allegories of life. 93 pp. sm. 4°. *Boston, Lee & Shepard,* 1872.

Adams (Nehemiah, *d. d.*) Church pastorals. Hymns and tunes for public and social worship. vii, 472 pp. 8°. *Boston, Ticknor & Fields,* 1864.

——— Evenings with the doctrines. 415 pp. 12°. *Boston, Gould & Lincoln,* 1861.

——— Remarks on the unitarian belief; with

Adams (Nehemiah, *d. d.*)—continued. a letter to a unitarian friend on the Lord's supper. viii, 5–175 pp. 16°. *Boston, Peirce & Parker*, 1832.

——— A voyage round the world. 152 pp. 3 pl. 16°. *Boston, H. Hoyt*, [1871].

Adams (Silas). The new era: a temperance poem. 19 pp. 12°. *Gardner, A. G. Bushnell & co.* 1870.

Adams (*Rev.* Thomas). The deuill's banket. Described in foure sermons. 1. The banket propounded; begunne. 2. The second seruice. 3. The breaking vp of the feast. 4. The shot or reckoning. The sinner's passing-bell. Together with phisicke from heauen. 4 p. l. 341 pp. sm. 4°. *London, R. Mab*, 1614.

Adams (William, *d. d. professor of divinity, Nashotah, Wisconsin*). A new treatise upon regeneration in baptism. xv, 384 pp. 8°. *Hartford (Conn.) M. H. Mallory & co.* 1871.

Adams (William, *m. d.*) On the reparative process in human tendons after subcutaneous division for the cure of deformities; also a series of experiments on rabbits, and a résumé of the english and foreign literature of the subject. xi pp. 7 l. 175 pp. 8 pl. 8°. *London, J. Churchill*, 1860.

Adams (William T.) Bivouac and battle; or, the struggles of a soldier. 16°. *Boston, Lee & Shepard*, 1872.

——— Cringle and cross-tree; or, the sea swashes of a sailor. By Oliver Optic. [*pseudon.*] 294 pp. 13 pl. 16°. *Boston, Lee & Shepard*, 1872.

[The upward and onward series, v. 4].

——— Desk and debit; or, the catastrophes of a clerk. By Oliver Optic. [*pseudon.*] 334 pp. 14 pl. 16°. *Boston, Lee & Shepard*, 1871.

[The upward and onward series, v. 3].

——— Northern lands; or, young America in Russia and Prussia. A story of travel and adventure. 360 pp. 5 pl. 16°. *Boston, Lee & Shepard*, 1872.

[Young America abroad, second series, no. 2].

——— Up the Baltic; or, young America in Norway, Sweden, and Denmark. A story of travel and adventure. 368 pp. 4 pl. 16°. *Boston, Lee & Shepard*, 1871.

Adcock (R. J.) Gravitation to the sphere and the two ellipsoids of revolution: ratio of the axes of a rotating fluid mass. 8 pp. 4°. *Cincinnati, Wilstach, Baldwin & co.* 1872.

Addey (Markinfield). "Stonewall Jackson." The life and military career of Thomas Jonathan Jackson, lieutenant general in the confederate army. 240 pp. 1 portrait. 12°. *New York, C. T. Evans*, 1863.

Additon (*Mrs.* J. H.) The operetta of Carlotta. In five acts. Music arranged by James Wright. 16 pp. 8°. *Rockland, Free Press*, 1870.

Address (The) of the episcopal clergy of Connecticut, to bishop Seabury; with the bishop's answer, and, a sermon before the convention at Middletown, August 3d, 1785, by the rev. Jeremiah Leaming, [etc.] Also, bishop Seabury's first charge, to the clergy of his diocess, [etc.] 8, 18, 15, 5 pp. 8°. *New-haven, T. & S. Green*, 1785.

[MISCELLANEOUS pamphlets, v. 197].

Address to a young lady on her entrance into the world. [*anon.*] 2 v. 1 p. l. 202 pp; 1 p. l. 216 pp. 8°. *London, Hookham & Carpenter*, 1796.

Address (An) to his excellency sir Charles Hardy, captain general and governor in chief of the province of New-York [etc.] By the author of a weekly paper, entitled, The watch-tower. [*anon.*] xiii pp. fol. *New York*, 1755.

[*With* INDEPENDENT (The) reflector].

Address (An) to major-general Tryon, written in consequence of his late expedition into Connecticut. [By Juvenis. *pseudon.*] 15 pp. 8°. [*n. p.*] 1779.

Address (An) to mothers, under the following heads: maternal authority, domestic attention, diligence and activity, œconomy, simplicity, objects of female pursuits, knowledge, virtue, and religion. [*anon.*] 2 p. l. 237 pp. 12°. *Oxford, Fletcher & son*, 1784.

Address (An) to the committee of correspondence in Barbadoes, occasioned by a late letter from them to their agent in London. By a North-American. [*anon.*] vi, 18 pp. 8°. *Philadelphia, W. Bradford*, 1766.

[HAZARD pamphlets, v. 20].

Address (An) to the freeholders and inhabitants of Pennsylvania; in answer to The plain dealer. [*anon.*] 12 pp. 8°. *Philadelphia, A. Armbruster*, 1764.

[HAZARD pamphlets, v. 76].

Address (An) to the freemen of South-Carolina, on the fœderal constitution, as proposed by the convention which met in Philadelphia, May, 1787. [*Signed* Civis. *anon.*] 12 pp. 16°. *Charleston, Bowen & co.* [1787]?

[HAZARD pamphlets, v. 105].

Address (An) to the inhabitants of the district of Maine, upon their separation from the present government of Massachusetts. By one of their fellow citizens. [*anon.*] 54 pp. 4°. *Portland, T. B. Wait,* 1791.

Adèle et Théodore; ou lettres sur l'éducation. *See* **Genlis** (S. F. D. de S. Aubin de).

Adelung (Johann Christoph). Fortsetzung und ergänzungen zu Jöcher's allgemeinem gelehrten-lexico. A–J. 2 v. viii l. 1248 pp; 1182 pp. 4°. *Leipzig, J. F. Gleditsch,* 1784–87.

—— Versuch eines vollständigen grammatisch-kritischen wörterbuches der hochdeutschen mundart, mit beständiger vergleichung der übrigen mundarten, besonders aber der oberdeutschen. Erster theil, von A–E. Dem noch beygefüget ist des herrn m. Fulda preisschrift über die beyden deutschen hauptdialecte. xvii, 1839 pp. 4°. *Leipzig, B. C. Breitkopf & sohn,* 1774.

Adler (G. J.) Handbook of german literature, containing: Schiller's Maid of Orleans, Goethe's Iphigenia in Tauris, Tieck's Puss in boots, The Xenia by Goethe and Schiller; with critical introductions and explanatory notes; to which is added an appendix, or specimens of german prose. 550 pp. 12°. *New York, D. Appleton & co.* 1854.

—— The poetry of the Arabs of Spain. Being the substance of a lecture read in the small chapel of the university of the city of New York, on the evening of March 28, 1867. 47 pp. 8°. *New York, Wynkoop & Hallenbeck,* 1867.

Adlerfeld (Gustav). Histoire militaire de Charles xii, roi de Suède, depuis l'an 1700 jusqu'à la bataille de Pultowa en 1709, écrite par ordre exprès de sa majesté. On y a joint une rélation exacte de la bataille de Pultowa, avec un journal de la retraite du roi à Bender. [Écrite en suédois et traduite en français par son fils, Carl Maximilian Adlerfeld]. 4 v. 12°. *Amsterdam, J. Wetstein & C. Smith,* 1740.

Adriano; or, the first of June. *See* **Hurdis** (*Rev.* James).

Adventures (The) of a king's page. *See* **White** (Charles).

Advertissemens novveaux, des roiavmes de la Chine et dv Giapon, escris sur la fin de l'an 1586. Auec le retour des princes giapponnois aux Indes. Le tout extraict des lettres des pères de la compagnie de Jésvs, et traduit d'italien en françois. [*anon.*] 111 pp. 16°. *Lion, J. Veyrat,* 1588.

[*With* MENDOZA (J. G. de). Histoire dv grand royaume de Chine, 1600].

Advys op de presentatie van Portugael. Het tweede deel. Met een remonstranci aen sijn konincklijcke majesteyt van Portugael by de inwoonders Portugesen van de Capitanie van Parnambocq overgelevert. [*anon.*] 1 p. l. 37 pp. sm. 4°. [*n. p.*] 1648.

Aedo y Gallart (Diego de). Le voyage dv prince don Fernande infant d'Espagne, cardinal, depvis le douzième d'auril de l'an 1632, qu'il partit de Madrit pour Barcelone avec le roy Philippe iv. son frère, jusques au jour de son entrée en la ville de Bruxelles le quatrième du mois de novembre de l'an 1634. Tradvict de l'espagnol, par le sr. Jvle Chifflet [etc.] 9 p. l. 204 pp. 1 tab. 2 pl. 8°. *Anvers, I. Cnobbaert,* 1635.

Ægineta (Paulus). *See* **Paulus** *ægineta.*

Aengemerckte voorvallen op de vredens articulen met Portugael. [*anon.*] 15 pp. sm. 4°. [*n. p.*] *anno* 1663.

Aenspraeck aen den ghetrouwen Hollander, nopende de proceduren der Portugesen in Brasill. [*anon.*] 15 pp. sm. 4°. *Graven-Hage, I. Burghoorn,* 1645.

Aenwysinge: datmen vande Oost en West-Indische compagnien, een compangie dient te maken. Mitsgaders twintich consideratien op de trafyque, zeevaert en commertie deser landen. [*anon.*] *b. l.* 18 l. sm. 4°. *Graven-haghe, I. Veeli,* 1644.

Ærodius (Petrus). *See* **Ayrault** (Pierre).

Æschines. Orations. *See* **Demosthenes** *and* **Æschines**.

Æschylus. The tragedies of Æschylus. Translated into english prose, from the texts of Blomfield and Scholefield. With notes. 3d ed. 2 p. l. 282 pp. 8°. *Oxford, H. Slatter,* 1840.

CONTENTS.

Prometheus.	Agamemnon.
Seven chiefs against Thebes.	The choëphoræ.
	The furies.
The Persians.	The supplicants.

—— Agamemnon. Denuo collato codice parisiensi recensuit, et annotationibus, siglisque metricis in margine scriptis, instruxit Fridericus Henricus Bothe. 140 pp. 8°. *Lipsiæ, sumtibus librariæ hahnianæ,* 1831.

—— The same. Ad optimorum librorum fidem denuo recensuit, integram lectionis varietatem notasque adiecit Augustus Wel-

Æschylus—continued. lauer. 1 p. l. 126 pp. 8°. *Lipsiæ, sumtibus F. C. G. Vogelii*, 1824.

——— The Prometheus of Æschylus, with notes; for the use of colleges in the United States. By T. D. Woolsey. viii, 90 pp. 12°. *Boston, J. Munroe & co.* 1837.

——— The seven before Thebes. Printed from the text of Schütz, under the care and direction of the senior class of Nassau Hall. 1 p. l. 40 pp. 8°. *Princeton press*, [*N. J.*] 1826.

Afgheworpen particuliere onderrichtinge vanden admirante aen den edelen Willem Rodewitz, capiteyn luytenant vant colonelschap vande duytsche ruyterie. 4 pp. sm. 4°. *Nemmeghen, A. Cornelissz.* [*about* 1607].

African methodist episcopal church. The african methodist episcopal church hymnbook. Selected from various authors. 512 pp. 32°. *Brooklyn, (N. Y.) G. Hogarth*, 1837.

——— Minutes of the general and annual conferences, [etc.] comprising four districts, for 1839-40. 47 pp. 12°. *Brooklyn, G. Hogarth*, 1840.

African (The) repository. [Monthly]. Jan. to Dec. 1871. v. 47. 8°. *Washington, American colonization society*, 1871.

African (The) traveller, or, prospective missions in Central Africa. By the author of "Village pastor." [*anon.*] 150 pp. 18°. *Boston, Mass sabbath-school society*, 1832.

Agassiz (Louis John Rudolph). An introduction to the study of natural history, in a series of lectures delivered in the hall of the college of physicians and surgeons, New York. 58 pp. 8°. *New York, Greeley & McElrath*, 1847.

——— Methods of study in natural history. viii, 319 pp. 12°. *Boston, Ticknor & Fields*, 1863.

Agathangelus *adrianopolites.* 'Αι καθ' 'Ομηρον αρχαιοτητες· και 'Αι κερκυραϊκαι αρχαιολογιαι· εκ της λατινιδος [A. M. Κυιρινου] επι την ἑλληνιδα φωνην αντιμετακληθεισαι ὑπο E. A. του B'. 6 p. l. 467 pp. 4°. *εν Μοσκα, εν τῳ της κοινοτητος τυπογραφειῳ*, 1804.

Agg (John). The ocean harp: a poem; in two cantos: with some smaller pieces; and a monody on the death of John Syng Dorsey, m. d. By the author of "Lord Byron's farewell to England." [*anon.* Preface subscribed J. A.] 182 pp. 18°. *Philadelphia, M. Thomas*, 1819.

Agnes [a novel]. *See* **Pike** (Mary H.)

Agostini (Leonardo). Le gemme antiche figvrate di L. Agostini. 2ª impressione. 2 parts. Eng. title. 52 pp. 116 pl; 4 p. l. 75 pp. 149 pl. 4°. *Roma, appresso G. B. Brvssotti*, 1686.

Agoult (Marie de Flavigny, *comtesse d'*). Esquisses morales. Pensées, réflexions et maximes par Daniel Stern. [*pseudon.*] 3ᵉ éd. revue et augmentée. 2 p. l. viii, 332 pp. 16°. *Paris, J. Techener*, 1859.

Agricoltura (L'). Giornale ed atti della società agraria di Lombardia. *See* **Milan.**

Agrippa von Nettesheim (Heinrich Cornelius). Female pre-eminence: or the dignity and excellency of that sex, above the male. An ingenious discourse: written originally in latine. Done into english, with additional advantages. By H[enry] C[ave]. 11 p. l. 83 pp. 16°. *London, T. R. & M. D.* 1670.

——— The same. Della nobiltà et eccellenza delle donne, nvovamente dalla lingva francese nella italiana tradotto [da Angelo Cocci. *anon.*] 30 l. 16°. *Vinegia, G. Giolito de Ferrarij*, 1544.

[*Note.*—This declamation was originally in latin, and addressed to Margaret of Austria. The french version was probably made by Louis Vivant].

——— The same. Dell' eccellenza e preeminenza del femmi nil sesso sopra il maschile. Trasportato dal latino nell' italiano. Da Giuseppe A. Graglia. 108 pp. 8°. *Londra, A. Grant*, 1776.

Aguecheek (*pseudon.*) *See* **Fairchild** (Charles B.)

Ahlfeld (Johann Friedrich). Predigten über die evangelischen perikopen. 7ᵉ aufl. viii, 690 pp. 8°. *Halle, R. Mühlmann*, 1863.

Ahn (Friedrich). Manual of german conversation. Revised by W. Grauert. viii, 205 pp. 12°. *New York, E. Steiger*, 1871.

Ahn (Johann Franz). Ahn's german handwriting. Being a companion to every german grammar and reader. With notes by W. Grauert. 62 pp. 12°. *New York, E. Steiger*, 1869.

Aïdé (Hamilton). Mr. & mrs. Faulconbridge. 2 v. 4 p. l. 279 pp; iv, 314 pp. 12°. *London, Smith, Elder & co.* 1864.

Aids to devotion, in three parts. Including Watts' guide to prayer. [*anon.* Subscribed E. L.] 288 pp. 16°. *Boston, Lincoln & Edmands*, 1831.

Aiken (J. B.) Harmonia ecclesiæ; or, companion to the christian minstrel: being

Aiken (J. B.)—continued.
a very choice collection of psalm and hymn tunes, anthems, chants, etc. Designed for choirs, singing schools, and singing societies. 336 pp. obl 8°. *Philadelphia, proprietor,* [1853].

——— The juvenile minstrel. A new system of musical notation; with a choice collection of moral and sacred songs. 208 pp. obl. 12°. *Philadelphia, E. C. & J. Biddle,* 1847.

Aiken (P. F.) A comparative view of the constitutions of Great Britain and the United States. In six lectures. viii, 192 pp. 16°. *London, Longman & co.* 1842.

Ailenroc (*pseudon.*) Musings of a middle-aged woman. 172 pp 12°. *Philadelphia, Claxton, Remsen & Haffelfinger,* 1872.

Ainslie (Hew). Scottish songs, ballads, and poems. 216 pp. 1 portrait. 16°. *New York, Redfield,* 1855.

Ainsworth (Luther). A practical system of english grammar. 144 pp. 12°. *Providence, B. Cranston & co. J. E. Brown,* 1837.

Aïssé (*Mademoiselle* Charlotte). Lettres à madame Calandrini. [Avec les lettres du chevalier d'Aydie, etc.] 5e éd. revue et annotée par m. J. Ravenel. Avec une notice par m. Sainte-Beuve. 2 p. l. 324 pp. 2 pl. 16°. *Paris, E. Dentu,* 1853.

Alabama educational almanac, 1872. 20 pp. 8°. *Montgomery, J. White,* 1872.

Alabaster (Henry). The wheel of the law. Buddhism illustrated from siamese sources by the modern Buddhist, a life of Buddha, and an account of the Phrabat. lix, 323 pp. 1 map. 8°. *London, Trübner & co.* 1871.

Albany. *Dudley observatory.* Annals of the Dudley observatory. v. 2. 8°. *Albany, the Argus co.* 1871.

CONTENTS.

Meteorological observations made at the Dudley observatory, during a period of nine years, from 1862 to 1871. Including hourly automatic printed records of the barometer for a continuous period of five years. G. W. Hough, director. Thomas E. McClure, Henry L. Foreman, assistants.

Albany institute. Transactions. v. i. viii, 250 pp. 1 l. 74 pp. 5 pl. 8°. *Albany, Webster & Skinners,* 1830.

Albarelli (Teresa). *See* **Vordoni** (Teresa Albarelli).

Albemarle (George, *duke of*). *See* **Monk** (George, *duke of Albemarle*).

Alberger (John). Monks, popes, and their political intrigues. 5 p. l. 5–376 pp. 12°. *Baltimore,* 1871.

Albèri (Eugenio). De Galilei Galileii circa Jovis satellites lucubrationibus quæ in pittianâ palatinâ bibliothecâ adservantur [etc.] 13 pp. 8°. *Florentiæ,* 1843.

——— Relazioni degli ambasciatori veneti al senato raccolte, annotate, ed edite da Eugenio Albèri. 3 series. 6 v. 8°. *Firenze, tipografia all' insegna di Clio,* 1839–44.

CONTENTS.

Serie 1a. Europa transalpina. 2 v. 1839–40.
2a. Relazioni d'Italia. 2 v. 1839–41.
3a. Stati ottomani. 2 v. 1840–44.

Alberti (Domenico Stanislao). Septenario de alabanzas en honra de la admirable, y noble virgen sta. Rosalia, natural, tutelar, y patrona de Palermo. Impresso en toscano, y traducido en castellano. 8 l. 18°. *Mexico, herederos de la viuda de F. R. Lupercio,* 1728.

Alberti (Leandro). Descrittione di tvutta Italia, nella quale si contiene il sito di essa, l'origine, & le signorie delle città, & de' castelli; co' nomi antichi, & moderni; i costumi de popoli, & de conditioni de paesi. Et di più gli huomini famosi, che l'hanno illustrata. Aggiuntaui la descrittione di tutte l'isole, all' Italia appartenenti. Nuouamente ristampata 2 v. in 1. 34 p. l. 495 l; 100, 5 l. 7 maps. sm. 4°. *Vinegia, A. Salicato,* 1588.

Albertus *magnus.* Les admirables secrets d'Albert le grand. Contenant plusieurs traités sur la conception des femmes, des vertus des herbes, des pierres précieuses, & des animaux. Augmenté d'un abrégé curieux de la phisionomie, & d'un préservatif contre la peste [etc.] Tirés et traduits sur des anciens manuscrits de l'auteur. 4 books in 1 v. 12 p. l. 312 pp. 5 pl. 16°. *Lyons, héritiers de Beringos fratres,* 1753.

——— Alberti magni compendium, oder kurtzer begriff vom ursprung und materia der metallen, worauff ein spagyrus seine gründliche principia festsetzen könne. 16°. *Hamburg, J. Naumann & G. Wolff,* 1675.

[*In* ALCHYMISTISCH sieben-gestirn. 1675. pp. 209–218].

——— Tractatvs de virtvtibvs herbarvm lapidvm et animalium. 18°. [*Franckfurt,* 1663]?

[*In* LONGINUS (Cæsar). Trinum magicum, pp. 241–345].

Albertus *stadensis.* Chronicon a condito orbe vsque ad a. c. 1256. fol. [*Argentorati, J. R. Dulssecker,* 1702].

[*In* KULPIS (Johann Georg von). Scriptores rervm germanicarvm. *Argentorati,* 1702. pp. 123–336].

Albinus *or* **Weiss** (Bernhard Siegfried). Oratio inauguralis de anatome comparata publice

Albinus *or* **Weiss** (B. S.)—continued.

habita, d. 2. Octobris 1719. Cum publicum anatomen & chirurgiam prælegendi munus in academia leidensi auspicaretur. 2 p. l. 46 pp. 4°. *Lugduni Batavorum, apud H. Mulhovium*, 1719.

[*With* NEANDER (Johann). Tabacologia. 1626].

——— Oratio qua in veram viam, quæ ad fabricae humani corporis cognitionem ducat, inquiritur, publice habita, quum ordinariam anatomes et chirurgiae professionem in academia lugduno-batava auspicaretur, a. d. 19 Novembris 1721. 2 p. l. 67 pp. 4°. *Lugduni Batavorum, apud H. Mulhovium*, 1721.

[*With* NEANDER (Johann). Tabacologia. 1626].

Albizzi (Bartolommeo degli). Liber conformitatum vite s. Frācisci ad uitā iesu xp̄i. [Ex recensione Fran. Zenonis]. Eng. tit. 3 p. l. 256 l. 4°. *Mediolani, per G. Ponticū*, 1510.

Albright (J. W.) Combination self-delineating patterns, contracting and expanding on parallel index-lines. Adapted to any fashion or style required. 4 pp. 3 pl. fol. *Philadelphia, Collins*, 1871.

Albrizzi (Isabella Teotochi). Ritratti. 4ª ed. Arrichita di due ritratti di due lettere sulla Mirra di Alfieri e della vita di Vittoria Colonna. 4 p. l. 193 pp. 24 portraits. 8°. *Pisa, N. Capurro*, 1826.

Album for postage and other stamps, american and foreign. [*anon.*] 208 pp. incl. 11 maps. 4°. *New York, D. Appleton & co.* 1863.

Albuquerque (The) republican review. [Weekly]. v. 1–2. *See* **Republican** (Albuquerque) review.

Alcaforada. *See* **Alcoforado.**

Alchymistisch sieben-gestirn, das ist, sieben schöne und ausserlesene tractätlein, vom stein der weisen, darinn der richtige weg zu solchem allerhöchsten geheimnüss zu kommen hell und klar gezeiget wird. Allen liebhabern der hoch-edlen wissenschafft zu gefallen und nützlichem unterricht, aus dem latein ins hoch-deutsche treulich übergesetzet. [*anon.*] 4 p. l. 232 pp. 16°. *Hamburg, J. Naumann & G. Wolff*, 1675.

CONTENTS.

ALBERTUS *magnus.* Compendium, oder kurtzer begriff vom ursprung und materia der metallen, pp. 209–218.
ARISTOTELES. Ein tractat Aristotelis des alchimisten an Alexandrum magnum vom stein der weisen, pp. 69–98.
DAUSTEN (John). Rosarivm, in welchem das aller

Alchymistisch, etc.—continued.

geheimeste geheimnüss vom stein der weissen verschlossen, pp. 99–208.
HERMES *trismegistus.* Gülden tractätlein, von der composition des steins der weisen, pp. 1–24.
LULLY (Raymond). Apertorium, von der wahren composition des steines der weisen, pp. 25–56.
——— Elvcidarivm, geschrieben über sein testament und codicill, wie die recht zu verstehen, pp. 57–68.
PONTAN (Johann). Ein sendbrief, darinn vom stein der weisen gehandelt wird, pp. 219–231.

Alciati (Andrea). Alciato de la manera de desafio, tradvzido de latin en romance castellano, por Iuan Martin Cordero valenciano. 113 l. numb. 115–118 pp. 18°. *Anvers, M. Nucio*, [1555].

Alcionio (Pietro). Petri Alcyonii medices legatvs de exsilio ad Nicolavm Schonbergvm pontificem campanvm. 66 l. 8°. *Venetiis, in ædibvs Aldi & A. Asvlani soceri*, 1522.

——— The same. 18°. [*Lipsiæ, apud J. F. Gleditsch*, 1707].

[*In* MENCKEN (J. B.) Analecta de calamitate litteratorum, 1707, pp. 1–250].

Alcock (Charles W.) The book of rules of the game of football, as adopted and played by the english football associations. 35 pp. 1 pl. 12°. *New York, Peck & Snyder*, [1871].

Alcoforado (Francisco). An historical account of the discovery of the island of Madeira, abridged from the portugueze original. [Edited by Francisco Manoel de Kello]. To which is added an account of the present state of the island [1748, and extracts from a voyage to Surat, in 1689, by John Ovington]. 1 p. l. x, 88 pp. 8°. *London, J. Payne and J. Bouquet*, 1750.

[*Note.*—First published in french, Paris, 1671; then in english, London, 1675].

Alcott (Louisa May). Aunt Jo's scrap-bag. My boys, etc. 3 p. l. 215 pp. 2 pl. 16°. *Boston Roberts brothers*, 1872.

——— Little men: life at Plumfield with Jo's boys. 2 p. l. 376 pp 4 pl. 16°. *Boston, Roberts brothers*, 1871.

——— Three proverb stories. (Kitty's class-day. Aunt Kipp. Psyche's art). 148 pp. 4 pl. 16°. *Boston, A. K. Loring*, [1868].

Alcott (William Alexander, *m. d.*) The beloved physician: or, the life and travels of Luke the evangelist. Revised by the editor, D. P. Kidder. 179 pp. 18°. *New York, G. Lane & C. B. Tippett*, 1845.

——— The first foreign mission; or journey of Paul and Barnabas to Asia Minor. 148 pp. 16°. *Boston, Mass. sabbath-school society*, [1840]?

——— The happy family made happier: or the resurrection of Lazarus. 60 pp. 1 map.

Alcott (William Alexander, *m.d.*)—continued. 16°. *Boston, Massachusetts sabbath-school society*, 1835.

——— A historical description of the first public school in Hartford, Conn. now under the superintendence of J. Olney, with a particular account of its methods of instruction and discipline. Accompanied by general remarks on common schools. 1 p. l. 102 pp. 12°. *Hartford, D. F. Robinson & co.* 1832.

——— The life of Peter the apostle. 188 pp. 1 pl. 18°. *Boston, Massachusetts sabbath-school society*, 1836.

——— The mother in her family: or sayings and doings at Rose hill cottage. [*anon.*] 16, 391 pp. 12°. *Boston, Weeks, Jordan & co.* 1838.

——— The mother's medical guide in children's diseases. 314 pp. 1 portrait. 16°. *Boston, T. R. Marvin*, 1842.

——— Paul's shipwreck. 126 pp. 18°. *Boston, Massachusetts sabbath-school society*, 1842.

——— The sabbath-school as it should be. 299 pp. 12°. *New York, J. Leavitt*, 1841.

——— The second foreign mission; or journey of Paul, Silas, Luke, and Timothy to Europe. 173 pp. 1 pl. 16°. *Boston, Massachusetts sabbath-school society*, 1835.

——— The story of Ananias and Sapphira. 72 pp. 18°. *New York, G. Lane & C. B. Tippett*, 1844.

——— Travels of our saviour, with some of the leading incidents of his life. 311 pp. 18°. *Boston, Mass. sabbath-school society*, 1840.

——— The young man's guide. 6th ed. Eng. title. 354 pp. 1 pl. 18°. *Boston, S. Colman*, 1835.

——— The same. 7th ed. 354 pp. 16°. *Boston, S. Colman*, 1835.

——— The same. 8th ed. Eng. title. 354 pp. 1 pl. 18°. *Boston, Perkins & Marvin*, 1836.

——— The same. 16th ed. Eng. title. 392 pp. 1 pl. 16°. *Boston, T. R. Marvin*, 1844.

——— The young missionary; exemplified in the life of Timothy. 175 pp. 18°. *Boston, Mass. sabbath-school society*, 1837.

——— The young mother, or management of children in regard to health. 2d ed. 332 pp. 12°. *Boston, Light & Stearns*, 1836.

Alcyonius (Petrus). *See* **Alcionio** (Pietro).

Alden (John B.) Bright side stories: gems of beauty in prose, poetry, and picture. 286 pp. incl. 15 pl. sm. 4°. *Chicago, J. S. Goodman & co.* 1871.

Alderete *or* **Aldrete** (Bernardo José). Del origen y principio de la lengva castellana ò romance que oy se vsa en España. 4 p. l. 89 l. numb. 1 l. fol. *Madrid, M. Sanchez*, 1674.

Aldine (The). A typographical art journal. [Monthly]. Sept. 1868, to Dec. 1871. v. 1–4. fol. *New York, J. Sutton & co.* 1868–72.

Aldine (The) press. *See* **Aldine** (The).

Aldrovandi (Ulisse). Cycni encomium. 18°. [*Lugd. Batavorum*, 1644].

[*In* DISSERTATIONVM lvdicrarvm et amœnitatvm scriptores varij, pp. 655–666].

Alessio *piemontese*. Les secrets dv seignevr Alexis piemontois. Reueu, corrigé, & augmenté d'vne infinité de rares secrets. Dernière éd. 912 pp. 40 l. 36°. *Roven, T. Reinsart*, 1600.

[*Note.*—Dr. Paget, of Bartholomew's hospital, in the article Alessio, in the biographical dictionary published by the society for useful knowledge, says there is no reason to identify this writer with Girolamo Ruscelli, as many have chosen to do].

Alexander (Alexander, *lieut. columbian service*). The life of Alexander Alexander: written by himself, and edited by John Howell. 2 v. 1 p. l. vii, iii, 339 pp. 1 portrait; 2 p. l. iii, 327 pp. 12°. *Edinburgh, W. Blackwood*, 1830.

Alexander (Archibald, *d. d.*) A brief outline of the evidences of the christian religion. 2d ed. 251 pp. 12°. *Princeton, D. A. Borrenstein*, 1825.

——— History of the Israelites, from the death of Joseph to the death of Moses. 212 pp. 18°. *Philadelphia, H. Perkins*, 1834.

——— A selection of hymns, adapted to the devotions of the closet, the family, and the social circle; and containing subjects appropriate to the monthly concerts of prayer for the success of missions and sunday schools; and other special occasions. xiv, 624 pp. 24°. *New-York, J. Leavitt*, 1831.

Alexander (A. J.) The short-horn record: containing the pedigrees of improved short horned cattle. v. 2. xvi, 184 pp. 5 pl. 8°. *Frankfort, Kentucky yeoman office*, 1871.

Alexander (Caleb, *d. d.*) A sermon occasioned by the death of George Washington. 23 pp. 8°. *Boston, S. Hall*, 1800.

[HAZARD pamphlets, v. 65].

Alexander (James Waddell, *d. d.*) Thoughts on preaching, being contributions to homiletics. xii, 514 pp. 12°. *New York, C. Scribner*, 1861.

Alexander (John Henry). Introïts: or ante-communion psalms for the sundays and holy-

Alexander (John Henry)—continued. days throughout the year. [*anon.*] 1 p. l. 187 pp. 12°. *Philadelphia, Lindsay & Blakiston*, 1844.

Alexander (Joseph Addison, *d. d.*) The gospel according to Matthew. *See* **Bible.** (*English*). *Matthew.*

——— Notes on new testament literature and ecclesiastical history. xvi, 319 pp. 12°. *New York, C. Scribner*, 1861.

——— Sermons. 2 v. 414 pp; 425 pp. 1 portrait. 12°. *New York, C. Scribner*, 1860.

Alexander (*Rev.* Samuel D.) History of the presbyterian church in Ireland. Condensed from the standard work of Reid and Killen. *See* **Reid** (James Seaton, *d. d.*) *and* **Killen.**

Alexander (William Lindsay, *d.d.*) Elisha's cry after Elijah. 16°. [*London, A. Fullerton & co.* 1854].

[*In* DISCOURSES and services on occasion of the death of the late rev. Ralph Wardlaw, d. d. 1854, pp. 45–87].

Alexandria (*Va.*) Boyd's directory. *See* **Washington City.** Directory.

Alexandria advertiser. v. 1. nos. 96–112, 114–281, 283–313. fol. *Alexandria*, 1797–98.

Alexandria (The) gazette and Virginia advertiser. [Tri-weekly]. May 13, 1840, to May 23, 1861. 21 v. fol. *Alexandria*, (*Va.*) 1840–61.

Alexandria (The) herald. [Tri-weekly]. March 15, 1816, to Aug. 20, 1817; Jan. 5 to Dec. 30, 1818; April 2, 1821, to Dec. 29, 1823. 5 v. fol. *Alexandria*, (*Va.*) *Corse & Rounsavell, and Rounsavell & Pittman*, 1816–23.

Alfio Balzani; or, extracts from the diary of a proscribed Sicilian. [*anon.*] 551 pp. 12°. *New York, Rudd & Carleton*, 1861.

Alfred (George). The american universal spelling book; containing a new and complete system of orthography, founded on the true principles of the english language. 192 pp. 16°. *Staunton*, (*Va.*) *I. Collett*, 1811.

Alger (Horatio, *jr.*) Paul the peddler; or, the adventures of a young street merchant. 281 pp. 3 pl. 16°. *Boston, Loring*, [1871].

[TATTERED Tom series, no. 2].

——— Sink or swim; or, Harry Raymond's resolve. 388 pp. 6 pl. 16°. *Boston, Loring*, [1871].

[LUCK and pluck series, no. 2].

——— Strong and steady; or, paddle your own canoe. 362 pp. 6 pl. 16°. *Boston, Loring*, [1871].

[LUCK and pluck series, no. 3].

Alger (Horatio, *jr.*)—continued.

——— Tattered Tom; or, the story of a street Arab. 282 pp. 3 pl. 16°. *Boston, Loring*, 1871.

[TATTERED Tom series, no. 1].

Ali bey. *See* **Bobowski** (Albert).

Allacci (Leone). De mensvra temporvm antiqvorvm, & præcipue Græcorvm, exercitatio. 4 p. l. 239 pp. 8°. *Coloniæ Agrippinæ, apud I. Kalcovivm & socios*, 1645.

[*With his* De templis Græcorvm recentioribvs. 1645].

——— De templis Græcorvm recentioribvs, ad Ioannem Morinum; de narthece ecclesiæ veteris, ad Gasparem de Simeonibus; nec non de Græcorvm hodie qvorvndam opinationibvs, ad Paullum Zacchiam. 8 p. l. 184 pp. 3 pl. 8°. *Coloniæ Agrippinæ, apud I. Kalcovivm & socios*, 1645.

——— Confvtatio fabvlæ de Ioanna papissa, ex monumentis græcis. Bartoldvs Nihvsivs recensuit, prologo atque epilogo auxit, nec non Telescopium adjunxit. 112 pp. 8°. *Coloniæ Agrippinæ, typis I. Kalcovii & sociorum*, 1645.

[*With his* De templis Græcorvm recentioribvs. 1645].

——— Drammaturgia, accresciuta e continuata fino all' anno mdcclv. 4 p. l. 1016 col. [on 254 l.] 4°. *Venezia, G. Pasquali*, 1755.

Allais (Denis Vairasse d'). *See* **Vairasse d'Allais.**

Allan (George). Life of sir Walter Scott, with critical notices of his writings. 411 pp. 1 pl. 8°. *Philadelphia, Crissy, Waldie & co.* 1835.

——— The same. 4°. *Philadelphia, Waldie*, 1836.

[WALDIE (A.) Select circulating library, v. 6, pp. 92–176].

Allatius. *See* **Allacci.**

Alleaume (—, *avocat*). Suite des caractères de Theophraste, et des mœurs de ce siècle. [*anon.*] 8, 437–662, 230 pp. 16°. *Paris, E. Michallet*, 1700.

[*Note.*—Appended is DISCOURS prononcé dans l'académie françoise, 1693. xliv pp.]

Allebach (J. C.) A complete organ and melodeon preceptor, on an easy and progressive method. Containing illustrations, in a clear and full explanation of the primary principles of musical science: with a variety of exercises, songs, etc. arranged for the most rapid advancement of learners. 56 pp. obl. 8°. *Philadelphia, S. C. Collins*, 1870.

Alleine (*Rev.* Joseph). Christian letters, full of spiritual instructions, tending to the promoting of the power of godliness, both in

Alleine (*Rev.* Joseph)—continued. persons and families. 12°. [*New York, R. Carter*, 1840].

[*In* BAXTER (R.) *and* ALLEINE (*Mrs.* T.) Life and death of the rev. Joseph Alleine. 1840. pp. 137–275].

——— The solemn warnings of the dead: or, an admonition to unconverted sinners. And, A call to the unconverted. By mr. Richard Baxter. 288 pp. 18°. *New York, J. Soule & T. Mason, for the methodist episcopal church in the United States*, 1818.

Alleine (*Mrs.* Theodosia). An account of the life and death of the late rev. Joseph Alleine. 18°. *Edinburgh, Waugh & Innes*, 1822.

[*In* MATHER (Increase). Lives of Cotton Mather and Joseph Alleine, 1822, pp. 121–242].

——— The same. *See* **Baxter** (*Rev.* Richard) *and* **Alleine** (*Mrs.* T.)

Allen (*Mrs.* Brasseya). Pastorals, elegies, odes, epistles, and other poems. 1 p. l. 163 pp. 16°. *Abingdon, (Md.) D. P. Ruff*, 1806.

Allen (Chester G.) Voice culture, 1871. *See* **Webb** (George James) *and* **Allen.**

Allen (Ethan). A brief narrative of the proceedings of the government of New York relative to their obtaining the jurisdiction of that large district of land, to the westward from Connecticut river, which, antecedent thereto, had been patented by his majesty's governor and council of the government of New Hampshire. Together with arguments demonstrating that the property of those lands was conveyed from the crown to the New Hampshire grantees by virtue of their respective charters. With remarks upon a pamphlet entitled "A state of the right of the colony of New York, etc." Bennington, 1774. 211 pp. 12°. *Hartford, Eben Watson, near the great bridge*, [1774]?

[HAZARD pamphlets, v. 47].

——— A narrative of colonel Ethan Allen's captivity, from 1775 to 1778, containing his voyages and travels. Written by himself. 64 pp. 16°. *Philadelphia, William Mentz*, 1779.

——— The same. 40 pp. 12°. *Boston, reprinted, Draper & Folsom*, 1799.

——— *and* **Fay** (Jonas). A concise refutation of the claims of New-Hampshire and Massachusetts-Bay, to the territory of Vermont; with occasional remarks on the claim of New York to the same. 29 pp. 8°. *Hartford, Hudson & Goodwin*, [1780]?

——— The same.

[HAZARD pamphlets, v. 45].

Allen (Ira). A vindication of the conduct of the general assembly of the state of Vermont, held at Windsor in October, 1778, against allegations and remarks of the protesting members; with observations on their proceedings at a convention held at Cornish, on the 9th day of December, 1778. 48 pp. 18°. *Dresden, Alden Spooner*, [1779]?

Allen (James, *secretary of the West India merchants*). Considerations on the present state of the intercourse between his majesty's sugar colonies and the dominions of the United States of America. 54 pp. 8°. *London*, 1784.

Allen (*Rev.* John, *of Boston*). An oration upon the beauties of liberty, or, the essential rights of the Americans. Delivered at the 2d baptist church in Boston, upon the last annual thanksgiving. Dedicated to the earl of Dartmouth. [By a british Bostonian. *anon.*] 3d ed. 23 pp. 8°. *New-London, printed by T. Green, for J. Knight*, 1773.

[HAZARD pamphlets, v. 45].

Allen (*Rev.* Joseph Henry). Hebrew men and times, from the patriarchs to the messiah. x, 435 pp. 12°. *Boston, Walker, Wise & co.* 1861.

Allen (Thomas Prentiss, *and* William Francis). A hand-book of classical geography, chronology, mythology, and antiquities. xii, 5–123 pp. 12°. *Boston, Swan, Brewer & Tileston*, 1861.

Allen (*Cardinal* William) *and others.* New testament, 1582. *See* **Bible.** (*English*).

Allen (William, *d. d.*) Poems of Nazareth and the cross. 60 pp. 12°. *Northampton, Bridgman & Childs*, 1866.

——— Psalms and hymns for public worship, containing all the psalms and hymns of dr. Watts, which are deemed valuable, together with a new version of all the psalms, and many original hymns, besides a large collection from other writers. Eng. title, xlvii, 690 pp. 18°. *Boston, W. Peirce*, 1835.

Alletz (Pons Augustin). Connoissance des poëtes les plus célèbres, ou moyen facile de prendre une teinture des humanités, contenant la vie de chaque poëte, le sentiment des sçavans sur le mérite de chaque auteur; les morceaux les plus estimés, avec la traduction, & des remarques historiques. 2 v. 7 p. l. 514 pp; 2 p. l. 536 pp. 1 l. 16°. *Paris, Didot*, 1752.

Allgemeine bibliographie. Monatliches verzeichniss der wichtigern neuen erscheinun-

Allgemeine bibliographie—continued. gen der deutschen und ausländischen literatur. Zusammengestellt von Paul Trömel. 1-2 jahrg. 8°. *Leipzig, F. A. Brockhaus,* 1856-57.

Allgemeine (Die) liedersammlung zum privat und öffentlichen Gottes-dienst. 410 pp. 24°. *Elkhart (Ind.) J. F. Funk & brud.* 1871.

Allgemeine monatsschrift für literatur. Herausgegeben von dr. L. Ross und dr. G. Schwetschke. 2 v. 8°. *Halle, C. A. Schwetschke & sohn,* 1850. s.

——— The same. Allgemeine monatsschrift für wissenschaft und literatur. Herausgegeben von J. G. Droysen [et al.] Jahrgang 1851-1854. 4 v. in 6. 8°. *Halle, Braunschweig, C. A. Schwetschke & sohn,* 1851-54. s.

Allgemeine zeitung. [Tägliche]. 1 Jan. 1798, to 31 Dec. 1871. 292 v. 4°. *Tübingen & Augsburg,* [1798-1871].

[1 Jan. to 8 Sept. 1798, v. 1-3, known as "Neueste weltkunde." *Wanting,* 1799].

Allibone (Samuel Austin). An alphabetical index to the new testament. Common version. Suitable to any edition, and useful to all ministers, teachers, and bible readers. [*anon.* By S. A. A.] 75 pp. 16°. *Philadelphia, American sunday-school union,* 1868.

——— The union bible companion: containing the evidences of the divine origin, preservation, credibility, and inspiration of the holy scriptures; an account of various manuscripts and english translations, all the books, and the chief doctrines of the bible; and plans of christian work: with a copious analytical index. 315 pp. 12°. *Philadelphia, American sunday school union,* [1871].

Allin (Thomas). Discourses on the immateriality and immortality of the soul; the character and folly of modern atheism; and the necessity of a divine revelation. x, 269 pp. 8°. *London, Hurst, Chance & co.* 1828.

Allman (George James, *m. d.*) A monograph of the gymnoblastic or tubularian hydroids. In two parts. 1. The hydroida in general. 2. The genera and species of the gymnoblasta. [Part 1]. xxiii, 154 pp. 12 l. 12 pl. fol. *London,* 1871.

[RAY society publications].

Allom (Thomas). Constantinople and the scenery of the seven churches of Asia Minor, illustrated, with an historical account by R. Walsh. 2 v. in 1. 2 p. l. xxxvi, 84 pp. 84 pl. 1 map; 100 pp. 93 pl. 1 map. 4°. *London, Fisher, son, & co.* [1850].

Allston (Robert F. W.) Essay on seacoast crops; read before the agricultural association of the planting states, on occasion of the annual meeting at Columbia, S. C. December 3d, 1853. 461 pp. 8°. *Charleston, (S. C.) A. E. Miller,* 1854.

Almanac for the use of navigators for 1870-74. *See* **United States.** (*Navy department*). *Nautical almanac office.*

Almanac for the year 1864, being bissextile, or leap year, and the fourth year of the independence of the Confederate States of America. Calculations made at university of Alabama. 20 pp. 12°. *Mobile, S. H. Goetzel,* 1864.

Almanach de Gotha. *See* **Gothaischer** hofkalender.

Almanach de la paix, pour l'année 1872. (1e année). Texte par F. Passy, M. Chevalier, É. Laboulaye, [et les autres]. Dessins de Bertall, Ratel et Nino. 64 pp. 16°. *Paris, Pichon & cie.* [1872].

Almon (John). The fugitive miscellany. Being a collection of such fugitive pieces, in prose and in verse, as are not in any other collection, [etc. *anon.*] 190 pp. 16°. *London, J. Almon,* 1774.

Aloe (Stanislao). Naples, ses monumens et ses curiosités, avec un catalogue détaillé du musée royal bourbon, suivi d'une description d'Herculanum, Pompéi, Stabies, Pestum, Pouzzoles, Cumes, Baïa, Capone, etc. 2e éd. augmentée. vii, 626 pp. 2 maps. 16°. *Naples, imprimerie du Virgile,* 1853.

Alsted (Johann Heinrich). Thesaurus chronologiæ. Ed. 4a. 692 pp. 23 l. 1 tab. 8°. *Herbornæ Nassoviorum,* 1650.

Alston (*Rev.* Philip William Whitmel). Sermons. With a biographical notice and funeral sermon, by the rt. rev. Jos. H. Otey, d. d. 456 pp. 1 portrait. 8°. *Philadelphia, H. Hooker,* 1854.

Alta (The) California, Pacific coast, and trans-continental railroad guide. 294 pp. 3 l. 1 map. sq. 16°. *San Francisco, F. McCrellish & co.* [1871].

Altar (The) at home. Second series. Selections and prayers for domestic worship. [*anon.*] xii, 336 pp. 12°. *Boston, Walker, Wise & co.* 1862.

Alting (Jacob). Opera omnia theologica; analytica, exegetica, practica, problematica: & philologica. 5 v. fol. *Amstelædami, excudit G. Borstius,* 1585-87.

[v. 1 and 5, 1587; v. 2-4, 1585-86].

Alting (Jacob)—continued.

CONTENTS.

v. 1. Jacobi Altingii vita. 4 p. l.
Analysis exegetica Geneseos, Exodi, Levitici, Numeri.
Commentarius theorico-practicus in Deuteronomium.
In xxiv priores Psalmos analysis exegetica.
In Jeremiam prophetam commentarius.
v. 2. Commentarius theorico-practicus in loca quædam selecta Pentateuchi; ex libris historicis veteris testamenti; in loca quædam selecta Psalmorum; et ex prophetis.
Parallelismus testimoniorum veteris testamenti quæ in euangelio suo citat s. Matthæus.
v. 3. Commentarius theorico-practicus in epistolam Pauli ad Romanos. [Capita 1–10].
v. 4. Commentarius theorico-practicus in caput undecimum epistolæ ad Romanos, ante hac editus sub titulo Spes Israelis.
Sermo academicus de Judæorum restitutione.
Commentarius in epistolam Pauli ad Romanos. [Capita 12–16].
Analysis exegetica in epistolam Pauli ad Colossenses.
In epistolam ad Hebræos commentarius.
Commentarius in loca quædam selecta novi testamenti.
v. 5. Sabbathum mere euangelicum, ecclesiæ utriusque testamenti proprium, ex verbo Dei propositum & assertum.
Schilo: seu de vaticinio patriarchae Jacobi, quod Genes. xlix, vers. 10 exstat.
Analysis exegetica catecheseos palatinæ.
Methodus theologiæ didacticæ.
Academicarum dissertationum tam philologicarum quam theologicarum heptades septem. Accesserunt orationum heptades duæ.
Sciagraphia biblica seu specimen oeconomiæ patriarcharum. Doctrina de sabbatho catecheseos palatinæ, et synodi nationalis Dordracenæ. Accedunt orationes duæ, prior recturæ academicæ auspicatæ; posterior terminatæ.
Epistolæ, et ex epistolis excerpta.
Mantissa miscellanea.
Fundamenta punctationis lingvæ sanctæ.
Synopsis institutionum Chaldæarum et Aramæarum.

Altmann (Johann Georg). État et délices de la Suisse, ou description historique et géographique des treize cantons suisses et leurs alliés. Nouv. éd. Corrigée & considérablement augmentée par plusieurs auteurs célèbres. [*anon.*] 2 v. 2 p. l. 455 pp. 32 pl. 7 maps; 2 p. l. 392 pp. 37 pl. 3 maps. 4°. *Neuchâtel, S Fauche*, 1778.

Altmeyer (Jean Jacques). Une succursale du tribunal de sang. [La prise de Mons, 1572]. 182 pp. 12°. *Bruxelles, C. Vanderauwera*, 1853.

Altolaguirre (Francisco Ignacio de). Relacion del milagro, que obró Dios por intercession de san Luiz Gonzaga a primero de marzo de 1765 en sor Maria Josepha Ramona de san Fermin Perez de Eulate, religiosa del Santa Clara a de la villa de Tolosa en Guipuzcoa. 4 l. 4°. *Madrid, M. Fernandez*, 1765.

Alunno (Francesco). Le ricchezze della lingva volgare sopra il Boccaccio. Di nuouo ristampate et ampliate. Con le dechiarationi, regole, asservationi, & aggiontoui le cadenze o uero definenze di tutte le uoci del detto Boccaccio, e del Petrarcha. [Ed. 4ª.] 396 pp. 4°. *Vinegia, P. Gherardo*, 1557.

Alzate y Ramirez (José Antonio de). *See* **Gacetas** de literatura de Mexico.

Amalteo (Giovanni Battista). Lycidas, [an eclogue]. Acon, [an eclogue]. Written in latin. [Translated into english by John Rooke]. 8°. [*London*, 1725].

[Rooke (John). Select translations, part 2, pp. 16–31. 1726].

Amaranth (The): or, religious poems. *See* **Harte** (Walter).

Amateurs' (The) annual, for 1872. Edited and compiled by Edwin Ballard and Frank Atwood. 64 pp. 7 photo. pl. 16°. *Boston, Annual publishing co.* 1872.

Amaury-Duval (Pineux). *See* **Baltard** (L. P.) Paris et ses monumens.

Ambrosius *mediolanensis* (*St.*) De officiis clericorum libros tres ad manuscriptorum et optimorum librorum fidem emendavit et selectam lectionum varietatem adiecit R. O. Gilbert. Praemissa est vita s. Ambrosii a Paulino scripta. vi, 188 pp. 12°. *Lipsiae, Tauchnitz*, 1839.

[Gersdorf (E. G.) Bibliotheca patrum ecclesiasticorum latinorum selecta, v. 8].

——— The same. Les devoirs de l'honnête-homme et du chrétien ou les offices de s. Ambroise. Traduits par m. l'abbé de Bellegarde. 18 p. l. 446 pp. 11 l. 16°, *Paris, A. Seneuse*, 1689.

——— Hexameri libros sex, emendavit et lectionum varietatem adjecit R. O. Gilbert. viii, 184 pp. 12°. *Lipsiae, Tauchnitz*, 1840.

[Gersdorf (E. G.) Bibliotheca patrum ecclesiasticorum latinorum selecta, v. 9].

——— Inni sinceri e carmi di sant' Ambrogio vescovo di Milano. Cavati specialmente da monumenti della chiesa milanese, e illustrati dal prete Luigi Biraghi. 158 pp. 8°. *Milano, E. Besozzi*, 1862. s.

Ambrosius (*pseudo-Ambrosius*). Sancti Ambrosii tractatus: in quo loca, doctrinam, ac mores Brachmanorum describit. 4°. [*Londini*, 1668].

[*In* Bysshe (Ed.) Palladius de gentibus Indiæ, pp. 57–84].

Ambulator; or, a pocket companion in a tour round London, within the circuit of twenty-five miles; including new catalogues of pictures, and illustrated by historical and biographical observations; to which is pre-

Ambulator—continued.
fixed, a concise description of the metropolis. [*anon.*] 4th ed. 2 p. l. 312 pp. 1 map. 12°. *London, J. Bew,* [*etc.*] 1792.

Amelot de la Houssaye (Abraham Nicolas). Réflexions, sentences et maximes morales, mises en nouvel ordre, avec des notes politiques et historiques. Nouvelle édition, corrigée et augmentée de maximes chrétiennes. 13 p. l. 276 pp. 3 l. 16°. *Paris, E. Ganeau* 1725.

America's appeal to the impartial world. Wherein the rights of Americans as men, as british subjects, and as colonists, the equity of the demand, and of the manner in which it is made, are considered, and the resorting to arms, vindicated. [*anon.*] 72 pp. 12°. *Hartford, Ebenezer Watson,* 1775.
[Imperfect].

——— The same.
[HAZARD pamphlets, v. 30].

——— The same.
[WOLCOTT pamphlets, v. 67].

American (The) agriculturist. [A monthly magazine] for the farm, garden, and household. Jan. to Dec. 1871. v. 30. 4°. *New York, O. Judd & co.* [1871].

——— The same. Der amerikanische agriculturist, gewidmet der belehrung aller klassen, welche in der bodencultur betheiligt sind, darin begriffen den farmer, gärtner, etc. Januar 1865 bis Dezember 1871. v. 24-30. 4°. *New York, O. Judd & co.* [1865-70].

——— Catalogue of rural books. Jan. 1870. 18 l. 4°. *New York, O. Judd & co.* [1870].
[*With* AMERICAN agriculturist, v. 29.]

American artisan and patent record: a weekly journal of arts, mechanics, manufactures, mining, engineering and chemistry, and repertory of patents. July 10, 1867, to Dec. 30, 1868. New series. v. 5-7. 4°. *New York, Brown, Coombs & co.* [1867-68]

——— The same. American artisan. A weekly journal of arts, mechanics, manufactures, engineering, chemistry, inventions, and patents. July 7, 1869, to Dec. 27, 1871. New series, v. 9-13. 4°. *New York, Brown, Coombs & co.* [1869-71].

American (The) bee journal. [Monthly]. Edited by Samuel Wagner. July, 1870, to June, 1871. v. 6. 8°. *Washington, S. Wagner,* 1871.

American (The) bibliopolist. [Monthly]. Jan. 1869, to Dec. 1871. v. 1-3. 8°. *New York, J. Sabin & sons,* 1869-71.

American (The) booksellers' guide. Monthly. Nov. 1, 1868, to Dec. 1, 1871. v. 1-3. 8°. *New York, American news co.* 1868-71.

American (The) cardinal. [*anon.*] 315 pp. 12°. *New York, Dodd & Mead,* 1871.

American (The) card-player: containing directions for euchre, whist, bezique, all-fours, pitch, commercial pitch, french fours, all fives, cassino, cribbage, straight and draw poker, and whiskey poker. [*anon.*] 151 pp. 16°. *New York, Dick & Fitzgerald,* [1866].

American (The) celt. A weekly journal of news, literature, and politics. Aug. 13, 1870, to June 17, 1871. v. 1-2. fol. *New York, M. J. Heffernan,* 1870-71.
[*Successor of* THE EMERALD. v. 2, incomplete: wanting, nos. 45-52].

American eclectic medical review. [Monthly]. Editors, R. S. Newton, m. d. P. A. Morrow, m. d. and A. Wilder, m. d. July, 1870, to June, 1871. v. 6. 8°. *New York, Russell's american steam-printing house,* 1870-71.

American educational monthly, devoted to popular instruction and literature. Jan. 1864, to Dec. 1871. v. 1-8. 8°. *New York, Schermerhorn, Bancroft & co.* 1864-71.

American (The) entomologist: an illustrated [monthly] magazine of popular and practical entomology. Edited by Benj. D. Walsh and Charles V. Riley. Sept. 1868, to Aug. 1869. v. 1. 8°. *St. Louis, R. P. Studley & co.* 1868. s.

——— The same. The american entomologist and botanist: an illustrated [monthly] magazine of popular and practical entomology and botany. Edited by Charles V. Riley and dr. George Vasey. Sept. 1869, to Dec. 1870. v. 2. 8°. *St. Louis, R. P. Studley & co.* 1870. s.
[Publication suspended].

American (The) ephemeris and nautical almanac for 1874. *See* **United States.** (*Navy department*).

American (The) exchange and review. A [monthly] miscellany of useful knowledge and general literature. Especially devoted to finance, mining and metallurgy, insurance, [etc.] Sept. 1870, to Feb. 1872. v. 18-20. 8°. *Philadelphia, Fowler & Moon, and Review publishing and printing co.* 1870-72.

American (The) farmer. [A weekly magazine] containing original essays and selections on agriculture, horticulture, rural and domestic economy, and internal improvements; with illustrative engravings and the

American (The) farmer—continued. prices of country produce. John S. Skinner, editor. March 23, 1827, to March 14, 1828. v. 9. 4°. *Baltimore, J. D. Toy*, 1827 [-28].

American homœopathic observer. *See* **American** observer.

American institute of architects. Incorporated, 1857. Proceedings of the third annual convention, held in New York, November 16 and 17, 1869. 4°. *New York, Western & co.* 1870.

American (The) journal of horticulture. *See* **Tilton's** journal of horticulture.

American (The) journal of medical sciences. [Quarterly]. Edited by Isaac Hayes, m. d. Jan. 1871, to April, 1872. New series. v. 61–63. 8°. *Philadelphia, H. C. Lea*, 1871–72.

American journal of numismatics, and bulletin of the American numismatic and archæological society. [Monthly]. May, 1868, to April, 1870. v. 3-4 in 1 v. 8°. *New York, American numismatic and archæological society*, [1868–70].

[*Note.*—Index to v. 1-4 in v. 4].

American (The) journal of science and arts. [Monthly]. Editors, James D. Dana and B. Silliman, [and others]. Jan. to Dec. 1871. 3rd series, v. 1–2. [Complete series], v. 101–102. 8°. *New Haven, editors*, 1871.

American (The) journal of syphilography and dermatology. [Quarterly]. Devoted to the consideration and treatment of venereal and skin diseases. Edited by M. H. Henry, m. d. Jan. 1870, to Oct. 1871. v. 1–2. 8°. *New York, F. W. Christern*, 1870–71. s.

American juvenile biography. The life of Christopher Columbus, the discoverer of America. [*anon.*] 233 pp. 1 pl. 16°. *Boston, B. H. Greene*, 1840.

——— The lives of Hernando Cortes, the discoverer of Mexico, and Francisco Pizarro, the conqueror of Peru. [*anon.*] 2 v. in 1. 194 pp. 2 pl. 16°. *Boston, B. H. Greene*, 1840.

American (The) life assurance magazine and journal of actuaries. [Quarterly]. Edited by G. E. Currie. July, 1862, to April, 1863, and Jan. 1870, to Dec. 1871. v. 4 and 11–12. 8°. *New York, G. E. Currie*, 1863–71.

American literary gazette and publishers' circular. [Semi-monthly]. Nov. 1, 1870, to Oct. 16, 1871. v. 16–17. 8°. *Philadelphia, G. W. Childs*, [1870–71].

American Lloyd's register, approved June 13, 1857. American and foreign shipping and

American Lloyd's register—continued. record of signal numbers, 1871. Compiled by Richard T. Hartshorne and John F. King. obl. 4°. *New York, board of american Lloyd's*, 1871.

——— The same, for 1872. obl. 4°. *New York, J. W. Pratt*, 1872.

——— The same. Appendix to the register of 1871, and supplement no. 10 to register of 1870, and supplement no. 1 to register of 1871. obl. 4°. [*New York*, 1871].

American (The) naturalist, an illustrated [monthly] magazine of natural history. Edited by A. S. Packard, jr. and F. W. Putnam. March, 1870, to Dec. 1871. v. 4-5. 8°. *Salem, (Mass.) Peabody academy of science*, 1870–71.

American normal school *and* National teachers' associations. Addresses and journal of proceedings of the American normal school and National teachers' associations at Cleveland, Ohio. Sessions of the year 1870. By authority of the publication committees. 222 pp. 8°. *Washington, J. H. Holmes*, 1871.

American observer; a monthly journal devoted to the dissemination of homœopathy, "the medicine of experience." Edwin A. Lodge, m. d. general editor. Jan. to Dec. 1871. v. 8. 8°. *Detroit, E. A. Lodge*, 1871.

American (The) orator: a manual of extemporaneous eloquence, including a course of discipline for the faculties of discrimination, arrangement, and oral discussion; and also practical exercises in reading, recitation, and declamatory debate. 288 pp. 6 pl. 18°. *Philadelphia, T. E. Zell*, 1871.

American (The) orator's own book. [*anon.*] Eng. title, xvi, 328 pp. 1 portrait. 18°. *Philadelphia, J. Kay, jr. & brother*, 1836.

American (The) philosophical society. *See* **Philadelphia.** *American philosophical society.*

American (The) poetical miscellany. Original and selected. 304 pp. 16°. *Philadelphia, R. Johnson*, 1809.

American (The) polytechnic journal; a new monthly periodical, devoted to science, mechanic arts, and agriculture. Conducted by Prof. Charles G. Page, m. d. J. J. Greenough, [and] Charles L. Fleischman. January to Dec. 1853. v. 1–2. 8°. *Washington*, 1853.

——— The same. v. 3. Greenough's American polytechnic journal; [etc.] Conducted by

American (The) polytechnic journal—continued. J. J. Greenough, m. d. [and] prof. Charles G. Page. January to June, 1854. v. 3. 8°. *New York, J. J. Greenough*, 1854.

American (The) psychological journal, devoted chiefly to the elucidation of mental pathology, and the medical jurisprudence of insanity. Conducted by Edward Mead, m. d. vol. 1, no. 1. January and March, 1853. 64 pp. 8°. *Cincinnati, Hygeia press*, 1852.

American (The) publisher. [Monthly]. Orion Clemens, editor. April, 1871, to March, 1872. v. i. fol. *Hartford, [American publishing co.* 1871–72].

American publisher and bookseller. A record of american and foreign literature. Monthly. May to Dec. 1868. Whole no. 6–13. Octavo series, nos. 1–8, in 1 v. 8°. *New York, G. R. Cathcart*, [1868].

American (The) quarterly observer. [Conducted by B. B. Edwards]. Jan. to Oct. 1834. v. 2–3. 8°. *Boston, Perkins & Marvin*, 1834.

American (The) racing record and turf guide, for 1871 and for 1872. Edited and published by W. G. Dorling. 2 v. 16°. *New York*, 1871–72.

American railroad journal. Steam navigation, commerce, finance, engineering, banking, mining, manufactures. John H. Schultz, editor. [A weekly magazine]. Jan. 7 to Dec. 30, 1871. Second quarto series, v. 27; or [complete series] v. 44. 4°. *New York, J. H. Schultz*, 1871.

American shipmaster's association. Record of American and foreign shipping, from surveys made and compiled with the sanction of the New York board of underwriters, to provide a standard american classification of vessels. 20 p. l. 656, 52 pp. 4°. *New York*, 1871.

——— The same. 20 p. l. 709, [2 l.] 53 pp. 4°. *New York*, 1872.

——— Rules for the construction and classification of iron vessels. 18 pp. 4°. [*New York*, 1871].

American society. Fashions, society, music, [etc. A weekly journal]. May 13 to 27, 1871. v. 1, nos. 1–3. fol. *New York*, 1871.

American turf register. *See* **Bruce** (S. D.) *and* **Carvalho** (E. N.)

Americo de Figueiredo e Melho (Pedro). Discurso academico proferido em presença de sua magestade o imperador no dia 22 de março de 1870. Por occasião da abertura do curso de esthetica professado pela primeira vez no Brasil. 19 pp 4°. *Rio de Janeiro, typographia nacional*, 1870.

Americus (*pseudon.*) A "new departure" for all parties. The mission of America. Is it prophecy? 96 pp. 8°. *Montgomery* (*Ala.*) 1872.

Amerikaan (De); blyspel. Gevolgd naar het Fransche. [*anon.*] 5 p. l. 80 pp. 16°. *Amsteldam, I. Duim*, 1733.

[DRAMATIC pamphlets, v. 1].

Amersham. *See* **Amundesham.**

Ames (Fisher). Speeches in congress, 1789–1796. Edited by Pelham W. Ames. 166 pp. 8°. *Boston, Little, Brown & co.* 1871.

Ames (*Mrs.* Mary Clemmer). Eirene; or, a woman's right. 2 p. l. 219 pp. 8°. *New York, G. P. Putnam & sons*, 1871.

Ames (William, *d. d.*) Bellarminvs enervatvs a Gvilielmo Amesio. Ed. nova ab auctore recognita et multis in locis aucta. 4 v. 24°. *Amstelodami, apud I. Ianssonium*, 1630.

——— Guiljelmi Amesij de conscientia, et eivs ivre, vel casibvs libri qvinqve. [Ed. 1ª.] Eng. title, 5 p. l. 432 pp. 11 l. 24°. *Amstelodami, apud I. Ianssonium*, 1631.

Amherst college. Opening of Walker hall, Amherst college, Amherst, Mass. Oct. 20, 1870. Address by W. A. Stearns, president, with other exercises. 77 pp. 8°. *Boston, Rand, Avery & Frye*, 1871.

Amici (Giovanni Battista). Collezione di alcune memorie e lettere del sig. ingegnere G. Amici. 11 memoirs in 1 v. 2 p. l. [196] pp. [11] pl. 4°. *Modena*, 1825.

[*Note.*—Academical memoirs separately reprinted and united by the author].

Amicus curiæ (*pseudon.*) *See* **Collier** (John Payne).

Amiot *or* **Amyot** (Joseph Marie). Abrégé historique des principaux traits de la vie de Confucius. Orné de 24 estampes in 4°, gravées par Helman, d'après des dessins originaux de la Chine envoyés à Paris par m. Amiot. 1 p. l. 24 l. 24 pl. 4°. *Paris, l'auteur*, [*about* 1790].

——— Lettre de Pékin, sur le génie de la langue chinoise, et la nature de leur écriture symbolique, comparée avec celle des anciens Égyptiens; on y a joint l'extrait de deux ouvrages nouveaux de mr. de Guignes, relatifs aux mêmes matières. Par un père de le

Amiot *or* **Amyot** (Joseph Marie)—continued. compagnie de Jésus, missionnaire à Pékin. [*anon.*] xxxviii, 50 pp. 3 l. 27 pl. 4°. *Bruxelles, J. L. de Boubers*, 1773.

[*Note.*—Prefixed is "Avis préliminaire par mr. Needham," that is John Forberville Needham, a Roman catholic divine, then resident at Brussels].

Ammirato (Scipione). Istorie fiorentine [sino all' ann. 1574]. Con l'aggivnti di Scipione Ammirato il giovane [Cristoforo Bianchi]. Con la tauola in fine delle cose più notabili. 2 v. in 3. 4 p. l. 1188 pp. 1 l; 4 p. l. 563 pp. 18 l. fol. *Firenze, Amador Massi*, 1641-47.

[*Note.*—This is the second edition of part first, which had been already printed in 1600. A private 2d ed. of part second was also printed, 53 lines on a page; but this is the legitimate issue, having 48 lines, like the other volumes].

——— The same. 2 parts in 11 v. 8°. *Firenze, L. Marchini & G. Becherini*, 1824-27.

[*Note.*—At the end of v. 11 is a Vita di Scipione Ammirato il seniore, del A. F. D. S.]

Amner (Richard). Considerations on the doctrines of a future state, and the resurrection, as revealed, or supposed to be so, in the scriptures: on the inspiration and authority of scripture itself; on some peculiarities in st. Paul's epistles: on the prophecies of Daniel and st. John, etc. [Also], some strictures on the prophecies of Isaiah. 3 p. l. 312 pp. 8°. *London, J. Johnson*, 1797.

Among the Alps. [*anon.*] 364 pp. 7 pl. 16°. *New York, American tract society*, [1871].

Amoretti (Carlo). Viaggio da Milano ai tre laghi Maggiore, di Lugano, e di Como, e ne' monti che li circondano. 6ª ed. corretta e corredata di antichi monumenti e della vita dell' autore, dal dottor Giovanni Labus. xl, 374 pp. 1 portrait. 16°. *Milano, G. Silvestri*, 1824.

Amoros y Ondeano (Francisco). Manuel d'éducation physique, gymnastique et morale. 2 v. 2 p. l. xvii, 488 pp; 2 p. l. 528 pp. 18°. *Paris, Roret*, 1834.

Amort (Eusebius). De revelationibus, visionibus et apparitionibus privatis regulæ tutæ ex scriptura, conciliis, ss. patribus, aliisque optimis authoribus collectæ, explicatæ et exemplis illustratæ. 8 p. l. 284, 588 pp. incl. 4 tab. 4°. *Augustæ Vindelicorum, sumptibus M. Veith*, 1744.

Amos (Andrew, *editor*). Gems of latin poetry, with translations by various authors; to which are added notes and illustrations. [Eng. and lat.] xxiii, 368 pp. 8° *Cambridge*, [*Eng.*] *J. Deighton*, 1851.

Amos (Sheldon). Difference of sex as a topic of jurisprudence and legislation. 43 pp. 8°. *London, Longmans, Green & co.* 1870.

Ampel en breed verhaal van de jongst-gewesene aardbevinge tot Port-Royal in Jamaica, op den $\frac{7}{17}$ Juny 1692. In twee brieven van den predikant der selver stad geschreven. [*anon.*] 8 pp. sm. 4°. *Rotterdam, B. Bos*, 1692.

[*Note.*—Another translation from the english of the same letters will be found under the title NAAUWKEURIG verhaal van de aardbeving. *Amsterdam*, 1692].

Ampelius (Lucius). Lucii Ampelii liber memorialis. 8°. [*Biponti, ex typographia societatis*, 1783].

[*In* FLORUS (Annæus). Epitome rerum romanarum, 1783, pp. 153-200].

Ampère (Jean Jacques Antoine). Histoire littéraire de la France avant le douzième siècle. 3 v. 8°. *Paris, L. Hachette*, 1839-40.

——— Histoire littéraire de la France sous Charlemagne et durant le xᵉ et xiᵉ siècle. 2ᵉ éd. 2 p. l. 468 pp. 8°. *Paris, Didier & cie.* 1868.

Ampzing (Samuel). West-Indische trivmphbasvyne, tot Godes ere ende roem der Batavieren gesteken, van wegen de veroveringe der Spaensche silver-vlote van Nova Hispania, inde baij van Matanca, door der schepen vande geoctroijeerde West-Indische compagnie, onder P. P. Heyn, generael, ende H. K. Lonk, admirael, geschied den 8. Sept. 1628. 6 p. l. 44 pp. sm. 4°. *Haerlem, A. Rooman*, 1629.

Amsterdam (*City of*). Conditien, die door de heeren bvrgermeesteren der stadt Amstelredam, volgens't gemaeckte accoordt met de West-Indische compagnie, ende d' approbatie van de staaten generael der Vereenighde Nederlanden daer op gevolght, gepresenteert werden aen alle de gene, die als colonier na Nieuw-Nederlandt willen vertrecken, etc. 7 l. sm. 4°. *Amsterdam, J. Banning*, 1656.

——— The same. 7 l. sm. 4°. *Amsterdam, weduwe van J. Banning*, 1659.

——— Copye vande resolutie van de heeren burgemeesters ende raden tot Amsterdam. Op't stuck vande West-Indische compagnie. Genomen in August 1649. 8 l. sm. 4°. [*Amsterdam*, 1649].

——— The same. 10 l. sm. 4°. *Uytrecht, I. Havick*, 1649.

Amsterdams dam-praetje, van wat outs en wat nieuws. En wat vreemts. [*anon.*] 20 l. sm. 4°. *Amsterdam, I. van Soest*, 1649.

Amsterdams tafel-praetje, van wat goets en wat quaets en wat noodichs. [*anon.*] *b. l.* 16 l. sm. 4°. *Gouda, I. Cornelisz*, 1649.

Amunátegui (Miguel Luis). Descubrimiento i conquista de Chile. viii, 534 pp. 8°. *Santiago, imprenta chilena*, 1862. s.

Amundesham *or* **Amersham** (John). Chronica monasterii s. Albani. Annales monasterii s. Albani, a Johanne Amundesham, monacho, ut videtur, conscripti, (a. d. 1421-1440). Quibus præfigitur chronicon rerum gestarum in monasterio s. Albani, (a. d. 1422-1431), a quodam auctore ignoto compilatum. Edited by Henry Thomas Riley. 2 v. 458 pp; 4, lxxvii, 498 pp. fac-sim. 8°. *London, Longman & co.* 1870-71.

[GREAT BRITAIN. *Master of the rolls.* Chronicles and memorials of Great Britain].

Amussat (Jean Zuléma). Amussat's lessons on retention of urine, caused by strictures of the urethra, and on the diseases of the prostate. Edited by A. Petit, (de l'isle de Re). Translated from the french by James P. Jervey, m. d. With notes. 3 p. l. 246 pp. iv pp. 4 pl. 12°. *Charleston, (S. C.) D. J. Dowling*, 1836.

Amyot (Joseph Marie). *See* **Amiot.**

Anacreon. Ανακρεοντος Τηϊου μελη. Anacreontis Teij odæ. Ab Henrico Stephano luce & latinitate nunc primum donatæ. 4 p. l. 110 pp. sm. 4°. *Lvtetiæ, apud Henricum Stephanum*, 1554.

[*Note.*—The fifty-five odes, here placed under the name of Anacreon, and first published by Henry Stephens, from manuscripts which no one else has seen (it is agreed among all modern critics), are not the work of Anacreon of Teos.—LEONHARD SCHMITZ].

——— The same. Carmina græce e recensione Gvlielmi Baxteri, cvm eivsdem Henr. Stephani et Tanegvidi Fabri notis. Accedvnt dvo Sapphvs odaria, atqve Theocriti anacreonticvm in mortvvm Adonin, cvravit Ioh. Frid. Fischervs. 17 p. l. 232 pp. 2 l. 1 portrait. 16°. *Lipsiæ, I. G. Mvller*, 1764.

——— The same. The odes of Anacreon, with the fragments of Sappho and Alcæus. 8°. [*London, Payne & Foss*, 1827].

[*In* TAYLOR (John). Poems on various subjects. 1827. pp. 259-308].

Anadol; the last home of the faithful. By the author of "The frontier lands of the christian and the Turk." [*anon.*] ii, 361 pp. 8°. *London, R. Bentley*, 1853.

Anales de la mineria mexicana, o sea: revista de minas, metalurgica mecanica, y de las ciencias de aplicacion a la mineria. Publicada por los antiguos profesores de la escuela practica de minas y a espensas del gobierno del Guanajuato. v. 1. 324 pp. 1 map, 8 pl. 12 tab. 8°. *Mexico, I. Cumplido*, 1861.

Analysis (An) of the talents and character of Napoleon Bonaparte; by a general officer. [*anon.*] xxix, 238 pp. 1 portrait. 8°. *London, W. Sams*, 1821.

Anania (Giovanni Lorenzo). De natvra dæmonvm. 12 p. l. 244 [144] l. numb. 18°. *Neapoli, apud I. B. Cappellum*, 1582.

Ancelot (Jacques Arsène François Polycarpe). Œuvres complètes de m. Ancelot, précédées d'une notice sur sa vie et ses ouvrages, par m. X. B. Saintine. xv, 672 pp. 1 l. 8°. *Paris, H. Delloye et V. Lecou*, 1838.

CONTENTS.

Louis IX, tragédie.
Le maire du palais, tragédie.
Fiesque, tragédie.
L'important, comédie.
Olga, tragédie.
Elisabeth, tragédie.
Un mariage d'amour, comédie.
Le roi fainéant, tragédie.
Lord Byron à Venise, drama.
Leontini, drama.
L'escroc du grand monde.
Marie de Brabant, poëme.
Épîtres.
Le chant de bataille de Lutzen, poëme
La montaigne des moineaux.
Six mois en Russie.
L'homme du monde.

Ancient devotional poetry. Now first published from a manuscript of the xvith or xviith century. [*anon.* Edited by George Stokes]. 75 l. sm. 4°. *London, religious tract society*, 1846.

Ancient Edom; and the fulfilment of prophecy in the present state of Arabia Petrea. [*anon.*] 139 pp. 7 pl. 2 maps. 18°. *Philadelphia, American sunday-school union*, [1839].

Ancient hymns of holy church. [*anon.* Dedication subscribed J. W.] 128 pp. 32°. *Hartford, Henry S. Parsons*, 1845.

Ancora (Gaetano d'). Guide du voyageur pour les antiquités, et curiosités naturelles de Pouzol, et des environs. [*anon.*] Traduit de l'italien par A. Barles de Manville. Eng. title, vi, 142 pp. 52 pl. 8°. *Naples, Zambraia*, 1792.

Ancourt (—— *abbé* d'). The lady's preceptor. Or, a letter to a young lady of distinction upon politeness. Taken from the french, and adapted to the religion, customs, and manners of the english nation. By a gentleman

Ancourt (—— *abbé* d')—continued. of Cambridge. [*anon.*] 4 p. l. 69 pp. 8°. *London, J. Watts*, 1743.

Anderde discovrs, by forma van messieve. Daer in kortelijck ende grondich verthoondt wort, de nootwendicheyt der Oost ende West Indische navigatie, oock met goede fondamentale redenen bewesen, dat door geen ander middel eenen vasten versekerden vrede en is te verwachten of te verhopen. [*anon.*] 12 l. sm. 4°. [*Amsterdam*]? 1622.

Andersen (Hans Christian). The ice-maiden: and other tales. Translated from the german, by Fanny Fuller. 189 pp. 18°. *Philadelphia, F. Leypoldt*, 1863.

—— Pictures of travel in Sweden, among the Hartz mountains, and in Switzerland, with a visit at Charles Dickens's house. Author's edition. vii, 293 pp. 12°. *New York, Hurd & Houghton*, 1871.

—— Stories and tales. Author's ed. xix, 532 pp. 19 pl. 12°. *New York, Hurd & Houghton*, 1871.

—— The story of my life. Now first translated into english, containing chapters additional to those published in the danish edition, bringing the narrative down to the Odense festival of 1867. Author's ed. 569 pp. 1 portrait. 12°. *New York, Hurd & Houghton*, 1871.

Andersen-Feldborg (J. Andreas). Poems from the danish. Selected and illustrated with historical notes. Translated into english verse, by William Sidney Walker. xvi, 9–174 pp. 16°. *London, Carpenter & son*, 1815.

Anderson (John J.) The historical reader, embracing selections from standard writers of ancient and modern history, interspersed with illustrative passages from british and american poets; with explanatory observations, notes, etc: to which are added a vocabulary of difficult words, and biographical and geographical indexes. 544 pp. 12°. *New York, Clark & Maynard*, 1871.

—— A pictorial school history of the United States; to which are added the declaration of independence and the constitution of the United States, with questions and explanations. 313, 38 pp. 1 pl. 12°. *New York, Clark & Maynard*, 1864.

—— The same. 363, 38 pp. 12°. *New York, Clark & Maynard*, 1867.

—— The same. 1 p. l. 364, 40 pp. 6 maps. 12°. *New York, Clark & Maynard*, 1871.

Anderson (John J.)—continued.

—— The same. 2 p. l. 380, 40 pp. 6 maps. 12°. *New York, Clark & Maynard*, 1872.

—— The United States reader, with explanatory observations, notes, etc. The whole arranged so as to form a complete class-manual of United States history. 1 p. l. 414 pp. 4 maps. 12°. *New York, Clark & Maynard*, 1872.

Anderson (J.) *and* **Howard** (S. B.) The social harp: containing a rich variety of scriptural songs, for the use of christians in their house of pilgrimage, adapted to all occasions & seasons. Compiled from various sources. 383 pp. 32°. *Louisville, Hull & brother*, 1854.

Andilly. *See* **Arnauld** d'Andilly.

Andover (*Mass.*) theological seminary. Triennial catalogue. 1870. 8°. *Andover, W. F. Draper*, 1870.

—— *Society of inquiry.* Memoirs of american missionaries, formerly connected with the society of inquiry respecting missions, in the Andover theological seminary: embracing a history of the society, etc. With an introductory essay by Leonard Woods, d. d. Published under the direction of the society. 367 pp. 1 pl. 12°. *Boston, Peirce & Parker*, 1833.

Andreas *ratisbonensis* (Joannes). Chronica de principibvs terræ Bavarorvm. fol. [*Argentorati, J. R. Dulssecker*, 1702].

[*In* Kulpis (Johann Georg von). Scriptores rervm germanicarvm. *Argentorati*, 1702. [Part 2]. pp. 1–98].

Andrelini (Publio Fausto). Epistolæ prouerbiales et morales longe lepidissime, nec minus sententiosæ: nuper a vicijs purgatæ. Quibus superaddite sunt recenter septem aliæ, ex farragine noua epistolarum Des. Erasmi excerptæ. [Ed. nova.] 19 l. 12°. *Parisiis, ex officina Prigentij Caluarini*, 1538.

Andres (Juan, *abâte*). Dell' origine, de' progressi e dello stato attuale d'ogni letteratura. Ed. prima venéta. 22 v. 8°. *Venezia, G. Vitto*, 1783–1800.

CONTENTS.

v. 1–3. Parte prima che contiene un generale prospetto della letteratura nelle diverse sue epoche.
4–9. Parte seconda che contiene le belle lettere.
10–12. Parte prima che contiene le scienze naturali.
13–16. Parte seconda che contiene le scienze naturali.
17–19. Parte prima delle scienze ecclesiastiche.
20–21. Parte seconda delle scienze ecclesiastiche.
22. Indice generale.

Andres de Uztarroz (Juan Francisco). Vida de san Orencio, obispo de Avx. 18 p. l. 233 pp. 4 l. 4°. *Zaragoça, P. Lanaja i Lamarca*, 1648.

Andrews (Eben A.) Ruth, the Moabitess. A sacred cantata, designed for musical conventions and festivals. 96 pp. obl. 8°. *St. Louis, author*, 1871.

Andrews (*Rev.* Emerson). Revival songs: a new collection of hymns and spiritual songs for closet and family worship, prayer, conference, revival, and protracted meetings. 172 pp. 16°. *Boston, J. H. Earle*, 1870.

——— Travels in bible lands: Italy, Egypt, Greece, Asia Minor, Syria, and Palestine. 192 pp. 2 pl. 1 portrait. 16°. *Boston, J. H. Earle*, 1872.

——— Youth's picture sermons for sunday schools and families. 124 pp. 1 portrait. 16°. *Boston, J. H. Earle*, 1871.

Andrews (E. B.) Report of labors in the second geological district [of Ohio], during the year 1870. 8°. [*Columbus*, 1871].

[OHIO (*State of*). Geological survey, 1870. Part 2, pp. 55–242].

Andrews (J. R.) Life of Oliver Cromwell to the death of Charles the first. xv, 426 pp. 8°. *London, Longmans, Green & co.* 1870.

Andrews (Stephen Pearl). The basic outline of universology. An introduction to the newly discovered science of the universe; its elementary principles; and the first stages of their development in the special sciences. Together with preliminary notices of alwato (*ahl-wah-to*), the newly discovered scientific universal language, resulting from the principles of universology. cxix, 764 pp. 8°. *New York, D. Thomas*, 1872.

——— Love, marriage, and divorce, and the sovereignty of the individual. A discussion by Henry James, Horace Greeley, and Stephen Pearl Andrews: including the final replies of mr. Andrews, rejected by the Tribune. Edited by Stephen Pearl Andrews. 103 pp. 12°. *New York, Stringer & Townsend*, 1853.

——— The primary synopsis of universology and alwato, the new scientific universal language. xviii, 224 pp. 12°. *New York, D. Thomas*, 1871.

Andrews (William S.) A treatise upon theological subjects, containing an exposition and defence of the great doctrines of natural and revealed religion; together with several prayers, written in conformity with the spirit of this work. viii, 202 pp. 12°. *Cambridge, (Mass.) Hilliard & Brown*, 1829.

Anecdotes of the american Indians. By the author of "Evenings in Boston," [etc. *anon.*] 252 pp. 16°. *New York, A. V. Blake*, 1844.

Anecdotes dramatiques. *See* **Laporte** (Clément *et l'abbé* Joseph de).

Anicetus (*pseudon.*) *See* **Clark** (William Adolphus).

Anichini (P.) A few remarks on the present laws of marriage, adultery, and seduction, in England. 2d ed. with considerable additions. xxix, 64 pp. 8°. *London, author*, 1836.

Annales de chimie et de physique, par mm. Chevreul, Dumas, Boussingault, Regnault et Wurtz, avec la collaboration de M. Bertin. [Mensuele]. Janv. 1865 jusqu'à déc. 1870. 4e série, v. 4–21. 8°. *Paris, V. Masson et fils*, 1865–70.

Annales de gestis Caroli Magni poetæ anonymi. fol. [*Argentorati, J. R. Dulssecker*, 1702].

[*In* KULPIS (Johann Georg von). Scriptores rervm germanicarvm. *Argentorati*, 1702. pp. 1–44].

Annales des voyages, de la géographie, de l'histoire et de l'archéologie, dirigées par M. V. A. Malte-Brun. [Mensuele]. Janv. 1869 jusqu'à sept. 1870. 7 v. 8°. *Paris*, 1869–70.

Annals of virgin saints. By a priest of the church of England. [*anon.*] xliii, 416 pp. 1 tab. 16°. *London, J. Masters*, 1846.

Annan (William). The difficulties of arminian methodism; embracing strictures on the writings of Wesley, drs. Clarke, Fisk, Bangs, and others, in a series of letters addressed to rev. * * * *. 2d ed. revised and enlarged. 196 pp. 18°. *Pittsburgh, D. M. Hogan & co.* 1836.

——— The same. Letters addressed to bishop Simpson, of Pittsburgh. 5th ed. 336 pp. 12°. *Philadelphia, W. S. & A. Martien*, 1861.

——— Letters on psalmody: a review of the leading arguments for the exclusive use of the book of psalms. 216 pp. 16°. *Philadelphia, W. S. & A. Martien*, 1859.

Annesley (*Miss* M.) Light in the valley; or, the life and letters of mrs. Hannah Bocking. 176 pp. 1 portrait. 18°. *New York, Carlton & Porter*, [1860].

Annuaire de l'économie politique et de statistique, par mm. Guillaumin, Joseph Garnier, Mce. Block, etc. 27e année. 1870. 18°. *Paris, Guillaumin & cie.* 1870.

Annual (The) illustrated catalogue and oarsman's manual, for 1871. 2 p. l. iii, 494 pp. 12 pl. 4°. *Troy (N. Y.) Waters, Balch & co* 1871.

Anspach (Elizabeth Fitzhardinge, *margravine of*). A journey through the Crimea to Constantinople. In a series of letters from Elizabeth lady Craven, to the margrave of Brandebourg, Anspach, and Bareith. Written in the year 1786. 4 p. l. 328 pp. 7 pl. 4°. *London, G. G. J. and J. Robinson*, 1789.

Anstice (Joseph). Selections from the choric poetry of the greek dramatic writers. Translated into english verse. 1 p. l. 246 pp. 8°. *London, B. Fellowes*, 1832.

Anstie (Francis E. *m. d.*) On the uses of wines in health and disease. 84 pp. 12°. *New York, J. S. Redfield*, 1870.

Answer (An) of the elders of the severall churches in New-England. *See* **Davenport** (*Rev.* John).

Answer (An) to the queries on the proprietary government of Maryland, inserted in the Public ledger. Also, an answer to remarks upon a message sent by the upper to the lower house of assembly of Maryland. [*anon.*] 1 p. l. 160 pp. 8°. [*n. p.*] 1764.
[MISCELLANEOUS pamphlets, v. 212].

Ante-nicene christian library. Translations of the writings of the fathers down to a. d. 325. Edited by the rev. Alexander Roberts, d. d and James Donaldson, ll. d. v. 17–20. 8°. *Edinburgh, T. & T. Clark*, 1870–71.

CONTENTS.

ARCHELAUS *carcharensis.* Acts of disputation with Manes, v. 20.
ARNOBIUS *afer.* The seven books of Arnobius adversus gentes, v. 19.
CLEMENS *romanus.* The Clementine homilies, v. 17, part 1.
——— The apostolical constitutions, v. 17, part 2.
COMMODIANUS. Instructions in favour of christian discipline, v. 18.
DIONYSIUS *alexandrinus.* Works, v. 20.
GREGORIUS *thaumaturgus.* Writings, v. 20.
PRATTEN (*Rev.* B. P.) Syriac documents attributed to the first three centuries, v. 20.
TERTULLIANUS (Q. S. F.) Writings, vol. iii. v. 18.
VICTORINUS *petavionensis.* A fragment on the creation of the world, v. 18.
——— A commentary on the apocalypse of st. John, v. 18.

Antes (John). Observations on the manners and customs of the Egyptians, the overflowing of the Nile and its effects; with remarks on the plague, and other subjects. 139 pp. 1 map. 4°. *London, J. Stockdale*, 1800.

Anthologia persica. 1778. *See* **Stürmer** (Ignaz von).

Antimachus *colophonius.* Reliquiæ. Primum a Schellenbergio, iterum ab I. A. Giles, auctius editæ. vii, 136 pp. 1 l. 8°. *Londini, J. Bohn*, 1838.

Antonini (Annibale). Nuovo dizzionario italiano-tedesco e tedesco-italiano. Ora con singolar essatezza migliorato e tradotto in tedesco. Ed. 2ª. 2 v. in 1. 7 p. l. 1536 col. (on 384 l.) 1 pl; 1 p. l. 704 col. (on 176 l.) 8°. *Lipsia, C. Fritsch*, 1777.

Antwoordt, op sekeren brief Evlaly, vervatende de redenen waerom datmen met den vyandt in geen conferentie behoort te treden. Door wien, ende met wat ordre de selve voor den dagh gebracht ende versocht is. Ende eyntlijck dat den treves in alle manieren schadelijk voor 't landt is, etc. [*anon.*] 8 l. sm. 4°. [*Graven-Hage*] ? 1629.

——— The same. [Another ed.] 8 l. sm. 4°. [*Graven-Hage*] ? 1629.

Antwoort vanden ghetrouwen Hollander. Op den aenspraeck van den heetgebaeckerden Hollander. [*anon.*] *b. l.* 8 l. sm. 4°. [*n. p.*] 1645.

Antwoort-brief, van een onpartijdigh coopman uyt Zeelant, aen sijn vrient in Engelant geschreven, op 't gene den selven onlanckx wiert toegesenden, rakende de pretensien der engelsche, van de nederlantsche ingesetenen, ende besonderlick d' engelsche seer onrechtmatige bekent-makinge vol injurien, ende illatien, korts door den engelschen Mercurius Publicus [etc. *anon.*] 24 pp. sm. 4°. *Vlissinge, Simoen Simoensz*, 1662.

Apcher de Saint-Flour (—). Le Jéhovah de Moïse, ou la divinité méconnue; ouvrage philosophique. 408 pp. 8°. *Bordeaux, Lavigne jeune*, 1830.

Apianus (Petrus). *See* **Bienewitz** (Peter).

Apicius (Caelius, *pseudon.*) Caelii Apitii de cvlinariæ rei disciplina libri decem. [Appendicvla de conditvris variis, ex Ioanne Damasceno]. 16°. *Lvgdvni*, 1541.
[*In* THORER (Albanus). [Selecta]. pp. 10–105].

Apollinaris. *See* **Sidonius Apollinaris.**

Apollonius *rhodius.* The loves of Medea and Jason. A poem, in three books: translated from the greek of Apollonius Rhodius's Argonautics, by the rev. J. Ekins. 111 pp. 4°. *London, J. & H. Hughs*, 1771.

——— The same. L'expédition des Argonautes, ou la conquête de la toison d'or, traduit par J. J. A. Caussin. 12°. [*Paris, Lefevre*, 1841].
[*In* MARTIN (Louis Aimé). Petits poëmes grecs. *Paris*, 1841. pp. 169–325].

Apologie der illuminaten. *See* **Weishaupt** (Adam).

Apologie (An) of the chvrches in New-England for chvrch-covenant. *See* **Mather** (*Rev.* Richard).

Apology (An) for the writings of Walter Moyle, esq. *See* **Hammond** (Anthony).

Appeal to the men of Great Britain in behalf of women. [*anon.*] 6 p. l. vi, 300 pp. 8°. [*London*], *J. Johnson & J. Bell*, 1798.
[Imperfect: wanting, pp. 291-298].

Appeal (An) to the parliament; or, Sion's plea against the prelacie. *See* **Leighton** (*Rev.* Alexander).

Appleton (Daniel) and co. Appleton's european guide book illustrated. Containing a map of Europe, and nine other maps, with plans of 20 of the principal cities, and 120 engravings. [By Montgomery Gibbs]. 732 pp. 12 (blank) l. 3 maps (in cover), and 27 other maps. 12°. *New York, D. Appleton & co.* 1870.

——— Appleton's general atlas of the world, containing maps of various countries, and particularly of the United States, its divisions, and the separate states; with full geographical sketches. 99 pp. 26 maps. 4°. *New York, D. Appleton & co.* 1872

———Appleton's journal of literature, science, and art. [Weekly]. Jan. 7 to Dec. 31, 1871. v. 5-6. 8°. *New York, D. Appleton & co.* 1871.

——— Illustrated trade list of domestic and foreign stationery. 64 pp. 4°. *New York, D. Appleton & co.* 1869.

——— The same. Complete illustrated trade list of domestic and foreign stationery. 62 pp. 4°. *New York, D. Appleton & co.* 1871.

Appleton (Nathaniel, *d. d*) Faithful ministers of Christ, the salt of the earth, and the light of the world. Illustrated in a sermon preach'd before the ministers of the province of the Massachusetts-Bay, at their annual convention in Boston, May 26, 1743. 56 pp. 8°. *Boston, S. Eliot*, 1743.
[MISCELLANEOUS pamphlets, v. 366].

——— A faithful and wise servant, had in honour throughout the churches. A discourse occasioned by the death of the rev. Edward Wigglesworth, d. d. 40 pp. 8°. *Boston, R. & S. Draper*, 1765.

——— God, and not ministers, to have the glory of all success given to the preached gospel. Two discourses on the preaching of

Appleton (Nathaniel, *d. d.*)—continued.
rev. mr. Whitefield. 44 pp. 8°. *Boston, Rogers & Fowle, for S. Eliot*, 1741.

——— Gospel ministers must be fit for the master's use, illustrated in a sermon at Deerfield, August 31, 1735, at the ordination of mr. John Sargent. 1 p. l. xiv, 32 pp. 12°. *Edinburgh (Scotland), Davidson & Trail*, 1736.

——— The great apostle Paul exhibited, and recommended as a pattern of gospel preaching: in a sermon preach'd at Roxbury, Nov. 7, 1750, at the ordination of rev. Oliver Peabody, jun'r. 36 pp. sm. 4°. *Boston, J. Draper*, 1751.

——— How God wills the salvation of all men; and their coming to the knowledge of the truth, from 1 Tim. ii, 4, as the means thereof. Illustrated in a sermon preached in Boston, March 27, 1753, at the ordination of rev. mr. Stephen Badger. Appended, the charge by dr. [Joseph] Sewall, and the right hand of fellowship by rev. mr. [Hull] Abbot. 2 p. l. 34 pp. 8°. *Boston, S. Kneeland*, 1753.

——— A sermon preached Oct. 9, being a day of public thanksgiving, occasioned by the surrender of Montreal, and all Canada, Sept. 8th, 1760, to the british troops under general Amherst. 36 pp. 8°. *Boston, J. Draper*, 1760.

——— A thanksgiving sermon on the total repeal of the stamp act. Preached in Cambridge, May 20th, [1766]. 32 pp. 8°. *Boston, Edes & Gill*, 1766.

Apurva Krishna (*Maha Raja, bahadur*). The history of the conquerors of Hind, from the most early period to the present time: containing an account of the religion, government, usages, and character of the inhabitants of that kingdom. [Chap. 2d.] 1 p. l. pp. 40-72; pp. 75-144 in Hindostanee. 8°. *Calcutta, Bengal catholic orphan press*, 1847.

Aquila (Serafino dell'). *See* **Serafino** dell, Aquila.

Arabian days' entertainments. Translated from the german, by Herbert Pelham Curtis. [*anon.*] 434 pp. 16 pl. 12°. *Boston, Phillips, Sampson & co.* 1858.

Arana (Diego Barros). *See* **Barros Arana.**

Aratus. The phenomena and diosemeia, translated into english verse, with notes, by John Lamb, d.d. 2 p. l. 128 pp. 8°. *London, J. W. Parker*, 1848.

Araucano (El). [Tri-semanal]. 3 de oct. 1861 hasta 28 de dic. 1867. Año 31-37.

Araucano (El)—continued.
7 v. fol. *Santiago, (Chile), imprenta nacional,* [1861–67].

Arber (Edward). English reprints. v. 1–13. 16°. *London, A. Murray & son,* 1868–71.

CONTENTS.

ADDISON (J.) Criticism on Milton's "Paradise lost." 1711–12. no. 8, v. 3.
ASCHAM (R.) Toxophilus. 1545. no. 7, v. 3.
——— The schoolmaster. 1570. no. 23, v. 10.
BACON (F.) A harmony of the essays, etc. of F. Bacon. [1597–1625]. no. 27, v. 13.
EARLE (G.) Micro-cosmographie. 1628. no. 12, v. 5.
GASCOIGNE (G.) The steele glas. 1576. no. 11, v. 5.
GOSSON (S.) The schoole of abuse. 1579. no. 3, v. 1.
——— A short apologie of the schoole of abuse. 1579. no. 3, v. 1.
HABINGTON (W.) Castara. 1640. no. 22, v. 10.
HOWELL (J.) Instructions for forreine travell. 1642. no. 16, v. 8.
JAMES I. *of Eng.* The essayes of a prentise, in the divine art of poesie. 1585. no. 19, v. 8.
——— A counterblaste to tobacco. 1604. no. 19, v. 8.
LATIMER (H.) Seven sermons before Edward vi. 1549. no. 13, v 6.
——— Sermon on the ploughers. 1549. no. 2, v. 1.
LEVER (T.) Sermons. 1550. no. 25, v. 12.
LYLY (J.) Euphues. The anatomy of wit. 1579. no. 9, v. 4.
——— Euphues and his England. 1580. no. 9, v. 4.
MILTON (J.) Areopagitica. 1644. no. 1, v. 1.
MORE (T.) Utopia. 1516. no. 14, v. 6.
NAUNTON (*Sir* R.) Fragmenta regalia. 1653. no. 20, v. 9.
PUTTENHAM (G.) The arte of English poesie. 1589. no. 15, v. 7.
REVELATION to the monk of Evesham. 1196–1482? no. 18, v. 8.
SELDEN (J.) Table-talk. 1689. no. 6, v. 2.
SIDNEY (*Sir* P.) An apologie for poetrie. 1595. no. 4, v. 2.
TOTTEL'S (R.) miscellany. Songes and sonettes by H. Howard earl of Surrey, Sir T. Wyatt, the elder, N. Grinald, and uncertain authors. 1557. no. 24, v. 11.
UDALL (N.) Roister Doister. 1553–66? no. 17, v. 8.
VILLIERS (G.) The rehearsal. 1672. no. 10, v. 5.
WATSON (T.) The 'Εκατομπαθια or passionate centurie of love. 1582. no. 21 v,. 9.
——— Melibœus, sive ecloga inobitum, &c. An eglogue upon the death of sir Francis Walsingham. 1590. no. 21, v. 9.
——— The tears of fancie. Or loue disdained. 1593. no. 21, v. 9.
WEBBE (E.) His trauailes. 1590. no. 5, v. 2.
WEBBE (W.) A discourse of English poetrie. 1586. no. 26, v. 12.

Arbuthnot (John, *m. d.*) An essay concerning the nature of aliments, and the choice of them, according to the different constitutions of human bodies. In which the different effects, advantages, and disadvantages of animal and vegetable diet, are explain'd. 2d. ed. To which are added, practical rules of diet, in the various constitutions and diseases of human bodies. 12 p. l. 430 pp. 8°. *London, J. Tonson,* 1732.

Archelaus *cascharensis.* The acts of the disputation of Archelaus, bishop of Caschar in Mesopotamia, with the heresiarch Manes. 8°. *Edinburgh,* 1871.
[*In* ANTE-NICENE christian library, v. 20].

Archer (George W.) More than she could bear: a story of the Gachupin war in Texas, 1812–13. By Hesper Bendbow. [*pseudon*]. 339 pp. 12°. *Philadelphia, Claxton, Remsen & Haffelfinger,* 1872.

Archer (*Rev.* James.) Sermons on various moral and religious subjects, for all the sundays, and some of the principal festivals of the year. v. 1. viii, 407 pp. 16°. *London, author,* 1785.

Archimedes. The arenarius, translated from the greek, with notes and illustrations. To which is added the dissertation of Christopher Clavius on the same subject from the latin. xvi, 63 pp. 1 pl. 8°. *London, J. Johnson,* 1784.

——— Des unvergleichlichen Archimedis kunstbücher oder heutigs tags befindliche schrifften, aus dem griechischen in das hoch-teutsche übersetzt, und mit nohtwendigen anmerkungen durch und durch erläutert von Johanne Christophoro Sturmio. Eng. title. 11 p. l. 428 pp. 4 l. 32 pp. fol. *Nürnberg, in verlegung T. Fürstens.* 1670.
[*Note.*—The commentary of Eutocius is presented as anmerkungen].

CONTENTS.

Von der kugel und rund-säule, zwey bücher, p. 1.
Von der kreiss- und scheiben- messung, ein buch, p. 161.
Von derer flächen gleichwichtigkeit, zwey bücher, p. 193.
Von der parabel-vierung, ein buch, p. 281.
Von denen regel- und kugel- ähnlichen figuren, ein buch, p. 313.
Von dennen schnekken-lineen und flächen, ein buch, p. 381.
Von einer zahl, welche grösser ist als die zahl alles sandes, wormit die höhe des ganzen firmamentes könnte ausgefüllet werden. 1667. 4 p. l. 32 pp.

Archives de flore. Journal botanique, rédigé par F. Schultz. 1re partie. Déc. 1854–déc. 1855. 8°. *Wissembourg, chez le rédacteur,* [1854–55]. S.

Arena (Antoine d'). Antonivs Arena ad suos compagnones studiantes qui sunt de persona friantes, bassas dansas in gallanti stilo bisognatas: & de novo per ipsum correctas, & joliter augmentatas, cum guerra romana totum ad longum signe require: & cum guerra neapolitana: & cum revolta genuensi: & guerra avenionensi: & epistola ad falotissimam garsam pro passado lo tempus alagramentum mandat. 18°. [*Lvgd. Batav. ex typographia rediviva,* 1648].
[*In* OBSOPŒUS (Vincenz). De arte bibendi. 1648. pp. 193–260].

Arend (J. P.) Algemeene geschiedenis des vaterlands, van de vroegste tijden tot op heden. 2 v. in 5. 4°. *Amsterdam, J. F. Schleijer,* 1840–51.

Argelander (Friedrich Wilhelm August). *See* **Bonn.** *Universitäts-sternwarte.*

Argens (Jean Baptiste de Boyer, *marquis* d'). Lettres cabalistiques ou correspondance philosophique, historique & critique, entre deux cabalistes, divers esprits élémentaires, & le seigneur Astaroth. Nouv. éd. [troisième], augmentée de lxxx nouvelles lettres, de quantité de remarques, & de plusieurs figures. 6 v. in 3. 18°. *La Haye, P. Paupie*, 1741.

——— La philosophie du bon-sens, ou réflexions philosophiques sur l'incertitude des connoissances humaines. Nouv. éd. Corrigée & augmentée par l'auteur. Avec un examen critique des remarques de m. l'abbé d'Olivet, [sur la théologie des philosophes grecs]. 3 v. 18°. *La Haye, P. Paupie*, 1755.

Argentine republic. Boletin de la exposicion nacional en Córdoba. (Publicacion oficial). Director, d. Bartolomé Victory y Suarez. v. 2, no. 1. 195 pp. 2 charts. 8°. *Buenos Aires*, 1871.

Argosy (The). [A monthly magazine] edited by mrs. Henry Wood. Jan. to Dec. 1871. v. 11-12. 8°. *London, J. Ogden & co.* [1871].

Arguello (Manuel de). Sermon panegyrico, en la celebridad de la dedicacion del templo nuevo de San Bernardo, titvlo Maria de Gvadalupe; dia tercero de la octaua. sm. 4°. [*Mexico, viuda de F. R. Lupercio*, 1691].

[*In* Ramirez de Vargas (A.) Sagrado padron y panegyricos sermones, etc. l. 19-35].

Argus (Arabella, *pseudon.*) The juvenile spectator: being observations on the tempers, manners, and foibles of various young persons: interspersed with such lively matter as it is presumed will amuse as well as instruct. xi, 225 pp. 4 pl. 12°. *London, W. Darton*, 1823.

Argyll (*Duke of*). *See* **Campbell** (George Douglas).

Ariosto (Lodovico). Choix d'élégies de l'Arioste, traduites de l'Italien; par m. [Pierre] Le Tourneur. 2 p. l. 139 pp. 12°. *Paris, Ph. D. Pierres*, 1785.

——— Orlando fvrioso. Nuouamente adornato di figure di rame da Girolamo Porro, padouano. Eng. title, 2 p. l. 654 pp. (incl. 51 pl.) 16 l. unp. 44 l. numb. 4°. *Venetia, Francesco de Franceschi & co.* 1584.

[*Note.*—In addition to the Orlando are I cinqve canti di m. Lodovico Ariosto, i quali seguono la materia del furioso. Tutti di nuouo reuisti e ricorretti da molti errori, con gli argomenti in rima o discorsi di m. Luigi Grotta d'Adria, con l'osservationi del sig. Alberto Lavezvola.

Next follows, Scontri de' luoghi i quali m. Lodovico Ariosto mutò doppo la prima impressione. Et la cagione perche facesse Raccolti dal s. Gio. Battista Pigna.

Also, Annotationi et avvertimenti di Jeronimo Ruscelli sopra i luoghi difficile et importanti del furioso.

Dichiaratione delle historie più importanti antichè et modernè toccate nel furioso, con una breve expositione delle favole raccolte da m. Niccolo Eugenico.

Alcune altre cose da avvertirsi nel furioso riconosciute de m. Simon Fornari.

Prefixed to the poem is La vita di m. Lodovico Ariosto tratta in compendio da i romanzi del s. Giovanbattista Pigna, and another life by Girolamo Garofalo.]

——— The same. Orlando furioso. Edito ad uso della gioventù con note ed un indice dal dott. G. B. Bolza. vi, 791 pp. 1 l. 8°. *Vienna, i. r. amministrazione per la vendità dé libri scolastici*, 1853.

Arislaüs *or* **Arisleus.** La tourbe des philosophes, ou l'assemblée des disciples de Pythagoras, appellée le code de vérité. [*anon.*] 12°. [*Paris, A. Cailleau*, 1741].

[*In* Salmon (William). Bibliothèque des philosophes chimique. 1741. v. 2, pp. 1-55.

Note.—A book having the same title is attributed to Philipp Morgenstern].

Aristeus (*Pseudo-*). The history of the seventy two interpreters: of their journey from Jerusalem to Alexandria: [etc. Also], the history of the angels, and their gallantry with the daughters of men. Written by Enoch the patriarch. Publish'd in greek by dr. Grabe. Made english by mr. Lewis, of Corpus Christi college, in Oxford. 2 p. l. xix, 196 pp. 16°. *London, J. Hooke & T. Caldecott*, 1715.

Aristoteles. Αριστοτελης. Aristotelis opera omnia graece ad optimorum exemplarium fidem recensuit, annotationem criticam, librorum argumenta, et novam versionem latinam adiecit Io. Theophilus Buhle. 5 v. 8°. *Biponti, ex typographia societatis*, 1791-1800.

CONTENTS.

v. 1. Aristotelis vitæ auctoribus Diogene Laertio Ammonio aliisque, pp. 1-104.
Commentatio de libris Aristotelis acroamaticis et exotericis, pp. 105-152.
Elenchus codicum et editionum librorum Aristotelis, pp. 153-274.
De librorum Aristotelis interpretibus, pp. 275-358.
Porphyrii Isagoge περι των πεντε φωνων, pp. 359-428.
Aristotelis categoriæ, pp. 429-548.

v. 2. Aristotelis liber de interpretatione, pp. 1-80.
Analyticorum libri quattuor, pp. 81-720.

v. 3. Aristotelis Topicorum libri octo, pp. 1-502.
De sophisticis elenchis liber, pp. 503-672.
Variæ lectiones coditis guelpherbytani, pp. 673-698.

v. 4. Aristotelis De arte rhetorica libri tres.

v. 5. Aristotelis Rhetorica ad Alexandrum, pp. 1-183.
De arte poetica liber, pp. 185-442.

——— Aristotle's poetics, literally translated, with explanatory notes and an analysis. xix, 76 pp. 12°. *London, G. & W. B. Whittaker*, 1819.

Aristoteles—continued.

——— Dissertation on rhetoric. Translated from the greek: with notes. By Daniel Michael Crimmin. 3d ed. corrected and greatly enlarged, to which is prefixed, a compendium of logic, by the rev. Julius Picquot. 1 p. l. 476 pp. 6 l. 116 pp. 8°. *London, J. J. Stockdale*, 1818.

——— Opvs magnorum moraliū Aristotelis, Girardo Ruffo Vaccariēsi interprete. Eidem nouę traductioni è graeco in latinum, adiectus ad literam cōmentarius. Altera eiusdē operis magnorum moralium interpretatio, per Georgium Vallam Placentinum. 114 l. fol. *Parisiis, ex officina S. Colinaei*, 1522.

[*With* NANI (Domenico). Polyanthea. *Argentina*, 1517].

——— The same. Aristotle of morals, to Nicomachus. Book the first. Translated by Edm[d] Pargiter; with a short account of the author prefixed and with notes from Andronicus, Eustratius and others. viii, 40 pp. 4°. *London, translator*, 1745.

——— Organum, hoc est libri omnes ad logicam pertinentes græce et latine. Ivl. Pacivs recensuit: e græca in latinam linguam conuertit: capitum & particularum distinctionibus, argumentisque: præterea variis lectionibus, necnō perpetuis notis, & tabulis synopticis illustrauit. Eng. title, 3 p. l. 831 pp. 4°. *Morgiis, G. Laimarius*, 1584.

[*Note.*—The Porphyrii isagoge occupies the first 34 pp. of the work].

——— Somma di tvtta la natvral filosofia di Aristotele. Raccolta da m. Lodovico Dolce; nella qvale si contengono. Della fisica libri viii. Del ciello libri iiii. Della generatione libri ii. Delle meteore libri iiii. Dell' anima libri iii. 98 l. numb. 16°. *Venetia*, [*about* 1560].

Aristoteles (*pseudo-Aristoteles*). Ein tractat Aristotelis des alchimisten an Alexandrum magnum vom stein der weisen vor zeiten geschrieben, und von einem christlichen philosopho zusammen gelesen. Aus dem latein ins deutsche übersetzet. 16°. [*Hamburg, J. Naumann & G. Wolff*, 1675].

[*In* ALCHYMISTISCH sieben-gestirn. 1675. pp. 69–98].

Armen-seelen-monat, oder betrachtungen und andachtsübungen für jeden tag des monats November, zum troste der leidenden seelen im fegfeuer. [*anon.*] 447 pp. 24°. *Einsiedeln, New-York & Cincinnati, C. & N. Benziger*, 1871.

Arminius *or* **Harmansen** (Jacob). Opera theologica. 12 p. l. 788 pp. 4°. *Francofurti, Anglus*, 1631.

CONTENTS.

Bertii oratio de vita et obitu Arminii.
Orationes de sacerdotio Christi, de objecto, authore ac fine, et de certitudine theologiæ ac denique de componendo religiones inter christianos dissidio.
Declaratio sententiæ authoris de prædestinatione, providentia Dei, libero arbitrio, gratia Dei, divinitate filii Dei, et de justificatione.
Apologia adversus articulos xxxi in vulgus sparsos.
Responsio ad quæstiones ix et ad eas anterotemata.
Disputationes publicæ et privatæ.
Amica collatio cum F. Junio de prædestinatione.
Examen prædestinationis perkinsianæ.
Analysis capitis ix, et dissertatio in caput vii epistolæ ad Romanos.
Epistola ad Hippolytum.
Articuli nonnulli diligenti examine perpendendi.

Armroyd (George). A connected view of the whole internal navigation of the United States, natural and artificial, present and prospective, corrected and improved from the edition of 1826. By a citizen of the United States. [*anon.*] 1 p. l. 617 pp. 2 pl. 1 map. 8°. *Philadelphia, Lydia R. Bailey*, 1830.

Armstrong (C. W.) Cases of contested elections. 1777 to 1871. *See* **New York** (*State of*). *Assembly*.

Armstrong (George, *m. d.*) An account of the diseases most incident to children. To which is added, an essay on nursing, with a particular view to infants brought up by hand. Also, a short account of the dispensary for the infant poor. New ed. with many additional notes, by A. P. Buchan, m. d. xxxv, 242 pp. 8°. *London, T. Cadell & W. Davies*, 1808.

Armstrong (George D. *d. d.*) The christian doctrine of slavery. 148 pp. 12°. *New York, C. Scribner*, 1857.

——— The doctrine of baptisms. Scriptural examination of the questions respecting 1. The translation of baptizo. 2. The mode of baptism. 3. The subjects of baptism. 322 pp. 12°. *New York, C. Scribner*, 1857.

Armstrong (*Rev.* Robert G.) Memoir of Hannah Hobbie; or, christian activity, and triumph in suffering. 255 pp. 18°. *New York, American tract society*, [1837].

Army and navy journal. *See* **United States** army and navy journal.

Arnalt and Lucenda, a historie. *See* **San Pedro** (Diego de).

Arnaud (François) *and* **Suard** (Jean Baptiste Antoine). Variétés littéraires ou recueil de pièces tant originales que traduites, concernant la philosophie, la littérature & les arts. [*anon.*] 4 v. 16°. *Paris, Le Jay*, 1770.

[*Note.*—On trouve dans ce recueil des lettres sur les

Arnaud (F.) *and* **Suard** (J. B. A.)—contin'd. animaux de Le Roy, et différens morceaux traduits par m. Turgot, l'abbé Morellet, et madame Necker.—*Quérard.*]

Arnaud (François Thomas Marie, Baculard d'). Fayel, tragédie. Nouv. éd. [Avec un Extrait de l'historie du châtelain de Fayel]. 126 pp. 2 pl. 8°. *Paris, Delalain*, 1777.

Arnaud (George d'). Lectionum graecarum libri duo, in quibus Graecorum scripta passim illustrantur & castigantur. Imprimis Hesychii, Arati, Theonis, Oppiani et Appollonii Rhodii. 4 p. l. 246 pp. 18 l. 8°. *Hagae Comitum, apud P. de Hondt*, 1730.

Arnauld (Antoine). Jugement équitable, sur les contestations présentés, pour éviter les jugemens téméraires & criminels. Tiré de S. Augustin. 8°. [*Cologne, P. Marteau*, 1683].
[*In* NICOLE (Pierre). Les imaginaires et les visionnaires. *Cologne*, 1683. pp. 648-83].

Arnauld d'Andilly (Robert). Vies de plvsievrs saints illvstres de divers siècles. Choisies & traduites par monsievr Arnavld d'Andilly. 4 p. l. 892 pp. 14 l. fol. *Paris, P. Le Petit*, 1664.

Arnault (Antoine Vincent). Les loisirs d'un banni. Pièces recueillies en Belgique, publiées avec des notes par Auguste Imbert. 2 v. 384 pp; 2 p. l. 374 pp. 8°. *Paris, l'éditeur*, 1823.

Arnobius *afer.* Arnobii oratoris adversus nationes libri septem. Recensuit, emendavit et adnotationibus illustravit F. Oehler. xxxi, 354 pp. 12°. *Lipsiae, B. Tauchnitz, jun.* 1846.
[GERSDORF (E. G.) Bibliotheca patrum ecclesiasticorum latinorum selecta, v. 12].

——— The same. The seven books of Arnobius adversus gentes. Translated by archd. Hamilton Bryce and Hugh Campbell. xx, 386 pp. 8°. *Edinburgh, T. & S. Clark*, 1871.
[ANTE-NICENE christian library, v. 19].

Arnold (*Major* Abraham K. *U. S. a.*) Notes on horses for cavalry service. Embodying the quality, purchase, care and diseases most frequently encountered. With lessons for bitting the horse, and bending the neck. 82 pp. 3 pl. 16°. *New York, D. Van Nostrand*, 1869.

Arnold (A. N. *d. d.*) One woman's mission, and how she fulfilled it. A memorial of mrs. Harriet E. Dickson. 272 pp. 16°. *Boston, H. A. Young & co.* 1871.

Arnold (Alexander S.) The Benson family. By the author of "Uncle Timothy Taber." [*anon.*] 196 pp. 12°. *Central Falls (R. I.) E. L. Freeman*, 1869.

Arnold (Alexander S.)—continued.

——— Children's catechism, for classes to recite in concert. By the author of "Uncle Timothy Taber." [*anon.*] 24 pp. 18°. *Central Falls (R. I.) E. L. Freeman*, 1871.

——— Uncle Timothy Taber; or, the new minister. By a sabbath-school superintendent. [*anon.*] 228 pp. 1 pl. 16°. *Augusta (Me.) G. W. Quinby*, 1868.

Arnold (Howard Payson). European mosaic. vii, 339 pp. 12°. *Boston, Little, Brown & co.* 1864.

Arnold (Nicolaus). Religio sociniana sev cathechesis racoviana maior, refutata. 13 p. l. 742 pp. 12 l. 4°. *Franequeræ, J. Wellens*, 1671.

Arnold (Samuel Greene). The life of George Washington. 228 pp. 18°. *New York, T. Mason & G. Lane*, 1840.

——— Memoir of Hannah More: with brief notices of her works, contemporaries, &c. 184 pp. 18°. *New York, T. Mason & G. Lane*, 1839.

Arnot (*Rev.* William). Laws from heaven for life on earth: illustrations of the book of proverbs. 430 pp. 8°. *London, T. Nelson & sons*, 1857.

Aromatarii (Giuseppe degli). Dialoghi di Falcidio Melampodio, in risposta a gli auuertimenti dati sotto nome di Crescentio Pepe [Alessandro Tassoni], intorno alle risposte fatte da lui alle considerationi del sig. Alessandro Tassoni sopra le rime del Petrarca. [*pseudon.*] 4 p. l. 348 pp. 2 l. 16°. *Venetia, per E. Deuchino*, 1613.

Aroux (Eugène). Dante hérétique, révolutionnaire et socialiste. Révélations d'un catholique sur le moyen âge. xvi, 472 pp. 8°. *Paris, J. Renouard & cie.* 1854.

Arrivabene (Ferdinando). Il secolo di Dante, commento storico necessario all' intelligenza della Divina commedia. Seconda ed. arricchita di tutte l'illustrazioni storiche da Ugo Foscolo stese sul poema di Dante, con indici accurati. 2 v. 476 pp; 362 pp. 16°. *Firenze, Ricordi & co.* 1830.

Arrivabene (Lodovico). Istoria della China. Nella quale si tratta di molte cose marauigliose di quell' amplissimo regno: onde s'acquista notitia di molti paesi, di varij costumi, di popoli, di animali, sì da terra, e sì da acqua. 12 p. l. 576 pp. 10 l. sm. 4°. *Verona, A. Tamo*, 1599.
[*Note.*—Questo è un romanzo, nel quale l'autore ha imitato assai bene lo stile del Boccaccio.—*Mazzuchelli*].

Arrowsmith (Aaron). A new and elegant general atlas. *See* **Morse** (Jedediah).

Arseos historico e analyse esthetigraphica do quadro de um episodio da batalha de Campo Grande, planejado e executado pelo dr. Pedro Americo de Figueiredo e Mello. 1 p. l. 101 pp. 1 portrait. 8°. *Rio de Janeiro, typographia nacional,* 1871.

Art [The] of conversation. With directions for self education. [*anon.*] 234 pp. 12°. *New York, Carleton,* 1864.

——— The same. 207 pp. sq. 16°. *New York, G. W. Carleton & co.* 1872.
[HAND-BOOKS of society, v. 4].

Art (The) of cookery, made plain and easy. [Also], one hundred and fifty new and useful receipts. New ed. With the order of a modern bill of fare, for each month. By a lady. [*anon.*] 1 p. l. xxx, 384 pp. 12 l. 8°. *London, W. Straban,* [*etc.*] 1774.
[Imperfect].

Art (The) of delivering written language; or, an essay on reading. *See* **Cockin** (William).

Art recreations, being a complete guide to pencil drawing, oil painting, water-color painting, etc. [*anon.*] 331 pp. 1 pl. 12°. *Boston, J. E. Tilton & co.* 1860.

Artaud (François). Notice des antiquités et des tableaux du musée de Lyon. 106 pp. 8°. *Lyon, Ballanche père & fils,* 1808.

——— Notice des inscriptions antiques du musée de Lyon. Par F. A. [*anon.*] 84 pp. 2 l. 8°. *Lyon, Pelzin,* 1816.

Arteaga (Stefano). Lettera alla signora Isabella Teotochi Albrizzi intorno la Mirra, tragedia del conte Alfieri. 8°. *Pisa, N. Capurro,* 1826.
[*In* ALBRIZZI (Isabella Teotochi). Ritratti, pp. 107–138].

Artephius *or* **Artefius.** Le livre d'Artephius, qui traite de l'art sécret, ou de la pierre philosophale. [Traduit du latin par Pierre Arnauld]. 12°. [*Paris, A. Cailleau,* 1741].
[*In* SALMON (William). Bibliothèque des philosophes chimiques. 1741. v. 2, pp. 112–174].

Arthur (Robert, *m. d.*) Treatment and prevention of decay of the teeth. 256 pp. 12°. *Philadelphia, J. B. Lippincott & co.* 1871.

Arthur (Timothy Shay). A christmas box for the sons and daughters of temperance. 133 pp. 12°. *Philadelphia, W. Sloanmaker,* 1847.

——— Family pride; or, the palace and the poor house: and pride or principle, or which makes the lady? 2 v. in 1. 71 pp; 71 pp. 18°. *Philadelphia, J. W. Bradley,* 1855.

Arthur (Timothy Shay)—continued.

——— Finger posts on the way of life 214 pp. 1 pl. 16°. *Philadelphia, J. W. Bradley,* 1853.

——— Lizzy Glenn: or, the trials of a seamstress. 1 p. l. 21–253 pp. 1 pl. 12°. *Philadelphia, B. Peterson & brothers,* [1859].

——— Lovers and husbands; a story of married life. 155 pp. 18°. *Philadelphia, J. W. Bradley,* 1855.

——— Madeline; or, a daughter's love and other tales. 158 pp. 18°. *Philadelphia, J. W. Bradley,* 1855.

——— Married and single; or, marriage and celibacy contrasted, in a series of domestic pictures. 157 pp. 18°. *Philadelphia, J. W. Bradley,* 1855.

——— The martyr wife: and other tales. [The ruined gamester. Improving stories for the young]. 3 v. in 1. 70 pp; 64 pp; 34 pp. 1 pl. 18°. *Philadelphia, J. W. Bradley,* [1855].

——— Mary Ellis; or, the runaway match: and Alice Melville; or, the indiscretion. 1 p. l. 72 pp. 1 l. 90 pp. 18°. *Philadelphia, J. W. Bradley,* 1855.

——— The mother. 141 pp. 18°. *Philadelphia, E. Ferrett & co.* 1846.

——— The same. 141 pp. 18°. *Philadelphia, J. W. Bradley,* 1855.

——— Six nights with the Washingtonians; and other temperance tales. 2 p. l. 21–536 pp. 11 pl. 1 portrait. 8°. *Philadelphia, T. B. Peterson & bros.* [1871].

——— Sweethearts and wives; or, before and after marriage. 163 pp. 18°. *Philadelphia, J. W. Bradley,* 1855.

——— Three years in a man-trap. By the author of "Ten nights in a bar-room." [*anon.*] 364 pp. 4. pl. 12°. *Philadelphia, J. M. Stoddart & co.* 1872.

——— Tired of housekeeping. 167 pp. 1 pl. 18°. *New York, D. Appleton & co.* [1842].

——— The wonderful story of Gentle Hand, and other stories. 144 pp. 4 pl. sm. 4°. *Philadelphia, J. M. Stoddart & co.* 1871.

Arthur (William). The successful merchant: sketches of the life of mr. Samuel Budgett. 7th ed. ix, 392 pp. 1 portrait. 12°. *London, Hamilton, Adams & co.* 1852.

Arwaker (Edmund). Thoughts well ememploy'd: or, the duty of self-observation. 6 p. l. 6, 152 pp. 1 pl. 16°. *London,* [*about* 1690].
[Imperfect: t. p. wanting].

Ascham (Roger). The scholemaster. Written between 1563-8. Posthumously published. 1st ed. 1570; collated with the second edition, 1571. By Edward Arber. 160 pp. 16°. *London*, 1870.

[ARBER'S English reprints, no. 23, in v. 10].

Ase-Neitha: an egyptian tale. [Translated from the german. *anon.*] 16°. [*London, D. Brewman for J. Searle*, 1789].

[*In* SENTIMENTAL love illustrated in Charmides and Theone [etc.] *London*, 1789. pp. 111-162].

Asher (Benjamin). Practice of architecture. Containing the five orders of architecture, and an additional column and entablature, with all their elements and details explained and illustrated, for the use of carpenters and practical men. 4th ed. 96 pp. 60 pl. 4°. *Boston, Perkins & Marvin*, 1840.

Asher & Adams' new commercial and statistical atlas and gazetteer of the United States, including portions of the provinces of Ontario and Quebec, with their lines of travel and avenues of trade, and comprising a concise description and the location of cities, villages, post-offices, railroad stations, etc. in the United States. v. 1 131 pp. 13 maps. fol. *New York, Asher & Adams*, 1872.

Ashhurst (John, *jr. m. d.*) The principles and practice of surgery. xxviii, 33-1011 pp. 8°. *Philadelphia, H. C. Lea*, 1871.

Ashmun (Jehudi). History of the american colony in Liberia from Dec. 1821, to 1823. 1 map, 43 pp. 8°. *Washington, Way & Gideon*, 1826.

——— The same.

[MARKOE pamphlets, v. 7 and 15].

——— The same.

[MISCELLANEOUS pamphlets, v. 411].

Ashton (Philip). An history of the strange adventures, and signal deliverances of mr. Philip Ashton, jun. of Marblehead. 38 pp 12°. *Boston, S. Gerrish*, 1725.

[*In* BARNARD (John). Ashton's memorial, etc. 1725].

Ashton (*Mrs.* Sophia Goodrich). The mothers of the bible. With an introductory essay, by rev. A. L. Stone. 335 pp. 1 pl. 12°. *Boston, J. P. Jewett & co.* 1855.

——— The same. x, 5-335 pp. 12°. *Boston, J. E. Tilton & co.* 1859.

Ashworth (T. M.) Tom Chips. 1871. *See* **Diekenga** (I. E.) *and* **Ashworth.**

Asiatic costumes; a series of forty-four coloured engravings, from designs taken from life: with a description to each subject. [*anon.*] 2 p. l. 88 pp. 44 pl. 12°. *London, R. Ackermann*, 1828.

Aspinwall (Edward, *d. d.*) An apology, being a series of arguments in proof of the christian religion. With a postscript address'd to all impartial free-thinkers. xxxviii, 384 pp. 8°. *London, A. Bettesworth & C. Hitch*, 1731.

Assassinat (L') de Pantin. [*anon.*] 256 pp. incl. 7 wood-cuts. 16°. *Paris, librairie des villes et des campagnes*, [1870]?

Assmann (Friedrich Wilhelm). Quellenkunde der vergleichenden anatomie. Als vorläufer einer pragmatischen geschichte der zootomie. Für naturforscher und anatomen. viii, 319 pp. 8°. *Braunschweig, F. Vieweg & sohn*, 1847. s.

Association monthly. Richard C. Morse, editor. Jan. to Dec. 1870. v. 1. 4°. *New York, executive committee of the young men's christian associations of the United States and British provinces*, 1870.

Astié (Jean Frédéric). Louis fourteenth, and the writers of his age; being a course of lectures delivered (in french) to a select audience in New York Introduction and translation by the rev. E. N. Kirk. xxiii, 413 pp. 12°. *Boston, J. P. Jewett & co.* 1855.

Astle (Thomas). The origin and progress of writing, as well hieroglyphic as elementary, illustrated by engravings taken from marbles, manuscripts and charters: also some account of the origin and progress of printing. Second ed. with additions. 4 p. l. xxiv, 240 pp. 33 pl. fol. *London, J. White*, 1803.

[*Note.*—With an autograph letter from the author to John Pinkerton].

Astrampsychus. Oneirocriticon, a Jos. Scaligero digestum & castigatum. Græce et latine. 4°. [*Amstelodami, apud H. & viduam T. Boom*, 1689].

[*In* GALLÉ (Servais). Σιβυλλιακοι χρησμοι, hoc est, sibyllina oracula. [etc.] *Amstelodami*, 1689. pp. 65-69].

Asylum (An) for fugitive pieces. 4 v. 1785-98. *See* **Debrett** (John).

Athenæum (The) journal of literature, science, the fine arts, music, and the drama. [Weekly]. Jan. to Dec. 1871. 2 v. 4°. *London, J. Francis*, 1871.

Atheos; or, the tragedies of unbelief. [*anon.*] 326 pp. 12°. *New York, Sheldon & co.* 1862.

Atherstone (Edwin). A midsummer day's dream. A poem. 1 p. l. 173 pp. 3 pl. 12°. *London, Baldwin, Cradock & Joy*, 1824.

Atkinson (*Rev.* Joseph M.) The true path, or the young man invited to the saviour. In

Atkinson (*Rev.* Joseph M.)—continued. a series of lectures. 300 pp. 12°. *Philadelphia, Presbyterian board of publication,* [1860].

Atkinson (*Rev.* Miles). Practical sermons. To which is prefixed a short memoir of the life and character of the author. 2 v. xii, lxxviii, 391 pp. 1 portrait; 5 p. l. 471 pp. 8°. *London, Longman,* [*& co.*] 1812.

Atkinson (Thomas). The chameleon. Second series. 327 pp. 16 l. music. 8°. *London, Longman,* 1833.

Atlantic (The) almanac. 1872. 8°. *Boston, J. R. Osgood & co.* 1871.

Atlantic (The) monthly. A magazine of literature, science, art, and politics. Jan. to Dec. 1871. v. 27–28. 8°. *Boston, J. R. Osgood & co.* 1871

Atlantis. Journal des neuesten und wissenswürdigsten aus dem gebiete der politik, geschichte [etc.] der nord- und südamerikanischen reiche, mit einschluss des westindischen archipelagus. Herausgegeben von Eduard Florens Rivinus in Philadelphia, 1826. 2 v. 400 pp; 370 pp. 8°. *Leipzig, J. C. Hinrichs,* 1826.
[MARKOE pamphlets, v. 63].

Atticus *secundus* (*pseudon.*) *See* **Sarrasin** (Jean François).

Atwood (*Rev.* Anthony). A manual on christian baptism: or, the nature, subjects, and mode of this divine ordinance pointed out and defended. xvi, 13–227 pp. 16°. *Philadelphia, Griggs & co.* 1840.

——— A pastor's legacy to those for whose benefit he has spent his life, or a final appeal to the carelesss, the inquiring, and the believing, in relation to life and usefulness. 211 pp. 16°. *Philadelphia, author,* 1866.

——— The young man's way to intelligence, respectability, honor and usefulness. 190 pp. 18°. *Philadelphia, Crolius & Gladding,* 1842.

Atwood (Daniel T.) Atwood's country and suburban houses. Illustrated. 287 pp. 12°. *New York, Orange Judd & co.* 1871.

Atwood (Frank). *See* **Amateurs'** (The) annual for 1872.

Atwood (J. Clement, *editor*). The canticles of the church. With the gloria in excelsis, nicene creed, nunc dimittis, kyrie eleison, and gloria tibi. Pointed for chanting, with prefatory remarks for the assistance of amateurs and congregations. 19 pp. 12°. *New York, J. C. Atwood,* 1870.

Aub (Theodor). Real estate transactions: as they are, and as they might be. A plan for the insurance of titles and mortgages. 38 pp. 8°. *New York, Baker, Voorhis & co.* 1871.

Auber (Daniel François Esprit). Black domino. [Libretto, without music]. *See* **Scribe** (Augustin Eugène).

——— Crown diamonds. Romantic opera in three acts. Containing text, overture and principal music (vocal and instrumental), as performed by english grand opera companies. Edited by G. W. Tryon, jr. 1 ill. title, 28 pp; music 64 pp. 1 portrait. 8°. *Philadelphia, American opera publishing co.* 1870.
[TRYON (George Washington, *jr.*) Gems of the lyric drama. v. 1, no. 2].

——— Fra Diavolo. Romantic opera in three acts. Containing text, overture, and principal music (vocal and instrumental), as performed by english grand opera companies. Edited by George W. Tryon, jr. 2 ill. titles, 29 pp; music 64 pp. 1 portrait. 4°. *Philadelphia, American opera publishing co.* 1869.
[TRYON (George W. *jr.*) Gems of the lyric drama. v. 1, no. 1].

——— Masaniello; a grand opera. Edited and translated by Manfredo Maggioni. 23 pp. 4°. *New York, Darcie & Corbyn,* 1855.

——— The principal musical gems of the opera of Masaniello, newly and expressly arranged as piano-forte solos. 5 pp. 8°. *New York, J. Darcie,* 1854.
[*With his* Masaniello].

Aublet de Maubuy (—). Histoire des troubles et des démêlés littéraires, depuis leur origine jusqu'à nos jours inclusivement. [*anon.*] 2 v. xii, 232 pp; 2 p. l. 310 pp. 8°. *Amsterdam,* 1786.

Auburn (*N. Y.*) Boyd's Auburn directory: 1871–72. Compiled by Andrew Boyd. 8°. *Auburn,* (*N. Y.*) *F. Allen* [*&*] *C. P. Williams,* [1870].

Auctentijck verhael van't remarcquabelste is voorgevallen in Brasil, tusschen den Hollandtschen admirael Willem Cornelisz. ende de spaensche vloot, [etc. *anon.*] 6 l. sm. 4°. *Amsterdam, I. van Hilten,* 1640.

Audiberti (Camillo Maria). Regiæ villæ poetice descriptæ. Apposita poematum, & epigrammatum appendice. Eng. tit. 8 p. l. 222 pp. 1 l. 4°. *Augustæ Taurinorum, ex typographia P. M. Dutti, & I. I. Ghringhelli soc.* 1711.

Audiguier (Vital d', *seigneur de la Ménor*). Love and valovr: celebrated in the person of the author, by the name of Adraste. Or, the

Audiguier (Vital d')—continued. divers affections of Minerva. One part of the unfained story of the true Lisander and Caliste. Translated out of the french by W. B. 11 p. l. 226 pp. sm. 4°. *London, T. Harper for T. Slater*, 1638.

Audouin (François Xavier). Histoire de l'administration de la guerre. v. 2–4. 8°. *Paris, Didot l'aîné*, 1811. s.
[v. 1 wanting].

Audouin (Jean Victor) *and* **Brullé** (Auguste). Histoire naturelle des insectes, traitant de leur organisation et de leurs moeurs en général, par V. Audouin, et comprenant leur classification et la description des espèces, par A. Brullé. v. 4–5. Coléoptères, v. 1–2. 8°. *Paris, F. D. Pillot*, 1834–38. s.
[Coléoptères, v. 3 wanting].

——— The same. v. 9. Orthoptères et hémiptères. 2 p. l. 415 pp. 5 col. pl. 8°. *Paris, F. D. Pillot*, 1835. s.

Audubon (John James). The birds of America, from drawings made in the United States and their territories. 500 colored plates. 8 v. 8°. *New York, G. R. Lockwood*, [1871].

Auer (Adelheid von). It is the fashion. From the german. By the translator of "Over yonder," etc. 293 pp. 12°. *Philadelphia, J. B. Lippincott & co.* 1872.

Auersperg (Anton Alexander, *count* von). The last knight, a romance-garland. From the german of Anastasius Grün. [*pseudon.*] Translated, with notes, by John O. Sargent. ix, 200 pp. sm. 4°. *New York, Hurd & Houghton*, 1871.

Auger (Athanase). Œuvres posthumes. 10 v. 12°. *Paris, l'imprimerie du cercle social*, 1792–93.

CONTENTS.

v. 1–5. De la constitution des Romains, sous le rois et aux tems de la république. 5 v. 1792–93.
v. 6–10. Discours de Cicéron, traduits.

Augusti (Johann Christian Wilhelm). Die schriften des alten testaments. 1809–11. *See* **Bible.** (*German*).

Augustinus (*St.* Aurelius). The works of Aurelius Augustine, bishop of Hippo. A new translation. Edited by the rev. Marcus Dods. v. 1–2. xvi, 557 pp; vi, 574 pp. 8°. *Edinburgh, T. & T. Clark*, 1871.

CONTENTS.

v. 1–2. The city of God.

——— Confessions, livres xiii [traduites par Arnault d'Andilly]. 8°. [*Paris, panthéon littéraire*, 1843].
[*In* BUCHON (J. A. C.) Choix d'ouvrages mystiques, pp. 33–233].

Augustinus (*St.* Aurelius)—continued.

——— Méditations [traduction par un anonyme]. 8°. [*Paris, panthéon littéraire*, 1843].
[*In* BUCHON (J. A. C.) Choix d'ouvrages mystiques, pp. 235–279].

Aunt Charity's legacy. Working for Jesus. [*anon.*] 29 pp. 1 pl. 18°. *New York, board of publication of r. c. a.* [1871].
[SEED corn series].

Ausland (Das). [Wöchentlich]. Ueberschau der neuesten forschungen auf dem gebiete der natur-, erd- und völkerkunde. 2. Januar 1868 bis 25. Dec. 1871. 41–44 jahrgang. fol. *Augsburg, J. G. Cotta*, 1868–71.

Austin (Arthur, *pseudon.*) *See* **Wilson** (John Mackay).

Austin (*Rev.* David). The millenium; or, the thousand years of prosperity, promised to the church of God, in the old testament and in the new, shortly to commence, and to be carried on to perfection. 426 pp. 1 portrait. 8°. *Elizabethtown, (N. J.) S. Kollock*, 1794.

CONTENTS.

AUSTIN (*Rev.* David). The downfall of mystical Babylon, or, a key to the providence of God in the political operations of 1793–94.
BELLAMY (*Rev.* Joseph). The millenium. [A sermon]. First published in Boston in 1753.
EDWARDS (*Rev.* Jonathan). An humble attempt to promote explicit agreement and visible union of God's people in extraordinary prayer.

Austin (Jane G.) Fairy dreams; or, wanderings in elf-land. With illustrations, by Hammatt Billings. 216 pp. sq. 16°. *Boston, J. E. Tilton & co.* 1859.

——— The shadow of Moloch mountain. 142 pp. 8°. *New York, Sheldon & co.* 1870.

——— The tailor boy. [*anon.*] 247 pp. 4 pl. 18°. *Boston, J. E. Tilton & co.* 1865.

Austin (William, *of Lincoln's inn*). Devotionis avgvstinianæ flamma, or, certaine devovt, godly, and learned meditations. Set forth by mrs. Anne Austin, as a surviving monument of some part of the great worth of her ever-honoured husband. 3 p. l. 292 pp. fol. *London, I. L. & R. Mab*, 1635.

Austria. (*Handels-ministerium*). Bericht über die allgemeine agricultur- und industrie-ausstellung zu Paris im jahre 1855. Nach den arbeiten und materialen der österreichischen berichterstatter und jury-mitglieder. Herausgegeben unter der redaction von dr. Eberhard A. Jonak. v. 3. 8°. *Wien, k. k. hof- und staats-druckerei*, 1857–58.

——— ——— Summarischer bericht betreffend die verhältnisse der industrie, des handels und verkehres Oberösterreich's in den jahren 1868

Austria—continued. und 1869. 188 pp. 3 tab. 8°. *Linz, handels- und gewerbekammer*, 1870. s.

——— (*Kaiserlich - königliche génie - comité*). Mittheilungen über gegenstände der ingenieur- und kriegswissenschaften. Jahrgang 1869. 1es–8es heft. 8 parts in 4. 8°. *Wien, C. Gerold's sohn*, 1869. s.

——— ——— The same. Inhaltsverzeichniss der bände i bis xiii, 1856–68. 2 p. l. 31 pp. 8°. *Wien, C. Gerold's sohn*, 1869.

——— ——— The same. Inhaltsverzeichniss. 1869. 8 pp. 1 l. 8°. *Wien, C. Gerold's sohn*, 1869.

——— (*Kriegs-ministerium*). Evolutions of the line, as practised by the austrian infantry, and adopted in 1853. Translated by lieut. C. M. Wilcox, 7th regiment, U. S. infantry. 132 pp. 8 pl. 12°. *New York, D. Van Nostrand*, 1860.

——— (*Ministerium des äussern*). Auswärtige angelegenheiten. Correspondenzen des kaiserlich - königlichen ministerium des äussern. no. 1–3. November, 1866, to July, 1869. 3 v. fol. *Wien, k. k. hof- und staatsdruckerei*, 1868–69. s.

——— (*Statistische central-commission*). Ausweise über den auswärtigen handel der österreichisch - ungarischen monarchie im sonnen-jahre 1868. xxix. jahrgang. lxxi, 173 pp. 4°. *Wien, k. k. hof- und staatsdruckerei*, 1870.

——— ——— Statistisches jahrbuch für das jahr 1869. 8°. *Wien, k. k. kof- und staatsdruckerei*, 1871.

Authentic and impartial narrative of the tragical scene in Southampton co. Va. on Monday, the 22d of August last, when fifty-five of its inhabitants were massacred by the blacks! [*anon.*] 38 pp. 12°. *New York, Warner & West*, 1831.

Auvigny (Jean du Castre d'). Memoirs of madame de Barneveldt. Translated from the french by miss Gunning. [*anon.*] 2 v. 2 p. l. 353 pp; 2 p. l. 325 pp. 8°. *London, S. Low*, 1795.

Averill (Anna S.) Annie Mason; or, the temple of shells. 420 pp. 16°. *New York, A. D. F. Randolph & co.* [1871].

Avery (A. S.) How to draw; the right and the wrong way. Illustrated with over one hundred figures. 30 pp. 8°. 14 pl. obl. fol. In 1 v. *New York, university publishing co.* 1872.

Avila (Josef de). Coleccion de noticias de muchas de las indulgencias plenarias y perpetuas que pueden ganar todos los fieles de Christo, que con la debida disposicion, visitaren en sus respectivos dias las iglesias que se irán nombrando en ellos, de esta corte de México. 10 p. l. 152 pp. 16°. *Mexico, F. de Zúñiga y Ontiveros*, 1787.

Avity (Pierre d'). The estates, empires and principallities of the world represented by ye description of countries, maners of inhabitants, riches of prouinces, forces, gouernment, religion: and the princes that haue gouerned in euery estate. With the begiñing of all militarie and religious orders. Translated out of french by Edw. Grimstone. Eng. title. 8 p. l. 1234 pp. fol. *London, M. Lownes and J. Bill*, 1615.

Avviso di Parnaso, difesa della patavinità di Givlio Paolo. *See* **Pignoria** (Lorenzo).

Ayerst (*Rev.* W.) The Jews of the nineteenth century. A collection of essays, reviews, and historical notices, originally published in the "Jewish intelligence." viii, 431 pp. 1 portrait. 8°. *London, London society's house*, 1848.

Ayesha, the maid of Kars. *See* **Morier** (James).

Aymon (Les quatre fils). *See* **Quatre** (Les) fils Aymon.

Ayrault (Pierre). Petri Ærodii de patrio jure ad filium pseudo-jesuitam dissertatio. 166 pp. 1 l. 18°. *Ultrajecti, apud J. Ribbium*, 1671.

Ayres (George B.) How to paint photographs in water-colors and in oil. Also, how to retouch negatives. 179 pp. 12°. *Philadelphia, Benerman & Wilson*, 1871.

Ayton (Richard). Essays and sketches of character. With a memoir of his life. xv, 274 pp. 1 portrait. 12°. *London, Taylor & Hessey*, 1825.

Azara (Felix de). Memorias sobre el estado rural del rio de la Plata en 1801; demarcacion de límites entre el Brasil y el Paraguay á últimos del siglo xviii, é informes sobre varios particulares de la América meridional española. Escritos postumos. Los publica su sobrino don Agustin de Azara, bajo la direccion de don Basilio Sebastian Castellanos de Losada. viii, 232 pp. 1 portrait. 8°. *Madrid, Sanchiz*, 1847.

——— The natural history of the quadrupeds of Paraguay and the river La Plata; translated from the spanish. With a memoir of the

Azara (Felix de)—continued.
author, a physical sketch, and notes ; by W. Perceval Hunter. v. 1. xxxii, 340 pp. 1 map. 8°. *Edinburgh, A. & C. Black,* 1838. s.
[No more published].

——— The same. Selections from the natural history of the quadrupeds of Paraguay and the river La Plata; comprising the most remarkable species of South America. Translated from the spanish. With notes, by W. P. Hunter. xix, 288 pp. 8°. *London, A. J. Valpy,* 1837.

Azara (José Nicolás de). Revoluciones de Roma que causaron la destitucion del papa Pio vii como soberano temporal, y el establecimiento de la última república romana, asi como la conquista de aquella parte de Italia por los franceses mandades por Napoleon ; y relacion de la política de España y de los sucesos de Francia posteriores á estos acontecimientos. Memorias. Obra póstuma que publica su sobrino el sr. d. Agustin de Azara, bajo la direccion de d. Basilio Sebastian Castellanos de Losada. 1 p. l. vii, 339 pp. 1 portrait. 8°. *Madrid, Sanchiz,* 1847.

Azeglio (Massimo Taparelli, *il marchese d'*). Ettore Fieramosca : or the challenge of Barletta. The struggles of an Italian against foreign invaders and foreign protectors. 1 p. l. 356 pp. 12°. *Boston, Phillips, Sampson & co.* 1859.

Azzolino (Pompeo, *il marchese*). Introduzione alla storia della filosofia italiana ai tempi di Dante, per la intelligenza dei concetti filosofici della divina commedia. 2 p. l. 125 pp. 8°. *Bastia,* 1839.

——— Pensieri sullo spirito della divina commedia di Dante. [*anon.*] 2 p. l. 37 pp. 8°. *Firenze, L. Pezzati,* 1837.

——— Sul veltro di Dante. Lettera al marchese Gino Capponi. 78 pp. 1 pl. 8°. *Firenze, L. Pezzati,* 1837.

B. (C. C.) France and her people. [*anon.*] 302 pp. 12°. *Philadelphia, W. B. Evans & co.* 1872.

B. (H.) Jesu-worship confuted ; or, certain arguments against bowing at the name of Jesus. Proving it to be idolatrous and superstitious, and so utterly unlawfull. With objections to the contrary fully answered. By H. B. [*anon.*] 38 pp. sm. 4°. *London, H. C.* 1660.

B. (H. N. W.) *See* **Baker** (Harriet Newell Woods).

B. (J.) *See* **Burrow** (*Sir* James).

B. (M. *le baron de*). *See* **Doris** (Charles).

B. (R. L.) An autobiography; being passages from a life now progressing in the city of Boston. [*anon.*] 240 pp. 16°. [*Boston*], *sold by subscription only,* 1871.

B. (W. S.) The origin and antiquity of engraving ; with some remarks on the utility and pleasures of prints. [*anon.*] 62 pp. 8°. *Philadelphia, G. Crabbie,* 1872.

Baarle (Caspar van). Casparis Barlæi antverpiani poemata. Ed. iv, altera plus parte auctior. 2 v. 11 p. l. 732 pp ; 4 p. l. 576 pp. 16°. *Amstelodami, apud I. Blaev,* 1645-6.

——— Caspari Barlæi oratio de ente rationis. 18°. [*Lugd. Batavorum,* 1644].
[*In* DISSERTATIONVM lvdicrarvm et amœnitatvm scriptores varij, pp. 304-332].

——— Nvptiæ peripateticæ, sive vniversæ philosophiæ ad statum conjugalem festiva applicatio. 18°. [*Lugd. Batavorum,* 1644].
[*In* DISSERTATIONVM lvdicrarvm et amœnitatvm scriptores varij, pp. 333-368].

Baars (Herman). Les pêches de la Norwége. 1 p. l. 61 pp. 7 l. 8°. *Paris, J. Bonaventure,* 1867.

Baber (*Rev.* Henry Hervey) Vetus testamentum græcum e codice ms. alexandrino. *See* **Bible.** (*Greek*).

Babington (Gervase, *bishop of Worcester, d.d.*) The workes of the right reverend father in God, Gervase Babington. Containing comfortable notes upon the five bookes of Moses. As also an exposition upon the creed, the commandements, the Lords prayer. With a conference betwixt mans frailtie and faith. And three sermons. 5 p. l. 1279 pp. fol. *London, G. Eld for T. Charde,* 1615.

Babington (Thomas). A practical view of christian education. From the 7th London edition. With a preliminary essay. By rev. T. H. Gallaudet. 4th American ed. 2 p. l. 212 pp. 16°. *Hartford, Cooke & co.* 1831.

Bach (Moriz). Das land Otuquis in Bolivia. *See* **Kriegk** (Georg Ludwig).

Bachaumont (François le Coigneux de). Pièces avec des éclaircissements. *See* **Chapelle** (Claude Emmanuel Lhuillier) *and* **Bachaumont.**

Bache (Richard Meade). American wonderland. 258 pp. 1 pl. 12°. *Philadelphia, Claxton, Remsen & Haffelfinger,* 1871.

Bachelet (A.) Les habitants du monde invisible ou les purs esprits, les anges déchus et les possédés, histoire récente dont les faits surnaturels sont démontrés. Ouvrage dont

Bachelet (A.)—continued. le but est de rattacher à la vie et de ranimer l'amour de vivre, chez les malheureux qui sont affectés d'hypocondrie, spleen ou maladie noire. 2 p. l. ii, 221 pp. 1 l. 8°. *Paris, Charpentier*, 1850.

Backer (Augustin *and* Alois de) *and* **Sommervogel** (Charles). Bibliothèque des écrivains de la compagnie de Jésus ou notices bibliographiques 1°. De tous les ouvrages publiés par les membres de la compagnie de Jésus depuis la fondation de l'ordre jusqu'à nos jours. 2°. Des apologies, des controverses religieuses, des critiques littéraires et scientifiques suscitées à leur sujet. Nouv. éd. refondue et considérablement augmentée. v. 1. A–G. fol. *Liége, l'auteur*, 1869.

Bacon (Francis). A harmony of the essays, etc. of Francis Bacon. [1597–1625. Reprinted]. Arranged by Edward Arber. 2 p. l. xl, 584 pp. 16°. *London*, 1871.
[ARBER'S English reprints, no. 27, in v. 13].

CONTENTS.

A harmony of the first group of ten essays. 1597. pp. 1–94.
Sacred meditations. The Latin version of 1597. Text 1. Placed on opposite pages to the English version of 1598. Text 2. pp. 95–131.
Of the colours of good and euill, 1597. pp. 132–154.
A harmony of the second group of twenty-four essays. pp. 155–416.
A harmony of the third group of six essays. First published in 1612. pp. 417–494.
A harmony of the fourth group of eighteen essays. First published in 1625. pp. 495–576.
A fragment of an essay of fame. First published by dr. Rawley, in Resuscitatio, in 1657. pp. 579–580.

Bacon (George Washington). Life and speeches of president Andrew Johnson. Embracing his early history, political career, speeches, proclamations, etc. With a sketch of the secession movement, and his course in relation thereto; also his policy as president of the United States. v, 137 pp. 1 portrait. 12°. *London, Bacon & co.* [1865]?

Bacon (*Rev.* Henry). The pastor's bequest. Selections from the sermons of rev. Henry Bacon. Edited by mrs. E. A. Bacon. 358 pp. 12°. *Boston, A. Simpkins*, 1857.

Bacon (*Rev.* Henry M.) Sermons on the Lord's prayer. 215 pp. 16°. *Auburn, W. J. Moses*, 1854.

Bacon (Leonard, *d. d.*) A historical discourse delivered at Worcester, in the old south meeting house, September 22, 1863; the hundredth anniversary of its erection. With introductory remarks by hon. Ira M. Barton. [etc.] And an appendix. 106 pp. 1 pl. 8°. *Worcester, E. R. Fiske*, 1863.

Bacon (*Rev.* Leonard Woolsey). The book of worship, for sunday schools and prayer meetings. Selections from psalms, hymns, and spiritual songs. [*anon.*] 72 l. 8°. *New York, Clark & Maynard*, 1871.

——— An inside view of the vatican council, in the speech of the most reverend archbishop [Peter Richard] Kenrick, of St. Louis. Edited, with notes and additional documents. 250 pp. 12°. *New York, American tract society*, [1872].

CONTENTS.

The syllabus of his holiness Pius ix.
The protest of father Hyacinthe.
The protest and speeches of bishop Strossmayer.
The apocryphal "speech of a bishop."
The acts of the council.
The appeal of father Hyacinthe.
The declaration of dr. Döllinger and his associates.
The programme of the anti-infallibility league.

Bacon (Roger). Le miroir d'alqvimie. Traduict de latin en françois, par vn gentilhomme du D'aulphiné. [Jacques Girard. Avec autres œuvres]. 627 pp. 18°. *Lyon, M. Bonhomme*, 1557.

CONTENTS.

BACON (Roger). De l'admirable povvoir et pvissance de l'art & de nature, où est traicté de la pierre philosophale. Traduict par Jacques Girard de Tournus. 95 pp.
——— Le miroir d'alqvimie. 33 pp.
CELESTINE (Claude). Des choses merveillevses en natvre, ov est traicté des erreurs des sens, des puissances de l'ame, & des influences des cieux. Traduict par Jacques Girard de Tournus. 191 pp.
CHALID BEN JESIKI. Le livre des secretz d'alqvimie. pp. 57–108.
HERMES *trismegistus.* La table d'esmeravde. pp. 34–56.
HORTULAIN. Petit commentaire sus la table d'esmeraude d'Hermes Trimegiste. pp. 39–56.
JOHN xxii. (Pope). L'elixir des philosophes, avtrement, l'art transmutatoire. 205 pp.
MEHUN (Jean de). Le miroir de maistre Iean de Mehun. pp. 109–134.

Bacon (Thomas H.) The literal staff: an attachment to the ordinary current index; facilitating reference to entries of any desired name, [etc.] 8 pp. 8°. *Hannibal, (Mo.) Winchell, Ebert & Marsh*, 1870.

Baden. Katalog der bibliothek des handelsministeriums in Karlsruhe Nach dem bestand am 1. Juli 1870. 8°. *Karlsruhe, C. F. Müller*, 1870. s.

——— Katalog der bibliothek der landesgewerbehalle in Karlsruhe. Nach dem bestand vom 1. Januar [-Dec.] 1870. 2 parts in 1 v. 8°. *Karlsruhe, C. F. Müller*, 1870. s.

——— Statistisches jahrbuch. 1. jahrgang, 1868. viii, 240 pp. 8°. *Karlsruhe, Macklot'sche druckerei*, 1869. s.

Baerle (Gaspard van). *See* **Baarle** (Caspar van).

Baffo (Giorgio). Raccolta universale delle opere di Giorgio Baffo veneto. 4 v. 8°. *Cosmopoli*, [*Venezia*], 1789.

Bagg (Joseph H.) Bagg on magnetism, or the doctrine of equilibrium: being an attempt to prove that not only the health of vegetables and animals, but all systems and principles in nature, depend upon an equilibrium of action between two extremes, and that the impulse or force by which they are produced, as well as destroyed, is owing to the magnetic fluids which operate both at the same time, on the same object or principle. x, 312 pp. 12°. *Detroit, Bagg & Harmon*, 1845.

Bagshaw (William, *m. a.*) On man; his motives, their rise, operations, opposition, and results. 2 v. xxvii, 387 pp; viii, 384 pp. 16°. *London, Longman*, 1833.

Baildon (John). A booke containing divers sorts of hands. 1581. *See* **Beauchesne** (John de) *and* **Baildon.**

Baile (J.) Wonders of electricity. Translated from the french. Edited, with numerous additions, by dr. John W. Armstrong. Eng. title, ix, 335 pp. 10 pl. 12°. *New York, Scribner, Armstrong & co.* 1872.
[Illustrated library of wonders].

Bailey (*Rev.* Benjamin). The duties of the christian ministry; with a view of the primitive and apostolical church, and the danger of departure from its doctrine and discipline. A sermon, preached at an ordination held in the church of st. Peter, Colombo, by George Trevor, lord bishop of Madras. With notes and an appendix, containing copious extracts from various authors. 1 p. l. iv, 390 pp. 12°. *London, W. E. Painter*, [1840]?

——— An exposition of the parables of our Lord; showing their connection with his ministry, their prophetic character, and their gradual development of the gospel dispensation. xvi, 512 pp. 8°. *London, J. Taylor*, 1828.

——— The house of bondage. A dissertation upon the nature of service or slavery under the levitical law, among the Hebrews in the earliest ages, and in the gentile world, until the coming of Christ. iv, 74 pp. 8°. *London, C. & J. Rivington*, 1824.
[MISCELLANEOUS pamphlets, v. 77].

Bailey (Joseph T.) & company. History of silver, ancient and modern. 53 pp. 1 pl. 18°. *Philadelphia, Bailey & co.* 1871.

Bailey (J. T.) An historical sketch of the city of Brooklyn, and the surrounding neighborhood, including the village of Williamsburgh and the towns of Flatbush, Flatlands, New Utrecht, and Gravesend. [With] an account of the battle of Long Island. 72 pp. 1 map. 12°. *Brooklyn, J. T. Bailey*, 1840.

Baines (T.) Shifts and expedients of camp life, travel, and exploration. 1871. *See* **Lord** (W. B.) *and* **Baines.**

Baird (Charles W.) Chronicle of a border town. History of Rye, Westchester county, New York, 1660–1870, including Harrison and the White Plains till 1788. xvii, 570 pp. 2 maps. 1 fac-simile. 8°. *New York, A. D. F. Randolph & co.* 1871.

Baird (*Rev.* Robert). Memoir of Anna Jane Linnard. With an introduction by the hon. Theodore Frelinghuysen, and a letter from the rev. William Neill, d. d 223 pp. 1 portrait. 16°. *Philadelphia, H. Perkins*, 1835.

——— Sketches of protestantism in Italy, past and present. Including a notice of the origin, history, and present state of the Waldenses. 418 pp. 1 portrait. 12°. *Boston, B. Perkins & co.* 1845.

——— Transplanted flowers, or memoirs of mrs. Rumpff, daughter of John Jacob Astor, and the duchess de Broglie, daughter of madame de Staël. With an appendix. 160 pp. incl. 2 pl. 12°. *New York, J. S. Taylor*, 1839.

Baker (Benjamin Franklin). Baker's theoretical and practical harmony: including a complete classification of intervals, common chords, discords, diatonic and fundamental harmonies, suspensions, and passing notes; with a treatment of thorough base, the affinity of chords, modulation, and pedal point. 112 pp. 8°. *Boston, O. Ditson & co.* 1870.

——— Camillus, the roman conqueror. A dramatic cantata, for mixed voices. Libretto by rev. I. N. Carman. Music by B. F. Baker. 76 pp. 8°. *Boston, H. Tolman & co.* 1865.

Baker (C. S. *m. d.*) Questions on the gospel according to st. John; or, the bible its own interpreter. 79 pp. 12°. *Norristown (Pa.) M. R. Wills*, 1871.

Baker (Harriet Newell Woods). Belle Clement's influence. A book for girls. 249 pp. 3 pl. 16°. *Boston, H. A. Young & co.* [1871].

——— Edith Withington; a book for girls. By H. N. W. B. [*anon.*] 249 pp. 3 pl. 16°. *Boston, H. A. Young & co.* [1871].

Baker (H. N. W.)—continued.

——— The happy home stories. For girls. By aunt Hattie. [*pseudon.*] 6 v. 18°. *Boston, H. A. Young & co.* 1871.

CONTENTS.

v. 1. Little Flyaway. 104 pp. 4 pl.
2. The spoiled picture. 105 pp. 3 pl.
3. Fleda's childhood. 105 pp. 4 pl.
4. The singing girl. 106 pp. 4 pl.
5. Molly and the wine-glass. 105 pp. 4 pl.
6. The twins. 103 pp. 4 pl.

——— Howard and his teacher, the sister's influence, and other stories. By mrs. Madeline Leslie. [*pseudon.*] 244 pp. 4 pl. 16°. *Boston, Shepard, Clark & Brown*, 1859.

——— Lulu Reed's pupil; a book for girls. By H. N. W. B. [*anon.*] 253 pp. 3 pl. 16°. *Boston, H. A. Young & co.* [1871].

——— Play and study. By mrs. Madeline Leslie. [*pseudon.*] 260 pp. 4 pl. 16°. *Boston, Shepard, Clark & Brown*, 1858.

——— Sophie's letter book; a book for girls. 248 pp. 3 pl. 16°. *Boston, H. A. Young*, [1871].

——— The twin brothers. [*anon.*] 243 pp. 18°. *New York, Harper & brothers*, 1843.

Baker (*Sir* Samuel White). Cast up by the sea. xiii, 456 pp. 9 pl. 16°. *London, Macmillan & co.* 1869.

Bakewell (Frederick C.) Natural evidence of a future life, derived from the properties and actions of animate and inanimate matter. xxiv, 372 pp. 8°. *London, Longman*, 1835.

——— Philosophical conversations: in which are familiarly explained the causes of many daily occurring natural phenomena. With notes and questions for review, by Ebenezer Bailey. xii, 286 pp. 9 pl. 12°. *Boston, Carter, Hendee & co.* 1833.

——— The same. 252 pp. 8 pl. 12°. *Boston, Carter, Hendee & co.* 1834.

Bakhtyar (The) nameh, or story of prince Bakhtyar and the ten viziers; a series of Persian tales. From a manuscript in the collection of sir William Ouseley. [*anon.*] vii, 119 pp. 8°. *London, the oriental press, for J. Debrett*, 1801.

Balance (The), and Columbian repository. [Weekly]. Jan. 1 to Dec. 24, 1805. v. 4. 4°. *Hudson, (N. Y.) H. Croswell*, 1805.

Balbi (Adrian). An abridgment of universal geography, modern and ancient: chiefly compiled from the Abrégé de géographie of Adrian Balbi. By T. G. Bradford. 520 pp. 24 pl. 12°. *Boston, W. D. Ticknor*, 1835.
[Atlas wanting].

Balcarcel y Formento (Domingo) *and* **Malo** (Felix Venancio). Lagrymas de la paz, vertidas en las exequias del señor d. Fernando de Borbon, vi. monarcha, de los que con tan esclarecido nombre ilustraron la monarchia española: celebradas en el augusto, metropolitano templo de esta imperial corte de Mexico. 3 p. l. 98 pp. 31 pl. sm. 4°. *Mexico, Colegio de San Ildefonso*, 1762.
[*Note.*—Contains emblematical plates engraved on copper by Antonio Moreno of Mexico].

Balch (Thomas). Les Français en Amérique pendant la guerre de l'indépendance des États-Unis, 1777–1783. viii, 277 pp. 1 map. 3 pl. 8°. *Paris, A. Sauton*, 1872.

Balch (*Rev.* Thomas Bloomer). Reminiscences of Georgetown, D. C. Second lecture delivered in the meth. protestant church, Georgetown, D. C. March 9, 1859. 26 pp. 8°. *Washington, H. Polkinhorn*, 1859. s.

Baldelli-Boni (Giovanni Batista). Del Petrarca e delle sue opere libri quatro. xxvi, 321 pp. 4°. *Firenze, G. Cambiahi*, 1797.

CONTENTS.

Brevi notizie intorno agli scrittori ed alle edizioni delle vite del Petrarca.
Del Petrarca e delle sue opere.
Notizie di Laura.
Del Virgilio di Milano.
Antenati congiunti e discendenti del Petrarca.
Calunnia apposta al Petrarca e confutazione della medesima.
Avvertimenti per una nuova edizione delle opere latine del Petrarca.
Notizie degli uomini illustri menzionati nell' opera.
Sommario cronologico della vita del Petrarca.

Baldi (Bernardino). Memorie concernenti la città di Urbino. 4 p. l. 148 pp. 148 pl. fol. *Roma, G. M. Salvioni*, 1724.

Baldi (Domenico). Dispvtatio de avro. 167 pp. 16°. *Florentiæ, typis F. Honofrij*, 1657.

Baldwin (Abraham C.) Themes for the pulpit: being a collection of nearly three thousand topics with texts, suitable for public discourses in the pulpit and lecture-room. Mostly compiled from the published works of ancient and modern divines. 324 pp. 12°. *New York, M. W. Dodd*, 1841.

Baldwin (John Dennison). Ancient America, in notes on american archæology. 299 pp. 12°. *New York, Harper & bros.* 1872.

Baldwin (Thomas, *d. d.*) A sermon delivered in Boston, Dec. 29, 1799, occasioned by the death of George Washington. 28 pp. 8°. *Boston, Manning & Loring*, [1800].
[HAZARD pamphlets, v. 64].

Balfe (Michael William). The Bohemian girl. [Libretto, without music]. *See* **Bunn** (Alfred).

——— The Rose of Castile. [Libretto, without

Balfe (Michael William)—continued. music.] 43 pp. 8°. [*New York*], *W. C. Bryant & co.* 1871.

[PAREPA-ROSA grand English opera].

——— Satanella; or, the power of love. [Libretto, without music.] *See* **Harris** (A.) *and* **Falconer** (E.)

Ballantyne (Randall). Rainy afternoons, or tales and sketches by the Howard family. 2 p. l. 267 pp. 11 pl. 12°. *Edinburgh, T. Constable & co.* 1853.

Ballard (*Rev.* Edward). Geographical names on the coast of Maine. From the coast survey report for 1868. 19 pp. 4°. [*Washington*], 1871.

Ballard (Edwin). *See* **Amateurs'** (The) annual, for 1872.

Ballard (Mrs. Julia P.) Building stones. 240 pp. 4 pl. 16°. *Boston, D. Lothrop & co.* 1871.

——— A little life. 112 pp. 2 pl. 18°. *Boston, I. P. Warren*, [1871].

Ballexserd (Jacques). Dissertation sur l'éducation physique des enfants, depuis leur naissance jusqu'à l'âge de puberté. 202 pp. 6 l. 18°. *Paris, Vallatla-Chapelle*, 1765.

Ballou (Hosea, 2d. *d. d.*, *b.* 1796, *d.* 1861). Ancient history of universalism, from the time of the apostles to the fifth general council, with an appendix, tracing the doctrine to the reformation. With notes, by rev. A. St. John Chambré, and T. J. Sawyer, d. d. [3d ed.] 313 pp. 12°. *Boston, universalist publishing house*, 1872.

Ballou (Maturin M.) Treasury of thought Forming an encyclopedia of quotations from ancient and modern authors. xii, 579 pp. 8°. *Boston, J. R. Osgood & co.* 1872.

Ballou's monthly magazine. Jan. 1871, to June, 1872. v. 33–35. 8°. *Boston, Thomes & Talbot*, [1871–72].

Balsacius (Joannes Ludovicus). *See* **Balzac** (Jean Louis Guez de).

Baltard (Louis Pierre). Paris et ses monumens, avec des descriptions historiques par Amaury-Duval. 3 parts in 1 v. fol. *Paris, auteur*, 1803–5.

CONTENTS.

Part 1. Le Louvre. 3 p. l. 53, 4 pp. 41 pl.
Saint Cloud. 20 pp. 11 pl.
Part 2. Château d'Écouen. 2 p. l. 14 pp. 14 pl.
Part 3. Fontainebleau. 1 p. l. 10 pp. 20 pl.
[No more published. Imperfect: pl. 6–9 of part 3 wanting].

Baltimore, (*Md.*) *Commissioners on Jones' falls.* Report of the joint standing committee on Jones' falls, to the first branch of the city council of Baltimore, October 7, 1870. Together with the ordinance as adopted Jan. 31, 1870. 186 pp. 4 maps. 8°. *Baltimore, city printers*, 1870.

Baltimore (*Md.*)—continued.

——— Wood's Baltimore city directory, 1871 and 1872. 2 v. 8°. *Baltimore, J. W. Woods*, 1871–72.

——— Business directory. 1871. *See* **Cleary** (William P.) & co.

Baltimore corn and flour exchange. Annual reports, for 1868, 1869, and 1871. 3 v. 8°. *Baltimore*, 1869–72.

Baltimore: past and present. With biographical sketches of its representative men. Illustrated by Bendann brothers. 1 p. l. 562 pp. 62 portraits. 8°. *Baltimore, Richardson & Bennett*, 1871.

Balzac (Jean Louis Guez, *seigneur* de). Le Barbon. 18°. *Norimbergæ*, 1665.

[*In* EPULUM parasiticum, pp. 221–315].

——— Socrate chrestien; & autres œuvres du mesme autheur. Eng. title, 14 p. l. 390, 178 pp. 20 l. 12°. *Paris, A. Covrbe*, 1657.

CONTENTS.

Le Socrate chrestien. Apologie contre le doctevr de Lovvain.
Devx discovrs envoyez à Rome, à monseignevr le cardinal Bentivoglio.
Trois discovrs envoyez à m. Descartes.
Dissertation ov diverses remarqves svr divers escrits, à m. Conrart.
Dissertation, ov responses à qvelqves qvestions. Av rev. pere Domandré de Saint Denis.

Bambagiuoli (Graziuolo). Roberto re di Gierusalemme sopra le virtù morali. [*pseudon.*] 8°. [*Turino, stamperia reale*, 1750].

[*In* UBALDINI (F.) Il trattato delle virtù morali, etc. pp. 1–32, ed. 1750].

Bampfield (Robert William). An essay on curvatures and diseases of the spine, including all the forms of spinal distortion. Edited by J. K. Mitchell, m. d. 223 pp. 8°. *Philadelphia, E. Barrington & G. D. Haswell*, 1845.

——— A practical treatise on tropical dysentery, more particularly as it occurs in the East Indies; [also], a practical treatise on scorbutic dysentery, with some facts and observations relative to scurvy. 2 p. l. x, 352, 11 pp. 1 tab. 8°. *London, Burgess & Hill*, 1819.

Bancroft (Albert L.) Bancroft's tourists' guide. The geysers. San Francisco, and around the bay, (north.) 227 pp. 2 l. lxxx pp. 16°. *San Francisco, A. L. Bancroft & co.* 1871.

——— The same. Yosemite. San Francisco

Bancroft (Albert L.)—continued. and around the bay, (south.) 256, lviii pp. 16°. *San Francisco, A. L. Bancroft & co.* 1871.

Bandello (Matteo). Romeo e Giulietta. Novella. 8°. [*Pisa, fratelli Nistri & co.* 1831].
[*In* PORTO (Luigi da). Giulietta e Romeo. 1831. pp. 75-122, 1 pl.]

Bandini (Angiolo Maria). Cl. Italorvm et Germanorvm epistolæ ad Petrvm Victorivm senatorem florentinvm nvnc primvm ex archetypis in lvcem ervtæ recensvit Victorii vitam adiecit et animadversionibvs illvstravit Ang. Mar. Bandinius. v. 1. civ, 176 pp. 1 pl. 4°. *Florentiæ*, 1758.

Bangor (*Maine*). Greenough, Jones & co.'s directory of the inhabitants, institutions, business firms, etc. in the city of Bangor, for 1871-2. [Also], a directory of Brewer. 3 p. l. 272, 60 pp. 1 l. 1 map. 8°. *Bangor, D. Bugbee & co.* 1871.

Bankers' (The) magazine, journal of the money market, and commercial digest. [London monthly]. April, 1844, to Dec. 1871. v. 1-31. 8°. *London, R. Groombridge and Groombridge & sons*, 1844-71.
[Wanting, v. 26 for 1866].

Bankers' (The) magazine and statistical register. [New York monthly]. Edited by I. Smith Homans. July, 1870, to June, 1871. Third series, v. 5. [Complete series], v. 25. 8°. *New York, I. S. Homans, jr.* 1870-71.

Banner of the church. [Weekly]. Joseph Cross, d.d. [and others], editors. Dec. 9, 1870, to Dec. 16, 1871. v. 1-2. fol. *Atlanta and Memphis*, [*W. S. Speirs*], 1870-71.

Banning (Edmund P. *m. d.*) Common sense on the mechanical pathology and treatment of chronic diseases of the male and female systems. 14th ed. With his lecture on the philosophy of the human voice, [and] on dress. 333 pp. 1 portrait. 12°. *New York, Wilson & co.* [1852].

Baptist (The) hymn book. [*anon.*] 590 pp. 16°. *Philadelphia, American baptist publication society*, [1871].

Baptist (The) praise book: for congregational singing. By Richard Fuller, E. M. Levy, S. D. Phelps, H. C. Fish, T. Armitage, E. T. Winkler, W. W. Everts, G. C. Lorimer, and Basil Manly, jr. J. P. Holbrook, special musical editor. xii, 9-640 pp. 8°. *New York, A. S. Barnes & co.* 1871.

Baptist (The) quarterly. Edited by prof. Lucius E. Smith, assisted by drs. Alvah Hovey, E. G. Robinson, A. N. Arnold, and

Baptist (The) quarterly—continued. J. M. Gregory. v. i. 1867. 512 pp. 8°. *Philadelphia, American baptist publication society*, 1867.

Baptist (The) teacher. A monthly journal for sunday-school workers. Editors, rev. A. E. Dickinson and rev. George A. Peltz. Jan. 1870, to Dec. 1871. v. 1-2. 4°. *Philadelphia, American baptist publication society*, [1870-71].

Bar (Jacques Charles). Recueil de tous les costumes des ordres religieux et militaires, avec un abrégé historique et chronologique. Enrichi de notes et de planches coloriées. 6 v. fol. *Paris, l'auteur*, 1778-89.

CONTENTS.

v. 1. Les costumes religieux et militaires des Mameluks, Arabes, Turcs, Orientaux, etc. [103 pl.]
v. 2. La suite des costumes des peuples de l'orient, des templiers, des chanoines et chevaliers de la Syrie, de la Palestine, d'Égypte, d'Éthiopie, d'Afrique, et de l'Inde. [92 pl.]
v. 3. Les ordres de chevalerie d'Europe. [110 pl.]
v. 4-5. Les ordres monastiques masculins. [96 pl; 100 pl.]
v. 6. Les ordres monastiques féminins. [116 pl.]

Barante (A. G. Prosper Brugière, *baron* de). A tableau of french literature during the eighteenth century. Translated from the 4th ed. xxxi, 216 pp. 16°. *London, Smith, Elder & co.* 1833.

Barbarigo (*Cardinale* Gregorio). Lettera pastorale alli molto rr. arcipreti, parrochi, e curati della città, e sua diocese, per promuovere alla sacra comunione li figliuoli, e figliuole idonei, ed arrivati agli anni, della discrezione. 10 pp. 16°. *Padova, stamperia del seminario*, 1770.
[*With* BELLARMINO (*Cardinale* Roberto). Dichiarazione più copiosa della dottrina christiana breve. 1770].

Barbaro (Daniello). Exqvisitæ in Porphirivm commentationes. 110 l. sm. 4°. *Venetiis, apud Aldi filios*, 1542.

Barbaro (Francesco). Prvdentissimi et gravi docvmenti circa la elettion della moglie al molto magnifico m. Lorenzo de Medici: nuouamente dal latino tradotti per m. Al berto Lollio. 62 l. numb. 4 l. unp. 16°. *Vinegia, G. Giolito de Ferrari*, 1548.

Barbaro (Hermolao, *the younger*). Epistole. 12°. [*Vinegia, G. Giolito de Ferrari*, 1548].
[*In* DOLCE (L.) Epistole. 1548. l. 139-152].

Barbee (William J. *m. d.*) The cotton question. The production, export, manufacture, and consumption of cotton. A condensed treatise on cotton in all its aspects: agricultural, commercial, and political. 251 pp. 6 pl. 12°. *New York, metropolitan record office*, 1866.

Barberino (Francesco da, *b.* 1264). Del reggimento e de' costumi delle donne. [Con annotazioni di Guglielmo Manzi, editore]. 4 p. l. xxxv, 407, 126 pp. 1 l. 1 portrait. 8°. *Roma, de Romanis*, 1815.

Barberino (Maffeo). *See* **Urban viii.**

Barberio (Giuseppe). De miseria poetarum græcorum. 18°. [*Lipsiæ, apud J. F. Gleditsch*, 1707].

[*In* MENCKEN (J. B.) Analecta de calamitate litteratorum. 1707. pp. 483-593].

Barbette (Paul, *m. d.*) Thesaurus chirurgiæ. Composed according to the doctrine of the circulation of the blood, and other new inventions of the moderns. With a treatise of the plague. Translated out of low-dutch into english. 3d. ed. To which is added the surgeon's chest [by Guil. Fabrice. Also], is adjoyned a treatise of diseases that for the most part attend camps and fleets. Written in high-dutch by Raymundus Mindererus. 3 v. in 1. Eng. title, 7 p. l. 394 pp. 7 l. 4 pl; 152 pp. 5 l. 16°. *London, M. Pitt*, 1676.

Barbier (Marie Anne). Les tragédies et autres poésies. Nouv. éd. 342 pp. 12°. *Leide, B. J. Van der Aa*, 1723.

Barbieri (Giovanni Maria). Dell' origine della poesia rimata. Opera, pubblicata ora per la prima volta e con annotazioni illustrata dal cav. ab. Girolamo Tiraboschi. 188 pp. 4°. *Modena, presso la società tipografica*, 1790.

Barbour (John, *archdeacon of Aberdeen*, 1375). The Bruce; or, the book of the most excellent and noble prince, Robert de Broyss, king of Scots: [etc.] With a preface, notes, and glossarial index, by the rev. Walter W. Skeat, [etc.] Part i. 8°. *London*, 1870.

[EARLY English text society. Extra series, no. 11].

Barcellini (Innocenzio). Industrie filologiche per dar risalto alle virtù del santissimo pontefice Celestino v., e liberare da alcune taccie Dante Alighieri creduto censore della celebre rinunzia fatta dal medesimo santo. 11 p. l. 342 pp. 16°. *Milano, G. P. Malatesta*, 1701.

Barchou de Penhoën (*Baron* Auguste Théodore Hilaire). Histoire de la philosophie allemande depuis Leibnitz jusqu'à Hegel. 2 v. 2 p. l. 412 pp; 2 p. l 308 pp. 1 l. 8°. *Paris, Charpentier*, 1836.

Barclay (John). Joannis Barclaii Argenis, figuris æneis adillustrata, suffixo clave, hoc est, nominum propriorum explicatione, atque indice locupletissimo. 11 p. l. 708 pp. 18 l. 37 pl. 18°. *Noribergæ, sumptibus W. M. Endteri*, 1703.

Barclay (John M.) Digest of the rules of the house of representatives U. S., the joint rules of the two houses, and of so much of Jefferson's manual as under the rules governs the house; of precedents of order and usages of the house: together with such portions of the constitution of the United States, laws of Congress, and resolutions of the house as relate to the proceedings of the house and the rights and duties of its members. 249 pp. 8°. *Washington, government printing office*, 1871.

[*With* UNITED STATES. Constitution. *Washington*, 1871].

Barclay (*Sir* Richard). A discovrse of the felicitie of man. Or his summum bonum. Written by sir Richard Barckley, knight, and now newly corrected and augmented. [2d. ed.] Eng. title, 7 p. l. 717 pp. sm. 4°. *London, W. Ponsonby*, 1603.

Barde (Alexandre). Histoire des comités de vigilance aux Attakapas. 428 pp. 16°. *Saint-Jean-Baptiste (Louisiane)*, 1861.

Bardwell (*Rev.* Horatio). Memoir of rev. Gordon Hall, one of the first missionaries of the amer. board of comm for for. missions, at Bombay. 260 pp. 1 pl. 12°. *Andover, Flagg, Gould & Newman*, 1834.

Barker (Fordyce, *m. d.*) On sea-sickness. 36 pp. 16°. *New York, D. Appleton & co.* 1870.

Barker (George Frederick, *m. d.*) The correlation of vital and physical forces. 36 pp. 12°. *New Haven (Conn.) C. C. Chatfield & co.* 1871.

[HALF hours with modern scientists, pp. 37-72, *or* no. 2, University series].

Barker (Joseph, *of Wortley*). Life of William Penn, the celebrated quaker and founder of Pennsylvania. 1 p. l. 9-320 pp. 1 portrait. 16°. *London, J. Chapman*, 1847.

Barker (Joseph, *esq.*) The authentic report of the theological discussion between the rev. William Cooke and Joseph Barker, 1845. *See* **Cooke** (William) and **Barker.**

Barker (R. P.) Texas; the "lone star state." Its lands, its soil, its productions, its climate and health, its inhabitants, railroads, harbors, seaports and rivers. 23 pp. 8°. *New York, C. D. Wynkoop*, 1871.

Barlow (John R.) John's trip, or a visit to Niagara. A serio-comic poem, in four cantos. 96 pp. 8°. *Niagara Falls, W. Pool*, 1871.

Barlow (Thomas, *d. d. bishop of Lincoln*). Genuine remains. Containing divers discourses theological, philosophical, historical, &c. Publish'd from his lordship's original papers. 12 p. l. 643 pp. 16°. *London, J. Dunton*, 1693.

Barnabas (*Saint*). The catholic epistle of st. Barnabas. 12°. [*Oxford*, 1840].

[*In* WAKE (William). The genuine epistles of the apostolical fathers, pp. 222–248].

Barnabas (*Pseudo-*) Η φερομενη του ἁγιου βαρναβα ἀποστολου επιστολη καθολικη. Sancti Barnabæ apostoli (vt fertvr) epistola catholica. Hanc primum e tenebris eruit, notisque et obseruationibus illustrauit Hugo Menardus monachus Sancti Mauri in Gallia. Opvs posthvmvm. 7 p. l. 246 pp. 1 l. 4°. *Parisiis, S. Piget*, 1645.

[*Note.*—It is not improbable that the author's name was Barnabas, and that the Alexandrian fathers came to the precipitate conclusion that it was composed by the associate of Paul.—*Smith's bib. dict.*]

Barnard (Charles). Gardening for money. How it was done, in flowers, strawberries, vegetables. 345 pp. 12°. *Boston, Loring*, [1869].

CONTENTS.

My ten-rod farm; or, how I became a florist.
The strawberry garden. How it was planted, what it cost, what came of it, financially and sentimentally.
John and Kate Wellson's successful experiment.
Farming by inches; or, "with brains, sir."
Mr. and Mrs. Robert Nellson's successful experiment.

——— The soprano: a musical story. By Jane Kingsford. [*pseudon.*] 179 pp. 12°. *Boston, Loring*, [1869].

Barnard (*Rev.* John, *of Marblehead, Mass b.* 1681, *d.* 1770). Ashton's memorial. An history of the strange adventures, and signal deliverances, of mr. Philip Ashton, with a short account of mr. Nicholas Merritt. To which is added a sermon on Dan. 3, 17. 2 p. l. 66 pp. 12°. *Boston, S. Gerrish*, 1725.

——— A new version of the psalms of David; fitted to the tunes used in the churches. With several hymns. 2 p. l. 278 pp. 1 l. 16°. *Boston, T. Leverett*, 1752.

——— Two sermons: the christian's behaviour under severe and repeated bereavements, and the fatal consequence of a peoples persisting in sin. [Preached to the very reverend dr. Mather's church in the time of the measels, 1713, 14]. 1 p. l. 68 pp. 16°. *Boston*, 1714.

[Title-page imperfect].

Barnes (*Rev.* Albert). An inquiry into the organization and government of the apostolic church: particularly with reference to the claims of episcopacy. 251 pp. 16°. *Philadelphia, Perkins & Purves*, 1843.

——— An inquiry into the scriptural views of slavery. 384 pp. 12°. *Philadelphia, Perkins & Purves*, 1846.

——— Life at three score and ten. [A sermon]. 148 pp. 16°. *New York, American tract society*, [1871].

——— Notes on the books of the new testament. *See* **Bible.** (*English*).

——— Practical sermons. 356 pp. 12°. *Philadelphia, H. Perkins*, 1841.

——— The scriptural argument for episcopacy examined. [*anon.*] 172 pp. 18°. *New-York, Leavitt, Lord & co.* 1835.

——— Sermons on revivals. With an introduction by rev. Joel Parker, d. d. 210 pp. 18°. *New-York, J. S. Taylor & co.* 1841.

Barnum (Phineas Taylor). Struggles and triumphs: or, forty years' recollections of P. T. Barnum. Author's ed. (Biography complete to April, 1871.) 856 pp. 28 pl. 1 portrait. 8°. *New York, American news co.* 1871.

Barnum (*Rev.* Samuel W.) Romanism as it is: an exposition of the roman catholic system, for the use of the american people; the whole drawn from official and authentic sources. 753 pp. 7 pl. 8°. *Hartford, (Conn.) Connecticut publishing co.* 1871.

Baroni Cavalcabó (Clemente). L'impotenza del demonio di trasportare a talento per l'aria da un luogo all' altro i corpi umani dimostrata. Dove anche si dimostra l'impossibilità di volare con artifizio umano. xxiv, 142 pp. 8°. *Rovereto, per il marchesani*, 1753.

Barrande (Joachim). Distribution des céphalopodes dans les contrées siluriennes. Extrait du syst. silur. du centre de la Bohême. v. 2. xviii, 480 pp. 8°. *Prague* [*et*] *Paris, l'auteur & éditeur*, 1870. s.

——— Documents anciens et nouveaux sur la faune primordiale et le système taconique en Amérique. 8°. *Paris*, 1861. s.

[Extrait du bulletin de la société géologique de France. 2e s. t. 17. pp. 203–321. pl. 4–5].

——— Trilobites. Extrait du supplément au vol. 1 du système silurien du centre de la Bohême. vi, 282 pp. 8°. *Prague* [*et*] *Paris, l'auteur & éditeur*, 1871. s.

Barré (Guillaume). History of the french consulate, under Napoleon Buonaparte; being an authentic narrative of his administration, including a sketch of his life, and a faithful

Barré (Guillaume)—continued. statement of interesting transactions, until the renewal of hostilities in 1803. viii, 535 pp. 1 portrait. 8°. *London, J. Cundee for T. Hurst*, 1804.

Barre (W. L.) Lives of illustrious men of America, distinguished in the annals of the republic as legislators, warriors, and philosophers. 906 pp. 28 portraits. 8°. *Cincinnati, W. A. Clarke*, 1859.

Barrell (George, *jun.*) The pedestrian in France and Switzerland. 312 pp. 12°. *New York, G. P. Putnam & co.* 1853.

Barrett (*Rev.* Benjamin F.) Episcopalianism. In three parts. 180 pp. 16°. *Philadelphia, J. B. Lippincott & co.* 1871.

——— The golden reed; or, the true measure of a true church. 311 pp. 12°. *New York, D. Appleton & co.* 1855.

——— Life of Emanuel Swedenborg, with some account of his writings. vii, 160 pp. 12°. *New York, S. Colman*, 1841.

——— The new view of hell. Showing its nature, whereabouts, duration, and how to escape it. 215 pp. 12°. *Philadelphia, J. B. Lippincott & co.* 1872.

Barrett (J. O.) Looking beyond: a souvenir of love to the bereft of every home. 101 pp. 12°. *Boston, W. White & co.* 1871.

——— The spiritual pilgrim: a biography of James M. Peebles. 303 pp. 1 portrait. 8°. *Boston, W. White & co.* 1871.

Barrière (Théodore) *and* **Sardou** (Victorien). A nervous set. Comedy in three acts. Translated from the french by S. M. Quincy, for the Boston amateur dramatic club. 96 pp. 12°. *Boston, Rand, Avery & Frye*, 1870.

Barros (Alonso de). Proverbi morali. Tradotti in italiano dal Alessandro Adimari. Col testo spagniolo a rincontro. 172 pp. 2 l. 18°. *Firenze, Zanobi Pignoni*, 1622.

Barros Arana (Diego). Compendio de historia de America. Partes i. (1) ii. America indijena. Descubrimiento i conquista. iv, 410 pp. 8°. *Santiago, Ferrocarril*, 1865. s.

——— Historia de la independencia de Chile durante los años 1811–12. 8°. *Santiago, imprenta nacional*, 1866. s.

[Valenzuela (J. S.) Historia jeneral de Chile. v. 1, pp. 267–471].

Barrows (*Rev.* E. P. *d.d.*) Sacred geography and antiquities. 685 pp. 22 pl. 5 maps. 12°. *New York, American tract society*, [1871].

Barruel (Auguste, *abbé*). The history of the clergy during the french revolution. xxiv, 396 pp. 8°. *Dublin, H. Fitzpatrick for P. Wogan*, 1794.

Barry (Charles A.) How to draw. Six letters to a little girl on the elementary principles of drawing. 57 pp. 16°. *Boston, J. R. Osgood & co.* 1871.

Barry (Herbert). Russia in 1870. xii, 418 pp. 12°. *London, Wyman & sons*, 1871.

Barry (P.) Barry's fruit garden. Revised, enlarged, and newly electrotyped. Illustrated. 491 pp. 12°. *New York, O. Judd & co.* [1872].

Barteau's new and improved sunday-school secretary's record. 1 p. l. 105 l. [blank]. 8°. *New York, Carlton & Lanahan*, [1872].

Barth (Heinrich). Sammlung und bearbeitung central-afrikanischer vokabularien. Collection of vocabularies of central-african languages. Parts 1–3. cccxxxiv, 295 pp. 8°. *Gotha, J. Perthes*, 1862–66. s.

Barthe (*Abbé* Eduard). Monument to the glory of Mary. Litany of the most Holy Virgin, accompanied with meditations. Translated from the french by an unworthy daughter of st. Joseph. 292 pp. 12°. *Philadelphia, P. F. Cunningham*, 1871.

Barthélemy (Jean Jacques). Carite and Polydorus. To which is prefixed, a treatise on morals. With the life of the author. xiv, 213 pp. 1 portrait. 16°. *London, Otridge & son*, 1799.

Barthez (Paul Joseph). Nouveaux élémens de la science de l'homme. 2e éd. 2 v. 4 p. l. 304, 238 pp; 2 p. l. 339, 244 pp. 8°. *Paris, Goujon*, 1806.

Bartholin (Albert). De scriptis Danorum, liber posthumus, auctior editus à fratre Thoma Bartholino. 6 p. l. 150 pp. 16°. *Hafniæ, P. Haubold*, 1666.

Bartholomew (*Elder* Jacob B.) A chronological chart of the old and new testaments. 1 l. folded. 8°. [*Eagleville (O.)* 1871].

Bartholomew (John). The handy atlas, consisting of maps of modern geography of all countries, embracing all the latest discoveries and changes in boundaries, and maps of ancient and historical geography. 2 p. l. 38 col. maps. 42 pp. 8°. *Chicago, Callaghan, Cockcroft & Warren*, 1871.

Bartholow (Roberts, *m. d.*) Spermatorrhœa: its causes, symptoms, results, and treatment. 3d ed. vi pp. 3 l. 120 pp. 12°. *New York, W. Wood & co.* 1871.

Bartlett (David W.) Cases of contested elections. *Washington*, 1870. *See* **United States.** *Congress.* Digest of election cases.

Bartlett (Elisha, *m. d.*) The history, diagnosis, and treatment of typhoid and of typhus fever; with an essay on the diagnosis of bilious remittent and of yellow fever. xvi, 393 pp. 8°. *Philadelphia, Lea & Blanchard*, 1842.

Bartlett (*Rev.* Thomas). Memoirs of the life, character, and writings, of Joseph Butler, late lord bishop of Durham. xxiv, 526 pp. 1 portrait. 8°. *London, J. W. Parker*, 1839.

Bartley (James Avis). Lays of ancient Virginia, and other poems. 204 pp. 12°. *Richmond, J. W. Randolph*, 1855.

Bartol (*Rev.* Cyrus Augustus). Pictures of Europe, framed in ideas. 2d ed. 2 p. l. 407 pp. 12°. *Boston, Crosby, Nichols & co.* 1856.

——— Radical problems. 2 p. l. 407 pp. 12°. *Boston, Roberts brothers*, 1872.

Barton (*Rev.* John). Perils of popery, especially considered with reference to the United States of America. 2 p.l. 236 pp. 16°. *Cincinnati, H. W. Derby & co.* 1845.

Barton (Richard). Farrago, containing essays, moral, philosophical, political, and historical: on Shakespeare, truth, boxing, kings, religion, commerce, governments, politeness, ennui, ingratitude, fortune, politics, &c. Abstracts and selections on various subjects. [*anon.*] 4 p. l. 414 pp. 8°. *Tewksbury, Dyde & son*, 1792.

Baruffaldi (Girolamo, *juniore*). Della tipografia ferrarese dall' anno mcccclxxi. al md. 96 pp. 8°. *Ferrara, G. Rinaldi*, 1777.

——— La vita di m. Lodovico Ariosto. 323 pp. 1 portrait. 4°. *Ferrara, pe' socj. bianchi e negri stamp. del seminario*, 1807.

Bascom (John). Æsthetics; or, the science of beauty. vii, 268 pp. 12°. *New York and Chicago, Woolworth, Ainsworth & co.* 1872.

——— Political economy: designed as a text-book for colleges. 366 pp. 12°. *Andover, W. F. Draper*, 1859.

——— Science, philosophy, and religion. Lectures delivered before the Lowell institute, Boston. iv, 311 pp. 12°. *New York, G. P. Putnam & sons*, 1871.

Bashfulness cured: ease and elegance of manner quickly gained. [*anon.*] 45 pp. 18°. *New York, S. Conly*, 1872.

Basilius Valentinus (*pseudon?*) Les douze clefs de philosophie de Basile Valentin. L'azoth, ou le moyen de faire l'or caché des

Basilius Valentinus—continued.

philosophes, de frère Basile Valentin. 12°. [*Paris, A. Cailleau*, 1741].

[*In* SALMON (Guillaume). Bibliothèque des philosophes chimiques. 1741. v. 3, pp. 1–180.

Note.—Andreas Solea is given in Jöcher as the real name of this alchemist; but all the best recent authorities give the name as above].

Basket (A) of barley loaves. By the author of "The high mountain apart." [*anon.*] 152 pp. 16°. *Philadelphia, Presbyterian board of publication*, [1870].

Basnage (Benjamin). De l'éstat visible et invisible de l'église. Servant de résponse à la demande, où estoit votre église, et de la parfaite satisfaction de Iésus Christ contre la fable du purgatoire. 8 p. l. 279 pp. 16°. *La Rochelle, Z. Le Cordier*, 1614.

Bastian (F.) Les abeilles. Traité théorique et pratique d'apiculture rationnelle. 3 p. l. iii, 328 pp. 16°. *Paris, librairie agricole de la maison rustique*, 1868.

Bastiat (Frédéric). Sophisms of the protectionists. Part i. Sophisms of protection—first series. Part ii. Sophisms of protection—second series. Part iii. Spoliation and law. Part iv. Capital and interest. Translated from the Paris edition of 1863. [By Horace White]. 3d ed. 1 p. l. xvi, 398 pp. 16°. *New York, American free trade league*, 1871.

Baston (William). Metrum de praelio apud Bannockburn. 8 pp. 4°. *Edinburgi, apud R. Fribarnium*, 1740.

[*With* MAJOR (John). Historia Majoris Britanniæ, 1740].

Batchelder (James L.) Societyism and its evils. The instrumentality of individuals and churches in the world's evangelization. By a Chicagoan. [*anon.*] 52 pp. 12°. *Chicago, Western news co.* 1871.

Bateman (Horatio). Biographies of two hundred and fifty distinguished national men. 1st ed. v. i. 5 p. l. xii, 250, 3 pp. 12°. *New York, J. T. Giles & co.* 1871.

Bateman (Newton). Eighth biennial report of the superintendent of public instruction. 1869–70. *See* **Illinois** (State of).

Bates (Samuel P.) History of Pennsylvania volunteers, 1861–5. v. 4. 8°. *Harrisburg, state printer*, 1870.

——— Lectures on mental and moral culture. 319 pp. 12°. *New York, A. S. Barnes & Burr*, 1860.

Bates (Thomas). The history of improved short-horn cattle, from the notes of the late Thomas Bates. *See* **Bell** (Thomas).

Bath (The) and Bristol magazine; or, western miscellany. v. 2-3. 1833-34. 8°. *Bath, E. Collings*, 1833-34.

Bathurst (*Rev.* Henry, *ll. b.*) Memoirs of the late dr. Henry Bathurst, lord bishop of Norwich. 2 v. xvi, 354 pp; 2 p. l. 356 pp. 8°. *London, A. J. Valpy*, 1837.

Bathurst (Ralph, *m. d.*) Literary remains. 296 pp. 8°. [*London*, 1761].

[*With* WARTON (Thomas). The life and literary remains of Ralph Bathurst].

Batjin (Nicolas). Histoire de l'empereur Napoléon i^er^ surnommé: le grand. 2 v. 660 pp. 3 pl; 640 pp. 8°. *Londres, Dulau et cie.* 1867.

Batkins (Jefferson S. *pseudon.*) Life of Jefferson S. Batkins, member from Cranberry Centre. Written by himself, assisted by the author of the "Silver spoon." [*pseudon.*] 496 pp. 1 portrait. 8°. *Boston, A. K. Loring*, [1871].

Battle (The) of the sexes. *See* **Wesley** (*Rev.* Samuel).

Bauclair. *See* **Beauclair** (P. L.)

Baudelot de Dairval (Charles César). De l'utilité des voyages, et de l'avantage que la recherche des antiquitéz procure aux sçavans. 2 v. 9 p. l. 361, xix pp. 1 l; 3 p. l. 361-732 pp. 9 l. 16°. *Paris, P. Auboüin & P. Emery*, 1686.

Baudens (Jean Baptiste Louis). La guerre de Crimée, les campements, les abris, les ambulances, les hôpitaux, etc. 2e éd. 3 p. l. 412 pp. 16°. *Paris, M. Lévy frères*, 1858.

Baudier (Dominique). Oratio fvnebris dicta honori & memoriæ maximi virorum Iosephi Ivsti Scaligeri. 23 pp. 4°. *Lvgdvni Batavorvm, apud L. Elzevirium & A. Cloncquium*, 1609.

[*With* HEINSIUS (D.) In obitum v. illustr. I. Scaligeri].

Baudius. *See* **Baudier.**

Baudrand (Michel Antoine). Geographia ordine litterarum disposita. 2 v. in 1. 12 p. l. 688 pp; 696 pp. 1 l. fol. *Parisiis, apud S. Michalct*, 1681-2.

Bauer (Eduin). Allgemeine predigtsammlung aus den werken der vorzüglichsten kanzelredner; zum vorlesen in landkirchen wie auch zur häuslichen erbauung. 3 v. 8°. *Leipzig, F. U. Brockhaus*, 1841-44.

CONTENTS.

v. 1. Evangelienpredigten auf alle sonn- und festtage des jahres. 1841.
v. 2. Epistelpredigten auf alle sonn- und festtage des jahres. 1843.
v. 3. Predigten über freie texte auf alle sonn- und festtage des jahres. 1844.

Bauer (Georg Lorenz). The theology of the old testament; or, a biblical sketch of the religious opinions of the ancient Hebrews. From the earliest times to the commencement of the christian era. Extracted and translated from the Theologie des alten testaments vii, 166 pp. 8°. *London, C. Fox*, 1838.

Bauer (Jacob). Gründlicher unterricht in der obstbaumzucht. Ein hand- und hausbuch für landwirthe und landschullehrer. xx, 259 pp. 2 pl. 16°. *Heidelberg, C. F. Winter*, 1833.

Bauhin (Caspar). De hermaphroditorum monstrosorumq: partuum natura, ex theologorum, jureconsultorum, medicorum, philosophorum, & rabbinorum sententia, libri duo hactenus non editi. 32; 572 pp. 12°. *Oppenheimi, typis H. Galleri, ære J. T. de Bry*, 1614.

[Eng. title and portrait of author on the 2d page. Title at the bottom reads *Francofvrti, excudebat M. Becker impensis I. T. & I. I. de Bry, frat.* 1600].

Baumann (Nicholas). Reynard the fox. A burlesque poem from the low-german original of the fifteenth century. [*anon.*] 202 pp. 12°. *Boston, De Vries, Ibarra & co.* 1865.

——— The same. Le roman du renard, traduit pour la première fois d'après un texte flamand du xiie siècle édité par J. F. Willems; augmenté d'une analyse de ce qu'ont écrit, au sujet des romans français du Renard, Legrand-d'Aussy, Robert, Raynouard, Saint Marc Girardin, Prosper Marchand, etc. Par Octave Delepierre. 2 p. l. iii, 335 pp. 8°. *Paris, Challamel*, [1837].

Baumbach (Adolph). Baumbach's new collection of sacred music. 219 pp. obl. 4°. *Chicago, Lyon & Healy*, [1871].

Baumhauer (Maria Matthias von). *Περι της ευλογου ἐξαγωγης.* Veterum philosophorum præcipue stoicorum doctrina de morte voluntaria. 4 p. l. 392 pp. 8°. *Trajecti ad Rhenum, tppis mandavit N. van der Monde*, 1842.

——— Disquisitio historico-juridica et critica de morte voluntaria. 2. p. l. 262 pp. 1 l. 8°. *Trajecti ad Rhenum, typis mandavit N. van der Monde*, 1843.

[*With his* Περι της ευλόγου ἐξαγωγης. *Trajecti ad Rhenum*, 1842].

Bausset (*Cardinal* Louis François de). Histoire de Bossuet, évêque de Meaux, composée sur les manuscrits originaux. 2e éd. revue et corrigée. 4 v. 8°. *Versailles, J. A. Lebel*, 1819.

Bavaria. (*K. statistisches bureau*). Die volkszählung im königreiche Bayern vom 3. Dezember 1867. 1. theil. Aufnahme der be-

Bavaria—continued.
völkerung nach den verabredungen des zollvereins mit hinweisung auf die resultate der früheren zählungen seit 1834 und der bewegung der bevölkerung von 1834 bis 1867, nebst einer kartographischen darstellung der dichtigkeit der bevölkerung. Summarischer ueberblick der religionsangehörigkeit der bevölkerung. Mit einer einleitung von dr. Georg Mayr. xxxii, 37 pp. 1 map. fol. *München, k. statistisches bureau*, 1868.
[XX. heft der beiträge zur statistik des königreichs Bayern].

——— ———. Verzeichniss der gemeinden des königreichs Bayern nach dem stande der bevölkerung im Dezember 1867, mit ausscheidung nach familien, geschlecht und religionsverhältnissen. vi, 265 pp. 1 l. 8°. *München, J. Gotteswinter & Mössel*, 1869. s.
[XXI. heft der beiträge zur statistik des königreichs Bayern].

Baxter (James). Technics for piano-forte. 64 pp. obl. 8°. *Friendship (N. Y.) J. C. Crandall*, 1870.

——— Technics for voice. 64 pp. obl. 8°. *Friendship (N. Y.) Baxter university of music*, [1871].

Baxter (*Rev.* Joseph). The duty of a people to pray to and bless God for their rulers. A sermon preached before the governour, council and representatives of Massachusetts-Bay, May 31, 1727. Being the day for the election of his majesty's council. 2 p. l. 36 pp. 16°. *Boston, B. Green*, 1727.

Baxter (Lydia). Gems by the wayside; or, religious and domestic poems. 283 pp. 1 portrait. 12°. *New York, Sheldon, Lamport & Blakeman*, 1855.

Baxter (*Rev.* Richard). A call to the unconverted. 18°. [*New York*, 1818].
[*In* ALLEINE (*Rev.* Joseph). The solemn warnings of the dead, pp. 183–288].

——— Paraphrase on the new testament. *See* **Bible.** (*English*).

——— *and* **Alleine** (*Mrs.* Theodosia). Life and death of the rev. Joseph Alleine, written by the rev. Richard Baxter, his widow, mrs. Theodosia Alleine, and other persons. [Also], his christian letters, full of spiritual instructions. With a preface by Alexander Duff, d. d. From the last Edinburgh ed. 275 pp. 12°. *New York, R. Carter*, 1840.

Baxter (R. Dudley). National debts. Partly read before the British association, at Liverpool. 2d ed. iv, 139 pp. 1 tab. 8°. *London, R. J. Bush*, 1871.

Bayer (Carl Robert). *See* **Byr.**

Bayle (Antoine Laurent Jessé). An elementary treatise on anatomy. Translated from the 4th edition of the french. By A. Sidney Doane, m. d. viii, 10–470 pp. 18°. *New York, Harper & brothers*, 1837.

——— *and* **Hollard** (Henri). A manual of general anatomy, containing a concise description of the elementary tissues of the human body. From the french. By S. D. Gross, m. d. x, 272 pp. 8°. *Philadelphia, J. Grigg*, 1828.

Bayle (Pierre). Projet et fragmens d'un dictionnaire critique. [*anon.*] 20 p. l. 400 pp. 4 l. 8°. *Rotterdam, R. Leers*, 1692.

Bayle (*Abbé, of Aix*). The pearl of Antioch. A picture of the east at the end of the fourth century. 355 pp. 1 pl. 12°. *Baltimore, Kelly, Piet & co.* 1871.

Bayley (*Rev.* John). Marriage as it is and as it should be. 175 pp. 12°. *New York, M. W. Dodd*, 1857.

Bayne (Peter). Essays in biography and criticism. Second series. 392 pp. 12°. *Boston, Gould & Lincoln*, 1858.

Bazancourt (César, *baron de*). Cinq mois au camp devant Sébastopol. 2e éd. 2 p. l. xxvii, 250 pp. 16°. *Paris, Amyot*, 1855.

Bazin (Antoine Pierre Louis). Théatre chinois ou choix de pièces de théatre composées sous les empereurs mongols, traduites pour la première fois sur le texte original. 2 p. l. lxiii, 409 pp. 1 l. 8°. *Paris, l'imprimerie royale*, 1838.

Bazin de Raucou (Anaïs). Notes historiques sur la vie de Molière. 2e éd. revue et augmentée. ix, 179 pp. 16°. *Paris, Techener*, 1851.

Beach (Alfred E.) The science record for 1872. A compendium of scientific progress and discovery during the past year. 400 pp. 4 pl. 12°. *New York, Munn & co.* 1872.

Beach (Elizabeth T. Porter). Pelayo: an epic of the olden time. 424 pp. 7 pl. 12°. *New York, D. Appleton & co.* 1864.

Beach (*Rev.* John). An appeal to the unprejudiced, in a supplement to the vindication of the worship of God according to the church of England. 106 pp. 16°. *Boston*, 1737.
[HAZARD pamphlets, v. 15].

——— A sermon, shewing that eternal life is God's free gift, bestowed upon all men who obey the gospel, and that free grace and free will concur in the affair of man's salvation.

Beach (*Rev.* John)—continued.
25 pp. 16°. *Newport, by the widow Franklin*, 1745.

——— Three discourses, casuistical and practical: Concerning the children's mocking the prophet Elisha, 2 Kings, ii, 23, 24. ii Explaining the true sense and meaning of those declarations the last shall be first, and the first last, and that many are called but few chosen, Matt. xx, 16. iii. Shewing the reason and propriety of rejoicing at the dissolution of the jewish state. Or, the destruction of Jerusalem and the temple, a proof of Christ's kingdom in heaven. From Luke, xxi, 28. 40 pp. 12°. *Boston, Mein & Fleming*, [*about* 1768].

——— Vindication of the worship of God according to the church of England, from the aspersions cast upon it by mr. Jonathan Dickinson, in a sermon preached at Newark, June 2, 1736. 58 pp. 16°. *New York, W. Bradford*, 1736.
[HAZARD pamphlets, v. 15].

Beadon (Richard, *lord bishop of Bath and Wells*). A commentary on the five books of Moses. 1694. *See* **Bible.** (*English*).

Beale (Anne). Nothing venture, nothing have. A novel. 3 v. 12° *London, R. Bentley*, 1864.

——— Simplicity and fascination; or, guardians and wards. 3 v. 12°. *London, R. Bentley*, 1855.

Beale (Francis). The game of chesse-play. [Introductory]. 18°. *London*, 1656.
[*In* GRECO (Gioachino). The royall game of chesse-play, pp. 1-16.
Note.—The English translation of this work is said to have appeared before the original in italian, which is not here given entire].

Beale (Lionel J.). A treatise on the distortions and deformities of the human body. Exhibiting a concise view of the nature and treatment of the principal malformations and distortions of the chest, spine and limbs. 2d ed. xv, 325 pp. 4 pl. 8°. *London, J. Churchill*, 1833.

Beaman (Charles C. *jr.*) The national and private "Alabama claims" and their "final and amicable settlement." xvi, 358 pp. 8°. *Washington, W. H. Moore*, [1871].

Bearcroft (Philip, *d. d.*) An historical account of Thomas Sutton; and of his foundation in Charter-house. xvi, 273 pp. 3 pl. 8°. *London, E. Owen*, 1737.

Beard (George). Minor poems: being a collection of fugitive pieces, principally com-

Beard (George)—continued.
posed in the West Indies; (with notes). xii, 169, xi pp. 16°. *London, J. C. Beard*, [*about* 1840].

Beard (George M. *m. d.*) Eating and drinking; a popular manual of food and diet in health and disease. xvii, 180 pp. 12°. *New York, G. P. Putnam & sons*, 1871.
[PUTNAM'S handy-book series, v. 4].

——— Stimulants and narcotics; medically, philosophically, and morally considered. xiv, 155 pp. 12°. *New York, G. P. Putnam & sons*, 1871.
[PUTNAM'S handy-book series].

——— *and* **Rockwell** (A. D. *m. d.*) A practical treatise on the medical and surgical uses of electricity, including localized and general electrization. xxxv, 698 pp. 8°. *New York, W. Wood & co.* 1871.

Beauchamps (Pierre François Godar de). Recherches sur les théâtres de France, depuis l'année onze cens soixante-un, jusques à présent. 6 p. l. [826] pp. 2 tab. 4°. *Paris, Prault père*, 1735.

Beauchesne (John de) *and* **Baildon** (John). A booke containing divers sortes of hands, as well the english as french secretarie with the italian, roman, chancelry & court hands. Also the true and iust proportiō of the capitall romāē. Eng. title, 43 l. unp. obl. 8°. *London, T. Vautrouillier*, 1581.

Beauclair (P. L. de). Anti-contrat social, dans lequel on réfute d'une manière claire, utile & agréable, les principes posés dans le Contrat social de J. J. Rousseau. ix, 272 pp. 16°. *La Haye, F. Staatman*, 1765.

Beaufort (Francis). Karamania, or a brief description of the south coast of Asia Minor and of the remains of antiquity. With plans, views, &c. collected in the years 1811 & 1812. 2d ed. xii, 309 pp. 3 l. 6 pl. 1 map. 8°. *London, R. Hunter*, 1818.

Beaufort d'Hautpoul (Anne-Marie, *comtesse de*). Arindal, ou le jeune peintre par mme. d'Hautpoult. 2 v. 2 p. l. 298 pp; 2 p. l. 368 pp. 16°. *Paris, H. Nicolle*, 1810.

Beaujour (Louis Félix, *baron de*). Aperçu des États-Unis, au commencement du xixe siècle, depuis 1800 jusqu'en 1810, avec des tables statistiques. 274 pp. 1 map. 17 tables. 8°. *Paris, L. G. Michaud*, 1814.

Beaumont (Gustave de). L'Irlande sociale, politique et religieuse. 5e éd. v. 1. 2 p. l. 408 pp. 12°. *Paris, C. Gosselin*, 1842. s.
[v. 2 wanting].

Beauties of the shamrock. Containing biography, eloquence, essays, and poetry. [*anon.*] v. 1. xxiv, 276 pp. 16°. *Philadelphia, B. Graves for W. D. Conway*, 1812.

Beaven (James). An account of the life and writings of s. Iræneus, bishop of Lyons and martyr : intended to illustrate the doctrine, discipline, practices, and history of the church, and the tenets and practices of the gnostic heretics, during the second century. xxviii, 334 pp. 8°. *London, author*, 1841.

Beccadelli *or* **Panormita** (Antonio). De dictis et factis Alphonsi regis Aragonvm et Neapolis libri qvatvor Antonii Panormitæ. Cvm respondentibus principum illius ætatis, Germanicorum potiss. dictis et factis similibus, ab Aenæa Sylvio collectis: et scholijs Iacobi Spiegelij : quibus chronologia vitæ Alphonsi et Lvdoici xii. Gall. regis, et Caroli v. imp. aliorumq̃ ; apophthegmata, et aliæ annotationes historicæ recens accesserunt. Editæ studio Davidis Chytræi. 4 p. l. 298 pp. 2 l. sm. 4°. *Witebergæ, typis hæredum Ioannis Cratonis*, 1585.

Beccadelli *or* **Beccatelli** (Lodovico). The life of cardinal Reginald Pole, written originally in italian, by Lodovico Beccatelli ; and now first translated into english. With notes critical and historical. [Also], an appendix, setting forth the plagiarisms, false translations, and false grammar in Thomas Phillips's History of the life of Reginald Pole. By the rev. Benjamin Pye. xxiv, 226 pp. 8°. *London, C. Bathurst*, 1766.

Béchard (Frédéric). Maurice. A novel. Translated from the original french, by mrs. Josephine Douglas. 305 pp. 12°. *New York, G. W. Carleton & co.* 1872.

Beck (Lewis C. *m. d.*) A manual of chemistry. 458 pp. 12°. *Albany, Webster & Skinner*, 1831.

——— The same. 3d ed. 483 pp. 12°. *New York, W. E. Dean*, 1838.

Becker (Wilhelm). Der verehrer Mariens in seinen häuslichen und öffentlichen andachten. 192, 48 pp. 18°. *Buffalo, F. Häfner*, 1872.

Beckett (Sylvester B.) Hester, the bride of the islands. A poem. 336 pp. 12°. *Portland, Bailey & Noyes*, 1860.

Beckwith (Arthur). International exhibition, London, 1871. Pottery. Observations on the materials and manufacture of terra-cotta, stone-ware, fire-brick, porcelain, earthen-ware, brick, majolica, and encaustic

Beckwith (Arthur)—continued.
tiles, with remarks on the products exhibited. 101 pp. 1 l. 8°. *New York, D. Van Nostrand*, 1872.

Bedell (Gregory Thurston, *d. d.*) Episcopacy : fact and law. Sermon preached at the consecration of rt. rev. M. A. De Wolfe Howe, d. d. bishop of the diocese of Central Pennsylvania, at St. Luke's church, Philadelphia. With explanatory notes. Printed by request. 48 pp. 8°. *Philadelphia, M'Calla & Stavely*, 1872.

Bedenckinge over d' antwoordt der heeren bewinthebbers vande Oost-Indische compagnie : aen d' edele gr. mog. heeren staten van Hollandt en West-Vrieslant, in twee schriften, overgelevert, belanghende de combinatie der twee compagnien. [*anon.*] *b. l.* 4 p. l. 32 pp. sm. 4°. *Graven-Haghe, J. Veeli*, 1644.

Bedenckinghen over den staet vande Vereenichde Nederlanden. 1608. *See* **Usselincx** (Willem).

Beecher (Catharine Esther). An appeal to the people in behalf of their rights as authorized interpreters of the bible. x, 380 pp. 12°. *New York, Harper & brothers*, 1860.

——— The moral instructor: containing lessons on the duties of life. Also designed as a reading book for schools. 194 pp. 12°. *Cincinnati, Truman & Smith*, 1838.

——— A treatise on domestic economy, for the use of young ladies at home, and at school. Revised ed. 383 pp. 12°. *Boston, T. H. Webb & co.* 1842.

Beecher (*Rev.* Charles). David and his throne. Pen pictures of the bible. With an introduction by Harriet Beecher Stowe. 315 pp. 16°. *New York, J. C. Derby*, 1855.

Beecher (*Rev.* Henry Ward). The life of Jesus, the Christ. Illustrated. xv, 387 pp. 1 l. 1 portrait. 15 pl. 2 maps. 4°. *New York, J. B. Ford & co.* 1871.

——— Morning and evening exercises: selected from published and unpublished writings of the rev. H. W. Beecher. Edited by Lyman Abbott. 560 pp. 1 portrait. 8°. *New York, Harper & brothers*, 1871.

——— The sermons of Henry Ward Beecher, in Plymouth church, Brooklyn. From verbatim reports by T. J. Ellinwood. "Plymouth pulpit." Sept. 25, 1869, to March 16, 1872. 3rd—7th series. 5 v. 8°. *New York, J. B. Ford & co.* 1870–72.

Beecher (*Rev.* Thomas K.) Our seven churches. viii, 167 pp. 16°. *New York, J. B. Ford & co.* 1870.

Beecher's illustrated magazine, [a monthly], original, pure, progressive, practical, popular. J. A. Beecher, editor. Jan. 1870, to Dec. 1871. v. 1-4 in 2 v. 8°. *Trenton (N. J.) J. A. Beecher*, 1870-71.

Beers (Frederick W, *editor*). Atlas of Franklin county, Massachusetts. 52 l. w. col. maps, etc. fol. *New York, F. W. Beers & co.* 1871.

——— Atlas of Jefferson county, Ohio. 37 l. w. col. maps. fol. *New York, F. W. Beers & co.* 1871.

——— Atlas of Worcester county, Massachusetts. From actual surveys by and under the direction of F. W. Beers, assisted by Geo. P. Sanford and others. 99 pp. 1 pl. 4°. *New York, F. W. Beers & co.* 1870.

——— *and others.* Atlas of Morris co. New Jersey, from actual surveys [etc.] 31 col. maps. 2 pl. fol. *New York, F. W. Beers, etc.* 1868.

Beger (Laurenz). Poenæ infernales Ixionis, Sisyphi, Ocni et Danaidum, ex delineatione Pighiana desumtæ, et dialogo illustratæ. 22 pp. 35 pl. fol. *Coloniæ Marchicæ, apud U. Liebpertum*, 1703. s.

Bégin (Louis-Jacques, *m. d.*) Application of the physiological doctrine to surgery. Translated from the French, by Wm. Sims Reynolds, m. d. 227 pp. 8°. *Charleston, E. J. von Brunt*, 1835.

Begin ('t) midden en eynde der zee-roveryen van den alder-fameusten zee-rover, Claas G[erritsz] Compaan. Van Oost-Zanen in Kennemer land. Vervattende zijn wonderlyke vreemde lands schadelyke dryf-togten. [*anon.*] 3 p. l. 42 pp. sm. 4°. *Amsterdam, G. de Groot*, 1726.

Beginning (The), progress, and conclusion of the late war, with other interesting matters considered, and a map of the lands, islands, gulphs, seas, and fishing-banks, comprising the cod fishery in America annexed. [*anon.*] 1 p. l. 32 pp. 1 map. 4°. *London, J. Almon*, 1770.

Bégon (*Comtesse* F. de). The house on wheels; (la maison roulante) or, the stolen child. Translated from the french of madame de Stolz by miss E. F. Adams. [*pseudon.*] 304 pp. 19 pl. 12°. *Boston, Lee & Shepard*, 1871.

Beidawi *or* **Beidhawi.** *See* **Nasir-ed-din** Abu Said Abdallah ben Omar ed-Beidhawi.

Belâgerung von Ostende. Iovrnal. Oder eigentlich tæglichs register von alle ghedenckwürdigste sachen, handlunghen vnd gheschichten so in der weith berhumbten vnwinlichen statt [etc.] 1601-04, sich zu beiden theilen haben zugetragen [etc.] In die hoochteudtsche sprache vertolmetscht. Durch I. S. [*anon.*] 35, 20, 6 l. 19 pl. sm. 4°. [*n. p.* 1604-05].

Belcher (William). The new Arcadia, a regular pindaric ode: (in imitation of Gray). 8 pp. 8°. [*London*, 1792].

[*In* Waldron (F. G.) Literary museum. *London*, 1792].

Belcher (*Lady*). The mutineers of the Bounty and their descendants in Pitcairn and Norfolk islands. With map and illustrations. 377 pp. 12°. *New York, Harper & brothers*, 1871.

Belden (George P.) Belden, the white chief; or, twelve years among the wild Indians of the plains. From the diaries and manuscripts of G. P. Belden. Edited by Gen. James S. Brisbin. 513 pp. 4 pl. 12°. *Cincinnati, C. F. Vent*, 1870.

Belfour (*Rev.* Okey). The lycæum of ancient literature; or, biographical and analytical account of the greek and roman classics. v. 1. viii, 422 pp. 12°. *London, R. Phillips*, 1809.

[No more published].

Belfrage (*Rev.* Henry, *d. d.*) Life and correspondence. *See* **M'Kerrow** (*Rev.* John) *and* **M'Farlance** (*Rev.* John).

Belgiojoso (*Mme.* Christine Trivulzio di). Histoire de la maison de Savoie. 2 p. l. viii, 544 pp. 8°. *Paris, M. Lévy frères*, 1860.

Belgravia. A London [monthly] magazine. Conducted by M. E. Braddon. Nov. 1870, to Feb. 1872. Second series, v. 3-6; first series, v. 13-16. 8°. *London*, [*Robson & sons*, 1870-72].

Belgravia (The) annual. [Edited] by M. E. Braddon. 1872. 8°. *London*, [*Robson & sons*, 1871].

Bell (A. N. *m. d.*) A knowledge of living things, with the laws of their existence. x, 318 pp. 2 col. pl. 12°. *New York, Baillière brothers*, 1860.

Bell (Mrs. Emma M.) Poems. 197 pp. 12°. *Philadelphia, J. B. Lippincott & co.* 1872.

Bell (George Hamilton, *m. d.*) Treatise on cholera asphyxia, or epidemic cholera, as it appeared in Asia, and more recently in Europe. With practical remarks on the dis-

Bell (George Hamilton, *m. d.*)—continued. ease in Europe; an appendix of cases; and the reports and regulations of the boards of health of London and Edinburgh. 2d ed. enlarged. xii, 244 pp. 1 map. 8°. *Edinburgh, W. Blackwood*, 1832.

Bell (*Major* James). Letters from Wetzlar, written in 1817, developing the authentic particulars on which the Sorrows of Werter are founded. To which is annexed, The stork; or, the herald of spring, a poem. vii, 109 pp. 1 portrait. 12°. *London, Rodwell & Martin*, 1821.

Bell (John, *m. d.*) Health and beauty. An explanation of the laws of growth and exercise. 253 pp. 18°. *Philadelphia, Carey & Hart*, 1838.

——— On regimen and longevity: comprising materia alimentaria, national dietetic usages, and the influence of civilization on health and the duration of life. 1 p. l. 13–420 pp. 12°. *Philadelphia, Haswell & Johnson*, 1842.

Bell (*Rev.* John Peden). Christian sociology, in two parts. 289 pp. 16°. *Aberdeen, G. & R. King*, 1853.

Bell (Robert). Rervm hispanicarum scriptorvm tomus posterior. 1 p. l. 611–1258 pp. 20 l. fol. *Francofvrti ad Moenum, apud A. Wechelvm*, 1579.

Bell (Thomas). The history of improved short-horn or Durham cattle, and of the Kirklevington herd, from the notes of the late Thomas Bates. With a memoir, by Thomas Bell. 1 p. l. ix, 371 pp. 1 l. 8 pl. 12°. *Newcastle-upon-Tyne, R. Redpath*, 1871.

Bell (William A.) New tracks in North America. A journal of travel and adventure whilst engaged in the survey for a southern railroad to the Pacific ocean during 1867–8. With contributions by gen. W. J. Palmer, major A. R. Calhoun, C. C. Parry, m. d. and capt. W. F. Colton. 2d ed. lxx, 565 pp. 24 pl. 1 map. 8°. *London, Chapman & Hall*, 1870.

Bellairs (Nona, *pseudon?*) Going abroad; or, glimpses of art and character in France and Italy. vi, 293 pp. 1 pl. 12°. *London, C. J. Skeet*, 1857.

Bellamy (E. W.) Four-oaks: a novel. By Kamba Thorpe. [*pseudon.*] 420 pp. 12°. *New York, Carleton*, 1870.

Bellamy (John). The history of all religions, comprehending the different doctrines, customs, and order of worship in the churches which have been established from the beginning of time to the present day. xxiv, 394 pp. 1 pl. 16°. *London, Longman & co.* [1812].

Bellamy (Joseph, *d. d. minister at Bethlem, N. E.*) An essay on the nature and glory of the gospel of Jesus Christ: as also on the nature and consequences of spiritual blindness: and the nature and effects of divine illumination. vi pp. 4 l. 254 pp. 16°. *Boston, S. Kneeland*, 1762.

——— The millenium. [A sermon]. First published at Boston in 1758. 8°. [*Elizabethtown, (N. J.) S. Kollock*, 1794].

[*In* AUSTIN. (*Rev.* David, *editor*). The millenium. 1794. pp. 9–49].

——— Remarks on the revd. mr. Croswell's letter to the reverend mr. Cumming. 36 pp. 8°. *Boston, S. Kneeland*, 1763.

——— A sermon delivered before the general assembly of the colony of Connecticut, at Hartford, on the day of the anniversary election, May 13th, 1762. 43 pp. 16°. *New-London, T. Green*, 1762.

——— That there is but one covenant, the covenant of grace; (proved from the word of God) and, the doctrine of an external graceless covenant, lately advanced, by the rev. Moses Mather: shewn to be an unscriptural doctrine. To which is prefixed, an answer, to a dialogue concerning The half-way covenant. 16, iv, 78 pp. 8°. *New-Haven, T. and S. Green*, 1769.

[Imperfect: leaves wanting at the close].

——— The wisdom of God in the permission of sin, vindicated; in answer to a pamphlet, intitled, An attempt, etc. 4 p. l. 87 pp. 16°. *Boston, S. Kneeland*, 1760.

Bellamy (Thomas). The life of Mr. William Parsons, comedian. To which are added his dramatic character, by John Litchfield, and a letter of intelligence, from Charles Dibdin. 76 pp. 1 portrait. 8°. *London, author*, 1795.

[*With his* Miscellanies, v. 2].

——— Miscellanies: in prose and verse. 2 v. 4 p. l. 248 pp; 131, 4 pp. 8°. *London, author*, 1794–5.

Bellanti (Lucio). Lvcii Belantii senensis physici liber de astrologica veritate, et in dispvtationes Ioannis Pici adversvs astrologos responsiones. 127 l. unp. 4°. *Florentie, Gherardus de Haerlem*, 1498.

[*Note.*—Two columns on a page, each of 42 lines].

Bellarmino (Roberto, *cardinale*). Dichiarazione più copiosa della dottrina cristiana

Bellarmino (Roberto)—continued. breve, composta per ordine di papa Clemente ottavo. Con l'editto della congregazione degli adulti. 192 pp. 16°. *Padova, stamperia del seminario*, 1770.

Bellegarde (Jean Baptiste Morvan, *l'abbé* de). Lettres curieuses de littérature et de morale. 10 p. l. 456 pp. 16°. *Paris, J. & M. Guignard*, 1702.

——— Models of conversation for persons of polite education. Selected and translated from the french. xvi, 312 pp. 8 l. 8°. *London, A. Millar*, 1765.

——— Politeness of manners and behaviour in fashionable society. From the french. ix, 168 pp. 1 l. 1 pl. 8°. *Paris, editor*, 1812.

——— Réflexions sur le ridicule, et sur les moyens de l'éviter. Où sont représentéz les différens caractères & les mœurs des personnes de ce siècle. 8e éd. augmentée. 6 p. l. 440 pp. 16°. *La Haye, G. de Voys*, 1720.

Bellin (Jacques Nicolas). Description des débouquemens qui sont au nord de l'isle de Saint-Domingue. [2e éd.] Eng. title, 4 p. l. 152 pp. 34 pl. 4°. *Versailles, département de la marine*, 1773.

[*Note.*—Plate 9 wanting].

——— [Mémoires publiés avec les cartes hydrographiques]. 4°. *Paris*, 1738-66.

CONTENTS.

Remarques sur le détroit de Belle-Isle, et les côtes septentrionales de la Nouvelle France. 16 pp. 1758.
Remarques sur la carte réduite de l'océan septentrionale, compris entre l'Asie et l'Amérique. 8 pp. 1766.
Observations sur la construction de la carte de l'océan meridional. 18 pp. 1739.
Observations sur la construction de la carte de l'archipel. 8 pp. 1738.
Remarques sur la carte réduite des parties connues du globe terrestre. 16 pp. 1755.

Belloguet (Dominique François Louis, *baron* Roget de). Ethnogénie gauloise, ou mémoires critiques sur l'origine et la parente des Cimmériens, des Cimbres, des Ombres, des Belges, des Ligures, et des anciens Celtes. Introduction—première partie, glossaire gauloise. xv, 286 pp. 1 l. 2 tab. 8°. *Paris, B. Duprat*, 1858.

Bellows (C. F. R.) Geometrical figures. Their properties, relations, and measurement; or a classification of geometrical facts. 2 p. l. 40 pp. 8°. *Ypsilanti, Pattison's steam printing house*, 1872.

Belot (Jean). Œvvres. Contenant la chiromence, physionomie, l'art de mémoire de Raymond Lulle; traicté des diuinations, augures & songes; les sciences steganographiques, paulines, armadelles & lullistes; l'art de doctement prescher & haranguer, &c. Dernière éd. augmentée de diuers traictez. 8 p. l. 343 pp. 1 pl. 16°. *Lyon, C. La Rivière*, 1649.

Belsham (*Rev.* Thomas). Memoirs of the rev. Theophilus Lindsey, including a brief analysis of his works; with anecdotes and letters of eminent persons, his friends and correspondents: also a general view of the progress of the unitarian doctrine in England and America. xxiii, 544 pp. 1 portrait. 8°. *London, J. Johnson & co.* 1812.

——— The same. 2d ed. corrected. xvi, 423 pp. 8°. *London, R. Hunter*, 1820.

Beltcher (William). *See* **Belcher.**

Beltran de Santa Rosa Maria (Pedro). Arte de el idioma maya, reducido a succintas reglas, y semilexicon yucateco. 8 p. l. 188 pp. 2 tab. sm. 4°. *Mexico, viuda de J. Bernardo de Hogal*, 1746.

Bembo (Pietro, *cardinale*). Degli asolani libri tre, [ne' quali si ragiona d'amore], con gli argomenti a ciascun libro, e con le postille di Tommaso Porcacchi. 3 p. l. 220 pp. 6 l. 12°. *Verona, P. A. Berno*, 1743.

——— Carmina. 16°. *Venetiis, ex officina Vincentii Valgrisii*, 1548.

[*In* CARMINA qvinqve illvstrivm poetarvm, pp. 7-21].

Bemis (George). Mr. Reverdy Johnson: the Alabama negotiations, and their just repudiation by the senate of the United States. 36 pp. 8°. *New York, Baker & Godwin*, 1869.

Bemmel. *See* **Van Bemmel** (Eugène).

Benci (Antonio). Elogio del conte Giulio Perticari. 16°. *Milano, G. Silvestri*, 1823.

[*In* PERTICARI (Giulio, *conte*). Opere, v. 1, pp. vii-xxiv].

Benci (Francesco). Oratio, ante ferias autumnales, cum studia proferrentur, habita. 18°. *Lugduni Batavorum, ex officina I. Maire*, 1655.

[ELEGANTIORES præstantium virorum satyræ, v. 1, part 2, 6 l. at the end].

Bendbow (Hesper, *pseudon.*) *See* **Archer** (George W.)

Benedetti (Alessandro). Il fatto d'arme del Tarro fra i principi italiani et Carlo ottavo re di Francia, insieme con l'assedio di Novara. Tradotto per messer Lodouico Domenichi. 59 l. 18°. *Vinegia, G. Giolito de Ferrari*, 1549.

Benedict (Hester A.) Vesta. 170 pp. 16°. *Philadelphia, Claxton, Remsen & Haffelfinger*, 1872.

Benedictus (Alexander). *See* **Benedetti.**

Benger (*Miss* Elizabeth Ogilvy). Memoirs of the life of Anne Boleyn, queen of Henry viii. From the third London edition. With a memoir of the author, by miss Aikin. 342 pp. 1 portrait. 12°. *Philadelphia, A. Hart*, 1850.

Benisch (Abraham). Jewish school and family bible. *See* **Bible**. (*English*).

Benivieni (Girolamo). Opere di Hierony. Benivieni [date in luce da Biagio Buonaccorsi]. 4 l. unp. 200 l. 16°. *Firenze, heredi di Philippo di Giunta*, 1519.

CONTENTS.

Vno canzona de lo amore celeste, & diuino col commento de lo ill. s. conte Iohan. Pico Mirandulano distincto in libri iii, l. 1.
Egloge viii con loro argumenti, l. 72.
Cantici, o uero capitoli, l. 104.
Canzone & sonetti di diuerse materie, l. 105.
Amore fugitiuo di Mosco poeta greco tradocto, l. 121.
Elegia di Propertio tradocta, l. 122.
Psalmi di Dauid tradocti, l. 125.
Sequentia de morti tradocta, [Dies irae], l. 129.
Laude & canzone morali, l. 130.
Stanze in passione Domini, l. 151.
Come si conoschi, & ami Dio per le sue creature stanze, l. 153.
Altre stanze di diuerse materie, l. 157.
Frottole, l. 165.

Benjamin (Asher). Elements of architecture, containing the tuscan, doric, ionic, and corinthian orders, with all their details and embellishments. Also, the theory and practice of carpentry. 232 pp. 28 pl. 8°. *Boston, B. B. Mussey*, 1843.

Benjamin ben Mordecai (*pseudon.*) *See* **Taylor** (*Rev.* Henry).

Bennet (*Rev.* George). Olam haneshamoth, or a view of the intermediate state, as it appears in the records of the old and new testament; the apocraphal books; in heathen authors; and the greek and latin fathers. With notes. iv, 419 pp. 8°. *Carlisle, B. Scott*, 1800.

Bennet (John). Collectio sententiarum, exemplorum, testimoniorum, nec non et similitudinum, in usum scholasticæ juventutis. Editio tertia, nuper recognita. 1 p. l. iv, 254 pp. 8°. *Cantabrigiæ, T. Fletcher & F. Hodson*, 1777.

Bennet (*Rev.* Thomas). A confutation of quakerism; or a plain proof the falsehood of what the principal quaker writers (especially Mr. R. Barclay in his Apology and other works) do teach. 6 p. l. 318 pp. 2 l. 8°. *Cambridge, (Eng.) university press, for E. Jeffery*, 1705.

Bennett (Solomon). The temple of Ezekiel: viz. an elucidation of the 40th, 41st, 42d, &c. chapters of Ezekiel, consistently with the hebrew original; and a minute description of the edifice, on scientific principles. Illustrated by a ground-plan and bird's-eye view. With an appendix, containing critical remarks on the authenticity of the book of Daniel; and an enquiry into the discrepancy between the jewish and the christian universal chronology. vii, 159 pp. 2 pl. 4°. *London, author*, 1824.

Bennett (William W. *d. d.*) Memorials of methodism in Virginia, from its introduction into the state, in the year 1772, to the year 1829. 741 pp. 1 portrait. 12°. *Richmond, author*, 1871.

Benning (Howe). Grace Courtney; or, seeking the shepherd. 225 pp. 3 pl. 16°. *Boston, I. P. Warren*, [1871].

Benson (The) family. *See* **Arnold** (Alexander S.)

Ben Syra. *See* **Jeschua ben Sira.**

Bentham (James). The history and antiquities of the conventual and cathedral church of Ely; from the foundation of the monastery, a. d. 673 to the year 1771. 4 p. l. 292, 70 pp. 50 pl. 4°. *Cambridge, J. Bentham*, 1771.

Bentley (Rensselaer). The new testament. *See* **Bible**. (*English*).

Bentley (Richard, *d. d.*) A dissertation upon the epistles of Themistocles, Socrates, Euripides, and others; and the fables of Aesop. 8°. *London*, 1705.

[*In* WOTTON (William, *d.d.*) Reflections upon ancient and modern learning, pp. 401–541].

——— Eight sermons preached at the hon. Robert Boyle's lecture, in the first year, 1692. fol. [*London*, 1739].

[BOYLE lectures, v. 1, 2 p. l. pp. 1-87].

Benzo (Ugo). Regole della sanità e natvra de' cibi. Arricchite di vaghe annotationi, & di copiosi discorsi, naturali, e morali dal sig. Lodovico Bertaldi. Et nuouamente in questa seconda impressione aggiontoui alle medeme materie i trattati di Baldasar Pisanelli, e sue historie naturali; & annotationi del medico Galina. 16 p. l. 898 pp. 1 l. 16°. *Torino, per gli eredi di G. D. Tarino*, 1620.

Beraud (*Dr.* B.) Éléments de physiologie de l'homme et des principaux vertébrés. Revus par M. Ch[arles Philippe] Robin. 2e éd. entièrement refondue. v. 2. 2 p. l. 864 pp. 16°. *Paris, G. Baillière*, 1857.

Bercheure *or* **Berchoire** (Pierre). Repertoriū morale perutile predicatoribus. Editū per fratrem Petrum berchariii pictauienī me-

Bercheure (Pierre)—continued. ritoque dictionarius appellatū. [Præcedit præfatio Johannis Bekenhaub]. *b. l.* 3 v. fol. *Ex officina A. Koberger, nurenbergensis,* 1489.

[*Note.*—Seventy lines in a column ; two columns on a page ; no catchwords].

Berdmore (Samuel, *d. d.*) Specimens of literary resemblance, in the works of Pope, Gray, and other celebrated writers; with critical observations: in a series of letters. 1 p. l. 127 pp. 8°. *London, G. Wilkie,* 1801.

Berean (The). A religious publication. February, 1824, to July, 1827. v. 1–3. 8°. *Wilmington, (Del.) Mendenhall & Walters,* [*etc.*] 1825–27.

Berettari (Sebastiano). Vita r. p. Josephi Anchietæ societatis Iesv sacerdotis in Brasilia defuncti. Ex iis qvæ de eo Petrus Roterigus lusitanico idiomate collegit. 2 p. l. 428 pp. 1 l. 18°. *Coloniæ Agrippinæ, I. Kinchius,* 1617.

Berg (F.) Der junge sänger, 1872. *See* **Robyn** (H.) *and* **Berg.**

Berg (Joseph F. *d. d.*) Lectures on romanism. With an introduction, by W. C. Brownlee, d. d. 300 pp. 12°. *Philadelphia, D. Weidner,* 1840.

——— The scripture history of idolatry, showing the connection between the traditions of pagan mythology and the bible. 184 pp. 8 pl. 18°. *Philadelphia, J. B. Lippincott & co.* 1838.

Bergamasque (Le), ou l'homme bon, doutant sans le vouloir & ennemi malgré lui de la vie sociale. [*anon.*] viii, 304 pp. 12°. *La Haye,* 1791.

Bergamo (*City of, Italy*). Atti del consiglio comunale della citta' di Bergamo. Fascicolo 9, 10. 1868–70. [Con allegati]. 2 v. 8°. *Bergamo, V. Pagnoncelli,* 1869–70. s.

Berger (Friederich Ludewig von). Gründliche erweisung dass ihro römisch-käyserl. majestät in dero oesterreichischen Niederlanden, nach allerhöchstem belieben commercia zu stabiliren, und zu aufrichtung einer Ost-und-West-Indischen compagnie behörige allergnädigste privilegia zu ertheilen berechtiget. 2 p. l. 59 pp. sm. 4°. *Regenspurg, J. C. Peetz,* 1723.

Berington (*Rev.* Joseph). Histoire littéraire des Grecs pendant le moyen age; ouvrage traduit de l'anglais, par A. M. H. Boulard. 2 p. l. 167 pp. 8°. *Paris, Debeausseaux,* 1822.

——— *and* **Kirk** (*Rev.* John). The faith of catholics on certain points of controversy, confirmed by scripture, and attested by the fathers of the five first centuries of the church. lviii, 462 pp. 8°. *London, J. Booker,* 1830.

Berkenhout (John, *m. d.*) Biographia literaria; or, a biographical history of literature: containing the lives of english, scotish, and irish authors, from the dawn of letters in these kingdoms to the present time, chronologically and classically arranged. 2 p. l. xxxiv, 537 pp. 2 l. 4°. *London, J. Dodsley,* 1777.

Bermingham (*Rev.* James). A memoir of the very rev. Theobald Mathew, with an account of the rise and progress of temperance in Ireland. Edited by P. H. Morris, m. d. and by whom is added The evil effects of drunkenness physiologically explained. 216 pp. 12°. *New York, A. V. Blake,* 1841.

Berna. *See* **Berni.**

Bernard *de Clairvaux* (*Saint*). Bernardus de cura rei familiaris, with some early scottish prophecies, etc. From a ms. Kk. 1. 5, in the Cambridge university library. Edited by J. Rawson Lumby. xi, 46 pp. 8°. *London,* 1870.

[EARLY English text society, no. 42].

——— Traité de la considération [traduit par Antoine de Saint-Gabriel]. 8°. [*Paris, panthéon littéraire,* 1843].

[*In* BUCHON (J. A. C.) Choix d'ouvrages mystiques, pp. 331–391].

Bernard (Charles de). L'écueil. Nouv. éd. 2 p. l. 382 pp. 1 l. 12°. *Paris, M. Lévy frères,* 1858.

——— Un homme sérieux. Nouv. éd. 2 p. l. 390 pp. 12°. *Paris, M. Lévy frères,* 1856.

Bernard (David). Light on free masonry. Revised edition. With an appendix revealing the mysteries of odd fellowship, by a member of the craft. 492 pp. 12°. *Dayton (O.) Vonneida & Sowers,* [1858].

Bernard (Nicholas, *d. d.*) The life and death of dr. James Usher, late arch-bishop of Armagh, and primate of all Ireland. Published in a sermon at his funeral at the abby of Westminster, April 17, 1656, and now reviewed with some other enlargements. 7 p. l. 119 pp. 2 l. 1 portrait. 16°. *London, E. Tyler,* 1656.

Bernard (*Rev.* Richard Boyle). A tour through some parts of France, Switzerland, Savoy, Germany and Belgium, during the summer and autumn of 1814. xx, 336 pp. 8°. *London, Longman,* 1815.

Bernardo *trévisano*. Le livre de la philosophie naturelle des métaux. La parole délaissée, traité philosophique. 12°. [*Paris, A. Cailleau*, 1741].
[*In* SALMON (William). Bibliothèque des philosophes chimiques. 1741. v. 2, pp. 325-436].

Berni, Berna, *or* **Bernia** (Francesco). Capitolo del gioco della primiera, col comento di messer Pietropaulo da San Chirico. [*anon.*] Eng. title, 37 l. 8°. *Roma, F. M. Caluo*, 1526.

——— Carmina. 16°. *Florentiæ, apvd Ivntas*, 1562.
[*In* CARMINA qvinqve Hetrvscorvm poetarvm, pp. 115-128].

Beroald (Philippe). Amores Guiscardi & Gismundæ; de duobus amantibus. E. Boccatio. Osculum Panthiæ omnium formosissimarum. Carmen amatorium. Diræ in maledicam Lenam. Quæstio, quis inter scortatorem, aleatorem, & ebriosum sit pessimus. 18°. [*Lvgd. Batav. ex typographia rediviva*, 1648].
[*In* OBSOPŒUS (Vincenz). De arte bibendi. 1648. pp. 102-168. Imperfect: wanting, pp. 169-190].

Berrien county (*Mich.*) directory and history, containing historical and descriptive sketches of the villages and townships within the county, and the names and occupations of persons residing therein, 1871. Ed. B. Cowles, compiler and publisher. 385 pp. 8°. *Niles (Mich.) E. B. Cowles*, 1871.

Berriman (William, *d. d.*) The gradual revelation of the gospel; from the time of man's apostacy. Set forth and explained in twenty-four sermons, preached in 1730, 1731, and 1732. fol. [*London*, 1739].
[BOYLE lectures, v. 3, pp. 581-784].

Berry (John W.) Uniac: his life, struggle, and fall. 217 pp. 8°. *Boston, A. Mudge & son*, 1871.

Bert (Pierre). Tabvlarvm geographicarvm contractarvm libri septem supra priores editiones auctiores. 8 p. l. 830 pp. 5 l. [including] 217 maps. obl. 18°. *Amsterodami, I. Hondius* [1616].

Bertaglia (Romualdo). Relazione delle paduli pontine, 1761. *See* **Manfredi** (Gabriel) and **Bertaglia.**

Bertaldi (Lodovico). *See* **Benzo** (Ugo). Regole della sanità e natvra de' cibi.

Berthre de Bourniseaux (P. Vict. J.) An historical sketch of the civil war in the Vendée, from its origin to the peace concluded at La Jaunaie. Translated from the french. xxxi, 286 pp. 12°. *Paris, J. Smith*, 1802.

Bertin (R. Joseph François Hyacinthe). Treatise on the diseases of the heart, and great vessels. Edited by J. Bouillaud. Translated from the french by Charles W. Chauncy, m. d. liii, 17-449 pp. 8°. *Philadelphia, Carey, Lea & Blanchard*, 1833.

Bertius (Petrus). *See* **Bert** (Pierre).

Bertolio (Antonio). Sopra gli aeroliti caduti il giorno 29 febbraio 1868. *See* **Denza** (Francesco).

Bertotti Scamozzi (Ottavio). Il forestiere istruito delle cose più rare di architettura, o di alcune pitture della città di Vicenza. Dialogo. 120 pp. 36 pl. 1 portrait. 4°. *Vicenza, G. B. Vendramini Mosca*, 1761.

Bertrand (—). Manuscript transmitted from St. Helena, by an unknown channel. [*anon.*] Translated from the french. 2 p. l. 148 pp. 8°. *London, J. Murray*, 1817.
[*Note.*—Professedly, an autobiography of Napoleon].

Berwick (George, *m. d.*) The forces of the universe. x, 127 pp. 12°. *London, Longmans, Green & co.* 1870. S.

Bescherelle (Louis Nicolas) *and* **Larcher** L. J.) La femme, jugée par les grands écrivains des deux sexes; ou la femme devant Dieu, devant la nature, devant la loi et devant la société. 2 p. l. vii, 586 pp. 3 l. 15 pl. 8°. *Paris, Simon*, 1846.
[*Note.*—Some of the plates are impressions from those originally published in Finden's Gallery of the Graces, retouched].

Beschreibung der münsterkirche und ihrer merkwürdigkeiten in Basel, mit abbildungen [die meisten von Constantin Guise. *anon.*] 1 p. l. 22 pp. 17 pl. 1 plan. fol. *Basel, Hasler & cie.* 1842.

Beschrijvinghe van Virginia, Nieuw Nederlandt, Nieuw Engelandt, en d' eylanden Bermudes, Berbados, en S. Christoffel. Met kopere figuren verciert. 88 pp. sm. 4°. *Amsterdam, J. Hartgers*, 1651.
[*Note.*—A reprint of some parts of van der Donck's Vertoogh, and of the second edition of de Laet.—*Asher*].

Beschryvinge van 't in-nemen vande stadt Salvador inde Baya de todos os sanctos in Brasil, door den admirael Iacob Willekes. [*anon.*] folded sheet, 1 pl. sm. 4°. *Amstelredam, C. I. Visscher*, 1624.

Besler (Basil). Hortvs Eystettensis, sive diligens et accvrata omnivm plantarvm, florum, stirpivm, ex variis orbis terrae partibvs, singvlari studio collectarvm, qvae in celeberrimis viridariis arcem episcopalem ibidem cingentibvs, hoc tempore conspicivntvr delinea-

Besler (Basil)—continued.
tio et ad vivvm repraesentatio. 2 v. fol. [*Norimbergae*], 1613.

CONTENTS.

v. 1. Classis aestiva.
Ordo collectarvm arborvm et frvcticvm aestivalivm. 14 pl.
Ordines collectarvm plantarvm aestivalivm, i-xiv. 169 pl. 8 l.
v. 2. Classis autumnalis.
Ordines collectarvm plantarvm avtumnalivm, i-iv. 42 pl. 3. l.
Classis hyberna.
Primus ordo collectarvm plantarvm hyemalivm. 7 pl. 1l.
Classis verna.
Ordo collectarvm arborvm et frvcticvm vernalivm. 14 pl.
Ordines collectarvm plantarvm vernalivm, i-ix. 120 pl. 7 l.

[*Note.*—There are wanting, according to Brunet, to make this a perfect copy, four leaves in the first part of v. 1, including a portrait of the author in the form of a medallion].

Besse (Joseph). The life and posthumous works of Richard Claridge. *See* **Claridge** (Richard).

Best (John Richard). Transrhenane memoirs. viii, 218 pp. 8°. *London, Longman*, 1828.

Bethlehemite order. (*Franciscans*). Regla, y constituciones de la sagrada religion bethlemitica, fundada en las Indias Occidentales por el v. p. fr. Pedro de San Joseph Betancur. 3 p. l. 90 pp. 1 pl. 4°. *Mexico, J. B. de Hogal*, 1751.

Bethune (*Rev.* C. J. S. *editor*). *See* **Canadian** (The) entomologist.

Béthune (Philippe de, *comte de Selles*). The covnsellor of estate. Contayning the greatest and most remarkeable considerations seruing for the managing of publicke affaires. Translated by E[dward] G[rimestone]. [*anon.*] 16 p. l. 336 pp. sm. 4°. *London, N. Okes*, 1634.

Betti (Pietro). Sul colera asiatico che contristò la Toscana nelli anni 1835-36-37-49, considerazioni mediche. Volume unico con documenti annessi. xx, 566 pp. 8°. *Firenze, tipografia delle Murate*, 1856. s.
[Considerazioni mediche sul colera asiatico, v. 1].

——— The same. Documenti annessi alle considerazioni sul colera asiatico che contristò la Toscana nelli anni 1835-36-37-49. 2 p. l. 564 pp. 8°. *Firenze, Murate*, 1857. s.
[Considerazioni mediche sul colera asiatico, v. 2].

——— The same. Prima appendice alle considerazione sul colera asiatico che contristò la Toscana, nelli anni 1835-36-37-49, comprendente la invasione colerica del 1854. xvii, 796 pp. 2 tab. 8°. *Firenze, Murate*, 1857. s.
[Considerazioni mediche sul colera asiatico, v. 3].

——— The same. Seconda appendice alle considerazioni sul colera asiatico che contristò la Toscana, comprendente la invasione colerica del 1855. 2 v. xx, 696 pp; 2 p. l. 811 pp. 2 l. 8°. *Firenze, Murate*, 1858. s.
[Considerazioni mediche sul colera asiatico, v. 4, 5].

Bettinelli (Saverio). Del risorgimento d'Italia negli studj, nelle arti e ne' costumi dopo il mille. 2 v. lx, 395 pp. 1 pl; viii, 430 pp. 8°. *Bassano, Remondini di Venezia*, 1775.

——— The same. 2 v. xlviii, 296, 84 pp; 391 pp. 8°. *Bassano, Remondini di Venezia*, 1786.

Beughem (Cornelius von). Apparatus ad historiam literariam novissimam variis conspectibus exhibendus, quorum quintus et ultimus elapsi seculi xvii. nunc prodit, qui est bibliographia eruditorum critico-curiosa. 5 p. l. 456 pp. 24°. *Amstelædami, J. Waesberg*, 1710. s.

Beugnot (Jacques Claude, *comte*). Mémoires du comte Beugnot ancien ministre (1783-1815). Publiés par le comte Albert Beugnot son petit-fils. 2e éd. 2 v. 2 p. l. 508 pp; 2 p. l. 419 pp. 2 l. 8°. *Paris, E. Dentu*, 1868.

Bevan (Joseph Gurney). Extracts from the letters and other writings of the late Joseph Gurney Bevan; preceded by a short memoir of his life. 3 p. l. 271 pp. 8°. *London, W. Phillips*, 1821.

Beverley (Thomas). The great soul of man, or, the soul in its likeness to God, its nature, operations, and everlasting state discoursed. 7 p. l. 317 pp. 8°. *London, W. Miller*, 1676.

Beyle (Marie Henri). Le rouge et le noir. Chronique du xixe siècle. Nouv. éd. 2 p. l. 504 pp. 12°. *Paris, M. Lévy frères*, 1857.

Bèze (Théodore de). Novum testamentum. *See* **Bible**. (*Latin*).

Biancardi (Bastiano *chiamato* Domenico Lalli). Le vite de' re di Napoli; raccolte succintamente con ogni accuratezza, e distese per ordine cronologico. 6 p. l. 475 pp. 32 pl. 4°. *Venezia, F. Pitteri*, 1737.

Bianchi (Noè). Viaggio del r. francesco Noè Bianco da Venezia al s. sepolcro, ed al monte Sinai. Aggiuntovi il modo di pigliar le sante indulgenze, ed a che chiese, monasterj, ed altri luochi siano concesse. 192 pp. 16°. *Bassano, G. A. Remondini*, 1742.

Bianconi (Giovanni Giuseppe). *See* **Repertorio** italiano per la storia naturale, 1853-54.

Bibaud (Michel). Histoire du Canada, sous la domination française. 370 pp. 12°. *Montreal, J. Jones*, 1837.

Biber (*Rev.* George Edward). Bishop Blomfield and his times. An historical sketch. xxvi, 421 pp. 12°. *London, Harrison,* 1857.

Bibiano (Frei.) Fabio. Annotado por um amigo. 77, 16 pp. 12°. *Rio de Janeiro, Aranha & Guimarães,* 1871.

Bible. (*Polyglot*). Biblia sacra qvadrilingvia novi testamenti graeci, cum versionibvs Syriaca, Graeca vvulgari, Latina et Germanica. Accurante m. Christiano Reineccio. Eng. title, 11 p. l. 968 pp. fol. *Lipsiae, svmtibus haeredvm Lanckisianorvm,* 1747.

——— (*Chinese*). Das evangelium des Matthaeus im volksdialekte der Hakka-Chinesen. Herausgegeben von R. Lechler. [In Roman letters]. 2 p. l. 91 pp. 12°. *Berlin, Unger,* 1860. s.

——— (*Dutch*). Bijbel, dat is de gansche heilige schrift, vervattende al de kanonijke bœken des ouden en nieuwen testaments. Op last van de h. m. heeren staten-generaal der Vereenigde Nederlanden, en volgens het besluit van de synode nationaal gehouden te Dordrecht, in de jaren 1618 en 1619, uit de oorspronkelijke talen in onze nederlandsche getrouwelijk overgezet. 2 v. in 1. 2 p. l. 868 pp; 272 pp. 8°. *Gravenhage, nederlandsche bijbelgenootschap,* 1860.

——— ——— *Isaiah.* De euangelische Jesaia: ofte des zelfs voorname euangelische prophetie. Door Abraham Hellenbroek. 4e druk. v. 4. 4°. *Amsterdam, H. Burgers,* 1736. s.
[v. 1-3 wanting].

——— ——— *New testament.* Het nieuwe testament ofte alle boeken des nieuwen verbonts onses heeren Jesu Christi door last van de h. m. heeren staten generaal der Vereenigde Nederl. en volgens het besluit van de sijnode nationael gehouden tot Dordrecht in de jaaren 1618 en 1619. Uit de grieksche tale in onze nederlandsche tale getrouwelijk overgezet. 1 p. l. 180 l. 18°. *Haarlem, J. Enschede & zonen,* 1819.

——— (*English*). Biblia. The bible, that is, the holy scripture of the olde and new testament, faithfully and truly translated in to Englishe. 1535. [By Myles Coverdale]. iv pp. 9 l. 816, 187, 266 pp. 1 portrait. 4°. *Reprinted, London, S. Bagster,* 1838.

——— ——— The same. [The byble in Englyshe of the largest and greatest volume, auctorysed and apoynted by the commaundemente of oure moost redoubted prynce, and soveraygne lorde kynge Henrye the viii. supreme heade of this his churche and

Bible (*English*)—continued.
realme of Englande: to be frequented and used in every churche wīn this his sayd realme, accordynge to the tenour of his former iniunctions geven in that behalfe. Oversene and perused at the cōmaundemēt of the kynges hyghnes, by the ryghte reverende fathers in God, Cuthbert [Tunstal] byshop of Duresme, and Nicolas [Heath] bisshop of Rochester]. *b. l.* 5 parts in 1 v. 72, 108, 116, 72 [for 70], 80 l. 65 lines to a page. fol. [*London, Edwarde Whitchurch,* 1541].
[*Note.*—Commonly known as Cranmer's bible. The edition of Nov. 1541. This copy is imperfect, and wants general title; calendar, 4 pp: prologue, 6 pp; part 1, title and l. 1, 37, and 40: part 4, title: part 5, (N. T.) l. 68 and 81–93, and tables of epistles 1 p: fol. 2 of part 1 is slightly imperfect].

——— ——— The same. [Genevan version]. *b. l.* 2-554 l. 4°. [*London, deputies of Christopher Barker, about* 1589].
[Imperfect: general title page, title-page of N. T. and leaves at beginning of text of old and new testaments wanting].

——— ——— The same. [Genevan version]. *b. l.* 1 p. l. 554 l. 4°. [*London, Christopher Barker,* 1584].
[Imperfect: general title-page wanting].

——— ——— The same. [Genevan version, and a translation of Beza's Greek testament by L. Tomson.] 190, 127, 121 l. 11 l. 4°. *London, deputies of Christopher Barker,* 1599.
[Imperfect: general title-page wanting].
[*Note.*—The apocrypha is omitted. The full title of the new testament is thus: "The new testament of our Lord Iesvs Christ, translated out of the greeke by Theod. Beza: with briefe summaries and expositions vpon the hard places by the said authour, Ioac. Camer, and P. Loseler, Villerius. Englished by L. Tomson, together with the annotations of Fr. Junius upon the revelation of s. John"].

——— ——— The same. The bible: that is, the holy scriptvres conteined in the old and new testament. [Genevan version and Tomson's New testament]. 4 p. l. 34 pp. 190, 197, 121 l. 11 l. 1 map. 4°. *London, Robert Barker,* 1610–11.

——— ——— The same. [Genevan version and Tomson's new testament]. *b. l.* 2 p. l. 554 l. 4°. *London, R. Barker,* 1613–14.

——— ——— The same. [Genevan version and Tomson's new testament]. 190, 181, 121 l. 11 l. 1 map. 4°. [*London, R. Barker,* 1615].
[Imperfect: general title-page wanting].

——— ——— The same. [Authorized version]. *b. l.* 8 p. l. 904 pp. 4°. *London, R. Barker and assignes of John Bill,* 1634.

——— ——— The same. [With Canne's preface and references, and tables of scripture

Bible (*English*)—continued.
weights and measures by Richard Cumberland, bp. of Peterborough]. 366 l. 12°. *Edinburgh, A. Kincaid*, 1766.

—— —— The same. With amendments of the language, by Noah Webster, ll. d. xvi, 907 pp. 8°. *New Haven, Durrie & Peck*, 1833.

—— —— The same. The right-aim school bible. And an annexment containing the free-debt-rule petitions. Also, the declaration of free-debtism. [By Rufus Davenport]. 510, 162 pp. 3 l. 12°. [*Boston, R. Davenport*], 1834.

—— —— The same. Stereotype ed. 669 pp. 12°. *New York, Amer. bible soc.* 1837.

—— —— The same. The English version, made by order of king James i. revised and amended. 2d ed. 2 v. in 1. iv, 632 pp. 2 l; iii, 192 pp. 8°. *Philadelphia, D. Bernard*, 1842.

—— —— The same. 968, 303 pp. 8°. *New York, Amer. bible soc.* 1843.

—— —— The same. The illuminated bible. Also, the apocrypha. To which are added, a chronological index, concordance, etc. Embellished with 1600 engravings by J. A. Adams, 1400 from original designs by J. G. Chapman. 4 p. l. 844 pp; 1 p. l. 128 pp; 2 p. l. 256, 56 pp. 2 pl. 4°. *New York, Harper & brothers*, 1846.

—— —— The same. And a selection of references and marginal readings: together with introductions to each book. 2 v. in 1. xxiv, 5–771 pp. 1 pl; x, 246 pp. 1 map. 8°. *New York, Carlton & Porter*, 1860.

—— —— The same. The family bible: with brief notes and instructions. Including the references and marginal readings of the polyglot bible. 1061 pp. [2 l.] 1063–1504 pp. 4 maps. 8°. *New York, American tract society*, [1861].

—— —— The same. With photographic record, or album. With the apocrypha, concordance and psalms. The text conformable to the original edition of 1610, and the American bible society's original standard edition of 1816. (Harding's fine ed.) 576, 116, [5 l.] 577–768, 41, 22 pp. 4°. *Philadelphia, W. W. Harding*, 1862.

—— —— The same. The illustrated polyglot family bible. With the apocrypha, concordance, and psalms in metre. Also, a history of the translation of the bible, and religious denominations, etc. Eng. title, [54], 768 pp. [193 pp.] 5 l. 10 pl. 4°. *Philadelphia, W. Flint*, [1869].

—— —— The same. The comprehensive and self-interpreting family bible: containing the old and new testaments and the apocrypha, including nearly one hundred thousand marginal readings and references, both parallel and explanatory, with an introduction, comprising an account of the english translation of the scriptures; a history of the canon of the old and new testaments, [etc.] Edited by prof. Calvin E. Stowe, d. d. To which is added an illustrated bible dictionary. Also a concordance, [etc.] viii, 96, 768, 104, 22, 41 pp. 5 l. 12 pl. 3 maps. 4°. *Hartford, (Conn.) Worthington, Dustin & co.* 1870.

—— —— The same. The holy bible, translated from the latin vulgate. Diligently compared with the hebrew, greek, and other editions, in divers languages, being the edition published by the english college at Rheims, 1582, and at Douay, 1609, as revised and corrected, in 1750, according to the clementine edition of the scriptures, by rev. Richard Challoner, bishop of Derba, with his annotations for clearing up the principal difficulties of holy writ. 2 p. l. 1532 pp. 14 col. pl. 16°. *New York, D. & J. Sadlier & co.* 1870.

—— —— The same. The pictorial home bible, devotional and explanatory: with the apocrypha, concordance, and marginal references. With companion articles; the whole forming a popular cyclopedia explanatory of the scriptures. By M. Laird Simons. xvi, 574, 116, 579–754, 42 pp. 4 l. 10 pl. 4°. *Philadelphia, W. Flint & co.* 1871.

—— —— *Bible with comment.* A commentary on the Holy Scriptures: critical, doctrinal, and homiletical, with special reference to ministers and students. By John Peter Lange, d. d. From the german, revised, enlarged, and edited by Peter Schaff, d. d. 3 v. 8°. *New York, C. Scribner & co.* 1870–72.

CONTENTS.

Old Testament.	v. 4.	Joshua, Judges, and Ruth.
	v. 13.	Jeremiah and Lamentations.
New Testament.	v. 3.	Gospel according to John.

—— —— —— The cottage bible, and family expositor; with practical expositions and explanatory notes, by Thomas Williams. To which are added, the references and marginal readings of the polyglott bible, together with original notes, [etc.] Edited

Bible (*English*)—continued.
by rev. William Patton, d. d. 2 v. 736 pp. 8 pl. 2 maps; 1 p. l. 737-1440 pp. 6 pl. 3 maps. 8°. *Hartford, Case, Lockwood & co.* 1862.

—— —— *Old testament.* Jewish school & family bible. Newly translated under the supervision of the rev. the chief rabbi of the united congregations of the british empire. By dr. A. Benisch. 2d ed. revised and improved. 4 v. 8°. *London, A. B. Davis,* 1852-61.

—— —— —— A harmony of the kings and prophets; or, an arrangement of the history contained in the books of kings and chronicles, together with the writings of the prophets introduced in chronological order as they were delivered, commencing with the revolt of the ten tribes and closing with the prophecy of Malachi. iv, 9-463 pp. 12°. *Boston, Mass. sabbath school union,* 1832.

—— —— *Pentateuch.* A commentary on the five books of Moses: with a dissertation concerning the author or writer of the said books, and a general argument to each of them. By Richard [Beadon], lord bishop of Bath and Wells. 2 v. in 1. lxxx, xx, 2 p. l. 468 pp; 2 p. l. 584 pp. 8°. *London, J. Heptinstall for W. Rogers,* 1694.

—— —— —— The pentateuch. Translated from the vulgate, and diligently compared with the original text, being a revised edition of the Douay version. With notes, critical and explanatory. By Francis Patrick Kenrick. 559 pp. 8°. *Baltimore, Kelly, Hedian & Piet,* 1860.

—— —— *Genesis.* Notes, critical and practical, on the book of Genesis; designed as a general help to biblical reading and instruction. By George Bush. 2 v. 354 pp; 1 p. l. 444 pp. 12°. *New York, E. French,* 1838.

—— —— —— Notes, critical and explanatory, on the book of Genesis. [v. 2.] From the covenant to the close. By Melancthon W. Jacobus. 266 pp. 12°. *New York, R. Carter & brothers,* 1866.

—— —— —— A critical and exegetical commentary on the book of Genesis. With a new translation. By J. G. Murphy, d. d. With a preface by J. P. Thompson, d. d. xvi, 535 pp. 8°. *Andover, W. F. Draper,* 1866.

—— —— *Joshua.* The book of Joshua. By F. R. Fay. Translated from the german, with additions, by George R. Bliss, d. d. 188 pp. 8°. *New York, Scribner & co.* 1872.

[BIBLE. (*English*). A commentary on the holy scriptures. By J. P. Lange. v. 4 (part 1), of the old testament].

—— —— *Judges.* The book of judges. By Paulus Cassell, d. d. Translated from the german, with additions, by P. H. Steenstra. 261 pp. 8°. *New York, C. Scribner & co.* 1872.

[BIBLE. (*English*). A commentary on the holy scriptures. By J. P. Lange. v. 4 (part 2) of the old testament].

—— —— *Ruth.* The book of Ruth. By Paulus Cassell, d. d. Translated from the german, with additions, by P. H. Steenstra. 53 pp. 8°. *New York, C. Scribner & co.* 1872.

[BIBLE. (*English*). A commentary on the holy scriptures. By J. P. Lange. v. 4 (part 3), of the old testament].

—— —— *Job.* Notes, critical, illustrative, and practical, on the book of Job: with a new translation, and an introductory dissertation. By Albert Barnes. 2 v. cxxvi, 311 pp; 312, 72 pp. 12°. *New York, Leavitt, Trow & co.* 1844.

—— —— —— The book of Job, and the prophets. Translated from the vulgate, and diligently compared with the original text, being a revised edition of the Douay version, with notes critical and explanatory, by Francis Patrick Kenrick, archbishop of Baltimore. 799 pp. 8°. *Baltimore, Kelly, Hedian & Piet,* 1859.

—— —— —— The book of Job paraphras'd. By Symon Patrick, d. d. 2d ed. corrected. 12 p. l. 335 pp. 12°. *London, J. Macock for R. Royston,* 1685.

—— —— *Psalms.* The psalms, books of wisdom, and canticle of canticles. Translated from the latin vulgate, diligently compared with the hebrew and greek, being a revised and corrected edition of the Douay version, with notes critical and explanatory, by Francis Patrick Kenrick. 584 pp. 8°. *Baltimore, Lucas brothers,* [1857].

—— —— —— A new translation of the book of psalms, with an introduction. By George R. Noyes. xxviii, 232 pp. 8°. *Boston, Gray & Bowen,* 1831.

—— —— *Proverbs.* Rills from the fountain of wisdom; or, the book of proverbs arranged and illustrated. By William M. Engles, d. d. 188 pp. 12°. *Philadelphia, Presbyterian board of publication,* 1845.

Bible (*English*)—continued.

——— ——— ——— A new translation of the proverbs of Solomon from the original hebrew, with explanatory notes. By William French, d. d. and the rev. George Skinner. 1 p. l. viii, 115 pp. 8°. *Cambridge, (Eng.) J. Smith,* 1831.

——— ——— *Ecclesiastes.* A commentary on ecclesiastes. By Moses Stuart. Edited and revised by R. D. C. Robbins. 346 pp. 12°. *Andover, W. F. Draper,* 1862.

——— ——— *Solomon's song.* Solomon's song: translated and explained. In three parts. i. The manuduction. ii. The version. iii. The supplement. By Leonard Withington. 4 p. l. 329 pp. 12°. *Boston, J. E. Tilton & co.* 1861.

——— ——— *Jeremiah.* The book of the prophet Jeremiah. Theologically and homiletically expounded by dr. C. W. Eduard Naegelsbach. Translated, enlarged, and edited by Samuel Ralph Asbury. 3 p. l. 446 pp. 8°. *New York, C. Scribner & co.* 1871.

[BIBLE. (*English*). Commentary. By J. P. Lange. v. 13 of the old testament].

——— ——— ——— The lamentations of Jeremiah. Theologically and homiletically expounded by dr. C. W. Eduard Naegelsbach. Translated, enlarged, and edited by Wm. H. Hornblower, d. d. 1 p. l. 196 pp. 8°. *New York, C. Scribner & co.* 1871.

[*With* Naegelsbach's Book of the prophet Jeremiah].

——— ——— *Daniel.* Commentaries of that diuine John Caluine, vpon the prophet Daniell, translated into englishe [by Arthur Golding]. 12 p. l. 120 l. 4°. *London, Iohn Daye,* 1570.

——— ——— *Minor prophets.* The minor prophets, with a commentary explanatory and practical, and introductions to the several books, by the rev. E. B. Pusey, d. d. Parts 1–3. 2 p. l. 300 pp. 4°. *Oxford, J. H. & J. Parker,* 1860–61.

[No more published].

——— ——— *Zechariah.* A short and sweete exposition vpon the first nine [ten] chapters of Zachary. By William Pemble. 3 p. l. 165 pp. sm. 4°. *London, R. Young for J. Bartlet,* 1629.

——— ——— *New testament.* Facsimile texts. The first printed english new testament. Translated by William Tyndale. Photolithographed from the unique fragment, now in the Grenville collection, British museum. [*Cologne,* 1526]. Edited by Edward Arber. 71, 62 pp. 1 pl. sm. 4°. *London,* 1871.

Bible (*English*)—continued.

——— ——— The same. The new testament of our Lord Iesus Christ. Printed by Conrad Badius, a. d. 1557. Together with king James' version of the new testament, in parallel columns, chapters, and verses, side by side. With an address to the people of God. By A. F. Uitts. 714 pp. 12°. *Indianapolis, R. I. Bright & co.* 1871.

——— ——— The same. The nevv testament of Iesus Christ, translated faithfvlly into english, out of the authentical latin, according to the best corrected copies of the same [by cardinal William Allen, and others]. In the english college of Rhemes. 14 p. l. 746 pp. 13 l. 4°. *Rhemes, J. Fogny,* 1582.

——— ——— The same. Translated out of the latin vulgate, diligently compared with the original greek, and first published by the english college of Rheims, anno 1582. With the original preface, arguments and tables, marginal notes, and annotations. [Also], an introductory essay, and a complete topical and textual index. 1 p. l. 458 pp. 8°. *New York, J. Leavitt,* 1834.

——— ——— The same. The text of the new testament of Iesus Christ, translated out of the vulgar latine by the papists of the traiterous seminarie at Rhemes. With arguments of bookes, chapters, & annotations, pretending to discouer the corruptions of diuers translations, & to cleare the controuersies of these dayes. Wherevnto is added [in parallel columns], the [bishops'] translation out of the original greeke, commonly vsed in the church of England. By W. Fvlke, d. in diuinitie. 4th ed. Eng. title, 29 p. l. 912 pp. 7 l. 1 portrait. fol. *London, by A. Mathewes, one of the assignes of H. Ogden,* 1633.

——— ——— The same. A new translation of those parts only of the new testament, which are wrongly translated in our common version, by Gilbert Wakefield. xvi, 141 pp. 8°. *London, J. Deighton,* 1789.

[MISCELLANEOUS pamphlets, v. 315].

——— ——— The same. 144 l. 8°. *New York, Whiting & Watson,* 1812.

——— ——— The same. With references and a key sheet of questions, historical, doctrinal, and practical. By Hervey Wilbur. ster. ed. 321 pp. 16°. *Boston, R. Bannister,* 1823.

——— ——— The same. Translated out of the original greek, and with the former translations diligently compared and revised. From which is selected an extensive vocabu-

Bible (*English*)—continued.
lary. [With] Walker's explanatory key. By Jeremiah Goodrich. 333 pp. 1 pl. 16°. *Albany, S. Shaw*, 1825.

——— ——— The same. A new self-interpreting testament, containing many thousands of various readings and parallel passages, collected from the most approved translators and biblical critics, with introductory arguments concerning the origin, occasion and character of each book; a reconciliation of seeming contradictions; and the meaning and pronunciation of scripture proper names. By the rev. John Platts. 4 v. 8°. *London, J. Robins & co.* 1827.

——— ——— The same. The text of the common translation arranged in paragraphs. By James Nourse. 373, xxiii pp. 18°. *New York, G. & C. Carvill*, 1827.

——— ——— ——— The same. By James Nourse. viii, 3–322 pp. 16°. *Boston, Perkins, Marvin & co.* 1834.

——— ——— The same. To which is added, a vocabulary of all the words therein contained. Likewise, a catalogue of all the proper names contained therein. By Rensselaer Bentley. 226, 62 pp. 16°. *Troy, (N. Y.) F. Adancourt*, 1828.

——— ——— The same. Being the English version made by order of king James i. carefully revised and emended. [By A. C. Kendrick]. 2 p. l. 192 pp. 4°. *Philadelphia, D. Bernard*, 1842.

——— ——— The same. Being the version of king James i. 2d ed. iii, 192 pp. 8°. *Philadelphia, D. Bernard*, 1842.

——— ——— The same. The commonly received version: with several hundred emendations. Edited by Spencer H. Cone and Wm. H. Wyckoff. 1 p. l. 394 pp. 8°. *New York, Lewis Colby*, 1850.

——— ——— The same. The emphatic new testament, according to the authorized version; with the various readings, in english, of the Vatican manuscript. [Edited, with an introductory essay on greek emphasis, by John Taylor]. 1 v. in 2. Eng. title, 4 p. l. 70, 449 pp. 8°. *London, S. Bagster & sons*, 1854.

——— ——— The same. The holy gospels and the acts of the apostles, in english: so printed as to show the sound of each word, without change of spelling; with tables representing english sounds by the alphabets of the principal languages of Europe and Asia. By Rev. Thomas Jarrett. xxi, 416 pp. 8°. *London, B. Quaritch*, 1857.

——— ——— The same. With chronological arrangement of the sacred books, and improved divisions of chapters and verses. By Leicester Ambrose Sawyer. 423 pp. 12°. *Boston, J. P. Jewett & co.* 1858.

——— ——— The same. Translated from the latin vulgate, and diligently compared with the original greek text, with notes, critical and explanatory, by Francis Patrick Kenrick, arch-bishop of Baltimore. 2d ed. 861 pp. 8°. *Baltimore, Kelly, Hedian & Piet*, 1862.

——— ——— The same. The new testament from the family bible: with brief notes and instructions. Including the references and marginal readings of the polyglot bible. 810 pp. 2 maps. 16°. *New York, American tract society*, [1862].

——— ——— The same. As revised and corrected by spirits. 320 pp. 8°. *New York, proprietors*, [1862].

——— ——— The same. The common english version, corrected by the final committee of the American bible union. iv, 326 pp. 18°. *New York, American bible union*, 1862.

——— ——— The same. With brief explanatory notes or scholia. By Howard Crosby, d. d. 2 p. l. 543 pp. 12°. *New York, C. Scribner*, 1863.

——— ——— The same. [Also, the book of psalms]. 303, 80 pp. 18°. *Augusta, (Ga.) Bible society of the Confederate States*, 1863.

——— ——— The same. In which all the proper names and words of two syllables and more are divided and accented as they should be pronounced. 372 pp. 24°. *New York, Carlton & Porter*, [1863].

——— ——— The same. Translated from the greek text of Tischendorf, by George R. Noyes, d.d. 570 pp. 12°. *Boston, American unitarian association*, 1869.

——— ——— *New testament with comment.* The new testament of our Lord and Savior Jesus Christ; translated out of the original greek, and with the former translation diligently compared and revised. With brief explanatory notes. [By J. and J. S. C. Abbott]. 586 pp. 8°. *Boston, Crocker & Brewster*, 1842.

——— ——— ——— A paraphrase on the new testament, with notes, doctrinal and practical. With an advertisement of diffi-

Bible (*English*)—continued.
culties in the Revelations. By the late rev. mr. Richard Baxter. 3d ed. corrected. [Also], mr. Baxter's account of his notes on some particular texts, for which he was imprison'd. 345 l. 8°. *London, T. Parkhurst,* [*etc.*] 1701.
[Imperfect: wanting several leaves].

——— ——— ——— The illustrated new testament; with notes, explanatory of the rites, customs, sects, phraseology, topography, and geography, referred to in this portion of the sacred pages. By Ingram Cobbin. viii, 528 pp. 23 pl. 8°. *New York, J. W. Goodspeed & co.* 1871.

——— ——— ——— The cottage testament: according to the authorized version, with notes, original and selected; likewise introductions and concluding remarks to each book, polyglott references and marginal readings, geographical index, chronological and other tables. By rev. William Patton, d. d. 2d ed. 718 pp. 3 maps. 18°. *New York, Mason brothers,* 1861.

——— ——— ——— The cottage polyglott testament: with notes, original and selected. Likewise introductory and concluding remarks to each book, polyglott references and marginal readings, chronological table, geographical index, and maps. By William Patton, d. d. 718 pp. 3 maps. 18°. *New York, J. S. Gilman,* 1860.

——— ——— ——— The village testament: with notes, original and selected; likewise introductions and concluding remarks to each book, polyglott references and marginal readings, geographical index, chronological and other tables. By William Patton, d. d. 2d ed. 718 pp. 2 maps. 18°. *New York, Mason brothers,* 1861.

——— ——— ——— Practical observations on the new testament. By rev. Thomas Scott. Arranged for family worship. With an introduction, by A. Alexander, d. d. xii, 532 pp. 5 pl. 8°. *Philadelphia, I. Ashmead & co.* 1842.

——— ——— ——— The sunday-school commentary. The new testament; with notes, pictorial illustrations, and references. The gospels and acts. By rev. Israel P. Warren, d. d. 10, 518 pp. 1 map. 8°. *Boston, Lee & Shepard,* 1871.

——— ——— ——— Commentary on the new testament. By D. D. Whedon, d. d. v. 3, Acts–Romans. 402 pp. incl. 9 pl. 1 map. 12°. *New York, Carlton & Lanahan,* 1871.

——— ——— ——— The new testament: carefully collated with the greek, and corrected; divided and pointed according to the various subjects treated of by the inspired writers, with the common division into chapters and verses in the margin; and illustrated with notes critical and explanatory. By Richard Wynne. 2 v. xviii, 489 pp; vi, 530 pp. 8°. *London, R. & J. Dodsley,* 1764.

——— ——— *Gospels.* A harmony of the four gospels in english, according to the authorized version, corrected by the best critical editions of the original. By Frederic Gardiner, d. d. xliii, 487 pp. 8°. *Andover, W. F. Draper,* 1871.

——— ——— ——— Notes, practical and expository, on the gospels: for the use of bible classes, sunday school teachers, catechists, and other pious laymen. By rev. Charles H. Hall. 2 v. 429 pp; 400 pp. 12°. *New York, D. Appleton & co.* 1857.

——— ——— ——— The same. 2d ed. 2 v. 429 pp; 400 pp. 12°. *New York, Hurd & Houghton,* 1871.

——— ——— ——— The four gospels, translated from the latin vulgate, and diligently compared with the original greek text, being a revision of the rhemish translation, with notes critical and explanatory. By Francis Patrick Kenrick, bishop of Philadelphia. 572 pp. 1 map. 8°. *New York, E. Dunigan & brother,* 1849.

——— ——— ——— The teacher's commentary on the gospel narrative of the last year of our Lord's ministry. By Henry C. McCook. xii, 515 pp. 6 pl. 1 map. 12°. *Philadelphia, Presbyterian board of instruction,* [1871].

——— ——— ——— A commentary on the gospels of Matthew and Mark, critical, doctrinal, and homiletical, embodying the results of german and english exegetical literature. With a general introduction, by William Nast, d. d. 760 pp. 1 portrait. 8°. *Cincinnati, Poe & Hitchcock,* 1864.

——— ——— ——— A translation of the gospels. With notes. By Andrews Norton. 2 v. vii, 443 pp; iv, 565 pp. 8°. *Boston, Little, Brown & co.* 1855.

——— ——— ——— A commentary on the new testament. By Lucius R. Paige. 2 v. 401 pp; 414 pp. 12°. *Boston, B. B. Mussey,* 1845.

CONTENTS.

v. 1. Matthew, Mark.
v. 2. Luke, John.

Bible (*English*)—continued.

——— ——— ——— The four gospels; with notes, chiefly explanatory. By Henry J. Ripley. 2 v. 297 pp. 1 map; 270 pp. 12°. *Boston, Gould, Kendall & Lincoln*, 1837.

——— ——— ——— Commentary on the gospels. By Thos. O. Summers, d. d. v. 3-4. Luke and John. 12°. *Nashville (Tenn.) publishing house of the methodist episcopal church south*, 1871-2.

——— ——— ——— A commentary on the gospels of Matthew and Mark. By D. D. Whedon, d. d. 422 pp. 1 map. 12°. *New York, Carlton & Porter*, 1860.

——— ——— ——— The four gospels in one. According to the authorized version. By a Chicago bible class teacher. [*anon.*] 283 pp. 12°. *Chicago, R. A. Campbell*, 1871.

——— ——— *Matthew.* The gospel according to Matthew. Explained by Joseph Addison Alexander. iv, 456 pp. 12°. *New York, C. Scribner*, 1861.

——— ——— ——— Disquisitions and notes on the gospels. Matthew. By John H. Morrison. 538 pp. 12°. *Boston, Walker, Wise & co.* 1860.

——— ——— ——— A catholike and ecclesiasticall exposition of the holy gospell after s. Mathewe, gathered out of all the singuler and approued deuines by Augustine Marlorate. And translated out of latine into englishe by Thomas Tymme. *b. l.* 5 p. l. 759 pp. 4 l. fol. *London, T. Marshe*, 1570.

——— ——— *Mark.* The gospel according to st. Mark: revised from the ancient greek mss. unknown to the translators of the authorized version. By a member of the university of Oxford [John Ivatt Briscoe, m. p.] 2 p. l. 34 pp. sm. 4°. *London, Longmans, Green & co.* 1870.

——— ——— ——— First gospel, being the gospel according to Mark; translated and arranged, with a critical examination of the book, its life of Jesus, and his religion. By Leicester Ambrose Sawyer. 175 pp. 12°. *Boston, Walker, Wise & co.* 1864.

——— ——— *John.* Notes on the gospels, critical and explanatory; incorporating with the notes, on a new plan, the most approved harmony of the four gospels. By Melancthon W. Jacobus. John. 348 pp. 1 pl. 12°. *New York, R. Carter & brothers*, 1856.

——— ——— ——— The gospel according to John. A commentary, critical, doctrinal, and homiletical. By John Peter Lange, d. d. Translated from the german, by Edward D. Yeomans, d. d. and Evelina Moore, with homiletical additions by E. R. Craven, d. d. Revised, enlarged, and edited by Philip Schaff, d. d. xv, 654 pp. 8°. *New York, Scribner, Armstrong & co.* 1872.

[Bible. (*English*). A commentary on the holy scriptures. By J. P. Lange. v. 3, of the new testament].

——— ——— ——— A commentary, critical, expository, and practical, on the gospel of John. By John J. Owen, d. d. xiv, 502 pp. 12°. *New York, Leavitt & Allen*, 1860.

——— ——— *Acts.* Actions of the apostles: translated from the original greek, by the rev. John Willis. xl, 295 pp. 8°. *London, Robson, Clarke & Faulder*, 1789.

——— ——— ——— Notes, explanatory and practical, on the acts of the apostles. By Albert Barnes. 20th ed. 356 pp. 1 map. 12°. *New York, Harper & brothers*, 1863.

——— ——— ——— The same. Revised ed. 418 pp. 1 map. 12°. *New York, Harper & brothers*, 1870.

——— ——— ——— A commentary on acts of apostles, with a revised version of the text. By J. W. McGarvey. 297 pp. 12°. *Cincinnati, Wrightson & co.* 1863.

——— ——— ——— The acts of the apostles; with notes, chiefly explanatory. By Henry J. Ripley. 334 pp. 12°. *Boston, Gould, Kendall & Lincoln*, 1844.

——— ——— *Epistles of Paul.* Commentaries on the epistles of Paul to the Galatians and Ephesians. By John Calvin. Translated from the original latin, by the rev. William Pringle. 383 pp. 8°. *Edinburgh, Calvin translation society*, 1854.

——— ——— ——— Commentaries on the epistles of Paul the apostle to the Philippians, Colossians, and Thessalonians. By John Calvin. Translated and edited from the original latin, and collated with the french version, by the rev. John Pringle. 490 pp. 8°. *Edinburgh, Calvin translation society*, 1851.

——— ——— ——— Commentaries on the epistles to Timothy, Titus and Philemon. By John Calvin. From the original latin, by rev. William Pringle. 398 pp. 8°. *Edinburgh, Calvin translation society*, 1856.

——— ——— ——— A paraphrase and notes on the epistles of st. Paul to the Colossians, Philippians, and Hebrews: after the manner of mr. Locke. [Also], several critical dis-

Bible (*English*)—continued.

sertations on particular texts of scripture. 2d ed. By the rev. mr. James Peirce. With a paraphrase and notes on the three last chapters of the Hebrews left unfinish'd by mr. Peirce; and an essay to discover the author of the epistle and language in which it was originally written. By Joseph Hallett, jun. 4 v. in 1. 4°. *London, J. Noon*, 1733–37.

——— ——— ——— Notes on the epistles of Paul the apostle to the Galatians and Ephesians. By Joseph Longking. 284 pp. 18°. *New York, Carlton & Porter, sunday-school union*, 1863.

——— ——— *Romans.* Notes, explanatory and practical, on the epistle to the Romans. Designed for bible-classes and sunday-schools. By Albert Barnes. 10th ed. revised and corrected. 367 pp. 12°. *New York, Harper & brothers*, 1871.

——— ——— ——— A critical commentary on the epistle of st. Paul the apostle to the Romans. By Robert Knight. xx, 640 pp. 8°. *London, S. Bagster & sons*, 1854.

——— ——— ——— A commentary on the epistle to the Romans. By Moses Stuart. Edited and revised by R. D. C. Robbins. 4th ed. 514 pp. 12°. *Andover, W. F. Draper*, 1859.

——— ——— ——— A commentary on the epistle to the Romans, with a translation and various excursus. By Moses Stuart. 576 pp. 8°. *Andover, Flagg & Gould*, 1832.

——— ——— *Corinthians.* Notes, explanatory and practical, on the first epistle of Paul to the Corinthians. By Albert Barnes. 357 pp. 12°. *New York, W. Robinson*, 1838.

——— ——— ——— The same. Revised ed. 319 pp. 12°. *New York, Harper & brothers*, 1872.

——— ——— ——— Notes, explanatory and practical, on the second epistle to the Corinthians, and the epistle to the Galatians. By Albert Barnes. Revised ed. 367 pp. 12°. *New York, Harper & brothers*, 1872.

——— ——— ——— An exposition of the second epistle to the Corinthians. By Charles Hodge, d. d. 1 p. l. 314 pp. 12°. *New York, R. Carter & brothers*, 1860.

——— ——— *Galatians.* A commentary on st. Paul's epistle to the Galatians, by Martin Luther. To which is prefixed Tischer's life of Luther. Abridged: a short sketch of the life of Zuingle; as also, a discourse on the glorious reformation, by S. S. Schmucker, d. d. 632 pp. 1 portrait. 8°. *Philadelphia, Quaker city publishing house*, 1872.

——— ——— *Ephesians.* A commentary, explanatory, doctrinal, and practical, on the epistle to the Ephesians. By R. E. Pattison, d. d. 244 pp. 12°. *Boston, Gould & Lincoln*, 1859.

——— ——— ——— A commentary on the epistle to the Ephesians. By Charles Hodge, d. d. 398 pp. 8°. *New York, R. Carter & brothers*, 1856.

——— ——— *Thessalonians.* Lectures on the epistles of Paul to the Thessalonians. [With text]. By John Lillie, d. d. 538 pp. 8°. *New York, R. Carter & brothers*, 1860.

——— ——— *Hebrews.* Commentaries on the epistle of Paul the apostle to the Hebrews. By John Calvin. Translated from the original latin and edited by the rev. John Owen. 448 pp. 8°. *Edinburgh, Calvin translation society*, 1853.

——— ——— ——— Popular lectures on the epistle of Paul, the apostle to the Hebrews. By Joseph Augustus Seiss. vi, 408 pp. 8°. *Baltimore, publication rooms*, 1846.

——— ——— *Catholic epistles.* Commentaries on the catholic epistles. By John Calvin. Translated and edited by rev. John Owen. 488 pp. 8°. *Edinburgh, Calvin translation society*, 1855.

——— ——— *Peter.* A practical commentary upon the first epistle general of Peter. By the rev. Robert Leighton, d. d. archbishop of Glasgow. To which is prefixed a brief memoir of the author. 2 v. 444 pp; 481 pp. 8°. *Philadelphia, Presbyterian board of publication*, [1864].

——— ——— *Revelation.* A revelation of the apocalyps. By T. Brightman. sm. 4°. *London*, 1644.

[*In* BRIGHTMAN (Thomas). Workes, pp. 1-611].

——— ——— ——— The revelation of John; with notes, critical, explanatory, and practical, designed for both pastors and people. By Henry Cowles, d. d. 254 pp. 12°. *New York, D. Appleton & co.* 1871.

——— ——— ——— A learned and complete commentary upon the book of the revelation. Delivered in several lectures, by mr. James Durham. As also, two sermons preached by the author, on Rev. xxii, 20. Together with a collection of some memorable things in his life. 810 pp. 7 l. 4°. *Glasgow, J. Bryce*, 1764.

Bible (*English*)—continued.

——— ——— ——— A dissertation on the book of revelation. By James Gray. 284 pp. 12°. *Newburgh, (N. Y.) B. F. Lewis & co. for R. Gray*, 1818.

——— ——— ——— The revelation of saint John the divine elucidated, from its commencement, a. d. 96, to the overthrow of the french empire under Napoleon Bonaparte: with some intimations concerning the predictions about to be accomplished; and an illustration of the New Jerusalem, and certain portions of Daniel and Ezekiel. By rev. James Ivory Holmes. 2 v. xx, 389 pp; 2 p. l. 508 pp. 8°. *London, J. Hatchard*, 1815.

——— ——— ——— The apocalypse; or, the revelation of saint John the divine: with a few notes and reflections. By the rev. Joseph Jones. xii, 182 pp. 12°. *London, Hamilton, Adams, and co.* [1852].

——— ——— ——— An exposition of the revelation of Jesus Christ to John. By John [Spinning? *anon.*] 256 pp. 12°. *New York, publisher*, 1834.

——— ——— ——— An attempt to translate the prophetic part of the apocalypse of saint John into familiar language, by James Winthrop. 79 pp. 8°. *Boston, Belknap & Hall*, 1795.

[Hazard pamphlets, v. 95].

——— (*French*). La sainte bible, qui contient l'ancien et le nouveau testament. Le tout reveu & conféré sur les textes hébreux & grecs, par les pasteurs & professeurs de l'église de Genève. 2 v. 4°. *Amsterdam, N. P. & J. Blasu pour Wolfgang*, [*etc.*] 1687.

——— ——— *New testament*. Le nouveau testament. Nouv. éd. Eng. title, 131 l. unp. 24°. *Amsterdam, F. G.* 1706.

——— ——— The same. 131 l. 24°. *Amsterdam, D. J. Changuion*, 1794.

——— ——— The same. Eng. title, 125 l. unp. 16°. *Amsterdam, D. J. Changuion*, 1794.

——— ——— The same. Revu sur les originaux, par David Martin. 444 pp. 16°. *New York, la société biblique américaine*, 1844.

——— ——— *Revelation*. Paraphrase et exposition svr l'apocalypse. Tirée des sainctes écritures & de l'histoire par Jonas Le Bvy s^{r}. de la Perie. [*pseudon.*] 4 p. l. 679 pp. 1 l. 4°. *Genève, P. Aubert*, 1651.

——— (*German*). Die illustrirte familien-bibel für häusliche erbauung und belehrung. Enthaltend das alte und neue testament, mit den apokryphen, der concordanz und randparallelen. Nach dr. Martin Luther's uebersetzung. Von M. Laird Simons. Eng. title, xvi, 175, 9–651, 88, 653–880 pp. 5 l. 11 pl. 1 map. 4°. *Philadelphia, W. Flint & co.* 1871.

——— ——— Historische bilder bibel. 1705. *See* **Krauss** (Johann Ulrich).

——— ——— *Old testament*. Die schriften des alten testaments. Neu übersetzt von J. C. W. Augusti und W. M. L. De Wette. 5 v. 8°. *Heidelberg, Mohr & Zimmer*, 1809–11.

——— ——— *Corinthians*. Vorlesungen über die beyden briefe Pauli an die Corinthier von Johann Friedrich von Flatt. Nach seinem tode herausgegeben von seinem sohne, C. D. F. Hoffmann. Nebst einem vorworte von C. C. von Flatt. iv, 448, 212 pp. 8°. *Tübingen, L. F. Fues*, 1827.

——— (*Greek*). *Old testament*. Vetus testamentum græcum e codice ms. alexandrino, qui Londini in bibliotheca musei britannici asservatur, typis ad similitudinem ipsius codicis scripturæ fideliter descriptum cura et labore Henrici Herveii Baber. 4 v. in 6. fol. *Londini, R. & A. Taylor*, 1816–28. s.

——— ——— *New testament*. Της καινης διαθηκης ἁπαντα. Novvm Iesv Christi testamentum. Cum notis Io. Scaligeri in locos aliquot difficiliores nunc primum editæ. 4 p. l. 453, 16 pp. 4°. *Genevæ, P. de la Rouiere*, 1620.

——— ——— The same. Jesu Christi domini nostri novum testamentum, sive novum fœdus, cujus græco contextui respondent interpretationes duæ, una vetus; altera, Theodori Bezæ. Ejusdem T. Bezæ annotationes. Accessit J. Camerarii in novum fœdus commentarius. 2 v. in 1. 18 p. l. 766 pp; 11 p. l. 125 pp. 2 l. fol. *Cantabrigiae, R. Daniel*, 1642.

——— ——— The same. Ἡ καινη διαθηκη. Novum testamentum. Juxta exemplar Joannis Millii accuratissime impressum. Ed. prima americana. 478 pp. 16°. *Wigorniæ, (Mass.) I. Thomas, jun.* 1800.

——— ——— The same. Ἡ καινη διαθηκη. The greek testament, with english notes, critical, philological, and exegetical, partly selected from the best commentators, ancient and modern, but chiefly original. By Samuel Thomas Bloomfield. 1st am. from the 2d Lond. ed. 2 v. xxxii, 597 pp; 631 pp. 8°. *Boston, Perkins & Marvin*, 1837.

——— ——— *Gospels*. Harmonia evangelica:

Bible (*Greek*)—continued.

a greek harmony of the four gospels. Consisting of selections from the four evangelists, arranged in chronological order, and forming a history of the saviour's life and ministry: with notes and a lexicon. By N. C. Brooks, ll.d. 210 pp. 18°. *Philadelphia, Claxton, Remsen & Haffelfinger*, 1871.
[BROOK'S classical series].

——— ——— ——— A harmony of the four gospels in greek, according to the text of Tischendorf; with a collation of the textus receptus, and of the texts of Griesbach, Lachmann, and Tregelles. By Frederic Gardiner, d. d. 268 pp. 8°. *Andover, W. F. Draper*, 1871.

——— ——— *Galatians.* A commentary, critical and grammatical, on st. Paul's epistle to the Galatians, with a revised translation. By C. J. Ellicott. And an introductory notice, by Calvin E. Stowe, d. d. 1 p. l. 183 pp. 8°. *Andover, W. F. Draper*, 1860.

——— ——— *Hebrews.* A critical commentary on the epistle to the Hebrews. By Francis S. Sampson, d. d. Edited from the manuscript notes of the author, by Robert L. Dabney, d. d. xv, 475 pp. 8°. *New York, R. Carter & brothers*, 1856.

——— (*Greek and english*). The emphatic diaglott: containing the original greek text of what is commonly styled the new testament, (according to the recension of dr. J. J. Griesbach,) with an interlineary word for word english translation; a new emphatic version, based on the various readings of the Vatican manuscript. By Benjamin Wilson. 16°. *Geneva (Ill.) author*, 1865.

——— ——— *John.* The gospel of st. John in greek: with an interlineal and analytical translation, on the principles of the Hamiltonian system, as improved by Thomas Clark, [etc. or,] The gospel according to st. John, in greek: to which is appended a critical annotation; also, the authorized english version of the protestant church, and a comparative view of the catholic translation from the vulgate; with historical and grammatical notes. By George William Heilig. 292 pp. 12°. *Philadelphia, C. Desilver*, 1861.

——— ——— *Galatians.* The epistle to the Galatians, in greek and english, with an analysis and exegetical commentary. By Samuel H. Turner, d. d. xiii, 98 pp. 8°. *New York, Dana & co.* 1856.

Bible (*Greek and english*)—continued.

——— ——— *Ephesians.* The epistle to the Ephesians, in greek and english. With an analysis and exegetical commentary. By Samuel H. Turner, d. d. xix, 198 pp. 8°. *New York, Dana & co.* 1856.

——— (*Hebrew*). Derek hakkodesh, sive Biblia sacra. Authore Elia Hvttero. 6 p. l. 1552 pp. fol. *Hambvrgi, typis Elianis*, 1587.

——— ——— *Old testament.* Vetus testamentum hebraicum, cum variis lectionibus. Edidit Benjaminus Kennicott. 2 v. xxiii, viii, 684 pp. 1 l; 2 p. l. 732, 129 pp. 3 l. fol. *Oxonii, e typographeo clarendoniano*, 1776–80.

——— (*Hebrew and english.*) Abridged school and family bible in hebrew and english. Elaborated by Jacob Levi Levinski, with the coöperation of rev. dr. H. Vidaver. 4 p. l. 414, 32 l. 6 l. 8°. *New York, L. H. Frank & co.* 1871.

——— (*Hebrew and latin*). *Apocrypha.* Tobias [seu Thobi ben Thobiel] hebraice vt is adhvc hodie apvd Ivdæos invenitur, omnia ex hebræo in latinum translata, in gratiam studiosorum linguæ sanctæ, per Pavlvm Fagivm. 24 l. 4°. *Isnæ*, 1542.
[*With* JESCHUA BEN SIRA. Sententiæ morales. *Isnæ*, 1542].

——— (*Italian*). Vecchio e nuovo testamento, secondo la volgata, tradotto in lingua italiana, e con annotazioni dichiaruto da Antonio Martini, arcivescovo di Firenze. v. 1–17, 19–24. 8°. *Firenze, G. Ducci*, 1827–30.
[Imperfect: wanting, v. 18 and v. 12, pp. 1–112].

——— (*Latin*). [Biblia sacra. Begins] Incipit epistola beati Hieronymi ad Paulinū presbyterū de omnib̄ diuine historie libris. [Ends] Expliciunt interpretatiōes hebraicorū nominū. 487 l. unp. 8°. *Basilee, per Johānem Froben de Hammelburck*, 1491.
[*Note.*—The first octavo ed. of the Vulgate. Commences with sign. a ij, and wants one leaf at the close].

——— ——— The same. Biblia latina cum commentariis Hvgonis de sancto Charo, seu postilla in Pentateuchem, Josue, Job, [etc.] 34 p. l. 436 l. numb. fol. *Basilea, A. Coberger*, 1504.
[*Note.*—Gothic type, in 2 columns, of 78 lines].

——— ——— The same. Biblia sacra vtrivsqve testamenti, ivxta hebraicam et graecam ueritatem, uetustissimorumq; ac emendatissimorum codicum fidem diligentissime recognita. Quibus tertius Machabæorum liber, paucissimiscognitus, iam recens accessit [edente Joanne Rudelio]. 414 l. unp. fol. *Coloniæ, Petrus Quentel*, 1527.

Bible (*Latin*)—continued.

——— ——— The same. Biblia sacrosancta veteris et novi testamenti. Iuxta vulgatem editionem. 8 p. l. 477 pp. 26 l. 12°. *Lvgdvni, Antonius Vincentius, ex officina typographica Michaelis Sylvii*, 1555.

[*Note.*—This appears to be the first bible in which the text is divided into distinct verses of separate paragraphs, as bibles are now printed].

——— ——— The same. [Biblia sacra cum praefatione Hentenii]. 529 l. 63 l. 12°. *Antverpiae, apvd Joan. Steelsium, typis Ioan. Withagius*, 1563.

[Imperfect: title-page and preface wanting, and l. 1-7, 10-24, supplied in *ms.*]

——— ——— The same. Biblia sacra vulgatae editionis Sixti v. pontificis max. jussu recognita, et Clementis viii. auctoritate edita, versiculis distincta, et ad singula capita argumentis aucta, pluribusque imaginibus, ornata. Eng. title, 11 p. l. 998 pp. 26 l. 8°. *Venetiis, Nicolavs Pezzana*, 1690.

——— ——— *New testament.* Novum testamentum domini nostri Jesu Christi. Interprete Theodoro Beza. 2 p. l. 291 pp. 16°. *Londini, impensis Harding & Lepard*, 1831.

——— ——— The same. Ex versione vulgata, cum paraphrasi et adnotationibus Henrici Hammondi ex anglica lingva in latinam transtulit, suisque animadversionibus illustravit, castigavit, auxit Joannes Clericus. Ed. 2a. 2 v. 6 p. l. 600 pp; 2 p. l. 724 pp. 6 l. fol. *Francofurti, T. Fritsch*, 1714.

——— ——— *Revelation* Apochalypsis Ihesv Christi. [Illustrated]. *b. l.* 16 l. fol. *Venetiis, per A. Pag[aninum]*, 1516.

[*Note.*—Sixteen wood engravings—one on the recto of each leaf,—mostly after designs by Albert Dürer. The text is printed on the reverse. The initial letters I. A. found on the plates are referred to Ioan Andrea, whom Brulliot and Nagler identify with Giovanni Andrea Valvassore, or Vavassore da Guadagnino].

Bible (George W.) Great european conflict. Franco-prussian war. Chassepot-rifle vs. zündnadelgewehr, or the needle gun. Real cause of the struggle. Name, title, and year of accession of the rulers of the european states. Kinds of governments. Armaments, military and naval. Rhenish provinces. Strategic points. Compiled and arranged from the latest european official sources and statistics. 164 pp. 4 portraits, 1 map. 12°. *New York, Bible brothers*, 1870.

Biblical (The) reason why: a family guide to scripture readings, and a hand-book for biblical students. By the author of "The reason why," etc. [*anon.*] xxiii, 324 pp. 12°. *New York, Dick & Fitzgerald*, [1859].

Bibliographie de la France. Journal général de l'imprimerie et de la librairie. 2e série. v. 13-14, 1869-70. 1e partie. Bibliographie. 2e partie. Chronique. 3e partie. Feuilleton commerciale. 4 v. 8°. *Paris, Pillet fils aîné*, 1869-70.

[CHRONIQUE *and* BIBLIOGRAPHIE bound together, for each year].

Bibliographie des ouvrages relatifs à l'amour. *See* I * * * (Le C. d').

Bibliophiles (Société des) françois. *See* **Paris.** (*Société des bibliophiles françois*).

Biblioteca de autores españoles, desde la formacion del lenguage hasta nuestros dias. v. 50 b. 8°. *Madrid, M. Rivadeneyra*, 1870.

CONTENTS.

OCHOA (E. de). Epistolario español. Colleccion de cartas de españoles ilustres antiguos y modernos, v. 2.

Biblioteca portátil española, ó colleccion de las mejores poesias, novelas, dramas, &c. de los escritores españoles del siglo xix hasta nuestros dias. v. 1. iv, 448 pp. 16°. *Brunsvico, E. Leibrock*, 1841. s.

[No more published].

Bibliotheca mejicana. A catalogue of an extraordinary collection of books and manuscripts, almost wholly relating to the history and literature of North and South America, particularly Mexico. [With printed list of prices at sale]. 2 p. l. 312, 41 pp. 8°. *London, Puttick & Simpson*, 1869.

Bibliotheca (The) sacra and theological eclectic. Edited by Edwards A. Park and George E. Day. [Quarterly]. Jan. to Oct. 1871. v. 28. 8°. *Andover (Mass.) W. F. Draper*, 1871.

Bibliothèque italique, ou histoire littéraire de l'Italie. Janvier, 1728 [à avril, 1729]. v. 1-4 in 2 v. 16°. *Genève, M. M. Bousquet & cie.* 1728-29.

[*Note.*—Par Bourguet, Cramer, Calendrini, &c.]

Bibliothèque des philosophes chimiques. *See* **Salmon** (William).

Bickersteth (*Rev.* Edward Henry). The two brothers, and other poems. 324 pp. 1 portrait. 12°. *New York, R. Carter & brothers*, 1871.

Bickham (George). Deliciae britannicae: or, the curiosities of Kensington, Hampton Court, and Windsor Castle, delineated; with additions. viii, 184 pp. 10 pl. 12°. *London, E. Owen*, [1742].

Bicknell (Alexander). Instances of the mutability of fortune, selected from ancient and modern history, and arranged according to their chronological order. xii, 453 pp. 8°. *London, J. S. Jordan*, 1792.

Bicknell (Alexander)—continued.

——— The life of Alfred the great, king of the Anglo-Saxons. xv, 404 pp. 1 portrait. 8°. *London, J. Bew*, 1777.

Bicknell (A. J.) Bicknell's village builder. Elevations and plans for cottages, villas, suburban residences, farm-houses, [etc.] also exterior and interior details for public and private buildings, with approved forms of contracts and specifications. Revised ed. 2 p. l. 20 l. 57 pl. 4°. *New York, A. J. Bicknell & co.* 1872.

——— The same. Supplement to Bicknell's village builder, containing eighteen modern designs for country and suburban houses at moderate cost, with elevations, plans, sections, [etc.] 6 l. 20 pl. fol. *New York, A. J. Bicknell & co.* [1871].

Bielfeld (Jacob Friedrich von). The elements of universal erudition, containing an analytical abridgment of the sciences, polite arts, and belles letters, by baron Bielfeld. Translated from the last edition printed at Berlin, by W. Hooper, m. d. 3 v. 8°. *London, G. Scott for J. Robson*, 1770.

Bienewitz (Peter). Cosmographia Petri Apiani, per Gemmam Frisium, iam demum ab omnibus vindicata mendis, ac nonnullis quoque locis aucta, figurisque nouis illustrata: additis eiusdem argumenti libellis ipsius Gēmæ Frisii. 2 p. l. 74 l. 1 pl. sm. fol. *Parisiis, apud Viuantium Gaultherot*, 1553.

Biffi (Serafino). Sui riformatorj pei giovani. 4 p. l. 189 pp. 1 l. fol. *Milano, G. Bernardoni*, 1870. s.

Bigelow (Andrew). Travels in Malta and Sicily, with sketches of Gibraltar, in 1827. xxii, 528 pp. 6 pl. 8°. *Boston, Carter, Hendee & Babcock*, 1831.

Bigelow (Henry Jacob, *m. d.*) Manual of orthopedic surgery, being a dissertation which obtained the Boylston prize for 1844, on the following question: "In what cases, and to what extent is the division of muscles, tendons, or other parts proper for the relief of deformity or lameness?" xiii, 211 pp. 6 pl. 8°. *Boston, W. D. Ticknor & co.* 1845.

Bigelow (Jacob, *m. d.*) Eolopoesis. American rejected addresses. [*anon.*] 240 pp. 12°. *New York, J. C. Derby*, [1855].

——— A history of the cemetery of Mount Auburn. 263 pp. 4 pl. 2 charts. 12°. *Boston and Cambridge, J. Munroe & co.* 1860.

Bigelow (John). France and hereditary monarchy. 2 p. l. 80 pp. 8°. *New York, C. Scribner & co.* 1871.

Bigelow (L. J.) Bench and bar: a complete digest of the wit, humor, asperities, and amenities of the law. New ed. greatly enlarged. 532 pp. 1 portrait. 8°. *New York, Harper & brothers*, 1871.

Bigelow (*Mrs.* M. A.) The last bird and other poems, for children. 126 pp. 18°. *New-York, author*, 1855.

Bigland (John). Essays on various subjects. 2d ed. 2 p. l. viii, 521 pp. 8°. *London, Longman*, 1811.

——— A natural history of birds, fishes, reptiles, and insects. 179 pp. 12 col. pl. 12°. *Philadelphia, J. Grigg*, 1828.

Biglia (Felice). Sui combustibili, e sul miglior modo adoperarli nelle macchine a vapore. 152 pp. 4 pl. 4°. *Torino, tipografia Ceresole e Panizza*, 1861. s.

Bigney (T. O.) Rocky mountain directory. *See* **Wallihan** (S. S.) *and* **Bigney**.

Bignon (Jean Paule, *abbé*). The adventures of Abdalla, son of Hanif, sent by the sultan of the Indies to make a discovery of the island of Borico, where the fountain which restores past youth is supposed to be found. Also an account of the travels of Rouschen, a persian lady, to the Topsy turvy island, undiscover'd to this day. Translated into french from an arabick manuscript found at Batavia by mr. de Sandisson, and now done into english by William Hatchett. [*pseudon.*] 3 p. l. vi, xviii, 169 pp. 8°. *London, T. Worrall*, 1729.

Bigot (*Mlle.* Stéphanie). Le chateau de Bois-Le-Brun, ou une famille mixté. 3e éd. 272 pp. 1 pl. 8°. *Lille, L. Lefort*, 1861.

Bigot de Morogues (*Baron* Pierre Marie Sebastien) Mémoire historique et physique sur les chutes des pierres tombées sur la surface de la terre à divers epoques. 1 p. l. iv, 360 pp. 8°. *Orléans, Jacob aîné*, 1812.

Bijdragen tot de natuurkundige wetenschappen, verzameld door H. C. Van Hall, W. Vrolik, en G. J. Mulder. 7 v. 8°. *Amsterdam, J. Vander Hey & zoon*, 1826–32. s. [No more published].

Bilderdijk (Willem). Poëzy. Eerste en tweede deel. 2e druk. xvi, 232 pp. 16°. *Rotterdam, J. Immerzeel*, 1822.

Bill (Ledyard). Minnesota; its character and climate. Likewise sketches of other resorts favorable to invalids; with copious notes on

Bill (Ledyard)—continued. health; also hints to tourists and emigrants. 205 pp. 1 pl. 12°. *New York, Wood & Holbrook*, 1871.

Billard (Charles Michel). A treatise on the diseases of infants. With notes by dr. Ollivier, of Angers. Translated from the third french edition, with an appendix by James Stewart, m. d. viii, 620 pp. 8°. *New York, G. Adlard*, 1839.

Billet (Anne Louise Françoise Delorme). Mémoires historiques de Stéphanie-Louise de Bourbon-Conti, écrits par elle-même· [*pseudon.*] 2 v. in 1. 2 p. l. 307 pp; 358 pp. 1 l. 8°. *Paris, l'auteur, an* vi [1798]·

[*Note.*—The work of an adventuress claiming to be "of the blood of the Bourbons," and written at her dictation by J. Corentin Royou].

Billingslea (Charles). The Addison reunion papers. viii, 270 pp. 12°. *Baltimore, J. C. Dulany & co.* 1871.

Billingsley (A. S.) Christianity in the war. Containing an account of the sufferings, conversions, prayers, dying requests, last words, and deaths of soldiers and officers in the hospital, camp, prison, and on the battle-field. Also, an account of distinguished christian men and their labors in the war. 1 p. l. xvi, 15–429 pp. 21 pl. 1 portrait. 12°. *Philadelphia, Claxton, Remsen & Haffelfinger*, 1872.

Billot (Albert). Droit international. De l'arrestation provisoire en vue d'extradition. 32 pp. 8°. *Paris, A. Durand & Pedone Lauriel*, 1868.

Billroth (Theodor). General surgical pathology and therapeutics, in fifty lectures. A text-book for students and physicians. Translated from the fourth german edition, with the special permission of the author, by Charles E. Hackley, m. d. xviii, 676 pp. 8°. *New York, D. Appleton & co.* 1871.

Bingham (J. Foote, *d. d.*) The christian marriage ceremony: its history, significance and curiosities: ritual, practical and archæological notes; and the text of the english, roman, greek and jewish ceremonies. 322 pp. 12°. *New York, A. D. F. Randolph & co.* 1871.

Bingham (Nathaniel). Observations on the religious delusions of insane persons; [also] a copious practical description of all the principal varieties of mental disease, and of its appropriate medical and moral treatment. xix, 213 pp. 8°. *London, J. Hatchard & son*, 1841.

Binghamton (*N. Y.*) Boyd's Binghamton city and Susquehanna railroad directory. 1871. 8°. *Binghamton (N. Y.) H. E. Pratt*, 1871.

Bingley (*Rev.* William). The economy of a christian life. viii, 4, 188 pp. 1 pl. 12°. *London, J. Sharpe*, 1822.

Biochimo. *See* **Greco** (Gioachino).

Birch (Samuel). Historical notices of the [Egyptian] monuments. *See* **Jones** (Owen) *and* **Goury** (Jules). Views on the Nile.

Birch (Thomas). The life of mrs. Catharine Cockburn. 8°. *London*, 1751.

[*In* COCKBURN (*Mrs.* Catharine) works, pp. i–xlviii].

Birchmore (*Rev.* John W.) Prophecy interpreted by history; including present events; being a brief & popular explanation of Daniel and of st. John. 279 pp. 12°. *New York, E. P. Dutton & co.* 1871.

Bird (Edward). Fate and destiny, inconsistent with christianity: or, the horrid decree of absolute and unconditional election and reprobation, fully detected. Shewing the grand error, of asserting, that Christ did not die for all men, but for an elect number only. 4 p. l. xxiii, 180 pp. 1 l. 8°. *London, C. Rivington*, 1726.

Bird (Frederick M.) Songs of the spirit. *See* **Odenheimer** (William Henry, *d. d.*) *and* **Bird.**

Birks (*Rev.* Thomas Rawson). The bible and modern thought. 436 pp. 12°. *Cincinnati, Poe & Hitchcock*, 1864.

——— The treasures of wisdom: or thoughts on the connection between natural science and revealed truth; with an essay on the analogy between mathematical and moral certainty. vii, 225 pp. 16°. *London, Seeley, Jackson & Halliday*, 1855.

Birmann (Pierre). Voyage pittoresque de Basle à Bienne par les vallons de Mottiers-Grandval. *See* **Bridel** (Philippe Syriach).

Biscioni (Antommaria). Vita di Antonfrancesco Grazzini, detto il Lasca. 12°. *Firenze, F. Moücke*, 1741.

[*In* GRAZZINI (Antonfrancesco). Rime, pp. xix–lxii].

Biscoe (E. L.) Katharine's experience. By the author of "The minister's wife," [etc. *anon.*] 372 pp. 3 pl. 16°. *Boston, Warren & Blakeslee*, [1869].

Bishop (*Rev.* Samuel). Poems on various subjects. The 3d ed. To which are prefixed, memoirs of the life of the author, [by Thomas Clare]. 2 v. xliv, 188 pp. 1 portrait; viii, 204 pp. 16°. *London, Cadell & Davies*, 1802.

Bisse (Thomas, *d. d.*) The beauty of holiness in the common-prayer: as set forth in four sermons preach'd at the Roll's chapel. 4 p. l. 173 pp. 8°. *London, W. B. for H. Clements*, 1716.

Bissell *or* **Bisselius** (Johann). Argonauticon americanorum sive historiae periculorum Petri de Victoria. *See* **Goveo de Victoria** (Pedro).

Bitaubé (Paul Jérémie). Joseph. A poem. In nine books. Translated from the french, by Kenneth Fergusson. 2 v. 1 p. l. 219 pp. 6 pl; 1 p. l. 199 pp. 4 pl. 12°. *Edinburgh, Ross & Blackwood*, 1801.

Bizarri (Bernardino). Discorso della generatione dell' hvomo in dialoghi. 4 p. l. 171 pp. 4°. *Urbino, appresso B. & S. Ragusij fratelli*, 1600.

Blaauw *or* **Blaeuw** (Willem Janszoon *and* Jan). Le grand atlas, ov cosmographie blaviane, en laquelle est exactement descritte la terre, la mer et le ciel. 12 v. fol. *Amsterdam, Jean Blaeu*, 1667.

CONTENTS.

v. 1. Introduction à la géographie, 16 p. l. iii pp. 1 map.
Arctique, qui est la première partie de la géographie.
v. 1. Groenlande, pp. 1–20, 1 map.
Jean Mayen, pp. 21–23, 1 map.
Spitzbergen, pp. 24–26, 1 map.
Nouvelle Zemla, pp. 27–34, 1 l. 1 map. 2 pl.
Destroit de Nassou et du Waygatz, pp. 35–46, 3 maps.
Islande, pp. 47–50, 1 map.
Europe, qui est la seconde partie de la géographie, xvii livres, 1 p. l. vii pp. 1 map.
v. 1. Norvegue, 1 p. l. 14 pp. 7 maps.
Danemarque, traduite du latin de J. I. Pontan, 1 p. l. 116 pp. 8 maps, 15 pl.
Slesvic, xlvi pp. 21 maps.
v. 2. Scandinavie, 1 p. 1 map.
Suède, par André Burée, etc. 61 pp. 9 maps.
Russie, 1 p. l. 35 pp. 7 maps, 1 pl.
Pologne, traduite du latin de Salomon Nevgebavere, etc. 1 p. l. 74 pp. 10 maps.
Régions orientales av delà de l'Alemagne près le Danube, 1 p. l. pp. 1–60, 5 maps.
Grèce, 1 p. l. pp. 61–112, 1 l. 6 maps.
v. 3. Alemagne, 1 p. l. 145 l. 1 l. 95 maps.
v. 4. Pays Bas. Belgique royale. 2 p. l. 193 pp. 35 maps.
Belgique confédérée, 1 p. l. vii, 106 pp. 1 l. 28 maps.
v. 5. Angleterre. [Par Guillaume Cambden et Jean Spead]. 6 p. l. 321 pp. 1 l. 58 maps.
v. 6. Escosse, [extraite du latin de R. Gordon, Buchanan, etc.] 6 p. l. 162 pp. 49 maps.
Irlande, 1 p. l. 50 pp. 1 l. 6 maps.
v. 7. France, 3 p. l. civ, 1–448 pp. 1 l. 36 maps.
v. 8. France, 1 p. l. pp. 449–786, 28 maps.
Suisse, 1 p. l. 58 pp. 1 l. 6 maps.
v. 9. Italie [incl. Sardinia and Sicily], 2 p. l. 206 pp. 1 l. 61 maps.
v. 10. Espagne, 2 p. l. xxx, 1–56 pp. 26 maps.
Portugal, pp. 57–70, 1 map.
Açores, pp. 71–75, 1 map.
Afrique, la troisième partie de la géographie, 1 p. l. pp. 1–10, 1 map.
v. 10. Barbarie, pp. 11–34, 1 map.
Marroc et Fez, pp. 35–55, 1 map.
Égypte, pp. 56–72, 1 map.
Nvmidie, pp. 73–80.
Libye ou Zaara, pp. 81–84.
Abyssinie, pp. 85–100, 1 map.
Les pays des nègres, pp. 101–113, 1 map.

Blaauw (W. J. *and* J.)—continued.

Gvinée, pp. 114–127, 1 map.
La basse Éthiopie, pp. 128–148, 1 map.
Congo, pp. 149–155, 1 map.
Malte, pp. 156–162, 1 map.
Canaries, pp. 163–168, 1 map.
Isles dv Cap Verd, pp. 169–171, 1 map.
Madagascar, pp. 172–180, 1 l. 1 map.
Asie, la quatrième partie de la géographie, 2 p. l. 1–4 pp. 1 map.
v. 11. Empire du Turc, pp. 5–48, 1 map.
Natalie ov Asie Minevre, pp. 49–72, 1 map.
Isle de Cyprus, pp. 73–80, 1 map.
Terre Saincte, pp. 81–110, 1 map.
Arabie, pp. 111–126, 1 map.
Perse, pp. 127–162, 1 map.
Inde Orientale, pp. 163–214, 1 map.
Estats dv Grand Mogol, pp. 215–236, 1 map.
Isles Molvqves, pp. 237–241, 1 map.
Tartarie, pp. 242–256, 1 map.
Chine, 4 p. l. pp. 1–160, 16 maps.
Japon, pp. 161–162, 1 map.
Table des degrez de longitvde et de latitvde, pp. 163–180.
Histoire de la guerre de Tartarie, pp. 181–214.
Catay. Par Jacques Gool. pp. 215–227, 1 l.
Amérique, la cinquième partie de la géographie. 1 p. l. xxviii pp. 1 map.
v. 12. Nouvelle France & terres adjacentes, pp. 1–16, 1 map.
Nouvelle Angleterre et Nouvelle Belgique, pp. 17–20, 1 map.
Virginie, pp. 21–24, 1 map.
Floride, pp. 25–28, 1 map.
Nouvelle Espagne et Nouvelle Galice, pp. 29–62, 1 map.
Yucatan et Gvatimala, pp. 63–81, 1 map.
Isles de l'Amérique, pp. 82–94, 1 map.
Isles Canibales, pp. 95–98, 1 map.
Isles de Bermvdez, pp. 99–101, 1 map.
Terre ferme, pp. 102–120, 1 map.
Granade, pp. 120–125.
Popajan, pp. 125–133.
Pérn, pp. 134–189, 1 map.
Chile, pp. 190–198, 1 map.
Magallanique, pp. 199–210, 1 map.
Paraguay, avec les régions adjacentes, pp. 211–224, 1 map.
Brasil, pp. 225–259, 3 maps.
Pernambuco, pp. 260–262, 2 maps.
Paraiba, pp. 263–276, 1 map.
Gvaiane, pp. 277–298, 1 map.
Novvelle Andalvzie, pp. 298–309, 1 l. 1 map.

Black (The) book of the admiralty. *See* **Great Britain.** *Master of the rolls.*

Black (The) crook. Feb. 1871. 13 pp. fol. *New York*, [*H. A. Elliott*], 1871.

Black (The) dwarf. A London weekly publication. Edited by T. J. Wooler, 1817–18. 2 v. 4°. *London, T. J. Wooler*, 1817–18.

Blackall (C. R.) Belshazzar, 1871. *See* **Butterfield** (J. A.)

Blackall (Offspring, *d. d. bishop of Exeter*). Eight sermons. fol. [*London*, 1739].
[BOYLE lectures, v. 1, pp. 525–625].

Blackburn (William Maxwell, *d. d.*) Judas the Maccabee, and the asmonean princes. 280 pp. 1 map. 18°. *Philadelphia, Presbyterian board of publication*, 1864.

——— The rebel prince, or lessons from the career of the young man Absalom. 264 pp. 12°. *Philadelphia, Presbyterian board of publication*, [1864].

——— The theban legion: a story of the

Blackburn (W. M. *d. d.*)—continued. times of Diocletian. 239 pp. 4 pl. 16°. *Philadelphia, Presbyterian board of publication,* [1871].

Blackburne (*Rev.* Francis). The works, theological and miscellaneous, including some pieces, not before printed; with some account of the life and writings of the author, by himself, completed by his son Francis Blackburne. 7 v. 8°. *Cambridge,* [*Eng.*] *B. Flower for the editor,* 1804.

CONTENTS.

v. 1. Some account of the author. cxxvi pp.
The use and advantage of the christian principle in the administration of human laws: a sermon. p. 1.
A serious enquiry into the use and importance of external religion. p. 91.
A sermon preached to a large congregation in the country, on Friday, Jan. 5, 1753, Old Christmas-day. p. 173.
A story of two Jews and the catacombs. Said to be translated from the french. p. 203.
A candid address to the Jews, occasioned by the repeal of a late act of parliament in their favour. With a postscript to the christian reader. p. 237.
A reply to dr. Tucker's strictures, on the preceding postscript. p. 283.
A letter to a friend, containing some remarks on dr. Sharpe's visitation charges. p. 327.
Notes, upon a paper intituled, "Some rules of caution for the more successful examination into the doctrine of the trinity."—By dr. Sharpe. p. 349.

v. 2. A critical commentary on archbishop Secker's letter to Horatio Walpole, concerning bishops in America. p. 3.
A letter written by a country clergyman to archbishop Herring. p. 101.
An apology for the authors of a book, intitled, Free and candid disquisitions relating to the church of England, &c. p. 135.
No proof in the scriptures of an intermediate state of happiness or misery between death and the resurrection. [Also], remarks on a letter in the gentleman's magazine for April, 1756, and on a paragraph in a sermon of archbishop Tillotson's. With a postscript, in answer to some remarks upon a late treatise relating to the intermediate state, &c. p. 179.
Remarks on dr. Warburton's account of the sentiments of the early Jews concerning the soul. p. 261.
A review of some passages in the last edition of The divine legation of Moses demonstrated. [Also], a defence of the above-mentioned remarks against the objections of Caleb Fleming. And a second postscript occasioned by the said mr. Fleming's late advertisement, &c. p. 339.

v. 3. An historical view of the controversy concerning an intermediate state and the separate existence of the soul between death and the general resurrection, deduced from the beginning of the protestant reformation to the present times. With some thoughts, in a prefatory discourse, on the use and importance of theological controversy. 2d ed.

v. 4. Considerations on the present state of the controversy between the protestants and papists of Great Britain and Ireland, particularly on the question how far the latter are entitled to toleration; being the substance of two discourses delivered in 1765-6. p. 1.
Four discourses, 1767-73: p. 261.
1. On the duty of a christian minister under the obligation of conforming to a national religion established by the civil powers.
2. On the questions, What is christianity; and, Where is it to be learned?
3. On the true meaning of the phrase, the interests of religion.
4. On the original principles of the first protestants.
A discourse on the study of the scriptures. Delivered in the year 1763. p. 405.

v. 5. The confessional: or, a full and free inquiry into the right, utility, edification, and success, of establishing systematical confessions of faith and doctrine in protestant churches. 3d ed.

v. 6. Remarks on the rev. dr. Powell's sermon in defence of subscriptions, preached before the university of Cambridge on the commencement sunday, 1757. p. 1.
Occasional remarks upon some late strictures on the confessional. p. 109.
The same. Part 2. Containing chiefly remarks on the first of three letters to the author of that work: and an examination of dr. Maclaine's defence of archbishop Wake. p. 163.

v. 7. Proposals for an application to parliament for relief in the matter of subscription to the liturgy and thirty-nine articles of the established church of England. p. 1.
Copy of the petition of the clergy, &c. relative to subscription to the thirty-nine articles, offered on the 6th of February, 1772, to the house of commons. p. 13.
A sketch of contradictions and inconsistencies in the obligations laid upon clergymen, in order to qualify themselves for ministering in the church of England. p. 21.
Reflections on the fate of a petition for relief in the matter of subscription, offered to the house of commons, Feby. 6th, 1772. With observations on the rev. dean Tucker's Apology for the present church of England, as by law established. p. 33.
Bishop Taylor's judgment on articles and forms of confession in particular churches. p. 271.
Bishop Taylor's judgment on subscription, &c. p. 323.
Index to the seven volumes. p. 351.
Table of texts of scripture referred to. p. 395.

Blacklock (Thomas, *d. d.*) Paraclesis; or, consolations deduced from natural and revealed religion: in two dissertations. The first supposed to have been composed by Cicero: the last originally written by T. Blacklock. 4 p. l. xxi, 357 pp. 8°. *Edinburgh, J. Dickson,* 1767.

[*Note.*—The Consolatio Ciceronis is a notorious forgery, ascribed usually to Carlo Sigonio].

Blackwall (Antony). An introduction to the classics: containing a short discourse on their excellencies; and directions how to study them to advantage. With an essay on the use of [rhetorical figures]. 6th ed. 4 p. l. 272 pp. 2 l. 16°. *London, J. & J. Rivington,* 1746.

——— The sacred classics defended and illustrated: or, an essay humbly offer'd towards proving the purity, propriety, and true eloquence of the writers of the new testament. 2d ed. 2 v. 432 pp. 8 l. 1 portrait; xxxi, 360 pp. 11 l. 8°. *London, C. Rivington,* 1827-31.

Blackwell (Antoinette Brown). The island neighbors. A novel of american life. 140 pp. 2 pl. 8°. *New York, Harper & brothers,* 1871.

Blackwell (J. Evert). Narrative of the discovery of the wine of Apocynum. 4 pp. 8°. [*New York, W. A. Willcox*, 1871].

Blackwell (Robert). Original acrostics, on some of the southern states, confederate generals, and various other persons and things. 75 pp. 4 pl. 12°. *Nashville*, 1870.

Blackwood's Edinburgh magazine. [Monthly]. Jan. to Dec. 1871. v. 109–110. 8°. *Edinburgh, W. Blackwood & sons*, 1871.

Blaeu (Jean). *See* **Blaauw** *or* **Blaeuw** (Willem Janszoon *and* Jan).

Blagrave (John). Astrolabium uranicum generale. A necessary and pleasaunt solace and recreation for nauigators in their long iorneying, containing the vse of an instrument or generall astrolabe: newly for them deuised by the author. 34 l. sm. 4°. [*London*], *T. Purfoot for W. Watts*, 1596.

Blair (*Rev.* David). The elements of natural and experimental philosophy. Revised, corrected, newly arranged and greatly improved, and enlarged. By E. A. Smith. 288 pp. 16°. *New York, McElrath, Bangs & Herbert*, 1834.

Blair (Hugh, *d. d.*) An abridgment of lectures on rhetorick. Revised and corrected. 264 pp. 12°. *Boston, J. T. Buckingham for Thomas & Andrews*, 1805.

——— The same. 264 pp. 16°. *Wilmington, M. R. Lockerman*, 1807.

——— Sermons. 3d American ed. v. 3. 16°. *Philadelphia, R. Campbell*, 1795.

Blair (Samuel, *d. d.* 1741–1818). An oration pronounced at Nassau-hall, January 14, 1761; on occasion of the death of king George ii. 8 pp. sm. 4°. *Woodbridge*, (*N. J.*) *J. Parker*, 1761.

——— The same.

[HAZARD pamplets, v. 39].

Blaisdale (*Rev.* Silas). First lessons in intellectual philosophy; or, a familiar explanation of the nature and operations of the human mind. 1st American ed. 358 pp. 12°. *Boston, Lincoln & Edmands*, 1829.

Blake (Andrew, *m. d.*) Aphorisms illustrating natural and difficult cases of accouchement; uterine hemorrhage, and puerperal peritonitis. 100 pp. 12°. *London, Longman* [*& co.*] 1817.

Blake (George). A masonic eulogy on the life of George Washington, pronounced before St. John's lodge, 4th Feb. [1800]. 2d ed. 23 pp. 8°. *Boston, J. Russell*, 1800.

[HAZARD pamplets, v. 64].

Blanc (Charles). Histoire des peintres français au dix-neuvième siècle. v. 1. 4 p. l. 445 pp. 8°. *Paris, Cauville frères*, 1845. s.

[No more published].

Blanc (Ludwig Gottfried). Vocabolario dantesco, o dizionario critico e ragionato delia divina commedia di Dante Alighieri. Ora per la prima volta recato in italiano da G. Carbone. xv, 464 pp. 12°. *Firenze, Barbèra, Bianchi & comp.* 1859.

Blancas (Jeronimo de). Regvm Aragoniæ series. 16°. *Coloniae Agrippinae, ex officina birckmannica*, 1602.

[*In* MYLIUS (Arnold). De rebvs hispanicis. pp. 138–154].

Blanchard (*Rev.* J.) *and* **Rice** (N. L. *d. d.*) A debate on slavery, held on the first, second, third and sixth days of October, 1845, in the city of Cincinnati, between rev. J. Blanchard, pastor of the sixth presbyterian church, and N. L. Rice, d. d. pastor of the central presbyterian church. 482 pp. 12°. *Cincinnati, W. H. Moore & co.* 1846.

Blanchard (Leone, *pseudon?*) Tried in the fire. 244 pp. 1 pl. 16°. *Boston, D. Lothrop & co.* 1871.

Blanchard (Pierre). Tableaux de la nature et des bienfaits de la providence, par Fénélon, Bossuet, Buffon, J. J. Rousseau, Barthélemy, etc. 3e éd. viii, 362 pp. 16°. *Paris, P. Blanchard*, 1824.

Blanche (August). The bandit. Translated from the swedish, and edited by Selma Borg and Marie A. Brown. 229 pp. 1 portrait. 8°. *New York, G. P. Putnam & sons*, 1872.

Blanchié y Palma (Francisco Javier). Margaritas. 1 p. l. xvi, 259 pp. 1 l. 8°. *Habana, Torres*, 1846.

[v. 1. No more published].

Blancus (Hieronymus). *See* **Blancas** (Jeronimo de).

Blandford (G. Fielding, *m. d.*) Insanity and its treatment. With a summary of the laws in force in the United States on the confinement of the insane. By Isaac Ray, m. d. viii, 17–471 pp. 8°. *Philadelphia, Henry C. Lea*, 1871.

Blanford (W. T.) Observations on the geology and zoology of Abyssinia, made during the progress of the british expedition to that country, in 1867–68. xii, 487 pp. 1 map, 13 pl. 8°. *London, Macmillan & co.* 1870.

Blasius (Johann Heinrich). Die wirbelthiere Europa's. *See* **Keyserling** (Alexander, *graf*) *and* **Blasius**.

Blaze de Bury (H.) Épisode de l'histoire du Hanovre.—Les Kœnigsmark. 2 p. l. xii, 383 pp. 16°. *Paris, M. Lévy frères*, 1855.

Bledsoe (Albert Taylor, *ll. d.*) An examination of president Edwards' inquiry into the freedom of the will. 234 pp. 12°. *Philadelphia, H. Hooker*, 1845.

——— Liberty and slavery: or, slavery in the light of moral and political philosophy. 8°. [*Augusta, (Ga.)* 1860].

[*In* ELLIOTT (E. N.) Cotton is king, pp. 269–458].

Blennerhasset (William). The universal and eternal system. Also, the principal points of the deists, against christianity, stated and answered. 1 p. l. vi, 327 pp. 8°. *Newcastle upon Tyne, author*, 1752.

Bliss (George). An address, delivered at the opening of the town-hall in Springfield March 24, 1828, containing sketches of the early history of that town, and those in its vicinity. With an appendix. 8°. [*Northhampton, (Ms.)* 1862].

[*In* CHAPIN (Orange). The Chapin genealogy, part v, or pp. 257–328].

Bliss (Philip P.) The charm: a collection of sunday-school music. 160 pp. obl. 16°. *Chicago, Root & Cady*, [1871].

Blitz (*Signor* Antonio). Fifty years in the magic circle; being an account of the author's professional life; his wonderful tricks and feats; with laughable incidents, and adventures as a magician, necromancer and ventriloquist. 432 pp. 17 pl. 12°. *Hartford, (Conn.) Belknap & Bliss*, 1871.

Blofeld (J. H.) Algeria, past and present. With a review of its history from the earliest periods to the present time. The whole carefully revised and corrected, from notes made during a personal visit in 1843, [etc.] 3 p. l. 402 pp. 8°. *London, T. C. Newby*, 1844.

Blois (François Louis de). Le directeur des âmes religieuses. [Traduction de Louis Jouard de La Nauze]. 8°. [*Paris, panthéon littéraire*, 1843].

[*In* BUCHON (J. A. C.) Choix d'ouvrages mistiques, pp. 719–752].

Bloomfield (Samuel Thomas, *d. d.*) Greek testament with notes. *See* **Bible.** (*Greek*).

Blount (Margaret). Barbara Home. 3 v. 12°. *London, J. Maxwell & co.* 1864.

Blount (Thomas). The academy of eloquence: containing a compleat english rhetorique, exemplified; common-places, and formula's digested into an easie and methodical way to speak and write fluently. 2d. ed. with additions. Eng. title, 4 p. l. 230 pp. 16°. *London, T. N. for H. Moseley*, 1656.

Bluett (J. C.) Duelling and the laws of honour examined, upon principles of common sense and revealed truth. xv, 156 pp. 16°. [*London*], *R. B. Seeley & W. Burnside*, 1835.

Blum (Georg) *and* **Wahl** (Louis). Seaside and fireside fairies. Translated from the german. By A. L. Wister. 292 pp. 3 pl. 12°. *Philadelphia, Ashmead & Evans*, 1864.

Blume (Carl Ludwig) *and* **Fischer** (Johann Baptist). Flora Javae nec non insularum adjacentium. Cum tabulis lapidi ærique incisis. 3 v. fol. *Bruxelles, J. Frank*, 1828.

CONTENTS.

v. 1. [Prooemium], 2 p. l. x pp. 1 pl.
Rhizantheæ, 26 pp. 6 pl. (3 col.)
Chloranthеæ, 14 pp. 2 pl. (col.)
Myriceæ, 8 pp. 1 pl. (col.)
Balsamifluæ, 12 pp. 2 pl. (1 col.)
Juglandeæ, 16 pp. 5 pl. (4 col.)
Cupuliferæ, 46 pp. 24 pl. (col.)
v. 2. (No title-page).
Anonaceæ, 108 pp. 53 pl. (47 col.)
Schizandreæ, 18 pp. 5 pl. (col.)
Magnoliaceæ, 40 pp. 12 pl. (10 col.)
Dipterscarpeæ, 24 pp. 6 pl. (col.)
v. 3. (*Incomplete* and no title-page).
Lorantheæ, 40* pp. 28* pl. (27 col.)
Filices, 196* pp. 94* pl. (col.)

——— The same. Nova series. v. i. Orchideae. 2 p. l. vi, 162 pp. 66, 5 pl. (56 col[d].) fol. *Lugduni Batavorum, impensis auctoris*, 1858 [-59].

Blumenbach (Johann Friedrich). Handbuch der naturgeschichte. 3e ausg. xvi, 715 pp. 1 pl. 16°. *Göttingen, J. C. Dieterich*, 1788.

Blumenthal (Louise Johanne Leopoldine). The life of general de Zieten, colonel of the royal prussian regiment of hussar-lifeguards. Translated from the german, by the rev. B. Beresford. 2 v. xiv, 317 pp. 1 map, 1 pl; x, 354 pp. 1 map, 1 pl. 8°. *Berlin, author*, 1803.

Blundeville (Thomas). M. Blundevile, his exercises, containing sixe treatises, the titles whereof are set down in the next printed page: which treatises are verie necessarie to be read and learned of all yoong gentlemen that haue not bene exercised in such disciplines, and yet are desirous to haue knowledge as well in cosmographie, astronomie, and geographie, as also in the arte of navigation, in which arte it is impossible to profite without the helpe of these, or such like instructions. *b. l.* 7 p. l. 350 l. 2 charts. 4°. *London, J. Windet*, 1594.

——— The order of dietynge of horses, as well when they reste as when they trauel, wherin is conteyned not only the kepers office, but also many preceptes necessarye too bee

Blundeville (Thomas)—continued. knowen of the ferrer or horseleche. *b. l.* Eng. title, 35 l. 1 portrait. 4°. *London, W. Seres,* 1565.

Boaden (J.) The man of two lives. A narrative written by himself. 2 v. in 1. 1 p. l. 273 pp; 1 p. l. 303 pp. 12°. *London, H. Colburn,* 1828.

Boardman (*Rev.* W. E.) Gladness in Jesus. xi, 164 pp. 16°. *Boston, Willard tract repository,* 1872.

Boas (Ben, *pseudon.*) The winged chariot: an allegory, [and other articles]. 300 pp. 2 pl. 12°. *Cincinnati, A. B. Volney,* 1858.

Bobovius. *See* **Bobowski.**

Bobowski (Albert). A treatise concerning the turkish liturgy, the pilgrimage to Mecca, circumcision, visiting the sick, &c. By Albertus Bobovius. With notes by Thomas Hyde. 8°. *London,* 1712.

[*In* FOUR treatises concerning the doctrine [etc.] of the Mahometans. *London,* 1712. pp. 103–150].

Boccaccio (Giovanni). Amores Guiscardi & Gismundæ: de duobus amantibus. Philippus Beroaldus e Boccatio. 18°. [*Lvgd. Batav. ex typographia rediviva,* 1643].

[*In* OBSOPŒUS (Vincenz). De arte bibendi. Variorum auctorum practica artis amandi, et declamationes Philip. Beroaldi. 1648. pp. 100–111].

——— "De preclaris mulieribus, that is to say in englyshe, of the ryghte renoumyde ladyes." Translated from "Bocasse," and dedicated to king Henry viii by "Henry Parcare, knight, lord Morley. From a manuscript on vellum. [Dedication and specimen pages]. vii, 8 pp. 8°. *London, for the editor,* 1789.

[*In* WALDRON (F. G.) Literary museum. *London,* 1792].

——— The novels and tales of the renowned John Boccacio: containing a hundred curious novels framed in ten days. 5th ed. much corrected and amended. 8 p. l. 483 pp. 1 portrait. sm. fol. *London, Awnsham Churchill,* 1684.

Boccalini (Trajano). Relation aus Parnasso, das ist allerhandt lustige, anmüthige, sowol politische, historische als moralische discurs. Sampt beygefügtem politischen probierstein. Erstlich in italianischer sprach beschrieben, jetzund aber in das teutsche übersetzt, [bey Johann Beyer. 3 parts in 1 v.] Eng. title, 21 p. l. 702 pp. 4°. *Franckfurt, J. Beyer,* 1644.

Boccardo (Gerolamo). Manuali di geografia e storia antica e nozioni elementari di antichità greche e romane, per le classi ginnasiali,

Boccardo (Gerolamo)—continued. secondo i nuovi programmi governativi. 3 v. 12°. *Torino, tipografia scolastica di A. Vecco e comp.* 1867–70. s.

CONTENTS.

Classe 1a ginnasiale. La storia e la geografia antica, dalle origine fino a Dario. 3a ed. 1867.
Classe 2a ginnasiale. La storia e la geografia della Grecia dalle origine fino alla guerra persiana. 4a ed. 1870.
Classe 3a ginnasiale. Geografia e storia della Grecia, dalla guerra persiana fino alla caduta sotto la dominazione romana. 4a ed. 1870.

Bôcher (Ferdinand). Progressive french reader. With notes, philological and grammatical; and references to Otto's french conversation grammar. 238 pp. 12°. *New York, Leypoldt & Holt,* 1871.

Bodecher (Jan). Jani Bodecheri, Benningi, sive Hermophili tanugriensis satyricon, in corruptæ juventutis corruptos. 18°. *Lugd. Batav.* 1655.

[ELEGANTIORES præstantium virorum satyræ, v. 2, pp. 579–676].

Bodenehr (Gabriel, *the elder*). Europens pracht und macht in 200 kupferstücken, worinnen nicht nur allein die berühmtest und ansehnlichste, sondern auch andere stätte, festungen, schlösser, &c. dises volkreichen welttheils, vermittelst anmuthiger und eigentlicher prospecte, sambt kurzer geographischer beschreibung vorgestellet werden. Eng. title, 2 p. l. 199 pl. obl. 4°. *Augsburg, G. Bodenehr,* [*about* 1710].

[Imperfect: wanting, pl. no. 84].

Bodin (Jean). De magorvm dæmonomania. Vom aussgelassnē wütigen teuffelsheer, allerhand zauberern, hexen und hexenmeistern, unholden, teuffelsbeschwerern, warsagern, schwartzkünstlern, vergifftern, augenverblendern, &c. Nun erstmals durch Johann Fischart auss frantzösischer sprach trewlich in teutsche gebracht. 8 p. l. 767 pp. 12°. *Strassburg, B. Jobin.* 1586.

Boèce. *See* **Boethius.**

Boemus *aubanus* (Joannes). *See* **Böhme** (Johann).

Boëthius (Anicius Manlius Torquatus Severinus). Consolation de la philosophie [traduite par Léon Colesse]. 8°. [*Paris, panthéon littéraire,* 1843].

[*In* BUCHON (J. A. C.) Choix d'ouvrages mystiques, pp. 281–330].

——— In Ciceronis topica commentariorum [libri septem. Adiungitur] de Diis et praesensionibus ex ipsius commento in topica Ciceronis fragmentum. 8°. [*Turici, typis Orellii,* 1833].

[*In* CICERO (Marcus Tullius) Opera ex recensione Orellii, v. 5, part 1, pp. 269–395].

Boggs (James). The resurrection of the redeemed; and hades. 145, 69 pp. 16°. *Philadelphia, J. B. Lippincott & co.* 1871.

Boggs (L. W. *jr.*) The farmer's account book. Based upon The farmer's day book. [Blank ruled]. 110 pp. 4°. *San Francisco, A. L. Bancroft & co.* 1872.

Böhm (Anton). Reiss-beschreibung auss Hispanien in Paraquariam. *See* **Sepp** (Anton) *and* **Böhm.**

Bohm (G.) Die sontagsschule. 1r–5r cursus. 5 v. 18°. *New York, E. Steiger,* 1871.

——— The same. Leitfaden für lehrer. 20 pp. 18°. *New York, E. Steiger,* 1871.

Böhme (Johann). I costvmi, le leggi, et l'vsanze di tutte le genti; divisi in tre libri. E tradotti per Lucio Fauno in questa nostra lingua volgare. Et aggiontoui di nuouo il quarto libro, nelqual si narra i costumi, et l'vsanze dell' Indie Occidentali, ouero Mondo Nuouo, da Gieronimo Giglio. 240 l. 18°. *Venetia, G. Bonadio,* 1564.

Bohndel (Henry). The rigger's assistant. A treatise on measuring, drafting, fitting rigging: rigging, stripping, and refitting vessels. 71 pp. 12°. *Boston, J. B. Chisholm,* 1871.

Boileau Despréaux (Nicolas). Œuvres [poétiques]. 2 p. l. 319 pp. 1 portrait. 32°. *Paris, Saintin,* 1822.

Boindin (Nicolas). A discourse upon the masks and habits used on ancient theatres. 4°. [*London,* 1740].

[*In* TURNBULL (George). Three dissertations, 1740. pp. 86–104, 1 pl.]

Boisguillebert *or* **Boisguilbert** (Pierre le Pesant de). Détail de la France, Factum de la France, opuscules divers. 8°. [*Paris, Guillaumin,* 1843].

[*In* DAIRE (Eugène). Économistes-financiers du 18e siècle. *Paris,* 1843. pp. 155–431].

——— The life of Mary Stewart, queen of Scotland and France. Written originally in french, and now done into english. With notes. By James Freebairn. lx, 328 pp. 8°. *Edinburgh, author,* 1725.

Boissard (Jean Jacques). Tractatus posthumus de divinatione et magiis præstigiis quorum veritas et vanitas solide exponitur per descriptionem deorum fatidicorum qui olim responsa dederunt; eorumque prophetarum, [etc. Cum effigiebus ab ipso autore delineatis, jam incisis per J. T. De Bry]. 14 p. l. 358 pp. 6 l. fol. *Oppenheimii, H. Galler,* 1615.

Boissat de Licieux (Pierre de). Histoire des chevaliers de l'ordre de s. Jean de Hiérusalem. *See* **Bosio** (Giacomo).

Boisseau (François Gabriel). Physiological pyretology; or, a treatise on fevers: according to the principles of the new medical doctrine. 1st amer. from the 4th french ed. Translated by J. R. Knox, m. d. xiv, 9–504 pp. 8°. *Philadelphia, Carey & Lea,* 1832.

Boissel (François). Le cathéchisme du genre humain, dénoncé par le ci-devant evêque de Clermont, à la séance du 5 novembre 1798, de l'assemblée nationale; précédé d'un discours sur les causes de la division, de l'esclavage et de la destruction des hommes, les uns par les autres, et sur les moyens d'en garantir les générations futures. 2e éd. 1 p. l. iv, 241, 40 pp. 8°. *Paris,* 1792.

Boissoudan (Jacques Élie Manceau de). Le fauconnier parfait, ou méthode pour dresser et faire voler les oi seaux. 2 p l. xii, 72 pp. 12°. *Paris, pour la société des bibliophiles,* 1866.

[*In* PARIS. Société des bibliophiles françois. 2e partie].

Boker (George H.) Poems of the war. 202 pp. 16°. *Boston, Ticknor & Fields,* 1864.

Bolanden (Conrad von). Gustav Adolph. Historischer roman. v. 4. [*or*] Schweden trank. Historischer roman über Gustav Adolph. 1 p. l. 651 pp. 16°. *Mainz, F. Kirchheim,* 1871.

Bolívar (Simon). Correspondencia genera del libertador Simon Bolívar. Enriquezida con la insercion de los manifiestos, mensages, exposiciones, proclamas, &c. Publicados por el heroe Colombiano desde 1810 hasta 1830. (Precede á esta coleccion interesante la vida de Bolívar, por Felipe Larrazabal). v. 1–2. [La vida de Bolívar]. xlii, 616 pp. 1 fac-simile, 1 portrait; 591 pp. 1 portrait. 8°. *New York, E. O. Jenkins,* 1871.

Bolton (Edmund). Hypercritica; or a rule of judgment for writing, or reading our history's. That according thereunto, a compleat body of our affairs, a corpus rerum anglicarum, may at last, and from ourselves, come happily forth. 8°. *Oxford, Antony Hall,* 1722.

[*In* TRIVET (Nicholas). Annalium continuatio, pp. 193–242].

Boltwood (Henry L.) English grammar, and how to teach it. 209 pp. 12°. *Chicago, G. Sherwood & co.* [1872].

Bolzani (Giovanni Pierio Valeriano). *See* **Valeriano Bolzani.**

Bombay geographical society. Catalogue of the library. Compiled by D. J. Kennelly. iv, 79 pp. 8°. *Bombay, education society*, 1862. s.

Bona (Giovanni, *cardinale*). Principes de la vie chrétienne [traduits par Lambert]. 8°. [*Paris, panthéon littéraire*, 1843].

[*In* BUCHON (J. A. C.) Choix d'ouvrages mystiques, pp. 489-556].

——— Le chemin du ciel [traduit par Louis Cousin]. 8°. [*Paris, panthéon littéraire*, 1843].

[*In* BUCHON (J. A. C.) Choix d'ouvrages mystiques, pp. 557-608].

Bonafos (H.) De l'extradition. xvi, 143 pp. 8°. *Lyon, A. Vingtrinier*, 1866.

Bonald (Louis Gabriel Ambroise, *vicomte* de). Essai analytique sur les lois naturelles de l'ordre social, ou du pouvoir, du ministre et du sujet dans la société. [*anon.*] 2 p. l. 260 pp. 8°. *Paris*, 1800.

Bonchamp (*Marchioness* de). Memoirs on La Vendée; edited by the countess [Félicité Ducrest] de Genlis. Translated from the french. 173 pp. 18°. *London, C. Knight & co.* 1823.

Bonichi (Bindo). Quattro canzoni. 8°. [*Torino, stamperia reale*, 1750].

[*In* UBALDINI (F.) Il tratato delle virtù, morali, etc. pp. 128-139. ed. 1750].

Bonn. *Universitäts-sternwarte.* Astronomische beobachtungen auf der sternwarte der königlichen rheinischen Friedrich-Wilhelms-universität zu Bonn, angestellt und herausgegeben von dr. Friedrich Wilhelm August Argelander. v. 2-7. 4°. *Bonn, A. Marcus*, 1852-69. s.

[Wanting, v. 1].

Bonnardot (Alfred). Histoire artistique et archéologique de la gravure en France. xvi, 302 pp. 8°. *Paris, Deflorenne neveu*, 1849.

Bonnell (J. M. *d. d.*) First lessons in english prose composition. 205 pp. 12°. *Louisville (Ky.) J. P. Morton & co.* 1871.

Bonnet (Charles). Contemplation de la nature. 2e ed. 2 v. 4 p. l. lxvi, 244 pp; xi, 301 pp. 8°. *Amsterdam, M. M. Rey*, 1769.

Bonney (*Mrs.* P. P.) Emma Wilfred: a gift for school girls. 427 pp. 4 pl. 18°. *Boston, Mass. sabbath-school society*, [1859].

——— Grace Bramen and other stories. 126 pp. 3 pl. 18°. *Boston, Mass. sabbath-school society*, [1863].

Bonsi (Bonso Pio). Versione letterale del saltero davidico in versi eroici toscani estratta dal testo originale ebraico con note che pongono in chiaro l'ebraico testo e la vulgata, e dei dièci cantici dei quali si serve la chiesa per le ore canoniche tradotti dai respettivi originali sullo stesso metro dei salmi. 2 v. xii, 235 pp; 244 pp. 4°. *Firenze, nella stamperià già Albizziniana da s. Maria in campo*, 1798.

Bonstetten (Charles Victor de). Pensées sur divers objets de bien public. 2 p. l. xvi, 254 pp. 8°. *Paris, J. J. Paschoud*, 1815.

Bontekoe van Hoorn (Willem Ysbrantsz.) Journael ofte gedenckwaerdige beschrijvinge van [zijn] ost-indische reyse, 1618-25. Waer by gevoeght is het journael van Dirck Alberss. Raven. 2 p. l. 76 pp. 8 pl. in text. sm. 4°. *Amsterdam, J. Hartgers*, 1650.

——— The same. 2 p. l. 76 pp. 6 pl. on 1 sheet. sm. 4°. *Amstelredam, J. Hartgers*, 1648.

[*In* HARTGERTS (J.) Oost-indische voyagien, v. 1, 10e stuck].

Book (The) of blunders; comprising hibernicisms, bulls that are not irish and typographic errors. Selected and edited by the compiler of "Gleanings for the curious." [*anon.*] 212 pp. 18°. *Philadelphia, Evans, Stoddart & co.* 1871.

Book of common prayer. *See* **Church** of England.

Book (A) of public prayer, compiled from the authorized formularies of worship of the presbyterian church, as prepared by the reformers Calvin, Knox, Bucer, and others. With supplementary forms. [*anon.*] 360 pp. 12°. *New York, C. Scribner*, 1857.

Book (The) of worship, 1871. *See* **Bacon** (Leonard Woolsey).

Book-buyer (The). A summary of american and foreign literature. [Monthly]. Oct. 15, 1870, to Sept. 15, 1871. v. 4. 8°. *New York*, [*C. Scribner & co.* 1871].

Bookseller (The). A handbook of british and foreign literature, [and] Bent's literary advertiser. [Monthly]. Jan. to Dec. 1871. [v. 14]. 8°. *London*, [*J. Whitaker*], 1871.

Boorde *or* **Borde** (Andrew). The fyrst boke of the introduction of knowledge. The which doth teache a man to speake parte of all maner of languages, and to knowe the vsage and fashion of al maner of cōtreys. And for to knowe the moste parte of all maner of coynes of money, ye which is curraunt in euery region. London, in Lothbury, W. Copland. *b. l.* 56 l. 4°. *Reprint-*

Boorde *or* **Borde** (Andrew)—continued. *ed, London, R. & A. Taylor, [for W. Upcott]*, 1814.

——— The same. The first boke of the introduction of knowledge made by Andrew Borde. A compendyous regyment or a dyetary of helth made in Mountpellier, compyled by Andrewe Boorde, [etc.] Barnes in the defence of the berde; a treatyse made, answeryng the treatyse of doctor Borde upon berdes. Edited by F. J. Furnivall [etc.] 384 pp. 8°. *London*, 1870.

[EARLY English text society, extra series, no. 10].

Booth (*Rev.* Abraham). The select works of Abraham Booth; comprising his Reign of grace, Essay on the kingdom of Christ, and Glad tidings. 3 v. in 1. 16°. *London, W. Jones*, 1825.

Bopp (Franz). Ardschuna's reise zu Indra's himmel, nebst anderen episoden des mahabharata. *See* **Maha-Bharata.** *Berlin*, 1824.

Borda (Jean Charles). Voyage fait par ordre du roi en 1771 et 1772. *See* **Verdun de la Crenne** (———) **Borda** *and* **Pingré.**

Borde (Andrew). *See* **Boorde.**

Bory de Saint-Vincent (Jean Baptiste George Marie). Guide du voyageur en Espagne. 2 p. l. xxxix, 666 pp. 2 maps. 8°. *Paris, L. Janet*, 1823.

Bosanden (Conrad von). Der alte Gott. Erzählung für das volk. 63 pp. 18°. *Mainz, F. Kirchheim*, 1871.

——— Die unfehlbaren. Volksnovelle. 3 p. l. 326 pp. 12°. *Mainz, F. Kirchheim*, 1871.

Boscan (Juan) *and* **Vega** (Garcilasso de la). Los amores de Ivan Boscan, y de Garcilasso de la Vega. 12 p. l. 769 pp. 18°. *Leon, I. A. Hvgvetan & M. A. Ravavd*, 1658.

Boscovich (Ruggiero Giuseppe). Esame del progetto de' signori Manfredi e Bertaglia in riguardo alle paludi pontine e porto di Terracina. 4°. [*Firenze, P. Allegrini*, 1785].

[*In* XIMENES (Leonardo). Raccolta delle perizie ed opuscoli idraulici, v. 1, pp. 73-116].

Bosio (Giacomo). Histoire des chevaliers de l'ordre de s. Jean de Hiervsalem, contenant levr admirable institution et police, la suitte des guerres de la Terre Saincte, où ils se sont trouuez, et leurs continuels voyages, entreprises, batailles, assauts et rencontres. Cydeuant escrite [ou plutôt traduite de l'italien] par le feu S.[ieur] D.[e] B.[oissat] S.[ieur] D.[e] L.[icieux]. Diuisée par chapitres, et augmentée des sommaires sur châque liure, [etc.] Par J. Bavdoin [Boissat lui-même]. Dernière éd. Où l'on a ajoinct les ordo-

Bosio (Giacomo)—continued. nances du chapitre général, tenu en l'an 1632. Illustrée d'une ample chronologie, des vies des grands-maistres, [etc.] Par frère Anne de Naberat. [*anon.*] 3 parts in 1 v. fol. *Paris, J. D'Allin*, 1658-59.

Bosredon Ransijat (*Le citoyen*). Journal du siége et blocus de Malte, depuis le 16 fructidor an 6, époque de la révolte des Maltais, jusqu'au 22 fructidor an 8, jour de l'évacuation de cette place par la garnison française. Paris, l'imprimerie de Valade, an 9. 2 p. l. xii, 368 pp. 12°. *Malte*, 1837.

Boss (Henry R.) Early newspapers in Illinois: read before the Franklin society of Chicago. 48 pp. 4°. *Chicago, Franklin society*, 1870.

[FRANKLIN society publications, no. 2].

Bosscha (Johannes). Het leven van Willem den tweede, koning der Nederlanden en groot-hertog van Luxemburg. 8 p. l. 752 pp. 9 maps and plans. 8°. *Amsterdam, C. M. Van Gogh*, 1852.

Boston (John, *monk of Bury*). Speculum coenobitarum. Nunc primo editum ab Antonio Hallio. 8°. *Oxonii, e theatro sheldoniano*, 1722.

[*In* TRIVET (Nicholas). Annalium continuatio, pp. 153-192].

Boston (*Mass.*) Annual report of the school committee of the city of Boston, 1870. 441 pp. 8°. *Boston, A. Mudge & son*, 1871.

——— An appeal to the world, or a vindication of the town of Boston from many false and malicious aspersions contained in certain letters and memorials written by governor Bernard, general Gage, commodore Hood, the commissioners of the american board of customs, and others, and by them respectively transmitted to the british ministry. Published by order of the town. 37 pp. 8°. *Boston, Edes & Gill*, 1769.

——— The same. 58 pp. 12°. *Boston, Edes & Gill*, 1770.

——— The same. 1 p. l. 58 pp. 8°. *London, J. Almon*, 1770.

[MISCELLANEOUS pamphlets, v. 108].

——— The same.

[MISCELLANEOUS pamphlets, v. 244].

——— Documents [of the city] for 1870. 126 v. in 3. 8°. *Boston, city printers*, 1871.

——— The mercantile agency reference book for the city of Boston, comprising a general list of the names in alphabetical order; also, the same classified according to kind of business. Corrected up to Oct. 1, 1871. 83, 168,

Boston—continued.
iv pp. obl. 8°. *Boston, E. Russell & co.* [1871].

——— (*Public library of the city of*). Lower hall. Class list for works in the arts and sciences, including theology, medicine, law, philosophy (moral, mental, political, and social), religious and devotional books, ecclesiastical history and missions, domestic and rural economy, recreative arts, trades, etc. 2d ed. September, 1871. 72 pp. 8°. *Boston,* 1871.

Boston (The) almanac and business directory for the years 1871-72. v. 36-37. 18°. *Boston, Sampson, Davenport & co.* 1871-72.

Boston business directory. Metropolitan directory and map of Boston and vicinity, no. 9. 8°. *Boston, D. Dudley & co.* 1871.

Boston business directory, 1870-71. *See* **Cleary** (William P.) & co.

Boston daily news. Aug. 9, 1870, to Dec. 31, 1871. 3 v. fol. *Boston,* [1870-71].

Boston (The) directory, embracing the city record, a general directory of the citizens, and a business directory. no. 67. For the year commencing July 1, 1871. 1248 pp. 1 map. 8°. *Boston, Sampson, Davenport & co.* [1871].

Boston dispensary. The seventy-fifth annual report of the Boston dispensary, with the by-laws, act of incorporation, &c. Prepared by Samuel A. Green, superintendent. 24 pp. 8°. *Boston,* 1871.

Boston (The gynæcological society of). Journal: A monthly journal devoted to the advancement of the knowledge of the diseases of women. Edited by Winslow Lewis, m. d. Horatio R. Storer, m. d. George H. Bixby, m. d. July, 1869, to Dec. 1871. v. 1-5. 8°. *Boston, J. Campbell,* [1869-71].

Boston (The) medical and surgical journal. [Weekly]. Edited by J. V. C. Smith, m. d. [and others]. Feb. 5, 1845, to Jan. 30, 1868. v. 32-77. 8°. *Boston, D. Clapp,* 1845-68.

——— The same. David W. Cheever, m. d. [and others], editors. Feb. 6, 1868, to Dec. 28, 1871. v. 78-85; new series, v. 1-8. 8°. *Boston, D. Clapp & son,* 1868-71.
[Wanting, v. 47 and 83 (n. s. 6)].

Boston (The) weekly magazine. Devoted to moral and entertaining literature, science, and the fine arts. Published by David H. Ela and John B. Hall. v. 2. Sept. 7, 1839, to Sept. 12, 1840. fol. *Boston, J. B. Hall,* 1839-40.

Botero (Giovanni). A treatise concerning the causes of the magnificencie and greatness of cities, in the italian tongue, now done into english by Robert Peterson. 3 p. l. 108 pp. 4 l. 4°. *London, R. Ockould & H. Tomes,* 1606.

Both (Carl, *m. d.*) Small-pox: the predisposing conditions and their prevention. 50 pp. 16°. *Boston, A. Moore,* 1872.

Bothwell (*Mrs.* Charlotte). The woman's confidential friend: a private book on midwifery. 2 p. l. ix, 80 pp. 8°. *Saint Louis, Levison & Blythe,* 1870.

Bott (Thomas). An answer to the reverend mr. Warburton's divine legation of Moses, in three parts. 4 p. l. 302 pp. 8°. *London, R. Manby,* 1743.

Botta (Carlo Giuseppe Guglielmo). History of the war of the independence of the United States of America. Translated from the italian, by George Alexander Otis. 3d ed. 2 v. 472 pp. 2 maps, 4 pl; 468 pp. 2 maps, 3 pl. 1 portrait. 8°. *New-Haven, N. Whiting,* 1834.

——— The same. 10th ed. 2 v. 472 pp. 3 portraits; 468 pp. 1 portrait, 1 pl. 8°. *Cooperstown (N. Y.) H. & E. Phinney,* 1848.

Botten-Hansen (P.) *and* **Petersen** (Siegwart). Norsk bog-fortegnelse. 1848-1865. Med anhang, indeholdende: 1. Indbydelses skrifter. 2. Politiske- og avertissements-tidender. 1 p. l. 302 pp. 8°. *Kristiania, den norske boghandler forenings forlag,* 1870.

Bottoni (Alberto). Albertini Bottonni nobilis patavini de morbis mvliebribvs libri secundus et tertius. 4 p. l. 100 l. 4°. *Venetiis, apud P. Meietum,* 1588.

Bouchereau (Louis). Statement of the sugar and rice crops made in Louisiana, in 1870-71, with an appendix. xx, 74 pp. 12°. *New Orleans,* 1871.

Bouchet (Jean). Histoire de Lovys, seignevr de la Trimoville, dit le cheualier sans reproche: dans laqvelle il y a qvelqves circonstances qui seruiront à éclaircir l'histoire du roi Charles viii. fol. [*Paris,* 1684].
[*In* GODEFROY (T. *and* D. de). Histoire de Charles viii. pp. 207-215].

Boudard (Jean Baptiste). Iconologie [françoise et italienne] tirée de divers auteurs. 3 v. in 1. fol. *Parme, auteur,* 1759.

Boudreaux (F. J.) The happiness of heaven. By a father of the society of Jesus. [*anon.*] 372 pp. 18°. *Baltimore, J. Murphy & co.* 1871.

Boufflers (Stanislas, *chevalier* de). Œuvres du chevalier de Boufflers. 2d éd. complète. 4 v. 18°. *Paris, Briand*, 1817.

CONTENTS.

v. 1. Poésies diverses, p. 1.
Traductions, p. 141.
v. 2. Discours académiques, p. 1.
Petits voyages en vers et en prose, p. 141.
v. 3. Contes et nouvelles en vers et en prose.
v. 4. Ah ! si, nouvelle allemande, p. 1.
Mélanges, p. 171.
Pièces fugitives de plusieurs personnes de la famille de l'auteur, p. 203.

Bougeant (Guillaume Hyacinthe). The wonderful travels of prince Fan-Feredin in the country of Arcadia. Interspersed with observations, historical, geographical, physical, critical, and moral. Translated from the original french. [*anon.*] viii, 197 pp. 16°. *Dublin, W. Gilbert*, 1789.

Bouhours (Dominique). Les entretiens d'Ariste et d'Eugène. Dernière éd. [*anon.*] Eng. title. 4 p. l. 438 pp. 5 l. 18°. *Amsterdam, J. le Jeune*, 1671.

——— La manière de bien penser dans les ouvrages d'esprit, dialogues; nouvelle édition. [*anon.*] viii, 459 pp. 16°. *Paris, libraires associés*, 1771.

——— Pensées ingénieuses des anciens et des modernes. Nouv. éd. 4 p. l. 334 pp. 12 l. 8°. *La Haye, M. Roguet*, 1721.

——— Pensées ingénieuses des pères de l'église. [Nouv. èd.] 12 p. l. 456 pp. 16 l. 16°. *Paris, L. Josse*, 1700.

Bouillon-Lagrange (Edme Jean Baptiste). L'art de composer facilement, et à peu de frais, les liqueurs de table, les eaux de senteurs, et autres objets d'économie domestique. Nouvelle éd. 2 p. l. 445 pp. 3 pl. 8°. *Paris, Dentu*, 1807.

Bouilly (Jean-Nicolas). Conseils à ma fille. [Contes]. 11e éd. 2 v. 1 p. l. 372 pp; 3 p. l. 354 pp. 10 pl. 16°. *Paris, L. Janet*, [1844]?

——— Les mères de famille. 2 v. 1 p. l. xvi, 439 pp. 8 pl; 2 p. l. 463 pp. 8 pl. 16°. *Paris, L. Janet*, [1823].

——— Tales for mothers. Translated from the french. 184 pp. 12°. *London, L. Relfe*, 1824.

Bouis (Amédée). Le whip-poor-will, ou les pionniers de l'Orégon. 2 p. l. xvi, 426 pp. 8°. *Paris, Comon & cie.* 1847.

Boulainvilliers (Henri, *comte de*). The life of Mahomet. Translated from the french original. 4 p. l. viii, 400 pp. 8°. *London, Hinchliffe*, 1731.

Boulard (S.) Traité élémentaire de bibliographie, contenant la manière de faire les inventaires, les prisées, les ventes publiques et de classer les catalogues. Les bâses d'une bonne bibliothèque, et la manière d'apprécier les livres rares et précieux. 2 v. in 1. 1 p. l. 140 pp; 2 p. l. 131 pp. 8°. *Paris, Boulard*, 1804–05.

Boulenger (Jules César). De conviviis libri qvattvor. 7 p. l. 394 pp. 7 l. 12°. *Lvgdvni, sumptibus L. Prost*, 1627.

——— De pictvra, plastice, statvaria libri dvo. 4 p. l. 162 pp. 3 l. 12°. *Lvgdvni, sumptibus L. Prost*, 1627.

[*With his* De conviviis, *Lvgdvni*, 1627].

——— De lvdis privatis, ac domesticis veterum liber vnicvs. 4 p. l. 80 pp. 3 l. 12°. *Lvgdvni, sumptibus L. Prost*, 1627.

[*With his* De conviviis. *Lvgdvni*, 1627].

Boulgaris (Eugenios). Ἡ *λογικη εκ παλαιωντε και νεωτερων συνερανισθεισα.* Ἡς *προτετακται αφηγησις προεισοδιωδης περι αρχης και προσοδου της κατα την φιλοσοφιαν ενστασεως, και προδιατριβαι τετταρες εισαγωγικαι εις ἁπασαν εν γενει την φιλοσοφιαν προτελεστικαι.* 18 p. l. 586 pp. 9 l. 8°. *Λειψιᾳ της Σαξονιας*, 1766.

Bouligny (*Mrs.* M. E. Parker). Bubbles and ballast. Being a description of life in Paris during the brilliant days of the empire; a tour through Belgium and Holland, and a sojourn in London. By a lady. [*anon.*] 372 pp. 12°. *Baltimore, Kelly, Piet & co.* 1871.

Bourbon (Louis Henri Joseph, *prince de Condé, duc de*). Memoirs of the life of the great Condé. Translated by Fanny Holcroft. x, 328 pp. 8°. *London, R. Juigné for Longman*, 1807.

Bourbon-Conti (Amilie Gabrielle Stéphanie Louise de, *pseudon.*) *See* **Billet** (Anne Louise Françoise Delorme).

Bourbourg (E. C. Brasseur de). *See* **Brasseur de Bourbourg.**

Bourgoigne (Antoine). Mvndi lapis lydivs siue vanitas per veritatē falsi accusata & conuicta. Eng. title, 3 p. l. 250 pp. 13 l. 4°. *Antuerp. typis viduæ I. Cnobbari*, 1639.

[*Note.*—Illustrated by 50 copperplates, engraved by Andreas Paul, or Pauli, after designs by Dieppenbeck].

Bourignon (Antoinette). An abridgement of the Light of the world; containing the conferences which m. Antonia Bourignon had with mr. Christian de Cort. [With] a preface to the unprejudiced reader, of every sect and party. By Joseph Whittingham Salmon. 8 p. l. 464 pp. 1 portrait. 8°. *London, R. Hindmarsh*, 1786.

Bourignon (Antoinette)—continued.

——— The renovation of the gospel spirit. Part 2d. Translated from the french. 6 p. l. 200 pp. 16°. *London*, [1707.]

[Imperfect: v. 1 wanting, and title-page of v. 2 without date].

Bournon (Jacques Louis, *comte de*). Traité complet de la chaux carbonatée, et de l'arragonite, auquel on a joint une introduction à la minéralogie en général, une théorie de la cristallisation, et son application, ainsi que celle du calcul, à la détermination des formes cristallines de ces deux substances. 3 v. 4°. *Londres, W. Phillips*, 1808.

Bourrit (Marc Théodore). Description des aspects du Mont-Blanc du côté de la Val-d'Aost, des glacières qui en descendent, de l'Allée-Blanche, de Cormayeur, de la cité d'Aoust, des marons ou crétins, du Grand St. Bernard, des réservoirs immenses d'eau au milieu des glaces, & de la découverte de la Martine. viii, 160 pp. 1 tab. 8°. *Lausanne, chez la société thypographique*, 1776.

Boussingault (Jean-Baptiste-Joseph Dieudonné). The chemical and physiological balance of organic nature. *See* **Dumas** (Jean-Baptiste) *and* **Boussingault.**

Bouvy (J.) Der stern des 19. jahrhunderts. Der heil. Ioseph. Sein leben, nebst einer achttägigen andacht zu ehren des hl. Joseph vom heil. kirchenlehrer Alphonsus. Nach der zweiten holländischen ausgabe. xxi, 225, 34 pp. 1 pl. 18°. *Baltimore, brüder Kreuzer*, 1872.

Bovee (C. Nestell). Thoughts, feelings, and fancies. 3 p. l. 451 pp. sq. 8°. *New York, Wiley & Halsted*, 1857.

Bowden (*Rev.* S.) Debarring and inviting service. 12°. [*Pittsburg*, 1872].

In REFORMED presbyterian church in North America. Memorial volume, pp. 128-138].

Bowdich (T. Edward). An account of the discoveries of the Portuguese in the interior of Angola and Mozambique. To which is added, a note by the author, on a geographical error of Mungo Park, in his last journal into the interior of Africa. 1 p. l. ii, 186 pp. 2 maps. 8°. *London, J. Booth*, 1824.

Bowdler (*Miss* H.) Poems and essays. 9th ed. vii, 274 pp. 8°. *Bath, R. Cruttwell*, 1797.

Bowdler (John). Poems divine and moral, many of them now first published. 2 v. xv, 276 pp; xiii, 304 pp. 8°. *London, T. Cadell*, 1821.

Bowen (Daniel). A history of Philadelphia, with a notice of villages, in the vicinity, etc. up to the year 1839; also, the state of society, in relation to science, religion, and morals; with an historical account of the military operations of the late war. [1812-14]. 1 p. l. iv, 200 pp. 8 l. 2 pl. 8°. *Philadelphia, D. Bowen*, 1839.

Bowen (*Rev.* George). Daily meditations. 429 pp. 12°. *Philadelphia, Presbyterian publication committee*, [1865].

Bowen (J. Burgoyne). Horatio and Anna; a tale of recent occurrences in the west [etc. A poem]. 100 pp. 18°. *Covington (Ky.) author*, 1842.

Bower (The) of bliss; with other amatory poems; including the loves of Abelard and Heloise. [*anon.*] 2 p. l. 258 pp. 8°. *London, E. Wilson*, 1814.

Bowers (*Capt.* A. *r. n. r.*) Bhamo expedition. Report on the practicability of re-opening the trade route, between Burma and western China. With an appendix. 2. p. l. 165 pp. 2 maps, 83 pl. 8°. *Rangoon, american mission press*, 1869. S.

Bowles (Oliver). De pastore evangelico tractatvs: in quo vniversum munus pastorale, tam quoad pastoris vocationem, & præparationem, quam ipsius muneris exercitium, accuratè proponitur. 11 p. l. 424 pp. 16°. *Genevæ, sumptibus I. H. Widerhold*, 1667.

Bowles (*Rev.* William Lisle). The missionary: a poem. 3d ed. viii, 206 pp. 16°. *London, J. Murray*, 1816.

Bowling (W. K. *m. d. editor*). *See* **Nashville** journal of medicine and surgery.

Bowman (Francis C.) *and* **Dana** (Charles A.) A household book of songs: for four voices. 1 p. l. 154 pp. 4°. *New York, D. Appleton & co.* 1872.

Box (Charles). The theory and practice of cricket, from its origin to the present time; with critical and explanatory notes upon the laws of the game. x, 165 pp. 16°. *London, F. Warne & co.* 1868.

Boxhorn (Marc Zuer). Allocvtio nvptialis, ad Gvilielmvm Goesivm, sponsum, cum domum duceret Elisabetham Heinsiam. 18°. [*Lugd. Batavorum*, 1644].

[*In* DISSERTATIONVM lvdicrarvm et amœnitatvm scriptores varij, pp. 369-382].

Boy (The) inventor; a memoir of Matthew Edwards. *See* **Bulfinch** (Thomas).

Boy life: being incidents from real life. [*anon.*] 216 pp. 3 pl. 18°. *Philadelphia, Presbyterian board of publication*, [1870].

Boyce (—). The art of lettering. *See* **Lyford** (—) *and* **Boyce.**

Boyd (Andrew). Boyd's business directory of Utica, Rome, Camden, Lowville, Washington Mills, Oriskany Falls, Clayville, Richfield Springs, Little Falls, Herkimer, Sherburne, Norwich, and intermediate railroad villages. 1871–72. 8°. *Utica (N. Y.) Gilbert & Salisbury,* [1871].

——— Boyd's directory of Astoria, East New York, Flatbush, Flushing, Glen Cove, Greenport, Hempstead, Huntington, Jamaica, Newtown, Patchogue, Port Jefferson, Riverhead, Sag Harbor, and Setauket, Long Island. With a business directory of patrons to the work. And an appendix of much general information. 1864–5. 12°. *New York,* [1864].

——— *See, also,* Directories, under—

Auburn, (*N. Y.*) **New York** state.
Binghamton. **Paterson,** (*N. J.*)
Elmira. **Syracuse,** (*N. Y.*)
Newport.

——— *and* **Boyd** (William Harry). *See* Directories, under—

Harrisburg. **Williamsport** city.
Wilkesbarre.

Boyd (*Mrs.* E. E.) *and* **Johnston** (Emma M.) The children's speaker, and anniversary gem. 154 pp. 18°. *Philadelphia, J. P. Skelly & co.* 1872.

Boyd (Francis A.) Columbiana; or, the north star. Complete in one volume. [A poem]. 69 pp. 12°. *Chicago, B. Hand,* 1870.

Boyd (*Rev.* James R.) Memoir of the life, character, and writings of Philip Doddridge, d. d. With a selection from his correspondence. 480 pp. 1 portrait. 12°. *New York, American tract society,* [1860].

Boyd (Mark). Reminiscences of fifty years. 390 pp. 12°. *New York, D. Appleton & co.* 1871.

Boyd (Robert, *d. d.*) None but Christ; or, the sinner's only hope. 360 pp. 12°. *Chicago, Church & Goodman,* 1864.

Boyd (William Harry). Business directory of the counties of Adams, Bucks, Chester, Cumberland, Dauphin, Delaware, Franklin, Lancaster, Montgomery, and York, Pa. With a general directory of all the inhabitants of Harrisburg, and an appendix of much useful information. 1860. 8°. *Philadelphia, W. H. Boyd,* 1860.

——— *See, also,* Directories, under—

District of Columbia. **Pottsville,** (*Pa.*)
Lancaster co. (*Pa.*) **Washington,** (*D. C.*)

Boyde (*Capt.* Henry). Several voyages to Barbary. Containing an historical and geographical account of the country. With the hardships, sufferings, and manner of redeeming christian slaves. Together with a curious description of Mequinez, Oran, and Alcazar. With a journal of the late siege and surrender of Oran. 2d ed. 3 p. l. 146, 158 pp. 4 pl. 3 maps. 8°. *London, O. Payne,* [*etc.*] 1736.

Boyer (Abel). Le grand théâtre de l'honneur & de la noblesse. Contenant: i. La sçience du blason. ii. Abbrêgé historique & chronologique des établissemens & des révolutions des monarchies & des souverainetez de l'Europe. iii. L'état présent de l'empire d'Allemagne. iv. Les armoiries & le blason des empereurs, rois, princes, & états souverains de la chrêtienté. En françois & en anglois. 2 v. in 1. xvi, 381 pp. 1 pl; 260 pp. 7 pl. 4°. *Londres, H. Woodfall,* 1729.

[*Note.*—With English title on reverse of title-page].

——— The history of king William the third. In iii parts. [*anon.*] 3 v. 8°. *London, A. Roper,* 1703.

Boyer (Pierre). Parallèle de la doctrine des payens avec celle des jésuites, et de la constitution du pape Clement xi. qui commence par ces mots: Unigenitus dei filius. [*anon.*] 7 p. l. 238 pp. 1 l. 16°. *Amsterdam, J. Roman,* 1726.

——— Portrait au naturel des jésuites et anciens et modernes: ou image véritable du premier et du dernier siècle de la société de Jésus; fin du Parallèle de la doctrine des payens avec celle des jésuites & de la bulle Unigenitus. [*anon.*] 84 pp. 8°. *Amsterdam, N. Potier,* 1731.

Boyle (Robert). Foundation lectures. A defence of natural and revealed religion; being a collection of the sermons preached at the lecture founded by hon. Robert Boyle; (from the year 1691 to 1732). With the additions and amendments of the several authors and general indexes. 3 v. fol. *London, D. Midwinter,* 1739.

CONTENTS.

Boyle (Robert)—continued.
IBBOT (Benjamin). v. 2, pp. 731–868.
KIDDER (Richard). v. 1, pp. 89–152.
LENG (John). v. 3, pp. 1–152.
STANHOPE (George). v. 1, pp. 627–836.
TURNER (John). v. 2, pp. 349–428.
WHISTON (William). v. 2, pp. 259–348.
WILLIAMS (John, *bishop of Chichester*). v. 1, pp. 153–274.
WOODWARD (Josiah). v. 2, pp. 491–564*.

Boylston (Zabdiel, *m. d.*) Historical account of the small-pox inoculated in New England, upon all sorts of persons, whites, blacks, and of all ages and constitutions. 2nd ed. corrected. vi, 53 pp. 16°. *Boston, S. Gerrish and T. Hancock,* 1730.

Boyne (William). The Yorkshire library. A bibliographical account of books on topography, tracts of the seventeenth century, biography, spaws, geology, botany, maps, views, portraits, and miscellaneous literature, relating to the county of York. With collations and notes on the books and authors. viii, 304 pp. 2 portraits. 4°. *London, Taylor & co.* 1869.

Boynton (Charles Brandon, *d. d.*) English and french neutrality and the anglo-french alliance, in their relations to the United States and Russia, including an account of the leading policy of France and of England for the last two hundred years—the origin and aims of the alliance—the meaning of the crimean war—and the reason of the hostile attitude of these two powers towards the United States, and of the movement on Mexico, with a statement of the general resources—the army and navy of England and France—Russia and America—showing the present strength and probable future of these four powers. 576 pp. 8°. *Cincinnati, C. F. Vent & co.* 1864.

Boys (*Rev.* Thomas). The suppressed evidence: or proofs of the miraculous faith and experience of the church of Christ in all ages, from authentic records of the fathers, Waldenses, Hussites, reformers, United brethren, &c. xi, 360 pp. 8°. *London, Hamilton, Adams & co.* 1832.

Boyse (Joseph). Discourses on the four last things, viz. death, judgment, heaven, and hell, and on some other subjects relating thereunto. 2 p. l. 607 pp. 8°. *Dublin, author,* 1724.

Brabant. Remontrance des trois états de ce pays et duché de Brabant à sa majesté impériale et catholique au sujet de ses lettres patentes d'octroy accordées pour l'établissement de la compagnie générale dans les Pays-Bas aûtrichiens pour le commerce et la navigation

Brabant—continued.
aux Indes. 18 pp. sm. 4°. *Bruxelles, E. de Grieck,* 1724.

Brabazon (Wallop). The deep sea and coast fisheries of Ireland, with suggestions for the working of a fishing company. Illustrated by William Cooper. 111 pp. 21 pl. 8°. *Dublin, J. McGlashan,* 1848.

Bradbury (William B.) Orio: all the sunday-school hymns from "Oriola, a complete hymn and tune book for sabbath schools." 2 p. l. 162 pp. 18°. *Cincinnati, Moore, Wilstach, Keyes & co.* 1860.

——— *and* **Main** (Sylvester). Cottage melodies; a hymn and tune book, for prayer and social meetings and the home circle. 320 pp. sq. 16°. *New York, Carlton & Porter,* [*etc.*] 1859.

Bradford (*Rev.* Samuel). The credibility of the christian revelation, from its intrinsic evidence; in eight sermons, preach'd in 1699. With a ninth sermon as an appendix. fol. [*London,* 1739].
[BOYLE lectures, v. 1, pp. 435–524].

Bradford (Sarah H.) The history of Peter the great, czar of Russia. 232 pp. 4 pl. 16°. *New York, D. Appleton & co.* 1858.

——— The Linton family; or, the fashion of this world. 320 pp. 12°. *New York, Pudney & Russell,* 1860.

——— The story of Columbus, simplified for young folks. 255 pp. 6 pl. 16°. *New York, C. Scribner,* 1857.

Bradford (William, *of Boston*). A dialogue, or third conference between some young men born in New England and some ancient men which came out of Holland and old England, concerning the church and the government thereof. Edited, with a preface and and notes, by Charles Deane. Reprinted from the proceedings of the Massachusetts historical society. xiii, 78 pp. 8°. *Boston, J. Wilson & son,* 1870.

Bradford (*Rev.* William). Sketches of the country, character, and costume, in Portugal and Spain, made during the campaign, and on the route of the British army, in 1808 and 1809. Esquisse du pays, du caractère et du costume, en Portugal et en Espagne, prises pendant la campagne et durant la marche de l'armée angloise, en 1808 et 1809. 39 l. 38 col. pl. fol. *London, J. Booth,* 1809.

——— Sketches of military costume in Spain and Portugal. Intended as a supplement to

Bradford (*Rev.* William)—continued. sketches of the country. 5 p. l. 24 pp. 13 col. pl. fol. *London, J. Booth,* [1809].
[*With* the preceding].

Bradlaugh (Charles). The bible: what it is. Book 1–5. pp. viii, 1–434. 12°. *London, Austin & co.* 1870.

—— Heresy: its utility and morality. A plea and a justification. 1 p. l. 65 pp. 12°. *London, Austin & co.* 1871.

Bradley (Stephen Row). Vermont's appeal to the candid and impartial world. A fair stating of the claims of Massachusetts Bay, New-Hampshire and New-York, the right of the state of Vermont to independence, etc. 50 pp. 8°. *Hartford, Hudson & Goodwin,* [1780].
[HAZARD pamphlets, v. 47].

Brady (William, *sailing-master, U. S. n.*) The naval apprentice's kedge anchor; or young sailor's assistant. 328 pp. 7 pl. 12°. *New York, Taylor & Clement,* 1841.

Brady (William). Glimpses of Texas: its divisions, resources, development and prospects. 104 pp. 1 l. 16°. *Houston,* 1871.

Bragge (Francis, *b. d.*) The works of Francis Bragge. A new ed. 5 v. 8°. *Oxford, university press,* 1833.

CONTENTS.

v. 1. On the miracles of our lord.
v. 2–3. On the parables of our lord.
v. 4. Thirteen sermons on undissembled religion.
v. 5. On the regulation of the passions.

Brailsford (*Rev.* Hodgson). An analysis of the literature of ancient Greece; together with critical remarks, elegant extracts, and biographical accounts. xx, 154 pp. 8°. *London, Longman & co.* 1833.

Brainard (John Gardner Calkins). Poems. A new and authentic collection, with an original memoir of his life. lxiv, 191 pp. 12°. *Hartford, E. Hopkins,* 1842.

Brainard (Mary). Esther Gray and other poems. 160 pp. 12°. *Rockford (Ill.) author,* 1871.

Braithwaite (Richard). *See* **Brathwait.**

Branagan (Thomas). The excellency of the female character vindicated; being an investigation relative to the cause and effects of the encroachments of men upon the rights of women, and the too frequent degradation and consequent misfortunes of the fair sex. By the author of the "Beauties of philanthropy." [*anon.* 3d ed.] 280 pp. 16°. *Harrisburg, T Wyeth,* 1828.

—— The penitential tyrant; a juvenile poem in two cantos. [With] compendious memoirs of the author. 122 pp. 18°. *Philadelphia, author,* 1805.

Branca (Carlo). Catalogo della libreria di Carlo Branca. xiii, 422 pp. 1 l. 8°. *Milano,* [*tipi fratelli Baroni*], 1870. s.

Brand (Hannah). Plays, and poems. xvi, 424 pp. 8°. *Norwich (Eng.) Beatniffe & Payne,* 1798.

Brand (John). The history and antiquities of the town and county, of the town of Newcastle upon Tyne, including an account of the coal trade of that place, and embellished with engraved views of the publick buildings, &c. 2 v. 1 p. l. xvi, 676 pp. 2 l. 22 pl. 1 map; 1 p. l. 724 pp. 4 l. 10 pl. 4°. *London, B. White & son,* 1789.

Brandreth (Benjamin, *m. d.*) The doctrine of purgation. Curiosities from ancient and modern literature. A collection of quotations on the use of purgatives, from Hippocrates, and other medical writers, covering a period of over two thousand years, proving purgation is the corner-stone of all curatives. 224 pp. 8°. *New York, Baker & Godwin,* 1871.

Brasilsche gelt-sack. Waer in dat claerlijck vertoont wordt, waer dat de participanten van de west-indische comp. haer gelt ghebleven is. [*anon.*] 14 l. sm. 4°. *Gedruct in Brasilien op't Reciff in de bree-bijl, anno* 1647.

Brasseur de Bourbourg (*L'abbé* E. Charles). Lettres pour servir d'introduction à l'histoire primitive des nations civilisées de l'Amérique Septentrionale, adressées à Monsieur le duc de Valmy. Cartas para servir de introduccion á la historia primitiva de las naciones civilizadas de la America Setentrional. [French and spanish]. 75 pp. 4°. *Mexico, M. Murguía,* 1851. s.

Brathwait (Richard). Barnabæ itinerarium; or, drunken Barnaby's four journeys to the north of England: in latin and english metre. Together with Bessy Bell. To which is now added the ancient ballad of Chevy Chase, in latin and english verse. [9th ed?] 1 p. l. xl, 324 pp. 1 pl. 18°. *York, T. Gent,* 1852.

—— A svrvey of history: or, a nursery for gentry. Contrived and comprized in an intermixt discourse upon historicall and poeticall relations. [1st ed.] 13 p. l. 416 pp. sm. 4°. *London, I. Okes for I. Emery,* 1638.

Brauer (Friedrich) *and* **Gerstäcker** (A.) Bericht über die wissenschaftlichen leistungen im gebiete der entomologie während der jahre 1867 und 1868. Erste hälfte. Insekten. Bearbeitet von Friedrich Brauer. 152 pp. 8°. *Berlin, Nicolaische verlagsbuchhandlung,* 1870. s.

Braun (Emil). Die ruinen und museen Roms. Für reisende, künstler und alterthumsfreunde. xxxiv, 860 pp. 16°. *Braunschweig, F. Vieweg & sohn,* 1854. s.

Braun (Johann). Vestitus sacerdotum hebræorum: sive commentarius amplissimus in Exodi cap. 28, ac 39, & Levit. cap. 16, aliaque loca s. scripturæ quam plurima. Altera ed. priori auctior & emendatior. 2 v. in 1. 36 p. l. 343 pp. 20 l. 4 pl; 2 p. l. pp. 345–752, 30 l. 16 pl. 4°. *Amstelodami, apud A. a Someren,* 1697–8.

Bray (*Mrs.* Anna Emma). The Talba, or moor of Portugal: a romance. 2 v. 201 pp; 193 pp. 12°. *New York, J. & J. Harper,* 1831.

Brayley (Edward Wedlake, *editor*). The graphic and historical illustrator: an original miscellany of literary, antiquarian, and topographical information; with 150 wood-cuts. iv, 416 pp. 4°. *London, J. Chidley,* 1834.

Brazil. *Chamber of deputies.* Annaes do parlamento brazileiro. Camara dos srs. deputados. Sesão de 1871. 4 v. fol. *Rio de Janeiro, J. Villeneuve & co.* 1871.

——— The empire of Brazil at the Paris international exhibition of 1867. 2 parts in 1 v. 139 pp; 1 p. l. iii, 197 pp. 1 map. 8°. *Rio de Janeiro, E. & H. Laemmert,* 1867. s.

Brazil (Portuguese) company. De instellinge van de generale compagnie, ghemaeckt in Portugael, na Brasil, toelatinge met de acte van sijn maiesteyt, gepasseert den 10 Meert, 1649. 12 l. sm. 4°. *Amsterdam, weduwe van Lief-houdt,* [1649].

Bread-winners. By a lady of Boston. [*anon.*] 295 pp. 16°. *Boston, Nichols & Hall,* 1871.

Breakenbridge (John). The crusades, and other poems. 327 pp. 8°. *Kingston, J. Rowlands,* 1846.

Breckinridge (John, *d. d.*) Discussion on the roman catholic religion, 1836. *See* **Hughes** (John, *archbishop of New York*) *and* **Breckinridge.**

Breckinridge (Robert Jefferson, *d. d.*) The knowledge of God, objectively considered, being the first part of theology considered as a science of positive truth, both inductive and deductive. xv, 530 pp. 8°. *New York, R. Carter & brothers,* 1858.

Breckinridge (R. J. *d. d.*)—continued.

Bree (*Rev.* William Thomas). The plain reader's help in the study of the holy scriptures, consisting of notes, explanatory and illustrative, chiefly selected or abridged from the family bible published by the society for promoting christian knowledge. 2 v. 3 p. l. 378 pp; 1 p. l. 336 pp. 4°. *Coventry, Rollason & Reader,* 1821–22.

Breed (*Rev.* William Pratt, *d. d.*) Christ liveth in me. 175 pp. 16°. *Philadelphia, Presbyterian board of publication,* [1871].

——— Grapes from the great vine for young fruit gatherers. 324 pp. 3 pl. 18°. *Philadelphia, Presbyterian board of publication,* [1864].

——— Hand-book for funerals. 95 pp. 16°. *Philadelphia, Presbyterian board of publication,* [1871].

——— Lessons in flying, for home birds. 164 pp. 3 pl. 18°. *Philadelphia, Presbyterian board of publication,* [1863].

Breeden-raedt aende vereenichde nederlandsche provintien. Gelreland. Holland. Zeeland. Wtrecht. Vriesland. Over-Yssel. Groeningen. Gemaeckt ende gestelt door I. A. [ende] G. W. C. [*anon.*] 24 l. sm. 4°. *Antwerpen, F. van Duynen,* 1649.

Bref recueil de l'assasinat, commis en la personne dv très illvstre prince, monseigneur le prince d'Orange, etc. par Jean Jauregui espaignol. [*anon.*] 33 l. sm. 4°. *Anvers, C. Plantin,* 1582.

Brégy (F. A.) A compendium of the grammatical rules of the french language. Parts 1–2. 61, 34 pp. 12°. *Philadelphia, Eldredge & brother,* 1872.

Brehm (Alfred Edmund). Cassell's book of birds. From the text of dr. Brehm. By Thomas Rymer Jones. v. 1–2. viii, 312 pp. 10 col. pl; viii, 320 pp. 10 col. pl. 4°. *London, Cassell, Petter & Galpin,* [1871].

Bremen. (*Bureau für bremische statistik*). Jahrbuch für die amtliche statistik des bremischen staats. iv. jahrgang. 1 heft: zur statistik des schiffs- und waarenverkehrs im jahre 1870. x, 196 pp. 4°. *Bremen, G. A. v. Halem,* 1871. s.

Bremen (The) lectures, on fundamental, living, religious questions. By various eminent european divines. Translated from the original german, by rev. D. Heagle. With an introduction, by Alvah Hovey, d. d. 308 pp. 12°. *Boston, Gould & Lincoln,* 1871.

Brennan (J. Fletcher). A general register of all the lodges and grand lodges of free masons in North America, which maintain mutual correspondence and recognition. 254 pp. 12°. *Cincinnati, American masonic publishing association*, 1871.

Brent (John). The Chelsea directory for 1872. *See* **Chelsea** (*City of*).

Brent (John Carroll, *editor*). Biographical sketch of the most rev. John Carroll, first archbishop of Baltimore: with select portions of his writings. 321 pp. 12°. *Baltimore, J. Murphy*, 1843.

Brentano (Lujo). On the history and development of gilds, and the origin of trade-unions. 8°. [*London*, 1870].

[EARLY english text society, no. 40. In SMITH (Toulmin). English gilds, pp. xlix–cxcix].

Brenz (Johann). A right godly and learned discourse vpon the booke of Ester. Written in latin by Iohn Brentius a german, and newly turned into english by Iohn Stockwood. *b. l.* 22 p. l. 178 pp. 16°. *London, I. Wolfe for I. Harrison the younger*, 1584.

Breslau. Zeitschrift für entomologie. *See* **Zeitschrift.**

Bretschneider (Carl Gottlieb). Handbuch der dogmatik der evangelisch-lutherischen kirche; oder, versuch einer beurtheilenden darstellung der grundsätze, welche diese kirche in ihren symbolischen schriften über die christliche glaubenslehre ausgesprochen hat. 3e verbesserte und vermehrte aufl. 2 v. xxii, 762, 71 pp; xii, 896 pp. 8°. *Leipzig, J. A. Barth*, 1828.

——— Henry and Antonio, or the proselytes of the romish and evangelical churches; translated from the german, with additional notes, by a minister of the lutheran church. 204 pp. 12°. *Baltimore, Lucas & Deaver*, 1834.

——— Lexicon manvale graeco-latinvm in libros novi testamenti. Ed. 2a. 2 v. 1 p. l. 708 pp; xiv, 662 pp. 1 l. 8°. *Lipsiae, sumptibus I. A. Barthii*, 1829.

Breugel (Johannes). Giovanni Brueghel pittor fiammingo e sue lettere. *See* **Crivelli** (Giovanni).

Brewer (*Rev.* E. Cobham, *ll. d.*) Dictionary of phrase and fable, giving the derivation, source, or origin of common phrases, allusions, and words that have a tale to tell. 2d ed. viii, 979 pp. 12°. *London, Cassell, Petter & Galpin*, [1871].

Brewster (Abel). Free man's companion; a new and original work, consisting of numerous moral, political and philosophical views, examples and explanations, tending to illustrate the general cause of truth, justice, virtue, liberty, and human improvement. 384 pp. 8°. *Hartford, A. Brewster*, 1827.

Brialmont (Alexis). Considérations politiques et militaires sur la Belgique. 3 v. 8°. *Bruxelles, Hayez*, 1851–52.

Brice (Germain). Nouvelle description de la ville de Paris, et de tout ce qu'elle contient de plus remarkable, [etc.] 8e éd. Tome 1. 4 p. l. 523 pp. 3 pl. 16°. *Paris, J. M. Gaudouin*, 1725.

Bricknell (*Rev.* William Simcox). Preaching: its warrant, subject, and effects, considered with reference to "The tracts for the times": in [three] sermons. With an appendix. xxiii, 213 pp. 8°. *London, F. Baisler*, 1841.

Bricktop (*pseudon.*) Parson Beecher and his horse. A humorous adventure. 96 pp. 12°. *New York, Winchell & Small*, 1871.

Bridel (L. *pasteur*). Récits américains ou conversions, réveils, expériences chrétiennes et entretiens sur la recherche du salut. Tirés des mémoires et journaux de trois pasteurs presbytériens des États-Unis [I. S. Spencer, d. d. rev. S. K. Kollock, W. Wisner, d. d.] 2 v. in 1. 2 p. l. iv, 258 pp; 1 p. l. 255 pp. 16°. *Paris, C. Meyrueis & cie.* 1854.

Bridel (Philippe Syriach) *and* **Birmann** (Pierre). Voyage pittoresque de Basle à Bienne par les vallons de Mottiers-Grandval. Les planches dessinées par Pierre Birmann. Accompagné d'un texte par l'auteur de la course de Basle à Bienne. [Philippe Syriach Bridel]. 1 p. l. 37 l. 36 pl. 1 map. fol. *Basle, P. Birmann*, 1802.

Bridgeport (*Conn.*) Bridgeport city directory, and Fairfield co. business record for 1871–72. no. 4. 8°. *Bridgeport, Standard association*, 1871.

Bridges (Sallie). Marble isle. Legends of the round table and other poems. 272 pp. 18°. *Philadelphia, J. B Lippincott & co.* [1864].

Bridgman (Eliza J. Gillett). The pioneer of American missions in China. The life and labors of Elijah Coleman Bridgman. With an introductory note, by Asa D. Smith, d. d. xv, 295 pp. 1 portrait. 12°. *New York, A. D. F. Randolph*, 1864.

Brief (A) discourse concerning regular singing, shewing from the scriptures, the neces

Brief (A) discourse, etc.—continued. sity and incumbency thereof in the worship of God. [*anon.*] 1 p. l. 18 pp. 16°. *Boston, John Elliot*, 1725.

Brief (A) examination of the rev. mr. Warburton's Divine legation of Moses. *See* **Morgan** (*Dr.* Thomas).

Brief remarks on the defence of the Halifax libel, on the british-american-colonies. [*anon.*] 40 pp. 8°. *Boston, Edes & Gill*, 1765. [HAZARD pamphlets, v. 19].

Brief review of the rise and progress, services and sufferings, of New England, especially Massachuset's-Bay. [*anon.*] 32 pp. 8°. *London, J. Buckland*, 1774.

Briefe (A) discoverie of doctor Allen's seditious drifts. *See* **D.** (G.)

Brierwood (Frank, *pseudon.*) Mabel Clifton. A novel. 304 pp. 12°. *Philadelphia, Claxton, Remsen & Haffelfinger*, 1869.

Briggs (Richard). The english art of cookery, according to the present practice; being a complete guide to all housekeepers, on a plan entirely new. With bills of fare for every month in the year. iv, xx, 656 pp. 12 pl. 8°. *London, G. G. J. & J. Robinson*, 1788.

——— The same. 2d ed. 1 p. l. iv, xx, 656 pp. 12 pl. 8°. *London, G. G. J. & J. Robinson*, 1791.

Brigham (Amariah, *m. d.*) Observations on the influence of religion upon the health and physical welfare of mankind. 331 pp. 12°. *Boston, Marsh, Capen & Lyon*, 1835.

——— Remarks on the influence of mental cultivation and mental excitement upon health. 3d ed. xxviii, 37–204 pp. 12°. *Philadelphia, Lea & Blanchard*, 1845.

Brigham (John C.) *and* **Morse** (Sidney Edwards). Nuevo sistema de geografia, antigua y moderna. 324 pp. 12°. *Nueva York, White, Gallaher & White*, 1827.

Bright (J. W. *m. d.*) Cancer: its classification and remedies. 191 pp. 8°. *Philadelphia, S. W. Butler, m. d.* 1871.

Brightman (Thomas, *puritan divine*). The workes of mr. Tho: Brightman: viz. a revelation of the apocalyps: containing an exposition of the whole book of the revelation of saint John. [Also], a most comfortable exposition of the last and most difficult part of the prophesie of Daniel. Together with a commentary on the whole book of canticles, or song of Solomon. [4th ed.] Eng. title, 4 p. l. 1088 pp. sm. 4°. *London, J. Field for S. Cartwright*, 1644.

Brignole Sale (Antonio Giulio). Maria Maddalena peccatrice, e convertita. 1 p. l. 216 pp. 18°. *Venetia, Turrini*, 1652.

Bril-gesicht voor de verblinde eyghen baetsuchtige handelaers op Brasil. Door een lief-hebber van't vaderlandt geschreven. [*anon.*] 7 pp. sm. 4°. [*n. p.*] 1638.

Brill (W. H.) Brill's family recipe book, containing several hundred practical receipts and general information in the arts, manufactures and trades, including medicine, pharmacy and domestic economy. 1 p. l. 96 pp. 12°. *Allegheny, (Pa.) W. H. Brill*, 1870.

Brincklé (J. G.) Poems. iv, 13–183 pp. 12°. *Philadelphia, Claxton, Remsen & Haffelfinger*, 1872.

Brinton (D. G.) An intermediate geography. *See* **Steinwehr** (A. *von*) *and* **Brinton.**

Brion de la Tour (Louis). Almanach intéressant dans les circonstances présentes, description abrégée des États-Unis de l'Amérique; des possessions anglaises, et des pays qui y sont contigus, dans les Indes Orientales. Eng. title, 72 pp. 2 maps, 1 pl. 32°. *Paris, Desnos*, 1780.

Briquet (*Madame* Marguerite Ursule Fortunée Bernier). Dictionnaire historique, littéraire et bibliographique des Françaises, et des étrangères naturalisées en France, connues par leurs écrits, ou par la protection qu'elles ont accordée aux gens de lettres, depuis l'établissement de la monarchie jusqu'à nos jours. xxiv, 347 pp. 1 portrait. 8°. *Paris, Treuttel & Würtz*, 1804.

Brisbane (William D.) Brisbane's golden ready reckoner; calculated in dollars and cents. To which are added, interest tables calculated in dollars and cents, for days and for months, at six per cent. and at seven per cent. per annum, alternately. 195 pp. 16°. *New York, Dick & Fitzgerald*, [1863].

Briscoe (John Ivatt). Gospel according to st. Mark. *London*, 1870. *See* **Bible.** (*English*).

Brisman (Sven). Engelskt och svenskt handlexicon med accentuation och pronunciation. Andra uplag. 2 p. l. 670 col. on 168 l.; 176 col. on 44 l. 4°. *Upsala, kongl. academiska bokhandeln*, 1801.

Brisse (*Baron* L.) Les 366 menus du baron Brisse. Nouv. éd. Par W. L. Townsend. xvi, 396 pp. 12°. *Paris, E. Donnaud*, 1868.

Bristed (John). The society of friends, or people commonly called quakers, examined.

Bristed (John)—continued.
xliv, 359 pp. 8°. *London, J. Mawman & J. White*, 1805.

——— Thoughts on the anglican and anglo-american churches. x, 500 pp. 8°. *London, reprinted for B. J. Holdsworth*, 1823.

British (The) almanac and companion for the years 1871 and 1872. 4 v. in 2. 16°. *London, J. Greenhill*, 1870–71.

British (The) american magazine. [A monthly magazine] devoted to literature, science, and art. May to Oct. 1863. v. 1. 8°. *Toronto, Rollo & Adam*, 1863.
[Imperfect: wanting, pp. 447–448].

British curiosities in art and nature; giving an account of rarities both antient and modern. Likewise an account of the posts, markets and fair-towns. [Also], a very useful scheme, containing a brief account of the state of each county in England, at one view. [*anon.*] 2d ed. with large additions. xvi, 248 pp. 1 table. 16°. *London, S. Illidge*, 1728.

British Guiana. Geological survey of British Guiana. Reports of the geological survey [by James G. Sawkins and Charles B. Brown] taken from the "Colonist" newspaper. December, 1869. 2 p. l. 166, iv pp. 8°. *Demerara, L. M'Dermott*, 1870.

British (The) magazine and monthly register of religious and ecclesiastical information, parochial history and documents respecting the state of the poor, progress of education, &c. v. 1–32. March, 1832, to December, 1847. 8°. *London, J. Turrill*, [*and others*], 1832–47.
[Incomplete: v. 33–36 wanting].

British (The) minstrel, and musical and literary miscellany; a selection of standard music, songs, duets, glees, choruses, etc. and articles in musical and general literature. [A periodical]. 3 v. 8°. *Glasgow, W. Hamilton*, 1843–45.

British museum. Acts and votes of parliament relating to the British museum, with the statutes and rules thereof, and the succession of trustees and officers, [1753–1805]. 129 pp. 8°. *London, W. Bulmer & co.* 1805.

——— Catalogue of lithophytes or stony corals. By J. E. Gray. 2 p. l. 51 pp. 18°. *London, trustees*, 1870.

——— Catalogue of monkeys, lemurs, and fruit-eating bats. By dr. J. E. Gray. viii, 137 pp. 8°. *London*, 1870.

——— Catalogue of sea-pens or pennatulari-

British museum—continued.
idæ. By J. E. Gray. 2 p. l. 40 pp. 8°. *London*, 1870.

——— Catalogue of syriac manuscripts in the British museum, acquired since the year 1838. By W. Wright, ll. d. Parts 1–2. 2 p. l. 1037 pp. 4°. *London, printed by order of the trustees*, 1870–71.

——— Catalogue of the collection of meteorites exhibited in the mineral department of the British museum. [By Neville Story Maskelyne]. 8 pp. 8°. *London*, 1871.

——— A catalogue of the greek and etruscan vases. 2 v. 2 p. l. 372 pp. 7 pl; viii, 332 pp. 2 l. 5 pl. 8°. *London, W. Nicol*, 1851.

——— Catalogue of the specimens of dermaptera saltatoria in the collection of the British museum. By F. Walker. Part 1–5. 8°. *London, printed for the trustees of the British museum*, 1869–71.

——— Catalogue of the specimens of hemiptera heteroptera in the collection of the British museum. By F. Walker. Part iv. iv, 211 pp. 8°. *London, printed for the trustees of the British museum*, 1871.

——— Catalogus codicum manuscriptorum orientalium qui in Museo britannico asservantur. Pars secunda, codices arabicos amplectans. [C. Rieu auctore]. 2 p. l. vi, 353–882 pp. fol. *Londini, impensis curatorum Musei britannici*, 1871.

——— A guide to that portion of the collection of prints bequeathed to the nation by the late Felix Slade, now on exhibition in the king's library. 31 pp. 16°. [*London*], 1869.

——— A guide to the autograph letters, manuscripts, original charters, and royal, baronial and ecclesiastical seals, exhibited to the public in the department of manuscripts. 48 pp. 16°. [*London*], *trustees*, 1869.

——— The same. 48 pp. 16°. [*London*], *trustees*, 1870.

——— A guide to the collection of minerals. [By N. S. Maskelyne]. 16 pp. 8°. [*London*], *trustees*, 1870.

——— A guide to the exhibition rooms of the departments of natural history and antiquities. iv, 142 pp. 1 table. 8°. [*London*], *trustees*, 1870.

——— A guide to the first vase room, in the department of greek and roman antiquities. 3d ed. 30 pp. 16°. *London*, 1869.

——— The same. 4th ed. 1 p. l. 31 pp. 12°. *London, trustees*, 1871.

British museum—continued.

——— A guide to the printed books exhibited in the Grenville library and king's library; to the autograph letters, manuscripts, charters, and seals, exhibited in the department of manuscripts; and to the drawings and prints exhibited in the king's library. 3 v. in 1. 1 p. l. 32 pp; 48 pp; 31 pp. 16°. *London*, 1867.

——— A guide to the printed books exhibited to the public. 32 pp. 16°. [*London*], 1869.

——— Hand-list of genera and species of birds, distinguishing those contained in the British museum. Part 3. Struthiones, grallæ, and anseres, with indices of generic and specific names. By G. R. Gray. xi, 350 pp. 8°. *London, printed by order of the trustees*, 1871.

——— Index to the collection of the minerals, with references to the table cases in which the species to which they belong are exhibited, [etc. By N. S. Maskeleyne]. 22 pp. 8°. *London, Woodfall & Kinder*, 1870.

——— A list of the books of reference in the reading room of the British museum. 2d ed. revised. xxviii, 349 pp. 2 pl. 8°. [*London*], *trustees*, 1871.

——— A selection from the miscellaneous inscriptions of Assyria. Prepared for publication by maj. gen. sir H. C. Rawlinson, assisted by George Smith. 13 pp. 70 pl. fol. *London, R. E. Bowler*, 1870.

——— Supplement to the catalogue of seals and whales in the British museum. By John Edward Gray. vi, 104 pp. 8°. *London, trustees*, 1871.

——— Supplement to the catalogue of shield reptiles in the collection of the British museum. Part 1. Testudinata. By J. E. Gray. ix, 120 pp. 4°. *London, trustees*, 1870.

British (The) quarterly review. Jan. 1868, to April, 1871. v. 47–53. 8°. *London, Jackson, Walford & Hodder, and Hodder & Stoughton*, [1868–71].

British (A) republic. [*anon.*] 2 p. l. 96 pp. 12°. *London, E. Truelove*, 1871.

British (The) trade journal. Morgan's british trade journal and export price current. [A monthly]. Jan. 1863, to Dec. 1869. v. 1, 8°. v. 2–7, 4°. *London, Morgan brothers*, 1863–69.

[*Note.*—Name changed in July, 1870].

——— The british trade journal. [Monthly]. Jan. 1870, to Dec. 1871. v. 8–9. 4°. *London*, [*S. V. Morgan*], 1870–71.

Brittan (N.) *and* **Sherwood** (L. H.) The school song and hymn book Designed for general use in schools, academies, and seminaries. 386 pp. 18°. *New York, A. S. Barnes & co.* 1855.

Britton (John). An historical account of Corsham house, etc. *See* **Methuen** (Paul Cobb).

Broad (J. Astor). The watch-word. A collection of sunday-school music. 160 pp. obl. 16°. *Boston, White, Smith & Perry*, [1871].

Broaddus (Andrew). The Dover selection of spiritual songs; with an appendix of choice hymns, on various occasions. 2 v. in 1. xvii, 275 pp; vii, 75 pp. 24°. *Richmond, Collins & co.* 1828.

——— The Virginia selection of psalms, hymns, and spiritual songs. From the most approved authors. In three parts. xxviii, 447 pp. 32°. *Richmond, (Va.) R. I. Smith*, 1836.

——— The same. pp. i–xvi, 368 l. pp. xvii–xl. 18°. *Richmond, (Va.) Smith & Palmer*, 1840.

——— The same. xv, 600 pp. 24°. *Richmond, (Va.) A. Morris*, 1856.

Broadluck (Cephas, *pseudon.*) *See* **Gazlay** (Allen W.)

Brockett (L. P. *m.d.*) The commercial traveller's guide book, being a complete manual for the use of commercial travellers and sellers of goods by sample. 346 pp. 1 map in cover. 12°. *New York, H. Dayton & co.* 1871.

——— Hospital training and nursing in the United States. 12°. [*New York, G. Routledge & sons*, 1872].

[*In* JONES (*Miss J.*) "Una and her paupers," pp. 471–497].

——— Paris under the commune; or, the red rebellion of 1871. 170 pp. 1 map, 27 pl. 8°. *New York, H. S. Goodspeed & co.* 1871.

——— The year of battles: or, the franco-german war of 1870–71. Comprising a history of its origin and causes, [etc.] With maps, plans of battles, [etc.] By Christian Weber. 404 pp. (incl. 25 pl.) 1 map. 8°. *New York, J. W. Goodspeed & co.* 1871.

Brockhaus (F. A. *bookseller*). Bibliotheca historica. Verzeichniss einer sammlung von werken aus dem gebiete der geschichte und deren hülfswissenschaften. viii, 374 pp. 8°. *Leipzig, F. A. Brockhaus*, 1866. S.

Brockmann (J. H.) Christian und Ernst. Eine besprechung über die lehre der oddfellows oder sonderbaren brüder auf grundlage heiliger schrift, nebst anhang enthaltend

Brockmann (J. H.)—continued. eine kurze aus den quellen geschöpfte mittheilung über den orden. 118 pp. 8°. *St. Louis, verfasser*, 1872.

Brodhead (John Romeyn). History of the state of New York. v. 2. 1st ed. xv, 680 pp. 8°. *New York, Harper & brothers*, 1871.

Broecke (Pieter van den). Wonderlijcke historische ende journaelsche aenteyckeningh, op sijne reysen, soo van Cabo Verde, Angola, Gunea, Oost-Indien. [1605–30]. 112 pp. 6 pl. on 1 sheet. sm. 4°. *Amstelredam, J. Hartgerts*, 1648.
[*In* HARTGERTS (J.) Oost-indische voyagien, v. 1, 7e stuck].

Broglie (Albert de). Questions de religion et d'histoire. 2 v. xx, 415 pp; 2 p. l. 429 pp. 1 l. 8°. *Paris, M. Lévy frères*, 1860.

Bronson (*Rev.* Asahel). A plain exhibition of methodist episcopacy. 259 pp. 12°. *Burlington, (Vt.) C. Goodrich*, 1844.

Brookes (James H. *d. d.*) The way made plain. 490 pp. 16°. *Philadelphia, American sunday-school union*, [1871].

Brookes (Matthew, *d. d.*) The sacred and most mysterious history of mans redemption. Wherein is set forth the gracious administration of Gods covenant with man-kind, at all times, from the beginning of the world unto the end. Historically digested into three books. 1 p. l. 276 pp. 4 l. fol. *London, W. Wilson, for author*, 1657.

Brookline (*Mass.*) The Brookline, Jamaica Plain and West Roxbury directory for 1871; containing a general directory of the residents, town registers, business directory, maps, &c. no. ii. 208, 40 pp. 1 map. 8°. *Boston, Dean Dudley & co.* 1871.

Brooklyn (*N. Y.*) The Brooklyn city and business directory for the year ending May 1st, 1872. Containing also a street and avenue directory and an appendix. Compiled by Geo. T. Lain. 2 p. l. [960] pp. 8°. *Brooklyn, Lain & co.* [1871].

——— Brooklyn street and avenue directory and guide. 81 pp. 12°. *Brooklyn, G. T. Lain*, [1871].

Brooks (Edward). The normal elementary algebra: containing the first principles of the science, developed with conciseness and simplicity. 287 pp. 12°. *Philadelphia, Sower, Barnes & Potts*, [1871].

Brooks (Jonathan). Antiquity; or the wise instructor. Being a collection of the most valuable admonitions and sentences, compendiously put together. xxviii, 324 pp. 12°. *Bristol, J. Brooks*, [1770].

Brooks (*Mrs.* Maria Gowen). Zophiel, a poem. [First canto]. 70 pp. 1 l. 16°. *Boston, Richardson & Lord*, 1825.

Brooks (Nathan Covington, *ll. d.*) Harmonia evangelica. 1871. *See* **Bible.** (*Greek*).

——— Scriptural anthology; or, biblical illustrations: designed as a christmas and birthday present. 1837. Eng. title, 180 pp. 9 pl. 18°. *Philadelphia, W. Marshall & co.* 1836.

——— The same. Eng. title, 180 pp. 9 pl. 8°. *Philadelphia, W. Marshall & co.* 1837.

Brooks (*Rev.* Thomas). The mute christian under the smarting rod: with sovereign antidotes for every case. 1 p. l. 246 pp. 18°. *Boston, S. Goldsmith*, 1841.

Brooks (William H.) A geography of Massachusetts. Also a geography of Middlesex co. *See* **Carter** (J. G.) *and* **Brooks.**

Brosses (Charles de). Traité de la formation méchanique des langues et des principes physiques de l'étymologie. 2 v. 1 p. l. lii, 452 pp. 9 pl; 498 pp. 12°. *Paris, Terrelonge an ix.* [1801].

Brot (Charles Alphonse). La comtesse aux trois galants, dernières amours. 2 v. 2 p. l. 286 pp; 2 p. l. 287 pp. 16°. *Bruxelles, Meline, Cans & cie*, 1839.

Brotherhead (Alfred P.) Himself his worst enemy: or, Philip duke of Wharton's career. 374 pp. 12°. *Philadelphia, J. P. Lippincott & co.* 1871.

Brougham (Henry, *baron Brougham and Vaux*). The critical and miscellaneous writings of Henry lord Brougham, to which is prefixed a sketch of his character. 2 v. ix, 25–349 pp; 330 pp. 12°. *Philadelphia, Lea & Blanchard*, 1841.

——— The life and times of Henry lord Brougham, written by himself. 3 v. 8°. *Edinburgh & London, W. Blackwood & sons*, 1871.

——— The same. 3 v. 12°. *New York, Harper & brothers*, 1871–72.

Broughton (*Rev.* Hugh). A concent of scripture. Eng. title, 37 l. 4 pl. 4°. [*London*, 1596]?
[*With* BIBLE. (*English*). Genevan version. *London, R. Barker*, 1610].

Broughton (Rhoda). "Good-bye, sweetheart!" A novel. 437 pp. 12°. *New York, D. Appleton & co.* 1872.

Broughton (*Rev.* Thomas). A prospect of futurity, in four dissertations on the nature and circumstances of the life to come: with a preliminary discourse on the natural and moral evidences of a future state; and an appendix on the general conflagration, or burning of the world. xvi, 519 pp. 8°. *London, T. Cadell*, 1768.

Broussais (François Joseph Victor). On irritation and insanity. A work, wherein the relations of the physical with the moral conditions of man are established on the basis of physiological medicine. Translated by Thomas Cooper, m. d. [With] two tracts on materialism, and an outline of the association of ideas. By Thomas Cooper, m. d. 408 pp. 8°. *Columbia (S. C.) S. J. McMorris*, 1831.

——— Principles of physiological medicine, in the form of propositions; embracing physiology, pathology, and therapeutics, with commentaries on those relating to pathology. Translated from the french, by Isaac Hays m. d. and R. Eglesfeld Griffith, m. d. 594 pp. 8°. *Philadelphia, Carey & Lea*, 1832.

Brown (Charles B.) Geological survey of British Guiana. *See* **British Guiana.**

Brown (*Rev.* George). The volume of creation; as illustrating the power, wisdom, and goodness of God. xix, 605 pp. 8°. *Berwick-upon-Tweed, author*, 1846.

Brown (James Baldwin). Memoirs of [John] Howard, compiled from his diary, his confidential letters, and other authentic documents. Abridged by a gentleman of Boston, from the London quarto edition. Eng. title, 4 l. 352 pp. 2 portraits. 16°. *Boston, Lincoln & Edmands*, 1831.

Brown (*Rev.* John, *of Haddington*). Sacred tropology: or, a brief view of the figures, and explication of the metaphors, contained in scripture. 417 pp. 12°. *London, W. Baynes*, 1802.

Brown (*Rev.* John, *of Haverhill, Mass.*) The examiner examin'd. An answer to the rev. mr. Prescott's examination of certain remarks. By the author of the remarks. [*anon.*] 105 pp. 12°. *Boston, printed by T. Fleet*, 1736.

——— Letter, to rev. John Cotton, containing a remarkable account of the extraordinary impressions made on the inhabitants of Haverhill, by the earthquake that shook New England, Nov. 1727. 5 pp. 12°. *Boston, S. Gerrish*, 1727.

[Cotton (*Rev.* John). A holy fear of God and his judgments, 1727].

Brown (*Rev.* John)—continued.

——— Ordination sermon preach'd at Arundel, Nov. 4, 1730. When rev. Thomas Prentice was ordained. 1 p. l. 5–30 pp. 16°. *Boston, T. Hancock*, 1731.

Brown (John, *d. d. of Edinburgh*). The aged minister's resolutions in the prospect of death. 16°. [*London, A. Fullarton & co.* 1854].

[*In* Discourses and services on occasion of the death of the late rev. Ralph Wardlaw, d. d. 1854. pp. 15–42].

Brown (*Rev.* John, *of Gartmore*). Vindication of the presbyterian form of church-government, as professed in the standards of the church of Scotland. In a series of letters, addressed to mr. Innes. With an appendix containing remarks on mr. Haldane's view of social worship. xii, 384 pp. 12°. *Edinburgh, H. Inglis*, 1805.

Brown (*Rev.* John Newton). Encyclopedia of religious knowledge: or, dictionary of the bible, theology, religious biography, all religions, ecclesiastical history, and missions. [With] a missionary gazetteer, containing descriptions of the various missionary stations throughout the globe; by rev. B. B. Edwards. Revised and corrected to date by rev. Geo. P. Tyler. Eng. title, 1275 pp. 19 pl. 4 maps. 8°. *Brattleboro' (Vt.) J. Steen & co.* 1858.

Brown (*Rev.* Moses B.) Elocution and voice-culture. 12°. [*Philadelphia, E. H. Butler & co.* 1872].

[*In* Lyons (Joseph A.) The American elocutionist, and dramatic reader, pp. 9–98].

Brown (Paul). An enquiry concerning the nature, end and practicability of a course of philosophical education; to which is subjoined a moral catechism. iv, 394 pp. 12°. *Washington, author*, 1822.

Brown (Rawdon, *editor*). Calendar of state papers and manuscripts, relating to english affairs, existing in the archives and collections of Venice, and in other libraries of northern Italy. v. 4. 1527–1533. 8°. *London*, 1871.

[Great Britain. *Treas. depart. Master of the rolls*].

Brown (Solyman). An essay on american poetry, with several miscellaneous pieces on a variety of subjects. 191 pp. 12°. *New Haven, H. Howe*, 1818.

Brown (*Capt.* Tarleton). Memoirs of Tarleton Brown, a captain in the revolutionary army, written by himself, with a preface and notes, by Charles I. Bushnell. 65 pp. 3 pl. 8° *New York, privately printed*, 1862.

Brown (Thurlow W.) Minnie Hermon; or, the night and its morning. 472 pp. 1 portrait. 12°. *Auburn & Buffalo, Miller, Orton & Mulligan*, 1854.

Brown (William Lawrence, *d. d.*) Philemon; or the progress of virtue; a poem. 2 v. 1 p. l. xxv, 206 pp; 2 p. l. 290 pp. 1 l. 16°. *Edinburgh, J. Ballantyne & co.* 1809.

Browne (Daniel J.) Letters from the Canary islands. 140 pp. 1 pl. 12°. *Boston, G. W. Light*, 1834.

Browne (Frances Elizabeth). Ruth: a sacred drama, and original lyrical poems. viii, 121 pp. 12°. *New York, Wynkoop & Hallenbeck*, 1871.

Browne (Henry H.) Insurance maps of the city of New York. v. 5, 1871. *See* **Perris** (William G.) *and* **Browne**.

Browne (Isaac Hawkins). The immortality of the soul: a poem from the latin: translated by John Lettice. [Also], the original poem; with a commentary and annotations, by the translator. 8 p. l. 312 pp. 8°. *Cambridge, J. Archdeacon & J. Burges*, 1795.

Browne (Matthew). Chaucer's England. 2 v. 3 p. l. 317 pp. 1 portrait; 3 p. l. 331 pp. 12°. *London, Hurst & Blackett*, 1869.

Browne (S. H.) The manual of commerce. Containing a concise account of the source, mode of production or manufacture of the principal articles of commerce. 429 pp. 12°. *Springfield (Mass.) Bill, Nichols & co.* 1871.

Browne (*Sir* Thomas, *m. d.*) Religio medici. A letter to a friend. Christian morals. Urn-burial, and other papers. xviii, 432 pp. 1 portrait. 16°. *Boston, Ticknor & Fields*, 1862.

——— The same. La religion du médecin, c'est à dire: description nécessaire par Thomas Brown, touchant son opinion accordante avec le pur service divin d'Angleterre. Eng. title, 11 p. l. 360 pp. 18°. [*Paris*], 1668.

Browne (William Hardcastle). Heart-throbs of eminent authors. 304 pp. 12°. *Philadelphia and Boston, G. Maclean*, 1872.

Browning (Elizabeth Barrett). Poems of memory and hope. With illustrations by Hennessy and Thwaites. 162 pp. 1 portrait. 12°. *New York, J. Miller*, 1872.

——— Poetical works. Complete in one volume. Corrected by the last London ed. 533 pp. 11 pl. 1 portrait. sq. 16°. *New York, J. Miller*, 1871.

Browning (Henry C.) Life of Goethe from his autobiographical papers. *See* **Goethe** (J. W. von).

Browning (Samuel). Poems. v. 1. 320 pp. 1 portrait. 8°. *London, author*, 1846.

Brownlee (William Craig, *d. d.*) The christian father at home; or, a manual of parental instruction. 252 pp. 1 pl. 18°. *New-York, R. Carter*, 1837.

——— The christian youths' book; and manual for young communicants. 480 pp. 1 portrait. 12°. *New York, R. Carter*, 1839.

——— Letters in the roman catholic controversy. 2d ed. xi, [364] pp. 1 portrait. 8°. *New York, author*, 1834.

Brown-Séquard (Charles Édouard). A course of lectures on the physiology and pathology of the central nervous system. xii, 276 pp. 3 pl. 8°. *Philadelphia, Collins*, 1860.

Brownson (Orestes Augustus). New views of christianity, society, and the church. xi, 116 pp. 12°. *Boston, J. Munroe & co.* 1836.

Bruce (Hamilton). The custom-house guide: a compendium of revenue laws and regulations governing the importations and exportations of merchandise; the registry, enrolling and licensing of vessels, with a general summary of the routine of business at custom-houses in the United States. To which is added a list of all the commercial ports of the world. 322 pp. 8°. *New York, E. & G. W. Blunt*, 1863.

——— The same. Commercial regulations of the port of New York and custom house guide. [With] the pilot and quarantine laws and harbor regulations of the port of New York. 2d and enlarged ed. 448 pp. 1 pl. 8°. *New York, E. & G. W. Blunt*, 1864.

——— The ware-house manual, and general custom house guide, with forms of entries, oaths, bonds, etc. Schedule of the rates of storage, adopted by the chamber of commerce of the city of New York, provisions relative to drawback, extracts from treasury regulations, etc. 216 pp. 8°. *New York, author*, 1862.

Bruce (John) *and* **Hamilton** (William Douglas) *editors*. Calendar of state papers, domestic series, of the reign of Charles i. 1638-39. *London*, 1871.

[Great Britain. *Treasury department. Master of the rolls*].

Bruce (S. D. *and* B. G.) Frank Forester's horse and horsemanship of the U. S. *See* **Herbert** (Henry William).

Bruce (S. D.) *and* **Carvalho** (E. N.) American turf register. A correct synopsis of turf events in the United States, embracing running, trotting and pacing, for 1870. 393 pp. 8°. *New York, Bruce & co.* 1871.

Bruciad (The), an epic poem, in six books. [*anon.*] xvi, 237 pp. 8°. *London, J. Dodsley*, 1769.

Brückmann (Franz Ernst). Relatio brevis historico-botanico-medica de avellana mexicana, vvlgo cacao dicta. Ed. secvnda priori avctior. 30 pp. 1 l. 2 pl. sm. 4°. *Brvnsvigae, L. Schroeder*, 1728.

Bruckner (William H.) American manures. *See* **Chynoweth** (J. B.) *and* **Bruckner**.

Brueghel (Johannes). *See* **Crivelli** (Giovanni).

Brugge (Jacob Segersz. van der). Twee journalen yeder gehouden by seven matroosen. In haer overwinteren op Spitsbergen, gelegen in Groenland, t'zedert het vertreck van de visschery-schepen der Geoctroyerde noortsche compagnie, [etc.] 36 pp. sm. 4°. *Amsterdam, G. J. Zaagman*, [*about* 1640].

Bruhier d'Ablaincourt (Jean Jacques). Caprices d'imagination, ou lettres sur différens sujets d'histoire, de morale, de critique, d'histoire naturelle, etc. [*anon.*] 6 p. l. 514 pp. 12°. *Paris, Briasson*, 1740.

Brullé (Auguste). Histoire naturelle des insectes. *See* **Audouin** (J. V.) *and* **Brullé**.

Brunet (*L'abbé* Ovide). Catalogue des végétaux ligneux du Canada pour servir à l'intelligence des collections de bois économiques envoyées à l'exposition universelle de Paris, 1867. 64 pp. 4 pl. 8°. *Québec, C. Darveau*, 1867. s.

——— Éléments de botanique et de physiologie végétale suivis d'une petite flore simple et facile pour aider à découvrir les noms des plantes les plus communes du Canada. 155 pp. 12°. *Québec, P. G. Delisle*, 1870. s.

——— Énumérations des genres de plantes de la flore du Canada, précédée des tableaux analytiques des familles (etc.) 45 pp. 12°. *Québec, G. & G. E. Desbarats*, 1864. s.

——— Histoire de picea qui se rencontrent dans les limites du Canada. 16 pp. 3 pl. 8°. *Québec, l'auteur*, 1866. s.

——— Notice sur le musée botanique de l'université Laval. Discours prononcé en séance solennelle le 8 juillet 1867. 14 pp. 8°. *Québec, A. Coté et cie.* 1867. s.

Brunet (*L'abbé* Ovide)—continued.

——— Notice sur les plantes de Michaux et sur son voyage au Canada et la baie d'Hudson d'après son journal manuscrit et autres documents inédits. 44 pp. 1 l. 8°. *Québec, bureau de L'abeille*, 1863. s.

Bruni *aretino* (Leonardo). Epistolarum libri viii, ad fidem codd. mss. suppleti, et castigati, et plusquam xxxvi epistolis, quae in editione quoque fabriciana deerant, locupletati recensente Laurentio Mehus. Accessere ejusdem epistolae populi florentini nomine scriptae. 2 v. 6 p. l. cxxviii, 142 pp; xxiv, 256 pp. 8°. *Florentiae, sump. J. Rigaccii*, 1741. s.

——— Libro della gverra de Ghotti, composto in lingua latina et fatto uulgare da Lodouico Petroni. Nuouamente stampato. 87 l. numb. 16°. *Firenze, per li heredi di P. di Giunta*, 1526.

Bruns (Victor). Lehrbuch der allgemeinen anatomie des menschen. Nach eigenen untersuchungen zum gebrauche bei vorlesungen, sowie zum selbststudium für practische ærzte und wundärzte. xxii, 398 pp. 8°. *Braunschweig, F. Vieweg & sohn*, 1841. s.

Bryant (Alfred). The attractions of the world to come. 308 pp. 12°. *New York, M. W. Dodd*, 1853.

Bryant (Thomas Sydenham, *m. d.*) Examinations in anatomy and physiology; being a complete series of questions and answers; to which are annexed, tables of the bones, muscles, and arteries. 404 pp. 2 tab. 12°. *Philadelphia, author*, 1835.

Bryant (William Cullen). A forest hymn. With illustrations by John A. Hums. 32 l. 8°. *New York, W. A. Townsend & co.* 1861.

——— The Odyssey of Homer translated into blank verse. *See* **Homer**.

Bryce (James). The holy roman empire. 3d ed. [Preceded by a chronological table of emperors and popes]. xxvii, 432 pp. 12°. *London, Macmillan & co.* 1871.

Bubbles and ballast. *See* **Bouligny** (*Mrs.* M. E. Parker).

Buchanan (George). Agrius, [an eclogue]. Amaryllis, [an eclogue]. Written in latin. [Translated into english, by John Rooke]. 8°. [*London*, 1725].

[Rooke (John). Select translations, part 2, pp. 44–62, 1726].

——— Baptistes: a sacred dramatic poem, in defence of liberty; as, written in latin, by mr. G. Buchanan: translated into english, by mr. John Milton: and first published

Buchanan (George)—continued.

1641. By order of the house of commons. 4°. *London*, 1740.

[*In* PECK (Francis). New memoirs of mr. John Milton. 1740. pp. 265–428.
Note.—"Ascribed by Peck, but on slender grounds, to Milton."—*Lowndes*].

——— Poemata in tres partes digesta. G. Buchanani, vita ab ipso scripto. Adjecta sunt paraphrasi psalmorum. Item collectanea. Etiam diversa carminum genera margini adjecta opera & studio N. Chytræi. 6 p. l. 592 pp. 16°. *Londini, B. Griffin*, 1686.

——— The same. Poemata quæ extant. Eng. title, 7 p. l. 556 pp. 6 l. 24°. *Amstelædami, apud H. Wetstenium*, 1687.

CONTENTS.

Psalmorum Davidis paraphrasis poetica.
Jephthes, sive votum, tragœdia.
Baptistes, sive calumnia, tragœdia.
Franciscanus et fratres.
Fratres fraterrimi.
Elegiarum liber 1.
Sylvarum liber 1.
Hendecasyllabon liber 1.
Jambon liber 1.
Epigrammatum libri 3.
Miscellaneorum liber 1.
De sphæra mundi libri 5.
Euripidis Medea & Alcestis latino carmine reddita.

Buchler (Johann). Laconicarvm epistolarvm thesavrvs bipartitvs: prior latinorvm, alter graecorvm breviores, easdemque argutas, iucundas & politulas continet epistolas. Opera m. Ioannis Bvchleri à Gladbach, collectus & digestus. 4 p. l. 662 pp. 1 l. 18°. *Coloniae, sumptibus B. Gualtheri*, 1606.

Büchner (Louis). Force and matter: empirico-philosophical studies, intelligibly rendered, with an additional introduction expressly written for the english edition. Edited, from the last edition of "Kraft und Stoff," by J. Frederick Collingwood. Second english, completed from the tenth german ed. ciii, 271 pp. 1 portrait. 12°. *London, Trübner & co.* 1870.

Buchon (Jean Alexandre C. *editor*). Choix d'ouvrages mystiques. Avec notices littéraires. 764 pp. 8°. *Paris, société du panthéon littéraire*, 1843.

CONTENTS.

AUGUSTINUS (*St.* Aurelius). Confessions, traduites par Arnault d'Andilly.
——— Méditations, traduction anonyme.
BERNARD (*St.*) Traité de la considération, traduite par Antoine de Saint Gabriel.
BLOIS (François Louis de). Le directeur des âmes religieuses, trad. par L. Jouard de Lanauze.
BOETHIUS (Anicius M. T. S.) Consolation de la philosophie, traduite par Léon Colesse.
BONA (Giovanni, *cardinale*). Principes de la vie chrétienne, traduit par Lambert.
——— Le chemin du ciel, traduit par Louis Cousin.
IMITATION de Jésus-Christ. Par Jean Gersen, traduction par Nicholas Beauzée.
TAULER (Johann). Institutions: traduction des frères-précheurs de Saint-Germain.

Buc'hoz (Pierre Joseph). Herbier, ou collecection des plantes médicinales de la Chine, d'après un manuscrit peint et unique qui se trouve dans la bibliothèque de l'empereur de la Chine, pour servir de suitte à la collection des fleurs qui se cultivent dans les jardins de la Chine et de l'Europe. 1 p. l. 100 pl. 1 l. fol. *Paris, auteur*, 1781.

Buck (*Rev.* Charles). The young christian's guide; or, suitable directions, cautions, and encouragement, to the believer, on his first entrance into the divine life. From the 2d London ed. [With selections]. 251 pp. 12°. *New Haven, for the subscribers*, 1812.

——— The same. With an introductory essay. By rev. T. T. Waterman. 180 pp. 18°. *Providence, Weeden & Cory*, 1834.

Buck (Dudley). Second motette collection. 188 pp. obl. 4°. *Boston, O. Ditson & co.* [1871].

Buck (*Rev.* William C.) The baptist hymn book. Original and selected. 350 l. 18°. *Louisville, J. Eliot & co.* 1842.

Bucke (Charles). On the life, writings, and genius of Akenside: with some account of his friends. 4 p. l. 312 pp. 1 portrait. 8°. *London, J. Cochrane & co.* 1832.

Buckingham (C. P.) A new arithmetic on the unit system: in which the fundamental principles of arithmetic are familiarly explained and illustrated. 447 pp. 12°. *Philadelphia, Claxton, Remsen & Haffelfinger*, 1869.

——— The principles of arithmetic, explained and illustrated. 447 pp. 12°. *Philadelphia, Claxton, Remsen & Haffelfinger* 1872.

Buckler (John Chessell). An historical and descriptive account of the royal palace at Eltham. 2 p. l. 108 pp. 1 pl. 8°. *London, J. B. Nichols & son*, 1828.

Buckminster (*Rev.* Joseph Stevens). Works; with memoirs of his life. 2 v. 435 pp; xiii, 435 pp. 12°. *Boston, J. Munroe & co.* 1839.

Buckwalter (P. W.) Machinists', engineers' and firemen's friend. The practical form to divide the valves and set the eccentric on a locomotive, link motion engine, and on a direct and a indirect motion, stationary engine. 93 pp. 1 pl. sq. 16°. *Pittsburgh (Pa.) E. Luft*, 1871.

Budd (*Rev.* Henry). Infant-baptism the means of national reformation according to

Budd (*Rev.* Henry)—continued. the doctrine and discipline of the established church. In nine letters to a friend. 3d ed. With a preface, in which it is designed to vindicate baptismal regeneration. viii, cclxxxiv, 520 pp. 12°. *London, R. B. Seeley & W. Burnside*, 1831.

——— The same. 3d ed. 1 p. l. viii, 520 pp. 12°. *London, Seeley, Burnside & Seeley*, 1843.

——— A memoir of the rev. Henry Budd: comprising an autobiography; letters, papers, and remains, &c. viii, 640 pp. 1 portrait. 12°. *London, Seeley, Jackson & Halliday*, 1855.

Buddicom (*Rev.* Robert Pedder). Friendship with God illustrated in the life of Abraham: a series of discourses. 2 v. xxiv, 482 pp; xii, 512 pp. 12°. *London, R. B. Seeley*, 1839.

Buddington (Zadel Barnes). Can the old love? A novel. 198 pp. 8°. *Boston, J. R. Osgood & co.* 1871.
[OSGOOD's library of novels, no. 4].

Budgen (L. M.) Live coals; or, faces from the fire. 1 p. l. xii, 78 pp. 35 col. pl. 4°. *London, L. Reeve & co.* 1867.

Budget (A) of humorous poetry. Comprising specimens of the best and most humorous productions of the popular american and foreign poetical writers of the day. By the author of the "Book of anecdotes and budget of fun." [*anon.*] 320 pp. 12°. *Philadelphia, G. G. Evans*, 1859.

Buffalo. *Board of trade.* Statement of trade and commerce for 1869. With comparisons of previous years; with important commercial statistics and statements. Reported by William Thurstone. 8°. *Buffalo, Warren, Johnson & co.* 1870.

——— The same. Statistics and information relative to the trade and commerce of Buffalo, 1871. 8°. *Buffalo, Warren, Johnson & co.* 1872.

Buffon's natural history. *See* **Wright** (John). Natural history.

Bugle (The) call; or, a summons to work in Christ's army. By a volunteer nurse. [*anon.*] 160 pp. 18°. *New York, American tract society*, [1871].

Buhle (Johann Gottlieb). Lehrbuch der geschichte der philosophie und einer kritischen literatur derselben. 8 v. in 9. 12°. *Göttingen, Vandenhoeck & Ruprecht*, 1796–1804.

Builder (The); an illustrated weekly magazine, for the architect, engineer, archæologist, constructor, sanitary reformer, and art-lover. Conducted by George Godwin. For 1870–71. v. 28–29. fol. *London*, [*Wyman & sons, printers*, 1870–71].

Buist (George, *d. d.*) Sermon. Matthew xiii, 55, 56. 12°. [*New Haven*, 1812].
[*In* BUCK (*Rev.* Charles). The young christian's guide. (Selections). pp. 203–220].

Bulenger. *See* **Boulenger.**

Bulfinch (Stephen Greenleaf, *d. d.*) Honor; or, the slave-dealer's daughter. 238 pp. 12°. *Boston, W. V. Spencer*, 1864.

——— Manual of the evidences of christianity, for classes and private reading. viii, 147 pp. 12°. *Boston, W. V. Spencer*, 1866.

Bulfinch (Thomas). The boy inventor; a memoir of Matthew Edwards, mathematical-instrument maker. [*anon.*] 110 pp. 1 pl. 1 portrait. 16°. *Boston, Walker, Wise & co.* 1860.

——— Legends of Charlemagne; or romance of the middle ages. xx, 373 pp. 6 pl. 12°. *Boston, J. E. Tilton & co.* 1863.

Bullar (John). Memoirs of the late rev. William Kingsbury. vii, 284 pp. 8°. *London, Black*, 1819.

Bulletin du bouquiniste. [Semi-mensuel]. 1er janvier 1857 jusqu' à 15 déc. 1871. 1e–15e année. v. 1–28. 8°. *Paris, A. Aubry*, 1857–71.
[*Note.*—Publication suspended, from Aug. 1, 1870 to July 15, 1871].

Bullinger (Henry). The christen state of matrymonye, wherin housbandes & wyfes maye lerne to kepe house together wyth loue. [*anon.* Translated by Myles Coverdale, bishop of Exeter]. *b. l.* 91 l. 4 l. unp. 24°. [*London*], 1543.

Bulwer-Lytton. *See* **Lytton.**

Bunbury (*Mrs.* Sarah Susanna). Life and letters of Robert Clement Sconce. Compiled for his grandchildren, by his daughter, Sarah Susanna Bunbury. 2 v. xv, 349 pp. 1 l; vii, 414 pp. 1 l. 8°. *London, Cox & Wyman*, 1861.

Bunce (J. Thackray). Cloudland and shadowland. 166 pp. 8 pl. sm. 4°. *London, Cassell, Petter & Galpin*, [1871]?

Bungener (Louis Félix). Calvin, sa vie, son œuvre et ses écrits. 515 pp. 16°. *Paris, J. Cherbuliez*, 1862.

——— Julien, ou la fin d'un siècle. 4 v. 12°. *Paris, J. Cherbuliez*, 1854.

Bungener (Louis Félix)—continued.

——— Trois sermons sous Louis xv. 3e éd. 3 v. 12°. *Paris, J. Cherbuliez*, 1854.

CONTENTS.

v. 1. Un sermon à la cour.
v. 2. Un sermon à la ville.
v. 3. Un sermon au désert.

——— Un sermon sous Louis xiv. suivi de deux soirées à l'hôtel de Rambouillet. 4e éd. 2 p. l. 341 pp. 12°. *Paris, J. Cherbuliez*, 1853.

Bunn (Alfred). The Bohemian girl. The music by M. N. Balfe. The words by A. Bunn. [Libretto, without music]. 40 pp. 8°. [*New York, W. C. Bryant & co.* 1871.
[PAREPA-ROSA grand english opera].

Bünting (Heinrich) *and* **Letzner** (Johann). Braunschweig-lüneburgische chronica, oder: historische beschreibung der durchlauchtigsten herzogen zu Braunschweig und Lüneburg; aus vielen gedruckten alten und neuen chronicken, getragen und beschrieben, fürnemlich aber durch des Letzneri gantzen Historia Caroli magni aus den chronicis mstis der städte Braunschweig, Lüneburg und Hannover vermehret. Mit gehörigen notis, documentis, sigillis, insignibus, nummis tam bracteatis quam solidis, & monumentis publicis bestärcket, und biss auf die jetzige zeiten continuiret, von Philippo Julio Rehtmeier. 3 v. fol. *Braunschweig, D. Detleffsen*, 1722.

Bunyan (John). The works of that eminent servant of Christ, John Bunyan, minister of the gospel. Illustrated edition. 2 v. in 1. 1015 pp. 15 pl. 1 portrait, 1 fac-simile. 8°. *Philadelphia, Bradley & co.* 1871.

——— Heart's ease in heart-trouble. Or, a sovereign remedy against all trouble of heart that Christ's disciples are subject to, under all kinds of afflictions in this life. 179 pp. 16°. *Brattleborough (Vt.) W. Fessenden*, 1813.

Burbury *or* **Burbery** (John). The history of the sacred and royal majesty of Christina Alessandra, queen of Swedland, with the reasons of her late conversion to the roman catholique religion. As also a relation of the severall entertainments given her by divers princes in her journey to Rome, with her reception in that city. [1st ed.] 15 p. l. 478 pp. 18°. *London, T. W.* 1658.

Burden-bearing: a story about Jenny Ellis. [*anon.*] 196 pp. 3 pl. 16°. *Philadelphia, American sunday school union*, 1870.

Burder (John). Life of Thomas Harrison Burder, m. d. with extracts from his correspondence. [*anon.*] viii, 206 pp. 18°. *Oxford, J. H. Parker*, 1845.
[*Note.*—This "is little more than an abridgement of the memoir published by" John Burder].

Burder (*Rev.* Samuel). Memoirs of eminently pious women. *See* **Gibbons** (Thomas, *d. d.*)

Burdett (Charles). Telemachus versified. *See* **Fénélon** (François de Salignac de La Mothe).

Burdett (*Rev.* Staunton S.) The baptist harmony: being a selection of choice hymns and spiritual songs for social worship. xx, 485 pp. 18°. *Philadelphia, T. W. Ustick*, 1834.

Burdon (Hannah D.) Seymour of Sudley; or, the last of the Franciscans. 3 v. 12°. *London, R. Bentley*, 1836.

Bureau (The): devoted to the commerce, manufactures, and general industries of the United States. [A monthly magazine]. Oct. 1869, to Sept. 1871. v. 1-2. 4° and 8°. *Chicago, the bureau printing co.* [1869-71].

Burgassi (Antonio Cesare). Serie dell' edizioni aldine, per ordine cronologico ed alfabetico. 3a ed. [con notizie da F. L. Baroni]. viii, 195 pp. 1 l. 2 portraits. 8°. *Firenzi, G. Molini*, 1803.

Bürger (Gottfried August). The wild huntsman. From the german, by Charles J. Lukens (etc.) 22 pp. 8°. *Philadelphia, Collins*, 1870.

Burgersdicius. *See* **Burgersdijk.**

Burgersdijk (Frenz). Institutionum logicarum libri duo. 9 p. l. 288, 62 pp. 18°. *Londini, ex officina R. Danielis*, 1651.

Burges (Bartholomew). A series of Indostan letters. Containing a striking account of the manners & customs of the gentoo nations, & of the Moguls and other mahomedan tribes in Indostan. xxv, 168 pp. 1 pl. 16°. *N. York, author*, [1790]?

Burgess (*Rev.* Ebenezer). What is truth? An inquiry concerning the antiquity and unity of the human race; with an examination of recent scientific speculations on those subjects. 424 pp. 12°. *Boston, I. P. Warren*, [1871].

Burgess (George, *d. d.*) The last enemy; conquering and conquered. 330 pp. 12°. *Philadelphia, H. Hooker*, 1850.

Burgess (Thomas). Observationes in Sophoclis Œdipum tyrannum, Œdipum coloneum, Antigonam: Euripidis Phœnissas, Æschyli

Burgess (Thomas)—continued.
Septem contra Thebas. 2 p. l. 143 pp. 8°. *Oxonii, J. & J. Fletcher,* 1778.
[*In* BURTON (John, *m. d.*) Pentalogia, v. 2].

Burgess (—, *d. d.*) Meditations, day by day. 126 pp. sq. 16°. *Boston, Gould & Lincoln,* 1871.

Burgundia (Antonius a). *See* **Bourgoigne** (Antoine).

Burk (James H.) First quarrels and first discords in married life: to which is added a matrimonial peace-offering. 291 pp. 12°. *Cincinnati, Applegate & co.* 1860.

Burke (*Sir* John Bernard). A genealogical and heraldic dictionary of the peerage and baronetage of the british empire. 33d ed. 1 p. l. xc, 1331 pp. 8°. *London, Harrison,* 1871.

——— A genealogical and heraldic history of the landed gentry of Great Britain and Ireland. 5th ed. 2 v. 2 p. l. iii, 746 pp; 2 p. l. pp. 747-1600. 8°. *London, Harrison,* 1871.

Burke's magazine for boys and girls. [Monthly]. Jan. to Dec. 1871. v. 1. 8°. *Macon, (Ga.) J. W. Burke & co.* 1871.
[Discontinued].

Burleigh (Joseph Bartlett, *ll. d.*) The constitution of the United States, with a complete index; and Washington's farewell address, to which are appended the one hundred and fifteen items and paragraphs in Washington's original manuscript, that he afterwards either omitted or amended. With a synopsis, parallel, and sphere of the national and state governments. 120 pp. 12°. *Philadelphia, Claxton, Remsen & Haffelfinger,* 1872.

——— New series of school readers. The thinker, in four numbers. v. 1-3. 18° and 12°. *Philadelphia, Claxton, Remsen & Haffelfinger,* 1872.

——— The same. The thinker, no. iv, or the american manual. Complete in itself. Containing an outline of the origin and progress of government; the law of nations; a clear explanation of the constitution of the United States. Stereotyped ed. 352, 44 pp. 12°. *Philadelphia, Claxton, Remsen & Haffelfinger,* 1872.

Burleigh (William Henry). Poems. 248 pp. 12°. *Philadelphia, J. M. M'Kim,* 1841.

——— The same. With a sketch of his life. By Celia Burleigh. xlviii, 306 pp. 1 portrait. 12°. *New York, Hurd & Houghton,* 1871.

——— The rum fiend and other poems. 46 pp. 3 pl. 12°. *New York, National temperance society & publication house,* 1871.

Burn (David). Plays, and fugitive pieces, in verse. v. 1. 3 p. l. 409 pp. 8°. *Hobart Town, W. Pratt,* 1842.
[No more published].

Burnap (George W. *d. d.*) Lectures on the doctrines of christianity, in controversy between unitarians and other denominations of christians. 394 pp. 12°. *Baltimore, W. R. Lucas & R. N. Wright,* 1835.

——— Miscellaneous writings. Collected and revised by the author. 343 pp. 12°. *Baltimore, J. Murray,* 1845.

Burnet (Gilbert, *bishop of Salisbury*). A sixth collection of papers relating to the present juncture of affairs in England. [*anon.*] 1 p. l. 34 pp. sm. 4°. *London, R. Janeway,* 1689.

CONTENTS.

i. Five letters from Scotland, giving account of expelling popery from thence.
ii. The prince of Orange's speech to Scots lords met at St. James's.
iii. A letter to a friend, advising how to free the nation from slavery.
iv. The application of the bishop and clergy of London to the prince of Orange, Sept. 21, 1688.
v. An address of the nonconformist ministers of London, to the prince of Orange.
vi. The address of the city of Bristol to the prince of Orange.
vii. A word to the wise, for setling the government.
viii. A modest proposal to the present convention.
ix. An historical account touching the succession of the crown.
x. A narrative of the miseries of New-England, by reason of an arbitrary government erected there.

Burnet (Thomas, *ll. d. master of the Charter-house*). A review of the theory of the earth and of its proofs: especially in reference to scripture. 1 p. l. 52 pp. fol. *London, W. Kettilby,* 1690.

——— The theory of the earth: containing an account of the original of the earth, and of all the general changes which it has already undergone, or is to undergo, till the consummation of all things. The two last books, concerning the burning of the world, and concerning the new heavens and new earth. 8 p. l. 224 pp. fol. *London, W. Kettilby,* 1690.

Burnet (Thomas, *d. d. rector of Westkington*). The demonstration of true religion, in a chain of consequences from certain and undeniable principles; wherein the necessity and certainty of natural and reveal'd religion, with the nature and reason of both, are prov'd and explain'd: and in particular, the authority of the christian revelation is establish'd. In sixteen sermons; preach'd at Bow-church, in the years 1724 and 1725 fol. [*London,* 1739].
[BOYLE lectures, v. 3, pp. 401-580].

Burnham (George P.) Burnham's new poultry book. A practical treatise on selecting, housing and breeding domestic fowls, and raising poultry and eggs for market. 342 pp. 5 pl. 12°. *New York, American news co.* 1871.

——— Memoirs of the United States secret service. [Compiled, by permission, from the department records]. With accurate portraits of prominent members of the detective force. Some of their most notable captures, and a brief account of the life of Col. H. C. Whiteley, chief of the division. 436 pp. 17 pl. 12°. *Boston, Lee & Shepard,* 1872.

Burnham (*Rev.* Richard). Pious memorials; or, the power of religion upon the mind in sickness, and at death: exemplified in the experience of many divines and other eminent persons at those important seasons. With a preface by the rev. mr. James Hervey A new ed. [with] a large appendix. 556 pp. 8°. *London, A. Millar,* [*etc.*] 1789.

Burns (Robert). The works of Robert Burns; with an account of his life, and a criticism on his writings. To which are prefixed, some observations on the character and condition of the scottish peasantry. [By James Currie, m. d.] 2d ed. 4 v. 8°. *London, T. Cadell, jun. & W. Davies,* 1801.

——— The same. 4 v. 18°. *Baltimore, F. Lucas, jr. & J. Cushing,* 1815.

——— Poems, chiefly in the scottish dialect. [1st Edinburgh ed.] xlviii, 343 pp. 1 portrait. 8°. *Edinburgh, author,* 1787.

——— The same. 3d ed. xlviii, 13-372 pp. 1 portrait. 8°. *London, A. Strahan,* 1787.

——— The same. [1st am. ed.] 304 pp. 16°. *Philadelphia, P. Stewart & G. Hyde,* 1788.

——— The same. 2d ed. considerably enlarged. 2 v. in 1. xi, 237 pp; 1 p. l. 283 pp. 8°. *Edinburgh, W. Creech,* 1793.

——— The same. [Also], several other pieces, not contained in any former edition of his poems; together with the life of the author, written by himself. xxxv, 312 pp. 12°. *Wilmington, (Del.) Bonsal & Niles,* 1804.

Burns (Robert, *jr.*) The caledonian musical museum, or complete vocal library of the best scotch songs, ancient and modern. Embellished with a portrait and fac-simile of the hand-writing of Burns, and containing upwards of two hundred songs by that immortal bard. The whole edited by his son. 3 v. 12°. *London, J. Dick,* 1809.

Burr (Enoch Fitch, *d. d.*) Ad fidem; or parish evidences of the bible. 1 p. l. ix, 353 pp. 12°. *Boston, Noyes, Holmes & co.* 1871.

Burr (Thomas Benge). The history of Tunbridge-wells. xii, 318 pp. 3 l. 8°. *London, M. Hingeston,* [*etc.*] 1766.

Burr (William Henry). Self-contradictions of the bible. 144 propositions, theological, moral, historical, and speculative; each proved affirmatively and negatively by quotations from scripture, without comment. [*anon.*] Revised and enlarged. 70 pp. 1 l. 16°. [*New York, American news co.*] 1872.

——— Sunday not the sabbath: all days alike holy. A controversy between the rev. dr. Sunderland, Wm. Henry Burr, and others. How the early fathers, reformers, and other eminent christian writers regarded sunday and the sabbath. Origin of the christian sabbath. Origin and abrogation of the jewish sabbath. 48 pp. 16°. *Washington, W. H. & O. H. Morrison,* 1872.

Burritt (Elihu). The children of the bible. 70 pp. sq. 16°. *New Britain, (Conn.) George L. Allen,* 1871.

——— Thoughts and things at home and abroad. With a memoir, by Mary Howitt. xxvi, 9-364 pp. 1 portrait. 12°. *Boston, Phillips, Sampson & co.* 1854.

Burrough bros. Formulary and descriptive catalogue of their fluid and solid extracts, with a complete botanical index. 180 pp. 12°. *Baltimore,* 1871.

Burroughs (John). Wake-Robin. iv, 231 pp. 16°. *New York, Hurd & Houghton,* 1871.

Burrow (*Sir* James). A few thoughts upon pointing and some other helps towards perspicuity of expression. By J. B. [*anon.* Appendix to his Essay on punctuation]. 1 p. l. 631-653 pp. 4°. [*London*]? *J. Worrall & B. Tovey,* 1768.

Burrows (George Mann, *m. d.*) An inquiry into certain errors relative to insanity, and their consequences; physical, moral, and civil. x, 320 pp. 1 pl. 8°. *London, T. & G. Underwood,* 1820.

Burthogge (Richard, *m. d.*) An essay upon reason, and the nature of spirits. 3 p. l. 280 pp. 12°. *London, J. Dunton,* 1694.

Burton (*Rev.* Edward). Testimonies of the ante-nicene fathers to the divinity of Christ. 2d ed. with additions. xviii, 489 pp. 3 l. 8°. *Oxford, university press,* 1829.

Burton (*Rev.* Edward)—continued.
——— Testimonies of the ante-nicene fathers to the doctrine of the trinity and of the divinity of the holy ghost. xviii, 151 pp. 8°. *Oxford, university press*, 1731.

Burton (John, *m. d.*) Πενταλογια, sive tragoediarum graecarum delectus: cum adnotatione J. Burton. Ed. altera. Cui observationes, indicemque græcum longe auctiorem et emendatiorem adjecit T. Burgess. 2 v. 2 p. l. 10, 52, 317 pp; pp. 318-513, 1 l. 142 pp. 321. 8°. *Oxonii, e typographeo clarendoniano apud J. & J. Fletcher*, 1779.

Burton (Juliette T.) The five jewels of the orient. 244 pp. 8 pl. 12°. *New York, Masonic publishing co.* 1872.

Burton (Leland). Burton's lightning arithmetic, especially adapted to class teaching. 110 pp. 1 l. 16°. *St. Louis, Bowman & Matthews*, 1871.

Burton (Richard *or* Robert). Historical remarks on the ancient and present state of the cities of London and Westminster. With an account of the most considerable occurrences, revolutions and transactions, as to wars, fires, plagues, etc. till the year 1681. New edition. 1 p. l. 178 pp. 1 pl. 4°. *Westminster, M. Stace*, 1810.

Bury (H. Blaze de). *See* **Blaze de Bury**.

Bury (Richard de). Histoire de la vie de Henri iv. roi de France et de Navarre. 2 v. xxiv, 468 pp. 6 portraits; 1 p. l. 459 pp. 4 portraits. 4°. *Paris, Didot l'aîné*, 1765.

Busch (William). Max and Maurice. A juvenile history in seven tricks. From the german by Charles T. Brooks. 56 pp. 12°. *Boston, Roberts brothers*, 1871.

Bush (Eliza C.) My pilgrimage to eastern shrines. xii, 317 pp. 1 pl. 8°. *London, Hurst & Blackett*, 1867.

Bush (George, *d. d.*) Illustrations of the holy scriptures, derived principally from the manners, customs, rites [etc.] of the eastern nations; with descriptions of the present state of countries and places mentioned in the sacred writings. 656 pp. 45 pl. 8°. *Brattleboro, Fessenden & co.* 1836.
——— Notes on genesis. *See* **Bible**. (*English*).
——— A treatise on the millennium. xv, 21-277 pp. 12°. *New-York, J. & J. Harper*, 1832.

Bush (Richard J.) Reindeer, dogs, and snow-shoes: a journal of siberian travel and explorations made in the years 1865, 1866, and 1867. 529 pp. 1 map. 8°. *New York, Harper & brothers*, 1871.

Bushby (*Rev.* Edward). The elements of logic. [*anon.*] 2 p. l. vi, 104 pp. 12°. *Cambridge, (Eng.) J. Smith*, 1826.
——— An introduction to the study of the holy scriptures. 2 p. l. 84 pp. 12°. *Cambridge, (Eng.) J. Smith*, 1829.
[*With his* Elements of logic. *Cambridge*, 1826].

Bushnell (Charles Ira). A narrative of the life and adventures of Levi Hanford, a soldier of the revolution. 80 pp. 1 l. 2 pl. 8°. *New York, privately printed*, 1863.

Bushnell (Horace, *d. d.*) The character of Jesus: forbidding his possible classification with men. 173 pp. 18°. *New York, C. Scribner*, 1861.

Business and diversion inoffensive to God. *See* **Seccomb** (*Rev.* Joseph).

Busnot (Dominique). The history of the reign of Muley Ismael, the present king of Morocco, Fez, Tafilet, Sous, &c. Translated from the original french now, first printed at Roan, 1714. 6 p. l. 250 pp. 16°. *London, A. Bell & J. Baker*, 1715.

Bussche (Alexandre Sylvain van den). Cinqvante ænigmes françoises d'A. Sylvain, avec les expositions d'icelles Ensemble quelques ænigmes espagnolles dudict autheur & d'autres. 2 v. in 1. 4 p. l. 54 l. numb; 4 p. l. 26 l. numb. 16°. *Paris, G. Beys*, 1582.

Butel-Dumont (George Marie). Histoire et commerce des Antilles angloises. [*anon.*] 1 p. l. x, 6 pp. 2 l. 284 pp. 1 map. 18°. [*Paris*], 1758.

Butler (Charles). The american gentleman. Eng. title, 288 pp. 1 pl. 18°. *Philadelphia, Hogan & Thompson*, 1836.
——— The american lady. 288 pp. 1 pl. 18°. *Philadelphia, Hogan & Thompson*, 1836.
——— The same. 288 pp. 2 pl. 12°. *Philadelphia, Hogan & Thompson*, 1839.

Butler (Clement Moore, *d. d.*) The book of common prayer interpreted by its history. 299 pp. 12°. *Boston, J. B. Dow*, 1845.
——— Lectures on the book of revelations. vi, 482 pp. 12°. *New York, R. Carter & brothers*, 1860.

Butler (John J. *d. d.*) Natural and revealed theology. A system of lectures, embracing the divine existence and attributes; authority of the scriptures; scriptural doctrine; institutions and ordinances of the christian church. 456 pp. 8°. *Dover, Freewill baptist printing establishment*, 1861.

Butler (Lilly, *d. d.*) Eight sermons preached in 1709. fol. [*London*, 1739].
[BOYLE lectures, v. 2, pp. 429–490].

Butler (*Mrs.* Marie R.) Riverside; or, winning a soul. 174 pp. 4 pl. 16°. *Cincinnati, Bosworth, Chase & Hall*, 1871.

Butler (Noble). The american spelling book. 160 pp. 12°. *Louisville, J. P. Morton & co.* [1871].

Butler (Samuel, *d. d.*) An atlas of antient geography. 3 p. l. 21 maps. 16 l. 8°. *Philadelphia, Carey & Lea*, 1832.

Butler (S. W. *m. d. editor*). *See* **Physician's** (The) annual for 1872.

Butler (*Rev.* Weeden). Memoirs of Mark Hildesley, d. d. lord bishop of Sodor and Man, and master of Sherburn hospital. viii, 691 pp. 8°. *London, J. Nichols*, 1799.

Butler (William, *teacher, London, Eng.*) Chronological, biographical, historical, and miscellaneous exercises, on a new plan. 9th ed. enlarged by Thomas Bourn. xi, 607 pp. 16°. *London, proprietor*, 1830.

Butler (William, *d. d.*) The land of the Veda: being personal reminiscences of India; its people, castes, thugs, and fakirs; its religions, mythology, principal monuments, palaces, and mausoleums: together with the incidents of the great sepoy rebellion, and its results to christianity and civilization. Also, statistical tables of christian missions, and a glossary of indian terms used in this work and in missionary correspondence. 550 pp. 1 map, 35 pl. 8°. *New York, Carlton & Lanahan*, 1872.

Butler (Willam Allen). Poems. vi, 263 pp. 16°. *Boston, J. R. Osgood & co.* 1871.

Butterfield (J. A.) Belshazzar. A historical cantata in four parts. Composed by J. A. Butterfield. Libretto by C. R. Blackall. Dramatized by E. M. Foote. 140 pp. fol. *Chicago, J. A. Butterfield*, 1871.

Buyr-praetjen: ofte tsamensprekinghe ende discours, op den brieff vanden agent Aerssens uyt Vranckrijck aende staten generael geschreven. Dienende tot ontdeckinge van der spaengiaerden ende hare adherenten listicheyt, trouweloosheyt, ende wreede wraeckgiericheydt. [*anon.*] *b. l.* 8 l. sm. 4°. [*n. p.* 1608].
[*In* NEDERLANDTSCHEN bye-corf].

Byford (William H. *m. d.*) A treatise on the chronic inflammation and displacements of the unimpregnated uterus. 215 pp. 8°. *Philadelphia, Lindsay & Blakiston*, 1854.

Byford (William H. *m. d.*)—continued.
——— The same. 2d ed. 248 pp. 8°. *Philadelphia. Lindsay & Blakiston*, 1871.

Bynæus (Antonius). De calceis Hebraeorum libri duo, cvris secundis recogniti, et aucti. Accedit ejusdem somnium, tertio recusum. 2 v. in 1. 9 p. l. 268 pp. 14 l; 4 p. l. 24 pp. 4°. *Dordraci, ex officina T. Goris*, 1715.

——— De morte Jesu Christi. 3 v. 4°. *Amstelaedami, G. Borstius*, 1691–98.

Byr *or* **Bayer** (Carl Robert). Sphinx; or, striving with destiny. A novel. Translated from the german. By Auber Forestier. 400 pp. 2 pl. 12°. *Philadelphia, New York, and Boston, G. Maclean*, 1871.

Byrne (William). Scottish scenery. *See* **Walker** (George, *landscape painter*).

Byron (George Gordon Noël, *6th baron Byron*). Historical illustrations of lord Byron's works in a series of etchings by Reveil, from original paintings, by A. Colin. 21 l. 20 pl. 8°. *London, C. Tilt*, 1833.

Bysshe *or* **Bissæus** (Edward). Παλλαδιου, περι των της Ινδιας εθνων. και των Βραγμανων. Palladius, de gentibus Indiæ et Bragmanibus. S. Ambrosius, de moribus Brachmanorum. Anonymus, de Bragmanibus. Quorum priorem et postremum nunc primum in lucem protulit, ex bibliotheca regia Edoardus Bissæus. 23 p. l. 104 pp. 4°. *London, T. Roycroft*, 1668.

C. (G. C.) 1724. *See* **Claudius** (Gottfried Christoph).

C. (J. *m. d.*) *See* **Cooke** (John, *m. d.*)

C (*m. l. d.*) Journal du voyage de Siam fait en 1685 et 1686 [1687]. *See* **Choisy** (François Timoléon de).

C. (R. *gent.*) The times' whistle: or a newe daunce of seven satires, and other poems: compiled by R. C. gent. [*anon.*] Now first edited, with introduction, notes and glossary, by J. M. Cowper. xxxviii, 178 pp. 8°. *London, N. Trübner & co.* 1871.
[EARLY english text society, no. 48].

Cabala, or the rites and ceremonies of the cabalist. National series. Arranged in accordance with the standard formula. [*anon.*] 198 pp. 18°. *New York, M. W. Redding & co.* 1872.

Cabinet (Le) dv roy Lovis xi. *See* **L'Hermite** (François, *dit* Tristan).

Cabinet (Le) jésuitique, contenant plusieurs pièces très curieuses des r. pères jésuites; avec un recueil des mystères de l'église romaine; le tout augmenté dans cette seconde

Cabinet (Le) jésuitique—continued. édition et enrichi de figures en taille douce. [*anon.*] 2 p. l. 184 pp. 24°. *Cologne, J. le Blanc*, 1678.

Cabrera (Paul Felix). Huehuetlaballan, Amerika's grosse urstadt in dem königreiche Guatimala. Neu entdeckt vom capitain don Antonio del Rio, und als eine phönizisch-cananäische und carthaginische pflanzstadt erwiesen. Mit 17 grossen zeichnungen in steind. Aus dem englischen von H. Berthoud. Abbildungen zu Huehuetlapallan, Amerika's grosser urstadt. [*anon.*] 1 p. l. 17 pl. fol. *Meiningen, P. Hartman*, 1823.
[Ms. title-page].

Cadogan (William Bromley). The life of the rev. William Romaine. iv, 96 pp. 1 portrait. 8°. *London, T. Bensley for Vernor & Hood*, [*etc.*] 1796.
[*Note.*—Appended is another brief memoir of Romaine, taken from the Evangelical magazine, for Nov. 1795; and another of Cadogan himself, from the same periodical, 1798].

Cæsarius *heisterbacensis*. Illvstrivm miracvlorvm, et, historiarvm memorabilivm lib. 12. ante annos ferè cccc. à Cæsario Heisterbachcensi, de iis, quæ sua ætate memoratu digna contigervnt, accuratè conscripti. [Editio nova]. 19 p. l. 902 pp. 19 l. 8°. *Coloniæ Agrippinæ, in officina birckmannica, sumptibus A. Mylii*, 1599.

Caffaro (Franciscus). Father Caffaro's letter upon the lawfulness or unlawfulness of the stage; with a brief introduction. 16°. [*New York*, 1826].
[*In* F. (D.) Defence of the drama, pp. 97-163].

Cailleux (Alphonse de). Voyages pittoresques et romantiques dans l'ancienne France. *See* **Nodier** (Charles) **Taylor** (J.) *and* **Cailleux**.

Calà (Carlo, *duca di Diano*). Memorie historiche dell' apparitione delle croci prodigiose. 6 p. l. 189 pp. 13 l. 4°. *Napoli, N de Bonis*, 1661.

Calamy (Edmund, *d. d.*) A practical discourse concerning vows; with a special reference to baptism and the Lord's supper. 4 p. l. 310 pp. 8°. *London, G. Larkin, jun.* 1697.

Calatayud y Borda (Cypriano Geronimo de). Oracion funebre que en las solemnes exequias de Maria Antonia de San Joseph, Larrea, Arispe, de los reyes: dixo xxx de Oct. 1782. 58 p. l. 144 pp. sm. 4°. *Lima, imprenta de los huerfanos*, 1783.

Calcutta (The) review. May, 1844, to December, 1857. v. 1-29. 28 v. 8°. *Calcutta and Serampore*, 1846-57.
[*Note.*—v. 1-2 are of 3d ed., and v. 26 is wanting].

Caldas (Francisco José de). Semanario de la Nueva Granada. *See* **Semanario**.

Caldecott (C.) Horæ sacræ. Divine ethics; or, the proverbs of Solomon, in verse. 8, 100 pp. 1 pl. 18°. *London, T. Harvey*, [*about* 1825].

Calder (Frederick). Memoirs of Simon Episcopius, the celebrated pupil of Arminius, who was condemned by the synod of Dort as a dangerous heretic, and, with several other ministers, was sentenced to perpetual banishment by the civil authorities of Holland; [also], a brief account of the synod of Dort; and of the sufferings to which the followers of Arminius were exposed. 1 p. l. 549 pp. 8°. *London, Simpkin & Marshall*, 1835.

Caldwall (Thomas). A select collection of ancient and modern epitaphs, and inscriptions. 1 p. l. iv, 416 pp. 1 portrait. 16°. *London, compiler*, 1796.

Caldwell (Anne). *See* **Marsh-Caldwell** (*Mrs.* Anne).

Caldwell (*Rev.* David). Parochial lectures on the psalms. Psalms 1-50. 586 pp. 12°. *Philadelphia, W. S. & A. Martien*, 1859.

Caldwell (S. L.) *and* **Gordon** (A. J.) The service of song for baptist churches. 480 pp. 8°. *Boston, Gould & Lincoln*, 1871.

——— ——— The same. 793 pp. 16°. *Boston, Gould & Lincoln*, 1871.

Caledonian (The) musical repository. 1811. *See* **Crosby's** caledonian musical repository.

Calendar. *See* **Kalendar**.

Calhoun (*Col.* A. R.) The color guard; a military drama in five acts, with accompanying tableaux. 43 pp. 16°. *Pittsburgh, A. A. Anderson & sons*, 1870.

Calid. *See* **Chalid ben Jesiki.**

California medical gazette. [Monthly]. J. D. B. Stillman, m. d. W. F. McNutt, m. d. etc. editors. Sept. 1869, to Aug. 1870. v. 2. 4°. *San Francisco, A. Roman & co.* [1870].

Calkins (N. A.) A manual to accompany Jeffers' panoramic apparatus for teaching reading, by object lesson exercises. 35 pp. 18°. *New York, Jeffers, Beecher & Jeffers*, 1871.

Calkins (Storrs Seabury). Calkins's business instructor. Also, the rules of commercial law epitomized for convenient reference. 156 pp. 1 l. 8°. *Oberlin, (O.) R. Butler*, 1871.

Callendar (George). Nautical remarks and observations for the chart of the harbour of Boston. Composed from different surveys; but principally from that taken in 1769. 11 pp. 4°. *London, for the author*, 1775.

Callender (*Rev.* John). An historical discourse on the affairs of Rhode-Island and Providence plantations from 1638 to the end of the first century. 14, 120 pp. 8°. *Boston, S. Kneeland & T. Green*, 1739.

[HAZARD pamphlets, v. 98.]

Callimachus. Inni tradotti da Dionigi Strocchi. 18°. [*Milano, G. Truffi*, 1831].

[*With* PINDARUS. Le odi. 1831. pp. 311–370].

Callistratus. Callistrati expositiones statvarvm. Ex Federici Morelli interpretatione. [Græce et latine]. fol. *Parisiis, apud M. Orry*, 1608].

[*In* PHILOSTRATUS. Opera qvæ exstant. *Parisiis*, 1608. pp. 864–883].

Callot (Jacques). Capitano de baroni. [Gueux ou mendiants]. 25 pl. obl. 8°. [*n. p. after* 1622].

[*Note.*—A collection of plates, evidently cut from an early work and pasted in this blank book. Numbered in the right-hand lower corner from 1 to 25. Title-page wanting].

Calvidius Letus (*pseudon.*) *See* **Quillet** (Claude).

Calvin (Jean). Calvin on secret providence. Translated by James Lillie. 1 p. l. 118 pp. 18°. *New York, R. Carter*, 1840.

——— Commentaries. *See* **Bible.** (*English*).

——— Ψυχοπαννυχία. 12°. *London, C. J. G. & F. Rivington*, 1829.

[*With* HUNTINGFORD (*Rev.* T.) Testimonies in proof of separate existence of the soul, pp. 393–500].

Calvo (Carlos). América latina. Coleccion histórica completa de los tratados, convenciones, capitulaciones, armisticios, cuestiones de límites y otros actos diplomáticos y políticos de todos los estados comprendidos entre el golfo de Méjico y el cabo de Hornos, desde el año de 1493 hasta nuestros dias. Primer período. v. 11. 8°. *Paris, A. Durand* [*etc.*] 1869.

Calvoli (Giovanni Cinelli). *See* **Cinelli Calvoli.**

Cambiaso y Verdes (Nicolas Maria de). Memorias para la biografia y para la bibliografia de la isla de Cadiz. v. 2. Desde J ante de U hasta Z. Con apéndices. 268 pp. 8°. *Madrid, viuda de Villalpando,* 1830.

Cambridge (Richard Owen). Works, including several pieces never before published with an account of his life and character, by his son. 1 p. l. vii, lxxviii, 507 pp. 4 pl. 12 portraits. 4°. *London, Cadell & Davies*, 1803.

CONTENTS.

Memoirs of the author.
Miscellaneous verses.
The scribleriad: an heroic poem in six books.
Essays published in The world.

Cambridge (*University of, England*). Gratulatio academiæ cantabrigiensis auspicatissimas Georgii iii. Magnæ Britanniæ regis, et serenissimæ Charlottæ principis de Mecklenburgh-Strelitz nuptias celebrantis. 64 l. fol. *Cantabrigiæ, J. Bentham*, 1761.

——— Oliva pacis. Ad illustrissimum celsissimumq; Oliverum, dominum protectorem; de pace cum fœderatis Belgis feliciter sancita, carmen cantabrigiense. [*anon.*] 36 l. 4°. *Cantabrigiæ, ex celeberrimæ academiæ typographeo*, 1654.

Cambridge (*Mass.*) The Cambridge directory and almanac for 1854. By John Ford. 1 p. l. 152 pp. 5 l. 1 map. 18°. *Cambridge, Chronicle office*, 1854.

——— The Cambridge directory for 1871 and 1872. By Dean Dudley. 2 v. 8°. *Cambridge, Sever, Francis & co. Boston, D. Dudley*, 1871–72.

Cambridge prize poems. Musæ seatonianæ: a complete collection of the Cambridge prize poems, from the first institution of that premium by the rev. Thomas Seaton, in 1750, to the year 1806. [Also], three poems, likewise written for the prize, by mr. Bally, mr. Scott, and mr. Wrangham. 2 v. vi, 332 pp; 2 p. l. 393 pp. 8°. *Cambridge, (Eng.) F. Hodson for J. Deighton*, 1808.

Camden (William). Annales: the true and royall history of the famous empresse Elizabeth, queene of England, France and Ireland &c. Wherein all such memorable things as happened during her blessed raigne, with such acts and treaties as past betwixt hir ma^tie^ and Scotland, France, Spaine, Italy, Germany, Poland, Sweden, Denmark, Russia, and the Netherlands, are exactly described. [*anon.* Englished by Abraham Darcie from the french translation of the original latin]. Eng. title, 46 p. l. 435 pp. 2 l. 292 pp. 4°. *London, B. Fisher*, 1625.

[Wants a portrait of queen Elizabeth].

——— La grande Bretagne. fol. *Amsterdam, Jean Blaeu*, 1667.

[BLAAUW (Willem Janszoon *and* Joan). Le grand atlas, v. 5].

Camden society. Publications. nos. 98, 103, and 104 in 2 v. 4°. *London*, 1868–71.

CONTENTS.

CAMDEN (The) miscellany. v. 6, (no. 104).
GARDINER (S. R.) Letters and other documents illustrating the relations between England and Germany at the commencement of the thirty years' war. 2d series. From the election of Fred. ii. to the conferences at Mühlhausen. (no. 98).
GREAT BRITAIN. (*Parliament*). Notes of debates in the house of lords, officially taken by Henry Elsing, 1621. Edited by S. R. Gardiner. (no. 103).

——— The same. New series, nos. 1–3 in 2 v. 4°. [*London*], *Camden society*, 1871.

CONTENTS.

FORTESCUE (The) papers; consisting chiefly of letters relating to state affairs, collected by John Packer. (no. 1).
GREAT BRITAIN. *Chapel royal*. The old cheque-book, or book of remembrance of the chapel royal, 1561–1744. Edited by E. F. Rimbault. (no. 3).
SHILLINGFORD (John). Letters and papers. Edited by S. A. Moore. (no. 2).

Camerarius (Joachim). Commentarius in novum fœdus. 11 p. l. 125 pp. 2 l. fol. *Cantabrigiae, ex officina R. Danielis*, 1642.

[*With* BIBLE. (*Greek*). Jesu Christi domini nostri testamentum. 1642].

——— Explicatio in dvos libros Nicomachi geraseni pythagorei deductionis ad scientiam numerorum. 1 p. l. 56 pp. sm. 4°. *Daventriæ, typis W. Wier*, 1667.

[*In* JAMBLICHUS *chalcidensis*. In Nicomachi geraseni arithmeticam introductionem, et de fato. 1668].

Camerarius (Philipp). Operæ horarvm svbcisivarvm, sive meditationes historicæ avctiores quam antea editæ. Continentes accuratum delectum memorabilium historiarum, & rerum tam veterum, quam recentium, [etc.] 3 v. in 1. 4°. *Francofvrti, typis E. Emmelij, impensis P. Kopfij*, 1618–24.

Cameron (Henry Clay). History of the American whig society. 8°. *Princeton, Stelle & Smith*, 1871.

[COLLEGE of New Jersey. Addresses [etc.] at the 100th anniversary of the American whig society, pp. 1–41].

Cameron (*Rev.* John). Ioannis Cameronis scoto-britanni theologi eximij τα σωζομενα, siue opera partim ab avctore ipso edita, partim post eius obitum vulgata, partim nusquam hactenus publicata, vel e gallico idiomate nunc primum in latinam linguam translata. In vnum collecta. 18 p. l. 864 pp. 20 l. fol. *Genevæ, in officina Iacobi Chouët*, 1642.

Cameron (*Rev.* William). Poems on several occasions. 8, 144 pp. 8°. *Edinburgh, D. Willison*, 1813.

Cametti (Ottaviano). Sectionum conicarum compendium. 108 pp. 14 pl. 16°. *Venetiis, ex typographia balleoniana*, 1765.

Camfield (*Rev.* Benjamin). A theological discourse of angels, and their ministries. Also an appendix containing some reflections upon mr. [John] Webster's Displaying supposed witchcraft. 8 p. l. 214 pp. 8°. *London, R. E. for H. Brome*, 1678.

Campagnes et croisières dans les états de Vénézuéla et de la Nouvelle-Grenade. *See* **Campaigns** and cruises.

Campaigns and cruises, in Venezuela and New Grenada, and in the Pacific ocean; from 1817 to 1830; with the narrative of a march from the river Orinoco to San Buenaventura on the coast of Chocò; and sketches of the west coast of South America, from the gulf of California to the archipelago of Chilöe. Also, tales of Venezuela. [*anon.*] 3 v. 12°. *London, Longman & co.* 1831.

[*Note.*—v. 2-3 entitled "Tales of Venezuela," parts i-ii].

——— The same. Campagnes et croisières dans les états de Vénézuéla et de la Nouvelle-Grenade; par un officier du 1er régiment de lanciers vénézuéliens. Traduit de l'anglais. [*anon.*] 2 p. l. 412 pp. 1 map, 1 portrait. 8°. *Paris, aux salons littéraires*, 1837.

Campanius (Johan, *pastor in New-Sweden*, 1642-48). Vocabularium barbaro-virgineorum. Additis passim locutionibus et observationibus historicis brevioribus ad linguæ pleniorem notitiam. [Indian and swedish]. 16°. *Stockholm, Burchard*, 1696.

[*In* LUTHER (Martin). Lutheri catechismus, öfwersatt på american-virginiske språket. 1696. pp. 133–160].

——— The same. Vocabulary and phrases in the american language of New-Sweden. [Indian and english]. 8°. *Philadelphia, McCarty & English*, 1834.

[*In* CAMPANIUS *holmensis* (Thomas). Short description of New Sweden, pp. 144–159].

Campbell (*Rev.* Alexander) *and* **Rice** (*Rev.* N. L.) A debate on the action, subject, design and administrator of christian baptism; also, on the character of spiritual influence in conversion and sanctification, and on the expediency and tendency of ecclesiastic creeds, as terms of union and communion. Reported by Marcus T. C. Gould, assisted by A. E. Draper. 1 p. l. 11–912 pp. 8°. *Lexington, (Ky.) A. T. Skillman & son*, 1844.

——— *and others.* Psalms, hymns, and spiritual songs, original and selected: compiled by A. Campbell, W. Scott, B. W. Stone, and L. T. Johnson. 248 pp. 4 l. 32°. *Bethany, (Va.) A. Campbell*, 1834.

Campbell (Archibald, *bishop of Aberdeen*). Some primitive doctrines reviv'd: or the intermediate or middle state of departed souls (as to happiness or misery) before the day of judgment. [*anon.*] xxxvi, 170 pp. 8°. *London, S. Keble,* 1713.

Campbell (Colin). History of the Balearick islands. *See* **Dameto** (Juan) *and* **Mut** (Vicente).

Campbell (Edward R.) The heroine of Scutari, and other poems. 334 pp. 12°. *New York, Dana & co.* 1857.

Campbell (George, *d. d.*) Lectures on systematic theology and pulpit eloquence. [Also], dialogues on eloquence, by M. de Fénélon. Edited by Henry J. Ripley. 2 v. in 1. 206 pp; 102 pp. 8°. *Boston, Lincoln & Edmands,* 1832.

Campbell (George Douglas, *duke of Argyll*). Iona. By the duke of Argyll. 2d ed. 2 p. l. 141 pp. 6 pl. 16°. *London, Strahan & co.* 1871.

Campbell (James). A treatise of modern faulconry: to which is prefixed an introduction shewing the practice of faulconry in certain remote times and countries. [By rev. Alex. Gillies]. 1 p. l. iv, 3–264 pp. 1 pl. 8°. *Edinburgh, author,* 1773.

Campbell (Jane C.) American evening entertainments; or, tales of city and country life. 353 pp. 12°. *New York, J. C. Derby,* 1856.

Campbell (John, *ll. d.*) Hermippus revived. *See* **Cohausen** (Johann Heinrich).

Campbell (J. L.) *and* **Hadley** (A. M.) The teacher's miscellany, a selection of articles from the proceedings of the College of professional teachers. 442 pp. 12°. *Cincinnati, Moore, Wilstach, Keys & co.* 1856.

Campbell (Robert). A pilgrimage to my motherland. An account of a journey among the Egbas and Yorubas of Central Africa, in 1859–60. 145 pp. 1 portrait. 12°. *New-York, T. Hamilton,* 1861.

Campbell (R. A. *editor*). Campbell's new atlas of the state of Illinois, with descriptions historical, scientific and statistical. Maps drawn by R. A. Campbell and H. F. Walling. Letter press descriptions by J. W. Foster, Newton Bateman, and others. 2 p. l. 51–86, 25, 7 pp. 34 col. maps. fol. *Chicago, R. A. Campbell,* 1870.

——— Campbell's shippers' guide and travelers' directory. 316 pp. 8°. *Chicago, R. A. Campbell,* 1869.

Campbell (R. A.)—continued.

——— The same. xx, 288 pp. 8°. *Chicago, R. A. Campbell,* 1871.

Camper (Charles) *and* **Kirkley** (Joseph W.) Historical record of the first regiment of Maryland infantry, with an appendix containing a register of the officers and enlisted men, biographies of deceased officers, etc. War of the rebellion, 1861–65. x, 312 pp. 12°. *Washington, Gibson brothers,* 1871.

Campolo (Giacinto). Tesoro del ss. rosario diviso in tre parti. 4 p. l. 521 pp. 1 l. 4°. *Messina, nella stamparia di V. d'Amico,* 1698.

Campomanes (Pedro Rodriguez). Antigüedad maritima de la republica de Cartago. Con el Periplo de Hannon, traducido del griego è ilustrado. 2 parts in 1 v. 16 p. l. 136 pp. 1 pl; 1 p. l. 132 pp. 1 l. 1 map. 8°. *Madrid, A. Perez de Soto,* 1756.

Camus (Jean Pierre, *évêque de Belley*). Nature's paradox: or, the innocent impostor. A pleasant polonian history: originally intituled Iphigines. Compiled in the french tongue. And novv englished by major VVright. 7 p. l. 372 pp. 4°. *London, J. C. for E. Dod & N. Exens,* 1652.

Canada (*Dominion of*). Journals of the senate and house of commons, 1871. Being the fourth session of the first parliament. v. 4. in 2 v. 8°. [*Ottawa,* 1871].

——— Sessional papers. Fourth session of the first parliament, 1871. [nos. 3–68]. v. 2–6. 8°. [*Ottawa,* 1871].

Canadian (The) entomologist. Edited by the rev. C. J. S. Bethune, m. a. Assisted by W. Saunders, E. B. Reed, and J. M. Denton, 1869–1871. v. 1–3. 8°. *Toronto, Copp, Clark & co. London (Ontario), Free press printing co.* 1869–71. s.

Canadian (The) parliamentary companion. Edited by Henry J. Morgan. 6th ed. 24°. *Montreal, Gazette steam printing house,* 1871.

Canale (Florian). De' secreti vniversali raccolti et sperimentali trattati nove. Ne' qvali si hanno rimedii per tutte le infermità de' corpi humani, come anco de caualli, boui, & cani. Con molti secreti appertinenti all' arte chemica, agricoltura & caccie. Nouamente posti in luce. 12 p. l. 269 pp. 16°. *Brescia, B. Fontana,* 1613.

Caner (Henry, *d. d.*) Joyfulness and consideration; or, the duties of prosperity and adversity. A sermon preached in Boston, before [the] governor, council, and representatives of Massachusetts-Bay, Jan. 1, 1761.

Caner (Henry, *d. d.*)—continued.
Upon occasion of the death of king George the second. 31 pp. 8°. *Boston, Green & Russell*, [1761].

Cannon (James Spencer, *d. d.*) Lectures on pastoral theology. 3 p. l. xxxvi, 617 pp. 1 portrait. 8°. *New York, C. Scribner*, 1853.

Cannon (Susan). Maidee, the alchemist; or, turning all to gold. 249 pp. 12°. *New York, M. Doolady*, 1871.

Cannon (Thomas). A close view of death and it's subsequent immortalities; giving a large account of the primitive christians, who conducted their lives by those views. With a previous discourse, demonstrating the truth of christianity. 304 pp. 16°. *London, E. Dilly*, 1740.
[Frontispiece wanting].

Canonici Fachini (Ginevra). Prospetto biografico delle donne italiane rinomate in letteratura dal secolo decimoquarto fino a' giorni nostri. Con una risposta a lady Morgan risguardante alcune accuse da lei date alle donne italiane nella sua opera L'Italie. 274 pp. 1 l. 8°. *Venezia, Alvisopoli*, 1824.

Cantemir (Demetrius). Histoire de l'empire othoman, où se voyent les causes de son aggrandissement et de sa décadence. Avec des notes très-instructives. Traduite en françois par m. de Joncquières. 2 v. 4 p. l. xlviii, 300 pp; 2 p. l. 390 pp. 4°. *Paris, Despilly*, 1743.

Cantoni (Gaetano). I comizi agrari del regno d'Italia. 3 v. 8°. *Torino*, 1870.
[ITALY. *Ministero di agricoltura, industria e commercio.* Annali. 1870.]

Cantù (Cesare). Margherita Pusterla. 2 p. l. 425 pp. 16°. *Leipzig, F. A. Brockhaus*, 1866.

Capèce (Scipione). De principiis rervm libri dvo. Ejusdem de vate maximo libri tres. 63 l. 16°. *Venetiis, Aldi filii*, 1546.

Capefigue (Jean Baptiste Honoré Raymond). Mesdemoiselles De Nesle et la jeunesse de Louis xv. 2 p. l. vii, 216 pp. 16°. *Paris, Amyot*, 1864.

Capel (Arthur, *baron Capel of Hadham*). Excellent contemplations, divine and moral. With some account of his life, and his letters to several persons, whilst he was prisoner in the Tower. Likewise his affectionate letters to his lady, the day before his death. With his pious advice to his son the late earl of Essex. [1st ed.] 1 p. l. 224 pp. 1 l. 18°. *London, N. Crouch*, 1683.

Capelle (Pierre). Dictionnaire de morale, de science et de littérature, ou choix de pensées ingénieuses et sublimes, de dissertations et de définitions. 2 v. 392 pp; 432 pp. 8°. *Paris, Capelle & Renaud*, 1810.

Capital (The). [Washington weekly]. Donn Piatt [and others], editors. March 12, 1871, to March 3, 1872. v. 1. fol. *Washington*, 1871-72.

Capitolo del gioco della primiera. 1526. *See* **Berni** (Francesco).

Caprices d'imagination. *Paris*, 1740. *See* **Bruhier d'Ablancourt** (Jean Jacques).

Capron (M. J.) Apron strings, and which way they pulled. By Archie Fell. [*pseudon.*] 270 pp. 2 pl. 16°. *Boston, Israel P. Warren*, [1871].

Caraccioli (Louis Antoine, *marquis* de). The true mentor; or, an essay on the education of young people of fashion. Translated from the french. xxi, 190 pp. 16°. *London, J. Coote*, 1760.

Caramuel Lobkowitz (Juan). Philippvs prvdens Caroli v. imp. filivs, Lvsitaniæ, Algarbiæ, Indiæ, Brasiliæ legitimvs rex demonstratvs. [Quinque libris]. Eng. title, 15 p. l. 430 pp. 13 l. 24 pl. fol. *Antverpiæ, ex officina B. Moreti*, 1639.

Cardano (Girolamo). Hieronymi Cardani castellionei mediolaniensis de consolatione libri tres. 132 l. numb. 16°. *Venetijs, apud H. Scotum*, 1542.
[Imperfect: wanting, l. 113-128.
Note.—The word castellioneus alludes to Cardano's pretence to being descended from the Castiglione family].

——— Podagrae encomium. 18°. [*Lugd. Batavorum*, 1644].
[*In* DISSERTATIONVM lvdicrarvm et amœnitatvm scriptores varij, pp. 41-66].

Cardoso (Luis). Portugal sacro-profano, ou catalogo alfabetico de todas as freguezias dos reinos de Portugal, e Algarve: das igrejas com seus oragos; do titulo das parocos, e annual rendimento de cada huma: [etc.] Composto, e ordenado por Paulo Dias de Niza. [*pseudon.*] 3 v. 16°. *Lisboa, M. M. da Costa*, 1757-68.

Carew (*Sir* George). Calendar of the Carew manuscripts. *See* **Great Britain.** *Treasury department.* (*Master of the rolls*).

Carey (*Mrs.* Eustace). Eustace Carey: a missionary in India. A memoir. xi, 566 pp. 1 portrait. 8°. *London, Pewtress & co.* 1857.

Carhart (John Wesley). Sunny hours: consisting of poems on various subjects. xi, 7–233 pp. 1 portrait. 12°. *New York, Pudney & Russell*, 1859.

Carleton (George, *bishop of Landaff*). The life of Bernard Gilpin, collected from his life written by George Carleton, from other printed accounts of the times he lived in, from original letters, and other authentic records. 1 p. l. 280, 52 pp. 6 l. 1 portrait. 8°. *London, author*, [1753].

Carleton (William M.) Poems. 145 pp. 12°. *Chicago, Lakeside publishing and printing company*, 1871.

Carlisle (Nicholas). Hints on rural residences. [*anon.*] Eng. title, 3 p. l. 107 pp. 4°. *London*, 1825.

Carlisle (*Rev.* S.) The messiah expecting his foes' subjection. 12°. [*Pittsburgh*, 1872].

[*In* REFORMED presbyterian church in North America, memorial volume, pp. 94–100].

Carlowitz (Aloïse Christine, *baronne de*). Le pair de France, ou le divorce. 3 v. 8°. *Paris, C. Lachapelle*, 1835.

Carlyle (Thomas). Collected works. Library ed. In 30 volumes. v. 19, 20, 23–30. 8°. *London, Chapman & Hall*, 1870–71.

CONTENTS.

v. 19. Latter-day pamphlets. [1850]. 3 p. l. 421 pp. 2 l.
v. 20. The life of John Sterling. [1851]. vii, 342 pp. 2 l. 1 portrait.
v. 23–30. History of Friedrich ii. of Prussia, called Frederick the great. [1858–1865]. In ten volumes.

——— The same. A general index to the library edition in thirty volumes. 2 p. l. 172 pp. 8°. *London, Chapman & Hall*, 1871.

——— Translations from the german. Uniform with his collected works. In three volumes. v. 1–2. 8°. *London, Chapman & Hall*, 1871.

CONTENTS.

GÖTHE (J. W. von). Wilhelm Meister's apprenticeship and travels, v. 1–2.

Carmichael (William M. *d. d.*) The early christian fathers: or memorials of nine distinguished teachers of the christian faith during the first three centuries: including their testimony to the three-fold ministry of the church. 406 pp. 1 l. 12°. *New York, A. V. Blake*, 1844.

Carmignani (Giovanni). Teoria delle leggi della sicurezza sociale. 4 v. 8°. *Pisa, presso i fratelli Nistri e ca.* 1831–32.

Carmina qvinqve Hetrvscorvm poetarvm [colligente F. Vinta seipso]. Nvnc primvm in lvcem edita. 4 p. l. 174 pp. 1 l. 16°. *Florentiæ, apvd Ivntas*, 1562.

CONTENTS.

Francisci Vinthæ Carminum libri ii. Ecloga i.
Fabii Segnii Carmina.
Francisci Bernii Carmina.
Benedicti Accolti car. Epigrammata.
Benedicti Varchii Epigrammata.
Insvper Pompeiani, et Evsthenii antiquorum, authorum, duo addita epigrammata.

Carmina qvinqve illvstrivm poetarvm. 275 pp. 2 l. 16°. *Venetiis, ex officina Vincentii Valgrisii*, 1548.

CONTENTS.

Petri Bembi liber i.
Andreæ Navgerii liber i.
Balthassaris Castilioni liber i.
Ioannis Cottæ liber i.
M. Antonii Flaminii libri iiii.
Eivsdem paraphrasis in triginta psalmos, versibvs scripta.

Caron (François). Beschrijvinghe van het machtigh coninckrijcke Japan, vervattende den aert eñ eygenschappen van t'landt, manieren der volckeren, als mede hare grouwelijcke wreedtheydt teghen de roomsche christenen. 1 p. l. 63 pp. sm. 4°. *Amsterdam, I. Hartgers*, 1648.

[*In* HARTGERTS (J.) Oost-indische voyagien, v. 1. 13e stuck].

Carpenter (*Prof.* G. T.) The bible vs. spiritualism: or, spiritualism condemned and the bible vindicated. In two parts. 107 pp. 16°. *Oskaloosa, (Iowa), Call & Bristol*, 1870.

Carpenter (Lant, *ll. d.*) Principles of education, intellectual, moral and physical. xxiii, 477 pp. 8°. *London, Longman* [*& co.*] 1820.

Carpenter (William). An introduction to the reading and study of the english bible. 3 v. 16°. *London, S. W. Partridge & co.* 1868.

——— Scripture natural history; containing a descriptive account of the quadrupeds, birds, fishes, insects, reptiles, serpents, plants, trees, minerals, gems, and precious stones, mentioned in the bible. First american ed. By rev. Gorham D. Abbott. [Also], sketches of Palestine, or the holy land. 408 pp. 12°. *Boston, Lincoln & Edmands*, 1833.

Carr (George P.) The river of life, and other poems. 2 p. l. 96 pp. 12°. *Baltimore, Turnbull brothers*, 1871.

Carr (John). A northern summer; or travels round the Baltic, through Denmark, Sweden, Russia, Prussia, and part of Germany, in the year 1804. xii, 480 pp. 11 pl. 4°. *London, R. Phillips*, 1805.

Carrière (*Abbé* Joseph). Prælectionum theologicarum compendium ad usum theologiæ

Carrière (*Abbé* Joseph)—continued. alumnorum. De matrimonio. Ed. 3a. 312 pp. 16°. *Dublinii*, [*ex typis J. F. Fowler*], 1847.

Carriere (Moriz). Die kunst im zusammenhang der culturentwickelung und die ideale der menschheit. v. 1-2. xxi, 569 pp; xvi, 612 pp. 8°. *Leipzig, F. A. Brockhaus*, 1863-66.

CONTENTS.

v. 1. Die anfänge der cultur und das orientalische alterthum in religion, dichtung und kunst. 1863.
v. 2. Hellas und Rom in religion und weisheit, dichtung und kunst. 1866.

Carroll (James). The american criterion of the english language; containing the elements of pronunciation. 120 pp. 16°. *New-London* (*Conn.*) *S. Green*, 1795.

Carroll (John, *archbishop of Baltimore*). Select portions of his writings. 12°. [*Baltimore, J. Murphy*, 1843].

[*In* BRENT (D. C.) Biographical sketch of the rev. John Carroll. *Baltimore*, 1843. pp. 222-321].

Carron (Guy Toussaint Julien). Vies des justes dans la profession des armes. [*anon.*] xii, 430 pp. 1 l. 16°. *Versailles, J. A. Lebel*, 1815.

Carruthers (*Rev.* E. W. *d. d.*) Revolutionary incidents: and sketches of character, chiefly in the "old north state." 431 pp. 12°. *Philadelphia, Hayes & Zell*, 1854.

Cartari (Vincenzo). Theatrum ethnico idololatricum politico-historicum ethnicorum idololatrias, simulacra, templa, sacrificia & deos, illorum origines, ritus et cæremonias, quæ in perficiendis sacris, fuerunt observata, quidque illis indicare voluerint, representans. Olim à Vincentio Chartario regiensi publicatum, postea à Paulo Hachemberg editum. 4 p. l. 228 pp. 8 l. 88 pl. sm. 4°. *Moguntiæ, L. Bourgeat*, 1699.

Carte (Thomas). A general history of England. 4 v. fol. *London, author*, 1747-55.

Carter (Edmund). Hand book of the Dutchess and Columbia railroad, and complete business directory of each place on the road. [*anon.*] 165 pp. sq. 16°. *Newburgh*, (*N. Y.*) *Carter, Fitzgerald & co.* 1871.

Carter (Elizabeth). Poems on several occasions. vii, 104 pp. 16°. *London, J. Rivington*, 1762.

[*Note.*—This includes only two pieces from the collection first published].

——— The same. 16°. *London, J. Rivington*, 1762.

[*With* GESNER (Solomon). Rural poems. *London*, 1762].

——— The same. 4th ed. vi, 118 pp. 16°. *Dublin, W. Watson*, 1777.

Carter (James Gordon) *and* **Brooks** (William H.) A geography of Massachusetts; for families and schools. x, 224 pp. 1 map. 18°. *Boston, Hilliard, Gray, Little & Wilkins*, 1830.

——— A geography of Middlesex county [Mass.] 106 pp. 2 pl. 18°. *Cambridge, Hilliard & Brown*, 1830.

Carter (*Rev.* John P.) The elements of general history. 317 pp. 1 map. 12°. *New York, University publishing co.* 1871.

Carter (St. Leger L.) Nugæ, by Nugator; or, pieces in prose and verse. 215 pp. 18°. *Baltimore, Woods & Crane*, 1844.

Carter (*Mrs.* Sarah C.) Lexicon of ladies' names, with their floral emblems. 208 pp. 6 col. pl. 18°. *Boston, J. Buffum*, [1852].

Carter (*Rev.* Thomas). History of the great reformation in England, Scotland, Ireland, Germany, France, and Italy. 1 p. l. 372 pp. 12°. *New York, Carlton & Porter*, 1860.

Carter (William C.) *and* **Glossbrenner** (Adam J.) History of York county [Pa.] from its erection to the present time. 183, 30 pp. 1 pl. 12°. *York*, (*Pa.*) *A. J. Glossbrenner*, 1834.

Cartwright (Peter, *d. d.*) Fifty years as a presiding elder. Edited by rev. W. S. Hooper. 281 pp. 1 portrait. 12°. *Cincinnati, Hitchcock and Walden*, 1871.

Cartwright (Samuel A. *m. d.*) Slavery in the light of ethnology. 8°. [*Augusta*, (*Ga.*) 1860].

[*In* ELLIOTT (E. N.) Cotton is king, pp. 689-728].

——— The education, labor, and wealth of the south. 8°. [*Augusta*, (*Ga.*) 1860].

[*In* ELLIOTT (E. N.) Cotton is king, pp. 875-892].

Carver (Robin, *pseudon?*) Anecdotes of natural history. 320 pp. 12°. *Boston, Lilly, Wait, Colman & Holden*, 1833.

——— The book of sports. 164 pp. sq. 16°. *Boston, Lilly, Wait, Colman & Holden*, 1834.

——— History of Boston. 160 pp. 1 pl. sq. 16°. *Boston, Lilly, Wait, Colman & Holden*, 1834.

——— Stories about Boston, and its neighborhood. Eng. title, 184 pp. 1 pl. sq. 16°. *Boston, Lilly, Wait & co.* 1833.

——— Stories of Poland. 142 pp. 12 pl. sq. 16°. *Boston, Carter, Hendee & co.* 1833.

Cary (*Rev.* Henry Francis). Lives of english poets, from Johnson to Kirke White, designed as a continuation of Johnson's lives. 3 p. l. 419 pp. 16°. *London, H. G. Bohn*, 1846.

Casa (Giovanni). Latina monimenta, quorum partim versibus, partim soluta oratione scripta sunt. 10 p. l. 275 [265] pp. 4°. [*Florentiæ*, 1564].

Casali (Giovanni Battista). De profanis et sacris veteribus ritibus, opus tripartitum, cujus prima pars agit de profanis Ægyptiorum ritibus, secunda pars agit de profanis Romanorum ritibus, tertia pars agit de sacris christianorum ritibus. 3 v. in 1. 4°. *Francofurti et Hanoverae, sumptibus T. H. Hauensteinii*, 1681.

Casas (Bartolomé de las). Breve relacion de la destruccion de las Indias Occidentales. 1 p. l. 140 pp. 18°. *Londres, Schulze y Dean*, 1812.

—— The same. Spieghel der spaenscher tyrannye, in West-Indien. Waer inne verhaelt wordt de moordadighe, schandelijcke, ende grouwelijcke feyten, die de selve spaenjaerden ghebruyckt hebben inde selve landen. In spaenscher talen beschreven. Mitsgaders de beschryvinge vander ghelegentheyt zeden ende aert van deself de lan den ende volcken. 42 l. sm. 4°. *Amstelredam, C. Claesz*, 1607.

—— The same. Den spieghel vande spaensche tierannie beeldelijcken afgemaelt. 18 l. including 18 pl. sm. 4°. *Amstelredam, C. Claesz*, 1609.

—— The same. 53 l. including 18 pl. sm. 4°. *Amsterdam, D. de Meijne aende Beurs*, 1612.

Casca llanna: (good news.) Love, woman, marriage: the grand secret! [*anon.*] 404 pp. 12°. *Boston, Randolph publishing co.* 1872.

Case (The) of the present possessors of the french lands in the island of St. Christophers. Humbly offered to the consideration of his majesty, and both houses of parliament. [*anon.*] 22 pp. 8°. *London, author*, 1721.
[MISCELLANEOUS pamphlets, v. 443].

Case (The) of ship mony briefly discoursed. *See* **Parker** (Henry).

Casella (Pietro Leone). Petri Leonis Casellæ de primis Italiæ colonis. De Tvscorvm origine & republica florentina. Elogia illvstrivm artificvm. Epigrammata et inscriptiones. 206 pp. 1 l. 12°. *Lvgdvni, sumptibus H. Cardon*, 1606.

Cassagnac (Adolphe Granier de). *See* **Granier de Cassagnac** (Adolphe).

Cassan (*Rev.* Stephen Hyde). Lives and memoirs of the bishops of Sherborne and Salisbury, from the year 705 to 1824. 3 parts in 1 v. 8°. *Salisbury, Brodie & Dowding*, 1824.

Cassas (Louis François). Voyage pittoresque et historique de l'Istrie et [de la] Dalmatie. [Rédigé par Joseph Lavallée, marquis de Bois-Robert]. 2 p. l. viii, 191 pp. 67 pl. 1 map. fol. *Paris, P. Didot*, 1802.

Cassas Zeinos (Diego de las). Sermon fvnebre a la traslacion de los huessos de el capitan d. Ioseph de Retes Largache, que se hizo de la iglesia cathedral de S. Bernardo, el dia 28 de Nov. 1690. sm. 4°. [*Mexico, viuda de F. R. Lupercio*, 1691].
[*In* RAMIREZ DE VARGAS (A.) Sagrado padron y panegyricos sermones, etc. l. 119-129].

Cassel (Paulus, *d. d.*) The book of judges. The book of Ruth. [Commentaries]. *See* **Bible.** (*English*).

Cassell (John). Book of birds. *See* **Brehm** (Alfred Edmund).

—— Cassell's popular natural history. [*anon.*] 4 v. 4°. *London, Cassell, Petter & Galpin*, [1864-67].

CONTENTS.

v. 1-2. Mammalia. 1864-65.
v. 3. Birds. 1866.
v. 4. Reptiles, fishes, insects, worms, crustaceans, molluscs, sea-stars, echinoderms, corallines, corals and animalcules. 1867.

Cassels (Samuel J.) Providence and other poems. 356 pp. 12°. *Macon, (Ga.) Griffin & Purse*, 1838.

Castagneda (Fernando Lopes de). *See* **Castañheda** (Fernão Lopes de).

Castaldo (Andres). Ceremonias de la iglesia en la uncion y coronacion del nuevo rey ó emperador. Escritas en latin, y traducidas al castellano. 1 p. l. 14 pp. 18°. *México, Valdés*, 1822.

Castañheda (Fernão Lopes de). Historia dell' Indie Orientali, scoperte, et conquistate da' Portoghesi, di commissione dell' inuitissimo re don Manuello [etc.] Distinta in libri vii. Et nuouamente di lingua portoghese in italiana tradotti dal signor Alfonso Vlloa. 2 v. 20 p. l. 518 l; 13 p. l. 366 l. 4°. *Venetia, F. e G. Ziletti*, 1578.

Castelvetro (Lodovico). Opere varie critiche, non più stampate, colla vita dell' autore scritta dal sig. proposto Lodovico Antonio Muratori. 6 p. l. 326 pp. 4°. *Berna, P. Foppens*, 1727.

Castiglione (*Conte* Baldassare). Carminvm liber. 16°. *Venetiis, ex officina Vincentii Valgrisii*, 1548.
[*In* CARMINA qvinqve illvstrivm poetarvm, pp. 59-85].

Castilhon *or* **Castillon** (Jean Louis). Le Diogène moderne, ou le désapprobateur, tiré en partie des manuscrits de sir Charles Wolban, & de sa correspondance avec sir George Bedfort, sir Olivier Stewart, &c. sur différens sujets de littérature, de morale & de philosophie. 2 v. xii, 395 pp; 2 p. l. 469 pp. 16°. *Bouillon, société typographique*, 1770.

Castilionæus (Balthassarus). *See* **Castiglione** (Baldassare).

Castle (Arthur). Phrénologie spiritualiste. Nouvelles études de psychologie appliquée. 2e éd. vii, 408 pp. 1 pl. 16°. *Paris, Didier & cie.* 1862.

Castle Avon. *See* **Marsh-Caldwell** (*Mrs.* Anne).

Castlemon (Harry, *pseudon.*) *See* **Fosdick** (Charles A.)

Castlen (Eppie Bowdre). Autumn dreams. By Chiquita. [*pseudon.*] 108 pp. 1 portrait. 12°. *New York, D. Appleton & co.* 1870.

Castro (Manuel Fernandez de). *See* **Fernandez de Castro.**

Cates (J. M. D.) Marriage and the married life. 292 pp. 12°. *Nashville (Tenn.) Graves, Marks & co.* 1860.

Cathara Clyde. [A novel]. *See* **Inconnu.**

Cathcart (George R.) Cathcart's youth's speaker. Selections in prose, poetry, and dialogues, for declamation and recitation. viii, 181 pp. 12°. *New York and Chicago, Ivison, Blakeman, Taylor & co.* 1872.

Cathcart (William). The papal system: from its origin to the present time. A historical sketch of every doctrine, claim and practice of the church of Rome. 478 pp. 1 portrait. 8°. *Philadelphia, Cathcart & Turner*, 1872.

Catholic mirror. Official organ of the archbishop of Baltimore, and bishops of Richmond, Wheeling, Wilmington, and vic. apost. North Carolina. [Weekly]. Jan. 7, to Dec. 30, 1871. v. 22. fol. *Baltimore, Kelly, Piet & co.* [1871].

Catholic (The) world. A monthly magazine of general literature and science. Oct. 1870, to March, 1872. v. 12–14. 8°. *New York, Catholic publication house*, 1871–72.

Catholic (The) youth's hymn book: containing the hymns of the seasons and festivals of the year, and an extensive collection of sacred melodies; by the christian brothers. 192 pp. 12°. *New York, P. O'Shea*, 1871.

Cattaneo (Alberto). Extrait d'vne histoire abbrégée (manvscrite) des roys de France. Principalement sur le sujet des Vaudois. fol. [*Paris*, 1684].
[*In* Godefroy (D.) Histoire de Charles viii. pp. 277–283].

Cattani da Diaccetto (Francesco, *the younger*). Breve raccolto della vita et costvmi di svor Catterina de Ricci. 20 l. sm. 4°. *Fiorenza, appresso G. Marescotti*, 1592.

——— L'essamerone. 4 p. l. 181 pp. 4 l. 4°. *Fiorenza, L. Torrentino*, 1563.

Catullus (Caius Valerius). The poems of Catullus: selected and prepared for the use of schools and colleges. By F. M. Hubbard. xii, 5–146 pp. 18°. *Boston, Perkins & Marvin*, 1836.

Cavanah (*Rev.* G. P.) General baptist hymn book: a collection of hymns for the use of christians in general, taken from the most approved authors. 456 pp. 24°. [*Evansville*], *author*, 1859.

Caverly (Robert B.) The bride of Burton, victory, and other poems. v. 2. 180 pp. 4 pl. 12°. *Lowell, (Ms.) Stone & Huse*, 1872.

——— The Merrimac and its incidents. An epic poem. 80 pp. 15 pl. 12°. *Boston, Innes & Niles*, 1866.

Caviceo (Giacopo). Libro del peregrino. Diligentemente in lingua toscha corretto. Et nouamente stampato, & hystoriato. Eng. title, 253 l. unp. 16°. *Venetia, H. di Rusconi & N. Zopino*, 1526.

——— The same. [2d ed.] 8 p. l. 232 l. 18°. *Vinegia, F. Bindoni & M. Pasini*, 1527.

Caxton (Laura, *pseudon?*) The Hartwell farm. Illustrated by the author. 200 pp. 4 pl. 12°. *Boston, A. K. Loring*, [1871].

Cayla (Jean Mamert). Le diable, sa grandeur et sa décadence. 2e éd. 402 pp. 1 l. 16°. *Paris, E. Dentu*, 1864.

Cayler (Charles). Out of the streets. A story of New York life. 360 pp. 12°. *New York, R. M. De Witt*, [1869].

Cayley (George John). Some account of the life and adventures of sir Regd. Mohun. Done in verse. 179 pp. 8°. *London, W. Pickering*, 1849.

C—d (A. *a. m.*) *and* **C.** (J. J.) A letter to the rev. mr. Foxcroft, being an examination of his apology for the rev. mr. Whitefield. By A. C—d, a. m. and J. J. C. [*anon.*] 19 pp. 4°. *Boston, T. Fleet*, 1745.
[*Note.*—Probably rev. Aaron Cleveland].

Cecil (*Rev.* Richard). A friendly visit to the house of mourning. 12°. [*New York, T. & J. Swords*, 1831].

[*In* NEW manual of private devotions, pp. 331–368].

——— Memoirs of the rev. John Newton, with general remarks on his life, connexions, and character. 258 pp. 12°. *New-York, T. A. Ronalds*, 1809.

Celestina (La), tragi-comedia. *See* **Rojas** (Fernando de) *and* **Cota** (Rodrigo de).

Celestine (Claude). Des choses merveillevses en natvre, où est traicté des erreurs des sens, des puissances de l'âme, & des influences des cieux, traduit en françois par Iaques Girard de Tournus. [*anon.*] 192 pp. 18°. *Lyon, M. Bonhomme*, 1557.

[*With* BACON (Roger). Le miroir d'alqvimie, 1557].

Cellarius (Christophorus). *See* **Keller** (Christoph).

Celsus (Aurelius *or* Aulus Cornelius). De re medica, libri octo. Q. Sereni medicinale poëma. Rhemnii poëma [de] pond. & mensuris. Cvm adnotationibvs et correctionibvs R. Constantini. 400 pp. 16°. *Venetijs, apud H. Scotum*, 1566.

Celtes *or* **Meissel** (Conrad). Conradi Celtis protvcii poete lavreati qvatvor libri amorvm secvndvm qvatvor latera Germanie feliciter incipivnt. [Ejusdem de origine, situ, moribus & institutio Norimbergæ libellus, etc.] lxxiii l. 47 l. unp. incl. 9 pl. 1 map. sm. fol. *Noribergæ*, 1500.

[*Note.*—34 lines on a page. Contains 2 woodcuts by Albert Dürer. In addition to the above, the vol. contains: Hymnos saphicvs in vitam sancti Sebaldi, Lvdvs Dyanae coram Maximiliano rege per sodalitatem litterariam danvbianam in Linzio; and Panegyricvs Vincencii Longini ad diuū Maximilianū, pro īstituto et erecto collegio poetarū et mathematicorū in Vienna].

Centinel (Vincent, *pseudon.*) Massachusetts in agony: or important hints to the inhabitants of the province, etc. 19 pp. sm. 4°. *Boston, D. Fowle*, 1750.

Cercada (Antonio Bera). Hebdomadario trino, exercicios devotos, y obsequiosos desagravios a la santissima trinidad. 3 p. l. 92 pp. 1 pl. 18°. *Mexico, J. B. de Hogal*, 1734.

[Imperfect: pp. 85–90 missing].

Ceremonies (The) for the healing of them that be diseased with the king's evil, used in the time of king Henry vii. [*anon.*] *London, H. Hills*, 1686. 8 pp. 8°. *London, reprinted for the editor*, 1789.

[*In* WALDRON (F. G.) Literary museum. *London*, 1792].

Ceremonies (The) of blessing cramp-rings on good-friday, used by the catholick kings of England. [From an old ms. *anon.*] 8 pp. 8°. [*London*, 1792].

[*In* WALDRON (F. G.) Literary museum. *London*, 1792].

Cerise (Laurent Alexandre Philibert). Exposé et examen critique du système phrénologique, considéré dans ses principes, dans sa méthode, dans sa théorie et dans ses conséquences. xxxi, 228 pp. 8°. *Paris, Trinquart*, 1836.

Cerneau (J.) Senda de las luces masónicas. 236 pp. 1 l. 1 pl. 18°. *New York, J. Kingsland & co.* a. l. 5821.

Cespedes (Christoval de). Vida, y virtudes de la venerable virgen Juana Maria de Estevan, religiosa de s. Clara en la ciudad de Santa-Fé, de Bogotà, en las Indias Occidentales. 10 p. l. 144 pp. sm. 4°. *Napoles, F. Mosca*, 1714.

Cessac (Girard Jean Lacuée, *comte* de). *See* **Lacuée.**

Chabanon (Michel Paul Guy de). Vie du Dante, avec une notice détaillée de ses ouvrages. 131 pp. 8°. *Amsterdam*, 1773.

Chabas (F.) Mélanges égyptologiques. 3e série. v. 1. Contenant sept mémoires et treize planches de textes hiératiques. Avec la collaboration de S. Birch et Ch. W. Goodwin. 2 p.l. 285 pp. 1 l. 13 pl. 8°. *Chalon, J. Dejussieu*, 1870. S.

Chabot (Charles). The handwriting of Junius, professionally investigated. With preface and collateral evidence, by the hon. Edward Twisleton. lxxviii, 300 pp. 137 l. facsimiles, 27 pl. 4°. *London, J. Murray*, 1871.

Chadbourne (Paul A. *ll. d.*) Lowell lectures: 1871. Instinct: its office in the animal kingdom, and its relation to the higher powers in man. 307 pp. 12°. *New York, G. P. Putnam & sons*, 1872.

Chalid ben Jesiki. Le livre des secretz d'alqvimie, translaté d'hébrieu en arabic, & d'arabic en latin, & de latin en françoys. 18°. [*Lyon, M. Bonhomme*, 1557].

[*In* BACON (Roger). Le miroir d'alqvimie. 1557. pp. 57–108].

——— *and* **Morienus** *romanus.* Entretien sur le magistère d'Hermès, rapporté par Galip, esclave de ce roi. 12°. [*Paris, A. Cailleau*, 1741].

[*In* SALMON (William). Bibliothèque des philosophes chimiques. 1741. v. 2, pp. 56–111].

Chalkley (Thomas). A collection of [his] works. [Preface by Israel Pemberton]. 2

Chalkley (Thomas)—continued. parts in 1 v. xiv, 590 pp. 12°. *Philadelphia, B. Franklin and D. Hall*, 1749.

CONTENTS.

Part i. A journal, or, historical account, of [his] life, travels, and christian experiences.
Part ii. God's great love unto mankind through Jesus Christ, our Lord.
Fruits of divine meditation at sea. 1699.
An exhortation to youth and others to follow.
A loving invitation to seek almighty God.
Forcing a maintenance, not warrantable from the holy scripture, for a minister of the gospel.
Some observations on Christ's sermon on the mount.
Some scruples of conscience about the common prayer.
A letter to a friend in Ireland; containing a relation of some sorrowful instances of the effects of intemperance.
A letter to Aquila Paca, high sheriff of Baltimore co. Maryland.
Christ's kingdom exalted.
Some considerations on the call, work, and wages, of the ministers of Christ.
Concerning personal election and reprobation.
A letter to Cotton Mather, in New-England.
Youth persuaded to obedience, gratitude, and honour, to God, and their parents.
Free thoughts communicated to freethinkers: in order to promote thinking on the name and works of God.

Challen (James). Igdrasil; or, the tree of existence. [A poem]. 170 pp. 12°. *Philadelphia, Lindsay & Blakiston*, 1859.

Chalmers (*Rev.* Peter). Two discourses on the sin, danger and remedy of duelling; with a view of the rise, progress, variations, prohibitions, and preventives, of single combat: with notes. x, 261 pp. 18°. *Edinburgh, Thomsons, brothers*, 1822.

Chalmers (*Rev.* Thomas). An introductory essay [to Baxter's Call to the unconverted]. 18°. *New York, American tract society*, [*about* 1840].

[*In* BAXTER (*Rev.* Richard). A call to the unconverted, [*about* 1840].

Chaluz de Vernevil (F. T. Alphonso). An original and condensed grammar of harmony, counterpoint and musical composition. *See* **Virués y Spínola** (José Joaquin de) *and* **Chaluz de Vernevil.**

Chambaud (Louis). The idioms of the french and english languages. New ed. carefully revised and improved. 262 pp. 16°. *London, F. Wingrave*, 1803.

Chamberlayne (Israel, *d. d.*) Saving faith; its rationale: with a demonstration of its presence in the organic condition of methodist-church membership. 216 pp. 12°. *New York, Carlton & Lanahan*, 1871.

Chamberlayne (William). Pharonnida; an heroic poem in five books. 2 v. viii, 192 pp; 1 p. l. 5–186 pp. 12°. *London, C. Chapple*, 1820.

Chamberlin (Everett). Chicago and the great conflagration, 1872. *See* **Colbert** (Elias) *and* **Chamberlin.**

Chambers (Reuben). The thomsonian practice of medicine; containing the names, and a description of the virtues and uses of the medicines belonging to this system of practice. 451 pp. 12°. *Bethania (Pa.)* 1843.

Chambers (Talbot W. *d. d.*) Hours of prayer in the noon prayer-meeting, Fulton street, New York. 212 pp. 1 pl. 16°. *New York, board of publication r. c. a.* [1871].

——— Memoir of the life and character of the late hon. Theo. Frelinghuysen, ll. d. 289 pp. 1 pl. 1 portrait. 12°. *New York, Harper & brothers*, 1863.

Chambers (William). France, its history and revolutions. vii, 336 pp. 12°. *Edinburgh and London, W. & R. Chambers*, 1871.

Chambers (William *and* Robert). Chambers's encyclopædia: a dictionary of universal knowledge for the people. v. 5–10. 8°. *Philadelphia, J. B. Lippincott & co.* 1871–72.

[Completed].

——— Chambers's journal of popular literature, science and arts. [Weekly]. Jan. 1 to Dec. 31, 1870. [Fourth series, v. 7]. 8°. *London and Edinburgh, W. & R. Chambers*, [1870].

——— Exemplary and instructive biography. For the study and entertainment of youth. 290 pp. 16°. *Edinburgh, W. & R. Chambers*, 1855.

[Chambers's educational course].

Champier (Symphorien). Extrait d'vne histoire des roys de France, intitvlée Francorvm regvm genealogia. [Aussi] extrait d'vne avtre histoire, dont le titre est Trophæum Gallorum, où est le traité de paix du roy Charles viii. auec le pape Alexandre vi. fol. [*Paris*, 1684].

[*In* GODEFROY (T. *and* D. de). Histoire de Charles viii. pp. 284–290].

Champion (The): containing a series of papers, humourous, moral, political, and critical. To each of which is added, A proper index to the times. [*anon.* By Henry Fielding and James Ralph]. 2 v. 1 p. l. x, 360 pp; 1 p. l. 360 pp. 12°. *London, J. Huggonson*, 1741.

Champlain (Samuel de). Œuvres, publiées sous le patronage de l'université Laval, par l'abbé C. H. Laverdière. 2e éd. 5 v. in 6. 4°. *Québec, G. E. Desbarats*, 1870.

CONTENTS.

v. 1. Preface. Notice biographique de Champlain. 1 p. l. lxxvi pp. 1 portrait.

Champlain (Samuel de)—continued.

Brief discovrs des choses plvs remarqvables qve Champlain a reconneues aux Indes Occidentalles au voiage qu'il en a faict en l'année 1599 et 1601. iv, 48 pp. 62 pl.
v. 2. Des savvages, ov voyage de Champlain, fait en la France Novvelle, 1603. *Paris, C. de Monstr'œil,* [1603]. viii, 63 pp.
v. 3. Les voyages de Champlain. *Paris, Iean Berjon,* 1613. xvi, 274 pp. 2 l. 24 pl.
Quatriesme voyage de Champlain, fait en 1613. pp. 279–327, 1 map.
v. 4. Voyages et discovvertvres faites en la Novvelle France, depuis l'anné 1615 iusques à la fin de l'année 1618. *Paris, C. Collet,* 1619. viii, 143 pp. 5 pl.
v. 5. 1e partie. Les voyages de la Novvelle France occidentale, dicte Canada, faits par Champlain, et toutes les descouuertes qu'il a faites en ce païs depuis l'an 1603, iusques en l'an 1629. *Paris, L. Sevestre,* 1632. 15, 328 pp.
v. 5. 2e partie. Seconde partie des voyages dv sievr de Champlain. 343, 8 pp. 1 map.
Traitté de la marine et dv devoir d'vn bon marinier. 55 pp.
Doctrine chrestienne dv Ledesme, traduicte en langage canadois. Par Brebœuf. [Avec] l'oraison dominicale, etc. 20 pp.
Pièces justificatives. 36 pp.
Table des matières. 30 pp.

Chandler (S. C.) The theology of the bible, or the true doctrines of the christian faith plainly stated and defended; with a key to the revelations. 408 pp. 1 portrait. 12°. *New York, author,* 1853.

Chandler (W. H.) Chandler's visitor's guide in and around Boston. 128 pp. 16°. *Boston, W. H. Chandler & co.* 1870.

Channing (William Ellery, *jr.*) The wanderer. A colloquial poem. 137 pp. 16°. *Boston, J. R. Osgood & co.* 1871.

——— The woodman, and other poems. iv, 92 pp. 16°. *Boston, J. Munroe & co.* 1849.

Chaos del tri per vno. *See* **Folengo** (Teofilo).

Chapel (The) of st. Mary. *See* **Evans** (Mary).

Chapelle (Claude Emmanuel Lhuillier) *and* **Bachaumont** (François le Coigneux de). Œuvres de Chapelle et de Bachaumont. [Publ. par Lefebvre de Saint Marc]. 1 p. l. lxxvi, 320 pp. 18°. *Paris, Quillau,* 1755.

Chapin (Orange). The Chapin genealogy, containing a very large proportion of the descendants of dea. Samuel Chapin, who settled in Springfield, Mass. in 1642. To which is added a "Centennial discourse," by E. B. Clark. Also, an address, by George Bliss. viii, 368 pp. 8°. *Northampton, Metcalf & co.* 1862.

Chapin (Walter). The missionary gazetteer, comprising a view of the inhabitants, and a geographical description of the countries and places, where protestant missionaries have labored; with an appendix, containing an alphabetical list of missionaries, their stations, the time of entering, removal, or decease. 420 pp. 1 map. 12°. *Woodstock, (Vt.) D. Watson,* 1825.

Chapin (William). A complete reference gazetteer of the United States of North America; containing a general view of the United States, and of each state and territory, and a notice of the various canals, railroads, and internal improvements. 371 pp. 8°. *New York, T. & E. H. Ensign,* 1843.

Chaplin (Jeremiah, *d. d.*) The evening of life; or, light and comfort amidst the shadows of declining years. A new edition, much enlarged. xvi, 281 pp. 1 pl. 12°. *Boston, Gould & Lincoln,* 1859.

——— Life of Henry Dunster. xx, 315 pp. 16°. *Boston, J. R. Osgood & co.* 1872.

——— The memorial hour; or the Lord's supper in its relation to doctrine and life. 283 pp. 12°. *Boston, Gould & Lincoln,* 1864.

Chapman (Alfred F.) Master's manual, adapted to the work and lectures as exemplified by the grand lodge of Massachusetts. 64 pp. 1 l. 32°. *Boston, Pollard & Leighton,* 1872.

Chapman (*Rev.* Ezekiel J.) Critical and explanatory notes, on many passages of scripture (of the new testament chiefly). 2d ed. 308 pp. 12°. *Utica, (N. Y.) Hastings & Tracy,* 1831.

Chapman (George). Cæsar and Pompey: a roman tragedy, declaring their vvarres. Out of whose euents is euicted this proposition. Only a iust man is a freeman. 37 l. unp. sm. 4°. *London, T. Harper for G. Edmonson,* 1631.

——— The tragedy of Alphonsus, emperour of Germany, as it hath been very often acted (with great applause) at the privat house in Black-Friers by his late maiesties servants. 2 p. l. 71 pp. sm. 4°. *London, H. Moseley,* 1654.

Chapman (George W.) A tribute to Kane: and other poems. 161 pp. 12°. *New York, Rudd & Carleton,* 1860.

Chapman (M. J.) Barbadoes, and other poems. x, 210 pp. 16°. *London, J. Fraser,* 1833.

Chapman (T. Ellwood). Philadelphia merchants' and artisans' directory for 1853. *See* **Philadelphia.**

Chapman (T. J. *compiler*). Schools and schoolmasters. From the writings of Dickens. *See* **Dickens** (Charles).

Chapone (Hester). The works of mrs. Chapone: now first collected. [Also], an account of her life and character, drawn up by her own family. 4 v. 16°. *London, J. Murray,* 1807.

Chaptal (Jean Antonin Claude, *comte de Chanteloup*). Chymistry applied to agriculture. 1st american ed. xl, 365 pp. 12°. *Boston, Hilliard, Gray & co.* 1835.

——— The same. With a preliminary chapter, on the organization, structure, etc. of plants, by sir Humphrey Davy. And an essay on lime as a manure, by M. Puvis; with observations, by James Renwick, ll. d. Translated and edited by rev. William Page. 359 pp. 18°. *New York, Harper & brothers,* 1839.
[School district library, no. 90].

Chardon de la Rochette (Simon). Mélanges de critique et de philologie. 3 v. 8°. *Paris, D'Hautel,* 1812.

Charistaeus (Joannes, *pseudon*?) De fide meretricvm, in svos amatores. Appendix ex orationibvs Ioannis Charistaei. [Auctore Jacobo Wimphelingio]? 18°. *Lvgd. Batav. ex typographia rediviva,* 1648.
[*In* OBSOPŒUS (Vincenz). De arte bibendi. 1648. pp. 265–280].

Charlatans (Les) célèbres. *See* **Gouriet** (Jean Baptiste).

Charles (*Mrs.* Elizabeth). Diary of mrs. Kitty Trevylyan: a story of the times of Whitefield and the Wesleys. By the author of "Chronicles of the Schonberg-Cotta family," [etc. *anon.*] With a preface, by the author, for the american edition. 436 pp. 12°. *New York, M. W. Dodd,* 1864.

Charleston (*S. C.*) The directory and stranger's guide; also a directory for Charleston Neck, for the year 1819. [Also], an almanack; the tariff of duties on all goods imported into the United States; rates of wharfage, weighing, storage, cartage and drayage, &c. 2 p. l. 98, 56 pp. 12°. *Charleston, Schenck & Turner,* 1819.

——— Directory for the year 1852. Containing the names, occupation, place of business and residence of the inhabitants generally, with other information of general interest. 12, 220 pp. 16°. *Charleston, J. H. Bagget,* 1851.

——— Charleston directory. 1866. Containing the names of the inhabitants, and an appendix of much useful information. Compiled by Burke and Boinest. 116 pp. 8°. *New York, M. B. Brown & co.* 1866.

Charlestown (*Mass.*) The Charlestown directory, 1872: containing the city record, the names of the citizens, and a business directory, with other useful information. By Sampson, Davenport & Co. no. xviii. 8°. *Charlestown, A. E. Cutter & co.* [1871].

Charleton (Walter, *m. d.*) Physiologia epicuro-gassendo-charltoniana: or a fabrick of science natural, upon the hypothesis of atoms, founded by Epicurus, repaired by Petrus Gassendus, augmented by Walter Charleton. 15 p. l. 475 pp. 2 l. fol. *London, T. Newcomb for T. Heath,* 1654.

Charlevoix (Pierre François Xavier de). History and general description of New France. Translated, with notes, by J. G. Shea. v. 5. 8°. *New York, J. G. Shea,* 1871.

Charpentier de Cossigny. *See* **Cossigny**.

Chartarius (Vincentius). *See* **Cartari** (Vincenzo).

Chase (Heber, *m. d.*) Treatise on the radical cure of hernia by instruments. With numerous illustrations. xiii, 195 pp. 8°. *Philadelphia, J. G. Auner,* 1836.

Chase (Mary Granger). Two christmas days. 154 pp. 1 pl. 18°. *New York, Gen. prot. episcopal s. s. union & ch. book society,* 1872.

——— Worth and riches. 206 pp. 18°. *New York, Gen. prot. episcopal s. s. union & ch. book society,* 1872.

Chase (Mary M.) Mary M. Chase and her writings. Henry Fowler, editor. xlvii, 336 pp. 12°. *Boston, Ticknor & Fields,* 1855.

Chase (S. C. *m. d.*) Mnemeology. Particularly devoted to the cultivation of the mental faculties; to which is added a treatise on physical culture. Also, a mental gymnasia, with miscellaneous chapters, prepared for lecturers and teachers. 221 pp. 12°. *Cincinnati, Moore, Wilstach, Keys & co.* 1862.

Chasles (Victor Euphémion Philarète). Études sur l'Espagne et sur les influences de la littérature espagnole en France et en Italie. 2 p. l. viii, 567 pp. 12°. *Paris, Amyot,* [1847].

——— Notabilities in France and England. With an autobiography. 277 pp. 12°. *New York, G. P. Putnam & co.* 1853.
[*Note.*—Translated from his "Studies upon men and manners of the nineteenth century"].

Chastel (Étienne Louis). Le christianisme et l'église au moyen âge. Coup-d'œil historique. xi, 358 pp. 1 l. 12°. *Paris, J. Cherbuliez,* 1859.

Chastel (Étienne Louis)—continued.

——— Histoire de la destruction du paganisme dans l'empire d'Orient. 2 p. l. 382 pp. 8°. *Paris, J. Cherbuliez*, 1850.

Chastellux (François Jean, *marquis* de). An essay on public happiness, investigating the state of human nature, under each of its particular appearances, through the several periods of history, to the present times. Translated by J. K. [*anon.*] 2 v. 6 p. l. 424, 23 pp; 2 p. l. 376, 2 pp. 29 l. 12°. *London, T. Cadell*, 1774.

Chastenet de Puységur (*Comte* Antoine Hyacinthe Anne). A treatise upon the navigation of St. Domingo: with sailing directions, for the whole extent of its coasts, channels, bays and harbours. Translated from the french by Charles de Monmonier. 2 p. l. 112 pp. 8°. *Baltimore, C. de Monmonier*, 1802.

——— The same.
[BAILEY pamphlets, v. 18].

Chastenet de Puységur (Armand Marie Jacques, *marquis* de). Appel aux savans observateurs du dixneuvième siècle de la décision portée par leurs prédécesseurs contre le magnétisme animal, et fin du traitement du jeune Hébert. 2 p. l. 11, 91, 110, 128 pp. 8°. *Paris, J. G. Dentu*, 1813.

——— An essay of instruction, on animal magnetism; translated from the french of the marquis de Puységur, together with various extracts upon the subject, and notes, by John King, m. d. 84 pp. 12°. *New York, J. C. Kelley*, [1837].

——— Du magnétisme animal, considéré dans ses rapports avec diverses branches de la physique générale. 2 p. l. 478 pp. 1 l. 8°. *Paris, Desenne*, 1807.

Chateaubriand (François Auguste de). The martyrs. A revised translation. Edited by O. W. Wight. 451 pp. 12°. *New York, Derby & Jackson*, 1859.

——— El siglo de oro del cristianismo. Traducido al castellano por el p. fr. Luis Fernandez de Santa Maria. 1ª ed. mexicana. 78 pp. 18°. *México*, 1845.

Chateauvieux. *See* **Lullin de Chateauvieux** (Jacob Frédéric).

Chatrian (Alexandre). *See* **Erckmann** (Émile) *and* **Chatrian.**

Chaucer (Geoffrey). A six-text print of Chaucer's Canterbury tales in parallel columns from the following mss: 1. The Ellesmere. 2. The Hengwrt. 3. The Cambridge univ. lib. 4. The Corpus Christi coll. Oxford. 5. The Petworth. 6. The Lansdowne. Edited by F. J. Furnivall. Parts 2–3. obl. fol. *London, N. Trübner & co.* 1870–71.
[CHAUCER society publications. 1st series, nos. 14–15].

——— The same. The Cambridge ms. (Cambridge univ. library, Gg. 4, 27) of Canterbury tales. Edited by Frederick J. Furnivall. Part iii. pp. 128–166, 2 l. 14 pl. 8°. *London, N. Trübner & co.* 1871.
[CHAUCER society publications. 1st series, no. 17].

——— The same. The Corpus ms. (Corpus Christi coll. Oxford) of Chaucer's Canterbury tales. Edited by Frederick J. Furnivall. Part iii. 23 l. 14 pl. 8°. *London, N. Trübner & co.* 1871.
[CHAUCER society publications. 1st series, no. 18].

——— The same. The Ellesmere ms. of Chaucer's Canterbury tales. Edited by Frederick J. Furnivall. Part iii. 12, 128–166 pp. 2 l. 14 pl. 8°. *London, N. Trübner & co.* 1871.
[CHAUCER society publications. 1st series, no. 16].

——— The same. The Lansdowne ms. (no. 851) of Canterbury tales. Edited by F. J. Furnivall. Part iii. 25 l. 14 pl. 8°. *London, N. Trübner & co.* 1871.
[CHAUCER society publications. 1st series, no. 20].

——— The same. The Petworth ms. of Chaucer's Canterbury tales. Edited by Frederick J. Furnivall. Part iii. 34 l. 14 pl. 8°. *London, N. Trübner & co.* 1871.
[CHAUCER society publications. 1st series, no. 19].

——— Gualtherus and Griselda; or, happiness properly estimated. A tale. sm. 4°. [*London, J. Hamilton & co.* 1794].
[*In* HAMILTON (John). Angelica's ladies' library, pp. 73–104].

——— A parallel-text edition of Chaucer's minor poems. Edited by Frederick J. Furnivall. Part i. 1 p. l. 121 pp. 1 pl. obl. fol. *London, Chaucer society*, 1871.
[CHAUCER society publications. 1st series, no. 21, part i].

——— The same. A one-text print of Chaucer's minor poems, edited by Frederick J. Furnivall. Part i. 100 pp. 1 pl. 8°. *London, N. Trübner & co.* 1871.
[CHAUCER society publications. 1st series, no. 24].

CONTENTS.

1. The dethe of Blaunche the duchesse, p. 1.
2. The compleynte to pite, p. 39.
3. The parlament of foules, p. 45.
4. The complaynt of Mars, p. 71.
5. The a b c, p. 83.

——— The same. Odd texts of Chaucer's minor poems, edited by Frederick J. Furni-

Chaucer (Geoffrey)—continued. vall. Part i. viii, 63 pp. 8°. *London, N. Trübner & co.* 1871.

[CHAUCER society publications. 1st series, no. 23].

CONTENTS.

1. Two bits of the parlament of foules, p. 1.
2. The two differing versions of the prologue of the legende of good women, p. 23.

Appendix of poems attributed to Chaucer:

1. The balade of pytee, a continuation of Chaucer's compleynte to pite, p. i.
2. The crouycle made by Chaucier, p. vi.

——— The same. Supplementary parallel-texts of Chaucer's minor poems. Edited by Frederick J. Furnivall. Part i. 1. The parlament of foules. 26 pp. obl. fol. *London, Chaucer society*, 1871.

[CHAUCER society publications. 1st series, no. 22].

Chaucer society. Publications. 1st series. nos. 1–24. 8°. and obl. fol. *London, society*, 1868–71.

CONTENTS.

CHAUCER (G.) A six text print of Chaucer's Canterbury tales in parallel columns from the following mss: 1. Ellesmere. 2. Hengwrt. 3. Cambridge. 4. Corpus Christi. 5. Petworth. 6. Lansdowne. Edited by F. J. Furnivall. Parts i–iii. obl. fol. (nos. 1, 14, and 15).
——— The same. Ellesmere ms. Parts i–iii. 8°. (nos. 2, 8, and 16).
——— The same. Hengwrt ms. Parts i–ii. 8°. (nos. 3 and 9).
——— The same. Cambridge ms. Parts i–iii. 8°. (nos. 4, 10, and 17).
——— The same. Corpus ms. Parts i–iii. 8°. (nos. 5, 11, and 18).
——— The same. Petworth ms. Parts i–iii. 8°. (nos. 6, 12, and 19).
——— The same. Lansdowne ms. Parts i–iii. 8°. (nos. 7, 13, and 20).
——— A parallel-text edition of Chaucer's minor poems. Edited by F. J. Furnivall. Part i. obl. fol. (no. 21).
——— The same. Supplementary parallel-texts of Chaucer's minor poems. Edited by F. J. Furnivall. Part i. obl. fol. (no. 22).
——— The same. Odd texts of Chaucer's minor poems, edited by F. J. Furnivall. Part i. (no. 23).
——— The same. A one-text print of Chaucer's minor poems, edited by F. J. Furnivall. Part i. (no. 24).

——— 2d series. nos. 1–6. 8°. *London, society*, 1868–71.

CONTENTS.

ELLIS (A. J.) On early english pronunciation with special reference to Shakespere and Chaucer. Parts i–iii. (nos. 1, 4, and 5).
ESSAYS on Chaucer. Part i. 1. Ebert's review of Sandras's Étude sur Chaucer. Translated by J. W. Van Rees Hoets. 2. A thirteenth-century latin treatise on the chilindre. (no. 2).
FURNIVALL (F. J.) A temporary preface to the six-text edition of Chaucer's Canterbury tales. Part i. (no 3).
——— Trial-forewords to my "Parallel-text edition of Chaucer's minor poems." (no. 6).

Chaulmer (Charles). Le novveav-monde ov l'Amérique chrestienne, avec le svpplément à l'abbrégé des Annales ecclésiastiqves et politiqves de l'ancien [par Cesar Barone], ou l'histoire des missions, & des autres affaires de l'Europe, de l'Asie et de l'Affrique. 6 p. l. 432 pp. 2 l. 360 pp. 3 l. 16°. *Paris, autheur & S. Piget*, 1659.

Chaumeix (Abraham Joseph de). La petite encyclopédie, ou dictionnaire des philosophes, ouvrage posthume d'un de ces messieurs. [*anon.*] 4 p. l. 136 pp. 12°. *Anvers, J. Gasbeck*, 1772.

Chaupy (Capmartin Bertrand de). Découverte de la maison de campagne d'Horace. Ouvrage utile pour l'intelligence de cet auteur, & qui donne occasion de traiter d'une suite considérable de lieux antiques. 3 v. 8°. *Rome, l'imprimerie de Zempel*, 1767–69.

Chauvenet (William). A manual of spherical and practical astronomy. With an appendix on the method of least squares. 2 v. 708 pp; 632 pp. 15 pl. 8°. *Philadelphia, J. B. Lippincott & co.* 1863.

Chavasse (Pye Henry). Physical life of man and woman: or, advice to both sexes. Advice to wife and mother, by P. H. Chavasse, and advice to a maiden, husband, and son, from the most recent french and german works; with notes and additions, by an american medical writer. 431 pp. 1 pl. 12°. *Cincinnati, National publishing co.* 1871.

——— Woman as a wife and mother. iv, 309 pp. 2 pl; 408 pp. 4 pl. 12°. *Philadelphia, W. B. Evans & co.* [1871].

——— *and* **Getchell** (F. H. *m. d.*) The physical training of children. By P. H. Chavasse. With a preliminary dissertation, by F. H. Getchell. 368 pp. 1 pl. 8°. *Philadelphia, New-world publishing company*, [1871].

Chazal (Flore Célestine Thérèse Henriette Tristan Moscoso, *madame*). Pérégrinations d'une paria (1833–1834), par mme. Flore Tristan. 2 v. xlvii, 400 pp; 2 p. l. 462 pp. 1 l. 8°. *Paris, A. Bertrand*, 1838.

Chazaud (A.) Étude sur la chronologie des sires de Bourbon (x^e–xiiie siècles). 2 p. l. iii, 244, xli pp. 1 l. 2 pl. 8°. *Moulins, C. Desrosiers*, 1865. S.

[MOULINS. Société d'émulation de l'Allier. Publications].

——— Fragments du cartulaire de la Chapelle-Aude. 2 p. l. xcv, 198 pp. 8°. *Moulins, C. Desrosiers*, [*etc.*] 1860.

[MOULINS. Société d'émulation de l'Allier. Publications].

Cheesbro (Caroline). *See* **Chesebro** (Caroline).

Cheever (George Barrell, *d. d.*) God's hand in America. With an essay, by the rev. dr. Skinner. 168 pp. 12°. *New York, M. W. Dodd*, 1841.

Cheever (G. B. *d. d.*)—continued.

——— Lectures on the life, genius and insanity of Cowper. 415 pp. 3 pl. 12°. *New York, R. Carter & brothers*, 1856.

——— Remarks on the life, character, and writings, of archbishop Leighton. 8°. [*Boston*, 1832].
[*In* LEIGHTON (Robert). Select works, pp. v–lx].

Chellis (Mary Dwinell). At lion's mouth. iv, 9–412 pp. 3 pl. 16°. *New York, National temperance society and publication house*, 1872.

——— Father Merrill. 410 pp. 3 pl. 16°. *Boston, I. P. Warren*, [1872].

——— The hermit of Holcombe. 336 pp. 4 pl. 16°. *Boston, H. A. Young & co.* [1871].
[STANDARD series of temperance tales].

Chelsea (*Mass.*) The Chelsea directory for 1872. no. 11. By John Brent. 8°. *Boston*, 1872.

Chemisches central-blatt. Repertorium für reine, pharmaceutische, physiologische und technische chemie. 3e folge. 1–2 jahrgang. 8°. *Leipzig, L. Voss*, 1870–71.

Cheney (*Mrs.* Ednah D.) Social games. A collection of 31 games with cards. 134 pp. sq. 24°. *Boston, Lee & Shepard*, [1871].

Chennechot (L. E.) Histoire philosophique et politique de Russie, depuis les temps les plus reculés jusqu'à nos jours. *See* **Esneaux** (J.) *and* **Chennechot**

Cherubini (Luigi Carlo Zanobi Salvatore Maria). The water-carrier. (Les deux journées). Lyric drama in three acts. Composed by Cherubini [without music]. Translated by Arthur Baildon. 31 pp. 8°. [*New York*], *W. C. Bryant & co.* 1871.
[PAREPA-ROSA grand english opera].

Chéruel (Adolphe). Saint-Simon considéré comme historien de Louis xiv. 3 p. l. x, 660 pp. 8°. *Paris, L. Hachette & cie.* 1865.

Chesebro (Caroline). Amy Carr; or, the fortune-teller. By Caroline Cheesbro. 226 pp. 3 pl. 16°. *New York, M. W. Dodd*, 1864.

——— The sparrow's fall; or, under the willow. And other stories. [Walter Martin. Sylva's garden. Tim Bernard's election. Ned and Nelly. Little Dick Weaver's great bonfire]. 178 pp. 18°. *New York, Carlton & Porter*, [1863].

——— Victoria; or, the world overcome. 465 pp. 12°. *New York, Derby & Jackson*, 1856.

Chevalet (Émile). Le livre de Job. 3 p. l. 280 pp. 12°. *Paris, P. Permain*, 1854.

Chevé (*Mme.* Émile). Méthode élémentaire de musique vocale. La partie théorique de cet ouvrage est rédigée par Émile Chevé. 2e éd. 320 pp. 8°. *Paris, l'auteur*, 1844.

Chevillier (André). L'origine de l'imprimerie de Paris. Dissertation historique et critique. 4 p. l. 448 pp. 4°. *Paris, J. de Laulne*, 1694.

Chiaramonti (Scipione). Difesa di Scipione Chiaramonti da Cesena al svo Antiticone, e libro delle tre nuoue stelle dall' oppositioni dell' avtore de' due massimi sistemi tolemaico, e copernicano. [*anon.*] 6 p. l. 344 pp. 2 l. 1 pl. 4°. *Firenze, appresso il Landini*, 1633.

Chicago (*Ill.*) Chicago census report; and statistical review, embracing a complete directory of the city, with a vast amount of valuable statistical, historical and commercial information, compiled from actual canvass. By Richard Edwards. 4 p. l. 1264 pp. 1 map. 8°. *Chicago, R. Edwards*, [1871].

——— Danenhower's Chicago city directory, for 1851. 264 pp. 1 map. 12°. *Chicago, W. W. Danenhower*, 1851. s.

——— Edwards' fourteenth annual directory of the inhabitants, institutions [etc.] of the city of Chicago, embracing a complete business directory for 1871. v. 14. 8°. *Chicago, R. Edwards*, 1871.

——— The guide: being a consolidation of Green's postal and Chandler's business guides. 4 p. l. 78 pp. 1 l. 8°. *Chicago, D. Green*, 1871.

——— A guide to the streets and avenues of the city of Chicago. 19 p. l. 104 pp. 4 l. 24°. [*Chicago*], *T. A. Hungerford & co.* [1871].

Chicago (The) fire. *See* **Goodsell** (J. H. *and* C. M.)

Child (Gilbert W). Essays on physiological subjects. 2d ed. With additions. xv, 300 pp. incl. 2 pl. 12°. *London, Longmans, Green & co.* 1869.

Child (Lydia Maria). The children of Mount Ida, and other stories. 282 pp. 1 pl. 12°. *New York, C. S. Francis*, 1871.

——— The Christ-child, and other stories. 190 pp. 2 pl. 18°. *Boston, D. Lothrop & co.* [1869].

——— The coronal. A collection of miscellaneous pieces, written at various times. vi, 285 pp. 1 pl. 16°. *Boston, Carter & Hendee*, 1832.

Child (Lydia Maria)—continued.

——— Good little Mitty, and other stories. 178 pp. 18°. *Boston, D. Lothrop & co.* [1869].

——— The magician's show box, and other stories. By the author of "Rainbows for children." [*anon.*] 295 pp. 6 pl. 16°. *Boston, Ticknor & Fields*, 1856.

——— Married women: biographies of good wives. 288 pp. 1 pl. 12°. *New York, C. S. Francis*, 1871.

——— The mother's book. xii, 168 pp. 12°. *Boston, Carter, Hendee & Babcock*, 1831.

——— The same. 6th ed. x, 175 pp. 12°. *New York, C. S. Francis & co.* 1844.

——— A new flower for children. 311 pp. 18°. *New York, C. S. Francis & co.* 1856.

——— Rose Marian, and the flower fairies. Adapted from the german legend. 46 pp. sq. 16°. *New York, C. S. Francis & co.* 1850.

Child (The) at home. [A monthly sunday-school paper. Colored edition]. July, 1864, to Dec. 1871. v. 5-12. 4°. *Boston, American tract society*, 1864-71.

Child-life in Italy; a story of six years abroad. [*anon.*] 363 pp. 12°. *Boston, J. E. Tilton & co.* 1866.

Children's catechism; for classes to recite in concert. 1871. *See* **Arnold** (Alexander S.)

Children's (The) friend. A monthly magazine, devoted to the best interests of the young. Edited by Esther K. Smedley. Jan. 1870, to Dec. 1871. v. 5-6. sm. 4°. *West-chester, (Pa.)* 1870-71.

Children's magazine. [Monthly]. Jan. to Dec. 1871. New series, v. 1; old series, v. 43. sm. 4°. *New York, Gen. prot. epis. sunday school union and church book society*, [1871].

Child's (The) preacher; a series of addresses to the young. Founded on scripture texts. [By Alexander Fletcher & others]. 451 pp. 6 pl. 18°. *New York, Carlton & Phillips*, 1855.

Chili. *Congress.* Documentos parlamentarios. Discursos de apertura en las sesiones del congreso, i memorias ministeriales correspondientes a la administracion publica. 1831-61. v. 1-9. 8°. *Santiago, Ferrocarril*, 1859-61. s.

——— *Departamento de hacienda.* Memoria que el ministro de estado en el departamento de hacienda presenta al congreso nacional de 1862-67. 6 v. 8°. *Santiago, imprenta nacional*, 1862-67. s.

Chili—continued.

——— *Departamento del interior.* Memoria que el ministro de estado en el departamento del interior presenta al congreso nacional. 1862-67. 6 v. 8°. *Santiago, imprenta nacional*, 1862-67. s.

——— *Departamento de relaciones exteriores.* Memoria que el ministro de estado en el departamento de relaciones exteriores presenta al congreso nacional. 1864-67. 4 v. 8°. *Santiago de Chile, imprenta nacional*, 1864-65. s.

Chimentellius. *See* **Cimentelli.**

China and foreign powers. Treaties of peace, etc. 101 pp. 8°. [*Canton*, 1846].
[Reprinted from the Chinese repository].

Chiquita (*pseudon.*) *See* **Castlen** (E. B.)

Chizzolini (Girolamo). *See* **Italia** (L') agricola, 1869-70.

Choerilus *samius.* Choerili samii qvae svpersvnt collegit et illvstravit de Choerili samii aetate vita et poesi aliisqve Choerilis disservit A. F. Naekius. Inest de Sardanapali epigrammatis dispvtatio. vi, 289 pp. 8°. *Lipsiæ, in libraria Wiedmannia*, 1817.

Choheleth, or the royal preacher, a poetical paraphrase of the book of Ecclesiastes. [*anon.*] 1 p. l. xxvi, 132 pp. 4°. *London, J. Wallis*, 1768.

Choiseul-Gouffier (*Comtesse* de, *née comtesse* de Tisenhauz). Halina Oginska, ou les Suédois en Pologne. 2 v. 2 p. l. 238 pp; 2 p. l. 219 pp. 16°. *Bruxelles, societé belge de librairie*, 1839.

Choisy (François Timoléon, *l'abbé* de). Journal du voyage de Siam fait en 1685 & 1686. 2e éd. 2 p. l. 652 pp. 18°. *Paris, S. Mabre-Cramoisy*, 1687.

Choix de maximes, pensées morales, et proverbes, tirés de divers philosophes anciens et de différens peuples. [*anon.*] 2 p. l. 284 pp. 24°. *Londres*, 1785.

Chokier (Jean Surlet de). *See* **Surlet** de Chokier (Jean).

Choquet (Charles). Traité de perspective linéaire, à l'usage des artistes; comprenant la perspective des ombres linéaires, et celle des réflexions produites par l'eau et les miroirs plans. 4 p. l. 184 pp. 28 pl. 4°. *Paris, A. André*, 1823.

Choses (Des) merveillevses en natvre. *See* **Celestine** (Claude).

Choveron (Bermond de). Bermondi Choveronii in lateranensis concilij titulum de publicis concubinarijs commentarij. 416 pp. 4°. *Lvgdvni, apud Sennetonios fratres*, 1550.

Christen (The) state of matrymonye. *See* **Bullinger** (Henry).

Christian (The). [A monthly religious newspaper]. Jan. 1866, to Dec. 1871. v. 1-6. fol. *Boston, W. L. Hastings*, 1866-71.

Christian (The) history, containing accounts of the revival and propagation of religion in Great-Britain, America, etc. for the year 1744. [Edited by Thomas Prince, jr.] v. 2. nos. 53-104. March 3, 1743-4 to Feb. 23, 1744-5. 1. p. l. vi, 416 pp. 8°. *Boston, S. Kneeland and T. Green for T. Prince, junr.* 1745.

Christian (The) lawyer: being a portraiture of the life and character of William George Baker. [*anon.*] 320 pp. 12°. *New York, Carlton & Porter*, 1859.

Christian (The) remembrancer. 1808. *See* **Serle** *or* **Searle** (Ambrose).

Christian songs for the sunday school. [*anon.*] 224 pp. obl. 16°. *New York and Chicago, Biglow & Main*, [1872].

Christian (The) treasury; containing prayers, with the epistles and gospels. [*anon.*] viii, 500 pp. 1 pl. 24°. [*New York, P. O'Shea*, 1867].
[Imperfect: title and 1 l. wanting].

Christian (The) union. [Weekly]. Henry Ward Beecher, editor. July 9, 1870, to Dec. 20, 1871. New series, v. 2-4. fol. *New York, J. B. Ford & co.* 1870-71.

Christian (The) year, a monthly magazine of church literature for the people. July to Oct. 1871. v. 1, nos. 1-4. 448 pp. 4 pl. 8°. *New York, P. F. Smith*, 1871.
[No more published].

Christiania. *Kongelige Frederiks universitets bibliothek.* Fortegnelse over den tilvæxt, 1866-69. 4 v. fol. *Christiania, Brogger & Christie*, 1868-71. s.

——— *Kongelige norske universitet.* Det kongelige norske Frederiks universitets aarsberetning for 1869-1870. Med bilage. Ved universitets secretair, [C. Holst]. 2 v. 8°. *Christiania, Brogger & Christie*, 1869-70. s.

——— *Königliche sternwarte.* Meteorologische beobachtungen an der königlichen universitäts-sternwarte zu Christiania. 1837-1863. obl. 4°. *Christiania, H. J. Jensen*, 1865. s.

——— *Polytekniske forening.* *See* **Polyteknisk** tidsskrift, 1869-70.

Christian's (The) daily companion: containing family and private devotions. Selected from the prayers of bishops Wilson and Andrews. [Also], a compilation from Palmer's and Cotterill's formularies. [*anon.*] 292 pp. 12°. *Georgetown, (D. C.) E. Weems for G. Nourse*, 1819.

Christian's (The), scholar's, and farmer's magazine. By a number of gentlemen. 2 v. 768 pp. 4 l; 736 pp. 4 l. 8°. *Elizabeth-town, (N. J.) S. Kollock*, 1789-90.

Christison (Robert). Manual of practical toxicology: condensed from dr. Christison's treatise on poisons. With notes and additions by J. T. Ducatel, m. d. xxiii, 21-341 pp. 12°. *Baltimore, W. & J. Neal*, 1839.

Christliche glaubenslehre. Herausgegeben von dem Calwer verlags-verein. [*anon.*] 2 v. in 3. 16°. *Calw, in der vereinsbuchhandlung, Stuttgart, J. F. Steinkopf*, 1854.

Christmas (The) locket. A holiday number of Old and new. [1870-71. nos. 1-2]. 1 p. l. 96 pp; 1 p. l. 96 pp. 8°. *Boston, Roberts brothers*, 1870-71.

Christy (David). Cotton is king: or, slavery in the light of political economy. 8°. [*Augusta, Ga.*] 1860.
[*In* ELLIOTT (E. N.) Cotton is king, pp. 17-267].

Chronicles (The) of Gotham. 1871-72. *See* **White** (Richard Grant).

Chronological (A) abridgement of the history of England, its constitution and laws, from the norman conquest to the revolution in 1688. [*anon.*] 1 p. l. 464 pp. 8°. *London, Payne & Foss*, 1815.

Chrysostomus (*S.* Joannes). Saint Chrysostom on the priesthood; translated from the original greek: with notes and a life of the father. By the rev. Henry M. Mason. 194 pp. 12°. *Philadelphia, E. Littell*, 1826.

Chrystal (*Rev.* James). A history of the modes of christian baptism, in vindication of the rubrics of the church of England since the reformation, and those of the american church. 324 pp. 12°. *Philadelphia, Lindsay & Blakiston*, 1861.

Church (Benjamin, *m. d.*) A poem occasioned by the death of the honourable Jonathan Law, esq; late governor of Connecticut. 8 pp. 4°. [*Boston*], 1751.

Church (John). A cabinet of quadrupeds: consisting of highly-finished engravings, by James Tookey; from drawings, by Julius Ibbetson; with historical and scientific descriptions, by John Church. 2 v. Eng. title, 115 l. 43 pl; eng. title, 104 l. 39 pl. 4°. *London, Darton and Harvey*, 1805.

Church (The) almanac. Compiled by William G. Farrington. 1871-72. 2 v. 16°. *New York, Protestant episcopal tract society, and Pott, Young & co.* [1871-72].

Church-government and church-covenant discvssed. *See* **Mather** (*Rev.* Richard).

Church (The) monthly. Edited by the rev. Benjamin B. Babbitt. Jan. to Dec. 1867. v. 12-13. 8°. *Boston, The church reading room*, 1867.

Church of England. [The booke of common prayer, and administration of the sacraments]. 29 l. 4°. [*London, R. Barker, about* 1580]?

[*With* BIBLE. (*English*). Genevan version. *London, R. Barker, about* 1580.
Note.—Imperfect: 11 l. wanting].

——— The same. 43 l. 4°. [*London, R. Barker*, 1584].

[*With* BIBLE. (*English*). Genevan version. *London, R. Barker*, 1584.
Note.—Imperfect: 2 l. wanting].

——— The same. 38 l. 4°. [*London, R. Barker*, 1614].

[*With* BIBLE. (*English*). Genevan version. *London, R. Barker*, 1614.
Note.—Imperfect: 2 l. wanting].

——— The same. 40 l. 4°. [*London, R. Barker*, 1615].

[*With* BIBLE. (*English*). Genevan version. *London, R. Barker*, 1615.
Note.—Imperfect: 2 l. wanting].

——— The same. 55 l. 4°. [*London, R. Barker*, 1634].

[*With* BIBLE. (*English*). Authorized version. *London, R. Barker*, 1634].

——— Certain sermons or homilies, appointed to be read in churches, in the time of queen Elizabeth, of famous memory. And now thought fit to be reprinted by authority from the king's most excellent majesty. With pious reflections and spiritual observations. By a divine of the church of England. [Also], the thirty-nine articles of religion, with bishop Beveridge's exposition of such of them as relate to divine faith and free salvation. 4th ed. 1 p. l. 537, 106 pp. 1 l. 4°. *London, editor*, 1766.

Church of Jesus Christ of the latter day saints. Doctrine and covenants of the church of the latter day saints: carefully selected from the revelations of God, and compiled by Joseph Smith, junior, Oliver Cowdery, Sidney Rigdon, Frederick G. Williams, presiding elders of said church, proprietors. 257, xxv pp. 16°. *Kirtland (Ohio), proprietors*, 1835.

——— Sacred hymns and spiritual songs, for the church of Jesus Christ of latter-day saints. 14th ed. 432 pp. 24°. *Salt Lake city, G. Q. Cannon*, 1871.

——— The saints' harp: a collection of hymns and spiritual songs for public and private devotion. Compiling committee: Joseph Smith, Mark H. Forscutt, David H. Smith, and Norman W. Smith. vi, 792 pp. 16°. *Plano, (Ill.) published by the reorganized church of Jesus Christ of latter day saints*, 1870.

Church psalmist; or psalms and hymns, for the public, social and private use of evangelical christians. [*anon.*] 653 pp. 16°. *New York, M. H. Newman*, 1843.

Churchill (George Cheetham). Die dolomitberge. *See* **Gilbert** (Josiah) *and* **Churchill.**

Churchman's (The) year book, with kalendar for the year of grace 1871. Compiled by William Stephens Perry, d. d. sq. 16°. *Hartford, Church press co.* 1871.

Churi (Joseph H.) Sea Nile, the Desert, and Nigritia: travels in company with captain Peel, r. n. 1851-52. With thirteen arabic songs, as sung by the egyptian sailors on the Nile. xii, 332 pp. 1 pl. 8°. *London, author*, 1853.

Chynoweth (James Bennett) *and* **Bruckner** (William H.) American manures; and farmers' and planters' guide. Comprising a description of the elements and composition of plants and soils. Also, chemical analyses of the principal manufactured fertilizers—their assumed and real value—and a full exposé of the frauds practiced upon purchasers. 260 pp. 12°. *Philadelphia, Chynoweth & co.* 1871.

——— The same. By W. H. Bruckner and J. B. Chynoweth. [2d ed.] viii, 3-260 pp. 12°. *Philadelphia, W. H. Bruckner*, 1872.

Chytræus *or* **Kochhaff** (David). De Carolo v. imperatore oratio. sm. 4°. *Wittebergae, typis hæredum Ioannis Cratonis*, 1585.

[*With* BECCADELLI (Antonio). De dictis et factis Alphonsi regis Aragonvm, pp. 167-199].

——— A soveraigne salve for a sick sovle. A treatise teaching the right vse of patient bearing the crosse, with the sundrie commodities that the same bringeth vnto christians, and the euils that come of impacience. [*anon.*] Englished by W. F. 28 l. unp. sm. 4°. *London, R. Field*, 1590.

Cicero (Marcus Tullius). M. Tullii Ciceronis opera quae supersunt omnia et deperditorum fragmenta ex recensione Io. Casp. Orellii.

Cicero (Marcus Tullius)—continued.

Ed. 2ª. emendatior. Curaverunt I. C. Orellius, Io. Georg Baiterus, [et Car. Halmius]. 11 v. in 8. 8°. *Turici, sumptibus ac typis Orellii, Füsslini et sociorum,* 1833–62.

CONTENTS.

v. 1. Incerti scriptoris rhetoricorum ad C. Herennium libri quattuor.
M. Tullii Ciceronis rhetoricorum libri duo qui sunt de inventione rhetorica.
De oratore libri tres.
De claris oratoribus liber qui dicitur Brutus.
Ad M. Brutum orator.
Topica.
De partitione oratoria dialogus.
Libellus de optimo genere oratorum.
v. 2. Orationes. Emendaverunt I. G. Baiterus et Car. Halmius.
v. 3. Epistolarum ad familiares libri xvi.
Epistolarum ad Quintum fratrem libri iii.
De petitione consulatus ad M. Tullium fratrem liber.
Epistolarum ad Atticum libri xvi.
Pseudociceronis epistolarum ad Brutum libri ii.
Pseudociceronis epistola ad Octavium.
v. 4. Libri qui ad philosophiam et ad rem publicam spectant. Emendaverunt I. G. Baiterus et Car. Halmius.
Part 1. Lucullus sive academicorum priorum liber ii.
Academicorum posteriorum liber i, et fragmenta.
De finibus bonorum et malorum libri v.
Tusculanarum disputationum ad M. Brutum libri v.
De deorum natura libri iii.
De divinatione libri ii. Recognovit G. Christ.
De fato liber ex recensione G. Christ.
Cato maior de senectute.
Laelius de amicitia.
De officiis libri iii.
Paradoxa stoicorum.
De re publica sex librorum reliquiae.
De legibus librorum reliquiae.
Part 2. A. Fragmenta orationum magnam partem superstitum.
B. Fragmenta orationum deperditorum xxii.
C. Tituli orationum deperditorum.
D. Fragmenta epistolarum.
E. Fragmenta deperditorum librorum philosophorum. Timaeus.
G. Fragmenta poëmatum.
H. Fragmenta librorum incertorum.
v. 5. M. Tullii Ciceronis scholiastae [latinae]. Ediderunt I. C. Orellius et I. G. Baiterus.
Part 1. C. Marii Victorini expositio in rhetorica Ciceronis. [Libri duo].
Versus Rufini v. c. litteratoris de compositione et de metris oratorum.
C. Iulii Victoris ars rhetorica Hermagorae, Ciceronis, Quintiliani, Aquilii, Marcomanni, Tatiani.
Anicii Manlii Severini Boethii commentarii in Ciceronis topica v, libri vi. [Atque] de diis et praesensionibus ex ipsius commento in topica Ciceronis fragmentum.
Favonii Eulogii disputatio de somnio Scipionis.
Part 2. Q. Asconii Pediani et pseudo-Asconii ad nonnullas M. Tullii Ciceronis orationes commentarii.
Scholia bobiensia sive ambrosiana et vaticana ad nonnullas M. Tullii Ciceronis orationes cum integris annotationibus Angeli Maii in editione romana et emendationibus Io. Casp. Orellii.
Scholiasta gronovianus in nonnullas M. Tullii Ciceronis orationes.
v. 6, 7, 8. Onomasticon tullianum [in partibus tribus] continens M. Tullii Ciceronis vitam, historiam litterariam, indicem geographicum et historicum, indicem legum et formularum, indicem graecolatinum, fastos consulares. Curaverunt I. C. Orellius et I. G. Baiterus.
v. 6. Onomastici tulliani pars prima.
M. Tullii Ciceronis historia per consules descripta et in annos lxiv. distincta per Franciscum Fabricium marcoduranum.
Memorabilia vitae Ciceronis per annos digesta a Schuetzio, emendata a L. Usterio.
Tabulae kalendarium romanorum vetus quale fuit ab a. u. 691 usque ad a. u. 709, comparantes cum forma anni iuliana. Ad illustrandis Ciceronis epistolas composuit. m. G. F. Korb.
Index editionum scriptorum M. Tullii Ciceronis. Scripta Ciceronem illustrantia.
Appendix. Petri Lazeri de Dionysio Lambino narratio.
v. 7. Onomastici tulliani pars secunda.
Onomasticon tullianum, varronianum, caesarianum, salustianum, asconianum et scholiastarum Ciceronis.
v. 8. Onomastici tulliani pars tertia.
Fasti consulares Romanorum [usque ad mortem Iustiniani imperatoris] ad fidem optimorum auctorum recogniti. [Per I. G. Baiterum].
Triumphi Romanorum usque ad Tiberium Cæsarem. [Ab eodem].
Index graeco-latinus.
Index legum romanarum quarum apud Ciceronem eiusque scholiastas item apud Livium, Velleium Paterculum, A. Gellium nominatim mentio fit.
Analecta. [Addenda vel corrigenda].
Index formularum. Epistolarum series.

——— Cato major de senectute, Laelius de amicitia. With explanatory notes. By E. P. Crowell, and H. B. Richardson. 171 pp. 16°. *Philadelphia, Eldredge & brother,* 1872. [CHASE and STUART'S classical series].

——— Consolatio Ciceronis. *See* **Blacklock** (Thomas, *d. d.*) Paraclesis.

——— De officiis libri tres. Ex editionibus Oliveti et Ernesti. Accedunt notæ anglicæ. Cura C. K. Dillaway. 297 pp. 16°. *Bostoniæ, Perkins & Marvin,* 1837.

——— The same. Tully's offices. In three books. Turned out of latin into english. By Ro. L'Estrange. 8 p. l. 208 pp. 16°. *London, H. Brome,* 1689.

——— Ciceronis selectae quaedam epistolae. Accedunt notulae & illustrationes anglicae. Cura M. L. Hurlbut. 336 pp. 12°. *Philadelphiae, H. Perkins,* 1836.

——— M. T. Ciceronis orationes quædam selectæ, notis illustratæ. [Curavit C. Folsom]. Ed. 4ª. 4 p. l. 403 pp. 12°. *Bostoniae, Hilliard, Gray, Little & Wilkins,* 1828.

——— The same. Cum interpretatione et historia succincta rerum gestarum et scriptorum M. T. Ciceronis. By John G. Smart. 2d ed. with a life of Cicero, in english. xvi, 367 pp. 8°. *Philadelphia, Towar & Hogan,* 1828.

——— The same. Editio stereotypa. 278 pp. 12°. *Bostoniae, Hilliard, Gray, Little & Wilkins,* 1831.

Cicero (Marcus Tullius)—continued.

——— The same. Select orations of Cicero. [Latin]. With english notes, critical and explanatory, and historical, geographical, and legal indexes. By Charles Anthon, ll. d. New ed. xl, 518 pp. 1 pl. 12°. *New York, Harper & brothers*, 1839.

——— The same. Oraisons choisies de Cicéron, traduction revue par m. de Wailly, avec le latin à côté, sur l'édition de l'abbé Lallemant, et avec des notes. Nouv. éd. v. 1, 3. 16°. *Paris, J. Barbou*, 1777–78.
[v. 2 wanting].

——— Orationes et epistolae selectae. With references to latin grammars; synonymes; notes critical and explanatory; and a vocabulary. By J. H. Hanson. iv, 363, 152 pp. 8°. *New York, Woolworth, Ainsworth & co.* 1871.

——— M. Tullii Ciceronis ad Quintum fratrem dialogi tres de oratore. Cum excerptis ex notis variorum. 2 p. l. 260 pp. 12°. *Novi-Portus, H. Howe*, 1832.

——— The same. De la composition oratoire; ou de l'invention, dans ses rapports généraux avec l'art de bien dire, et principalement avec l'éloquence du barreau. Ouvrage traduit avec des éclaircissemens, par S. Abel-Lonquêue. 2 p. l. 320 pp. 12°. *Paris, Testu & cie.* 1813.

——— M. Tullii Ciceronis pro A. Cluentio habito oratio ad iudices. With english notes, by Austin Stickney. x; 144 pp. 12°. *Cambridge, Sever & Francis*, 1860.

——— Cicero's prince. The reasons and counsels for settlement and good government of a kingdom, collected out of Cicero's works. By T. R. 4 p. l. 88 pp. 16°. *London, S. Mearne*, 1668.

Cicognara (*Conte* Leopoldo, *editor*). Omaggio delle provincie venete alla maestà di Carolina Augusta, imperatrice d'Austria. 18 l. 17 pl. fol. *Venezia, Alvisopoli*, 1818.

Cieszkowski (*Comte* Auguste). Du crédit et de la circulation. 2e éd. 2 p. l. 404 pp. 1 l. 8°. *Paris, Guillaumin & cie.* 1847.

Cimentelli (Valentino). Marmor pisanvm de honore Bisellii. Parergon inseritur de veterum sellis, synopsis appenditur de re donatica antiquorum. Accedit myiodia, siue de muscis odoris pisanis epistola. 4 p. l. 272 pp. 5 pl. 4°. *Bononiæ, ex typographia hæredis V. Benatii*, 1666.

Cincinnati (*City of*). Williams' Cincinnati directory and business advertiser for 1850–51. 2d annual issue. 317 pp. 1 map. 8°. *Cincinnati, C. S. Williams*, 1850. s.

——— The same. Williams' Cincinnati directory. June, 1871. M. V. Williams, superintendent. 8°. *Cincinnati, Cincinnati directory office*, [1871].

——— (*Public library*). Catalogue of the public library of Cincinnati. [By W. F. Poole]. xii, 644 pp. 8°. *Cincinnati, Wilstach, Baldwin & co.* 1871.

Cincinnati (The) almanac, for the year 1846; being a complete picture of Cincinnati and its environs, accompanied by a new and accurate plan of the city. 160 pp. 1 map. 18°. *Cincinnati, Robinson & Jones*, 1846.

Cincinnati (The) commercial. [Daily]. Jan. 1 to Dec. 31, 1871. 2 v. fol. *Cincinnati, M. Halstead & co.* 1871.

Cincinnati daily chronicle. Jan. 1 to April 30, 1871. fol. *Cincinnati, Chronicle company*, 1871.
[Consolidated with the Cincinnati times, May 1, 1871. *See* CINCINNATI times and chronicle].

Cincinnati (The) daily enquirer. Jan. 1 to Dec. 31, 1871. 2 v. fol. *Cincinnati, Faran & McLean*, 1871.

Cincinnati (The) medical repertory. Edited by J. A. Thacker, m. d. [A monthly]. v. 1. [1868]. 388 pp. 8°. *Cincinnati, The medical journal association*, [1869].

Cincinnati times and chronicle. [Daily]. May 1 to Dec. 30, 1871. fol. *Cincinnati, Chronicle company*, 1871.
[*See* Cincinnati daily chronicle].

Ciocchi (Giovanni Maria). La pittura in Parnaso. xxiv, 310 pp. 4°. *Firenze, M. Nestenus*, 1725.

Cionacci (Francesco). Storia della beata Vmiliana de' Cerchi, vedova fiorentina del terz' ordine di San Francesco. Distinta in qvattro parti, nelle qvali si da' svfficiente contezza 1. Della vita, 2. Del culto e fama immemorabile, 3. Degli scrittori, e 4. Delle apparenti notizie della medesima beata. 1 p. l. x, 456 pp. 4°. *Firenze, Santi Franchi*, 1682.

Circignano (Niccolo, *cavalière dalle Pomerancia*). Ecclesiae anglicanae trophaea, sive sanctorum martyrum qui pro Christo catholicae q' fidei veritate asserenda, antiquo recentioriq' persecutionum tempore, mortem in Anglia subierunt. Per Io. Bapt. de Caualleriis æneis typis repraesentatæ. 1 p. l. 36 pl. fol. *Romae, B. Grassi*, 1584.

Circle (The) of the sciences, v. 4–5. *See* **Logic**, ontology, and the art of poetry. 1776.

Circleville (*Ohio*). Williams' Circleville and Lancaster directory, city guide, and business mirror. v. 1. 1859–60. Compiled by C. S. Williams. 8°. *Circleville, L. N. Olds; Lancaster, J. Searles*, 1859.

Circular (The). Published weekly by the Oneida and Wallingford communities. March 21 to Dec. 26, 1870. v. 7. fol. *Oneida community* (*N. Y.*) 1870.
[*Title changed* January, 1871, to ONEIDA circular. *See* ONEIDA circular].

Cisano (Giovanni). Tesoro di concetti poetici: scelti da' piv illvstri poeti toscani, e ridotto sotto capi per ordine d'alfabeto. Parte 1ª. 36 p. l. 1200 pp. 16°. *Venetia, appresso E. Deuchino & G. B. Pulciani*, 1610.

Citizen (The). Being the great outline of political science; and a defence of the british constitution, from the writings of Montesquieu, Blackstone, Hume, Paley, Gibbon, &c. [*anon.* By dr. Thornton] ? vi, 19–286 pp. 2 l. 8°. *London, T. Cox*, 1794.

Cittadini (Celso). Delle antichita' delle armi gentilizie. Colle annotazioni di Giovan Girolamo Carli. 1 p. l. xxvi, 144 pp. sm. 4°. *Lucca, S. & G. D. Marescand*, 1741.

Civiale (Jean). Traité pratique sur les maladies des organes génito-urinaires. 3e partie. Maladies du corps de la vessie. 2e éd. considérablement augmentée. 2 p. l. 612 pp. 8°. *Paris, J. B. Baillière*, 1851.

Civil (The) engineer and architect's journal. [Monthly]. Jan. to May, 1868. v. 31. 4°. *London, W. Kent & co.* 1868.
[Discontinued from above date].

Civil, military and naval gazette. [A weekly magazine] devoted to the interests of the citizen, soldier and sailor. W. F. Davidson, editor. Sept. 12, 1850, to March 13, 1851. v. 1. 4°. *Annapolis,* (*Md.*) *J. B. T. M'Neir*, 1850–51.
[Wanting, no. 25, for March 6, 1851, pp. 193–200].

Cizeron Rival (François Louis). Recréations littéraires; ou anecdotes et remarques sur différents sujets. 3 p. l. 264 pp. 12°. *Lyon, J. M. Bessiat*, 1765.

Claflin (Tennie C.) Constitutional equality a right of woman; with her duties to herself,—together with a review of the constitution of the United States, showing that the right to vote is guaranteed to all citizens. Also a review of the rights of children. 3 p. l. 148 pp. 1 portrait. 8°. *New York, Woodhull, Claflin & co.* 1871.

Claims of the Africans: or the history of the American colonization society. By the author of Conversations on the Sandwich Islands mission, etc. [*anon.*] 252 pp. 18°. *Boston, Massachusetts sabbath school union*, 1832.

Clap (*Rev.* Thomas, *president of Yale college*). The annals; or history of Yale-college, in New-Haven, in the colony of Connecticut, from the founding thereof, in the year 1700, to the year 1766: with an appendix, containing the present state of the college. 2 p. l. 122 pp. 8°. *New-Haven, J. Hotchkiss & B. Mecom*, 1766.

——— A brief history and vindication of the doctrines received and established in the churches of New-England, with a specimen of the new scheme of religion beginning to prevail. 2d ed. 40 pp. 1 l. 12°. *Boston, S. Kneeland*, 1757.

——— A letter to the rev. mr. Edwards [respecting mr. Whitefield's "design to turn out the generality of ministers in the country"]. 11 pp. sm. 4°. *Boston, T. Fleet*, 1745.

——— The religious constitution of colleges, especially of Yale-college in New-haven, in Connecticut. 20 pp. 12°. *New London, T. Green*, 1754.

Clara Harrington. A domestic tale. [*anon.*] 3 v. 12°. *London, Colburn & co.* 1852.

Clare (Thomas). Memoirs of the life of the rev. mr. Bishop. 16°. *London, Cadell & Davies*, 1802.
[*In* BISHOP (*Rev.* Samuel). Poems, v. 1, pp. xiii–xliv].

Claremont; or, the undivided household. [*anon.*] 206 pp. 12°. *Philadelphia, Parry & McMillan*, 1857. s.

Clarendon (Edward Hyde, 1*st earl of*). *See* **Hyde** (Edward).

Claridge (Richard). The life and posthumous works of Richard Claridge, being memoirs and manuscripts relating to his experiences and progress in religion: his changes in opinion, and reasons for them. With essays in defence of several principles and practices of the people call'd quakers. Collected by Joseph Besse. 12 p. l. 576 pp. 6 l. 8°. *London, assigns of J. Sowle*, 1726.

Claridge (*Captain* R. T.) Hydropathy; or, the cold water cure, as practised by Vincent Priessnitz, at Graefenberg, Silesia, Austria. 4th ed. 1 p. l. 318 pp. 1 pl. 8°. *London, J. Madden & co.* 1842.

Claridge (*Captain* R. T.)—continued.
——— The same. 1st Amer. ed. With notes by dr. P. Lapham. 285 pp. 12°. *New York, proprietor*, 1843.

Clark (Charles Cowden). Adam, the gardener. Revised by the editors of the Popular library. 2 p. l. 252 pp. 16°. *Boston, J. Allen & co.* 1835.

Clark (Daniel). A newly discovered system of electrical medication. 141 pp. 16°. *Chicago, Rounds & James*, 1869.

Clark (D. W. *d. d.*) Man all immortal; or, the nature and destination of man as taught by reason and revelation. 464 pp. 12°. *Cincinnati, Poe & Hitchcock*, 1864.

Clark (Ewan). Miscellaneous poems. xxviii, 317 pp. 8°. *Whitehaven, (Eng.) J. Ware & son*, 1779.

Clark (E. B.) A centennial discourse delivered before the First congregational society in Chicopee, Sept. 26, 1852. 8°. [*Northampton*, 1862].
[*In* CHAPIN (Orange). The Chapin genealogy, part iv, or pp. 235-253].

Clark (Frederick Le Gros). The practical anatomy and elementary physiology of the nervous system; designed for the use of students in the dissecting room. xxiv, 367 pp. 8°. *London, Longman, Rees, etc.* 1836.

Clark (James, *m. d.*) The influence of climate in the prevention and cure of chronic diseases, more particularly of the chest and digestive organs: comprising an account of the principal places resorted to by invalids in England and the south of Europe. With an appendix, containing a series of tables on climate. xxvii, 328 pp. incl. 6 tables. 8°. *London, T. & G. Underwood*, 1829.

Clark (John A. *d. d.*) Awake, thou sleeper! A series of awakening discourses. 244 pp. 12°. *New York, R. Carter*, 1844.
——— Gathered fragments. Eng. title, 408 pp. 1 pl. 12°. *Philadelphia, W. Marshall & co.* 1836.
——— The same. 408 pp. 12°. *New York, R. Carter & brothers*, 1860.
——— Gleanings by the way. 352 pp. 12°. *Philadelphia, W. J. & J. K. Simon*, 1842.
——— The pastor's testimony. 333 pp. 12°. *Philadelphia, Marshall, Clark & co.* 1834.
——— The same. 2d ed. 240 pp. 12°. *Philadelphia, W. Marshall & co.* 1835.
——— The same. 7th ed. 240 pp. 12°. *New York, R. Carter & brothers*, 1859.

Clark (John A. *d. d.*)—continued.
——— The young disciple; or, a memoir of Anzonetta R. Peters. 328 pp. 12°. *New York, R. Carter & brothers*, 1860.

Clark (John Heaviside). Practical illustration of Gilpin's day. *See* **Gilpin** (*Rev.* William).

Clark (*Rev.* Rufus W.) Life scenes of the messiah. 330 pp. 1 pl. 12°. *Boston, J. P. Jewett & co.* 1855.
——— The same. The true prince of the tribe of Judah; or, life scenes of the messiah. To which is added, from dr. Adam Clarke, an account of the lives of all the writers of the new testament. Also, the religious creed and history of the Jews. xii, 355 pp. 6 pl. 12°. *Boston, A. Colby & co.* 1859.
——— The same. The life of our Lord and Saviour Jesus Christ; also, the religious creed and history of the Jews; the true christian religion, or plain and easy road to heaven; and a complete history of the bible. [2d ed.] compiled and published by Albert Colby. xii, 355 pp; 1 l. 58 pp; 39 pp. 12°. *Lowell, A. Colby*, 1871.
——— Romanism in America. 271 pp. 16°. *Boston, J. E. Tilton & co.* 1859.

Clark (Samuel A.) Memoir of the rev. Albert W. Duy. 8°. [*Philadelphia*, 1846].
[*In* DUY (*Rev.* Albert W.) Sermons, pp. 17-96].

Clark (Thomas). The anabasis of Xenophon; with an interlinear translation. *See* **Xenophon.**

Clark (William Adolphus). The cannonade. By Anicetus. [*pseudon.*] 148 pp. 12°. *Boston, A. Williams & co.* 1861.
——— Hard knocks; or, who is first? A satire. By Anicetus. [*pseudon.*] 118 pp. 5 pl. 12°. *Boston, A. W. Levering*, 1872.
——— The learned world. By Anicetus. [*pseudon.*] xvii, 270 pp. 12°. *Boston, W. H. Piper & co.* 1864.

Clark (W. S.) Elements of geography and history, containing a geography of the world, and historical sketches of different countries. Illustrated by stereoscopic views. 401 pp. 8°. *Rockford, (Ill.) Clark, Lake & co.* 1871.
[Stereoscopic views wanting].
——— Illustrated history, comprising in a condensed form a history of the United States, a geography of the western continent, and the chief objects of interest on the eastern continent, including a historical and descriptive sketch of the Holy Land. Illustrated by stereoscopic views, published by E. and H. T.

Clark (W. S.)—continued.
Anthony, New York. iv, 440 pp. 8°. *Rockford, (Ill.) J. H. Clark & co.* 1870.
[Stereoscopic views wanting].

Clarke (*Rev.* Adam). An account of the infancy, religious and literary life, of Adam Clarke, ll. d. written by one who was intimately acquainted with him from his boyhood to the sixtieth year of his age, [i. e. himself]. 24, 178 pp. 12°. *New-York, B. Waugh & T. Mason*, 1833.

Clarke (Cuthbert). The true theory and practice of husbandry. [Also], a compendium of mechanics: to assist the husbandman in the choice and construction of every implement peculiar to his business. xii, 360 pp. 4°. *London, author*, 1777.

Clarke (Dorus, *d. d.*) Orthodox congregationalism and the sects. 169 pp. 12°. *Boston, Lee & Shepard*, 1871.

Clarke (*Rev.* James Freeman). Ten great religions: an essay in comparative theology. 1 p. l. x, 528 pp. 8°. *Boston, J. R. Osgood & co.* 1871.

Clarke (James Stanier). Naufragia or historical memoirs of shipwrecks and of the providential deliverance of vessels. 2 v. xvi, 421 pp. 1 pl; xxi, 445 pp. 1 map. 12°. *London, J. Mawman*, 1805–06.

Clarke (John, *d. d.*) An enquiry into the cause and origin of evil: in which the principal phænomena of nature are explained, according to the true principles of philosophy; more particularly in answer to mr. Bayle, and other defenders of the ancient manichæan scheme of two independent principles. fol. [*London*, 1739].
[Boyle lectures, v. 3, pp. 153–276].

Clarke (John, *of Hull*). An essay upon study. Wherein directions are given for the due conduct thereof, and the collection of a library. 2d ed. vi, 340 pp. 1 l. 12°. *London, A. Bettesworth & C. Hitch*, 1737.

Clarke (*Mrs.* Mary G.) Home garner; or, the intellectual and moral store house: gathered for the family circle from the rich experience of many faithful reapers. 414 pp. 8°. *Philadelphia, J. B. Lippincott & co.* [1856].

Clarke (*Mrs.* R. S.) Aunt Madge's story. By Sophie May. [*pseudon.*] 214 pp. 3 pl. 18°. *Boston, Lee & Shepard*, 1872.
[Little Prudy's flyaway series, no. 3].

——— The doctor's daughter. By Sophie May. [*pseudon.*] 330 pp. 11 pl. 16°. *Boston, Lee & Shepard*, 1872.

Clarke (Samuel, *d. d.*) A demonstration of the being and attributes of God. fol. [*London*, 1739].
[Boyle lectures, v. 2, 2 p. l. pp. 1–55].

——— A discourse concerning the unchangeable obligations of natural religion, and the truth and certainty of the christian revelation. Being eight sermons preached in 1705. fol. [*London*, 1739].
[Boyle lectures, v. 2, pp. 57–196].

Clarke (Thomas). The battle and other poems, patriotic and humorous. 216 pp. 1 portrait. 12°. *Chicago, Clarke & co.* 1871.

Clasen (Daniel). De oraculis gentilium et in specie de vaticiniis sibyllinis libri tres. In fine adivncta svnt carmina sibyllina e versione Sebastiani Castalionis [Châteillon], vt et Onuphrii Panvinii tractatvs de sibyllis. 2 v. in 1. 8 p. l. 824 pp; 4 p. l. 104 pp. 22 l. 4°. *Helmstadii, apud H. Mullerum*, 1673.

Claude (Jean). Explication de la section liii. du catéchisme. 56 pp. 8°. *Charenton, E. Lucas*, 1682.

——— La parabole des noces, expliquée en cinq sermons sur le chapitre xxiie de s. Matthieu, jusqu'au verset 14e. Prononcéz à Charenton [en 1675], par Iean Clavde. Avec trois autres sermons du même autheur. 3 p. l. 292 pp. 8°. *Saumur, R. Péan*, 1683.
[*With his* La parabole des noces, etc. 1683].

——— Sermon sur le vers. xiv. du chapit. vii. de l'Ecclésiaste. Prononcé à la Haye le 21. novembre, 1685. 32 pp. 8°. *Londres, B. Griffin*, 1686.
[*With his* La parabole des noces, etc. 1683].

Clauder (Gabriel). Gabrielis Clauderi methodus balsamandi corpora humana, aliaqve majora sine evisceratione et sectione hucusqve solita. Adnexa item est methodus parandi varias essentias atque spiritus chymicos extemporaneé, sine igne aut destillatione. 8 p. l. 216 pp. 6 l. 4°. *Altenburgi, apud G. Richterum*, 1679.

Clausen (Henri Frédéric Charles de). Traits caractéristiques de l'histoire de Russie. xx, 187 pp. 8°. *Paris, Didot, jeune*, 1804.

Clausing (Lewis). A treatise on the jesuits. 16°. [*New York, Van Nostrand & Dwight*, 1836].
[*In* Morse (S. F. B.) The proscribed german student, etc. pp. 59–244].

Claustre (André de). Dizionario mitologico, ovvero della favola, storico, poetico, simbolico ec. Tradotta dal francese, ed in questa nuova edizione arrichita di figure. v. 1–3

Claustre (André de)—continued. in 1 v. A to I. [Illustrated]. 8°. *Venezia, A. Savioli*, 1785–6.

Clavis apocalyptica, 1632. *See* **Mede** (*Rev.* Joseph).

Clavius (Christoph). Dissertation on the possibility of numbering the sands. pp. 49–63. 8°. *London, J. Johnson*, 1784.

[*With* ARCHIMEDES. Arenarius. ed. 1784].

Clayton (W. H.) A collection of psalms and hymns, for social and private worship. [*anon.*] 206 l. unp. 12°. *New-York, C. S. Van Winkle*, 1820.

Cleary (William P.) & co. Business directory of the cities of New York, Philadelphia, Boston, and Baltimore; and a business register of the principal manufacturers in the United States. 1870–71. 8°. *New York, W. P. Cleary & co.* [1871].

Cleaver (*Rev.* Robert). Ten sermons [on] the Lords svpper. *See* **Dod** (*Rev.* John) *and* **Cleaver.**

Cleeton (G. E.) The annual directory of poultry breeders and fanciers in the United States and Canadas, for 1870. 45 pp. 1 pl. 8°. *New Haven, G. E. Cleeton*, [1870].

Cleland (John). The way to things by words, and to words by things, being a sketch of an attempt at the retrieval of the antient celtic, or, primitive language of Europe. [With] a succinct account of the sanscort, or learned language of the bramins. Also, two essays, the one on the origin of the musical waits at christmas. The other on the real secret of the free masons. [*anon.*] 1 p.l. vii, 123 pp. 8°. *London, L. Davis & C. Reymers*, 1766.

Clemens *romanus* (*S.*) The apostolical constitutions. Edited, with notes, by James Donaldson, ll. d. 2 p. l. 280 pp. 8°. *Edinburgh, T. & T. Clark*, 1870.

[ANTE-NICENE christian library, v. 17].

——— The Clementine homilies. 2 p. l. 340 pp. 8°. *Edinburgh, T. & T. Clark*, 1870.

[ANTE-NICENE christian library, v. 17].

——— [The epistles of St. Clement to the Corinthians. 12°. *Oxford*, 1840].

[*In* WAKE (William). The genuine epistles of the apostolical fathers, pp. 57–91, 366–372].

——— Recognitiones. Rufino aquilei. presb. interprete. Ad librorum mss. et edd. fidem expressae. Curante E. G. Gersdorf. x, 254 pp. 12°. *Lipsiae, B. Tauchnitz, jun.* 1838.

[GERSDORF (E. G.) Bibliotheca patrum ecclesiasticorum latinorum selecta, v. 1].

Clemens (Samuel Langhorne). Roughing it. By Mark Twain. [*pseudon.*] 591 pp. 8 pl. 8°. *Hartford, American publishing co.* 1872.

Clement v. (*Pope. Bertrand de Goth*). Constitutiones una cum apparatu J. Andreæ. [*In fine*] per Petruz schoiffher de gernschem. [2d ed.] 65 l. fol. *Moguntiae.* Auno dñice incar‖nacõnis m.cccc.lxvij. Octaua die mensis octobris.

[*Note.*—Gothic type, colored initials, two columns of 70 lines on the first 61 leaves, and of 49 lines on the last 4 leaves. The colophon is on the recto of the 61st leaf. The 4 leaves at the close contain the rule of St. Francis, and the constitution of John xxii].

Clement of Rome. *See* **Clemens** *romanus.*

Clement (Clara Erskine). A handbook of legendary and mythological art. iv, 497 pp. 1 pl. 12°. *New York, Hurd & Houghton*, 1871.

Clement (J.) Memoir of Adoniram Judson: being a sketch of his life and missionary labors. 336 pp. 1 portrait. 12°. *Auburn, Derby & Miller*, 1852.

Clerc. *See* **Le Clerc** (Nicolas Gabriel Clerc, *dit*).

Clericus (Joannes). *See* **Leclerc** (Jean).

Clermont-Tonnerre (Stanislas, *comte de*). Recueil des opinions. 4 v. 8°. *Paris, Migneret*, 1791.

Cleveland (Charles Dexter). A compendium of classical literature; comprising choice extracts translated from the best greek and roman writers, with biographical sketches, accounts of their works, and notes directing to the best editions and translations. Part i. From Homer to Longinus. Part ii. From Plautus to Boëthius. 622 pp. 12°. *Philadelphia, E. C & J. Biddle & co.* 1861.

Cleveland (H. W. S.) Hints to riflemen. 260 pp. 1 pl. 12°. *New York, D. Appleton & co.* 1864.

Cleverskercke (J. P. V. Brande van). Mehrmaliges schreiben des holländischen ambassadeurs in Engelland, herrn von Cleverskercke, an ihro hoch mögende die herren general-staaten der Vereinigten Niederlanden, den erfolg, nach entdeckter conspiration in Engelland, wider des königs leben, betreffend. 4 l. sm. 4°. [*Franckfurt am Mayn, M. Beckern*, 1606].

[*With* Warhafftige unnd eygentliche beschreibung der allerschrecklichsten und grauesamsten verrätherey so jemals erhört worden, wider die königliche maiestat [etc.] 1606].

Clifford (George, 3*d earl of Cumberland*). Voyage to the Azores. *See* **Wright** (Edward).

Cliffton (William). A poetical epistle to [William Gifford]. 12°. [*Philadelphia, W. Cobbett*, 1799].

[*In* GIFFORD (William). The Baviad, and Mæviad. 1799. pp. v–xi].

Clizia (*pseudon ?*) L' infelice amore dei due fedelissimi amanti Giulia e Romeo, scritto in ottava rima ad Ardèo suo. 8°. [*Pisa, fratelli Nistri & cc.* 1831].

[*In* PORTO (Luigi da). Giuletta e Romeo. 1831. pp. 143-204].
Note.—Il modo misterioso con cui lo stampatore Giolito nomina il cav. Gherardo Bolderi, ha fatto supporre ad alcuni che possa questo componimento esser opera appunto del predetto cavaliere.—*Torri*].

Clopinel (Jehan de). *See* **Meun** (Jehan de).

Clowes (*Rev.* John). A memoir of the late John Clowes, written by himself: with a history of the commencement in Great Britain of the new church, called the New Jerusalem. [Also], a selection of letters, on various subjects of christian life and doctrine. xiv, iv, 313 pp. 3 pl. 8°. *Manchester, J. Gleave*, 1834.

Clute (John J.) The school geography. viii, 5-363 pp. 12°. *New York, S. Wood & sons*, 1833.

Coach - makers' international journal, devoted to the interests of the trade. I. D. Ware, editor. [A monthly magazine]. Oct. 1870, to Sept. 1871. v. 6. 4°. *Philadelphia, I. D. Ware*, 1871.

Coale (Josiah). Books and divers epistles; collected and published, as it was desired by him [etc.] 344 pp. sm. 4°. [*London*], 1671.

CONTENTS.

An invitation of love to the hungry and thirsty.
A salutation to the suffering seed.
To all the babes in Christ, etc.
A warning to the king and both houses of parliament.
England's sad estate lamented.
The whore unvail'd, or the mystery of the deceit of the church of Rome, reveal'd.
A testimony concerning Richard Farnsworth.
A song of the judgments and mercies of the Lord.
A vindication of the light within, against John Newman.
Epistles, [etc. interspersed throughout the collection].
A testimony concerning Lodowick Muzzleton.

Coate (Samuel). A guide to true happiness. 177 pp. 18°. *Philadelphia, S. W. Conrad*, 1804.

Coates (Reynell, *m.d.*) Physiology for schools. 333 pp. 12°. *Philadelphia, Marshall, Williams & Butler*, 1840.

——— Popular medicine; or, family adviser. 614 pp. 8°. *Philadelphia, Carey, Lea & Blanchard*, 1838.

Cobb (Joseph B.) Leisure labors; or, miscellanies historical, literary, and political. 1 p. l. 408 pp. 12°. *New York, D. Appleton & co.* 1858.

Cobbe (Frances Power). Religious duty. 2 p. l. 331 pp. 12°. *London, Trübner & co.* 1864.

Cobbet (*Rev.* Thomas, *of New England*). A fruitfull and usefull discourse, tovching the honour due from children to parents, and the duty of parents towards their children. 6 p. l. 243 pp. 16°. *London, J. Rothwell*, 1656.

Cobbett (James Paul). A ride of eight hundred miles in France; [also], a general view of the finances of that kingdom. 1 p. l. 202 pp. 5 l. 12°. *London, author*, 1824.

Cobbett (John M.) Letters from France; containing observations made in that country during a journey from Calais to the south, as far as Limoges. viii, 288 pp. 12°. *London, Mills, Jowett & Mills*, 1825.

Cobbett (William). Cobbett's annual register. 1802-03. v. 1-4. 8°. *London, Cox & Baylis*, 1802-03.

——— The same. Cobbett's political register. 1804 to 1811. v. 5-20. 8°. *London, R. Bagshaw & author*, 1804-11.

Cobbin (Ingram). The illustrated new testament. *New York*, 1871. *See* **Bible.** (*English*).

Cobbold (*Rev.* Richard). The history of Margaret Catchpole, a Suffolk girl. 3d ed. xi, 393 pp. 8 pl. 12°. *London, H. Colburn*, 1846.

Cobden (Paul, *pseudon.*) The turning wheel. 364 pp. 4 pl. 16°. *Boston, Lee & Shepard*, 1872.

[BECKONING series, v. 3].

Cobia (*Rev.* Daniel). Sermons. With an introduction, and a sermon on the occasion of his death, by William W. Spear. xl, 542 pp. 8°. *Charleston, J. P. Beile*, 1838.

Coccejus. *See* **Coch.**

Cocconi (Pietro Giovanni). Epilogo di notizie storiche concernenti la vita dell' abate Carlo Innocenzo Frugoni. 8°. *Brescia, D. Berlendis*, 1782.

[*In* FRUGONI (Carlo Innocenzo). Poesie scelte, v. 1, pp. i-xl].

Coch, Cock *or* **Coccejus** (Johann). Duo tituli thalmvdici sanhedrin et maccoth: quorum ille agit de synedriis; judiciis, suppliciis capitalibus Ebræorum; hic de pœna falsi testimonii, exsilio & asylis, flagellatione: cum excerptis ex utriusque gemara, versa & annotationibus, illustrata. 16 p. l. 436 pp. 2 l. 4°. *Amstcrodami, apud I. Ianssonivm*, 1629.

Cochem (Martin von). Heiliger zeiten gebetbuch oder andachten und gebete auf alle heiligen zeiten und tage des ganzen jahres nebst allen übrigen gewöhnlichen andachten.

Cochem (Martin von)—continued.
Neu herausgegeben und verbessert von P. Friedrich Willam. 432 pp. 1 pl. 18°. *Einsiedeln, New York and Cincinnati, K. & N. Benziger,* 1870.

Cochin (Augustin). L'abolition de l'esclavage. 2 v. 2 p. l. xxxviii, 483 pp; 2 p. l. 534 pp. 8°. *Paris, J. Lecoffre,* 1861.

Cockburn (*Mrs.* Catharine). The works of mrs. Catharine Cockburn, theological, moral, dramatic and poetical. Revised and published, with an account of the life of the author, by Thomas Birch. 2 v. 2 p. l. xlviii, 455 pp; 2 p. l. 576 pp. 1 portrait. 8°. *London, J. & P. Knapton,* 1751.

Cockin (William). The art of delivering written language; or, an essay on reading. In which the subject is treated philosophically as well as with a view to practice. [*anon.*] xx, 152 pp. 8°. *London, H. Hughs for J. Dodsley,* 1775.

Cocles (Barthelemy). La physionomie naturelle, et la chiromance. Avec les figures. 287 pp. 18°. *Rouen, J. B. Besongne,* 1700.

Codman (John, *d. d.*) A narrative of a visit to England. 248 pp. 16°. *Boston, Perkins & Marvin,* 1836.

Codman (*Capt.* John). Ten months in Brazil; with notes on the paraguayan war. 2d ed. 218 pp. 4 pl. 12°. *New York, J. Miller,* 1872.

Codrington (Robert). The second part of Youths behaviour, or decency in conversation amongst women. Whereunto is added a collection of select proverbs. Together with severall letters. 7 p. l. 230 pp. 15 l. 18°. *London, W. Lee,* 1664.

[*With* HAWKINS (Francis). Youths behavior, or decency in conversation amongst men].

Codronchi (Giovanni Battista). Baptistæ Codronchi imolensis commentarivs de annis climactericis, ac ratione vitandi eorum pericula, vitamque producendi. 8 p. l. 174 pp. 1 l. 16°. *Bononiae, typis B. Cochij,* 1620.

Coffin (Robert Barry). Castles in the air, and other phantasies. By Barry Gray. [*pseudon.*] x, 352 pp. 12°. *New York, Hurd & Houghton,* 1871.

Cogswell (William, *d. d.*) The harbinger of the millenium; with an appendix. x, 13-362 pp. 12°. *Boston, Peirce & Parker,* 1833.

——— Letters to young men preparing for the christian ministry. 236 pp. 16°. *Boston, Perkins & Marvin,* 1837.

Cogswell (William, *d. d.*)—continued.

——— The theological class book; containing a system of divinity, in the form of question and answer, accompanied with scripture proofs. x, 172 pp. 16°. *Boston, Crocker & Brewster,* 1832

Cohausen (Johann Heinrich). Ermippo redivivo, o sia il metodo di prolungar la vita e il vigore. Traduzione dall' inglese. [Di F. P. *anon.*] xii, 210 pp. sm. 4°. *Livorno, A. Santini & comp.* 1756.

[*Note.*—The original of this singular book appeared at Francfort in 1742. It was republished at Sorau, in 1753, as Der wieder lebende Hermippus; oder physicalische und medicinische abhandlung sein leben durch das anhauchen junger mädchen auf 115 jahre zu verlängern. Dr. John Campbell translated it into english, with additions, a circumstance which has caused its authorship to be attributed to him].

Cohen (—). New Orleans directory, 1854-55. *See* **New Orleans.**

Coignet (Matthieu, *sieur de la Thuillerie*). Politiqve discovrses vpon trveth and lying. An instrvction to princes to keepe their faith and promise: containing the summe of christian and morall philosophie, and the dutie of a good man in sundrie politique discourses vpon the trueth and lying. First composed by sir Martyn Cognet. Newly translated out of french into english, by sir Edward Hoby. 6 p. l. 246 pp. 4°. *London, R. Newberie,* 1586.

Coin (The) book. 1872. *See* **Homans** (I. Smith).

Coit (Thomas Winthrop, *d. d.*) Lectures on the early history of christianity in England. With sermons delivered on several occasions. xi, 334 pp. 12°. *New York, D. Dana, jr.* 1859.

——— A theological common-place book. With a copious index. 3d ed. iv, 320 pp. 4°. *New York, D. Dana, jr.* 1857.

Colange (L.) Zell's popular encyclopedia, a universal dictionary of english language, science, literature and art. By L. Colange, ll. d. 2 v. 1196 pp; 1 p. l. 1152 pp. 4°. *Philadelphia, T. E. Zell,* 1870-71.

Colburn (Zerah) *and* **Holley** (Alexander L.) The permanent way and coal-burning locomotive boilers of european railways; with a comparison of the working economy of european and american lines, and the principles upon which improvement must proceed. xxiii, 168 pp. 51 pl. fol. *New York, Holley & Colburn,* 1858.

Colburn's new monthly magazine. *See* **New monthly** magazine.

Colburn's united service magazine, and naval and military journal. [Monthly]. Jan. 1871, to April, 1872. 4 v. 8°. *London, Hurst & Blackett*, [1871–72].

Colby (Albert). Life of Jesus Christ. *See* **Clark** (*Rev.* R. W.)

Colby (Charles). The world in miniature: with descriptions of every nation and country. Together with a treatise on physical geography. The western hemisphere. 239 pp. 46 maps, 11 charts. 4°. *New Orleans, (La.) A. B. Griswold*, 1857.

Cole (*Rev.* Albert). Sermon before the Maine missionary society at its sixty-fourth anniversary. 1871. 8°. [*Portland*, 1871].

[*In* MAINE. General conference of the congregational churches, minutes of the forty-fifth annual meeting, pp. 75–83].

Cole (Samuel W.) The muse; or, flowers of poetry. 216 pp. 18°. *Cornish, (Maine), author*, 1827.

Coleman (*Mrs.* Chapman). The life of John J. Crittenden, with selections from his correspondence and speeches. Edited by his daughter. 2 v. 389 pp. 1 portrait; 392 pp. 1 portrait. 8°. *Philadelphia, J. B. Lippincott & co.* 1871.

Coleman (H.) Notes on mental and moral philosophy; with an appendix, containing a selection of questions set at the India civil service examinations, between the years 1856 and 1864. x, 207 pp. 16°. *London, Harrison*, 1865.

Coleman (*Rev.* Lyman). An historical geography of the bible. xii, 17–489 pp. 6 maps. 12°. *Philadelphia, E. H. Butler & co.* 1849. S.

Colenso (John William, *d. d. bishop of Natal*). The pentateuch and book of Joshua critically examined. Part 6. [The later legislation of the pentateuch]. xxxix, 644, 174 pp. 8°. *London, Longmans, Green, & co.* 1871.

Coles (*Rev.* George). The antidote, or revelation defended, and infidelity repulsed; in a course of lectures. 395 pp. 8°. *Hartford, P. Canfield*, 1836.

—— Lectures on the book of proverbs. By the author of "Lectures to children." [*anon.*] 173 pp. 18°. *New York, T. Mason & G. Lane*, 1840.

—— The supernumerary. *See* **Woolsey** (*Rev.* Elijah).

Colesworthy (D. C.) The old bureau, and other tales. 408 pp. 12°. *Boston, Antique book store*, 1861.

Colet (Claude). The famous, pleasant, and delightful history of Palladine of England. Discoursing of honourable adventures, of knightly deeds of arms and chivalry: interlaced likewise with the love of sundry noble personages, as time and affection limited their desires. [*anon.*] Translated out of french by A[nthony] M[unday]. 2d ed. 3 p. l. 160 pp. 1 pl. 18°. *London, J. Marshall*, [*about* 1600].

Colgan (William James). Poems. vi, 112 pp. 12°. *New-York, Leavitt, Trow & co.* 1844.

Colin (A.) Historical illustrations of lord Byron's works, 1833. *See* **Byron** (George Gordon).

Collection de documents inédits sur l'histoire de France. *See* **France.** *Ministère de l'instruction publique.*

Collection (A) of anthems, [from the psalms, without musical score], as the same are now performed in his majesty's chapels royal. [*anon.*] 1 p. l. 214 pp. 3 l. 12°. *London, J. Bettenham for D. Barker*, 1749.

Collection (A) of psalms and hymns, for social and private worship. [*anon.*] 2d ed. 420 pp. 12°. *New-York, A. Paul*, 1823.

—— The same. Revised edition. With supplement. [*anon.* By H. D. S.] 520 pp. 16°. *New York, C. S. Francis & co.* 1845.

Collet (Pierre, *s. t. d.*) Traité des devoirs des gens du monde, et surtout des chefs de famille. xxxii, 412 pp. 16°. *Paris, J. Debure l'aîné*, [*etc.*] 1764.

Collette (Charles Hastings). A reply to Cobbett's "History of the protestant reformation in England and Ireland." 2 p. l. 347 pp. 8°. *London, S. W. Partridge & co.* 1869.

Collier (*Rev.* Jeremy). Pearls of great price; or, maxims, reflections, characters and thoughts, on miscellaneous subjects. Selected from the works of the rev. J. Collier, by the editor of "Sir William Jones's discourses," [J. E.] xxvii, 127 pp. 18°. *London, J. Rickerby*, 1838.

Collier (John). Essays on the progress of the vital principle from the vegetable to the animal kingdoms and the soul of man, introductory to contemplations on deity. xv, 376 pp. 8°. *London, author*, 1800.

Collier (John Payne). Criticisms on the bar; including strictures on the principal counsel practising in the courts of king's bench, common pleas, chancery, and exchequer.

Collier (John Payne)—continued. By Amicus curiæ. [*pseudon.*] 2 p. l. xii, 308 pp. 16°. *London, W. Simpkin & R. Marshall*, 1819.

——— Traditionary anecdotes of Shakespeare. Collected in Warwickshire, in the year 1693. Now first published from the original manuscript. 19 pp. 8°. *London, T. Rodd*, 1838.

Collier (Mary A.) The christian statesman. Memoirs of William Wilberforce. 325 pp. 1 pl. 16°. *New York, R. Carter & brothers*, 1855.

Collier (*Rev.* William). The gospel treasury: volume the first, containing a great variety of interesting anecdotes, remarkable providences, and precious fragments. Selected chiefly from the London evangelical magazine. 2d ed. v. 1. 324 pp. 12°. *Charlestown, (Mass.) S. T. Armstrong*, 1810.

Collin de Plancy (Jacques Auguste Simon). Anecdotes du dix-neuvième siècle, ou collection inédite d'historiettes et d'anecdotes récentes [etc.] pour servir à l'histoire des mœurs et de l'esprit du siècle où nous vivons, comparé aux siècles passés. 2 v. x, 319 pp; 2 p. l. 312 pp. 8°. *Paris, C. Painparré*, 1821.

——— Les contes noirs ou les frayeurs populaires; nouvelles, contes, aventures merveilleuses, bizarres et singulières, anecdotes inédites, etc; sur les apparitions, les diables, les spectres, les revenans, les fantômes, les brigands, etc; par J. S. C. de Saint Albin. [*pseudon.*] 2 v. 2 p. l. 180 pp. 2 l. 1 pl; 2 p. l. 182 pp. 1 l. 1 pl. 16°. *Paris, P. Mongie, l'aîné*, 1818.

——— Dictionnaire critique des reliques et des images miraculeuses. 3 v. 8°. *Paris, Guien & cie.* 1821–22.

Collins (T. K. *jr.*) The timbrel of Zion: a choice collection of psalm and hymn tunes, anthems, and chants. 352 pp. obl. 8°. *Philadelphia, T. K. Collins, jr.* 1853. s.

Collins (Thomas Wharton). Humanics. 2 p. l. 358 pp. 1 table. 8°. *New York, D. Appleton & co.* 1860.

Collins (Wilkie). Poor miss Finch. 1 p. l. 9–196 pp. 1 pl. 1 portrait. 8°. *New York, Harper & brothers*, 1872.

Collot (*Rev.* P.) Doctrinal and scriptural catechism. Translated from the french, by mrs. J. Sadlier. New ed. vi, 416 pp. 16°. *New York, D. & J. Sadlier & co.* 1871.

Collyer (Joseph). A new system of geography. *See* **Fenning** (Daniel) *and* **Collyer**.

Collyer (*Rev.* Robert). The life that now is; sermons. 351 pp. 1 portrait. 16°. *Boston, Horace B. Fuller*, 1871.

Colombia (United States of). Coleccion de tratados publicos, convenciones y declaraciones diplomaticas de los Estados Unidos de Colombia. 378 pp. 1 l. 8°. *Bogotá, Echeverría hermanos*, 1867.

——— Ordenanzas para el regimen, disciplina, subordinacion y servicio de la guardia colombiana. 175 pp. 7 l. iv pp. 8°. *Bogotá, Echeverría hermanos*, 1863.

——— Reglamento de administracion i contabilidad militar de los Estados Unidos de Colombia. 2 parts in 1 v. 54 pp. 11 l. 2 tab; 76 pp. 8°. *Bogotá, imprenta de la nacion*, 1862.

——— Reglamento e instruccion de la infanteria de linea i tiradores, para el servicio de los cuerpos de la guardia colombiana i la milicia de los estados. 259 pp. 9 l. music. 8°. *Bogotá, Echeverría hermanos*, 1862

——— *Congress.* Actos legislativos del congreso de los Estados Unidos de Colombia en sus sesiones de 1867. Edicion oficial. 8°. *Bogotá*, 1867.

——— *National convention.* Actos lejislativos de la convencion nacional de los Estados Unidos de Colombia. Instalada en Rionegro, el 4 de Febrero de 1863. 12°. *Bogotá, imprenta de la nacion*, 1863.

Colombo (Ferdinando). Vita di Cristoforo Colombo, descritta da Ferdinando, suo figlio, e tradotta da Alfonso Ulloa. Nuova ed. xxxii, 370 pp. 8°. *Londra, Dulau & co.* 1867.

Colonne *or* **Colonna** (Guido dalle). The avncient historie and onely trewe and syncere cronicle of the warres betwixte the Grecians and the Troyans, and subsequently of the fyrst euercyon of the auncient and famouse cytye of Troye vnder Lamedon the king, and of the laste and fynall destruction of the same vnder Pryam, wrytten by Daretus a Trojan and Dictus a Grecian both souldiours and present in all the sayde warres and digested in latyn by the lerned Guydo de Columpnis and sythes translated in to englyshe verse by John Lydgate moncke of Burye. Newly imprinted. [Edited by Robert Braham]. *b. l.* 160 l. sm. fol. *London, Thomas Marshe*, 1555.

[*Note.*—Two columns on a page; 49 lines in each column].

Colorado gazetteer, 1871. *See* **Wallihan** (S. S.) *and* **Bigney** (T. O.)

Colt (*Mrs.* S. S.) The tourist's guide through the empire state. Embracing all cities, towns and watering places, by Hudson river and New York central route. v, 239 pp. 44 pl. 8°. *Albany, S. S. Colt*, 1871.

Colthrop (*Sir* Henry). The liberties, usages, and customes of the city of London; confirmed by especiall acts of parliament, with the time of their confirmation. Also, divers ample, and most beneficiall charters, granted by king Henry the 6. king Edward the 4. and king Henrie the 7th, not confirmed by parliament as the other charters were, and where to find every particular grant and confirmation at large. 1 p. l. 25 pp. sm. 4°. *London, B. Alsop for N. Vavasour*, 1642.

Colton (*Rev.* Calvin). Thoughts on the religious state of the country; with reasons for preferring episcopacy. 2 p. l. 10–208 pp. 12°. *New-York, Harper & brothers*, 1836.

Colton (John). Original poetical works. 192 pp. 8°. *Hartford, G. L. Coburn*, 1871.

Colton (Joseph H.) Colton's new introductory geography. 85 pp. incl. 18 col. maps. 4°. *New York, Sheldon & co.* 1872.
[COLTON's new series].

Columbia college. (*New York city*). Catalogue of the governors, trustees, and officers, and of the alumni and other graduates, of Columbia college, from 1754 to 1870. 163 pp. 8°. *New York, D. Van Nostrand*, 1871.

Columbia (*District of*). *See* **District of Columbia.**

Columbia (*United States of*). *See* **Colombia.**

Columbian (The) preacher. v. 1. 1808. *See* **Elliot** (Nathan).

Columella (Lucius Junius Moderatus). De re rvstica libri xiii. 530 pp. 9 l. 16°. *Lvgdvni, apvd S. Gryphivm*, 1537.

Coluthus. L'enlèvement d'Hélène, traduit du grec par Scip. Allut. 12°. [*Paris, Lefèvre*, 1841].
[*In* MARTIN (Louis Aimé). Petits poëmes grecs. *Paris*, 1841. pp. 97–110].

——— The same. Il rapimento di Elena di Colutho tebano e Le avventure di Ero e di Leandro di Museo grammatico. Poemetti greci portati in poemetti italiani dal prof. Baccio dal Borgo, con note ed illustrazioni. xix, 168 pp. 8°. *Pisa, typografia nistri*, 1837.

Comazzi (Giovanni Battista). The morals of princes; or, an abstract of the most remarkable passages contain'd in the history of all the emperors who reign'd in Rome. With a moral reflection drawn from each quotation. Done into english by William Hatchett. xvi, 391 pp. 8°. *London, T. Worrall*, 1729.
[Imperfect: pp. vii–viii wanting].

Combe (Andrew, *m. d.*) Observations on mental derangement: being an application of the principles of phrenology to the elucidation of the causes, symptoms, nature, and treatment of insanity. 1st amer. ed. with notes and bibliography, by an american physician. 336 pp. 8°. *Boston, Marsh, Capen & Lyon*, 1834.

Combe (George). The constitution of man considered in relation to external objects. With an additional chapter on the harmony between phrenology and revelation. By Joseph A. Warne. 4th american from the 2d english ed. xii, 412 pp. 12°. *Boston, W. D. Ticknor*, 1835.

——— Lectures on moral philosophy. iv, 183 pp. 12°. *Boston, Marsh, Capen & Lyon*, 1836.

Combe (William). The history of Johnny Quæ Genus, the little foundling of the late doctor Syntax: a poem, by the author of the Three tours. [*anon.*] 2 p. l. 260 pp. 23 col. pl. 8°. *London, R. Ackermann*, 1822.

Comfort (George F.) A manual of german conversation: to succeed the german course. viii, 239 pp. 12°. *New York, Harper & brothers*, 1871.

——— The teacher's companion to the german course. 110 pp. 12°. *New York, Harper & brothers*, 1870.

Comfort (J. W. *m. d.*) The practice of medicine on thomsonian principles. And a materia medica, adapted to the work. xv, 514 pp. 8°. *Philadelphia, A. Comfort*, 1843.

——— Thomsonian practice of midwifery, and treatment of complaints, peculiar to women and children. viii, 215 pp. 8°. *Philadelphia, A. Comfort*, 1845.

Comines *or* **Commines** (Philippe de La Clide de). The historie of Philip de Commines knight. [Translated by Thomas Dannett]. Eng. title, 7 p. l. 366 pp. fol. *London, I. Bill*, 1614.

Commelin, Commelyn, *or* **Commelinus** (Johannes *and* Casparus). Horti medici amstelodamensis rariorum tam Orientalis, quàm Occidentalis Indiæ, aliarumque peregrinarum plantarum, descriptio et icones

Commelin (J. *and* C.)—continued.
ad vivum æri incisæ. Auctore Joanne Commelino. Opus posthumum, latinitate donatum, notisque et observationibus illustratum, à F. Ruyschio, et F. Kiggelario; [*or*], Beschryvinge en curieuse afbeeldingen van rare vreemde oost-west-indische en andere gewassen vertoont in den amsterdamsche kruyd-hof [etc. Latin and dutch]. 12 p. l. 220 pp. 110 pl. fol. *Amstelaedami, P. & J. Blaeu, etc.* 1697.

——— The same. Part ii. Horti medici amstelædamensis rariorum tam Africanarum, quàm utriusque Indiæ, aliarumque plantarum descriptio et icones ad vivum æri incisæ. Pars altera; [*or*], Beschryvinge en curieuse afbeeldingen van rare vreemde africanische, oost-west-indische en andere gewassen vertoont in den amsterdamsche kruyd-hof. Tweede deel. [Latin and dutch]. 9 p. l. 224 pp. 2 l. 113 pl. fol. *Amstelædami, P. & J. Blaeu*, 1701.

Comment l'esprit vient aux tables. 1854. *See* **Morin** (Alcide).

Commercial (The) and financial chronicle, and Hunt's merchants' magazine, a weekly newspaper representing the industrial and commercial interests of the United States. Jan. 7 to Dec. 30, 1871. v. 12–13. fol. *New York, W. B. Dana*, 1871.

Commercial (The) statistical annual, containing full statistical reports on the leading articles of commerce, for the year 1871, compared with several preceding years. 81 pp. fol. *New York, Daily bulletin association*, 1872.

Commines. *See* **Comines.**

Commodianus *gazæus.* Instructionum per litteras versuum primas libri duo. Recensuit F. Oehler. 12°. *Lipsiae, B. Tauchnitz, jun.* 1847.

[GERSDORF (E. G.) Bibliotheca patrum ecclesiasticorum latinorum selecta, v. 13, pp. 156–191].

——— The same. The instructions of Commodianus in favour of christian discipline, against the gods of the heathens. (Expressed in acrostics). 8°. [*Edinburgh, T. & T. Clark*, 1870].

[ANTE-NICENE christian library, v. 18, pp. 434–474].

Common events. [A novel]. *See* **Galt** (John).

Common (A) place-book to the holy bible: or, the scripture's sufficiency practically demonstrated. Wherein the substance of scripture, respecting doctrine, worship, and manners, is reduced to its proper head. 3d ed. improved with twelve intire additional chapters. [*anon.*] 8 p. l. 440 pp. 6 l. 4°. *London, R. & J. Bonwicke, & R. Wilkin*, 1725.

[*Note.*—Commonly ascribed to Locke].

Complete (The) farmer: or, a general dictionary of husbandry in all its branches; containing the various methods of cultivating and improving every species of land, according to the precepts of both the old and new husbandry. By a society of gentlemen. 4th ed. 362 l. unp. 34 pl. fol. *London, T. Longman*, [*etc.* 1793].

Comstock (Andrew, *m. d.*) Practical elocution, or a system of vocal gymnastics. 2d ed. 300 pp. 1 pl. 12°. *Philadelphia, Kay & brother*, 1837.

Comstock (John Lee, *m. d.*) An introduction to the study of botany. 260 pp. 12°. *Hartford, D. F. Robinson & co.* 1832.

——— The same. Including a treatise on vegetable physiology. 15th ed. 485 pp. 12°. *New York, Pratt, Woodford & co.* 1847.

——— Outlines of geology. xii, 336 pp. 12°. *Hartford, D. F. Robinson & co.* 1834.

——— Primary lessons in natural philosophy. 224 pp. 24°. *New York, Pratt, Woodford, & co.* 1850. s.

——— Youth's book of astronomy. 136 pp. sq. 16°. *Boston, W. Peirce*, 1835.

Comte (François Charles Louis). Histoire de la garde nationale de Paris, depuis l'époque de sa fondation jusqu'à l'ordonnance du 29 avril 1827. vii, 534 pp. 1 l. 8°. *Paris, A. Sautelet & cie.* 1827.

Concanen (Edward). A new matrimonial ladder. Eng. title, 20 l. 19 pl. 4°. *London, Read & co.* [*about* 1830].

Concha i Toro (Melchior). Chile durante los años de 1824 a 1828. Memoria historica. xxvii, 376 pp. 8°. *Santiago, imprenta nacional*, 1862. s.

Condé (*Prince* de). *See* **Bourbon** (Louis Henry Joseph, *prince de Condé, duc* de).

Cone (Spencer Houghton, *d. d.*) New testament. 1850. *See* **Bible.** (*English*).

Coney (Thomas, *d. d.*) The devout soul; consisting of meditations, poems, hymns and prayers. 2 v. in 1. xvii, 270 pp; 1 p. l. vii, 262 pp. 8°. *London, R. Wilkin* [*etc.*] 1722.

Confession. [A novel]. *See* **Simms** (William Gilmore).

Confessions of a french catholic priest. To which are added, warnings to the people of

Confessions of a french catholic priest—con'd. the United States. By the same author. Edited by Samuel F. B. Morse, [*anon.*] xiv, 255 pp. 12°. *New York, J. S. Taylor*, 1837.

Congressional directory. *See* **United States.** *Congress.*

Conlin (Johann Rudolph). Roma sancta sive Benedicti xiii pontificis maximi & eminen tissimorum & reverendissimorum s. r. e. cardinalium viva virtutum imago, aeri & literis in perennaturum virtutum memoriam incisa. Continentur vitae, familiae, patriae, legationes, aliáque scitu & memoratu digna omnium s. r. e. cardinalium qui ultimo conclavi anno 1724 interfuêre. Praeter eos qui à sanctissimo patre Benedicto xiii, neo-denominati fuêre. Quibus supplementi loco in singulos 6 menses post creationem accedent quotquot s. r. e. cardinales denominari contigerit. Eng. title, 4 p. l. 266 pp. 94 pl. fol. *Augustae Vindelicorum*, 1726.
[*Note.*—Plate 82 wanting].

Connected (A) view of the whole internal navigation of the United States. *See* **Armroyd** (George).

Connecticut (*State of*). Annual report of the board of education, presented to the general assembly, May session, 1871. With the annual report of the secretary of the board. 252 pp. 2 pl. 1 chart. 8°. *New Haven, Tuttle, Morehouse & Taylor*, 1871.

——— Journal of the senate and house of representatives, May session, 1871. 2 v. 8°. *Hartford, Case, Lockwood & Brainard*, 1871.

——— Public documents of the legislature, May session, 1871. Printed by order of the general assembly. 32 docs. in 1 v. 8°. *Hartford*, 1871.

Connecticut (The) business directory, for 1871. 8°. *Boston, Briggs & co.* 1871.

Connecticut (The) gazette. April 3 [to] Dec. 25, 1762. Num. 365–403. 4°. [*New-Haven, Ct.*] 1762.

Connecticut (The) mutual life insurance company, of Hartford, Conn. Manual of instructions and rates. 89 pp. 18°. *Hartford*, 1872.

Connoissance des poëtes les plus célèbres. *See* **Alletz** (Pons Augustin).

Conquest and self-conquest. *See* **McIntosh** (Maria J.)

Consideratien op de cautie van Portugael. [*anon.*] 26 pp. 3 l. sm. 4°. [*n.p.*] *gedruct anno* 1647.

Considerations on the nature and the extent of the legislative authority of the british parliament. [*anon.*] 35 pp. 16°. *Philadelphia, W. & T. Bradford*, 1774.

——— The same.
[HAZARD pamphlets, v. 44].

Considerations on the sovereignty, independence, trade and fisheries of New-Ireland (formerly known by the name of Nova-Scotia) and the adjacent islands. [*anon.*] 24 pp. 18°. [*n.p.* 1782].

Considerations upon the act of parliament, whereby a duty is laid of six pence sterling per gallon on molasses, and five shillings per hundred on sugar of foreign growth, imported into any of the british colonies. Shewing some of the many inconveniences necessarily resulting from the operation of the said act. [etc. *anon*] 28 pp. 8°. *Boston, Edes & Gill*, 1764.

——— The same.
[HAZARD pamphlets, v. 36].

Considerations upon the rights of the colonists to the privileges of british subjects. [*anon.*] 27 pp. 8°. *New-York, J. Holt*, 1766.
[HAZARD pamphlets, v. 5].

Consoni (Taddeo dei). La esistenza e spiritualità dell' anima distinta dallo spirito sensitivo prodotto del meccanismo organico contro i materialisti. 2ª ed. toscana. xvi, 368 pp. 1 portrait. 8°. *Firenze, F. Bencini*, 1855.

Constitution (The) of society, as designed by God. [Appendix, by Veritas. *anon.*] xiv, 639 pp. 8°. *London, E. Wilson*, 1835.

Contemporary (The) review. [Monthly]. January, 1866. to May, 1872. v. 1–19. 8°. *London, A. Strahan and Strahan & co.* 1866–72.

Contra manifest van signor Fernando Telles de Faro, voor desen geweest ambassadeur extraordinaris van Portugael in Hollandt. Waer in ontdeckt sijn de valsche pretexten van sijn wegh loopen uyt s'Gravenhage, door een brief [etc. *anon.*] 12 pp. sm. 4°. [*n.p.*] 1659.

Conversations on war and general culture. *See* **Helps** (Arthur).

Conyngham (Kate, *pseudon.*) The sunny south; or, the southerner at home, embracing five years' experience of a northern governess in the land of the sugar and the cotton. Edited by prof. J. H. Ingraham, of Mississippi. 526 pp. 12°. *Philadelphia, G. G. Evans*, 1860.

Cooke (Belle W.) Tears and victory, and other poems. 253 pp. 12°. *Salem, (Oregon), E. M. Waite*, 1871.

Cooke (Edward). The character of warre, or the image of martiall discipline: contayning many vsefull directions for musters & armes, and the very first principles in discipline. 41 l. unp. sm. 4°. *London, T. Purfoot*, 1626.

Cooke (George Alexander). Topographical and statistical description of the county of Buckingham. To which is prefixed, a copious travelling guide. 156 pp. 1 map. 18°. *London, C. Cooke*, [1816].

Cooke (George Wingrove). History of party; from the rise of the whig and tory factions, 1666, to the passage of the reform bill, 1832. 3 v. 8°. *London*, 1836–37.

Cooke (John, *m. d.*) The new theory of generation, according to the best and latest discoveries in anatomy, farther improved and fully displayed. By J. C. m. d. [*anon.*] v. 1. xxiv, 340 pp. 8°. *London, J. Buckland*, 1762.

[No more published].

Cooke (John Esten). A life of gen. Robert E. Lee. vi, 577 pp. 11 pl. 3 portraits, 10 maps. 8°. *New York, D. Appleton & co.* 1871.

——— Out of the foam. A novel. 340 pp. 12°. *New York, Carleton*, 1871.

Cooke (Josiah P. *jr.*) Religion and chemistry; or, proofs of God's plan in the atmosphere and its elements. ix, 348 pp. 8°. *New York, C. Scribner*, 1864.

[GRAHAM lectures, v. 3].

Cooke (M. C. *editor*). *See* **Hardwicke's** science gossip.

Cooke (*Rev.* Parsons). A history of german anabaptism, gathered mostly from german writers, living in the age of the lutheran reformation, and embracing a full view of the peasants' wars, the celestial prophets, and other fanatics of that day, and of the historical connection between the present baptists and the anabaptists. 412 pp. 1 l. 18°. *Boston, C. Tappan*, 1845.

——— Recollections of rev. E. D. Griffin, or incidents illustrating his character. 205 pp. 1 portrait. 16°. *Boston, Mass. sabbath school society*, [1855].

Cooke (William, *of Lincoln's Inn*). The elements of dramatic criticism, containing an analysis of the stage under the following heads, tragedy, tragi-comedy, comedy, pantomime, and farce. With a sketch of the education of the greek and roman actors; concluding with some general instructions for succeeding in the art of acting. 3 p. l. xi, 216 pp. 8°. *London, G. Kearsly and G. Robinson*, 1775.

Cooke (*Rev.* William) *and* **Barker** (Joseph). The authentic report of the theological discussion between the rev. W. Cooke and mr. Jos. Barker, held during ten nights in Newcastle. iv, 450 pp. 12°. *London, J. Bakewell*, 1845.

——— The same. The supplement, or companion to the discussion. By Wm. Cooke. 451–474 pp. 12°. [*London*, 1845].

[*With* the preceding].

Coole (Benjamin). A testimony to the truth of God, as held by the people, called, Quakers. *See* **Penn** (William) *and* **Coole.**

Cooley (Timothy Mather, *d. d.*) Sketches of the life and character of the rev. Samuel Haynes. With some introductory remarks by William B. Sprague, d. d. 345 pp. incl. 1 portrait. 12°. *New York, Harper & brothers*, 1837.

Coolidge (Susan, *pseudon.*) *See* **Woolsey** (Sarah C.)

Coolie (The), his rights and wrongs. *See* **Jenkins** (Edward).

Cooney (Robert). A compendious history of the northern part of the province of New Brunswick, and of the district of Gaspe, in Lower Canada. 4 p. l. 288 pp. 8°. *Halifax, (N. S.) J. Howe*, 1832.

Cooper (Anthony Ashley, *3d earl of Shaftesbury*). A character of Augustus, Maecenas and Horace; with some reflections on the works of Horace. 4°. [*London*, 1740].

[*In* TURNBULL (George). Three dissertations. 1740. pp. 20–67, 1 pl.]

Cooper (Charles Henry *and* Thompson). Athenae cantabrigienses. 2 v. 1500–1609. viii, 589 pp; viii, 569 pp. 8°. *Cambridge, (Eng.) Deighton, Bell & co.* 1861.

Cooper (John). An appendix to Placidus de Titus's Primum mobile. 8°. [*London, Davis & Dickson*, 1815].

[*In* TITI (Placido de). Primum mobile, pp. 425–462].

Cooper (Robert). The infidel's text-book, being the substance of thirteen lectures on the bible. 1st american ed. iv, 265 pp. 12°. *Boston, J. P. Mendum*, 1858.

——— Spiritual experiences, including seven months with the brothers Davenport. 2 p. l. 219 pp. 18°. *London, Heywood & co.* 1867.

Cooper (Samuel, *m. d.*) A dictionary of practical surgery: revised, corrected, and enlarged with numerous notes and additions, embracing all the principal improvements and greater operations introduced and performed by american surgeons. By David Meredith Reese, m. d. 3 v. in 1. 8°. *New York, Harper & brothers*, 1842.

——— The first lines of the theory and practice of surgery; including the principal operations. With notes and additions, by Willard Parker, m. d. 4th american, from the 7th London ed. 2 v. 540 pp; 531 pp. 8°. *New York, S. S. & W. Wood*, 1844.

Cooper (Thomas, *m. d.*) The scripture doctrine of materialism. 1823. A view of the metaphysical and physiological arguments in favor of materialism. First published in 1781. Outline of the association of ideas. 8°. *Philadelphia, A. Small*, 1823.

[*In* BROUSSAIS (F. J. V.) On irritation and insanity. 1831. pp. 293–408].

Cooper (Thomas, *the chartist*). Wise saws and modern instances. 2 v. x, 258 pp; 234 pp. 8°. *London, J. How*, 1845.

Coote (Charles, *ll. d.*) The life of Caius Julius Caesar; drawn from the most authentic sources of information. iv, 278 pp. 3 l. 1 portrait. 12°. *London, author*, 1796.

Cope (Edward Drinkard). On the hypothesis of evolution: physical and metaphysical. 71 pp. 12°. *New Haven, (Conn.) C. C. Chatfield & co.* 1871.

[HALF hours with modern scientists, pp. 145–215].

Copello (Juan). Memoria sobre la profilaxis de la tisis pulmonar tuberculosa. 267 pp. 12°. *Lima, J. Enrique del Campo*, 1867.

Copenhagen. *Det kongelige danske videnskabernes selskab.* Regesta diplomatica historiæ danicæ. Index chronologicus diplomatum et literarum, historiam danicam inde ab antiquissimis temporibus usque ad annum 1660. [*Or*] Chronologisk fortegnelse over hidtil trykte diplomer og andre brevskaber til oplysning af den danske historie fra de ældste tider indtil aar 1660, met kort angivelse af indholdet. 2 v. in 3. xxxv, 887 pp; xxxiii, pp. 1–834; 2 p. l. pp. 835–1639. 4°. *Kjöbenhavn, J. D. Quist & comp.* 1847–70. s.

Copland (Alexander). Mortal life; and the state of the soul after death; conformable to divine revelation, as interpreted by the ablest commentators, and consistent with the discoveries of science. By a protestant layman. [*anon.*] 3 p. l. 572 pp. 8°. *London, Smith, Elder & co.* 1833.

Copland (Robert). Jyl of Breyntford's testament. 8°. [*London, for private circulation*, 1871].

[*In* FURNIVALL (F. J. *editor*). Jyl of Breyntford's testament [etc.] 1871. pp. 1–19].

Coquereau (J. B. L.) Mémoires de l'abbé Terrai, controlleur-général des finances; avec une relation de l'émeute arrivée à Paris en 1775, & suivis de quatorze lettres d'un actionnaire de la compagnie des Indes. [*anon.*] 2 p. l. 398 pp. 16°. *Londres*, 1776.

Coquerel (Athanase Laurent Charles). Le christianisme expérimental. xx, 529 pp. 12°. *Paris, J. Cherbuliez*, 1847.

——— Histoire sainte et analyse de la bible, avec un critique sacrée élémentaire et un ordre de lecture des livres saints. xx, 484 pp. 16°. *Paris, Cherbuliez et cie.* 1839.

——— The same. 2e éd. revue et corrigée. xx, 484 pp. 16°. *Paris, Cherbuliez et cie.* 1842.

——— La mort seconde et les peines éternelles. Deux sermons sur l'apocalypse, ii, 11. 2 p. l. 72 pp. 12°. *Paris, J. Cherbuliez*, 1850.

——— Sermons. ier et iie recueils, et sermons détachés. Nouvelle édition. xv, 564 pp. 8°. *Paris, Marc-Aurel, frères*, 1842.

Corancez (Louis Alexandre Olivier de). Histoire des Wahabis, depuis leur origine jusqu'à la fin de 1809; par L. A. [*anon.*] 2 p. l. viii, 222 pp. 1 l. 8°. *Paris, Crapart*, 1810.

Coras (Jean de). Arrest mémorable dv parlement de Tholose. Contenant vne histoire prodigieuse d'vn svpposé mary, aduenüe de nostre temps: enrichié de cent et onze belles et doctes annotations. 1560. 8 p. l. 160 pp. 16°. *Paris, Galliot du Pré*, 1572.

Corbaux (François). Dictionnaire des arbitrages simples, considérés par rapport à la France, dans les changes entre les villes commerçantes, tant de l'Europe que des autres parties du monde, et qui ont une correspondance mutuelle. 2 v. viii, 210 pp. 1 l. 159 pp; xiv, 744 pp. 4°. *Paris, l'auteur*, 1802.

Corbin (P. *and* F.) Corbin's illustrated catalogue and price list of builders', cabinet, and miscellaneous hardware, including locks, latches, and ornamental bronze goods. xv, 398 pp. 4°. *Hartford, Case, Lockwood & Brainard*, 1871.

Cordemoy (Louis Géraud de). A philosophicall discourse concerning speech, conformable to the cartesian principles. Englished out of french. 11 p. l. 125 pp. 18°. [*London*], *J. Martin*, 1668.

Cordemoy (Louis Géraud de)—continued.

——— Traité des saintes reliques. 8°. *Paris, Guien et comp.* 1822.

[COLLIN DE PLANCY (J. A. S.) Dictionnaire des reliques, etc. v. 3, pp. 331-361].

Coriat junior. [*pseudon.*] *See* **Paterson** (Samuel).

Corneille (Pierre). The first act of the tragedy of Pompey, translated from the french of m. Corneille. [By Edmund Waller]. 4°. [*London, I. Tonson*, 1729].

[*In* WALLER (Edmund). Works. *London*, 1729. pp. 377-396].

Cornelius (*Mrs.* Mary H.) The young housekeeper's friend. Revised and enlarged. 254 pp. 12°. *Boston, Taggard & Thompson*, 1864.

——— The same. Revised and enlarged. 312 pp. 12°. *Boston, Thompson, Bigelow & Brown*, 1871.

Cornell (J. H.) The congregational tune-book. A selection of hymn-tunes, old and new. iv, 148 pp. 8°. *New York, Pott, Young & co.* 1872.

Cornhill (The) magazine. [Monthly]. Jan. to Dec. 1871. v. 23-24. 8°. *London, Smith, Elder & co.* 1871.

Cornutus (Lucius Annæus). Phurnuti de natura deorum commentarius. [Græce et latine]. 8°. [*Amstelædami, apud H. Wetstenium*, 1688].

[*In* GALE (Thomas). Opuscula mythologica, pp. 137-236].

Cornwallis (Kinahan). Adrift with a vengeance: a tale of love and adventure. 319 pp. 12°. *New York, Carleton*, 1870.

——— Pilgrims of fashion. A novel. xvi, 337 pp. 12°. *New York, Harper & brothers*, 1862.

Coronelli (Marco Vincenzo). An historical and geographical account of the Morea, Negropont, and the maritime places, as far as Thessalonica. Written in italian. Englished by R. W. 4 p. l. 230 pp. 41 maps. 16°. *London, M. Gillyflower & W. Canning*, 1687.

Correspondent (The), a selection of letters, from the best authors; together with some originals, adapted to all the periods and occasions of life. [*anon.*] 2 v. xi, 343 pp. 6 l; 1 p. l. 348 pp. 3 l. 12°. *London, T. Cadell, jun. & W. Davies*, 1796.

Corson (Hiram). Hand-book of anglo-saxon and early english. xv, 572 pp. 8°. *New York, Holt & Williams*, 1871.

Cort verhael, hoe den admirael Dirck Symonsz. voor de west-indische compagnie den 30 October 1628, ontrent Farnabocque vijf schepen met een gallioentjen heeft verovert ende verdestrueert. [*anon.*] Folded sheet. sm. 4°. *Amsterdam, I van Hilten*, 1629.

Cort verhael vande ordre die sijne coninncklicke majesteyt van Spagnien aen sijn generalissimo den graef [Fernando Mascarenhas] de la Torre inde Bay de todos los Sanctos gegeven heeft, om int werck te stellen al t'ghene hy tot recuparatie van Brasil noodigh achten soude. Mitsgaders 't remarcabelste dat op de custe van deselve capitania, soo int ghevecht vande spaensche vlote stercke 87 zeylen [etc. *anon.*] *b. l.* 6 l. sm. 4°. *Amsterdam, I. van Hilten*, [1640].

Cort verhael van den staet en gelegentheyt vande saecken, tusschen d'engelsche en nederlantsche oost-indische compagnie, altans controvers zijnde. [*anon.*] 16 pp. sm. 4°. *Amsterdam, P. Guldemont*, 1664.

Corte (Gottlieb). *See* **Kortte** (Gottlieb).

Corte (J. B. de). Leçons de littérature anglaise, ou morceaux en prose et en vers tirés des meilleurs auteurs anglais. Vers. 1e éd. 275 pp. 12°. *Roulers, D. Vanhee*, 1841.

Cortese (Isabella). Varietà di secreti, ne' quali si contengono cose minerali, medicinali, profumi, belletti, artifitij, & alchimia; con altre belle curiosità aggiunte Di nvovo ristampati. 8 p. l. 206 pp. 16°. *Venetia, L. Spineda*, 1614.

Cospi (Ferdinando). Mvseo cospiano annesso à quello del famoso Vlisse Aldrovandi e donato alla sua patria dal signor Ferdinando Cospi march. di Petriolo. Descrizione di Lorenzo Legati. 12 p. l. 532 pp. 1 pl. fol. *Bologna, G. Monti*, 1677.

Cossigny (Joseph François Charpentier de). Voyage à Canton, capitale de la province de ce nom, à la Chine; par Gorée, le cap de Bonne-Espérance, et les Isles de France et de la Réunion; suivi d'observations sur le voyage à la Chine, de lord Macartney et du citoyen Van-Braam, et d'une esquisse des arts des Indiens et des Chinois. viii, 607 pp. 8°. *Paris, André*, [1799].

Costa (Giovanni). Poema Alexandri Pope de homine, Jacobi Thomson & Thomæ Gray selecta carmina, ex britanna in latinam linguam translata a Joanne Costa. Cum nonnullis ejusdem poeticis scriptionibus. 4 p. l. 128 pp. 4°. *Patavii, typis seminarii*, 1775.

Costa (Margherita). Istoria del viaggio d'Alemagna del serenissimo gran duca di Toscana Ferdinando secondo. 392 pp. 2 l. 4°. *Venezia*, [1630]?

Costanzo (Giuseppe Giustino, *abate* di). Di un antico testo a penna della divina commedia di Dante, con alcune annotazioni su le varianti lezioni e sulle postille del medesimo. Lettera di Eustazio Dicearcheo ad Angelio Sidicino. [*pseudon.*] 112 pp. 4°. *Roma, Fulgoni*, 1801.

Coster (Charles de). Légendes flamandes [etc.] Précédées d'une préface par Émile Deschanel. 2 p. l. iv, 251 pp. 1 l. 12 pl. 8°. *Paris, M. Lévy frères*, 1858.

Coster (Jacques). Manual of surgical operations; containing the new methods of operating devised by Lisfranc. The translation and notes by John D. Godman, m. d. 265 pp. 2 tab. 12°. *Philadelphia, Carey & Lea*, 1825.

Cota (Rodrigo de). La Celestina. 1822. *See* **Rojas** (Fernando de) *and* **Cota.**

Coton (Pierre). Institvtio catholica in qua exponitur fidei veritas et comprobatur adversus hæreses et svperstitiones huius ævi, in quatuor divisa libros qui totidem J. Caluini voluminibus et institutioni opponi queant. E gallico vertit L. C. R. 24 p. l. 872 pp. 22 l. 4°. *Moguntiae, sumptibus P. Henningii*, 1618.

Cotta (Giovanni). Carmina. 16°. *Venetiis, ex officina Vincentii Valgrisii*, 1548.
[*In* CARMINA qvinqve illvstrivm poetarvm, pp. 87-95].

Cottom (Peter). The american star. Being a choice collection of the most approved patriotic and other songs. Together with many original ones, never before published. 2d ed. 1 p. l. 215 pp. 1 pl. 18°. *Richmond, P. Cottom*, 1817.

Cotton (Charles). Burlesque upon burlesque: or, the scoffer scoft. Being some of Lucian's dialogues, newly put into english fustian. 2d ed. 3 p. l. 200 pp. 1 l. 1 portrait. 8°. *London, C. Brome*, 1687.

Cotton (*Rev.* John, *of Boston*). The controversie concerning liberty of conscience in matters of religion truly stated, by way of answer to some arguments to the contrary sent unto him. 1 p. l. 14 pp. sm. 4°. *London, T. Banks*, 1646.
[*Note.*—The "arguments" replied to fill pp. 1-6, and are said to have been written long since by a witness of Jesus Christ, close prisoner in Newgate].

Cotton (*Rev.* John, *of Newton*). A holy fear of God, and his judgments, exhorted to: in a sermon preach'd at Newton, Nov. 3, 1727. On a day of fasting and prayer, occasion'd by the terrible earthquake, on the Lords-day night before. With an appendix containing an account of the impressions made on the inhabitants of Haverhill [by rev. John Brown]. 2 p.l. xvi, 24, 7 pp. 16°. *Boston, S. Gerrish*, 1727.

Cotton (*Rev.* John)—continued.

——— Two sermons preach'd at Dorchester, April 9, 1727. With a preface by the rev. mr. Danforth, of Dorchester. 1 p. l. vi, 464 pp. 18°. *Boston, S. Gerrish*, 1727.

Counting-house (The) monitor. A weekly business journal, containing notices of dividends, interest, coupons, etc. when due and where payable; meetings, and closing of transfer books, of stock co's: etc. Jan. 1, 1869, to Jan. 2, 1870. v. 1. 8°. *New York, E. W. Bullinger*, 1869.

Country (The) gentleman's magazine. [Monthly]. July, 1870, to Dec. 1871. v. 5-7. 8°. *London, Simpkin, Marshall & co.* 1870-71.

Couper (Robert, *m. d.*) Poetry, chiefly in the scottish language. [2d ed.]? 2 v. 285 pp; 310 pp. 16°. *Inverness, by J. Young*, 1804.

——— Speculations on the mode and appearance of impregnation in the human female; with an account of the principal ancient, and an examination of the modern, theories of generation. 2d ed. xiii, 194 pp. 8°. *Edinburgh, P. Hill*, 1797.

Cournault (Édouard). Exposition des principes actuels de la philosophie, ou examen historique et discussion critique des principes subjectif, spiritualiste, et éclectique, sur lesquels repose de nos jours la philosophie. 3 p. l. 320 pp. 8°. *Paris, Ladrange*, 1843.

Court (Charles Caton de). Relation de la bataille donnée auprès de Fleurus par l'armée du roy, le 1. iuillet. 1690. sous les ordres de m. le maréchal duc de Luxembourg. Avec un plan qui marque tous les mouvemens que ce général a faits pour la gagner. [*anon.*] 10 p.l. 274, 76 pp. 1 map. 18°. *Paris, M Guerout*, 1690.

Court (The) journal and fashionable gazette. [London weekly]. Jan. to Dec. 1871. fol [*London, W. Rayner*, 1871].

Court (The) magazine, [and la belle assemblée]. From June, 1832, to December, 1836. v. 1-8. 8°. *London, E. Bull*, [1832-36].
[Incomplete: v. 3 and 9 wanting].

Court (The) magazine—continued.

——— The same. The court magazine, and monthly critic. From January to December, 1837. v. 10–11. 8°. *London, E. Churton*, 1837.

——— The same. The court magazine, and monthly critic, and lady's magazine, and museum of the belles lettres, etc. United series. From January, 1838, [to] June, 1846. v. 12–28. 8°. *London, Dobbs & co.* [1838–46].

[*Note.*—This periodical was begun in the year 1756, under the title of "The lady's magazine"].

Courte de la Blanchardière (*L'abbé*). A voyage to Peru; performed by the [ship] Conde of St. Malo, in the years 1745 [to] 1749. Written by the chaplain [*anon.*] To which is added, An appendix, containing the present state of the spanish affairs in America, in respect to mines, trade, and discoveries. [By the english editor. *anon.*] xv, 173 pp. 16°. *London, R. Griffiths*, 1753.

Courtilz de Sandras (Gatien de). La guerre d'Espagne, de Bavière, et de Flandre, ou mémoires du marquis D * * *. Contenant ce qui s'est passé de plus sécret & de plus particulier depuis le commencement de cette guerre, jusqu'à la fin de la campagne de 1706. 264 pp. 7 maps, 3 pl. 16°. *Cologne*, [*La Haye*], *P. Marteau*, 1707.

——— Mémoires de Gaspard comte de Chavagnac. [1624-95. *anon.*] 3 p. l. 504 pp. 16°. *Amsterdam, J. Malherbe*, 1700.

Courtoy (Henry). Guide to Holyroodhouse. *See* **Macmillan** (James).

Cousin (Victor). Essays on the destiny of modern philosophy, and an exposition of eclecticism. 136 pp. 16°. *Edinburgh, T. & T. Clark*, [*about* 1850].

——— Madame de Longueville. Nouvelles études sur les femmes illustres, et la société du xviie siècle. 2e éd. xii, 484 pp. 1 portrait. 8°. *Paris, Didier*, 1853.

——— Madame de Sablé. Études sur les femmes illustres et la societé du xviie siècle. xii, 464 pp. 8°. *Paris, Didier*, 1854.

Cousin Alice: a memoir of Alice B. Haven. [*anon.*] 392 pp. 1 portrait. 12°. *New York, D. Appleton & co.* 1865.

Cousin Alice. [*pseudon.*] *See* **Haven** (*Mrs.* Alice Bradley).

Cousins (The). *See* **McIntosh** (Maria J.)

Couteau (James Baptiste, *pseudon.*) *See* **Jephson** (Robert).

Covarrubias (Juan de Horoźco y). *See* **Horoźco y Covarrubias.**

Covarrubias Horoźco (Sebastian de). Tesoro de la lengva castellana, o española. 2 v. in 1. 6 p. l. 274 l. numb. 1 l; 213 l. numb. 2 l. fol. *Madrid, M. Sanchez*, 1673–74.

[*With* ALDERETE (Bernardo José). Del origen y principio de la lengva castellana].

Cove (*Rev.* Morgan). An essay on the revenues of the church of England. 2d ed. 390 pp. 8°. *London, T. Cadell, jun. & W. Davies*, 1797.

Covent (The) garden journal. 2 v. 1 p. l. 816 pp. 4 pl. 8°. *London, J. J. Stockdale*, 1810.

[*Note.*—Only two volumes published].

Coverdale (Myles, *bishop of Exeter*). Biblia. 1535. Reprint, 1838. *See* **Bible.** (*English*).

Coward (William, *m. d.*) Second thoughts concerning human soul. Demonstrating the notion of human soul, as believ'd to be a spiritual and immaterial substance, united to human body, to be an invention of the heathens, and not consonant to the principles of philosophy, reason, or religion. 2d ed. corrected and enlarg'd. 10 p. l. 344 [435] pp. 8°. *London, A. Baldwin*, 1704.

Cowles (Edward B.) Berrien county directory and history, 1871. *See* **Berrien** county.

Cowles (Henry, *d. d.*) The revelation of John. *See* **Bible.** (*English*).

Cowper (J. Meadows, *editor*). *See* **Furnivall** (Frederick J.) *and* **Meadows.**

Cowper (William, *m. d.*) Myotomia reformata: or an anatomical treatise on the muscles of the human body. Illustrated with figures after the life. To which is prefixed an introduction concerning muscular motion. [Edited by Richard Mead]. 6 p. l. lxxvii, 2 l. 194 pp. 67 pl. fol. *London, R. Knaplock*, 1724.

Cowtan (Robert). Memories of the british museum. vii, 428 pp. 1 pl. 8°. *London, R. Bentley & son*, 1872.

Cox (Edward W.) The arts of writing, reading, and speaking. 264 pp. sq. 16°. *New York, G. W. Carleton & co.* 1872.

[HAND-BOOKS of society, v. 3].

Cox (*Rev.* Melville Beveridge). Remains of Melville B. Cox, late missionary to Liberia. With a memoir, by the rev. Gershom F. Cox. 250 pp. 1 portrait. 18°. *New York, T. Mason & G. Lane*, 1839.

Cox (*Rev.* Robert). The life of the rev. John William Fletcher, vicar of Madeley. 1st am. ed. with introduction, and a selection

Cox (*Rev.* Robert)—continued. from the correspondence of mr. Fletcher, by rev. George A. Smith. xxvii, 240 pp. 12° *Philadelphia, George & Byington*, 1837.

Cox (*Mrs.* W. N.) Richard Peters: or, could he forgive him. By Percy Curtiss. [*pseudon.*] 356 pp. 3 pl. 16°. *Boston, Graves & Ellis*, 1872.

Coxe (Arthur Cleveland, *bishop of western New York*). Advent, a mystery. 132 pp. 12°. *New York, J. S. Taylor*, 1837.

——— Athanasion. Second edition, with notes and corrections. Also, miscellaneous poems. By the author of "Christian ballads." [*anon.*] 2 p. l. 187 pp. 12°. *New-York, Wiley & Putnam*, 1842.

——— Christian ballads. [*anon.*] 138 pp. 12°. *New York, Wiley & Putnam*, 1840.

——— The same. Illustrated by John A. Hows. Revised edition. 235 pp. 14 pl. 8°. *New York, D. Appleton & co.* 1865.

——— The signs of the times as connected with the Vatican council: a series of lectures, delivered in Rochester, and other places. With a letter on christian unity by the late bishop of western New York. 56 pp. 8°. *Rochester, (N. Y.) D. M. Dewey*, 1870.

Coxe (John Redman, *m. d.*) The american dispensatory, containing the natural, chemical, pharmaceutical and medical history of the different substances employed in medicine; together with the operations of pharmacy; illustrated and explained, according to the principles of modern chemistry. 6th ed. iv, 766 pp. 8°. *Philadelphia, H. C. Carey & Lea*, 1825.

Coxe (Margaret). Claims of the country on american females. [*anon.*] iv, 15-243 pp; iv, 244 pp. 12°. *Columbus, I. N. Whiting*, 1842.

[Imperfect: wanting "introduction," pp. 1-12].

——— Floral emblems; or, moral sketches from flowers. 144 pp. 4 pl. 16°. *Cincinnati, H. W. Derby & co.* 1845.

——— The life of John Wycliffe, d. d. 216 pp. 16°. *Columbus, I. N. Whiting*, 1840.

——— The young lady's companion: in a series of letters. 1 p. l. viii, 342 pp. 12°. *Columbus, I. N. Whiting*, 1839.

——— The same. The young lady's companion, and token of affection; in a series of letters. x, 348 pp. 8°. *Columbus, I. N. Whiting*, 1846.

Cracroft (Bernard). Essays, political and miscellaneous. Reprinted from various

Cracroft (Bernard)—continued. sources. 2 v. xvi, 322 pp; xvi, 320 pp. 12°. *London, Trübner & co.* 1868.

Craig (*Rev.* Robert). A refutation of certain primary doctrines of popery, in which it is demonstrated, that the italian or roman church has long since ceased to be orthodox; also, a demonstrative argument, that St. Peter never was bishop of Rome. 2 v. 1 p. l. xxiv, 93, iv, 86, 114 pp; 1 p. l. xxiv, 93, iv, 86, 114 pp. 8°. *Dublin, J. Porter*, 1823.

Craig (W. Marshall). Essay on painting. 4°. *London*, 1817.

[*In* LAIRESSE (Gérard de). Treatise on painting, v. 2, pp. 273-294].

Craik (Dinah Maria Mulock). Fair France. Impressions of a traveller. By the author of "John Halifax, gentleman," [etc. *anon.*] 238 pp. 12°. *New York, Harper & brothers*, 1871.

——— Hannah. By the author of "John Halifax, gentleman," [etc. *anon.*] 310 pp. 2 pl. 12°. *New York, Harper & bros.* 1872.

Craik (James, *d. d.*) Old and new. 1 p. l. 284 pp. 12°. *New York, D. Dana, jr.* 1860.

Crakanthorp (Richard, *s. t. d.*) Defensio ecclesiæ anglicanæ, [contra M. Antonii de Dominis, d. archiepiscopi spalatensis iniurias. Iohanne Barkham, s. t. d. in lucem editum]. xxiv, 603 pp. 8°. *Oxonii, apud J. H. Parker*, 1847.

[LIBRARY of anglo-catholic theology].

Cranmer (Thomas, *archbishop of Canterbury*). Cranmer's bible. 1541. *See* **Bible.** (*English*).

Cranz (David). Alte und neue brüder-historie oder kurz gefasste geschichte der evangelischen brüder-unität in den ältern zeiten und insonderheit in dem gegenwärtigen jahrhundert. 8 p. l. 868 pp. 28 l. 12°. *Barby, H. D. Ebers*, 1771.

Crashaw (Richard). Carmen Deo nostro, te decet hymnvs. Sacred poems, collected, corrected, avgmented [etc.] 131 pp. 16°. *Paris, P. Targa*, 1652.

Craven (*Mrs.* Augustus). Anna Severin. Erzählung. Deutsch von J. B. Kälin. Autorisirte uebersetzung. 352 pp. 16°. *New York and Cincinnati, G. K. & N. Benziger*, 1871.

Crawford (*Mrs.* M. J. E.) Songs of early and later years. 180 pp. 16°. *Philadelphia, author*, 1872.

Credner (Carl August). Geschichte des neutestamentlichen kanon. Herausgegeben von dr. G. Volkmar. viii, 424 pp. 8°. *Berlin, G. Reimer*, 1860.

Credner (Heinrich). Über die gliederung der oberen juraformation und der wealdenbildung im nordwestlichen Deutschland. Nebst einem anhange über die daselbst vorkommenden nerineen und chemnitzien. xi, 192 pp. 11 pl. 1 map, 3 tab. 8°. *Prag, F. A. Credner*, 1863.

Crell (A. F. *m. d.*) *and* **Wallace** (W. M.) The family oracle of health; economy, medicine, and good living; adapted to all ranks of society, from the palace to the cottage. 5 v. 8°. *London, J. Walker, etc.* 1824–28.

Crell (Johann). The two books of John Crellius francus, touching one God, the Father. Translated out of the latine into english. 5 p. l. 315 pp. 10 l. sm. 4°. *Kosmoburg*, [*London*], 1665.

Crelle (August Leopold). Handbuch des feldmessens und nivellirens in den gewöhnlichen fällen. vi, 372 pp. 12 tab. 8°. *Berlin, G. Reimer*, 1826.

Cremer (J. J.) Ein tag in der residenz. 16°. *Braunschweig, F. Vieweg & sohn*, 1866. s.
[GLASER (Adolf). Niederländische novellen, pp. 99–142].

——— Der vetter vom lande. 16°. *Braunschweig, F. Vieweg & sohn*, 1866. s.
[GLASER (Adolf). Niederländische novellen, pp. 199–235].

Crescimbeni (Giovanni Mario). L'istoria della volgar poesia. Nella seconda impressione, fatta l'anno 1714, d'ordine della ragunanza degli Arcadi, corretta, riformata, e notabilmente ampliata; e in questa terza pubblicata unitamente co i comentarj intorno alla medesima, riordinata, ed accresciuta. 6 v. 4°. *Venezia, L. Basegio*, 1730–31.

——— Vita dell' abbate Alessandro Guidi. 16°. *Venezia, P. Piotto*, 1787.
[*In* GUIDI (Alessandro). Poesie, pp. 9–40].

Cresswell (Daniel). An elementary treatise on the geometrical and algebraical investigation of maxima and minima: [also], a selection of propositions deducible from Euclid's elements. iv, 273, 58 pp. 8°. *Cambridge, W. Metcalfe for J. Deighton*, 1812.

Cretan (The). [Monthly]. April to Dec. 1868, nos. 1–7 in 1 v. 4°. *Boston*, 1868.

Creyton (Paul, *pseudon.*) *See* **Trowbridge** (John Townsend).

Crimes (Les) de la philosophie. *See* **Piestre** (J. L.)

Crinesius (Christoph). Bavel; sive discursus de confusione linguarum, tum orientalium: hebraice [etc.]: tum occidentalium, nempe græcæ [etc.], statuens hebraicam, omnium esse primam et ipsissimam matricem, concinnatus. 6 p. l. 144 pp. 2 l. sm. 4°. *Noribergæ, typis & sumptibus S. Halbmayeri*, 1629.

Crinito *or* **Riccio** (Pietro). Petri Criniti commentarii de honesta disciplina. 137 l. unp. 4°. *Florentie, impensa P. de Giunta*, 1504.
[*With his* Libri de poetis latinis].

——— Petri Criniti de honesta disciplina, lib. xxv. [De] poëtis latinis, lib. v, et poëmaton, lib. ii. Cum indicibus. 864 pp. 2 l. 24°. *Lvgdvni, apvd haered. S. Gryphii*, 1561.

——— Petri Criniti libri de poetis latinis. 47 l. unp. 4°. *Florentie, per P. Iuntam*, 1505.
[*Note.*—No pagination; 39 lines on a page].

Cririe (James, *d. d.*) Scottish scenery: or, sketches in verse, descriptive of scenes chiefly in the highlands of Scotland. xxxv, 412 pp. 20 pl. 4°. *London, T. Cadell, jun. and W. Davies*, 1803.

Crisp (Tobias, *d. d.*) Christ alone exalted; in the perfection and encouragements of the saints, notwithstanding sins and trials. Being the complete works of T. Crisp, containing fifty-two sermons on several select texts of scripture. To which are added notes explanatory, with memoirs of the doctor's life, etc. by the late dr. Gill. 4th ed. corrected. 2 v. 1 p. l. lxxxvi, 583 pp. 1 portrait; 1 p. l. viii, 648 pp. 8°. *London, J. Murgatroyd*, 1791.

——— The same. 7th ed. 2 v. viii, v–xliv, 366 pp. 1 portrait; iv, 412 pp. 1 portrait. 8°. *London, J. Bennett*, 1832.

Critical observations on the sixth book of the Æneid. [*anon.*] 1 p. l. 56 pp. 8°. *London, P. Elmsley*, 1770.
[*With* DELAFAYE (Theodore). An essay on Virgil's celebrated gates of sleep. *London*, 1743].

Crittenden (John Jordan). Correspondence and speeches. *See* **Coleman** (*Mrs.* Chapman).

Crivelli (Giovanni). Giovanni Brueghel [Breugel] pittor fiammingo, o sue lettere e quadretti esistenti presso l'Ambrosiana. xii, 403 pp. 3 fac-similes. 8°. *Milano, tipografia e libreria arcivescorille*, [*a spese dell' Ambrosiana*], 1868. s.

Croft (John). Excerpta antiqua; or, a collection of original manuscripts. 2 p. l. 112 pp. 8°. *York, W. Blanchard*, 1797.

Croll (Oswald). Bazilica chymica, & praxis chymiatricæ. Or, royal and practical chym-

Croll (Oswald)—continued.
istry. In three treatises. Wherein all those excellent medicines and chymical preparations are fully discovered, from whence our modern chymists have drawn their choicest remedies. Augmented and inlarged by John Hartman. To which is added his Treatise of signatures of internal things, or a true and lively anatomy of the greater and lesser world. As also, the practice of chymistry of John Hartman, m. d. augmented and inlarged by his son. All faithfully englished by a lover of chymistry. 3 v. in 1. fol. *London, J. Starkey & T. Passinger*, 1670.

Croly (*Rev.* George). The theory of baptism. The regeneration of infants in baptism vindicated on the testimony of holy scripture, christian antiquity, and the church of England. xxii, 223 pp. 8°. *London, F. & J. Rivington*, 1850.

Croly (*Mrs.* Jennie). Jennie Juneiana. Talks on women's topics. By Jennie June. [*pseudon.*] 240 pp. 12°. *Boston, Lee & Shepard*, 1864.

Cromek (R. H.) Reliques of Robert Burns; consisting chiefly of original letters, poems, and critical observations on scottish songs. xv, 322 pp. 18°. *Baltimore, F. Lucas, jr. & J. Cushing*, 1815.

[BURNS (Robert). The works of Robert Burns, [Edited by J. Currie, 1815], v. 4].

Crosby (Alpheus). A compendious grammar of the greek language. 370 pp. 12°. *New York, Woolworth, Ainsworth & co.* 1871.

——— A grammar of the greek language. For the use of schools and colleges. Revised ed. 475 pp. 12°. *New York, Woolworth, Ainsworth & co.* 1871.

——— Greek lessons: consisting of selections from Xenophon's anabasis, with a vocabulary, notes, directions for the study of the grammar, sentences for translation into greek, and suggestions for greek dialogue. Revised ed. iii, 13–133 pp. 12°. *New York and Chicago, Woolworth, Ainsworth & co.* 1872.

——— Greek tables for the use of students. Revised, with the addition of many references and latin analogies, a catalogue of verbs, an outline of sentential analysis, &c. 120 pp. 12°. *New York, Woolworth, Ainsworth & co.* 1871.

——— An outline of sentential analysis, with other grammatical sketches: reprinted from a grammar of the greek language. 1 p. l. 99–111 pp. 12°. *New York, Woolworth, Ainsworth & co.* 1871.

Crosby (Howard, *d. d.*) The healthy christian: an appeal to the church. 163 pp. 18°. *New York, American tract society*, [1871].

——— Jesus: his life and work, as narrated by the four evangelists. 551 pp. 22 pl. 8°. *New York, University publishing co.* 1871.

——— The new testament, with notes. 1863. *See* **Bible.** (*English*).

Crosby's caledonian musical repository; [or] The caledonian musical repository: a choice collection of esteemed scottish songs, adapted for the voice, violin, and german flute. Eng. title, 1 p. l. pp. 7–286, 1 pl. 16°. *Edinburgh, Oliver & Boyd*, 1811.

Cross (James C.) Parnassian bagatelles; being a miscellaneous collection of poetical attempts. [Also], a comic sketch in one act, called The way to get unmarried. And the village doctor, or killing no cure. 4 p. l. 157 pp. 8°. *London, Burton & co.* 1796.

Cross (John A.) *and* **Dudley** (Charles E.) Our sunday-school hymnody. 144 pp. obl. 12°. *Brooklyn, E. F. DeSelding*, [1871].

Cross (Joseph, *d. d.*) Headlands of faith; a series of dissertations on the cardinal truths of christianity. Edited by Thomas O. Summers, d. d. 341 pp. 12°. *Nashville, E. Stevenson & I. E. Evans*, 1856.

Cross (*Rev.* Marcus E.) The mirror of intemperance, and history of the temperance reform. To which is added the life and death of king Alcohol, and original and selected anecdotes. 240 pp. 12°. *Philadelphia, J. T. Lange*, 1849.

——— *editor.* The museum of religious knowledge; designed to illustrate religious truth. 264 pp. 1 pl. 12°. *Philadelphia, J. Whetham*, 1869.

Cross (Nicolas). The cynosura, or a saving star that leads to eternity. Discovered amidst the celestial orbs of David's psalms by way of paraphrase upon the Miserere. 6 p. l. 450 pp. 3 l. fol. *London, T. Rooks*, 1670.

Crosse (H.) Études sur les mollusques terrestres et fluviatiles du Mexique et du Guatémala. 1870. *See* **Fischer** (P.) *and* **Crosse.**

Crosswell (William, *d. d.*) Poems, sacred and secular. Edited, with a memoir, by A. Cleveland Coxe. xlvii, 284 pp. 1 portrait. 16°. *Boston, Ticknor & Fields*, 1861.

Crouch (Julia). Three successful girls. vii, 382 pp. 12°. *New York, Hurd & Houghton*, 1871.

Crousaz (Jean Pierre). New maxims concerning the education of youth. And a discourse concerning pedantry. Both translated from french into english by the rev. George Stephen Tacheron. xi, 167, 58 pp. 16°. *London, translator*, 1740.

Crowe (*Rev.* William). Lewesdon hill, considerably enlarged: with other poems. 3d ed. x, 115 pp. 16°. *London, T. Cadell*, 1804.

Crowell (John, *d. d.*) Republics; or, popular government an appointment of God. 238 pp. 16°. *Philadelphia, Presbyterian board of publication*, [1871].

Crown (A) from the spear. *See* **Hamilton** (C. V.)

Croxall (Samuel, *d. d.*) Scripture politics: being a view of the original constitution, and subsequent revolutions, in the government religious and civil, of that people, out of whom the saviour of the world was to arise: as it is contained in the bible. 1 p. l. x, 503 pp. 8°. *London, J. Tonson & J. Watts*, 1735.

——— *See, also,* **Novelist** (The).

Cruden (*Rev.* William). Nature spiritualised, in a variety of poems, containing pious and practical observations on the works of nature, and the ordinary occurrences in life. xv, 295 pp. 12°. *J. & W. Oliver*, 1766.

Cruveilhier (Jean). The anatomy of the human body. 1st american, from the last Paris edition. Edited by Granville Sharp Pattison, m. d. xv, 907 pp. 8°. *New York, Harper & brothers*, 1844.

Cudmore (P.) The irish republic. A historical memoir on Ireland and her oppressors. 331 pp. 8°. *Saint Paul, (Minn.) Pioneer printing co.* 1871.

Cujas (Jacques). Iacobi Cviacii observationvm et emendationvm lib. xxviii. Accessere avctorvm citationes, locorum graecorum interpretationes. Praefationem praemisit Io. Gottl. Heineccivs. 1 p. l. xxxiv, 928 pp. 44 l. 4°. *Halae, impensis Orphanotrophei*, 1737.

Culbertson (*Rev.* M. Simpson). Darkness in the flowery land; or, religious notions and popular superstitions in north China. 235 pp. 1 pl. 12°. *New York, C. Scribner*, 1857.

Cullen (Alexander). The history of Scotland, from the earliest period of authentic record, to the present time, including biographical memoirs of the most illustrious

Cullen (Alexander)—continued.
men, that have adorned that kingdom. Eng. title, 437 pp. 11 pl. 4°. *London, T. Crabb*, [1815].

Cullis (Charles, *m d.*) Faith hymns. 160 pp. 24°. *Boston, Willard street tract repository*, [1870].

Cullum (*Brig-gen.* George W. *U. S. a.*) Systems of military bridges in use by the United States army, those adopted by the great european powers, and such as are employed in British India. With directions for the preservation, destruction, and re-establishment of bridges. vi, 226 pp. 7 pl. 8°. *New York, D. Van Nostrand*, 1863.

Cultivator (The) and country gentleman. Devoted to the practice and science of agriculture and horticulture at large, and to all the various departments of rural and domestic economy. [Weekly]. Jan. 5 to Dec. 28, 1871. v. 36. fol. *Albany, L. Tucker & son* 1871.

Cumberland (George Clifford, 3*d earl of*). *See* **Clifford** (George).

Cumming (*Rev.* John, *d. d.*) Moses right and bishop Colenso wrong; being popular lectures on the pentateuch. 271 pp. 12°. *New York, J. Bradburn*, 1863.

Cumming (W. F. *m. d.*) Notes of a wanderer, in search of health, through Italy, Egypt, Greece, Turkey, up the Danube, and down the Rhine. 2 v. xix, 415 pp. 1 pl. 1 map; xv, 360 pp. 1 pl. 8°. *London, Saunders & Otley*, 1839.

Cunningham (Allan). Sir Marmaduke Maxwell, a dramatic poem; The mermaid of Galloway; The legend of Richard Faulder; and twenty scottish songs. xi, 209 pp. 16°. *London, Taylor & Hessey*, 1822.

——— Songs: chiefly in the rural language of Scotland. xx, 83 pp. 12°. *London, author*, 1813.

Cunningham (John, *d. d.*) The quakers from their origin till the present time: an international history. xv, 335 pp. 12°. *Edinburgh, J. Menzies & co.* 1868.

Cunningham (*Rev.* J. W.) Sancho, or the proverbialist. [*anon.*] 2d ed. 2 p. l. vi, 178 pp. 12°. *London, T. Cadell*, 1816.

Cunningham (Timothy). The history of the customs, aids, subsidies, national debts, and taxes, of England, from William the conqueror, to the present year 1778. 3d ed. 2 p. l. 359 pp. 2 l. 8°. *London, J. Johnson*, 1778.

Cuper, Couper *or* **Kuyper** (Frenz). Arcana atheismi revelata, philosophice & paradoxe refutata, examine tractatus theologico-politici. 2 v. in 1. 8 p. l. 304 pp. 4°. *Roterodami, apud I. Næranum*, 1676.

Cupples (*Mrs.* George). Singular creatures, and how they were found: being stories and studies from the domestic zoölogy of a scotch parish. 333 pp. 4 pl. 16°. *Boston, Lee & Shepard*, 1872.

Curicke *or* **Küricke** (Reinhold). Der stadt Dantzig historische beschreibung, worinnen von dero uhrsprung, situation, regierungs-art, geführten kriegen, religions- und kirchenwesen aussführlich gehandelt wird. Verfasset and zusamen getragen im jahr 1645. Anitzo aber mit sonderbahrem fleiss, nebts vielen dazu gehörigen kupferstücken in öffentlichen druck ausgegeben von Georg Reinhold Curicken, anno 1686. Und mit vielen newen additionibus vermehret und continuiret biss auf die gegenwertige zeit. Eng. title, 5 p. l. 432 pp. 4 l. 17 pl. fol. *Amsterdam & Dantzigk, J. & G. Janssons von Waesberge*, 1688.

Curling (T. B. *m. d.*) A practical treatise on the diseases of the testis, and of the spermatic cord and scrotum. Edited by P. B. Goddard, m. d. 568 pp. 8°. *Philadelphia, Carey & Hart*, 1843.

Currie (Helen). Poems. viii, 5–150 pp. 18°. *Philadelphia, T. H. Palmer*, 1818.

Currie (James, *m. d.*) The life of Robert Burns; with a criticism on his writings. To which are prefixed some observations on the scottish peasantry. 8°. *London, T. Cadell*, 1801.

[*In* BURNS (Robert). The works of Robert Burns, v. 1. *London*, 1801].

——— The same. 18°. [*Baltimore*, 1815].

[*In* BURNS (Robert). The works of Robert Burns. *Baltimore*, 1815. v. 1, pp. 23–267].

Currier (Ephraim). The second coming of Christ, and the resurrection. 188 pp. 12°. *Skowhegan, M. Littlefield*, 1841.

Curtin (D.) Curtin's directory of Long Island [32 towns], with a business directory of patrons of the work. 1871–72. 499 pp. 12°. *New York, D. Curtin*, 1871.

Curtis (*Rev.* Thomas F.) The progress of baptist principles in the last hundred years. 422 pp. 12°. *Boston, Gould & Lincoln*, 1855.

Curtis's botanical magazine. By J. D. Hooker. [Monthly]. 3d series. v. 26–27, (or v. 96–97 of the whole work). 8°. *London, L. Reeve & co.* 1870–71.

Curtiss (Percy, *pseudon.*) *See* **Cox** (*Mrs. W. N.*)

Curtius (Ernst). The history of Greece. Translated by Adolphus William Ward. Revised, after the last german ed. by W. A. Packard. v. 2–3. 12°. *New York, C. Scribner & co.* 1871–72.

Cushing (*Mrs.* Caroline W.) Letters, descriptive of public monuments, scenery, and manners in France and Spain. 2 v. xii, 342 pp. 1 portrait; x, 344 pp. 12°. *Newburyport, (Mass.) E. W. Allen & co.* 1832.

Cutter (Ephraim, *m. d.*) Monograph. Phyrotomy, for the removal of laryngeal growths, modified. 30 pp. 8°. *Boston, J. Campbell*, 1871.

Cutting (*Rev.* Sewall S.) Historical vindications: a discourse on the province and uses of baptist history. With appendixes, containing historical notes and confessions of faith. 224 pp. 12°. *Boston, Gould & Lincoln*, 1859.

Cuyler (*Rev.* Theodore L.) The cedar christian: and other practical papers and personal sketches. 215 pp. 16°. *New York, R. Carter & brothers*, 1864.

——— Heart-life. 191 pp. 1 portrait. 18°. *New York, American tract society*, 1871.

——— Thought-hives. 341 pp. 1 portrait. 12°. *New York, R. Carter & bros.* 1872.

Cyfaill (**Y**) o'r hen wlad. [Welsh monthly]. Cylchgrawn misol y methodistiaid calfinaidd yn America. Dan olygiaeth y parch. William Roberts, d. d. a'r parch. Morgan A. Ellis. Ionawr–Rhagfyr 1871. Old series, v. 34; new series, v. 2. 8°. *New York, H. J. Hughes*, 1871.

Cypress (J. *jr. pseudon.*) *See* **Hawes** (William Post).

Cyprianus *carthaginensis* (*S.* Thascius Cæcilius). Opera genuina. Ad optimorum librorum fidem expressa brevique adnotatione instructa curante D. I. H. Goldhorn. 2 v. viii, 254 pp. 1 l; viii, 279 pp. 12°. *Lipsiae, B. Tauchnitz, jun.* 1838–39.

[GERSDORF (E. G.) Bibliotheca patrum ecclesiasticorum latinorum selecta, v. 2–3].

CONTENTS.

v. 1. Epistolæ. v. 2. Tractatus.

——— Trattato di San Cipriano vescouo, & martire, di dua sorte di martirio. Tradotto di lingua latina, in volgare per don Raffaello [Castrucci] monacho della badia di Firenze. Con la vita, & passione del medesimo, [per Paolo diacono monaco cassinese]. Et altre testimonanze di santissimi dottori della sua

Cyprianus—continued.
santità & dottrina. 140 pp. 1 l. 16°. *Firenze, [figluoli di L. Torrentini]*, 1567.

[*Note.*—Following the Trattato, is a sermone di S. Cipriano del gran bene che patorisce la pazienza].

Czechowski (*Rev.* Michael B.) Thrilling and instructive developments: an experience of fifteen years as a roman catholic clergyman and priest. 286 pp. 16°. *Boston, author*, 1862.

Czvittinger (David). Specimen Hungariæ literatæ, virorvm ervditione clarorvm natione Hungarorvm, Dalmatarvm, Croatarvm, Slavorvm, atque Transylvanorvm, vitas, scripta, elogia et censvras ordine alphabetico exhibens. Accedit bibliotheca scriptorum qui extant de rebus hungaricis. 7 p. l. 408, 80 pp. 2 l. 4°. *Francofvrti et Lipsiæ, typis et sumptibus J. G. Kohlesii*, 1711.

D. (A. J. S.) *See* **Sigaud de la Fond** (Joseph Aignan).

D. (A. K.) Trifles. [*anon.*] 297 pp. 3 pl. 16°. *Boston, D. Lothrop & co.* 1871.

D. (C. L.) Vollständiges lehrgebäude der ganzen optik, oder der sehe-, spiegel- und strahlbrech-kunst, darinn die gründe derselben theoretisch und praktisch vorgetragen, die verfertigung der maschinen und instrumente, die zubereitung aller arten von spiegeln und optischen gläsern, deutlich gelehret, auch der gebrauch derselben bey den experimenten gezeiget wird. 9 p. l. 772 pp. 2 l. 89 pl. 4°. *Altona, D. Iversen*, 1757.

D. (G.) A briefe discoverie of doctor Allens seditious drifts, contriued in a pamphlet written by him, concerning the yeelding vp of the towne of Deuenter, (in Ouerrissel) vnto the king of Spain by sir William Stanley, [etc. *anon.* subscribed G. D.] 3 p. l. 128 pp. 4°. *London, F. Coldock*, 1588.

D. (S. M.) Life of Sidney. *See* **Davis** (*Mrs.* S. M.)

Dabney (R. L. *d. d.*) Syllabus and notes of the course of systematic and polemic theology, taught in Union theological seminary, Virginia. Published by the students. 2 parts in 1 v. vi, 303 pp; 323 pp. 8°. *Richmond, Shepperson & Graves*, 1871.

Dacier (André). An essay upon satyr. 16°. [*London*, 1719].

[*In* Le Bossu (Réné). Treatise of the epick poem, v. 2, pp. 298–315].

——— Fragments taken from remarks upon passages of Aristotle's poetry. 16°. [*London*, 1719].

[*In* Le Bossu (Réné). Treatise of the epick poem, v. 2, pp. 352–354].

Dagg (John L. *d. d.*) Manual of theology. A treatise on christian doctrine. 379 pp. 8°. *Philadelphia, American baptist publication society*, [1871].

Daheim. [Ein deutsches familienblatt, mit illustrationen. Wöchentlich]. 1. Oct. 1870 bis 23. Sept. 1871. v. 7. 4°. *Leipzig, R. König*, 1871.

Dahlgren (John A. *rear-admiral U. S. n.*) Memoir of Ulric Dahlgren. By his father. [Edited by his mother]. 308 pp. 1 portrait. 12°. *Philadelphia, J. B. Lippincott & co.* 1872.

Dähne (August Ferdinand). Geschichtliche darstellung der jüdisch-alexandrinischen religions-philosophie. 2e abth. xx, 498 pp. 1 l; viii, 266 pp. 1 l. 8°. *Halle, buchhandlung des waisenhauses*, 1834.

Dahuron (Réné). Vollständiger garten-bau, darinnen sowohl von einheimischen als ausländischen gewächsen, blumen und bäumen gründliche nachricht gegeben wird. Nebst einem nützlichen unterricht von der bienen wartung; vom baum-beschneiden; und der rechten baumzucht. 7e aufl. 7 p. l. 684 pp. 9 l. 10 pl. 12°. *Weimar, S. H. Hoffmann*, 1757.

Daily morning chronicle. [Washington]. John M. Morris, editor. Jan. 2 to Dec. 30, 1871. 2 v. fol. *Washington, Chronicle publishing co.* 1871.

Daily (The) national republican. [Washington]. W. J. Murtagh, editor. Jan. 2 to Dec. 30, 1871. 2 v. fol. *Washington, W. J. Murtagh*, 1871.

Daily (The) patriot. [Washington]. Nov. 1870, to Dec. 30, 1871. 2 v. fol. *Washington, The patriot newspaper association*, 1870–71.

Daily Richmond whig. Jan. 1 to Oct. 6, 1864. fol. *Richmond (Va.)* 1864.

Daire (Eugène). Économistes-financiers du 18e siècle. Précédés de notices historiques sur chaque auteur, et accompagnés de commentaires et de notes explicatives. vii, 1008 pp. 1 portrait. 8°. *Paris, Guillaumin*, 1843.

CONTENTS.

Boisguillebert (Pierre le Pesant de). Détail de la France, Factum de la France, opuscules divers.
Dutot. Réflections politiques sur le commerce et les finances.
Law (John). Considérations sur le numéraire et le commerce: Mémoires et lettres sur les banques: Opuscules divers.
Melon (Jean François). Essai politique sur la commerce.
Vauban (Sébastien le Prestre de). Projet d'une dime royale.

Dairval. *See* **Baudelot de Dairval.**

Dake (Orsamus Charles). Nebraska legends and poems. 165 pp. 12°. *New York, Pott & Amery*, 1871.

Dale (Antonius van, *m. d.*) De oraculis ethnicorum dissertationes duæ: quarum prior de ipsorum duratione ac defectu, posterior de eorundem auctoribus. Accedit et schediasma de consecrationibus ethnicis. [Editio princeps]. Eng. title, 15 p. l. 510 pp. 8 l. 1 pl. 16°. *Amstelædami, apud H. & viduam T. Boom*, 1683.

[Slightly imperfect].

——— Dissertationes de origine ac progressu idololatriæ et superstitionum: de vera ac falsa prophetia; uti et de divinationibus idololatricis Judæorum. 1 v. in 2. 26 p. l. 762 pp. 7 l. 4°. *Amstelodami, apud H. & viduam T. Boom*, 1696.

Dale (Fanny). Household words for girls and boys, original and selected. 216 pp. 18°. *Philadelphia, G. Collins*, 1855.

Dall (Caroline H.) "Woman's right to labor;" or, low wages and hard work: in three lectures delivered in Boston, November, 1859. xv, 185 pp. 12°. *Boston, Walker, Wise & co.* 1860.

Dallas (George Mifflin) Life and writings of Alexander James Dallas. 487 pp. 8°. *Philadelphia, J. B. Lippincott & co.* 1871.

Dalmazzoni (Angelo). The antiquarian, or the guide for foreigners to go the rounds of the antiquities of Rome. 312 pp. 12°. *Rome, author*, 1803.

Dalton (John C. *m. d.*) A treatise on human physiology; designed for the use of students and practitioners of medicine. 5th ed. revised and enlarged. xxiv, 33–728 pp. 8°. *Philadelphia, H. C. Lea*, 1871.

Dalzell (Andrew). *Αναλεκτα ἑλληνικα ἡσσονα.* Or, collectanea græca minora; with explanatory notes, collected or written by Andrew Dalzell. 6th Cambridge ed. in which the notes and lexicon are translated from the latin into english. xi, 328 pp. 1 pl. 8°. *Boston, Cummings, Hilliard & co.* 1825.

Dameto (Juan) *and* **Mut** (Vicente). The ancient and modern history of the Balearick islands; or of the kingdom of Majorca; which comprehends the islands of Majorca, Minorca, Yviça, Formentera and others. With their natural and geographical description. Translated from the original spanish [by Colin Campbell]. 8 p. l. 304 pp. 8 l. 2 maps. 12°. *London, W. Innys*, 1716.

Damianus a Goes. *See* **Goes** (Damiaõ de).

Dammapadam. Buddha's dhammapada, or "path of virtue." Translated from pâli. By F. Max. Müller. 12°. [*New York, C. Scribner & co.* 1872].

[*In* MÜLLER (Frederic Maximilian). Lectures on the science of religion, pp. 149–300].

Dampier (William). Nieuwe reize naa de Zuidzee, en verder rondom de waereld. *See* **Rogers** (Woodes).

Damsel (The) of Darien. *See* **Simms** (William Gilmore).

Damvilliers (*Sieur* de, *pseudon.*) *See* **Nicole** (Pierre).

Dana (Charles A.) A household book of songs. *See* **Bowman** (Francis C.) *and* **Dana.**

Dana (Daniel, *d. d.*) A discourse on the character and virtues of general George Washington: delivered February 22, 1800, the day of national mourning for his death. 31 pp. 8°. *Newburyport, A. March*, 1800.

[MOORE pamphlets, v. 28].

Dana (E.) Sacred and household poetry, gathered from the highways and byways. By the compiler of "Life and letters of miss Mary C. Greenleaf." 224 pp. 12°. *Newburyport, Moulton & Clark*, 1858.

Dana (James Dwight). Corals and coral islands. [Illustrated]. 398 pp. 3 maps, 4 pl. 8°. *New York, Dodd & Mead*, 1872.

——— A text-book of geology. vi, 354 pp. 12°. *Philadelphia, T. Bliss & co.* 1864.

——— The same. vi, 354 pp. 12°. *Philadelphia, T. Bliss & co.* 1869.

Dana (Mary S. B.) Charles Morton, or the young patriot. A tale of the American revolution. 236 pp. 18°. *New York, Dayton & Newman*, 1843.

——— Forcastle Tom; or, the landsman turned sailor. 216 pp. 18°. *New York, Harper & brothers*, 1846.

——— The parted family, and other poems. 312 pp. 12°. *New York, Dayton & Saxton*, 1842.

Danby (William). Thoughts, chiefly on serious subjects. 2 v. 4 p. l. 281 pp. 6 l. 1 portrait; 4 p. l. 216 pp. 4 l. 8°. *Exeter, author*, 1822.

[*Note.*—v. 1, 2d ed. with additions].

Dancourt (Florent Carton). Œuvres choisies [comédies]. Ed. stéréotype. 5 v. 24°. *Paris, Didot*, 1810.

CONTENTS.

v. 1. Notice sur Dancourt.
Le chevalier à la mode.
La femme d'intrigues.

Dancourt (Florent Carton)--continued.
v. 2. Les bourgeoises à la mode.
La fête de village.
Les trois cousines.
v. 3. Les agioteurs.
La maison de campagne.
L'été des coquettes.
La Parisienne.
L'impromptu de garnison.
v. 4. Le tuteur.
Les vendanges de Suresne.
Le moulin de Javelle.
Les vacances.
Le charivari.
v. 5. Le retour des officiers.
Les curieux de Compiègne.
Le mari retrouvé.
Colin-maillard.
Le galant jardinier.

Daneau (Lambert). Trve and christian friendshippe. With all the braunches, members, parts, and circumstances thereof, godly and learnedly described. Written first in latine, and now turned into english. Together also with a right excellent inuectiue of the same author, against the wicked exercise of dice-play, and other prophane gaming. *b. l.* 2 v. in 1. 25 l; 36 l. unp. 18°. *London, A. Veale*, 1586.

Danenhower (W. W.) Danenhower's Chicago directory. *See* **Chicago.**

Dangers of coquetry. A novel. [*anon.*] 2 v. 2 p. l. 144 pp; 2 p. l. 133 pp. 18°. *London, W. Lane*, 1790.

Daniel (Gabriel). Voiage du monde de Descartes. [*anon.* 2e éd?] 8 p. l. 308 pp. 16°. *Paris, veuve de S. Bénard*, 1691.

——— The same. A voyage to the world of Cartesius. Translated into english by T. Taylor. [*anon.*] 2d ed. 8 p. l. 298 pp. 3 l. 12°. *London, T. Bennet*, 1694.

Daniel (*Mrs.* Mackenzie, *pseudon.*) *See* **Pickering** (*Miss* Ellen).

Daniel (Samuel). Works newly augmented. 3 p. l. 97 l. 78 l. unp. sm. 4°. *London, S. Waterson*, 1602.
[Imperfect: leaf 83 in ms.]

Daniele (Francesco). Monete antiche di Capva, con alcune brievi osservazioni. Si aggiunge un discorso del culto prestato da' Capuani a' Numi lor tutelari. xxi, 129 pp. 4°. *Napoli, nella stamperia simoniana*, 1802.

Daniell (John Frederic). Familiar illustrations of natural philosophy. Selected principally from Daniell's chemical philosophy. By James Renwick, ll. d. 403 pp. 16°. *New York, Harper & brothers*, 1839.

Daniell (William). Interesting selections from animated nature, with illustrative scenery. 2 v. in 1. 62 l. 60 pl; 62 l. 60 pl. obl. 4°. *London, T. Cadell & W. Davies*, [1807-12].

Daniels (*Mrs.* Eunice True). Poems. With a memoir of her life. 184 pp. 12°. *New York, J. F. Trow*, 1843.

Dannhauer (Johann Conrad). Præadamita vtis sive fabula primorum hominum ante Adamum conditorum explosa. 8 p. l. 574 pp. 6 l. 16°. *Argentorati, ex officina J. Stædelii*, 1656.

Dantès (Alfred Langue). Tables biographiques et bibliographiques des sciences, des lettres et des arts, indiquant les œuvres principales des hommes les plus connus en tous pays et à toutes les époques, avec mention des éditions les plus estimées. vii, 646 pp. 1 l. 8°. *Paris, Delaroque frères*, 1866.

Danti (Antonino). Osservationi di diverse historie et d'altri particolari degni di memoria: con un cumulo di sententie notabili di molti huomini famosi: & con una raccolta di lettioni sententiose & pie, tolte da piu auttori illustri. 4 p. l 168 l. numb. 4°. *Venetia, M. Boselli*, 1573.

D'Arblay (Frances Burney). Memoirs of madame D'Arblay. Compiled from her voluminous diaries and letters, and from other sources. By mrs. Helen Berkeley. [A. C. Mowatt Ritchie]. 2 v. in 1. 143 pp; 144 pp. 16°. *New York, J. Mowatt & co.* 1844.
[*With* BROWNING (Henry C.) Life of Goethe, 1844].

Darby (John, *pseudon.*) Odd hours of a physician. [Essays]. 256 pp. 16°. *Philadelphia, J. B. Lippincott & co.* 1871.

Darc (Jeanne, *pseudon.*) Jeanne d'Arc, par elle-même. *See* **Dufaux** (Ermance). Vies dictées d'outre tombe.

Darling (Henry, *d. d.*) The closer walk, or the believer's sanctification. 226 pp. 16°. *Philadelphia, J. B. Lippincott & co.* 1862.

Darling (Mary G.) In the world. A sequel to "Battles at home." 330 pp. 4 pl. 16°. *Boston, H. B. Fuller*, 1871.

Darling (Ralph). A poetical version of the four gospels. 2 p. l. iii, 391 pp. 4°. *Hull, R. Peck*, [*about* 1800].

Darrow (Jason). The new light; or, discourses on the christian church; or the evils of sectarianism; and on the true manner of becoming christians. Also, dissertations on infants, idiots, and pagans: with inquiries into the origin of the negro race, essays on abolitionism, free-masonry, odd-fellowship, [etc.] 480 pp. 12°. *Covington (Ky.) author*, 1846.

Darrow (Pierce). The artillerist; comprising the drill without arms, and exercises and movements of the light and horse artillery. With a sword exercise for the light artillery. Also, rules for the formation of companies and regiments. 2d ed. 156 pp. 8 pl. 12°. *Hartford, O. D. Cooke*, 1821.

——— Cavalry tactics; comprising the modern mode of discipline and sword exercise, for the cavalry generally. Adapted to the rules and regulations of infantry, as prepared by gen. Scott, and established by a resolve of Congress. To which is added the review exercise. In five parts. 155 pp. 8 pl. 12°. *Hartford, O. D. Cooke*, 1822.

Daru (Pierre Antoine Noël Bruno, *comte*). Des chemins de fer, et de l'application de la loi du 11 juin 1842. 2 p. l. 400 pp. 8°. *Paris, L. Mathias*, 1843. S.

Darwin (Charles). The descent of man, and selection in relation to sex. 2 v. viii, 423 pp; viii, 475 pp. 12°. *London, J. Murray*, 1871.

——— The same. 2 v. vi, 409 pp; viii, 436 pp. 12°. *New York, D. Appleton & co.* 1871.

Darwin (Robert Waring). Principia botanica: or, a concise and easy introduction to the sexual botany of Linnæus. 3d ed. 6 p. l. 326 pp. 8°. *Newark, M. Hage*, 1810.

Dash (*La comtesse, pseudon.*) *See* **Saint-Mars** (N. Cisterne de Courtiras, *vicomtesse* de).

Dati (Carlo Roberto). Lepidezze di spiriti bizzari, e cvriosi avvenimenti. [Pubblicati da Domenico Moreni]. xxxii, 182 pp. 8°. *Firenze, Magheri*, 1829.

Daumas (Melchior Joseph Eugène). Le sahara algérien. Études géographiques, statistiques, et historiques sur la région au sud des établissements français en Algérie. xvi, 339 pp. 8°. *Paris, Fortin, Masson & cie.* 1845.

Dauncey (John). A compendious chronicle of the kingdom of Portugal, from Alfonso the first king, to Alfonso the sixth, now reigning. With a cosmographical description of the dominions of Portugal. [1st ed.] 7 p. l. 216 pp. 16°. *London, T. Johnson for F. Kirkman*, 1661.

Dausten (John). Johannis Daustenij angli rosarivm, in welchem das aller geheimeste geheimniss vom stein der weisen verschlossen. Aus dem latein ins deutsche gebracht.

Dausten (John)—continued.
16°. [*Hamburg, J. Naumann & G. Wolff*, 1675].
[*In* ALCHYMISTISCH sieben-gestirn. 1675. pp. 99–208].

Davenport (*Rev.* John, *minister in Boston*). An answer of the elders of the severall chvrches in New-England unto nine positions sent over to them (by ministers in England) to declare their judgments therein. Written in the yeer, 1639. [*anon.*] 30 pp. sm. 4°. *London, B. Allen*, 1643.
[*With* MATHER (*Rev.* Richard). Church-government and church-covenant].

Davenport (Rufus). The right-aim school bible. 1834. *See* **Bible.** (*English.*)

Davenport (R. A.) A dictionary of biography; comprising the most eminent characters of all ages, nations, and professions. First american edition, with numerous additions, corrections, and improvements. 527 pp. 8°. *Boston, Gray & Bowen*, 1832.

David (C. G.) A positivist primer: being a series of familiar conversations on the religion of humanity. 141 pp. 12°. *New York, D. Wesley & co.* 1871.

David (Jules A.) La bande noire. 2 v. 228 pp; 234 pp. 16°. *Bruxelles, Meline, Cans et cie.* 1837.

——— Le dernier marquis. 2 v. 266 pp. 1 l; 270 pp. 1 l. 16°. *Bruxelles, Meline, Cans et cie.* 1838.

——— La duchesse de Presles. 2 v. 248 pp; 266 pp. 16°. *Bruxelles, A. Wahlen*, 1836.

——— Frédéric le lion. 2 v. 259 pp; 293 pp. 16°. *Bruxelles, Meline, Cans et cie.* 1840.

——— Un prétendant. 2 p. l. 240 pp. 16°. *Bruxelles, Meline, Cans et cie.* 1841.

——— Les protecteurs. 2 v. 296 pp; 280 pp. 16°. *Bruxelles et Leipzig, Meline, Cans et cie.* 1840.

——— Le serment. 2 p l. 176 pp. 16°. *Bruxelles, Société belge de librairie*, 1841.

David (Toussaint Bernard Éméric). *See* **Éméric David.**

David Joriszoon. *See* **Joris** (David).

Davidson (Lucretia Maria). Poems. With illustrations by F. O. C. Darley. Edited by M. Oliver Davidson. xxvi, 270 pp. 10 pl. 2 portraits. 12°. *New York, Hurd & Houghton*, 1871.

Davidson (*Rev.* Peter). The pentateuch vindicated from the objections and misrepresentations of bishop Colenso. xx, 205 pp. 16°. *Edinburgh, A. Elliot*, 1863.

Davidson (Robert, *d. d.*) Elijah, a sacred drama, and other poems. 184 pp. 12°. *New York, C. Scribner*, 1860.

Davies (Samuel, *d. d, president coll. of N. J.*) The curse of cowardice: a sermon preached to the militia of Hanover county, in Virginia, at a general muster, May 8, 1758. With a view to raise a company for capt. Samuel Meredith. 3 p. l. 36 pp. 12°. *London, J. Buckland*, 1758.

——— The duty of christians to propagate their religion among heathens, earnestly recommended to the masters of negroe slaves in Virginia. Sermon preached in Hanover, [Va.] Jan. 8, 1757. 46 pp. 16°. *London, J. Oliver*, 1758.
[HAZARD pamphlets, v. 105].

——— A sermon before the presbytery of New Castle, Oct. 11, 1752. 38 pp. 8°. *Philadelphia, B. Franklin & D. Hall*, 1753.
[HAZARD pamphlets, v. 20].

——— A sermon delivered at Nassau-hall, January 14, 1761, on the death of George ii. [with] a brief account of the life, character and death of the author. By David Bostwick. 32 pp. 8°. *Boston, R. Draper*, [1761].

——— The state of religion among the protestant dissenters in Virginia; in a letter to Rev. Joseph Bellamy. 44 pp. 8°. *Boston, S. Kneeland*, 1751.
[HAZARD pamphlets, v. 111].

Davis (Almond H.) The female preacher, or memoir of Salome Lincoln, afterwards the wife of elder Junia S. Mowry. 162 pp. 1 portrait. 16°. *Providence (R. I.) J. S. Mowry*, 1843.

Davis (Andrew Jackson). Mental disorders; or, diseases of the brain and nerves, developing the origin and philosophy of mania, insanity, and crime, with full directions for their treatment and cure. Special edition. 487 pp. 1 pl. 12°. *New York, American news co.* 1871.

——— Morning lectures. Twenty discourses, delivered before the friends of progress in the city of New York, in the winter and spring of 1863. 434 pp. 12°. *New York, C. M. Plumb & co.* 1865.

Davis (*Mrs.* Caroline E. Kelly). Faithful in least. 360 pp. 3 pl. 16°. *Boston, H. Hoyt*, [1871].

——— Friday Lowe. 346 pp. 1 pl. 16°. *Philadelphia, J. C. Garrigues & co.* 1869.

Davis (*Mrs.* Caroline E. Kelly)—continued.

——— The same. Sequel to Friday Lowe. 347 pp. 1 pl. 16°. *Philadelphia, J. C. Garrigues & co.* 1870.

——— Penny Rust's christmas. [Also, "Toady." *anon.*] 2 v. in 1, 117 pp. 2 pl; 150 pp. 1 pl. 16°. *Boston, H. Hoyt*, [1871].

——— Two books. 206 pp. 2 pl. 16°. *Boston, H. Hoyt*, [1871].

Davis (Charles Henry Stanley, *m. d.*) History of Wallingford, Conn. from its settlement in 1670 to the present time, including Meriden, which was one of its parishes until 1806, and Cheshire, which was incorporated in 1780. viii, 955 pp. 10 pl. 20 portraits. 8°. *Meriden, (Conn.) author*, 1870.

Davis (I. B. *m. d.*) The ancient and modern history of Nice; comprehending an account of the foundation of Marseilles: [with] descriptive observations on the nature, produce, and climate, of the former city, and its adjoining towns: with an introduction, containing hints of advice to invalids. xxxii, 348 pp. 1 pl. 8°. *London, Tipper & Richards*, 1807.

Davis (J.) History of the welsh baptists. 204 pp. 12°. *Pittsburgh, D. M. Hogan*, 1835.

Davis (Joseph Barnard, *m. d.*) Thesaurus craniorum. Catalogue of the skulls of the various races of man, in the collection of J. B. Davis, m. d. xxii, 374 pp. 2 pl. 1 tab. 8°. *London, for the subscribers*, 1867. s.

Davis (*Mrs.* Rebecca Harding). Margret Howth. A story of to-day. [*anon.*] 1 p. l. 266 pp. 12°. *Boston, Ticknor & Fields*, 1862.

Davis (*Mrs.* S. M.) The life and times of sir Philip Sidney. [*anon.* Preface subscribed S. M. D.] 281 pp. 3 pl. 12°. *Boston, Ticknor & Fields*, 1859.

Dawson (John, *d. d.*) Dissertations on the following subjects; viz. Samuel's appearance at Endor. Pilate's wife's dream concerning Christ. Moses and Elias appearing to three disciples. St. Peter's deliverance by an angel. Abraham's reply to Dives. 4 p. l. 184 pp. 8°. *London, W. & J. Innys*, 1727.

Dawson (J. W.) The fossil plants of the devonian and upper silurian formations of Canada. 1 p. l. 92, 8 pp. 20 pl. 8°. *Montreal, Dawson bros.* 1871. s.
[CANADA. Geological survey].

Day (Francis). The fishes of Malabar. 1 p. l. xxxii, 293 pp. 20 col. pl. 4°. *London, B. Quaritch*, 1865.

Day (George T.) The life of rev. Martin Cheney. 471 pp. 1 portrait. 12°. *Providence, G. H. Whitney*, 1853.

Day (Henry N.) Rhetorical praxis. The principles of rhetoric exemplified and applied in copious exercises for systematic practice, chiefly in the development of thought. 309 pp. 12°. *Cincinnati, Moore, Wilstach, Keys & co.* 1861.

Day (Robert). Free thoughts in defence of a future state. With occasional remarks on a book intituled, An inquiry concerning virtue. And a refutation of the reviv'd hylozoicism of Democritus and Leucippus. [*anon.*] 2 p. l. 111 pp. 8°. *London, D. Brown*, 1700.

Daza (Antonio). Istoria, vita miracoli estasi, e revelationi della bene avventvrata vergine, svor Giovanna della croce del terzo ordine del S. Francesco di nuouo corretta et emendata per frà Antonio Dazza. Tradotta di spagnuolo in italiano da Paolo Brusantini. 24 p. l. 258 pp. 3 l. 18°. *Modono, G. Cassiani*, 1616.

Déageant de Saint Martin (Guichard). Mémoires de monsievr Déageant, envoyez à monsievr le cardinal Richeliev. Contenans plusievrs choses particulières & remarquables arriuées depuis les dernières années du roy Henry iv. insques au commencement du ministère de monsieur le cardinal de Richelieu. 4 p. l. 398 pp. 1 l. 18°. *Grenoble, P. Charvys*, 1668.

Dean (*Rev.* Paul). A course of lectures in defence of the final restoration. 190 pp. 8°. *Boston, E. M. Stone*, 1832.

Deane (H. Bargrave). The law of blockade: its history, present condition, and probable future. An international law essay. 1870. 2 p. l. ii, 55 pp. 8°. *London, Longmans, Green, Reader & Dyer*, 1870.

Débat des héraulx darmes de frãce et dengleterre. England and France in the fifteenth century. The contemporary french tract entitled "The debate between the heralds of France and England," presumed to have been written by Charles, duke of Orleans: translated for the first time into english; with an introduction, notes, an inquiry into the authorship, etc. xx, 225 pp. 8°. *London, Longmans, Green & co.* 1870.

Debate (The) between the heralds of France and England. *See* **Débat** des héraulx darmes de frãce et dengleterre.

Debay (A.) Hygiène de la voix, et gymnastique des organes vocaux. Histoire de la musique, depuis son origine jusqu'à nos jours. 2 p. l. 356 pp. 12°. *Paris, Moquet*, 1852.

——— Les mystères du sommeil et du magnétisme ou physiologie anecdotique du somnambulisme naturel et magnétique. Physique des tables tournantes, explication naturelle de leurs mouvements. 5ᵉ éd. 2 p. l. 387 pp. 12°. *Paris, E. Dentu*, 1854.

De Bosis (Francesco). Il gabinetto di scienze naturali e l'osservatorio meteorologico nel r. istituto industriale e professionale di Ancona. Con appendice sugli studi di storia naturale anconitana di F. De-Bosis e Luigi Paolucci. 157 pp. 8°. *Ancona, F. Gabrielli & comp.* 1867.

——— Meteorologia anconitana dal 1° decembre 1863 al 30 novembre 1868. 123 pp. 4°. *Ancona, G. Cherubini*, 1869. s.

Debouchel (Victor). Histoire de la Louisiane, depuis les premières découvertes jusqu'en 1840. 1 p. l. 197 pp. 16°. *Nouvelle-Orléans, J. F. Lelievre*, 1841.

Debraux (Paul Émile). Chansons complètes, augmentées d'une notice et d'une chanson sur Debraux par m. de Béranger. 3 v. 18°. *Paris*, 1835-36.

Debrett (John). An asylum for fugitive pieces, in prose and verse, not in any other collection: with several pieces never before published. [*anon.*] 4 v. 16°. *London, J. Debrett*, 1785-98.

Decker (Johann Heinrich). Spectrologia, h. e. discursus ut plurimum philosophicus de spectris. Eng. title, 10 p. l. 198 pp. 9 l. 16°. *Hamburgi, apud G. Liebernickel*, 1690.

De Costa (*Rev.* B. F.) Sketches of the coast of Maine and Isles of Shoals, with historical notes. 221 pp. 1 photo. sm. 4°. *New York*, 1869.

Dedekind (Friedrich). Grobianvs et grobiana, de morvm simplicitate, libri tres, in gratiam omnium rusticitatis amantium conscripti. 96 l. numb. 16°. *Francoforti ad Moenvm, apud hære C. Egen*, 1575.

Deductie ingestelt tot onderrichtinge van den coningh van Groot Brittannien op verscheyden poincten vervatt in seeckere antwoorde van wegen syne majesteyt gegeven aenden ambassadeur vande staten generael der Vereenighde Nederlanden. [Dutch and French]. 52 l. sm. 4°. *Graven-hage*, 1664.

Dedvctie, waer by onpartijdelijk over-vvogen ende bevvesen vvort, vvat het beste voor de

Dedvctie, etc.—continued.
compagnie van West-Indien zy: den handel te sluyten of open te laten. [*anon.*] 32 pp. sm. 4°. *Graven-Hage, I. Burchoorn*, [1639]?

Defence (A) of the answer and arguments of the synod at Boston, 1662. *See* **Mather** (*Rev.* Richard) *and* **Mitchell** (*Rev.* Jonathan).

Defence (A) of the letter from a gentleman at Halifax, to his friend in Rhode-Island. [*anon.*] 30 pp. sm. 4°. *Newport, S. Hall*, 1765.

De Forest (John W.) Kate Beaumont. 165 pp. 6 pl. 8°. *Boston, J. R. Osgood & co.* 1872.

——— Overland. A novel. 209 pp. 1 portrait. 8°. *New York, Sheldon & co.* [1872].

De Kroyft (*Mrs.* S. Helen). Little Jakey. 132 pp. 8 pl. 12°. *New York, Hurd & Houghton*, 1872.

Delacour (*Rev.* James). A prospect of poetry, with other poems. 1 p. l. 112 pp. 2 l. 8°. *Cork, J. Harris*, 1807.

Delafaye (Theodore). An essay on Virgil's celebrated gates of sleep. Containing besides a very particular enquiry into this intricate subject, as well as into Homer's similar gates, a solution of Virgil's falso damnati crimine mortis; and at the close of it a true key to the Æneis. 1 p. l. 105 pp. 8°. *London, J. Robinson*, 1743.

Delafond (A. S. S.) A dictionary of the wonders of nature. Translated principally from the works of Delafond. With considerable additions from original manuscripts. 2 p. l. 416 pp. 6 l. 1 portrait. 18°. *London, T. Hurst*, 1803.

Delamalle (Gasparin Gilbert). Essai d'institutions oratoires à l'usage de ceux qui se destinent au barreau. [1e éd.] 2 v. in 1. xxxii, 246 pp; 2 p. l. 303 pp. 8°. *Paris, Delaunay*, 1816.

Delany (*Rev.* Patrick). Reflections upon polygamy, and the encouragement given to that practice in the scriptures of the old testament. By Phileleutherus dubliniensis. 2d ed. With a preface, in which the main objection against the work is obviated, and the author's views in publishing it at this time, accounted for. 2 p. l. xvi, 188 pp. 8°. *London, C. Rivington* [*etc.*] 1739.

[*Note.*—Preceded by the title-page of the first ed. 1737].

Delaporte (Léon). Études sur la société. 1 p. l. xxxii, 307 pp. 8°. *Paris, L. Hachette & cie.* 1855.

De la Ramé (Louise). Folle-farine. By Ouida. [*pseudon.*] 530 pp. 12°. *Philadelphia, J. B. Lippincott & co.* 1871.

Delaware river and West Jersey railroad commercial directory for 1872. Embracing all the commercial, manufacturing and business houses in every city and town located on the Delaware river, from the capes to Trenton, N. J. with those upon the line of the West Jersey railroad. With a list of the leading firms in the city of Philadelphia, carefully compiled from a reliable canvass. 8°. *Philadelphia, Bessonett & Moran*, [1871].

De Leon (T. C.) What might have been; or, the old love and the new. By the author of "Cross purposes." [*anon.*] 3 v. 12°. *London, T. C. Newby*, 1856.

Delepierre (Octave). La parodie chez les Grecs, chez les Romains, et chez les modernes. 1 p. l. 182 pp. 4°. *Londres, N. Trübner & cie.* 1870.

——— Résumé analytique et historique des divers romans ou poèmes du Renard, principalement en ce qui concerne les ouvrages français de ce nom. 8°. [*Paris, Challamel*, 1837].

[*In* BAUMANN (Nicholas). Le roman du Renard, d'après un texte flamand du xiie siècle, édité par J. F. Willems, pp. 53–142, ed. 1837].

Delisle de Sales (Jean Baptiste Claude Isoard). Éponine, ou de la république, ouvrage de Platon découvert et publié par l'auteur de la Philosophie de la nature. Nouvelle éd. 6 v. 8°. [*Paris*, 1793].

——— Philosophie du bonheur. Manuscrit de Platon, publié par l'auteur de la Philosophie de la nature; et servant de supplément à ce dernier ouvrage. [*anon.*] Nouv. éd. 2 v. 4 p. l. 1–16, cclviii, 17–182 pp. 1 l. 1 portrait; 2 p. l. 383 pp. 2 l. 16 pp. music. 8°. *Paris, Goujon*, 1800.

Delitzsch (Franz). A system of biblical psychology. Translated from the German, (2d ed.) by the rev. Robert Ernest Wallis. xvi, 585 pp. 8°. *Edinburgh, T. & T. Clark*, 1867.

[Foreign theological library].

Delius *or* **Delen** (Matthæus). De arte jocandi, libri qvatvor. 18°. [*Lvgd. Batav. ex typographia rediviva*, 1648].

[*In* OBSOPŒUS (Vincenz). De arte bibendi, 1648, pp. 65–136].

Delort (Joseph). Mes voyages aux environs de Paris. 2 v. vi, 322 pp. 9 facs. 2 pl. 1 map; 2 p. l. 335 pp. 17 facs. 2 pl. 8°. *Paris, Picard-Dubois*, 1821.

Delta kappa epsilon song book. [With notes]. Apud Upsilon edition. 168 pp. 1 pl. 8°. [*Boston, O. Ditson & co.* 1871].

Deltuf (Paul). Les petits malheurs d'une jeune femme. 2 p. l. 295 pp. 12°. *Paris, M. Lévy frères,* 1860.

Demangeon (J. B.) Physiologie intellectuelle, ou l'esprit de l'homme, considéré dans ses causes physiques et morales, d'après la doctrine de Gall, de Spurzheim et d'autres auteurs, avec un rapprochement comparatif des instincts qui remplacent l'intelligence dans les brutes. 3e éd. enrichie de plusieurs observations nouvelles. xv, 606 pp. 1 pl. 8°. *Paris, Fortin, Masson & cie.* 1843.

Demidoff de San Donato (Anatole, *comte*). La Crimée. Illustrée par Raffet. 2e éd. 268 pp. 12 pl. 16°. *Paris, E. Bourdin,* 1855.

De Mille (James). The american baron. A novel. 132 pp. 8°. *New York, Harper & brothers,* 1872.

—— The cryptogram. A novel. With illustrations. 261 pp. 8°. *New York, Harper & brothers,* 1871.

—— Fire in the woods. 423 pp. 4 pl. 16°. *Boston, Lee & Shepard,* 1872.

—— The young dodge club. Among the brigands. 328 pp. 3 pl. 16°. *Boston, Lee & Shepard,* 1872.

Democrates *philosophus.* Democratis philosophi aureæ sententiæ. [Græce et latine]. 8°. [*Amstelaedami, apud H. Wetstenium,* 1688].

[*In* GALE (Thomas). Opuscula mythologica, pp. 626–632].

Demophilus *philosophus.* Demophili similitudines, seu vitæ curatio, ex pythagoreis. [Græce et latine]. 8°. [*Amstelaedami, apud H. Wetstenium,* 1688].

[*In* GALE (Thomas). Opuscula mythologica, pp. 613–625].

Demorest's illustrated monthly, and mme. Demorest's mirror of fashions. Jan. to Dec. 1871. v. 8. 4°. [*New York, W. J. Demorest,* 1871].

Demorest's Young America. A boys and girls monthly magazine. Jan. to Dec. 1871. v. 5. 8°. *New York,* [*W. J. Demorest,* 1871].

Demosthenes. *Δημοσθενους περι του στεφανου λογος.* 4°. [*Lvtetiae,* 1564].

[*In* LAMBIN (Denis). Oratio de laudibus litterarum. 1564. pp. 81–171].

—— Orationes. 8°. *Oxonii,* 1835.

[*In* HISTORIA græca, ed. secunda, pp. 343–407].

Demosthenes *and* **Æschines.** Cinqve orationi di Demosthene et vna di Eschine, tradotte [da Girolamo Ferro] di lingua greca in italiana, secondo la uerità de' sentimenti. 255 l. 12°. *Venetia, Aldvs,* 1557.

CONTENTS.

Oratione della falsa ambascieria, l. 2.
Oratione contro Media, del pvgno, l. 64.
Oratione contro Androtione, l. 104.
Oratione di Eschine contro Tesifonte, l. 120.
Oratione della corona, l. 167.
Oratione contra la legge di Lettine, in materia dell' esentioni, l. 225.

Demoustier (Charles Albert). Cours de morale et opuscules en vers et en prose. 2 p. l. 408 pp. 1 portrait. 8°. *Paris, A. A. Renouard,* 1804.

[*Note.*—Appended are—
Les consolations.
Notice sur la vie et les ouvrages de madame Dubocage.
Le voyage de l'amitié : fragment.
Fragmens du dix-huitième siècle.
Poésies diverses.

—— Lettres à Émilie sur la mythologie. 6 v. in 3. 24°. *Paris, A. A. Renouard,* 1824.

—— Théatre. 2 v. in 1. 2 p. l. 225 pp; 2 p. l. 200 pp. 1 l. 24°. *Paris, A. A. Renouard,* 1804.

CONTENTS.

v. 1. Le conciliateur.
Les femmes.
v. 2. Alceste ou le misanthrope corrigé.
Le divorce.
La toilette de Julie.
L'amour filial.

Dempster (Francis). Papismus lucifugus. *See* **Menzies** (John) *and* **Dempster.**

Denison (*Mrs.* Mary Andrews). The days and ways of the cocked hats: or the dawn of the revolution. 383 pp. 1 pl. 12°. *New York, S. A. Rollo,* 1860.

—— The master. iv, 270 pp. 12°. *Boston, Walker, Wise & co.* 1862.

—— The Talbury girls. By Clara Vance. [*pseudon.*] 487 pp. 3 pl. 16°. *Boston, D. Lothrop & co.* 1871.

Dennys (N. B.) The treaty ports of China and Japan. A complete guide to the open ports of those countries, together with Peking, Yedo, Hongkong and Macao. Forming a guide book and vade mecum for travellers, merchants, and residents in general. ix, 668, xlix, 26 pp. 29 maps. 8°. *London, Trübner & co.* 1867.

Denon (*Baron* Dominique Vivant). Description des objets d'arts qui composent le cabinet de feu m. le baron V. Denon. Monuments antiques, historiques, modernes ; ouvrages orientaux, etc. Par L. J. J. Dubois. 2 p. l. v, 308 pp. 8°. *Paris, H. Tilliard,* 1826.

Dent (Arthur). The ruin of Rome; or, an exposition upon the whole revelation: wherein is plainly shewed and proved that the popish religion, together with all the power and authority of Rome, shall decay more and more throughout all the churches of Europe, and shall be utterly destroyed before the end of the world. xxi, 302 pp. 3 pl. 8°. *London, T. Kelly*, 1841.

Denza (Francesco, *editor*). Sopra gli aeroliti caduti il giorno 29 febbraio 1868 nel territorio di Villanova e Motta dei Conti, Piemonte, circondario di casale. Memoria dei professori Agostino Goiran, Antonio Bertolio, Arturo Zanneti, Luigi Musso. xxii, 89 pp. 3 pl. 12°. *Torinio, collegio degli artigianelli*, 1868. s.

[Estratto dal Bulletino meteorologico del r. collegio Carlo Alberto in Moncalieri].

Depping (Georges Bernard). Histoire de la Normandie sous le règne de Guillaume-le-conquérant et de ses successeurs, depuis la conquête de l'Angleterre jusqu'à la réunion de la Normandie au royaume de France. 2 v. viii, 524 pp; 2 p. l. 478 pp. 1 l. 8°. *Rouen, É. Frère*, 1835.

——— Histoire des expéditions maritimes des Normands, et de leur établissement en France au dixième siècle. 2 v. 2 p. l. li, 464 pp; 2 p. l. 348 pp. 8°. *Paris, Ponthieu*, 1826.

——— Histoire générale de l'Espagne, depuis les tems les plus reculés jusqu'au règne des rois maures. Édition sortie des presses de D. Colas, en 1811. 2 v. 1 p. l. xl, 439 pp. 1 map; 1 p. l. 444 pp. 8°. *Paris,. T. Dabo*, 1814.

——— Introduction sur la littérature, la mythologie, les moeurs des hommes du nord. 8°. [*Rouen, É. Frère*, 1835].

[*In* Licquet (F. T.) Histoire de Normandie, v. 1, pp. xiii-cxcii, ed. 1835].

De Puy (W. H. *d. d*) Threescore years and beyond; or, experiences of the aged. A book for old people, describing the labors, home life, and closing experiences of a large number of representative men and women. Illustrated ed. 512 pp. 1 tab. 5 pl. 8°. *New York, Carlton & Lanahan*, 1872.

——— *See, also*, **Methodist** (The) almanac.

De Quincey (Thomas). Beauties selected from [his] writings. 432 pp. 1 portrait. 12°. *Boston, Ticknor & Fields*, 1862.

——— Klosterheim; or, the masque. With a biographical preface, by dr. Shelton Mackenzie. xxiv, 258 pp. 12°. *Boston, Whittemore, Niles & Hall*, 1855.

Dereume (A.) Notices bio-bibliographiques sur quelques imprimeurs, libraires, correcteurs, compositeurs, fondeurs, lithographes, etc. qui se sont fait connaître à divers titres, principalement comme auteurs; avec indication de leurs portraits. [Première série]. 2 p. l. 65 pp. 8°. *Bruxelles, E. Devroye*, 1858.

Derham (William, *d. d.*) Life of John Ray. 8°. *London, J. Dodsley & J. Walter*, 1760.

[*In* Ray (John). Select remains, 1760, pp. 1-100].

——— Physico-theology: or, a demonstration of the being and attributes of God, from his works of creation. Being the substance of sixteen sermons preached in 1711 and 1712. With large notes and many curious observations. fol. [*London*, 1739].

[Boyle lectures, v. 2, 5 p. l. pp. 561-729. 1 pl.]

Desbillons (François Joseph Terasse). Nouveaux éclaircissements sur la vie et les ouvrages de Guillaume Postel. 162 pp. 16°. *Liége, J. J. Tutot*, 1773.

De Schweinitz (Edmund). The life and times of David Zeisberger, the western pioneer and apostle of the Indians. 747 pp. 8°. *Philadelphia, J. B. Lippincott & co.* 1870.

——— The moravian manual; containing an account of the protestant church of the Moravian united brethren, or Unitas fratrum. 178 pp. 12°. *Philadelphia, Lindsay & Blakiston*, 1859.

Description de la Brasil, et de la ville de Pernambuco; aussi de tout les païs, et des moulins de sucre, [etc.] [*anon.*] Folded sheet, 1 pl. sm. 4°. *Anuers, A. Verhoeuen*, [1625].

Description de la reprise de la ville de S. Salvador, située en la Baye de Todos os sanctos, en Brasil, nouuellement faicte par l'armade et gensdarmerie de sa majesté catholicque d'Espaigne. [*anon.*] Folded sheet, 1 pl. sm. 4°. *Anuers, A. Verhoeuen*, 1625.

Desforges (P. J. B. Choudard). Eugène et Eugénie, ou la méprise conjugale, histoire de deux enfans d'une nuit d'erreur et de leur parens. 4 v. 12°. *Paris, Chaignieau aîné*, an vii, [1799].

Des Guidi (*Comte* Sebastian). Lettre aux médecins français sur la médecine homœopathique. Troisième édition enrichie des préfaces des traducteurs [etc.] Par le docteur F. Perrussel. 144 pp. 2 portraits. 8°. *Paris, Baillière*, 1852.

Desjardins (Abel, *editor*). Négociations diplomatiques de la France avec la Toscane.

Desjardins (Abel)—continued.
Documents recueillis par Giuseppe Conestrini, et publiés par Abel Desjardins. v. 3. *Paris, imprimerie impériale*, 1865.
[FRANCE. *Ministère de l'instruction publique.* Collection de documents inedits sur l'histoire de France, 1re série].

Desmerliers (Jean). Iridis coelestis, et coronæ luculenta descriptio. Per Ioannem Demerlierivm ambianum. 13 l. unp. 4°. *Parisiis, ex typographia Diomysij à Prato*, 1567.

Desperriers (Bonaventure). Cymbalum mundi, ou dialogues satiriques sur différens sujets. Avec une lettre critique dans laquelle on fait l'histoire, l'analyse, & l'apologie de cet ouvrage. Par Prosper Marchand. Nouv. éd. [faite d'après la première de 1537], augmentée de notes et de remarques par plusieurs savans [Falconnet et Lancelot]. 2 p. l. xxxi, 244 pp. 2 l. 16°. *Amsterdam, P. Marchand*, 1732.
[*Note.*—The original title-page was: Cymbalum mundi, en Françoys, contenant iv dialogues poëtiques, fort antiques, joyeux & facetieux. md.xxxvii].

——— The same. Cymbalum mundi: or satirical dialogues on various subjects. With a critical letter containing the history and analysis of the work, together with an apology for it. [By Prosper Marchand]. Done into english from the original [from the copy printed in the year 1537]. 8 pp. 3 l. xliii, 77 pp. 12°. *London, J. Newton*, 1723.

Despréaux (Nicolas Boileau). *See* **Boileau-Despréaux.**

Desrey (Pierre, *de Troyes*). Relation dv roy Charles viii. povr la conqveste dv royavme de Naples. Qui sert de supplément au iournal précedent [par André de la Vigne], où le commencement semble manquer. fol. [*Paris*, 1684].
[*In* GODEFROY (T. *and* D.) Histoire de Charles viii, pp. 190-206.

Dessert (The) book; a complete manual from the best american and foreign authorities. With original economical recipes By a Boston lady. [*anon.*] 202 pp. 12°. *Boston, J. E. Tilton & co.* 1872.

Desultory reminiscences of a tour through Germany, Switzerland, and France. By an American. [*anon.*] xx, 364 pp. 8°. *Boston, W. D. Ticknor*, 1836.

Detroit (*City of*). The Detroit city directory and advertising gazetteer of Michigan, for 1855-6. James Dale Johnston, compiler. 304 pp. 8°. *Detroit, R. T. Johnstone & co.* 1855.

Deusing (Anton). Foetus mussipontani, extra uterum in abdomine geniti, secundinæ detectæ: quibus multa naturæ admiranda & abstrusa in lucem eruuntur. Accessit historia partus infelicis: quo gemellorum ex utero in abdominis cavum elapsorum, ossa sensim, multis annis post, per abdomen ipsum in lucem prodierunt. 312 pp. 1 l. 24°. *Groningæ, typis J. Draper*, 1662.

Deutsch (Solomon). A key to the pentateuch; explanatory of the text and the grammatical forms. Part 1. Genesis. 104, xxiii pp. 8°. *New York, Holt & Williams*, 1871.

Deutsch-amerikanisches conversations-lexicon. Mit specieller rücksicht auf das bedürfnisz der in Amerika lebenden Deutschen, (bearbeitet) unter mitwirkung vieler hervorragender deutschen schriftsteller Amerika's. A.-Jud. v. 1-5. 8°. *New York, F. Gerhard*, 1869-71.

Deutsche vierteljahrs-schrift. Januar 1860 bis Oct. 1870. 23-33 jahrgang. no. 89-132 in 22 v. 8°. *Stuttgart, J. G. Cotta*, 1860-70.
[*Note.*—v. 30, heft 2, no. 120, *contains* Register no. 1-120].

Deuxponts (Guillaume de Forbach, *comte* des). My campaigns in America: a journal kept by count William de Deux-Ponts, 1780-81. Translated from the french manuscript, with an introduction and notes, by Samuel Abbott Green. xvii, 176 pp. 8°. *Boston, J. K. Wiggin & W. P. Lunt*, 1868.

De Vere (*Sir* Aubrey). A song of faith. Devout exercises and sonnets. xv, 286 pp. 16°. *London, W. Pickering*, 1842.

De Vere (M. Schele). *See* **Schele de Vere.**

Devereux (George H.) Sam Shirk: a tale of the woods of Maine. iv, 391 pp. 12°. *New York, Hurd & Houghton*, 1871.

Devereux (Robert, *2d earl of Essex*). An apologie of the earle of Essex, against those which iealovsly, and maliciovsly, tax him to be the hinderer of the peace and qviet of his covntry. Penned by himselfe in anno 1598. 23 l. unp. sm. 4°. *London, R. Bradocke*, 1603.

De Wette (Wilhelm Martin Leberecht). Human life; or, practical ethics. Translated from the german. By rev. Samuel Osgood, d. d. 2 v. xx, 368 pp; viii, 409 pp. 16°. *Boston & Cambridge, J. Munroe & co.* 1856.

——— Die schriften des alten testaments. *See* **Bible.** (*German*).

Deyeux (Théophile). Les deux faussaires. 2 v. 2 p. l. 387 pp; 2 p. l. 390 pp. 8°. *Paris, Houdaille,* 1836.

Diaccetto. *See* **Cattani da Diaccetto.**

Dialoghi tra' il diavolo zoppo e il diavolo guercio, trattenimenti curiosi del signor Le Noble. [*pseudon?*] Tradotti dal francese nella lingua italiana. 5 p. l. 263 pp. 16°. *Venezia, F. Storti,* 1723.

Dialogue (A) of polygamy, written originally in italian: rendred into english by a person of quality. [*etc. anon.*] 10 p. l. 89 pp. 18°. *London, J. Garfeild,* 1657.

Diamond (The) fields of South Africa; with notes of journey there and homeward, and some things about diamonds and other jewels. By one who has visited the fields. [*anon.*] 238 pp. 12°. *New York, American news co.* 1872.

Diano (Carlo Cala, *duca* di). *See* **Cala.**

Diatessaron: or the history of our Lord Jesus Christ, compiled from the four gospels, according to the authorized version. [*anon.*] 6 p. l. 211 pp. 8°. *Oxford, S. Collingwood for J. H. Parker,* 1837.

Diavolo (Il) storico critico politico esposto sotto la figura del diavolo guercio in lega col diavolo zoppo contro 'l diavolo gobbo, trattenimento curioso, e morale di venti, e una sera; ricavato dal francese. [*anon.*] 4 p. l. 216 pp. 1 pl. 16°. *Venezia, T. Bettinelli,* 1744.

Diaz (*Mrs.* A. M) William Henry and his friends. 1 p. l. 265 pp. 1 pl. 16°. *Boston, J. R. Osgood & co.* 1872.

Diaz de Niza (Paolo, *pseudon.*) *See* **Cardoso** (Luis).

Dibdin (Charles). A letter of intelligence, [respecting William Parsons, comedian]. 8°. [*London, T. Bellamy,* 1795].

[*In* BELLAMY (Thomas). The life of mr. William Parsons, comedian, 1795, pp. 59-76].

Dicearcheo (Eustazio, *pseudon.*) *See* **Costanzo** (Giuseppe Giustino).

Dickens (Charles). A child's history of England. 2 v. 278 pp; 307 pp. 16°. *New York, Harper & brothers,* 1855.

——— The same. Also a holiday romance, and other pieces. xx, 583 pp. 8 pl. 12°. *Boston, J. R. Osgood & co.* 1871.

——— Schools and schoolmasters. From the writings of Charles Dickens. Edited by T. J. Chapman. 215 pp. 2 pl. 12°. *New York and Chicago, A. S. Barnes & co.* [1871].

Dickenson. *See* **Dickinson.**

Dickinson (Ellen E.) Emmanuel and other stories. 123 pp. 1 pl. 16°. *New York, T. Whittaker & co.* [1871].

Dickinson (James, *quaker*). A journal of [his] life, travels, and labour of love in the work of the ministry. xxvii, 172 pp. 16°. *London, T. S. Raylton,* 1745.

Dickinson (Jonathan, *chief justice of Penn.*) God's protecting providence man's surest help and defence, evidenced in the deliverance of Robert Barrow, with diverse other persons from the waves of the sea; among which they suffered shipwrack [Sept. 23, 1696], and also from the cruel devouring jaws of the inhuman canibals of Florida. 4th ed. 4 p. l. 80 pp. 12°. *Philadelphia, W. Bradford,* 1751.

[HAZARD pamphlets, v. 111].

——— The same. 6th ed. 95 pp. 18°. *Stanford (N. Y.) D. Lawrence,* 1803.

——— The same. Ongelukkige schipbreuk en yslyke reystogt, van etlyke engelschen, in den jaare 1696 van Jamaika in West Indiën, na Pennsylvania t'scheep gegaan, en in de golf van Florida gestrand [etc.] In't engelsch beschreeven. En daaruyt vertaald door W. Sewel. 100 pp. 4 l. 1 map, 2 pl. 16°. *Leyden, P. van der Aa,* [*about* 1710].

Dickinson (Rodolphus). A compendium of the religious doctrines, religious and moral precepts, historical and descriptive beauties of the bible; with a separate moral selection from the apocrypha. Being a transcript of the received text. 2d ed. 274 pp. 18°. *Greenfield (Mass.) compiler,* 1815.

Dictionnaire des athées anciens et modernes. *See* **Maréchal** (Pierre Sylvain).

Dictionnaire historique des anecdotes de l'amour. *See* **Maréchal** (Pierre Sylvain).

Didot (Ambroise Firmin). [Bibliothèque grecque, avec traduction latine en regard]. v. 56. 8°. *Parisiis, Didot,* 1860.

CONTENTS.

v. 56. Mullachius. Fragmenta philosophorum græcorum.

Didymus *clericus.* *See* **Foscolo** (Niccolo Ugo).

Diekenga (I. E.) *and* **Ashworth** (T. M.) Tom Chips. 236 pp. 12°. *Philadelphia, J. B. Lippincott & co.* 1871.

Dieta (La) di vari avtori, o verò ravnanza di varie opere politiche modernissime. Sopra li correnti, ed emergenti affari, ed interessi di tutti li potenti dell' Europa, che regnano al presente. Nuovamente ristampata con

Dieta (La) di vari avtori, etc.—continued. aggiunta. [*anon.*] 3 p. l. 785 pp. 18°. *Cologna, per L. Tivoglio*, 1675.

CONTENTS.

Instrvttione a monsignor vescovo d'Anglone, destinato da nostro signore suo nvntio in Toscana. 1 p. l. 18 pp.
La monarchia di Spagna crescente e calante, in dialogo in forma di sogno. [Scritta da Gregorio Leti]. pp. 1-102.
Instrvttione a gl'ambasciadori, che assisteranno nella corte di Roma per la maestà catolica, & il modo, che deuono vsare in esercitar la loro ambasciaria. [Scritta da G. Leti] ? pp. 103-120.
Relatione di tvtto cio' che passo' tra il pontefice Alesandro vii. e la maestà del re christianissimo, nell' anno 1662, li 20. Agosto, per l'insulto fatto da' papalini al duca di Crechì regio ambasciatore. [Scritta da Gregorio Leti]. 168 pp.
Forma del governo giesvitico, con vna instrvtione & auuiso a' potentati, del modo, con il quale si gouernano li giesviti. Per ridurre la loro compagnia ad vna parfetta monarchia. 101 pp.
Lettera amfibologica, e persvasiva di vn giesvita ad vn cavaliero suo discepolo. 42 pp.
Risposta del cavaliere discepolo alla lettera persvasiva del giesvita maestro. 48 pp.
Il lamento de' monaci, et frati contro la corte di Roma, per vedersi priui di quelle dignità ecclesiastica da loro per lungo tempo possedure. 60 pp.
Risposta della corte al lamento de' monaci, et frati. 36 pp.
Il processo della critica contro gli auttori ignoranti, e mercenari, che compongono libri in questi tempi. 72 pp.
Diario, e lettera sopra gli affari correnti di don Giovanni d'Avstria. Con vn ritratto della sua vita, cioè, nascita, qualità, costumi, attioni, e gouerni.

Dieterich (Johann Conrad). Φυλλοβολία, seu sparsio florum. 18°. [*Francofvrti ad Mœnum, sumpt. G. H. Ohrlingii*, 1698].

[*In* NICOLAI (Johann). Tractatus de phyllobolia. 1698. pp. 126-185].

Dieu (Louis de). Rvdimenta lingvæ persicæ. Accedvnt duo priora capita Geneseos, ex persica translatione Iac. Tawusi. 4 p. l. 95 pp. 4°. *Lvgdvni Batavorvm, ex officina elseviriana*, 1639.

[*With* XAVIER (Hieronymus). Historia Christi, persice conscripta].

Digby (John, *earl of Bristol*). The earl of Bristol's defence of his negotiations in Spain. Edited, from mss. in the Bodleian library and the public record office, by Samuel Rawson Gardiner. 1 p. l. xxxix, 56 pp. sm. 4°. [*London*], *Camden society*, 1871.

[*In* CAMDEN miscellany, v. 6].

Digges (Leonard). A geometrical practical treatize named pantometria, diuided into three bookes, longimetra, planimetra, and stereometria. First published by Thomas Digges. With a mathematicall discourse of the fiue regular platonicall solides, and their metamorphosis into other fiue compound rare geometricall bodyes. Lately reviewed by the avthor himselfe, and augmented with sundrie additions, diffinitions, problemes and rare theoremes. 3 p. l. 196 pp. 1 l. fol. *London, A. Jeffes*, 1591.

Dillon (John B.) Notes on historical evidence in reference to adverse theories of the origin and nature of the government of the United States of America. 141 pp. 8°. *New York, S. W. Green*, 1871.

Dillon (John Talbot). Letters from an english traveller in Spain, in 1778, on the origin and progress of poetry in that kingdom; with occasional reflections on manners and customs; and illustrations of the romance of don Quixote. [*anon.*] x, 322 pp. 3 pl. 8°. *London, R. Baldwin*, 1781.

Dimmick (*Rev.* Luther F.) Memoir of mrs. Catharine M. Dimmick. 214 pp. 12°. *Boston, T. R. Marvin*, 1846.

Dindorf (Wilhelm, *editor*). *See* **Pollux** (Julius). Onomasticon. 1824.

Dingley (Charles, *editor*). *See* **Euterpiad** (The). 1830.

Diogenes *laertius*. Incomincia el libro de La vita de philosophi, et delle loro elegantissime sententie, extracto da D. Lahertio et altri antiqvissimi avctori. 71 l. unp. 8°. *Venetiis, per B. Celerivm*, 1480.

[*Note.*—Derived in part from Walter Burley].

Diogenianus. Diogeniani vvlgaria proverbia, græcè nunc primùm eruta, latinè reddita ac scholiis illustrata ab Andrea Schotto. 4°. [*Antverpiae, ex officina plantiniana, apud viduam & filios I. Moreti*, 1612].

[*In* SCHOTT (Andreas). Παροιμίαι ἑλληνικαί. *Antverpiae*, 1612. pp. 169-257].

Dionysius *alexandrinus*. The extant fragments of the works and the epistles of Dionysius, bishop of Alexandria. 8°. *Edinburgh, T. & T. Clark*, 1871.

[ANTE-NICENE christian library, v. 20].

Dionysius *carthusianus*, *or* **Dionysius de Leewis** *or* **Leuwis**, *alias* **Rikel** *or* **Ryckel**. Dialogo, overo ragionamento del giudicio particolar dell' anime dopo la morte. Di Dionisio cartusiano. Con vn' aggionta di letanie, d'orationi, & di raccommandationi; con le quali i cartusiani son soliti di aiutar i suoi morienti. Tradotto di latino in volgare dal Rafaello da Sauignano. 12 p. l. 312 pp. 18°. *Venetia, D. Imberti*, 1590.

——— D. Dionysii carthvsiani summae fidei orthodoxae libri dvo. Primvs, agit de Deo eiusq; attributis, de angelis, de rerum omnium creatione, statu, gubernatione, de animæ potentiis, dæmonum impugnatione & fato. Secvndvs, de beatitvdine hominis, de passionibus animæ, de habitibus virtutum, de legibus ac præceptis, gratiaque & merito. Nusquam ante hac typis excusi.

Dionysius *carthusianus*—continued. 14 p. l. 243 l. numb. 8°. *Parisiis, apud H. & D. de Marnef*, 1548.

Dionysius *halicarnassensis*. Traité de l'arrangement des mots, traduit du grec de Denys d'Halicarnasse ; avec des réflexions sur la langue françoise, comparée avec la langue grecque ; et la tragédie de Polyeucte de P. Corneille, avec des remarques ; par l'abbé Batteux. xliv, 424 pp. 16°. *Paris, Nyon l'aîné et fils*, 1788.

Dionysius *periegetes*. Dionysii orbis descriptio, cum veterum scholiis, et Eustathii commentariis. Accedit Periegesis Prisciani, cum notis Andreæ Papii. [Græce et latine]. 6 p. l. 314, 48 pp. 22 l. 1 pl. 5 maps. 8°. *Oxoniæ, e theatro sheldoniano*, 1697.

Discours by forme van remonstrantie : vervatende de noodsaeckelickheyd van de oosindische navigatie. 1608. *See* **Usselincx** (Willem).

Discours de la paix, contre le Portugais. [*anon.*] 15 pp. sm. 4°. [*Graven-Haghe*? 1647].

Discovrs merveillevx de la vie, actions & déportemens de Catherine de Médicis. *See* **Estienne** (Henri).

Discovrs op verscheyde voorslaghen rakende d'oost en west-indische trafyken. Het eerste deel. Waerinne ghehandelt wert van't prolongeren of vernieuwen van't oost-indische octroy. [*anon.*] 20 l. sm. 4°. [*Graven-Haghe*]? 1645.

Discovrs véritable de ce qvi est advenv à trois blasphématevrs ordinaires dv nom de Diev iovans avx cartes dans vn cabaret, distant de quatre lieuës de Troyes en Champagne, sur le grand chemin de Paris. [*anon.*] 1 p. l. 6 pp. 16°. *Troyes, G. Mazot*, 1599.

Discourses and services on occasion of the death of the late rev. Ralph Wardlaw, d. d. 2 p. l. 147 pp. 16°. *London, A. Fullarton & co.* 1854.

CONTENTS.

ALEXANDER (W. L. *d. d.*) Elisha's cry after Elijah, p. 45.
BROWN (John, *d. d.*) The aged minister's resolutions in the prospect of death, p. 15.
MACFARLANE (John, *ll. d.*) Tribute to dr. Wardlaw, p. 137.
MCLEOD (*Rev.* Norman). The nature of future happiness, p. 89.
THOMSON (*Rev. prof.*) Address at the funeral, p. 1.

Discovery (A) of new worlds. From the french. *See* **Fontenelle** (Bernard Le Bouyer de).

Discussion (The) : or the character, education, prerogatives, and moral influence of woman. [*anon.*] 288 pp. 12°. *Boston, C. C. Little & J. Brown*, 1837.

Disraeli (Isaac). A dissertation on anecdotes ; by the author of Curiosities of literature. [*anon.*] vii, 83 pp. 8°. *London, C. & G. Kearsley*, 1793.

Dissertation (A) on anecdotes. *See* **Disraeli** (Isaac).

Dissertationvm lvdicrarvm et amœnitatvm, scriptores varij. Ed. nova et aucta. Eng. title, 3 p. l. 666 pp. 18°. *Lvgd. Batavor. apud F. Hegerum*, 1644.

CONTENTS.

ALDROVANDI (U.) Cycni encomium, pp. 655–666.
BAERLE (G. van). Oratio de ente rationis, pp. 304–332.
——— Nuptiæ peripateticæ, pp. 333–368.
BOXHORN (M. Z.) Allocvtio nvptialis, pp. 369–382.
CALCAGNINI (C.) Encomivm pvlicis, pp. 67–82.
CARDANO (G.) Podagrae encomium, pp. 41–66.
DOËS (Jan van der). In lavdem vmbræ declamatio et carmen, pp. 270–300.
ESCRIVA (Fr.) Muscæ encomivm, pp. 555–578.
GUERNA (A.) Grammaticale bellvm, pp. 400–446.
GUTHERIERRES (J.) Cæcitatis encomivm, pp. 519–554.
HEINSIUS (D.) Lavs pedicvli, pp. 383–399.
LIPSIUS (J.) Lavs elephantis, pp. 447–473.
MAJORAGIO (M. A.) Lvti encomivm, pp. 209–254.
MELANCHTHON (P. S.) Lavs formicæ, pp. 190–208.
MENAPIUS (W.) Encomivm febris quartanæ, pp. 474–518.
PASSERAT (J.) Encomivm asini, pp. 259–269.
PIRCKHEIMER (W.) Apologia, sive lavs podagrae, pp. 1–39.
PUTTEN (H. van der). Democritvs, pp. 579–593.
——— Ovi encomivm, pp. 595–654.
SCALIGERO (G. C.) De lavdibus anseris, pp. 255–258.
WINMANN (N.) De arte natandi, pp. 83–189.

District of Columbia. Boyd's directory of the district of Columbia, together with a compendium of its governments, institutions, and trades. Wm. H. Boyd, compiler. 1872. 555 pp. 8°. *Washington (D. C.) Daily republican office*, 1872.

——— Gazetteer of the district of Columbia for 1871–2, embracing the names and address of the principal business and professional firms in the district, and the laws of the district of Columbia relating to hacks, vehicles, and license, taxes, and trades ; also an illustrated sketch of the district of Columbia. 173 pp. 8°. *Washington, Morris & Drysdale*, [1871].

——— Report of the committee on the indebtedness of the district, on the affairs of the police court, August 14, 1871. 27, 97 pp. 8°. *Washington, Republican print*, 1871. S.

Disturnell (John). The great lakes, or inland seas of America. Together with a guide to the upper Mississippi river. 252 pp. 8 pl. 1 map. 16°. *Philadelphia, W. B. Zieber*, 1871.

Disturnell (John)—continued.

——— Official census of the United States and territories by counties, etc. for 1860 and 1870, and of British America, from the latest enumeration; also, the constitution of the United States. 64 pp. 8°. *Philadelphia, J. Disturnell,* 1872.

Ditson (George Leighton, *m. d.*) The federati of Italy: a romance of caucasian captivity. 319 pp. 12°. *Boston, W. White & co.* 1871.

Ditzler (*Rev.* Jacob) *and* **Wilkes** (Elder L. B.) The Louisville debate: a discussion of the question, What is christian baptism? including its proper subjects and design. Held between [them] in "Weisiger hall," Louisville, Ky. December, 1870. 708 pp. 8°. *Lexington (Ky.) J. D. Trapp,* 1871.

Dixon (Edward H. *m. d.*) The kidney: its structure, functions, and diseases; Bright's disease; the urine. 44 pp. 1 l. 12°. *New York, J. S. Redfield,* 1871.

Dixon (Francis B.) Hand-book of marine insurance and average. 301 pp. 20 l. 8°. *New York, H. Spear,* 1862.

Dixon (John). A key to the prophecies; containing an explanation of the symbols used for prophetic declarations in the bible; also remarks upon the prophecies contained in the book of Daniel and revelation [etc.] 342 pp. 12°. *Boston, author,* 1844.

Dixon (Joshua). Scriptural examinations on the church catechism. Revised and adapted to the liturgy of the protestant episcopal church, with notes and an appendix. By the rev. George A. Smith. xii, 231 pp. 18°. *Philadelphia, W. Marshall & co.* 1836.

Dixon (William Hepworth). Her majesty's tower. v. 3-4. 8°. *London, Hurst & Blackett,* 1871.

Doane (William Croswell). A memoir of the life of George Washington Doane, d. d. ll. d. bishop of New Jersey. By his son. v. 1. 9-577 pp. 8°. *New York, D. Appleton & co.* 1860.

Dobbins' family companion. 1870. v. 1. no. 1. 12 pp. 8°. *Philadelphia, Ringwalt & Brown,* 1870.
[No more published].

Dobson (*Mrs.* Susannah). Historical anecdotes of heraldry and chivalry, tending to shew the origin of many english and foreign coats of arms, circumstances and customs. [*anon.*] 2 p. l. 3; 316 pp. 5 pl. 4°. *Worcester, (Eng.) Barker & son,* [1796].

Dockham (C. Augustine). A directory of the city of Newburyport, for 1854. *See* **Newburyport** (*Mass.*)

Dod (Charles Roger). Dod's parliamentary companion. 1871 and 1872. 2 v. 32°. *London, Whittaker & co.* 1871-72.

Dod (*Rev.* John) *and* **Cleaver** (*Rev.* Robert). Ten sermons, tending chiefly to the fitting of men for the worthy receiving of the lord's svpper. The sixe first, by I. Dod. The foure last, by R. Cleaver. Whereunto is annexed a plaine and learned metaphrase on the epistle to the Colossians, written by a godly and judicious preacher. Newly printed and inlarged. 4 p. l. 288 pp. 8°. *London, T. Harper for J. Harrison,* 1634.

Dodd (*Rev.* Philip Stanhope). A view of the evidence, afforded by the life and ministry of st. Peter, to the truth of the christian revelation. viii, 415 pp. 8°. *London, J. G. & F. Rivington,* 1837.

Dodd (William, *ll. d.*) The beauties of history; or, pictures of virtue and vice; drawn from examples of men eminent for their virtues, or infamous for their vices. 244, viii pp. 16°. *Philadelphia, B. & T. Kite,* 1807.

——— Thoughts in prison, and other miscellaneous pieces, with the life of the author. Cooke's ed. Eng. title, xiv, 125 pp. 3 pl. 18°. *London, C. Cooke,* 1810.

——— The same. 177 pp. 1 portrait, 1 pl. 16°. *Philadelphia, B. & T. Kite,* 1808.

Doddridge (Philip, *d. d.*) Practical discourses on regeneration. In ten sermons. [Also], two sermons, on the scripture doctrine of salvation by grace through faith. 3d american ed. 216, 36 pp. 16°. *Boston, E. Lincoln,* 1803.

——— Sermons to young persons. 6th ed. 196 pp. 16°. *Philadelphia, W. Young,* 1793.

Döderlein (Christian Albert). Animadversiones historico-criticae de Thaletis et Pythagoræ theologica ratione. 231 pp. 8°. [*n. p.*] *J. F. Hager,* 1750.

Dodge (David Low). Memorial of mr. David L. Dodge, consisting of an autobiography, prepared at the request and for the use of his children; with a few selections from his writings. 325 pp. 8°. *Boston, published only for the family,* 1854.

Dodge (Mary Abigail). Country living and country thinking, by Gail Hamilton. [*pseudon.*] vi, 461 pp. 12°. *Boston, Ticknor & Fields,* 1862.

Dodge (Mary Abigail)—continued.

——— Gala-days, by Gail Hamilton. [*pseudon.*] 2 p. l. 436 pp. 12°. *Boston, Ticknor & Fields*, 1863.

——— Stumbling-blocks. By Gail Hamilton. [*pseudon.*] 2 p. l. 435 pp. 12°. *Boston, Ticknor & Fields*, 1864.

——— Woman's worth and worthlessness. The complement to "A new atmosphere." By Gail Hamilton. [*pseudon.*] 291 pp. 12° *New York, Harper & brothers*, 1872.

Dodsley (Robert). Poems. [*anon.*] 2 p. l. 242 pp. 1 l. 4°. *London, author*, 1780.

——— Trifles: viz. The toy-shop. The king and the miller of Mansfield. The blind beggar of Bethnal-Green. Rex & pontifex. The chronicle of the kings of England. The art of preaching, in imitation of Horace's art of poetry. The right of mankind to do what they will, asserted. With several others. 2d ed. 1 p. l. vi, 350 pp. 8°. *London, J. Dodsley*, 1777.

Dodson (Michael). Memoirs of the life and writings of the late rev. and learned Hugh Farmer. [Also], a piece of his, never before published, printed from the only remaining manuscript of the author. Also, some original letters, and an extract from his essay on the case of Balaam. Taken from his manuscript, since destroyed. ix, 159 pp. 8°. *London, T. N. Longman & O. Rees*, 1804.

Dodsworth (William). Clarendon. A novel. 3 v. 12°. *London, Simpkin, Marshall & co.* 1852.

Dodsworth (William, *verger*). A guide to the cathedral church of Salisbury. With a particular account of the great improvements made therein. [1st ed.] 2 p. l. 84 pp. 8°. *Salisbury, B. C. Collins*, 1792.

[*With* HISTORY (The) and description of Guildford, 2d ed. [1801]].

——— The same. 2d ed. 2 p. l. 84 pp. 8°. *Salisbury, B. C. Collins*, 1792.

Dodwell (Henry). Annales velleiani, qvintilianei, statiani, seu vitæ P. Velleii Paterculi, M. Fabii Quintiliani, P. Papinii Statii, (obiterque Juvenalis,) pro temporum ordine, dispositæ. 6 p. l. 306 pp. 21 l. 8°. *Oxonii, e theatro sheldoniano*, 1698.

——— A discourse concerning the obligation to marry within the true communion, following from their style of being called a holy seed. 4 p. l. 254 pp. 8°. [*London*, 1702].

——— A treatise concerning the lawfulness of instrumental music in holy offices. [Also], a preface concerning the lawfulness and use of organs in the christian church. The 2d ed. with large additions. 1 p. l. 87, 143 pp. 8°. *London, W. Haws*, 1700.

Doës (Jan Van der). Iani Dovsæ in lavdem vmbræ declamatio et carmen. 18°. [*Lugd. Batavorum*, 1644].

[*In* DISSERTATIONVM lvdicrarvm et amœnitatvm scriptores varij, pp. 270-300].

Doggett (Henry). Life and campaigns of Napoleon Bonaparte, emperor of France, etc. iv, 285 pp. 18°. *Baltimore, J. G. Hanzsche*, 1822.

Doings in Maryland, or Matilda Douglas. [*anon.*] 316 pp. 12°. *Philadelphia, J. B. Lippincott & co.* 1871.

Dolce (Lodovico). Il capitano. Comedia. Con alcvne stanze nella favola d'Adone. 57 l. 16°. *Vinegia, G. Giolito de Ferrari*, 1545.

——— Dialogo, nel qvale si ragiona della qualità, diuersità, e proprietà de i colori. 87 l. numb. 1 l. unp. 16°. *Venetia, G. B. & M. Sessa fratelli*, 1565.

[*With his* Libri tre delle gemme, 1565].

——— Dialogo, nel quale si ragiona del modo di accrescere e conseruar la memoria. Eng. title, 3 p. l. 120 l. numb. 16°. *Venetia*, [*G. B. & M. Sessa fratelli*, 1562].

——— Epistole di G. Plinio, di m. Franc. Petrarca, del s. Pico della Mirandola et d'altri eccellentiss. hvomini. Tradotte per m. Lodovico Dolce. 4 p. l. 164 l. 12°. *Vinegia, G. Giolito de Ferrari*, 1548.

——— Libri tre ne i qvali si tratta delle diuersi sorti delle gemme, che produce la natura, della qvalità, grandezza, vellezza, & virtù loro. 99 l. 16°. *Venetia, G. B., M. Sessa & fratelli*, 1565.

——— Le prime imprese del conte Orlando. Da lvi composte in ottava rima, et nvovamente stampate. Con argomenti et allegorie per ogni canto. 8 p. l. 212 pp. sm. 4°. *Vinegia, G. Giolito de' Ferrari*, 1572.

——— I qvattro libri delle osservationi di m. Lodovico Dolce, di nvovo ristampate, & con somma diligenza corrette. 238 pp. 16°. *Vinegia, A. Salicato*, 1585.

Dole (Felicien Capron de). Blues and carmines of indigo; a practical treatise on the fabrication of every commercial product derived from indigo. Translated from the french, with extensive and important additions, by prof. H. Dussauce. xvi, 25-216 pp. 12°. *Philadelphia, H. C. Baird*, 1863.

Döllen (Johann Heinrich Wilhelm). The portable transit instrument in the vertical of the pole star, translated from the original memoir of Wm. Döllen, by Cleveland Abbe. 48 pp. 8°. *Washington, government printing office*, 1870.

Döllinger (Johann Joseph Ignatz). Declaration of prof. Döllinger and his associates. [Translated from the authorized french version]. 8°. [*New York, American tract society*, 1872].
[*In* BACON (L. W.) An inside view of the vatican council, pp. 232–240].

Dolomieu (Guy Sylvestre Tancrède Gralet Déodat de). Mémoire sur les Iles Ponces, et catalogue raisonné des produits de l'Etna; pour servir à l'histoire des volcans: suivis de la description de l'éruption de l'Etna, du mois de juillet 1787. Ouvrage qui fait suite au Voyage aux îles de Lipari. 1 p. l. vi, 526 pp. 1 l. 4 maps, 1 table. 8°. *Paris, Cuchet*, 1788.
[*With his* Voyage aux îles de Lipari, 1783].

——— Voyage aux îles de Lipari, fait en 1781, ou notices sur les Iles Æoliennes, pour servir à l'histoire des volcans; suivi d'un mémoire sur une espèce de volcan d'air, & d'un autre sur la température du climat de Malthe, & sur la différence de la chaleur réelle & de la chaleur sensible. 208 pp. 8°. *Paris*, 1783.

Domeier (William, *m. d.*) Observations on the climate, manners, and amusements of Malta; principally intended for the information of invalids. 1 p. l. 116 pp. 8°. *London, J. Callow*, 1810.

Domestic (The) missionary. [A semimonthly religious newspaper]. March 1, 1869, to February 15, 1870. v. 1. fol. *New York*, [*domestic missions, protestant episcopal church*], 1869–70.
[No more published: succeeded by the Domestic and foreign missionary, or home and abroad].

Donaldson (James, *ll. d. editor*). *See* **Antenicene** christian library.

Donaldson (John). Agricultural biography; containing a notice of the life and writings of the British authors on agriculture, from 1480 to the present time. viii, 137 pp. 8°. *London, author*, 1854.

Donaldson (Paschal). The odd-fellows' textbook and manual. An elucidation of the theory of odd-fellowship. Revised and corrected by p. g. George Bertram. Revised ed. 1871. 1 p. l. 366 pp. 17 pl. 1 portrait. 12°. *Philadelphia, Moss & co.* 1872.

Donaldson (S. J. *jr.*) Lyrics and other poems. 208 pp. 12°. *Philadelphia, Lindsay & Blakiston*, 1860.

Donaldson (Thomas). Poems, chiefly in the scottish dialect; both humorous and entertaining. 225 pp. 12°. *Alnwick, W. Davison*, 1809.

Donan de Vizé (Jean). The history of the siege of Toulon. With an account of the political reasons that induced the confederates to undertake it. Together with all the transactions, from the duke of Savoy's entrance into Provence, to his going out of it. With a most exact, and curious plan of Toulon, never before publish'd. Done into english by mr. A[bel] Boyer. 2 parts in 1 v. 4 p. l. 71 pp; 40 pp. 4°. *London, A. Collins*, 1708.

Donck (Adriaen van der). Vertoogh van Nieu-Neder-Land, weghens de gheleghentheydt, vruchtbaerheydt, en soberen staet desselfs. 49 pp. sm. 4°. *Graven-Hage, M. Stael*, 1650.

Dondini (Guglielmo). Historia de rebus in Gallia gestis ab Alexandro Farnesio Parmæ et Placentiæ duce iii. 3 p. l. 537 pp. 19 l. 5 pl. 4°. [*n. p. n. d.*]
[*Note.*—Probably printed at Nuremberg, 1675].

Donesmondi (Ippolito). Dell' istoria ecclesiastica di Mantova. Parte 1ª. 6 p. l. 396 pp. 6 l. 4°. *Mantova, A. & L. Osanna fratelli*, 1612.

Doni (Antonio Francesco). Mondi celesti, terrestri, et infernali, de gli academici pellegrini. Mondo piccolo, grande, misto, resibile, imaginato, de' pazzi et massimo. Inferno de gli scolari, de mal maritati, delle puttane, et ruffiani, soldati et capitani, poltroni, dottor cattiui, legisti, artisti, de gli vzarai, de poeti, e compositori ignoranti. 8 p. l. 431 pp. 16°. *Venetia, appresso N. Moretti*, 1583.

——— Pittvre del Doni, academico pellegrino. Diuise in due trattati. Libro primo. 64 l. numb. 4°. *Padova, G. Perchacino*, 1564.

Donizetti (Gaetano). Anna Bolena. [Libretto, without music]. 46 pp. 8°. [*New York*], *W. C. Bryant & co.* 1871.
[PAREPA-ROSA grand english opera].

——— The daughter of the regiment. A grand opera in three acts. The music by Donizetti. Words specially translated by Arthur Baildon. [Libretto, without music]. 29 pp. 8°. *New York, W. C. Bryant & co.* 1871
[PAREPA-ROSA grand english opera].

Donizetti (Gaetano)—continued.

——— Lucretia Borgia. [Libretto, without music]. 35 pp. 8°. [*New York*], *W. C. Bryant & co.* 1871.

[PAREPA-ROSA grand english opera].

Donkersley (*Rev.* Richard). Facts about boys, for boys. 194 pp. 5 pl. 18°. *New York, Carlton & Porter*, [1859].

——— Facts about girls, for girls. 220 pp. 6 pl. 18°. *New York, Carlton & Porter*, [1860].

Donn (Rob.) Songs and poems, in the gaelic language. *See* **Mackay** (Robert).

Donne (John, *d. d. dean of St. Pauls*). Letters to severall persons of honour. Published by John Donne, dr. of the civill law. 3 p. l. 318 pp. sm. 4°. *London, R. Marriot*, 1651.

Donovan (Edward). Descriptive excursions through South Wales and Monmouthshire, [1800–1804]. 2 v. xxvii, 404 pp. 19 pl; ix, 396 pp. 12 pl. 8°. *London, author*, 1805.

Doolittle (*Rev.* N.) *and* **Power** (*Rev.* John H.) A discussion of the subject of universalism, held in Laport, Lorain county, Ohio, from July 29th, to August 6th, 1845: between rev. N. Doolittle and rev. John H. Power. Reported by mr. A. A. Wetmore. 360 pp. 16°. *Columbus (O.) Tribune office print*, 1846.

Doolittle (*Rev.* Thomas). A call to delaying sinners: or the danger of delaying, in matters concerning our souls. 14th ed. 10 p. l. 134 pp. 1 portrait. 18°. *London, R. Ware*, [*etc.*] 1750.

Doomed (The) city! Chicago. *See* **Mackintosh** (Charles H.)

Dora Darling; the daughter of the regiment. [*anon.*] 370 pp. 5 pl. 12°. *Boston, J. E. Tilton & co.* 1865.

Doré (Gustave). Le capitaine Fracasse. Illustré. *See* **Gautier** (Théophile).

——— Fierabras. Traduite par Mary Lafon. Illustré. *See* **Fier a bras**.

——— L'habitation du désert, par le capitaine Mayne Reid. Illustré par Gustave Doré. *See* **Reid** (*Capt.* Mayne).

Dorgan (John A.) Studies. viii, 223 pp. 12°. *Philadelphia, author*, 1862.

Doris (Charles). Amours secrettes de Napoléon Buonaparte, par m. le baron de B***. [*anon.*] 5e éd. 4 v. 16°. *Paris, G. Mathiot*, 1817.

——— Amours secrettes des quatre frères de Napoléon, par m. le baron de B***. [*anon.*] 5e éd. 4 v. 16°. *Paris, G. Mathiot*, 1817.

——— Chagrins domestiques de Napoléon Buonaparte à l'îsle Sainte-Hélène; précédé de faits historiques de la plus haute importance; le tout de la main de Napoléon, ou écrit sous sa dictée. Papiers enlevés de son cabinet dans la nuit du 4 au 5 mai 1821, et publiés par Edwige Santine, ex-huissier du cabinet de N. B. à Sainte-Hélène. Suivi de notes précieuses sur les six derniers mois de la vie de Napoléon. [*pseudon.*] 2 p. l. iv, 236 pp 8°. *Paris, G. Mathiot*, 1821.

——— Mémoires secrets sur Napoléon Buonaparte. Par m. le baron de B. 7e éd. 2 v. 16°. *Paris, G. Mathiot*, 1817.

Dorling (W. G.) *See* **American** (The) racing record for 1871.

Dorner (H.) Führer durch den zoologischen garten zu Hamburg. 17e aufl. viii, 104 pp. 1 map. 16°. *Hamburg, verlag der zoologischen gesellschaft*, 1871. S.

Dornfeld (J.) Die geschichte des weinbaues in Schwaben. viii, 272 pp. 12°. *Stuttgart, Cohen & Risch*, 1868. S.

Dorr (Benjamin, *d. d.*) A historical account of Christ church, Philadelphia, from its foundation, 1695, to 1841; and of St. Peter's and St. James's until the separation of the churches. xii, 430 pp. 12°. *New York, Swords, Stanford & co.* 1841.

Dörr (*Dr.* Friedrich). Der deutsche krieg gegen Frankreich im jahre 1870. Auf grund amtlicher und anderer zuverlässiger quellen. 7er abdruck. v. 1. 460 pp. 12 portraits. 1 map, 1 chart. 8°. *Berlin, gebrüder Paetel*, 1870.

Dorr (*Mrs.* Julia C. R.) Lanmere. 447 pp. 12°. *New York, Mason brothers*, 1856.

——— Poems. 192 pp. 12°. *Philadelphia, J. B. Lippincott & co.* 1872.

Dorsey (Sarah Anne). Athalie, or, a southern villeggiatura: "a winter's tale." By "Filia." [*pseudon.*] 109 pp. 8°. *Philadelphia, Claxton, Remsen & Haffelfinger*, 1872.

Dortous de Mairan. *See* **Mairan.**

Dorward (B. I.) Wild flowers of Wisconsin. Poems. x, 248 pp. 16°. *Milwaukee, Catholic news co.* 1872.

Dossie (Robert). Observations on the potash brought from America, [with] processes for making potash and barilla in North America. 41 pp. 8°. *London*, 1767.

Doten (Lizzie). Poems of progress. 252 pp. 1 portrait. 12°. *Boston, W. White & co.* 1871.

Dougherty (*Mrs.* Elizabeth C.) The city out of sight. no. 5, new series. 86 pp. 24°. *Memphis (Tenn.) Sunday-school board, southern baptist convention*, 1871.

Doughty (*Rev.* John). A manual of New church doctrine. 47 pp. 12°. *Philadelphia, J. B. Lippincott & co.* 1871.

Douglas (Amanda M.) Kathie's stories. 6 v. 16°. *Boston, Lee & Shepard*, 1871–72.

CONTENTS.

v. 1. Kathie's three wishes. 260 pp. 4 pl.
2. Kathie's aunt Ruth. 278 pp.
3. Kathie's summer at Cedarwood. 257 pp. 4 pl.
4. Kathie's soldiers. 262 pp.
5. In the ranks. 272 pp.
6. Kathie's harvest days. 278 pp.

——— Lucia: her problem. 315 pp. 12°. *New York, Sheldon & co.* 1872.

Douglas (Marian). Picture poems for young folks. vi, 104 pp. sm. 4°. *Boston, J. R. Osgood & co.* 1872.

Douglas (R. K.) Poems and songs, chiefly scottish. viii, 160 pp. 16°. *Edinburgh, A. Macredie*, 1824.

Douglas (*Rev.* William). Annals of the first african church in the United States of America, now styled the African episcopal church of St. Thomas, Philadelphia, in its connection with the early struggles of the colored people to improve their condition, with the co-operation of the Friends, and other philanthropists. 172 pp. 12°. *Philadelphia, King & Baird*, 1862.

Douglas' (W. & B.) descriptive catalogue and price list of patent pumps, hydraulic rams, chain pumps, garden engines, and other hydraulic machines, hardware, etc. manufactured at their works in Middletown, Conn. 188 pp. 1 pl. 8°. *Middletown, (Conn.)* 1872.

Douglass (R.) Infant baptism; including a series of conversations on the subject and mode of baptism, designed, chiefly for the benefit of the young. 150 pp. 18°. *Philadelphia, King & Baird*, 1851.

Douglass (William, *m. d.*) The practical history of a new epidemical fever, which prevailed in Boston in the year 1735 and 1736. 18 pp. 12°. *Boston, T. Fleet*, 1736.

Dover (George J. W. Agar-Ellis, *baron*). *See* **Ellis.**

Dover (*New Hampshire*). The Dover, Great Falls, and Rochester directory for 1871–72. Compiled, printed, and published by Dean Dudley & co. 8°. *Boston*, 1871.

Dowling (John, *d. d.*) The history of romanism, from the earliest corruptions of christianity; with chronological table, indexes, glossary. A new edition, with supplements continuing the history from the accession of pope Pius ix. to his proclamation of papal infallibility, and his deposition as a temporal sovereign, a. d. 1870. 2 p. l. 940 pp. 2 pl. 8°. *New York, E. Walker*, [1871].

Dowling (Morgan E.) Southern prisons: or, Josie, the heroine of Florence. Four years of battle and imprisonment. 506 pp. 16 pl. 2 portraits. 8°. *Detroit, W. Graham*, 1870.

Downes (John). Roscius anglicanus, or, an historical review of the stage, after it had been suppress'd in 1641, 'till the time of king Charles the ii's restoration, in May, 1660. Giving an account of its rise again: [etc.] *London, H. Playford*, 1708. With additions by the late Thomas Davies. 70 pp. 1 l. 27 pp. 8°. *London, for the editor*, 1789.

[*In* WALDRON (F. G.) Literary museum. *London*, 1792.

Downing (Andrew Jackson). Selected fruits: from Downing's Fruits and fruit-trees of America. With some new varieties; including their culture, propagation and management in the garden and orchard. By Charles Downing. 678 pp. 12°. *New York, J. Wiley & son*, 1871.

Downing (*Rev.* Joshua Wells). Remains, with a brief memoir. Edited by Elijah H. Downing. 329 pp. 12°. *New York, G. Lane & P. P. Sandford*, 1841.

Downward and upward. *See* **Venner** (Lizzie).

Doyle (Martin). The flower garden, or monthly calendar of practical directions for the culture of flowers. 1st amer. ed. With notes and observations by L. D. Gale, m. d. 180 pp. 3 col. pl. 12°. *New York, Moore & Payne*, 1835.

Doylé (William). Some account of the british dominions beyond the Atlantic, particularly the question about the northwest passage. xvi, 87 pp. 1 map. 8°. *London, J. Browne*, [1770].

Dozy (F.) *and* **Molkenboer** (J. H.) Bryologia javanica, seu descriptio muscorum frondosum archepelagi indici iconibus illustrata. v. 1. xii, 161 pp. 130 pl. 4°. *Lugduni Batavorum, A. W. Sythoff, E. J. Brill*, 1854–67. s.

Drake (Benjamin). Sketches of the services of William Henry Harrison. *See* **Todd** (Charles S.) *and* **Drake.**

Drake (Francis S.) Dictionary of american biography, including men of the time; containing nearly ten thousand notices of persons of both sexes, of native and foreign birth, who have been remarkable, or prominently connected with the arts, sciences, literature, politics, or history, of the american continent. xvi, 1019 pp. 8°. *Boston, J. R. Osgood & co.* 1872.

Drake (Joseph Rodman). The culprit fay: a cantata. 1872. *See* **Ensign** (J. L.)

Dramatic (The) censor; or, critical companion. [*anon.*] 2 v. 4 p. l. 480 pp; 4 p. l. 499 pp. 1 pl. 8°. *London, J. Bell*, 1770.

Draper (*Rev.* Bourne Hall). Bible illustrations; or, a description of manners and customs peculiar to the east, especially explanatory of the holy scriptures. American edition, with many improvements. 215 pp. sq. 16°. *Boston, Carter, Hendee & co.* 1832.

——— Conversations of a father with his son, on some leading points in natural philosophy; [etc.] 162 pp. sq. 16°. *New York, N. B. Holmes*, [1833].

Draper (Edmund S.) Prof. Draper's 600 easy, profitable, and pleasant ways to make money, a compendium of valuable receipts for making articles in constant demand, and of ready sale. 144 pp. 16°. *Cincinnati, Adderley & Harpel*, 1871.

Drayton (Michael). England's heroical epistles, written in imitation of the stile and manner of Ovid's epistles: with annotations of the chronicle history. Newly corrected and amended. 4 p. l. 225 pp. 1 pl. 16°. *London, S. Smethwick*, [*about* 1632].

——— The same. 8 p. l. 272 pp. 1 pl. 16°. *London, J. Hazard*, 1737.

Dresdner gewerbevereins-zeitung. Organ der sächsischen gewerbevereine und des sächsischen baugewerkevereins. Herausgeber: August Walter. Erscheint monatlich zweimal. 1–3 jahrg. 1868–70. 3 v. fol. *Dresden, H. Henkler*, 1868–70. s.

Dressler (William). Christmas chimes. 27 pp. obl. 8°. *New York, J. L. Peters*, [1871.]

——— The ne plus ultra glee and chorus book. A collection of popular glees, trios, quartets, and choruses. 324 pp. obl. 8°. *New York, J. L. Peters*, [1871].

Dreux du Radier (Jean François). Récréations historiques, critiques, morales, et d'érudition; avec l'histoire des fous en titre d'office. Par m. D. D. A. 2 v. xx, 381 pp. 1 l; 2 p. l. 358 pp. 1 l. 12°. *Paris, Robustel & la veuve Duchesne*, 1767.

Drew (Benjamin). Pens and types: or, hints and helps for those who write, print, or read. 128 pp. 2 l. 12°. *Boston, Lee & Shepard*, 1872.

Drew (Samuel). The life of the rev. Thomas Coke. [With] his travels and missionary exertions, in England, Ireland, America, and the West Indies; with an account of his death, on the 3d of May, 1814, and an abstract of his writings and character. xix, 391 pp. 1 portrait. 8°. *London, T. Cordeux*, 1817.

——— An original essay on the immateriality and immortality of the human soul, founded solely on physical and rational principles. 2d ed. enlarged. 306 pp. 8°. *Bristol, R. Edwards*, 1803.

Drey (*Dr.* Johann Sebastian von). Neue untersuchungen über die constitutionen und kanones der apostel. Ein historisch-kritischer beitrag zur literatur der kirchengeschichte und des kirchenrechts. xvi, 446 pp. 1 l. 8°. *Tübingen, H. Laupp*, 1832.

Dridoens (Jean). De concordia liberi arbitrij, & prædestinationis diuinæ, liber unus. 6 p. l. 242 pp. 1 l. 4°. *Lovanii, ex officina R. Rescii*, 1537.

——— De gratia & libero arbitrio, libri duo. 2 v. in 1. 12 p. l. 272 pp; 115 pp. 4°. *Lovanii, ex officina R. Rescii*, 1537.
[*With his* De concordia liberi arbitrij, 1537].

Droom-gesicht eenes metter herten tot Godt op-getrockenen mensches: in hem veroorzaeckt (zoo 't schijnt) door voor-gaende overdenckinge van Godes goetheyt (bijzonder nu door d'aenmerckinghe der goeder hope tot den long gewenschten vrede vernieut zijnde) ende der menschen quaetheyt. Bly-eynd-spelswijze in druck uyt-ghegeven. [*anon.*] 34 l. sm. 4°. [*n. p.*] 1607.
[*In* NEDERLANDTSCHEN bye-corf].

Drouineau (Gustave). L'ironie. 2 v. 298 pp; 266 pp. 16°. *Bruxelles, J. P. Meline*, 1834.

Drown (Daniel A.) Fragrant flowers and other poems. 236 pp. 12°. *Boston, Walker, Wise & co.* 1860.

Droz (François Xavier Joseph). The art of being happy: from the french of Droz, Sur l'art d'être heureuse; in a series of letters from a father to his children: with observations and comments. By Timothy Flint. viii, 313 pp. 12°. *Boston, Carter & Hendee*, 1832.

——— The same. By Bourne Hall Draper.

Droz (F. X. J.)—continued.
A new ed. xii, 269 pp. 2 pl. 18°. *London, W. Darton & son,* [1844].

Droz (Gustave). Around a spring. Translated from the french, by M. S. 150 pp. 8°. *New York, Holt & Williams,* 1871.
[Leisure hour series].

Druid (The); a series of miscellaneous essays. [*anon.*] iv, 236 pp. 8°. *Glasgow, R. Chapman,* 1812.

Drummond (Henry). Social duties on christian principles. 4th ed. enlarged. xv, 203 pp. 16°. *London, J. Hatchard & son,* 1839.

Drummond (*Rev.* James). Thoughts for the christian life. With an introduction by J. G. Holland. xvi, 9–371 pp. 12°. *New York, C. Scribner,* 1864.

Drury (Anna H.) Deep waters. A novel. 3 v. 12°. *London, Chapman & Hall,* 1863.

Du Bartas (Guillaume de Sallust). The vranie, or heavenly mvse. [Translated by king James i. of England. Edinburgh, 1585. Reprinted by Edward Arber. French and english. 16°. *London,* 1869].
[ARBER's english reprints, v. 8, no. 19. *In* JAMES I. *of England.* The essayes of a prentise, in the divine art of poesie, pp. 19–39].

Dublin (*Archbishopric of*). Constitutiones provinciales et synodales ecclæsiae metropolitanae et primatialis dubliniensis. 148 pp. 1 l. 16°. [*Dublin*]? 1770.

Dublin international exhibition of arts and manufactures, 1865. Official catalogue. Published by authority of the executive committee. 2d ed. xxvi, 202 pp. interleaved. 8°. *Dublin, for the committee,* 1865. S.

Dublin (The) review. [Quarterly]. July, 1867, to Oct. 1871. New series, v. 9–17. [Complete series, v. 61–69]. 8°. *London, Burns, Oates & co.* 1867–71.

Dublin university magazine, a literary and political journal. [Monthly]. Jan. to Dec. 1871. v. 77–78. 8°. *Dublin, G. Herbert,* 1871.

Dubois (L. J. J.) Description des objets d'arts qui composent le cabinet de feu m. le baron V. Denon. Monuments antiques, etc. *See* **Denon** (Dominique Vivant).

Dubosc (Jacques). The accomplish'd woman. Written in french by m. du Boscq in 1630. Translated by a gentleman of Cambridge, L[awrence] M[aydwell]? 2 v. 12 p. l. 273 pp. 7 l; 2 p. l. 296 pp. 5 l. 16°. *London, J. Watts,* 1753.

Du Cerceau (Jean Antoine). The history of the revolution of Persia. *See* **Krusinski** (Judasz Tadeusz).

Du Chaillu (Paul B.) The country of the dwarfs. 314 pp. 18 pl. 12°. *New York, Harper & brothers,* 1872.

——— Explorations and adventures in equatorial Africa; with accounts of the manners and customs of the people, and of the chase of the gorilla, the crocodile, leopard, elephant, hippopotamus, and other animals. Revised and enlarged ed. 535 pp. 26 pl. 8°. *New York, Harper & brothers,* 1871.

Duchatel (Pierre). Petri Castellani ludus, sive convivium saturnale. 18°. [*Lugduni Batavorum,* 1655].
[ELEGANTIORES præstantium virorum satyræ, v. 2, pp. 409–462].

Duchesne (Jean). Bibliothèque impériale. Description des estampes exposées dans la galerie de la bibliothèque impériale, attribuée au cabinet depuis l'année 1854, et formant un aperçu historique des produits de la gravure. xxxvii, xvi, 210 pp. 1 l. 8°. *Paris, J. Renouard et cie.* 1855.

——— Notice des estampes exposées à la bibliothèque du roi; contenant des recherches historiques et critiques sur ces estampes et sur les auteurs. xxiii, 119 pp. 16°. *Paris, De Bure frères,* 1823.

Duchillon (*pseudon.*) *See* **Dutens** (Louis). Memoirs of a traveller.

Ducrest (Gargette). Mémoires sur l'impératrice Joséphine, sur la ville, la cour et les salons de Paris sous l'empire. 2 p. l. 160 pp. sm. fol. *Paris, G. Barba,* [*about* 1860].
[Chroniques populaires].

Dudevant (Amantine Lucile Aurore Dupin, *madame*). Cesarine Dietrich. By George Sand. [*pseudon.*] Translated by Edward Stanwood. 138 pp. 8°. *Boston, J. R. Osgood & co.* 1871.

——— Handsome Lawrence. A sequel to "A rolling stone." By George Sand. [*pseudon.*] Translated from the french by Carroll Owen. 122 pp. 8°. *Boston, J. R. Osgood & co.* 1871.

——— The marquis de Villemer. By George Sand. [*pseudon.*] Translated from the french by Ralph Keeler. 1 p. l. 130 pp. 8°. *Boston, J. R. Osgood & co.* 1871.

——— The miller of Angibault. A novel. By George Sand. [*pseudon.*] Translated from the french by miss Mary E. Dewey. vi, 320 pp. 16°. *Boston, Roberts brothers,* 1871.

——— A rolling stone. By George Sand. [*pseudon.*] Translated from the french, by Carroll Owen. 113 pp. 8°. *Boston, J. R. Osgood & co.* 1871.

Dudevant (A. L. A. D. *madame*)—continued.
——— The snow man. A novel. By George Sand. [*pseudon.*] Translated from the french by Virginia Vaughan. 2 p. l. 555 pp. 16°. *Boston, Roberts brothers*, 1871.

Dudevant (Maurice)? Callirhoé. By Maurice Sand. [*pseudon.*] Translated from the french by S. A. DaPonte. 325 pp. 12°. *Philadelphia, Claxton, Remsen & Haffelfinger*, 1871.

Dudley (Charles E.) Our sunday-school hymnody. *See* **Cross** (J. A.) *and* **Dudley.**

Dudley (Dean). Cambridge directory. *See* **Cambridge** (*Mass.*)

Duel (Le). [*anon.*] 175 pp. 16°. *Paris, P. Lebigre-Duquesne*, 1868.
[Bibliothèque des curiosités].

Duellist (The), or a cursory review of the rise, progress, and practice of duelling, with illustrative anecdotes from history. [*anon.*] viii, 205 pp. 8°. *London, Longman*, 1822.

Du Faur (Guy, *de Pibrac*). *See* **Pibrac** (Guy du Faur, *seigneur* de).

Dufaux (*Mlle.* Ermance). Vies dictées d'outre-tombe à Ermance Dufaux, agée de 14 ans, et publiées par elle. Jeanne d'Arc, par elle-même. 392 pp. 12°. *Melun, Desrues*, 1855.

Duffield (*Rev.* George). Dissertations on the prophecies relative to the second coming of Jesus Christ. xv, 9–434 pp. 12°. *New York, Dayton & Newman*, 1842.

Duffy (Charles Gavan). The ballad poetry of Ireland. 252 pp. 24°. *Dublin, J. Duffy*, 1845.

Du Four de Longuerue (Louis). *See* **Longuerue.**

Dufrénoy (Adélaïde Gillette Billet) *and* **Tastu** (Sabine Casimir Amable Voiart). Le livre des femmes, choix de morceaux extraits des meilleurs écrivains français, sur le caractère, les mœurs et l'esprit des femmes. 2 v. 1 p. l. xii, 352 pp; 2 p. l. 381 pp. 2 pl. 16°. *Paris, Persan* [*etc.*] 1823.

Dugan (James). History of Hurlbut's fighting fourth division; and especially the marches, toils, privations, adventures, skirmishes, and battles of the fourteenth Illinois infantry. 265 pp. 4 portraits. 12°. *Cincinnati, E. Morgan & co.* 1863.

Duguet (Jacques Joseph). The principles of the christian religion. [*anon.*] Translated from the french by the revd. Thomas Lally. 3 v. 8°. *London, J. Nourse*, 1749.

Duhamel du Monceau (Henri Louis). Art du chandelier. 1 p. l. 41 pp. 3 pl. fol. [*Paris*], 1764.
[*With* Malouin (Paul Jacques). Description et détails des arts du meunier. 1767].

Du Hautchamp (—). Histoire générale et particulière du visa fait en France pour la réduction et l'extinction de tous les papiers royaux et des actions de la compagnie des Indes, que le système des finances avoit enfantez. On y a joint un état des actionaires et des Mississippiens compris au rôle des taxes du 15. septembre 1722, avec des remarques sur leur fortunes présentes. [*anon.*] 2 v. in 1. xii, 240 pp; 1 p. l. 286 pp. 16°. *La Haye, F. H. Scheurleer*, 1743.

Duhring (Henry, *m. d.*) Essays on human happiness. 1 p. l. vi, 87 pp. 16°. *London, Longman, Green, Brown & Longmans*, [1848].

Dulwich gallery. A series of plates, from the most celebrated pictures in this collection, executed by R. Cockburn, custodian. 50 col. pl. fol. in port-folio. [*London, n. d.*]

Dumas (Alexandre). Ange Pitou. Nouvelle éd. 2 v. 2 p. l. 342 pp; 2 p. l. 338 pp. 16°. *Paris, M. Lévy frères*, 1860.
——— Aventures de Lyderic. 280 pp. 16°. *Bruxelles, Meline, Cans & cie.* 1842.
——— Les compagnons de Jéhu. 2 v. 2 p. l. 380 pp; 1 p. l. 395 pp. 12°. *Paris, librairie nouvelle*, 1859.
——— De Paris à Astrakan. Nouvelles impressions de voyage. 1e–3e série. 3 v. 16°. *Paris, librairie nouvelle*, 1860.
——— Jehanne la pucelle. 1429–31. 2 p. l. 275 pp. 16°. *Bruxelles, Meline, Cans & cie.* 1842.
——— Louis quinze. 4 v. 16°. *Bruxelles, Meline, Cans & cie.* 1849–50.
——— Les mille et un fantômes. 3 v. 16°. *Bruxelles, Meline, Cans & cie.* 1849.
——— La régence et Louis quinze. Deux parties. 2 p. l. 466 pp. 1 l. 15 pl. 8°. *Paris, Malmenayde & de Riberolles*, 1855.

Dumas (Alexandre, *fils*). La dame aux perles. 2 p. l. 383 pp. 16°. *Paris, librairie nouvelle*, 1855.

Dumas (Jean Baptiste) *and* **Boussingault** (Jean Baptiste Joseph Dieudonné). The chemical and physiological balance of organic nature: an essay. Edited by D. P. Gardner, m. d. From the 3d edition, with new documents. 174 pp. 16°. *New York, Saxton & Miles*, 1844.

Dumersan (Théophile Marion). Notice des monumens exposés dans le cabinet des mé-

Dumersan (T. M.)—continued.
dailles et antiques de la bibliothèque du roi; suivie d'une description des objets les plus curieux que renferme cet établissement, de notes historiques sur sa fondation, ses accroissemens, etc Et d'un catalogue, d'empreintes de pierres gravées. 76 pp. 12 pl. 8°. *Paris, Journé*, 1819.

Dummer (Edward). Hand book for beginners in mechanical drawing. 1 p. l. 42 pp. 18°. *Newburyport (Mass.)* 1871.

Dummer (*Rev.* Jeremiah). A letter to a noble lord, concerning the late expedition to Canada. [*anon.*] 26 pp. 12°. *London, A. Baldwin*, 1712.

Dumolard (Henri François Élisabeth Étienne Orcel). Notice historique sur la vie de Charles Simon Favart. 8°. *Paris, L. Collin*, 1808.

[*In* FAVART (Charles Simon). Mémoires et correspondance, v. 1, pp. i–lxxxvi].

Dumont (Étienne). Souvenirs sur Mirabeau et sur les deux premières assemblées législatives. Ouvrage posthume publié par m. J. L. Duval. xxxii, 479 pp. 12 l. facs. 8°. *Paris, C. Gosselin*, 1832.

Dumont (George Marie Butel–). *See* **Butel-Dumont.**

Dumont (*Mrs.* Julia L.) Life sketches from common paths: a series of american tales. 286 pp. 12°. *New York, D. Appleton & co.* 1856.

Dumoulin (Alain). Grammatica latino-celtica, doctis ac scientiarum appetentibus viris composita. 6 p. l. 194 pp. 2 tables. 8°. *Pragæ Bohemorum*, 1800.

Du Moulin (Pierre). A vindication of the sincerity of the protestant religion in the point of obedience to sovereignes. Opposed to the doctrine of rebellion, authorised and practised by the pope and the jesuites. In answer to a jesuitical libel, entituled Philanax anglicvs. 12 p. l. 142 pp. 1 l. sm. 4°. *London, I. Redmayne*, 1664.

Du Moulin (Pierre, *fils*). A treatise on peace of soul, and content of mind. First corrected, improved, and re-published with notes, by M. Sartoris. And now translated into english, with additional notes, by John Scrope, d. d. 2 v. 6 p. l. xxxii, 295 pp; 2 p. l. 444 pp. 8°. *Salisbury, Millar*, 1765.

Dun (R. G.) and co. The mercantile agency reference book, (and key,) containing ratings of the merchants, manufacturers, and traders generally, throughout the United States and

Dun (R. G.) and co.—continued.
Canada. July, 1871; January, 1872. 2 v. 4°. *Philadelphia, R. G. Dun & co.* 1871–72.

Duncan (Archibald, *r. n.*) The british trident; or, register of naval actions; including authentic accounts of all the most remarkable engagements at sea, in which the british flag has been eminently distinguished; from the period of the memorable defeat of the spanish armada, to the present time. Chronologically arranged. 5 v. 12°. *London, J. Cundee*, 1805–09.

Duncan (Henry, *d. d.*) Sacred philosophy of the seasons; illustrating the perfections of God in the phenomena of the year. With important additions and some modifications to adapt it to american readers. By F. W. P. Greenwood. 4 v. 12°. *Boston, Marsh, Capen & Lyon*, 1839.

Duncan (*Rev.* John M.) An essay on the origin, character, and tendency of creeds and confessions of faith, as instruments of ecclesiastical power. 262 pp. 12°. *Baltimore, Cushing & sons*, 1834.

Duncan (John Shute). Botano-theology, an arranged compendium, chiefly from [James Edward] Smith, [rev. Patrick] Keith, and [Anthony Todd] Thomson. [With three appendices. *anon.*] iv, 112 pp. 8°. *Oxford, J. Parker*, 1825.

Duncan (William). The elements of logic. In four books. 239 pp. 12°. *New York, E. Duyckinck*, 1818.

Duncan (William C. *d. d.*) The tears of Jesus of Nazareth. 172 pp. 12°. *New York Sheldon & co.* 1860.

Dunglison (Robley, *m. d.*) History of medicine from the earliest ages to the commencement of the nineteenth century. Arranged and edited by Richard J. Dunglison, m. d. xii, 17–287 pp. 8°. *Philadelphia, Lindsay & Blakiston*, 1872.

—— History of the moxa. *See* **Larrey** (Dominique Jean). On the use of the moxa.

—— The medical student, or aids to the study of medicine. Including a glossary of the terms of the science, and of the mode of prescribing,—bibliographical notices of medical works; the regulation of different medical colleges of the union, etc. xii, 323 pp. 8°. *Philadelphia, Carey, Lea & Blanchard*, 1737.

—— New remedies: the method of preparing and administering them; their effects on

Dunglison (Robley, *m. d.*)—continued. the healthy and diseased economy, etc. 429 pp. 8°. *Philadelphia, A. Waldie*, 1839.

——— The same. 3d ed. xii, 9–541 pp. 8°. *Philadelphia, Lea & Blanchard*, 1841.

Dunham (Samuel Ashley). Lives of the most eminent literary and scientific men of Great Britain. Early writers. [*anon.*] 2 p. l. 392 pp. 16°. *London, Longman*, [*etc.*] 1840.

CONTENTS.

St. Columba, and the introduction of christianity and of civilization into North Britain.
Alfred the great, english civilization in the ninth century.
Chaucer, 1328–1400.

[*Note.*—Same as The cabinet cyclopædia, v. 36].

Dunlap (William). Thirty years ago; or the memoirs of a water-drinker. [*anon.*] 2 v. vii, 5–208 pp; 220 pp. 12°. *New York, Bancroft & Holley*, 1836.

Dunn (*Rev.* L. R.) The mission of the spirit; or, the office and work of the comforter in human redemption. 303 pp. 16°. *New York, Carlton & Lanahan*, 1871.

Dunn (Nathan). A descriptive catalogue of the chinese collection, in Philadelphia. With miscellaneous remarks upon the manners, customs, trade, and government of the celestial empire. 1 p. l. 120 pp. 8°. *Philadelphia, proprietor*, [1839].

Dunning (*Mrs.* A. K.) Bessie Haven, or the little girl who wanted to shine. By Nellie Grahame. [*pseudon.*] 72 pp. 2 pl. 18°. *Philadelphia, Presbyterian board of publication*, [1864].

——— Bet and Bounce. By Nellie Grahame. [*pseudon.*] 72 pp. 2 pl. 18°. *Philadelphia, Presbyterian board of publication*, [1871].

——— Carrie Trueman, or the girl who disobeyed her parents. By Nellie Grahame. [*pseudon.*] 107 pp. 3 pl. 18°. *Philadelphia, Presbyterian board of publication*, [1864].

——— Charlie Evans, or the boy who could not keep his temper. By Nellie Grahame. [*pseudon.*] 107 pp. 2 pl. 18°. *Philadelphia, Presbyterian board of publication*, [1864].

——— Diamonds reset. By Nellie Grahame. [*pseudon.*] Eng. title, 192 pp. 12°. *Philadelphia, Presbyterian board of publication*, 1863.

——— Fred. Wilson's sled. By Nellie Grahame. [*pseudon.*] 59 pp. 2 pl. 18°. *Philadelphia, Presbyterian board of publication*, 1869.

——— Grace and Polly. By Nellie Grahame. [*pseudon.*] 72 pp. 2 pl. 18°. *Philadelphia, Presbyterian board of publication*, [1871].

Dunning (*Mrs.* A. K.)—continued.

——— Harry Edwards, or the boy who told lies. By Nellie Grahame. [*pseudon.*] 72 pp. 2 pl. 18°. *Philadelphia, Presbyterian board of publication*, [1864].

——— Hattie Winthrop, or the little girl who could not guard her tongue. By Nellie Grahame. [*pseudon.*] 106 pp. 1 pl. 18°. *Philadelphia, Presbyterian board of publication*, [1864].

——— Jack Myers, or the boy who stole a penny. By Nellie Grahame. [*pseudon.*] 72 pp. 2 pl. 18°. *Philadelphia, Presbyterian board of publication*, [1864].

——— Little Annie's first bible lessons. By Nellie Grahame. [*pseudon.*] 175 pp. 3 pl. 18°. *Philadelphia, Presbyterian board of publication*, [1863].

——— Mary's new friends. By Nellie Grahame. [*pseudon.*] 72 pp. 2 pl. 18°. *Philadelphia, Presbyterian board of publication*, [1871].

——— Mrs. Latimer's meetings. By Nellie Grahame. [*pseudon.*] 72 pp. 2 pl. 18°. *Philadelphia, Presbyterian board of publication*, [1869].

——— Ned Turner, or the boy who said, "Wait a minute." By Nellie Grahame. [*pseudon.*] 140 pp. 18°. *Philadelphia, Presbyterian board of publication*, [1863]?

——— Rebella, or the shining way. By Nellie Grahame. [*pseudon.*] 144 pp. 3 pl. 18°. *Philadelphia, Presbyterian board of publication*, [1863].

——— Ruth Cummings, or the girl who could not deny herself. By Nellie Grahame. [*pseudon.*] 108 pp. 3 pl. 18°. *Philadelphia, Presbyterian board of publication*, [1864].

——— The step-mother's recompense, or mrs. Ellerton's trials and reward. By Nellie Grahame. [*pseudon.*] 283 pp. 16°. *Philadelphia, Presbyterian board of publication*, [1864].

——— Stories for the little ones. By Nellie Grahame. [*pseudon.*] 8 v. 16°. *Philadelphia, Presbyterian board of publication*, [1868].

CONTENTS.

Alice Townsend's garden. 60 pp. 1 pl.
Carrie's hard lesson. 60 pp. 1 pl.
The casket of gems. 60 pp. 1 pl.
Contrasts. 60 pp. 1 pl.
The golden rule. 60 pp. 1 pl.
Little home missionaries. 60 pp. 1 pl.
Shining lights. 60 pp. 1 pl.
Stray lambs. 60 pp. 1 pl.

——— The three homes, or three ways of spending the sabbath. By Nellie Grahame.

Dunning (*Mrs.* A. K.)—continued. [*pseudon.*] 216 pp. 3 pl. 18°. *Philadelphia, Presbyterian board of publication,* [1863].

——— Tim Harrison, or the boy that couldn't say no. By Nellie Grahame. [*pseudon.*] 108 pp. 3 pl. 18°. *Philadelphia, Presbyterian board of publication,* [1864].

Dunton (John). Heavenly pastime, or, pleasant observations on all the most remarkable passages throughout the holy bible, of the old and new testament. Newly allegoriz'd in several delightful dialogues, poems, similitudes, and divine fancies. 2d ed. 136 pp. 18°. *London, J. Dunton,* 1685.

Dupaty (Charles Marguerite Jean Baptiste Mercier). Lettres sur l'Italie. 2 v. viii, 252 pp; 1 p. l. 263 pp. 12°. *Rome,* 1789.

——— The same. Travels through Italy, in a series of letters; written in 1785. Translated from the french by an english gentleman. xii, 403 pp. 8°. *London, G. G. J. & J. Robinson,* 1788.

Dupin (François Pierre Charles). Force militaire de la Grande-Bretagne. 2 v. in 1. xvi, 280 pp; ix, 274 pp. 4°. *Paris, Bachelier,* 1820.

——— Force navale de la Grande-Bretagne. 2 v. in 1. xvi, 280 pp; vii, 284 pp. 4°. *Paris, Bachelier,* 1821.

Duplais (*Mm. aîné et jeune*). A treatise on the manufacture and distillation of alcoholic liquors. Translated and edited from the french. By M. McKennie, m. d. To which are added the United States internal revenue regulations for the assessment and collection of taxes on distilled spirits. xxviii, 17–743 pp. 15 pl. 8°. *Philadelphia, H. C. Baird,* 1871.

Duponcet (J. N.) Histoire de Gonsalve de Cordouë, surnommé le grand capitaine. 2 v. 17 p. l. 367 pp; 1 p. l. 342 pp. 5 l. 16°. *Paris, J. Mariette,* 1714.

Dupouy (F. C.) Raccolta di massime e pensieri tirati dai migliori autori antichi e moderni. Tradotte in lingua italiana. vii, 130 pp. 12°. *London, E. R. Bentley,* 1820.

Dupré (August). A treatise on the origin, nature, and varieties of wine. *See* **Thudichum** (J. L. W.) *and* **Dupré.**

Dupré de Saint-Maure (Émile). Anthologie russe, suivie de poésies originales. 3 p. l. xlv, 360 pp. 8°. *Paris, G. J. Trouvé,* 1823.

Dupuy (*Miss* Eliza A.) The cancelled will. 1 p. l. pp. 19–403. 12°. *Philadelphia, T. B. Peterson & brothers,* [1872].

Dupuy (*Rev.* Starke). Hymns and spiritual songs, selected and original. 7th ed: enlarged and greatly improved. 527 pp. 18°. *Louisville, (Ky.) Morton & Smith,* 1832.

Du Radier (J. F. Dreux). *See* **Dreux du Radier.**

Durand (David, *d. d.*) Poème sur la chute de l'homme, et les ravages de l'or et de l'argent. fol. *Londres,* 1729.

[*In* PLINIUS *secundus* (Caïus). Histoire naturelle de l'or et de l'argent, 2 p. l. pp. i–lxxii].

——— La vie de Jean Frédéric Ostervald, pasteur de Neufchâtel en Suisse. 2 p. l. xv, 307 pp. 8°. *Londres, T. Payne & fils,* 1778.

Durand (— *l'abbé*) **Melton** (Louis) *and* **Preti** (Jean). Stratégie raisonnée des ouvertures du jeu d'échecs, illustrée de nombreux diagrammes. xxiv, 444 pp. 8°. *Paris, J. Preti,* 1862.

Dürer (Albrecht). Albert Durer's designs of the prayer book. (1515. Reprint). 1 p. l. 8 pp. 44 pl. sm. fol. *London, R. Ackermann's lithographic press,* 1817.

——— The same. Oratio dominica delineationibus Alberti Düreri cincta. 4°. *Monachii, J. B. Dreselly,* [1839].

[*In* STOEGER (F. X.) Oratio dominica polyglotta].

Durham (*Rev.* James). Commentary upon revelation. *See* **Bible.** (*English*).

Durivage (Francis Alexander). A popular cyclopedia of history, ancient and modern, forming a copious historical dictionary of celebrated institutions, persons, places and things; with notices of the present state of the principal cities, countries and kingdoms of the known world: [also] a chronological view of memorable events. 1 p. l. 708 pp. 31 pl. 8°. *Boston, E. R. Broaders,* 1835.

Durkee (Silas, *m. d.*) A treatise on gonorrhœa and syphilis. xi, 442 pp. 8 col. pl. 8°. *Boston, J. P. Jewett & co.* 1859.

Du Rondel (Jacques). La vie d'Epicure. 5 p. l. 83 pp. 18°. *Paris, A. Cellier,* 1679.

Dussauce (H.) A general treatise on the manufacture of vinegar: theoretical and practical; as well as the fabrication of pyroligneous acid, wood vinegar, etc. etc. and a treatise on acetometry. With illustrations. 392 pp. 8°. *Philadelphia, H. C. Baird,* 1871.

——— A practical treatise on the fabrication of matches, gun cotton, colored fires and fulminating powders. 336 pp. 12°. *Philadelphia, H. C. Baird,* 1864.

Dutens (Louis). Des pierres précieuses et des pierres fines, avec les moyens de les connoître et de les évaluer. Nouv. éd. revue et

Dutens (Louis)—continued. augmentée par l'auteur. 152 pp. 1 l. 12°. *Florence, J. Molini,* [1780]?

——— Tables généalogiques des héros des romans; avec un catalogue des principaux ouvrages en ce genre. [*anon.* 2e éd.] 1 p. l. 21 tables. sm. 4°. *Londres, M. Edwards,* [1796].

——— Journal of travels made through the principal cities of Europe. Translated from the french, by John Highmore. [Also], an appendix: containing the roads of Italy; with some useful tables and hints to strangers who travel in France. 2 p. l. xxxi, 177, 26 pp. 8°. *London, J. Wallis,* 1782.

——— Memoirs of a traveller now in retirement. Written by himself. Interspersed with historical, literary and political anecdotes, relative to many of the principal personages of the present age. Translated from the french [of Duchillon, *pseudon.*] under the superintendence of the author. 5 v. 16°. *London, R. Phillips,* 1806.

[*Note.*—Vol. v entitled "Dutensiana; intended as a sequel to the Memoirs of a traveller," etc.]

Dutot (—). Réflexions politiques sur le commerce et les finances. 8°. [*Paris,* 1843].

[*In* DAIRE (Eugène). Économistes-financiers du 18e siècle. *Paris.* 1843. pp. 837–1008].

Duval (Amaury Pineux). Paris et ses monumens. *See* **Baltard** (Louis Pierre).

Du Verdier (Antoine). Prosopographie, ov description des hommes illvstres, et avtres renomméz. Auec vne ample chronique de ce qui s'est passé en toutes les parties du monde, depuis la création d'iceluy iusques à présent. Enrichie de figvres. 3 v. fol. *Lyon, P. Frelon,* 1603.

Du Verdier (Gilbert Saulnier). The love and armes of the greeke princes. Or, the romant of romants. Written in french by M. Verdere, and translated for Philip, earle of Pembroke and Montgomery. 3 v. in 1. fol. *London, T. Harper for T. Walkley,* 1640.

Duvillers (François). Les parcs et jardins créés et exécutés par F. Duvillers. 1e et 2e partie. 14 livraisons in portfolio. 56 pp. 28 pl. fol. *Paris, auteur,* [1867–70].

Duy (*Rev.* Albert William). Sermons. With a biographical sketch of the author, containing extracts from his papers. By Samuel A. Clark. 4 p. l. 17–355 pp. 8°. *Philadelphia, R. S. H. George,* 1846.

Dwyer (Edward). A compendium of the principal laws and regulations relating to the militia of Great Britain and Ireland; and of the duties of lords-lieutenants, [etc.] in connexion therewith. Preceded by a short history of the force from the period of its earliest organization to the present time. viii, 146 pp. 1 l. 12°. *London, Butterworths,* [1871].

Dyason (William). Philosophical and literary essays. A new ed. with considerable additions. 1 p. l. 175 pp. 16°. *London, T. Tegg,* 1808.

——— Poetry in letters, relative to books, men, and manners. v. 2. 2 p. l. 201 pp. 12°. *London, author,* [1804].

[*With his* Philosophical essays; imperfect, v. 1 wanting].

Dyche (*Rev.* Thomas). A new general english dictionary; peculiarly calculated for the use and improvement of such as are unacquainted with the learned languages. [Also], a compendious english grammar. Together with a supplement of the proper names of the most noted kingdoms, provinces, cities, towns, rivers, &c. throughout the known world. As also of the most celebrated emperors, kings, queens, &c. Finished by the late William Pardon. 16th ed. with the addition of the several market towns in England and Wales, [etc.] 456 l. 8°. *London, C. Bathurst,* 1777.

Dyckman (Jacob, *m. d.*) A dissertation on the pathology of the human fluids. 248 pp. 8°. *New York, author,* 1814.

Dyke (*Rev.* Daniel). The mystery of selfedeceiuing: or, a discovrse and discouery of the deceitfulnesse of mans heart. Published since his death, by his brother I. D. And now by him augmented and inlarged. 7 p. l. 438 pp. 6 l. 4°. *London, W. Stansby,* 1630.

Dyke (*Rev.* Jeremy). A worthy communicant: or a treatise, shewing the due order of receiving the sacrament of the Lord's supper. 527 pp. 16°. *London, J. Macock for L. Favvn,* 1657.

Dymond (Jonathan). Essays on the principles of morality, and on the private and political rights and obligations of mankind. With a preface, by the rev. George Bush. x, 19–432 pp. 8°. *New-York, Harper & brothers,* 1834.

——— The same. The principles of morality, and the private and political rights and obligations of mankind. Abridged, and provided with questions, by Caroline M. Kirkland.

Dymond (Jonathan)—continued. 263 pp. 16°. *New York, C. S. Francis & co.* 1842.

——— An inquiry into the accordancy of war with the principles of christianity; and an examination of the philosophical reasoning by which it is defended. With notes, by Thomas Smith Grimké. Together with an appendix. xx, 13–300 pp. 12°. *Philadelphia, I. Ashmead & co.* 1834.

Eadie (John, *d.d.*) An analytical concordance to the holy scriptures; or the bible presented under distinct and classified heads or topics. lxiv, 776 pp. 8°. *Boston, Gould & Lincoln*, 1857.

Eadmerus, Edmar, Edimerus, *or* Edmundus. Opera. 2 p. l. 216 pp. fol. *Lutetiae Parisiorum, Montalant*, 1721.

CONTENTS.

De vita S. Anselmi.
Historiæ novorum libri sex cum notis Johannis Seldeni.
De excellentia virginis Mariæ.
De quatuor virtutibus beatæ virginis Mariæ.
De beatitudine cœlestis patriæ.
De S. Anselmi similitudinibus.
[*In* ANSELMUS *cantuariensis* (*S.*) Opera. Ed. Lutetiae Parisiorum, 1721].

Eagle crag. By the author of the "Golden-ladder" series. [*anon.*] 203 pp. 3 pl. 16°. *New York, R. Carter & brothers*, 1871.
[Drayton-hall series, no. 5].

Eames (Jane Anthony). The budget closed. xiv, 368 pp. 12°. *Boston, Ticknor & Fields*, 1860.

Earle (*Rev.* A. B.) The rest of faith. 96 pp. 24°. *Boston, J. H. Earle*, 1871.

Earle (John, *bishop of Salisbury*). Micro-cosmographie, [or, a peace of the world discovered in essays and characters]. 1628. With additional characters from the 5th ed. of 1629; and the 6th ed. of 1633. Carefully edited by Edward Arber. 104 pp. 16°. *London, A. Murray & son*, 1868.
[ARBER's english reprints, v. 5, no. 12].

Earle (John, *rector of Swanswick*). The philology of the english tongue. viii, 599 pp. 16°. *Oxford, Clarendon press*, 1871.

Earle (Pliny, *m. d.*) Marathon, and other poems. 120 pp. 12°. *Philadelphia, H. Perkins*, 1841.

Early english text society. Publications. 11 v. 8°. *London, N. Trübner & co.* 1870–71.

CONTENTS.

BERNARD *de Clairvaux* (*Saint*). De cura rei familiaris, with some early scottish prophecies. Edited by J. R. Lumbey. (no. 42).
C. (R. *gent.*) The times' whistle: or a newe daunce of seven satires, and other poems. Now first edited by J. M. Cowper. (no. 48).

Early english text society—continued.

ELLIS (A. J.) An early english pronunciation. Part iii. Illustrations of the pronunciation of the 14th and 16th centuries. (Extra series, xiv).
FURNIVALL (F. J.) *and* Cowper (J. M.) *editors*. A supplicacyon for the beggers. Written about the year 1529 by Simon Fish. Now re-edited by F. J. Furnivall. With A supplycacion to our moste soueraigne lorde kynge Henry the eyght (1544), A supplication of the poore commons (1546), The decaye of England by the great multitude of shepe, 1550–3, edited by J. M. Cowper. (Extra series, xiii).
GREGORY I. *the great* (*Saint*). King Alfred's west-saxon version of Gregory's Pastoral care. With an english translation, the latin text, notes and an introduction. Edited by H. Sweet. Part i. (no. 45).
LAUDER (W.) Extant minor poetical works. Edited by F. J. Furnivall. (no. 41).
LUMBY (J. R. *editor*). Ratis raving, and other moral and religious pieces in prose and verse. (no. 43).
LYNDESAY (*Sir* D.) Minor poems. Edited by J. A. H. Murray. (no. 47).
MORRIS (R. *editor*). Legends of the holy rood; symbols of the passion and cross-poems. In old english of the 11th, 14th, and 15th centuries. (no. 46).
SMITH (T. *editor*). English gilds. The original ordinances of more than one hundred english gilds: [etc.] With a preliminary essay on the history and development of gilds, by Lujo Brentano. (no. 40).
STARKEY (T.) England in the reign of king Henry the eighth. A dialogue between cardinal Pole and Thomas Lusset. Edited by J. M. Cowper. Part ii. (Extra series, xii).

Early (The) life, campaigns, and public services of Robert E. Lee; with a record of the campaigns and heroic deeds of his companions in arms. By a distinguished southern journalist. [*anon.*] 26, 33–851 pp. 7 pl. 8°. *New York, E. B. Treat & co.* 1870.

Early (The) Saxons; or, the character and influence of the saxon race, illustrated in a history of the introduction of christianity into England. [*anon.*] 144 pp. 5 pl. 18°. *Philadelphia, American sunday school union*, [1842].

Eastburn (Robert). A faithful narrative of dangers and sufferings during his late captivity among the Indians. 45 pp. 8°. *Philadelphia, W. Dunlap*, 1758.
[HAZARD pamphlets, v. 9].

Eastlake (Charles Locke, *architect*). A history of the gothic revival. An attempt to show how the taste for mediæval architecture which lingered in England during the two last centuries has since been encouraged and developed. xvi, 427 pp. 36 pl. 4°. *London, Longmans, Green & co.* 1872.

Eastman (F. S.) A history of Vermont, from its first settlement to the present time. With a geographical account of the country, and a view of its original inhabitants. 110 pp. 16°. *Brattleboro, Holbrook & Fessenden*, 1828.

Eastman (Julia A.) The Romneys of Ridgemont. A story of the hills. 346 pp. 3 pl. 16°. *Boston, D. Lothrop & co.* 1871.

Eastman (J. R.) Report on observations of the eclipse, &c. made at Syracuse, Sicily. 4°. [*Washington*, 1871].

[*In* UNITED STATES. *Navy department*. (*Naval observatory*). Report on observations of the total solar eclipse of Dec. 22, 1870, pp. 121–132].

Eastman & co.'s guide book for the eastern coast of New England. *See* **Waite** (Otis F. R.)

Easton (Peter Z.) The scripture doctrine in reference to the seat of sin in the regenerate man. 125 pp. 16°. *New York, A. D. F. Randolph & co.* [1872].

Eastwood (Frances). Marcella: the fearless christian maiden. A tale of the early church. 329 pp. 2 pl. 16°. *New York, Dodd & Mead*, [1870].

Easy (An) introduction to the knowledge of nature. Adapted to the capacities of children. [*anon.*] 167 pp. 1 pl. 18°. *Philadelphia, American sunday school union*, [1846].

Eaton (Amos). Manual of botany for North America: containing generic and specific descriptions of the indigenous plants and common cultivated exotics, growing north of the gulf of Mexico. 6th ed. With the addition of the most approved natural arrangement of genera: also their etymologies and accentuation. 2 v. in 1. 401 pp; 138 pp. 12°. *Albany, O. Steele*, 1833.

——— Prodromus of a practical treatise on the mathematical arts: containing directions for surveying and engineering. 4 p. l. 192 pp. 12°. *Troy (N. Y.) E. Gates*, 1838.

Eaton (David). Scripture the only guide to religious truth. A narrative of the proceedings of the society of baptists in York, in relinquishing the popular systems of religion, from the study of the scriptures. [Also], a brief account of their present views. [1st ed.] viii, 134 pp. 8°. *York, author*, 1800.

Eaton (James H.) A key of solutions to examples in Eaton's Common school arithmetic. 143 pp. 12°. *Boston, Thompson, Bigelow & Brown*, [1871].

Eaton (Joseph H.) The army paymaster's manual. *See* **United States.** *War department.*

Eaton (*Rev.* T. R.) Shakespeare and the bible. iv, 188 pp. 8°. *London, J. Blackwood*, 1858.

——— The same. Shakespeare and the bible: showing how much the great dramatist was indebted to holy writ for his profound knowledge of human nature. Third thousand. 226 pp. 12°. *London, J. Blackwood*, [1860]?

Eatto (Timothy). Collection of hymns. *See* **Richardson** (Jacob D.) *and* **Eatto.**

Eberhard (Johann August). Charakteristik des freiherrn von Leibnitz. 1 p. l. 194 pp. 4 pl. 8°. *Leipzig, in der Jacobäerschen buchhandlung*, [1817].

——— Neue apologie des Sokrates, oder untersuchung der lehre von der seligkeit der heiden. Neue [3te] und verbesserte aufl. 2 v. xvi, 512 pp; xvi, 528 pp. 16°. *Berlin & Stettin, F. Nicolai*, 1776–78.

——— The same. Examen de la doctrine touchant le salut des payens, ou nouvelle apologie pour Socrate. Traduit de l'allemand [par Charles Guillaume Frédéric Dumas]. 4 p. l. 414 pp. 1 l. 8°. *Amsterdam, E. van Harrevelt*, 1773.

Eberle (John, *m. d.*) A treatise of the materia medica and therapeutics. 2d ed. with corrections. 2 v. xi, 327 pp; 401 pp. 8°. *Baltimore, S. & W. Meeteer*, 1825.

——— The same. 3d ed. enlarged and corrected. 2 v. xvi, 416 pp; 445 pp. 8°. *Philadelphia, J. Grigg*, 1830.

Ebers (George) The daughter of an egyptian king. Translated from the german by Henry Reed. 368 pp. 12°. *Philadelphia, J. B. Lippincott & co.* 1871.

Ebert (*Prof.*) Review of E. G. Sandras' Étude sur Chaucer considéré comme imitateur des trouvères (Paris, Durand, 1859), from the "Jahrbuch für romanische und englische literatur", Oct. - Dec. 1861, pages 85–106, translated by John W. Van Rees Hoets, and revised by the author. 2 p. l. 28 pp. 8°. *London, N. Trübner & co.* 1868.

[CHAUCER society publications. 2d series, no. 2. Essays on Chaucer, part 1.

Ebony (The) idol. *See* **Flanders** (*Mrs.* G. M.)

Ecce homo. 1827. *See* **Holbach** (Paul Henri Thiry, *baron* d').

Ecce orienti. *See* **Redding** (M. Wolcott).

Eccentric (The) magazine; or, lives and portraits of remarkable persons. 2 v. in 1. viii, 280 pp. 39 pl; viii, 304 pp. 37 pl. 4°. *London, G. Smeeton*, 1814.

Ecclesiastical (The) history society. Publications. 7 v. 8°. *Cambridge, university press*, 1847–52.

CONTENTS.

FIELD (Richard, *d. d.*) Of the church. Five books. 4 v. (no. 1).

HEYLIN (Peter, *d. d.*) Ecclesia restaurata; or, the history of the reformation of the church of England. With life of the author by John Barnard. Edited by J. C. Robertson. 2 v. (no. 4).

WOOD (Anthony à). Athenæ oxonienses. v. 1. Life of A. à Wood, written by himself. New ed. by P. Bliss. (no. 3).

[*Note.*—This society has been dissolved].

Echard (Laurence). Gazetteer. *See* **Ladvocat** (Jean Baptiste). Dictionnaire géographique.

Eck (Johann von). Der drit thail christenlicher predigen an den hohen festen vnd hochzeytlichen tagen, der hayligen, durch das ganntz jar, nach gebrauch christenlicher kirchen, zů gůt vnd nutz den frommen alten christen. 8 p. l. cccv l. fol. [*Ingolstat, Jörg Krapffen & Jacob Vogkers*, 1531].

Eckard (*Rev.* James Read). A personal narrative of residence as a missionary in Ceylon and southern Hindoostan, with statements respecting those countries and the operations of missionaries there. 254 pp. 18°. *Philadelphia, Perkins & Purves*, 1844.

Eclectic (The) magazine of foreign literature, science, and art. W. H. Bidwell, editor. [Monthly]. Jan. to Dec. 1871. New series, v. 13–14. [Complete series, v. 76–77]. 8°. *New York, E. R. Pelton*, 1871.

Eclectic (The) medical journal, edited by John M. Scudder, m. d. [Monthly]. Jan. to Dec. 1871. v. 31. 8°. *Cincinnati, J. M. Scudder*, 1871.

Economist (The), weekly commercial times, bankers' gazette, and railway monitor: a political, literary, and general newspaper. Jan. 7 to Dec. 30, 1871. v. 29. fol. *London, T. H. Meredith*, 1871.

Eddy (A. D.) The christian citizen. The obligations of the christian citizen, with a review of high church principles in relation to civil and religious institutions. 164 pp. 12°. *New York, J. S. Taylor*, 1843.

Eddy (Daniel Clarke, *d. d.*) The Percy family. 5 v. 16°. *Boston, A. F. Graves*, 1859–61.

CONTENTS.

v. 1. A visit to Ireland. 255 pp.
v. 2. Through Scotland and England. 256 pp.
v. 3. Paris to Amsterdam. 256 pp. 9 pl.
v. 4. The Baltic to Vesuvius. 256 pp.
v. 5. The Alps and the Rhine. 248 pp. 2 pl.

——— Roger Williams and the baptists. An historical discourse delivered before the Young men's christian union, in Hollis street church, Dec. 2, 1860. 146 pp. 16°. *Boston, A. F. Graves*, 1861.

——— Walter's tour in the east. 3 v. 16°. *New York, Sheldon & co.* 1863.

CONTENTS.

Walter in Athens. 226 pp. 4 pl.
Walter in Jerusalem. 220 pp. 4 pl.
Walter in Egypt. 229 pp. 3 pl.

[*Note.*—Three vols. wanting to complete the series].

Edgar (A. H.) John Bull and the papists; or, passages in the life of an anglican rector. 1 p. l. 472 pp. 12°. *London, T. Richardson & son*, 1846.

Edimerus. *See* **Eadmer.**

Edinburgh medical journal, combining The Monthly journal of medicine and the Edinburgh medical and surgical journal. [Monthly]. July, 1868, to June, 1871. v. 14–16 in 6 v. 8°. *Edinburgh, Oliver & Boyd*, 1869–71.

Edinburgh (The) review, or critical journal. [Quarterly]. Jan. 1871, to Oct. 1871. v. 133–134. 8°. *London, Longmans*, 1871–71.

Edinburgh (Royal college of physicians of). Supplement to catalogue of the library of the royal college of physicians of Edinburgh, 1863–70. viii, 279 pp. 1 pl. 8°. *Edinburgh, Crawford & M'Cabe*, 1870.

Edinburgh. (Royal infirmary). Pharmacopoeia pauperum, in usum nosocomii regii edinburgensis. [Interleaved, with notes in ms.] 76 pp. 16°. *Edinburgi, apud Hamilton, Balfour & Neill, sumptibus nosocomii*, 1752.

Edith; or, the quaker's daughter. A tale of puritan times. By one of her descendants. [*anon.*] 407 pp. 12°. *New York, Mason brothers*, 1856.

Edkins (*Rev.* Joseph). The religious condition of the Chinese: with observations on the prospects of christian conversion amongst that people. viii, 288 pp. 16°. *London, Routledge, Warnes & Routledge*, 1859.

Edkins (Joshua). A collection of poems, mostly original, by several hands. 2 v. xxxix, 328 pp; xii, 364 pp. 8°. *Dublin, editor*, 1789–90.

Edmar. *See* **Eadmerus.**

Edmund (*Mrs.* A. M.) Memoir of mrs. Sarah D. Comstock, missionary to Arracan. 228 pp. 1 portrait. 12°. *Philadelphia, American baptist publication society*, [1854].

Edmunds (A. C.) Pen sketches of Nebraskans, with photographs. 510 pp. 20 photographs. 8°. *Lincoln (Nebraska), R. & J. Wilbur*, 1871.

Edmundus. *See* **Eadmer.**

Edna Harrington; or, the daughter's influence in the home circle. [*anon.*] 311 pp. 5 pl. 16°. *New York, American tract society*, [1871].

Edson (Ambrose). The key-stone: or a familiar illustration of important scripture

Edson (Ambrose)—continued. truth. 159 pp. 16°. *Hartford, D. Burgess*, 1835.

——— Memoir of Charlotte Hamilton, illustrating the reality and power of godliness in childhood. 3d ed. 162 pp. 18°. *Boston, Massachusetts sabath-school society*, [1853].

Educational (The) year-book, 1872. A handbook of reference, comprising a digest of american public school laws, systems of instruction, and interesting matters pertaining to schools and colleges, ranging from professional anecdotes to educational statistics. Published annually. [By William B. Smith]. 222 pp. 12°. *New York, A. S. Barnes & co.* 1872.

Edward and Miriam. A tale of Iceland. [*anon.*] 204 pp. 16°. *Philadelphia, American sunday-school union*, [1836].

Edward Clifford; or, memories of childhood. [*anon.*] 342 pp. 6 pl. 16°. *New York, R. Carter & brothers*, 1856.

Edward Wortley Montagu. An autobiography. [*anon.*] 3 v. 8°. *London, F. C. Newby*, 1869.

——— The same. 540 pp. 12°. *Philadelphia, Turner & co.* 1870.

Edwards (*Rev.* Bela Bates). Memoir of the rev. Elias Cornelius. 360 pp. 1 portrait. 12°. *Boston, Perkins & Marvin*, 1833.

——— Missionary gazetteer. 8°. [*Brattleboro', (Vt.)* 1858].

[*In* BROWN (*Rev.* J. Newton). Encyclopedia of religious knowledge, pp. 1187–1275].

Edwards (*Mrs.* C. M.) Benjie and his friends; or, coming up and going down. 196 pp. 18°. *New York, Carlton & Porter*, [1860].

——— Helpful Susan: the story of a girl who made herself useful. 288 pp. 18°. *New York, Carlton & Porter*, [1862].

——— The little brown jug; or, the power of prayer. 216 pp. 18°. *New York, Carlton & Porter*, [1863].

——— Minnie Ray: a story of faith and good works. 198 pp. 18°. *New York, Carlton & Porter*, 1857.

——— My sister Margaret. A temperance story. 328 pp. 4 pl. 16°. *New York, Carlton & Porter*, 1859.

——— Sammy Seymour, the drunkard's boy. A story for boys. 219 pp. 18°. *New York, Carlton & Porter*, [1861].

——— Soft words; or, gentle Susan. A tale of every day life. 144 pp. 18°. *Boston, Mass. sabbath-school soc.* [1853].

Edwards (*Mrs.* C. M.)—continued.

——— Sylvia Austin; or, the girl who stole a cent: and Benny Blubber, the crying boy. 130 pp. 2 pl. 18°. *New York, Carlton & Porter*, [1859].

——— A winter at Quakerville; or, Lizzie's history of herself. Being incidents at the close of the late war. 126 pp. 18°. *Boston, Mass. sabbath-school soc.* [1853].

Edwards (Henri Milne). Leçons sur la physiologie et anatomie comparée de l'homme et des animaux faites à la faculté des sciences de Paris. v. 1–7. 8°. *Paris, V. Masson*, 1857–62. s.

CONTENTS.

v. 1. Introduction. Du sang. De la respiration.
v. 2. De la respiration. [Suite].
v. 3. De la circulation du sang.
v. 4. De la circulation du sang. [Suite]. De la transsudation. Du système lymphatique.
v. 5. De l'absorption. De la digestion.
v. 6. De la digestion. [Suite]. Des organes complémentaires du canal intestinal des vertébrés.—Appareil hépatique. Appareil pancréatique.
v. 7. Des phénomènes chimiques de la digestion. De l'absorption des produits du travail digestif. Des sécrétions. Des excrétions. De la nutrition.

——— Recherches zoologiques pour servir à l'histoire de la faune de l'Amérique centrale et du Mexique. *See* **France.** *Ministère de l'instruction publique.*

——— Outlines of anatomy and physiology, translated from the French. By J. F. W. Lane, m. d. 312 pp. 8°. *Boston, C. C. Little & J. Brown*, 1841.

Edwards (John, *d. d.*) The preacher. A discourse, shewing, what are the particular offices and employments of those of that character in the church. With a free censure of the most common failings and miscarriages of persons in that sacred employment. 1 p. l. xxxviii pp. 13 l. 358 pp. 5 l. 1 portrait. 8°. *London, J. Robinson*, [*etc.*] 1705.

——— Veritas redux. Evangelical truths restored: namely, those concerning God's eternal decrees, the liberty of man's will, grace and conversion, the extent and efficacy of Christ's redemption, and perseverance in grace. 1 p. l. xxxviii, 558 pp. 1 l. 8°. *London, J. Robinson*, [*etc.*] 1707.

Edwards (Jonathan, *d. d. president of the coll. of N. J.*) The life and character of the late rev. Jonathan Edwards. [By Samuel Hopkins]. Together with a number of his sermons on various important subjects. 5 p. l. 97 pp. 4 l. 279 pp. 12°. *Boston, S. Kneeland*, 1765.

——— Two dissertations, i. Concerning the end for which God created the world. ii,

Edwards (Jonathan)—continued. The nature of true virtue. 1 p. l. v, 191 pp. 12°. *Boston, S. Kneeland*, 1765.
[*With his* Life and character, 1765].

Edwards (Jonathan, *d. d. president of Union college*). Works: with a memoir of his life and character. By Tryon Edwards. 2 v. xl, 518 pp. 1 portrait; 556 pp. 8°. *Andover, Allen, Morrill & Wardwell*, 1842.

——— An humble attempt to promote explicit agreement and visible union of God's people in extraordinary prayer, for the revival of religion and the advancement of Christ's kingdom on earth, pursuant to scripture-promises and prophecies concerning the last time. With a preface by several ministers. [Reprint]. 8°. *Elizabethtown, (N. J) S. Kollock*, 1794.
[*In* AUSTIN (*Rev.* David, *editor*). The millenium. *Elizabethtown*, 1794. pp. 51–321].

Edwards (Richard). Chicago census report, 1871. *See* **Chicago**.

——— Directories. *See* **Memphis, New Orleans, St. Louis.**

Edwards (Tryon, *d. d.*) Memoir of Jonathan Edwards, d. d. 8°. [*Andover*, 1842].
[*In* EDWARDS (Jonathan, *pres. Union coll.*) Works. v. 1. pp. 9–40].

——— Pearls; or, the world's laconics. Being choice thoughts of the best authors, in prose and poetry. With an introduction by William B. Sprague, d. d. 432 pp. 1 pl. 12°. *Boston, B. B. Russell*, 1872.

Edwards (William). The book-keeper's atlas: or, a perfect system of book keeping, by double entry; founded on principles of real business. 205 pp. 4°. *New York, Harper & brothers*, 1834.

Effigies poeticae: or the portraits of the british poets illustrated by notes biographical, critical, and poetical. [*anon.*] 2 p. l. ii, 112 pp. 12°. *London, J. Carpenter & son*, 1834.

Effinger (Conrad Maria). Geistlicher wegweiser für jünglinge. Ein lehr- und gebetbuch für christliche jünglinge. 512 pp. 24°. *Einsiedeln, New York & Cincinnati, C. & N. Benziger*, 1871.

——— Die sternenkrone der allezeit unbefleckten gottesmutter Maria. Betrachtungen über ihr heiligstes leben als vorbild jeder tugend. Mit einer Maiandacht, [etc.] 430 pp. 2 pl. 18°. *Einsiedeln, New York & Cincinnati, C. & N. Benziger*, 1870.

Egerton (Harriet Catherine Greville, *viscountess of Ellesmere*). Journal of a tour in the holy land, in May and June, 1840. With

Egerton (H. C. G.)—continued. lithographic views, from original drawings, by lord Francis Egerton. 4 p. l. 141 pp. 1 l. 4 pl. 8°. *London, Harrison & co.* 1841.

Egerton (John). Egerton's theatrical remembrancer, containing a complete list of all the dramatic performances in the english language; their several editions, dates and sizes, and the theatres where they were originally performed: together with an account of those which have been acted and are unpublished, and a catalogue of such latin plays as have been written by english authors, from the earliest production of the english drama to the end of the year 1787. [Also] notitia dramatica, being a chronological account of events relative to the english stage. vii, 354 pp. 12°. *London, T. & J. Egerton*, 1787.

Eggleston (Edward, *d. d.*) The hoosier schoolmaster. A novel. 226 pp. 12 pl. 12°. *New York, O. Judd & co.* 1871.

Egleston (T.) Tables of weights, measures, coins, &c. of the United States and England, with their equivalents in the french decimal system. ix, 60 pp. 16°. *New York, J. Wiley & son*, 1871.

Egliseau (S. S.) Gleanings from real life. 180 pp. 1 pl. 18°. *Philadelphia, Presbyterian board of publication*, [1856].

——— Lizzie Ferguson, or the sabbath-school scholar. 180 pp. 4 pl. sq. 18°. *Philadelphia, Presbyterian board of publication*, [1856].

——— Lucy Dunlevy, a sketch from life. 156 pp. 2 pl. sq. 18°. *Philadelphia, Presbyterian board of publication*, [1856].

Egyptisches traumbuch. *See* **Mönches** (Des) Aegydius Lebrecht egyptisches traumbuch.

Ehinger (Elias). Thesavrvs antiqvitatvm eruditione ecclesiastica refertissimus, h. e. opus historicum omnibus omnino, cujuscunque sint religionis, utilissimum, [etc.] 6 p. l. 849 pp. 4°. *Francofurti, sumpt. T. M. Götzii*, 1662.

Eibergen (Rutgerus). Swymel-klacht des spaenschen konincks Philippi qvarti, over het eerste verlies van sijn silver-vlote, [8 Sept. 1628]: waer mede dese landen, door Gods hulpe, verrijckt heeft den zee-ridder generael Pieter Pietersen Heyn. 16 pp. sm. 4°. *Amstelredam, W. I. Stam*, 1629.

Eigendliche beschreibung des lands Guiana, welches gelegen an der vesten meergrentzenden landschafft America. [*anon.*] 63 pp. 1 map. sm. 4°. *Bärn, S. Kneubüler*, 1677.

Einault (Louis). Christine. From the french. 171 pp. 16°. *New York, J. S. Redfield*, 1871.

Einstein (Morris). Origin and development of religious ideas and beliefs, as manifested in history and seen by reason. 2 p. l. 270 pp. 12°. *Titusville (Pa.) Daily Courier steam print*, 1871.

Eirenæus *philoponos philalethes* (*pseudon.*) A true light of alchymy. Containing i. A correct edition of the Marrow of alchymy. ii. The errors of a late tract called, A short discourse of the quintessence of philosophers. iii. The method and materials pointed at, composing the sophick mercury, and transmuting elixir. 3 p. l. 98 pp. 16°. *London, I. Dawks for the author*, 1709.

[*With* URBIGERUS (Baro). Aphorismi urbigerani. 1690. Imperfect: pp. 93–96 wanting.

Note.—Sir George Ripley wrote a Medulla alchemiae translated into english by William Salmon, in 1692. The pseudonym Eirenæus philoponus philalethes has been explained as indicating George Starkey].

Eisenlohr (G. W.) Leitfaden zum religionsunterricht in den evangelisch-protestant. kirchen Amerika's. 48 pp. 12°. *Cincinnati*, 1869.

Ekman (Fredric Joachim). Beskrifning om Runö i Liffland. 4 p. l. 326, x pp. 8°. *Tavastehus, G. Nordenswan*, 1847.

[Imperfect: 1 plate wanting].

Elci (*Count* d'). The present state of the court of Rome: containing the life and character of the late pope Clement xi. and a short account of his elevation to the papacy, and of the most remarkable occurrences in his pontificate; with the lives and characters of all the cardinals who assisted at the last conclave, [etc.] Translated from an italian manuscript never yet publish'd. With a preface on the rise and nature of the college of cardinals. xlvii, 400 pp. 12°. *London, G. Strahan*, 1721.

Eldad *had-dani.* Relation d'Eldad le danite voyageur du ixe siècle; traduite en français suivie du texte hébreu et d'une lettre chaldéenne. Par E. Carmoly. 2 p. l. 59 pp. 20 l. 8°. *Paris, la librairie orientale de mad. ve. Dondey-Dupré*, 1838.

Elder (Walter). The cottage garden of America; containing practical directions for the culture of flowers, fruits, and vegetables. 233 pp. 12°. *Philadelphia, Moss & brother*, 1849. S.

Elderhorst (William, *m. d.*) A manual of blowpipe-analysis, and determinative mineralogy. 2d ed. xviii, 11–176 pp. 12°. *Philadelphia, T. E. Zell*, 1861.

Eldon (Abraham). The continental traveller's oracle; or, maxims for foreign locomotion. Edited by his nephew. 2 v. viii, 277 pp; 1 p. l. 285 pp. 16°. *London, H. Colburn*, 1828.

Eldridge (Abby, *pseudon*) Kate Stanley, or the power of perseverance. 200 pp. 2 pl. 18°. *Philadelphia, Presbyterian board of publication*, [1863].

——— Walter and Alice, or the mother's prayer answered. 179 pp. 3 pl. 18°. *Philadelphia, Presbyterian board of publication*, [1863].

Eldridge (C. S. *m. d.*) Self-enervation: its consequences and [homœopathic] treatment. With an introduction by prof. Joseph Hooper, m. d. 64 pp. 12°. *Chicago, C. S. Halsey*, 1869.

Elegantiores præstantium virorum satyræ. 2 v. [v. 1 in two parts]. Eng. title, 5 p. l. 170, [12 l.], 280 pp. 6 l; 1 p. l. 281–940 pp. 18°. *Lugduni Batavorum, ex officinâ I. Maire*, 1655.

CONTENTS.

BENCI (F.) Oratio, ante serias autumnales.
BODECHER (Jan). Satyricon in corruptæ juventutis mores corruptos.
DUCHATEL (P.) Ludus, sive convivium saturnale.
FABRICUS (V.) Satyra, pransus paratvs.
FERRARI (O.) Satyrica quædam. Momus, sive satyra varroniania.
JULIANUS *imp.* (F. C.) Cæsares, sive satyra in romanos imperatores. [P. Martin et C. Comteclair, interpretibus]. Misopogon.
KUN (P. van der). Sardi venales, in hujus saeculi homines plerosque inepte eruditos.
LIPSIUS (Justus). Satyra menippæa. Somnium.
NANNINCK (P.) Somnium, sive paralipomena Virgili.
PUTTEN (H. van der). Comus, sive phagesiposia cimmeria.
RIGAULT (N.) Funus parasiticum.
SANGENESIUS (J.) De Parnasso.
SENECA (L. A.) Clavdii Cæsaris apocolocyntosis.

Elements (The) of logic. *See* **Bushby** (*Rev.* Edward).

Elements of mythology; or, classical fables of the Greeks and Romans; to which are added some notices of syrian, hindu, and scandinavian superstitions, together with those of the american nations; the whole comparing polytheism with true religion. By the author of "American popular lessons." [*anon.*] xii, 348 pp. 18°. *Philadelphia, Towar J. & D. M. Hogan*, 1830.

Élie de Beaumont (Jean Baptiste Armand Louis Léonce). Leçons de géologie pratique. v. 1. xi, 557 pp. 9 pl and maps. 8°. *Paris, P. Bertrand*, 1845. S.

[v. 2-3 wanting].

Eliot (Charles W.) *and* **Storer** (Francis H.) An elementary manual of chemistry. Abridged from Eliot and Storer's manual,

Eliot (C. W.) *and* **Storer** (F. H.)—continued. with the co-operation of the authors. By Wm. Ripley Nichols. xii, 287, lxiii pp. 12°. *New York, Ivison, Blakeman, Taylor & co.* 1872.

Eliot (*Rev.* Jared). A continuation of the essay upon field-husbandry, as it is, or may be ordered in New-England. 5th part. 44 pp. 16°. *New York, J. Parker & W. Weyman,* 1754.
[HAZARD pamphlets, v. 104].

——— The same. The sixth essay on field-husbandry in New-England. 34 pp. 8°. *New Haven, J. Parker & co.* 1759.
[HAZARD pamphlets, v. 50].

——— The two witnesses; or, religion supported by reason and divine revelation. Being the substance of a lecture-sermon, preach'd at the North-society in Lyme, October 29, 1735, before the Association of the county of New-London; and published at their desire. 1 p. l. 79 pp. 16°. *N. London, T. Green,* 1736.

Eliot (Samuel). Passages from the history of liberty. viii, 278 pp. 12°. *Boston, W. D. Ticknor & co.* 1847.

Eliot (W. G. *d. d.*) A manual of prayer, for public and private worship; with a collection of hymns. [*anon.* Preface subscribed W. G. E.] 2d ed. 314 pp. 12°. *Boston, J. Munroe & co.* 1845.

Eliot. *See* **Elyot.**

Eliza Woodson. [A novel]. *See* **Farnham** (Eliza W.)

Elkswatawa; or, the prophet of the west. *See* **French** (James S.)

Ellery (Robert L. J.) Astronomical observations at the Melbourne observatory. *See* **Victoria.** (*Australia*). *Melbourne observatory.*

Ellesmere (Harriet C. G. Egerton, *viscountess of*). *See* **Egerton.**

Ellet (*Mrs.* Elizabeth Fries Lummis). The new cyclopædia of domestic economy, and practical housekeeper. 603 pp. 8°. *Norwich* (*Conn.*) *H. Bill,* 1872.

——— Poems, translated and original. 229 pp. 16°. *Philadelphia, Key & Biddle.* 1835.

——— Rambles about the country. 257 pp. 18°. *Boston, Marsh, Capen, Lyon & Webb,* 1840.

——— Scenes in the life of Joanna of Sicily. 256 pp. 12°. *Boston, Marsh, Capen, Lyon & Webb,* 1840.

Ellicott (Charles John, *bishop of Gloucester and Bristol*). A commentary, critical and grammatical, on st. Paul's epistle to the Galatians. *See* **Bible.** (*Greek*).

——— Historical lectures on the life of our Lord Jesus Christ, being the Hulsean lectures for the year 1859. With notes, critical, historical, and explanatory. 382 pp. 12°. *Boston, Gould & Lincoln,* 1862.

Elliot (Nathan, *editor*). The columbian preacher; or, a collection of original sermons, from preachers of eminence in the United States. Embracing the distinguishing doctrines of grace. v. 1. 304 pp. 8°. *Cattskill,* (*N. Y.*) *N. Elliot,* 1808.

Elliotson (John, *m. d.*) The principles and practice of medicine. Edited by Nathaniel Rogers, m. d. and Alexander Cooper Lee. 1st amer., from the 2d London ed. With notes and additions by Thomas Stewardson, m. d. 1046 pp. 8°. *Philadelphia, Carey & Hart,* 1844.

Elliott (*Rev.* David). Letters on the general structure, government, laws and discipline of the church; embracing some remarks on creeds and confessions of faith. 200 pp. 12°. *Chambersburg, author,* 1826.

——— The life of the rev. Elisha Macurdy. With an appendix, containing brief notices of various deceased ministers of the presbyterian church in western Pennsylvania. 323 pp. 1 portrait. 12°. *Allegheny, Kennedy & brother,* 1848.

Elliott (E. N. *ll. d.*) Cotton is king, and pro-slavery arguments: comprising the writings of Hammond, Harper, Christy, Stringfellow, Hodge, Bledsoe, and Cartwright, on this important subject. With an essay on slavery in the light of international law, by the editor. 908 pp. 5 portraits. 8°. *Augusta* (*Ga.*) *Pritchard, Abbott & Loomis,* 1860.

Ellis (Alexander J.) On early english pronunciation, with especial reference to Shakspere and Chaucer, containing an investigation of the correspondence of writing with speech, in England, from the anglosaxon period to the present day, preceded by a systematic notation of all spoken sounds by means of the ordinary printing types. Including a re-arrangement of Prof. F. J. Child's memoirs on the language of Chaucer and Gower, and reprints of the rare tracts by Salesbury on english, 1547, and welch, 1567, and by Barcley on french, 1521. Parts 1-3. 8°. *London, Trübner & co.* 1869-70.

Ellis (Alexander J.)—continued.

CONTENTS.

Part 1. On the pronunciation of the xivth, xvith, xviith, and xviiith centuries.
Part 2. On the pronunciation of the xiiith and previous centuries, of anglosaxon, icelandic, old norse and gothic, with chronological tables of the value of letters and expression of sounds in english writing.
Part 3. Illustrations of the pronunciation of the xivth and xvith centuries. Chaucer, Gower, Wycliffe, Spencer, Shakspere, Salesbury, Barcley, Hart, Bullokar, Gill. Pronouncing vocabulary.

[CHAUCER society publications. 2d series, nos. 1, 4, and 5].

——— The same. Part 3. 8°. *London, Trübner & co.* 1871.

[EARLY english text society publications, extra series, no. 14].

Ellis (*Rev.* George Edward). A collection of psalms and hymns for the sanctuary. xxvii, 90 pp. 238 l. unp. 16°. *Boston, J. Munroe & co.* 1845.

——— The same. A collection of hymns for the sanctuary. Revised ed. with a supplement. xxxii, 90 pp. 275 l. unp. 16°. *Boston & Cambridge, J. Munroe & co.* 1860.

Ellis (George James Welbore Agar-, *baron Dover*). Lives of the most eminent sovereigns of modern Europe. From the second London edition. Eng. title, pp. 13–260. 16°. *New York, A. V. Blake*, 1844.

Ellis (Hercules). Romances and ballads of Ireland. xxxi, 432 pp. 18°. *Dublin, J. Duffy*, 1850.

Ellmaker (Elias E.) The revelation of rights. 202 pp. 8°. *Columbus, (O.) publisher*, 1841.

——— The same. 2d ed. 152 pp. 12°. *Pittsburgh, A. A. Anderson*, 1847.

Elmira (*N. Y.*) Boyd's directory: (etc.) A business directory of Elmira, Horseheads, Wellsburg, and other towns. 1871–72. 8°. *A. & H. W. Boyd*, [1870].

Elmwood; or, the inalienable inheritance. [*anon.*] 284 pp. 2 pl. 16°. *Boston, Congregational publishing society*, [1870].

Elogj di Dante Alighieri [etc.] *See* **Fabroni** (Angelo).

Elphinston (James). Forty years' correspondence between geniusses ov boath sexes and James Elphinston: in six pocket-vollumes: foar ov oridginal letters, two' ov poetry. 6 v. in 3. 12°. *London, W. Richardson*, 1791.

——— The same. v. 7–8. 12°. *London, W. Richardson*, 1794.

Elsing (Henry). Notes of the debates in the house of lords, a. d. 1621. *See* **Great Britain.** (*Parliament*).

Elvert (Christian, *ritter* d'). Geschichte der k. k. mähr.-schles. gesellschaft zur beförderung des ackerbaues, der natur- und landeskunde, mit rücksicht auf die bezüglichen cultur-verhältnisse Mährens und österr. Schlesiens. Verlag der genannten gesellschaft. 2 p. l. 503, 384 pp. 8°. *Brünn, R. M. Rohrer*, 1870. s.

[*Note.*—"Bildet den 4. band seiner beiträge zur cultur-geschichte Mährens und Schlesiens"].

Elwes (Alfred). Ralph Seabrooke: or, the adventures of a young artist in Piedmont and Tuscany. xv, 366 pp. 1 l. 6 pl. 16°. *London, Griffith & Farran*, 1861.

Ely (*Mrs.* Caroline T. Holmes). Memoir of Harriet Ann Holmes, by her sister. 108 pp. 16°. *Philadelphia, Perkins & Purves*, 1844.

Elyot *or* **Eliot** (*Sir* Thomas). The castel of helth corrected and in some places augmented by the fyrste authour therof. [3d ed.] 8 p. l. 94 l. sm. 4°. *Londini, T. Berthelet*, 1541.

Elysium: a prelude. As acted on her majesty's birth-day, by his majesty's royal company of comedians at Hanover. [Translated from the german. *anon.*] 16°. [*London, D. Brewman for J. Searle*, 1789].

[*In* SENTIMENTAL love illustrated in Charmides and Theone [etc.] *London*, 1789. pp. 163–204].

Elze (Carl). Lord Byron, a biography. With a critical essay on his place in literature. Translated with the author's sanction, and edited with notes. xxii, 516 pp. 1 fac-simile, 1 portrait. 8°. *London, J. Murray*, 1872.

Emblemata amatoria: iam demum emendata. [*anon.*] Eng. title, 30 l. incl. 24 pl. obl. 8°. *Amstelredam, D. Pietersz*, 1612.

Embury (*Mrs.* Emma Catharine Manley). Constance Latimer; or, the blind girl. With other tales. 169 pp. 18°. *New-York, Harper & brothers*, 1838.

Emerald (The): an illustrated journal. [Weekly]. Feb. 8, 1868, to Aug. 6, 1870. v. 1–6. fol. *New York, D. O'Sullivan & co. and Emerald publishing co.* 1868–70.

[*Note.*—No more published: *succeeded by* The American celt. v. 3, 4, and 5 incomplete].

Éméric-David (Toussaint Bernard). Histoire de la peinture au moyen âge, suivie de l'histoire de la gravure, du discours sur l'influence des arts du dessin, et du musée olympique. Avec une notice sur l'auteur par P. L. Jacob, bibliophile [Paul Lacroix]. 2 p. l. xxx, 318 pp. 1 l. 16°. *Paris, Charpentier*, 1852.

Emerson (George B.) *and* **Flint** (Charles Louis). Manual of agriculture, for the school, the farm, and the fireside. vi, 306 pp. 12°. *Boston, Swan, Brewer & Tileston,* 1862.

Emerson (L. O.) The national chorus book. A choice collection of oratorio and opera choruses, glees, etc. 203 pp. 8°. *Boston, O. Ditson & co.* [1871].

——— *and* **Mathews** (W. S. B.) The Emerson method for reed organs; containing easy and progressive lessons, scales and studies; voluntaries, interludes, songs and quartettes, [etc.] 160 pp. obl. 4°. *Boston, O. Ditson & co.* 1872.

——— *and* **Tilden** (W. S.) The hour of singing, a book for high schools; seminaries, and the social choir. 240 pp. obl. 8°. *Boston, O. Ditson & co.* [1871].

Emerson (Ralph, *d. d. prof. at Andover*). Life of rev. Joseph Emerson, pastor of the third congregational church, in Beverly, Ms. and subsequently principal of a female seminary. 454 pp. 12°. *Boston, Crocker & Brewster,* 1834.

Emmerich (Anna Catherine). Vie de n. s. Jésus Christ d'après les visions de la sœur Anne-Catherine Emmerich, recueillies par Clémente Brentano. [Traduite et] précédée d'une introduction [par l'abbé Edmond de Cazalis]. 6 v. 16°. *Paris, H. Casterman,* 1860.

Emmons (Samuel B). The vegetable family physician: containing a description of the roots and herbs common to this country, with their medicinal properties and uses: also directions for the treatment of diseases incident to human nature, by vegetables alone; embracing many valuable indian recipes. 5 p. l. 7–176 pp. 16°. *Boston, G. P. Oakes,* 1836.

Emory (John, *d. d. bishop m. e. church*). The episcopal controversy reviewed. Edited by his son, from an unfinished manuscript. 183 pp. 1 portrait. 8°. *New York, T. Mason & G. Lane,* 1838.

Emory (*Rev.* Robert). History of the discipline of the methodist episcopal church. 350 pp. 12°. *New York, G. Lane & P. P. Sandford,* 1844.

——— The life of the rev. John Emory, d. d. By his eldest son. With an appendix. 380 pp. 1 portrait. 8°. *New York, G. Lane,* 1841.

Empie (Adam, *d. d.*) Sermons on various subjects, written and preached at different places and times during his public ministry of forty-four years. 511 pp. 12°. *New York, Dana & co.* 1856.

Énault (Louis). The pupil of the legion of honor. Translated from the french, by mrs. Rebecca L. Tuft. 1 p. l. 185 pp. 8°. *Philadelphia, Porter & Coates,* [1871].

Enchanted (The) plants. *See* **Montolieu** (*Mrs.*)

Encyclopädisches wörterbuch der medicinischen wissenschaften. Herausgegeben von den professoren der medicinischen facultät zu Berlin. 36 v. 8°. *Berlin, J. W. Boike et al.* 1828–47. s.

Enfield (William). Young artist's assistant, or elements of the fine arts. 6th ed. 2 p. l. 319 pp. 6 pl. 12°. *London, T. Tegg,* [*about* 1812].

Engagement (The): a novel. [*anon.*] 3 v. 12°. *London, H. Colburn,* 1841.

Engel (Johann Jakob). Essays and tales, moral, literary, and philosophical. From the original german, by Thomas Horne. ix, 336 pp. 1 pl. 16°. *London, J. Coxhead,* 1808.

Engelbrecht (Hans *or* Johann). Eine warhafftige geschicht und gesicht vom himmel und der hellen. Diss ist nun die historie und gesicht, das erste gesichte, da Gott der heilige geist mir Hans Engelbrecht hat wieder vom todte erwecket. Diese wunder aber sindt geschehen im jahre 1622. 22 l. sm. 4°. [*n. p.*] 1625.

Engelmayr (F. Angelus). Series impedimentorum matrimonii dirimentium juxta principia theologiæ moralis, et juris pontificii ordinata, & divulgata anno, quo glacialis hyems: nix avxerat vudas. Ed 2ª aucta appendice de dispensatione super impedimentis. 7 p. l. 224 pp. 12°. *August. Vind. & Græcii, P. J. Veith & Wolff,* 1745.

——— Series impedimentorum matrimonii impedientium juxta principia theologiæ moralis, et juris pontificii ordinata, & divulgata anno, quo czechis Avgvstæ vertex redimitvr ab axe. Ed. 1ª aucta appendice de dispensatione super impedimentis. 4 p. l. 288 pp. 12°. *August. Vind. & Graecii, P. J. Veith & Wolff,* 1744.

[*With* the above].

England. *See* **Great Britain.**

England (Church of). *See* **Church** of England.

England (Royal agricultural society of). Journal. Second series, v. 7. 8°. *London, J. Murray*, 1871.

England and France in the 15th century. *See* **Débat** des héraulx darmes de frãce et dengleterre.

Engles (William M. *d.d.*) Rills from the fountain of wisdom, or the book of Proverbs illustrated. *See* **Bible.** (*English*).

English (The) catalogue of books for 1870 and 1871, containing a complete list of all the books published in Great Britain and Ireland [etc.] also, of the principal books published in the United States, with an index of subjects. 2 v. 8°. *London, S. Low, Marston,* [*etc.*] 1871-72.

Englishman (The). *See* **Steéle** (Richard).

Englmayr. *See* **Engelmayr.**

Ennemoser (Joseph). Der magnetismus im verhältnisse zur natur und religion. xvi, 272 pp. 8°. *Stuttgart and Tübingen, J. G. Cotta,* 1842.

Ennius (Quintus). Quinti Ennii poetæ inter Romanos vetustissimi reliquiæ quæ extant omnes, ex editionibus variis conquisitæ a J. A. Giles. 2 p. l. 84 pp. 8°. *Oxoniæ, D. A. Talboys*, 1834.

Enoch (*Pseudo-*). The history of the angels, and their gallantry with the daughters of men. Written by Enoch the patriarch. Publish'd in greek by dr. Grabe. Made english. 16°. *London*, 1715.

[*In* Aristæus. The history of the seventy-two interpreters. 1715. pp. 175-196].

Ensign (J. L.) The culprit fay: a cantata, for female voices. Words from the poem by Joseph Rodman Drake. Music composed by J. L. Ensign. 78 pp. 8°. *Boston, O. Ditson & co.* [1872].

Enter into thy closet. *See* **Wetenhall** (Edward).

"**Entered** at stationers' hall." A sketch of the history and privileges of the company of stationers. With notes on Francis Moore, John Partridge, and other distinguished personages. [*anon.*] 2 p. l. 32 pp. 12°. *London, M. Thomas*, 1871.

Entertainer (The), containing remarks upon men, and manners, religion, and policy. [*anon.*] [Nos. i-xliii, Nov. 6, 1717, to Aug. 27, 1718. Bi-weekly]. 3d ed. 16 p. l. 297 pp. 18°. *London, J. Osborn*, 1734.

[No more published].

Entertaining (The), moral, and religious repository; containing, upwards of three

Entertaining (The), etc.—continued.

score separate performances, written for the amusement and instruction of the youth of both sexes. Published by a society in Great Britain for the suppression of vice and immorality. [v. 2]. 1 p. l. 324 pp. 12°. *Elizabeth-town (N. J.) S. Kollock for C. Davis*, 1799.

Entomologische zeitung. Herausgegeben von dem entomologischen vereine zu Stettin. 1er-32er jahrgang. 1840-71. 32 v. 8°. *Stettin*, 1840-71. s.

Entretiens (Les) d'Ariste et d'Eugène. *See* **Bouhours** (Dominique).

Entwerffung von eroberung der stadt Olinda, so in der hauptmannschafft Pharnambuco gelegen, vnd durch Heinrich Cornelis Lonck, general und colonell Wartenburg, eingenommen: welche eygentlich abgebildet, vnd mit dem jagd schiff der Braeck genannt, überschicket worden. [*anon.*] Sheet, folded in sm. 4°. [*Amsterdam?* 1630].

Eolopoesis—American rejected addresses. *See* **Bigelow** (Jacob, *m. d.*)

Éon de Beaumont (Charles Geneviève Louis August André Timothée d'). Les loisirs du chevalier d'Éon de Beaumont, sur divers sujets importans d'administration, &c. pendant son séjour en Angleterre. 13 v. 8°. *Amsterdam*, 1774.

CONTENTS.

v. 1. Tableau historique & politique de la république de Pologne.
Recherches historiques sur la province d'Alsace.
v. 2. Recherches sur les royaumes de Naples et de Sicile.
v. 3. Abrégé chronologique de l'histoire sainte et ecclésiastique.
v. 4. Recherches sur le commerce et la navigation.
Observations sur les droits d'entré, [et] sur les péages de France.
Sur le célibat.
Examen de la banque de Law, ou l'avantage du crédit public.
v. 5. Recherches sur les lois russes. Mémoire sur le commerce de Russie.
v. 6. Histoire d'Eudoxie Fœderowna première femme de Pierre le grand.
Revenus & les dépenses de la république de Gênes.
De l'excellence d'un état libre. [Par M. Needham]. Traduit de l'anglois.
v. 7. Observations sur le royaume d'Angleterre.
v. 8. Détails sur l'Écosse.
Tableau des possessions de l'Angleterre dans l'Amérique.
Actes du parlement pour l'Amérique.
Établissements des Anglois aux Indes Orientales.
v. 9. Dissertation sur les bleds.
Sur les mendians et les enfants trouvés.
Éclaircissemens historiques sur le domaine du roi de France.
Considérations sur la gabelle, les aides et le tabac en France.
v. 10. Origine, droits et prérogatives des principaux emplois qui relèvent de la couronne de France.

Éon de Beaumont—continued.

Impôts sur le clergé de France.
v. 11. Origine et progrès de la taille en France.
v. 12. Détail général des finances de France.
Mémoire sur le domaine d'occident.
Détail de l'hôtel-royal des invalides.
État des troupes de France.
Des maréchaussées de France.
Recherches historiques sur les trois évêchés, Metz, Toul, et Verdun.
Situation de la France dans l'Inde avant la guerre.
v. 13. Table des matières.

Epicurus. Epicurvs' morals, collected partly out of his own greek text, in Diogenes Laertius, and partly out of the rhapsodies of Marcvs Antonivs, Plvtarch, Cicero, & Seneca, and faithfully englished [by Walter Charleton]. 18 p. l. 201 pp. 16°. *London, H. H.* 1670.

Epigrammatum delectus ex omnibus tum veteribus, tum recentioribus poetis, accurate decerptus cum dissertatione de verâ pulchritudine & adumbratâ. Adjectæ sunt elegantes sententiæ ex antiquis poëtis parcè, sed severiore judicio, selectæ. Cum brevioribus sententiis ac proverbiis ex autoribus græcis & latinis. [*anon.*] Ed. 12a. 23 p. l. 311, 24 pp. 12°. *Londini, G. Innys*, 1752.

Episcopal (The) manual: or an attempt to explain and vindicate the doctrine, discipline and worship of the protestant episcopal church, as taught in her public formularies, and the writings of her approved divines. [Also], observations on family and public devotion. By a clergyman of the protestant episcopal church. [*anon.*] 322 pp. 1 l. 18°. *Philadelphia, E. Earle & W. W. Woodward*, 1815.

Epulum parasiticum, quod eruditi conditores, instructoresq̄ Car. Feramusius, Ægid. Menagius, Jo. Franc. Saracenus, Nic. Rigaltius, et Jo. Lud. Balsacius, hilarem epulantibus in modum, Macrino parasitogrammatico, Gargilio Mamurræ parasitopædagogo, Gargilio Macroni parasitosophistæ, G. Orbilio Muscæ, L. Biberio Curculioni, atq; Barboni, jucundé appararunt & comiter. 28 p. l. 315 pp. 6 pl. 18°. *Norimbergæ*, 1665.

Erasmus *or* **Gerhardt** (Desiderius). Witt against wisdom, or a panegyrick upon folly. Penn'd in latin [and now] render'd into english. 23 p. l. 157 pp. 12°. *Oxford, L. Lichfield for A. Stephens*, 1683.

Eratosthenes *cyrenæus.* Ἐρατοσθένους κυρηναίου καταστερισμοί. Eratosthenis cyrenæi catasterismi. [Græce et latine]. 8°. *Amstelædami, apud H. Wetstenium*, 1688].

[*In* GALE (Thomas). Opuscula mythologica, pp. 97-136].

Erber (Bernardin). Notitia illustris regni Bohemiæ scriptorum, geographica et chorographica. 4 p. l. 146 pp. 1 l. 1 pl. fol. *Vindobonæ, apud A. Bernardum*, 1760.

Erckenbald. Erckenbaldi de antecessoribvs svis in episcopatv carmen. Ex codice augustanæ bibliothecæ. fol. [*Argentorati, J. R. Dulssecker*, 1702].

[*In* KULPIS (Johann Georg von). Scriptores rervm germanicarvm. *Argentorati*, 1702. pp. 120-122].

Erckmann (Émile) *and* **Chatrian** (Alexandre). The blockade of Phalsburg: an episode of the end of the empire. Translated from the french of Erckmann-Chatrian. 1 p. l. 308 pp. 16°. *New York, C. Scribner & co.* 1871.

Erdan (Alexandre). La France mystique, tableau des excentricités religieuses de ce temps. 3e éd. revue par l'auteur, et augmentée d'une nouvelle préface par Charles Potvin. 2 v. 2 p. l. xxiii, 291 pp. 1 pl; 2 p. l. 347 pp. 3 pl. 1 table. 12°. *Amsterdam, R. C. Meijer*, 1860.

Erdmann (Carl Gottlieb Heinrich). Lehrbuch der chemie und pharmacologie für aerzte, thierärzte und pharmaceuten. v. 2. Organische chemie und pharmakologie. viii, 1042 pp. 1 pl. 8°. *Berlin, Veit & co.* 1854. S.

[v. 1, 1841, wanting].

Erdmann (Johann Eduard). Grundriss der psychologie. viii, 96 pp. 12°. *Leipzig, F. C. W. Vogel*, 1840.

——— Psychologische briefe. 2e vermehrte aufl. xix, 334 pp. 12°. *Leipzig, C. Geibel*, 1865.

[*With his* Grundriss der psychologie, 1840].

——— Versuch einer wissenschaftlichen darstellung der geschichte der neuern philosophie. 1 v. in 2 parts. xi, cxii, 336 pp. 1 l; 257 pp. 8°. *Leipzig, Riga & Dorpat, E. Frantzen*, 1834-36.

CONTENTS.

v. 1. Darstellung und kritik der philosophie des Cartesius nebst einer einleitung in die geschichte der neuern philosophie.
v. 2. Malebranche, Spinoza, und die skeptiker und mystiker des siebzehnten jahrhunderts. Darstellung und kritik ihrer systeme.

Erdmann (Otto Linné). Erdmann-König, grundriss der allgemeinen waarenkunde. 7te, völlig umgearbeitete und stark vermehrte auflage von dr. Christian Rudolph König. xii, 472 pp. 1 pl. 8°. *Leipzig, J. A. Barth*, 1871. S.

Erhard (*Dr.* —). Fauna der cycladen. 1er theil. Die wirbelthiere der cycladen. Nebst einem anhange über deren pflanzendecke. Mit einer karte über die verbreitung der

Erhard (*Dr.* —)—continued. hasen und kaninchen. v, 116 pp. 1 l. 1 col. map. 8°. *Leipzig, Voigt & Günther*, 1858. s.

Ermippo redivivo. *Livorno*, 1756. *See* **Cohausen** (J. W.)

Ernest Carroll, or artist-life in Italy. A novel. [*anon.*] 2d ed. 344 pp. 16°. *Boston, Ticknor & Fields*, 1859.
[*Note.*—Ascribed in some catalogues to a mr. Greenough].

Ernst (Henry). Accountant and bookseller's manual of commercial calculations, reduced to their utmost simplicity. In two parts. 200 pp. 8°. *New York, Harper & brothers*, 1871.

Erpen (Thomas van). Historia Iosephi patriarchæ, ex Alcorano, arabice. *See* **Mohammed.**

——— Proverbiorvm arabicorvm centuriæ duæ, ab anonymo quodam Arabe collectæ & explicatæ: cum interpretatione latina & scholiis Iosephi Scaligeri et Thomæ Erpenii. 4 p. l. 126 pp. sm. 4°. *Leidæ, in officina raphelengiana*, 1614.

Ersch (Johann Samuel) **Gruber** (J. G.) *and others*. Allgemeine encyclopädie der wissenschaften und künste. 1e section. A–G. Herausgegeben von Hermann Brockhaus. v. 90–91. Gregorius-Grizio. 4°. *Leipzig, F. A. Brockhaus*, 1871.

Erxleben (Johann Christian Polycarp). Anfangsgründe der naturlehre. 12 p. l. 648 pp. 8 pl. 4°. *Göttingen & Gotha, J. C. Dieterich*, 1772.

Escosura (Patricio de la). Ni rei, ni roque. Episodio historico del reinado de Felipe ii. Año de 1595. Novela original. 372 pp. 12°. *Nueva York, J. de la Granja*, 1841.

Escriva (Francisco). Francisci Scribanii muscæ encomivm. 18°. [*Lugd. Batavorum*, 1644].
[*In* DISSERTATIONVM lvdicrarvm et amœnitatvm scriptores varij, pp. 555–578].

Esneaux (J.) *and* **Chennechot** (L. E.) Histoire philosophique et politique de Russie, depuis les temps les plus réculés jusqu'à nos jours. 5 v. 8°. *Paris, J. Corréard, je.* 1830.

Esperanza; my journey thither and what I found there. [*anon.*] 332 pp. 12°. *Cincinnati, V. Nicholson*, 1860.

Espinola (Nicolas de). Via dolorosa. 11 l. 18°. *Mexico, herederos de la viuda de F. R. Lupercio*, 1724.

Espinosa (Juan). La herencia española de los americanos. Seis cartas criticas a Isabel segunda. Seguidas de otros escritos de interes público. 350 pp. 1 l. 16°. *Lima, imprenta del Correo*, 1852.

Esprit des meilleurs écrivains français. 1777. *See* **Pélée de Chenouteau** (Blaise Louis).

Esputa (John). Musical instructor, calculated to impart a complete knowledge of music in a rapid and thorough manner, to which is added scales and exercises for brass instruments. 79 pp. 8°. *Washington, J. Esputa*, [1870].

Espy (Josiah). Memorandums of a tour made by J. Espy in the states of Ohio and Kentucky and Indiana territory, in 1805. viii, 29 pp. 8°. *Cincinnati, R. Clarke & co.* 1870.
[OHIO valley historical series. Miscellanies, no. 1].

Esquivel (Antonio Maria). Tratado de anatomía pictórica, inspeccionado por la real academia de nobles artes de s. Fernando, y aprobado por el gobierno de s. m. para el estudio de los pintores y escultores. Eng. title, 99 pp. 20 l. 18 pl. fol. *Madrid, F. Andrés y co.* 1848.

Essai analytique sur les lois naturelles de l'ordre social. *See* **Bonald** (Louis Gabriel Ambroise, *vicomte* de).

Essais de morale. *See* **Nicole** (Pierre).

Essay (An) on immortality. *See* **Fearn** (John).

Essay (An) on pvblic happiness. *See* **Chastellux** (François Jean, *marquis* de).

Essay (An) on the life, character, and writings of dr. Samuel Johnson. *See* **Towers** (Joseph, *ll. d*).

Essay on shooting: the whole interspersed with summary observations on the various subjects of the sport. [*anon.*] 2d ed. xxxii, 313 pp. 8°. *London, T. Cadell*, 1791.

Essay (An) upon the present state of the theatre in France, England and Italy. With reflections upon dramatic poetry in general, and the characters of the principal authors and performers of those nations. [*anon.*] 4 p. l. 220 pp. 16°. *London, I. Pottinger*, 1760.

Essays. By a barrister. [*anon.*] (Reprinted from the Saturday Review). iv, 335 pp. 12°. *London, Smith, Elder & co.* 1862.
[*Note.*—Ascribed to James Fitz-James Stephen].

Essays on the sources of the pleasures received from literary compositions. *See* **Greenfield** (William).

Essenus (*pseudon.*) *See* **Scott** (John).

Esser (Hermann). Draughtsman's alphabets: a series of plain and ornamental alphabets, designed especially for engineers, architects, draughtsmen, engravers, painters, etc. 2 p. l. 25 l. obl. 8°. *New York, Keuffel & Esser*, [1871].

Essex (Robert Devereux, 2*d earl of*). *See* **Devereux** (Robert).

Este (Charles). A journey in the year 1793, through Flanders, Brabant, and Germany, to Switzerland. [With appendix, containing four letters of Linnæus to Lord Baltimore, and Spallanzani's tour to Vesuvius, Ætna, etc.] 2 p. l. 381 pp. 6 l. 8°. *London, J. Debrett*, 1795.

Estell and co. Commercial lists.
See **Glasgow.** **Manchester.**
Liverpool. **Yorkshire.**
London.

Estienne (Charles). De re hortensi libellvs, vulgaria herbarum, florum, ac fruticum, qui in hortis conseri solent, nomina latinis uocibus effere docens ex probatis autoribus. [Ed. 2a.] 98 pp. 7 l. 12°. *Lugduni, apud Seb. Gryphium*, 1539.

——— *and* **La Rivière** (Estienne de). De dissectione partium corporis humani libri tres, à Carolo Stephano, doctore medico editi, vnà cum figuris, & incisionum declarationibus, à Stephano Riuerio chirurgo cōpositis. Eng. title, 11 p. l. 375 pp. incl. 62 pl. fol. *Parisiis, apud S. Colinæum*, 1545.

Estienne (Henri). Discovrs merveillevx de la vie, actions, et déportemens de Catherine de Médicis, royne mère; déclarant tovs les moyens qu'elle a tenus pour usurper le gouuernement du royaume de France & ruiner l'éstat d'iceluy. [*anon.*] 138 pp. 12°. *Selon la copie imprimée à Paris*, 1649.

——— Legenda s. Catharinae Mediceæ reginæ matris, vitae, actorum, & consiliorum, qvibvs vniversvm regni gallici statum turbare conata est, stupenda eaque vera enarratio. [*anon.*] 103 pp. 16°. [*n. p.*] 1575.

——— Parodiæ morales H. Stephani in poetarum vet. sententias celebriores, totidē versibus gr. ab eo redditas. Eng. title, 7 p. l. 150, 187 pp. 16°. [*Genevae*], *H. Stephanus*, 1575.

État et délices de la Suisse. *See* **Altmann** (Johann Georg).

État (De l') et du sort des colonies des anciens peuples. *See* **Sainte-Croix** (G. E. J. G. de Clermont-Lodève, *baron* de).

État présent de l'église réprésenté par le prophète Isaïe dans les chapitres 1, 3, 5. [*anon.*] 36 pp. 18°. [*Amsterdam, N. Potier*, 1731.]
[*With* BOYER (Pierre). Portrait au naturel des jésuites. *Amsterdam*, 1731].

Etereo (Ardente). Tesoro delle gioie trattado cvrioso, nel quale se dichiara breuemente la virtù, qualità, & proprietà delle gioie. Et delle altre cose più famose. Reuisto, & accresciuto dall' academico casinense inquieto. [Giovanni Batista Ardemanio]. 12 p. l. 212 pp. 1 l. 16°. *Padova, P. P. Tozzi*, 1626.

Etheridge (Robert). Appendix v. to the geological survey of [the island of] Jamaica, and summary of the palæontology of the carribean area. 8°. [*London*, 1869.] s.
[*In* GREAT BRITAIN. *Geological survey.* Geology of Jamaica. Memoirs, pp. 306–339].

Etiquette for ladies; with hints on the preservation, improvement, and display of female beauty. [*anon.*] 224 pp. 18°. *Philadelphia, Carey, Lea and Blanchard*, 1838.

Etonian (The). [A series of essays]. 3d ed. [*anon.*] 3 v. 8°. *London, H. Colburn & co.* 1823.

Ettrick (*Rev.* William). The second exodus; or reflexions on the prophesies of the last times, fulfilled by late events and now fulfilling, by the scourge of popery, and the conversion and restoration of Israel. 2 v. xvii, 470 pp; 7 p. l. 565 pp. 8°. *Sunderland, author*, 1810.

Eugenius; or, the infidel reclaimed. [*anon.*] 2 v. 285 pp; 290 pp. 8°. *London, printed for the booksellers*, 1830.

Euripides. The Alcestis of Euripides, with notes. By T. D. Woolsey. ix, 124 pp. 12°. *Cambridge, (Mass.) J. Munroe & co.* 1834.

——— Euripidis Electra. Ad optimarum editionum fidem emendavit et annotationibus in usum juventutis instruxit Hastings Robinson. 2 p. l. viii, 121 pp. 8°. *Cantabrigiæ* [*Angl.*] *typis academicis*, 1822.

——— Euripidis Hippolytus coronifer. Ad fidem manuscriptorum ac veterum editionum emendavit et annotationibus instruxit Jacobus Henricus Monk. Ed. 2a. xvi, 188 pp. 8°. *Cantabrigiæ* [*Angl.*] *typis academicis*, 1813.

——— The same. Evripidis tragœdia Hippolytvs, qvam latino carmine conversam a Georgio Ratallero adnotationibvs instrvxit Lvdov. Casp. Valckenaer. [Græce et latine]. xxxii, 416 pp. 8°. *Lipsiæ, sumptibus C. H. F. Hartmanni*, 1823.

Euripides—continued.

——— Euripidis Phœnissæ edidit Fridericus Henricus Bothe. In usum scholarum. 86 pp. 8°. *Lipsiæ, sumtibus librariæ hahnianæ*, 1825.

——— The same. Phœnissæ. 8°. [*London, C. & J. Rivington*, 1825].
[*In* TROLLOPE (William). Pentalogia græca, pp. 299-403].

——— The same. 8°. [*Oxonii, apud J. & J. Fletcher*, 1779.]
[*In* BURTON (John, *m. d.*) Pentalogia, v. 2, pp. 319-432].

——— Ευριπιδου Τρῳάδες. Euripidis Troades. Notis Porsoni, Burneii, Musgravii, Barnesii, Seidleri, aliorumque illustrata. 2 p. l. 192 pp. 8°. *Glasguæ, excudebant A. & J. Duncan*, 1819.

Eusebius *pamphilus*. Evsebii cæsariensis liber contra Hieroclem, qvi ex Philostrati historia comparauit Apollonium tyaneum saluatori nostro Iesv Christo. Zenobio Acciolo Florentino interprete. [Græce et latine]. fol. [*Parisiis, apud M. Orry*, 1608].
[*In* PHILOSTRATUS. Opera quæ exstant. *Parisiis*, 1608. pp. 433-483].

——— Eusebii caesariensis prooemium et capita priora demonstrationis evangelicæ, quæ in editionibus hactenus desiderantur, latine reddita. [Græce et latine]. 4°. *Hamburgi, sumtu T. C. Felginer*, 1725.
[*In* FABRICIUS (Johann Albrecht). Delectus argumentorum, [etc.] *Hamburgi*, 1725. pp. 1-22].

——— The same. Leaves from Eusebius. Selected from his celebrated work, The evangelical preparation, and translated from the original greek by the rev. Henry Street. xxiv, 288 pp. 12°. *London, E. Bull*, 1842.

Eustathius *thessalonicensis*. Επιστολη και υπομνηματα επι τηΔιονυσιου του Περιηγητου οικουμενης περιηγεσει. 262 pp. 8°. Βιεννη, 1808.
[Συλλογη των εν επιτομη τοις παλαι γεωγραφηθεντων. v. 2].

——— Ευσταθιου παρεκβολαι εις Διονυσιου περιηγσιν. 8°. [*Oxoniæ, e theatro sheldoniano*, 1697].
[*In* DIONYSIUS *periegetes*. Orbis descriptio, pp. 101-291. *Oxoniæ*, 1697].

Euterpiad (The): an album of music, poetry, and prose. Edited by Charles Dingley. [A fortnightly]. v. 1. Eng. title, 240 pp. 3 pl. 4°. *New York, G. W. Bleecker*, 1830.

Evan Dale. [A novel]. *See* **Keyes** (F.)

Evangelical lutheran church. The christian book of concord, or symbolical books of the evangelical lutheran church; comprising the three chief symbols, the unaltered Augsburg confession, the apology, the Smalcald articles, Luther's smaller and larger catechisms, the formula of concord, and an appendix. To which is prefixed an historical introduction. Second edition. Translated from the german. 780 pp. 8°. *Newmarket (Va.) S. D. Henkel & brs.* 1854.

——— A collection of hymns and a liturgy, for the use of the evangelical lutheran churches; to which are added prayers for families and individuals. New and enlarged stereotype edition. 2 v. in 1. vi, 488 pp; 172 pp. 16°. *New-York, H. Ludwig*, 1834.

——— A liturgy for the use of the evangelical lutheran church. By authority of the ministerium of Pennsylvania and adjacent states. 220 pp. 12°. *Philadelphia, Lindsay & Blakiston*, 1860.

Evans (Augusta J.) Inez: a tale of the Alamo. [New ed.] 298 pp. 12°. *New York, G. W. Carleton & co.* 1871.

Evans (Hugh Davey, *ll. d.*) Essays to prove the validity of anglican ordinations; in answer to the rt. rev. Peter Richard Kendrick, r. c. bishop of St. Louis. By a layman. 328 pp. 12°. *Baltimore, J. Robinson*, 1844.

Evans (John, *printer*). A chronological outline of the history of Bristol, and the stranger's guide through its streets and neighborhood. xxxiv, 376 pp. 1 map. 4°. *Bristol, author*, 1824.

Evans (John, *ll. d.*) History of all christian sects and denominations; their origin, peculiar tenets, and present condition. With an introductory account of atheists, deists, jews, mahometans, pagans, etc. With the addition of the most recent statistics relating to religious sects in the United States. By the american editor. 2d ed. 288 pp. 12°. *New York, J. Mowatt & co.* 1844.

Evans (John, *lieutenant r. n.*) A revision and explanation of geographical and hydrographical terms, and those of a nautical character, relating thereto; with descriptions of winds, storms, clouds, etc. 1 p. l. xi, 179 pp. 7 pl. 12°. *London, Longman*, 1824.

Evans (John M.) The baptist hymn and tune book. Music. 1871. *See* **Plymouth** collection.

Evans (Mary). The chapel of st. Mary. By the author of "The rectory of Moreland." [*anon.*] 396 pp. 12°. *Boston, J. E. Tilton & co.* 1861.

Evans (R. M.) The story of Joan of Arc. 2d ed. vi, 182 pp. 24 pl. 16°. *London, W. Smith*, 1847.

Evans (*Rev.* Robert Wilson). Biography of the early church. 1 p. l. v, 414 pp. portrait. 16°. *London, J. G. & F. Rivington*, 1837.

Evans (*Rev.* Warren F.) The mental-cure, illustrating the influence of the mind on the body, both in health and disease, and the psychological method of treatment. 364 pp. 12°. *Boston, H. H. & T. W. Carter*, 1869.

Evanson (Edward). Reflections upon the state of religion in christendom; particularly in the countries situated within the limits of the western roman empire, at the commencement of the xixth century of the christian era. 163 pp. 8°. *Exeter, S. Woolmer*, 1802.

Evelyn Harcourt. A novel. By the author of "Temptation, or, a wife's perils," [etc. *anon.*] 3 v. 12°. *London, H. Colburn*, 1847.

Evening (The) journal almanac. 1860 and 1865. 2 v. 12°. *Albany, Weed, Parsons & co.* 1860–65.

Evening (The) post. [New York daily]. Jan. 2 to Dec. 30, 1871. 2 v. fol. *New York, W. C. Bryant & co.* 1871.

Evening recreations: a series of dialogues on the history and geography of the bible. In four parts. [*anon.*] 4 v. 18°. *Philadelphia, American sunday school union*, 1830–32.

Evening (The) star. [Washington daily]. Crosby S. Noyes, editor. Jan. 2 to Dec. 30, 1871. 2 v. fol. *Washington, Evening star newspaper co.* 1871.

Everest (Cornelius). The singing teacher. A manual containing an original theoretical and practical course of elementary instruction in vocal music. nos. 1–2. 2 v. 64 pp; 32 pp. obl. 12°. *Philadelphia, Lee & Walker*, [1871].

Everest (C. W.) The snow-drop: a gift for a friend. 128 pp. 32°. *New York, J. S. Redfield*, 1845.

——— Vision of death; and other poems. 128 pp. 32°. *Hartford, Robins & Smith*, 1845.

Everhart (James B.) Miscellanies. 4 p. l. 300 pp. 1 pl. 12°. *Westchester, E. F. James*, 1862.

Evershaw (Mary). Five years in Pennsylvania. 1 p. l. 227 pp. 12°. *London, W. Strange*, 1840.

Every body's (The) album: a humorous collection of tales, quips, quirks, anecdotes, and facetiæ. 2 v. 432 pp; 436 pp. 8°. *Philadelphia, C. Alexander*, 1836.

Every Saturday, an illustrated weekly journal. Jan. 7 to Dec. 30, 1871. New [illustrated] series. v. 2–3. fol. *Boston, J. R. Osgood & co.* [1871].

Ewald (*Rev.* Ferdinand Charles, *ll. d.*) Journal of missionary labours in the city of Jerusalem, during the years 1842–4. xvi, 239 pp. 2 l. 1 map. 16°. *London, B. Wertheim*, 1845.

Ewald (Georg Heinrich August von). Grammatica critica linguae arabicae, cum brevi metrorum doctrina. 2 v. x, 394 pp. 1 l. 1 tab; viii, 348 pp. 8°. *Lipsiae, sumtibus librariae hahnianae*, 1831–33.

——— The history of Israel. Translated from the german. Edited by J. Estlin Carpenter. v. 3–4. 8°. *London, Longmans, Green & co.* 1871.

Ewald (Johann Ludwig). Christelijk huisen handboek of bespiegelingen voor elken dag des jaars. Nieuwe uitgave. 4 v. 8°. *Amsterdam, J. van der Hey & zoon*, 1826.

Examen over het Vertoogh tegen het ongefondeerdè ende schadelijck sluyten der vryen handel in Brasil. Door een ondersoecker der waerheyt. [*anon.*] 16 pp. sm. 4°. [*Gravenhage*]? 1637.

Examen vande valsche resolutie vande heeren burgemeesters ende raden tot Amsterdam. Op't stuck vande west-indische compagnie. [*anon.*] 36 pp. sm. 4°. *Amsterdam, A. de Bruyn*, 1649.

Examination (An) of canon Liddon's Bampton lectures on the divinity of our Lord and Saviour Jesus Christ. By a clergyman of the church of England. [*anon.*] xii, 427 pp. 12°. *Boston, Little, Brown & co.* 1872.

Examiner (The) examin'd. *See* **Brown** (*Rev.* John, *of Haverhill, Mass.*)

Excell (*Rev.* J. J.) An essay on the family. 224 pp. 12°. *Wooster (O.)* 1859.

——— The mysteries and beauties of redemption. 440 pp. 12°. *Wooster (O.)* 1860.

Excellency (The) of the female character vindicated. 1828. *See* **Branagan** (Thomas).

Excelsior (The) monthly magazine, [and Public spirit]. Devoted to the elevation of the race. [Rev. M. N. Olmsted, editor]. June, 1868, to March, 1869. v. 1–2. 8°. *New York, Olmsted & Welwood*, [1869].

Excelsior (The) monthly magazine—cont'd.

——— The same. The excelsior monthly magazine. Rev. M. N. Olmsted, editor. Jan. to June, 1870. v. 3. [New series, v. 1]. 8°. *New York*, 1870.

——— The same. The excelsior monthly magazine and Home monthly. July, 1870, to Dec. 1871. v. 4-6. [New series v. 2-4, Excelsior; v. 8-11, Home monthly]. 8°. *New York, C. L. Van Allen*, [1870-71].

[*Note.*—"Public spirit" consolidated with the Excelsior monthly magazine, Sept. 1868].

Exercicios para andar en la presencia de Dios, y meditaciones de la sagrada passion, y muerte de n. redemptor Jesu-Christo. [*anon.*] 20 l. 1 pl. 18°. *Mexico, Colegio de S. Ildefonso*, 1759.

Explication des cérémonies de la fête-Dieu d'Aix en Provence. *See* **Grégoire** (Gaspard)

Exposition universelle. 1855, 1862, 1867. *See* **France.** *Commission impériale.*

Extrait d'vne histoire de France, manvscrite, qui commence l'an 1270. & finit l'an 1510. *See* **Saint-Gélais** (Jean de).

Eynatten (Maximilian van). Manvale exorcismorvm: continens instrvctiones, & exorcismos ad eiiciendos e corporibus obsessis spiritus malignos. 8 p. l. 314 pp. 1 l. 16°. *Antverpiæ, ex officina plantiniana*, 1619.

Eyriès (Jean Baptiste Benoît). Fantasmagoriana, ou recueil d'histoires d'apparitions de spectres, revenans, fantômes, etc; traduit de l'allemand, par un amateur. [*anon.*] 2 v. xv, 276 pp; 2 p. l. 304 pp. 16°. *Paris, F. Schoell*, 1812.

F. (D.) A defence of the drama, containing Mansel's free thoughts, extracts from the most celebrated writers, and a discourse on the lawfulness & unlawfulness of plays, by the celebrated father Caffaro, divinity professor at Paris. 2 p. l. 294 pp. 16°. *New York, G. Champley*, 1826.

F. (E. E.) Little people whom the Lord loved. 251 pp. 3 pl. 16°. *Boston, I. P. Warren*, [1871].

F. (J. S.) Demonologia; or, natural knowledge revealed; being an exposé of ancient and modern superstitions. [*anon.*] xvi, 438 pp. 12°. *London, J. Bumpus*, 1827.

F. (L. A.) Daisy Seymour. [*anon.*] 270 pp. 3 pl. 16°. *Boston, D. Lothrop & co.* 1871.

F. (S. A.) Great success. *See* **Flint** (S. A.)

F. (S. K. P.) Familiar letters on subjects interesting to the minds and hearts of females. By a lady. [*anon.* Subscribed S. K. P. F.] 7 pp. 13-340 pp. 12°. *Boston, Crocker & Brewster*, 1834.

F. (S. K. P.)—continued.

Faber (Frederick William, *d. d.*) The creator and the creature; or, the wonders of divine love. With an introduction, by an american clergyman. 414 pp. 12°. *Baltimore, Murphy & co.* 1857.

Faber (*Rev.* George Stanley). A treatise on the genius and object of the patriarchial, the levitical, and the christian, dispensations. 2 v. xxiii, 431 pp; xix, 439 pp. 8°. *London, C. & J. Rivington*, 1823.

Fabian (Bentham). Australia: being a brief compendium of the geographical position, topography, characteristic features, description of the principal rivers, headlands, productions, etc. A guide to the gold regions. [With appendix]. 112 pp. 1 map. 8°. *New York, editors*, 1852.

Fabri (Augustin). Continuatio i-ii Romae sanctae. fol. *Augustae Vind.* 1729.

[*In* CONLIN (Joan Rudolph). Roma sancta, 1726, pp. 203-266, pl. 72-94.
Note.—Imperfect: plate 82 wanting].

Fabrice *or* **Fabri de Hildan** (Guillaume). Cista militaris, or a military chest, furnished either for sea, or land, with convenient medicines and necessary instruments. Amongst which is also a description of dr. Lower's lancet, for the more safe bleeding. Written in latin by Gulielmus Fabritius hildanus. Englished for publick benefit. 1 p. l. 30 pp. 16°. *London, W. Godbid*, 1674.

[*With* BARBETTE (Paul). Thesaurus chirurgiæ. *London*, 1676].

Fabricius (Franz). M. Tullii Ciceronis historia per consules descripta et in annos lxiv. distincta. 8°. *Turici, typis Orellii*, 1836].

[*In* CICERO (M. T.) Opera ed. Orellius, v. 6, pp. 1-109].

Fabricius (Johann Albrecht). Delectus argumentorum et syllabus scriptorum qui veritatem religionis christianæ adversus atheos, epicureos [etc.] lucubrationibus suis asseruerunt. Præmissa sunt Eusebii cæsariensis prooemium et capita priora demonstrationis evangelicæ, quæ in editionibus hactenus desiderantur, et latine redita. 5 p. l. 756 pp. 14 l. 1 pl. 4°. *Hamburgi, sumtu T. C. Felginer*, 1725.

Fabricius (Vincenz). Vincenti Fabrici satyra, pransvs paratvs, in poëtas, et eorum contemptores. 18°. 1655.

[ELEGANTIORES præstantium virorum satryæ, v. 2 pp. 677-738].

Fabritius Hildanus (Gulielmus). *See* **Fabrice** *or* **Fabri de Hildan** (Guillaume).

Fabroni (Angelo). Elogj di Dante Alighiori, di Angelo Poliziano, di Lodovico Ariosto, e di Torquato Tasso. [*anon.*] 3 p. l. 380 pp. 8°. *Parma, dalla stamperia reale*, 1800.

——— Historia academiae pisanae. 3 v. 4°. *Pisis, excudebat C. Mugnainius in aedibus auctoris*, 1791-95.

——— Laurentii Medicis magnifici vita. 2 v. viii, 234 pp. 1 portrait; 399 pp. 4°. *Pisis, J. Gratiolius*, 1784.

——— Leonis x. pontificis maximi vita. 330 pp. 4°. *Pisis, A. Landius*, 1797.

——— Lettere inedite di uomini illustri, per servire d'appendice all' opera intitolata Vitae Italorum doctrina excellentium. 2 v. viii, 364 pp. 1 pl; viii, 352 pp. 12°. *Firenze, F. Moücke*, 1773-75.

——— Magni Cosmi Medicei vita. 2 v. viii, 194 pp. 1 l. 1 portrait; 264 pp. 4°. *Pisis, A. Landi*, 1788-89.

——— Vitae Italorum doctrina excellentium qui saeculis xvii. et xviii. floruerunt. 20 v. 8°. *Pisis, C. Ginesius* [*et al.*] 1778-99; *Lucae, typis D. Marescandoli*, 1804-05.

[*Note.*—v. 20 contains the life of Fabroni, and a selection of letters of contemporaries to Fabroni].

Fabronius (Hermann). Geographia historica: newe summarische welt historia, oder beschreibung aller keyserthumb, königreiche, fürstenthumb, vnd völcker heutiges tages auff erden. 5e ed. 2 v. in 1. 11 p. l. 590 pp. 1 map; 96 pp. sm. 4°. *Schmalkalden, W. Ketzeln*, 1627.

Fabry (Jean Baptiste Germain). Itinéraire de Buonaparte de l'île d'Elbe à l'île Sainte-Hélène, ou mémoires pour servir à l'histoire de la seconde usurpation, avec le recueil des principales pièces officielles de cette époque. 2e éd. considérablement augmentée. Par l'auteur de la Régence à Blois, [etc. *anon.*] 2 v. 1 p. l. xvi, 486 pp; xi, 460 pp. 8°. *Paris, Le Normant*, 1817.

Facts for the people. [A monthly anti-slavery periodical]. G. Bailey, editor. June, 1853, to May, 1854. v. 1. 4°. *Washington, G. Bailey*, 1853-54.

——— The same. May, 1855, to April, 1856. New series, v. 1. 8°. *Washington, G. Bailey*, 1855-56.

Facts, illustrative of the treatment of Napoleon Buonaparte in Saint Helena. Being the result of minute inquiries and personal research in that island. [*anon.*] 1 p. l. 146 pp. 3 pl. 8°. *London, W. Stockdale*, 1819.

"Fadette" (*pseudon.*) *See* **Rodney** (*Mrs.* Minnie Reeves).

Fairbanks (George R.) History of Florida from its discovery by Ponce de Leon, in 1512, to the close of the Florida war, in 1842. 350 pp. 12°. *Philadelphia, J. B. Lippincott & co.* 1871.

Fairbanks (Lorenzo). A practical business arithmetic. 430 pp. 12°. *New York, University publishing co.* 1871.

Fairchild (Charles B.) Aguecheek. [*anon.*] 336 pp. 12°. *Boston, Shepard, Clark & Brown*, 1859.

Fairfield (Caroline E.) Our bible-class, and the good that came of it. 352 pp. 12°. *New York, Derby & Jackson*, 1860.

Fairfield (*Rev.* Harrison). The wreck and the rescue. A memoir of the rev. Harrison Fairfield. Written chiefly by himself. Edited by Enoch Pond, d. d. 157 pp. 2 pl. 18°. *Boston, Massachusetts sabbath school society*, [1858].

Fairfield (Sumner Lincoln). The cities of the plain. A scripture poem. 58 pp. 1 l. 16°. *Boston, C. G. Green*, 1827.

[MISCELLANEOUS pamphlets, v. 410].

Fairmount park. Sketches of its scenery, waters, and history. [*anon.*] 1871. *See* **Keyser** (Charles S.)

Faithful and true. *See* **Robbins** (S. S.)

Falbaire de Quingey. *See* **Fenouillot de Falbaire de Quingey.**

Falcâo (Jozé Anastacio). De l'état actuel de la monarchie portugaise, et des cinq causes de sa décadence. viii, 276 pp. 1 portrait. 8°. *Paris, C. de Behr*, 1830.

Falcidio Melampodio (*pseudon.*) *See* **Aromatarii** (Giuseppe degli).

Falda (Giovanni Battista). Il nvovo teatro delle fabriche, et edificii, in prospettiva di Roma moderna. Date in luce da Gio. Iacomo Rossi. 3 v. in 1. 2 eng. titles, 33 pl; 1 p. l. 16 pl; 1 p. l. 34 pl. obl. fol. *Roma, G. I. Rossi*, 1665.

Fale (Thomas). Horologiographia. The art of dialling: teaching an easie and perfect way to make all kinds of dials vpon any plaine plat howsoeuer placed. 4 p. l. 60 l. numb. 16 l. unp. sm. 4°. *London, Felix Kyngston*, 1626.

Falkenstein (Carl Constantin). Thaddäus Kosciuszko, nach seinem öffentlichen und häuslichen leben geschildert. 2e aufl. xxiii, 376 pp. 2 pl. 8°. *Leipzig, F. A. Brockhaus*, 1834.

Fall (The) of man: or, the loves of the gorillas. *See* **White** (Richard Grant).

Fallows (Samuel). Constitutions of the United States and of the state of Wisconsin; with questions, adapted to the use of common schools. 164 pp. 12°. *Madison (Wis.) Atwood & Culver*, 1871.

Fame (The) and glory of England vindicated. *See* **Libertas.**

Familiar letters on subjects interesting to females. *See* **F.** (S. K. P.)

Family (The) doctor, or the home book of health and medicine. A popular treatise on the means of avoiding and curing diseases, and of preserving the health and vigor of the body to the latest period. By a physician of Philadelphia. [*anon.*] 630 pp. 8°. *New York, C. M. Saxton, Barker & co.* 1859.

Famous (The), pleasant, and delightful history of Palladine of England. *See* **Colet** (Claude).

Fane (Julian Charles Henry). Original poems. *See* **Lytton** (Robert Bulwer). Julian Fane.

Fantoni (Giovanni, *fra gli arcadi Labindo*). Opere. [Ed. 2ª.] 3 v. 16°. *Lugano*, 1823-24.

CONTENTS.

v. 1. Memorie istoriche sulla vita di Giovanni Fantoni, p. 5.
Osservazioni sui metri oraziani delle odi di Labindo, p. 71.
Delle odi di Labindo, libro i-iv.
v. 2. Idilj, p. 3.
Egloghe virgiliane, p. 47.
Notti, p. 63.
Poemetti, p. 77.
Scherzi, p. 127.
v. 3. Epithalmj, p. 3.
Sonnetti, p. 19.
Prose letterarie, p. 97.

Faria e Sousa (Manuel de). Epitome de las historias portvgvesas. 2 v. in 1. 6 p. l. 696 pp. 12 l. sm. 4°. *Madrid, F. Martinez*, 1628.

Farmer (C. M.) The fairy of the stream, and other poems. 167 pp. 16°. *Richmond (Va.) Harrold & Murray*, 1847.

Farmer-freund (Der). 1871. Landwirthschaftlicher kalender für die deutschen farmer in Nordamerika, bearbeitet von H. Nicholas Jarchow. 88 pp. 4°. *New York, Farmer-zeitung-company*, 1871.

Farmer's (The) magazine. Third series. January, 1870, to December, 1871. v. 37-40. 8°. *London, Rogerson & Tuxford*, 1870-71.

Farnham (Eliza W.) Eliza Woodson; or, the early days of one of the world's workers. A story of american life. [*anon.*] 425 pp. 12°. *New York, A. J. Davis & co.* 1864.

Farquharson (Martha). *See* **Finley** (Martha).

Farr (Edward). Select poetry, chiefly devotional, of the reign of queen Elizabeth. Collected and edited for the Parker society. 2 v. lvi, 256 pp; 1 p. l. 257-559 pp. 16°. *Cambridge, university press*, 1845.

——— Select poetry, chiefly sacred, of the reign of king James the first. xliv, 360 pp. 16°. *Cambridge (Eng.) J. & J. J. Deighton*, 1847.

Farr (*Rev.* Jonathan). Forms of morning and evening prayer, composed for the use of families. viii, 168 pp. 16°. *Boston, J. Munroe & co.* 1836.

——— Sermons, designed to teach plainly the doctrines of the gospel, and earnestly to enforce the precepts of Jesus Christ. 280 pp. 16°. *Boston, L. C. Bowles*, 1833.

Farrago (The). Containing essays, etc. *See* **Barton** (Richard).

Farrar (C. C. S.) The war, its causes and consequences. 260 pp. 12°. *Cairo (Ill.) Blelock & co.* 1864.

Farrar (Eliza Rotch). The young lady's friend. By a lady. [*anon.*] xi, 432 pp. 12°. *Boston, American stationers' co.* 1836.

Farrar (*Rev.* John). An ecclesiastical dictionary, explanatory of the history, antiquities, heresies, sects, and religious denominations of the christian church. iv, 560 pp. 1 chart. 12°. *London, J. Mason*, 1853.

Farren (George). Observations on the laws of mortality and disease, and on the principles of life insurance. With an appendix, containing illustrations of the progress of mania, melancholia, craziness, and demonomania, as displayed in Shakespeare's characters of Lear, Hamlet, Ophelia, and Edgar. 1 pl. 132 pp. 8°. *London, author*, 1829.

Fastré (J. A. M.) The acts of the early martyrs. First series. 282 pp. 12°. *Philadelphia, P. F. Cunningham*, 1871. [Messenger series, no. 3].

——— The same. 2d series. 1 p. l. 271 pp. 12°. *Philadelphia, P. F. Cunningham*, 1871. [Messenger series, no. 4].

Father Butler, or sketches of Irish manners. [*anon.*] 218 pp. 18°. *Philadelphia, T. Latimer*, 1835.

Fatherland series. 27 v. 16°. *Philadelphia, Lutheran board of publication*, 1869-72.

CONTENTS.

HOFFMANN (Franz). Adventures of Leo Rembrandt. 241 pp. 4 pl.
——— Anton, the fisherman. 172 pp. 2 pl.
——— Buried in the snow. 161 pp. 2 pl.

Fatherland series—continued.

HOFFMANN (Franz). Dominic. 246 pp. 4 pl.
——— Fritz; or filial obedience. 125 pp. 1 pl.
——— Geyer Wältz. 196 pp. 6 pl.
——— The greek slave. 239 pp. 2 pl.
——— The iron age of Germany. 236 pp. 4 pl.
——— The iron head, a story of Charles xii. 239 pp.
——— Maternal love. 200 pp. 2 pl.
——— Prince Wolfgang. 316 pp. 4 pl.
——— René. 176 pp.
——— The story of father Miller. 176 pp. 2 pl.
——— The story of the old schoolmaster. 231 pp. 3 pl.
——— The treasure of the Inca. 169 pp. 2 pl.
——— Under the earth. 134 pp. 1 pl.
NIERITZ (Gustav). Faithful unto death. 287 pp. 3 pl.
——— Gottlieb Frey. 226 pp. 4 pl.
——— The three kings. 223 pp. 3 pl.
OERTEL (P. F. W.) Leonhard, the runaway. 74 pp.
——— Olaf Thorlaksen. From the German of van Horn. [*pseudon.*] 211 pp. 2 pl.
PETZEL (Rosa). The cottage by the lake. By Martin Claudius. [*pseudon.*] 160 pp. 1 pl.
REDENBACHER (W.) The little cloister ruin. 130 pp. 2 pl.
ROSKOWSKA (M.) Die halligen; or, in the midst of the North Sea. 159 pp. 2 pl.
SCHMID (Christoph von). The hop blossoms. 174 pp. 2 pl.
SEPPELI the swiss boy. 123 pp. 2 pl.
WILD (Carl). The valley mill. 227 pp. 1 pl.

Faunce (*Rev.* D. W.) Questions on the words and works of the apostles. 106 pp. 16°. *Boston, A. F. Graves,* 1871.

Faure (*Mlle.* H.) Nouveaux synonymes français. xii, 346 pp. 1 l. 12°. *Paris, madame Huzard,* 1819.

Favart (Charles Simon). Mémoires et correspondance littéraires, dramatiques et anecdotiques. Publiés par A. P. C. Favart, son petit-fils; et précédés d'une notice historique, par H. F. Dumolard. 3 v. 8°. *Paris, L. Collin,* 1808.

Favourite english poems of modern times unabridged. Illustrated. [*anon.*] xii, 372 pp. sm. 4°. *London, S. Low, son & co.* 1862.

Fawcett (Edgar). Short poems for short people. 95 pp. 12°. *New York, F. B. Felt & co.* 1872.

Fawcett (Henry). Pauperism: its causes and remedies. viii, 270 pp. 12°. *London and New York, Macmillan & co.* 1871.

Fay (Andreas). Originelle fabeln und aphorismen. Aus dem ungarischen übersetzt von L. Petz. 4 p. l. 150 pp. 3 l. 1 pl. 12°. *Raab, S. Ludvigh,* 1825.

Fay (*Rev.* F. R.) The book of Joshua. *See* **Bible.** (*English*).

Fay (Jonas). A concise refutation of the claims of New-Hampshire and Massachusetts-Bay, to the territory of Vermont. *See* **Allen** (Ethan) *and* **Fay** (Jonas).

Faye (H.) Leçons de cosmographie, rédigées d'après les programmes officiels. 2e éd. 2 p. l. iv, 422 pp. 15 pl. 8°. *Paris, L. Hachette & cie.* 1854.

Fazello (Tommaso). De rebvs sicvlis decades dvae, nvnc primvm in lvcem editae. 10 p. l. 664 pp. 14 l. 4°. *Panormi, typis excvdebant, I. M. Mayda, & F. Carrara,* 1560.

Fearn (John). An essay on immortality. [*anon.*] vii, 328 pp. 8°. *London, D. Cock & co. for Longman,* [*etc.*] 1814.

——— A letter to professor Stewart, on the objects of general terms, and the axiomatical laws of vision. viii, 32 pp. 4°. *London, Longman & co.* 1817.

Fearon (Henry Bradshaw). Thoughts on materialism: and on religious festivals, and sabbaths. iv, 214 pp. 8°. *London, Longman,* 1833.

Featley (*Rev.* John). A fountain of tears emptying it self into three rivolets, viz. of 1. Compunction. 2. Compassion. 3. Devotion. Or sobs of nature sanctified by grace. Jer. ix, 1. Eng. title, 6 p. l. 603 pp. 2 l. 18°. *London, O. Blagrave & R. Northcot,* 1683.

Fedeli (Fedele). Storia naturale e medica delle acque minerali dell' alta val di Nievole. 1870. *See* **Savi** (Paolo) *and* **Fedeli.**

Federalist (The). Le fédéraliste, ou collection de quelques écrits en faveur de la constitution proposée aux États-Unis de l'Amérique, par la convention convoquée en 1787; publiés dans les États-Unis de l'Amérique par mm. Hamilton, Madisson et Gay [Jay]. 2 v. 2 p. l. xxi–lij, 366 pp; 2 p. l. 511 pp. 8°. *Paris, Buisson,* 1792.

Feijo (*Rev.* Diogo Antonio). Demonstration of the necessity of abolishing a constrained clerical celibacy; exhibiting the evils of that institution, and the remedy. Translated from the portuguese, with an introduction and appendix, by rev. D. P. Kidder. 128 pp. 18°. *Philadelphia, Sorin & Ball,* 1844.

Feith (Rhijnvis van). Oden en gedichten. 3 v. 16°. *Zwolle, H. As. zoon, Doyer,* 1824.

Feldborg (J. A. Andersen-). *See* **Andersen-Feldborg.**

Féline (Adrien). Manual of french pronunciation; with extracts from the french classics, written in phonetic characters. Revised, with additions, by William Watson. xvi, 159 pp. 16°. *Boston, Lee & Shepard,* 1866.

Felix *of Croyland.* The anglo-saxon version of the life of st. Guthlac, hermit of Crowland. Now first printed from a ms. in the cottonian library. With a translation and notes, by Charles Wycliffe Goodwin. [Anglo-saxon and english]. vi, 125 pp. 12°. *London, J. R. Smith,* 1848.

Felix *of Croyland*—continued.
——— The same. Vita s. Guthlaci presb. anachoretæ Croylandiæ in Anglia. [Cum annotatis]. Subjunguntur analecta excerpta ex historia Ingulfi abbatis croylandensis. Etiam translatio s. Guthlaci, ex mss. anglicanis. fol. [*Parisiis*, 1866].
[*In* ACTA sanctorum, v. 11, pp. 38-60].

Fell (Archie, *pseudon.*) *See* **Capron** (M. J.)

Fell (Ralph). Vie politique, littéraire et privée de Charles James Fox. Ouvrage traduit de l'anglais sur la quatrième édition originale, par J. Martinet. [*anon.*] 2 p. l. 324 pp. 1 portrait. 8°. *Paris, Parsons, Galignani & cie.* 1807.
[*Note.*—Abridged from the original English ed.]

Fellowes (J.) Reminiscences. Moral poems and translations. With an appendix. 275 pp. 16°. *Exeter (N. H.) Gerrish & Tyler*, 1824.

Fellowes (*Rev.* Robert). A body of theology, principally practical. In a series of lectures. 2 v. xxiii, 549 pp; viii, 530 pp. 12 l. 8°. *London, J. Mawman*, 1807.
——— Religion without cant: or, a preservative against lukewarmness and intolerance; fanaticism, superstition, and impiety. lx, 404 pp. 8°. *London, J. White*, 1801.

Fellows (John). The veil removed; or reflections on David Humphrey's essay on the life of Israel Putnam. Also, notices of Oliver W. B. Peabody's life of the same, S. Swett's sketch of Bunker Hill battle, etc. 231 pp. 12°. *New York, J. D. Lockwood*, 1843.

Feltham (John). A tour through the island of Mann, in 1797 and 1798; comprising sketches of its ancient and modern history, constitution, laws, commerce, agriculture, fishery, &c. including whatever is remarkable in each parish, its population, inscriptions, registers, &c. 294 pp. 3 pl. 8°. *Bath, C. Dilly*, 1798.

Felton (Samuel). Imperfect hints towards a new edition of Shakespeare, written chiefly in the year 1782. [*anon.*] 2 parts in 1 v. 4 p. l. xxxii, 126 pp; 4 p. l. xxiii, 173 pp. 4°. *London, J. Walter for the author*, 1787-88.

Felton (S.) On the portraits of english authors on gardening, with biographical notices. 2d ed. with considerable additions. xxxix, 221 pp. 8°. *London, E. Wilson*, 1830.

Female life among the Mormons. [*anon.*] *See* **Ferris** (*Mrs.* B. G.)

Fendt (Tobias). Monvmenta sepvlcrorvm cvm epigraphis ingenio et doctrina excellentivm virorvm; aliorvmq. tam prisci quam

24

Fendt (Tobias)—continued.
nostri secvli memorabilivm; de archetypis expressa. Eng. title, 5 p. l. 129 plates. fol. [*Vratislaviæ*], 1574.

Fénélon (François de Salignac de la Mothe). Part of the spiritual works of the celebrated Francis Fenelon. Translated by Richard Houghton. 2d ed. 2 v. viii, 272 pp; x, 352 pp. 8°. *Dublin, C. Bentham*, 1822.
——— Reflections and meditations selected from the writings of Fenelon; with a memoir of his life. By J. R. G. Hassard. And an introduction, by rev. Thomas S. Preston. 374 pp. 12°. *New York, P. O'Shea*, 1865.
——— Telemachus versified. By [Charles Burdett]. 2 p. l. 209 pp. portrait. 8°. *London, W. Spiers*, [*about* 1820].
——— Thoughts on spiritual subjects. Translated from the writings of Fenelon. ix, 148 pp. 1 portrait. 16°. *Boston, S. G. Simpkins*, 1843.

Fenestella (Lucius, *pseudon.*) *See* **Fiocchi** (Andrea Domenico).

Fenning (Daniel) **Collyer** (Joseph) *and others.* A new system of geography: or, a general description of the world. Containing a particular and circumstantial account of all the countries, kingdoms, and states of Europe, Asia, Africa, and America. With the birds, beasts, reptiles, insects, the various vegetables, and minerals found in different regions. 2 v. 2 p. l. xliv, 519 pp. 4 l. 15 pl. 9 maps; 784 pp. 10 l. 15 pl. 19 maps. fol. *London, for S. Crowder*, 1764-65.

Fenouillot de Falbaire de Quingey. (Charles Georges). Œuvres de m. de Falbaire de Quingey. 2 v. 4 p. l. 375 pp. 1 portrait; 2 p. l. 248, 242 pp. 8°. *Paris, veuve Duchesne*, 1787.

CONTENTS.

v. 1. L'honnête criminel, ou l'amour filial, drame en cinq actes et en vers, p. 1.
Le premier navigateur, pastorale-lyrique, en trois actes, avec un prologue, p. 119.
Dissertation sur les ballets-pantomimes, et particulièrement sur celui du premier navigateur, p. 181.
Les deux avares, comédie en deux actes en prose, mêlée d'ariettes, p. 215.
De l'insensibilité, p. 289.
Sur les salines de Franche-Comte, p. 294.
Pièces fugitives, p. 359.
v. 2 (*a*). Le fabricant de Londres, drame en cinq actes et en prose, p. 1.
L'école des mœurs, ou les suites du libertinage; drame en cinq actes et en vers, p. 125.
v. 2 (*b*). Les jammabos, ou les moines japonois; tragédie, dédiée aux manes de Henri iv. et suivie de remarques historiques. 242 pp.

Feramo (Carolo). Macrini parasitogrammatici ἡμερα ad Celsum. [*pseudon.*] 18°. *Norimbergae*, 1665.
[*In* EPULUM parasiticum, pp. 1-32, 1 pl.]

Feramusius (Carolus). *See* **Feramo** (Carolo).

Féraud-Giraud (L. J. D.) Droit international. France & Sardaigne. Exposé des lois et traités. vii, 558 pp. 8°. *Paris, A. Durand*, 1859.

Fernald (Woodbury M.) Universalism against partialism: in a series of lectures delivered in Newburyport, Mass. 270 pp. 18°. *Boston, B. B. Mussey*, 1840.

Fernandez de Castro (Manuel). Estudio sobre las minas de oro de la isla de Cuba. 105 pp. 1 map. 8°. *Havana, imprenta "el Iris,"* 1864. s.

Fernandez de Medrano (Sebastian). Geographia o moderna descripcion de el mundo, enriquezida de algunas relaciones de los payses orientales. 8 p. l. 412, 85 pp. 8 pl. 25 maps. 16°. *Brusselas, L. Marchant*, 1701.

Fernandez Vallejo (Francisco Antonio). Oracion funebre en las solemnes exequias, que en la muerte de Fernando de Borbon rey de las Españas, sexto de este nombre; se celebraron en la ciudad de Mexico, 15 de Marzo de 1760. 1 p. l. 25 pp. sm. 4°. *Mexico, colegio de S. Ildefonso*, 1760.

[*With* BALCARCEL Y FORMENTO (D.) *and* MALO (F. V.) Lagrymas de la paz].

Fernwood; or, Hattie's birth-day visit. By the author of "Fruit gathering," [etc. *anon.*] 204 pp. 3 pl. 16°. *Philadelphia, American s. s. union*, [1871].

Ferrari (Francesco Bernardino). De vetervm acclamationibvs et plavsv libri septem. 18 p. l. 407 pp. 20 l. 4°. *Mediolani, ex ambrosiani collegii typographia*, 1627.

Ferrari (Giovanni). Histoire de la raison d'état. xi, 464 pp. 8°. *Paris, M. Lévy frères*, 1860.

——— Histoire des revolutions d'Italie ou Guelfes et Gibelins. 4 v. 8°. *Paris, Didier & cie.* 1858.

Ferrari (Ottavio). Momus, sive satyra varroniana, poësi, poëtisque, cognoscendis accommodata. [*anon.*] 18°. [*Lugd. Batavorum*, 1655].

[ELEGANTIORES præstantium virorum satyræ, v. 2, pp. 463-578].

——— Octavii Ferrarii satyrica qvædam. 18°. [*Lugd. Batavorum*, 1655].

[ELEGANTIORES præstantium virorum satyræ, v. 2, pp. 739-906].

CONTENTS.

De nuptiis philologiae.
Artium et disciplinarum ductio.
Suppetiae criticis Catae.
De causis pereuntium litterarum.
Quopraetio viri principes literas ac literatos habuerint.
Literatorum funus.
Juventutis otium negotiosum. Literatorum infelicitas.

Ferraz (*M. professor at Strasburg*). De la psychologie de saint Augustin. 2 p. l. 494 pp. 8°. *Paris, Durand*, 1862.

Ferrer (*S.* Vicente). Profetie certissime stvpende et admirabili, dell' antichristo, et innvmerabili mali al mondo (se presto non si emendera) preparati, et donde hanno da venire, et dove hanno da cominciare. 40 l. 16°. [*Florentia, about* 1520].

CONTENTS.

Operetta mirabile di San Vincentio intitolato del fine del mondo.
Predica di Francesco da Monte Polzano.

Ferretti (Giovanni Battista). Mvsae lapidariae antiqvorvm in marmoribvs carmina, seu deorum donaria, hominumque illustrium oblitterata monumenta, & deperdita epitaphia: cum rerum perpetratarum publicis incisis lapidibus, quibus templorum aræ, votiua in tabellis, iconum stylobatæ, mortuorum sepulchra, facinorumque diagliphica, notata insunt: visa in vrnis, vasculis, loculis, lucernis, columnis, obeliscis, plumbeis laminis, tabulisque æneis. Eng. title, 4 p. l. 10, 372 pp. fol. *Veronæ, typis A. de Rubeis*, 1672.

Ferris (*Mrs.* Benjamin G.) Female life among the Mormons. A narrative of many years personal experiences. By the wife of a mormon elder, recently from Utah. [*anon.*] x, 9-449 pp. 1 pl. 12°. *New York, J. C. Derby*, 1855.

Ferronius (Arnoldus). *See* **Le Ferron** (Arnoul).

Fessler (Ignatius Aurelius, *called* Innocentius). Innocentii Fessler Anthologia hebraica e sacris Hebraeorum libris depromta. Adiecta est versio latina et adnotationes. 4 p. l. 63, 168 pp. 4°. *Leopoli, T. Piller*, 1787.

Fetridge (W. Pembroke). Hand-book for travellers. *See* **Harpers'** hand-book for travellers in Europe and the east.

Feuchère (Léon). L'art industriel, recueil de dispositions et de décorations intérieures, comprenant des modèles pour toutes les industries d'ameublement et de luxe. 72 planches composés et dessinées par L. Feuchère, gravées par Varin frères et précédées d'une introduction sur l'application de l'art à l'industrie. 2 p. l. 73 pl. fol. *Paris, Goupil & cie.* [*about* 1840].

Feuchtwanger (Lewis). A hand-book on silex, embraced in three practical treatises: 1. On soluble glass, and all its applications in the arts. 2. On glass making, in all its details. 3. A guide for soap making, the manufacture of all soaps and their manipula-

Feuchtwanger (Lewis)—continued. tions. 347 pp. 1 portrait. 12°. *New York, L. & J. W. Feuchtwanger*, 1871.
[*Note.*—A second edition of his "Practical treatise on soluble glass"].

Feudal tyrants; or, the counts of Carlsheim and Sargans. A romance. Taken from the german. By M. G. Lewis. [*anon.*] 2d ed. 4 v. 12°. *London, J. F. Hughes*, 1807.

Feudge (*Mrs.* Fannie R.) Enlisted for life; or, the boy-soldier in the king's army. 294 pp. 4 pl. 16°. *New York, American tract society*, [1871].

Feuerbach (Ludwig Andreas). Qu'est-ce que la religion d'après la nouvelle philosophie allemande. Par Hermann Ewerbeck [traducteur]. viii, 590 pp. 8°. *Paris, Ladrange*, 1850.

Feuerbach (Paul Joseph Anselm von). Nachgelassene schriften. 4 v. 12°. *Braunschweig, F. Vieweg & sohn*, 1853.

CONTENTS.

v. 1. Anselm Feuerbach's leben, briefe und gedichte. Herausgegeben von Henriette Feuerbach.
v. 2–3. Geschichte der griechischen plastik. Herausgegeben von Hermann Hettner.
v. 4. Kunstgeschichtliche abhandlungen. Herausgegeben von Hermann Hettner.

Feuillet (Octave). Monsieur de Camors. 9e éd. 2 p. l. 377 pp. 12°. *Paris, M. Lévy frères*, 1868.

Feuquières (Antoine de Pas, *marquis* de). Memoirs of the late marquis de Feuquieres, lieutenant-general of the french army. Written for the instruction of his son. Being an account of all the wars in Europe, from the year 1672, to the year 1710. Translated from the french. 2 v. xl, 408 pp. 4 l. 1 map; 2 p. l. 368 pp. 50 l. 8°. *London, T. Woodward*, [*etc.*] 1737.

Feykes Haan (Lourens). *See* **Haan.**

Ficino (Marsiglio). Epistole. 12°. [*Vinegia, G. Giolito de Ferrari*, 1548].
[*In* DOLCE (L.) Epistole. 1548. l. 155–157].

Fickes (David Gray). Oliver Cromwell Gray. A sketch of his life. *See* **Gray** (O. C.)

Field (David Dudley). Draft outlines of an international code. 2 p. l. 32, 463 pp. 8°. *New York, Diossy & co.* 1872.

Field (Richard, *d. d. dean of Gloucester*). Of the church, five books. [Reprint. From the 3d (Oxford) ed. 1635]. 4 v. 8°. *Cambridge (Eng.) The university press*, 1847–52.
[ECCLESIASTICAL history society publications, no. 1].

Fielding (Henry, *editor*). *See* **Champion** (The). 1741.

Fields (James Thomas). Yesterdays with authors. 5 p. l. 352 pp. 12°. *Boston, J. R. Osgood & co.* 1872.
[*Note.*—The authors are Pope, Thackeray, Hawthorne, Dickens, Wordsworth, and Miss Mitford].

Fier a bras. Der roman von Fierabras, provenzalisch. [*anon.*] Herausgegeben von Immanuel Bekker. lxviii, 5–186 pp. 4°. *Berlin, G. Reimer*, 1829.

——— The same. Fierabras. Légende nationale, traduite par Mary Lafon et illustrée de gravures dessinées par G. Doré. xv, 179 pp. 2 l. 12 pl. 8°. *Paris, librairie nouvelle*, 1857.

Fight (The) at dame Europa's school. *See* **Pullen** (Henry William).

Figueroa (Joseph Vidal de). *See* **Vidal de Figueroa.**

Figuier (Guillaume Louis). Mammalia. Their various orders and habits popularly illustrated by typical species. xii, 606 pp. 8°. *London, Chapman & Hall*, 1870.

——— The to-morrow of death; or, the future life according to science. Translated from the french by S. R. Crocker. viii, 395 pp. 12°. *Boston, Roberts bros.* 1872.

Filelfo (Francesco). Epistolae familiares domini Francisci Philelphi. lxxxvii l. numb. 1 l. fol. *Venetiis, per I. de Cereto alias Tacuinum de Tridino*, 1498.
[*With his* Orationes cum aliis opusculis. 1496.
Note.—Sixty-two lines on a page].

——— Orationes Philelphi cum aliis opusculis. lxxix l. fol. *Venetiis, per P. de Pinzis*, 1496.
[*Note.*—Sixty-one lines usually on a page].

Filelfo (Giovanni Maria). Vita Dantis Aligherii. Nvnc primvm ex codice lavrentiano in lvcem edita et notis illvstrata [studio et cura Dominici Morenii]. xliv, 144 pp. 8°. *Florentiae, ex typographia magheriana*, 1828.

"**Filia.**" [*pseudon.*] *See* **Dorsey** (S. A.)

Filicaia (Vincenzio da). Poesie toscane. 2 v. 1 p. l. 279 pp; 318 pp. 16°. *Firenze, N. Conti*, 1819.

Finch (Anne Hatton, *countess of Winchilsea*). Poems on several occasions. 4 p. l. 390 pp. 12°. *London, W. Taylor*, 1714.

Finch (*Sir* Henry, *of Gray's inn*). Νομοτεχνια; cestascavoir, vn description del common leys d Angleterre solonqve les rules del art. Parallelees ove les prerogatives le roy. Ovesque auxq le substance & effect de les estatutes (disposes en lour proper lieux) per le quels le common ley est abridge, enlarge, ou ascunment alter, del commencement de

Finch (*Sir* Henry)—continued.
Magna Charta, fait 9. H. 3, tanque a cest jour. 5 p. l. 149 l., fol. *London, for the societie of stationers*, 1613.
[There are 9 l. unp. between l. 22 and l. 23].

Finlay (George). The hellenic kingdom, and the greek nation. With an introduction by S. G. Howe. xii, 11–110 pp. 12°. *Boston, Marsh, Capen & Lyon*, 1837.

Finlay (William). Poems, humorous and sentimental. x, 278 pp. 16°. *Paisley, Murray & Stewart, & W. Wotherspoon*, 1846.

Finlayson (William). Simple scottish rhymes. 168 pp. 16°. *Paisley, S. & A Young*, 1815.

Finley (Martha). Lilian; or, did she do right? 104 pp. 1 pl. 8°. *Philadelphia, W. B. Evans & co.* [1871].

——— An old-fashioned boy. By Martha Farquharson. 346 pp. 4 pl. 16°. *Philadelphia, Evans, Stoddart & co.* [1871].

——— Wanted—a pedigree. 528 pp. 1 pl. 12°. *Philadelphia, W. B. Evans & co.* [1871].

Finney (*Rev.* Charles G.) Lectures on systematic theology, embracing lectures on moral government, together with atonement, moral and physical depravity, regeneration, philosophical theories, and evidences of regeneration. xix, 587 pp. 8°. *Oberlin (O.) J. M. Fitch*, 1846.

——— Lectures to professing christians. Delivered in the city of New-York, in the years 1836 and 1837. From notes by the editor of the New York Evangelist, revised by the author. 348 pp. 12°. *New-York, J. S. Taylor*, 1837.

Fiocchi (Andrea Domenico). L. Fenestellæ de magistratibus, sacerdotiisqve Romanorvm libri ii. [*pseudon.*] 37 l. 8°. *Lvtetiæ, apud Vascosanum*, 1550.
[*With* LETO (Giulio Pomponio). De romanis magistratibvs, 1550].

Fioravanti (V.) Columella's return from his studies at Padua. Composed by V. Fioravanti. Translated and adapted by Arthur Baildon. [Libretto, without music]. 35 pp. 8°. [*New York*], *W. C. Bryant & co.* 1871.
[PAREPA-ROSA grand english opera].

Fiordibello (Antonio). De vita Iacobi Sadoleti s. r. e. presbyteri card. commentarius. 16°. [*Lvgdvni*, 1560].
[*In* SADOLETO (Jacopo). Epistolarum libri sexdecim, pp. 697–716].

Fiore (Pasquale). Nouveau droit international public suivant les besoins de la civilisation moderne. Traduit de l'italien, annoté,

Fiore (Pasquale)—continued.
précédé d'une introduction historique, et suivi d'une table analytique et alphabétique des matières par P. Pradier-Fodéré. 2 v. 2 p. l. cxvi, 526 pp; 2 p. l. 695 pp. 8°. *Paris, A. Durand & Pedone-Lauriel*, 1868–69.

Fiori (Giorgio). Georgii Flori mediolanensis de expeditione Caroli viii. in neapolitanum regnum, libri dvo. fol. [*Paris*, 1684].
[*In* GODEFROY (T. *and* D. de) Histoire de Charles viii. pp. 216–237].

Fire (The) insurance register. *See* **Goodsell** (J. H. *and* C. M.)

Firenze antica, e moderna. *See* **Follini** (Vincenzo) *and* **Rastrelli** (Modesti).

Firenzuola (Agnolo). Opere. 5 v. 8°. *Milano, dalla società tipographica de' classici italiani*, 1802.

CONTENTS.

v. 1. Vita, dialogo dello bellezza delle donne. Lettere diverse. Discorsi degli animali.
v. 2. Ragionamenti amorosi. Novelle.
v. 3. Giornata prima dell' asino d'oro di Apulejo, traslato di latino.
v. 4. Le rime.
v. 5. La Trinuzia comedia. I Lucidi comedia.

——— Prose. 65 l. 18°. *Fiorenza, B. Giunti*, 1548.
[*With his* Rime, ed. 1549].

——— Le rime. 136 l. 18°. *Fiorenza, B. Giunti*, 1549.

Fireside (The) companion. *See* **New York** fireside companion.

Firmacus Maternus *junior* (Julius). De errore profanarum religionum ad Constantium et Constantem Augustos liber. Recensuit F. Oehler. 12°. *Lipsiae, B. Tauchnitz, jun.* 1847.
[GERSDORF (E. G.) Bibliotheca patrum ecclesiasticorum latinorum selecta, v. 1, pp. 57–120.]

Firmianus Lactantius. *See* **Lactantius.**

Firmianus Symposius (Cælius). Cælii Symposii ænigmata. Hanc novam editionem, juxta lectiones optimas diligenter congestam, curavit Lucius M. Sargent. 35 pp. 12°. *Bostoniæ, Nov-Angl. prelo Belcher & Armstrong*, 1807.

First help in accidents and sickness. A guide in the absence, or before the arrival, of medical assistance. Published with the recommendation of the highest medical authority. [*anon.*] 264 pp. 16°. *Boston, A. Moore*, 1871.

Fischer (Johann Baptist). Flora Javae nec non insularium adjacentium. *See* **Blume** (Carl Ludwig).

Fischer (P.) *and* **Crosse** (H.) Études sur les mollusques terrestres et fluviatiles du

Fischer (P.) *and* **Crosse** (H.)—continued. Mexique et du Guatémala. 152 pp. 6 pl. 4°. [*Paris, imprimerie impériale*, 1870]. s.
[FRANCE. *Ministère de l'instruction publique.* Mission scientifique au Mexique. Recherches zoologiques, 7e partie].

Fisgrave (Antony, *ll. d. pseudon?*) Midas; or, a serious inquiry concerning taste and genius; including a proposal for the certain advancement of the elegant arts. [Also], by way of illustration, a fragment of ancient history. xvi, 208 pp. 18°. *London, J. Murray*, 1808,

Fish (Henry C. *d. d.*) The price of soul-liberty, and who paid it. 152 pp. 18°. *New York, Sheldon & co.* 1860.
——— Primitive piety revived, or the aggressive power of the christian church. A premium essay. xii, 249 pp. 12°. *Boston, Congregational board of publication*, 1855.

Fish (*Rev.* Joseph). Christ Jesus the physician, and his blood the balm, [etc.] In a sermon preach'd before the general assembly of Connecticut, on the day of their anniversary election, May 8, 1760. 66 pp. 16°. *New-London, Timothy Green*, [*etc.*] 1760.
——— The examiner examined. Remarks on a piece wrote by mr. Isaac Backus; printed in 1768. (Called, "An examination of nine sermons," by mr. Joseph Fish). Wherein those sermons are vindicated. 127 pp. 8°. *New-London (Conn.) T. Green*, 1771.

Fish (Simon). A supplicacyon for the beggers. Written about the year 1529. Now re-edited by Frederick J. Furnivall. 8°. *London, N. Trübner & co.* 1871.
[EARLY english text society. Extra series, xiii, pp. 1–18].

Fisher (Frances C.) Mabel Lee. A novel. By the author of "Valerie Aylmer," [etc. *anon.*] 162 pp. 4 pl. 8°. *New York, D. Appleton & co.* 1872.
——— Morton house. A novel. By the author of "Valerie Aylmer." [*anon.*] 2 p. l. 266 pp. 4 pl. 8°. *New York, D. Appleton & co.* 1872.

Fisher (George Adams). The yankee conscript; or eighteen months in Dixie. With an introduction by rev. William Dickson. 251 pp. 1 portrait. 12°. *Philadelphia, J. W. Daughaday*, 1864.

Fisher (Jonathan). Scenery of Ireland illustrated in a series of select views. v. 1. 2 p. l. iv pp. 53 l. unp. 6 pp. 60 pl. obl. fol. *London, author*, 1795.
[Wanting 4 pl.: nos. 5, 6, 30, 51].

Fisher (Richard Swainson, *m. d.*) A chronological history of the civil war in America. Illustrated with A. J. Johnson's and J. H. Colton's steel plate maps and plans of the southern states and harbors. 160 pp. 10 maps. 8°. *New York, Johnson & Ward*, 1863.

Fisher (*Rev.* Samuel R.) Exercises on the Heidelberg catechism. Revised ed. 256 pp. 16°. *Chambersburg (Pa.) publication office of the German reformed church*, 1854.
——— The family assistant; or book of prayers for the use of families. 308 pp. 16°. *Chambersburg (Pa.) M. Kieffer & co.* 1855.

Fisher (Samuel W. *d. d.*) Occasional sermons and addresses. 568 pp. 8°. *New York, Mason brothers*, 1860.

Fisher (Theodore W. *m. d.*) Plain talk about insanity: its causes, forms, symptoms, and the treatment of mental diseases. With remarks on hospitals and asylums, and the medico-legal aspect of insanity. 3 p. l. 17–97 pp. 3 pl. 8°. *Boston, A. Moore*, 1872.

Fiske (William O.) The offertorium: a complete collection of music for the sunday and holyday services of the catholic church. 247 pp. obl. 8°. *Boston, O. Ditson & co.* [1872].

Fitch (Eleazar T. *d. d.*) Sermons, practical and descriptive, preached in the pulpit of Yale college. [Edited by Lucius W. Fitch]. viii, 365 pp. 8°. *New Haven, Judd and White*, 1871.

Fitch (Samuel Sheldon, *m. d.*) A system of dental surgery. In three parts. i. Dental surgery as a science. ii. Operative dental surgery. iii. Pharmacy connected with dental surgery. 2d ed. 553 pp. 14 pl. 1 tab. 8°. *Philadelphia, Carey, Lea & Blanchard*, 1835.

Fitch (*Captain* William E.) Manual of the tenth regiment infantry n. g. s. N. Y. comprising forms of all the books and blanks used by the regiment. 62 pp. 12°. *Albany, The argus co.* 1872.

Fitchburg (*Mass.*) The Fitchburg directory, for the year commencing July, 1871. 244 pp. 3 l. 8°. *Fitchburg (Mass.) L. G. Corbin*, [*etc.*] 1871.

Fitzball (E.) Maritana. [Libretto]. *See* **Wallace** (W. V.)

Fitzgerald (Edward). A hand-book for the Albany rural cemetery, with an appendix of emblems. 1 p. l. 141 pp. 12 pl. 1 map. 12°. *Albany, Van Benthuysen printing house*, 1871.

Fitzinger (Leopold Joseph). Bilder-atlas zur wissenschaftlich-populären naturgeschichte der amphibien in ihren sämmtlichen hauptformen. 1 p. l. [108 col. pl.] 200 fig. 4°. *Wien, k. k. hof- und staatsdruckerei,* 1864. s.

——— Bilder-atlas zur wissenschaftlich-populären naturgeschichte der fische in ihren sämmtlichen hauptformen. 1 p. l. [7 col. pl.] 193 fig. 4°. *Wien, k. k. hof- und staatsdruckerei,* 1864.

Fitzwilliam (William Wentworth-, *viscount* Milton). A history of the San Juan water boundary question, as affecting the division of territory between Great Britain and the United States. Collected and compiled from official papers and documents printed under the authority of the governments respectively of Great Britain and Ireland and of the United States of America, and from other sources. 2 p. l. 442 pp. 2 maps. 8°. *London, Cassell, Petter & Galpin,* 1869.

Five years in the Alleghanies. [By a colporteur. *anon.*] 206 pp. 1 pl. 18°. *New York, American tract society,* [1863].

Flamel (Nicolas). Le livre de Nicolas Flamel, contenant l'explication des figures hyérogliphiques qu'il a fait mettre au cimetière des ss. innocens à Paris. Petit traité d'alchymie, intitulé le sommaire philosophique [poëme]. Le désir désiré de N. Flamel. 12°. [*Paris, A. Cailleau,* 1741].

[*In* SALMON (Guillaume). Bibliothèque des philosophes chimiques. 1741. v. 2, pp. 195-324].

Flaminio (Marco Antonio). Carminvm libri qvattvor. 16°. *Venetiis, ex officina Vincentii Valgrisii,* 1548.

[*In* CARMINA qvinqve illvstrivm poetarvm, pp. 97-227].

——— De rebus divinis. [With a translation by Tho. Morell]. 8°. [*London, E. Owen,* 1736].

[*In* VIDA (Marco Girolamo). Poems on divine subjects. *London,* 1736. pp. 221-237].

——— M. Antonii Flaminii paraphrasis in triginta psalmos, versibvs scripta. 16°. *Venetiis, in officina Vincentii Valgrisii,* 1548.

[*In* CARMINA qvinqve illvstrivm poetarvm, pp. 229-275].

Flanders (*Mrs.* G. M.) The ebony idol. [*anon.*] 2 p. l. 283 pp. 1 pl. 18°. *New York, D. Appleton & co.* 1860.

Flatt (Johann Friedrich von). Vorlesungen über die beyden briefe Pauli an die Corinthier. *See* **Bible.** (*German*).

Flaux (A. de). Du Danemarck. Impressions de voyage, aperçus historiques, et considérations sur le passé, le présent et l'avenir de ce pays. 2 p. l. 363 pp. 8°. *Paris, F. Didot frères, fils et comp.* 1862.

Flavel (*Rev.* John). The great design and scope of the gospel opened. An extract from [his] "England's duty." Recommended as a word peculiarly seasonable for the present day. With a preface by the rev. mr. Byles. 3 p. l. 28 pp. 1 l. 16°. *Boston, H. Foster,* 1741.

——— Husbandry spiritualized; or the heavenly uses of earthly things. [Also], occasional meditations upon birds, beasts, trees, flowers, &c. Also, the touchstone of sincerity. And extracts from A token for mourners. 392 pp. 12°. *Middletown,* [*Conn.*] *J. A. Boswell,* 1824.

——— Sacramental meditations upon divers passages of scripture. 1st american, from the 6th London edition, with corrections and translations. iv, 156 pp. pp. 161-176. 12°. *Richmond, J. Martin,* 1824.

——— Two treatises: the first of fear, from Isa. 8: v. 12, 13, 14. The second, the righteous man's refuge in the evil day, from Isaiah 26: v. 20. 7 p. l. 285 pp. 12°. *London, H. H. for R. Boulter,* 1682.

——— A word to the well wishers of the good work of God in this land. 23 pp. 16°. *Boston, Rogers & Fowle,* 1742.

[*Note.*—An extract from his Blow at the root, etc.]

Flechere (*Rev.* John William de la). *See* **Fletcher** (*Rev.* John William).

Fleetwood (William). Inscriptionum antiquarum sylloge in duas partes distributa. Quarum prior inscriptiones ethnicas singulares & rariores pene omnes continet. Altera christiana monumenta antiqua quæ hactenus innotuerunt omnia complectitur. 7 p. l. 536 pp. 6 l. 8°. *Londini, impensis G. Graves,* 1691.

Fleischmann (Charles L.) *See* **American** (The) polytechnic journal.

Fleming (Caleb). A survey of the Search after souls, by dr. Coward, dr. S. Clarke, and others. Wherein the principal arguments for and against the materiality are collected: and the distinction between the mechanical and moral system stated. With an essay to ascertain the condition of the christian, during the mediatorial kingdom of Jesus. 2 p. l. xiii, 314 pp. 8°. *London, C. Henderson,* 1758.

Fleming (Lorenzo D.) The new-testament companion, designed for bible classes, sabbath school teachers, and young students of the scriptures. With an introduction. 196 pp. 1 pl. 24°. *Portland (Me.) S. H. Colesworthy*, 1839.

Fleming (M.) Political annals of Lower Canada; being a review of the political and legislative history of that province, under the act of the imperial parliament, which established a house of assembly and legislative council. With an introductory chapter on the previous history of Canada, and an appendix of documents, etc. By a british settler. [*anon.*] lxxviii, 180 pp. 8°. *Montreal, Montreal Herald office*, 1828.

Fleming (*Rev.* Robert, *sr.* 1630–94). The fulfilling of the scripture. Or an essay shewing the exact accomplishment of the word of God in his works performed and to be performed. Containing [at the close] some rare histories of the works and the servants of God in the church of Scotland. With a preface by mr. Foxcroft. xxiv, xii, 522 pp. 16°. *Boston, W. McAlpine*, 1743.

Fleming (*Rev.* Robert, *jr. d.* 1716). Discourses on several subjects. The first containing a new account of the rise and fall of the papacy. The second upon God's dwelling with men. The third concerning the ministerial office. The fourth being a brief account of religion as it centers in the lord Jesus Christ. 4 p. l. clxxvii, 248 pp. 7 l. 8°. *London, A. Bell*, 1701.

Fletcher (Giles, *ll. d.*) Christs victorie, and triumph in heauen, and earth, over, and after death. 8 p. l. 84 pp. 16°. *Cambridge (Eng.) C. Legge*, 1610.

Fletcher (*Rev.* John William). Beauties of Fletcher; being extracts from his Checks to antinomianism. By rev. T. Spicer. 315 pp. 1 pl. 12°. *New York, T. Mason & G. Lane*, 1840.

——— Letters, from his posthumous works, edited by the rev. Melville Horne. 12°. [*Philadelphia*, 1837].

[*In* COX (Robert). The life of the rev. J. W. Fletcher, 1837, pp. 175–240].

——— The posthumous pieces of the late rev. John William de la Flechere. By the rev. Melville Horne. 384 pp. 16°. *Albany, Barber & Southwick for T. Spencer & A. Ellison*, 1794.

——— The same. The posthumous works of the rev. John Fletcher, compiled by the rev. Melville Horne. [Also], a dialogue, selected

Fletcher (*Rev.* J. W.)—continued.

from mr. Fletcher's papers, and furnished by the rev. Joseph Benson. 432 pp. 1 portrait. 12°. *Baltimore, Harrod & Buel*, 1814.

Fletcher (Joseph, *d. d.*) Lectures on the principles and institutions of the roman catholic religion: with an appendix containing critical and historical illustrations. 5th ed. Edited by the rev. Joseph Fletcher, [son]. vii, 325 pp. 16°. *London, W. Kent & co.* 1851.

Fleury (*Rev.* Anthony). A short essay on the general resurrection: wherein it is proved, that we shall rise with those same bodies that we now have; and the objections to this opinion are candidly examined and answered. 350 pp. 8°. *Dublin, S. Powell*, 1752.

Fleury (Édouard). Biographie de Camille Desmoulins. Études révolutionnaires. 396 pp. 8°. *Laon, E. Fleury & A. Chevergny*, [*about* 1854].

Flint (Charles Louis). Manual of agriculture. *See* **Emerson** (George B.) *and* **Flint.**

Flint (S. A.) Great success. By F. S. A. author of "The silver lining." [*anon.*] 397 pp. 3 pl. 16°. *Boston, H. A. Young & co.* [1871].

Flögel (Carl Friedrich). Geschichte der komischen litteratur. 4 v. 8°. *Liegnitz und Leipzig, D. Siegert*, 1784–87.

Florebellus (Antonius). *See* **Fiordibello** (Antonio).

Florence. (*Galerie impériale*). Galerie impériale et royale de Florence. Nouv. éd. ornée des planches de la Vénus de Médicis, de celle de Canova et de l'Apollon. 193 pp. 1 l. 3 pl. 16°. *Florence, Albizzi*, 1819.

Flores (Juan de). L'histoire d'Aurélio & Isabelle fille du roy d'Escoce, mieux corrigée que por cy deuant, mise en español & françois. [Par Maurice Scèvi? *anon.*] 96 l. 24°. *Anuers, I. VVithage*, 1556.

Florian (Jean Pierre Claris de). Estelle, roman pastoral. 2 v. in 1. 116 pp; 142 pp. 16°. *Paris, Bailly*, 1788.

——— Numa Pompilius. 2 v. in 1. 2 p. l. 176 pp; 183 pp. 2 pl. 24°. *Paris, Lebigre frères*, 1833.

——— Claudine; or, the girl of Savoy. A tale. 16°. [*Georgetown* (D. C.) *Richards & Mallory*, 1813].

[*In* GENLIS (S. F. D. de Saint Aubin, *comtesse* de). Sainclair, or the victim to the arts and sciences, 1813. pp. 195–246].

Florian (J. P. C. de)—continued.
——— New tales. From the french. 2 p. l. 283 pp. 16°. *London, T. & J. Egerton*, 1792.

CONTENTS.

Seymour; an english tale, p. 1.
Selico; an african tale, p. 60.
Claudina; a savoyard tale, p. 89.
Zulbar; an indian tale, p. 142.
Camira; an american tale, p. 175.
Valeria; an italian tale, p. 235.

Florio (Giovanni). Vocabolario italiano & inglese, a dictionary italian & english. Formerly compiled by John Florio, and since his last edition, 1611, augmented by himself in his life time, with many thousand words, and thuscan phrases. Now most diligently revised, corrected, and compared, with La Crusca, and other approved dictionaries. [With] a dictionary english & italian, with severall proverbs and instructions for the speedy attaining to the italian tongue. By Gio: Torriano. 388 l. 40 pp. fol. *London, T. Warren*, 1659.

Florus (Annæus). L. Annaei Flori epitome rerum romanarum. L. Ampelii liber memorialis. Praemittitur notitia literaria studiis societatis bipontinae. 1 p. l. 229 pp. 14 l. 8°. *Biponti, ex typographia societatis*, 1783.

Flotow (Friedrich von). Martha. [Libretto, without music]. 43 pp. 8°. [*New York*], *W. C. Bryant & co.* 1871.
[Parepa-Rosa grand english opera].

Flower (Benjamin). The french constitution; with remarks on some of its principal articles; in which their importance in a political, moral and religious point of view, is illustrated; and the necessity of a reformation in church and state in Great Britain, enforced. viii, 501 pp. 8°. *London, G. G. J. & J. Robinson*, [*etc.*] 1792.

Flower (William Henry, *m. d.*) Diagrams of the nerves of the human body; exhibiting their origin, divisions and connections, with their distribution to the various regions of the cutaneous surface and to all the muscles. Edited, with additions, by William W. Keen, m. d. 12 pp. 6 pl. 4°. *Philadelphia, T. Hamilton*, 1872.

Floyd (*Rev.* M.) Travels in France and the british islands. 383 pp. 12°. *Philadelphia, J. B. Lippincott & co.* 1859.

Fluctibus (Robertus de). *See* **Fludd** (Robert).

Fludd (Robert). Integrvm morborvm mysterivm. 2 v. Eng. title, 12 p. l. 503 pp; 2 p. l. 413 pp. fol. *Francofvrti, typis excusus W. Hofmanni, prostat in officina G. Fitzeri*, 1631.

Fludd (Robert)—continued.
——— Philosophia moysaica. In qua sapientia & scientia creationis & creaturarum sacra veréque christiana ad amussim & enucleate explicatur. 4 p. l. 152 l. numb. fol. *Govdæ, P. Rammazenius*, 1638.

——— Pvlsvs, seu nova et arcana pvlsvvm historia, e sacro fonte radicaliter extracta. Hoc est, portionis tertiæ pars tertia, de pvlsvvm scientia. 94 pp. fol. [*Francofvrti*, 1631].
[*With his* Integrvm morborvm mysterivm, v. 2].

——— Responsvm ad Hoplocrisma-spongvm M. Fosteri presbiteri, ab ipso, ad vngventi armarii validitatem delendam ordinatvm, hoc est, spongiæ M. Fosteri expressio sev elisio. 30 l. numb. fol. *Govdæ, P. Rammazenius*, 1638.
[*With his* Philosophia moysaica].

——— Utriusque cosmi maioris scilicet et minoris metaphysica, physica atqve technica historia [etc.] v. 1. 1 p. l. 788 pp. 5 l. 4 pl. fol. *Oppenhemii, ære J. T. de Bry, typis H. Galleri*, 1617.

Fluviatulis piscator. [*pseudon.*] *See* **Seccomb** (*Rev.* Joseph). Business and diversion inoffensive etc.

Focher (Juan). Itinerarivm catholicvm proficiscentium, ad infideles cōuertendos. Nu per summa cura et diligētia auctū, expurgatum, limatū ac prælo mādatū, per fratrem Didacum Valadesium. 8 p. l. 99 l. 8 l. sq. 18°. *Hispali, apud Alfonsum Scribanum*, 1574.
[Imperfect: last leaf wanting].

Focke (Gustav Waldemar). Physiologische studien. A. Wirbellose thiere. 1. Polygastrische infusorien. Parts 1–2 in 1 v. 2 p. l. 64 pp. 3 l. 3 col. pl; 2 p. l. 64 pp. 3 pl. 8°. *Bremen, C. Schünemann*, 1847–54. s.

Foglietta (Uberto). Uberti Folietæ clarorvm Ligvrvm elogia. 4 p. l. 265 pp. 1 l. sm. fol. *Romae, apud heredes Antonii Bladii*, 1573.

Foigny *or* **Cogny** (Gabriel). Nieuwe reize na het Zuid-land, behelzende de gewoontens en zeden der Zuidlanders, der selver godtsdienst, oeffeningen, studien, oorlogen, gediertens, en alle de voornaamste zeldsaamheden welke aldaar gevonden worden. Door Jaques Sadeur. [*pseudon.*] 48 pp. 1 pl. sm. 4°. *Amsterdam, W. de Coup*, 1701.
[*Note.*—Translated from the french and abbreviated].

Folengo (Teofilo, *baptised* Girolamo). Chāos del tri per vno. [*anon.*] 112 l. 16°. *Vinc-*

Folengo (Teofilo)—continued. *gia, G. A. & P. fratelli de Nicolini da Sabio,* 1546.

[*Note.*—Chiefly in italian, partly latin and macaronic].

——— [Selections] from the Phantasiæ macaronicæ of Theoph. Folengi (Merlin Cocaius). [Reprint]. 16°. [*New York, Hurd & Houghton,* 1872].

[*In* MORGAN (James Appleton). Macaronic poetry, pp. 195-198].

Folieta (Ubertus). *See* **Foglietta** (Uberto).

Folio. A journal of music, art, and literature. Edited by Dexter Smith. [Monthly]. Sept. 1869-Dec. 1871. v. 1-5 in 2 v. 4°. *Boston, White, Smith & Perry,* 1869-71.

Folkingham (William). Fevdigraphia. The synopsis or epitome of svrveying methodized. 4 p. l. 88 pp. sm. 4°. *London, R. Moore,* 1610.

Follen (Eliza Lee). Home dramas for young people. vii, 441 pp. 12°. *Boston & Cambridge, J. Munroe & co.* 1859.

——— Little songs, for little boys and girls. By the author of The well-spent hour, etc. [*anon.*] 66 pp. sq. 24°. *Boston, L. C. Bowles,* 1833.

Follini (Vincenzo) *and* **Rastrelli** (Modesti). Firenze antica e moderna illustrata. [*anon.*] 8 v. 8°. *Firenze, P. Allegrini,* 1789-90.

[*Note.*—v. 1-2 by Follini; v. 3-8 by Rastrelli].

Fonblanque (Albany). Cut adrift. A novel. 3 v. 12°. *London, R. Bentley,* 1869.

Fonfrède (Henri). Questions d'économie publique, recueillies et mises en ordre par Ch. Al. Campan, son collaborateur. 2 v. vii, 416 pp; 450 pp. 8°. *Bordeaux, C. Gayet & Lawalle jeune,* 1846.

Fontaine (*Rev.* Edward). How the world was peopled. Ethnological lectures. 341 pp. 12°. *New York, D. Appleton & co.* 1872.

Fontani (Francesco). Viaggio pittorico della Toscana. Ed. 3ª, con ritratto dell' autore. 6 v. 18°. *Firenze, G. Marenigh,* 1822.

Fontenelle (Bernard Le Bouyer *or* Le Bovier de). Entretiens sur la pluralité des mondes, augmentés des dialogues des morts. Nouvelle éd. xvi, 410 pp. 1 pl. 18°. *Paris, J. Bossange & Tenon,* 1821.

——— The same. A discovery of new worlds. From the french. Made english by mrs. A[phra] Behn. With a preface by way of essay upon translated prose, wholly new. 22 p. l. 159 pp. 12°. *London, W. Canning,* 1688.

Fontenelle (Bernard Le B. de)—continued.

——— Fontenelle's Dialogues of the dead, in three parts. i. Dialogues of the antients. ii. The antients with the moderns. iii. The moderns. Translated from the french by the late John Hughes. With a reply to some remarks in a critique, call'd The judgment of Pluto, &c. and two original dialogues. 2d ed. 1 p. l. lxvi, 256 pp. 16°. *London, J. Tonson,* 1730.

——— Of pastorals. English'd by mr. Motteux. 16°. [*London,* 1795].

[*In* Le Bossu (René). Treatise of the epick poem, v. 2, pp. 316-351].

Foot (Jessé). The life of John Hunter. 2 p. l. 288 pp. 8°. *London, T. Becket,* 1794.

——— The life of Arthur Murphy. iv, 464 pp. 3 portraits, 4 facs. 4°. *London, J. Faulder,* 1811.

Foot (Joseph I. *d. d.*) Sermons. With a brief biographical sketch, by rev. George Foot. 600 pp. 8°. *Philadelphia, Hooker & Agnew,* 1841.

Foote (Edward B. *m. d.*) Plain home talk about the human system—the habits of men and women—[etc.] embracing medical common sense applied to causes, prevention, and cure of chronic diseases. 909 pp. 1 portrait. 12°. *New York, Wells & Coffin,* 1870.

Foote (E. M.) Belshazzar. 1871. *See* **Butterfield** (J. A.)

Foote (John P.) Memoirs of the life of Samuel E. Foote, by his brother. 307 pp. 12°. *Cincinnati, R. Clarke & co.* 1860.

For everybody. [An illustrated family paper. Monthly]. Feb. to Dec. 1871. v. 1. 4°. *Buffalo, H. H. Sage,* [1871].

Forbes (James David). Notice biographique sur L. A. Necker. 12°. [*Genève, J. Cherbuliez,* 1864].

[*In* NECKER (L. A.) Mémoire sur les oiseaux des environs de Genève, pp. 5-45, ed. 1864].

Forbes (Patrick, *m. d.*) A full view of the public transactions in the reign of q. Elizabeth [1558-1563]: or a particular account of all the memorable affairs of that queen, transmitted in a series of letters and other papers of state. Published from manuscripts in the Paper office, Cottonian library, and other public and private repositories, at home and abroad. 2 v. 2 p. l. xii, 507 pp. 8 l; 6 p. l. 500 pp. 10 l. fol. *London, G. Hawkins,* 1740-41.

Forcadel (Étienne). Penvs ivris civilis, sive de alimentis tractatvs. Item Auiarium iuris ciuilis Ad haec, Ardua sapientis cuiusdam

Forcadel (Étienne)—continued. græci cum stulto romano disputatio nutu habita. 71, 50 pp. 4°. *Lvgdvni, apvd I. Tornaesivm & G. Gazeivm*, 1550.
[*With* CHOVERON (Bermond de). De publicis concubinarijs].

Ford (John). The Cambridge directory, 1854. *See* **Cambridge** (*Mass.*)

Ford (*Mrs.* Sallie Rochester). Grace Truman; or, love and principle. 499 pp. 1 portrait. 12°. *New York, Sheldon, Blakeman & co.* 1857.

——— Mary Bunyan, the dreamer's blind daughter. A tale of religious persecution. 1 p. l. 11–488 pp. 1 pl. 12°. *New York, Sheldon & co.* 1860.

Ford (Theodosia). Christmas fairies. 2 p. l. 11–199 pp. 4 pl. 16°. *Philadelphia, Claxton, Remsen & Haffelfinger*, 1872.

Forest hills cemetery: its establishment, progress, scenery, monuments, etc. [*anon.*] 237 pp. 10 pl. 12°. *Roxbury,* [*Mass.*] *J. Backup*, 1855.

Forester (Frank, *pseudon.*) *See* **Herbert** (Henry William).

Forgues (Émile Dauran). La Chine ouverte. Aventures d'un fankouei dans le pays de Tsin. Par Old Nick. [*pseudon.*] Ouvrage illustré par Auguste Borget. Eng. title, vi, 396 pp. 49 pl. 8°. *Paris, H. Fournier*, 1845.

Formby (*Rev.* Henry). A visit to the east; comprising Germany and the Danube, Constantinople, Asia Minor, Egypt, and Idumea. 5 p. l. 387 pp. 5 pl. 12°. *London, J. Burns*, 1843.

Formey (Jean Henri Samuel). Le philosophe chrétien. 2e éd. 4 v. 16°. *Leide, E. Luzac, fils*, 1752–57.

——— Le philosophe payen, ou pensées de Pline; avec un commentaire littéraire & moral. 3 v. 16°. *Leide, E. Luzac, fils*, 1759.

Forrest (Chris.) De Witt's complete american farrier and horse doctor. With copious notes from the best english and american authorities. 208 pp. 16°. *New York, R. M. De Witt*, [1870].

Forrest (Neil, *pseudon?*) Fiddling Freddy. 228 pp. 4 pl. 16°. *New York, A. D. F. Randolph & co.* [1871].

Försch (Johann August). Leben, thaten, und meinungen des Ulrich Zwingli. 3 p. l. 156 pp. 1 l. 1 portrait. 16°. *Chambersburg (Pa.) V. Scriba*, 1837.

Forster (George). A journey from Bengal to England, through the northern part of India, Kashmire, Afghanistan, and Persia, and into Russia, by the Caspian-sea. 2 v. xv, 315, pp. 1 map; 2 p. l. 297 pp. 4°. *London, R. Faulder*, 1798.

Forster (Johann Reinhold). Manuel pour servir à l'histoire naturelle des oiseaux, des poissons, des insectes et des plantes; où sont expliqués les termes employés dans leurs descriptions, et suivant la méthode de Linné; traduit du latin: augmenté d'un mémoire de Murray sur la conchyliologie, traduit de la même langue, et de plusieurs additions considérables extraites des ouvrages des cit. Lacépède, Jussieu, Lamarck, Cuvier, etc. Par J. F. B. Léveillé. xxiv, 437 pp. 8°. *Paris, Villier*, [1799].

CONTENTS.

1e partie. Ornithologie.
2e partie. Ichthyologie.
3e partie. Testacéologie. [Par A. Murray].
4e partie. Entomologie.
5e partie. Terminologie botanique.

Forster (John). The life of Charles Dickens. v. 1. 1812–1842. xix, 398 pp. 2 portraits. 8°. *London, Chapman & Hall*, 1872.

——— The same. v. 1. 1812–1842. 418 pp. 1 portrait, 1 pl. 6 facs. 12°. *Philadelphia, J. B. Lippincott & co.* 1872.

Forster. *See* **Foster.**

Fort (G.) Coos-coo-soo; or letters from Tangier, in Africa. 299 pp. 1 pl. 12°. *Philadelphia, J. S. M'Calla*, 1859.

Fortescue (The) papers; consisting chiefly of letters relating to state affairs, collected by John Packer, secretary to George Villiers, duke of Buckingham. Edited, from the original mss. in the possession of the hon. G. M. Fortescue, by Samuel Rawson Gardiner. 2 p. l. xxxv, 225 pp. 4°. [*London*], *Camden society*, 1871.
[CAMDEN society publications, new series, v. 1, no. 1].

Fortis (Alberto). Travels into Dalmatia; containing general observations on the natural history of that country and the neighboring islands; the natural productions, arts, manners and customs of the inhabitants: in a series of letters. To which are added by the same author, observations on the island of Cherso and Osero. Translated from the italian under the author's inspection. With an appendix, and additions. 1 p. l. x, 584 pp. 19 pl. 1 map. 4°. *London, J. Robson*, 1778.

Fortnightly (The) review. Edited by John Morley. [Monthly]. Jan. 1, 1871, to Dec. 1, 1871. New series, v. 9–10; old series, v. 15–16. 8°. *London, Chapman & Hall*, 1871.

Fosbery (Thomas Vincent). Hymns and poems for the sick and suffering. xlii, 333 pp. 16°. *London, Rivingtons,* 1871.

Foscolo (Niccolò Ugo). Didymi clerici prophetæ minimi Hypercalypseos liber singularis. [Con una Notizia intorno a Didimo chierico, stampata al volumetto intitolato Viaggio sentimentale di Yorick, versione di Didimo, Pisa, 1813, e Clavis Hypercalypseōs]. xvi, 64, 12 pp. 8°. [*Pisis, in ædibus sapientiæ,* 1815].

[No title-page: in its place are these words:—Hujus libelli duplex facta est editio, quarum una exemplis xii, altera xcii. Imperfect: p. 1-2 wanting].

Fosdick (Charles A.) Go ahead; or, the fisher-boy's motto. By Harry Castlemon. [*pseudon.*] 16°. *Cincinnati, R. W. Carroll & co.* 1872.

Foster (*Rev.* Elon). New cyclopædia of poetical illustrations, adapted to christian teaching: embracing poems, odes, legends, lyrics, hymns, sonnets, extracts, etc. A companion volume to New cyclopædia of illustrations. 696 pp. 8°. *New York, W. C. Palmer, jr. & co.* 1872.

Foster (G. W.) Sacred crown. *See* **Hodges** (D. F.) *and* **Foster.**

Foster (*Rev.* John, *of Bristol, Eng.*) Considerations addressed to the unbeliever, to young men, and to men of the world; being the introductory essay to "Doddridge's Rise and progress of religion in the soul." 203 pp. 16°. *Glasgow, W. Collins,* [*about* 1847].

Foster (*Rev.* John O.) Life and labors of mrs. Maggie Newton Van Cott, the first lady licensed to preach in the methodist episcopal church in the United States. With an introduction, by rev. Gilbert Haven, and rev. David Sherman. xxxix, 339 pp. 1 portrait. 12°. *Cincinnati, Hitchcock & Walden, for the author,* 1872.

Foster (Lillian). Way-side glimpses, north and south. 250 pp. 12°. *New York, Rudd & Carleton,* 1860.

Foster (Samuel). The sector altered; and other scales added: with the description and use thereof. sm. 4°. *London, A. Clark,* 1673.

[*In* GUNTER (Edmund). Works, pp. 157-195].

Foster *or* **Forster** (Thomas). A narrative of the proceedings of the society called quakers, within the quarterly meeting for London and Middlesex, against Thomas Foster, for openly professing their primitive doctrines concerning the unity of God. xl, 372 pp. 8 l. 8°. *London, printed by C. Stower, Hackney, J. Johnson & co.* [*etc.*] 1813.

Foster. *See* **Forster.**

Fothergill (John, *quaker*). An account of the life and travels, in the work of the ministry, of John Fothergill. [Also], divers epistles to friends in Great-Britain and America, on various occasions. iv, 280 pp. 16°. *Philadelphia, J. Chattin,* 1754.

Fothergill (Samuel). Eleven discourses, delivered extempore, at several meeting-houses of the people called Quakers. 263 pp. 12°. *Wilmington (Del.) Coale & Rumford,* 1817.

Foucher de Careil (*Comte* Louis Alexandre). Hegel et Schopenhauer, études sur la philosophie allemand moderne depuis Kant jusqu'à nos jours. 2 p. l. xxxix, 386 pp. 1 l. 8°. *Paris, L. Hachette & cie.* 1862.

Foudras (Théodore Louis Auguste, *marquis* de). Un caprice de grande dame. 3 v. 16°. *Paris, A. Cadot,* 1852.

Foulaines (F. N. de). Harmonie des cultes catholique, protestant et mosaïque avec les constitutions de l'empire français. Par m. ****, jurisconsulte. [*anon.*] 460 pp. 8°. *Paris, Gautier & Bretin,* 1808.

Foulston (John, *architect*). The public buildings erected in the west of England, as designed by John Foulston. 1 p. l. 86 pp. 118 pl. 4°. *London, author,* 1838.

Found dead. By the author of "Married beneath him." [*anon.*] 2d ed. 2 p. l. iv, 348 pp. 12°. *London, Chapman & Hall,* [1869].

Fountain (The) and the bottle; comprising thrilling examples of the opposite effects of temperance and intemperance. Edited by a son of temperance. [*anon.*] Eng. title, 448 pp. 18 pl. 8°. *Hartford, Case, Tiffany & co.* 1850.

Four treatises concerning the doctrine, discipline and worship of the mahometans. To which is prefix'd The life and actions of Mahomet, extracted chiefly from mahometan authors. 96; 254 pp. 8°. *London, J. Darby for B. Lintott,* 1712.

CONTENTS.

An abridgment of the mahometan religion: translated out of arabick [of Abu Shoja] into latin by H. Reland, and from thence into english.

A defence of the mahometans from several charges falsly laid against them by christians: written in latin by H. Reland, and translated into english.

A treatise of Bobovius [Bobowski] concerning the liturgy of the Turks, their pilgrimage to Mecca, &c. Translated from the latin.

Historical and critical reflections on mahometanism and socinianism, translated from the french.

Four years at Yale. By a graduate of '69. [*anon.*] xiv, 713 pp. 12°. *New Haven, C. C. Chatfield & co.* 1871.

Fourmont (Étienne, *dit l'aîné*). Réflexions critiques sur les histoires des anciens peuples, Chaldéens, Hébreux, Phéniciens, Égyptiens, Grecs, &c. jusqu'au tems de Cyrus. [1e éd.] 2 v. 4 p. l. viii, iii–lvi, 88, 384 pp. 2 l; 1 p. l. 503 pp. 1 l. 4°. *Paris, M. Père,* [*etc.*] 1735.

Fourth (The) book of one hundred pictures. [*anon.*] 108 pp. 18°. *Philadelphia, American s. s. union,* [1871].

Fourth (The) progressive reader. [*anon.*] 312 pp. 18°. *New York, P. O'Shea,* 1871.
[ILLUSTRATED (The) progressive series].

Fous (Les) douteux et les fous sublimes, recueil des scènes dialoguées, d'anecdotes tantôt historiques, tantôt supposées, et de considérations philosophiques tendant à dévoiler et à combattre bien des erreurs, bien des préjugés et bien des abus; par l'auteur du Pourvoyeur d'une maison d'aliénés. [*anon.*] 186 pp. 12°. *Paris, G. Pissin,* [1844].

Fovargue (Stephen). A new catalogue of vulgar errors. 2 p. l. viii, 203 pp. 8°. *Cambridge,* [*Eng.*] *author,* 1767.

Fowle (Daniel). A total eclipse of liberty: being a true and faithful account of the arraignment, and examination of Daniel Fowle before the honorable house of representatives of the province of Massachusetts-Bay in New-England, Octob. 24th 1754, barely on suspicion of his being concern'd in printing and publishing a pamphlet, intitled, The monster of monsters. Written by himself. 32 pp. 16°. *Boston,* [*D. Fowle*], 1755.
[*With* THUMB (Thomas). Monster of monsters. 1754].

——— The same. An appendix to the late Total eclipse of liberty. 24 pp. 16°. *Boston,* [*D. Fowle*], 1756.
[*With his* Total eclipse of liberty].

Fowler (Henry, *editor*). Sketch of the life of Mary M. Chase. 12°. [*Boston,* 1855].
[*In* CHASE (Mary M.) Writings, pp. xi–xlvi].

Fowler (Orson Squire). Life: its science, laws, faculties, functions, conditions, philosophy, and improvement: including the organism, health, social affections, moral sentiments, intellect, memory, self-education, autobiography, miscellany, &c. as taught by phrenology. [v. 1. Physiological science]. 1 p. l. vii, 375 pp. 8°. *Boston, O. S. Fowler,* 1871.

——— Maternity; or bearing, confinement, and the treatment of infants: including the analysis, preservation, and restoration of female health and beauty; the causes and cures of feminine ailments, [etc.] as taught by phrenology and physiology. v, 87–236 pp. 8°. *Boston, O. S. Fowler,* 1870.

——— Physiology, animal and mental; applied to the preservation and restoration of health of body, and power of mind. 312 pp. 12°. *New York, Fowlers & Wells,* 1847.

Fowls (The) of the air. *See* **Warner** (Susan). Stories of Vinegar hill, v. 2.

Fox (Charles). The american text book of practical and scientific agriculture. Including analyses by the most eminent chemists. x, 354 pp. 8°. *Detroit, Elwood & co.* 1854. S.

Fox (Edward). The pleasure paths of travel. [Europe]. vi, 342 pp. 12°. *London, T. C. Newby,* 1857.

Fox (*Rev.* Thomas B.) The ministry of Jesus Christ; compiled and arranged from the four gospels, for families and sunday schools. With poetical illustrations and notes. By T. B. Fox. v. 1. 247 pp. 18°. *Boston, Weeks, Jordan & co.* 1837.

——— The same. 3d ed. viii, 13–261 pp. 16°. *Boston, Crosby & Nichols,* 1845.

Fox (*Rev.* Wm. Johnson). Memorial edition of [his] collected works. 12 v. 8°. *London, C. Fox,* 1865–68.

CONTENTS.

v. 1. Lectures, sermons, etc. prior to 1824.
v. 2. Christ and christianity.
v. 3. Miscellaneous lectures and sermons: and twenty sermons on the principles of morality inculcated in the holy scriptures.
v. 4. Anti-corn-law speeches, chiefly reprinted from the "League" newspaper; and occasional speeches.
v. 5. Letters on the corn laws, by "a Norwich weaver-boy"; and extracts from letters by "Publicola."
v. 6. Miscellaneous essays, political, literary, critical and biographical.
v. 7–10. Reports of lectures at South-place chapel, Finsbury.

Fraa by og bygd. Tidskrift aat vestmannalaget. v. 1–3. 16°. *Bjorgvin, E. B. Giertsen,* 1870–71. S.

Fragments of ancient poetry, translated from the gaelic. *See* **Macpherson** (James).

Fraguier (Claude François). The gallery of Verres. 4°. [*London,* 1740].
[*In* TURNBULL (George). Three dissertations. 1740, pp. 68–85].

Fraichot (Casimir). Supplementum ad annales et chronicon Philippi Brietii ab anno 1663. usque ad annvm 1692. [*anon.*] 162 pp. 6 l. 18°. [*n. p. about* 1700].

Français de Nantes (*Comte* Antoine). Le manuscrit de feu M. Jerome, contenant son

Français de Nantes (*Comte* A.)—continued. oeuvre inédite, une notice biographique sur sa personne, un fac-simile de son écriture, et le portrait de cet illustre contemporain. [*pseudon.*] 2 p. l. 463 pp. 1 fac-sim. 8°. *Paris, Bossange frères*, 1825.

France. Recueil des édits, déclarations, lettres patentes, arrests, et autres pièces concernant la compagnie des Indes [Occidentales, 1709-1728]. 3 v. 4°. *Paris, veuve Saugrain*, 1720-30.

——— *Commission impériale.* Exposition universelle de 1855. Explication des ouvrages de peinture, sculpture, gravure, lithographie et architecture des artistes vivants étrangers et français exposés au palais des beaux-arts. lx, 616 pp. 12°. *Paris, Panis*, 1855.

——— ——— Exposition universelle de 1862 à Londres. Section française. Catalogue officiel publié par ordre de la commission impériale. 272, 182, 54 pp. 1 l. 8°. *Paris, imprimerie impériale*, 1862.

——— ——— Exposition universelle de 1867 à Paris. Commission de l'histoire du travail. Rapport de m. E. du Sommerard. 112 pp. 8°. *Paris, P. Dupont*, 1867.

——— *Ministère de l'agriculture, du commerce et des travaux publics.* Annuaire pour l'année 1869. État du personnel au 1er mars 1869. 8°. [*Paris*, 1869].

[ANNALES des ponts et chaussées. Personnel, 4e série, v. 9].

——— ——— Exposition universelle à Londres en 1862.—Empire français.—Notice sur les modèles, cartes et dessins relatifs aux travaux publics, réunis par les soins du ministère de l'agriculture, du commerce, et des travaux publics. 3 p. l. 263 pp. 8°. *Paris, E. Thunot & cie.* 1862. S.

——— *Ministère de la guerre.* Annuaire militaire de l'empire française pour l'année 1869, 1870. 2 v. 12°. *Paris, veuve Berger-Levrault et fils*, 1869-70.

——— ——— Catalogue explicatif et raisonnée de l'exposition permanente des produits de l'Algérie, suivie du catalogue méthodique des produits algériens à l'exposition universelle de Paris en 1855. [Rédigé par Jules Duval]. 207 pp. 8°. *Paris, F. Didot frères*, 1855.

——— *Ministère de l'instruction publique.* Annuaire de l'instruction publique pour l'année 1870. Publié par J. Delalain. 16°. *Paris, J. Delalain & fils*, 1870.

——— ——— Archives des missions scientifiques et littéraires, choix de rapports et instructions. 6 v. 8°. *Paris, imprimerie nationale*, 1850-56. S.

——— ——— The same, 2e série. v. 1-2. 8°. *Paris, imprimerie impériale*, 1864. S.

[v. 2, liv. 3, et seq. wanting].

——— ——— Collection de documents inédits sur l'histoire de France. Première série. Histoire politique. 3 v. 4°. *Paris, imprimerie impériale*, 1865-71.

CONTENTS.

DESJARDINS (Abel). Négociations diplomatiques de la France avec la Toscane. Documents recueillis par Giuseppe Conestrini, et publiés par Abel Desjardins. v. 3. 1865.

REY (G,) Étude sur les monuments de l'architecture militaire des croisés en Syrie et dans l'île de Chipre, par G. Rey. 1871.

THIERRY (J. N. Augustin). Recueil des monuments inédits de l'histoire du tiers état. Première série. Chartes, coutumes, actes municipaux, statuts des corporations d'arts et métiers des villes et communes de France. Région du nord. t. 4. Contenant les pièces relatives à l'histoire municipale d'Abbeville et à celle des villes, bourgs et villages de la basse Picardie. 1870.

——— ——— Description physique de l'île de Crète. Par V. Raulin. 3 v. 8°. *Paris, A. Bertrand*, 1869.

——— ——— Recherches zoologiques pour servir à l'histoire de la faune de l'Amérique centrale et du Mexique. Publiées sous la direction de Milne Edwards. 7e partie. 3 p. l. 152 pp. 6 l. 6 pl. 4°. *Paris, imprimerie impériale*, 1870. S.

CONTENTS.

Études sur les mollusques terrestres et fluviatiles du Mexique et du Guatémala. Par P. Fischer et H. Crosse.

——— ——— Revue des sociétés savantes des départements. 4e série. v. 1-2. 8°. *Paris, imprimerie impériale*, 1865. S.

——— *Ministère de la marine.* Statistique des pêches maritimes. 1866 et 1867. Extrait de la Revue maritime et coloniale. 2 v. 8°. *Paris*, 1868. S.

——— ——— Annales hydrographiques, recueil d'avis, instructions, documents et mémoires relatifs à l'nydrographie et à la navigation. 1849-1858. v. 1-15. 8°. *Paris, P. Dupont*, 1849-58. S.

France (Institut impériale de). Annuaire pour 1870 et 1871. 2 v. 16°. *Paris, imprimerie nationale*, 1870-71.

Frances (Margaret). Rose Carleton's reward. 283 pp. 4 pl. 16°. *Cincinnati, Bosworth, Chase & Hall*, 1871.

Francesco da Monte Polzano. Predica di Francesco da Monte Polzano. 16°. [*Florentia, about* 1520].

[*In* FERRER (S. Vicente). Profetie certissime stvpendo et admirabili. [*about* 1520]. l. 30-40].

Francia (Louis). Studies of landscapes by T. Gainsborough, T. Hoppner, r. a. T. Girtin, Wm. Owen, r. a. A. Calcot, S. Owen, I. Varley, I. S. Hayward and L. Francia. Imitated from the originals by L. Francia. 25 pl. obl. fol. [*London*], 1810.

Francini (Jean Nicolas de) **Gaureault** (Hyacinthe de) *and others*. Recueil général des opera représentéz par l'académie royale de musique, depuis son établissement. 16 v. 16°. *Paris, J. B. C. Ballard*, 1703–45.

Franciscus *rothomagensis*. *See* **Harlay** (François de).

Franck (Sebastian). Werelt-spiegel, ofte beschryvinge des gehelen aert-bodems, met sijn vier gedeelten, Europa, Asia, Africa, America, etc. Verbetert, vermeerdert, verrijckt met verscheydene annotatien [etc.] Door Joh. Phocylides Holwarda. *b. l.* Eng. title, 3 p. l. 652 pp. 5 l. sm 4°. *Bolswart, S. van Haringhouck*, 1649.

Franck. *See* **Francke.**

Francke (August Hermann). A letter to a friend concerning the most useful way of preaching. Written in german. Translated into latin by order of [G. A.] Franck, and into english by David Jennings. 16°. *Boston*, 1740.

[*With* JENNINGS (*Rev.* John). Two discourses. *Boston*, 1740. pp. 55–86].

——— The same. Of the most useful way of preaching. 12°. [*Philadelphia, W. W. Woodward*, 1810.]

[*In* WILLIAMS (Edward, *d. d.*) The christian preacher. 1810. pp. 77–91].

Francklin (*Captain* William). The history of the reign of Shah-Aulum, the present emperor of Hindostaun. Containing the transactions of the court of Delhi, and the neighbouring states, during a period of thirty-six years: interspersed with geographical and topographical observations on several of the principal cities of Hindostaun. With an appendix. xxiv, 254 pp. 1 map. 4°. *London, author*, 1798.

——— Military memoirs of mr. George Thomas; who rose from an obscure situation to the rank of a general, in the service of the native powers of the north-west of India. Compiled and arranged from mr. Thomas's original documents. 383 pp. 2 pl. 1 map. 8°. *London, J. Stockdale*, 1805.

Franco (*Rev.* John Joseph). Simon Peter and Simon Magus, a legend of the early days of christianity in Rome. 239 pp. 12°. *Philadelphia, P. F. Cunningham*, 1871.

["MESSENGER" series, no. 2].

Franco (Niccolò). Le pistole vvlgari di m. Nicolò Franco. 267 l. 1 l. 16°. *Venetijs, apud A. Gardane*, 1542.

Frank Leslie's boy's and girl's weekly, [and other periodicals]. *See* **Leslie** (Frank).

Frank Warrington. *See* **Harris** (*Mrs.* Sidney S.)

Frankfort (*Germany*). Handelskammer zu Frankfurt am Main. Jahresbericht für 1869 und 1870. 2 v. 8°. *Frankfurt a. M. Mahlu & Waldschmidt*, 1870–71. s.

Frankfurt. *See* **Frankfort.**

Franklin (Benjamin). The examination of Benjamin Franklin, before an august assembly, relating to the repeal of the stamp act, &c. 16 pp. 8°. [*n. p.* 1766].

[HAZARD pamphlets, v. 16].

——— The same. Interrogatoire de mr. Franklin, deputé de Pensilvanie au parlement de la Grande Bretagne. De l'anglois par Ch.... D. H.... 35 pp. 8°. *Strasbourg, Simon Kürsner*, [1766].

——— Proposals relating to the education of youth in Pensilvania. [*anon.*] 32 pp. 8°. *Philadelphia*, [*Benjamin Franklin*], 1749.

[HAZARD pamphlets, v. 45].

——— Remarks on a late protest against [his] appointment as agent for [Pennsylvania]. 7 pp. 8°. [*Philadelphia*, 1764]?

——— The same.

[HAZARD pamphlets, v. 20].

Franklin (*Rev.* Benjamin, *of Cincinnati*). The gospel preacher: a book of twenty sermons. 500 pp. 12°. *Cincinnati, Franklin & Rice*, 1869.

Franklin (Josephine). Rachel: a romance. 300 pp. 12°. *Boston, Thayer & Eldridge*, 1860.

Franklin (*Rev.* Samuel). A critical review of wesleyan perfection, in twenty-four consecutive arguments, in which the doctrine of sin in believers is discussed. 614 pp. 8°. *Cincinnati, Methodist book concern*, 1866.

Franklin society. Publications, nos. 1–2. 4°. *Chicago, Franklin society*, 1869–70.

CONTENTS.

BOSS (H. R.) Early newspapers in Illinois. 48 pp. (no. 2).
SHEAHAN (J. W.) The printer: what he might be. 20 pp. (no. 1).

Frankreich und der deutsch-französische krieg in den jahren 1870–71. [Aus dem vierten bande des Deutsch-amerikanischen conversations-lexicons. *anon.* By Alex. J. Schem]? 2 p. l. 86 pp. 8°. *New York*, 1871.

Fraser (Charles). Reminiscences of Charleston. 119 pp. 8°. *Charleston (S. C.) J. Russell*, 1854.

Fraser *or* **Frazer** (*Rev.* John). Δεττεροσκοπιά; or a brief discourse concerning the second sight; commonly so called. Published by mr. Andrew Sympson, with a short account of the author. *Edinburgh*, 1707. 48 pp. 16°. [Reprinted]. *Edinburgh, D. Webster*, 1820.
[*With* STEWART (William Grant). The popular superstitions of the highlanders. 1823].

Fraser's magazine. Edited by James Anthony Froude. [Monthly]. Jan. to June, 1871. New series, v. 3-4; [complete series, v. 83-85]. 8° *London, Longmans, Green & co.* 1871.

Frauds (The) of the New York city government exposed. [*anon.*] *See* **Genung** (Abram P.)

Frazer. *See* **Fraser.**

Freckleton (George, *m. d.*) Outlines of general pathology. 267 pp. 12°. *London, J. W. Parker*, 1838.

Freelance (Radical, *pseudon.*) The philosophers of Foufouville. 297 pp. 12°. *New York, G. W. Carleton*, 1868.

Freeman (Edward Augustus). Historical essays. vii, 406 pp. 8°. *London, Macmillan & co.* 1871.

——— The history of the norman conquest of England, its causes and its results. v. 4. The reign of William the conqueror. xxvi, 827 pp. 3 pl. 1 map. 8°. *Oxford, the Clarendon press*, 1871.

——— Old english history for children. xxxii, 372 pp. 5 maps. 16°. *London, Macmillan & co.* 1869.

Freeman (William P.) Biography of Isaac W. Ambler. 2d ed. 240 pp. 12°. *Biddeford (Me.) Horton brothers*, 1860.

Freemasons. Constitutions of the antient fraternity of free and accepted masons. Containing the charges, regulations, &c. &c. Published, by the authority of the united grand lodge, by William Henry White. [New ed.] viii, 147 pp. 12 pl. 8°. *London, Norris & son*, 1847.

——— The same. Part 2. Published, by the authority of the united grand lodge, by William Williams. 4 p. l. 142 pp. 1 l. 8°. *London, W. P. Norris & son*, 1827.

——— *Grand chapter of Minnesota.* Proceedings of the grand royal arch chapter of Minnesota, at its grand annual convocations, in the city of St. Paul, from December 17th, 1859, to January 12th, 1871. Compiled by William S. Combs, grand secretary. 234 pp. 8°. *Saint Paul, Pioneer printing co.* 1871.

Freemasons—continued.

——— ——— The same. Proceedings, at the tenth annual convocation, Jan. 12, 1871. 111 pp. 8°. *St. Paul*, 1871.
[*With* the proceedings of grand chapter, 1859-71].

——— *Grand lodge of Minnesota.* Proceedings of the grand lodge of ancient free and accepted masons, of Minnesota, at its grand annual communications, in the city of St. Paul, from Feb. 25, A.·. L.·. 5823, to January 14, A.·. L.·. 5869. 1 p. l. 695 pp. 1 tab. 8°. *Saint Paul, Pioneer book and job printing co.* 1869.

——— ——— The same. Proceedings, 1869-71. 3 v. 8°. *Saint Paul, Pioneer book and job printing co.* 1870-71.

——— *Grand chapter of Pennsylvania.* Constitution, rules and regulations of the grand holy royal arch chapter of Pennsylvania. With an appendix, containg the ceremonial, prayers, charges, and forms; [also] a list of the subordinate chapters, lodges, etc. 145 pp. 8°. *Philadelphia, coöperative printing co.* [1872].

——— *Knights templar.* The grand encampment of knights templar, and appendant orders, of Massachusetts and Rhode Island. Its history; edicts; past and present grand officers; and organizations of its subordinates. 68 pp. 8°. *Boston, J. Wilson & son*, 1864.

——— ——— Proceedings of the grand encampment of knights templars and appendant orders of Massachusetts and Rhode Island, for 1864. 8°. *Boston, J. Wilson & son*, 1864.

——— ——— The same. Abstract of the proceedings of the grand encampment of knights templars and appendant orders of Massachusetts and Rhode Island, for the years ending October 1865-1871. 7 v. 8°. *Boston, press of the Freemasons' magazine, [etc.]* 1865-72.

——— ——— Proceedings of the general grand encampment of the knights templar of the United States of America, from its formation, 1816 to 1856. 1 p. l. 361, xxvii pp. 8°. *New Orleans, The bulletin office*, 1860.

——— *Knights of the red cross.* General statutes of the imperial, ecclesiastical, and military order of the knights of the red cross of Rome and Constantine, and the laws of the k. h. s. [Also] a sketch of the history of the

Freemasons—continued. red cross order, and the by-laws of the Rose of Sharon conclave, no. 60, Rouseville, Pa. By C. L. Stowell. 127 pp. 18°. *Titusville (Pa.) Morning herald office*, 1872.

—— *Scottish rite.* Constitutions [of 1867] of the supreme council of the ancient accepted scottish rite, for the northern masonic jurisdiction of the U. S. orient, Boston, Mass. 28 pp. 8°. *New York, Masonic publishing co.* 1870.

—— —— Morals and dogma of the ancient and accepted scottish rite of freemasonry. Prepared for the supreme council of the thirty-third degree, for the southern jurisdiction of the United States, and published by its authority. iv, 861 pp. 8°. *Charleston (S. C.)* [1871].

—— —— Proceedings of the supreme council of sovereign grand inspectors-general of the thirty-third and last degree, ancient accepted scottish rite, for the northern masonic jurisdiction of the United States of America, at its grand east, in annual session, held at Boston, Mass. 1863-70. With accompanying documents. v. 3-10. 8 v. 8°. *Boston & New York*, 1863-70.

Freemason's (The) quarterly review. April 1, 1834, to Dec. 31, 1842. v. 1-9. 8°. *London, Sherwood, Gilbert & Piper*, [1834-42].

—— The same. March 31, 1843, to Dec. 31, 1849. Second series, v. 1-7; [complete series, v. 10-16]. 8°. *London, Sherwood, Gilbert & Piper, and W. & T. Piper*, [1843-49].

—— The same. The freemasons' quarterly magazine and review. March 30, 1850, to Dec. 31, 1852. [Third series], v. 1-3; [complete series, v. 17-19]. 8°. *London, R. Spencer*, [1850-52].

—— The same for March 31, 1853. New [fourth] series, v. 1, no. 1. 8°. *London, G. Routledge & co.* [1853].

Free-thinker (The). [no. 1-159]. From Lady-day, 1718, to Michaelmas, 1719. 3 v. 8°. *London*, 1722-23.

[*Note.*—A very superior collection of essays, by Ambrose Phillips, Hugh Boulter, abp. Zachary Pearce, bp. Richard West, George Stubbs, Gilbert Burnet, bp. and Henry Steele.—LOWNDES.
The 2d ed. 1733, had the additional title: "Essays on ignorance, superstition, bigotry, enthusiasm, craft, etc. with several pieces of wit and humour"].

Free thoughts in defence of a future state. *See* **Day** (Robert).

Free-trader (The). [Organ of the American free-trade league. Monthly]. June, 1869, to Dec. 1871. v. 3-5. sm. fol. *New York, J. Sarell*, 1869-71.

[*Note.*—Discontinued; succeeded by the People's pictorial tax-payer].

—— The same. Supplement. Report of the special commissioner of the revenue upon the industry, trade, commerce, etc. of the United States, for the year 1869. Prefaced by a scheme for a purely revenue tariff, which would yield $127,500,000 gold. Prepared by the American free-trade league. 42 pp. fol. *New York, Am. free-trade league*, 1870.

[*With* FREE-TRADER (The), v. 3].

Free-will Baptists. Hymns for christian melody. Selected from various authors. [By Henry Hobbs, Samuel Beede, and William Burr, publishing committee of the Free-will baptist connection]. 608 pp. 24°. *Boston, D. Marks*, 1832.

Freijlinghausen (*Rev.* Theodorus Jacobus). Sermons. Translated from the dutch. And prefaced by a sketch of the author's life, by rev. William Demarest. With an introduction by the rev. Thomas De Witt, d. d. vi, 3-422 pp. 12°. *New York, board of publication of the reformed protestant dutch church*, 1856.

Freinsheim (Johann). Excerptiones chronologicae ad L. A. Florum. 8°. [*Biponti, ex typographia societatis*, 1783].

[*In* FLORUS (Annæus). Epitome rerum romanorum. 1783. pp. 201-229].

Frelinghuysen (Frederick). An oration on the death of George Washington, delivered in New-Brunswick, 22d Feb. 1800. 23 pp. 8°. *New-Brunswick, A. Blauvelt*, 1800.

[HAZARD pamphlets, v. 65].

Frelinghuysen. *See* **Freijlinghausen.**

French (Gilbert J.) Practical remarks on the minor accessories to the services of the church, with hints on the preparation of altar cloths, pede cloths, and other ecclesiastical furniture. 179 pp. 1 pl. 16°. *Leeds, T. W. Green*, 1844.

French (James S.) Elkswatawa; or, the prophet of the west. A tale of the frontier. [*anon.*] 2 v. 246 pp; 254 pp. 12°. *New York, Harper & brothers*, 1836.

French (John H. *ll. d.*) Key to French's common school arithmetic. 176 pp. 16°. *New York, Harper & brothers*, 1872.

[FRENCH's mathematical series].

—— Key to French's elementary arithmetic, for the slate. 85 pp. 16°. *New York, Harper & brothers*, [1871].

[FRENCH's mathematical series].

French (L. Virginia). My roses: the romance of a June day. 3 p. l. 13–278 pp. 12°. *Philadelphia, Claxton, Remsen & Haffelfinger*, 1872.

French (William, *d. d.*) A new translation of the proverbs of Solomon. 1831. *See* **Bible.** (*English*).

French (The) family cook: being a complete system of french cookery. Translated from the french. [*anon.*] 3 p. l. xxiv, 342 pp. 8°. *London, J. Bell*, 1793.

Freneau (Philip). A journey from Philadelphia to New-York, by way of Burlington and South-Amboy. [In verse]. By Robert Slender, stocking weaver. [*pseudon.*] 28 pp. 8°. *Philadelphia, F. Bailey*, 1787.
[HAZARD pamphlets, v. 41].

——— Letters on various interesting and important subjects; many of which have appeared in the Aurora. By Robert Slender, o. s. m. [*pseudon.*] 142 pp. 8°. *Philadelphia, R. Slender*, 1799.
[THORNDIKE pamphlets, v. 7].

——— A poem on divine revelation, delivered at the commencement at Nassau-Hall, Sept. 28, 1774. 3 l. 22 pp. 8°. *Philadelphia, R. Aitken*, 1774.
[HAZARD pamphlets, v. 116].

——— A poem, on the rising glory of America; delivered at the public commencement at Nassau-Hall, Sept. 25, 1771. [*anon.*] 27 pp. 16°. *Philadelphia, R. Aitken*, 1772.
[HAZARD pamphlets, v. 101].

Fréville (Charles Ernest de). Mémoire sur le commerce maritime de Rouen, depuis les temps les plus reculés jusqu'à la fin du xvie siècle. Ouvrage couronné et publié par l'académie impériale des sciences, belles-lettres et arts de Rouen. 2 v. xxxv, 402 pp; 2 p. l. 552 pp. 8°. *Rouen*, 1857. s.

Frey (Heinrich) *and* **Leuckart** (Rudolph). Beiträge zur kenntniss wirbelloser thiere, mit besonderer berücksichtigung der fauna des norddeutschen meeres. 4 p. l. 170 pp. 2 pl. 4°. *Braunschweig, F. Vieweg & sohn*, 1847. s.

——— The same. s.
[Zoological pamphlets, v. 1].

Frey (*Rev.* Joseph Samuel Christian Frederick). Essays on christian baptism. 124 pp. 12°. *Boston, Lincoln & Edmands*, 1829.

——— The same. 5th ed. 311 pp. 1 portrait. 12°. *New York, author*, 1843.

Freylinghausen (Johann Anastasius). An abstract of the whole doctrine of the christian religion, with observations. From a manuscript in her majesty's possession. The first book stereotyped by the new process. xi, 216 pp. 8°. *London, E. Harding*, 1804.

Freylinghausen. *See* **Freijlinghausen.**

Freytag (Friedrich Gotthilf). Analecta litteraria de libris rarioribvs. 4 p. l. 1138 pp. 12°. *Lipsiæ, in officina weidemanniana*, 1750.

Frianoro (Raffaele, *pseudon.*) *See* **Nobili** (Giacinto de').

Frick (*Dr.* J.) Physical technicks; or practical instructions for making experiments in physics, and the construction of physical apparatus with the most limited means. Translated by John D. Easter, ph. d. 467 pp. 8°. *Philadelphia, J. B. Lippincott & co.* 1861.

Friderici. *See* **Friedrich** (Johann).

Friedrich (Friedrich). The lost despatch. Translated from the german. By L. A. Williams. 107 pp. 8°. *Boston, J. R. Osgood & co.* 1871.

Friedrich (Johann). Panegyricus secularis, complectens originem incrementa et fortunam academiæ lipsicæ 47 pp. 1 l. 12°. *Martisburgi*, 1689].
[*With* PEIFFER (David). Lipsia, ed. 1689].

Fries (Jakob Friedrich). Versuch einer kritik der principien der wahrscheinlichkeitsrechnung. viii, 236 pp. 8°. *Braunschweig, F. Vieweg & sohn*, 1842. s.

Frisbie (*Rev.* Levi). An eulogy on the character of George Washington, delivered at Ipswich, 7 Jan. 1800. [With] general Washington's [Farewell] address. 61 pp. 8°. *Newburyport, E. M. Blunt*, 1800.
[HAZARD pamphlets, v. 64].

Frisch (Ch.) Vita Johannis Kepleri. 8°. [*Francofurti a. M. Heyder & Zimmer*, 1870]. s.
[*In* KEPLER (Johann). Opera omnia, v. 8, part 2, pp. 698–1028].

Friuli. *Associazione agraria friulana.* Bullettino. Anno xiv–xv. Presidenza dell' associazione agraria friulana, editrice. 8°. *Udine G. Seitz*, 1869–70. s.

Froidour (Louis de). Lettre à monsievr Barrillon Damoncourt, contenant la relation & la description des travaux qui se font en Languedoc, pour la commvnication des devx mers. 3 p. l. 101 pp. 11 maps. 12°. *Tovlovse, I. D. Camvsat*, 1672.

Froissart (*Sir* John). Stories from Froissart. By the late Barry St. Leger. 3 v. 8°. *London, H. Colburn*, 1832.

Frontinus (Sextus Julius). Strategematicon libri iv. 34 l. unp. fol. *Bononiae, Plato de Benedictis*, 1495.
[*In* VETERES scriptores de re militari. *Bononiae*, 1496].

Frossard (Benjamin Sigismond). La cause des esclaves nègres et habitans de la Guinée, portée au tribunal de la justice, de la religion, de la politique; ou histoire de la traite & de l'esclavage des nègres, preuves de leur illégitimité, moyens de les abolir sans nuire ni aux colonies ni aux colons. 2 v. 1 p. l. vi, 367 pp; 1 p. l. vii, 403 pp. 8°. *Lyon, Aimé de la Roche*, 1789.

Frost (John, *ll. d.*) Historical collections of all nations; comprising notices of the most remarkable events and distinguished characters in the history of the world; with anecdotes of heroes, statesmen, patriots and sovereigns; with special notices of the heroes of the west. 1008 pp. (incl. 71 pl.) 8°. *Hartford, Tiffany & co.* 1852.

——— History of the United States; for the use of common schools. 324 pp. 16°. *Philadelphia, E. C. Biddle*, 1837.

——— The same. New ed. 432 pp. 12°. *Philadelphia, E. C. Biddle*, 1837.

——— Indian battles, captivities, and adventures. From the earliest period to the present time. 408 pp. 2 pl. 12°. *New York, J. C. Derby*, 1856.

——— Lardner's outlines of universal history. *See* **Keightley** (Thomas).

——— The life of William Penn, with a sketch of the early history of Pennsylvania. 239 pp. 1 pl. 18°. *Philadelphia, Orrin Rogers*, 1839.

——— Pictorial history of the middle ages, from the death of Constantine the great to the discovery of America by Columbus. 360 pp. 8°. *Philadelphia, C. J. Gillis*, 1846.

——— Outlines of history. *See* **Keightley** (Thomas).

Frost (Joseph *and* Isaac, *editors*). Divine songs of the Muggletonians, in grateful praise to the only true God, the Lord Jesus Christ. xxiv, 621 pp. 1 portrait. 16°. *London, R. Brown*, 1829.

Frost (*Mrs.* L. J. H.) Lynda Newton; or life's discipline. 410 pp. 4 pl. 16°. *Boston, A. F. Graves*, [1871].

Frost (Maria Goodell). Gospel fruits: or, bible christianity illustrated; a premium essay. 188 pp. 4 pl. 18°. *Cincinnati, Am. reform tract and book society*, [1856].

Frost (Sarah Annie). How to write a composition. 178 pp. 16°. *New York, Dick & Fitzgerald*, 1871.

Frothingham (*Rev.* Octavius B.) Stories from the lips of the teacher. Retold by a disciple. vi, 193 pp. 1 pl. sq. 16°. *Boston, Walker, Wise & co.* 1863.

Frothingham (Richard). A tribute to Thomas Starr King. 247 pp. 12°. *Boston, Ticknor & Fields*, 1865.

Frugoni (Carlo Innocenzo). Poesie scelte. [Con la vita sua descritta da P. G. Cocconi]. 2 v. xl, xli, 374 pp; viii, 424 pp. 8°. *Brescia, D. Berlendis*, 1782.

Fry (Caroline). Scripture principles of education. Revised from the London edition. 160 pp. 16°. *Philadelphia, George, Latimer & co.* 1823.

Fry (Edward). Essays on the accordance of christianity with the nature of man. 2 p. l. 216 pp. 12°. *Edinburgh, T. Constable & co.* 1857.

Fry (Frinkle, *pseudon.*) "Wooden nutmegs" at Bull Run. A humorous account of some of the exploits and experiences of the three months Connecticut brigade, and the part they bore in the national stampede. 86 pp. 8°. *Hartford, G. L. Coburn*, 1872.

Fryer (John, *m. d.*) A new account of East India and Persia, in eight letters. Being nine years travels, begun 1672. And finished 1681. 4 p. l. xiv, 427, xxiv pp. 4 pl. 1 portrait, 3 maps. fol. *London, R. Chiswell*, 1698.

Fryxell (Anders). Lebensgeschichte Karl's des zwölften, königs von Schweden. Nach dem schwedischen originale frei übertragen von G. F. von Jenssen-Tusch. 5 v. 8°. *Braunschweig, F. Vieweg & sohn*, 1861. s.

Fuentes (José Mor de). *See* **Mor de Fuentes**.

Fugitive (The) miscellany. *See* **Almon** (John).

Fulke (William, *d. d.*) A defense of the sincere and trve translation of the holy scriptvres into the english tongve, against the manifold cavils, frivolous quarrels, and impudent slanders of Gregorie Martin, of Rhemes. [Also] a briefe confutation of all such quarrels and cavils, as haue beene uttered against the writings of W. Fvlke. 2 p. l. 26, 206, 17 pp. fol. *London, by A. Mathewes, one of the assignes of H. Ogden*, 1633.

[*With* Bible. (*English*). The text of the new testament (translation of Rheims and of the church of England). *London*, 1633].

Fuller (Edwin W.) The angel in the cloud. 167 pp. 12°. *New York, E. J. Hale & son*, 1871.

Fuller (Hiram). Sparks from a locomotive; or, life and liberty in Europe. By the author of "Belle Brittan's Letters." [*anon.*] 305 pp. 12°. *New York, Derby & Jackson*, 1859.

Fuller (Jane Gay). Bending willow: a tale of missionary life in the north-west. 305 pp. 3 pl. 16°. *New York, R. Carter & brothers*, 1872.

Fuller (Metta Victoria). *See* **Victor** (*Mrs.* Metta V. Fuller).

Fuller (Richard, *d. d.*) Sermons. 384 pp. 12°. *New York, Sheldon & co.* 1860.

——— *and* **Wayland** (*Rev.* Francis) Domestic slavery considered as a scriptural institution: in a correspondence between the rev. Richard Fuller and the rev. Francis Wayland. viii, 254 pp. 18°. *New York, L. Colby*, 1845.

Fuller (Richard F.) Chaplain Fuller: being a life sketch of a New England clergyman and army chaplain [Arthur B. Fuller]. vi, 342 pp. 1 portrait. 12°. *Boston, Walker, Wise & co.* 1863.

Fuller (*Rev.* Thomas). The holy and profane states. With some account of the author and his writings. xxxix, 293 pp. 16°. *Cambridge* (*Mass.*) *Hilliard & Brown*, 1831.
[LIBRARY of the old english poets. *Cambridge*, 1831. v. 1].

Fulton (*Rev.* Justin D.) The true woman. To which is added woman vs. ballot. 214, 50 pp. 16°. *Boston, Lee & Shepard*, 1869.

Fulvio Pellegrino. *See* **Morato.**

Furness (*Rev.* William H.) Domestic worship. 275 pp. 12°. *Philadelphia, J. Kay, jr. & brother*, 1840.

——— Remarks on the four gospels. 340 pp. 12°. *Philadelphia, Carey, Lea & Blanchard*, 1836.

Furniss (William). The old world; or scenes and cities in foreign lands. 290 pp. 4 pl. 1 map. 12°. *New York, D. Appleton & co.* 1850.

Furnivall (Frederick J. *editor*). Early english treatises and poems on education, precedence, and manners in olden time. From mss. in the British museum and Bodleian libraries, etc. 1 p. l. xxiv, 128 pp. 8°. [*London*, 1869].
[EARLY english text society. Extra series, v. 8, part 1].

——— Jyl of Breyntford's testament, by Robert Copland, The wyll of the deuyll and his last testament, A talk of ten wives on their husbands' ware, a balade or two by Chaucer,

Furnivall (Frederick J.)—continued.
and other short pieces. 44 pp. 8°. *London, for private circulation*, 1871.

——— Trial-forewords to my "Parallel-text edition of Chaucers minor poems." (With a try to set Chaucer's works in their right order of time,) by F. J. Furnivall. 1 p. l. v, 123 pp. 1 pl. 8°. *London, Chaucer society*, 1871.
[CHAUCER society publications, 2d series, no. 6, part 1].

——— *and* **Cowper** (J. Meadows) *editors.* A supplicacyon for the beggers. Written about the year 1529 by Simon Fish. Now re-edited by Frederick J. Furnivall. With A supplycacion to our moste soueraigne lorde kynge Henry the eyght (1544), A supplication of the poore commons (1546), The decaye of England by the great multitude of shepe (1550–3), edited by J. Meadows Cowper. xviii, 115 pp. 8°. *London, N. Trübner & co.* 1871.
[EARLY english text society. Extra series, xiii].

Future (The). A journal of philosophical research and criticism. [Edited by Luke Burke. A monthly]. no. 1–14. 1860–61. 8°. *London*, [*Trübner & co.* 1860–61].
[*With* The reasoner, v. 26].

Fysh (*Rev.* Frederic). An examination of "Anastasis," the late work of professor Bush; exposing the fallacy of the arguments therein advanced, and proving the doctrine of the resurrection of the body to be a scriptural and a rational doctrine. xx, 400 pp. 12°. *London, Seeley, Burnside & Seeley*, 1847.

G. (A.) Ansvver to Gardiner. 1547. *See* **Gilby** *or* **Gilbie** (Anthony).

G. (A. S.) Original poetic effusions, religious, moral and sentimental. [*anon.*] Eng. title, 2 pl. vi, 206 pp. 16°. *Boston*, 1822.

G. (B.) A newyeares gifte. 1570. *See* **Garter** (Bernard).

G. (*Capt.* J. C.) Lee's last campaign. By capt. J. C. G. [*anon.*] 59 pp. 24°. *Raleigh* (*N. C.*) *W. B. Smith & co.* 1866.

G. (J. L.). Fables diverses. *Paris*, 1807. *See* **Grenus** (Jacques Louis).

G. (L. E.) Irish Amy. *See* **Guernsey** (Lucy Ellen).

Gaboriau (Émile). Le dossier no. 113. 5e éd. 2 p. l. 487 pp. 12°. *Paris, E. Dentu*, 1869.

——— The mystery of Orcival. Translated from the french. By George M. Towle. 168 pp. 8°. *New York, Holt & Williams*, 1871.
[LEISURE hour series, no. 4].

Gabriac (*Comte* de). Promenade à travers l'Amérique du sud, Nouvelle-Grenade, Équateur, Pérou, Brésil. 3 p. l. 304 pp. 21 pl. 2 maps. 8°. *Paris, M. Lévy frères*, 1868.

Gabrini (Francis). Saturday, the day consecrated to Mary ; or, meditations on the greatness, the virtues, and the glories of the most holy virgin. Translated from the german by rev. Eugene O'Keeffe. xx, 434 pp. 1 pl. 12°. [*New York*], 1872.

Gaby (Jean Baptiste). Relation de la Nigritie. [etc.] Avec la découverte de la rivière du Senega, dont on a fait une carte particulière. 5 p. l. 90 pp. 1 l. 1 map. 18°. *Paris, E. Couterot*, 1689.

Gacetas de literatura de Mexico : por d. José Antonio Alzate [y] Ramirez. [1789-1799. Reimpresas]. 4 v. sm. 4°. *Puebla, M. Buen Abad*, 1831.

Gachard (Louis Prosper). Analectes belgiques, ou recueil de pièces inédites, mémoires, notices, faits et anecdotes concernant l'histoire des Pays-Bas. v. 1. 2 p. l. 8, 492 pp. 1 facsim. 8°. *Bruxelles, A. Wahlen*, 1830.

——— Relations des ambassadeurs vénitiens sur Charles-quint et Philippe ii. 2 p. l. lxxx, 330 pp. 8°. *Bruxelles, M. Hayez*, 1855.

Gaertner (Carl). The art of singing, by C. Gaertner, for the pupils of his national conservatory of music. vi, 77 pp. 4°. *Philadelphia, author*, 1871.

——— Melodious exercises for the pianoforte. 56 pp. 4°. *Philadelphia*, 1869.

Gage (Annie O.) The bible standard of duty, a question book of practical religion. With an introduction by rev. William L. Gage. 1 p. l. 106 pp. 16°. *Hartford, Brown & Gross*, [1871].

Gage (*Rev.* William Leonard). The land of sacred mystery, or the bible read in the light of its own scenery. Eng. title, 610 pp. 5 pl. 5 maps. 8°. *Hartford (Conn.) Worthington, Dustin & co.* 1871.

Gaine's universal register, or, columbian kalendar, for the year 1787 : and the 12th of american independence after the 4th July. 2 p. l. 200 pp. 1 l. 18°. *New-York, H. & J. R. Gaine*, [1786].

Gainsforde (Thomas). The historie of Trebizond, in foure bookes. 3 p. l. 360 pp. 4°. *London, T. Downe and E. Dawson*, 1616.

Galaxy (The). An illustrated magazine of entertaining reading. [Monthly]. Jan. to Dec. 1871. v. 11-12. 8°. *New York, Sheldon & co.* 1871.

Gale (Leonard D. *m. d.*) Elements of natural philosophy : embracing the general principles of mechanics, hydrostatics, hydraulics, pneumatics, acoustics, optics, electricity, galvanism, magnetism, and astronomy. 276 pp. 12°. *New York, Collins, Keese & co.* 1837.

Gale (*Rev.* Nahum, *d. d.*) Memoir of rev. Bennet Tyler, d. d. 8°. [*Boston*, 1859].

[*In* TYLER (Bennet, d. d.) Lectures on theology, pp. 11-149].

Gale (S. *of Charleston, S. C.*) An essay on the nature and principles of public credit. vi, 234 pp. 8°. *London, B. White*, 1784.

Gale (Thomas). Opuscula mythologica, physica et ethica. Græce et latine. [Cum notis variis]. Eng. title, 11 p. l. 752 pp. 4 l. 8°. *Amstelaedami, apud H. Wetstenium*, 1688.

CONTENTS.

ANONYMI longe Heraclito recentioris liber de incredibilibus.
CORNUTUS (A.) Phurnuti de natura deorum commentarius.
DEMOCRATIS philosophi aureæ sententiæ.
DEMOPHILI similitudines, seu vitæ curatio ex pythagoreis.
ERATOSTHENIS cyrenæi catasterismi.
Ex quorundam pythagoreorum libris fragmenta, in quibus de philosophia morali agitur.
HERACLIDIS pontici allegoriæ Homeri.
HERACLITUS de incredibilibus.
HOMERI poëtæ vita.
OCELLUS lucanus philosophus de universi natura.
PALÆPHATUS de incredibilibus historiis.
SALLUSTII philosophi de diis et mundo liber.
SECUNDI atheniensis sophistæ sententiæ.
SEXTI pythagorei sententiæ, e græco in latinum a Ruffino versæ.
THEOPHRASTI notationes morum.
TIMÆUS locrus de anima mundi & natura.

Galenus (Claudius). Œuvres anatomiques, physiologiques, et médicales de Galien, traduites sur les textes imprimés et manuscrits accompagnées de sommaires, de notes, de planches et d'une table des matières, précédées d'une introduction, par le dr. Ch. Daremberg. v. 1-2. 2 p. l. xvi, 706 pp. 1 l ; 2 p. l. 786 pp. 8°. *Paris, J. B. Baillière*, 1854-56.

[No more published].

CONTENTS.

v. 1. Que le bon médecin est philosophe.
Exhortation à l'étude des arts.
Que les mœurs de l'âme sont la conséquence des tempéraments du corps.
Des habitudes.
v. 1-2. De l'utilité des parties du corps humain.
v. 2. Des facultés naturelles.
Du mouvement des muscles.
Des sectes aux étudiants.
De la meilleure secte, à Thrasybule.
Des lieux affectés.
De la méthode thérapeutique, à Glaucon.

Galien. *See* **Galenus.**

Gallaeus. *See* **Gallé.**

Gallé (Servais). Σιβυλλιακοι χρησμοι, hoc est, sibyllina oracula, ex veteribus codicibus

Gallé (Servais)—continued. emendata, ac restituta et commentariis diversorum illustrata. Accedunt etiam oracula magica Zoroastris, Jovis, Apollinis, &c. Astrampsychi oneiro-criticum, &c. Græce & latine. Eng. title, 13 p. l. 792 pp. 12 l. 127 pp. 4°. *Amstelodami, apud H. & viduam T. Boom*, 1689.

Gallenga (Antonio). The Blackgown papers. By L. Mariotti. [*pseudon.*] 2 v. vii, 256 pp. 1 pl; 3 p. l. 276 pp. 1 pl. 12°. *London, Wiley & Putnam*, 1846.

Gallien (F.) L'escamoteur habile, ou l'art d'amuser agréablement une société. [etc.] 266 pp. 4 l. 16°. *Pesth, C. A. Hartleben*, 1816.

Galloway (Joseph). Brief commentaries upon such parts of the revelation and other prophecies as immediately refer to the present times. With the prophetic, or anticipated history of the church of Rome. [Also], a pill for the infidel and atheist. [Reprint]. 2 v. x, 382 pp; 1 p. l. 414 pp. 12°. *Trenton (N. J.) J. Oram for D. Fenton*, 1809.

[Imperfect: v. 1 wanting all after p. 382, and v. 2 the first and last leaves].

Galloway (William Brown) Philosophy and religion with their mutual bearings comprehensively considered, and satisfactorily determined, on clear and scientific principles. xvi, 544 pp. 8°. *London, Smith, Elder & co.* 1837.

Galos (Henri). Enquête sur la marine marchande. 2 p. l. 84 pp. 8°. *Paris, Amyot*, 1865.

Galt (John). Common events: a continuation of rich and poor. [*anon.*] 2 p. l. 382 pp. 12°. *Edinburgh, W. Blackwood*, 1825.

——— The member: an autobiography. By the author of "The Ayrshire legatees," etc. etc. [Archibald Jobbry, *pseudon.*] viii, 272 pp. 16°. *London, J. Fraser*, 1832.

——— The tragedies of Maddalen, Agamemnon, lady Macbeth, Antonia and Clytemnestra. vi, 262 pp. 1 pl. 4°. *London, Cadell & Davis*, 1812.

Gambara (Lorenzo). Lavrentii Gambaræ brixiani, rervm sacrarvm liber. Cvm argumentis Iacobi Pacti. 194 pp. 1 l. sm. 4°. *Antverpiæ, ex officina C. Plantini*, 1577.

Gandini (Marc Antonio). *See* **Xenophon.** Le opere tradotte dal greco. 1736.

Gandouet (F. *pseudon.*) The french politick detected, with the characters of the french politicians display'd; in iv parts. By way of allegory. Where the maxims of both governments of that nation, ecclesiastical and civil, are prov'd immutable from its legislators, druides or priests of the Guals [Gauls] to this day; notwithstanding the usurp'd name of christian. 7 p. l. 16, 176 pp. 1 l. 16°. *Bristol, W. Bonny*, 1709.

Gangooly (Joguth Chunder). Juthoo and his sunday school; or child life in India. By a native brahmin. With an appendix of "Short stories." 90 pp. 18°. *Boston, Walker, Wise & co.* 1861.

Ganilh (*Rev.* Anthony). Odes, and fugitive poetry. 36 pp. 12°. *Boston, W. Smith*, 1830.

Ganilh (Charles). De la contre-révolution en France, ou de la restauration de l'ancienne noblesse et des anciennes supériorités sociales dans la France nouvelle. xvi, 238 pp. 1 l. 8°. *Paris, Béchet aîné*, 1823.

Ganyard (A. O.) The talisman of battle and other poems. 120 pp. 12°. *Rochester (N. Y.) W. S. King*, 1864.

Garat (Dominique Joseph). Mémoires historiques sur la vie de m. Suard, sur ses écrits, et sur le xviiie siècle. 2 v. 5 p. l. xliv, 363 pp; 1 p. l. 451 pp. 8°. *Paris, A. Belin*, 1820.

Garcia (Juan Antonio). Al asombro de los desiertos, horror de las penitēcias, muger fuerte, Santa Maria Egypciaca novena. 15 l. 18°. *Mexico, heredero de la viuda de M. de Rivera*, 1722.

Garcilaso de la Vega (*The inca*). First part of the royal commentaries of the yncas. Translated and edited, with notes and introduction, by Clements R. Markham. v. 2. (Containing books 5, 6, 7, 8, & 9). 8° *London, Hakluyt society*, 1871.

[HAKLUYT society publications, v. 43].

——— Histoire des guerres civiles des Espagnols, dans les Indes, entre les Piçarres & les Almagres, qui les avoient conquises. Traduite de l'espagnol de l'ynca par J. Baudoin. 4 parts in 2 v. Eng. title, 9 p. l. 768 pp. 2 pl. 2 maps; eng. title, 5 p. l. 648 pp. 1 pl. 16°. *Amsterdam, G. Kuyper*, 1706.

Garcin de Tassy (Joseph Héliodore). Manuel de l'auditeur du cours d'hindoustani, ou thèmes gradués pour exercer à la conversation et au style épistolaire; accompagnés d'un vocabulaire français-hindoustani. 2 p. l. 92 pp. 8°. *Paris, imprimerie royale*, 1836. S.

Gardeners' (The) chronicle and agricultural gazette. [Weekly]. Jan. 7 to Dec. 30, 1871. fol. *London,* [*W. Richards*] *for the proprietors,* 1871.

Gardiner (David). Chronicles of the town of Easthampton, county of Suffolk, New York. 4 p. l. 121 pp. 8°. *New York,* [*Bowne & co.*] 1871.

Gardiner (Frederic). Diatessaron. The life of our lord; in the words of the gospels. viii, 259 pp. 16°. *Andover, W. F. Draper,* 1871.

——— Harmony of the four gospels [in english]. *See* **Bible.** (*English*).

——— A harmony of the four gospels in greek. *See* **Bible.** (*Greek*).

Gardiner (*Mrs.* H. C.) A king's daughter: with other stories from real life. 379 pp. 16°. *New York, Carlton & Lanahan,* [1871].

Gardiner (James T.) The sign painter's guide. 70 pp. 16°. *Cincinnati, author,* 1871.

Gardiner (*Captain* Richard, *editor*). *See* **Memoirs** of the siege of Quebec.

Gardiner (Samuel Rawson, *editor*). Letters and other documents illustrating the relations between England and Germany at the commencement of the thirty years' war. 2d series. From the election of the emperor Ferdinand ii. to the close of the conferences at Mühlhausen. xi, 194 pp. sm. 4°. *London, Camden society,* 1868.

[CAMDEN society publications, no. 98].

Gardner (Augustus K. *m. d.*) Our children: their physical and mental development. 340 pp. 6 pl. 12°. *Hartford* (*Conn.*) *Belknap & Bliss,* 1872.

Gardner (Celia E.) Stolen waters. 326 pp. 12°. *New York, G. W. Carleton & co.* 1871.

Gardner (F. B.) The carriage painters' illustrated manual. 126 pp. 18°. *New-York, S. R. Wells,* 1871.

Gardner (*Mrs.* H. C.) Extracts from the diary of a country pastor. 240 pp. 16°. *Cincinnati, Poe & Hitchcock,* 1864.

Gardner (Samuel Jackson). Autumn leaves. vii, 301 pp. 12°. *New York, Hurd & Houghton,* 1865.

Garengeot (René Jacques Croissant de). Splanchnologie, ou l'anatomie des viscères; avec des figures originales tirées d'après les cadavres, suivie d'une dissertation sur l'origine de la chirurgie. 2e éd. revue, corrigée & augmentée par l'auteur. 2 v. 2 p. l. xlv, 352 pp. 9 pl; 4 p. l. 372 pp. 1 l. 11 pl. 16°. *Paris, C. Osmont,* 1742.

Garfield (Ellery Irving). Knights templar tactics and drill with the working text and burial service of the orders of knighthood, as adopted by the grand commandery of the state of Michigan. 183 pp. 1 pl. 18°. *Detroit, E. B. Smith & co.* 1871.

Garfield (*Miss* Emma). Principles of elocution. vii, 146 pp. 12°. [*n. p.*] *author,* 1871.

Garlandia (Johannes de, *called* Hortulanus). Le commentaire sur La table d'émeraude de Hermes. *See* **Hermes** *trismegistus.* La table d'émeraude. 1741.

Garnett (Catharine Grace). The night before the bridal. A spanish tale. Sappho, a dramatic sketch, and other poems. xii, 220 pp. 8°. *London, Longman,* 1824.

Garrard (Edmund). The covntrie gentleman moderator. Collections of such intermarriages, as haue beene betweene the two royall lines of England and Spaine, since the conquest. With diuers reasons to moderate the country peoples passions, concerning the prince his royall match. 3 p. l. 67 pp. sm. 4°. *London, Edward Allde,* 1624.

——— The same.

[MISCELLANEOUS pamphlets, v. 101].

Garrard (*Maj. gen.* Kenner). Nolan's system of training cavalry horses. 1 p. l. 114 pp. 24 pl. 12°. *New York, D. Van Nostrand,* 1862.

Garrard (Thomas). Edward Colston, the philanthropist, his life and times; including a memoir of his father; the result of a laborious investigation into the archives of the city. Edited by Samuel Griffiths Tovey. xi, 507 pp. 1 l. 1 portrait. 4°. *Bristol, J. Chilcott,* 1852.

Garratt (Alfred C. *m. d.*) Electro-physiology and electro-therapeutics; showing the best methods for the medical uses of electricity. 2d. ed. 2 p. l. 716 pp. 2 pl. 8°. *Boston, Ticknor & Fields,* 1861.

Garrett (Augusta Browne). The precious stones of the heavenly foundations. With illustrative selections in prose and verse. 328 pp. 12°. *New York, Sheldon & co.* 1859.

Garrett (Edward). The occupations of a retired life. 2d ed. viii, 472 pp. 16°. *London, Strahan & co.* 1869.

Garrett (L.) A collection of hymns and spiritual songs, generally used at camp and prayer meetings. 278 pp. 5 l. 32°. *Nashville* (*Tenn.*) *Western methodist office,* 1834.

Garrett (L.)—continued.

——— Recollections of the west. To which are added Fletcher's six letters on the spiritual manifestation of the son of God. 240 pp. 24°. *Nashville, Western methodist office*, 1834.

Gartenlaube (Die). Illustrirtes familienblatt. [Wöchentlich]. Januar bis Dec. 1871. v. 19. 4°. *Leipzig, E. Keil*, 1871.

Garter (Bernard). A newyeares gifte, dedicated to the pope's holinesse, and all catholikes addicted to the sea of Rome: preferred the first day of Januarie, one thousand, fiue hundreth, seauentie and nine, by B. G. citizen of London: in recompence of diuers singular and inestimable reliques, of late sent by the said pope's holinesse into England, the true figures and representations whereof, are heereafter in their places dilated. [*anon.*] 52 l. unp. 4°. *London, H. Bynnemann*, 1579.

[*Note.*—Sometimes attributed to Barnaby Googe, but the weight of authority is in favor of Garter].

Garzoni (Tommaso). Il seraglio de gli stupori del mondo. Diuiso in diece appartamenti, secondo gli vari, & ammirabili oggetti. Cioè di mostri, prodigii, prestigii, sorti, oracoli, sibille, sogni, cvriosità astrologica, miracoli in genere, e maraviglie in spetie. Arricchita di varie annotationi dal m. r. p. d. Bartolomeo Garzoni suo fratello. 30 p. l. 788 pp. 4°. *Venetia, A. & B. Dei, fratelli*, 1613.

Gascoigne *or* **Gascoyne** (George). 1. Certayne notes of instruction in english verse. 1575. 2. The steele glas. 1576. 3. The complaynt of Philomene. 1576. Preceded by George Whetstone's A remembrance of the well imployed life, and godly end of George Gascoigne. Carefully edited by Edward Arber. 119 pp. 16°. *London, A. Murray & son*, 1868.

[ARBER's english reprints, v. 5, no. 11].

——— A delicate diet, for daintie mouthde droonkardes. Wherein the fowle abuse of common carowsing, and quaffing with heartie draughtes, is honestlie admonished. *London, Richard Jhones*, 1576. 24 pp. 8°. *London, reprinted for the editor*, 1789.

[*In* WALDRON (F. G.) Literary museum. *London*, 1792].

Gaskins (James). The farmer's guide, or a new theory of agriculture; founded on philosophical and practical principles, and adapted to all climates. 215 pp. 12°. *Baltimore, S. Sands*, 1838.

Gasparin (Agenor Étienne, *comte* de). Le bonheur. Troisième série de discours prononcés à Genève. 226 pp. 1 l. 12°. *Paris, C. Meyrueis & cie.* 1859.

Gassendi (Pierre). Three discourses of happiness, virtue, and liberty. Collected from the works of the learned Gassendi, by m. [François] Benier. Translated out of french. 3 p. l. 452 pp. 2 l. 8°. *London, A. & J. Churchill*, 1699.

Gaston (*Rev.* Hugh). A scripture account of the faith and practice of christians; consisting of an extensive collection of pertinent texts of scripture, illustrative of the various articles of revealed religion: reduced into distinct sections. 4th ed. 370 pp. 8°. *Philadelphia, Hogan & Thompson*, 1834.

Gastrell (Francis, *d. d.*) The certainty of the christian revelation, and the necessity of believing it, established. In opposition to all the cavils and insinuations of such as pretend to allow natural religion, and reject the gospel. 12 p. l. 357 pp. 8°. *London, T. Bennet*, 1699.

——— Eight sermons. fol. [*London*, 1739].

[*In* BOYLE lectures, v. 1, pp. 275-352].

——— A moral proof of the certainty of a future state. 4 p. l. 102 pp. 8°. *Dublin, S. Brock*, 1737.

Gataker (*Rev.* Thomas). Certaine sermons, first preached, and after published at severall times. 2 v. in 1. 3 p. l. 347 pp; 3 p. l. 320 pp. fol. *London, E. Brewster*, 1637.

Gates (*Mrs.* Rozina). A panoramic view of the creation! in the light of geology. 56 pp. 16°. *St. Joseph (Mich.) T. L. Reynolds*, 1871.

Gatta (Costantino). Memorie topographico-storiche della provincia di Lucania compresa al presente nelle provincie Basilicata, e di principato-citeriore. Colla serie genealogica de' serenissimi principi di Salerno, e di Bisignano dell' illustre famiglia Sanseverino. Divise in tre parti. 14 p. l. 488 pp. 8 l. 3 pl. 4°. *Napoli, G. Muzio*, 1732.

Gattel (Claude Marie). Dictionnaire universel de la langue française, avec la prononciation figurée. 3e éd. 2 v. 2 p. l. xxxii, 880 pp; 2 p. l. 868 pp. 8°. *Lyon, mm. J. Buynand*, 1819.

Gauden (John, *bishop of Worcester*). Hieraspistes; a defence by way of apology for the ministry and ministers of the church of England. 23 l. 594 pp. 6 l. 4°. *London, A. Crooke*, 1653.

Gauden (John)—continued.

——— Ἱερὰ δάκρυα. Ecclesiæ anglicanæ suspiria. The tears, sighs, complaints, and prayers of the church of England: setting forth her former constitution, compared with her present condition; also the visible causes, and probable cures, of her distempers. In iv books. 5 p. l. 711 pp. fol. *London, J. G. for R. Royston*, 1659.

——— Κακωυργοι sive Medicastri: slight healings of publique hurts. A sermon preached before the [corporation] of London, February 28, 1659. 4 p. l. 112 pp. sm. 4°. *London, A. Crook*, 1660.

Gaudin (Jacques). Les inconvéniens du célibat des prêtres, prouvés par des recherches historiques. [*anon.*] 3 p. l. xvi, 439 pp. 8°. *Genève, J. L. Pellet*, 1781.

Gaudy Le Fort (—). Promenades historiques dans le canton de Genève. 2e éd. corrigée et augmentée. 2 v. 216 pp; 235 pp. 16°. *Genève, J. Cherbuliez*, 1849.

Gaureault (Hyacinthe de). Recueil général des opéra représentéz par l'académie royale de musique. *See* **Francini** (Jean Nicolas de) *and* **Gaureault**.

Gaussen (S. R. Louis). Theopneusty, or, the plenary inspiration of the holy scriptures. Translated by E. N. Kirk. 2 p. l. 343 pp. 12°. *New-York, J. S. Taylor & co.* 1842.

Gautier (César). The idioms of the french language. In french and english. 3d ed. 2 p. l. vii, 455 pp. 12°. *London, J. Souter*, 1818.

Gautier (Hubert *or* Henri). La bibliothèque des philosophes, et des sçavans, tant anciens que modernes, avec les merveilles de la nature, où l'on voit leurs opinions sur toute sorte de matières physiques; comme aussi tous les systèmes qu'ils ont pû imaginer jusqu'à présent sur l'univers, & leurs plus belles sentences sur la morale; et enfin, les nouvelles découvertes que les astronomes ont faites dans les cieux. 3 v. 8°. *Paris, A. Cailleau*, 1723–34.

——— Traité de la construction des chemins, où il est parlé de ceux des Romains, des pavez des grands chemins, la carte de l'ancienne Gaule, etc. Nouv. éd. 4 p. l. 334 pp. 1 l. 8 pl. 1 map. 8°. *Paris, A. Cailleau*, 1721.

Gautier (Théophile). Le capitaine Fracasse. Illustré de 60 dessins de Gustave Doré. 4 p. l. 496 pp. 60 pl. 8°. *Paris, Charpentier*, 1866.

Gautier (Théophile)—continued.

——— Un trio de romans. [Militona, Jean et Jeannette, Arria Marcella]. 2 p. l. 353 pp. 1 l. 12°. *Paris, V. Lecou*, 1852.

Gayarré (Charles). Fernando de Lemos. Truth and fiction. A novel. 486 pp. 12°. *New York, G. W. Carleton & co.* 1872.

Gayton (Edmund). The art of longevity, or, a diæteticall institution. 8 p. l. 94 pp. 4°. *London, author*, 1659.

Gazet (Nicolas). Le miroir des vevfves. [etc.] Autre miroir de la vie (en estat de viduité) et mort de la sérénissime princesse Loyse de Lorraine, royne doüairière de France et de Poloigne décédée en l'an 1601. 2 v. in 1. 8 p. l. 133 l. 3 l. unp; 5 p. l. 21 l. 18°. *Paris, G. Lombard*, 1601.

Gazette de Leyde. *See* **Nouvelles** extraordinaires de divers endroits.

Gazlay (Allen W.) Races of mankind; with travels in Grubland. By Cephas Broadluck. [*pseudon.*] 310 pp. 2 pl. 16°. *Cincinnati, Longley brothers*, 1856.

Gazlay (J. W.) Sketches of life and social relations, with other poems. 317 pp. 8°. *Cincinnati, author*, 1860.

Gazlay (Theodore). The practical printers' assistant: containing numerous schemes of imposition, definite directions for making composition rollers, and many useful tables. 135 pp. (incl. 1 pl.) 12°. *Cincinnati, J. A. James & co.* 1836.

Geber. *See* **Abú** Músá Jábir ben Hayyan et-Tarsusé.

Gebhard (Janus). Antiqvarvm lectionvm libri duo. [Selecta]. 112 pp. 16°. *Herbornæ Nassoviorum*, 1618.

Gee (*Rev.* Joshua). A letter to the rev. mr. Nathanael Eells, moderator of the late convention of pastors, containing some remarks on their printed testimony. 17 pp. 8°. *Boston, J. Draper for N. Proctor*, 1743.

Geer (*Capt.* John J.) Beyond the lines: or a yankee prisoner loose in Dixie. With an introduction, by rev. Alexander Clark. 285 pp. 4 pl. 1 portrait. 16°. *Philadelphia, J. W. Daughaday*, 1863.

Géhant (J. B. Victor). Le livre des principes ou plan nouveau d'éducation d'accord avec la raison et les traditions catholiques. 1 p. l. 380 pp. 12°. *Paris, J. Renouard & cie.* 1849.

Gelasius di Cilia. Himmlischer blumengarten. Katholisches gebet- und erbauungsbuch für heilsbegierige seelen. Neu bear-

Gelasius di Cilia—continued. beitet von A. Maier. 432 pp. 24°. *Einsiedeln, New-York & Cincinnati, C. & N. Benziger*, 1871.

Gems of beauty: or, literary gift for mdcccl. Edited by Emily Percival. Illuminated title, 296 pp. 7 pl. 8°. *Boston, Phillips, Sampson & co.* 1850.

General (A) history of the county of Norfolk, [Eng.] intended to convey all the information of a Norfolk tour, with the more extended details of antiquarian, statistical, pictorial, architectural, and miscellaneous information; including biographical notices, original and selected. [*anon.*] 3 v. 8°. *Norwich, J. Stacy*, 1829.

General (A) history of the Turks, Moguls, and Tatars, vulgarly called Tartars. Together with a description of the countries they inhabit. Made english from the french, with additions. 1 v. in 2. 2 p. l. xliii, 792 pp. 2 maps. 8°. *London, J. & J. Knapton*, [*etc.*] 1729–30.

CONTENTS.

v. 1. The genealogical history of the Tatars, translated from the tatar manuscript written in the mogul language by Abu'l Ghazi bahader, khan of Khowarazm.

v. 2. An account of the present state of the northern Asia and Siberia; with some observations relating to great Russia, Turky, Arabia, Persia, India and China.

Génin (François). Lexique comparé de la langue de Molière et des écrivains du xviie siècle, suivi d'une lettre à m. A. F. Didot, sur quelques points de philologie française. 2 p. l. lxxxvii, 463 pp. 8°. *Paris, F. Didot frères*, 1846.

Genlis (Stéphanie Félicité Ducrest de Saint-Aubin, *comtesse* de). Adèle et Théodore, ou lettres sur l'éducation, contenant tous les principes relatifs aux trois differens plans d'éducation des princes, des jeunes personnes, & des hommes. [*anon.*] 3 v. 18°. *Paris, J. F. Bassompierre*, 1785.

——— The same. Adelaide and Theodore; or letters on education: containing all the principles relative to three different plans of education; to that of princes, and to those of young persons of both sexes. Translated from the french. 2d ed. 3 v. 16°. *London, C. Bathurst*, 1784.

——— De l'influence des femmes sur la littérature française, comme protectrices des lettres et comme auteurs; ou précis de l'histoire des femmes françaises les plus célèbres. 2 p. l. xl, 373 pp. 8°. *Paris, Maradan*, 1811.

Genlis (*Comtesse* de)—continued.

——— Manuel du voyageur, or the traveller's pocket companion, in six languages. 9th ed. enlarged and greatly improved, by P. A. Cignani. viii, 560, x pp. obl. 18°. *London, S. Leigh*, [*about* 1830]?

[Imperfect: wanting from p. 560 to the end].

——— Religion considered as the only basis of happiness, and of true philosophy. [Translated from the french]. 2 v. xxi, 296 pp; 3 p. l. 291 pp. 12°. *London, T. Payne & son*, 1787.

——— Sainclair, or the victim to the arts and sciences; and Hortense, or the victim to novels and travel. Translated from the french. By Archibald Haralson. [Also], a tale of m. Florian, entitled Claudine, or the Savoyarde. 246 pp. 16°. *Georgetown (D. of C.) Richards & Mallory*, [*etc.*] 1813.

——— Zuma, or the tree of health. [Also], the fair Pauline,—Zeneida,—the reeds of the Tiber,—and the widow of Luzi. 180 pp. 16°. *New-York, W. B. Gilley*, 1818.

Genoa. (*Consiglio provinciale*). Atti. Sessioni ordinaria e straordinaria, anno 1870. 112, 115 pp. fol. *Genova, Ferrando*, [1871]. s.

——— (*Regio istituto tecnico industriale-professionale e di marina mercantile della provincia di Genoa*). Atti. Pubblicati per cura ed a spese del municipio di Genoa. 2 v. 2 p. l. 1020 pp. 1 pl; 1 p. l. 836 pp. 15 pl. 8°. *Genova, coi tipi del r. i. de' sordo-muti*, 1868–69. s.

Genova. *See* **Genoa.**

Gentleman's (The) magazine. [Monthly]. Dec. 1870, to Dec. 1871. Entirely new [6th] series, v. 6–7; [complete series, v. 230–231]. 8°. *London, W. H. Allen & co. and Grant & co.* 1871.

Genung (Abram P.) The frauds of the New York city government exposed. Sketches of the members of the ring and their confederates; with a list of checks, copied from the books in the office of the comptroller, representing millions of dollars paid out on fraudulent claims. [*anon.*] 52 pp. 8°. *New York, author*, 1871.

Geographical (A) history of Nova Scotia. Containing an account of the situation, extent and limits thereof, as also of the various struggles between the two crowns of England and France for the possession of that province. [*anon.*] 110 pp. 1 l. 12°. *London, P. Vaillant*, 1749

Geographical (A) present; being descriptions of the several countries of Africa. Compiled from the best authorities [*anon.*] iv, 130 pp. 12 col. pl. 16°. *New-York, W. Burgess,* 1831.

Geographical (A) view of the United States. [*anon.*] 130 pp. 1 l. 8°. *Boston, A. K. White,* 1827.

George (*Rev.* Augustus C.) Counsels to converts. 357 pp. 12°. *Cincinnati, Poe & Hitchcock,* 1864.

George (*Rev.* H. H.) Covenanting a duty in new testament times. 12°. [*Pittsburgh,* 1872].

[*In* REFORMED presbyterian church in North America. Memorial volume, pp. 27-39].

George (*Rev.* Nathan D.) An examination of universalism, embracing its rise and progress, and the means of its propagation. 210 pp. 1 l. 12°. *Boston, Waite, Peirce & co.* 1846.

Georget (Étienne Jean). De la folie. Considérations sur cette maladie. x, 511 pp. 8°. *Paris, Crevot,* 1820.

Georgetown (*D. C.*) Boyd's directory of Washington, Georgetown, and Alexandria, [etc.] 1871. 17 p. l. 388, xcvi pp. 1 l. 8°. *Washington* (*D. C.*) 1871.

Georgia (*State of*). The constitution of the state of Georgia. 11 pp. 4°. *Savannah, W. Lancaster,* 1777.

[HAZARD pamphlets, v. 33].

——— Journal of the house of representatives, at the annual sessions of the general assembly, at Milledgeville, 1861, 1862, and Atlanta, 1869. 3 v. 8°. *Milledgeville, Boughton, Nisbet & Barnes; Atlanta, public printer;* 1861-69.

——— Journal of the senate [and] house of representatives, at the called session of the general assembly, 1868, and annual session, 1870. 7 v. 8°. *Macon, J. W. Burke & co.; Atlanta, public printer;* 1869-70.

Georgia (The) gazette. Jan. 7, 1790, to Dec. 29, 1791. nos. 363-466. fol. *Savannah, J. & N. Johnston,* 1790-91.

Georgirenes (Joseph). A description of the present state of Samos, Nicaria, Patmos, and mount Athos. Translated by one that knew the author in Constantinople. [With a greek preface]. 10 p. l. 112 pp. 12°. *London, M. Pitt,* 1678.

Georgius Pachymeres. *See* **Pachymeres.**

Gérando (Joseph Marie, *baron* de). Self-education; or the means and art of moral progress. Translated from the french of m. le baron Degérando. 3d ed. vii, 386 pp. 12°. *Boston, Marsh, Capen & Lyon,* 1833.

Gérando (J. M. *baron* de)—continued.

——— The visitor of the poor. Translated from the french, by a lady of Boston. With an introduction, by Joseph Tuckerman. 2d ed. xxxiii, 211 pp. 12°. *Boston, Marsh, Capen & Lyon,* 1833.

Gerbert (Martin). De Rudolpho Suevico, comite de Rhinfelden, duce, rege deque eius inlustri familia, ex augusta ducum Lotharingiae prosapia, apud D. Blasii sepulta; cryptae huic antiquae, nova Austriacorum principum adiuncta. 6 p. l. 166 pp. 1 l. 1 pl. 4°. [*Saint-Blaise*], *typis San-Blasianis,* 1785.

Gerdes (Daniel). Florilegium historico-critico librorum rariorum. Ed. 3a. 6 p. l. 384 pp. 6 l. 8°. *Groningæ & Bremæ, apud H. Spandaw & G. W. Rump,* 1763.

Gerhard (Johann). Gerard's meditations, written originally in the latine tongue. Translated and revised by Ralph Winterton. 4th ed. 11 p. l. 323 pp. 18°. *Cambridge* (*Eng.*) *printed by the printers to the universitie,* 1635.

——— Gerard's prayers: or, a daily practise of pietie. Written originally in the latine tongue. Translated and revised by Ralph Winterton. 5th ed. 6 p. l. 155 pp. 18°. *Cambridge* (*Eng.*) *printed by the printers to the universitie,* 1631.

[*With his* Meditations, 1635].

Gerhard (William W. *m. d.*) Clinical lectures, delivered at the Philadelphia medical institute, and at the Philadelphia hospital. 8°. [*Philadelphia,* 1842].

[*In* GRAVES (R. J.) Clinical lectures, pp. 429-560].

——— Lectures on the diagnosis, pathology, and treatment of the diseases of the chest. 158 pp. 1 pl. 8°. *Philadelphia, Haswell & Barrington,* 1842.

Gerlach (G. C. F.) Logen-hierarchie, besonders in bezug auf Krause's, Heldmanns und Gädike's freimaurer-schriften. viii, 150 pp. 16°. *Freiberg, Craz & Gerlach,* 1819.

German reformed church. Das neue und verbesserte gesangbuch, worinnen die psalmen Davids samt einer sammlung alter und neuer geistreicher lieder enthalten sind. Nebst einem anhang des heydelbergischen catechismus. 2te aufl. 3 p. l. 148, 586, 26 pp. 8 l. 16°. *Germantown,* [*Pa.*] *M. Billmeyer,* 1799.

——— Psalms and hymns for the use of the German reformed church, in the United States of America. Published by the synod of the said church. 2d ed. iv, 626 pp. 12 l. 24°. *Philadelphia, C. Sherman & co.* 1834.

Germany. Brief des keyserlijcke majest. van Duytslandt aende heeren staten vande Gheunieerde Provintien gheschreven. Op't stuck vande nederlantsche vredehandeling. Midtsgaders d'antwoort vande staten. *b. l.* 4 l. sm. 4°. [*n. p.*] 1608.
[*In* NEDERLANDTSCHEN bye-corf].

——— Débats de l'assemblée de Francfort sur les questions de l'église et de l'instruction publique. Traduits par N. Reyntiens. 2 p. l. iv, 247 pp. 8°. *Bruxelles, A. Decq*, 1849.

——— General instructions for consuls of the german empire, on the 6. June 1871. The english portion translated from the german original, by Charles Kirchhoff. 44 pp. 4°. *New York, W. H. Waterman*, 1872.

——— Lettres patentes d'octroy accordées par sa majesté impériale et catholique, pour le terme de trente années à la compagnie générale à établir dans les Pays-Bas aûtrichiens, pour le commerce et la navigation aux Indes. 1 p. l. 36 pp. sm. 4°. *Bruxelles, E. H. Fricx*, 1723.

Gerrish (Andrew). A synopsis on the prevention and cure of disease. 208 pp. 12°. *Boston, Saxton & Peirce*, 1841.

Gersdorf (E. G.) Bibliotheca patrum ecclesiasticorum latinorum selecta. Ad optimorum librorum fidem edita. 13 v. 12°. *Lipsiae, B. Tauchnitz, jun.* 1838–47.

CONTENTS.

AMBROSIUS (*S.*) De officiis clericorum libros tres emendavit R. O. Gilbert. Praemissa est vita s. Ambrosii a Paulino scripta. v. 8.
——— Hexaemeri libros sex emendavit R. O. Gilbert. v. 9.
ARNOBIUS. Adversus nationes libri septem. v. 12.
CLEMENS *romanus* (*S.*) Recognitiones. v. 1.
COMMODIANUS. Instructionum per litteras versuum primas libri duo. v. 13.
CYPRIANUS (Th. C.) Opera genuina. v. 2–3.
FIRMACUS Maternus (Julius). De errore profanarum religionum liber. v. 13.
LACTANTIUS Firmianus. Opera. v. 10–11.
MINUCIUS Felix (M.) Octavius. v. 13.
PAULINUS *nolanus* (M. P. A.) Poema adversus paganos. v. 13.
TERTULLIANUS (Q. S. F.) Opera. v. 4–7.

Gerstaecker (A.) Bericht über die wissenschaftlichen leistungen im gebiete der entomologie, 1867–68. *See* **Brauer** *and* **Gerstaecker.**

Geruzez (Nicolas Eugène). Essais de littérature française. 1re série. Moyen âge. Renaissance. 2 p. l. iv, 498 pp. 1 l. 16°. *Paris, Garnier frères*, [1863].

——— The same. 2e série. Temps modernes. 3e éd. 2 p. l. 510 pp. 1 l. 16°. *Paris, Garnier frères*, [1863].

Geruzez (Nicolas Eugène)—continued.

——— Histoire abrégée de la littérature française. viii, 360 pp. 1 l. 16°. *Paris, J. Delalain*, 1862.

——— Histoire de la littérature française depuis ses origines jusqu'à la révolution. 2 v. 4 p. l. 488 pp; 2 p. l. 507 pp. 8°. *Paris, Didier & cie.* 1861.

——— Histoire de la littérature française pendant la révolution, 1789–1800. viii, 423 pp. 16°. *Paris, Charpentier*, 1859.

Gesenius (William, *d. d.*) A hebrew and english lexicon of the old testament, including the biblical chaldee. Translated from the latin, by Edward Robinson, d. d viii, 1092 pp. 8°. *Boston, Crocker & Brewster*, 1836.

Gesner (Solomon, *poet*, 1730–88). Rural po ems. Translated from the original german of m. Gesner. xxiv, 106 pp. 1 pl. 16°. *London, T. Becket & P. A. De Hondt*, 1762.

Gess (W. F.) The scripture doctrine of the person of Christ. Freely translated from the german, with many additions, by J. A. Reubelt, d. d. 456 pp. 12°. *Andover*, [*Ms.*] *W. F. Draper*, 1870.

Getchell (F. H. *m. d.*) Physical training of children. *See* **Chavasse** (P. H.) *and* **Getchell.**

Ghazi (Abu'l) *bahader*. *See* **Abu'l Ghazi** *bahader*.

Giannone (Pietro). Anecdotes ecclésiastiques, contenant la police & la discipline de l'église chrétienne, depuis son établissement jusqu'au xi. siecle; les intrigues des évêques de Rome, et leurs usurpations sur le temporel des souverains. Tirées de L'histoire du royaume de Naples, de Giannone, brulée à Rome en 1726. [Traduites par Jacob Vernet]. xxiv, 360 pp. 16°. *Amsterdam, J Catuffe*, 1738.

Gibbon (John, *brig. gen. U. S. a.*) The artillerist's manual. Compiled from various sources, and adapted to the service of the United States. 568 pp. 14 pl. 8°. *New York, D. Van Nostrand*, 1860.

——— The same. 2d ed. 478 pp. 28 pl. 8°. *New York, D. Van Nostrand*, 1863.

Gibbons (Thomas, *d. d.*) Memoirs of eminently pious women, who were ornaments to their sex, blessings to their families, and edifying examples to the church and world. 2 v. lxiv, 436 pp. 6 pl; 2 p. l. 528 pp. 5 portraits. 8°. *London, J. Buckland*, 1777.

——— The same. Memoirs of eminently pious women, of the british empire. New ed.

Gibbons (Thomas, *d. d.*)—continued. [*anon.*] Corrected and enlarged by the rev. Samuel Burder. v. 3. viii, 515 pp. 7 portraits. 8°. *London, Ogles, Duncan & Cochrane*, 1815.

——— Rhetoric; or, a view of its principal tropes and figures, in their origin and powers: with a variety of rules to escape errors and blemishes, and attain elegance and propriety in composition. 8 p. l. 478 pp. 1 pl. 8°. *London, J. Buckland & J. Payne*, 1767.

Gibbons (William). Practical logic, or an assistant to theme writers. 100 pp. 12°. *Cleveland,* [*O.*] *Sandford & Lott*, 1840.

Gibbs (John). Letters from Græfenberg, in the years 1843–46. With the report, and extracts from the correspondence, of the Enniscorthy hydropathic society. xxiv, 280 pp. 12°. *London, C. Gilpin*, 1847.

Gibson (H. S.) A collection of miscellaneous poems, moral, religious, sentimental, and amusing. 156 pp. 16°. *Philadelphia, J. Crissy*, 1834.

Gibson (John). Odes and other poems. 127 pp. 16°. *Edinburgh, Fairbairn & Anderson*, 1818.

Gibson (John Mason). A condensation of matter upon the anatomy, surgical operations, and treatment of diseases of the eye, together with remarks. 204 pp. 12 pl. 4°. *Baltimore, W. R. Lucas*, 1832.

Gibson (William, *m. d.*) Institutes and practice of surgery; being outlines of a course of lectures. 6th edition, much enlarged and improved. 2 v. xii, 25–502 pp. 21 pl; 540 pp. 13 pl. 8°. *Philadelphia, J. Kay, jun. & brother*, 1841.

Gibson (*Rev.* William). The year of grace: a history of the revival in Ireland, a. d. 1859. With an introduction by rev. Baron Stow, d. d. 464 pp. 12°. *Boston, Gould & Lincoln*, 1860.

Gibson (William Sidney). An essay on the filial duties; in which their divine obligation is established from holy scripture, and their importance to social happiness and public welfare is enforced; with anecdotes and illustrations from ancient and modern history. iv, 104 pp. 8°. *London, W. Pickering*, 1848.

Giddings (Daniel). *See* **Gittins** *or* **Giddings.**

Giebel (Christoph Gottfried Andreas). Die nützlichen vögel unserer aecker, wiesen, gärten und wälder. Nothwendigkeit ihrer pflege and schonung, widerlegung der bisherigen vorurtheile gegen dieselben, und ihre hohe bedeutung für die vertilgung schädlicher thiere. 2r abdruck. 2 p. l. 162 pp. 12°. *Berlin, Wiegandt & Hempel*, 1868. s.

Gifford (William). The Baviad, and Mæviad. [Also], a poetical epistle to the author, by an american gentleman. [William Cliffton]. A new edition revised. xxi, 145 pp. 12°. *Philadelphia, W. Cobbett*, 1799.

Giglio (Gieronimo). Costumi et l'vzanze dell' Indie Occidentali, ouero Mondo Nuouo. 18°. *Venetia, G. Bonadio*, 1564.

[*With* Böhme (Johann). I costvmi [etc.] di tutte le genti, 1564. l. 193–240].

Giglioli (Enrico Hillyer). I Tasmaniani, cenni storici ed etnologici di un popolo estinto. (Estratto dall' archivio di antropologia e di etnologia). 118 pp. 3pl. 8°. *Firenze, G. Pellas*, 1871. s.

Gihon (Albert Leary, *m. d.*) Practical suggestions in naval hygiene. 151 pp. 12°. *Washington, government printing office*, 1871.

Gilbert (Davies). The parochial history of Cornwall, founded on the manuscript histories of mr. Hals and mr. Tonkin; with additions and various appendices, by Davies Gilbert. 4 v. 8°. *London, J. B. Nichols & son*, 1838.

Gilbert (D. *d. d.*) The love of Jesus; or, visits to the blessed sacrament, for every day in the month: to which is added the devotion of the forty hours. 1st am. from last London ed. 336 pp. 24°. *Baltimore, John Murphy & co.* 1871.

Gilbert (Grove Karl). Report on the geology of Williams, Fulton and Lucas counties, [Ohio]. 8°. [*Columbus*, 1871].

[Ohio (*State of*). Geological survey, 1870. Part 7, pp. 485–499].

Gilbert (*Rev.* Jesse S.) The mystery of iniquity; or, romanism not christianity. 244 pp. 16°. *Newark (N. J.) Ward & Tichenor*, 1872.

Gilbert (John T.) A history of the city of Dublin. 3 v. 8°. *Dublin, J. Duffy*, 1861.

Gilbert (Josiah) *and* **Churchill** (George Cheetham). Die dolomitberge. Ausflüge durch Tirol, Kärnten, Krain und Friaul, 1861–63. Mit einem geologischen abschnitte. Aus dem englischen von G. A. Zwanziger. Abtheil. i. xvi, 304 pp. 8°. *Klagenfurt, F. v. Kleinmayr*, 1865. s.

[Abtheil. 2–3 wanting].

Gilbert (Walter B.) The church chorister; being a manual for training singing boys. 108 pp. 16°. *New York, E. P. Dutton & co.* 1872.

Gilby *or* **Gilbie** (Anthony). An ansvver to the deuillish detection of Stephane Gardiner, bishoppe of Wynchester, published to the intent that such as be desirous of the truth should not be seduced by hys errours, nor the blind & obstinate excused by ignorance. *b. l.* 216 l. 16°. [*London, Grafton*], 1547.

Gilchrist (John). The oriental fabulist or polyglot translations of Esop's and other ancient fables from the english language, into hindoostanee, persian, arabic, brij bhakha, bongla, and sunkrit, in the roman character, by various hands, under the direction of J. Gilchrist. 1 p. l. xlvii, 316 pp. 8°. *Calcutta, Hurkaru office*, 1803.

Gilder (William H.) The sabbath scholar's offering: a present for the holidays. 108 pp. 18°. *Philadelphia, I. Rogers*, 1841.

Gildersleeve (Basil L. *ll. d.*) A latin exercise-book; with references to Gildersleeve's latin grammar. 164 pp. 12°. *New York, University publishing co.* 1871.

Giles (*Rev.* Charles). Pioneer: a narrative of the nativity, experience, travels, and ministerial labors of rev. C. Giles. With incidents, observations, and reflections. 333 pp. 1 portrait. 12°. *New York, G. Lane & P. P. Sandford*, 1844.

——— The triumph of truth; or, the vindication of divine providence. A poem; in which philosophy, theology, & description are combined. In fourteen books. vii, 13–276 pp. 1 portrait. 18°. *New York, Harper & brothers*, 1838.

——— The same. 2d ed. 288 pp. 18°. *New York, G. Lane & P. P. Sandford*, 1843.

Gilfillan (George). The martyrs, heroes and bards of the scottish covenant. 2d ed. 251 pp. 16°. *London, A. Cockshaw*, 1853.

Gilfillan (Robert). Original songs. viii, 152 pp. 16°. *Edinburgh, J. Anderson, jun.* 1831.

Gill *or* **Gil** (Alexander). The sacred philosophie of the holy scriptvre, laid downe as conclusions in the articles of our faith, commonly called the apostles' creed. [Also, a treatise concerning the trinitie of persons in vnitie of the deitie. 2d ed.] Eng. title, 13 p. l. 196, 232 pp. fol. *London, A. Griffin for I. Norton & R. Whitaker*, 1635.

Gillespie (William). An exposure of the unchristian and unphilosophical principles set forth in mr. Combe's "Constitution of man;" being an antidote to the poison of that publication. 3d ed. 1 p. l. 132 pp. 8°. *Edinburgh, T. Clark*, 1837.

Gillespie (W. M. *ll. d.*) A treatise on levelling, topography and higher surveying. Edited by Cady Staley. xiv, 171 pp. 8°. *New York, D. Appleton & co.* 1870.

Gillet (Ransom H.) The federal government; its officers and their duties. 444 pp. 12°. *New York, Woolworth, Ainsworth & co.* 1871.

Gillette (*Rev.* E. H.) Life lessons in the school of christian duty. By the author of "The life and times of John Huss." [*anon.*] 407 pp. 12°. *New York, A. D. F. Randolph*, 1864.

Gillham (*Rev.* William B.) The æolian lyrist: a new collection of psalm and hymn tunes adapted to the various metres in general use; with a few anthems and set pieces. 248 pp. obl. 8°. *Cincinnati, Applegate & co.* 1853. s.

Gillies (*Rev.* Alexander). An introduction, shewing the practice of faulconry in certain remote times and countries. 8°. [*Edinburgh*, 1773].

[*In* CAMPBELL (James). A treatise of modern faulconry, pp. 29–118].

Gillmore (*Rev.* Hiram). Lectures on christianity: wherein its necessity, authenticity, and utility, are supported by evidences historical, philosophical, experimental, and miscellaneous. 308 pp. 12°. *Cleveland,* [*O.*] *F. B. Penniman*, 1837.

Gilly (William Stephen). A memoir of Felix Neff, pastor of the high Alps. 128 pp. 18°. *Boston, Mass. sabbath-school society*, 1833.

Gilman (Caroline). Love's progress. By the author of "The recollections of a New-England housekeeper," [etc. *anon.*] 171 pp. 12°. *New York, Harper & brothers*, 1840.

——— Recollections of a southern matron. 272 pp. 12°. *New-York, Harper & brothers*, 1838.

——— Tales and ballads. 190 pp. 12°. *Boston, W. Crosby & co.* 1839.

Gilmer (George R.) Sketches of some of the first settlers of upper Georgia, of the Cherokees, and the author. 587 pp. 1 portrait. 8°. *New York, D. Appleton & co.* 1855.

Gilmore (J. H.) Declamations and dialogues for the sunday-school. 251 pp. 18°. *Boston, H. A. Young & co.* [1871].

Gilmore (Patrick S.) History of the national peace jubilee and great musical festival, held in the city of Boston, June, 1869, to commemorate the restoration of peace throughout the land. x, 758 pp. 4 pl. 1 portrait. 8°. [*Cambridge*], *author*, 1871.

Gilmore (Quincy Adams). Practical treatise on limes, hydraulic cements and mortars, containing reports of numerous experiments conducted in New York city, during the years 1858 to 1861 inclusive. 333 pp. 8°. *New York*, *D. Van Nostrand*, 1863.

[UNITED STATES. *Engineer department*. Papers on practical engineering, no. 9].

—— The same. 4th ed. 334 pp. 1 pl. 8°. *New York*, *D. Van Nostrand*, 1872.

Gilpin (*Rev.* Joshua). An account of the rev. John Fletcher. 16°. [*New-York*, *E. Cooper & J. Wilson*, 1805].

[*In* WESLEY (*Rev.* John). A short account of the life and death of the rev. John Fletcher. 1805. pp. 147-276].

lpin (*Rev.* William). A practical illustration of Gilpin's day, representing the various effects on landscape scenery from morning till night, in thirty designs from nature. With instructions in, and explanation of, the improved method of colouring, and painting in water colours, by John Heaviside Clark. 2 p. l. vi, 17 l. 30 pl. fol. *London*, *Priestley and Weale*, 1824.

Gilroy (Clinton G.) The art of weaving, by hand and by power, with an introductory account of its rise and progress in ancient and modern times. 4 p. l. 574 pp. 35 pl. 8°. *New York*, *G. D. Baldwin*, 1844.

Ginsburg (Charles D. *ll. d.*) The moabite stone; a fac-simile of the original inscription, with an english translation, and a historical and critical commentary. 2d ed. revised and enlarged. 1 p. l. 57 pp. 3 pl. 1 map. 4°. *London*, *Reeves & Turner*, 1871.

Ginx's baby. *See* **Jenkins** (Edward).

Giovio (Paolo). Compendio dell' historie di Paolo Giovio [1494-1544], fatto per m. Vincentio Cartari da Reggio, [etc.] 14 p. l. 422 pp. 1 l. 16°. *Vinegia*, *G. Giolito de Ferrari*, 1562.

—— The same. P. Jovii Warhafftige beschreibunge aller chronickwirdiger namhafftiger historien vnd geschichten, so sich bey menschen gedächtnuss von 1494 biss 1547, hin vñ wider in der gantzen welt, zugetragen vnd verlauffen. In lateinischer sprach gantz ordenlich, gründtlich vnd vollkōmlich beschrieben. Zum theil durch Georgium

Giovio (Paolo)—continued.

Forberger vnd Hieronymū Haluerium in die hohe teutsche sprach verdolmetscht. 2 v. in 1. 2 p. l. 427, lxxx pp. 10 l; 514 pp. 7 l. fol. *Franckfurt am Mayn*, *G. Raben in verlegung P. Perne*, 1570.

[Imperfect].

Giraffi (Alessandro). An exact historie of the late revolutions in Naples; and of their monstrous successes. Published in italian; and rendred to english, by J[ames] H[owell]. 3 p. l. 146 pp. 18°. *London*, *J. G. for J. Williams*, 1650.

Giraldi (Giglio Gregorio). Philosophi Pythagoræ symbolorum interpretatio. 18°. *Londini*, 1673.

[*In* HIEROCLES. De providentia & fato, 1673, pp. 85-171].

Giraldo (Mathias de, *pseudon.*) Histoire curieuse et pittoresque des sorciers, devins, magiciens, astrologues, voyants, revenants, âmes en peine, vampires, spectres, fantômes, apparitions, visions, gnomes, lutins, esprits malins, sorts jetés, exorcismes, etc. depuis l'antiquité jusqu'à nos jours. Revue et augmentée par m. Fornari. 2 p. l. 256, 56 pp. 5 pl. 8°. *Paris*, *B. Renault*, 1846.

Girard (Guillaume). The history of the life of [Jean Louis de la Vallette] the duke of Espernon, the great favourite of France. Englished by Charles Cotton. Wherein the history of France is continued from the year 1598, where d'Avila leaves off, down to our own times, 1642. [*anon.*] 10 p. l. 651 pp. 2 portraits. fol. *London*, *E. Cotes*, *& A. Clark*, *for H. Brome*, 1670.

Girard (S. François). Socialisme. Trois leçons du professeur E. Cherbuliez sur Fourier, son école et son système, reproduites et réfutés par un ministre du saint évangile. xii, 490 pp. 8°. *Paris*, *à la librairie de l'école sociétaire*, 1844.

Giraud (L. J. D. Féraud-). *See* **Féraud-Giraud**.

Giraudeau (Bonaventure). Histoires et paraboles pensées et maximes de l'évangile médité. Mises en léçons par E. A. Giraudeau. Précédées d'une notice inédite sur la vie et les écrits du p. Bonav. Giraudeau. 2 p. l. 352 pp. 8°. *Paris*, *l'éditeur*, 1845.

Girault (A. Napoléon). Vie de George Washington. Traduit de l'anglais. 321 pp. 6 pl. 18°. *Philadelphia*, *American sunday-school union*, [1834].

—— The same. 4e éd. 321 pp. 18°. *Philadelphia*, *H. Perkins*, 1836.

Girolami (Flavio). Nvova minera d'oro. Nella quale si dimostra, l'arte chimica esser verissima, e con la piera filosofica potersi far l'oro. Con le risposte à quelli c'hanno scritto contra tal' arte, & alle obiettioni, che si possono far' all' auttore. 4 p. l. 172 pp. 6 l. 4°. *Venetia, appresso B. Barezzi*, 1590.

[*With* QUATTRAMI (Evangelista). La vera dichiaratione di tvtte le metafore, similitudini, & enimmi de gl'antichi filosofi alchimisti, 1587].

Gittins *or* **Giddings** (Daniel). Remarks on the tenets and principles of the quakers, as contained in the Theses theologicæ of Robert Barclay. [*anon.*] lii, 348 pp. 8°. *London, J. Bettenham by E. Withers*, 1758.

Giusti (Giuseppe, *editor*). Raccolta di proverbi toscani, con illustrazioni. Ora ampliata ed ordinata. 2 p. l. xii, 423 pp. 12°. *Firenze, F. le Monnier*, 1853.

Giustiniani (Lorenzo). De perfectionis gradibus, *or* De gradibvs: qvibvs ad perfectionem anima provehitvr. 38 l. fol. [*n. p. n. d.*]

[*Note.*—41 lines to a page. This work was probably printed at Venice between 1475 and 1490. It is not mentioned in any of the standard authorities. The text begins, "Diui Laurentii Iustiniani Venetia℞ prothopatriarchæ opus"].

Gladwin (Francis). A dictionary persian, hindoostanee and english: including synonyma. 2 v. 4 p. l. 608 pp; 1 p. l. 609-1066, vi pp. 8°. *Calcutta, T. Hubbard*, 1809.

Glanius (—). Relation du naufrage d'un vaisseau hollandois, nommé Ter Schelling, vers la côte de Bengala. [*anon.*] Eng. title, 2 p. l. 80 pp. 4°. *Amstredam, veuve de J. van Meurs*, 1681.

[*With* STRUYS (Jan Janszen). Voyages en Moscovie, etc. 1681].

Glanvill (Joseph). Lux orientalis, or an inquiry into the opinion of the eastern sages, concerning the præexistence of souls: being a key to unlock the grand mysteries of providence, in relation to man's sin and misery. [*anon.*] 19 p. l. 192 pp. 18°. *London*, 1662.

——— Plus ultra: or, the progress and advancement of knowledge since the days of Aristotle. In an account of some of the most remarkable late improvements of practical, useful learning: to encourage philosophical endeavours. 17 p. l. 150 pp. 2 l. 16°. *London, J. Collins*, 1668.

——— The vanity of dogmatizing: or confidence in opinions. Manifested in a discourse of the shortness and uncertainty of our knowledge, and its causes; with some reflexions on peripateticism; and an apology for philosophy. 16 p. l. 250 pp. 3 l. 18°. *London, E. C. for H. Eversden*, 1661.

Glareanus (Henricus Loritus). *See* **Loritz** (Heinrich).

Glaser (Adolf). Niederländische novellen, den originalen nacherzählt. 3 p. l. 235 pp. 16°. *Braunschweig, F. Vieweg & sohn*, 1866. s.

CONTENTS.

CREMER (J. J.) Ein tag in der residenz.
——— Der vetter vom lande.
HILDEBRAND. Die familie Stastock.
——— Die familie Kegge.

Glasgow (The) & Greenock commercial list, 1871-72, third and fourth years. By Estell & co. fol. *London*, [*Seyd & co.*] 1871.

Glauber (Johann Rudolph). Explicatio tractatuli, qui Miraculum mundi inscribitur, tam plana quam solida. 71 pp. 16°. *Amstelodami, apud J. Janssonium*, 1656.

[*With his* Miraculum mundi, 1658].

——— Miraculum mundi, sive plena perfectaque descriptio admirabilis naturæ, ac proprietatis potentissimi subiecti, ab antiquis menstruum universale sive mercurius philosophorum dicti: quo vegetabilia, animalia & mineralia facillime in saluberrima medicamenta, & imperfecta metalla in permanentia ac perfecta transmutari possunt. Ex germanico latinum factum. 64 pp. 16°. *Amsterodami, apud J. Janssonium*, 1658.

——— The same. Miraculi mundi pars altera in qua adventus jam dudum prædicti Eliæ artistæ magnificus describitur, adeoque ipsum sal artis mirificum, philosophorum esse, vegetabilium, animalium, mineraliumve, medicinam præstantissimam demonstratur. 101 pp. 16°. *Amsteldami, apud J. Janssonium*, 1660.

[*With his* Miraculum mundi, 1658].

——— The same. Miraculi mundi continuatio, in qua tota natura denudatur, & toti mundo nude ob oculos ponitur; immo dilucide & aperte demonstratur, fieri posse, ut ex sale petræ omnium vegetabilium, animalium & mineralium summa medicina paretur [etc.] 133 pp. 16°. *Amstelodami, apud J. Janssonium*, 1658.

[*With his* Miraculum mundi, 1658].

Glennie (*Rev.* Alexander). Sermons preached on plantations to congregations of negroes. viii, 161 pp. 18°. *Charleston*, [*S. C.*] *A. K. Miller*, 1844.

Glossary (A) of provincial words used in Herefordshire and some of the adjoining counties. [*anon.*] xii, 132 pp. 12°. *London, J. Murray*, 1839.

Glossbrenner (Adam J.) History of York county, (Pa.) *See* **Carter** (W. C.) *and* **Glossbrenner**.

Goad (John). Astro-meteorologica, or aphorisms and discourses of the bodies cœlestial, their natures and influences. 4 p. l. 509 pp. fol. *London, J. Rawlings for O. Blagrave*, 1686.

Gobineau (Arthur, *comte* de). The rose of Typhaines; a tale of the commune in the twelfth century. Translated by Charles D. Meigs, m. d. 438 pp. 12°. *Philadelphia, Claxton, Remsen & Haffelfinger*, 1872.

[*Note.*—The same work was published in 1869 under the title of Typhaine's abbey].

Goch (— von). Die heutige historie oder der gegenwärtige staat von Indostan und Ceilon. *See* **Salmon** (Thomas).

Goddard (Paul B. *m. d.*) Plates of the arteries, with references; for the use of medical students. 49 pp. incl. 12 pl. 4°. *Philadelphia, J. G. Auner*, 1839.

Goddard (William). The partnership: or, the history of the rise and progress of the Pennsylvania chronicle. 2 nos. in 1 v. 72 pp. 8°. *Philadelphia, W. Goddard*, 1770.

[HAZARD pamplets, v. 27].

Godefroy (Théodore *and* D.) Histoire de Charles viii. roy de France, par Guillaume de Jaligny, André de la Vigne, & autres historiens de ce temps-là. Où sont décrites les choses les plus mémorables arrivées pendant ce règne, depuis 1483. jusques en 1498. Enrichie de plusieurs mémoires, observations, contracts de mariage, traitéz de paix, & autres titres & pièces historiques non encore imprimées. Le tout recueilli par feu monsieur Godefroy. 8 p. l. 759 pp. fol. *Paris, de l'imprimerie royale, par S. Mabre-Cramoisy*, 1684.

CONTENTS.

BOUCHET (J.). Histoire de Lovys, seignevr de Trimoville, dit le cheualier sans reproche, pp. 207-215.

CHAMPIER (J.) Extrait d'vne histoire (abrégée) des royes de France, intitvlée Francorvm regvm genealogia, [et] d'vne autre histoire, où est le traité de paix du roy Charles viii. auec le pape Alexandre vi. pp. 284-290.

CATTANEO (A.) Extrait d'vne histoire abregée,—sur le sujet des Vaudois, pp. 277-283.

DESREY (P.) Relation dv voyage dv roy Charles viii. povr la conqveste dv royavme de Naples, pp. 190-206.

EXTRAIT de l'histoire de Lovys, dvc d'Orléans pour ce qui regarde celle du roy Charles viii. pp. 253-277.

EXTRAITS de différens ouvrages, qui ont rapport au roi Charles viii. & à son règne, par plusieurs auteurs, pp. 290-304.

FIORI (G.) De expeditione Caroli viii. in neapolitanum regnum libri duo, pp. 216-237.

JALIGNY (G. de). Histoire de plvsievrs choses mémorables aduenuës du règne de Charles viii. és années 1486, '87, '88, & '89, pp. 3-90.

LA VIGNE (A. de). Extrait de l'histoire dv voyage de Naples dv roy Charles viii. en forme de iovrnal (1494-1495), pp. 114-189.

LEGATIO gallicana de expeditione italica regis Francorum Caroli viii. ad pontificem romanvm [etc.] pp. 238-253.

Godefroy (T. *and* D.)—continued.

SAINT-GÉLAIS (J.) Extrait d'vne histoire de France, qui commence l'an 1270. & finit l'an 1510. pp. 91-113.

TRAITEZ de paix, négotiations, contracts de mariages, testamens, lettres historiques, & autres actes: servant de preuves à l'histoire du roy Charles viii. pp. 305-759.

Godman (John D. *m. d.*) American natural history. Part 1. Mastology. 2 v. 362 pp. 16 pl; 331 pp. 16 pl. 8°. *Philadelphia, H. C. Carey & I. Lea*, 1826.

——— The same. 2d ed. v. 1. 362 pp. 17 pl. 8°. *Philadelphia, Key & Mickle*, 1831. s.

Godsmark (Samuel). Poems. An experimental treatise on the facts and theories of life. 1st ed. 104 pp. 12°. *New York, Russell brothers*, 1871.

Godwin (*Rev.* B.) Lectures on the atheistic controversy; delivered in 1834, at Sion chapel, Bradford, Yorkshire, forming the first part of a course of lectures on infidelity. xvi, 280 pp. 8°. *London, Jackson & Walford*, 1834.

Goes (Damiaõ de). De bello cambaico secvndo commentarii tres. 16°. *Coloniae Agrippinae, ex officina birckmannica*, 1602.

[*In* MYLIUS (Arnold). De rebvs hispanicis, pp. 311-376].

——— Deploratio lappianae gentis. 16°. *Coloniae Agrippinae, ex officina birckmannica*, 1602.

[*In* MYLIUS (Arnold). De rebvs hispanicis, pp. 247-254].

——— Diensis nobilissimae Carmaniae sev Cambaiae vrbis oppvgnatio. 16°. *Coloniae Agrippinae, ex officina birckmannica*, 1602.

[*In* MYLIUS (Arnold). De rebvs hispanicis, pp. 270-310].

——— Fides, religio, moresqve Aethiopvm. 16°. *Coloniae Agrippinae, ex officina birckmannica*, 1602.

[*In* MYLIUS (Arnold). De rebvs hispanicis, pp. 154-246].

——— Hispania. 30 l. sm. 4°. *Lovanii, R. Rescius*, 1542.

——— The same. 16°. *Coloniae Agrippinae, ex officina birckmannica*, 1602.

[*In* MYLIUS (Arnold). De rebvs hispanicis, pp. 1-48].

——— Orbis Olisiponis descriptio. 16°. *Coloniae Agrippinae, ex officina birckmannica*, 1602.

[*In* MYLIUS (Arnold). De rebvs hispanicis, pp. 53-94].

Goes (Willem van der). Wilelmi Goesii vindiciæ, pro recepta de mutui alienatione sententia. Accedit specimen ejusdem controversiæ. 6 p. l. 241 pp. 16°. *Lugduni Batavorum, ex officina A. Wyngaerden*, 1646.

Goethe (Johann Wolfgang von). Faust. A tragedy. Translated by Lewis Filmore. vi, 64 pp. 8°. [*London, C. Griffin & co.* 1866]?

——— The same. Faust, a dramatic poem. Translated by John Wynniatt Grant. 162 pp. 8°. *London, Hamilton, Adams & co.* 1867.

[*Note.*—With corrections in the handwriting of the translator].

——— The same. Faust, a tragedy. The second part. Translated, in the original metres, by Bayard Taylor. xvi, 536 pp. 8°. *Boston, J. R. Osgood & co.* 1871.

——— Goethe's elective affinities: with an introduction by Victoria C. Woodhull. vii, 325 pp. 12°. *Boston, D. W. Niles*, 1872.

——— Goetz von Berlichingen with the iron hand. A drama in five acts. From the german of Goethe. [*anon.*] xxxvi, 9-185 pp. 12°. *Philadelphia, Carey, Lea & Blanchard*, 1837.

——— Iphigenie auf Tauris. 12°. *New York, D. Appleton & co.* 1854.

[*In* ADLER (G. J.) Handbook of german literature, pp. 241-317].

——— Life of Goethe. From his autobiographical papers and the contributions of his contemporaries. By Henry C. Browning. 2 v. in 1. 142 pp; 143 pp. 16°. *New York, J. Mowatt & co.* 1844.

——— Stella; translated from the german of m. Goethe. 1 p. l. 4, 113 pp. 8°. *London, Hookham & Carpenter*, 1798.

——— Torquato Tasso. Ein schauspiel. 2 p. l. 149 pp. 1 pl. 18°. *Stuttgart & Tübingen, J. G. Cotta*, 1854.

——— Werther, opera di sentimento. Nuova traduzione coll' aggiunta di un' apologia in favore dell' opera medesima. 2 v. 107 pp; 1 p. l. 122 pp. 18°. *Livorno, P. Meucci*, 1808.

——— Wilhelm Meister's apprenticeship and travels. Translated from the german by Thomas Carlyle. 2 v. xvi, 351 pp; 4 p. l. 344 pp. 8°. *London, Chapman & Hall*, 1871.

[*In* CARLYLE (Thomas). Translations from the german, v. 1-2].

Goiran (Agostino). Sopra gli aeroliti caduti il giorno 29 febbraio 1868, etc. *See* **Denza** (Francesco).

Gold (*Capt.* Charles). Oriental drawings: sketched between the years 1791 and 1798. 97 l. 48 col. pl. 4°. *London, G. and W. Nicoll*, 1806.

Golden (The) age. Theodore Tilton, editor. [Weekly]. March 4 to Dec. 30, 1871. v. i. fol. *New York, T. Tilton*, 1871.

Golden thorns. *See* **Warner** (Susan). Stories of Vinegar hill, v. 3.

Gold-headed (The) cane. *See* **Macmichael** (William).

Goldsmith (Christabel, *pseudon.*) *See* **Smith** (Julie P.)

Goldsmith (Oliver). Essays. [1st ed.] 1 p. l. vii, 236 pp. 16°. *London, W. Griffin*, 1765.

——— The same. 2d ed. 1 p. l. vi, 248 pp. 16°. *London, W. Griffin*, 1766.

——— The same. [5th ed?] 1 p. l. vi, 248 pp. 16°. *London, I. & F. Rivington, etc.* 1775.

——— Poems, plays and essays. With a critical dissertation on his poetry, by John Aikin, m. d. and an introductory essay, by Henry T. Tuckerman. xxvii, 530 pp. 1 portrait. 12°. *Boston, Phillips, Sampson & co.* 1854.

——— The traveller, the deserted village, and other poems. 1 p. l. 154 pp. 6 pl. 16°. *London, J. Sharpe*, 1826.

——— El vicario de Wakefield. Traducida al castellano por M. Dominguez. 312, x pp. 16°. *Nueva-York, C. S. Van Winkle*, 1825.

Gölis (Leopold Anthony). A treatise on the hydrocephalus acutus, or inflammatory water in the head. Translated from the german, by Robert Gooch, m. d. x, 279 pp. 8°. *London, Longman, Orme & Brown*, 1821.

[*With* HALL (Marshall). Descriptive essay on disorders of the digestive organs].

Goltz (Hubert). Fastos magistratvvm et trivmphorvm romanorvm ab vrbe condita ad Avgvsti obitvm ex antiqvis tam nvmismatvm qvam marmorvm monvmentis restitvtos. 12 p. l. 288 pp. 22 l. fol. *Brvgis Flandrorvm*, 1566.

Gomara (Francisco Lopez de). La historia general de las Indias, con todos los descubrimientos, y cosas notables que han acaescido enellas, dende que se ganaron hasta agora. Añadiose de nueuo la descripcion y traça de las Indias, con vna tabla alphabetica de las prouincias [etc.] 16 p. l. 287 l. 16°. *Anvers, Iuan Steelsio*, 1554.

[Parte primera].

——— The same. Histoire générale des Indes Occidentales, et terres neuues, qui iusques à present ont esté descouuertes. 5ᵉ éd. Augmentée de la descripcion de la Nouuelle Espagne [etc.] 4 p. l. 485 l. 18 l. 16°. *Paris, Michel Sonnius*, 1605.

[*Note.*—Part two of the work, but greatly abbreviated].

Good (John Mason). Good's book of nature. Abridged from the original work. 224 pp. sq. 16°. *Boston, Allen & Ticknor*, 1834.

Good cheer. Edited by Norman Macleod. The christmas no. of Good words. Christmas, 1871. 48 pp. 1 pl. 8°. *London, Strahan & co.* [1871].

[*With* Good words for 1871].

Good health: a popular annual of the laws of correct living, as developed by medical science, etc. [Monthly]. June, 1869, to May, 1872. v. 1-3. 8°. *Boston, A. Moore*, 1870-72.

Good words. [A monthly religious magazine]. Edited by Norman Macleod, d. d. Jan. to Dec. 1871. [v. 12]. 8°. *London, Strahan & co.* [1871].

Goodall (Walter). An examination of the letters, said to be written by Mary, queen of Scots, to James, earl of Bothwell: shewing by intrinsick and extrinsick evidence, that they are forgeries. Also, an inquiry into the murder of king Henry. 2 v. 2 p. l. xxix, 418 pp; 1 p. l. 392 pp. 12°. *Edinburgh, T. & W. Ruddimans*, 1754.

——— An introduction to the history and antiquities of Scotland. Written originally in latin. 2 p. l. 122 pp. 18°. *Edinburgh, C. Herriott*, 1773.

Goode (*Rev.* William H.) Outposts of Zion, with limnings of mission life. 464 pp. 1 portrait. 12°. *Cincinnati, Poe & Hitchcock*, 1863.

Goodfellow (Gabriel, *pseudon.*) The book of liberals: a book for liberals and anti-liberals; being a looking-glass for the former, and an eye-glass (or spy-glass) for the latter. xvi, 271 pp. 16°. *London, author*, 1849.

Goodhue (*Rev.* J. A.) The crucible; or, tests of a regenerate state. With an introduction by rev. Edward N. Kirk, d. d. 2 p. l. 352 pp. 12°. *Boston, Gould & Lincoln*, 1860.

Goodrich (Charles Augustus). A history of the church, from the birth of Christ to the present time. To which is added an account of the religious rites and ceremonies of all nations. Also, a view of the most efficient missionary societies. 504 pp. 1 map, 1 chart. 8°. *New York, A. K. White & co.* 1834.

——— A history of the United States of America, on a plan adapted to the capacity of youths. New stereotype ed. 352 pp. 16° *Boston, Carter, Hendee & co.* 1834.

——— The influence of mothers on the character, welfare, and destiny of individuals,

Goodrich (Charles Augustus)—continued. families and communities, illustrated in a series of anecdotes: with a preliminary essay on the same subject. 193 pp. 18°. *Boston, Crocker & Brewster*, 1835.

——— Lectures to children, on the last hours of our Lord Jesus Christ. 186 pp. 16°. *Hartford, D. Burgess & co.* 1835.

Goodrich (Chauncey A.) Travels and sketches in North and South America; embracing an account of their situation, origin, plan, extent, their inhabitants, manners, customs, and amusements, and public works, institutions, edifices, &c. together with sketches of historical events. Illustrated with engravings. 704 pp. 2 pl. 8°. *Hartford, Case, Tiffany & co.* 1852.

Goodrich (Jeremiah). The new testament. *Albany*, 1825. *See* **Bible.** (*English*).

Goodrich (Samuel Griswold). A book of quadrupeds, for youth. [*anon.*] 324 pp. 16°. *New York, P. Hill*, 1832.

——— Fireside education. By the author of Peter Parley's tales. [*pseudon.*] 1 p. l. 396 pp. 1 pl. 12°. *New York, F. J. Huntington*, 1838.

——— The first book of history. By the author of Peter Parley's tales. [*pseudon.*] 180 pp. 16 maps. sq. 12°. *Cincinnati, C. D. Bradford & co.* 1831.

——— The same. Revised ed. 183 pp. 16 maps. sq. 12°. *Boston, C. J. Hendee*, 1837.

——— A history of all nations, from the earliest periods to the present time; or, universal history: in which the history of every nation, ancient and modern, is separately given. 2 v. 600 pp; x, 601-1207 pp. 8°. *Boston, Wilkins, Carter & co.* 1849-51.

——— Parley's panorama; or curiosities of nature and art, history and biography. A new ed. 608 pp. 2 pl. 8°. *Hartford, House & Brown*, 1857.

——— Peter Parley's book of anecdotes. [*anon.*] 144 pp. sq. 16°. *Boston, Russell, Shattuck & co.* 1836.

——— Peter Parley's common school history. 407 pp. 12°. *Boston, American stationers' company*, 1838.

——— Peter Parley's method of teaching arithmetic to children. [*pseudon.*] 144 pp. sq. 16°. *Boston, Carter & Hendee*, 1833.

——— Peter Parley's method of telling about geography to children. 122 pp. 1 pl. 6 maps. sq. 16°. *Hartford, H. & F. J. Huntington*, 1829.

Goodrich (Samuel Griswold)—continued.

——— Peter Parley's tales about Great Britain: including England, Wales, Scotland, and Ireland. [*pseudon.*] 160 pp. 1 map. sq. 16°. *Baltimore, J. Jewett*, 1832.

——— Peter Parley's tales about South America. [*pseudon.*] 166 pp. 1 map. sq. 16°. *Baltimore, J. Jewett*, 1832.

——— Peter Parley's tales of animals, containing descriptions of three hundred quadrupeds, birds, fishes, reptiles and insects. Revised edition, with questions, and other improvements. [*pseudon.*] 360 pp. 12°. *Louisville, Morton & Smith*, 1836.

——— A pictorial history of ancient Rome. With sketches of the history of modern Italy. 333 pp. 1 pl. 3 maps. 12°. *Philadelphia, E. H. Butler & co.* 1855.

——— The same. 336 pp. 12°. *Philadelphia, E. H. Butler & co.* 1871.

——— A pictorial history of England. 448 pp. 12°. *Philadelphia, E. H. Butler & co.* 1871.

——— A pictorial natural history: embracing a view of the mineral, vegetable, and animal kingdoms. 415 pp. 12°. *Boston, J. Munroe & co.* 1842.

——— Sketches from a student's window. 311 pp. 12°. *Boston, W. D. Ticknor*, 1841.

——— Sow well and reap well; or, fireside education. 3d ed. 343 pp. 12°. *Albany, E. H. Pease*, 1846.

——— A system of universal geography, popular and scientific, comprising a physical, political, and statistical account of the world and its various divisions, [etc.] 920 pp. 1 l. 8°. *Cincinnati, Roffe & Young*, 1832.

——— The travels, voyages, and adventures of Gilbert Go-ahead, in foreign parts. [Asia]. Edited by Peter Parley. [*pseudon.*] 1 p. l. 295 pp. 6 pl. 12°. *New York, J. C. Derby*, 1856.

——— The young American: or book of government and law; showing their history, nature and necessity. 2 p. l. 282 pp. 16°. *New York, W. Robinson*, 1842.

Goodsell (J. H. *and* C. M.) The Chicago fire and the fire insurance companies. An exhibit of the capital, assets, and losses of the companies, together with a graphic account of the great disaster. [*anon.*] 78 pp. 1 map. 8°. *New York & Chicago, J. H. & C. M. Goodsell*, 1871.

——— ——— The fire insurance register and index to the resources, condition, and standing of the principal american fire insurance companies. For 1872. 1 sheet. 16°. *New York, J. H. & C. M. Goodsell*, 1872.

——— ——— Life insurance in the United States. The business and standing of sixty-four life insurance companies as shown by official tables from the report of the Massachusetts life insurance commissioner. 11 pp. 12°. *New York & Chicago, J. H. & C. M. Goodsell*, 1871.

Goodspeed (*Rev.* E. J. *d. d.*) History of the great fires in Chicago and the west. With a history of the rise and progress of Chicago, the "young giant." To which is appended a record of the great fires in the past. 667 pp. 1 pl. 1 map. 8°. *New York, H. S. Goodspeed & co.* [1871].

Goodwin (Edward C.) Wayside songs 185 pp. 12°. *New York, Mason brothers*, 1856.

Goodwin (E. J. *m. d.*) The family medical guide. 102 pp. 12°. *Louisville (Ky.) J. C. Webb & co.* 1871.

Goodwin (George). Babels balm; or the honey-combe of Romes religion. With a neate straining-out of the rammish honey thereof. Sung in latine. And translated into english, by Iohn Vicars. 7 p. l. 111 pp. 2 l. sm. 4°. *London, N. Browne*, 1624.

[*Note.*—The title of the latin original is "Melissa religionis pontificiæ ejusdemque apostropo, x elegiis"].

Goodwin (Thomas). Christ set forth in his death, resurrection, ascension, sitting at God's right hand, intercession, as the cause of iustification. Object of justifying faith. Together with a treatise discovering the affectionate tendernesse of Christ's heart now in heaven, unto sinners on earth. 18 p. l. 288 pp; 6 p. l. 201 pp. 18°. *London, C. Greene*, 1642.

——— A discourse of the punishment of sin in hell; demonstrating the wrath of God to be the immediate cause thereof. [Also], a sermon, proving a state of glory for the spirits of just men upon dissolution. 5 p. l. 337 pp. 16°. *London, J. Robinson*, 1680.

Goodwin (William W.) An elementary greek grammar. 2d ed. xx, 1 l. 242 pp. 12°. *Boston, Ginn brothers*, 1871.

Googe (Barnaby). A newyeares gift. *See* **Garter** (Bernard).

——— The whole art and trade of hvsbandry. *See* **Heresbach** (Conrad).

Gordon (A. J.) Service of song for baptist churches. 1871. *See* **Caldwell** (S. L.) *and* **Gordon.**

Gordon (*Miss* Helen). Questions on the life of our saviour, for the use of sunday-schools in the protestant episcopal church. Infant series. viii, 86 pp. 18°. *New York, E. P. Dutton & co.* 1872.

Gordon (John). Poems. viii, 114 pp. 16°. *Edinburgh, J. Ballantyne & co.* 1807.

Gordon (William R. *d. d.*) Particular providence, in distinction from general, necessary to the fulfillment of the purposes and promises of God; illustrated by a course of lectures on the history of Joseph. 492 pp. 10 pl. 12°. *New York, R. & R. Brinkerhoff,* 1855.

——— A three-fold test of modern spiritualism. 408 pp. 12°. *New York, C. Scribner,* 1856.

Gore (*Mrs.* Catherine Grace). Peers and parvenus. A novel. 3 v. 12°. *London, H. Colburn,* 1846.

Gorham (B. W.) Choral echoes from the church of God in all ages. 296 pp. 22 l. 18°. *Boston, H. V. Degen,* 1864.

Gorostiza (Manuel Eduardo de). Contigo pan y cebolla. Comedia original en cuatro actos. 16°. *Brunsvico, E. Leibrock,* 1841.

[BIBLIOTECA portátil español. v. 1. pp. 345-448].

Gorrie (*Rev.* P. Douglass). The Black River conference memorial: containing sketches of the life and character of the deceased members of the Black River conference of the m. e. church. With portraits and an introduction. 351 pp. 10 portraits. 12°. *New York, Carlton & Phillips,* 1852.

Goslicki (Wawrżyniec Grimald). The accomplished senator. In two books. Written originally in latin, by L. G. Gozliski. Done into english from the ed. printed at Venice in 1568. By mr. Oldisworth. 7 p. l. xxxii, 330 pp. 3 l. 4°. *London, author, [translator],* 1733.

Gothaischer genealogischer hofkalender nebst diplomatisch-statistischem jahrbuch. 108-109 jahrgang. 1871-1872. 2 v. 24°. *Gotha, J. Perthes,* 1870-71. s.

——— The same. Almanach de Gotha. Annuaire généalogique, diplomatique et statistique. 108-109 année. 1871-1872. 2 v. 24°. *Gotha, J. Perthes,* 1870-72.

Göthe. *See* **Goethe.**

Gother (*Rev.* John). The spiritual works of the rev. John Gother. 16 v. 16°. *Newcastle, F. Coates,* [1790].

CONTENTS.

v. 1-2. Instructions on the epistles and gospels of the sundays.
v. 3. Instructions on the epistles and lessons, and gospels on sundays.
v. 4-5. Instructions on all the feasts.
v. 6-7. Afternoon-instructions for sundays, holydays, and other feasts.
v. 8. Instructions for the afflicted, sick, and prisoners: and masters, traders, labourers, servants, youth, and children.
v. 9. Instructions for particular states and conditions of life.
v. 10. Instructions and devotions for hearing mass; for confession, communion, and confirmation.
v. 11. Principles and rules of the gospel.
v. 12. A practical catechism, divided into fifty-two lessons for each sunday in the year: with an appendix.
v. 13 and 15. Prayers for sundays and festivals.
v. 14. Prayers for every day in lent, easter-week, and festivals in lent.
v. 16. The sinners complaints to God; being devout entertainments of the soul with God.

Gotthard (Johann Christian). Authentische beschreibung von dem merkwürdigen bau des tiefen Georg-Stollens am Oberharze. 7 p. l. 280 pp. 1 pl. 16°. *Wernigerode, C. S. Struck,* 1801.

Gouernayle (The) of helthe: with the medecyne of yͤ stomacke. Reprinted from Caxton's edition, (circa m.cccc.xci,) with introductory remarks and notes, by William Blades. 1 p. l. viii, 110 pp. 8°. *London, Blades, East & Blades,* 1858.

[*Note.*—55 copies only printed. The work has been attributed to John de Burdeux or Bourdeaux].

Gould (*Mrs.* Adeline E.) The evergreen chaplet. A christmas gift. 2 p. l. 146 pp. 13 pl. sq. 16°. *Boston, Hilliard, Gray & co.* 1841.

Gould (Augustus Addison). Otia conchologica: descriptions of shells and mollusks, from 1839 to 1862. 2 p. l. 256 pp. 8°. *Boston, Gould & Lincoln,* 1862. s.

CONTENTS.

Expedition shells described for the work of the United States exploring expedition, commanded by Charles Wilkes, [etc.] 1846.
Shells of the North Pacific exploring expedition, commanders Ringgold and Rodgers; mostly collected by William Stimpson. [1859-61].
Collectanea.—Descriptions of shells and mollusks. Reprinted from various scientific periodicals, with revisions.

Gould (Edward S.) John Doe and Richard Roe; or, episodes of life in New York. 312 pp. 12°. *New York, Carleton,* 1862.

Gould (Hannah Flagg). The golden vase; a gift for the young. 224 pp. 3 pl. 16°. *Boston, B. B. Mussey,* 1843.

——— Poems. viii, 174 pp. 1 pl. 16°. *Boston, Hilliard, Gray, Little & Wilkins,* 1832.

——— The youth's coronal. 200 pp. 12°. *New York, D. Appleton & co.* 1851.

Goulding (*Rev.* F. R.) The young maroon-ers, on the Florida coast; or Robert and Harold. New and enlarged ed. 446 pp. 11 pl. 16°. *Philadelphia, J. S. Claxton*, 1866.

Gouraud (Charles). Histoire de la politique commerciale de la France et de son influence sur le progrès de la richesse publique depuis le moyen âge jusqu'à nos jours. 2 v. 2 p. l. 388 pp; 2 p. l. 459 pp. 8°. *Paris, A. Durand*, 1854.

Gourgaud (Gaspard, *baron*). Napoleon and the grand army in Russia, or a critical examination of the work of count Ph. de Segur 2 p. l. xvi, 453, 54 pp. 8°. *London, M. Bossange & co.* 1825.

Gouriet (Jean Baptiste). Les charlatans célèbres, ou tableau historique des bateleurs, des baladins [etc.] et généralement de tous les personnages qui se sont rendus célèbres dans les rues et sur les places publiques de Paris, depuis une haute antiquité jusqu'à nos jours. [*anon.*] 2e éd. 2 v. in 1. 2 p. l. 336 pp. 1 pl; 1 p. l. 346 pp. 8°. *Paris, Lerouge*, 1819.

Gourlay (William, *m. d.*) Observations on the natural history, climate, and diseases of Madeira, during a period of eighteen years. viii, 158 pp. 8°. *London, J. Callow*, 1811.

Goury (Jules). Views on the Nile. *See* **Jones** (Owen) *and* **Goury.**

Goveo de Victoria (Pedro). Joannis Bisselii, Argonauticon americanorum, sive Historiæ periculorum Petri de Victoria, ac sociorum eius, libri. 11 p. l. 480 pp. 6 l. 1 pl. 1 map. 12°. *Monachii, formis L. Straubii, sumptibus I. VVagneri*, 1647.

Gozliski (Laurence Grimald). *See* **Goslicki** (Wawrżyniec Grimald).

Graauwhart (Hendrik). Leerzame zinnebeelden, bestaande in christelyke bedenkingen door vergelykinge eeniger schepselen, als dieren, vogels, gewassen, &c. Eng. title, 15 p. l. 218 pp. 3 l. 110 pl. in text. 16°. *Amsterdam, A. Cornelisse en J. Verheyde*, 1758.

Grace King; or, recollections of events in the life and death of a pious youth: with extracts from her diary. [*anon.*] 228 pp. 24°. *New York, T. Mason & G. Lane*, 1840.

Gracian (Baltasar). Réflexions politiques, sur les plus grands princes, et particulièrement sur Ferdinand le catholique. Ouvrage traduit de l'espagnol, avec des notes historiques & critiques [par de Silhouette]. 6 p. l. 350 pp. 11 l. 16°. *Paris, B. Alix*, 1730.

Grafton (Richard). [A chronicle at large and meere history of the affayres of Englande and kinges of the same. Deduced from the creation of the world vnto the first habitation of thys islande and so by continuance vnto the first yere of quuene Elizabeth. Collected out of sundry aucthors]. *b. l.* 1 v. in 2. 6 p. l. 192 pp. 4 l; 1369 pp. 15 l. fol. [*London, Henry Dunham for R. Tottyl and H. Toye*, 1569].

[Imperfect: v. 1. has title, 4 l. and pp. 1-2, 5-8 in *ms*; v. 2. wants title and 6 l. at end].

Graham (Andrew J.) Second standard phonographic reader. 184 pp. 12°. *New York, A. J. Graham*, [1861].

Graham (*Mrs.* Isabella). The power of faith, exemplified in the life and writings of the late mrs. Isabella Graham. A new ed. enriched by her narrative of her husband's death, and other select correspondence. [*anon.* Compiled by Joanna Bethune]? 440 pp. 12°. *New York, American tract society*, 1843.

——— The unpublished letters and correspondence of mrs. Isabella Graham, from 1767 to 1814. Selected and arranged by her daughter, mrs. Bethune. 314 pp. 12°. *New York, J. S. Taylor*, 1838.

Graham (*Rev.* John, *presbyterian minister in the U. S.*) Autobiography and reminiscences of rev. John Graham, late pastor of the associate, now the united presbyterian congregation of Bovina, Delaware co. N. Y. [With] sermons. vi, 206 pp. 12°. *Philadelphia, W. S. Rentoul*, 1870.

Graham (*Rev.* John, *rector in the diocess of Derry*). Poems, chiefly historical. x, 359 pp. 8°. *Belfast, Stuart & Gregg*, 1829.

Graham (Patrick, *d. d.*) Essay on the authenticity of the poems of Ossian; in which the objections of Malcolm Laing, are particularly considered and refuted. [With] an essay on the mythology of Ossian's poems, by prof. Richardson. 1 p. l. xxiv, 471 pp. 8°. *Edinburgh, J. Ballantyne & co. for P. Hill, A. Constable & co.* [*etc.*] 1807.

Grahame (James). British georgics. 2 p. l. viii, 342 pp. 4°. *Edinburgh, J. Ballantyne & co.* 1809.

Grahame (Nellie, *pseudon.*) *See* **Dunning** (*Mrs.* A. K.)

Grainger (James, *m. d.*) A poetical translation of Tibullus; and of Sulpicia. *See* **Tibullus** (Albius) *and* **Sulpicia.**

Grammar school hymn-book; for normal and grammar schools, and families. [*anon.*]

Grammar school hymn-book—continued. xxvii, 240 pp. 16°. *New York, Woolworth, Ainsworth & co.* [1871].

Grand (A) exposé of the science of gambling. Containing a complete disclosure of the secrets of the art, as practiced by professional gamblers. Written by an adept. [*anon.*] 194 pp. 18°. *New York, F. A. Brady*, [1860].

Grandeau (Louis). Notice sur la vie et les travaux de Pierre Gratiolet. 16°. [*Paris, J. Hetzel*, 1865].
[*With* GRATIOLET (P.) De la physionomie, pp. 389–438].

Grandes ombres sur le sentier de la vie. Par l'auteur de Doing and suffering, traduit de l'anglais par m[lle] Rilliet de Constant. [*anon.*] 2 p. l. 306 pp. 16°. *Neuchâtel, C. Leidecker*, 1864.

Grandmaison (Millin de). *See* **Millin** (Aubin Louis).

Grandpré (*Madame* Pauline de, *editor*). The prisoners of St. Lazare. By madame * * *. Translated from the french by mrs. E. M. McCarthy. 12°. *New York, D. Appleton & co.* 1872.

Granger (*Rev.* Thomas). Syntagma logicvm. Or, the divine logike. Serving especially for the vse of divines in the practise of preaching, etc. 8 p. l. 387 pp. sm. 4°. *London, Wm. Jones for A. Johnson*, 1620.

Granier de Cassagnac (Adolphe). History of the working and burgher classes. Translated by Ben. E. Green. 352 pp. 8°. *Philadelphia, Claxton, Remsen & Haffelfinger*, 1871.

Grant (*Mrs.* Anne, *of Laggan*). Poems on various subjects. 1 p. l. 10, 17–447 pp. 8°. *Edinburgh, author*, 1803.

Grant (James). The newspaper press: its origin—progress—and present position. 2 v. xiv, 456 pp; x, 462 pp. 8°. *London, Tinsley brothers*, 1871.

Grant (John Wynniatt). Faust. Translated, 1867. *See* **Goethe** (Johann Wolfgang von).

Granucci (Niccolò). La piacevol notte, et lieto giorno, opera morale. 186 l. numb. 2 l. unp. 16°. *Venetia, I. Vidali*, 1574.

Granville (George, *viscount Lansdowne*). Genuine works in verse and prose. 2 v. 6 p. l. 563 pp; 4 p. l. 337 pp. 1 pl. 4°. *London, J. Tonson* [*etc.*] 1732.

Grapaldi (Francesco Maria). De partibus ædium cum additamentis, [etc.] [Ed. 3[a]]? 16 p. l. 157 [147] l. sm. 4°. [*Parma*], *F. Vgoletus parmensis*, 1506.

Gratianus. *See* **Graziani.**

Gratiolet (Pierre). De la physionomie et des mouvements d'expression. Suivi d'une notice sur sa vie et ses travaux, et de la nomenclature de ses ouvrages par Louis Grandeau. vi, 438 pp. 1 portrait. 16°. *Paris, J. Hetzel*, [1865].

Grauert (E. F.) A new method of learning the portuguese language. 346 pp. 12°. *New York, D. Appleton & co.* 1863.

Grauert (William). Second german reader. With notes and vocabulary. 2 p. l. 180 pp. 12°. *New York, E. Steiger*, 1871.

——— Viertes deutsches lesebuch. Herausgegeben durch den vorort des nordamerikanischen turnerbundes unter begutachtung einer commission von schulmännern. 404 pp. 12°. *New York, E. Steiger*, 1871.
[Turner-schulbücher, iv].

Gravenweert (J. van). Essai sur l'histoire de la littérature néerlandaise. 4 p. l. 251 pp. 8°. *Amsterdam, S. Delachaux*, 1830.

Graves (Richard, *d. d.*) Select scriptural proofs of the trinity. To which are annexed notes and illustrations. 119 pp. 8°. *Dublin, W. Curry, jr. & co.* 1840.

Graves (Robert J. *m. d.*) Clinical lectures. 2d american ed. with notes and a series of lectures, by W. W. Gerhard, m. d. 560 pp. 8°. *Philadelphia, E. Barrington & G. D. Haswell*, 1842.

Gray (Alonzo). Elements of chemistry; containing the principles of the science, both experimental and theoretical. 360 pp. 16°. *Andover, Gould, Newman & Saxton*, 1840.

Gray (Asa, *m. d.*) The botanical text-book. Comprising part i. An introduction to structural and physiological botany. Part ii. The principles of systematic botany. 413 pp. 12°. *New York, Wiley & Putnam*, 1842.

——— First lessons in botany and vegetable physiology. To which is added a copious glossary, or dictionary of botanical terms. xii, 236 pp. 12°. *New York, Ivison, Phinney & co.* 1862.

——— Manual of the botany of the northern United States, including Virginia, Kentucky, and all east of the Mississippi; arranged according to the natural system. 3d revised ed. with garden botany, etc. xcviii, 606 pp. 13 l. 6 pl. 12°. *New York, Ivison, Phinney & co.* 1862.
[*With his* First lessons in botany and vegetable physiology].

Gray (Barry, *pseudon.*) *See* **Coffin** (Robert Barry).

Gray (*Rev.* Edward P.) The apostolic treasury: its nature, history, and restoration. With appended extracts from bishop Doane of Albany, and dr. Adams, of Nashotah. 79 pp. 16°. *San Francisco, Libby & Swett*, 1871.

Gray (George H. *sen.*) The mystic circle, and american hand-book of masonry. xxiv, 11-430 pp. 1 portrait. 8°. *Cincinnati, E. Morgan & co.* 1850.

Gray (George Robert). Catalogues of zoological collections in the British museum. *See* **British** museum.

Gray (George Zabriskie). The children's crusade: an episode of the thirteenth century. xiii, 238 pp. sq. 12°. *New York, Hurd & Houghton*, 1870.

Gray (James, *of Longford, Ireland*). Dissertation on revelation. *See* **Bible.** (*English*).

Gray (John Edward). Catalogues of zoological collections in the British museum. *See* **British** museum.

Gray (Oliver Cromwell). A sketch of his life: with his fragmentary writings. Edited by his nephew, David Gray Fickes. 213 pp. 1 portrait. 12°. *Philadelphia, J. B. Lippincott & co.* 1872.

Gray (O. W.) New topographical atlas of the state of Pennsylvania. *See* **Walling** (Henry F.) *and* **Gray.**

Gray (Samuel Octavus). British sea-weeds: an introduction to the study of the marine algæ of Great Britain, Ireland, and the Channel islands. xxiv, 312 pp. 16 l. 16 pl. 12°. *London, L. Reeve & co.* 1867.

Gray (Thomas). Selecta carmina. 4°. [*Patavii*, 1775].
[*In* COSTA (G.) Poema, pp. 61-81].

Graziani (Antonio Maria). De casibus virorum illustrium. Opera ac studio D. Flecherii. 4 p. l. 412 pp. 6 l. 4°. *Lutetiæ Parisiorum, apud A. Cellier*, 1680.

Graziani (Girolamo). Il conqvisto di Granata. Poema heroico. Con gli argomenti del signor Flaminio Calvi. 4 p. l. 256 pp. 4°. *Modana, B. Soliani*, 1650.

Grazzini (Antonfrancesco, *detto il Lasca*). Rime. [Con la vita di Grazzini, scritta dal dottore Antommaria Biscioni]. 2 v. lxiii, 380 pp. 1 portrait; xxvii, 392 pp. 16°. *Firenze, F. Moücke*, 1741.

Great Britain. *Chapel royal.* The old cheque-book, or book of remembrance, of the chapel royal, from 1561 to 1744. Edited, from the original ms. preserved among the muniments of the chapel royal, st. James's palace, by Edward F. Rimbault. 2 p. l. xx, 250, 5 pp. 1 fac-simile. sm. 4°. [*London*], *for the Camden society*, 1872.
[CAMDEN society publications. New series, no. 3].

Great Britain—continued.

—— *Civil service commission.* Sixteenth report of her majesty's civil service commissioners, together with appendices. 8°. *London, G. E. Eyre & W. Spottiswoode*, 1871.

—— *Emigration commission.* Thirteenth general report of the emigration commissioners. 1870. 8°. *London, h. m. stationery office*, 1870.

—— *India department.* A catalogue of the arabic, persian and hindustany manuscripts, of the libraries of the king of Oudh, compiled under the orders of the government of India by A. Sprenger. v. 1. Containing persian and hindustany poetry. viii, 645 pp. 1 l. 8°. *Calcutta, J. Thomas*, 1854.
[*Note.*—No more published].

—— *Naval department.* Extracts from the report of her britannic majesty's commissioners, appointed to inquire into the condition and management of lights, buoys and beacons. Submitted March 5, 1861, and presented to both houses of parliament by command of her majesty. Republished for the use of the U. S. light-house establishment. 254 pp. 8°. *Washington, government printing office*, 1871.

—— —— The nautical almanac and astronomical ephemeris for the years 1874 [and] 1875; with an appendix containing elements and ephemerides of Ceres, Pallas, Juno, Vesta, and Astræa. Published by order of the lords commissioners of the admiralty. 2 v. 8°. *London, G. E. Eyre & W. Spottiswoode*, 1870-71.

—— —— The navy list, corrected to the 20th March, 1871. 16°. *London, J. Murray*, 1871.

—— —— The same. Corrected to the 20th September, 1871. 16°. *London, J. Murray*, 1871.

—— *Parliamentary papers.* Ephemeris parliamentaria; or a faithfull register of the transactions in parliament, in the third and fourth years of the reign of king Charles. [1627-28. Edited by Thomas Fuller, d. d.] 10 p. l. 269 pp. 1 l. sm. fol. *London, J. Williams and F. Eglesfield*, 1654.

—— —— Further reports from her majesty's diplomatic and consular agents abroad respecting the condition of the industrial

Great Britain—continued.
classes and the purchase power of money in foreign countries. v, 946 pp. 8°. *London, Harrison & sons,* 1871.

—— ——Hansard's parliamentary debates, third series: commencing with the accession of William iv. 34° Victoriæ, 1871. Comprising the period from the 9th day of February, 1871, [to] the 21st day of August, 1871. [Five volumes of the session]. v. 204–208. 8°. *London, C. Buck,* 1871.

—— —— Notes of the debates in the house of lords, officially taken by Henry Elsing, clerk of the parliaments, a. d. 1621. Edited, from the original ms. in the possession of lieut.-col. Carew, by Samuel Rawson Gardiner. ix, 158 pp. sm. 4°. [*London*], *Camden society,* 1870.

[CAMDEN society publications, no. 103].

—— —— Report from the select committee on letters patent; together with the proceedings of the committee, minutes of evidence, appendix, and index. x, 242 pp. 1 l. fol. [*London,* 1871].

—— —— Statistical abstract for the united kingdom in each of the last fifteen years, from 1856 to 1870. 18th no. 132 pp. 8°. *London, G. E. Eyre & W. Spottiswoode,* 1871.

—— *Royal observatory* (*Greenwich*). Astronomical and magnetical and meteorological observations made at the royal observatory, Greenwich, in the year 1869: under the direction of George Biddell Airy. 5 p. l. civ, 712 pp. 1 map. 4°. *London, G. E. Eyre & W. Spottiswoode,* 1871. S.

—— *Treasury. Geological survey.* Memoirs of the geological survey. Reports on the geology of Jamaica; or, part ii. of the west indian survey. By James G. Sawkins, with contributions from G. P. Wall, Lucas Barrett, Arthur Lennox, and C. B. Brown. And an appendix by Robert Etheridge. Published by order of the lords commissioners of her majesty's treasury. vi, 339 pp. 10 pl. 1 map. 8°. *London, Longmans, Green & co.* 1869.

CONTENTS.

BARRETT (L.) Analyses and assays, pp. 292–302.
ETHERIDGE (R.) Appendix v. to the geological survey of Jamaica, area and summary of the palæontology of the Caribbean sea, pp. 306–339.
SAWKINS (J. G.) Geological report on the island of Jamaica, pp. 1–262.
WILSON (N.) Outline of the flora of Jamaica, pp. 263–291.

—— —— *Master of the rolls.* Calendar of state papers and manuscripts, relating to english affairs, existing in the archives and collections of Venice, and in other libraries of northern Italy. v. 4. 1527–1533. Edited by Rawdon Brown. 8°. *London, Longman & co.* 1871.

—— —— —— Calendar of state papers, domestic series, of the reign of Elizabeth, addenda, 1566–1579; preserved in her majesty's public record office. Edited by Mary Anne Everett Green. 8°. *London, Longman & co.* 1871.

—— —— —— Calendar of state papers, domestic series, of the reign of Charles i. 1638–1639. Preserved in her majesty's public record office. Edited by John Bruce, and William Douglas Hamilton. 8°. *London, Longman & co.* 1871.

—— —— —— Chronicles and memorials of Great Britain during the middle ages. 4 v. 8°. *London, Longman & co.* 1871.

CONTENTS.

AMUNDESHAM *or* AMERSHAM (John). Chronica monasterii s. Albani. Annales monasterii s. Albani, a Johanne Amundesham, monacho, ut videtur, conscripti, (a. d. 1421–1440). Quibus præfigitur chronicon rerum gestarum in monasterio s. Albani, (a. d. 1422–1431), a quodam auctore ignoto compilatum. Edited by Henry Thomas Riley. 2 v.
MONUMENTA juridica. The black book of the admiralty, with an appendix. v. 1. Edited by sir Travers Twiss.
ROGER DE HOVEDEN. Chronica magistri Rogeri de Houedene. v. 4. Edited by W. Stubbs.

—— *War department.* The new army list, militia list, and Indian civil service list; exhibiting the rank, standing, and various services of every regimental officer in the army serving on full pay, the dates of every officer's commissions, and distinguishing those obtained by purchase. By col. H. G. Hart. no. cxxx. 510 pp. 8°. *London, J. Murray,* 1871.

—— —— Revised army regulations. v. 2. The queen's regulations and orders for the army. vii, 395 pp. 8°. *London,* 1868.

Great Britain *and* **Spain.** Articulen van het contract ende accoort ghemaeckt tusschen Jacobus den eersten, coninck van Enghelandt ter eenre, ende Philips den derden, coninck van Spaengnien: midtsgaders de eertshertoghen Albertus ende Isabella Clara Eugenia. Gemaect den 18 Augusti 1604. VVt het enghels in het neder-duytsch overgheset. *b. l.* 8 l. sm. 4°. *London, R. Barker,* 1604. [*Reprinted, n. p.* 1608].

[*In* NEDERLANDTSCHEN bye-corf].

Great Falls (*New Hampshire*). Directory for 1871–72. *See* **Dover** (*N. H.*)

Great (The) industries of the United States: being an historical summary of the origin, growth, and perfection of the chief industrial

Great (The) industries, etc.—continued. arts of the country. By Horace Greeley, Leon Case, [and others. *anon.*] 1304 pp. 8°. *Hartford, J. B. Burr & Hyde*, 1872.

Greatorex (Thomas). Psalms, extracted from the old and new versions, for the use of the parish church, st. Mary-le-bone. With a selection of tunes, harmonized and arranged for three voices, and applicable to congregational singing; with an accompaniment for the organ or piano-forte. 104 pp. 8°. *London, J. Booth*, [1828].

Greco (Gioachino). The royal game of chesse-play. Illustrated with almost an hundred gambetts. Being the study of Biochimo the famous Italian. [Translated by Francis Beale]. 9 p. l. 120 pp. 1 l. 18°. *London, H. Herringman*, 1656.

Greeley (Horace). What I know of farming: a series of brief and plain expositions of practical agriculture as an art based upon science. 335 pp. 12°. *New York, G. W. Carleton & co.* 1871.

——— *See, also*, **Great** (The) industries of the United States. 1872.

Green (Ashbel, *d. d.*) A historical sketch or compendious view of domestic and foreign missions in the presbyterian church of the United States of America. 214 pp. 12°. *Philadelphia, W. S. Martien*, 1838.

——— Lectures on the shorter catechism of the presbyterian church in the United States of America. 2 v. 451 pp; 476 pp. 12°. *Philadelphia, Presbyterian board of publication*, 1841.

Green (Benjamin E.) The irrepressible conflict between labor and capital: a brief summary of some of the chief causes and results of the late civil war in the United States, as presented in the translator's preface to Adolphe Granier de Cassagnac's History of the working and burgher classes, in which the origin, nature, and objects of the much calumniated french commune are historically explained. lxv, 329-352, 13 pp. 1 l. 8°. *Philadelphia, Claxton, Remsen & Haffelfinger*, 1872.

Green (Duff). How to pay off the national debt, regulate the value of money, and maintain stability in the values of property and labor. 216 pp. 12°. *Philadelphia, Claxton, Remsen & Haffelfinger*, 1872.

Green (Joseph Henry). Mental dynamics, or groundwork of a professional education.

Green (Joseph Henry)—continued. The Hunterian oration, 15th February, 1847. 65 pp. 8°. *London, W. Pickering*, 1847.

——— Vital dynamics. The Hunterian oration before the royal college of surgeons in London, 14th February, 1840. xxxi, 135 pp. 8°. *London, W. Pickering*, 1840.

Green (Lewis Warner, *d. d.*) Sermons. 12°. [*New York*, 1871].

[*In* HALSEY (Leroy J.) Memoir of L. W. Green, pp. 101-491].

Green (Mary Anne Everett, *editor*). Calendar of state papers, domestic series, of the reign of Elizabeth, addenda, 1566-1579. 8°. *London*, 1871.

[GREAT BRITAIN. *Treasury department. Master of the rolls*].

Green (Richard W.) An arithmetical guide; in which the principles of numbers are inductively explained: and applied to the every-day business of life. 288 pp. 18°. *Philadelphia, H. Perkins*, 1836.

Green (Samuel Abbott, *m. d.*) Introduction and notes to Deuxponts' My campaigns in America. *See* **Deuxponts** (Guillaume de Forbach, *comte* des).

Green (William Henry, *d. d.*) An elementary hebrew grammar, with reading and writing lessons and vocabularies. 2d ed. viii, 194 pp. 12°. *New York, J. Wiley & son*, 1871.

——— The pentateuch vindicated from the aspersions of bishop Colenso. vi, 9-195 pp. 12°. *New York, J. Wiley*, 1863.

Greene (David). Manual of christian psalmody. *See* **Mason** (Lowell) *and* **Greene**.

Greene (Edward Burnaby, *editor, etc.*) *See* **Pindar**. The pythian, nemean and isthmian odes, translated into english verse. 1778.

Greene (George Washington). The life of Nathaniel Greene, major general in the army of the revolution. v. 2-3. 8°. [*New York, Hurd & Houghton*, 1871.

Greene (John H.) A catechism of irish geography and topography, physical, social, historical and biographical, for schools and families. 3 p. l. 200 pp. 8°. *Cincinnati, W. Doyle*, 1859.

Greene (William Batchelder). The blazing star; with an appendix treating of the jewish cabbala. Also, a tract on the philosophy of mr. Herbert Spencer, and one on New-England transcendentalism. 180 pp. 12°. *Boston, A. Williams & co.* 1872.

Greenfield (William). Essays on the sources of the pleasures received from literary com-

Greenfield (William)—continued. positions. [*anon.*] vii, 379 pp. 8°. *London, J. Johnson*, 1809.

——— The same. [*anon.*] 2d ed. 2 p. l. 390 pp. 8°. *London, Longman*, 1813.

Greenock (The) commercial list. 1871-72. *See* **Glasgow.**

Greenough (A. J.) The boys and girls of Beech Hill. 298 pp. 3 pl. 16°. *Boston, I. P. Warren*, [1871].

Greenough (S. L.) Lilian. [*anon.*] 312 pp. 12°. *Boston, Ticknor & Fields*, 1863.

Greenough (*Mrs.* Richard S.) Arabesques: Monarè. Apollyona. Domitia. Ombra. 3 p. l. 213 pp. 12°. *Boston, Roberts brothers*, 1872.

Greenough, Jones & co.'s directory of the cities and towns on the line of the Boston and Providence, Taunton and New Bedford, and Providence and Worcester railroads. 458 pp. 8°. *Boston, Greenough, Jones & co.* 1871.

——— Directory of the city of Bangor, for 1871-2. *See* **Bangor** (*Maine*).

Greenwald (E. *d. d.*) Questions on the gospels for the church year. vi, 205 pp. 18°. *Lancaster (Pa.) school association of the church of the holy trinity*, 1869.

Greenwood (*Rev.* Charles). The child and the man, or the children, the sabbath school, and the world. With an introduction by rev. E. N. Kirk. xv, 13-423 pp. 12°. *Boston, S. K. Whipple & co.* 1855.

Greenwood (Francis William Pitt, *d. d.*) Sermons of consolation. xii, 335 pp. 12°. *Boston, C. C. Little & J. Brown*, 1842.

——— The same. A new ed. xii, 329 pp. 16°. *Boston, Little, Brown & co.* 1864.

——— (*editor*). Sacred philosophy of the seasons. *See* **Duncan** (Henry, *d. d.*)

Greenwood (Grace, *pseudon.*) *See* **Lippincott** (*Mrs.* Sarah Jane Clarke).

Gregg (Rollin H. *m. d. editor*). *See* **Homœopathic** (The) quarterly.

Grégoire (Gaspard). Explication des cérémonies de la fête-dieu d'Aix en Provence, ornée de figures et des airs notés, consacrés à cette fête. [*anon.*] 1 p. l. 220 pp. 14 pl. 16°. *Aix, E. David*, 1777.

Grégoire (Pierre, *of Toulouse*). De repvblica libri sex et viginti in dvos tomos distincti. Ex relectione authoris, nunc emendati, & additionibus aucti. 2 v. in 1. 6 p. l. 480 pp; 4 p. l. 227 pp. 24 l. fol. *Lvgdvni, I. S. Pillehotte*, 1609.

Grégoire de Tours (*Saint*). *See* **Gregorius** *turonensis.*

Gregorius *nazianzenus* (*S.*) Tributes to the dead; in a series of ancient epitaphs, translated from the greek by Hugh Stuart Boyd. xl, 78 pp. 8°. *London, G. B. Whittaker*, 1826.

Gregorius *thaumaturgus.* Writings of Gregory thaumaturgus. 8°. *Edinburgh*, 1871.
[ANTE-NICENE christian library, v. 20, pp. 1-156].

Gregorius *turonensis* (Georgius Florentius). Histoire ecclésiastique des Francs, par saint Grégoire. Suivie d'un sommaire de ses autres ouvrages, et précédée de sa vie écrite au xe siècle par Odon, abbé de Cluni. Traduction nouvelle par Henri Bordier. 2 v. 2 p. l. xxxix, 291 pp; 2 p. l. 481 pp. 16°. *Paris, F. Didot frères*, 1859-61.

Gregory i. *the great* (*Saint and pope*). King Alfred's west-saxon version of Gregory's pastoral care. With an english translation, the latin text, notes, and an introduction. Edited by Henry Sweet. Part i. 3 p. l. 288 pp. 8°. *London, N. Trübner & co.* 1871.
[EARLY english text society publications, no. 45].

Gregory (George, *d. d.*) Dr. Gregory's history of the christian church; from the earliest periods to the present time. Revised and improved, with additions; exhibiting the present state and prospects of the christian world. By Martin Ruter, s. t. d. 1 p. l. 637 pp. 8°. *Cincinnati, Roff & Young*, 1832.

——— The same. [New ed.] Containing a general view of missions, and exhibiting the state of religion in different parts of the world. Compiled by Martin Ruter, d. d. 2 p. l. 9-447 pp. 8°. *New York, B. Waugh & T. Mason*, 1834.

——— Letters on literature, taste, and composition, addressed to his son. 2 v. vii, 287 pp; iv, 321 pp. 16°. *London, R. Phillips*, 1808.

Gregory (George, *m. d.*) Treatise on the theory and practice of physic. With notes and additions, by Nathaniel Potter, m. d. and S. Colhoun, m. d. 2 v. 5 p. l. xxxiv, 532 pp; 2 p. l. 546 pp. 3 l. 8°. *Philadelphia, Towar & Hogan*, 1826.

Gregory (H. D.) An index to Mitchell's new school atlas, containing over 17,000 names. 41 pp. 4°. *Philadelphia, author*, 1871.
[*With* MITCHELL (S. A.) New school atlas].

——— The same. 112 pp. 8°. *Philadelphia, author*, 1871.

Gregory (John, *m. d.*) A comparative view of the state and faculties of man with those of the animal world. 6th ed. 2 v. 2 p. l. xxiii, 172 pp. 4 l; 2 p. l. 208 pp. 2 l. 16°. *London, J. Dodsley*, 1774.

Gregory (John M.) School funds and school laws of Michigan. 1859. *See* **Michigan.**

Grenus (Jacques Louis). Fables diverses, tant originales qu'imitées des fabulistes étrangers, et quelques autres poésies. Par J. L. G. 2 v. viii, 292 pp. 4 pl; 2 p. l. 336 pp. 4 pl. 18°. *Paris, Bossange, Masson & Besson*, 1807.

Grenville (*Sir* Richard). Two authentick journals of sir Richard Grenville, afterwards general in the west for king Charles i. viz. 1. of the expedition to Cadiz in Spain, anno 1625; 2. of the expedition to the isle of Rhee in France, anno 1627. 4°. [*London, J. Tonson* [*etc.*] 1732].

[*In* GRANVILLE (George, *lord Lansdowne*). Genuine works in verse and prose. v. 2. pp. 249–337].

Grenville. *See* **Granville.**

Greppin (J. Baptiste). Description géologique du Jura bernois et de quelques districts adjacents compris dans la feuille vii de l'atlas fédéral. Avec un carte, une planche de profils géologiques et sept de fossils. 4 p. l. xx, 357 pp. 7 pl. 1 map. 4°. *Berne, J. Dalp*, 1870.

[SWITZERLAND. Matériaux pour la carte géologique de la Suisse, v. 8].

Gresley (*Rev.* William). Church Clavering, or the schoolmaster. New ed. 2 p. l. 280 pp. 1 pl. 16°. *London, J. Burns*, [1846].

——— Ecclesiastes anglicanus; being a treatise on preaching, as adapted to a church of England congregation. 1st american, from the 2d english ed. with notes by the rev. Benjamin I. Haight. xvi, 340 pp. 12°. *New York, D. Appleton & co.* 1843.

Gresset (Jean Baptiste Louis). Œuvres. Nouv. éd. revue, corrigée, considérablement augmentée, & donnée au public par l'auteur. 2 v. xxiv, 336 pp; 360 pp. 16°. *Londres, É. Kelmarneck*, 1765.

CONTENTS.

v. 1. Discours prononcé à l'académie françoise par l'auteur, le jour de sa réception.
Poëmes, etc.
v. 2. Discours sur l'harmonie.
Édouard iii. tragédie.
Sidnei, comédie.
Le méchant, comédie.

Gretschel (Heinrich). *See* **Jahrbuch** der erfindungen.

Grey (A. M. *or Mrs. col.* E. C.) An old country house. A novel by the author of "The gambler's wife," [etc. *anon.*] 3 v. 12°. *London, T. C. Newby*, 1850.

Grey (Mary G.) *and* **Shirreff** (Emily). Thoughts on self-culture, addressed to women. 2 v. xii, 280 pp; viii, 291 pp. 8°. *London, E. Moxon*, 1850.

Gridley (Selah, *m. d.*) The mill of the muses. 267 pp. 18°. *Exeter, T. Gridley*, 1828.

Grier (*Rev.* Richard). An answer to Ward's errata of the protestant bible; [also] an appendix, containing a review of the preface to the fourth edition of the errata. xxxvi, 168 pp. 4°. *London, T. Cadell & W. Davies*, 1812.

Grierson (Henry). Delineations of St. Andrews; being a particular account of everything remarkable in the history and present state of the city and ruins, the university, [etc.] viii, 244 pp. 4 pl. 12°. *Edinburgh, P. Hill*, 1807.

Grierson (*Rev.* Thomas). Autumnal rambles among the scottish mountains: or, pedestrian tourist's friend. 2d ed. 232 pp. 2 pl. 16°. *Edinburgh, J. Hogg*, 1851.

Griffet (Henri). Traité des différentes sortes de preuves qui servent à établir la vérité de l'histoire. 4 p. l. 456 pp. 16°. *Liége, J. F. Bassompierre*, 1769.

Griffith (*Mrs.* Elizabeth). A series of genuine letters between Henry and Frances. *See* **Griffith** (Richard *and* Elizabeth).

Griffith (Richard *and Mrs.* Elizabeth). A series of genuine letters between Henry and Frances. [*pseudon.*] 6 v. 12°. *London, W. Johnston*, 1767–70.

[*Note.*—v. 1-2 are of 3d ed.]

Griffiths (John, *m. d.*) Travels in Europe, Asia Minor, and Arabia. xx, 396 pp. 4 pl. 1 map, 1 portrait. 4°. *London, T. Cadell & W. Davies*, 1805.

Grimaldi (Francesco Antonio). La vita di Diogene cinico. 3 p. l. 260 pp. 1 portrait. 12°. *Napoli, V. Mazzola-Vocola*, 1777.

Grimes (J. Stanley). Etherology; or, the philosophy of mesmerism and phrenology; including a new philosophy of sleep and of consciousness, with a review of the pretensions of neurology and phreno-magnetism. 350 pp. 12°. *New York, Saxton & Miles*, 1845.

——— Outlines of geonomy: a treatise on the physical laws of the earth and the creation of the continents. Founded on recent discoveries. 168 pp. 12°. *Boston, Phillips, Sampson & co.* 1858.

Grimestone (Edward, *translator*). *See* **Béthune** (Philippe de).

Grimke (Frederick). The works of Frederick Grimke. 2 v. in 1. 3 p. l. 733 pp; 261 pp. 8°. *Columbus (O.) Columbus printing co.* 1871.

CONTENTS.

v. 1. Nature and tendency of free institutions. 3d ed.
v. 2. Letters. Reflections on the present crisis. Essays. Apothems.

Grimoald (Nicolas). Songes. [1557. Reprinted]. 16°. [*London*, 1870].

[ARBER'S English reprints, v. 11, no. 24, pp. 96-125].

Grimshaw (William). The history of South America, from the discovery of the new world by Columbus, to the conquest of Peru by Pizarro. 252 pp. 12°. *New-York, Collins & Hannay*, 1830.

——— The life of Napoleon, with the history of France, from the death of Louis xvi. to 1821. 285 pp. 12°. *Philadelphia, Towar & Hogan*, 1829.

Grindle (Wesley, *m. d.*) The sexual system, and medical companion. 377 pp. 12°. *Philadelphia*, 1864.

Grinfield (Edward William). The jesuits: an historical sketch. Eng. title, xx, 471 pp. 16°. *London, Seeleys*, 1853.

Griswold (Rufus Wilmot). The cypress wreath: a book of consolation for those who mourn. 128 pp. 32°. *Boston, Gould, Kendall & Lincoln*, 1844.

——— Gems from american female poets, with brief biographical notices. 160 pp. 1 pl. 32°. *Philadelphia, H. Hooker*, 1842.

Griswold (*Mrs.* Stephen M.) A woman's pilgrimage to the holy land; or, pleasant days abroad. Being notes of a tour through Europe and the east. 423 pp. 1 pl. 12°. *Hartford, J. B. Burr & Hyde*, 1871.

Grivel (Guillaume). L'isle inconnue, ou mémoires du chevalier des Gastines. Nouvelle éd. 4 v. 16°. *Paris, Moutard*, 1784.

Grondich discours over desen aen-staenden vrede-handel. 1608. *See* **Usselincx** (Willem).

Gronow (J.) A review of England and Wales: in which the historical events of every town, village, and place are briefly expressed. xx, 375 pp. 1 map. 12°. *London, Simpkin and Marshall*, 1849.

Grose (Francis). Lexicon balatronicum. A dictionary of buckish slang, university wit, and pickpocket eloquence. Compiled originally by captain Grose. And now considerably altered and enlarged, with the modern changes and improvements, by [Hewson Clarke] a member of the Whip club. Assisted by Hell-fire Dick, and James Gordon, esqrs. of Cambridge; and William Soames, esq. of the hon. society of Newman's hotel. viii pp. 112 l. 1 pl. 8°. *London, C. Chappel*, 1811.

Gross (*Rev.* Joseph B.) The heathen religion in its popular and symbolical development. xvi, 372 pp. 12°. *Boston, J. P. Jewett & co.* 1856.

Gross (Samuel D. *m. d.*) Elements of pathological anatomy. 2d ed. revised and greatly enlarged. 822 pp. 6 col. pl. 8°. *Philadelphia, E. Barrington & G. D. Haswell*, 1845.

——— **Richardson** (T. G. *m. d.*) *and* **Gross** (S. W. *m. d.*) *editors*. *See* **North** (The) american medico-chirurgical review.

Grosvenor (*Mrs.* H. S.) Right and wrong. 216 pp. 18°. *Boston, Mass. sabbath-school society*, [1855].

Grotius (Hugo). De rebus belgicis: or, the annals, and history of the low-countrey-warrs. Wherein is manifested, that the United Netherlands, are indebted for the glory of their conquests, to the valour of the english. Faithfully rendered into english, by T. M. 4 p. l. 974 pp. 18 l. 16°. *London, H. Twyford & R. Paulet*, 1665.

——— Eclogue [Myrtilus] translated from the latin. [By John Rooke]. 1 p. l. 15 pp. 8°. *London*, 1725.

[ROOKE (John). Select translations, part 2, ed. 1726].

——— Poemata, collecta & magnam partem nunc primùm edita à fratre Gvilielmo Grotio. Eng. title, 11 p. l. 548 pp. 1 l. 16°. *Lugdun. Batav. apud A. Clouquium*, 1617.

Grout (*Rev.* Lewis). Zulu-land; or, life among the Zulu-Kafirs of Natal and Zululand, South Africa. 351 pp. 9 pl. 1 map. 12°. *Philadelphia, Presbyterian publication committee*, [1864].

Grove (Henry). Some thoughts concerning the proofs of a future state, from reason. xvi, 211 pp. 8°. *London, R. Hett*, 1730.

Grove (John). Epidemics examined and explained: or, living germs proved by analogy to be a source of disease. ix, 192 pp. 8°. *London, J. Ridgway*, 1850.

Gruber (J. G. *editor*). Allgemeine encyclopädie der wissenschaften und künste. *See* **Ersch** (J. S.) **Gruber** *and others*.

Grün (Anastasius, *pseudon.*) *See* **Auersperg** (Anton Alexander, *count* von).

Grund (Francis J.) Elements of chemistry, with practical exercises. xii, 384 pp. 12°. *Boston, Carter, Hendee & co.* 1833.

Grundy (John). The stranger's guide to Hampton court palace and gardens. 96 pp. 12°. *London, Bell & Daldy*, 1857.

Gruner (Willam H. L.) Caryatides from the "Stanza dell' Eliodoro" in the Vatican. 1852. *See* **Raffaelle d'Urbino.**

Grüner (M. L.) The manufacture of steel. Translated from the french, by Lenox Smith, with an appendix on the Bessemer process in the United States, by the translator. 193 pp. 9 pl. 2 tab. 8°. *New York, D. Van Nostrand*, 1872.

Guaccio (Francesco Maria). Compendivm maleficarvm, ex quo nefandissima in genus humanum opera venefica, ac ad illa vitanda remedia conspiciuntur. In hac autem secunda æditione ab eodem authore pulcherrimis doctrinis ditatum, exemplis auctum, & remedijs locupletatum. His additus est exorcismus potentissimus ad soluendum omne opus diabolicum; nec non modus curandi febricitantes. Eng. title, 7 p. l. 391 pp. 4°. *Mediolani, ex collegij ambrosiani typographia*, 1626.

Guadaloupe: a tale of love and war. By one who served in the late war with Mexico. [*anon.*] 156 pp. 1 pl. 12°. *Philadelphia, J. B. Smith & co.* 1860.

Guarini (Giovanni Battista). Pastor fido di G. B. Guarini. Euridice di Ottavio Rinuccini. 3 p. l. 328 pp. 16°. *Venezia, A. Zattae figli*, 1783.

Guasco (Francisco Eugenio, *marchese* di). Musei capitolini antiquae inscriptiones. 3 v. fol. *Romae, J. G. Salomonius*, 1775.

Guazzi *or* **Guazzo** (Marco). Historie di tvtte le cose degne di memoria nel mondo per terra et per acqua successe, qual hanno principio l'anno m.d.ix, [etc.] 4 p. l. 105 pp. 16°. *Venetia, Comin da Trino di Monferrato*, 1548.

[*With* GIOVIO (Paolo). Compendio dell' historie, etc.]

Guerike (Heinrich Ernst Ferdinand). The life of Augustus Herman Franke, founder of the orphan-house in Halle. Translated from the german: by Samuel Jackson. With an introductory preface by the rev. E. Bickersteth. viii, 296 pp. 1 portrait. 16°. *London, H. G. Bohn*, 1847.

Guerna (Andrea). Grammaticale bellvm nominis & verbi regum. 18°. [*Lugd. Batavorum*, 1644].

[*In* DISSERTATIONVM lvdicrarvm et amœnitatvm scriptores varij, pp. 400-446].

Guernsey (Clara F.) Alice Fenton; or, alone in the world. 235 pp. 3 pl. 16°. *Philadelphia, American s. s. union*, [1871].

——— The silver rifle: a story of the Saranac lakes. 256 pp. 3 pl. 16°. *Philadelphia, American sunday-school union*, [1871].

Guernsey (Lucy Ellen). The dark night; or, "The fear of man bringeth a snare." 135 pp. 2 pl. 18°. *Philadelphia, American s. s. union*, [1871].

——— Ethel's trial in becoming a missionary. 336 pp. 3 pl. 16°. *Philadelphia, American s. s. union*, [1871].

——— The Fairchilds; or, "Do what you can" 223 pp. 3 pl. 16°. *Philadelphia, American sunday-school union*, [1871].

——— Irish Amy. [*anon.* Preface subscribed L. E. G.] 312 pp. 4 pl. 18°. *Philadelphia, American sunday school union*, [1854].

——— Lady Betty's governess; or, the Corbet chronicles, [1637]. 369 pp. 12°. *New York, T. Whittaker*, 1872.

——— Only in fun; or, Henry Willson's voyage. 168 pp. 2 pl. 18°. *Philadelphia, American s. s. union*, [1871].

——— The sign of the cross; or, Edah Champlin. 309 pp. 16°. *New York, General protestant episcopal s. s. union and church book society*, 1856.

Guettier (A.) A practical guide for the manufacture of metallic alloys; comprising their chemical and physical properties, with their preparation, composition and uses. Translated from the french, by A. Fesquet. xxiv, 13-293 pp. 12°. *Philadelphia, H. C. Baird*, 1872.

Guevara (Antonio de). Oratorio de i religiosi, et esercitio de i virtvosi. Tradotto di spagnvolo in italiano per m. Pietro Lauro, & di nuouo aggiontoui le apostille nell margine, & con tre tauole. 14 p. l. 296 pp. 4°. *Vinegia, G. Giolito de' Ferrari*, 1559.

Guiana *See* **British Guiana.**

Guibert (Jacques Antoine Hippolyte, *comte* de). Journal d'un voyage en Allemagne, fait en 1773. Ouvrage posthume, publié par sa veuve, et précédé d'une notice historique sur la vie de l'auteur, par F. E. Toulongeon. 2 v. 2 p. l. 326 pp. 1 pl.; 2 p. l. 300 pp. 1 pl. 8°. *Paris, Treuttel et Würtz*, 1803.

Guicciardini (Lodovico). Descrittione di tvtti i Paesi Bassi, altrimenti detti Germania Inferiore. Riueduta di nuouo, & ampliata per tutto la terza volta. 4 frontispieces, 9 p. l. 432 pp. 9 l. 73 pl. fol. *Anversa, C. Plantino*, 1588.

Guide (The) to domestic happiness. [*anon.*] 1st american from the 5th London ed. 185 pp. 1 pl. 16°. *New-Haven, Sidney's press for I. Cooke & co.* 1804.

Guide (A) to the Mount's Bay and the Land's End. *See* **Paris** (John Ayrton).

Guidi (Alessandro). Poesie di Alessandro Guidi, con la sua vita descritta da Gio. Mario Crescimbeni, con altre aggiunte. Ed. 4ta, recorretta e ripurgata da molti errori corsi nelle passate edizioni. 382 pp. 16°. *Venezia, P. Piotto*, 1787.

Guignes (Joseph de). Extrait de deux ouvrages nouveaux relatifs [au génie de la langue chinoise]. 4°. *Bruxelles, J. L. de Boubers*, 1773].

[*In* AMIOT *or* AMYOT (J. M.) Lettre de Pékin. 1773. pp. ix-xxxviii].

Guild (A. E.) Hymns of the ages. *See* **Whitmarsh** (Caroline S.) *and* **Guild.**

Guild (Curtis). Over the ocean; or, sights and scenes in foreign lands. viii, 558 pp. 8°. *Boston, Lee & Shepard*, 1871.

Guillaume *le breton.* Philippide. Extraits concernant les guerres de Flandre. Texte latin et français. Avec une introduction et des notes. Par Octave Delepierre. xxii, 150 pp. 170 l. 4°. *Bruges, V. Werbrouck*, 1841.

[BRUGES. (*Société d'émulation*). Recueil de chroniques, etc.]

Guimarães (Luiz, *jr.*) Galeria brazileira. Pedro Americo. 128 pp. 18°. *Rio de Janeiro, H. Brown e J. de Almeida*, 1871.

Guirey (*Rev.* William). A funeral sermon, on the death of George Washington, delivered before the methodist episcopal church at Lynn, [Mass.] Jan 7, 1800. 22 pp. 8°. *Salem, J. Cushing*, 1800.

[HAZARD pamphlets, v. 64].

Guizot (Élisabeth Charlotte Pauline de Meulan, *madame*). Les enfants. Contes à l'usage de la jeunesse. 4e éd. 2 v. 2 p. l. viii, 349 pp. 4 pl.; 2 p. l. 358 pp. 1 l. 4 pl. 16°. *Paris, Didier*, 1838.

——— The same. Tales in french. For young persons. By madame Guizot. iv, 163 pp. 16°. *Boston, Allen & Ticknor*, 1833.

——— The young student; or, Ralph and Victor. From the french, by Samuel Jackson.

Guizot (E. C. P. de M.)—continued.
3 v. in 1. 18°. *New York, D. Appleton & co.* 1844.

Guizot (François Pierre Guillaume). Nouveau dictionnaire universel des synonymes de la langue française, contenant les synonymes de Girard, Beauzée, Roubaud, d'Alembert, etc. 2 v. in 1. 2 p. l. xl, 548 pp; 2 p. l. 549-1007 pp. 8°. *Paris, Maradan*, 1809.

——— The history of France from the earliest times to the year 1789. Translated by Robert Black. v. 1. xii, 617 pp. (incl. 38 pl.) 1 map. 8°. *London, S. Low, Marston, Low & Searle*, 1872.

Guldberg (C. M. *editor*). *See* **Polyteknisk** tidsskrift, 1869-70.

Guldenstubbé (*Baron* Louis de). Pneumatologie positive et expérimentale. La réalité des esprits et le phénomène merveilleux de leur écriture directe demontrées. xxxvi, 216 pp. 15 pl. 8°. *Paris, A. Franck*, 1857.

Guldin (Johannes C.) "Altes und neues" aus dem schatz des göttlichen wortes in einer sammlung von predigten und predigtentwürfen. xxxi, 606 pp. 1 l. 8°. *New-York, A. W. Steinhaus*, 1853.

Gully (James Manley, *m. d.*) A guide to domestic hydrotherapeia, the water cure in acute disease. xv, 283 pp. 16°. *London, Simpkin, Marshall & co.* 1863.

Gummere (John). An elementary treatise on astronomy. In two parts. To which are added, solar, lunar, and other astronomical tables. 2d ed. 373, 104 pp. 7 pl. 8°. *Philadelphia, Kimber & Sharpless*, 1837.

——— The same. 3d ed. improved. 359, 112 pp. 8 pl. 8°. *Philadelphia, Kimber & Sharpless*, 1842.

Gunter (Edmund). Works: containing the description and vse of the sector, cross-staff, bow, quadrant, and other instruments. With a canon of artificial sines and tangents to a radius of 10.00000 parts, and the logarithms from an unit to 10000. To which is added, the description and use of another sector and quadrant, both of them invented by mr. Sam. Foster. The 5th ed. diligently corrected, and divers matters added. By William Leybourn. 10 p. l. 313; 224 pp. 86 l. 2 pl. sm. 4°. *London, F. Eglesfield*, 1673.

Günther (Friedrich August). Der homöopathische thierarzt. Ein hülfsbuch für cavallerie-offiziere, gutsbesitzer oekonomen und alle hausväter. 2e aufl. 2 v. 240 pp; viii,

Günther (Friedrich August)—continued. 252 pp. 8°. *Sondershausen, F. A. Eupel*, 1839–40.

CONTENTS.

v. 1. Die krankheiten des pferdes und ihre homöopathische heilung. Mit beiträgen von Johann Friedrich Kerl.
v. 2. Die krankheiten der rinder, schafe, schweine, ziegen und hunde und ihre homöopathische heilung.

Gurdon (*Rev.* Brampton). The pretended difficulties in natural or reveal'd religion no excuse for infidelity. Sixteen sermons preached in 1721 and 1722. fol. [*London*, 1739].

[BOYLE lectures, v. 3, pp. 277–399].

Gurley (*Mrs.* E. S.) Edith Somers; or, a child's influence. 267 pp. 5 pl. 18°. *New York, American tract society*, [1871].

Gustavus iii. *king of Sweden.* Collection des écrits politiques, littéraires et dramatiques de Gustave iii, roi de Suède; suivie de sa correspondance. [Par Dechaux]. 5 v. 8°. *Stockholm, C. Delén*, 1804–05.

CONTENTS.

v. 1. Discours littéraires et politiques.
v. 2. Amusemens dramatiques, t. 1. Plan de Gustave Vasa, tragédie lyrique en trois acts. Gustave Adolphe et Ebba Brahe, drame héroïque en trois actes.
v. 3. Siri Brahe, ou les curieuses, drame en trois actes. Amusemens dramatiques, t. 2. Helmfelt, drame en cinq actes. Le jaloux Napolitain, drame en trois actes. Marthe Bauer et Laurent Sparre, drame en trois actes. Alexis Michaelowitsch et Natalie Narischkin, comédie en deux actes.
v. 4–5. Correspondance.

Gutherius. *See* **Guthierres.**

Guthierres (Jacques). Tiresias, sev cæcitatis encomivm. 18°. [*Lugd. Batavorum*, 1644].

[*In* DISSERTATIONVM lvdicrarvm et amœnitatvm scriptores varij, pp. 519–554].

Guthry (Henry, *bishop of Dunkeld*). Memoirs of Henry Guthry: wherein the conspiracies and rebellion against king Charles i. to the time of the murther of that monarch, are briefly and faithfully related. 7 p. l. 255 pp. 8°. *London, W. B. for J. Nutt*, 1702.

Gwynne (Talbot). The school for fathers. An old english story. 205 pp. 12°. *New York, Harper and brothers*, 1852.

H. (F. D.) Helps to a holy lent. *See* **Huntington** (*Rev.* Frederick D.)

H. H. *See* **Hunt** (Helen Maria Fiske).

H. (H. B.) Plea for the heathen: or, heathenism ancient and modern. [*anon.* Subscribed H. B. H.] vii, 5–199 pp. 18°. *Boston, Massachusetts sabbath school society*, 1832.

H. (H. H.) The Caverley family; or, mrs. Linden's teachings. [*anon.*] 251 pp. 16°. *New York, D. Dana, jr.* 1860.

H. (H. L.) Little Ada; or, the three new years. [*anon.*] 267 pp. 4 pl. 16°. *Philadelphia, Claxton, Remsen & Haffelfinger*, 1872.

H. (M. A.) Cosmo's visit to his grandfather By M. A. H. [*anon.*] 206 pp. 1 pl. 18° *New York, R. Carter & brothers*, [1860].

H. (T.) Behemoth, 1680. *See* **Hobbes** (Thomas).

H * * * * (Therese). Bemerkungen über Holland aus dem reisejournal einer deutschen frau. Von Therese H * * * * [Herbst? *anon.*] viii, 400 pp. 16°. *Leipzig, G. Fleischer*, 1811.

Haan (Lourens Feykes). Beschryving van de straat Davids, van de Zuydbay, tot om het eyland Disko. Als meede van de Z. O. bogt tot door het Waygat. *b. l.* 14 pp. sm. 4°. *Amsterdam, G. van Keulen*, 1719.

[*With* the following].

——— The same. Beschryving van de straat Davids, benevens des zelven inwooners, zede, gestalte, en gewoonte, misgaders hunne visvangst, [etc.] Als mede een verhaal van de westkust van de straat, of anders Noord Amerika. 40 pp. sm. 4°. *Amsteldam, G. van Keulen*, 1720.

Habersham & co. Grocers' telegraphic cypher. 107 pp. 16°. *Baltimore, J. Cox*, 1871.

Habert (Philippe). The temple of death. By [H. P. Phipps] the earl of Mulgrave. A translation out of french. 16°. *London*, 1695.

[*In* SAUNDERS (Francis). The temple of death, etc pp. 33–48].

Habesci (Elias). The present state of the ottoman empire. Containing a more accurate and interesting account of the turks than any yet extant. Including a particular description of the court and seraglio of the grand signor. Translated from the french. 1 p. l. xxiii, 443 pp. 8°. *London, R. Baldwin*, 1784.

Habington (William). Castara. The 3d ed. of 1640; edited and collated with the earlier ones of 1634, 1635. By Edward Arber. 144 pp. 16°. *London*, 1870.

[ARBER'S English reprints, v. 10, no. 22].

Habits (The) of good society: a handbook for ladies and gentlemen. [*anon.*] 320 pp. sq. 16°. *New York, G. W. Carleton & co.* 1872.

[HAND-BOOKS of society, v. 2].

Häcker (Ludwig). Amerikanische reiseskizzen aus dem gebiete der technik, landwirthschaft und des socialen lebens. x, 200 pp. 8°. *Braunschweig, F. Vieweg & sohn*, 1867. S.

Hacket (J. T.) The student's assistant in astronomy and astrology. Also a discourse on the harmony of phrenology, astrology, and physiognomy. 170 pp. 1 pl. 18°. *London, Bray & King*, 1836.

Hadassah, [or Esther], the jewish orphan. [*anon.*] 112 pp. sq. 16°. *Philadelphia, American sunday school union*, [1834].

Haddock (Thomas M.) Haddock's Savannah, Ga. directory, 1871. *See* **Savannah.**

Hadermann (Jeannette R.) Dead men's shoes. A romance. 420 pp. 12°. *Philadelphia, J. B. Lippincott & co.* 1872.

Hadley (A. M.) The teacher's miscellany. *See* **Campbell** (J. L.) *and* **Hadley.**

Hadley (Hiram). Lessons in language: an introduction to the study of english grammar. 138 pp. 12°. *Chicago, Hadley brothers*, 1871.

Hadrawa (Norbert). Freundschaftliche briefe über verschiedene auf der insel Capri entdeckte und ausgegrabene alterthümer. Aus dem italiänischen übersezt, [von R. S. Walther]. 144 pp. 9 pl. 4°. *Dresden, Walther*, 1794.

Hadrianus (Junius Hornanus). *See* **Junius** *or* **Jonghe** (Adriaan).

Haen (Antoonije van). Antonii de Haen de magia liber. Ed. 2a. xxiv, 184 pp. 8°. *Lipsiæ, svmptibvs I. P. Kravs*, 1777.

Häfener (Franz). Der wiesenbau in seinem ganzen umfange nebst anleitung zum nivelliren, zur erbauung von schleuszen, wehren, brücken, etc. xvi, 717 pp. 4 l. 8°. *Reutlingen, C. Mäcken*, 1847.

Hagar (D. B.) A common school arithmetic. 324 pp. 12°. *Philadelphia, Cowperthwait & co.* 1871.

——— An elementary arithmetic. 208 pp. 12°. *Philadelphia, Cowperthwait & co.* 1871.

——— Primary lessons in numbers. 112 pp. 16°. *Philadelphia, Cowperthwait & co.* 1871.

Hagen (John Cole). Affection's gift, for the loving and the loved. 144 pp. 3 pl. 12°. *Philadelphia, J. E. Potter*, 1859.

Hagen (Steven van der). Beschrijvinghe van de tweede voyagie, ghedaen naer d'Oost-Indien. Onder den admirael Steven van der Hagen. [1603–05]. Waer inne verhaelt het veroveren der portugeser forten op Amboyna.

Haven (Steven van der)—continued.
62–96 pp. sm. 4°. [*Amsterdam, J. Hartgers*, 1648].

[*In* HARTGERTS (J.) Oost-indische voyagien, v. 1. 5e stuck].

Hager (Joseph, *d. d.*) An explanation of the elementary characters of the Chinese; with an analysis of their ancient symbols and hieroglyphics. 1 p. l. lxxvi, 1 l. 44 pp. 2 pl. fol. *London, R. Phillips*, 1801.

Hague (James D.) Mining industry. With geological contributions by Clarence King. xv, 647 pp. 37 [38] pl. 4°. *Washington, government printing office*, 1870.

[UNITED STATES. *War department.* (*Engineer corps*). Exploration of the fortieth parallel, v. 3].

Hague (William, *d. d.*) Home life. Twelve lectures. 271 pp. 12°. *New York, S. Dickerson*, 1855.

Hähn (Johann Friedrich). Anweisung zur krieges-bau-kunst worinnen die beschaffenheit und anlegung, wie auch der angriff und die vertheidigung der festungen, schantzen und linien nach theorie und praxis abgehandelt wird. 6 p. l. xxxii, 480 pp. 22 tab. 8°. *Berlin, im buchladen der realschule*, 1757.

Hahn (Ludwig). Geschichte der auflösung der jesuiten-congregationen in Frankreich im jahre 1845. xiii, 218 pp. 8°. *Leipzig, Brockhaus & Avenarius*, 1846.

Hahnemann (Samuel C. F.) The chronic diseases: their specific nature and homœopathic treatment. Translated and edited by Charles J. Hempel, m. d. With a preface by Constantine Hering, m. d. xii, 202 pp. 1 l. 12°. *New York, W. Radde*, 1846.

Hails (William Anthony). Remarks on Volney's Ruins, or a survey of the revolutions of empires. x, 390 pp. 8°. *London, L. B. Seeley & son*, 1825.

Haines (Isaac S. *m. d.*) Catechism on chemistry, adapted to the course of lectures delivered in the university of Pennsylvania. 2d ed. 144 pp. 16°. *Philadelphia, J. G. Auner*, 1839.

——— The same. 3d ed. 160 pp. 16°. *Philadelphia, J. G. Auner*, 1845.

Haldar (Neel-rutna). *See* **Neel-rutna** Haldar.

Haldeman (Samuel S.) Affixes in their origin and application, exhibiting the etymologic structure of english words. Revised ed. 292 pp. 12°. *Philadelphia, E. H. Butler & co.* 1871.

Hale (Anne G.) Fanny and Robbie. A year book for the children of the church. 138 pp. 1 pl. 16°. *Boston, E. P. Dutton & co.* 1867.

Hale (*Rev.* Benjamin). Scriptural illustrations of the daily morning and evening service, and litany of the protestant episcopal church, with notes. By rev. Benjamin Hale. xi, 9-102 pp. 16°. *Boston, Perkins, Marvin & co.* 1835.

Hale (B. E.) Familiar conversations upon the constitution of the United States. 132 pp. 18°. *West Bradford,* [*Ms.*] *Hale & co.* 1835.

Hale (*Rev.* Edward Everett). How to do it. 2 p. l. 269 pp. 16°. *Boston, J. R. Osgood & co.* 1871.

——— The rosary of illustrations of the bible. Edited by rev. Edward E. Hale. 293 pp. 6 pl. 8°. *Boston, Phillips & Sampson,* 1849.

Hale (Edwin M. *m. d.*) Lectures on diseases of the heart. xi, 19-206 pp. 8°. *New York, Boericke & Tafel,* 1871.

Hale (Sarah Josepha). Flora's interpreter: or, the american book of flowers and sentiments. 6th ed. improved. 262 pp. 1 l. 1 col. pl. 12°. *Boston, Marsh, Capen & Lyon,* 1838.

——— The same. Flora's interpreter, and fortuna flora. 3d revision. 288 pp. 2 col. pl. 12°. *Boston, Chase, Nichols & Hill,* 1860.

——— The ladies' wreath: a selection from the female poetic writers of England and America. With original notices and notes; prepared especially for young ladies. 408 pp. 12°. *Boston, Marsh, Capen & Lyon,* 1837.

——— Traits of American life. 298 pp. 12°. *Philadelphia, Carey & Hart,* 1835.

Hales (John). The works of the ever memorable mr. John Hales, of Eaton. Now first collected together. 3 v. 18°. *Glasgow, J. Tonson,* 1765.

——— Several tracts. viz. 1. Concerning the sin against the holy ghost. 2. Of the sacrament of the Lord's supper. 3. Paraphrase on s. Matthew's gospel. 4. Of the power of the keys. 5. Of schism and schismaticks. 6. Miscellanies. [Also], his letter to archbishop Laud, occasion'd by his tract of schism; never before published among his works. 228 pp. 1 portrait. 16°. [*London*], 1716.

Hales (William, *d. d.*) The inspector, or select literary intelligence for the vulgar a. d. 1798, but correct a. d. 1801. [*anon.*] 1 p. l. xii, xix, 259 pp. 8°. *London, J. White,* 1799.

Haley (*Rev.* William D.) Words for the workers: in a series of lectures to working-men, mechanics and apprentices. xi, 146 pp. 12°. *Boston, Crosby, Nichols & co.* 1855.

Half hours with modern scientists. Huxley—Barker—Stirling—Cope—Tyndall. 4 p. l. 288 pp. 12°. *New Haven* (*Conn.*) *C. C. Chatfield & co.* 1871.

[UNIVERSITY scientific series].

CONTENTS.

BARKER (G. F. *m. d.*) Correlation of vital and physical forces.
COPE (E. D.) On the hypothesis of evolution.
HUXLEY (T. H.) On the physical basis of life.
STIRLING (J. H.) As regards protoplasm—reply to Huxley.
TYNDALL (John). Scientific addresses. On the methods and tendences of physical investigation.—On haze and dust.—On the scientific use of the imagination.

Haliburton (Thomas Chandler). The clockmaker: sayings and doings of Samuel Slick of Slickville. xi, 271 pp. 6 pl. 16°. *New York, Hurd & Houghton,* 1872.

Halifax (George Saville, *marquis of*). *See* **Saville** (George, *marquis of Halifax*).

Halkerston (Peter). A treatise on the history, law, and privileges of the palace and sanctuary of Holyroodhouse; with appendix, list of cases, and index materiarum. xi, 236 pp. 8°. *Edinburgh, Maclachlan & Stewart,* 1831.

Hall (Alfred G. *m. d.*) Views of the new theory of disease and of treatment and cure, based upon the nutritive principle: illustrative of the science of fluid physiology and the chemical properties of the blood. 135 pp. 1 portrait. 8°. *Washington* (*D. C.*) *author,* 1852.

Hall (*Miss* Arethusa). Life and character of the rev. Sylvester Judd. [*anon.*] xii, 591 pp. 12°. *Boston, Crosby, Nichols & co.* 1854.

——— The literary reader: consisting of selections in prose and verse. Including remarks on the art of reading. 408 pp. 12°. *Boston, J. P. Jewett & co.* 1850. s.

Hall (A. H.) Equal rights of the rich and poor. 148 pp. 18°. *Boston, J. French & co.* 1855.

Hall (*Mrs.* Anna Maria Fielding). The way of the world. By the author of "De Lisle" and "The trials of life." [*anon.*] 3 v. 12°. *London, E. Bull,* 1831.

Hall (Baynard R.) Exercises, analytical and synthetical; arranged for the new and compendious latin grammar. 140 pp. 12°. *Philadelphia, the author,* 1836.

Hall (Charles H. *d. d.*) Notes on the gospels, *See* **Bible.** (*English*).

Hall (David). Some brief memoirs of the life of David Hall; with an account of the life

Hall (David)—continued.
of his father John Hall. [Also], divers of his epistles to friends, on various occasions. 1 p. l. 222 pp. 8°. *London, L. Hinde*, 1758.

Hall (Fanny W.) Rambles in Europe; or, a tour through France, Italy, Switzerland, Great Britain, and Ireland, in 1836. 2 v. xi, 228 pp; viii, 246 pp. 12°. *New-York, E. French*, 1848.

Hall (*Rev.* James, *of North Carolina*). A brief history of the Mississippi territory, to which is prefixed a summary view of the country between the settlements on the Cumberland river and the territory. 1 p. l. 70 pp. 12°. *Salisbury, F. Coupee*, 1801.

——— The same.

[HAZARD pamphlets, v. 110].

Hall (*Judge* James, *of Cincinnati*). Legends of the west. Author's revised edition. 435 pp. 12°. *New York, G. P. Putnam & co.* 1853.

Hall (John, *d. d. of New York*). Papers for home reading. 365 pp. 1 portrait. 12°. *New York, Dodd & Mead*, 1871.

Hall (John, *teacher*). The reader's guide, containing a notice of the elementary sounds in the english language; instructions for reading both prose and verse, with numerous examples for illustration, and lessons for practice. 360 pp. 12°. *Hartford, Canfield & Robins*, 1836.

Hall (Joseph, *d. d. bishop of Norwich*). A defence of the Humble remonstrance, against the frivolous and false exceptions of Smectymnvvs. Wherein the right of leiturgie and episcopacie is clearly vindicated from the vaine cavils, and challenges of the answerers. By the author of the Humble remonstrance. Seconded (in way of appendance) with the judgment of D. Abrahamvs Scvltetvs, concerning the divine right of episcopacie, and the no-right of lay-eldership. Translated out of his latine. 3 p. l. 200 pp. 4°. *London, N. Butter*, 1641.

[MISCELLANEOUS pamphlets, v. 102].

——— Letters to archbishop Usher [and] A latin sermon preached before the synod of Dort, Nov. 19, 1618. 8°. *London, B. Seeley & son*, 1826.

[*In* JONES (*Rev.* John). Bishop Hall, his life and times, pp. 461-492].

——— Resolutions and decisions of divers practicall cases of conscience in continuall use amongst men. 3d ed. with some additionalls. 11 p. l. 399 pp. 3 l. 18°. *London, R. Hodgkinson & J. Grismond*, 1654.

Hall (Joseph, *d. d.*)—continued.

——— Select devotional and practical works of bishop Hall. With an introductory notice of the life and writings of the author. 238 pp. 18°. *Hartford, Belknap & Hamersley*, 1835.

Hall (Louisa J. Park). Joanna of Naples, by the author of "Miriam." [*anon.*] 2 p. l. 213 pp. 12°. *Boston, Hilliard, Gray & co.* 1838.

——— Miriam; a dramatic poem. [*anon.*] viii, 124 pp. 12°. *Boston, Hilliard, Gray & co.* 1837.

Hall (Marshall, *m. d.*) A descriptive, diagnostic and practical essay on disorders of the digestive organs and general health; being an attempt to prosecute the views of dr. Hamilton and mr. Abernethy, and a second edition of the essay on the mimoses, with additions. 5 p. l. 184 pp. 8°. *London, Longman*, 1820.

Hall (Samuel Carter, *editor*). The book of british ballads. With preliminary remarks to each ballad, and an introduction, by Park Benjamin. xi, 153 pp. 8°. *New York*, [*Douglas*, 1844].

——— The book of gems. The poets and artists of Great Britain. [With illustrations]. 2 v. xvi, 304 pp. 2 l. facsim; 5 p. l. 302 pp. 2 l. facsim. 8°. *London, Fisher, son & co.* 1844.

——— The same. The modern poets and artists of Great Britain. [With illustrations]. xvi, 304 pp. 2 l. facsim. 8°. *London, H. G. Bohn*, 1846.

Hall (Samuel R. *teacher*). The arithmetical manual. vii, 13-288 pp. 12°. *Andover, Flagg, Gould & Newman*, 1832.

——— The child's friend: or things which every boy can do. 132 pp. sq. 16°. *Boston, Carter, Hendee & co.* 1833.

——— Practical lectures on parental responsibility, and the religious education of children. vii, 13-176 pp. 12°. *Boston, Peirce & Parker*, 1833.

Hall (*Mrs.* Sarah E.) Conversations on the bible, between a mother and her children. 5th ed. 360 pp. 12°. *Philadelphia, H. Hall*, 1837.

——— Selections from the writings of mrs. Sarah Hall, with a memoir of her life. [By Harrison Hall]. 1 portrait, xxv, 180 pp. 16°. *Philadelphia, H. Hall*, 1833.

Hall (Theophilus D.) English-latin dictionary. *See* **Smith** (William H.) *and* **Hall**

Hall (William W. *m. d.*) Fun better than physic; or, everybody's life-preserver. 333 pp. 1 portrait. 12°. *Springfield (Mass.) D. E. Fisk & co.* [1871].

Hall (*Captain, of the Indian army*). Songs and occasional poems, on various subjects. 2d ed. xviii, 230 pp. 1 l. 16°. *London, Black & co.* 1815.

Hallenbeck (William E.) Directory of life insurance companies transacting business in the United States, Great Britain, Germany, and other countries. Compiled from official and other sources. 3 p. l. 291 pp. 12°. *New York, Wynkoop & Hallenbeck*, 1871.

Haller (Albert von). Nomenclator ex historia plantarum indigenarum Helvetiae excerptus. iv, 216 pp. 8°. *Bernæ, sumptibus societatis typographicæ*, 1769. s.
[BOTANICAL pamphlets, v. 11].

Hallett (A. R.) The orphean. 1871. *See* **Perkins** (W. O.) *and* **Hallett**.

Halliday (Samuel B.) The lost and found; or life among the poor. 356 pp. 1 pl. 12°. *New York, Blakeman & Mason*, 1859.

Halliwell (James Orchard). A brief account of the life, writings, and inventions of sir Samuel Morland. 32 pp. 8°. *Cambridge*, [*Eng.*] *E. Johnson*, 1838.

——— Rara mathematica; or, a collection of treatises on the mathematics and subjects connected with them, from ancient inedited manuscripts. viii, 120 pp. 1 l. 8°. *London, J. W. Parker*, 1839.
[*With his* Brief account of the life of sir Samuel Morland. *Cambridge*, 1838].

Hallock (*Rev.* William A.) "Light and love."—A sketch of the life and labors of the rev. Justin Edwards, d. d. the evangelical pastor; the advocate of temperance, the sabbath, and the bible. 556 pp. 1 portrait. 12°. *New York, American tract society*, [1855].

Halpine (Mary Grace). Ernest Richmond and his little mother. 296 pp. 5 pl. 18°. *New York, Carlton & Porter*, [1863].

——— The prayer of faith. 111 pp. 1 pl. 18°. *Boston, Mass. sabbath school society*, [1864].

Hals (William). The parochial history of Cornwall. *See* **Gilbert** (Davies).

Halsey (Harlan P.) Annie Wallace; or, the exile of Penang. A tale. xiii, 304 pp. 12°. *New York, Miller & Holman*, 1859.

Halsey (Le Roy J. *d. d.*) The beauty of Immanuel. 204 pp. 12°. *Philadelphia, Presbyterian board of publication*, [1860].

——— Memoir of the life and character of rev. Lewis Warner Green, d. d. With a selection from his sermons. xi, 491 pp. 2 portraits. 12°. *New York, C. Scribner & co.* 1871.

Halsted (Caroline A.) The obligations of literature to the mothers of England. xv, 178 pp. 1 pl. 8°. *London, Smith, Elder & co.* 1840.

Halton (*Rev.* Thomas). A historical and practical exposition of the catechism of the church of England. viii, 215 pp. 16°. *London, J. Burns*, 1843.

Halyburton (*Rev.* Thomas). The great concern of salvation. 176 pp. 18°. *Philadelphia, Presbyterian board of publication*, [1838].

——— Memoirs of the life of the rev. Thomas Halyburton. With an appendix, embracing an account of the church of Scotland during the times of Halyburton. 320 pp. 1 pl. 12°. *Edinburgh, J. Johnstone*, [1847].

Hamblin (George W.) The Kansas guide. Facts and practical suggestions to those who intend seeking new homes in the "far west." 62 pp. 1 l. 8°. *Ottawa, G. W. Hamblin*, 1871.

Hamburg. (*Verein für hamburgische statistik*). Beiträge zur statistik Hamburg's. (Mit besonderer rücksicht auf die jahre 1821–1852). i. Bevölkerung. ii. Armenwesen. iii. Accise und konsumption. iv. Staatshaushalt. 2 p. l. 180 pp. sm. fol. *Hamburg, Perthes-Besser & Mauke*, 1854.

Hamburg und Altona. Eine zeitschrift zur geschichte der zeit, der sitten und des geschmaks. 1r–4r jahrgang. 16 v. in 8. 8°. *Hamburg, F. H. Nestler*, 1801-05. s.

Hamerton (Philip Gilbert). The isles of Loch Awe and other poems of my youth. xiv, 374 pp. 15 pl. 16°. *London, W. E. Painter*, 1855.

———(*editor*). The portfolio, an artistic periodical. [Monthly]. v. 1–2. 2 p. l. 192 pp. 26 pl; 2 p. l. 196 pp. 38 pl. fol. *London, Seeley Jackson, & Halliday*, 1870–71.

Hamilton (Alfred, *d. d.*) May I believe? or the warrant of faith. 138 pp. 18°. *Philadelphia, Presbyterian board of publication*, [1859].

Hamilton (C. V.) A crown from the spear. By the author of "Woven of many threads." [*anon.*] vi, 172 pp. 8°. *Boston, J. R. Osgood & co.* 1872.

Hamilton (Gail, *pseudon.*) *See* **Dodge** (Mary Abigail).

Hamilton (*Rev.* Hugh, *bishop of Ossory*). The works of the right rev. Hugh Hamilton; collected and published, with some alterations and additions from his manuscripts, by Alexander Hamilton, his eldest son. 2 v. xxxvi, 273 pp. 1 portrait, 19 pl; 2 p. l. 371 pp. 8°. *London, W. Bulmer & co. for G. & W. Nicol*, 1809.

CONTENTS.

v. 1. De sectionibus conicis, tractatus geometricus, in quo, ex natura ipsius coni, sectionum affectiones facillime deducuntur methodo nova.

v. 2. Introduction to the essay on the existence and attributes of God, p. 5.

An attempt to prove the existence of the supreme unoriginated being, p. 81.

An essay on the permission of evil; and the necessary connection between intelligence and free agency, p. 135.

Philosophical essays, p. 163.

Four introductory lectures on natural philosophy. p. 295.

Hamilton (James, *jun.*) An account of the late intended insurrection among a portion of the blacks of this city. [Charleston]. 48 pp. 8°. *Charleston (S. C.) A. E. Miller*, 1822.

[WOLCOTT pamphlets, v. 88].

——— The same. Negro plot. An account of the late intended insurrection among a portion of the blacks of the city of Charlestown, S. C. 30 pp. 8°. *Boston, J. W. Ingraham*, 1822.

[MOORE pamphlets, v. 36].

Hamilton (John, *editor*). Angelica's ladies library; or, parents and guardians present. Eng. title, vi, 440 pp. 7 pl. sm. 4°. *London, J. Hamilton & co.* 1794.

Hamilton (Joseph). The only approved guide through all the stages of a quarrel: containing the royal code of honor; reflections upon dueling; and the outline of a court for the adjustment of disputes. 4 p. l. 12; 254 pp. 12°. *London, Hatchard & sons*, 1829.

Hamilton (J. A.) Hamilton's celebrated dictionary; comprising an explanation of 3,500 italian, french, german, english, and other musical terms, phrases, and abbreviations. Also a copious list of musical characters. With an appendix, consisting of a reprint of John Tinctor's "Terminorum musicæ diffinitorium," the first musical dictionary known. Edited by John Bishop. viii, 202 pp. 24°. *London, R. Cocks & co.* [1849].

Hamilton (Kate W.) Chinks of Clannyford. 380 pp. 4 pl. 16°. *Philadelphia, Presb. board of pub.* [1872].

Hamilton (P. S.) Nova-Scotia considered as a field for emigration. Published by authority of the provincial parliament of Nova-Scotia. 2 p. l. 91 pp. 1 map. 8°. *London, J. Weale*, 1858.

Hamilton (William, *d. d.*) The mourner in Zion comforted. Revised and improved, from the 2d Edinburgh ed. by the author of The comforter. 240 pp. 12°. *Pittsburgh, Cook & Schoyer*, 1834.

Hamilton (William Douglas, *editor*). Calendar of state papers, of the reign of Charles i. 1638–39. *See* **Bruce** (John) *and* **Hamilton.**

Hamilton (*Rev.* William T.) Infant baptism, a scriptural ordinance; and baptism by sprinkling lawful. 116 pp. 12°. *Newark (N. J.) W. Tuttle*, 1831.

Hammann (J. M. Herman). Des arts graphiques destinés à multiplier par l'impression, considérés sous le double point de vue historique et pratique. xii, 489 pp. 12°. *Genève, J. Cherbuliez*, 1857. s.

Hammen y Leon (Lorenzo van der). Don Felipe el prvdente, segvndo deste nombre, rey de las Españas y Nvevo-Mvndo. 8 p. l. 192, 1 l. sm. 4°. *Madrid, vivda de A. Martin*, 1625.

Hammer (Julius). Schau um dich und schau in dich. Dichtungen. 5e auflage. xiii, 174 pp. 18°. *Leipzig, F. A. Brockhaus*, 1856.

Hammond (*Mrs.* Adelaide F.) Josephine Eloise, a novel. 93 pp. 8°. *Baltimore, Baltimore news co.* 1872.

Hammond (Anthony). An apology for the writings of Walter Moyle, esq; in answer to the groundless aspersions of mr. Hearne and dr. Woodward. With a word or two concerning the frivolous cavils of messieurs Whiston and Woolston, relating to the thundering legion. [*anon.*] 1 p. l. 22 pp. 8°. *London*, 1727.

[*With* MOYLE (Walter). Whole works. *London*, 1727].

Hammond (Henry, *d. d. canon of Christ's church, Oxford*). Of fundamentals in a notion referring to practise. 1 p. l. 244 pp. 3 l. 16°. *London, J. Flesher for R. Royston*, 1654.

——— Novum testamentum, cum paraphrasi et adnotationibvs H. H. *See* **Bible.** (*Latin*). *New testament.*

Hammond (James Hamilton). Slavery in the light of political science. 8°. [*Augusta (Ga.)* 1860].

[*In* ELLIOTT (E. N.) Cotton is king, pp. 627–688].

Hammond (William A. *m. d.*) A treatise on diseases of the nervous system. 754 pp. 8°. *New York, D. Appleton & co.* 1871.

Hampson (John). The poetics of Marcus Hieronymus Vida. *See* **Vida** (Marco Girolamo).

Hanaford (*Mrs.* Phebe A.) From shore to shore, and other poems. 277 pp. 1 portrait. 12°. *Boston, B. B. Russell*, 1871.

——— The young captain: a memorial of capt. Richard C. Derby, fifteenth reg. Mass. volunteers, who fell at Antietam. 226 pp. 1 pl. 18°. *Boston, Degen, Estes & co.* 1865.

Hanaford (William G. *m. d.*) Lectures on chemistry, with familiar directions for performing experiments with a small apparatus. vi, 3–140 pp. 12°. *Boston, Richardson, Lord & Holbrook*, 1831.

Hanbury (Benjamin, *editor*). An enlarged series of extracts from the diary, meditations and letters of mr. Joseph Williams. *See* **Williams** (Joseph).

Hancarville (Pierre François Hugues, *dit* d'). Recherches sur l'origine, l'esprit et les progrès des arts de la Grèce ; sur leurs connections avec les arts et la religion des plus anciens peuples connus ; sur les monumens antiques de l'Inde, de la Perse, du reste de l'Asie, de l'Europe et de l'Égypte. [*anon.*] 3 v. 4°. *Londres, B. Appleyard*, 1785.

Hancock (John, *d. d.*) Arguments to prove the being of God. With objections against it answered. Being several sermons preached in the year 1706. fol. [*London*, 1739].
[BOYLE lectures, v. 2, pp. 197–258].

Hand (W. M.) The home surgeon and physician : designed to assist heads of families, travellers, and sea-faring people, in discerning, distinguishing, and curing diseases ; with concise directions for the preparation and use of a numerous collection of the best american remedies. With an introduction, by J. L. Comstock, m. d. 3d. ed. 256 pp. 12°. *Hartford, S. Andrus & son*, 1847.

Handbook of the Dutchess and Columbia railroad. *See* **Carter** (Edmund).

Hand-books of society. 3 v. sq. 16°. *New York, G. W. Carleton & co.* 1872.

CONTENTS.

ART (The) of conversation, v. 1.
COX (Edward W.) The arts of writing, reading, and speaking, v. 3.
HABITS (The) of good society, v. 2.

Haney's journal for the farm, household, workshop, store and factory. [Monthly]. Jan. 1868, to Dec. 1870. v. 1–3. 4°. *New York, Jesse Haney & co.* 1868–70.

Hanger (Charles Henry). Proverbial and moral thoughts. In a series of essays. iv, 204 pp. 16°. *London, J. Cornish*, 1857.

——— The same. 2d ed. viii, 204 pp. 16°. *London, J. Cornish*, 1858.

Hanks (*Rev.* Stedman W.) The black valley: the railroad and the country ; with an account of the introduction of water. An allegory. 186 pp. 16 pl. 1 diagram. 16°. *Boston, Congregational publishing society*, [1871].

——— Light on the ocean. 204 pp. 1 pl. 18°. *Boston, Mass. sabbath-school society*, [1862].

Hannah (John). Discourses on the fall and its results. viii, 289 pp. 12°. *London, Rivingtons*, 1857.

Hanno *carthaginiensis.* Hannonis carthaginiensivm dvcis navigatio, qva maximam Libycae orae partem ultra Herculis columnas lustrauit: è greco sermone in latinum, Conrado Gesnero interprete, nũc primum conuersa. Adjecta svnt etiam scholia. 21 pp. 16°. *Tigvrivm, A. Gesnervs*, 1559.
[*With* LEO *africanus* (Joannes). De totivs Africae descriptione libri ix. ed. 1559].

——— The same. El Periplo de Hannon ilustrado por Pedro Rodriguez Campomanes. [Greek and spanish texts]. Con notas latinas de Juan Hudson. 8°. [*Madrid*, 1756].
[CAMPOMANES (P. R.) Antigüedad maritima de la republica de Cartago. Part 2, pp. 1–132].

Hannover (Adolph). Über die entwickelung und den bau des säugethierzahns. 133 pp. 8 pl. 4°. *Breslau, Grass, Barth & comp.* [1856]. S.
[Aus den Verhandlungen des kaiserl. Leopold.-Carol. akademie der naturforscher, v. xxv, p. ii].

Hanover. *Statistisches bureau.* Zur statistik des königreichs Hannover 1^{es}–8^{es} heft. Schifffahrts-statistik für die jahre 1849 bis 1860 incl. fol. *Hannover, F. Culemann*, 1862. S.

Hansen (P. Botten-). *See* **Botten-Hansen.**

Hanson (J. H.) Preparatory latin prosebook : containing all the latin prose necessary for entering college. With references to latin grammars ; synonymes ; notes critical and explanatory ; and a vocabulary. 23d ed. enlarged and improved. xi, 609, 152 pp. 1 map. 8°. *New York, Woolworth, Ainsworth & co.* 1871.

Hanway (Jonas). Letters on the importance of the rising generation of the laboring part of our fellow-subjects. 2 v. 2 p. l. xxiv, 246 pp. 1 table ; 2 p. l. x, 319 pp. 8°. *London, A. Millar & T. Cadell*, 1767.

Happel (Eberhard Werner). Fortuna brittannica, oder brittannischer glückswechsel: fürstellend eine kurtzbündige beschreibung aller königen von Engelland, und des schier stets unglückseeligen hauses Stuart. Insonderheit aber den ausführlichen lebens-lauf Caroli ii. und des jüngst unglücklich entwichenen königs Jacobi ii. Fortgesetzet biss zur erhebung des jetzigen grossmächtigen königs Wilhelm von Oranien. [1st ed?] 4 p. l. 220 pp. 8 l. 4°. *Hamburg, T. von Wiering*, 1689.

Happiness (The) of heaven. By a father of the society of Jesus. *See* **Boudreaux** (F. J.)

Hapstone (Dalman). The ancient psalms in appropriate metres: a strictly literal translation from the hebrew, with explanatory notes. x, 316 pp. 8°. *Edinburgh, W. Oliphant & co.* 1867.

Harbaugh (*Rev.* Henry). Poems. 285 pp. 12°. *Philadelphia, Lindsay & Blakiston*, 1860.

——— Union with the church, the solemn duty, and the blessed privilege, of all who would be saved. 2d ed. 127 pp. 18°. *Philadelphia, Lindsay & Blakiston*, 1856.

Harden (Edward I.) The life of George M[ichael] Troup. 536, xxii pp. 1 portrait. 8°. *Savannah, E. I. Purse*, 1859.

Harding (Chester). My egotistigraphy. Prepared for his family and friends, by one of his children. 185 pp. 12°. *Cambridge, J. Wilson & son*, 1866.

Hardinge (Nicholas). Poems, latin, greek, and english; to which is added an historical enquiry and essay upon the administration of government in England during the king's minority. Collected and revised by George Hardinge. 3 p. l. xvi, 332 pp. 1 portrait. 8°. *London, J. Nichols, son, & Bentley*, 1818.

Hardwicke's science-gossip: an illustrated medium of interchange and gossip for students and lovers of nature. Edited by M. C. Cooke. [Monthly]. Jan. to Dec. 1871. v. 7. 8°. *London, R. Hardwicke*, 1872.

Hare (Francis, *d. d. bishop of Chichester*). The works of the late dr. Francis Hare. 2 v. viii, 480 pp; 2 p. l. 472 pp. 8°. *London, E. Owen*, 1746.

Harington (*Sir* John). A briefe view of the state of the church of England, as it stood in q. Elizabeths and king James his reigne, to the yeere 1608. Being a character and history of the bishops of those times. 5 p. l. 211 pp. 1 l. 18°. *London, J. Kirton*, 1653.

Harirí al-basrí. *See* **Abu** Mohammed al Kasim ben Ali al-Harirí.

Harlay (François de, *archbishop of Rouen*). Francisci archiepiscopi rothomagensis ecclesiasticæ historiæ liber primvs. 2 p. l. 152 pp. 8°. *Parisiis, apud M. Le Blanc*, 1629.

Harles (Gottlieb Christoph). Christoph. Cellarii orthographia latina ex vetvstis monvmentis nec non recentivm ingeniorvm cvris excerpta digesta novisqve observationibvs illvstrata qvam denvo recensvit emendavit observationibvs Longolii [et aliorvm] svisqve avxit et Cortii Dispvtationes de vsv orthographiæ cvm orthographia norisiana typis repetendas cvravit Theoph. Christophorvs Harles. Cvm præfatione Christiani Adolphi Klotzii. 2 v. in 1. 23 p. l. 390 pp. 1 pl; 298 pp. 7 l. 8°. *Altenbvrgi, ex officina richteria*, 1768.

Harley (*Dr.* A. J.) The young Crusoe; or, adventures of a shipwrecked boy. 270 pp 6 pl. 12°. *Boston, Walker, Wise & co.* 1864.

Harmansz (Wolfert). Zee-getogt na de Oost-Indien. 1601–03. *See* **West-Zanen** (Willem van).

Harmonie des cultes catholique, protestant, et mosaïque avec les constitutions de l'empire français. *See* **Foulaines** (F. N. de).

Harness (The) and carriage journal. Devoted to the trade in harness, carriages, trunks, coach and saddlery hardware, accoutrements, etc. [Weekly]. Aug. 6, 1870, to July 29, 1871. v. 14. 4°. *New York*, [*etc.*] *Dexter & co.* [1870–71].

Harper (William). Slavery in the light of social ethics. 8°. [*Augusta* (*Ga.*) 1860]. [*In* ELLIOTT (E. N.) Cotton is king, pp. 547–626].

Harper's bazar. A repository of fashion, pleasure, and instruction. [Weekly]. Jan. 7 to Dec. 30, 1871. v. 4. fol. *New York, Harper & brothers*, 1871.

Harpers' hand-book for travellers in Europe and the east. By W. Pembroke Fetridge. 10th year. 12°. *New York, Harper & brothers*, 1871.

Harper's new monthly magazine. Dec. 1870, to Dec. 1871. v. 42–43. 8°. *New York, Harper & brothers*, 1871.

Harper's weekly. A journal of civilization. Jan. 7 to Dec. 30, 1871. v. 15. fol. *New York, Harper & brothers*, [1871].

Harriott (John). The religion of philosophy, as contra-distinguished from modern french philosophy; and as an antidote to its pernicious effects, lately so evident in the preva

Harriott (John)—continued. lence of assassination & suicide. xvii, 152 pp. 8°. [*London*], *Maurice*, 1812.

——— Struggles for life, exemplified in the various travels and adventures in Europe, Asia, Africa and America. 3d ed. 3 v. 12°. *London, author*, 1815.

Harris (Alexander). A geographical hand book. With a copious index. Adapted as an aid to the student of history. 427 pp. 12°. *Lancaster* (*Pa.*) *Daily express office*, 1862.

Harris (A.) *and* **Falconer** (E.) Satanella; or, the power of love, a romantic opera in four acts, by A. Harris and E. Falconer. The music by M. W. Balfe. [Libretto without music]. 44 pp. 8°. [*New York*], *W. C. Bryant & co.* 1871.
[PAREPA-ROSA grand english opera].

Harris (Chapin A. *m. d.*) The dental art, a practical treatise on dental surgery. 383 pp. 3 pl. 8°. *Baltimore, Armstrong & Berry*, 1839.

——— The principles and practice of dentistry, including anatomy, physiology, pathology, therapeutics, dental surgery and mechanism. 10th ed. Revised and edited by Philip H. Austen, m. d. 794 pp. 8°. *Philadelphia, Lindsay & Blakiston*, 1871.

Harris (John, *d. d.* 1667–1719). Eight sermons. fol. [*London*, 1739].
[BOYLE lectures, v. 1, pp. 353–434].

Harris (John, *d. d.* 1804–56). The great commission: or, the christian church constituted and charged to convey the gospel to the world. With an introductory essay, by William R. Williams, d. d. xlvi, 37–484 pp. 12°. *Boston, Gould, Kendall & Lincoln*, 1842.

——— Union; or the divided church made one. Revised american ed. 301 pp. 16°. *Boston, Gould, Kendall & Lincoln*, 1838.

Harris (*Mrs.* Sidney S. *formerly* Miriam Cole). Frank Warrington. By the author of "Rutledge," [etc. *anon.*] 478 pp. 12°. *New York, C. Scribner & co.* 1871.

——— Louie's last term at St. Mary's. [*anon.*] 239 pp. 12°. *New York, Derby & Jackson*, 1860.

——— The same. 239 pp. 12°. *New York, C. Scribner & co.* 1871.

——— Richard Vandermarck. A novel. 1 p. l. 330 pp. 12°. *New York, C. Scribner & co.* 1871.

——— A rosary for lent; or, devotional readings, original and compiled, by the author of

Harris (*Mrs.* Sidney S.)—continued. "Rutledge." [*anon.*] 360 pp. 12°. *New York, C. Scribner & co.* 1872.

——— Roundhearts and other stories. By the author of Rutledge. [*anon.*] 185 pp. 4 pl. 12°. *New York, C. Scribner & co.* 1871.

——— St. Philip's. By the author of "Rutledge," [etc. *anon.*] 340 pp. 12°. *New York, C. Scribner & co.* 1871.

——— Rutledge. By the author of "The Sutherlands," [etc. *anon.*] 21st ed. 504 pp. 12°. *New York, C. Scribner & co.* 1872.

——— The Sutherlands. By the author of "Rutledge," [etc. *anon.*] 11th ed. 2 p. l. 9–474 pp. 12°. *New York, C. Scribner & co.* 1871.

Harris (*Rev.* Thomas L.) Regina: a song of many days. 239 pp. 12°. *London, W. White*, 1860.

——— Truth and life in Jesus. Sermons, preached in the Mechanics' institution, David street, Manchester, Oct. Nov. and December, 1859. viii, 199 pp. 16°. *New York, New church publishing association*, 1860.

Harris (Walter, *m. d.*) A treatise of the acute diseases of infants. [Also], medical observations on several grievous diseases. Written originally in latin. Translated into english by John Martyn. xxviii, 228 pp. 12°. *London, T. Astley*, 1742.
[*With* WALKER (Sayer, *m. d.*) Observations on the constitution of women].

Harris (*Capt.* William Cornwallis). Portraits of the game and wild animals of southern Africa, delineated from life in their native haunts, during a hunting expedition from the Cape Colony as far as the tropic of Capricorn, in 1836 and 1837, with sketches of the field sports. Eng. title, 4 p. l. 175 pp. 2 l. 30 col. plates. fol. *London, W. Pickering*, 1840.

Harris (Wm. T. *editor*). *See* **Journal** (The) of speculative philosophy.

Harrisburg (*Penn.*) The Harrisburg business directory, and stranger's guide, with a sketch of its first early settlement. By H. Napey. 64 pp. 1 map. 8°. [*n. p.*] *author*, 1842.

——— "The patriot" Harrisburg directory, and a business directory of Carlisle, Chambersburg, Greencastle, Middletown, Mechanicsburg, Newville, Shippensburg, etc. 1871–72. 8°. [*Harrisburg*], *A. & W. H. Boyd*, [1871].

Harrison (George). Adversaria; or, selections and reflections on civil, political, moral, and religious subjects. xv, 382 pp. 8°. *London, Darton, Harvey, & Darton*, 1818.

Harrison (Henry, *d. d.*) The weary traveller his eternal rest, being a discourse of that blessed rest here, which leads to endless rest hereafter. 5 p. l. 256 pp. 1 pl. 12°. *London, A. G.& J. P. for R. Clavell*, 1681.

Harrison (Jennie, *pseudon?*) The old back room. 392 pp. 2 pl. 16°. *New York, Dodd & Mead*, [1871].

——— The right way, and how Agnes Turner walked in it. 121 pp. 1 pl. 18°. *New York, A. D. F. Randolph*, 1864.

Harrison (John P. *m. d.*) Essays and lectures on medical subjects. 192 pp. 12°. *Philadelphia, J. Crissy*, 1835.

Harrod (John J.) The academical reader, comprising selections from the most admired authors, designed to promote the love of virtue, piety, and patriotism. 323 pp. 1 pl. 12°. *Baltimore, J. J. Harrod*, 1830.

——— The new and most complete collection of camp, social, and prayer meeting hymns and spiritual songs, now in use. 318 pp. 32°. *Baltimore, J. J. Harrod*, 1830.

Harry and his pony. By the author of "Little Kitty's library." [*anon.*] 180 pp. 6 pl. 16°. *New York, R. Carter & brothers*, 1871.

Harry's summer in Ashcroft. [*anon.*] 204 pp. sq. 16°. *New York, Harper & brothers*, 1860.

Harsha (David A.) The life of Charles Sumner; with choice specimens of his eloquence, a delineation of his oratorical character, and his great speech on Kansas. 329 pp. 1 portrait, 1 pl. 12°. *New York, Dayton & Burdick*, 1856.

——— The star of Bethlehem: a guide to the saviour. 528 pp. 12°. *New York, Sheldon & co.* 1861.

Harsha (*Rev.* J. W.) The song of the redeemed, salvation to God, and to the lamb. vii, 446 pp. 1 portrait. 12°. *New York, Sheldon & co.* 1861.

Hart (*Colonel* H. G.) New army list, 1871. *See* **Great Britain.** *War department.*

Hart (John). The svmme of the conference betvveene Iohn Rainoldes and Iohn Hart. *See* **Reynolds** (John) *and* **Hart** (John).

Hart (John S. *ll. d.*) A grammar of the english language. 201 pp. 12°. *Philadelphia, E. H. Butler & co.* 1862.

——— A manual of english literature. 636 pp. 8°. *Philadelphia, Eldridge & brother*, 1872.

Hart & Anderson, *publishers. See* **World** (The) in the stereoscope. 1872.

Harte (Francis Bret). Condensed novels. iv, 212 pp. 1 pl. 12°. *Boston, J. R. Osgood & co.* 1871.

——— East and west poems. 171 pp. 16°. *Boston, J. R. Osgood & co.* 1871.

——— The luck of Roaring camp, and other sketches. 75 pp. 6 pl. 4°. *Boston, J. R. Osgood & co.* 1872.

——— The pliocene skull. Sketches by E. M. Schaeffer, m. d. 1 p. l. 8 pp. 4°. *Washington, Peters & Rehn*, [1871].

——— The poetical works of Bret Harte. Complete ed. 333 pp. 17 pl. sq. 16°. *Boston, J. R. Osgood & co.* 1872.

Harte (Walter). The amaranth: or, religious poems; consisting of fables, visions, emblems, &c. [*anon.*] xv, 295 pp. 1 pl. 8°. *London, Robinson & Roberts*, 1767.

Hartford (*Conn.*) Geer's Hartford city directory, for 1871-72; together with a classified business directory, and a newly engraved map of the city; also a full reprint of the contents of our 1841 directory. No. xxxiv. July, 1871, to July, 1872. 292 pp. 1 map. 8°. *Hartford, Hartford steam printing co.* 1871.

——— The Hartford city guide for 1871-72; also a classified directory of many of the business firms, with a new map of the city. 380 pp. 1 map. 12°. *Hartford, Coburn & Jenison*, 1871.

Hartgerts *or* **Hartgers** (Joost). Oost indische voyagien, door dien begin en voortgangh van de Vereenighde nederlandtsche oost-indische compagnie. Vervatende de voornaemste reysen, by de inwoonderen der selver provintien derwaerts ghedaen. v. 1. Eng. title, 11 p. l. 13 parts. sm. 4°. *Amstelredam, J. Hartgerts*, 1648.

CONTENTS.

BONTEKOE VAN HOORN (Willem Ysbrantz). Journael van reyse, 1618-25. 10e stuck.
BROECKE (Peter van den). Wonderlijcke aenteyckeningh, op sijne reysen, 1605-30. 7e stuck.
CARON (François). Beschrijvinghe van Japan. 13e stuck.
HAGEN (Steven van der). Beschrijvinge van de tweede voyage, [1603-05]. 5e stuck.
HOUTMAN VAN ALCKMAER (Cornelis). Erste schipvaert der Hollanders naer Oost-Indien, 1595. 2e stuck.
L'HERMITE (Jacques) *and* SCHAPENHAM (G. H.) Journael vande nassausche vloot, 1623-26. 9e stuck.
MATELIEF (Cornelis, *de jonge*). Journael vande reyse, 1605-08. 6e stuck.
NECK (Jacob van). Verhael van de schip-vaert, 1598-1600. 3e stuck.
NOORT (Olivier van). Wonderlijcke voyagie, 1598-1601. 4e stuck.
PELSAERT (François). Ongeluckige voyagie van't schip Batavia, 1628-29. 11e stuck.
ROELOFSZ (Roelof). Kort verhael vande tweede voyagie onder Jacob van Neck, 1601-04. 4e stuck.

Hartgerts (Joost)—continued.

SCHOUTEN (Ioost). Beschrijvinghe van Siam. 13e stuck.

SCHOUTEN (Willem Cornelisz). Journael van de reyse, 1615-17. 8e stuck.

SPILBERGHEN (Joris van). Journael van de voyagie, 1601-04. 5e stuck.

——— Oost- en west-indische voyagie, 1615-17. 8e stuck.

TWIST (Johan van). Generale beschrijvinge van Indien. 12e stuck.

VEER (Gerrit de). Verhael van de erste schipvaert der hollandische schepen na Cathay ende China, 1594. 1e stuck.

WEERT (Sebald de). Verhael van t' gene seeckere vijf schepen, in't jaer 1598, nae de straet Magalanes. 3e stuck.

[*Note.*—With the above is bound, WEST-ZANEN (Willem van). Derde zee-getogt na de Oost-Indien, onder Iacob Heemskerk, 1601-04; though not belonging to the Hartgerts collection].

Hartley (Cecil B.) The gentleman's book of etiquette, and manual of politeness; being a complete guide for a gentleman's conduct in all his relations towards society. From the best french, english, and american authorities. 332 pp. 12°. *Philadelphia, G. G. Evans*, 1860.

——— Heroes and patriots of the south; comprising lives of general Francis Marion, general William Moultrie, general Andrew Pickens, and governor John Rutledge. With sketches of other distinguished heroes and patriots who served in the revolutionary war in the southern states. 320 pp. 1 pl. 12°. *Philadelphia, G. G. Evans*, 1860.

——— The three mrs. Judsons, the celebrated female missionaries. A new edition. 419 pp. 2 portraits. 12°. *Philadelphia, G. G. Evans*, 1860.

Hartmann (Anton Theodor). Biblisch-asiatischer wegweiser zu Oluf Gerhard Tychsen oder wanderungen durch die merkwürdigsten gebiete der biblisch-asiatischen literatur, und den merkwürdigen beilagen. 1 p. l. cccviii, 114 pp. 8°. *Bremen, J. G. Heyse*, 1823.

Hartmann (Johann, *m. d.*) Praxis chymiatricæ: or the practise of chymistry. Augmented and enlarged by his son with considerable additions. Faithfully rendered into english. 2 p. l. 184 pp. 10 l. fol. *London, J. Starkey & T. Passinger*, 1670.

[*With* CROLL (Oswald). Bazilica chymica, 1670].

Hartmann (Moritz). Zeitlosen. Gedichte. xi, 336 pp. 12°. *Braunschweig, F. Vieweg & sohn*, 1858. S.

Hartmann (Theodore). Charity Green, or the varieties of love. 601 pp. 12°. *New York, J. W. Norton*. 1859.

Hartshorne (Richard T. *editor*). *See* **American Lloyd's register.**

31

Hartstonge (Matthew Weld). Minstrelsy of Erin, or poems lyrical, pastoral and descriptive. vii, 198 pp. 16°. *Edinburgh, J. Ballantyne & co.* 1812.

Hartwig (George, *m. d.*) The polar and tropical worlds: a description of man and nature in the polar and equatorial regions of the globe. Edited, with additional chapters, by dr. A. H. Guernsey. xx, 17-761 pp. 8°. *Springfield*, [*Ms.*] *Bill, Nichols & co.* [1871].

Harvard college (*Cambridge, Mass.*) Annual reports of the president and treasurer of Harvard college. 1869-70 and 1870-71. 2 v. 8°. *Cambridge, university press*, 1871-72.

——— *Museum of comparative zoology.* Illustrated catalogue of the Museum of comparative zoology, at Harvard college. 8°. *Cambridge, printed for The museum of comparative zoology*, 1871. S.

CONTENTS.

no. 4. Deep-sea corals. By L. F. de Pourtalès.

Harvey (Joseph). An examination of the pelagian and arminian theory of moral agency as advocated by dr. Beecher in his "Views in theology." 1 p. l. 224 pp. 12°. *New York, E. Collier*, 1837.

Harvey (*Rev.* M. *of St. John's, Newfoundland*). Lectures, literary and biographical. viii, 512 pp. 12°. *Edinburgh, A. Elliot*, 1864.

Harwood (Edward, *d. d.*) A view of the various editions of the greek and roman classics, with remarks. 2d ed. corrected and enlarged. xxviii, 234 pp. 3 l. 12°. *London, T. Becket*, 1778.

——— The same. 4th ed. [Also], a view of the prices of the early editions of the classics at the late sale of the Pinellian library. 1 p. l. xxviii, 340 pp. 3 l. 12°. *London, G. G. J. & J. Robinson*, 1790.

Hasenmüller (Elias). Historia iesvitici ordinis, das ist: gründtliche vnd aussführliche beschreibung dess jesuitischen ordens, vnnd ihrer societet. Auss dem latein ins teudtsche gebracht, durch Melchiorem Leporinvm. *b. l.* 18 p. l. 660 pp. 4°. *Franckfurt am Mayn*, 1594.

Haskel (Daniel). A chronological view of the world; exhibiting the leading events of universal history; together with an account of the appearance of comets, and a complete view of the fall of meteoric stones, in all ages; a continuation to the present time. 278 pp. 12°. *New York, J. H. Colton*, 1853.

Haskins (*Rev.* David Greene). Selections from the scriptures of the old and new testaments for families and schools. xv, 401 pp. 12°. *Boston, C. P. Dutton & co.* 1861.

Haslam (John, *m. d.*) Illustrations of madness: exhibiting a singular case of insanity, [that of J. T. Mathews], and a no less remarkable difference in medical opinion. xi, 81 pp. 8°. *London, G. Hayden*, 1810.
[MEDICAL pamphlets, v. 3].

——— Sound mind; or, contributions to the natural history and physiology of the human intellect. xiii, 192 pp. 8°. *London, Longman*, 1819.
[MEDICAL pamphlets, v. 3].

Hassard (J. R. G.) Memoir of Fenelon. 12°. [*New York*, 1865].
[*In* FÉNELON (François de Salignac de La Mothe). Reflections and meditations, pp. 13-42].

Hasse (Hermann Gustav). Über die vereinigung der geistlichen und weltlichen obergewalt im römischen kirchenstaate. xx, 248 pp. 4°. *Haarlem, F. Bohn*, 1852.

Hasselt (*Dr.* A. W. M. van). Die lehre von dem tode und scheintode. Erster band. Allgemeiner theil. xii, 176 pp. 8°. *Braunschweig, F. Vieweg & sohn*, 1862. s.

Hastings (Anna). The Russel family. 201 pp. 16°. *New York, M. W. Wood*, 1857.

Hastings (Flora Elizabeth Rawdon). Poems by the lady Flora Hastings. Edited by her sister. xv, 282 pp. 8°. *Edinburgh, W. Blackwood & sons*, 1841.

Hastings (Horace L.) Clover hill stories. 192 pp. 18°. *Boston, H. L. Hastings*, 1866.

——— Pleasant hours with good children. Stories written and selected. 190 pp. 1 pl. 18°. *Boston, H. L. Hastings*, 1867.

——— Reasons for my hope. 128 pp. 12°. *Providence (R. I.) H. L. Hastings*, 1860.

——— Thessalonica; or, the model church. A sketch of primitive christianity. 168 pp. 12°. *New York, Rudd & Carleton*, 1861.

Hastings (Thomas). The presbyterian psalmodist; a collection of tunes adapted to the psalms and hymns of the presbyterian church in the United States of America. Approved by the general assembly. 368 pp. 4 l. obl. 8°. *Philadelphia, Presbyterian board of publication*, [1852]. s.

——— (*editor*). *See* **Musical** (The) miscellany.

——— *and* **Bradbury** (William B.) The New York choralist; a new and copious collection of psalm and hymn tunes, adapted to all the metres in general use. With a large

Hastings (Thomas)—continued.
variety of anthems and set pieces. 352 pp. obl. 8°. *New York, M. H. Newman & co.* 1847. s.

——— *and* **Mason** (Lowell). Spiritual songs, for social worship. 5th ed. 328 pp. 16°. *Utica, [N. Y.] G. Tracy*, 1837.

——— *and* **Patton** (William). The christian psalmist; or, Watts' psalms and hymns, with copious selections from other sources. The whole carefully revised and arranged, with directions for musical expression. By Th. Hastings and Wm. Patton. 626 pp. 16°. *New York, D. Fanshaw*, 1839.

Haswell (Charles H.) Book-keeping by double entry. In two parts. 2 v. 203 pp. 1 tab; 43 pp. 4°. *New York, D. Appleton & co.* 1871.

——— Journal [and ledger] of part ii, of a set of books "B," containing the record of a series of commercial and financial transactions, for a period of three months. 2 v. 1 p. l. 24 pp; 1 p. l. 13 pp. fol. *New York, D. Appleton & co.* 1871.

Haswell (James M.) The man of his time. Part 1. The story of Napoleon iii. By James M. Haswell. Part 2. The same story as told by popular caricaturists of the last thirty years. [Edited by J. C. Hotten]. 1 p. l. iv, 17-319 pp. 67 col. pl. 12°. *London, J. C. Hotten*, [1871].

Hatch (Cora L. V.) *See* **Tappan** (Cora L. V. Hatch).

Hatch (*Rev.* Reuben). Bible servitude reexamined; with special reference to proslavery interpretations and infidel objections. 284 pp. 12°. *Cincinnati, Applegate & co.* 1862.

Hatfield (*Rev.* Edwin F.) Patient continuance in well-doing; a memoir of Elihu W. Baldwin, d. d. With an introduction by Samuel Hanson Cox, d. d. 404 pp. 1 portrait. 12°. *New York, J. Leavitt*, 1843.

Hathaway (Levi). The narrative of Levi Hathaway, giving an account of his life, experience, call to the ministry of the gospel of the son of God, and travels as such to the present time. 140 pp. 12°. *Providence, author*, 1820.

Hattie (Aunt, *pseudon.*) *See* **Baker** (*Mrs.* H. N. Woods).

Hauchecorne (*L'abbé*). Abrégé latin de philosophie, avec une introduction et de notes françoises. 2 v. 8 p. l. lii, 290 pp. 1 l; 4 p. l. 279 pp. 8 pl. 16°. *Paris, l'auteur*, 1784.

Haudicquer de Blancourt (Jean *ou* François). De l'art de la verrerie, [etc.] 8 p. l. 602 pp. 3 l. 8 pl. 16°. *Paris, J. Jombert*, 1697.

Haughton (*Sir* Graves Chamney). Prodromus, or an enquiry into the first principles of reasoning; including an analysis of the human mind. 4 p. l. viii, 264 pp. 8°. *London, W. H. Allen & co.* 1839.

Haus- und landwirthschafts-kalender des landwirthschaftlichen vereins in Bayern auf das gemeine jahr 1871. 100 pp. 1 map. 4°. *München, M. Pössenbacher*, 1870. s.

Hautpoul (Anne Marie, *comtesse* de Beaufort d'). *See* **Beaufort d'Hautpoul.**

Hauxley (Edward). Navigation unvail'd; or, a new and complete system of navigation in all its branches. 2 v. viii, 464 pp. 1 pl; 2 p. l. 236, 199 pp. 4 pl. 8°. *London, author*, 1743.

Havana (*Cuba*). *Real colegio de Belen.* (*Observatorio magnético y meteorologico.*) Observaciones magnéticas y meteorológicas hechas por los alumnos del colegio de Belen. Año meteorologico de 30 noviembre de 1869 a 30 de noviembre de 1870. 8°. *Habana, imprenta y libreria religiosa*, 1870. s.

Haven (*Mrs.* Alice Bradley). Loss and gain; or, Margaret's home. 315 pp. 1 pl. 12°. *New York, D. Appleton & co.* 1860.

——— Out of debt, out of danger. By cousin Alice. [*pseudon.*] 251 pp. 3 pl. 16°. *New York, D. Appleton & co.* 1856.

——— A place for everything; and everything in its place. 215 pp. 4 pl. 16°. *New York, D. Appleton & co.* 1857.

Haven (*Rev.* Elias). Christ's agony improved. In a sermon preached at a public lecture in Attleborough, Jan. 5th, 1741, 2. 31 pp. 12°. *Boston, S. Kneeland and T. Green*, 1742.

Haven (*Rev.* Gilbert) *and* **Russell** (Thomas). Father Taylor, the sailor preacher. Incidents and anecdotes of rev. Edward T. Taylor. 445 pp. 2 pl. 2 portraits. 12°. *Boston, B. B. Russell*, 1872.

Haven (Marion). Joanna; or, learning to follow Jesus. 280 pp. 3 pl. 16°. *Boston, I. P. Warren*, 1871.

Haverhill (*Mass.*) Greenough, Jones & co.'s directory of the inhabitants, institutions, manufacturing establishments, societies, business, business firms, etc. in the city of Haverhill, for 1872, [also] a directory of Bradford. 8°. *Boston, Greenough Jones & co.* 1872.

Haweis (*Rev.* H. R.) Music and morals. 478 pp. 12°. *New York, Harper & brothers*, 1872.

Haweis (*Rev.* Thomas). The communicant's spiritual companion; or, an evangelical preparation for the Lord's supper. viii, 128 pp. 18°. *Cork, R. Tivy*, 1818.

Hawes (*Mrs.* A. H.) The grafted bud; a memoir of Angelica Irene Hawes. 102 pp. 1 pl. 16°. *New York, Redfield*, 1853.

Hawes (Joel, *d. d.*) Lectures to young men, on the formation of character, etc. 4th ed. With an additional lecture on reading. 172 pp. 18°. *Hartford, Cooke & co.* 1830.

——— The religion of the east, with impressions of foreign travel, 215 pp. 2 pl. 12°. *Hartford, Belknap & Hamersley*, 1845.

Hawes (Noyes P.) The United States spelling book, and english orthoepist. 2d ed. 251 pp. 16°. *Augusta, author*, 1826.

Hawes (Stephen). New testament manual: embracing an historical tabular view of the gospels; tables of the parables, discourses, and miracles of Christ; predictions in the old testament, with their fulfilment in the new; classification of the books of the new testament, with observations on each; biographical sketches, descriptions of places. 175 pp. 1 map. 16°. *Boston, Lee & Shepard*, 1871.

Hawes (William Post). Sporting scenes and sundry sketches; being the miscellaneous writings of J. Cypress, jr. [*pseudon.*] Edited by Frank Forester. [*pseudon.*] 2 v. vi, 241 pp. 2 pl; vi, 231 pp. 2 pl. 12°. *New York, Gould, Banks & co.* 1842.

Hawkins (Francis, *editor*). Youth's behaviour, or decency in conversation amongst men. Composed in french by grave persons, for the use and benefit of their youth. Now newly turned into english. With the addition of twenty-six new precepts. 8th impression. [Also], the first entrance of a youth in the university. 3 p. l. 70 pp. 25 l. 18°. *London, W. Lee*, 1663.

Hawkins (Francis Bisset, *m. d.*) Germany; the spirit of her history, literature, social condition, and national economy; illustrated by reference to her physical, moral, and political statistics, and by comparison with other countries. xx, 475 pp. 8°. *London, J. W. Parker*, 1838.

Hawkins (George). An essay on female education: containing an account of the present state of the boarding schools for young

Hawkins (George)—continued. ladies in England: in which the errors are pointed out, and a plan laid down for a complete reformation on a principle never before attempted. 3 p. l. 92 pp. 16°. *London, G. Wilkie*, 1781.

Hawkins (Henry). Partheneia sacra, or the mysteriovs and deliciovs garden of the sacred Parthenes; symbolically set forth and enriched with piovs devises and emblemes for the entertainment of devovt sovles. Contriued al to the honovr of the incomparable virgin Marie mother of God. By H. A. [*anon.*] Eng. title, 7 p. l. 271 pp. 12°. [*Rouen*]? *I. Covstvrier*, 1633.

[*Note.*—This work has been wrongly attributed to Henry Annesley].

Hawkins (*Sir* John, *pseudon.*) Probationary odes for the laureatship: with a preliminary discourse. xlvi, 131 pp. 8°. *London, J. Ridgway*, 1785.

[*Note.*—A travesty, in the name of Hawkins, directed chiefly against Thomas Wharton, jr. containing an original anon. ms. letter of presentation of the author, subscribed "The editor of The probationary odes"].

Hawkins (Lætitia Matilda). The countess and Gertrude; or, modes of discipline. 2d ed. 4 v. 8°. *London, F. C. & J. Rivington*, 1812.

Hawkins (*Sir* Richard). Observations, in his voyage into the South Sea. 1593. 3 p. l. 169 pp. 3 l. sm. fol. *London, for Iohn Iaggard*, 1622.

Hawks (J. M. *m. d.*) The Florida gazetteer, containing also a guide to and through the state; complete official and business directory; state and national statistics. 214 pp. 8°. *New Orleans, J. M. Hawks, Bronze pen office*, 1871.

Hawley (Z. K.) Congregationalism and methodism. 311 pp. 12°. *New York, Leavitt, Trow & co.* 1846.

Hawthorne (Nathaniel). Passages from the french and italian note-books of Nathaniel Hawthorne. 2 v. 1 p. l. 307 pp; 1 p. l. 306 pp. 12°. *Boston, J. R. Osgood & co.* 1872.

Hay (*Rev.* Alexander). Treatise on baptism, with a preface by the rev. dr. Shelton, and a letter recommendatory, by bishop Chase, with a sketch of the life of the author by rev. Charles Dresser. 131 pp. 18°. *New York, J. A. Sparks*, 1842.

Hay (John). Castilian days. 3 p. l. 414 pp. 16°. *Boston, J. R. Osgood & co.* 1871.

——— Jim Bludso of the Prairie Belle, and Little Breeches. With illustrations by S. Eytinge, jr. 23 pp. 8 pl. 12°. *Boston, J. R. Osgood & co.* 1871.

——— Pike county ballads and other pieces. 167 pp. 16°. *Boston, J. R. Osgood & co.* 1871.

Hayden (*Mrs.* C. A.) Carry Emerson; or, life at Cliftonville. 2d ed. 360 pp. 12°. *Boston, J. French & co.* 1856.

Hayden (Ferdinand Vanderveer). Preliminary report of the United States geological survey of Wyoming. *See* **United States.** (*Interior department*).

Hayden (*Rev.* William B.) Ten chapters on marriage: its nature, uses, duties, and final issues. vii, 160 pp. 16°. *Boston, W. Carter & brother*, 1863.

Hayes (Isaac I. *m. d.*) The land of desolation: being a personal narrative of observation and adventure in Greenland. 357 pp. 12°. *New York, Harper & brothers*, 1872.

Hayes (William). Portraits of rare and curious birds, with their descriptions, from the menagery of Osterly Park, in the county of Middlesex. By W[illiam] Hayes and family. 2 v. in 1. 3 p. l. 1–50 pp; 2 p. l. 51–101 pp. 100 col. pl. 4°. *London, R. Faulder*, 1794–99.

[*Note.*—The majority of the copies of this work have only 80 pl.]

Haygood (Atticus G.) *and* **McIntosh** (R. M.) The amaranth: a book of songs, hymns, anthems, chants, and concert pieces for the sunday-school; with occasional pieces for the choir. 160 pp. obl. 16°. *Nashville (Tenn.) A. H. Redford*, 1871.

Hayley (William). An essay on history; in three [poetical] epistles to Edward Gibbon, esq. with notes. 2d ed. 1 p. l. 123 pp. 12°. *Dublin, P. Byrne*, 1782.

Haym (Niccolà Francesco). Biblioteca italiana, o sia notizia de' libri rari nella lingua italiana. Annessovi tutto il libro [lettera] dell' eloquenza italiana di Giusto Fontanini. In questa seconda edizione aggiuntovi altri autori moderni. 11 p. l. 266 pp. 4°. *Venezia, F. Ricciardo*, 1736.

Hayne (Paul H.) Avolio; a legend of the island of Cos. With poems, lyrical, miscellaneous, and dramatic. xi, 244 pp. 12°. *Boston, Ticknor & Fields*, 1860.

——— Legends and lyrics. 183 pp. 12°. *Philadelphia, J. B. Lippincott & co.* 1872.

Haynes (D. C.) The baptist denomination: its history, doctrines, and ordinances. With

Haynes (D. C.)– continued. an introduction by John Dowling, d. d. 356 pp. 12°. *New York, Sheldon, Blakeman & co.* 1856.

Hayward (Aaron S.) Nature's laws in human life: an exposition of spiritualism; embracing the various opinions of extremists, pro and con; together with the author's experience. By the author of "Vital magnetic cure." [*anon.*] 308 pp. 12°. *Boston, W. White & co.* 1872.

Hayward (George, *m. d.*) Outlines of human physiology. 6, 13–217 pp. 12°. *Boston, Marsh, Capen & Lyon*, 1834.

Hayward (John). The book of religions. To which are added church and missionary statistics, together with biographical sketches. 432 pp. 12°. *Boston, J. Hayward*, 1842.

——— The New England gazetteer; containing descriptions of all the states, counties and towns in New England: also descriptions of the principal mountains, rivers, lakes, capes, bays, harbors, [etc.] Alphabetically arranged. 255 l. unp. 3 pl. 8°. *Boston, J. Hayward*, 1839.

Hazard (Rowland G.) Essay on language, and other papers. Edited by E. P. Peabody. 348 pp. 12°. *Boston, Phillips, Sampson & co.* 1857.

——— Freedom of mind in willing; or, every being that wills a creative first cause. 455 pp. 12°. *New York, D. Appleton & co.* 1864.

Hazeltine (Silas Wood). The traveller's dream and other poems. 150 pp. 1 l. 12°. *Boston, author*, 1860.

Hazen (Edward). The panorama of professions and trades. 320 pp. sm. 4°. *Philadelphia, M. Hunt & son*, [1836].

——— A practical grammar of the english language; or, an introduction to composition; in which sentences are classified into verbal forms and phrases. 240 pp. 12°. *New York, Huntington & Savage*, 1842.

Head (*Rev.* Nelson). Daily walk with wise men; or, religious exercises for every day in the year. xx, 782 pp. 12°. *New York, Harper & brothers*, 1861.

Headley (Joel T.) The Adirondack; or, life in the woods. New and enlarged ed. 8 p. l. 451 pp. 8 pl. 12°. *New York, C. Scribner*, 1869.

——— Mountain adventures in various parts of the world. Selected from the narratives of celebrated travellers. With an introduction and additions. vi, 356 pp. 26 pl. 16°. *New York, C. Scribner & co.* 1872.

Headrich (John). Arcana philosophica: or, chymical secrets, containing the noted and useful chymical medicines of dr. Wil. and Rich. Russel chymists. As also several curious chymical processes and spagerick preparations of natural things for the use of medicin; likewise four curious small treatises, by dr. Aurelius Philipus Theophrastus Paracelsus. 8 p. l. 128 pp. 4 l. 16°. *London, H. Hills*, 1697.

Heady (Morrison). The farmer boy, [Washington], and how he became commander-in-chief. By uncle Juvinell. [*pseudon.*] Edited by William M. Thayer. 321 pp. 3 pl. 12°. *Boston, Walker, Wise & co.* 1864.

Heaney (J. M. P.) A short treatise on the rosary; together with six reasons for being devout to the blessed virgin; also true devotion to her. 232 pp. 1 pl. 18°. *New York, D. & J. Sadlier & co.* 1863.

Heard (Franklin Fiske). Curiosities of the law reporters. 2 p. l. 212 pp. 12°. *Boston, Lee & Shepard*, 1871.

Hearn (William). The combination gameboard and its games. 1 p. l. 13 pp. 8°. *New York, Union printing co.* 1872.

Hearne (Thomas). Ductor historicus: or, a short system of universal history, and an introduction to the study of it. 2d ed. augmented. 2 v. Eng. title, 9 p. l. 494 pp. 6 l; 8 p. l. 405 pp. 7 l. 12°. *London, T. Childe*, 1704–5.

Heart (The) of the west: an american story. By an Illinoian. [*anon.*] 232 pp. 8°. *Chicago, Hand & Hart*, 1871.

Hearth and home. [Weekly]. Jan. 7 to Dec. 30, 1871. v. 3. fol. *New York, O. Judd & co.* 1871.

Heath (Benjamin). Notæ sive lectiones ad tragicorum græcorum veterum Aeschyli, Sophoclis, Euripidis, quæ supersunt dramata diperditorumque relliquias. 5 p. l. xiv, 505 pp. 4°. *Oxonii, e typographeo clarendoniano*, 1762.

[Imperfect: pp. 97–100 of Sophocles wanting].

Heath (Laban). Description of United States treasury notes, known as greenbacks; national bank notes; and the new treasury notes, series of 1869. [*anon.*] 36 pp. 1 l. 1 pl. 8°. *Boston, L. Heath & co.* [1871].

Heath (Nicholas, *bishop of Rochester*). The byble in englyshe. 1541. *See* **Bible.** (*English*).

Heath (*Sir* Robert). Maxims and rules of pleading; in actions real, personal and mixt, popular and penal, [etc. 1st ed.] 4 p. l. 332 pp. 14 l. 8°. *London, A. Roper*, 1694.

Heavenly hymns for heavy hearts. Compiled for the Presbyterian board of publication. 216 pp. 12°. *Philadelphia, Presbyterian board of publication*, [1864].

Hébrard (J.) De la librairie, son ancienne prospérité, son état actuel, causes de sa décadence, moyens de régénération. 61 pp. 8°. *Paris, J. Hébrard & cie.* 1847.

Hecht (P. Laurenz). Die lilie im garten Gottes. Ein unterrichts- und gebetbuch für katholische jungfrauen. 6e aufl. 381 pp. 4 pl. 32°. *Einsiedeln, New York & Cincinnati, C. & N. Benziger*, 1870.

Heckford (William). Characters or historical anecdotes of all the kings and queens of England, from William the conqueror to the present time. With an appendix, containing the characters of Oliver Cromwell, admiral Blake, duke of Marlborough, king of Prussia, Voltaire. 1 p.l. xvi, 272 pp. 16°. *London, G. G. J. & J. Robinson*, 1787.

Heemskerk (Jacob). Zee-getogt na de Oost-Indien. 1601–03. *See* **West-Zanen** (Willem van).

Heereboord (Adriaan). Ermeneia logica; seu synopseos logicæ burgersdicianæ explicatio, tum per notas tum per exempla. Editio nova accurata. Accedit ejusdem authoris praxis logica. 4 p. l. 311 pp. 18°. *Londini, R. Danielis*, 1662.

[*With* BURGERSDIJK (Frenz). Institutionum logicarum libri duo. 1651. Imperfect: pp. 167–170 wanting].

Heilbrunner (Jakob). Dæmonomania pistoriana, magica et cabalistica morborum curandorum ratio, a Ioanne Pistorio niddano, ex lacunis iudaicis ac gentilitiis hausta, post christianis propinata. Cum antidoto prophylactico. 26 p. l. 134 pp. 16°. *Lauingæ, typis palatinis*, 1601.

Heilig (George William). The gospel according to st. John, in greek. *See* **Bible.** (*Greek and english*).

Heiligen (Die) Gottes in ihren gebeten vollständiges andachts- und gebetbuch für katholische christen. Aus den schriften der heiligen: [etc.] Von einem priester der

Heiligen (Die) Gottes, etc.—continued. diözese Freiburg. [*anon.*] 432 pp. 18°. *Einsiedeln, New York & Cincinnati, K. & N. Benziger*, 1871.

Heine (Heinrich). Buch der lieder. viii, 261 pp. 18°. *Rotterdam, H. Nijgh*, 1863.

[HEINE's sämmtliche werke. Fünfter band].

——— [Poems. Translated by Julian Fane]. 12°. [*London, J. Murray*, 1872].

[*In* LYTTON (Robert Bulwer). Julian Fane. A memoir. 1872. pp. 70–93].

Heinsius (Daniel). In obitum v. illvstr. Ioseph Scaligeri. Ivl. Cæs. [Scaligeri] a Bvrden f[ilii], eruditorum principis orationes duæ. Accedunt Epicedia eiusdem & aliorum: effigies item ac monumentum Scaligeri. 3 p. l. 100 pp. 3 pl. 4°. *Lugd. Bat. apud L. Elzeuirium & A. Cloncquium*, 1609.

——— Lavs pedicvli, ad conscriptos mendicorum patres. 18°. [*Lugd. Batavorum*, 1644].

[*In* DISSERTATIONVM ludicrarvm et amœnitatvm scriptores varij, pp. 383–399].

——— Thyrsis, [an eclogue]. Written in latin. [Translated into english, by John Rooke]. 8°. [*London*, 1725].

[ROOKE (John). Select translations. Part 2. pp. 32–43. ed. 1726].

Heiress (The) of Haughton. *See* **Marsh-Caldwell** (*Mrs.* Anne).

Heis (Eduard, *editor*). *See* **Wöchentliche** unterhaltungen, etc.

Heiton (John). The castes of Edinburgh. 2d ed. enlarged. vii, 263 pp. 16°. *Edinburgh, J. Menzies*, 1860.

Helfenstein (*Rev.* J. C. Albertus). A collection of choice sermons. Translated from the german by I. Daniel Rupp. xi, 261 pp. 12°. *Carlisle, C. Helfenstein*, 1832.

Helffenstein (Samuel, *d. d.*) The doctrines of divine revelation, as taught in the holy scriptures, exhibited, illustrated, and vindicated. Designed for the use of christians generally, and for young men, preparing for the gospel ministry, in particular. 394 pp. 1 portrait. 8°. *Philadelphia, J. Kay, jr. & brother*, 1842.

Heliodorus. Æthiopicorum libri decem. Graece et latine [interprete Warschewiczkio]. 1 v. in 2. xxxiv, 267 pp; 416 pp. 8°. *Argentorati*, [1798].

[MITSCHERLICH (C. W.) Scriptores erotici græci, v. 2–3].

Hellenbroek (Abraham). De euangelische Jesaia. *See* **Bible.** (*Dutch*).

Helmers (Jan Frederik). Gedichten. 3de druk. 3 v. 16°. *Rotterdam, J. Immerzeel, jr.* 1822–3.

Helmers (Jan Frederik)—continued.

——— De hollandsche natie, in zes zangen. 6e druk. 2 p. l. 147 pp. 16°. *Gravenhage, weduwe J. Allart & comp.* 1822.

——— Nagelaten gedichten. 2 v. 2 p. l. viii, 202 pp. 1 portrait; xxiv, 168 pp. 8°. *Haarlem, F. Bohn,* 1814–15.

Helmont (Johann Baptist van). Deliramenta catarrhi: or, the incongruities, impossibilities, and absurdities couched under the vulgar opinion of defluxions. The translator and paraphrast dr. Charleton. 6 p. l. 75 pp. 4°. *London, E. G. for W. Lee,* 1650.

[*With his* Ternary of paradoxes. *London,* 1650. Imperfect: pp. 73–74 mutilated].

——— Oriatrike or, physick refined. The common errors therein refuted, and the whole art reformed and rectified: [etc.] Rendered into english; by J. C. sometime of Oxon. 22 p. l. 1161 pp. 11 l. fol. *London, L. Loyd,* 1662.

——— A ternary of paradoxes. The magnetick cure of wounds, nativity of tartar in wine, image of God in man. Translated, illustrated, and ampliated by Walter Charleton. [2d ed.] Eng. title, 25 p. l. 147 pp. 4°. *London, J. Flesher for W. Lee,* 1650.

Helper (Hinton Rowan). Noonday exigencies in America. (With an appendix, to be read in advance of the text, in the perusal of these pages, by all such inattentive persons as may have been, some years ago, in the habit of reading with eyes askant). 211 pp. 12°. *New York, Bible brothers,* 1871.

Helps (Arthur). Conversations on war and general culture. By the author of "Friends in council." [*anon.*] 2 p. l. 306 pp. 12°. *London, Smith, Elder & co.* 1871.

——— Thoughts upon government. viii, 245 pp. 8°. *Boston, Roberts brothers,* 1872.

Helsham (Richard, *m. d.*) A course of lectures in natural philosophy. Published by Bryan Robinson, m. d. 3d ed. x, 404 pp. 11 pl. 8°. *London, J. Nourse,* 1755.

Hemans (Felicia Dorothea). The poetical works of mrs. Felicia Hemans. With a critical preface. xx, 49–361 pp. 1 portrait. 8°. *Philadelphia, T. T. Ash,* 1836.

Hemmenway (Moses, *d. d.*) A discourse at Wells, 22 Feb. 1800, [on] the death of George Washington. 16 pp. 8°. *Portsmouth (N. H.) C. Peirce,* 1800.

[Hazard pamphlets, v. 64].

Hemming (Nicolaus). Libellvs de coniugio, repudio, & diuortio. In gratiam fratrvm, qvi iudices cavsarvm matrimonialium in regnis Dania & Noruegia constituti sunt. 1 p.l. 231 pp. 15 l. 16°. *Lipsiæ, J. Steiman,* 1581.

Henck (E. C.) Spirit voices: odes, dictated by spirits of the second sphere, for the use of harmonial circles. 2d ed. 144 pp. 18°. *Philadelphia, G. D. Henck,* 1854.

Henderson (J.) The horsemen's guide and farrier, the external and internal structure of the horse, and the diseases and lameness to which he is liable in the domesticated condition, [etc.] 166 pp. sq. 16°. *Albion (N. Y.) A. Bruner,* 1868.

Hengstenberg (Ernst Wilhelm). Egypt and the books of Moses, or the books of Moses illustrated by the monuments of Egypt; with an appendix. From the german by R. D. C. Robbins. xii, 300 pp. 12°. *Andover, Allen, Morrill & Wardwell,* 1843.

Hénin de Cuvillers (Étienne Félix, *baron* d'). Le magnétisme éclairé, ou introduction aux archives du magnétisme animal. 2 p. l. 252 pp. 8°. *Paris, Barrois l'aîné,* 1820.

Henkel (*Rev.* Paul). Church hymn book; consisting of hymns and psalms, original and selected. 2d ed. xiv, 527 pp. 18°. *New-market (Va.) Solomon Henkel,* 1838.

Henkel (*Professor* —). Waaren-lexicon für droguisten, apotheker und kaufleute, enthaltend eine specielle characteristik der gangbaren droguen, colonialwaaren, chemikalien und farbwaaren. vi, 478 pp. 8°. *Stuttgart, G. Weise,* 1869.

Henkle (*Rev.* M. M.) The life of Henry Bidleman Bascom, d. d. ll. d. late bishop of the methodist episcopal church south. 408 pp. 1 portrait. 12°. *Louisville, Morton & Griswold,* 1854.

Hennepin (Louis). Relacion de un pais que nuevamente se ha descubierto en la America Septentrional de mas estendido que es la Europa. Saca à luz en Castellano, d. Sebastian Fernandez de Medrano. [*anon.*] 4 p. l. 86 pp. 16°. *Brusselas, L. Marchant,* 1699.

Hennequin (Joseph François Gabriel). Dictionnaire de maximes, ou choix de maximes, pensées, sentences, réflexions et définitions, extraites des moralistes et des écrivains tant anciens que modernes. 3 p. l. 520 pp. 8°. *Paris, A. J. Kilian,* 1828.

Hennessy (W. J. *artist*). Edwin Booth in twelve dramatic characters. *See* **Winter** (William).

Hennet (Albert Joseph Ulpien). Théorie du crédit public. viii, 587 pp. 4°. *Paris, Testu & co.* 1816.

Henniker (*Sir* Frederick). Notes, during a visit to Egypt, Nubia, the Oasis Bœris, Mount Sinai, and Jerusalem. 2d ed. vii, 352 pp. 3 pl. 8°. *London, J. Murray*, 1824.

Henry (Caleb S. *d. d.*) Considerations on some of the elements and conditions of social welfare and human progress. Being academic and occasional discourses and other pieces. x, 415 pp. 12°. *New York, D. Appleton & co.* 1861.

Henry (James P.) Resources of the state of Arkansas, with description of counties, railroads, mines, and the city of Little Rock. 134 pp. 1 l. 8°. *Little Rock (Ark.) Price & McClure*, 1872.

Henry (John Joseph). Campaign against Quebec; being an accurate and interesting account of the hardships and sufferings of that band of heroes who traversed the wilderness, by the route of the Kennebec, and Chaudiere river, to Quebec, in the year 1775. Revised ed. 212 pp. 16°. *Watertown (N. Y.) Knowlton & Rice*, 1844.

Henry (*Rev.* Matthew). The communicant's companion; or, instructions and helps for the right receiving of the Lord's supper. 303 pp. 16°. *Carlisle (Pa.) J. McCarrell*, 1826.

——— The life of the rev. Philip Henry. Abridged. 258 pp. 18°. *Philadelphia, Presbyterian board of publication*, 1840.

Henry (Sarepta Irish). Victoria: with other poems. 186 pp. 12°. *Cincinnati, Poe & Hitchcock*, 1865.

Henry (Thomas Charlton, *d. d.*) Letters to an anxious inquirer, designed to relieve the difficulties of a friend under serious impressions. With a biographical sketch of the author. 4th ed. 309 pp. 1 pl. 18°. *Philadelphia, Presbyterian board of publication*, [1840].

Henry *and* **Frances.** A series of genuine letters between Henry and Frances. *See* **Griffith** (Richard *and* Elizabeth).

Henry Morris; or, living for an object. [*anon.*] 193 pp. 4 pl. 16°. *Philadelphia, American sunday-school union*, [1856].

Henshaw (John Prentiss Kewley, *d. d.*) An inquiry into the meaning of the prophecies relating to the second advent of our lord Jesus Christ; in a course of lectures, delivered in St. Peter's church, Baltimore. 228 pp. 12°. *Baltimore, D. Brunner*, 1842.

Henshaw (J. P. K. *d. d.*)—continued.

——— Memoir of the life of the rt. rev. Richard Channing Moore, d. d. bishop of the protestant episcopal church in the diocese of Virginia. Accompanied by a selection of the sermons of the late bishop. 1 p. l. x, 9–503 pp. 1 portrait. 8°. *Philadelphia, W. Stavely & co.* 1843.

——— Theology for the people: in a series of discourses on the catechism of the protestant episcopal church. 576 pp. 1 portrait. 8°. *Baltimore, D. Brunner*, 1840.

Hentz (*Mrs.* Caroline Lee). Aunt Patty's scrap-bag. With illustrations by Darley. 2 p. l. 23–322 pp. 6 pl. 12°. *Philadelphia, T. B. Peterson & bros.* [1872].

——— The banished son; and other stories of the heart. 2 p. l. 17–277 pp. 12°. *Philadelphia, T. B. Peterson & brothers*, [1870].

Hentz (Nicholas Marcellus). A manual of french phrases and french conversations: adapted to Wanostrocht's grammar. 154 pp. 12°. *Boston, Richardson & Lord*, 1822.

Hephæstion *alexandrinus.* *Εγχειριδιον περι μετρων και ποιηματος. Εις το αυτο σχολια.* Enchiridion de metris et poemate. Cum scholiis antiquis et animadversionibus Joannis Cornelii de Pauw. [Greek text with latin scholia]. 2 p. l. 188 pp. 4 l. 4°. *Trajecti ad Rhenum, apud M. L. Charlois*, 1726.

Heraclides *ponticus.* *Ἡρακλειδου του ποντικου ἀλληγοριαι ὁμηρικαι.* Heraclidis pontici allegoriæ Homeri. [Græce et latine]. 8°. [*Amstelaedami, apud H. Wetstenium*, 1688].

[*In* Gale (Thomas). Opuscula mythologica, pp. 405–498.

Note.—This work was probably, some say certainly, not written by Heraclides, although commonly attributed to him].

Heraclitus. *Ἡρακλειτου περι ἀπιστων.* Heracliti de incredibilibus. [Græce et latine Leone Allatio interprete]. 8°. [*Amstelædami, apud H. Wetstenium*, 1688].

[*In* Gale (Thomas). Opuscula mythologica, pp. 67–82].

Herald (The) of health and journal of physical culture, advocates higher type of manhood—physically, intellectually, and morally. [1870]. Old series, v. 49–50. New series, v. 15–16. M. L. Holbrook, m. d. editor. 8°. *New York, Wood & Holbrook*, 1870.

Herberay (Nicolas de, *seigneur des Essarts*). The most excellent history of the valiant, and renowned knight, Donflores of Greece, knight of the swans, second sonne to Esplandran, emperour of Constantinople. Be-

Herberay (Nicolas de)—continued. ing, a supplement to Amadis de Gaule. Translated into english by W. P. 2 p. l. 62 pp. 4°. *London,* [*for R. I.* 1664].
[Title-page slightly imperfect].

Herbert (Charles). Italy and italian literature. xx, 376 pp. 1 pl. 12°. *London, Sherwood, Gilbert & Piper,* 1835.

Herbert (Henry, *10th earl of Pembroke*). Military equitation: or, a method of breaking horses, and teaching soldiers to ride. 4th ed. 4 p. l. 140 pp. 17 pl. sm. 4°. *London, G. & T. Wilkie,* 1793.

Herbert (Henry William). Frank Forrester's horse and horsemanship of the United States and british provinces of North America. Revised, corrected, enlarged, and continued to 1871, by S. D. and B. G. Bruce. 2 v. 657 pp. 5 l. 12 pl; 601 pp. 16 pl. 8°. *New York, G. E. Woodward,* 1871.

——— Wager of battle; a tale of saxon slavery in Sherwood forest. 336 pp. 12°. *New York, Mason brothers,* 1855.

Herbert (Thomas). A relation of some yeares travaile, begvnne anno 1626. Into Afrique and the greater Asia. Of their religion, language, habit, discent, ceremonies, and other matters concerning them. Together with the proceedings and death of the three late ambassadours: as also the two great monarchs, the king of Persia, and the Great Mogol. Eng. title, 4 p. l. 225 pp. 7 l. fol. *London, W. Stansby,* 1634.

Herder (Ferdinand von). Bemerkungen über die wichtigsten bäume, sträucher und stauden des k. botanischen gartens in St. Petersburg, und der St. Petersburger flora, mit rücksicht auf ihre periodische entwicklung. 1 p. l. 134 pp. 8°. *Moskau, buchdruckerei der k. universität,* 1865. S.
[*With his* Mittheilungen].

——— Mittheilungen über die periodische entwicklung der pflanzen im freien lande des k. botanischen gartens zu St. Petersburg, nebst notizen aus der Petersburger flora. 2 parts in 1 v. 1 p. l. 351 pp; 1 p. l. 8 pp. 13 tab. 8°. *Moskau, buchdruckerei der k. universität,* 1864-66. S.

Herder (Johann Gottlieb). Idées sur la philosophie de l'histoire de l'humanité. Traduit de l'allemand et précédé d'une introduction par Edgar Quinet. 3 v. 8°. *Paris, F. G. Levrault,* 1827-28.

Herdman (John). An essay on the causes and phenomena of animal life. xii, 236 pp. 8°. *Edinburgh, W. Creech,* [*etc.*] 1795.

Hereby (Nicholas de, *m. de Essule*). History of Donflores. *See* **Herberay** (Nicolas de, *seigneur des Essarts*).

Heresbach (Conrad). The whole art and trade of hvsbandry, contained in foure bookes. [*anon.*] Enlarged by Barnaby Googe. *b. l.* 11 p. l. 182 l. numb. sm. 4°. *London, T. S. for R. Moore,* 1614.
[Imperfect: wanting all after l. 182].

Hering (Constantine, *m. d.*) C. Hering's domestic physician. Third american edition, comprising the former editions of the homœopathist, or domestic physician, revised, with additions from the author's manuscript of the fifth german edition, together with the additions of drs. Goullon, Gross & Stapf, to which is added a chapter on the diseases of women. xvi pp. 4 l. 412 pp. 2 tab. 1 portrait. 16°. *Philadelphia,* 1845.

Hermas. The shepherd of st. Hermas. 12°. [*Oxford,* 1840].
[*In* WAKE (William). The genuine epistles of the apostolical fathers, pp. 263-364].

Hermes *trismegistus.* Asclepius dialogus & philosophia magna. 18°. [*Hambvrgi,* 1593].
[*In* PATRIZZI (Francesco). Magia philosophica, 1593. pp. 45-253].

——— Hermetis trismegisti gülden tractätlein, von der composition des steins der weisen. 24 pp. 16°. *Hamburg, J. Naumann & G. Wolff,* 1674.
[*In* ALCHYMISTISCH sieben-gestirn. 1675. pp. 1-24].

——— Hermes Mercurius trismegistus; his divine pymander. Also, the asiatic mystery, the smaragdine table and the song of Brahm. Edited by Paschal Beverly Randolph. 148 pp. 8°. *Boston, Rosicrucian publishing company,* 1871.

——— La table d'esmeravde. Περι χημειας. [Avec un petit commentaire de l'Hortvlain]. 18°. [*Lyon, M. Bonhomme,* 1557].
[*In* BACON (Roger). Le miroir d'alqvimie. 1557. pp. 34-56].

——— The same. La table d'émeraude, avec le commentaire de l'Hortulain. Les sept chapitres attribuéz à Hermes. 12°. [*Paris, A. Cailleau,* 1741].
[*In* SALMON (William). Bibliothèque des philosophes chimiques. 1741. v. 1. pp. 1-76].

Hermitage (The), or views of life and manners. A poem, with notes. [*anon.*] 3 p. l. 102 pp. 16°. *London, Longman,* 1809.

Herodes Atticus (Tiberius Claudius). Herodis Attici qvæ svpersvnt adnotationibvs illvstravit Raphael Fiorillo. Præfixa est epistola Chr. G. Heynii ad avctorem. 1 p. l. xxvi, 216 pp. 8°. *Lipsiæ, svmtibvs C. Fritsch,* 1801.

Herodianus. Herodiani historiæ de imperio post Marcvm, vel de svis temporibvs, e græce translatæ, Angelo Politiano interprete. [1493]. 182 pp. 12°. *Parisiis, ex officina Rob. Stephani,* 1544.
[*Note.*—Italian type].

Herodotus. Herodıtı hıstorıcı ıncıpıt. Laurentıı Vall'. conuersıo de Greco ın Latınum. 245 l. fol. *Rome, ın domo Petrı de Maxımıs,* 1475.
[*Note.*—This is the second impression of Valla's version of Herodotus. Dibdin says: "It is supposed to have been executed by Pannartz alone, and is among the latest productions 'in domo Petri Maximis.'" 38 lines to a page. The letter i rarely has a dot. No pagination, signature, or catchwords].

——— The same. Clio. 1. Terpsichore, 5. 8°. *Oxonii,* 1835.
[*In* HISTORIA græca, ed. 2a, pp. 1–136].

Heroes and hunters of the west; comprising sketches and adventures of Boone, Kenton, Brady, Logan, Whetzel, Fleehart, Hughes, Johnston, etc. [*anon.*] 300 pp. 12°. *Philadelphia, H. C. Peck & T. Bliss,* 1853.

Herold (Louis Joseph Ferdinand). Zampa, an opera, in three acts. [Libretto, without music]. 46 pp. 8°. *New York, G. F. Nesbitt & co.* 1872.
[PAREPA-ROSA grand english opera].

Herrera (Christoval Perez de). *See* **Perez de Herrera.**

Herrera (Fernando de). Rimas. Por don Ramon Fernandez. [Libro 1–2]. 2 v. 1 p. l. 89, 231 pp; 1 p. l. 253 pp. 16°. *Madrid, la imprenta real,* 1786.
[*Note.*—v. 4–5 of Herrera's collected works].

Herrey (Robert F.) Two right profitable and fruitfull concordances, or large and ample tables alphabeticall. The first conteyning the interpretation of the hebrue, caldean, greeke, and latine wordes and names throughout the whole bible: and the second comprehending all such other principall wordes and matters, as concerne the sense and meaning of the scriptures. *b. l.* 82 l. 4°. *London, deputies of Christopher Barker,* [*about* 1580]?
[*With* BIBLE. (*English*). Genevan version. *London, C. Barker,* [*about* 1580].

——— The same. 92 l. 4°. *b. l.* *London, Christopher Barker,* [1584].
[*With* BIBLE. (*English*). Genevan version. *London, C. Barker,* 1584].

——— The same. 82 l. 4°. *London, R. Barker,* 1613.
[*With* BIBLE. (*English*). Genevan version. *London, R. Barker,* 1614].

Herrich-Schäffer (Gottlieb August). Nomenclator entomologicus. Verzeichniss der

Herrich-Schäffer (G. A.)—continued.
europäischen insecten; zur erleichterung des tauschverkehrs mit preisen versehen. 2 v. in 1. iv, 116 pp; viii, 244 pp. 8 pl. 16°. *Regensburg, F. Pustet,* 1835–40. s.

Herrmann (Carl). Bibliotheca erfurtina. Erfurt in seinen geschichts- und bild-werken. xii, 500 pp. 8°. *Erfurt, selbstverlag des verfassers,* 1863.

Herron (James P.) American grammar: adapted to the national language of the United States; with an accompanying panorama. 312 pp. 12°. *Columbus (O.) Osgood & Pearce,* 1859.
[Imperfect: panorama wanting].

Hersee (William). Poems. 3d ed. To which are added a tribute of gratitude to the memory of the late William Hayley, esq. and several other pieces. xvii, 332 pp. 8°. *London, T. Cadell,* 1822.
[*Note.*—pp. 237–238 and 247–248 wanting].

Hertslet (Edward). A complete collection of the treaties and conventions, and reciprocal regulations at present subsisting between Great Britain and foreign powers; and of the laws, decrees, orders in council, &c. concerning the same; so far as they relate to commerce and navigation, the slave-trade, post-office communications, copyright, &c. and to the privileges and interests of the high contracting parties. Compiled from authentic documents. v. 11–12. With an index of subjects to the entire series. 8°. *London, Butterworths,* 1864–71.

Hertz (Wilhelm). Der practische landschaftsgärtner. Eine einleitung zur anlegung oder verschönerung von gärten verschiedener grösse. 1 p. l. 146 pp. 24 (21 col.) pl. 8°. *Stuttgart, Hoffmann,* 1840. s.

Hervey (*Rev.* Henry). Discourses to different ages and classes. 112 pp. sq. 16°. *Springfield (O.) office of the "Presbyterian of the west,"* 1845.

——— A series of lectures on old testament miracles. 301 pp. 1 l. 16°. *Springfield (O.) Presbyterian of the west,* 1844.

Hervey (*Rev.* James). Letters to the right honourable lady Frances Shirley. 4 p. l. 320 pp. 16°. *London, J. Rivington, jun. for J. F. & C. Rivington,* 1782.

——— Meditations and contemplations. 2 v. in 1. 310 pp. 16°. *Philadelphia, B. & T. Kite,* 1808–9.

Hervey (Thomas K.) The amaranth; a miscellany of original prose and verse. Con-

Hervey (Thomas K.)—continued. tributed by distinguished writers, and edited by T. K. Hervey. Eng. title, xv, 96 pp. 12 pl. fol. *London, A. H. Baily & co.* 1839.

Herzog (J. J. *editor*). The protestant theological and ecclesiastical encyclopedia: being a condensed translation of Herzog's real encyclopedia. By rev. J. H. A. Bomberger, assisted by distinguished theologians. Parts 1-6 (752 pp.) 8°. *Philadelphia, Lindsay & Blakiston,* 1856-58. s.
[Parts 7 et seq. wanting].

Hesekiel (John George Louis). The life of Bismarck, private and political; with descriptive notices of his ancestry. Translated and edited, with introduction, notes, and appendices, by Kenneth R. H. Mackenzie. 491 pp. 11 pl. 4 portraits. 8°. *New York, Harper & brothers,* 1870.

Hesiodus. La théogonie, Les travaux et les jours, et Le bouclier d'Hercule. Traduction de m. Bignan. 12°. [*Paris,* 1841].
[*In* MARTIN (Louis Aimé). Petits poëmes grecs. 1841. pp. 17-96].

Heude (*Lieut.* William). A voyage up the persian gulf, and a journey overland from India to England, in 1817. x, 252 pp. 4 pl. 8°. *London, Longman,* 1819.

Heustis (Jabez Wiggins, *m. d.*) Medical facts and inquiries, respecting the causes, nature, prevention, and cure of fever: more expressly in relation to the endemic fevers of summer and autumn in the southern states. With a history of the bilious remitting fever of Alabama, as it appeared in 1821-2. 1 p. l. 442 pp. 8°. *Cahawba,* [*Ala.*] *W. B. Allen,* 1825.

Hey (Richard, *ll. d.*) Three dissertations; on the pernicious effects of gaming, on duelling, and on suicide. First published in 1783, 1784, 1785. Prize essays. Revised and corrected, in 1811, by the author. xxi, 269 pp. 8°. *Cambridge, J. Smith,* 1812.

Heydon (*Sir* Christopher). An astrological discourse with mathematical demonstrations, proving the powerful and harmonical influence of the planets and fixed stars upon elementary bodies, in justification of the validity of astrology. With an astrological judgment upon the great conjunction of Saturn & Jupiter, 1603. Published by N. Fiske. 8 p. l. 111 pp. 18°. *London, J. Macock for N. Brooks,* 1650.

Heyl (Lewis). United States duties on imports, 1871. *See* **United States.** *Treasury department.*

Heylin (Peter). Bibliotheca regia, or, the royal library, containing a collection of such of the papers of his late maiesty king Charls, the second monarch of Great Britain, as have escaped the wrack and ruines of these times. Not extant in the Reliquiæ carolinæ, or the Exact collection of Edward Husbands. 2 books in 1 v. The first relating to the concernments of the church, the second unto those of the civil state. 7 p. l. 600 pp. 1 l. 1 pl. 12°. *London, H. Seile,* 1659.

——— Cosmographie in foure bookes. Contayning the chorographie and historie of the whole world, and all the principall kingdomes, provinces, seas, and isles, thereof. 3d [6th] ed. corrected and inlarged by the author. Eng. title, 7 p. l. 1110 (paged 1095) pp. 6 l. 4 maps. fol. *London, P. Chetwind,* 1670.
[*Note.*—The title-pages of the separate books are dated from 1662-67].

Heywood *or* **Haywood** (*Mrs.* Eliza). A spy on the conjurer. Or, a collection of surprising and diverting stories, with merry and ingenious letters. By way of memoirs of the famous mr. Duncan Campbell. 7 p. l. 259 pp. 8°. *London, W. Ellis,* [*etc.*] 1725.

Heywood (Elizabeth). The grocer's boy; or, the young american who did not want to be extraordinary. 192 pp. 4 pl. 16°. *New York, Carlton & Lanahan,* [1871].

Heywood (James). The recommendations of the Oxford university commissioners, with selections from their report; and a history of the university subscription tests, including notices of the university and collegiate visitations. xxxvi, 559 pp. 1 tab. 8°. *London, Longman, Brown, Green & Longmans,* 1853.

Heywood (John). A mery playe betwene the pardoner and the frere the curate and neybour Pratte. Imprynted by Wyllyam Rastell, 1533. *b. l.* 8 l. unp. sm. fol. [*London*], *reprinted by G. Smeeton,* [1819]?

——— Of gentylnes and nobylyte. A [poetical] dyaloge betwen the marchaūt, the knyght, and the plowman, dysputyng who is a verey gentylman, and who is a noble man, and how men shuld come to auctoryte. [*At end*]: Iohēs Rastell me fieri fecit [1535]. Reprint. 51 pp. 4°. [*n. p. about* 1820].
[*Note.*—Only 23 copies printed].

Heywood (J. C.) How will it end? A romance. 301 pp. 12°. *Philadelphia, J. B. Lippincott & co.* 1872.

Heywood (Mark, *pseudon?*) Mr. Christopher Katydid (of Casconia). A tale. Edited by Mark Heywood. 2 v. xxiv, 318 pp; viii, 323 pp. 8°. *London, Saunders, Otley & co.* 1864.

Heywood (*Rev.* Oliver). The whole works of the rev. Oliver Heywood, now first collected, including some tracts extremely scarce, and others from unpublished manuscripts: with memoirs of his life. 5 v. 8°. *Idle, J. Vint, for editor*, 1825-27.

CONTENTS.

v. 1. Life of mr. O. Heywood, [by rev. Richard Slate]. Extracts from his diary, soliloquies, letters, etc. Life of mr. N. Heywood. Life of mr. Angier. Lives of mr. O. H.'s relatives.
v. 2. Heart treasure. Sure mercies of David.
v. 3. Closet prayer. Intercession of Christ. Life in God's favour. Israel's lamentation after the Lord. Job's appeal.
v. 4. Baptismal bonds. A family altar. The best entail. Heavenly converse.
v. 5. A new creature. The two worlds. Meetness for heaven. The general assembly. Original sermons. Youth's monitor.

Heywood (Thomas). The king in the country. A dramatic piece, in two acts. [Adapted from Heywood's King Edward the fourth, by F. G. Waldron]. 28 pp. 8°. *London, for the editor*, 1789.

[*In* WALDRON (F. G.) Literary museum. *London*, 1792].

Hibbard (*Rev.* Freeborn G.) Christian baptism: its mode, obligation, import, and relative order. 218 pp. 12°. *New-York, G. Lane & P. P. Sandford*, 1841.

——— A treatise on infant baptism. 1 p. l. 328 pp. 12°. *New York, G. Lane & P. P. Sandford*, 1843.

Hibbard (John B. *m. d.*) American practical physician. A condensed treatment with new principles for acute, chronic, and surgical diseases, by clinical experience of more than twenty-five years, without poisons. 204 pp. 3 pl. 1 portrait. 12°. *New York, P. B. Bergen & Tripp*, 1860.

Hickman (Edwin C.) Scraps of poetry and prose. 200 pp. 18°. *Lexington (Ky.) A. W. Elder*, 1854.

Hickman (William A.) Brigham's destroying angel: being the life, confession, and startling disclosures of the notorious Bill Hickman, the danite chief of Utah. Written by himself, with explanatory notes by J. H. Beadle. 219 pp. 1 portrait. 16°. *New York, G. A. Crofutt*, 1872.

Hickok (Laurens P. *d. d.*) Creator and creation: or, the knowledge in the reason of God and his work. 360 pp. 8°. *Boston, Lee & Shepard*, 1872.

Hickok (Laurens P. *d. d*)—continued.

——— Rational psychology; or, the subjective idea and objective law of all intelligence. A new and revised edition. 343 pp. 8°. *New York, Ivison, Phinney & co.* 1861.

Hicks (Elias *and* Edward). Sermons delivered in friends' meetings, New York, in 5th month, 1825. Taken in short-hand, by L. H. Clarke, and M. T. C. Gould. 138 pp. 8°. *New-York, J. V. Seaman*, 1825.

Hicks (*Rev.* George). Spinoza reviv'd: or, a treatise, proving the book, entitled, The rights of the christian church, etc. (in the most notorious parts of it) to be the same with Spinoza's Rights of the christian clergy, etc. And that both of them are grounded upon downright atheism. [Also], a preliminary discourse relating to the same books. 36 p. l. 179 pp. 8°. *London, J. Morphew*, 1709.

Hierocles *alexandrinus.* Commentarius in aurea Pythagoreorum carmina. Joan. Curterio interprete. [Græce et latine]. 16 p. l. 433 pp. 1 l. 18°. *London, J. R. for J. Williams*, 1673.

——— Hierocles de providentia & fato: una cum fragmentis ejusdem; et Lilii Gyraldi interpretatione symbolorum Pythagoræ; notisque Merici Casauboni ad commentarium Hieroclis in aurea carmina. [Græce et latine]. 32 p. l. 271 pp. 18°. *London, J. R. for J. Williams*, 1673.

[*With his* Commentarius in aurea carmina. *London*, 1673].

Hieronymus (*S.* Eusebius). Epistole de san hieronymo vulgare. cclxix l. 1 l. unp. 2 frontispieces. fol. *Ferrara, Lorenzo di Rossi*, 1497.

[*Note.*—Appended to the Epistole is the work De lordine del uiuere neli monasterii de monache et temporale et spirituale. At its termination we read, Questa sopra scripta regula di scõ hieronymo fu finita di scriuere et di uulgarigiar̃ da mi fratte Matheo da Ferrara pouero iesuato. Many wood-cuts after designs of Mantegna. 2 columns on a page, 48 lines in a column].

Hieronymus *pragensis.* Historia et monumenta. 1558. *See* **Huss** (Johannes) *and* **Hieronymus** *pragensis.*

Hiestand (*Rev.* Henry). Travels in Germany, Prussia and Switzerland. Including some account of his early life, conversion, and ministerial labours in the United States. Edited by a minister of the gospel in New-York. 294 pp. 12°. *New York, J. S. Taylor*, 1837.

Higgins (W. Mullinger). The book of geology: an elementary treatise on that science. [Also], an account of the geology of the

Higgins (W. Mullinger)—continued. english watering-places. viii, 365 pp. 1 chart, 5 col. pl. 16°. *London, R. Tyas*, 1842.

Higginson (Thomas Wentworth). Atlantic essays. 2 p. l. 341 pp. 12°. *Boston, J. R. Osgood & co.* 1871.

High school hymn book. 1871. *See* **Lewis** (*Mr. of Waterbury, Conn.*)

Highmore (Nathaniel, *m. d.*) Corporis hvmani disqvisitio anatomica; in qva sangvinis circvlationem in quavis corporis particula plurimis typis novis, ac ænygmatum medicorum succinctâ dilucidatione ornatam prosequutus est. Eng. title, 6 p. l. 262 pp. 4 l. fol. *Hagæ-Comitis, ex officina S. Broun*, 1651.

——— The history of generation. Examining the several opinions of divers authors, especially that of sir Kenelm Digby, in his discourse of bodies. [Also] a discourse of the cure of wounds by sympathy. 7 p. l. 141 pp. 2 pl. 16°. *London, R. N. for J. Martin*, 1651.

Hildebrand (*Dr.* Bruno). Statistik Thüringens. *See* **Thüringia**.

Hildebrand (—). Die familie Kegge. 16°. *Braunschweig, F. Vieweg & sohn*, 1866.
[GLASER (Adolf). Niederländische novellen, pp. 1–98].

——— Die familie Stastock. 16°. *Braunschweig, F. Vieweg & sohn*, 1866.
[GLASER (Adolf). Niederländische novellen, pp. 143–198].

Hildeburn (*Mrs.* Mary J.) Gaffney's tavern, and the entertainment it afforded. 284 pp. 4 pl. 16°. *Philadelphia, Presbyterian board of publication*, [1872].

Hildreth (Betsey P.) Jerusalem's pilgrim, or, a journey from the kingdom of darkness, to the New Jerusalem: set forth under the similitude of a dream. 173 pp. 16°. *Lowell (Ms.) N. L. Dayton*, 1842.

Hildreth (*Rev.* Hosea). A book for Massachusetts children, in familiar letters from a father, for the use of families and schools. [*anon.*] iv, 132 pp. 1 map. 12°. *Boston, Hilliard, Gray, Little & Wilkins*, 1829.

——— A view of the United States; for the use of schools and families. 162 pp. 1 map. 16°. *Boston, Carter & Hendee*, 1830.

Hildreth (Samuel P. *m. d.*) Contributions to the early history of the northwest, including the moravian missions in Ohio. 240 pp. 16°. *Cincinnati, Poe and Hitchcock*, 1864.

Hill (A. F.) Our boys. The personal experiences of a soldier in the army of the Potomac. 412 pp. 12°. *Philadelphia, J. E. Potter*, 1864.

Hill (*Rev.* Brian). Observations and remarks in a journey through Sicily and Calabria, in the year 1791: with a postscript, containing some account of the ceremonies of the last holy week at Rome, and of a short excursion to Tivoli. 306 pp. 1 map. 8°. *London, J. Stockdale*, 1792.

Hill (B. L. *m. d.*) An epitome of the homœopathic healing art. 160 pp. 2 l. 18°. *Cleveland (O.) J. Hall*, [1859].

Hill (Daniel H.) The crucifixion of Christ. 345 pp. 12°. *Philadelphia, W. S. & A. Martien*, 1859.

Hill (Isabel). Holiday dreams; or, light reading, in poetry and prose. vii, 184 pp. 8°. *London, T. Cadell*, 1829.

Hill (*Sir* John). Eden: or, a compleat body of gardening. Containing plain and familiar directions for raising the several useful products of a garden. Compiled and digested from the papers of the late celebrated Mr. Hale, by the authors of the compleat body of husbandry. 1 p. l. iv, ii, 714 pp. 60 pl. fol. *London, T. Osborne*, 1757.

Hill (Joseph). The interest of these United provinces. Being a defence of the Zeelanders choice. With severall remarkes, upon the present; and conjectures, on the future state of affaires, in Europe: especially as relating to this republick. By a wellwisher to the reformed religion, and the welfare of these countries. [*anon.*] 120 pp. 4°. *Middleburg, T. Berry*, 1673.

Hill (Samuel, *rector of Killmington*). A vindication of the primitive fathers against the imputations of Gilbert [Burnett], lord bishop of Sarum. 7 p. l. 175 pp. 12°. [*London*], *J. Whitlock*, 1695.
[*With* MALEBRANCHE (Nicolas de). Christian conferences. 1695].

Hill (S. S.) A short account of Prince Edward island, designed chiefly for the information of agriculturist and other emigrants of small capital. By the author of the Emigrant's introduction to an acquaintance with the british american colonies, &c. [*anon.*] 2 p. l. vi, 89 pp. 1 l. 1 map. 8°. *London, Madden & co.* 1839.
[MISCELLANEOUS pamphlets, v. 289].

Hill (*Rev.* Thomas). Jesus, the interpreter of nature; and other sermons. 241 pp. 12°. *Boston, Walker, Wise & co.* 1860.

Hill *or* **Hylle** (Thomas, *of London*). The moste pleasaunte arte of the interpretacion of dreames, whereunto is annexed sundry pro-

Hill *or* **Hylle** (Thomas)—continued. blemes with apte aunsweares neare agreeing to the matter, and very rare examples, not the like extant in the english tongue. Gathered by the formor auctour Thomas Hill Londoner: and now newly imprinted. *b. l.* 106 l. 16°. *London, T. Marsh,* 1576.

Hillard (George Stillman). The Franklin fifth reader for the use of public and private schools with an introductory treatise on elocution by prof. Mark Bailey. x, 374 pp. 1 pl. 12°. *Boston, Brewer and Tileston,* [1871].

——— Life and campaigns of George B. McClellan, major-general U. S. army. 396 pp. 1 portrait. 12°. *Philadelphia, J. B. Lippincott & co.* 1864.

Hiller (*Rev.* O. Prescott). Pocahontas; or the founding of Virginia. A poem. In three cantos. 107 pp. 16°. *London, Hatchard & co.* 1865.

Hillhouse (*Rev.* James). A sermon concerning the life, death, and future state of saints on the occasion of the death of Rachel Hillhouse, of Londonderry, Ireland, Jan. 7th, 1716. [With a preface by Increase and Cotton Mather]. 4 p. l. 135 pp. 18°. *Boston, B. Green,* 1721.

Himes (Joshua V.) Memoir of William Miller. 18°. [*Boston,* 1841].

[*In* MILLER (William). View of the prophecies and prophetic chronology, pp. 7–14].

Himmel (Enoch, *the elder*). De antichristis, præter primarivm, in ecclesia visibili plvrimis, adversvs criminationes cvivsdam Antonii Probi, [etc.] pro veritate et clarissimo Hermanno Rennechero, [etc.] Theologica et scholastica disputatio, cui accessit appendix eiusdem argumenti, ostendens ubiqvitatis patronos antichristos, et compendium omnium hæreticorum esse. 94, 50 l. 16°. [*Wittenberg*] ? 1591.

[MISCELLANEOUS pamphlets, v. 513].

Hincks (William B.) Historical notes respecting the parish of Stratfield and Newfield, now Bridgeport, Conn. 8°. [*Bridgeport, Standard association,* 1871].

[*In* BRIDGEPORT (*Conn.*) Bridgeport city directory, 1871–72, pp. 25–77].

Hind (John Russell). The solar system: a descriptive treatise upon the sun, moon, and planets, including an account of all the recent discoveries. 198 pp. 1 pl. 12°. *New York, G. P. Putnam,* 1852.

Hinds (*Rev.* Samuel). An enquiry into the proofs, nature, and extent of inspiration, and into the authority of scripture. vii, 191 pp. 8°. *Oxford, W. Baxter for J. Parker,* 1831.

Hine (Edward). The english and american nation identified with the lost house of Israel, by twenty-seven identifications. viii, 44 pp. 8°. *New York, T. Weekes,* 1871.

Hingston (Edward P.) The genial showman. Being reminiscences of the life of Artemus Ward, and pictures of a showman's career in the western world. New ill'd ed. x, 519 pp. 19 pl. 12°. *London, J. C. Hotten,* [1870].

Hinrichs (Gustavus). The elements of physical science, demonstrated by the student's own experiments and observations. v. 1–2. 3 p. l. 170 pp. 64 blank l. 1 pl; 3 p. l. 170 pp. 40 blank l. 8°. *Davenport (Iowa) Griggs, Watson & Day,* 1870–71.

CONTENTS.

v. 1. The elements of physics.
2. The elements of chemistry and mineralogy.

Hinrichs (Johann Conrad). Verzeichnisz der bücher, landkarten, &c. welche vom Januar bis zum December 1871 neu erschienen oder neu aufgelegt worden sind. 2 v. 12°. *Leipzig, J. C. Hinrichs,* 1871.

Hinton (Isaac Taylor). A history of baptism, both from the inspired and uninspired writings. 372 pp. 12°. *Philadelphia, American baptist publication and s. s. society,* 1840.

Hinton (*Rev.* John Howard). The active christian: a series of lectures. 1st am. ed: with an introduction by the rev. Ezra Stiles Ely, d. d. viii, 235 pp. 18°. *Philadelphia, French & Perkins,* 1833.

——— The means of a religious revival. With an introductory essay. 103 pp. 16°. *Boston, Lincoln & Edmands,* 1831.

Hints for the young. [*anon.*] *See* **Woodward** (Samuel, *m. d.*)

Hints to a fashionable lady. By a physician. [*anon.*] 242 pp. 18°. *New York, C. S. Francis,* 1831.

Hints to my countrymen. By an American. [*anon.*] vii, 216 pp. 12°. *New York, J. Seymour,* 1826.

Hints to sunday school teachers, in a series of familiar lectures. By a pastor. [*anon.*] 100 pp. 16°. *Boston, J. Monroe & co.* 1840.

Hippeau (Célestin, *editor*). *See* **Tillières** (Tanneguy Leveneur, *comte* de). Mémoires inédits.

Hippocrates. The prognostics and prorrhetics of Hippocrates, translated from the original Greek; with large annotations, critical and explanatory. To which is prefixed a short account of the life of Hippocrates, by

Hippocrates—continued.
John Moffat. xx, 292 pp. 8°. *London, C. Elliot, T. Kay & co.* 1788.
[Imperfect: wanting pp. 1-16].

Hirjeebhoy Merwanjee. Journal of a residence of two years and a half in Great Britain. *See* **Nowrojee** (Jehangeer) *and* **Merwanjee** (Hirjeebhoy).

Hirsch (Meier). A collection of arithmetical and algebraic problems and formulæ: translated from the original German. By Francis J. Grund. xii, 342 pp. 12°. *Boston, Carter, Hendee & Babcock,* 1831.

Hirst (Henry B.) The coming of the mammoth, the funeral of time, and other poems. 188 pp. 12°. *Boston, Phillips & Sampson,* 1845.

Hirten-brief an die wahren und ächten freymäurer alten systems. [*anon.*] Neue auflage. viii, 224 pp. 16°. [*Leipzig, Cnobloch*], 5785, [1785].

—— The same. [Anhang]. Etwas über den hirten-brief an die wahren und ächten freymäurer alten systems. Hrn. d. J. S. Semler gewidmet. [*anon.*] 10 p. l. 96 pp. 16°. *Germanien,* [*Leipzig, Cnobloch*], 5786, [1786].
[*With* the preceding].

Hirzel (*Dr.* Christoph Heinrich). *See* **Jahrbuch** der erfindungen.

Hislop (*Rev.* Alexander). The two Babylons; or, the papal worship proved to be the worship of Nimrod and his wife. 2d ed. xv, 478 pp. 16°. *Edinburgh, W. Whyte & co.* 1858.

Histoire (L') d'Aurélio & Isabelle fille du roy d'Escoce. *See* **Flores** (Juan de).

Histoire des chevaliers de l'ordre de s. Jean de Hierusalem. *See* **Bosio** (Giacomo).

Histoire des comtes de Flandre, depuis l'établissement de ses souverains, jusques à la paix générale de Ryswick, en 1697. [*anon.*] Eng. title, 21 p. l. 454 pp. 9 l. 16°. *La Haye, M. Uytwerf & L. & H. van Dole,* 1698.

Histoire (L') des impératrices [romaines. *anon.*] Eng. title, 8 p. l. 340 pp. (incl. 54 pl.) 4°. *Paris, N. de Sercy,* 1646.

Histoire des pyramides de Quito, élevées par les académiciens envoyés sous l'équateur par ordre du roi, 1751. *See* **La Condamine** (Charles Marie de).

Histoire des troubles et des démêlés littéraires. *See* **Aublet de Maubuy.**

Histoire des Wahabis. *See* **Corancez** (Louis A. O. de).

Histoire générale et particulière du visa fait en France pour l'extinction de tous les papiers royaux et des actions de la compagnie des Indes. *See* **Du Hautchamp** (—).

Historia crítica de Jesu Cristo. 1822. *See* **Holbach** (Paul Henri Thiry, *baron* d').

Historia græca, ex insignioribus fere historicis et oratoribus, qui græce scripserunt. [*anon.*] Ed. alt. v, 484 pp. 8°. *Oxonii, S. Collingwood,* 1835.

CONTENTS.

DEMOSTHENES. Orationes, [8].
HERODOTUS. Clio, 1. Terpsichore, 5.
LYSIAS. Oratio funebris. Oratio in Eratosthenem.
POLYBIUS. Historiæ ex lib. 1, 3.
THUCYDIDES. Historiæ lib. 1, 2.
XENOPHON. Historiæ lib. 3.

Historia s. Petri, persice conscripta. Latine reddita a Ludovico de Dieu. *See* **Xavier** (Geronimo).

Historical and critical reflections upon mahometanism and socinianism. [From the french. *anon.*] 8°. *London,* 1712.
[*In* FOUR treatises concerning the doctrine [etc.] of the mahometans. *London,* 1712. pp. 151-254].

Historical and descriptive lessons, embracing sketches of the history, character and customs of all nations, [etc. *anon.*] 336 pp. 18°. *Brattleboro'* [*Vt.*] *Holbrook & Fessenden,* 1828.

Historical anecdotes of heraldry and chiv alry. *See* **Dobson** (*Mrs.* Susannah).

History (The) and description of Guildford, the county-town of Surrey. [*anon.*] 2d ed. corrected & enlarged. 1 p. l. 40 pp. 8°. *Guildford, J. & S. Russell,* [*about* 1801].

History (The) of America, in two books. Containing, 1. A general history of America, 2. A concise history of the late revolution. [*anon.*] New ed. 455 pp. 1 map. 12°. *Philadelphia, J. Webster,* 1819.
[*Note.*—Original edition published 1798, and reprinted from the "Encyclopaedia; or a dictionary of arts and sciences, and miscellaneous literature. Published by Thomas Dobson," in 21 v. 1798-1803].

History (The) of Isuf [Vascovich] bassa, captain general of the ottoman army at the invasion of Candia. [*anon.*] 4 p. l. 196 pp. 4 l. 16°. *London, R. Kettlewel,* 1684.

History (The) of Johnny Quæ Genus. *See* **Combe** (William).

History (The) of Joseph and his brethren. Genesis, chap[rs] xxxvii, xxxviii. [With illuminated illustrations]. xl pp. 26 col. pl. 4°. *London, Day & son,* [1870].

History of king William the third. *See* **Boyer** (Abel).

History of Madagascar; embracing the progress of the christian mission and an account of the persecution of the native christians. [*anon.*] 342 pp. 1 pl. 18°. *Philadelphia, American sunday school union*, [1839].

History (The) of miss Pamela Howard. By the author of Indiana Danby. [*anon.*] 2 v. 1 p. l. 215 pp; 1 p. l. 228 pp. 16°. *London, T. Lowndes*, 1773.

History of nations spoken of in the old testament. By the author of "Jewish history." [*anon.*] 144 pp. 16°. *Boston, Peirce & Parker*, 1832.

History of Pennsylvania Hall, which was destroyed by a mob, on the 17th of May, 1838. [*anon.* By Samuel Webb]? 200 pp. 3 pl. 8°. *Philadelphia, Merrihew & Gunn*, 1838.

History (A) of popery, including its origin, progress, doctrines, practice, institutions, and fruits, to the commencement of the 19th century. By a watchman. [*anon.*] With an introductory essay, by Samuel Miller, d. d. 1 p. l. 416 pp. 1 pl. 12°. *New York, J. P. Haven*, 1834.

History of roman catholicism: from the reign of Constantine the great, a. d. 325, down to the present time, exhibiting a full and impartial detail of the superstitions, corruptions, and tyranny of the papal church. Including also a correct account of the rise and progress of jesuitism, monachism, and the inquisition. Together with a full disclosure of the secret designs and operations of popery in the United States. Compiled and abridged from the most authentic sources. [*anon.*] 600 pp. 8°. *New-York, S. L. Holbrook & co.* 1836.

History of Susan Ellmaker; or, an answer to the question, "If a man die, shall he live again?" [*anon.*] 155 pp. 1 pl. sq. 16°. *Philadelphia, American sunday-school union*, [1836].

History (The) of the American education society. [*anon.*] 105 pp. 16°. *Boston, Massachusetts sabbath school society*, 1835.

History of the church in the fifth century. [*anon.*] 106 pp. 18°. *Philadelphia, American sunday school union*, 1832.

History of the Delaware and Iroquois Indians formerly inhabiting the middle states. With various anecdotes illustrating their manners and customs. [*anon.*] 153 pp. 1 pl. 1 map. 8°. *Philadelphia, American sunday school union*, 1832.

History (A) of the holy catholic inquisition. Compiled from various authors. With an introduction by the rev. Cyrus Mason. [*anon.*] xi, 5–192 pp. 12°. *Philadelphia, H. Perkins*, 1835.

History (The) of the life of the duke of Espernon. *See* **Girard** (Guillaume).

History (The) of the pilgrims; or a grandfather's story of the first settlers of New England. [*anon.*] 142 pp. 1 pl. 16°. *Boston, Massachusetts sabbath-school union*, 1831.

History (The) of the remarkable siege of Toulon. Attacked by the English and Dutch by sea, and prince Eugene and the duke of Savoy by land, in the year 1707. With the political reasons that moved the confederates to undertake it. Collected from the original papers and personal knowledge of some gentlemen concerned in the expedition. [*anon.*] 1 p. l. 198 pp. 12°. *London, editor*, 1746.

History of the Sandwich Islands: with an account of the american mission established there in 1820. 197 pp. 1 map. 16°. *Philadelphia, American sunday school union*, 1831.

History of the Sioux or Dakota Indian mission. 94 pp. 1 pl. 18°. *Boston, Massachusetts sabbath school society*, 1841.

History of the United States, from their first settlement as colonies, to the close of the war with Great Britain, in 1815. [*anon.*] 2 p. l. 337 pp. 12°. *New-York, C. Wiley*, 1825.

History of two celebrated Thebans, Pelopidas and Epaminondas. [*anon.*] 84 pp. 16°. [*Fairhaven, J. Lyon*, 1798]?

[*With* PRIDEAUX (Humphrey, *d. d.*) The true nature of imposture fully displayed in the life of Mahomet. ed. 1798].

History of Verulam and St. Alban's: containing an historical account of the decline of Verulam and the origin of St. Alban's, and of the present state of the town, the abbey, and other churches, public buildings, [etc. *anon.*] xiv, 239 pp. 13 l. 1 plan, 3 pl. 16°. *St. Alban's, S. G. Shaw*, 1815.

Hitchcock (Charles H.) *See* **New Hampshire** (*State of*). Geological survey.

——— *See, also*, **Mount** Washington in winter. 1871.

Hitchcock (David). The shade of Plato: or, a defence of religion, morality & government. A poem, in four parts. To which is prefixed, a sketch of the author's life. 107 pp. 18°. *Hudson (N. Y.) printed at the Balance-press*, 1805.

Hoadly (E. S.) A system for beginners in the art of playing upon the piano-forte. *See* **Mason** (W.) *and* **Hoadly** (E. S.)

Hobart (John Henry, *p. e. bishop of New York*). Instruction and encouragement for lent. 227 pp. 12°. *New York, D. Dana*, 1859.

Hobart (*Rev.* Noah). An attempt to illustrate and confirm the ecclesiastical constitution of the consociated churches, in the colony of Connecticut. Occasioned by a late "Explanation of the Saybrook platform." 44 pp. 8°. *New-Haven, B. Mecom*, 1765.
[*Note.*—Title and pp. 3–4 slightly imperfect].

Hobbes (Thomas). Behemoth. The history of the civil wars of England, from the year 1640, to 1660. Purged from the errours of former editions. By T. H. [*anon.*] 1 p. l. 286 pp. 16°. *London*, 1680.

Hobler (J. Paul). The words of the favourite pieces, as performed at the Glee club, held at the Crown and Anchor tavern, Strand. Compiled from their library. 2 p. l. 116 pp. 16°. *London, editor*, 1794.

Hoddeson (John). Sion and Parnassus, or epigrams on severall texts of the old and new testament. [Also], a poem on the passion, a hymn on the resurrection, ascention, and feast of pentecost. 4 p. l. 128 pp. 1 portrait. 16°. *London, R. Daniel for G. Eversden*, 1650.

Hodge (Archibald Alexander, *d. d.*) Outlines of theology. 522 pp. 8°. *New York, R. Carter & brothers*, 1860.

Hodge (Charles, *d. d.*) The bible argument on slavery. 8°. [*Augusta* (*Ga.*) 1860].
[*In* ELLIOTT (E. N.) Cotton is king, pp. 837–873].

——— Essays and reviews. Selected from the Princeton review. 2 p. l. 633 pp. 8°. *New York, R. Carter & brothers*, 1857.

——— An exposition of second Corinthians. A commentary on Galatians. *See* **Bible**, (*English*).

——— The fugitive slave law. 8°. [*Augusta* (*Ga.*) 1860].
[*In* ELLIOTT (E. N.) Cotton is king, pp. 805–836].

——— Systematic theology. v. 1–2. xiii, 648 pp; xi, 732 pp. 8°. *New York, Scribner & co.* 1872.

Hodges (D. F.) *and* **Foster** (G. W.) Sacred crown: new hymn tunes, anthems, sentences, motets and chants for public and private worship. 384 pp. obl. 8°. *Boston, Lee & Shepard*, 1871.

Hodges (W.) An historical account of Ludlow castle. Compiled from original manuscripts, etc. with an appendix. [Also], Comus, a mask presented at Ludlow castle, 1634, before the earl of Bridgewater: by John Milton. 1 p. l. vi, 84, 40 pp. 1 pl. 8°. *Ludlow, W. Felton*, 1803.

Hodgson (*Rev.* Francis). An examination of the system of new divinity; or new school theology. 416 pp. 12°. *New York, T. Mason & G. Lane*, 1839.

Hodgson (William, jr.) Select historical memoirs of the religious society of friends, commonly called quakers. 420 pp. 12°. *Philadelphia, author*, 1844.

Hoffman (Charles Fenno). The echo: or, borrowed notes for home circulation. 48 pp. 8°. *Philadelphia, Lindsay & Blakiston*, 1844.

Hoffman (Mary I.) Agnes Hilton; or, practical views of catholicity. A tale of trials and triumphs. 477 pp. 12°. *New York, P. O'Shea*, 1864.

Hoffman (Murray). The ritual law of the church; with its application to the communion and baptismal offices. [Also] notes upon orders, the articles, and canons of 1603. xiv, 394 pp. 8°. *New York, Pott, Young & co.* 1872.

Hoffman (William). The monitor; or, jottings of a New York merchant during a trip round the globe. xiv, 448 pp. 8 pl. 1 portrait. 12°. *New York, Carleton*, 1863.

Hoffman. *See* **Hoffmann** *and* **Hofmann.**

Hoffmann (Franz). The iron head; or, an old soldier's story of Charles xii. king of Sweden. From the german by M. A. Anderson. 239 pp. 16°. *Philadelphia, Lutheran board of publication*, 1871.
[FATHERLAND series].

Hofland (Barbara, *or Mrs.* Thomas Christopher). The son of a genius; a tale, for the use of youth. By the author of The history of an officer's widow and family. [*anon.*] 216 pp. 16°. *Boston, T. Wells*, 1826.

——— The young pilgrim, or Alfred Campbell's return to the east; and his travels in Egypt, Nubia, Asia Minor, Arabia Petræa, &c. xii, 211 pp. 6 pl. 12°. *New-York, O. A. Roorbach*, 1828.

Hofmann - Peerlkamp (Peder). Liber de vita, doctrina et facultate Nederlandorum qui carmina latina composuerunt. Ed. altera emendata et aucta. xii, 576 pp. 8°. *Lugduni-Batavorum, apud H. W. Hazenberg & socios*, 1843.

Hogg (James). The pilgrims of the sun; a poem. 135 pp. 1 l. 16°. *Philadelphia, M. Thomas*, 1815.

Hogrewe (Johann Ludwig). Theoretische und praktische anweisung zur militairischen aufnahme oder vermessung im felde. Zum gebrauch für officiers und angehende ingenieurs. 8 p. l. 320 pp. 9 tab. 8°. *Hannover, C. W. H. Pockwitz, jun.* 1785.

Hohenheim (Philipp Aureolus Theophrastus Bombast von). *See* **Paracelsus.**

Hohenlohe-Waldenburg-Schillingsfürst (Alexander Leopold Franz Emmerich von). Prince Hohenlohe's prayer book; or, the christian praying in the spirit of the catholic church. Translated from the german. 1st american ed. 335 pp. 1 pl. 18°. *Baltimore, J. Myers*, 1827.

Holbach (Paul Henry Thiry, *baron* d'). Ecce homo! or, a critical inquiry into the history of Jesus of Nazareth; being a rational analysis of the gospels. First american ed. [*anon.*] 412 pp. 8°. *New York, printed for the proprietors of the philosophical library*, 1827.

[*Note.*—The first english edition, (*Edinburgh*, 1799), was announced as a translation from the french. The original was entitled, Histoire critique de Jésus Christ, ou analyse raisonnée des évangiles. *Amsterdam, M. M. Rey, about* 1770.]

——— The same. Historia crítica de Jesu Cristo, ó analísis razonado de los evangelios. Traducida del francés por el P. F. de T. exjesuita. [*anon.*] 2 v. lv, 202 pp; 2 p. l. 280 pp. 16°. *Londres, Davidson*, 1822.

Holbrook (Alfred). School management. [Lectures]. 270 pp. 1 l. 8°. *Lebanon (O.) J. Holbrook*, 1871.

Holbrook (Martin L. *m. d.*) Parturition without pain; a code of directions for escaping from the primal curse. 113 pp. 16°. *New York, Wood & Holbrook*, 1871.

Holcombe (William H. *m. d.*) Southern voices: poems. 164 pp. 12°. *Philadelphia, J. B. Lippincott & co.* 1872.

Holcraft (Richard, *editor*). Tales of humour and romance, selected from popular german writers. 1 p. l. xvi, 304 pp. 8°. *London, Longman*, 1829.

——— The same. 215 pp. 8°. *New York, C. S. Francis, [etc.]* 1829.

Holdich (Joseph). The wesleyan student; or memoirs of Aaron Haynes Hurd, late a member of the Wesleyan university, Middletown, Conn. 281 pp. 18°. *Middletown (Conn.) E. Hunt & co.* 1839.

Holdich (*Mrs.* L. A.) Meadowside; or, aunt Grace and Dora. An autobiography. 153 pp. 18°. *New York, Carlton & Porter*, [1861].

——— Sally Grafton and her teacher. 106 pp. 18°. *New York, Carlton & Porter*, [1861].

——— Victor; or, Paris troubles and Provence roses. 142 pp. 18°. *New York, Carlton & Porter*, [1861].

Holdsworth (Edward). Remarks and dissertations on Virgil; with some other classical observations. Published, with several notes, and additional remarks, by Mr. Spence. v, 620 pp. 10 pl. 2 maps. 4°. *London, J. Dodsley*, 1768.

Holdsworth *or* **Holsworth** (Richard, *d. d.*) The valley of vision, or, a clear sight of sundry sacred truths. Delivered in twenty sermons. 5 p. l. 539 pp. 11 l. sq. 12°. *London, R. Tomlins*, 1651.

Hole (Matthew, *d. d.*) Practical discourses on the nature, properties, and excellencies of charity, above all the gifts and graces of the holy spirit, as they are described in the 13th chapter of the first epistle of St. Paul to the Corinthians. [Also], a visitation sermon, with an appendix subjoin'd. 6 p. l. 360, 150, 6 pp. 8°. *Oxford, L. Lichfield for the author*, 1725.

Hole (*Rev.* Richard). Arthur; or, the northern enchantment. A poetical romance, in seven books. xvi, 254 pp. 8°. *London, G. G. J. & J. Robinson*, 1789.

[*With* BRUCIAD (The). ed. 1769].

——— Remarks on the Arabian nights' entertainments; in which the origin of Sindbad's voyages, and other oriental fictions, is particularly considered. iv, 258 pp. 16°. *London, T. Cadell*, 1797.

Holgate (Jerome B.) Noachidæ: or, Noah, and his descendants. 354 pp. 12°. *Buffalo, Breed, Butler & co.* 1860.

Holiday (The) gem: for boys. [*anon.*] 192 pp. 18°. *Philadelphia, American sunday school union*, [1843].

Holiday (The) gem: for girls. [*anon.*] 184 pp. 18°. *Philadelphia, American sunday school union*, [1843].

Holiday stories. [*anon.*] 178 pp. 14 pl. 18°. *Boston, W. Crosby & co.* 1839.

Holiness; or the legend of st. George, a tale from Spencer's faerie queene, by a mother. [*anon.*] iv, 182 pp. 16°. *Boston, E. R. Broaders*, 1836.

Holinshed (Raphael). Chronicles, comprising 1 The description and historie of England, 2 The description and historie of Ireland, 3 The description and historie of Scotland: first collected and published by Raphaell Holinshed, William Harrison, and others: now newlie augmented and continued to the yeare 1586, by Iohn Hooker alias Vowell and others. With conueniunt tables. [2d ed.] *b. l.* 3 v. in 2. fol. *London, Iohn Harrison [and others]*, 1585-87.

[*Note.*—Collation, v. 1, 4 l. 250 pp. 2 l. 202 pp; v. 2 183 pp. 3 l. 464 pp. 27 l; v. 3, 3 l. 1592 pp. 29 l. Complete with the exception of the title of v. 3 The historie of Scotland was continued by Francis Thin, and that of England by John Stow, Abraham Fleming, etc.]

——— The same. The castrations of the last edition of Holinshed's chronicle, both in the scotch and english parts, containing forty-four sheets. [Published by dr. Francis (?) Drake]. fol. *London, W. Meares*, 1723.

Holland (*Rev.* Elihu G.) Memoir of rev. Joseph Badger. 4th ed. 473 pp. 1 portrait. 12°. *New York, C. S. Francis & co.* 1854.

Holland (*Sir* Henry). Recollections of past life. x, 351 pp. 12°. *New York, D. Appleton & co.* 1872.

Holland (Josiah Gilbert). The bay-path; a tale of New England colonial life. 418 pp. 12°. *New York, G. C. Putnam*, 1857.

——— Letters to the Joneses. By Timothy Titcomb. [*pseudon.*] 347 pp. 12°. *New York, C. Scribner*, 1863.

Hollandsche oprechtigheid, tegen de Engelse redenloose onrechtveerdigheid. Bewezen en verhandeld in een t'zamenspraak; waar in ook vertoond is de engelscher trouweloosheid, moorderijen [etc.] in Guinea. [*anon.*] 2 v. in 1. 40 pp; 4 p. l. 32 pp. sm. 4°. *Amsterdam, J. Van Dalen*, 1665.

Hollar (Wenzel). The kingdome of England, & principality of Wales, exactly described whith euery sheere, & the small townes in euery one of them, in six mappes, portable for every man's pocket. 1 l. 6 maps. obl. 8°. *London, J. Garrett*, [1644].

Hollard (Henri). A manual of general anatomy. *See* **Bayle** (Antoine-Laurent-Jessé) *and* **Hollard.**

Holley (Alexander L.) Locomotive boilers of european railways. *See* **Colburn** (*Zerah*) *and* **Holley.**

Hollick (Frederick, *m. d.*) The diseases of woman, their causes and cure familiarly explained, etc. 103rd ed. 466 pp. 3 pl. 16°. *New York, T. W. Strong*, [1855]?

Hollick (Frederick, *m. d.*)—continued.

——— The male generative organs, in health and disease, from infancy to old age. 120th ed. 467 pp. 3 pl. 16°. *New York, T. W. Strong*, [1848]?

——— The marriage guide, or natural history of generation. 200th ed. 483 pp. 4 pl. 16°. *New York, T. W. Strong*, [1860]?

——— The matron's manual of midwifery, and the diseases of women during pregnancy and in childbed. 47th ed. xii, 469 pp. 3 pl. 16°. *New York, T. W. Strong*, [1848]?

——— A popular treatise on venereal diseases, in all their forms, embracing their history and probable origin; and the best modes of treating them. 413 pp. 6 pl. 16°. *New York, T. W. Strong*, [1852].

Hollingbery (William). A history of his late highness Nizam Alee Khaun, soobah of the Dekhan. With an appendix. [xc], 73, 38 pp. 2 l. 4°. *Calcutta, J. Greenway*, 1805.

Hollingworth (R.) Mancuniensis; or, an history of the towne of Manchester, and what is most memorable concerning it. 126 pp. 1 map. 16°. *Manchester, W. Willis*, 1839.

Hollis *or* **Holles** (Denzil, *lord*). Memoirs of Denzil lord Holles, from the year 1641, to 1648. [1st ed.] xvi, 214 pp. 9 l. 8°. *London, T. Goodwin*, 1699.

Holloway (Henry H.) Mental geometry, or generalizations of geometrical demonstrations in planes, solids, and spherics. iv, 243 pp. 12°. *Philadelphia, J. B. Lippincott & co.* 1865.

Holloway (W. R.) Indianapolis. A historical and statistical sketch of the railroad city, a chronicle of its social, municipal, commercial, and manufacturing progress, with full statistical tables. viii, 390 pp. 24 pl. 1 map. 8°. *Indianapolis journal print*, 1870.

Holly (H. Hudson). Church architecture. Illustrated with thirty-five lithographic plates, from original designs. 1 illumin. title, 258 pp. 4°. *Hartford, (Conn.) M. H. Mallory & co.* 1871.

Holmes (Abiel, *d. d.*) A sermon preached at Cambridge, Dec. 29, 1799, [on] the death of George Washington. 22 pp. 8°. *Boston, S. Hall*, 1800.

[HAZARD pamphlets, v. 64].

Holmes (George). Sketches of some of the southern counties of Ireland, collected during a tour in the autumn, 1797. viii, 210 pp. 1 l. 7 pl. 8°. *London, Longman & Rees, [etc.]* 1801.

Holmes (George F. *ll. d.*) A grammar of the english language. 1 p. l. 246 pp. 12°. *New York, University publishing co.* [1871.]

——— The southern elementary spelling book. For schools and families. Prepared under the supervision of prof. Geo. F. Holmes, ll. d. 150 pp. 12°. *New York, Richardson & co.* 1866.

——— The southern pictorial primer, or first reader. 60 pp. 16°. *New York, Richardson & co.* 1866.

——— The southern pictorial third reader. For schools and families. Prepared under the supervision of prof. G. F. Holmes. 168 pp. 12°. *New York, Richardson & co.* 1866.

Holmes (*Rev.* James Ivory). The revelation of saint John elucidated. *See* **Bible**. (*English*).

Holmes (*Mrs.* Mary J.) Darkness and daylight. A novel. 384 pp. 12°. *New York, Carleton,* 1864.

——— Edna Browning; or, the Leighton homestead. A novel. 423 pp. 16°. *New York, G. W. Carleton & co.* 1872.

——— The english orphans; or, a home in the new world. 331 pp. 12°. *New York, D. Appleton & co.* 1855.

——— The homestead on the hillside, and other tales. 379 pp. 12°. *New York & Auburn,* 1856.

——— The same. 379 pp. 12°. *New York, Miller, Orton & Mulligan,* 1857.

——— Hugh Worthington. Of a novel. 370 pp. 12°. *New York, Carleton,* 1865.

——— Marian Grey; or, the heiress of Redstone hall. 400 pp. 12°. *New York, Carleton,* 1863.

——— Millbank; or, Roger Irving's ward. 402 pp. 12°. *New York, G. W. Carleton & co.* 1871.

Holmes (Oliver Wendell, *m. d.*) Homœopathy and its kindred delusions; two lectures delivered before the Boston society for the diffusion of useful knowledge. v, 72 pp. 12°. *Boston, W. D. Ticknor,* 1842.

——— Mechanism in thought and morals. An address delivered before the Phi Beta Kappa society of Harvard university, June 29, 1870. With notes and afterthoughts. 101 pp. 16°. *Boston, J. R. Osgood & co.* 1871.

——— Soundings from the Atlantic. 3 p. l. 468 pp. 12°. *Boston, Ticknor & Fields,* 1864.

——— Urania: a rhymed lesson, [etc.] 32 pp. 8°. *Boston, W. D. Ticknor & co.* 1846.

Holstein (Lucas). De vita & scriptis Porphyrii philosophi dissertatio. 87 pp. 16°. *Cantabrigiæ, G. Morden,* 1655.

[*With* PORPHYRIUS. De abstinentia ab animalibus necandis. *Cantabrigiæ,* 1655].

Holstenius. *See* **Holstein.**

Holtrop (Jan Willem). Monuments topographiques des Pays-Bas au quinzième siècle. Collection de fac-simile d'après les originaux conservés à la bibliothèque royale de La Haye et ailleurs. Publiée avec l'autorisation de son excellence le ministre de l'intérieur. xiii, 126 pp. 6 l. 133 pl. 1 map. 4°. *La Haye, M. Nijhoff,* 1857–68.

Holwell (John). Catastrophe mundi; or, Europe's many mutations until the year, 1701. Being an astrological treatise of the effects of the triple conjunction of Saturn and Jupiter 1682 and 1683, [etc.] Wherein the fate of Europe for these next 20 years is more than probably conjectured. Also, an ephimeris of all the comets that have appeared from the year 1603, to 1682. [With] the hieroglyphicks of Nostrodamus. 2 p. l. 91 pp. 6 pl. 4°. *London, author,* 1682.

——— The same. An appendix to Holwel's Catastrophe mundi, being an astrological discourse of the rise, growth, and continuation of the Othoman family, with the nativities of the present french king, emperors of Germany and Turky. [With] a supliment of the judgment of comets. 4 p. l. 40 pp. 4°. *London, J. G. for F. Smith,* 1683.

[*With his* Catastrophe mundi. *London,* 1682].

Holyoake (George Jacob). Public speaking and debate. With an essay on sacred eloquence, by Henry Rogers. Revised, with introduction and notes, by L. D. Barrows, d. d. 2d ed. 234 pp. 12°. *New York, Carlton & Porter,* 1863.

Holyoke (Hetty, *pseudon.*) Never mind the face: or, the cousin's visit. iv, 9–211 pp. 4 pl. 16°. *New York, C. Scribner,* 1857.

——— The surprise; or, Blanche and her friends. By Hetty Holyoke. [*pseudon.*] 168 pp. 6 pl. 18°. *Boston, Putnam & brother,* 1856.

Holywood (John)? Johannis de Sacro-Bosco tractatus de arte numerandi. [Reprint]. 8°. [*London,* 1839].

[*In* HALLIWELL (James Orchard). Rara mathematica. 1839. pp. 1–26].

Homans (Isaac Smith). The coin book, comprising a history of coinage [by R. Mushet]; a synopsis of the mint laws of the United States; statistics of the coinage from 1792 to

Homans (Isaac Smith)—continued. 1870; list of current gold and silver coins, and their custom house values; a dictionary of all coins known in ancient and modern times, with their values; the gold and silver product of each state to 1870; list of works on coinage; the daily price of gold from 1862 to 1871. With engravings of the principal coins. [*anon.*] 2 p. l. 139, 5 pp. 33 pl. 8°. *Philadelphia, J. B. Lippincott & co.* 1872.

Home (Daniel Douglas). Incidents in my life. v. 2. viii, 374 pp. 12°. [*London, Whittingham & Wilson*], 1872.

Home (Henry, *lord* Kames). An abridgment of elements of criticism. Edited by John Frost. 300 pp. 12°. *Philadelphia, Towar, J. & D. M. Hogan*, 1831.

Home games for the people: a collection of family amusements for the fireside, parlour, or picnic parties. For the use of the old and young. [*anon.*] 160 pp. 4 pl. sq. 16°. *New York, P. J. Cozans*, [1855].

Home (The) of the gileadite, and other tales. 161 pp. 1 pl. 18°. *Philadelphia, American sunday school union*, [1841].

Homeri poetæ vitæ. Ὁμηρου του ποιητου βιος. [Græce et latine. *anon.*] 8°. [*Amstelædami, apud H. Wetstenium*, 1688].
[*In* GALE (Thomas). Opuscula mythologica, physica et ethica. *Amstelædami.* pp. 281-404].

Homerus. Homeri Iliadis libri novem priores librique xviii. et xxii. Ex recensione C. G. Heyne. Cum notis brevibus, quas ex Heyne et aliis præcipue collegit, nonnullas adjecit E. Robinson. 352 pp. 8°. *Catskill (N. Y.) N. Elliott*, 1822.

——— The same. Homeri Ilias. Nova editio stereotypa iteratis curis castigata et expolita. 2 v. 1 p. l. 301 pp. 1 l. 1 pl; 1 p. l. 320 pp. 18°. *Lipsiæ, sumtibus et typis C. Tauchnitii*, 1828.

——— The same. Ὁμηρου Ἰλιας. Homeri Ilias, ex recensione C. G. Heynii; cum notis anglicis, curante J. D. Ogilby. iv, 415, 110 pp. 8°. *Novi Eboraci, Collins & Hannay*, 1832.

——— The same. Homer. His Iliads, translated, adorn'd with sculpture, and illustrated with annotations, by John Ogilby. 21 p. l. 518 pp. 52 pl. fol. *London, T. Roycroft*, 1660.

——— The same. The first six books of Homer's Iliad, with english notes, a metrical index, and homeric glossary. By Charles Anthon, ll. d [Greek]. viii, 897 pp. 1 portrait. 12°. *New York, Harper & brothers*, 1847. s.

——— The same. Iliade di Omero, traduzione del cav. Vincenzo Monti. 3 v. 8°. *Firenze, L. Ciardetti*, 1825.

——— His Odysses, translated, adorn'd with sculpture, and illustrated with annotations, by John Ogilby, esq. 2 p. l. 358 pp. 24 pl. fol. *London, J. Flesher for the authour*, 1669.

——— The same. The Odyssey of Homer translated into english blank verse, by William Cullen Bryant. 2 v. xi, 324 pp; v, 311 pp. 4°. *Boston, J. R. Osgood & co.* 1871-72.

——— La batrachomyomachie, ou combat des rats et des grenouilles. 12°. [*Paris*, 1841].
[*In* MARTIN (Louis Aimé). Petits poëmes grecs. 1841. pp. 5-16].

——— Volgarizzamento dell' inno a Cerere, scoperto ultimamente e attribuito ad Omero. Si aggiunge un breve discorso sul gusto presente delle belle lettere in Italia [dar Ippolito Pindemonte]. xxiv, 188 pp. 8°. *Bassano, G. Remondini*, 1785.
[MOORE pamphlets, v. 104].

Homes of the west, and how they were made happy. By the author of "Johnny Wright," [etc. *anon.*] 288 pp. 1 pl. 18°. *Philadelphia, Presbyterian board of publication*, [1864].

Homme (De l'). 1761. *See* **Panckoucke** (Charles Joseph).

Homo versus Darwin: a judicial examination of statements recently published by mr. Darwin regarding "The descent of man." [*anon.*] 155 pp. 12°. *London, Hamilton, Adams & co.* [1871].

Homœopathic (The) quarterly. A journal devoted to the interests of pure homœopathy. Rollin H. Gregg, editor. Jan. to Oct. 1869. v. 1. 8°. *Buffalo, printing office of Matthews & Warren*, 1869.

Homolle (E.) *and* **Quevenne** (T. A.) Mémoire sur la digitaline et la digitale. 376 pp. 8°. *Paris, G. Baillière*, 1854. s.
[Archives de physiologie, no. 1].

Honoring God in the daily life of childhood. [*anon.*] 139 pp. 18°. *Philadelphia, American sunday-school union*, [1863].

Honorius *augustodunensis.* D. Honorii avgvstvdvnensis presbyteri libri septem. Antehac in lucem non editi. 23 p. l. 474 pp. 19 l.

Honorius *augustodunensis*—continued. 16°. [*At end*] *Basileae, apvd haered. A. Cratandri*, 1544.

CONTENTS.

1. De imagine mundi.
2. De temporibus mathesis.
3. De philosophia mundi, lib. 4.
4. De affectionibus solis.
5. De ætatibus mundi chronicon.
6. De luminaribus siue scriptoribus ecclesiasticis.
7. De hæresibus.

Hood (Edwin Paxton). Representative wo men; queens, heroines, peasants, confessors, and philanthropists. 3 p. l. 280 pp. 16°. *London, Partridge & Oakey*, 1853.

Hood (Thomas). The miscellaneous poems of T. Hood, containing Lamia, the Epping hunt, odes and addresses, and poems of sentiment, wit, and humor, with notes. Edited by Epes Sargent. 359 pp. 8°. *Boston, Phillips, Sampson & co.* 1858.

——— Whims and waifs. Now first collected. 479 pp. 12°. *New York, Derby & Jackson*, 1860.

Hook (James). Pen Owen. 3 v. 12°. *Edinburgh, W. Blackwood*, 1822.

Hooker (*Rev.* Herman). The child's book on the sabbath. 279 pp. sq. 16°. *New York, Leavitt, Lord & co.* 1835.

——— The family book of devotion; containing daily morning and evening prayers, for four weeks; a sermon or contemplation, and an evening prayer, for every sunday in the year: and an appendix of prayers for particular occasions. With an introduction on the importance of family religion. 507 pp. 8°. *Philadelphia, Key & Biddle*, 1836.

——— Popular infidelity. 286 pp. 12°. *Philadelphia, W. Marshall & co.* 1836. [THE LIBRARY of christian knowledge, v. 5].

Hooker (*Rev.* Thomas, *of Hartford, Conn.*) The sovles hvmiliation. 2nd ed. [*anon.*] 223 pp. 12°. *London, A. Crooke*, 1638.

——— The soules implantation. A treatise containing, The broken heart, on Esay 57, 15, The preparation of the heart, on Luk. 1, 17, The soules ingraffing into Christ, on Mal. 3, 1, Spirituall love and joy, on Gal. 5, 22. [*anon.*] 1 p. l. 266 pp. sm. 4°. *London, Fulke Clifton*, 1637.

Hooker (Worthington, *m. d.*) First book in chemistry. For the use of schools and families. 231 pp. 1 pl. sq. 16°. *New York, Harper & brothers*, 1862.

——— Science for the school and family. Part 1. Natural philosophy. 346 pp. 12°. *New York, Harper & brothers*, 1863.

Hoole (John). An account of the life and writings of John Scott. 8°. *London, J. Phillips*, 1785. [*In* SCOTT (John). Critical essays on the poems of several english poets, pp. i-lxxxix].

Hoop (A. van der, *jr.*) William Tell. Switsersche tafereelen. 8 p. l. 187 pp. 8°. *Amsterdam, van Kempen*, 1833.

Hooper (Lucy Hamilton). Poems. 196 pp. 1 portrait. 12°. *Philadelphia, J. B. Lippincott & co.* 1871.

Hoorn (Willem Cornelisz. Schouten van). *See* **Schouten van Hoorn.**

Hoorn (Willem Ysbrantsz. Bontekoe van). *See* **Bontekoe van Hoorn.**

Hope (George H. *m. d.*) Till the doctor comes, and how to help him. 99 pp. 12°. *New York, G. P. Putnam & sons*, 1871.

Hopkins (Caleb). An easy instructor in the most useful knowledge: containing a first book, spelling book, and dictionary. Together with chronological tables of remarkable events, discoveries, and improvements, and an abridgement of geography. 2 v. in 1. 108 pp; xxxvi, 162 pp. 18°. *New York, J. & J. Harper*, 1830.

Hopkins (John). Book of psalms in metre. *See* **Sternhold** (Thomas) **Hopkins** (John) *and others.*

Hopkins (John Henry, *bishop of Vermont*). Christianity vindicated, in seven discourses on the external evidences of the new testament, with a concluding dissertation. xii, 174 pp. 12°. *Burlington, E. Smith*, 1833.

——— The primitive creed, examined and explained. In two parts. xv, 415 pp. 12°. *Burlington, E. Smith*, 1834.

——— Sixteen lectures on the causes, principles, and results, of the british reformation. viii, 387 pp. 12°. *Philadelphia, J. M. Campbell & co.* 1844.

Hopkins (Josiah, *d. d.*) The christian's in structor. Containing a summary explanation and defence of the doctrines and duties of the christian religion. 3d ed. 336 pp. 1 portrait. 12°. *Auburn (N. Y.) J. C. Derby & co.* 1847.

Hopkins (Mark, *d. d.*) The law of love and love as law; or, christian ethics. With an appendix, containing strictures by dr. McCosh, with replies. 3d ed. xxv, 400 pp. 12°. *New York, C. Scribner & co.* 1871.

——— Lectures on the evidences of christianity, before the Lowell institute, January, 1844. 383 pp. 8°. *Boston, T. R. Marvin*, 1846.

Hopkins (Mark, *d. d.*)—continued.
——— The same. Evidences of christianity. Revised as a text-book. viii, 13-356 pp. 8°. *Boston, T. R. Marvin & son*, 1863.

Hopkinson (John P. *m. d.*) Engravings of the arteries. 15 pp. 9 col. pl. 8°. *Philadelphia, J. G. Auner*, 1833.

Hopper (Edward). The fire on the hearth in Sleepy Hollow. A christmas poem of the olden time. 105 pp. 16°. *New York, Hurd & Houghton*, 1865.

Hoppin (Augustus). Ups and downs on land and water. [A book of illustrations]. 48 l. numb. obl. fol. *Boston, J. R. Osgood & co.* 1871.

Hopton (Arthur). Speculum topographicum: or the topographicall glasse. Containing the vse of the topographicall glasse, theodeliters, plaine table, and circumferentor. With many rules of geometry, [etc.] 7 p. l. 204 pp. 3 l. 4°. *London, S. Waterson*, 1611.

Horæ poeticæ. Part 1. The spiritual application of the classics. Part 2. A paraphrase of the Proserpine of Claudian. Part 3. Lyrics on various subjects. To which is appended, A popular epistle on the utility of the classics. [*anon.* By a retired physician]. xvii, 225 pp. 8°. *London, privately printed*, 1841.

Horæ solitariæ. *See* **Serle** *or* **Searle** (Ambrose).

Horatius Flaccus (Quintus). Quinti Horatii Flacci opera. Accedunt clavis metrica et notæ anglicæ. Cura B. A. Gould. iv, 380 pp. 12°. *Bostoniæ, Hilliard, Gray, Little & Wilkins*, 1828.
——— The same. Q. Horatii Flacci poëmata. The works of Horace, with explanatory notes. Selected from the larger edition. By Charles Anthon, ll. d. xxxiii, 681 pp. 12°. *New York, G. & C. & H. Carvill*, 1833.
——— The same. Horatius restitutus [in illum librorum ordinem quo sunt olim ab ipso in vulgus edita secundum Bentleii sententiam]: or the books of Horace arranged in chronological order according to the scheme of dr. Bentley, from the text of Gesner, corrected and improved. With a preliminary dissertation, very much enlarged, on the chronology of the works, on the localities, and on the life and character of that poet. By James Tate. 2d ed. [Also], an original treatise on the metres of Horace. xx, 205, 250 pp. 8°. *London, Baldwin & Cradock*, 1837.

Horatius Flaccus (Quintus)—continued.
——— The same. The works of Horace, with english notes, critical and explanatory, by Charles Anthon. A new edition, with corrections and improvements. xxxiii, 681 pp. 1 pl. 12°. *New York, Harper & brothers*, 1839.
——— The same. Q. Horatii Flacci opera, illustrated from antique gems by C. W. King. The text revised, with an introduction, by H. A. J. Munro. xxxiv, 456 pp. 8°. *London, Bell & Daldy*, 1869.
——— The same. Les poésies d'Horace, traduites en françois. Nouv. éd. 2 v. xl, 314 pp; iv, 406 pp. 24°. *Paris, Saillant*, 1777.
——— The same. Odes d'Horace, traduites en vers françois, avec des notes, par m. Chabanon de Maugris; livre troisième. 303 pp. 16°. *Paris, Lacombe*, 1773.
[*With* BEAUCLAIR (P. L.) Anti-contrat social. 1765].
——— Horace of the art of poetry, made english by the earl of Roscommon, [Wentworth Dillon]. 16°. [*London*, 1695].
[*In* SAUNDERS (Francis). The temple of death, a poem; etc. 1695. pp. 5-32].
——— The lyric works of Horace, translated into english verse. *See* **Parke** (*Col.* John).
——— Satires. 8°. [*Bruxelles*, 1842].
[*In* RAOUL (L. V.) Les trois satiriques latins, v. 2, pp. 111-374].

Horbery (*Rev.* Matthew). An enquiry into the scripture-doctrine concerning the duration of future punishment. Occasion'd by some late writings, and particularly mr Whiston's Discourse of hell-torments. xii, 313 pp. 8°. *London, J. Fletcher*, 1744.

Hordynski (Joseph). History of the late polish revolution, and the events of the campaign. xvi, 406 pp. 18 pl. 8°. *Boston, Carter & Hendee*, 1832.

Horler (Joseph). An apology for the ministers of Jesus Christ, and preachers of his gospel: together with a vindication of that gospel itself, from the misrepresentations of mr. Tho. Chubb; in a book, lately published in his name, falsely called, The true gospel of Jesus Christ asserted. xxiv, 176 pp. 8°. *London, author*, [1739].

Horn (Georg). Kerkelyke en wereldlyke historie, van de scheppinge des werelts, tot t'jaer 1666. In het Nederduyts vertaalt. Waer aen is by gevoegt de historie sedert 1666 tot 1684, door Balthasar Bekker. Den laetsten druk nevens een derde verfolg tot, 1696 door Melchior Leydekker. 7 p. l. 392 pp. 15 l. 78, 62 pp. 1 l. 146 pp. 5 l. 16°. *Amsterdam, J. Rotterdam*, 1746.

Horn (W. O. van, *pseudon.*) *See* **Oertel** (P. F. Wilhelm).

Hornanus (Adrianus Junius). *See* **Junius** *or* **Jonghe.**

Hornblower (*Mrs.*) Nellie of Truro. By the author of "Vara." [etc. *anon.*] 432 pp. 1 pl. 12°. *New York, R. Carter & brothers*, 1856.

Horne (George, *d. d.*) [Thoughts on a variety of subjects]. 8°. *London, G. G. & J. Robinson*, 1795.

[*In* JONES (William). Memoirs of the life, studies, etc. of the right rev. G. Horne. Appendix, or pp. 189–413].

Hornstein (Carl). Magnetische und meteorologische beobachtungen, 1870. *See* **Prague.** (*k. k. sternwarte*).

Horozco y Covarrubias (Juan de). Emblemas morales, [etc.] 88, 4, 217 l. sm. 4°. *Çaragoça, A. Rodriguez, a costa de Juan de Bonilla*, 1603–04.

Horrebov (Peder). The natural history of Iceland. To which is added, a meteorological table. Translated from the danish original. xx, 207 pp. 1 map. fol. *London, A. Linde, etc.* 1758.

Horsford (Mary Gardiner). Indian legends and other poems. 167 pp. 12°. *New York, J. C. Derby*, 1855.

Horst (C.) Das hebungs- und steuerwesen für die herzogthümer Holstein und Schleswig. 95 pp. 4°. *Kiel, C. Schröder & comp.* 1857.

Hortensius (Lambert). Lamberti Hortensij Montfortij secessionum ciuiliū vltraiectinarum, & bellorum, ab ann. xxiiij. supra m.ccccc usque ad translationem episcopatus ad Burgundos, libri septem. 3 p. l. 256 pp. 6 l. fol. *Basileæ, ex officina I. Oporini*, 1546.

——— Verhaal van de oproeren der wederdoopers, voorgevallen te Amsterdam, Munster en in Groeninger-land. In't duyts vertaald. Eng. title, 5 p. l. 162 pp. (incl. 17 pl.) 16°. *Amsterdam, P. Wittebol*, 1699.

Hortensius (*pseudon.*) Deinology; or, the union of reason and elegance: being instructions to a young barrister. With a postscript, suggesting some considerations on the viva voce examination of witnesses at the english bar. By Hortensius. 2d ed. 2 p. l. vii, 234 pp. 8°. *London, W. Clarke & sons*, 1801.

Horticulturist (The) and journal of rural art and rural taste. Edited by Henry T. Williams. [Monthly]. Jan. to Dec. 1871. v. 26. 8°. *New York, H. T. Williams*, 1871.

Hortigosa (Tomas Lopez de). Solemnas exequias del señor dr. d. José Gregorio Alonzo de Hortigosa. *See* **Manero** (José Mariano de) *and* **Hortigosa.**

Hortulanus. *See* **Garlandia** (Joannes de).

Hosford (*Rev.* B. S.) Paul, and the chief cities of his labors. xviii, 257 pp. 12°. *Boston, Massachusetts sabbath school society*, 1857.

Hosken (*Rev.* C. H.) Infant baptism weighed in the balances and found wanting; being an examination and refutation of the rev. dr. Brownlee, on the mode and subjects of baptism. 196 pp. 1 l. 16°. *Troy (N. Y.) Bardwell & Kneeland's press*, 1843.

Hosmer (*Mrs.* Margaret). Blanche Gilroy. A girl's story. 330 pp. 12°. *Philadelphia, J. B. Lippincott & co.* 1871.

Hospital life; being incidents from the prayer meeting and hospital. [*anon.*] 180 pp. 3 pl. 18°. *New York, board of publication of the Reformed protestant dutch church*, 1863.

Hospital transports. A memoir of the embarkation of the sick and wounded from the peninsula of Virginia, in the summer of 1862. Compiled and published at the request of the sanitary commission. [*anon.*] 167 pp. 16°. *Boston, Ticknor & Fields*, 1863.

Höst (Georg). Efterretninger om Marókos og Fes, samlede der i landene fra ao. 1760 til 1768. 10 p. l. 292 pp. 12 l. 34 pl. 1 portrait. 4°. *Kiobenhavn, N. Möller*, 1779.

Hotel guests' (The) guide for the city of New York. 1871–2. [*anon.*] 4 p. l. 187 pp. 8°. *New York, W. P. Cleary & co.* 1871.

Hotman *or* **Hotomann** (François). De fvroribvs gallicis, horrenda et indigna amirallij Castillionei, nobilivm atq; illustrium virorum cæde, scelerata ac inaudita piorum strage passim edita per complures Galliæ ciuitates, sine vllo discrimine generis, sexus, ætatis et conditionis hominum: vera et simplex narratio. Ernesto Varamvndo frisio avctore. [*pseudon.*] ccxii pp. 16°. *Londini, ex officina Henrici Bynneman*, 1573.

[*Note.*—This work has been falsely attributed to Theodore de Beza and to Hubert Languet].

——— Franco-Gallia: or, an account of the ancient free state of France, and most other parts of Europe, before the loss of their liberties. Written originally in latin by Francis Hotoman, in 1574. And translated into english by the author of the Account of Denmark [Robert Molesworth]. 2 p. l. xii, 10, vi, 144 pp. 8°. *London, T. Goodwin*, 1711.

Hotten (John Camden). Literary copyright. Seven letters addressed by permission to the right hon. the earl Stanhope. 155 pp. 12°. *London, J. C. Hotten*, 1871.

——— The man of his time. [Napoleon iii]. Part 2. *See* **Haswell** (James M.)

Hottinger (Johann Heinrich). Historia orientalis: quae ex variis orientalium monumentis collecta, agit. 1. De muhammedismo. 2. De saracenismo, seu religione veterum arabum. 3. De chaldaismo. 4. De statu christianorum & iudæorum tempore orti & nati muhammedismi. 5. De variis inter ipsos muhammedanos. 6. Accessit, ex occasione genealogiæ Muhammedis, plenior illustratio Taarich Bene Adam. 8 p. l. 374 pp. 11 l. sm. 4°. *Tiguri, typis J. J. Bodmeri*, 1651.

——— Smegma orientale: sordibus barbarismi, contemtui præsertim linguarum orientalium oppositum. 6 p. l. 550 pp. 4°. *Heidelbergæ, A. Wyngaerden*, 1658.

Hotze (C. L.) First lessons in physics. 172 pp. 12°. *St. Louis, Hendricks & Chittenden*, 1871.

Hough (G. W.) Meteorological observations made at the Dudley observatory, from 1862 to 1871. *See* **Albany**. *Dudley observatory*. Annals, v. 2.

Hours of devotion: translated from the 13th german edition. By a member of the American institute of letters. [*anon.*] 251 pp. 12°. *New York, Bliss & Wadsworth*, 1834.

[*Note.*—The original compiler of this valued manual was Georg Victor Keller. It is mainly known from the part taken in it by Zschokke].

House (Erwin). The homilist: a series of sermons for preachers and laymen. Original and selected. 496 pp. 12°. *New York, Carlton & Porter*, 1860.

——— The missionary in many lands: a series of interesting sketches of missionary life. 393 pp. 12°. *New York, Carlton & Porter*, 1860.

House (E. G.) The botanic family friend: being a complete guide to the new system of thomsonian medical practice. In three parts. 300 pp. 12°. *Boston, author*, 1844.

House (The) in town. *See* **Warner** (Susan).

Household (The) book of irish eloquence; containing the select speeches of Daniel O'Connell, Richard Lalor Sheil, John Philpot Curran, Henry Grattan, Edmund Burke, Richard Brinsley Sheridan, Charles Phillips, Robert Emmet, Whiteside, Meagher, McGee. With biographical notes by a member of the New York bar. 704 pp. 3 pl. 7 portraits. 8°. *New York, J. A. McGee*, 1871.

Household (The) treasure, or, the young housewife's companion. [etc.] 158 pp. 6 pl. 12°. *Philadelphia, J. T. Huey & co.* 1871.

Housekeeper's (The) book; with a complete collection of receipts for economical domestic cookery. By a lady. [*anon.*] xvi, 13–217 pp. 12°. *Philadelphia, W. Marshall & co.* 1837.

Housekeeper's (The) magazine, and family economist. 1 p. l. 528 pp. 9 pl. 8°. *London, Knight & Lacey*, 1826.

Housman (*Mrs.* C.) Letter to Charles Empson, esq. [concerning the "winged globe," and other symbols of the ancient Hebrews]. 1 p. l. 108 pp. 14 pl. 8°. *London, Hughes & Robinson*, 1848.

Houstoun (James). Some new and accurate observations and accounts of the coast of Guinea. 62 pp. 8°. *London, J. Peele*, 1725.

Houtman van Alckmaer (Cornelis). Eerste schip-vaert der Hollanders naer Oost-Indien, met vier schepen onder t'beleydt van Cornelis Houtman van Alckmaer, uyt Texel t'zeylgegaen 1595. 1 p. l. 102 pp. (7 pl. in text). sm. 4°. *Amsterdam, I. Hartgers*, 1650.

——— The same. 1 p. l. 102 pp. 6 pl. on 1 sheet. sm. 4°. *Amsterdam, I. Hartgers*, 1648.

[*In* HARTGERS (J.) Oost-Indische voyagien, v. 1, 2e stuck].

Houzé (A.) Atlas universel historique et géographique, composé de cent une cartes donnant les différentes divisions et modifications territoriales des diverses nations aux principales époques de leur histoire. 3 p. l. 101 maps. 4°. *Paris, librairie universelle*, [1837–38].

Hovell-Thurlow (*Hon.* T. J.) *See* **Thurlow** (*Hon.* T. J. Hovell).

Hoven (Erniest). Neither Rome nor Judah. 251 pp. 4 pl. 16°. *Philadelphia, Presbyterian board of publication*, [1872].

Hovenden (Robert). A tract of future times, or the reflections of posterity on the excitement, hypocrisy, and idolatry of the nineteenth century. viii, 190 pp. 16°. *London, C. Gilpin*, 1851.

Hovey (Alvan, *d. d.*) God with us; or, the person and work of Christ, with an examination of "The vicarious sacrifice" of dr. Bushnell. 275 pp. 12°. *Boston, Gould & Lincoln*, 1872.

——— Outlines of christian theology; for the use of students in the Newton theological institution. 206 pp. 8°. *Boston, author*, 1861.

How (Charles). Devout meditations; or, a collection of thoughts on religious and philosophical subjects. 1st american ed. 189 pp. 18°. *New-York, S. Wood*, 1807.

How (William Walsham). Pastor in parochiâ. 5th ed. xv, 288 pp. 16°. *New York, Pott, Young & co.* [1871].

How the kingdom came to little Joy. [*anon.*] 196 pp. 3 pl. 16°. *Philadelphia, American s. s. union*, [1871].

How to get a farm, and where to find one. *See* **Morris** (Edmund).

Howard (George, *esq. pseudon.*) *See* **Laird** (Francis Charles).

Howard (Gorges Edmond). Miscellaneous works in verse and prose. 3 v. 8°. *Dublin, R. Marchbank*, 1782.

Howard (Henry, *earl of Surrey*). Songes and sonettes, 1557. [Reprinted]. 16°. [*London*, 1870].

[ARBER'S english reprints, v. 11, no. 24, pp. 1–32, 217–222].

Howard (Horton, *m. d.*) Howard's domestic medicine: being a revised edition of Horton Howard's anatomy and physiology, and midwifery, diseases of women and children. Practice of medicine and materia medica. New enlarged ed. 3 v. in 1. 989 pp. 8°. *Cincinnati, H. M. Rulison*, 1859.

——— An improved system of botanic medicine, founded upon correct physiological principles: a concise view of anatomy and physiology; with an illustration of the new theory of medicine. 2 v. 139, 24 pp; 444 pp. 12 pl. 8°. *Columbus, author*, 1832.

——— The same. To which is added, a treatise on female complaints, midwifery, and the diseases of children. 2d ed. 3 v. 8°. *Columbus (Ohio), author*, 1833.

Howard (John, *m. d.*) Practical observations on the natural history and cure of the venereal disease. 2d ed. 2 v. xxxviii, 396 pp. 2 pl; 2 p. l. 334 pp. 8°. *London, C. & R. Baldwin*, 1806.

Howard (Joseph Theophilus, *m. d.*) Gynecology; or, treatise on midwifery and physical ailments of women and children. 276 pp. 12°. *Washington, W. H. & O. H. Morrison*, 1871.

Howard (Leonard, *d. d.*) Miscellaneous pieces in prose and verse. To which are added, the letters, &c. of that well-known facetious gentleman Henry Hatsell, esq. deceased; and several tracts, poems, &c. of some eminent personages of wit and humour.

Howard (Leonard, *d. d.*)—continued. 2 v. 347 pp; 1 p. l. 120, 99 pp. sm. 4°. *London*, 1765.

Howard (Philip). The scriptural history of the earth and of mankind, compared with the cosmogonies, chronologies, and original traditions of ancient nations; with an attempt to explain philosophically, the mosaical account of the creation and the deluge, and to deduce from this last event the causes of the actual structure of the earth. 3 p. l. 602 pp. 1 l. 4°. *London, R. Faulder*, 1797.

Howard (*Sir* Robert). The duel of the stags. 16°. [*London*, 1695].

[*In* SAUNDERS (Francis). The temple of death, a poem; etc. 1695. pp. 65–82].

——— Five new plays, viz. The surprisal, Committee, comedies. And The Indian-queen, Vestal-virgin, Duke of Lerma, tragedies. 2d ed. corrected. 5 p. l. 252 pp. 1 l. fol. *London, H. Herringman*, 1700.

Howard (W. W.) Aids to french composition; or, progressive and instructive exercises for the practical application of grammatical rules to writing french. 309 pp. 12°. *New York, Ivison & Phinney*, 1854.

Howe (Elisha P.) The young citizen's catechism, explaining the duties of district, town, city, county, state, and United States officers. Together with rules for parliamentary and commercial business. 189 pp. 16°. *New York, A. S. Barnes & Burr*, 1861.

Howe (E. D.) Mormonism unvailed: or, a faithful account of that singular imposition and delusion, from its rise to the present time. With sketches of the characters of its propagators, and a full detail of the manner in which the famous golden bible was brought before the world. [Also], inquiries into the probability that the historical part of the said bible was written by one Solomon Spalding, more than twenty years ago, and by him intended to have been published as a romance. 290 pp. 16°. *Painesville, author*, 1834.

[Imperfect: wanting 1 pl.]

Howe (George, *d. d.*) A discourse on theological education: delivered on the bicentenary of the Westminster Assembly of divines, July, 1843. To which is added, advice to a student preparing for the ministry. 243 pp. 18°. *New York, Leavitt, Trow & co.* 1844.

Howe (*Rev.* John). The blessedness of the righteous opened, and further recommended from the consideration of the vanity of this

Howe (*Rev.* John)—continued. mortal life: in two treatises. 12 p. l. 514 pp; 6 p. l. 96 pp. 1 l. 12°. *London, A. Maxwell for S. Gellibrand*, 1673.

Howe (Joseph W. *m. d.*) Emergencies, and how to treat them. The etiology, pathology, and treatment of the accidents, diseases, and cases of poisoning, which demand prompt action. 265 pp. 8°. *New York, D. Appleton & co.* 1871.

Howe (Samuel L.) The high-school philotaxian grammar, being a concise and lucid guide to a knowledge of the english language. 154 pp. 12°. *Chicago, Bassett brothers*, 1871.

Howell (James). Instructions for forreine travell. 1642. Collated with the 2d ed. of 1650. Carefully edited by Edward Arber. 88 pp. 16°. *London*, 1869.
[ARBER's english reprints, v. 8, no. 16].

Howell (*Rev.* Robert Boyte C.) Terms of sacramental communion. 296 pp. 12°. *Philadelphia, American baptist publication and sunday school society*, 1841.

Howells (William D.) Their wedding journey. With illustrations by Augustus Hoppin. 2 p. l. 287 pp. 12°. *Boston, J. R. Osgood & co.* 1872.

Howells' *and* **Durham's** annual register of lawyers, bankers, and real estate agents, throughout the United States and Canadas, designed to facilitate general intercourse and correspondence on matters pertaining to law, land, and money. 1871. 116 pp. 8°. *New York, Howells & Durham*, [1871].

Howison (James, *m. d.*) A dictionary of the malay tongue, as spoken in the peninsula of Malacca, &c. In two parts, english and malay, and malay and english. To which is prefixed the grammar of that language. xi, 224 pp; 1 p. l. 188 pp. 1 map. 4°. *London, Arabic and persian press*, 1801.

Howitt (Mary). A memoir of Elihu Burritt. *See* **Burritt** (Elihu). Thoughts and things at home and abroad.

——— The seven temptations. xi, 373 pp. 12°. *London, R. Bentley*, 1834.

Howitt (William). A boy's adventures in the wilds of Australia; or, Herbert's note-book. 359 pp. 5 pl. 16°. *Boston, Ticknor & Fields*, 1855.

——— The life and adventures of Jack of the mill. A fireside story. 2d ed. 2 v. in 1. xvi, 263 pp; 1 p. l. 276 pp. 16°. *London, Longman*, 1845.

Howitt (William)—continued.

——— Madam Dorrington of the Dene: the story of a life. 5 v. 12°. *London, H. Colburn*, 1851.

Howland (Henry J.) Business directory of the city of Worcester for 1871–2. *See* **Worcester** (*Mass.*)

Howland (*Mrs.* —). The infant school manual, or teacher's assistant. Containing a view of the system of infant schools. Also a variety of useful lessons; for the use of teachers. 3d ed. 274 pp. 1 pl. 12°. *Boston, Richardson, Lord & Holbrook*, 1831.

Hows (John W. S.) The ladies' book of readings and recitations: a collection of approved extracts from standard authors. 449 pp. 12°. *Philadelphia, E. H. Butler & co.* 1864.

Howship (John, *m. d.*) Practical observations on the symptoms, discrimination, and treatment of some of the most important diseases of the lower intestines and anus, [etc.] To which are added, some suggestions upon a new and successful mode of correcting habitual confinement in the bowels, [etc.] 3d ed. with numerous additions. xvi, 282 pp. 8°. *London, Longman, Hurst, Rees, Orme, Brown & Green*, 1824.

Howson (H. *and* C.) A brief inquiry into the principles, effect, and present state of the american patent system. Together with the laws of the United States relating to patents, trade-marks and copyrights. 1 p. l. 112 pp. 8°. *Philadelphia, Sherman & co.* 1872.

Howson (John S. *d. d.*) The metaphors of st. Paul, and companions of st. Paul. With an introduction by H. B. Hackett, d. d. 2 v. in 1. vii, 91 pp; 211 pp. 4 pl. 16°. *Boston, American tract society*, 1872.

Hoyle (William). Our national resources; and how they are wasted. An omitted chapter in political economy. 4th ed. xiii, 160 pp. 8°. *Manchester*, [*Eng.*] *J. Heywood*, [1871].

Hoyt (*Rev.* James). "The mountain society:" a history of the First presbyterian church, Orange, N. J. 281 pp. 3 pl. 12°. *New York, C. M. Saxton, Barker & co.* 1860.

Hoyt (*Rev.* Ralph). A chaunt of life, and other poems, with sketches and essays. In six parts. Part 1. 1 p. l. 32 pp. 1 pl. 8°. *New-York, Piercy & Reed*, 1844.

Hub (The). A journal for the carriage and car shop. [Edited by Geo. W. W. Houghton. Monthly]. April, 1870, to Feb. 15, 1871. v. 2. fol. *Boston and New York, Valentine & co.* [1871].

Hub (The)—continued.

——— The same. The hub and New York coachmakers' magazine. [Edited by Geo. W. W. Houghton. Monthly]. March 15, 1871, to March 15, 1872. v. 13 [of the New York coachmakers' magazine]. New series, v. i. fol. *New York,* [*Valentine & co.*] 1872.

Hudson (*Rev.* Charles). Questions on select portions of scripture. 170 pp. 1 map. 16°. *Boston, press of the Independent messenger,* 1832.

Hudson (*Rev.* Henry N.) Plays of Shakespeare, selected and prepared for use in schools. *See* **Shakespeare** (William).

——— Shakespeare: his life, art, and characters. With an historical sketch of the origin and growth of the drama in England. 2 v. 474 pp; 495 pp. 12°. *Boston, Ginn brothers,* 1872.

Hudson (Peter). Guide pour ceux qui commencent à apprendre la langue françoise. Ou moyen aisé et facile pour traduire le françois en anglois. [Or], The french scholar's guide: or, an easy help for translating french into english. 8th ed. xxviii, 347 pp. 12°. *Dublin, T. Webb & P. Byrne,* 1783.

Huet (Pierre Daniel, *bishop of Avranches*). A philosophical treatise concerning human understanding. 2d ed. 5 p. l. xxvi, 224 pp. 1 portrait. 8°. *London, J. Stone,* 1729.

Hugbald *or* **Hucbald**. Hugbaldi monachi ecloga de laudibus calvitii. Ad Carolum calvum imperatorem. [1853]. 16°. *New York, Hurd & Houghton,* [*reprint*], 1872.
[*In* MORGAN (James Appleton). Macaronic poetry, pp. 134–142].

Hughan (William James). Masonic sketches and reprints. 1. History of freemasonry in York. 2. Unpublished records of the craft. With valuable appendices, containing mss. from the British museum, etc. Never before published. 224 pp. 1 fac-simile. 8°. *New York, Masonic publishing co.* 1871.

Hughes (Henry). Treatise on sociology, theoretical and practical. 292 pp. 12°. *Philadelphia, Lippincott, Grambo & co.* 1854.

Hughes (John, *archbishop of New York*) *and* **Breckinridge** (John, *d. d.*) A discussion of the question, Is the roman catholic religion, in any or in all its principles or doctrines, inimical to civil or religious liberty? and of the question, Is the presbyterian religion, in any or in all its principles or doctrines, inimical to civil or religious liberty? [Before the union literary and debating institute, of Philadelphia]. 22, 31–546 pp. 8°. *Philadelphia, Carey, Lea & Blanchard,* 1836.

Hughes (William, *m. a. of Clapham*). Disputationes grammaticales cum super regulis lilianis, de nominum generibus, verborumque præteritis & supinis, tum robinsonianis, de heteroclitis. 8 p. l. 110 pp. 18°. *Londini, typis G. R.* 1671.

Hughs (Thomas). The american popular reader; or, lessons for junior classes. 214 pp. 16°. *Philadelphia, Key & Mielke,* 1831.

Hugo de S. Caro, *cardinalis S. Sabinæ. See* **Hugues de Saint Cher.**

Hugo (Hermann). Pia desideria. Lib. iii. Ad Urbanum viii. Editio 6 emendata. Eng. title, 14 p. l. (including 2 pl.) 442 pp. (including 44 pl.) 2 l. 1 pl. 16°. *Antverpiae, H. Aertssens,* 1632.

——— De prima scribendi origine et universa rei literariæ antiquitate, cui notas, opusculum de scribis, apologiam pro Wæchtlero, præfationem et indices adjecit C. H. Trotz. 20 p. l. 40, 612 pp. 33 l. 6 pl. 8°. *Trajecti ad Rhenum, apud H. Besseling,* 1738.

Hugo (Minor, *pseudon?*) Hints and reflections for railway travellers and others; or, a journey to the phalanx. 3 v. 12°. *London, G. Earle,* 1843.

Hugo (Victor Marie). Les travailleurs de la mer. 3 v. 8°. *Bruxelles, A. Lacroix, Verboekhoven & cie.* 1866.

Huguenots (The) of France; or, the times of Henry iv. By the author of Ilverton rectory. [*anon.*] 198 pp. 2 pl. 18°. *New York, American tract society,* [1864].

Hugues de Saint Cher. Commentariis seu postilla in Pentateuchum. *See* **Bible.** (*Latin*).

Huidekoper (Frederic). The belief of the first three centuries concerning Christ's mission to the underworld. 187 pp. 12°. *Boston, Crosby, Nichols & co.* 1854.

Huidekoper. *See* **Huydecoper.**

Huigens. *See* **Huygens.**

Huish (Anthony). Priscianus ephebus: or a more full and copious explanation of the rules of syntax: heretofore briefly delivered and printed under the name of Priscianus nascens. Clearing and smoothing the way to the syntax, both english and latin, of Lilies grammar. 171 l. 16°. *London, I. Redmayne for W. Garret,* 1663.

Hulbert (Charles). Cheshire antiquities, roman, baronial, and monastic: being a republication of genuine original copper plates, engraved by J. Strutt. With historical and illustrative descriptions: also, a re-print of

Hulbert (Charles)—continued.
"The county palatine of Chester," by John Speed; an original memoir of that eminent historian, &c. &c. 68 pp. 18 pl. 4°. *Shrewsbury & Providence grove, C. Hulbert*, 1838.

Hull (Robert, *m. d.*) Essays on determination of blood to the head. xlvii, 154 pp. 8°. *London, Churchill*, 1842.

Hullah (John). A course of lectures on the third or transition period of musical history, delivered at the Royal institution of Great Britain. xvi, 302 pp. 8°. *London, Longman*, 1865.

Hulls (Jonathan). A description and draught of a new-invented machine for carrying vessels or ships out of, or into any harbour, port or river, against wind and tide, or in a calm. 48 pp. 1 pl. 16°. *London, printed for the author*, 1737. [*Reprinted, London, for I. Sheepshanks*, 1855].
[*Note.*—Only 39 copies reprinted].

Hulse (Georgie A.) Sunbeams and shadows, and buds and blossoms; or, leaves from aunt Minnie's portfolio. 262 pp. 12°. *New York, D. Appleton & co.* 1851.

Hulsius (Levinus). Chronologia, hoc est, brevis descriptio rervm memorabilivm, in provinciis hac adivncta tabvla topographica comprehensis gestarum, [id est Europae orientalis et australis] usq. ad hunc mdiiic annum præsentem. 3 p. l. 89 pp. 8 maps. sm. 4°. *Noribergæ, typis C. Lochneri*, 1597.

Human (The) heart. [A collection of tales. *anon.*] xiii, 370 pp. 12°. *London, Taylor & Hessey*, 1824.

Humble (William). The monitor; or, useful extracts on moral and religious subjects. viii, 335 pp. 8°. *London, C. & J. Rivington*, 1825.

Humboldt (Friedrich Heinrich Alexander, *baron* von). Selections from [his] works, relating to the climate, inhabitants, productions, and mines of Mexico. With notes by John Taylor. 2 p. l. xxviii, 3 l. 310 pp. 1 pl. 8°. *London, Longman*, 1824.

Humboldt (Gay). Poems and letters to Don Brown by Gay Humboldt, alias Burr Lington, d. ll. xi, 252 pp. 12°. *Albany, E. H. Bender*, 1857.

Hume (David). An enquiry concerning the principles of morals. 4 p. l. 253 pp. 16°. *London, A. Millar*, 1751.

Hume (*Rev.* John). The seed and the harvest. [Temperance anecdotes]. xiv, 166 pp. 18°. *Edinburgh, Gall & Inglis*, [1850].

Humphrey (Heman, *d. d.*) The life and labors of the rev. T. H. Gallaudet. 440 pp. 1 portrait. 12°. *New York, R. Carter & brothers*, 1857.

——— Revival sketches and manual. In two parts. 476 pp. 12°. *New York, American tract society*, [1859].

Humphreys (F. *m. d.*) Manual of veterinary specific homœopathy, comprising diseases of horses, cattle, sheep, hogs, and dogs, and their specific homœopathic treatment. 240 pp. 16°. *New York, J. A. Gray*, 1860.

Humphry (*Rev.* William Gilson). The doctrine of a future state: in nine sermons, preached before the university of Cambridge in the year 1849. At the lecture founded by the rev. John Hulse. 1 p. l. xi, 285 pp. 8°. *London, J. W. Parker*, 1850.

Hundredfold (An). *See* **Warner** (Susan). Stories of Vinegar hill. v. 5.

Hunnewell (James F.) The lands of Scott. 508 pp. 1 portrait, 3 maps. 12°. *Boston, J. R. Osgood & co.* 1871.

Hunt (Helen Maria Fiske). Bits of travel. By H. H. [*anon.*] 2 p. l. 304 pp. sq. 16°. *Boston, J. R. Osgood & co.* 1872.

Hunt (Henry). [Memoirs]. To the radical reformers, male and female, of England, Ireland, and Scotland. [Letters, petitions, addresses, debates, editorials, correspondence, etc. relative to his trial, and imprisonment at Ilchester]. 34 nos. April 1, 1821, to July 15, 1823. 8°. *London, T. Dolby*, 1821–23.
[Imperfect: 16 nos. wanting, between the dates above mentioned.
Note.—The letters were issued on the 1st and 15th of each month].

Hunt (Leigh, *or* James Henry Leigh). The feast of the poets, with other pieces in verse. 2d ed. xii, 177 pp. 12°. *London, Gale & Fenner*, 1815.

——— Juvenilia; or, a collection of poems: written between the ages of twelve and sixteen. 3 p. l. 216 pp. 18°. *Philadelphia, author*, 1804.

——— A legend of Florence. A play. In five acts. 2d ed. xix, 82 pp. 8°. *London, E. Moxon*, 1840.

——— The months, descriptive of the successive beauties of the year. 136 pp. 16°. *London, C. & J. Ollier*, 1821.

——— (*editor*). The reflector. *See* **Reflector** (The).

——— The story of Rimini, a poem. xvii, 85 pp. 16°. *Boston, Wells & Lilly*, 1816.

Hunt (*Rev.* Thomas P.) The book of wealth: in which it is proved from the bible, that it is the duty of every man, to become rich. 119 pp. 18°. *New York, E. Collier*, 1836.

——— The pillow, a selection of daily texts on a new plan. 110 pp. sq. 16°. *New York, E. Collier*, 1836.

Hunt's Merchants' magazine year book. 1871. 452 pp. 1 portrait. 8°. *New York, W. B. Dana*, 1871.

Hunter (Alexander, *m. d.*) Men and manners: or, concentrated wisdom. 4th ed. 263 pp. 12°. *York, T. Wilson & son*, 1809.

Hunter (*Rev.* Joseph). A disquisition on the scene, origin, date, etc. of Shakespeare's Tempest. In a letter to Benjamin Heywood Bright, esq. 2 p. l. 151 pp. 8°. *London, C. Whittingham*, 1839.

Hunter (Thomas). Elements of plane geometry. Part 1. With an appendix on mensuration. 132 pp. 12°. *New York, Harper & brothers*, 1871.

Hunter (*Rev.* Thomas). An historical account of earthquakes extracted from the most authentic historians. And a sermon preached at Weaverham, in Cheshire, on Friday the 6th of February last [1756]. 2 p. l. 159 pp. 8°. *Liverpool, R. Williamson*, 1756.

Hunter's (The) guide, and trapper's companion. A complete guide in all the various methods by which to capture all kinds of game, fur animals, &c. Also, full directions how to cure and tan all kinds of skins, &c. together with numerous arts, secrets, and much other valuable and interesting reading matter not to be obtained elsewhere. By an experienced woodsman. [*anon.*] 74 pp. 18°. *Hinsdale (N. H.) Hunter & co.* 1871.

Hunting, trapping and fishing made easy. A concise and practical guide for amateurs and professionals, including gunning and rifle shooting, the manufacture and use of traps, snares, nets, baits, etc. with full instructions for preserving, tanning and dyeing skins and furs, and much other valuable information. [*anon.* By John David Hardin]? 70 pp. 16°. *New York, J. Haney & co.* [1871].

Huntingford (*Rev.* Thomas). Testimonies in proof of the separate existence of the soul in a state of self-consciousness between death and the resurrection. Accedit Johannis Calvini *ψυχοπαννυχια*. 3 p. l. 500 pp. 12°. *London, C. J. G. & F. Rivington*, 1829.

Huntington (*Rev.* Frederick Dan). Helps to a holy lent. By the bishop of central New York. [F. D. H. *anon.*] 208 pp. 16°. *New York, E. P. Dutton & co.* 1872.

Huntington (*Rev.* Gurdon). The shadowy land, and other poems, (including The guests of Brazil). 506 pp. 1 l. 8°. *New York, J. Miller*, 1861.

Huntington (Jedediah Vincent). Alban. A tale. By the author of "Lady Alice." [*anon.*] 3 v. 12°. *London, Colburn & co.* 1851.

Huntington (Joshua). Gropings after truth: a life journey from New England congregationalism to the one catholic and apostolic church. 1 p. l. 167 pp. 16°. *New York, Catholic publication society*, 1868.

Huntington (J. H.) *See* **Mount** Washington in winter. 1871.

Huntington (*Rev.* William Reed). Questions on the fourth gospel. By the rev. William Reed Huntington. [With text]. 108 pp. 18°. *New York, E. P. Dutton & co.* 1872.

Huntington (William S.) The roadmaster's assistant and section-master's guide; a manual of reference for all having to do with the permanent way of american railroads. viii, 95 pp. 18°. *Chicago, A. N. Kellogg*, 1871.
[RAILROAD gazette series].

Hurdis (James, *d. d*). Adriano; or, the first of June. A poem. By the author of The village curate. [*anon.*] 2d ed. 1 p. l. 105 pp. 8°. *London, J. Johnson*, 1792.
[HURDIS' Poems, v. 2].

——— Lectures shewing the several sources of that pleasure which the human mind receives from poetry. [1st ed.] 1 p. l. 330 pp. 4°. *Bishopstone (Sussex), author's own press*, 1797.

——— Poems by the author of The village curate, and Adriano. [*anon.*] vii, 254 pp. 1 table. 8°. *London, J. Johnson*, 1790.
[HURDIS' Poems, v. 1].

——— Sir Thomas More: a tragedy. By the author of The village curate, and other poems. [*anon.*] 2d ed. 132 pp. 8°. *London, J. Johnson*, 1793.
[HURDIS' Poems, v. 1].

——— Tears of affection, a poem, occasioned by the death of a sister tenderly beloved. 59 pp. 8°. *London, J. Johnson*, 1794.
[HURDIS' Poems, v. 2].

——— The village curate, a poem. A new and improved ed. (being the 4th). [*anon.*]

Hurdis (James, *d. d.*)—continued.
2 p. l. 136 pp. 8°. *Bishopstone* (*Sussex*), *author's own press*, 1797.
[HURDIS' Poems, v. 2].

Hurrion (*Rev.* John). Whole works; now first collected. 3 v. 16°. *London, R. Baynes*, 1823.

CONTENTS.

v. 1. The life of the author.
The knowledge of Christ and him crucified, in eight sermons.
v. 2. The knowledge of Christ glorified, in twelve sermons.
Sermons.
v. 3. The scripture doctrine of the real personality and the internal and extraordinary work of the Holy Spirit, stated and defended, in sixteen sermons.

Hurtley (Thomas). A concise account of some natural curiosities, in the environs of Malham, in Craven, Yorkshire. 68, 199 pp. 3 pl. 8°. *London, at the logographic press by J. Walter*, 1786.

Huss (Johannes) *and* **Hieronymus** *pragensis or* **Jerome** *of Prague.* Ioannis Hus, et Hieronymi pragensis historia et monvmenta, partim annis svperioribvs pvblicata, partim nvnc demum in lucem prolata & edita, cum scriptis & testimonijs multorum nobilitate, eruditione, atque pietate præstantium. [Additæ svnt narrationes de eorum condemnatione inivsta, et indigno svpplicio ab incertis avctoribus et a Poggio florentino]. 2 v. 8 p. l. cccccxxi l; 2 p. l. ccclxvi l. 1 unp. l. fol. *Noribergæ, in officina I. Montani & V. Neuberi*, 1558.

Hutchins (*Rev.* Charles L.) The sunday school hymnal. [With music]. 2 p. l. 204 pp. 8°. *Buffalo, Breed, Lent & co.* 1871.

Hutchinson (Benjamin). Biographia medica; or, historical and critical memoirs of the lives and writings of the most eminent medical characters that have existed from the earliest account of time to the present period; with a catalogue of their literary productions. 2 v. xvi, 510 pp; 1 p. l. 546 pp. 8°. *London, J. Johnson*, 1799.

Hutchinson (C. C.) Resources of Kansas. Fifteen years experience. 288 pp. 1 map. 12°. *Topeka* (*Kansas*), *author*, 1871.

Hutchinson (Enoch). Music of the bible; or, explanatory notes upon those passages in the sacred scriptures which relate to music, including a brief view of hebrew poetry. 513 pp. 8°. *Boston, Gould & Lincoln*, 1864.

Hutchinson (Francis, *bishop of Down and Connor*). A defence of the antient historians: with a particular application of it to the history of Ireland and Great Britain, and other northern nations. In a dialogue between a protestant and a papist, an Englishman and an Irishman. [Also], two sermons, the first preached on occasion of the union, [1707], and the other at a publick commencement at Cambridge. xv, 270 pp. 8°. *Dublin, S. Powell for J. Smith & W. Bruce*, 1734.

Hutchinson (James H. *m. d. editor*). *See* **Medical** (The) times.

Hutchinson (Samuel, *of Boston, N. E.*) A declaration of a future glorious estate of a church to be here upon earth, at Christs personal appearance for the restitution of all things, a thousand years before the ultimate day of the general judgement. Set forth by S. H. of Boston in New-England. 36 pp. sm. 4°. *London*, 1667.

Hutchinson (*Gov.* Thomas). The witchcraft delusion of 1692. From an unpublished manuscript (an early draft of his history of Massachusetts) in the Massachusetts archives. With notes by William Frederick Poole. 43 pp. 4°. *Boston, privately printed*, 1870.
[*Note.*—Reprinted from "The New-England historical and genealogical register"].

Hutchinson (William). An excursion to the lakes in Westmoreland and Cumberland; with a tour through part of the northern counties, in the years 1773 and 1774. 1 p. l. 382 pp. 2 l. 18 pl. 8°. *London, J. Wilkie*, 1776.

Hutter (Elias). Derek hakkodesh; sive biblia sacra. *See* **Bible.** (*Hebrew*).

Hutton (Charles). The diarian miscellany: both mathematical and poetical, extracted from the Ladies' diary, from the beginning of that work in the year 1704, down to the end of the year 1773. With many additional solutions and improvements. In five volumes. vols. 4 & 5. Being the poetry. [Enigmas, etc.] 2 v. 12°. *London, G. Robinson & R. Baldwin*, 1775.

Hutton (Richard Holt). The incarnation and principles of evidence: a theological essay. With an introduction by Samuel Osgood, d. d. ix, 85 pp. 16°. *New York, Pott & Amery*, 1871.

Hutton (William). A trip to Coatham, a watering place in the north extremity of Yorkshire. vii, 318 pp. 2 pl. 1 map, 1 portrait. 8°. *London, J. Nichols & son*, 1810.

Huxley (Thomas Henry). On the physical basis of life. 12°. *New Haven (Conn.) C. C. Chatfield & co.* 1871.

[HALF hours with modern scientists, pp. 3-35].

Huydecoper (Balthazar). Proeve van taalen dichtkunde; in vrymœdige aanmerkingen op Vondels vertaalde herscheppingen van Ovidius. 2e uitgave. Door F. van Lelyweld. Met byvœgsels en vermeerderingen van den schryver, en eenige aanteckeningen van den uitgever. 4 v. 8°. *Leyden, A. & J. Honkoop*, 1782-91.

Huyghens, *or* **Hugenius** (Christiaan). De la pluralité des mondes; ouvrage dans le goût de celui de mr. de Fontenelle, sur le même sujet. Traduit du latin. xxxvi, 276 pp. 12 l. 4 pl. 16°. *La Haye, J. Neaulme*, 1724.

Hyacinth (The); or, affection's gift. A christmas, new year, and birthday present. For 1845, 1846, and 1854. 3 v. 18°. *Philadelphia, H. F. Auners*, [1844-53].

Hyde (Anna M.) A ladder to learning for little climbers. Showing how play and study may be combined. 137 pp. 18°. *Philadelphia, J. Challen & son*, 1860.

Hyde (Edward, 1*st earl of Clarendon*). A brief view and survey of the dangerous and pernicious errors to church and state, in mr. Hobbes's book, entitled Leviathan. 4 p. l. 322 pp. 4°. [*Oxon*], *theater*, 1676.

——— The same. 2d impression. 4 p. l. 322 pp. 1 pl. 4°. *Oxon: theater*, 1676.

Hyginus (Caius Julius). De mundi et sphere ac utriusqz partium declaratione cũ planetis et varijs signis historiatis. 47 l. 4°. *Venetijs, M. Sessa*, 1512.

Hymn, tune, and service book for sunday schools. [*anon.*] 131 pp. 8°. *Boston, American unitarian association*, 1869.

Hymns and chants; with offices of devotion. Arranged according to the church year. For use in [schools. *anon.*] 348 pp. 24°. *Lebanon (Pa.) sunday-school of St. John's church*, [1861].

Hymns for sunday schools. Selected from various authors. 208 pp. 24°. *New York, G. Lane & P. P. Sandford*, 1842.

Hymns for the vestry and the fireside. [*anon.*] xvi, 200 pp. 18°. *Boston, Gould, Kendall & Lincoln*, 1841.

Hymns of the ages. *See* **Whitmarsh** (Caroline Snowden) *and* **Guild** (A. E.)

Hymns to the supreme Being: in imitation of the eastern songs. 1795. *See* **King** (Edward).

Hymns written for the use of hebrew congregations. [*anon.*] 2d ed. xvi, 212 pp. 16°. *Charleston (S. C.) congregation Beth Elohim*, 1856.

Hyperides. Ὑπεριδου λογος ἐπιταφιος. The funeral oration of Hyperides over Leosthenes and his comrades in the lamian war. The text edited with notes and an introduction by Churchill Babington. 2d ed. corrected. 1 p. l. 58 pp. 1 l. 8°. *Cambridge (Eng.) Deighton, Bell & co.* 1859.

Hyrtl (Carl Joseph). Das vergleichend-anatomische museum an der wiener medicinischen facultät im jubiläumsjahre 1865. Nebst einem anhang: Catalog der, in der privatsammlung des herausgebers befindlichen skelete, gehörorgane, und mikroskopischen injections-präparate. xiii, 213, 41 pp. 8°. *Wien, W. Braumüller*, 1865. s.

I*** (Le C. D') Bibliographie des ouvrages relatifs à l'amour, aux femmes, au mariage et des livres facétieux, pantagruéliques, scatologiques, satyriques, etc. 3e éd. considérablement augmentée. v. 1-3. A—Hamilton. 16°. *Turin, J. Gay & fils*, 1871.

Ibbetson (Julius). A cabinet of quadrupeds. 1805. *See* **Church** (John).

Ibbetson (Nathaniel N.) Revival hymns, chiefly selected from various authors. 4th ed. 126 pp. 18°. *Philadelphia, S. Probasco*, 1823.

Ibbot (Benjamin, *d. d.*) A course of sermons preach'd in 1713, and 1714. Wherein the true notion of the exercise of private judgment, or free-thinking, in matters of religion, is stated. fol. [*London*, 1739].

[BOYLE lectures, v. 2, 2 p. l. pp. 731-868].

Ideen (Marie A.) Changing the crosses and winning the crown. 123 pp. 1 pl. 16°. *Philadelphia, J. B. Lippincott & co.* 1872.

Ignatius (*Saint*). [The epistles of st. Ignatius]. 12°. *Oxford, T. Tegg*, 1840.

[*In* WAKE (William). The genuine epistles of the apostolical fathers, pp. 125-167].

Ignis (The) fatuus: or, a voice from the clouds. Comprising the climax of iniquity, an opera; the quinciad, and other poems. [*anon.* By James Care Price]? 136 pp. 12°. *Richmond*, [*Va.*] *author*, 1827.

Ihne (Wilhelm). The history of Rome. English edition. 2 v. xxxv, 575 pp; xix, 490 pp. 8°. *London, Longmans, Green & co.* 1871.

Ihre (Johann von). Glossarium suiogothicum, in quo tam hodierno usu frequentata vocabu-

Ihre (Johann von)—continued. la, quam in legum patriarum tabulis aliisque ævi medii scriptis obvia explicantur. 2 v. 1 p. l. xlviii pp. 298 l; 1 p. l. 286 l. fol. *Upsaliæ, typis edmannianis*, 1769.

Illiger (Johann Carl Wilhelm). Prodromus systematis mammalium et avium. xviii, 302 pp. 8°. *Berolini, C. Salfeld*, 1811. s.
[ZOOLOGICAL pamphlets, v. 36].

Illinois (*State of*). Constitution. Adopted August 26, 1818. 24 pp. 8°. *Kaskaskia,* [*Ill.*] *Blackwell & Berry*, 1818.
[WOLCOTT pamphlets, v. 86].

——— Eighth biennial report of the superintendent of public instruction of the state of Illinois. [By Newton Bateman]. 1869–70. viii, 392 pp. 8°. [*Springfield*, 1870].

——— *Industrial university.* Third annual report of the board of trustees of the Illinois industrial university, for the academic year 1869–70. With a report of the agricultural lectures and discussions, at Champaign, Centralia and Rockford, etc. xiv, 407, iii pp. 1 table. 8°. *Springfield, State journal printing office*, 1870.

Illustrated (The) annual register of rural affairs and cultivator almanac, for 1872. no. 18. 12°. *Albany, L. Tucker & son*, 1872.

Illustrated (The) catholic family almanac for the United States, for 1872. 112 pp. 12°. *New York, Catholic publication society*, [1871].

Illustrated (The) christian weekly. April 15 to Dec. 30, 1871. v. 1. fol. *New York, American tract society*, [1871].

Illustrated library of travel, exploration, and adventure. 12°. *New York, Scribner, Armstrong & co.* 1872.

CONTENTS.

TAYLOR (Bayard). Travels in Arabia.

Illustrated library of wonders. 2 v. 12°. *New York, C. Scribner & co.* 1872.

CONTENTS.

MARION (F.) The wonders of vegetation. From the french. Edited by Schele de Vere.
TISSANDIER (G.) The wonders of water. From the french.

Illustrated (The) London news. [Weekly]. July, 1870, to December, 1871. v. 57–59. fol. *London, G. C. Leighton*, 1870–71.

Illustrations of scripture for the children of the new church. Published by the general convention of the new church in the United States. [*anon.*] 2 p. l. 258 pp. 12°. *New York, New-church book depository*, 1857.

Illustrirter kalender für 1852, 1856–1868, 1871. Jahrbuch der ereignisse, bestrebungen und fortschritte im völkerleben und im gebiete

Illustrirter kalendar—continued. der wissenschaften, künste und gewerbe. v. 7, 11–23, and 26. 8°. *Leipzig, J. J. Weber*, 1852–70. s.

Imaginaires (Les), et les visionnaires. *See* **Nicole** (Pierre).

Imbert (Auguste). Mon rêve ou le gouvernement des animaux. 8°. [*Paris*, 1823].
[*In* ARNAULT (A. V.) Les loisirs d'un banni, v. 2, pp. 305–374].

Imbonati (Carlo Giuseppe). Chronicon tragicum sive de eventibus tragicis principum, tyrannorum, virorumque fama vel nobilitate illustrium. A primo in orbe terrarum monarcha vsque ad xvii. seculum Christi. Two parts in 1 v. 7 p. l. xlviii, 140 pp. 4 l. 1 pl; 364 pp. (incl. 1 pl.) 8 l. 4°. *Romæ, typis hæredum Corbelletti*, 1696.

Imitatione (De) Christi. Imitation de Jésus-Christ. Par frère Jean Gersen. [Traduction de Nicolas Beauzée]. 8°. [*Paris, Panthéon littéraire*, 1843].
[*In* BUCHON (J. A. C.) Choix d'ouvrages mystiques, pp. 393–488].

Imlah (John). May flowers. Poems and songs: some in the scottish dialect. xxiv, 232 pp. 16°. *London, Baldwin, Cradock & Joy*, 1827.

Immortals (The): or, the heroes of the eighteenth century. [*anon.*] 2 p. l. 73, 7 pp. 4°. *Jamaica* (*W. I.*) *W. Smart*, [1760]?

Imogen, and other poems. [*anon.*] 81 pp. 12°. *Boston, B. B. Russell*, 1871.

Impartial (An) account of lt. col. Bradstreet's expedition to fort Frontenac. By a volunteer on the expedition. [*anon.*] 60 pp. 8°. *London, T. Wilcox* [*and others*], 1759.
[HAZARD pamphlets, v. 37].

Impartial (An) enquiry into the right of the french king to the territory west of the great river Mississippi, in North America, not ceded by the preliminaries, including a summary account of that river, and the country adjacent. [*anon.*] 1 p. l. 58 pp. 12°. *London, W. Nicoll*, [1762].

Impartial (An) enquiry into the state and utility of the province of Georgia. [*anon.*] 1 p. l. 104 pp. 12°. *London, W. Meadows*, 1741.
[MISCELLANEOUS pamphlets, v. 220].

Imperfect hints towards a new edition of Shakespeare. *See* **Felton** (Samuel).

Improved question-book, and studies on the parables and other instructions of the Saviour. With the text. 120 pp. 24°. *Philadelphia, American sunday school union*, [1871].

Improved question-book on the life of Christ. [*anon.*] 134 pp. 24°. *Philadelphia, American sunday-school union*, [1868].

Incidents in the life of president Dwight, illustrative of his moral and religious character. [*anon.*] 156 pp. 16°. *New-Haven, A. H. Maltby*, 1831.

Incledon (Charles V.) The Taunus, or doings and undoings, being a tour in search of the picturesque, romantic, fabulous and true; the roman antiquities of the Taunus, and the Donnersberg, [etc.] with reflections on the character, manners and habits of the people. xvi, 636 pp. 1 l. 1 pl. 8°. *Mentz, Kirchheim, Schott & Thielmann*, 1837.

Inconnu (*pseudon.*) Cathara Clyde: a novel. By Inconnu. 377 pp. 12°. *New York, C. Scribner*, 1860.

Inconvéniens (Les) du célibat des prêtres. 1781. *See* **Gaudin** (Jacques).

Independent (The). [A religious weekly newspaper. Henry C. Bowen, editor. Jan. 5 to Dec. 28, 1871. v. 23. fol. *New York, H. C. Bowen*, 1871].

Independent (The) reflector. nos. 1-52. Nov. 1752-Nov. 1753. 212 pp. fol. *New York, J. Parker*, 1752-53.
[HAZARD pamphlets, v. 31].

India (British). *Trigonometrical survey.* Account of the operations of the great trigonometrical survey of India. v. 1. The standards of measure and the base-lines. Also an introductory account of the early operations of the survey, during the period 1800-1830. By colonel J. T. Walker, superintendent of the survey. 1 p. l. xxxv, 1, 104, [333], 60 pp. 33 pl. 1 map. 4°. *Dehra Doon, office of the great trigonometrical survey*, 1870. s.

——— ——— Tables of heights in Sind, the Punjab, n. w. provinces, and central India, determined by the great trigonometrical survey of India, trigonometrically and by spirit leveling operations, to May, 1862. 196 pp. 1 table, 1 map. 8°. *Calcutta, Public works, department press*, 1863. s.

India (French) company. *See* **France.** Recueil des édits, etc. concernant la compagnie des Indes.

Indiana (*State of*). *General assembly.* Brevier legislative reports: embracing shorthand sketches of the journals and debates of the general assembly, session of 1871. v. 12. 8°. *Indianapolis, W. H. Drapier*, 1871.

Indiana (*State of*)—continued.

——— ——— [Documentary journals]. 1853-1871. 18 v. 8°. *Indianapolis, state printer*, 1853-71.

[*Note.*—Entitled as follows:
Documentary journal of the general assembly of the state of Indiana. Part 1, for 1867-68. Part 2, for 1869. v. 1, for 1870-71. 3 v. 1869-71.
Documents of the general assembly of Indiana, at sessions 1850 [-'51], '57, part 2, '61, '63 (42d session, part 2, v. 1, and 43d session), '65, '67, part 1. 9 v. 1851-67.
Documents and annual reports of the officers and public institutions of the state of Indiana, for the year 1864. 1865].
Reports of the officers of the state of Indiana, for the years 1853, '55, '59 and '6J, '63, '69. 5 v. 1854-69.

——— ——— Journal of the house of representatives. 1826-27, 1829-30, 1832-36, 1838-42, 1843-44, 1847-49, 1855, 1857, 1861-71. 23 v. 8°. *Indianapolis, state printer*, 1827-71.

——— ——— Journal of the senate. 1825-44, 1847-48, 1861-71. 27 v. 8°. *Indianapolis, state printer*, 1826-71.

——— *Geological survey.* Second report of the geological survey of Indiana, made during the year 1870, by E. T. Cox, state geologist, assisted by prof. John Collett, and dr. G. M. Levette. 304 pp. 8 pl. 3 maps. 8°. *Indianapolis, R. J. Bright*, 1871.

——— *State board of agriculture.* Twelfth annual report. 8°. *Indianapolis, state printer*, 1870.

——— *State library.* Catalogue of the rules and regulations of the Indiana state library, arranged by James De Sanno, state librarian. 100 pp. 8°. *Indianapolis, state printer*, 1872.

Inett (John, *d. d.*) Origines anglicanæ: or, a history of the english church. Beginning where bishop Stillingfleet has ended his history of the british church. And containing an account of the affairs thereof, from the first planting of the christian religion amongst the English Saxons, [till the death of king John]. 2 v. 2 p. l. xxiv, 390 pp. 5 l; 2 p. l. xxiv, 503 pp. 3 l. fol. *London, T. H. for M. Watton, & Oxford, theater*, 1704-10.

Ingersoll (Charles M.) Conversations on etymology and syntax; to which exercises in false syntax are annexed. viii, 172 pp. 18°. *Philadelphia, Bennett & Walton*, 1822.

Inglis (James). One with Christ in glory. Thoughts on John xvii, with a revised version from a critical greek text, and the authorized version illuminated. 127 pp. 1 pl. sq. 12°. *New York, J. Inglis & co.* [1871].

Ingraham (*Rev.* Joseph Holt). The prince of the house of David, or, three years in the

Ingraham (*Rev.* Joseph Holt)—continued. holy city. Carefully revised. 472 pp. 1 pl. 12°. *Philadelphia, G. G. Evans*, 1860.

——— The throne of David; from the consecration of the shepherd of Bethlehem, to the rebellion of prince Absalom. In a series of letters addressed by an assyrian ambassador, resident at the court of Saul and David, to his lord and king on the throne of Nineveh. 603 pp. 4 pl. 12°. *Philadelphia, G. G. Evans*, 1860.

Inman (John). History of the United States. 8°. [*New York*, 1845].

[*In* MAUNDER (Samuel). The Treasury of history, v. 2].

Inquiry (An) into the nature, cause and cure of the present epidemick fever. Together with observations concerning the difference betwixt nervous and inflammatory fevers, and the method of treating each. In a letter to a physician. [*anon.*] 128 pp. 8°. *London, T. Astley*, 1742.

[MEDICAL pamphlets, v. 5].

Inquiry (An) into the present state of the british navy, with reflections on the late war with America, [etc.] By an Englishman. [*anon.*] xv, 166 pp. 8°. *London, C. Chapple*, 1815.

Inquiry (An) into the scripture meaning of the word satan, and its synonimous terms, the devil, or the adversary, and the wicked-one. Wherein also, the notions concerning devils, or demons, are brought down to the standard of scripture. The whole interspersed with remarks on various terms, passages, and phrases in the old and new testaments. [*anon.*] 2 p. l. iii, 40, 77 pp. 8°. *London, J. Wheble*, 1772.

Insaurralde (Joseph). Ara poru aguĭyey haba [ò Buen uso del tiempo]: conico, quatia poromboe ha marângâtu. Ang ramò mbĭa reta mêmêngatu Parana hae Uruguaĭ ĭgua upe yquabeê mbĭ [etc.] 2 v. 12 p. l. 464 pp; 7 p. l. 368 pp. 18°. *Madrid, J. Ibarra*, 1759–60.

Inside Paris during the siege. By an Oxford graduate. [*anon.*] viii, 342 pp. 12°. *London, Macmillan and co.* 1871.

Inspector (The), or select literary intelligence. *See* **Hales** (William, *d. d.*)

Institut de France. Annuaire, 1870–1871. 2 v. 16°. *Paris, imprimerie impériale et imprimerie nationale*, 1870–71.

Insurance (The) monitor. Devoted to the interests of insurance; fire, marine, life, casualty and otherwise. C. C. Hine, editor. [Monthly]. Jan. to Dec. 1871. v. 19. 4°. *New York*, [*C. C. Hine*, 1871].

Insurance reporter. C. Albert Palmer, editor. [Weekly]. Jan. 5 to Dec. 28, 1871. v. 13. fol. *Philadelphia, C. A. Palmer*, [1871].

Insurance (The) times. A journal solely devoted to life, fire and marine insurance. Stephen English, editor. [Monthly]. Jan. to Dec. 1871. v. 4. 4°. *New York, S. English*, [1871].

Insurgents (The): an historical novel. [*anon.*] 2 v. vii, 13–284 pp; 1 p. l. 5–276 pp. 12°. *Philadelphia, Carey, Lea & Blanchard*, 1835.

Intelligencer (The). [*anon.* Reprint]. 3 p. l. 217 pp. 8°. *London, A. Moor*, 1729.

Interest (The) of these United provinces. Being a defence of the Zeelanders choice. *See* **Hill** (Joseph).

Interior (The). [A weekly religious newspaper]. Arthur Swazey, editor. March 17, 1870, to Dec. 28, 1871. v. 1–2. fol. *Chicago, Western presbyterian publishing co.* [1870–71].

Internal (The) revenue record and customs journal. A weekly register of official information on internal revenue and customs. Jan. 1 to Dec. 31, 1871. v. 13–14. 4°. *New York, W. C. & F. P. Church*, [1871].

Interpretation (The) of the bible. [*anon.*] 124 pp. 18°. *Boston, Mass. sabbath school society*, 1844.

Introits. *See* **Alexander** (John Henry).

Investigator (The); or, quarterly magazine. Edited by the rev. William Bengo Collyer, d. d., the rev. Thomas Raffles, ll. d., and James Baldwin Brown, ll. d. v. 1–3, 5–8. 1820–24. 8°. *London, T. & G. Underwood*, 1820–24.

[v. 4 wanting].

Investor's (The) monthly manual, a newspaper for investors in british, colonial and foreign stocks, [etc.] Jan. 28 to Dec. 30, 1871. New series, v. 1; [complete series, v. 7]. fol. *London*, [*T. H. Meredith*, 1871].

Iournael, ofte kort discours, nopende de rebellye ende verradelijcke desseynen der Portugesen, alhier in Brasil voorgenomen, 't welck in Junio 1645 is ontdeckt. Ende wat vorder daer nae ghepasseert is, tot den 28 April 1647. Beschreven door een lief-hebber, die selfs int begin der rebellye daer te lande is gheweest [etc. *anon.*] 40 l. sm. 4°. *Arnhem, J. Jacobsz.* 1647.

Iovrnal de ce qvi s'est passé en la navigation de la flote du parlement d'Angleterre vers l'isle des Barbades, et en la réduction de ladite isle: et le iûne général ordonné dans les Provinces-vnies des Païs-Bas. pp. 541–552. sm. 4°. *Paris*, 1652.

[GAZETTE de France. Supplément. No. 68, 7 juin, 1652].

Iowa (*State of*). *Auditor of state's office.* First annual report of the insurance department. Fire insurance: 1868–1869. 8°. *Des Moines, state printer*, 1870. s.

—— *Census board.* The census of Iowa, as returned in the year 1869: showing, in detail, the population, agricultural statistics, domestic and general manufactures, and other items of interest. Published under direction of the census board. 8°. *Des Moines, state printer*, 1869. s.

—— *Department of public instruction.* Fifteenth biennial report of the superintendent of public instruction, [A. S. Kissell, 1869–71]. 8°. *Des Moines, state printer*, 1872.

—— *General assembly.* Journal of the house of representatives [and] senate of the thirteenth general assembly. 2 v. 8°. *Des Moines, state printer*, 1870.

—— —— Legislative documents, submitted, to the thirteenth general assembly. 1870. 2 v. 8°. *Des Moines, state printer*, 1870.

—— *Geological survey.* Report on the geological survey of the state of Iowa, to the thirteenth general assembly, Jan. 1870, containing results of examinations and observations made within the years 1866, 1867, 1868, and 1869. By Charles A. White, m. d. geological corps; Charles A. White, state geologist; Orestes H. St. John, assistant; Rush Emery, chemist. 2 v. viii, 391 pp. 12 pl; viii, 443 pp. 5 pl. 2 maps. 4°. *Des Moines, Mills & co.* 1870.

Iowa railroads. Guide, etc. 1871. *See* **Wolfe** (J. M.)

Ireland (John B.) Wall-street to Cashmere. A journal of five years in Asia, Africa, and Europe; comprising visits, during 1851, 2, 3, 4, 5, 6, to the Danemora iron mines, the "seven churches," plains of Troy, Palmyra, Jerusalem, Petra, Seringapatam, Surat. 531 pp. 73 pl. 1 map. 8°. *New York, S. A. Rollo & co.* 1859.

Ireland (Samuel). A picturesque tour through Holland, Brabant, and part of France; made in the autumn of 1789. Illustrated. [1st ed.] 2 v. xvi, 213 pp. 28 pl; vi, 209 pp. 16 pl. 8°. *London, T. & J. Egerton*, 1790.

—— Picturesque views on the river Thames, from its source in Glocestershire to the Nore; with observations on the public buildings and other works of art in the vicinity. [1st ed.] 2 v. xvi, 210 pp. 28 pl. 1 map; viii, 259 pp. 26 pl. 1 map. 8°. *London, T. & J. Egerton*, 1792.

—— Picturesque views on the river Wye, from its source at Plinlimmon hill, to its junction with the Severn below Chepstow: with observations on the public buildings, and other works of art in the vicinity. [1st ed.] xii, 159 pp. 31 pl. 1 map. 8°. *London, R. Faulder*, 1797.

Ireland (William Henry). Neglected genius. A poem. Illustrating the untimely and unfortunate fate of many british poets; from the period of Henry the eighth to the æra of the unfortunate Chatterton. Containing imitations of their different styles, &c. xxiv, 152 pp. 8°. *London, G. Cowie & co.* 1812.

Iris (The); a journal of literature, science, and the fine arts. v. 2. [no. 28–54, July 9, 1825, to January 7, 1826]. sm. 4°. *London, J. Gifford*, 1826.

Irish (*Rev.* William Norman). Hebrew charts; containing the elements of the language. 79 pp. 4°. *Albany (N. Y.) Weed, Parsons & co.* 1872.

Irish Amy. *See* **Guernsey** (Lucy Ellen).

Irish (The) people. A weekly journal of news, politics and literature. Peter McCorry, editor. Jan. 14, 1871, to Jan. 6, 1872. v. 6. fol. *New York, M. J. O'Leary & co.* 1871–72.

Irving (David, *ll. d.*) The elements of english composition. 12th ed. viii, 357 pp. 12°. *Edinburgh, W. Whyte & co.* 1852.

Isabel, (*pseudon.*) *See* **Simms** (William Gilmore). Pelayo.

Isham (Warren). The mud cabin; or, the character and tendency of british institutions, as illustrated in their effect upon human character and destiny. 312 pp. 4 pl. 12°. *New York, D. Appleton & co.* 1853.

Isidorus *hispalensis.* [Soliloquia seu synonyma de homine et ratione. Begins] Incipit prologus Isidori episcopi in soliloquia eiusdem. [Ends] Sancti Isidori Ispalensis archiep̄i sinonima expliciūt. *b. l.* 18 l. unp. 4°. [*Norimbergæ, Joh. Sensenschmidt*, 1470]. s.

Israelitisches gebetbuch. *See* **Jewish** church.

Isreels (Joseph). Ezekiel's temple; being an attempt to delineate the structure of the holy edifice, its courts, chambers, gates, &c. as described in the last nine chapters of the book of Ezekiel. 3 p. l. v, 60 pp. 1 l. 3 pl. 4°. *London, author*, 1826.

Italia (L') agricola. Giornale dedicato al miglioramento morale ed economico delle popolazione rurali. Instituito e diretto dal cav. G. Chizzolini. Anni 1-2. 2 v. sm. fol. *Milano, stabilimento redaelli dei fratelli Rechiedei*, 1869-70. s.

Italian (The) girl. *See* **McLain** (Mary Webster).

Italian (The) sketch book. *See* **Tuckerman** (Henry Theodore).

Italy. *Ministero di agricoltura, industria e commercio.* Annali. I comizi agrari del regno d'Italia. 3 v. 8°. *Torino, stamperia dell' unione tipografico-editrice*, 1870. s.

CONTENTS.

Parte prima. Operato e proposte negli anni 1867, 1868, 1869.
Parte seconda. I quesiti sullo stato dell' agricoltura negli anni 1866, 1867 e 1868. Relazione del prof. Gaetano Cantoni.
Parte terza. Allegati. Relazione del prof. Gaetano Cantoni.

——— Atti ufficiali della prima sessione del congresso delle camere di commercio e proposta di programma presentata al signor ministro d'agricultura, industria e commercio dal dottor Pietro Maestri. 122 pp. 8°. *Firenze, Tofani*, 1867. s.

——— ——— [Statistica del regno d'Italia]. Acque minerali. Anno 1868. xix, 176 pp. sm. fol. *Firenze, tipografia Tofani*, 1869. s.

——— ——— ——— Industria manifattrice. Trattura della seta. Anni 1867-68. 2 v. 8°. *Firenze, tipografia Tofani*, 1869-70. s.

——— ——— Statistica forestale. Parte prima. fol. *Firenze, tipografia cenniniana*, 1870. s.

——— *Camera dei deputati.* Relazione del deputato [Quintano] Sella alla commissione d'inchiesta composta dei deputati Depretis, Ferracciù, Macchi, Mantegazza, Sella, Tenani, sulle condizioni dell' industria mineraria nell' isola di Sardegna. 125 pp. 4°. [*Firenze, tip. eredi Botta*], 1871. s.

——— ——— Relazione della commissione parlamentare d'inchiesta sul corso forzoso dei biglietti di banca deliberata nella tornata del 10 marzo 1868, composta dei deputati Seismit-Doda, Cordova, Rossi Alessandro, Sella, Messedaglia, Lampertico, Lualdi. (Sessione 1867-68. 3 v. 4°. *Firenze, per gli eredi Botta*, 1868-69.

Italy—continued.

——— *Commissione reale dell' esposizione italiana nel* 1861. Esposizione italiana tenuta in Firenze nel 1861. [Relazioni]. 3 v. 8°. *Firenze, G. Barbèra*, 1864-67. s.

——— *Direzione della statistica generale.* Statistica del regno d'Italia. Amministrazione publica. Bilanci comunali, anni 1867-69. Bilanci provinciali, anno 1869. 2 v. sm. fol. *Firenze, tipografia Tofani*, 1870. s.

——— ——— ——— Gli asili infantili nel 1869. xv, 40 pp. 4°. *Firenze, tipografia Tofani*, 1870. s.

——— ——— ——— Popolazione. Movimento dello stato civile nel anno 1867, [1868, 1869]. Compilato per cura del ministero d'agricoltura, industria e commercio. 3 v. sm. fol. *Firenze, tipografia Tofani*, 1868-71. s.

——— ——— ——— Sanità publica. Il cholera morbus nel 1866 e 1867. xix, 72 pp. sm. fol. *Firenze, tipografia Tofani*, 1870. s.

——— ——— ——— Morti violente. Anno 1867. sm. fol. *Firenze, tipografia Tofani*, 1869. s.

——— *Direzione generale delle strade ferrate dello stato.* Traforo delle Alpi tra Bardonnèche e Modane. Relazione della direzione tecnica alla direzione generale delle strade ferrate dello stato, [da G. Sommeiller]. 3 p. l. 113 pp. 10 pl. sm. fol. *Torino, Ceresole & Panizza*, 1863. s.

——— *Ministero dell' interno.* [Statistica del regno d'Italia]. Istituti di previdenza. Le casse di risparmio 1866-67. 2 v. sm. fol. *Firenze, tipografia Tofani*, 1869-70. s.

——— ——— ——— Le opere pie nel 1861. [v. 4, 5, 6, 9, 15]. fol. *Firenze, tipografia Tofani, [etc.]* 1869-70. s.

——— ——— Relazione sull' andamento delle amministrazioni dipendenti dal ministero dell' interno nell' anno 1866. Presentata dal ministro al parlamento il 22 dicembre. 1 p. l. 228 pp. 1 l. 9 tables. 4°. *Firenze, eredi Botta*, 1866. s.

——— *Ministero della marina.* [Statistica del regno d'Italia]. Movimento della navigazione italiana all' estero. Anni 1867-68. 2 v. sm. fol. *Firenze, Tofani*, 1869-70. s.

——— ——— ——— Movimento della navigazione nei porti del regno. Pesca del pesce e del corallo — marineria mercantile, costruzione navali—infortuni marittimi. Anni 1867-68. 2 v. sm. fol. *Firenze, G. Civelli, [etc.]* 1868-69. s.

Itinéraire complet de l'empire français, 1811. *See* **Langlois** (Hyacinthe).

Ives (Levi Silliman, *d. d.*) "The apostles' doctrine and fellowship." Five sermons preached in the principal churches of his diocese, during his spring visitation, 1844. 190 pp. 16°. *New York, D. Appleton & co.* 1844.

——— "The obedience of faith." Seven sermons delivered on his visitations to the churches in his diocese, during 1848-9. 2 p. l. 161 pp. 16°. *New York, Stanford & Swords*, 1849.

——— (*editor*). *See* **New** manual of private devotions.

J. (F. M.) Allan Leslie: or, the young missionaries. [*anon.*] 223 pp. 1 l. 1 pl. 18°. *New York, General prot. episcopal sunday school union & church book society*, 1860.

J. (L. B.) Heavenly watchwords; or promises and countersigns. By L. B. J. [*anon.*] 125 pp. 16°. *Philadelphia, Presbyterian board of publication*, [1861].

Jaccard (Auguste). Supplément à la description géologique du Jura vaudois et neuchâtelois. Avec une carte (feuille vi de l'atlas fédéral) et quatre planches de profils géologiques. 2 p. l. 79 pp. 4 pl. 4°. *Berne, J. Dalp*, 1870.
[SWITZERLAND. Matériaux pour la carte géologique de la Suisse, v. 7].

Jackson (Charles D. *d. d.*) Suffering here—glory hereafter. Sermons. 190 pp. 1 portrait. 12°. *New York, E. P. Dutton & co.* 1872.

Jackson (Edward P.) A mathematical geography, with a supplement containing an outline of astronomy, and a manual for the stellar tellurian. 110, 28 pp. 3 l. sm. 4°. *Hartford (Conn.) The stellar tellurian manufacturing co.* 1872.

Jackson (James, *m. d.*) Letters to a young physician just entering upon practice. iv, 344 pp. 12°. *Boston, Phillips, Sampson & co.* 1855.

Jackson (James C. *m. d.*) Consumption: how to prevent it, and how to cure it. vii, 400 pp. 1 portrait. 8°. *Boston, B. L. Emerson*, 1862.

——— The sexual organism, and its healthful management. 279 pp. 1 portrait. 8°. *Boston, B. L. Emerson*, 1861.
[*With* TRALL (Russell T. *m. d.*) Pathology of the reproductive organs].

Jackson (*Rev.* John). Chronological antiquities: or, the antiquities and chronology of the most ancient kingdoms. 3 v. 4°. *London, author*, 1752.

Jackson (*Rev.* John)—continued.

——— A defense of human liberty, in answer to the principal arguments which have been alledged against it; and particularly to Cato's letters on that subject. In which defense the opinion of the antients, concerning fate, is also distinctly and largely considered. 2d ed. To which is added, A vindication of human liberty: in answer to a dissertation on liberty and necessity. Written by A[nthony] C[ollins]. 2 v. in 1. 4 p. l. 207 pp; viii, 63 pp. 8°. *London, J. Noon*, 1730.

Jackson (Samuel, *m. d.*) The principles of medicine, founded on the structure and functions of the animal organism. xx, 9-631 pp. 8°. *Philadelphia, Carey & Lee*, 1832.

Jackson (*Major* William). Eulogium on the character of general Washington; pronounced before the Pennsylvania society of the Cincinnati, 22 Feb. 1800. 44 pp. 8°. *Philadelphia, J. Ormrod*, 1800.
[HAZARD pamphlets, v. 65].

——— The same.
[WOLCOTT pamphlets, v. 60].

Jackson (*Rev.* William). The christian's legacy; with an appendix, containing a compendium of the holy bible. 420 pp. 12°. *Providence, author*, 1841.

——— Man of sorrows; or, the providence of God displayed: as experienced by the author. 339 pp. 12°. *Baltimore, W. Wooddy*, 1834.

——— The same. 2d ed. 360 pp. 12°. *Boston, C. D. Strong*, 1838.

——— The same. 3d ed. enlarged. 420 pp. 1 portrait. 12°. *Boston, author*, 1842.

Jackson (*Rev.* William M.) Baptismal obligations; or the duties and responsibilities of god-parents and baptized persons. 176 pp. 12°. *Philadelphia, Hooker & Agnew*, 1841.

Jackson (*Mich.*) Jackson city directory, for 1869-70, also including the villages of Grass Lake, Parma, Brooklyn, Napoleon, Concord, Leoni, and Norvell. Compiled and published by James M. Thomas. 3 p. l. 295 pp. 8°. *Jackson (Mich.) J. M. Thomas*, 1869.

——— The same. For 1871, with a complete portrait of Jackson. Statistical tables, etc. 224 pp. 8°. *Battle Creek (Mich.) J. M. Thomas*, 1871.

Jacksonville (*Florida*). Jacksonville city directory, and business advertiser, for 1871. 12°. *Jacksonville (Fla.) Florida union job office*, 1871.

Jacob (Hildebrand). The works of Jacob. Containing poems on various subjects, and occasions; with the Fatal constancy, a trag-

Jacob (Hildebrand)—continued.
edy; and several pieces in prose. The greatest part never published before. 8 p. l. 461 pp. 1 l. 8°. *London, W. Lewis,* 1735.

Jacob (P. L. *bibliophile; pseudon.*) *See* **Lacroix** (Paul).

Jacobite minstrelsy; with notes illustrative of the text, and containing historical details in relation to the house of Stuart, from 1640 to 1784. [*anon.*] 1 p. l. viii, xiv, 362 pp. 2 pl. 12°. *Glasgow, R. Griffin & co.* 1829.

Jacobs (Heyman). Zondagse school, of uitlegginge op de evangeliën van de zondagen, met schoone gebeden vermeerderd na den roomschen text. 548 pp. 2 l. 16°. *Antwerpen, F. J. van Tetroode,* [*about* 1750].

Jacobs (J. A.) Lessons for the deaf and dumb. 192 pp. 16°. *Lexington (Ky.) W. M. Todd & W. D. Skillman,* 1834.

Jacobs (Sarah S.) Nonantum and Natick. 336 pp. 1 pl. 12°. *Boston, Massachusetts sabbath school society,* 1853.

Jacobus (Melancthon W. *d. d.*) Notes on Genesis. Notes on the gospels. *See* **Bible.** (*English*).

Jacobus *januensis* de Voragine. *See* **Voragine.**

Jacobus magnus *parisiensis.* *See* **Legrand** (Jacques).

Jacopone da Todi. Li cantici del b. Iacopone da Todi, e sva vita, con li discorsi del padre Gio. Battista Modio, et in qvesta nostra impressione aggiontoui alcuni cantici di esso beato, cavati da vn manoscritto antico, non più stampati. 2 p. l. 300 pp. 8 l. 16°. *Napoli, L. Scoriggio,* 1615.

Jacquier (François). *See* **Le Seur** (T.) *and* **Jacquier.**

Jacquin (Nicolas Joseph, *baron*). Dreyhundert auserlesene amerikanische gewächse nach linneischer ordnung. 300 col. pl. 6 v. in 3. 8°. *Nürnberg, Rospische buchhandlung,* 1786-9.

[*Note.*—Composed chiefly of reduced copies of the plates (264) of Jacquin's "Selectorum stirpium americanarum historia," with explanations of the plates].

Jäger (Friedrich Georg von). Über die fossilen säugethiere Würtembergs. Als nachtrag zu dem 1839 unter gleichem titel erschienenen werke. Besonders abgedruckt aus dem 22 bande der Nova acta naturae curiosorum. 170 pp. 1 l. 5 pl. 4°. *Breslau,* 1850.

[PALÆONTOLOGICAL pamphlets, v. 13].

Jahr (Georg Heinrich Gottlieb). New homœopathic pharmacopœia and posology, or the preparation of homœopathic medicines and the administration of doses. Translated, with additions, by James Kitchen, m. d. xxii, 9-306 pp. 8°. *Philadelphia, J. Dobson,* 1842.

Jahrbuch der erfindungen und fortschritte auf den gebieten der physik und chemie, der technologie und mechanik, der astronomie und meteorologie. Herausgegeben von dr. H. Hirzel und H. Gretschel. 1865-1869. v. 1-5. 12°. *Leipzig, Quandt & Händel,* 1865-69. s.

Jahrbücher für wissenschaftliche botanik. Herausgegeben von dr. N. Pringsheim. v. 1-2. 8°. *Berlin, A. Hirschwald,* 1858-60. s.

Jaligny (Guillaume de). Histoire de plvsievrs choses mémorables aduenuës du règne de Charles viii, roy de France, és années 1486, 1487, 1488, & 1489. fol. [*Paris,* 1684].

[*In* GODEFROY (T. *and* D.) Histoire de Charles viii, pp. 3-90].

Jamaica Plain (The) and West Roxbury directory for 1871. *See* **Brookline** (*Mass.*)

Jamblichus *chalcidensis.* Jamblichi chalcidensis in Nicomachi geraseni arithmeticam introductionem [liber quartus] et de fato. Nunc primum editus, in latinum sermonem conversus, notis perpetuis illustratus a Samuele Tennulio. Accedit Joachimi Camerarii explicatio in duos libros Nicomachi. [Græce et latine]. Eng. title, 6 p. l. 181 pp. 1 l. 239 pp. sm. 4°. *Arnhemiæ, apud J. F. Hagium,* 1668.

[*Note.*—The notes were printed at Deventer, by Willem Wier, 1667].

James i. *of England.* The essayes of a prentise, in the divine art of poesie. Edinburgh, 1585. A counterblaste to tobacco. London, 1604. Carefully edited by Edward Arber. 120 pp. 16°. *London,* 1869.

[ARBER's english reprints, v. 8, no. 19].

CONTENTS.

Twelf sonnets of inuocations to the goddis.
The Vranie [of Du Bartas] translated.
Ane metaphoricall invention of a tragedie called Phoenix.
Ane schort treatise conteining some revlis and cautelis to be obseruit and eschewet in scottis poesie.
The CIII psalme, translated out of Tremellius.
Ane schort poeme of tyme.

James (Charles). Poems. 4th ed. 2 v. 5 p. l. xlvii, 215 pp. 3 pl. 2 l. music, 1 portrait; 6 p. l. 288 pp. 2 pl. 1 portrait. 8°. *London, T. Egerton (etc.)* 1817.

James (*Rev.* David). The patriarchal religion of Britain; or a complete manual of ancient british druidism. 100 pp. 8°. *London, Whittaker and co.* 1836.

[MISCELLANEOUS pamphlets, v. 107].

James (*Rev.* John Angell). The church member's guide. Edited by J. O. Choules. New edition. With an introductory essay, by Hubbard Winslow. xxxv, 9–240 pp. 16°. *Boston, Gould, Kendall & Lincoln,* 1838.

——— Pastoral addresses. With an introduction by rev. William Adams. 213 pp. 18°. *New York, D. Appleton & co.* 1861.

James (Joseph). A compendious hebrew and english lexicon. xxx, 145 pp. 16°. *Philadelphia, Wm. Brown,* 1826.

Jameson (William). Spicilegia antiquitatum Ægypti atque ei vicinarum gentium. 22 p. l. 472 pp. 16°. *Glasguæ, typis J. & G. Duncan,* 1720.

Jamieson (Alexander). A grammar of logic and intellectual philosophy, on didactic principles. 1st american ed. 304 pp. 12°. *New-Haven, A. H. Maltby & co.* 1822.

——— The same. 2d ed. xx, 358 pp. 1 l. 12°. *London, for G. & W. B. Whittaker,* 1824.

Janes (*Rev.* Edwin L.) Wesley his own historian. *See* **Wesley** (John).

Janes (*Rev.* Thomas). The beauties of the poets: being a collection of moral and sacred poetry, from the most eminent authors. viii, 304 pp. 3 pl. 16°. *London, Scatcherd & Letterman,* 1806.

Janet (Paul). La crise philosophique, mm. Taine, Renan, Littré, Vacherot. 2 p. l. 180 pp. 16°. *Paris, G. Baillière,* 1865.

Janeway (Jacob J. *d. d.*) An exposition of a portion of the epistle to the Romans, in the form of questions and answers. 135 pp. 18°. *New-York, R. Carter,* 1838.

——— The internal evidence of the holy bible, or the bible proved from its own pages to be a divine revelation. 287 pp. 12°. *Philadelphia, Presbyterian board of publication,* 1845.

——— Letters explaining the abrahamic covenant, with a view to establish, on this broad and ancient basis, the divine right of infant baptism; and the question relative to the mode of administering this christian ordinance. 2 p. l. 302 pp. 16°. *Philadelphia, author,* 1812.

Janeway (*Rev.* James, 1636–74). The life of the rev. John Janeway. Abridged for the board. [*anon.*] 18°. *Philadelphia, Presbyterian board of publication,* 1840.

[*In* ORME (*Rev.* William). The life of the rev. John Owen, pp. 225–256].

——— A seasonable and earnest address to the citizens of London, soon after the dreadful fire in 1666. By rev. James Janeway. [With] dr. Smollett's account of the said conflagration. Together with a particular relation of the great fire of Boston, in New-England; March 20, 1760. 55 pp. 16°. *Boston, B. Mecom,* [1760].

Janiçon (François Michel). Lettres sérieuses et badines, sur un livre intitulé, État présent de la république des Provincies-Unies. Et sur d'autres ouvrages. 1re partie. v. 1. lvi, 292 pp. 16°. *La Haye, J. van Duren,* 1729.

——— Lettres sérieuses et badines sur les ouvrages des savans, et sur d'autres matières. v. 2–4. Part 1. 5 v. 16°. *La Haye, J. van Duren,* 1729–30.

Janney (Samuel M.) The last of the Lenapé, and other poems. 180 pp. 12°. *Philadelphia, H. Perkins,* 1839.

——— A teacher's gift. Consisting of original essays in prose and verse, and translations from the french. 1 p. l. iv, 9–170 pp. 1 pl. 18°. *Philadelphia, T. E. Chapman,* 1840.

Janson (Baldwin). A practical grammar of the dutch language, with exercises to each rule. 3d ed. 1 p. l. 304 pp. 12°. *London, T. Boosey,* 1803.

Jarratt (*Rev.* Devereux). Sermons on various and important subjects, in practical divinity, adapted to the meanest capacities, and suited to the family and closet. v. 3. 321 pp. 1 l. 16°. *Philadelphia, W. W. Woodward,* 1794.

Jarrett (*Rev.* Thomas). The holy gospels and the acts of the apostles. *London,* 1857. *See* **Bible.** (*English*).

Jaudon (Daniel). A system of polite learning, being an epitome of the arts and sciences, for the use of schools. 5th american ed. improved. Frontispiece, 214 pp. 18°. *Philadelphia, B. Warner,* 1816.

[Title-page imperfect].

Jauffret (Louis François). Fables nouvelles. 2 v. 1 p. l. xxviii, 211 pp. 3 pl; 2 p. l. 210 pp. 3 pl. 16°. *Paris, Maradan,* 1815.

Jay (*Rev.* William). Memoirs of the life and character of the late rev. Cornelius Winter. 1st amer. ed. xii, 371 pp. 12°. *New York, S. Whiting & co.* 1811.

Jay (W. M. L.) My winter in Cuba. 296 pp. 12°. *New York, E. P. Dutton & co.* 1871.

Jeaffreson (John Cordy). Annals of Oxford. 2 v. vi, 356 pp; vi, 328 pp. 8°. *London, Hurst & Blackett,* 1871.

Jeake (Samuel, *senior*). *Λογιστικηλογία*, or arithmetick surveighed and reviewed: in four books. Wherein the nature of numbers ab-

Jeake (Samuel)—continued. solutely abstract, generally and specially contract, with their simple and comparative elements, are plainly declared, and fully handled. 9 p. l. 664 pp. 10 l. fol. *London, J. R. & R. D. for W. Kettilby*, 1696.

Jeanie's scrap-book. [*anon.*] 216 pp. 2 pl. 18°. *Philadelphia, Presbyterian board of publication*, [1861].

Jeffers (William N.) Nautical surveying. 292 pp. 9 pl. 8°. *New York, D. Van Nostrand*, 1871.

Jeffreys (John Gwyn, *f. r. s.*) British conchology, or an account of the mollusca which now inhabit the British isles and the surrounding seas. v. 5. Marine shells, and naked mollusca to the end of the gastropoda, the pteropoda, and cephalopoda; with a supplement and other matter, concluding the work. 1 p. l. 258 pp. 1 l. 103 col. pl. 12°. *London, J. Van Voorst*, 1869.

Jeffries (B. Joy, *m. d.*) Animal and vegetable parasites of the human skin and hair. 102 pp. 16°. *Boston, A. Moore*, 1872.

——— The eye in health and disease: being a series of articles on the anatomy and physiology of the human eye, and its surgical and medical treatment. 119 pp. 8°. *Boston, A. Moore*, 1871.

Jeffries (David). A treatise on diamonds and pearls; in which their importance is considered; and plain rules are exhibited for ascertaining the value of both; also the true method of manufacturing diamonds. 4th ed. with large improvements. 1 p. l. xvi, 116 pp. 30 pl. 16°. *London, E. Lumley*, [*about* 1860].

Jelinek (Carl). Die temperatur-verhältnisse der jahre 1848–1863 an den stationen des österreichischen beobachtungsnetzes, durch fünftägige mittel dargestellt. Auf kosten der kaiserlichen academie der wissenschaften herausgegeben. 1 p. l. 146 pp. 2 pl. 4°. *Wien, druck der k. k. hof- und staatsdruckerei*, 1869.

Jelliffe (W. M.) Good selections, in prose and poetry. 166 pp. 12°. *New York, J. W. Schermerhorn & co.* 1872.

Jencke (Johann Friedrich). Freie gaben für geist und gemüth. Zur erweiterung des unterstützungsfonds für arme erwachsene taubstumme. Zweiter jahrgang, 1853. 398 pp. 1 l. 1 pl. 1 map. 8°. *Dresden, herausgeber*, 1853.

Jenkin (Robert, *d. d.*) The reasonableness and certainty of the christian religion. 6th ed. corrected. 2 v. 4 p. l. lii, 422 pp; 1 p. l. lxx, 560 pp. 8°. *London, J. J. & P. Knapton*, [*etc.*] 1734.

Jenkins (Alexander). The history and description of the city of Exeter, and its environs, ancient and modern, civil and ecclesiastical. 5 p. l. 451 pp. 2 l. 12 pl. 8°. *Exeter*, [*Eng.*] *P. Hedgeland*, 1806.

Jenkins (Amaziah). Systematic lectures on english grammar. 256 pp. 16°. *Rochester (N. Y.) W. Alling & co.* 1836.

Jenkins (*Capt.* Charles). England's triumph: or, spanish cowardice expos'd. Being a compleat history of the many signal victories gain'd by the royal navy and merchants ships of Great Britain, for the term of four hundred years past, over the insulting and haughty Spaniards. 300 pp. 2 pl. 1 table. 12°. *London*, 1739.

Jenkins (Edward). The coolie, his rights and wrongs. Notes of a journey to British Guiana, with a review of the system and of the recent commission of inquiry. By the author of "Ginx's baby." [*anon.*] xii, 446 pp. 8°. *London, Strahan & co.* 1871.

——— Ginx's baby. His birth and other misfortunes. A satire. [*anon.*] 3d american from the 5th London ed. xii, 224 pp. 16°. *New York, G. Routledge & sons*, 1871.

——— Lord Bantam. A satire. By the author of "Ginx's baby." [*anon.*] viii, 243 pp. 16°. *New York, G. Routledge & sons*, 1872.

Jenkins (Thornton A.) The rule of the road at sea and in inland waters; or, steering and sailing rules. *See* **United States.** *Navy department. Bureau of navigation.*

Jenks (A. S.) The heart and voice; or, songs of praise for the sanctuary. Hymn and tune book, designed for congregational singing in the methodist episcopal church, and for congregations generally. 448 pp. 8°. *Philadelphia, Perkinpine & Higgins*, [1865].

Jenks (*Rev.* George H.) The Lord's day of the early church; what it was, and how observed,—proved by christian writers of the first three centuries. 67 pp. 16°. *San Francisco, Libby & Swett*, 1871.

Jenner (*Rev.* David). The prerogative of primogeniture: shewing, that the right of succession to an hereditary crown, depends not upon grace, religion, &c. but onely upon birth-right and primogeniture; and that the chief cause of all, or most, rebellions in christendom, is a fanatical belief, that, temp-

Jenner (*Rev.* David)—continued. oral dominion is founded in grace. 8 p. l. 192 pp. 2 l. 16°. *London, J. Hindmarsh*, 1685.

Jennings (Edward, *lieut. r. n.*) Hints on sea-risks, containing some practical suggestions for diminishing maritime losses both of life and property; addressed to merchants, ship-owners, and mariners. xvi, 102 pp. 1 pl. 8°. *London, R. B. Bate*, 1844.

Jennings (*Rev.* John). Two discourses; the first, of preaching Christ; the second, of particular and experimental preaching. With a preface by dr. Isaac Watts. 4th ed. [With] a letter concerning the most useful way of preaching, by dr. A. H. Franck. 86 pp. 16°. *Boston, J. Edwards and H. Foster*, 1740.

——— The same. Of preaching Christ. Of particular and experimental preaching. 12°. [*Philadelphia, W. W. Woodward*, 1810].

[*In* WILLIAMS (Edward, *d. d.*) The christian preacher. 1810. pp. 45–76].

Jennings (Robert). Cattle and their diseases, embracing their history and breeds, crossing and breeding, and feeding and management; with the diseases to which they are subject, and the remedies best adapted to their cure. 340 pp. 12°. *Philadelphia, J. E. Potter*, 1863.

——— The horse and his diseases. To which are added, Rarey's method of taming horses, and the law of warranty as applicable to the purchase and sale of the animal. 384 pp. 12°. *Philadelphia, J. E. Potter*, 1860.

Jennings (W. J.) The lumberman and builder. 62 pp. 8°. *St. Louis, E. F. Hobart & co.* 1871–72.

Jephson (Henry L.) Notes on irish questions. 1 p. l. ix, 336 pp. 8°. *Dublin, W. McGee*, 1870.

Jephson (Robert). The confessions of James Baptiste Couteau, citizen of France, written by himself; and translated from the original french by R. Jephson. [*pseudon.* 1st ed.] 2 v. 7 p. l. 257 pp. 7 pl; 3 p. l. 232 pp. 2 pl. 12°. *London, J. Debrett*, 1794.

Jepson (B.) The elementary music reader. Book first. 168 pp. 8°. *New Haven (Conn.) C. C. Chatfield & co.* 1871.

Jerment (*Rev.* George). Life of bishop Leighton. 8°. *London, R. Ogle*, 1811.

[*In* LEIGHTON (Robert). Remains, pp. i–c].

——— Parental duty: or, the religious education of children, illustrated and urged in several discourses. viii, 169 pp. 12°. *London, author*, 1791.

[HAZARD pamphlets, v. 71].

Jerningham (Edward). Poems on various subjects. Viz. The nunnery, The magdalens, The nun, Ruins of an abbey, Yarico to Inkle, Il latte, fugitive pieces. 2 p. l. 119 pp. 16°. *London, J. Robson*, 1767.

Jerome *of Prague.* *See* **Huss** (Johann).

Jerome (M. *pseudon.*) *See* **Français de Nantes** (*comte* Antoine).

Jerome (Stephen). Seaven helpes to heaven. 3d. ed. 11 p. l. 537 pp. 16°. *London, I. W. & A. M. for R. Iackson*, 1620.

Jerrold (W. Blanchard). Cent per cent. A story written upon a bill stamp. 268 pp. 5 pl. 12°. *London, J. C. Hotten*, [1869].

Jerusalem (Johann Friedrich Wilhelm). Betrachtungen über die vornehmsten wahrheiten der religion. 2 v. in 3. 8°. *Braunschweig, Waisenhaus-buchhandlung*, 1776–91.

Jervis (John B.) Railway property. A treatise on the construction and management of railways. 341 pp. 12°. *New York, Phinney, Blakeman & Mason*, 1861.

Jeschua ben Sira. Sententiæ morales ben Syrae, vetvstissimi avthoris hebræi, qui a Iudæis nepos Hieremiæ prophetæ fuisse creditur, cum succincto commentario. [Hebrew and latin]. 32 l. 4°. *Isnæ*, 1542.

Jesse (Edward). A summer's day at Hampton court, being a guide to the palace and gardens; with an illustrative catalogue of the pictures. viii, 135 pp. 9 pl. 16°. *London, J. Murray*, 1839.

Jesuits' (The) morals. *See* **Perrault** (Nicolas).

Jesus (Society of). Le journal des jésuites, [1645–1668]. *See* **Journal** (Le) des jésuites.

Jésus-Christ sous l'anathème et l'excommunication. [*anon.*] ix, 61 pp. 1 l. 8°. *Amsterdam, N. Potier*, 1731.

[*With* BOYER (Pierre). Portrait au naturel des jésuites et anciens et modernes. *Amsterdam*, 1731].

Jesus! der getreueste gefehrte u. helffer, zu wasser und lande, darinnen tägliche morgen- und abend-seegen, buss- beicht- comūnion- reise- und andere gebete und lieder enthalten; wobey auch allerhand rechen-tafeln zum waaren-einkauff und verkauff, auch zinss-tafeln, &c. Nebst dem wegweiser, sonnen-zeiger, wind- und see-compass, &c. [*anon.*] 2 v. 3 p. l. 170 pp. 1 l. 1 pl; 250 pp. 1 l. 18°. *Leipzig & Waldenburg, G. Hofmann*, [1747]?

Jesus meine liebe. Katholisches gebetbuch für kirche und haus. [*anon.*] 432 pp. 18°. *Einsiedeln, New York & Cincinnati, K. & N. Benziger*, 1871.

Jesus (The) of history. [*anon.*] xx, 426 pp. 8°. *London, Williams & Norgate*, 1869.

Jeter (Jeremiah B. *d. d.*) Scriptural communion. 70 pp. 18°. *Philadelphia, American baptist publication society*, [1871].

——— The seal of heaven: or the impression of divine truth on a candid mind. 204 pp. 12°. *New York, American tract society*, [1871].

Jevons (W. Stanley). The theory of political economy. xvi, 267 pp. 8°. *London, Macmillan & co.* 1871.

Jewel (John, *bishop of Salisbury*). A defense of the Apologie of the churche of Englande. Conteininge an answeare to a certaine booke lately set foorthe by M. Hardinge, and entituled, A confutation of the Apology of the church of England. Whereunto there is also newly added an answeare unto another like booke, written by the saide M. Hardinge, entituled, A detection of sundrie foule errours &c. Printed at Louiane, anno 1568. 21 p. l. 801 pp. fol. *London, H. Wykes*, 1570.

Jewett (Charles, *m. d.*) A forty years' fight with the drink demon, or a history of the temperance reform as I have seen it, and of my labor in connection therewith. 409 pp. 8 pl. 12°. *New York, National temperance society and publishing house*, 1872.

Jewett (*Rev.* Milo P.) The mode and subjects of baptism. 3d ed. 129 pp. 16°. *Boston, Gould, Kendall & Lincoln*, 1840.

Jewett (Moses, *m. d.*) Jewett's family physician. The iatroleptic practice of medicine, or the curing of diseases principally by external application and friction. 534 pp. 8°. *Columbus (O.) author*, 1838.

Jewett (*Mrs.* Susan W.) From fourteen to fourscore. iv, 416 pp. 12°. *New York, Hurd & Houghton*, 1871.

Jewish church. Gesänge und gebete für den öffentlichen gottesdienst der Israeliten. 1 p. l. iv, 106 pp. 12°. [*Baltimore, Deutsch & Golderman*, 1871].

[*With* JEWISH church. Israelitisches gebetbuch. 1871].

——— Israelitisches gebetbuch für den öffentlichen gottesdienst im ganzen jahre geordnet und übersetzt von Benjamin Szold. [Hebrew and german]. 2te aufl. viii, 592 pp. 12°. *Baltimore, Deutsch & Golderman*, 1871.

Jewry (*Miss* Laura). Audrey. A novel. 3 v. 12°. *London, T. C. Newby*, 1853.

Joanna of Naples. [A novel]. *See* **Hall** (Louisa J. Park).

Joannes *actuarius*. Opera. De actionibvs et spiritus animalis affectibȝ eiusqȝ nutritione lib. ii. [Julio Alexandrino tridentino interprete]. De vrinis lib. vii. [Ambrosio Leone interprete]. Methodi medendi lib. vi. [Cornelio Henrico Mathesio interprete]. 2 v. in 1. 9 p. l. 408 pp; 653 pp. 16°. *Parisiis, apud Bernardum Turrisanum in aldina bibliotheca*, 1556.

Jobbry (Archibald, *pseudon.*) *See* **Galt** (John).

Jobert (Louis). La science des médailles, pour l'instruction de ceux qui commencent à s'appliquer à la connoissance des médailles antiques & modernes. [*anon.*] 4 p. l. 304 pp. 11 l. 16°. *Paris, L. Lucas*, [*etc.*] 1692.

Jobson (David Wemyss). Outlines of the anatomy and physiology of the teeth, etc. Their diseases and treatment. With practical observations on artificial teeth. viii, 270 pp. 4 pl. 8°. *Edinburgh, W. Tait*, 1834.

Jobson (Richard). The golden trade: or, a discouery of the riuer Gambra, and the golden trade of the Aethiopians. Also, the commerce with a great blacke merchant, called Buckor Sano, and his report of the houses couered with gold, and other strange obseruations for the good of our owne countrey; set downe as they were collected in trauelling, part of the yeares, 1620, and 1621. 3 p. l. 166 pp. sm. 4°. *London, N. Okes*, 1623.

Johlson (J.) Instruction in the mosaic religion. Translated from the german. By Isaac Leeser. viii, 139 pp. 8°. *Philadelphia, A. Waldie*, 5590, [1830].

John xxii (*pope*, Jacques d'Euse). L'élixir des philosophes, avtrement, l'art transmutatoire, attribué au pape Iean xxii. de ce nom: nõ encores veu, ny imprimé par cy deuant. 205 pp. 18°. *Lyon, M. Bonhomme*, 1557.

[*With* BACON (Roger). Le miroire d'alqvimie. 1557].

John *of Austria*. Diario, e lettera sopra gli affari correnti. Con vn ritratto della sua vita, cioè, nascità, qualità, costumi, attioni, e gouerni. 120 pp. 16°. [*Cologna, per L. Tivoglio*, 1675].

[*In* DIETA (La) di vari avtori. 1675].

John, *the hermit*. The hermit of Erving castle, Erving, Mass. [*anon.*] 60 pp. 12°. *Erving, published for the benefit of the hermit*, 1871.

John Amundesham. *See* **Amundesham** (John).

John Bull. [London weekly]. Jan. 7 to Dec. 30, 1871. v. 51. fol. *London, J. H. Batty*, 1871.

John Bull's scientific (?) man-machine, 1871. *See* **Wood** (L. A.)

Johnny Wright, the boy who tried to do right. By the author of "Little boy True." [etc. *anon.*] 300 pp. 2 pl. 18°. *Philadelphia, Presbyterian board of publication,* [1861].

Johns (*Rev.* Bennett George). The land of silence and the land of darkness. xi, 194 pp. 16°. *London, Longman,* 1857.

Johnson (Alexander B.) The philosophy of human knowledge, or a treatise on language. vi, 3–200 pp. *New York, G. & C. Carvill,* 1828.

——— Religion in its relation to the present life. 180 pp. 16°. *New York, Harper & brothers,* 1841.

——— A treatise on language: or the relation which words bear to things. [2d ed.] xxvi, 33–274 pp. 8°. *New York, Harper & brothers,* 1836.

Johnson (Anna C.) The Iroquois; or, the bright side of indian character. By Minnie Myrtle. [*pseudon.*] 317 pp. 8 pl. 12°. *New York, D. Appleton & co.* 1855.

Johnson (A. N.) The american choir: a collection of church music; to which is prefixed Johnson's new system for conducting choirs and teaching singing schools. 384 pp. obl. 8°. *New York, H. G. Abbey,* 1858. s.

——— Domestic concert collection, no. 1. For social singing associations. 80 pp. 1 l. obl. 8°. *Cincinnati, J. Church & co.* [1871].

——— Instructions in thorough base; being a new and easy method for learning to play church music upon the piano forte or organ. iv, 120 pp. obl. 8°. *New York, S. T. Gordon,* [1871].

——— The key-stone collection of church music: a complete collection of hymn tunes, anthems, psalms, chants, &c. [Also] the physiological system, for training choirs and teaching singing schools; and the cantata, The morning of freedom. 352 pp. obl. 8°. *Lancaster city (Pa.) Murray, Young & co.* 1856. s.

——— The true psalmist: a collection of psalm-tunes, chants and anthems, for public worship, and of social music, set pieces and choruses. Containing also Johnson's method for teaching the art of reading music, and Johnson's method for training chorus choirs. 384 pp. obl. 8°. *Cincinnati, J. Church & co.* [1871].

Johnson (A. N.)—continued.

——— The true singing school text book. 192 pp. obl. 8°. *Cincinnati, J. Church & co.* [1871].

Johnson (E.) The judge's pets. Stories of a family and its dumb friends. v, 206 pp. 16°. *New York, Hurd & Houghton,* 1872.

Johnson (Howard F. *m. d.*) The treatment of incurable diseases. 2 p. l. 159 pp. 1 pl. 8°. *London, Longman, Brown, Green and Longmans,* 1851.

Johnson (I. D. *m. d.*) Therapeutic key; or, practical guide for the homœopathic treatment of acute diseases. 179 pp. 24°. *Philadelphia, F. E. Boericke,* 1872.

Johnson (James, *surgeon*). The oriental voyager; or, descriptive sketches and cursory remarks, on a voyage to India and China, in his majesty's ship Caroline, performed in the years 1803–4–5–6. Interspersed with extracts from the best modern voyages and travels. xvi, 388 pp. 6 l. 1 table. 8°. *London, J. Asperne,* 1807.

Johnson (Jeremiah, *jr.*) The young singer's friend; or, the Lee avenue collection of hymns and songs, sacred and secular. Compiled by the superintendent, Jeremiah Johnson, jr. 3 parts. 4 p. l. 316, 210, 137 pp. 24°. *New York, A. S. Barnes & co.* 1859.

Johnson (James C.) Flower festival on the banks of the Rhine: a cantata for floral and other concerts, together with conversations on the elements of music. 112 pp. obl. 12°. *Boston, J. R. Miller,* [1855]. s.

——— Juvenile oratorios: a collection of songs designed for floral and other concerts, juvenile classes, schools, etc. 176 pp. obl. 12°. *Boston, Wilkins, Carter & co.* 1849.

——— (*editor*). Carmina melodia: a song book for schools and seminaries, including a complete elementary course, by A. N. Johnson, a large collection of new songs, by J. C. Johnson, and chorals for elementary practice, by William Tillinghast. 192 pp. obl. 12°. *Boston, J. R. Miller,* 1855.

Johnson (Jesse Zimmerman). The young student: or, literary remains of J. Zimmerman Johnson, with a brief sketch of his life, by his father. Edited by J. Newton Brown, d. d. 192 pp. 1 portrait. 16°. *Philadelphia, J. A. Wagenseller,* 1865.

Johnson (M. R.) *and* **Kennedy** (P. W.) The accountant's guide, a practical work on double entry book-keeping. 212 pp. 8°. [*New York, Johnson & Kennedy,* 1871].

Johnson (Nathaniel Emmons). Household consecration. 192 pp. 12°. *New York, E. Collier,* 1836.

——— The sacred seal; or the wanderer restored, a poem. 80 pp. 1 pl. 12°. *New York, J. S. Taylor & co.* 1843.

Johnson (Robert B.) A history of rowing in America, containing a treatise on rowing, training and exercise, with all necessary information for amateur and professional oarsmen. With contributions from William Blaikie, Joshua Ward, C. P. Kunhardt, Benj. F. Brady, Stephen Roberts, A. McC. Duncan, Robert Fulton. 270 pp. 1 l. 12°. *Milwaukee, Corbitt & Johnson,* 1871.

Johnson (Rosa Vertner). Poems. 334 pp. 1 portrait. 12°. *Boston, Ticknor & Fields,* 1857.

Johnson (Samuel, *ll. d.*) The life of Johnson [*anon.* By Arthur Murphy]: with maxims and observations, moral, critical, and miscellaneous, accurately selected from the works of dr. Samuel Johnson, and arranged in alphabetical order. From the 5th London edition. 285 pp. 18°. *Boston, Marsh, Capen & Lyon, & B. H. Greene,* 1833.

——— The plan of a dictionary of the english language; addressed to the right hon. Philip Dormer [Stanhope], earl of Chesterfield. 1 p. l. 34 pp. 4°. *London, J. & P. Knapton,* [*etc.*] 1747.

Johnson (*Mrs.* Susannah). A narrative of the captivity of mrs. Johnson. Containing an account of her sufferings, during four years with the Indians and French. [1754-58. 1st ed.] 144 pp. 16°. *Walpole, New Hampshire, David Carlisle, jun.* 1796.

Johnson (*Mrs.* S. O.) Every woman her own flower gardener. A handy manual of flower gardening for ladies. 148 pp. 1 pl. 4°. *New York, H. T. Williams,* 1871.

Johnson (Virginia W.) What the world made them. By the author of "Travels of an american owl." [*anon.*] 284 pp. 12°. *New York, G. P. Putnam & son,* 1871.

Johnson (Walter R.) The scientific class-book. *See* **Moffat** (John M.)

Johnson & Lund. Catalogue of dentists' materials. 253 pp. 8°. *Philadelphia,* 1871.

Johnston (Emma M.) The children's speaker. *See* **Boyd** (*Mrs.* E. E.) *and* **Johnston.**

Johnston (James Dale). Detroit directory, 1855. *See* **Detroit.**

Johnston (John, *d. d.*) The autobiography and ministerial life of rev. John Johnston, d. d. Edited and compiled by the rev. James Carnahan, d. d. Together with an appendix. 225 pp. 2 portraits, 1 pl. 12°. *New York, M. W. Dodd,* 1856.

Johnston (John, *prof. in Wesleyan university*). A manual of natural philosophy. New and revised ed. 379 pp. 1 pl. 12°. *Philadelphia, Thomas, Cowperthwait & co.* 1851. s.

Johnston (R. M.) The English classics: a historical sketch of the literature of England from the earliest times to the accession of king George iii. 275 pp. 12°. *Philadelphia, J. B. Lippincott & co.* 1860.

Johnston (William, *m. d.*) The good samaritan; or, sick man's friend: intended as a pocket companion, for thomsonians, and all others who would wish to prevent, or cure their own diseases. 288 pp. 18°. *Philadelphia,* 1841.

Johonnot (Jackson). The remarkable adventures of Jackson Johonnot, of Massachusetts, who served as a soldier in the western army, in the expedition under gen. Harmer and gen. St. Clair, containing an account of his captivity, sufferings, and escape from the Kickappoo Indians. Written by himself. 24 pp. 8°. *Greenfield (Mass.) A. Phelps,* 1816.

Jolliffe (Thomas Robert). Narrative of an excursion from Corfu to Smyrna; comprising a progress through Albania and the north of Greece; with some account of Athens. To which is annexed, a translation of the Erastae, of Plato. By the author of "Letters from Palestine." [*anon.*] 1 p. l. xvi, 272 pp. 8°. *London, Black, Young & Young,* 1827.

Jolly (The) angler; or water-side companion, containing an account of all the best places for angling, as well as the tackle, baits, & other requisites to form an expert angler. [*anon.*] 4th ed. Frontispiece, 100 pp. 12°. *London, J. March,* [1842].

Jolly (*Baron* M. L.) Monographie de la chapelle de Bourgogne à Anvers. [French, german, dutch, and english texts]. 10 l. 12 pl. fol. *Vienne, imprimerie impériale,* 1858. s.

Jonak (Eberhard A. *editor*). Bericht über die allgemeine-ausstellung zu Paris, 1855. *See* **Austria.** (*K. k. ministerium für handel*).

Jonas (Justus). Apology of the Augsburg confession. [1531]. *See* **Melanchthon** (Philip) *and* **Jonas.**

Jones (Abner). Church melodies: a collection of psalms, hymns, and spiritual songs;

Jones (Abner)—continued. adapted to public and social worship, from dr. Watts and other authors. With directions for musical expression. 736 pp. 24°. *New-York, Moore & Payne*, 1833.

Jones (Charles C. *jr.*) Historical sketch of Tomo-chi-chi, mico of the Yama Craws. 133 pp. 8°. *Albany (N. Y.) J. Munsell*, 1868.

——— Reminiscences of the last days, death and burial of general Henry Lee. 43 pp. 1 portrait. 4°. *Albany (N. Y.) J. Munsell*, 1870.

Jones (Charles L. S.) American lyrics: comprising The discovery, a poem; sapphic, pindaric and common odes; songs and tales of american and patriotic subjects. And also imitations from the greek, latin, french, and spanish. 306 pp. 12°. *Mobile, Pollard & Dade*, 1834.

Jones (Charles P.) Roman catholicism scripturally considered; or, the church of Rome the great apostasy. 396 pp. 12°. *New York, M. W. Dodd*, 1856.

Jones (Edward C.) The harp of Sylva. 218 pp. 12°. *Philadelphia, R. S. George*, 1841.

Jones (Frederick). History [of the world] from 1831 to 1840. 8°. [*Philadelphia*, 1841].

[*In* ROTTECK (Carl von). General history of the world, v. 4, pp. 342–393].

Jones (Henry). Poems on several occasions. xxxi, 212 pp. 8°. *London, R. Dodsley*, 1749.

Jones (James A.) Haverhill; or, memoirs of an officer in the army of Wolfe. 2 v. 2 p. l. 228 pp; 1 p. l. 263 pp. 12°. *New-York, J. & J. Harper*, 1831.

Jones (Jesse H.) The kingdom of heaven; what it is; where it is; and the duty of american christians concerning it. xix, 362 pp. 12°. *Boston, author*, 1871.

Jones (Joel, *ll. d.*) Notes on scripture. 584 pp. 8°. *Philadelphia, W. S. & A. Martien*, 1861.

Jones (*Rev.* John). Bishop Hall, his life and times: or, memoirs of the life, writings and sufferings, of the rt. rev. Joseph Hall, d. d; with a view of the times in which he lived; and an appendix, containing some of his unpublished writings, his funeral sermon, [by rev. J. Whitefoot], &c. xvi, 582 pp. 8°. *London, L. B. Seeley & son*, 1826.

Jones (John B.) Wild southern scenes. A tale of disunion! and border war! 502 pp. 1 pl. 12°. *Philadelphia, T. B. Peterson & brothers*, [1859].

Jones (*Rev.* Joseph). The apocalypse. *See* **Bible.** (*English*).

Jones (*Miss* J.) "Una and her paupers:" memorials of Agnes Elizabeth Jones, by her sister. With an introduction by Florence Nightingale. 1st am. from the 2d Lond. ed. With an introductory preface by the rev. Henry Ward Beecher. And a supplementary chapter on hospital nursing and training in the United States, by the author of "Woman's work in the civil war," [L. P. Brockett]. xlvi, 497 pp. 12°. *New York, G. Routledge & sons*, 1872.

Jones (Joseph Huntington, *d. d.*) The brazen serpent, or faith in Christ illustrated. 108 pp. 2 pl. 18°. *Philadelphia, Presbyterian board of publication*, 1864.

——— Man, moral and physical: or the influence of health and disease on religious experience. xviii, 7–300 pp. 12°. *Philadelphia, W. S. & A. Martien*, 1860.

——— Outline of a work of grace in the presbyterian congregation at New Brunswick, N. J. during the year 1837. 148 pp. 16°. *Philadelphia, H. Perkins*, 1839.

Jones (Joshua). English grammar, in two parts. The first, a brief analysis of the english language. The second, a practical system of etymology and syntax. xii, 7–172 pp. 16°. *West-Chester (Penn.) S. Siegfried*, 1833.

Jones (Judson). The alphabet of orthoëpy and its application to monosyllables. 96 pp. 16°. *St. Paul, Press printing co.* 1870.

Jones (*Rev.* Lot). Memoir of mrs. Sarah Louisa Taylor; or an illustration of the work of the holy spirit, in awakening, renewing, and sanctifying the heart. Eng. title, 324 pp. 1 portrait. 12°. *New York, J. S. Taylor*, 1838.

Jones (L. J.) The southern minstrel: a collection of psalm and hymn tunes, odes and anthems: in three parts, selected from eminent authors, together with a number of new tunes, never before published, suited to nearly every metre. 280 pp. 1 l. obl. 8°. *Philadelphia, Grigg, Elliot & co.* 1849. s.

Jones (Owen). Examples of chinese ornament selected from objects in the South Kensington museum and other collections. Eng. title, 15 pp. 100 pl. fol. *London, S. & T. Gilbert*, 1867.

——— *and* **Goury** (Jules). Views on the Nile: from Cairo to the second cataract: drawn on stone by George Moore, from sketches taken in 1832 and 1833 by Owen

Jones (O.) *and* **Goury** (J.)—continued. Jones and the late Jules Goury; with historical notices of the monuments by Samuel Birch. Eng. title, 33 l. 30 pl. fol. *London, Graves and Warmsley*, 1843.

Jones (Silas). Practical phrenology. 336 pp. 12°. *Boston, Russell, Shattuck & Williams*, 1836.

Jones (Stephen). Masonic miscellanies, in poetry and prose. Containing i. The muse of masonry, comprising one hundred and seventy masonic songs. ii. The masonic essayist. iii. The freemason's vade-mecum. xi, 328 pp. 18°. *London, Vernor & Hood*, 1797.

——— A new biographical dictionary: containing a brief account of the most eminent persons and remarkable characters in every age and nation. 8th ed. 2 p. l. 464 pp. 18°. *London, Longman, Orme & co.* [*etc.*] 1840.

Jones (S. S.) The sunday question, and self-contradictions of the bible. Also, a lecture by Parker Pillsbury on "the sabbath." 123 pp. 12°. *Chicago, Religio-philosophical publishing house*, 1871.

Jones (Thomas). The principles and practice of book-keeping. 2 p. l. 160 pp. 8°. *New York, Wiley & Putnam*, 1841.

Jones (*Sir* William). Poeseos asiaticæ commentariorum libri sex, cum appendice; subjicitur limon, seu miscellaneorum liber. 2 p. l. xxxii, 542 pp. 1 l. 1 pl. 8°. *Londini, e typographeo richardsoniano, veneunt apud T. Cadell*, 1774.

Jones (*Rev.* William, *f. r. s.*) Physiological disquisitions; or, discourses on the natural philosophy of the elements. viii, xxxii, 627 pp. 8 pl. 4°. *London, J. Rivington & sons*, 1781.

——— Memoirs of the life, studies, and writings of the rt. rev. George Horne, d. d. [Also], his lordship's own collection of his thoughts on a variety of great and interesting subjects. 2 p. l. 418 pp. 1 portrait. 8°. *London, G. G. & J. Robinson*, 1795.

Jones (*Rev.* William, 1762–1846). Some account of the life and writings of [Samuel Stennett, d. d.] 8°. *London, T. Tegg*, 1824.

[*In* STENNETT (*Samuel, d. d.*) *Works. v. 1, pp.* v–xxxviii].

Jones (Willoughby). The life of James Fisk, jr. including the great frauds of the Tammany ring. With brilliant pen pictures in the lights and shadows of New York life. Illustrated. 512 pp. 8°. *Philadelphia, Union publishing co.* 1872.

Jonghe. *See* **Junius.**

Jongtys (Daniel). Tooneel der jalouzijen, waar op vertoont werden veel treurige gevallen, wonderlijke geschiedenissen, en schrikkelijke wreede uitwerkselen der jaloersheid. 2e druk. v. 2. Eng. title, 3 p. l. 836 pp. 8 l. 16°. *Amsterdam, Willem de Coup*, [*etc.*] 1699.

Jonson (Ben). Execration against Vvlcan. With divers epigrams by the same author to severall noble personages in this kingdome. Never published before. 28 l. unp. 4°. *London, J. Benson*, 1640.

——— Works. [Specimen of a proposed new ed.] v. 1. Containing, [a part of] Every man in his humour. 64 pp. 8°. [*London*, 1792].

[*In* WALDRON (F. G.) Literary museum. *London*, 1792].

Jordan (Cornelia J. M.) Richmond: her glory and her graves. A poem. In two parts. xxxix pp. 8°. *Richmond* (*Va.*) *Medical journal print*, 1867.

Jordan (H. J. *m. d.*) The philosophy of marriage, being eight important lectures on the functions and disorders of the nervous system, reproductive organs and special diseases. xi, 176 pp. 18°. *New York*, [1871].

Joris *or* **Jorisz** (David). Alle vaten sichtmen wtgheuen wat sy inhebben: alsoe moeten alle natuerē der kruyden, creatueren vnde ruchten der aerden van ghelijck, haer vermoeghen vnde aert na, voortbrenghen, weer sy willen oder niet: euen is my dit ten ghoede gheschiet. [*anon.*] *b. l.* 1 p. l. 40 l. fol. [*n. p.* 1556].

[*With his* Verklaringke der scheppenissen].

——— Een leerlijk vñ christlijck ghespreck tusschen een godtgheleert, bibelschgheleerdt vnde sophistgeleert. [*anon.*] *b. l.* 39 l. fol. [*n. p.* 1555] ?

[*With his* Verklaringke der scheppenissen].

——— Een seer schoon vnde heerlyck tractaet off onderwys, van Godes gheest, liefde vnde stemme, mit de verlooren mensche. [*anon.*] *b. l.* 57 l. fol. [*n. p.* 1553].

[*With his* Verklaringke der scheppenissen].

——— Verklaringke der scheppenissen, an v mijn veminde kinderen vnde ghebroeders, liefhebberen Christi alleen verschreuen. [*anon.*] *b. l.* 1 p. l. 137 l. numb. 10 l. unnumb. fol. [*n. p.* 1553].

[*Note.*—This famous fanatic founded the anabaptist sect].

Josephus (Flavius). [De bello Judaico] Historiarum Iosephi libri nvmero vii. Platyna [Bartolommeo de Sacchi] emendavit.

Josephus (Flavius)—continued.
1761. fol. *Impressit Arnoldvs Pannartz in domo Petri de Max. civis romani*, 1475.
[*Note.*—This is the first separate publication of the treatise De bello Judaico. The translation is probably that once attributed to Rufinus, but really made by Ambrosius. 38 lines to a page. No pagination, signatures, or catchwords].

—— The destruction of Jerusalem; abridged from the history of the jewish wars, by Flavius Josephus. With a description of Palestine; together with an epitome of its modern history. By rev. Daniel Smith. 206 pp. 1 pl. 18°. *New York, T. Mason & G. Lane*, 1840.

Jouffroy (Thomas Simon). Moral philosophy: extracts from Jouffroy. Translated by Robert N. Toppan. 318 pp. 12°. *New York, W. H. Tinson*, 1862.

Jourdan (Jean Baptiste). The life and military exploits of Pyrrhus, king of Epire. In six books. Written originally in french. And now render'd into english, by Thomas Mortimer. xvi, 462 pp. 8°. *London, C. Say, for the author*, 1751.

Journal britannique, par M. Maty. v. 1-18. 1750-55. 18°. *La Haye, H. Scheurleer, jun.* 1750-55.
[*Note.*—v. 19-21 wanting.
"Maty n'a rédigé que les dix-huit premiers volumes, les trois autres l'ont été par Mauvius. Joncourt a donné une continuation à ce recueil, sous le titre de Nouvelle bibliothèque anglaise."—*Quérard*].

Journal (A) by one of the suite of Thomas Beckington, during an embassy to negociate a marriage between Henry vi. and a daughter of the count of Armagnac, a. d. 1442. With notes and illustrations, by Nicholas Harris Nicolas. [*anon.*] lxxix, 130 pp. 8°. *London, W. Pickering*, 1828.

Journal des économistes. Revue de la science économique et de la statistique. 29e - 30e année. Janvier 1870-sept. 1871. 3e série. v. 17-23. 8°. *Paris, Guillaumin & cie.* 1870-71.

Journal (Le) des jésuites [1645-1668], publié d'après le manuscrit original conservé aux archives du séminaire de Québec, par m. m. les abbés Laverdière et Casgrain. x, 12 l. 403 pp. 4°. *Québec, L. Brousseau*, 1871.

Journal of a tour round the southern coasts of England. *See* **Manners** (John Henry).

Journal of a tour through North and South Wales, &c. *See* **Manners** (John Henry).

Journal of a tour to the northern parts of Great Britain. *See* **Manners** (John Henry).

Journal (The) of applied chemistry. Devoted to chemistry as applied to the arts, manufactures, metallurgy and agriculture. [Monthly]. Jan. to Dec. 1871. v. 6. 4°. *New York, Philadelphia, and Boston, Dexter & co.* 1871.

Journal (The) of applied science, and record of progress in the industrial arts. Edited by P. L. Simmonds. [Monthly]. Jan. 1870 to Dec. 1871. v. 1-2. fol. *London, W. Kent & co.* [1870-71].

Journal (The) of education for Ontario, edited under the direction of the rev. Egerton Ryerson, d. d. chief superintendent of education, by J. George Hodgins, deputy superintendent. [Monthly]. Jan. to Dec. 1871. v. 24. 4°. *Toronto, Hunter, Rose & co.* 1871.

Journal (The) of entomology. Descriptive and geographical. v. 1. 8°. *London, Taylor & Francis*, 1862. s.

Journal (The) of speculative philosophy. Edited by Wm. T. Harris. [Quarterly]. Jan. to Oct. 1871. v. 5. 8°. *St. Louis, R. P. Studley & co.* 1871.

Journal of the gynæcological society of Boston. [Monthly]. *See* **Boston** (Gynæcological society of).

Journal of the telegraph. A semi-monthly record of the progress of the telegraph, and of electric science. James D. Reid, editor. Dec. 1, 1870, to Nov. 15, 1871. v. 4. 4°. *New York, J. D. Reid*, [1871].

Journal. *See* **Iournal** *and* **Iournael.**

Journey-book (The) of England. *See* **Knight** (Charles).

Jousse (J.) A compendious dictionary of italian and other terms used in music; illustrated by numerous examples. 4 p. l. 147 pp. 8°. *London, Clementi & co.* [1829].

Jouy (Victor Joseph Étienne, *dit*). Bélisaire, tragédie en cinq actes et en vers. 4 p. l. xxxii, 87 pp. 8°. *Paris, Corréard & Alexis-Eymery*, 1818.
[*With* PLANARD (F. A. E. de). Le pré aux clercs. 1833].

Jovius (Paulus). *See* **Giovio** (Paolo).

Juan Bautista (*Fray*). Advertencias. Para los confessores de los naturales. Primera parte. 8 p. l. 112 l. 57 l. unp. 18°. *Mexico, en el conuento de Sanctiago Tlatilulco, M. Ocharte*, 1600.
[*Note.*—Imperfect: leaves wanting at the close of the Tabla.
With his Confessionario en lengva mexicana].

—— Confessionario en lengva mexicana y castellana. 8 p. l. 112 l. 2 l. unp. 18°. *Santiago Tlatilulco, [Mexico], Melchior Ocharte*, 1599.

Juan de San Bernardo. Devocion, y novena de la esclarecida virgen, y martyr s. Barbara. 3 p. l. 21 l. 18°. *Mexico, uiuda de F. R. Lupercio*, 1695.

Juarros (Domingo). Compendio de la historia de la ciudad de Guatemala. 2 v. 3 p. l. 385 pp; 1 p. l. xv, 361 pp. 8°. *Guatemala, I. Beteta*, 1808–18.

CONTENTS.

v. 1. i. Descripcion geografica del reyno de Guatemala. Geografia eclesiastica.
ii. Cronicon de la ciudad de Guatemala.
iii. Indice cronologico de los varones illustres, que ha tenido esta ciudad.
v. 2. iv. Parte 1a en que se discurre sobre algunos puntos de la historia de este reyno en general. [Historia de los Indios].
Parte 2a. De la historia de las provincias, que se hallan situadas en la parte austral del reyno de Guatemala.
v. De las provincias situades acia la mar del Norte.
vi. De las provincias situades en el medio.

Jubeltöne für sonntagschulen und den familienkreis. [*anon.*] 160 pp. obl. 16°. *Cleveland*, [*O.*] *Sonntagschul- und tractverein der evangelischen gemeinschaft*, [1871].

Judson (*Mrs.* Emily Chubbuck). [Letters]. 12°. [*New York*, 1860].
[*In* KENDRICK (A. C.) The life and letters of mrs. Judson].

Judson (L. Carroll). The masonic advocate: being a concise exposition and full defence of free masonry. With an appendix, containing an abridgment of Mackey's and Oliver's lexicons of free masonry. 2d ed. 2 p. l. 13–323 pp. 2 portraits. 12°. *Philadelphia, author*, 1859.

——— The probe, or one hundred and two essays on the nature of men and things. With an appendix, containing the declaration of independence, the constitution of the United States, Washington's farewell address, and a miniature biography of Washington and the signers. 272, 48 pp. 12°. *Philadelphia, G. B. Zieber & co.* 1846.

——— The same. The moral probe, or one hundred and two common-sense essays on the nature of men and things. With an appendix. 5th ed. 272, 64 pp. 12°. *Philadelphia, J. M. Stoddart & co.* 1872.

Julian (George W.) Speeches on political questions. With an introduction by L. Maria Child. xx, 472 pp. 1 portrait. 8°. *New York, Hurd & Houghton*, 1872.

Julianus *imperator* (Flavius Claudius). Juliani imp. misopogon, vel antiochensis, [graece et latine]. Interprete Petro Martinio. [Præfatio, vbi authoris vita ex variis,

Julianus *imperator* (F. C.)—continued.
præcipuè Marcellini, locis disseritur]. 18°. [*Lugduni Batavorum*, 1655].
[ELEGANTIORES præstantium virorum satyræ, v. 1, part 2, 12 l. pp. 106–213].

——— Cæsares, sive satyra in romanos imperatores: interprete Petro Cunæo, [P. Van der Kun]. In limine est ejusdem præfatio in Iulianum. 18°. [*Lugduni Batavorum*, 1655].
[ELEGANTIORES præstantium virorum satyræ, v. 1, pp. 111–168].

——— The same. [Graece et latine]. C. Cantoclaro [Charles Canteclair] interprete. 18°. [*Lugduni Batavorum*, 1655].
[ELEGANTIORES præstantium virorum satyræ, v. 1, part 2, 7 p. l. 12–105 pp.]

——— The same. Les Césars de l'empereur Julien, traduits du grec, par feu mr. le baron de Spanheim. 4 p. l. xliii, 288, 196 pp. 2 pl. 4°. *Amsterdam, F. l'Honoré*, 1728.

——— Œuvres complètes de l'empereur Julien, traduites, pour la première fois, du grec en français, accompagnées d'argumens et de notes, et précédées d'un abrégé historique et critique de sa vie; par R. Tourlet. 3 v. 8°. *Paris, auteur*, 1821.

——— Two orations of the emperor Julian; one to the sovereign sun, and the other to the mother of the gods; translated from the greek. With notes, and a copious introduction, in which some of the greatest arcana of the grecian theology are unfolded. lxviii, 204 pp. 1 l. 8°. *London, E. Jeffrey*, 1793.

Julianus *toletanus*. Prognosticon fvtvri saeculi, etc. 54 l. sm. 4°. *Lipsiae, M. Blum*, 1536. s.

Juncker (Christian). Schediasma historicum, e ephemeridibus sive diariis eruditorum, in nobilioribus Europæ partibus hactenus publicatis. In appendice exhibetur centuria foeminarum eruditione et scriptis illustrium, ab eòdem collecta. 2 v. 9 p. l. 306 pp. 6 l; 3 p. l. 138 pp. 18°. *Lipsiæ, J. F. Gleditsch*, 1692.

June (Jennie, *pseudon.*) *See* **Croly** (*Mrs.* Jennie).

Junius *or* **Jonghe** (Adriaan). Hadriani Ivnii Hornani Batavia. In qua præter gentis & insulæ antiquitatem, originem, decora, mores, aliaque ad eam historiam pertinentia, declaratur quæ fuerit vetus Batauia, quæ Plinio, Tacito, & Ptolemæo cognita: quæ item genuina inclytæ Francorum nationis fuerit sedes. 10 p. l. 411 pp. 4°. *Lvgdvni Batavorvm, apud F. Raphelengium*, 1588.

Junius unmasked: or, Thomas Paine the author of the letters of Junius, and the declaration of independence. [*anon.*] 322 pp. 12°. *Washington (D. C.) J. Gray & co.* 1872.

Junkin (David X. *d. d.*) The good steward, or systematic beneficence an essential element of christianity. 118 pp. 1 l. 12°. *Philadelphia, Presbyterian board of publication,* [1864].

——— The reverend George Junkin, d. d. ll. d. A historical biography. 609 pp. 1 portrait. 8°. *Philadelphia, J. B. Lippincott & co.* 1871.

Junkin (George, *d. d.*) A treatise on sanctification. 160 pp. 16°. *Philadelphia, Presbyterian board of publication,* [1864].

Junot (Laure Permon, *duchesse* d'Abrantes). L'amirante de Castille. 2 v. 351 pp; 360 pp. 16°. *Bruxelles, J. P. Meline,* 1832.

——— Blanche. 2 v. in 1. 276 pp; 275 pp. 16°. *Bruxelles, Meline, Cans & cie.* 1839.

——— La duchesse de Valombrai. 2 v. 2 p. l. 353 pp; 2 p. l. 284 pp. 16°. *Bruxelles, Hauman & comp.* 1839.

——— Souvenirs d'une ambassade et d'un séjour en Espagne et en Portugal, de 1808 à 1811. 2 v. 289 pp. 1 l; 326 pp. 16°. *Bruxelles, Hauman, Cattoir & cie.* 1838.

Jurieu (Pierre). The accomplishment of the scripture prophecies, or the approaching deliverance of the church. In two parts. Faithfully englished from the new french ed. corrected and enlarged, with the explication of the visions of Daniel, and the revelation. 2 v. in 1. 24 p. l. 271, 396 pp. 12°. *London,* 1687.

——— The same. A continuation. To which is added, A confirmation of the exposition of the sixteenth chapter of the revelation. Faithfully englished. 11 p. l. 256, 30 pp. 12°. *London,* 1688.

[NOTE.—With the preceding. Imperfect].

——— A critical history of the doctrines and worships (both good and evil) of the church from Adam to our saviour Jesus Christ; giving an account of the origin of all the idolatries of the ancient pagans, as far as they relate to the jewish worship. Written in french. And faithfully done into english. 2 v. Eng. title, 14 p. l. 592 pp; 6 p. l. 224, 302 pp. 14 l. 8°. *London, J. Taylor & G. Sawbridge,* 1705.

——— Les soupirs de la France esclave, qui aspire après la liberté. [*anon.*] 228 pp. 4°. *Amsterdam,* 1690.

[*Note.*—"Attribué par les uns à Levassor et par d'autres à Gatien de Courtilz, cet ouvrage est bien réellement de Jurieu."—*Michel Nicolas,* in Nouv. biog. gen. xxviii, 271].

Jussieu (Adrian de). Die botanik. Aus dem französischen von prof. G. Kissling. 4 v. in 1. 18°. *Stuttgart, Scheible, Rieger & Sattler,* 1844.

[Populäre naturgeschichte der drei reiche, von F. S. Beudant, Milne-Edwards, A. v. Jussieu, v. 9-12].

Justinianus (Laurentius). *See* **Giustiniani** (Lorenzo).

Juvenalis (Decimus Junius). Juvenal's sixteen satyrs or, a svrvey of the manners and actions of mankind. With arguments, marginall notes, and annotations clearing the obscure places out of the history, lawes and ceremonies of the Romans. By sir Robert Stapylton. Eng. title, 8 p. l. 287 pp. 1 portrait. 18°. *London, H. Mosely,* 1647.

——— The same. Mores hominum. The manners of men, described in sixteen satyrs, by Juvenal: as he is published in his most authentick copy, lately printed by command of the king of France. Whereunto is added the invention of seventeen designes in picture; with arguments to the satyrs. As also explanations to the designes in english and latine. Together with a large comment, clearing the author in every place, wherein he seemed obscure, out of the laws and customes of the Romans, and the latine and greek histories. By sir Robert Stapylton. Published by authority. 12 p. l. 522 pp. 14 l. 17 pl. 1 portrait. fol. *London, R. Hodgkinsonne,* 1660.

——— The same. Satires. 8°. *Bruxelles,* 1842. s.

[RAOUL (L. V.) Les trois satiriques latins, v. 1].

——— *and* **Persius Flaccus** (Aulus). Satiræ expurgatæ, notis illustratæ. Curavit, F. P. Leverett. 1 p. l. 252 pp. 12°. *Bostoniæ, Hilliard, Gray, Little & Wilkins,* 1832.

——— Les satyres de Juvenal, et de Perse, de la traduction de me. de Martignac. Avec des remarques. [Latin text with prose french translation]. 5 p. l. 532 pp. 1 pl. 12°. *Paris, J. B. Coignard,* 1682.

Juvenile (The) forget-me-not, a christmas, new year's and birth day present: for 1841. 180 pp. 4 pl. 18°. *Philadelphia, H. F. Anners,* 1840.

Kalendar (The) of the protestant episcopal church in the United States of America, for 1872. 12 l. 12°. *New York, Pott, Young & co.* [1871].

Kane (Robert, *m. d.*) Elements of chemistry, including the most recent discoveries and applications of the science to medicine and pharmacy, and to the arts. American ed. with additions and corrections, by John William Draper, m. d. 704 pp. 8°. *New York, Harper & brothers,* 1842.

Kansas (*State of*). Constitution, adopted at Wyandot, July 29th, 1859. 16 pp. 8°. [*Wyandot*, 1859]?

Kansas (The) farmer. Devoted to the farm, the shop and the fireside. George T. Anthony, editor. [Monthly]. Jan. 15 to Dec. 15, 1871. v. 8. 4°. *Leavenworth*, [1871].

Kapp (Friedrich). Friedrich der grosse und die Vereinigten Staaten von Amerika. Mit einem anhang: die Vereinigten Staaten und das seekriegsrecht. iv, 202, xxx pp. 8°. *Leipzig, Quandt & Händel*, 1871.

Karlsruhe. Katalog der bibliothek des handelsministerium. *See* **Baden.**

Karoli Magni Francorvm regis et imp. vita descripta, vt videtur, magne parte a monacho cœnobii egolismensis s. Eparchii. [*anon.*] fol. [*Argentorati, J. R. Dulssecker*, 1702].
[*In* KULPIS (Johann G. von). Scriptores rervm germanicarvm. *Argentorati*, 1702, pp. 45-65].

Kastell (J.) Catalog, nebst einigen merkwürdigen theils noch ungedruckten schriften und notizen über das concilium im jahr 1414 in Konstanz. [*anon.*] 2 p. l. 52 pp. 2 l. 18°. [*Konstanz, J. Kastell*], 1832.

Kastner (August). Geschichte der stadt Neisse mit besonderer berücksichtigung des kirchlichen lebens in der stadt und dem fürstenthume Neisse. v. 2. 1608 to 1655. 2 p. l. viii, 599 pp. 1 map. 8°. *Neisse, im selbstverlage des verfassers*, 18[53-]54. s.
[v. 1. not published].

——— Der neisser geschichts-freund. v. 2. Geschichte der neisser schützengilde. 4 p. l. 229* pp. 1 pl. 8°. *Neisse, J. Graveur*, 1850. s.

Kate Felton; or, a peep at realities. By an american lady. [*anon.*] vi, 444 pp. 1 portrait. 12°. *Boston, E. P. Weston*, 1859.

Kate Kilborn; or, sowing and reaping. By the author of "Jeanie Morrison." [*anon.*] 1 title, 284 pp. 3 pl. 16°. *New York, R. Carter & bro.* 1856.

Kate Morgan and her soldiers. [*anon.*] 190 pp. 4 pl. 18°. *Philadelphia, American sunday-school union*, [1862].

Katharine's experience. [*anon.*] *See* **Biscoe** (E. L.)

Katholisches gebet- und gesangbuchlein zum gebrauche für kirche und haus. [*anon.*] 288 pp. 24°. *Einsiedeln, New York & Cincinnati, C. & N. Benzinger*, 1871.

Katie and her mother; or, the widow's trust. [*anon.*] 126 pp. 1 pl. 18°. *New York, Carlton & Porter*, [1861].

Katie Hildreth; or, trials of temper. [*anon.*] 142 pp. 3 pl. 18°. *Boston, Mass. sabbath school society*, [1861].

Katie's secret; or, the boys and girls of Otter-Creek. [*anon.*] 352 pp. 4 pl. 18°. *Boston, Mass. sabbath school society*, [1861].

Kaufmann (Franz Joseph). Der Pilatus, geologisch untersuch und beschrieben. 1867. *See* **Switzerland.** *Geologische commission*, [*etc.*]

Kaufmann (Theodore). Kaufmann's american painting book. The art of painting, or of imitating the effects of color in nature. 22 pp. 4 col. pl. 4°. *Boston, L. Prang & co.* 1871.

Kaup (Jacob). Skizzirte entwickelungs-geschichte und natürliches system der europäischen thierwelt. 1r theil, welcher die vogelsäugethiere und vögel, nebst andeutung der entstehung der letzteren aus amphibien enthält. xii, 204 pp. 12°. *Darmstadt, C. W. Leske*, 1829. s.

Kautz (*Capt.* August V.) The company clerk: showing how and when to make out all the returns, reports, rolls, and other papers, and what to do with them. 142 pp. 3 tab. 12°. *Philadelphia, J. B. Lippincott & co.* 1863.

——— Customs of service for non-commissioned officers and soldiers, as derived from law and regulations, and practised in the army of the United States. 303 pp. 18°. *Philadelphia, J. B. Lippincott & co.* 1864.

Kavanagh. *See* **Cavanah.**

Kaye (Matilda Arbuthnot, *lady* Lister-). *See* **Lister-Kaye.**

Keach (*Rev.* Benjamin). The travels of true godliness. Revised and improved; with occasional notes, and a memoir of his life; by Howard Malcom. 2d ed. Eng. title, 212 pp. 3 pl. 16°. *Boston, Lincoln & Edmands*, 1831.

Keatinge (*Col.* Maurice). Travels in Europe and Africa: comprising a journey through France, Spain, and Portugal, to Morocco: with a particular account of that empire. Also, a second tour through France in 1814. 2 v. in 1. xvi, 346, 274 pp. 34 pl. 4°. *London, H. Colburn*, 1816.

Keble (*Rev.* John). The christian year. Thoughts in verse for the sundays and holydays throughout the year. 288 pp. 16°. *Philadelphia, D. Ashmead*, [1869]?

——— Miscellaneous poems. 2d ed. xxxii, 310 pp. 16°. *Oxford & London, J. Parker & co.* 1869.

Keene (Edwin). Sydney Fielding: the domestic history of a gentleman who served under their late majesties, George iv. and William iv. 2 v. 1 p. l. 328 pp; 1 p. l. 338 pp. 12°. *London, R. Bentley*, 1857.

Keene (*Mrs.* Sarah F. Prince). Guy's life lesson. 366 pp. 3 pl. 16°. *Boston, H. Hoyt*, [1872].

——— The island home; or, the illuminated text. [*anon.*] 318 pp. 3 pl. 16°. *Boston, Cong. sabbath-school and publishing society*, [1870].

——— Orient boys. 408 pp. 3 pl. 16°. *Boston, H. Hoyt*, [1870].

Keene (Surrey). Sophie Krantz; or the cot and the castle. By Surrey Keene. [*pseudon.*] 248 pp. 1 pl. 18°. *Philadelphia, Burns & Sieg*, 1859.

Keightley (Thomas). The history of Greece. To which is added, a chronological table of contemporary history. By Joshua Toulmin Smith. xii, 490 pp. 12°. *Boston, Hilliard, Gray & co.* 1839.

——— History of the roman empire, from the accession of Augustus to the end of the empire of the west; being a continuation of The history of Rome. Edited by Joshua Toulmin Smith. xii, 438 pp. 12°. *Boston, Hilliard, Gray & co.* 1841.

——— Lardner's outlines of universal history: embracing a concise history of the world, from the earliest period to the present time. [*anon.*] Edited by John Frost. 466 pp. 12°. *Philadelphia, Hogan & Thompson*, 1835.

——— Outlines of history: embracing a concise history of the world from the earliest period to the pacification of Europe in 1815. 2d american ed. with additions, etc. by John Frost. [*anon.*] 466 pp. 12°. *Philadelphia, Carey & Lea*, 1831.

Keil (Georg). New fairy stories for my grandchildren. Translated from the german, by S. W. Lander. 84 pp. 4 pl. sq. 16°. *New York, D. Appleton & co.* 1861.

Keith (George, *quaker*). A journal of travels from New-Hampshire to Caratuck, [North Carolina]. 2 p. l. 92 pp. sm. 4°. *London, B. Aylmer*, 1706.

Keller (Christoph). Christophori Cellarii chaldaismvs, siue grammatica noua linguæ chaldaicæ, copiosissimis exemplis, & vsu multiplici, quem chaldæa lingua theologiæ & sacræ scripturæ interpretationi præstat,

Keller (Christoph)—continued.
illustrata. 2 p. l. 90 pp. 1 l. 4°. *Cizæ, sumtu Bielckiano*, 1685.

——— Christophori Cellarii geographia antiqua in compendium redacta, novis praefationibus nunc exornata a Francisco Tirolio et Joanne Baptista Ghisio communi sumptu atque labore, amplioribus tabulis aucta, et accuratioribus catalogis locupletata. 2 p. l. x pp. 25 l. 35 maps, (appendix), x, 40 pp. 1 pl. obl. fol. *Romae*, 1774. s.

——— Christoph. Cellarii orthographia latina ex vetvstis monvmentis hoc est nvmmis marmoribvs tabvlis membranis vetervmqve grammaticorvm placitis. 8°. *Altenbvrgi, ex officina richteria*, 1768.

[*In* HARLES (Gottlieb C.) Christoph. Cellarii orthographia latina. *Altenbvrgia*, 1768, v. 1, pp. 7–390].

Kelley (J. Clawson, *m. d.*) Key to medical science. 239 pp. 12°. *New York, J. A. Fraetas & J. W. Kelley*, 1842.

Kelley (Owen). Choice selection of family recipes for man and beast. 1 p. l. 58 pp. 16°. *Bay city, Culbert, Warren & Krœncke*, 1871.

Kelley (William Darrah). Speeches, addresses and letters on industrial and financial questions. [With] an introduction, copious notes, and an index. xxx, 5–514 pp. 8°. *Philadelphia, H. C. Baird*, 1872.

Kellie (*Sir* Thomas). Pallas armata, or militarie instructions for the learned: and all generous spirits, who affect the profession of armes. 1st part. Containing the exercise of infanterie, as well antient as moderne. 10 p. l. 121 pp. sm. 4°. *Edinburgh, heires of A. Hart*, 1627.

Kellogg (*Rev.* Elijah). The pleasant cove series. v. 1–3. 16°. *Boston, Lee & Shepard*, 1872.

CONTENTS.

1. Arthur Brown, the young captain, 288 pp. 4 pl.
2. The young deliverers, 304 pp. 2 pl.
3. The cruise of the Casco, 326 pp. 3 pl.

Kelly (Caroline E.) *See* **Davis** (Caroline E. Kelly).

Kelly (Fanny). Narrative of my captivity among the Sioux Indians. 285 pp. 10 pl. 1 portrait. 12°. *Cincinnati, Wilstach, Baldwin & co.* 1871.

Kelly (Hall J.) A geographical sketch of that part of North America, called Oregon: containing an account of the indian title: discoveries, climate, mountains, rivers, soil, animals, &c. [with] a map of the country. 80 pp. 1 map. 8°. *Boston, J. Howe*, 1830.

[MISCELLANEOUS pamphlets, v. 371].

Kelly (Hugh). The works of Hugh Kelly. [With] the life of the author. xix, 492 pp. 1 portrait. 4°. *London, author's widow*, 1778.

CONTENTS.

False delicacy: a comedy.
A word to the wise: a comedy.
Clementina: a tragedy.
The school for wives: a comedy.
The romance of an hour: a comedy.
Thespis: or a critical examination into the merits of the principal performers belonging to Drury-Lane theatre.
Thespis: or a critical examination into the merits of the principal performers belonging to Covent Garden theatre.
An elegy, to the memory of the right hon. William, earl of Bath.
Fugitive pieces.

Kelly (James, *of London*). A complete collection of scotish proverbs explained and made intelligible to the english reader. 7 p. l. 400 pp. 8 l. 8°. *London, W. & J. Innys & J. Osborn*, 1721.

Kelly (James, *of N. Y.*) The american catalogue of books (original and reprints) published in the United States from Jan. 1866, to Jan. 1871; with supplement, containing names of learned societies and other literary associations, with a list of their publications, 1866 to 1871. v. 2. 2 p. l. 488 pp. 8°. *New York, J. Wiley & son*, 1871.

Kelly (Patrick, *ll. d.*) Oriental metrology; comprising the monies, weights, and measures of the East Indies, and other trading places in Asia, reduced to the english standard by verified operations. To which is added, an appendix, on oriental measures of time. 2 p. l. xi, 178 pp. 8°. *London, Longman*, 1832.

Kelly (Thomas). Hymns on various passages of scripture. 6th ed. with many new hymns. xii, 424 pp. 18°. *Dublin, R. M. Tims*, 1826.

Kelly Nash, or, "I didn't think." By the author of The blue flag. [etc. *anon.*] 138 pp. 3 pl. 18°. *New York, American tract society*, [1863].

Kelsall (Charles). Esquisse de mes travaux, de mes voyages, et de mes opinions: dans une lettre à son ami Agathomerus, par Mela britannicus. vii, 234 pp. 12°. *Londres, A. J. Valpy*, 1830.

——— Phantasm of an university: with prolegomena. 4 p. l. 174 pp. 1 l. 21 pl. 4°. *London, J. Moyes for White, Cochrane & co.* 1814.

Kelvey (Henry, *editor*). The poetical review, or select specimens of british poetry; illustrated by numerous and elegant critiques, &c. xvi, 353 pp. 1 l. 12°. *Sheffield, J. Pearce*, 1829.

Kelvin (Kit, *pseudon.*) Kit Kelvin's kernels. 270 pp. 4 pl. 12°. *New York, Rollo*, 1860.

Kemble (Francis Anne). Poems. 312 pp. 12°. *Boston, Ticknor & Fields*, 1859.

Kemble (John Mitchill). Ueber die stammtafel der Westsachsen. 36 pp. 12°. *München*, 1836.

Kemper (Frederic Augustus). Consolations of the afflicted. 258 pp. 12°. *Cincinnati, W. J. Ferris & co.* 1831.

Kempis (Thomas à). The little garden of roses and valley of lilies. Now first correctly translated from the original latin. xxii, 295 pp. 1 pl. 32°. *New York, Casserly & sons*, 1844.

Kendall (E. Otis). Atlas of the heavens; showing the places of the principal stars, clusters, and nebulae; designed to accompany the uranography; or a description of the heavens. 18 pl. 4°. *Philadelphia, Butler & Williams*, 1844.

Kendall (George Wilkins). Sheep raising in Texas. 8°. [*New York*, 1860].

[*In* RANDALL (Henry S.) Sheep husbandry, pp. 320–322].

Kendall (John, *of Colchester*). Letters on religious subjects, written by divers friends, deceased. First published in London, by John Kendall, 1802. [*anon.*] 288 pp. 16°. *Burlington (N. J.) D. Allinson*, 1805.

Kendall (Thomas). A grammar and vocabulary of the language of New Zealand. Published by the church missionary society. [Edited by Samuel Lee]. 4 p. l. 230 pp. 12°. *London, R. Watts*, 1820.

Kendrick (Asahel C. *d. d.*) The life and letters of mrs. Emily C[hubbuck] Judson. 426 pp. 1 portrait. 12°. *New York, Sheldon & co.* 1860.

——— New testament. *Phila.* 1842. *See* **Bible.** (*English*).

Kenealy (Edward). Brallaghan, or the deipnosophists. xi, 336 pp. 16°. *London, E. Churton*, 1845.

Kennaquhom (Colin, *esq. pseudon.*) Money. A novel. 3 v. 12°. *London, Hurst & Blackett*, 1860.

Kennedy (Donald). Kennedy on diseases of the skin. 2d ed. 1 p. l. 128 pp. 3 pl. 8°. *Roxbury (Mass.) D. Kennedy*, 1871.

Kennedy (Edward Shirley). Thoughts on being; suggested by meditation upon the infinite, the immaterial, and the eternal. xv, 302 pp. 8°. *London, Longman*, 1850.

Kennedy (Grace). Father Rowland, a north american tale. [*anon.*] 2d ed. 195 pp. 18°. *Baltimore, F. Lucas, jr.* [1831].

Kennedy (*Rev.* James). Humiliation for sin a preparation for enjoying divine favor. 12°. [*Pittsburgh,* 1872].

[*In* REFORMED presbyterian church in North America. Memorial volume, pp. 40–57].

Kennedy (P. W.) The accountant's guide, 1871. *See* **Johnson** (M. R.) *and* **Kennedy.**

Kenney (John Henry). The burniad; an epistle to a lady, in the manner of Burns. With poetic miscellanies, original and imitative. vii, 144 pp. 16°. *London, Vernor, Hood & Sharpe,* 1808.

Kennicott (Benjamin.) Dissertatio generalis in vetus testamentum hebraicum; cum variis lectionibus, ex codicibus manuscriptis et impressis. 129 pp. fol. *Oxonii,* [*e typographeo clarendoniano*], 1780.

[*In* BIBLE. (*Hebrew*). Vetus testamentum hebraicum, cum variis lectionibus. Edidit B. Kennicott. 2 v. *Oxonii,* 1776–80].

——— Two dissertations: the first on the tree of life in Paradise, with some observations on the creation and fall of man; the second on the oblations of Cain and Abel. 2d ed. with an appendix. ix, 254 pp. 8°. *Oxford, author,* 1747.

——— Vetus testamentum hebraicum. *See* **Bible.** (*Hebrew*).

Kenrick (Francis Patrick, *archbishop of Baltimore*). The catholic doctrine on justification. Explained and vindicated. 255 pp. 12°. *Philadelphia, E. Cummiskey,* [1841].

——— The pentateuch. Job and the prophets. The psalms, book of wisdom, and canticles. New testament. The four gospels. *See* **Bible.** (*English*).

Kenrick (John). A biographical memoir of the late rev. Charles Wellbeloved. vii, 256 pp. 8°. *London, E. T. Whitfield,* 1860.

Kenrick (Peter Richard, *archbishop of St. Louis*). The new month of Mary, or reflections for each day of the month, on the different titles applied to the holy mother of God, in the litany of Loretto: principally designed for the month of May. 273 pp. 16°. *Philadelphia, E. Cummiskey,* 1840.

——— Speech, prepared for speaking, but not spoken, in the vatican council, [in Rome, 1870]. 8°. Naples, de Angelis brothers. 12°. [*New York, reprinted,* 1872].

[*In* BACON (Leonard Woolsey). An inside view of the vatican council, pp. 91–174].

——— The validity of anglican ordinations examined; or, a review of certain facts regarding the consecration of Mathew Parker, first protestant archbishop of Canterbury. 227 pp. 12°. *Philadelphia, E. Cummiskey,* 1841.

Kenrick (William). The american silk grower's guide; or the art of raising the mulberry and silk, and the system of successive crops in each season. 2d ed. 167 pp. 16°. *Boston, Weeks, Jordan & co.* 1839.

——— The new american orchardist, or an account of the most valuable varieties of fruit, adapted to cultivation in the climate of the United States, from the latitude of 25° to 54°. Also, a brief description of the most ornamental forest trees, shrubs, flowers, &c. xxxvi, 25–423 pp. 12°. *Boston, Carter, Hendee, & co.* 1833.

Kentucky. A report of the history and management of the Kentucky penitentiary. *See* **Sneed** (William C.)

Kenyon (John). Poems: for the most part occasional. xvi, 200 pp. 8°. *London, E. Moxon,* 1838.

Kepler (Johann). Opera omnia. Edidit dr. Ch. Frisch. 8 v. in 9. 8°. *Francofurti a. M. Heyder & Zimmer,* 1858–70. s.

Kératry (Auguste Hilarion). Examen philosophique des considérations sur le sentiment du sublime et du beau, dans le rapport des caractères, des tempéraments, des sexes, des climats, et des religions, d'Emmanuel Kant. xxviii, 380 pp. 8°. *Paris, Bossange frères,* 1823.

——— Inductions morales et physiologiques. 2d éd. revue et augmentée. 2 p. l. xiv, 467 pp. 8°. *Paris, Maradan,* 1818.

Kerhallet (Charles Philippe de). General examination of the Atlantic ocean. With nautical directions for avoiding hurricanes, and a memoir on the currents of the Atlantic. Translated from the 3d french ed. by R. H. Wyman. xiii, 217 pp. 5 maps. 8°. *Washington, government printing office,* 1870.

[UNITED STATES. *Navy department. Bureau of navigation. Hydrographic office*].

——— General examination of the Pacific ocean, followed by nautical directions for avoiding hurricanes. Translated from the second french edition, under the direction of commander Charles Henry Davis, U. S. n. by authority of the author. xv, 212 pp. 3 charts. 8°. *New York, E. & G. W. Blunt,* 1861.

Kerr (Hugh). A poetical description of Texas, and narrative of many interesting events of that country; also, an appeal to those who oppose the union of Texas with the United States. To which is added, The Texas heroes, nos. 1 and 2. 122 pp. 18°. *New York, author,* 1838.

Kerr (William C.) Rip-raps: or, drift thoughts wide apart. 256, 117 pp. 3 pl. 12°. *New York, De W. C. Lent & co.* 1871. s.

Kervyn de Lettenhove (Joseph Marie Bruno Constantin). Froissart. Étude littéraire sur le xive siècle. 2 v. 2 p. l. xii, 334 pp; 2 p. l. 348 pp. 16°. *Paris, A. Durand,* 1857.

Ketteler (Wilhelm Emmanuel, *freiherr* von, *bishop of Mentz*). Freiheit, autorität und kirche. Erörterungen über die grossen probleme der gegenwart. 2e aufl. xii, 259 pp. 8°. *Mainz, F. Kirchheim,* 1862.

Ketten (Johannes Michael von der). Apelles symbolicus exhibens seriem amplissimam symbolorum, poetisque, oratoribus, ac verbi Dei prædicatoribus conceptus subministrans varios. 2 v. Eng. title, 11 p. l. 898 pp. [including 42 pl.]; 10 p. l. 568 pp. [including 16 pl.] 14 l. 12°. *Amstelaedami & Gedani, apud J. Waesbergios,* 1699.

Keyes (Emerson W.) A history of savings banks in the state of New York from 1819 to 1869. To accompany the annual report of the superintendent relative to savings banks. 334 pp. 8°. *Albany, Argus co. prs.* 1870.

Keyes (F.) Evan Dale. [*anon.*] iv, 387 pp. 12°. *Boston, A. Williams & co.* 1864.

Keyes (Frederick J.) A life-poem, and other poems. 120 pp. 12°. *Boston, Phillips, Sampson & co.* 1855.

Keys (*Rev.* Charles C.) The class-leader's manual. To which is prefixed an introductory chapter on the history and scriptural basis of class-meetings. 224 pp. 18°. *New-York, Lane & Scott,* 1851.

Keyser (Charles S.) Fairmount park. Sketches of its scenery, waters, and history. [*anon.*] 144 pp. 1 pl. 12°. *Philadelphia, Claxton, Remsen & Haffelfinger,* 1871.

Keyserling (Alexander, *graf*) *and* **Blasius** (Johann Heinrich). Die wirbelthiere Europa's. Erstes buch: Die unterscheidenden charactere. 7 p. l. xcviii, 248 pp. 8°. *Braunschweig, F. Vieweg & sohn,* 1840. s.
[*Note.*—No more published].

Kidder (Daniel Parish, *d. d.*) The christian pastorate: its character, responsibilities, and duties. 569 pp. 12°. *Cincinnati, Hitchcock and Walden,* 1871.

—— The sunday school reciter: a collection of addresses and dialogues on moral and religious subjects. 168 pp. 18°. *New York, G. Lane & C. B. Tippett,* 1846.

Kidder (Daniel Parish, *d.d.*)—continued.

—— A treatise on homiletics: designed to illustrate the true theory and practice of preaching the gospel. 495 pp. 12°. *New York, Carlton & Porter,* 1864.

Kidder (J. B.) Elements of ancient history: arranged in clear and connected order, for the use of the junior classes of students. 1 p. l. 113 pp. 18°. *New York, H. & S. Raynor,* 1836.

Kidder (Richard, *bishop of Bath and Wells*). That part of [his] demonstration of the Messias, preached at the hon. Robert Boyle's lecture. fol. [*London,* 1739].
[BOYLE lectures, v. 1, pp. 89–152].

Kieffer (Aldine S.) Glad hosannas: a collection of new sabbath school and revival music, comprising a variety of new and beautiful hymns with appropriate tunes. 96 pp. obl. 16°. *Singer's Glen, Rockingham co. (Va.) J. Funk's sons,* 1871.

Kiehl (Emilie M.) Golden grains. 82 pp. 1 portrait. 12°. *Philadelphia, J. B. Lippincott & co.* 1871.

Kiel (*University library of*). Verzeichniss der handschriften der Kieler universitätsbibliothek, welche die geschichte der herzogthümer Schleswig und Holstein betreffen. Von H. Ratjen. 2 v. in 1. 296 pp; 1 p. l. 40 pp. 8°. *Kiel,* 1847.
[Imperfect: v. 1, pp. 217–249 wanting].

Kilham (*Rev.* Alexander). Life, extracts of letters (in favour of reform), written by a number of preachers to Mr. Kilham, during the time of his undertaking the cause of religious liberty. [Edited by John Grundell and Robert Hall]. xxvii, 222 pp. 16°. *Nottingham, C. Sutton,* [1799].
[MISCELLANEOUS pamphlets, v. 190].

Kime (William Thomas). Albert the good; a nation's tribute of affection to the memory of a truly virtuous prince. xii, 461 pp. 5 pl. 4°. *London, J. F. Shaw & co.* 1862.

Kincaid (*Capt.* John). Random shots from a rifleman. 192 pp. 12°. *Philadelphia, E. L. Carey & A. Hart,* 1835.

Kind (Friedrich). Der freischütz. [Libretto]. *See* **Weber** (C. M. von).

Kindling; or, a way to do it. By a sabbath school teacher. [*anon.*] With an introductory note by the rev. R. S. Storrs, jun. d. d. 384 pp. 12°. *New York, M. W. Dodd,* 1856.

King (Alonzo). Facts not fiction; in a series of letters addressed to his children. 106 pp. 18°. *Boston, New England sabbath school union,* 1837.

King (Alonzo)—continued.

——— Memoir of George Dana Boardman, late missionary to Burmah. Containing much intelligence relative to the Burman mission. With an introductory essay, by a distinguished clergyman. New ed. Eng. title, xxxv, 319 pp. 1 portrait. 12°. *Boston, Gould, Kendall & Lincoln,* 1836.

King (*Rev.* Charles William). Q. Horatii Flacci opera, illustrated from antique gems. *See* **Horatius Flaccus** (Quintus).

King (Clarence). Mountaineering in the Sierra Nevada. 3 p. l. 292 pp. 12°. *Boston, J. R. Osgood & co.* 1872.

——— Geological contributions. *See* **United States.** *War department.* (*Corps of engineers*). Exploration of the fortieth parallel.

King (*Rev.* David). An exposition and defence of the presbyterian form of church government. 2d ed. 2 p. l. 358 pp. 16°. *Edinburgh, Johnstone & Hunter,* 1854.

King (Dexter S.) Fireside poetical readings, illustrative of american scenery, rural life, and historical incidents, and also of religious feelings, designed as a domestic and religious offering. 1 p. l. 313 pp. 12°. *Boston, D. S. King,* 1843.

King (Edward, 1735-1807). Hymns to the supreme Being. In imitation of the eastern songs. [*anon.*] vii, 168 pp. 8°. *London, Darton & Harney,* 1795.

——— The same. New ed. viii, 190 pp. 12°. *London, T. Bensley for J. White,* 1798.

——— The same. New ed. vi, 263 pp. 8°. *London, T. Bensley for J. White,* 1808.

——— Morsels of criticism; tending to illustrate some few passages in the holy scriptures upon philosophical principles and an enlarged view of things. 2d ed. To which is now added, A second and supplemental part, designed to shew the perfect consistency of philosophical discoveries, and of historical facts, with the revealed word of God. 3 v. 8°. *London, J. White,* 1800.

King (John, *m. d.*) An essay of instruction, on animal magnetism. *See* **Chastenet de Puységur** (Antoine M. J. *marquis de*).

——— Women: their diseases and their treatment. 366 pp. 8°. *Cincinnati, Longley brothers,* 1858.

King (John F.) *See* **American** Lloyd's register.

King (*Rev.* Josiah). Mr. [Charles] Blount's oracles of reason, examined and answered, in nine sections. In which his many hete

King (*Rev.* Josiah)—continued.

rodox opinions are refuted, the holy scriptures and revealed religion are asserted, against deism and atheism. 8 p. l. 236 pp. 16°. *Exeter, S. Darker for P. Bishop,* 1698.

King (*Mrs.* Maria M.) The brotherhood of man, and what follows from it. In two lectures. 41 pp. 8°. *Boston, W. White & co.* 1871.

King (Peter, *lord King, baron Ockham*). An inquiry into the constitution, discipline, unity, and worship, of the primitive church. With an introduction by the american editor. 300 pp. 12°. *New York, G. Lane & P. P. Sandford,* 1841.

King (William, *archbishop of Dublin*). An admonition to the dissenting inhabitants of the diocess of Derry: concerning a book lately published by mr. J. Boyse, entituled, Remarks on a late discourse of William, lord bishop of Derry; concerning the inventions of men in the worship of God. 2 p. l. 58 pp. 16°. *London, W. Keblewhite,* 1694.

[*With his* Discourse concerning the inventions of men in the worship of God. 3d ed. 1696].

——— The same. A second admonition. With an appendix, containing an answer to mr. B's objections against the sign of the cross. 2 p. l. 281 pp. 16°. *London, R. Clavel,* 1696.

[*With his* Discourse concerning the inventions of men in the worship of God. 3d ed. 1696].

——— A discourse concerning the inventions of men in the worship of God. 3d ed. 2 p. l. 188 pp. 16°. *London, W. Keblewhite,* 1696.

King (The) of the commons. *See* **White** (James).

Kingdom (The) of grace; or, the millenarian theory rigidly examined and demonstrated to be false. By an anti-millenarian. [*anon.*] 216 pp. 12°. *Cincinnati, E. Goodman,* 1843.

Kingsford (Jane, *pseudon.*) *See* **Barnard** (Charles).

Kingsley (*Rev.* Charles). At last: a christmas in the West Indies. xii, 402 pp. 13 pl. 12°. *London, Macmillan and co.* 1871.

——— Sermons on national subjects, preached in a village church. viii, 312 pp. 16°. *London, J. J. Griffin & co.* 1852.

——— The voyages and adventures of sir Amyas Leigh, knight, of Burrough, in the county of Devon, in the reign of her most glorious majesty, queen Elizabeth. vi, 588 pp. 12°. *Boston, Ticknor & Fields,* 1855.

Kingston (William H. G.) Our sailors: or, anecdotes of the engagements and gallant deeds of the british navy, during the reign

Kingston (W. H. G.)—continued. of her majesty queen Victoria. 2d ed. xv, 282 pp. 1 pl. 16°. *London, Griffith & Farran*, 1865.

Kinker (Jan). Le dualisme de la raison humaine; ou le criticisme de Em. Kant, amélioré sous le rapport de la raison pure, et rendu complet sous celui de la raison pratique. Publié par les soins et sous les auspices, et avec des notes de J. D. Cocheret de la Morinière. 2 v. xxvii, 266 pp. 3 l. 1 portrait; viii, 372 pp. 1 l. 8°. *Amsterdam, Weytingh & Van der Haart*, 1850-52.

Kirby (John). The Suffolk traveller, first published by mr. John Kirby, who took an actual survey of the whole county, in the years 1732-34. 2d ed. with many alterations and large additions, by several hands. xvi, 340 pp. 5 maps. 8°. *London, J. Shave*, 1764.

Kircher (Athanasius). Latium. Id est, nova et parallela Latii tum veteris tum novi descriptio. Qua quaecunque vel natura, vel veterum Romanorum ingenium admiranda effecit, geographico-historico-physico ratiocinio, juxta rerum gestarum, temporumque seriem exponitur et enucleatur. Eng. title, 7 p. l. 263 pp. 7 l. 25 pl. 1 portrait. fol. *Amstelodami, J. J. à Waasberge*, 1671.

Kirk (*Rev.* John, *of Lichfield, Eng.*) The faith of catholics, on certain points of controversy. *See* **Berington** (*Rev.* Joseph) *and* **Kirk.**

Kirk (*Rev.* John). The cloud dispelled: or, the doctrine of predestination examined. With an introduction by rev. Daniel Curry, d. d. 293 pp. 12°. *New York, N. Tibbals & co.* 1860.

Kirkaldy (David). Results of an experimental inquiry into the tensile strength and other properties of various kinds of wrought iron and steel. 2d ed. 1 p. l. 227 pp. 16 pl. 8°. *London, author*, 1866.

Kirke (Henry). The first english conquest of Canada; with some account of the earliest settlements in Nova Scotia and Newfoundland. xi, 227 pp. 1 map. 8°. *London, Bemrose & sons*, 1871.

Kirke (Robert). A sketch of the case and sufferings of mr. Robert Kirke, his majesty's late consul at Algiers. 63, 128 pp. 8°. *London*, 1781.

Kirkham (Samuel). A compendium of english grammar, accompanied by an appendix in familiar lectures; containing a new systematic mode of parsing; likewise exercises in false syntax, and a key to the exercises.

Kirkham (Samuel)—continued. 84 pp. 1 tab. 16°. *Frederick-town*, [*Md.*] *author*, 1823.

——— An essay on elocution. 324 pp. 12°. *Baltimore, J. W. Woods*, 1833.

——— The same. 3d ed. enlarged and improved. 357 pp. 12°. *New York, Robinson, Pratt & co.* 1836.

Kirkland (*Mrs.* Caroline M.) Memoirs of Washington. xiii, 516 pp. 3 pl. 1 portrait. 12°. *New York, D. Appleton & co.* 1857.

Kirkley (Joseph W.) Historical record of the first Maryland infantry. *See* **Camper** (Charles) *and* **Kirkley.**

Kirkpatrick (J. *m. d.*) The analysis of inoculation: comprizing the history, theory, and practice of it: with an occasional consideration of the most remarkable appearances in the small pox. xxiv, 288 pp. 6 l. 8°. *London, J. Millan, etc.* 1754.

Kirkton (*Rev.* James). The secret and true history of the church of Scotland, from the restoration to the year 1678. [Also], an account of the murder of archbishop Sharp, by James Russell, an actor therein. Edited from the mss. by Charles Kirkpatrick Sharpe. [With his sermons]. 1 p. l. lxix, 484 pp. 3 pl. 4°. *Edinburgh, J. Ballantyne & co.* 1817.

Kissam (Richard S. *m. d.*) The nurse's manual, and young mother's guide. 143 pp. 16°. *Hartford, Cooke & co.* 1834.

Kist (Leopold). Amerikanisches. xi, 820 pp. 8°. *Mainz, F. Kirchheim*, 1871.

Klaczko (Julian). Une annexion d'autrefois. L'union de la Pologne et de la Lithuanie. 177 pp. 1 l. 16°. *Paris, librairie du Luxembourg*, 1869. S.

Kladderadatsch. Humoristisch-satyrisches wochenblatt. 1. Januar bis 31. Dec. 1871. 24° jahrgang. 4°. *Berlin, A. Hofmann u. co.* [1871].

Klaer licht, ofte vertoogh van's lants welvaeren, aengaende de combinatie van de Oost en West-Indische compagnien. [*anon.*] 6 l. sm. 4°. [*n. p.*] 1644.

Klauer - Klattowski (Wilhelm). Popular songs of the Germans, with a translation of all unusual words and difficult passages, and explanatory notes. xvi, 248 pp. 16°. *London, Simpkin, Marshall & co.* 1836.
[*Note.*—German poetical anthology, v. 1].

Klein (Jacob Theodor). Historia avivm prodromvs cvm praefatione de ordine animalivm in genere. Accessit historia mvris alpini

Klein (Jacob Theodor)—continued. et vetvs vocabvlarivm animalivm, msc. 8 p. l. 238 pp. 8 pl. 4°. *Lvbecae, apvd I. Schmidt*, 1750.

Klippart (John H.) Agricultural survey [of Ohio]. 8°. [*Columbus*, 1871].

[OHIO. *Geological survey*. 1870. Part 4, pp. 311-400].

Klitz (Philip). Sketches of life, character, and scenery in the New forest: a series of tales, rural, domestic, legendary, and humorous. ix, 233 pp. 3 l. 8°. *London, Orr & co.* 1850.

Klügel (Georg Simon). Encyclopädie, oder zusammenhängender vortrag der gemeinnützigsten, insbesondere aus der betrachtung der natur und des menschen gesammelten kenntnisse. 2e auflage. v. 3-4. 8°. *Berlin & Stettin, F. Nicolai*, 1793-4.

CONTENTS.

v. 3. Die astronomie mit der mathematischen geographie, (etc.)
v. 4. Die seewissenschaften, die kriegswissenschaften und die philosophie.

Knatchbull (*Sir* Norton). Annotations upon some difficult texts in all the books of the new testament. 8 p. l. 320 pp. 8°. *Cambridge, W. Graves*, 1693.

Kneeland (Abner). National hymns, original and selected; for the use of those who are "slaves to no sect." 2 p. l. 140 pp. 18°. *Boston, office of the Investigator*, 1834.

——— A series of [eight] lectures on the doctrine of universal benevolence. 204 pp. 12°. *Philadelphia, author*, 1818.

——— *and* **McCalla** (*Rev.* William L.) Minutes of a discussion on the question "Is the punishment of the wicked absolutely eternal? or is it only a temporal punishment in this world, for their good, and to be succeeded by eternal happiness after death?" Taken in short-hand, by R. L. Jennings. 336 pp. 8°. [*Philadelphia*], *for the publisher*, 1824.

Kneeland (Samuel, *m. d.*) The wonders of the Yosemite valley, and of California. With original photographic illustrations, by John P. Soule. 71 pp. 10 phot. 8°. *Boston, A. Moore*, 1871.

Knight (Charles). The journey-book of England. Derbyshire. [*anon.*] 3 p. l. 150 pp. 1 map. sm. 4°. *London, C. Knight & co.* 1841.

Knight (Paul Slade, *m. d.*) Observations on the causes, symptoms, and treatment of derangement of the mind, founded on an extensive moral and medical practice in the treatment of lunatics. Together with the particulars of the sensations and ideas of a gentleman during his mental alienation, written by himself during his convalescence. viii, 167 pp. 2 pl. 8°. *London, Longman*, 1827.

——— The same.

[MEDICAL pamphlets, v. 3].

Knight (Robert). Commentary on Romans. *See* **Bible.** (*English*).

Knight (Thomas F.) Pamphlets on the fishes and fisheries of Nova Scotia. 2 v. in 1. 8°. *Halifax, printer to the queens most excellent majesty*, 1866-67. S.

CONTENTS.

No. 1. Descriptive catalogue of the fishes of Nova Scotia. [With Supplementary paper on sea-mammals and shell fish. 1 p. l. 54 pp].
No. 2. Shore and deep sea fisheries of Nova Scotia. 1 p. l. vii, 113 pp.

Knight (William, "*student in astrology*"). Vox stellarum: or, the voyce of the stars; being a brief and easie introduction, to the knowledge of the number, names and characters of the planets and signs, aspects, [etc.] Likewise how to judge of the affairs of the world, by revolutions, eclipses, great conjunctions and blazing stars. Also, something touching the popish plot, and other remarkable affairs of the year, 1678. 6 p. l. 156 pp. 18°. *London, E. T. & R. H. for T. Passinger*, 1681.

Knight (William, *of London*). Oriental outlines of a rambler's recollections of a tour in Turkey, Greece, & Tuscany, in 1838. [xiv], 342, xiv pp. 1 map. 16°. *London, S. Low*, 1839.

Knights of the red cross. *See* **Freemasons.**

Knights templar. *See* **Freemasons.**

Knobloch (Johann, *editor*). Sammlung der vorzüglichsten schriften aus der thierarzney. v. 1. xxviii, 452 pp. 2 pl. 12°. *Prag, J. E. Diesbach*, 1785. S.

Knöfel (Henry). Viertes deutsches lesebuch. Ein lesebuch für die höhern klassen der deutschamerikanischen schulen und zur selbstbelehrung. 348 pp. 12°. *Louisville* (*Ky.*) *H. Knöfel*, [1867].

Knolles (Richard). The generall historie of the Turkes, from the first beginning of that nation to the rising of the othoman familie: [etc.] Together with the lives and conqvests of the othoman kings and emperours. 4th ed. 5 p. l. 1512 pp. 24 l. fol. [*London*], *A. Islip*, 1631.

——— The same. The turkish history, comprehending the origin of that nation, and the

Knolles (Richard)—continued.
growth of the othoman empire, with the lives and conquests of their several kings and emperors. Written by mr. Knolles, and contin'u'd by sir Pavl Rycavt, to the peace at Carlowitz, in the year 1699. And abridg'd by mr. [John] Savage. 2 v. 5 p. l. 495 pp. 15 pl. 1 portrait; 1 p. l. 407 pp. 12 l. 10 pl. 8°. *London, I. Cleave,* 1701.

Knorr (George Wolfgang). Les délices des yeux et de l'esprit, ou collection générale des différentes espèces de coquillages que la mer renferme. 6 v. 4°. *Nuremberg,* 1760–73.

——— *and* **Walch** (Johann Ernst Immanuel). Recueil des monumens des catastrophes que le globe terrestre a éssuiées, contenant des pétrifacations dessinées, gravées et enluminées d'aprés les originaux, commencé par feu mr. George Wolfgang Knorr, et continué par ses heritiers avec l'histoire naturelle de ces corps par mr. Jean Ernest Emmanuel Walch. Traduit de l'allemand. 5 parts in 4 v. fol. *Nuremberg,* 1767–78.

Knowles (*Rev.* James Davis). Memoir of mrs. Ann H. Judson, late missionary to Burmah. Including a history of the American baptist mission in the burman empire. 324 pp. 1 map, 1 portrait. 12°. *Boston, Lincoln & Edmands,* 1829.

Knowles (James Sheridan). A collection of poems on various subjects. 4 p. l. 72 pp. 8°. *Waterford, author,* 1810.

——— A debate on the character of Julius Cæsar. 12°. [*Boston,* 1838].
[*In* RUSSELL (William). Rudiments of gesture, pp. 73–120].

Knowles (Sarah E.) Orlean Lamar, and other poems. 167 pp. 12°. *New York, D. Appleton & co.* 1864.

Knox (Alexander, *m. d.*) The irish watering places, their climate, scenery, and accommodations; including analyses of the principal mineral springs, by dr. R. Kane, and remarks on the various forms of disease to which they are adapted. viii, 336 pp. 1 pl. 8°. *Dublin, W. Curry, jun. & co.* 1845.

Knox (*Rev.* Hugh). Discourses on the truth of revealed religion and other important subjects. 2 v. xxiii, 345 pp; 1 p. l. 347 pp. 8°. *London, T. Cadell,* 1768.

Koch (Johann). Oracula metrica Jovis, Apollinis, Hecates, Serapidis, et aliorum deorum ac vatum tam virorum quam fœminarum a Joanne Opsopœo collecta. Item Astrampsychi oneirocriticon, a Jos. Scaligero, digestum

Koch (Johann)—continued.
& castigatum. Græce et latine. 127 pp. 4°. [*Amstelodami, apud H. & viduam T. Boom,* 1689].
[*With* GALLÆUS (Servatius). Σιβυλλιακοι Χρησμοι, hoc est, sibyllina oracula. *Amstelodami,* 1689].

Koettig (R. F.) Geschichtliche, technische, und statistische notizen über den steinkohlenbergbau Sachsens. 3 p. l. 85 pp. 4°. *Leipzig, W. Engelmann,* 1861. S.
[SAXONY. Die steinkohlen des königreichs Sachsen, 4e abth.]

Kolberg (Oskar). Lud. Jego zwyczaje, sposób życia, mowa, podania, przysłowia, obrzędy, gusta, zabawy, pieśni, muzyka i tańce. Serya 5. Krakowskie. Część pierwsza. viii, 384 pp. 2 col. pl. 8°. *Krakow, w drukarni uniwersytetu jagiellońskiego,* 1871.

Koliades (Constantinos). Ulysse-Homère, ou du véritable auteur de l'Iliade et de l'Odyssée. 1 p. l. viii, 102 pp. 1 l. 14 pl. 5 maps, 1 portrait. fol. *Paris, Bure frères,* 1829.

——— The same. Ulysses Homer; or a discovery of the true author of the Iliad and Odyssey. xxiii, 68 pp. 8°. *London, J. Murray,* 1829.

Kolk (Jacobus Lodewijck Coenraad Schroeder van der). Seele und leib in wechselbeziehung zu einander. Sechs vorträge. ix, 192 pp. 8°. *Braunschweig, F. Vieweg & sohn,* 1865. S.

Kollmann (Augustus Frederic Christopher). A new theory of musical harmony, according to a complete and natural system of that science. 2 p. l. viii, 80, xxxvi pp. 4°. *London, author,* 1823.

Konewka (Paul). Falstaff and his companions. Twenty one illustrations in silhouette. *See* **Shakespeare** (William).

Koning (Jacob). Dissertation sur l'origine, l'invention et le perfectionnement de l'imprimerie. Traduite du hollandois. xii, 180 pp. 8 pl. 8°. *Amsterdam, S. Delachaux,* 1819.

——— The same.
[*With* NÉE DE LA ROCHELLE (J. F.) Éloge historique de Jean Gensfleisch, dit Guttenberg. 1811].

Koppiers (Pieter Hendrik). Observata philologica in loca qvaedam Antiphonis, Theocriti, Pavli apostoli, Eratosthenis, et Propertii. 10 p. l. 178 pp. 5 l. 8°. *Lvgdvni Batavorvm, apud P. Delfos, ivn.* 1771.

Kornmann (Heinrich). De miracvlis mortvorvm: in quo mirabilia Dei miracula & exempla mortuorum ex veteri & nouo testamento, ex ecclesiasticis & prophanis historicis, summa opera & studio collecta habentur,

Kornmann (Heinrich)—continued. quæstiones naturales, physicæ, medicæ, theologicæ & iuridicæ traduntur & artificiose pertractantur. Nunc primum in lucem editum. 176 l. unnumb. 16°. [*Darmstadii*]? *sumptibus I. I. Porsii*, 1610.

Kort ende warachtich verhael vande heerlijcke victorie te weghe ghebracht by de xii schepen afghevaren wt Hollandt, onder tghebiedt van Hugo Verhaghen, in de eylanden vande Moluckes. [*anon.*] *b. l.* 2 l. sm. 4°. *Rotterdam, J. Janssz*, 1606.

Korte observatien op het vertoogh, door een ongenaemden uyt-gegeven, aende staten generael der Vereenighde Nederlanden. Nopende de voor-gaende ende tegenwoordige proceduren van Brasil. Ingestelt door een lief-hebber des vaderlants. [*anon.*] 4 l. sm. 4°. *Amsterdam, P. van Marel*, 1647.

Kortte *or* **Corte** (Gottlieb). M. Gottlieb Kortte tres dissertationes criticæ de vsv orthographiæ latinæ qvas recensvit, emendavit, ac observationibvs ipsivs avctoris, et cel. Longolii svisqve avxit Theophilvs Christophorvs Harles. Accessit orthographia norisiana. 8°. [*Altenbvrgi, ex officina richteria*, 1768].

[*In* HARLES (Gottlieb). Christoph. Cellarii Orthographia latina, [etc.] *Altenbvrgi*, 1768. v. 2. pp. 1-154].

Kortüm (Carl Arnold). The jobsiad, a grotesco-comico-heroic poem. From the german. By C. S. Brooks. xviii, 181 pp. 12°. *Philadelphia, F. Leypoldt*, 1863.

Kotzebue (August Friedrich Ferdinand von). The history and surprising adventures of Joseph Pignata, who was confined in the dungeons of the holy inquisition. Translated from the german. By G. Beech. 1 p. l. 5–26 pp. 1 col. pl. 16°. *London, Dean & Munday*, 1821.

——— Léontine de Blondheim. Traduit de l'allemand, avec notes, par H. L. C. 3 v. 12°. *Londres, B. Dulau & co.* 1808.

Kraatz (*Dr.* G.) Verzeichniss der käfer Deutschlands. Herausgegeben von dem Entomologischen verein in Berlin. vi, 84 pp. 1 l. 1 pl. 8°. *Berlin, Nicolai'sche verlagsbuchhandlung*, 1869. s.

[Beiheft zum jahrgange 1869 der Berliner entomologischen zeitschrift].

Krause (William E. F.) The german-french war of 1870, and its consequences upon future civilization. iv, 142 pp. 8°. *San Francisco, J. Winterburn & co.* 1872.

Krauss (Johann Ulrich). Historische bilder bibel. 1-5 theil. 135 pl. 6 l. fol. *Augspurg*, 1705.

Krauth (Charles Porterfield, *d. d.*) The conservative reformation and its theology: as presented in the Augsburg confession, and in the history and literature of the Evangelical lutheran church. xvi, 840 pp. 8°. *Philadelphia, J. B Lippincott & co.* 1871.

Kreuter (Franz). Praktisches handbuch der drainage, oder anleitung zur trockenlegung nasser und kalter gründe und zur dauernden boden-verbesserung nach englischer art. xx, 218 pp. 2 tables. 8°. *Wien, C. Gerold*, 1851.

Krieger (Jacob, *sr.*) Compound discount and exchange tables: by the use of which may be found the amount to be added to a bill of exchange, draft, or note, to produce, when discounted, the entire net amount, either at simple discount from 3 to 18 per cent. or with collection, exchange, brokerage or commission, and the discount combined: also tables showing how much exchange a certain amount of money will buy. 299 pp. fol. *Louisville (Ky.) J. P. Morton & co.* 1871.

Kriegk (Georg Ludwig). Das land Otuquis in Bolivia. Nach einem originalberichte des herrn Moriz Bach, [etc.] mit beziehung auf allgemeine südamerikanische verhältnisse. ix, 54 pp. 1 map. 8°. *Frankfurt am Main, S. Schmerber*, 1838.

Krohn (Henrik). Fraa Vestlandet. 111 pp. 16°. *Bjørgvin, E. B. Giertsen*, 1868. s.

——— Minne fraa ei Stokkholmsferd. 2 p. l. 148 pp. 16°. *Bjørgvin, E. B. Gjertsen*, 1867. s.

——— Svein og Gudveig. [A poem]. 108 pp. 1 l. 16°. *Bjørgvin, E. B. Giertsen*, 1869. s.

Krummacher (Friedrich Wilhelm). Elisha. From the german. Revised by the rev. R[obert] F[rancis] Walker. 4 p. l 251 pp. 12°. *London, Religious tract society*, 1838.

Krusinski (Judasz Tadeuz). The history of the revolution of Persia: taken from the memoirs of father Krusinski, procurator of the jesuits at Ispahan. Done into english, from the original, just published at Paris, by father Du Cerceau, who has prefix'd a short history of the Sophies; with curious remarks on the accounts given by Tavernier, sir John Chardin, [etc.] 1 p. l. xxiv, 274 pp; 4 p. l. 199, xxiv pp. 8°. *London, J. Pemberton*, 1728.

[*Note.*—Map wanting].

Kulpis (Johann Georg von). Scriptores rervm germanicarvm a Carolo M. usq; ad Fridericvm iii. inclusive: partim denuo, desiderati hactenus in tabernis, partim auctiores, partim de novo in unvm volvmen collecti. una cvm omni re diplomatica Friderici imp. & indicibus convenientibus. Accessit etiam praefatio Jo. Schilteri. 6 p. l. 378, 98 pp. 27 l. 148 pp. 11 pl. 320 pp. fol. *Argentorati, apud J. R. Dulsseckerum*, 1702.

[*Note.*—Though the title-page bears only the name of Schilter, this is but a new edition of the work of Kulpis, first printed 1685, under the title Æneae Sylvii historia Friderici iii. etc. That life is here included, accompanied by abundant illustrations].

CONTENTS.

ÆNEÆ SILUII historia rerum Friderici iii. imperatoris.
ALBERTI *stadensis* chronicon a condito orbe vsque ad a. c. 1256.
ANDREÆ *ratisbonensis* chronicon. [Chronica de principibvs terrae Bavarorvm].
ANNALES de gestis Caroli magni poetæ anonymi.
DIPLOMATA et documenta Friderici iii. imp.
ERCKENBALDI de antecessoribvs svis in episcopatv carmen.
INDEX diplomatvm Friderici iii. et docvmentorvm variorvm eo pertinentivm.
INDEX rerum memorabilium in hoc volumine obviarum.
KAROLI MAGNI vita descripta, magna parte a monacho, [anonymo].
MARTINI *poloni* chronicon. [Chronologia romanorum pontificum et imperatorum].
NITHARDI de dissensionibus filiorum Lodhvvici Pii ad annum usq. 843.
THEGANI *trevirensis* opvs de gestis domini Ludiwici imp.

Kumo (O ke) Leomele, no na himeni a me na halelu e hoolea aku ai i ke akua. [Sandwich island hymn book]. 360 pp. sq. 18°. *Oahu, na na misionari*, 1834.

Kun (Pieter van der). Sardi venales. Satyra menippæa in hujus saeculi homines plerosque inepte eruditos. Petrus Cvnævs, scripsit. 18°. [*Lugduni Batavorum*], 1655.

[ELEGANTIORES præstantium virorum satyrae, pp. 35-110].

Kurtz (Benjamin, *d. d.*) Arguments, derived from sacred scripture and sound reason, exhibiting the necessity and advantages of infant baptism; and proving sprinkling or affusion to be the most scriptural and appropriate mode of administering it; together with a number of essays on important subjects connected with baptism. 370 pp. 12°. *Baltimore, at the publication rooms*, 1840.

Küttner (Carl Gottlob) *and* **Nicholson** (William). New and complete dictionary of the german language for Englishmen, according to the german dictionary of mr. J. C. Adelung; [or], Neues und vollständiges deutsch-englisches wörterbuch, zu J. C. Adelung's englisch-deutschem wörterbuche. 3 v. 8°. *Leipzig, E. B. Schwickert*, 1805.

L. Sybelle and other poems. By L. [*anon.*] 192 pp. 12°. *New York, Carleton*, 1862.

L. (E.) Treasures of. *See* **Lloyd** (Elizabeth).

L. (E. Y.) The bible story told for children; from the time of Abraham to the time of Christ. By a teacher. Edited by E. Y. L. 100 pp. 16°. *Boston, Walker, Fuller and co.* 1866.

L. (G. D.) The first voyage of Rodolph the voyager. *See* **Sewell** (*Rev.* William).

L. (H.) Chants chrétiens. [*anon.*] 6e éd. 2 p. l. iv, 368 pp. 8°. *Paris, M. Doucloux & cie.* 1851.

L. (L. E.) *See* **Landon** (Letitia Elizabeth).

L. (S. J.) Consolation; or, a winter's gleaning. In a poem. [*anon.*] 114 pp. 12°. *Boston, B. B. Russell*, 1871.

L . . . . (The) family at Washington; or, a winter in the metropolis. [*anon.*] 2 p. l. 13-159 pp. 12°. *Washington, Davis & Force*, 1822.

La Barre de Beaumarchais (Antoine de). Les virtus païennes. 16°. [*La Haye, Schurleer*, 1729].

[*In* STEELE (Richard). Le héros chrétien, pp. 175-231].

Labberton (Robert H.) An historical atlas containing a chronological series of one hundred maps, at successive periods, from the dawn of history to the present day. xvi pp. 40 col. maps. obl. 4°. *Philadelphia, Claxton, Remsen & Haffelfinger*, 1872.

——— Historical questions, logically arranged and divided. The companion-book to Labberton's Outlines of history. xvi, 248 pp. obl. 4°. *Philadelphia, Claxton, Remsen & Haffelfinger*, 1872.

La Bédollière (Émile Gigault de). Mother Michel and her cat. Translated from the french by Fanny Fuller. 104 pp. 16°. *Philadelphia, F. Leypoldt*, 1865.

La Bédoyère (Charles Angélique François Huchet, *comte* de). Memoirs of the public and private life of Napoleon Bonaparte; from the ms. of count Labédoyère. Preceded by an analysis of the french revolution. 2 v. viii, 1052 pp. 2 pl. 8°. *London, G. Virtue*, [1827].

Labindo (*pseudon.*) *See* **Fantoni** (Giovanni).

La Bissachère (Pierre Jacques Lemonnier de). Exposé statistique du Tunkin, de la Cochinchine, du Camboge, du Tsiampa, du Laos, du Lac-Tho. Par m. M—n [Montyon]. Sur la relation de m. de La Bissa-

La Bissachère (P. J. L. de)—continued. chère, missionnaire dans le Tunkin. 2 v. 1 p. l. 364 pp. 1 l; 1 p. l. 169 pp. 8°. *Londres, Vogel & Schulze*, 1811.

La Blanchardière (*L'abbé* Courte de). *See* **Courte de La Blanchardière.**

La Boëssière (*maître d'armes*). Traité de l'art des armes, à l'usage des professeurs et des amateurs. xxii, 309 pp. 20 pl. 8°. *Paris, Didot l'aîné*, 1818.

Laborde (*Col.* Étienne). [The emperor Napoleon's journey] from Elba to Paris. 8°. [*Dublin, Grant & Bolton*, 1841].

[*In* USSHER (*Capt. sir* Thomas). A narrative of events connected with the first abdication of Napoleon. *Dublin*, 1841, pp. 83–100].

Laborde (Jean Benjamin de). Essai sur l'histoire chronologique de plus de 80 peuples de l'antiquité. Composé pour l'éducation de monseigneur le dauphin. v. 2. Abrégé chronologique des principaux faits arrivés depuis la naissance d'Hénoch, l'an du monde 622, jusqu'à la naissance de Jésus-Christ. 2 v. 2 p. l. 554 pp. 1 l; 4 p. l. 719 pp. 7 tables. 4°. *Paris, Didot l'aîné*, 1788–89.

Laborde (Léon Emmanuel Simon Joseph *comte* de). Notice des émaux, bijoux et objets divers exposés dans les galeries du Louvre. *See* **Paris.** (*Musée du Louvre*).

La Bouillerie (— *abbé* de). Hours before the altar; or, meditations on the holy eucharist. 209 pp. 24°. *New-York, E. Dunigan & brother*, 1856.

Labus (Giovanni). Vita di Carlo Amoretti. 16°. *Milan, per G. Silvestri*, 1824.

[*In* AMORETTI (Carlo). Viaggio da Milano ai tre laghi, [etc.] pp. ix–xl].

Labutte (A.) Histoire des ducs de Normandie jusqu'à la mort de Guillaume le conquérant. Préface par Henri Martin. 2e éd. 2 p. l. xii, 368 pp. 12 pl. 8°. *Paris, Furne, Jouvet & cie.* 1866.

La Caille (Jean de). Histoire de l'imprimerie et de la librairie, où l'on voit son origine et son progrès, jusqu'en 1689. 2 p. l. 322 pp. 13 l. 4°. *Paris, J. de la Caille*, 1689.

Lacey (William B. *d. d.*) An illustration of the principles of elocution. 2d ed. 300 pp. 12°. *Pittsburgh, D. M. Hogan*, 1833.

——— A system of moral philosophy; or, christian ethics. 2d ed. 312 pp. 12°. *Pittsburgh, Patterson, Forrester & co.* 1837.

La Condamine (Charles Marie de). Histoire des pyramides de Quito, élevées par les académiciens envoyés sous l'équateur par ordre du roi. [*anon.*] 1 p. l. 53 pp. 1 chart. 4°. [*Paris*], 1751.

Lacordaire (Jean Théodore). Histoire naturelle des insectes. Genera des coléoptères. t. 2e, contenant les familles des Paussides-hétérocérides. 2 p. l. 548 pp. 8°. *Paris, Roret*, 1854. S.

[v. 1 and 3–7 wanting].

——— Introduction à l'entomologie, comprenant les principes généraux de l'anatomie et de la physiologie des insectes, des détails sur leurs mœurs et un résumé des principaux systèmes de classification. 2 v. 463 pp; 684 pp. 8°. *Paris, Roret*, 1834–38. S.

[Imperfect: wanting in v. 1, pp i–xxxiii and 12 pl; in v. 2, pp. xvi and 12 pl.]

Lacroix (Jean Pascal). *See* **Pascal Lacroix.**

Lacroix (Paul). La danse macabre, histoire fantastique du quinzième siècle par P. L. Jacob, bibliophile. [*pseudon.*] 232 pp. 1 l. 16°. *Bruxelles, H. Dumont*, 1832.

——— Une femme malheureuse. Fille-femme. Par Paul L. Jacob. [*pseudon.*] 2 v. 320 pp; 284 pp. 18°. *Bruxelles, J. P. Meline*, 1836.

La Croze (Mathurin Veyssière de). Thesavrus epistolicus lacrozianus. Ex bibliotheca iordaniana edidit Io. Lvdovicvs Vhlivs. 3 v. in 2. 8°. *Lipsiæ, impens. I. F. Gleditschii*, 1742–46.

Lactantius Firmianus (Lucius Cœlius *or* Cæcilius). Opera omnia qvae exstant, cvm notis integris C. Cellarii et selectis avt excerptis, [aliorum]. Omnia recensvit et notis criticis instrvxit I. L. Bvnemann. 2 v. in 1. 27 p. l. 1528 pp. 40 l. 1 pl. 2 spec. m. 8°. *Lipsiae, impensis S. B. Waltheri*, 1739.

CONTENTS.

v. 1. Divinarvm institutionvm libri septem.
v. 2. De ira Dei. De opificio Dei vel formatione hominis. Epitome institvtionvm divinarvm. De mortibvs persecvtorvm. Symposivm. Carmen de Phœnice. Carmen de pascha. De passione Domini.

——— The same. Opera. Ad optimorum librorum fidem emendavit et cum selecta lectionum varietate edidit O. F. Fritzsche. 2 v. 12°. *Lipsiae, B. Tauchnitz*, 1842–44.

[GERSDORF (E. G.) Bibliotheca patrum ecclesiasticorum latinorum selecta. v. 10–11].

——— De opifitio Dei. fol. *Bologna*, 1684.

[*In* SCARLATINI (Ottavio). L'hvomo, e sve parti figvrato, e simbolico. Part 2. pp. 251–267].

——— Diuinarum institutionum libri vii. De ira Dei, liber i. De opificio Dei, liber i. Epitome in libros suos liber acephalos, Phœnix. Carmen de dominica resurrectione. Carmen de passione Domini. 10 p. l. 434 pp. 8°. *Basileæ, apvd A. Cratandrvm*, 1521.

Lactantius Firmianus (L. C.)—continued.
——— A summary of the writings of Lactantius. By the rev. Jacob Henry Brooke Mountain. xx, 154 pp. 8°. *London, J. G. & F. Rivington*, 1839.

Lacuée (Gérard Jean, *comte de Cessac*). Guide de l'officier particulier en campagne. 3e éd. 2 v. xlvi, 351 pp. 13 pl; 2 p. l. 363 pp. 7 pl. 8°. *Paris, Barrois l'aîné*, 1816. s.

Lacy (Nathan, *m. d.*) De podagra. 5 p. l. 97 pp. 16°. *Venetiis, apud A. Poleti, svmptibvs avthoris*, 1692.

Ladd (William). The hero of Macedon, or history of Alexander the great, viewed in the light of the gospel. 108 pp. 18°. *Boston, J. Loring*, 1832.

Ladies diary. *See* **Hutton** (Charles.) The diarian miscellany, 1775.

Ladies' gems, or poems on the love of flowers, kindness to animals, and the domestic affections. From the most approved authors. 108 pp. 16°. *New-York*, 1855.

La Dixmerie (Nicolas Bricaire de). La sibyle gauloise, ou la France, telle qu'elle fut, telle quelle est, & telle, à peu-près, qu'elle pourra être. Ouvrage traduit du celte, & suivi d'un commentaire. xxviii, 276 pp. 1 pl. 8°. *Londres*, 1775.

Ladreyt (Casimir). Chrestomathie de la littérature française, ou morceaux choisis des meilleurs écrivains français depuis 1520 jusqu'en 1845, avec 176 notices biographiques, littéraires et bibliographiques. Nouvelle éd. x, 355 pp. 12°. *New York, W. E. Dean*, 1845.
——— The study of french simplified; or, new elements, of the french language, methodically displayed in a complete course of progressive practical lessons, [etc.] xii, 163 pp. 12°. *New York, H. & S. Raynor*, 1844.

Ladvocat (Jean Baptiste). Dictionnaire géographique, ou description des quatre parties du monde, par Vosgien. [*pseudon.*] Seconde édition, augmentée et entièrement refondue, renfermant les changemens survenus par suite des différens traités, jusqu'à ce jour. Par Giraud. 3 p. l. 792 pp. 8 maps. 8°. *Lyon, Yvernault & Cabin*, 1811.
[*Note.*—The first edition (1747) purports to be translated from the thirteenth edition of the english gazeteer of Laurence Echard, but a comparison between the present edition and Echard's gazetteer shows no specific resemblance].

Lady's (The) almanac for 1872. 32°. *Boston, G. A. Coolidge*, [1871].

Lady's (The) friend. Edited by mrs. Henry Peterson. [Monthly]. Jan. to Dec. 1871. v. 8. 8°. *Philadelphia, Deacon & Peterson*, [1871].

Lady's (The) pocket library. 3d american ed. 312 pp. 2 l. 16°. *Chambersburg*, [*Pa.*] *Dover & Harper for M. Carey, Philadelphia*, 1797.

CONTENTS.

1. Miss More's essays.
2. Dr. Gregory's legacy to his daughters.
3. Lady Pennington's unfortunate mother's advice to her daughters.
4. Rudiments of taste, by the countess of Carlisle.
5. Mrs. Chapone's letter on the government of the temper.
6. Swift's letter to a young lady newly married.
7. Moore's fables for the female sex.

Lætus (Pomponius). *See* **Leto** (Giulio Pomponio).

La Farina (Giuseppe). Studi storici nove sul secolo decimo-terzo. 2a ed. viii, 980 pp 1 l. 8°. *Bastia, a spese dell' editore*, 1857. s.
——— Rischiarazioni e documenti sopra nove studi storici del secolo xiii. 2a ed. 1 p. l. 662 pp. 8°. *Bastia, a spese dell' editore*, 1857.

La Feuille (Daniel de). Livre nouveav et utile pour toutes sortes d'artistes, [etc.] Contenant quatre alphabets de chiffres fleuronnez au premier trait avec quantité de devises, d'emblêmes et de nœuds d'amour. (etc.) 1 p. l. 29 pl. 2 l. 16°. *Amsterdam*, 1690.

La Fond (Jean Réné Sigaud de). *See* **Sigaud de la Fond.**

La Fontaine (Jean de). Les amours de Psyché et de Cupidon. Édition ornée de figures imprimées en couleurs, d'après les tableaux de M. Schall. 163 pp. 4 col. plates. 4°. *Paris, Defer de Maisonneuve*, 1791.
——— Fables. Illustrated by J. J. Grandville. Translated from the french, by Elizur Wright, jr. 2 v. 1 p. l. vi, 13-245 pp; 1 p. l. 351 pp. 12°. *New York, Derby & Jackson*, 1860.

Lagrange (Edme Jean Baptiste Bouillon-). *See* **Bouillon-Lagrange.**

La Grange (Frédéric de). Le grand livre du destin. Répertoire général des sciences occultes d'après Albert-le-grand, N. Flamel, Paracelse, Roger Bacon, Corneille Agrippa, le pape Jean xxii. Ch. Fourrier, Eteilla, madame Lenormand, Gall, Lavater, etc. 3e éd. précédée de la prophétie du solitaire Dorval. viii, 388 pp. 8°. *Paris, Lavigne*, 1850.

Lagrange (*Rev.* J.) The philosophy of moral necessity and moral freedom, in two parts.

Lagrange (*Rev.* J.)—continued.
Part first. Principles of necessity and of freedom. Part second. Principles of harmony; reconciling particularly man's moral freedom with divine foreknowledge and predestination. 270 pp. 12°. *Auburn (N. Y.) W. J. Moses,* 1854.

La Grave (Guillaume Poncet de). *See* **Poncet de La Grave.**

La Harpe (Jean François). Œuvres [dramatiques] choisies. Éd. stéréotype. 2 v. 2 p. l. xi, 257 pp; 223 pp. 24°. *Paris, P. Didot l'aîné, & F. Didot,* 1819.

La Hontan (N. *baron* de). Reizen in het Noordelyk America. [Med verfolg van] gedenkschriften. Vertaalt door G. Westerwyk, [etc.] 2 v. 6 p. l. 582 pp. 1 map, 3 pl; 1 p. l. 552 pp. 1 map, 6 pl. 16°. *Gravenhage, I. Beauregard,* 1739.

Lai de Melion. [*anon.*] 8°. [*Paris, Silvestre,* 1832].
[*In* MONMERQUÉ (L. J. N.) *and* MICHEL (F.) Lai d'Ignaurés, pp. 43–67].

Lai du Trot. [*anon.*] 8°. *Paris, Silvestre,* 1832].
[*In* MONMERQUÉ (L. J. N.) *and* MICHEL (F.) Lai d'Ignaurés, pp. 69–83].

Laidlaw (Alexander H.) An american pronouncing dictionary of the english language. 600 pp. sq. 16°. *Philadelphia, Crissy & Markley,* [1859].

Laighton (Albert). Poems. 135 pp. 12°. *Boston, Brown, Taggard & Chase,* 1859.

——— The poets of Portsmouth. *See* **Payson** (Aurin M.) *and* **Laighton.**

Laighton. *See* **Leighton.**

Lain (George T.) Brooklyn directory, 1872. *See* **Brooklyn** (*N. Y.*)

Laird (Francis Charles, *lieut. r. n.*) Lady Jane Grey, and her times. By George Howard, esq. [*pseudon.*] vii, 392 pp. 1 portrait. 12°. *London, Sherwood, Neely & Jones,* 1822.

Lairesse (Gérard de). A treatise on the art of painting in all its branches; accompanied by seventy engraved plates, and exemplified by remarks on the paintings of the best masters. Revised, corrected, and accompanied with an essay, by W. M. Craig. 2 v. Eng. title, iv, 296 pp. 35 pl; iv, 294 pp. 36 pl. 4°. *London, E. Orme,* 1817.

La Jonchère (C. de). Nouveau dictionnaire portatif français-suédois. Nytt franskt och swenskt hand-lexicon. 5e uppl. 4 p. l. 754 pp. 2 l. sm. 4°. *Orebro, N. M. Lindhs' boktryckeri,* 1838.

Lakeside (The) monthly. Jan. 1871, to June, 1872. v. 5–7. 8°. *Chicago, Reed, Browne & co. and University publishing co.* 1871–72.
[*Note.*—v. 1–4 *known as* The western monthly. No numbers issued for Nov. and Dec. 1871].

Lamar (J. S.) The organon of scripture: or, the inductive method of biblical interpretation. 324 pp. 12°. *Philadelphia, J. B. Lippincott & co.* 1860.

La Marche (C. F. S. de). Russische anekdoten von der regierung und tod Peters des dritten; imgleichen von der erhebung und regierung Catharinen der andern. Ferner von dem tode des kaysers Iwan, welchen zum anhange beygefüget die lebensgeschichte Catharinen der ersten. 304 pp. 16°. *Petersburg,* 1764.

Lamartine (Alphonse Marie Louis Prat de). Raphaël. Pages de la vingtième année. 1 p. l. 300 pp. 12°. *Bruxelles, Meline, Cans, & ce.* 1849.

——— Graziella. Nouvelle éd. 191 pp. 16°. *Paris, librairie nouvelle,* 1852.

——— Twenty-five years of my life, and memoirs of my mother. Translated by lady [Mary Elizabeth] Herbert. 2 v. x, 385 pp; ix, 356 pp. 8°. *London, R. Bentley & son,* 1872.

La Martinière (Pierre Martin de). Voyage des pais septentrionavx. Dans lequel se void les mœurs, manière de vivre, et superstitions des Norweguiens, Lappons, Kiloppes, Borandiens, Syberiens, Samojedes, Zembliens, et Islandois. 8 p. l. 201 pp. 18°. *Paris, L. Vendosme,* 1671.

——— The same. Neue reise in die nordischen landschafften. Das ist: eine beschreibung der sitten, gebräuche, aberglauben, gebäuden, und kleidung der Norweger, Lapländer, Killopen, Borandianer, Siberianer, Samojeden, Zemblaner and Eissländer, sampt einem bedencken über den irrthum unser erdbeschreiber, wo nemlich Grönland und Nova Zembla liegen, und wie weit sie sich erstrecken. Aus dem englischen ins deutsche übersetzet durch I. Langen. 4 p. l. 80 pp. 4°. *Hamburg, Nauman & Wolff,* 1675.

Lamb (Jonathan). The child's instructor, or second book for primary schools. 180 pp. 16°. *Burlington,* [*Vt.*] *A. & D. Day,* 1829.

——— The practical spelling-book, and child's instructor: or, second book for primary schools. 144 pp. 12°. *Boston, T. Webb & co.* 1844.

Lambarde (William). Dictionarium Angliae topographicum et historicum. An alphabetical description of the chief places in England and Wales, with an account of the most memorable events which have distinguish'd them. Now first publish'd. 1 p. l. iv, xiv, 498 pp. 1 portrait. 4°. *London, F. Gyles*, 1730.

Lambert (Anne Thérèse de Marguenat de Courcelles, *marquise* de). The works of the marchioness de Lambert. A new ed. from the french. 2 v. 2 p. l. 264 pp ; 1 p.l. 238, xx pp. 16°. *London, W. Owen*, 1769.

——— Advice of a mother to her daughter. [From the french]. sm. 4°. [*London, J. Hamilton & co.* 1794].

[*In* HAMILTON (John). Angelica's ladies' library, pp. 169–212].

——— The marchioness de Lambert's letters to her son and daughter, on true education, etc. Translated by mr. Rowell. xxiv, 200 pp. 8°. *London, M. Cooper*, 1749.

——— New reflexions on the fair sex. Written originally in french, (and suppress'd). Translated into english, by J. Lockman. xxiv, 72 pp. 16°. *London, N. Prevost*, 1729.

Lambert (Edward R.) History of the colony of New Haven, before and after the union with Connecticut. 216 pp. 16 pl. 12°. *New Haven, Hitchcock & Stafford*, 1838.

Lambin (Denis). Dionysii Lambini oratio de laudibus litterarum, pridie quàm nobileis Æschinis in Ctesiphontem, & Demosthenis pro Ctesiphōte orationes inter se contrarias explicare inciperet. 8 l. 4°. *Lvtetiae, apud viduā G. Morelii*, 1564.

Lamborn (E.) The practical teacher, or familiar explanations and illustrations of the modus operandi of the school room. 2 p. l. 113 pp. 8°. *Lancaster* [*Pa.*] *Murray & Stoek*, 1855.

Lamé-Fleury (Jules Raymond). L'histoire sainte, racontée aux enfants. 10e éd. 2 p. l. iv, 350 pp. 24°. *Paris, Borrani & Droz, etc.* 1853.

Lami (Giovanni). Lezione di antichità toscane, e spezialmente della città di Firenze, recitate nell' Accademia della crvsca. 1 v. in 2. cxcvi, 718 pp. 12 pl. 2 portraits. 4°. *Firenze, A. Bondvcci*, 1766.

Lamon (Ward H.) The life of Abraham Lincoln ; from his birth to his inauguration as president. xv, 547 pp. 13 portraits, 2 pl. 1 fac-simile. 8°. *Boston, J. R. Osgood & co.* 1872.

La Monnoye (Bernard de). Œuvres choisies. [Publiées par J. A. Rigoley de Juvigny]. 3 v. 8°. *La Haye, C. Le Vier*, 1770.

Lamont (*Mrs.* Æneas). Poems, and tales in verse. iv, 179 pp. 12°. *London, author*, 1818.

Lamp (A) for the feet. [*anon.*] 190 pp. 32°. *Philadelphia, American sunday school union*, [1863].

Lancaster (*Rev.* Thomas William). The harmony of the law and the gospel with regard to the doctrine of a future state. xvi, 470 pp. 8°. *Oxford, University press for J. Parker*, 1825.

Lancaster (*Mass.*) Catalogue of Lancaster town library. 2 p. l. 108, 31 pp. 16°. *Clinton,* [*Mass.*] *W. J. Coulter*, 1868.

Lancaster (*Ohio*). Williams' Circleville and Lancaster directory. *See* **Circleville.**

Lancaster county (*Pa.*) Boyd's Lancaster county business directory. 1859–60. Compiled by William H. Boyd. 40 l. unp. 41–316 pp. 12°. *Lancaster (Penn.) Sprenger & Westhaeffer*, [1859].

Lance (William). Georgii Washingtonis vita. (1a pars, ad 1777]. xi, 75 pp. 1 portrait. 12°. *Carolopoli, in Carolina australi, D. J. Dowling*, 1836.

Lancelot (Claude). Le jardin des racines grecques, mises en vers françois, avec un traité des prépositions et autres particules, et un recueil des mots françois tirez de la langue grecque. [*anon.*] Nouv. éd. 14 p. l. 394 pp. 1 l. 20 pp. 16°. *Paris, Thiboust*, 1740.

——— The same. The greek primitives, of the messieurs de Port-Royal. To which are added rules for derivation, or the formation of words ; selected principally from Buttmann's greek grammar. [*anon.*] viii, 184 pp. 16°. *Boston, Perkins & Marvin*, 1831.

Lancet (The). A journal of british and foreign medicine, physiology, surgery, chemistry, criticism, literature, and news. [Weekly]. Edited by J. G. Wakley, m. d. July 2, 1870, to Dec. 30, 1871. 3 v. fol. *London, office of "The lancet,"* [1870–71].

Lanciego y Eguilaz (Joseph de, *arçobispo de Mexico*). Carta pastoral que escribe â sus amadas hijas las religiossas de toda su filiacion. 1 p. l. 46 l. 18°. *Mexico, herederos de la viuda de M. de Ribera*, 1716.

Lanctot (Benoni). Chinese and english phrase book, with the chinese pronunciation indicated in english, specially adapted for the use of merchants, travelers and families. 80 pp. 12°. *San Francisco, A. Roman & co.* 1867.

Land (The) owner. A journal of real estate. Devoted to landed interests, building and improvement. [Monthly]. Jan. 1870, to Sept. 1871. v. 2-3. 4°. *Chicago, J. M. Wing & co.* [1870-71].
[Incomplete: wanting, Oct. 1870-Jan. 1871; none published for Oct.-Dec. 1871].

Land (The) without the sabbath. A grandmother's tale. By the author of "Edward and Miriam," [etc. *anon.*] 198 pp. 1 pl. 18°. *Philadelphia, H. Perkins*, 1841.

Landais (Napoléon). Dictionnaire général et grammatical des dictionnaires français: extrait et complément de tous les dictionnaires anciens et modernes les plus célèbres. 7e éd. 2 v. 848 pp; 816 pp. 4°. *Paris, Didier*, 1843.

Landels (William, *d. d.*) Woman: her position and power. iv, 288 pp. 12°. *London, Cassell, Petter & Galpin*, [1870].

Lander (Meta, *pseudon?*) Fading flowers. xiv, 288 pp. 2 pl. sq. 12°. *Boston, J. E. Tilton & co.* 1860.

——— Marion Graham; or, "higher than happiness." 506 pp. 12°. *Boston, Crosby, Nichols, Lee & co.* 1861.

Lander (Sarah W.) Spectacles for little eyes. [*anon.*] viii, 198 pp. 12°. *Boston, Walker, Wise & co.* 1862.

——— Spectacles for young eyes. 3 v. 16°. *Boston, Walker, Wise & co.* 1863-64.

CONTENTS.

Pekin. 218 pp. 4 pl.
St. Petersburg. 203 pp. 8 pl.
Moscow. 202 pp. 6 pl.

Landis (Robert Wharton). The cross. A poem. 462 pp. 8°. *New York and Cincinnati, C. F. Vent*, 1870.

——— A plea for the catholic doctrine of the trinity. ix, 227 pp. 12°. *Philadelphia*, 1832.

Landon (Letitia Elizabeth, *mrs.* McLean). Traits and trials of early life. By L. E. L. [*anon.*] 240 pp. 8°. *Philadelphia, E. L. Carey & A. Hart*, 1837.

Landscapes in verse. Taken in spring. *See* **Pratt** (Samuel Jackson).

Landwirthschaftliches centralblatt für Deutschland. Repertorium der wissenschaftlichen forschungen und praktischen erfahrungen im gebiete der landwirthschaft. Herausgegeben von dr. Adolf Wilda, [etc.] 4er zu 8er jahrgang, 1856-1870. 30 v. in 15. 8°. *Berlin, K. Wiegandt*, [*etc.*] 1856-70.

Lane (Horace). The wandering boy, careless sailor, and result of inconsideration. A true narrative. 224 pp. 1 pl. 18°. *Skaneateles, [N. Y.] Luther A. Pratt*, 1839.

Laneton parsonage. *See* **Sewell** (Elizabeth Missing).

Lanfrey (Pierre). Histoire de Napoléon 1er. 2e éd. v. 1-4. 16°. *Paris, Charpentier*, 1868-70.

——— The same. The history of Napoleon the first. [From the french]. v. 1. vii, 496 pp. 8°. *London and New York, Macmillan & co.* 1871.

Lang (John Dunmore, *d. d.*) Transportation and colonization; or, the causes of the comparative failure of the transportation system in the australian colonies: with suggestions for ensuring its future efficiency in subserviency to extensive colonization. viii, 244 pp. 12°. *London, A. J. Valpy*, 1837.

Langdon (William B.) A descriptive catalogue of the chinese collection, now exhibiting at St. George's place, Hyde Park corner, London, with condensed accounts of the genius, government, history, literature, agriculture, arts, trade, manners, customs and social life of the people of the celestial empire. 19th english ed. 1 p. l. 163 pp. 16 pl. 8°. [*London*], *for the proprietor*, 1843.

Lange (John Peter, *d. d.*) Commentary on the holy scriptures. *See* **Bible.** (*English*).

Langenes (Bernardt). Caert-thresoor, inhoudende de tafelen des gantsche werelts landen, met beschryvinghen verlicht, nu van nieus toegereet. 2 v. in 1. 7 p. l. 462 pp. 118 maps, 1 pl; 196 pp. 58 maps. obl. 16°. *Amsterdam, C. Claesz*, 1599.

Langewald (Ferdinand A.) Neueste praktische lehr-methode der weberei zum selbstunterricht auf hand- und maschinenstühlen. 2 p. l. vii, 118 pp. 1 l. 4°. *North Oxford (Mass.) F. Langewald*, [1871].

Langford (John Alfred). Religious scepticism and infidelity; their history, cause, cure, and mission. v, 245 pp. 12°. *London, J. Chapman*, 1850.

Langhorne (John). Poetical works. 2 v. 4 p. l. 164 pp. 1 pl; 2 p. l. 181 pp. 16°. *London, T. Becket*, 1766.

Langlé (Joseph Adolphe Ferdinand). Maître Pathelin. *See* **Leuven** (Adolphe de) *and* **Langlé.**

Langley (Batty *and* Thomas). The builder's jewel: or, the youth's instructor and workman's remembrancer. New ed. to which is added, a dictionary of terms used in architecture. 62 pp. 100 pl. sq. 16°. *Haddington, G. Miller*, 1805.

Langley (B. *and* T.)—continued.
——— Gothic architecture, improved by rules and proportions, in many grand designs of columns, doors, windows, &c. With plans, elevations, and profiles, geometrically explained. 1 p. l. 64 pl. 4°. *London, J. Millan*, 1747.

Langley (Henry G.) The San Francisco directory. *See* **San Francisco.**

Langley (Thomas). An abridgemēt of the workc of Polidore Virgile. *See* **Virgilio** (Polidoro).

Langlois (Hyacinthe). Itinéraire complet de l'empire français, comprenant la Hollande, une partie de l'Allemagne, l'Italie, et les provinces illyriennes. [*anon.*] 2e éd. 3 v. 16°. *Paris, H. Langlois*, 1811.

Lanman (Charles). Essays for summer hours. 4 p. l. 175 pp. 12°. *Boston, Hilliard, Gray & co.* 1841.
——— The same. 2 p. l. 250 pp. 12°. [*Boston*, 1842].
——— The Japanese in America. 1 p. l. 352 pp. 3 phot. 12°. *New York, University pub. co.* 1872.
——— Letters from a landscape painter. By the author of "Essays for summer hours." [*anon.*] 2 p. l. 265 pp. 12°. *Boston, J. Munroe & co.* 1845.
[Imperfect: wanting pp. 169–190].

La Noue (François de, *dit Bras-de-fer*). Correspondance de François de La Noue, surnommé Bras-de-fer, accompagnée de notes historiques et précédée de la vie de ce grand capitaine, par Ph. Kervyn de Volkaersbeke. 2 p. l. x, 275 pp. 2 pl. 1 portrait. 8°. *Gand, Duquesne*, 1854.

Lanz (Alois). Inscriptionum et carminum libri tres. xxiv, 144 pp. 4°. *Florentiae, typis Carli & soc.* 1807.

La Pommeraye (A. Texier de). *See* **Texier de la Pommeraye.**

Laporte (Clément *and l'abbé* Joseph de). Anecdotes dramatiques. [*anon.*] 3 v. 12°. *Paris, veuve Duchesne*, 1775.

Laporte (J.) A new series of Laporte's progressive lessons in landscape. 24 pl. obl. fol. *London, Griffiths, fancy repository*, 1816.

Lara (Mariano Aniceto de). Resumen historico de los hechos notables de los partidos Yorkino, Escoces y Santanista, desde la independencia hasta la toma de Mexico por los Norte-americanos, [poema]. 70 pp. 18°. *Mexico, S. Perez*, 1852.

Larcher (L. J.) La femme. *See* **Bescherelle** (Louis Nicolas) *and* **Larcher.**
——— Satires et diatribes sur les femmes, l'amour et le mariage. Avec une réfutation. 2 p. l. 282 pp. 1 l. 16°. *Paris, A. Delahays*, 1860.

Lardner (Dionysius, *ll. d.*) The steam engine familiarly explained and illustrated; with an historical sketch of its invention and progressive improvement; its applications to navigation and railways; with plain maxims for railway speculators. With additions and notes, by James Renwick, ll. d. 2d amer. from the 5th Lond. ed. 325 pp. 13 pl. 8°. *Philadelphia, E. L. Carey & A. Hart*, 1836.
——— Lardner's outlines of universal history. *See* **Keightley** (Thomas).

Lardner (Nathaniel, *d. d.*) Memoirs of the life and writings of the late rev. Nathaniel Lardner, d. d. [by Andrew Kippis], containing a catalogue of his works, with several letters relating to them, and other original papers. [*anon.*] Also eight sermons upon various subjects. viii, 374 pp. 8°. *London, J. Buckland*, [*etc.*] 1769.

Larenaudière (Philippe de). Anglo-saxonica. *See* **Wright** (Thomas).

La Rivière (Étienne de). De dissectione partium corporis humani. *See* **Estienne** (Charles) *and* **La Rivière.**

Larkin (Martin). The rival collection of prose and poetry. 504 pp. 12°. *New York, J. W. Schermerhorn & co.* 1872.

Larned (*Mrs.* L.) The american nun; or the effects of romance. vi, 142 pp. 16°. *Boston, Otis, Broaders & co.* 1836.

La Rochefoucauld (François, *duc* de). Moral maxims and reflections. Now made english. Eng. title, 23 p. l. 196 pp. 18°. *London, M. Gillyflower*, [*etc.*] 1694.

La Rochefoucault Liancourt (François Alexandre Frédéric, *duc* de). Des prisons de Philadelphie. Par un européen. [*anon.*] 44 pp. 8°. *Philadelphie, Moreau de St. Méry*, 1796.

La Rochette (Simon Chardon de). *See* **Chardon de la Rochette.**

La Roque (Gilles André de). Traité de l'origine des noms et des surnoms. 10 p. l. 304 pp. 16°. *Paris, E. Michallet*, 1681.

La Roque (Jean de). A voyage to Arabia the happy, by way of the Eastern ocean, and the streights of the Red-sea: perform'd by the french for the first time, 1708–10.

La Roque (Jean de)—continued.
Together with a particular relation of a journey from the port of Moka to the court of the king of Yemen, in the second expedition, 1711-13. Also, an account of the coffee-tree, and its fruit. xii, 312 pp. 4 pl. 16°. *London, G. Strahan*, 1726.

Larousse (Pierre). Grand dictionnaire universel du xixe siècle français, historique, géographique, mythologique, bibliographique, littéraire, artistique, scientifique, etc. v. 5-6. Con-dzo. 4°. *Paris, Larousse & Boyer*, 1870.

Larra (Mariano José de). No mas mostrador, comedia original en cinco actos. 16°. *Brunsvico, E. Leibrock*, 1841.
[BIBLIOTECA portatil español, v. 1, pp. 69-149].

Larrazábal (Felipe). La vida de Bolivar, escrita cuidadosamente, con presencia de documentos autentícos y muchos inéditos, de grande interes. 2 v. 8°. [*New York*, 1871].
[BOLIVAR (Simon). Correspondencia general, v. 1-2].

Larrey (Dominique Jean, *baron*). Observations on wounds, and their complications by erysipelas, gangrene and tetanus, and on the principal diseases and injuries of the head, ear and eye. Translated from the french by E. F. Rivinus, m. d. viii, 332 pp. 2 pl. 8°. *Philadelphia, Key, Mielke & Biddle*, 1832.

——— On the use of the moxa as a therapeutical agent. Translated from the french, with notes, and an introduction containing a history of the substance, by Robley Dunglison. 4 p. l. lxxvi, 148 pp. 8°. *London, T. & G. Underwood*, 1822.

Lasca (A. F. Grazzini, detto *il*). *See* **Grazzini.**

Las Casas (Bartolomé de). *See* **Casas.**

La Serre (Jean Puget de). The mirrour which flatters not. Transcrib'd into english from the french, by T. C. 14 p. l. 58, 71-228 pp. 8 l. 2 pl. 16°. *London, E. P. for R. Thrale*, 1639.

——— El sepulcro de las delicias del mundo: traducido al castellano é ilustrado con un compendio histórico por Nicolas Antonío. 159 pp. 8°. *Madrid, imprenta real*, 1792.

——— Panégyriques des hommes illustres de nostre siècle, [dédiez au cardinal Mazarin]. Eng. title, 9 p. l. 67 pp. 5 pl. fol. [*Paris*, 1655].
[*Note.*—The five persons commemorated here are Pierre Seguin, Matthieu de Molé, Pomponne de Bellièvre, Abel Servien, marquis de La Sablé, and Nicolas Fouquet].

Lasicki (Jan). De Rvssorvm Moscovitarvm et Tartarorvm religione, sacrificiis, nvptiarvm,

Lasicki (Jan)—continued.
fvnervm ritv. E diversis scriptoribvs, [etc.] Nunc primum in lucem edita. 4 p. l. 296 pp. 14 l. sm. 4°. *Spirae Nemetvm, B. d'Albinus*, 1582.

Lasso *or* **Lassus** (Roland de Lattre, *called* Orlando de). Magnum opvs mvsicvm Orlandi de Lasso. Complectens omnes cantiones qvas motetas vulgo vocant, tam antea editas quam hactenus nondum publicatas. A Ferdinando & Rvdolpho, authoris filiis, collectum, & impensis eorundem typis mandatum. Cantvs. Eng. title, 289 l. fol. *Monachii, ex typographia N. Henrici*, 1604.

Last (The) sensation. [Weekly]. Dec. 28, 1867, to May 30, 1868. v. 1. fol. *New York, J. Carter*, [1867-68].
[*Note.*—Title changed to the Days' doings].

Lastarria (José Victorino). Investigaciones sobre la influencia social de la conquista i del sistema colonial de los Españoles en Chile. 8°. *Santiago, imprenta nacional*, 1866. s.
[*In* VALENZUELA (J. S.) Historia jeneral de Chile, v. 1, pp. 1-101].

Latimer (*Miss* E.) Idyls of Gettysburg. 126 pp. 8°. *Philadelphia, G. Maclean*, 1872.

Latin phrase book, consisting of colloquial phrases and dialogues. To which is added a list of geographical and other proper names systematically arranged. By a teacher. [*anon.*] 116 pp. 18°. *Boston, J. Munroe & co.* 1836.

Latin (A) treatise on the chilindre (13 century). Edited with translation by Edmund Brock. 8°. [*London*, 1868].
[*With* EBERT (Prof.) Review of E. G. Sandras' Étude sur Chaucer, pp. 29-52].

Latinais-Suomalainen sanakirja. *See* **Rothsten** (F. W.)

Latini (Brunetto). Il tesoretto. 8°. [*Torino, stamperia reale*, 1750].
[*In* UBALDINI (F.) Il trattato delle virtu' morali, etc. pp. 33-127. ed. 1750].

La Tour (Louis Brion de). *See* **Brion de La Tour.**

Latrobe (John H. B.) A lost chapter in the history of the steamboat. 44 pp. 8°. *Baltimore*, 1871.
[MARYLAND historical society. Fund-publication, no. 5].

Latter-day saints. *See* **Church** of Jesus Christ of latter-day saints.

Latude (Henri Masers de). Memoirs of Henry Masers de Latude, who was confined during thirty-five years, in the different state prisons of France. Arranged from the original documents, by m. Thierry. Published

Latude (Henri Masers de)—continued. in France in 1790, and now first translated into english, by John William Calcraft. vii, 364 pp. 16°. *Dublin, W. F. Wakeman,* 1834.

Lauder (*Sir* Thomas Dick). Highland rambles, and long legends to shorten the way. 2 v. ix, 361 pp. 3 pl; 2 p. l. 380 pp. 1 l. 4 pl. 12°. *Edinburgh, A. & C. Black,* 1837.

Lauder (William). The extant [minor] poetical works of William Lauder, playwright, poet, and minister of the word of God. Edited by Fitzedward Hall [and] F. J. Furnivall. 2 p. l. xxxii, 48 pp. 8°. *London, N. Trübner & co.* 1870.
[EARLY english text society, no. 41].

Launay (Pierre de, *sieur de la Motte et de Vauferlan*). Remarqves svr le texte de la bible; ov explication des mots, des phrases, et des figvres difficiles de la s. écriture. 25 p. l. 553 pp. 46 l. 4°. *Genève, I. A. & S. De Tournes,* 1667.

——— Paraphrase et exposition svr l'apocalypse. Par Jonas Le Buy. [*pseudon.*] *See* **Bible.** (*French*).

Laurent (François). Histoire du droit des gens et des relations internationales. v. 15–17. 8°. *Paris, librairie internationale,* 1869–70.

CONTENTS.

v. 15. L'empire.
v. 16. La réaction religieuse.
v. 17. La religion de l'avenir.

Lauri (Jacopo). Ecclesiæ et palatia vrbis Romæ et aliarṽ civitṽm. Liber primvs. Eng. title, 54 pl. obl. fol. *Romæ,* 1633.

Laurie (Joseph, *m. d.*) The parent's guide: containing the diseases of infancy and childhood, and their homœopathic treatment. Edited, with additions, by Walter Williamson, m. d. 458 pp. 12°. *Philadelphia, Rademacher & Sheek,* 1854.

Laurie (Thomas, *d. d.*) Dr. Grant and the mountain Nestorians. [A biography]. 418 pp. 1 portrait, 1 map. 12°. *Boston, Gould & Lincoln,* 1853.

Lavallée (Joseph). Histoire des inquisitions religieuses d'Italie, d'Espagne et de Portugal, depuis leur origine jusqu'à la conquête de l'Espagne. 2 v. 400 pp. 2 pl; 415 pp. 4 pl. 8°. *Paris, Capelle & Renand,* 1809.

——— Voyage de l'Istrie et de la Dalmatie. 1802. *See* **Cassas** (Louis François).

——— Letters of a mameluke; or a moral and critical picture of the manners of Paris. With notes by the translator. 2 v. xi, 300 pp. 1 p. l. 276 pp. 12°. *London, J. Murray,* 1804.

Lavater (Louis). De spectris, lemuribus, et magnis atque insolitis fragoribus, variisque praesagitionibus, quae plerunque obitum hominum, magnas clades, mutationesque imperiorum praecedunt, liber unus. Editio tertia prioribus multo emendatior. Eng. title, 7 p. l. 314 pp. 3 l. 8 pl. 18°. *Gorichemi, P. Vink,* 1683.

Laveaux (Jean Charles Thiébault de). Les nuits champêtres. xvi, 240 pp. 12°. *Lausanne, J. P. Heubach & comp.* 1784.

La Vigne (André de). Extrait de l'histoire dv voyage de Naples dv roy Charles viii, mis par escrit, en forme de iovrnal, [septembre 1494 au novembre 1495], de son exprés vouloir & commandement. fol. [*Paris,* 1684].
[*In* GODEFROY (T. and D. de). Histoire de Charles viii, pp. 114–189].

Law (Edmund, *bishop of Carlisle*). Considerations on the theory of religion. To which is prefixed, a life of the author, by the late William Paley, d. d. A new ed. by George Henry Law, d. d. xvi, 536 pp. 8°. *London, Rodwell & Martin,* [*etc.*] 1820.

——— An enquiry into the ideas of space, time, immensity, and eternity; as also the self-existence, necessary existence, and unity of the divine nature; in answer to a book lately publish'd by mr. Jackson, entitled The existence and unity of God proved from his nature and attributes. [Also], a dissertation upon the argument a priori for proving the existence of a first cause. By a learned hand. 2 p. l. 196, 98 pp. 8°. *Cambridge, W. Fenner & R. Beresford for W. Thurlbourn,* 1734.

Law (John). Considérations sur le numéraire et le commerce. Mémoires et lettres sur les banques, opuscules divers. 8°. [*Paris,* 1843].
[*In* DAIRE (Eugène). Économistes-financiers du 18e siècle. *Paris,* 1843. pp. 433–698].

Law (*Rev.* William). A serious call to a devout and holy life. From the 15th London ed. [Also], some account of the author, and three letters to a friend, not before published in any of his works. Also, his character, by Edward Gibbon. 345 pp. 12°. *Harrisburg, W. Gillmor,* 1816.

Lawrence (Annie M.) Olive Loring's mission. 279 pp. 3 pl. 16°. *Boston, D. Lothrop & co.* 1871.

Lawrence (James). The empire of the Nairs; or, the rights of women. An utopian romance, in twelve books. 4 v. 16°. *London, T. Hookham, jun. & E. T. Hookham,* 1811.

Lawrence (Jonathan, jr.) A selection from the writings of the late Jonathan Lawrence, junior. vi, 172 pp. 12°. *New York, Sleight & Van Norden*, 1833.

Lawrence (Samuel). The moral design of freemasonry, deduced from the old charges of a freemason. [With] The vision of Achmed; a masonic allegorical poem. 240 pp. 12°. *Atlanta (Georgia) "Signet and journal" office*, 1860.

Lawrence (William Beach, *ll. d.*) The treaty of Washington. Letters. 25 pp. 8°. *Providence, Hammond, Angell & co.* 1871.

Lawson (*Rev.* Deodat). Christ's fidelity the only shield against satan's malignity. Asserted in a sermon deliver'd at Salem-village, the 24th of March, 1692. A time of publick examination, of some suspected for witchcraft. 2d ed. 6 p. l. 120 pp. 16°. *London, for the author*, 1704.

Lawson (George, *d. d.*) Lectures on the history of Joseph. 2d ed. 2 v. 388 pp; viii, 408 pp. 12°. *Edinburgh, J. Pillans & sons for Oliphant, Waugh & Innes*, 1812.

Lawson (John, *surveyor general of N. C.*) Allerneuste beschreibung der provintz Carolina in West-Indien. Samt einem reise-journal von mehr als tausend meilen unter allerhand indianischen nationen. Aus dem englischen übersetzet durch M. Vischer. 7 p. l. 365 pp. 1 l. 1 map, 1 pl. 16°. *Hamburg, Thomas von Wierings erben*, 1712.

Lawson (John.). The maniac, with other poems. xv, 101 pp. 16°. *Philadelphia, Hellings & Aitken*, 1811.

Lawson (L. M. *m. d.*) A practical treatise on phthisis pulmonalis; embracing its pathology, causes, symptoms, and treatment. 557, 40 pp. 8°. *Cincinnati, Rickey, Mallory & co.* 1861.

Lay (Henry C. *d. d.*) Studies in the church; being letters to an old-fashioned layman. 255 pp. 16°. *New York, Pott, Young & co.* 1872.

Layton (Henry). A search after souls: or, the immortality of a humane soul, theologically, philosophically, and rationally considered. With the opinions of ancient and modern authors. By a lover of truth. [*anon.*] 2 v. in 1. 1 p. l. 278 pp; 1 p. l. 188, 215, 55, 23 pp. sm. 4°. [*London*], 1706.

Lazarus (Emma). Admetus and other poems. vii, 229 pp. 12°. *New York, Hurd & Houghton*, 1871.

Lea (Matthew Carey). A manual of photography: intended as a text book for beginners and a book of reference for advanced photographers. 336 pp. 8°. *Philadelphia, Benerman & Wilson*, 1868.

—— The same. 2d ed. revised and enlarged. 439 pp. 8°. *Philadelphia, author*, 1871.

Leal (*pseudon.*) Fables for little folks. 176 pp. 4 pl. 16°. *New York, D. W. C. Lent & co.* 1872.

Lear (Edward). Nonsense songs, stories, botany, and alphabets. With one hundred and fifty illustrations. 70 l. unp. 4°. *Boston, J. R. Osgood & co.* 1871.

Learmont (John). Poems, pastoral, satirical, tragic, and comic. Carefully corrected by the author. xvi, 414 pp. 8°. *Edinburgh, author*, 1791.

Learn to say no, or the city apprentice. [*anon.*] 122 pp. 3 pl. 18°. *Philadelphia, Presbyterian board of publication*, [1856].

Leatherman (P. R.) Elements of moral science. 414 pp. 12°. *Philadelphia, J. Challen & son*, 1860.

Leaves from the tree of life. A verse of scripture with words of comment or illustration, for every day in the year. [*anon.*] 249 pp. 18°. *Philadelphia, American sunday school union*, [1859].

Leavitt's farmer's almanac, and miscellaneous year book, for the year of our Lord 1872. No. 76. By Dudley Leavitt. 8°. *Concord, E. C. Eastman & co.* 1871.

Lebelle (F. M.) The Fairfields. 175 pp. 16°. *Chicago, L. H. Kimball*, 1871.

Lebens-beschreibungen der biblischen scribenten. *See* **Serpilius** (Georg).

Lebert (Sigmund) *and* **Stark** (Ludwig). Grosse theoretisch-praktische klavierschule für den systematischen unterricht nach allen richtungen des klavierspiels vom ersten anfang bis zur höchsten ausbildung. Mit einem im vierten theil enthaltenen anhang, bestehend aus vier grossen original-beiträgen von dr. Franz v. Liszt. 4e aufl. (v. 1–2) und 3e aufl. (v. 3–4). 4 v. 4°. *Stuttgart, verlag der I. G. Cotta'schen buchhandlung*, 1869–71.

Le Blond (Alexandre). The theory and practice of gardening: wherein is fully handled all that relates to fine gardens, commonly called pleasure-gardens, consisting of parterres, groves, bowling-greens, &c. Together with remarks and general rules in all that concerns the art of gardening. Done

Le Blond (Alexandre)—continued. from the late edition printed at Paris, by John James. 2d ed. with additions. vii, 297 pp. 9 l. 36 pl. 4°. *London, B. Lintot,* 1728.

Lebon (Hubert). Beauties of the sanctuary. From the french. 211 pp. 1 pl. 18°. *Baltimore, Kelly & Piet,* [1860].

——— The holy communion, it is my life! Translated from the french by M. A. Garnett. 315 pp. 18°. *Baltimore, John Murphy & co.* 1871.

Le Bosquet (John). The congregational manual; or a concise exposition of the belief, government, and usages, of the congregational churches. With an introduction, by rev. Benjamin P. Stone. 127 pp. 18°. *Boston, Otis, Broaders & co.* 1841.

Le Bossu (René). Treatise of the epick poem: containing many curious reflexions, very useful and necessary for the right understanding and judging of the excellencies of Homer and Virgil. Made english by W. J. To which are added, an essay upon satyr, by mons. [André] D'Acier, and a treatise upon pastoral, by mons. Fontanelle. [Also, fragments of mr. Dacier upon Aristotle's poetry]. 2d ed. with some memoirs of the life of the author. 2 v. in 1. 30 p. l. xxxvi, 224 pp; 1 p. l. 354 pp. 16°. *London, J. Knapton,* 1719.

Le Boutillier de Rancé (Armand Jean). Maximes chrétiennes et morales. 2 v. 7 p. l. 384 pp; 2 p. l. 376 pp. 8 l. 16°. *Paris, D. Mariette,* 1698.

Le Brethon (J. J. P.) Guide to the french language. 1st american from the 7th London ed. corrected, enlarged, and improved by P. Bekeart. 3 p. l. 388 pp. 12°. *New York, W. E. Dean,* 1839.

Le Brun (Charles). La galerie de monsr. le président Lambert, représentant l'apothéose d'Hercule. Le lieu paroit préparé pour le mariage de ce héros avec Hébé, déesse de la jeunesse; & il est orné de trophées élévéz à sa gloire, où sont représentéz tous ses travaux. Gravé par les soins de B. Picart. 2 p. l. 36 pl. fol. *Paris, Du Change,* [1713–19].

[*Note.*—2 pl. bear the name of Eustache Le Sueur].

Lebrun (Pierre Antoine). Œuvres. v. 1. 2 p. l. xxxviii, 423 pp. 8°. *Paris, Perrotin,* 1844. s.

CONTENTS.

Ulysse. Marie Stuart. Le cid d'Andalousie.

LeBuy (Jonas, *sieur de La Perie, pseudon.*) *See* **Launay** (Pierre).

Lechler (R.) Das evangelium des Matthaeus im volksdialekte der Hakka-Chinesen. *See* **Bible.** (*Chinese*).

Leclerc (Jean). Bibliothèque ancienne et moderne. 29 v. 16°. *Amsterdam, D. Mortier,* [*etc.*] 1714–30.

——— Bibliothèque choisie, pour servir de suite à la Bibliothèque universelle. 28 v. 16°. *Amsterdam, H. Schelte,* [*etc.*] 1703–18.

——— Bibliothèque universelle et historique. 2e éd. revue & corrigée. 26 v. 16°. *Amsterdam, Wolfgang,* [*etc.*] 1687–1718.

——— Joannis Clerici opera philosophica in quatuor volumina digesta. Ed. quarta auctior & emendatior. v. 1. 12 p. l. 377 pp. 16°. *Amstelodami, apud J. L. de Lorme,* 1710.

——— The lives of the primitive fathers, viz, Clemens alexandrinus, Eusebius, bishop of Cæsarea, Gregory Nazianzen, and Prudentius, the christian poet. With their several opinions about the deity of Christ. Also, a short history of pelagianism. Written in french. Now done into english. 4 p. l. 389 pp. 8°. *London, T. Ballard,* 1701.

[*Note.*—It is doubtful whether their lives were written by Leclerc].

——— Reflections upon what the world commonly call good-luck and ill-luck, with regard to lotteries. And of the good use which may be made of them. Done into english. 13 p. l. 199 pp. 12°. *London, M. Gilliflower,* 1699.

——— A treatise of the causes of incredulity. With two letters, containing a direct proof of the truth of christianity. Translated from the french. viii, 327 pp. 16°. *London, A. & J. Churchill,* 1697.

Le Clerc (Nicolas Gabriel Clerc, *dit*). Yu le grand et Confucius, histoire chinoise: par m. Clerc. [1e éd.] xviii, 702 pp. 3 l. 8 tables. 4°. *Soissons, P. Courtois,* 1769.

Le Clerc (Sébastien). Métamorphoses d'Ovide, ornés de 138 gravures. *See* **Ovidius Naso** (Publius).

Leclerc de Sept-Chênes (—). Essai sur la religion des anciens Grecs. 2 v. xii, 271 pp; 2 p. l. 226 pp. 12°. *Genève, Barde, Manget & cie.* 1787.

Lecomte (Ferdinand). The war in the United States. Report to the Swiss military department; preceded by a discourse to the Federal military society assembled at Berne, Aug. 18, 1862. Translated from the French. 118 pp. 12°. *New York, D. Van Nostrand,* 1863.

Le Courayer (Pierre François). *See* **Relation** des deux rebellions.

Lecturas inglesas escogidas, ó sea trozos de los mejores escritores ingleses y americanos, en prosa y verso, arreglados en lecciones con notas gramaticales y fraseológicas, traduccion interlinear y un vocabulario con la pronunciacion y definiciones. Por un profesor. [*anon.*] 431 pp. 12°. *Nueva York, G. R. Lockwood,* [1871].

Lectures, historical, expository, and practical, on the communion service of the protestant episcopal church in the United States. By a presbyter of the church. [*anon.*] xiv, 13-273 pp. 12°. *Philadelphia, J. B. Lippincott & co.* 1865.

Lectures on the book of proverbs. *See* **Coles** (*Rev.* George).

Lecturess (The): or woman's sphere. By the author of "My cousin Mary." [*anon.*] 124 pp. 18°. *Boston, Whipple & Damrell,* 1839.

Lederer (Julius). Die noctuinen Europa's, mit zuziehung einiger bisher meist dazu gezählter arten des asiatischen Russland's, Kleinasien's, Syrien's und Labradors. xv, 252 pp. 4 pl. 8°. *Wien, F. Manz,* 1857. s.

——— (*editor*). See **Wiener** entomologische monatschrift, 1857-63.

Ledesma (Diego de). Doctrine chrestienne. Traduicte en langage canadois, autre que celuy des Montagnars, pour la conuersion des habitans dudit pays. Par le r. p. [Jean de] Brebœuf. [Avec] l'oraison dominicale, [et prières ordinaires], tradvite en langage des Montagnars de Canada, par le r. p. [Énemond] Massé. 20 pp. 4°. *Québec, reprinted, G. E. Desbarats,* 1870.

[CHAMPLAIN (S. de). Oeuvres. v. 5, part 2. *Québec,* 1870].

Ledesme. *See* **Ledesma** (Diego de).

Lee (Arthur T. *col. U. S. a.*) Army ballads, and other poems. 160 pp. 3 pl. 16°. [*New York*], 1871.

Lee (Charles A. *m. d.*) The elements of geology for popular use; containing a description of the geological formations and mineral resources of the United States. viii, 375 pp. 4 l. 1 pl. 16°. *New York, Harper & brothers,* 1839.

[*Note.*—School district library, no. 86].

——— Human physiology; for the use of elementary schools. 224 pp. 18°. *New York, American common school union,* 1838.

Lee (Francis). Once a second. *See* **Locke** (Una) *and* **Lee.** Isabel's trials, and Once a second.

Lee (Hannah F.) Historical sketches of the old painters. [*anon.*] 4 p. l. 296 pp. 12°. *Boston, Hilliard, Gray & co.* 1838.

——— The life and times of Thomas Cranmer. By the author of "Three experiments in living," [etc. *anon.*] viii, 277 pp. 12°. *Boston, Hilliard, Gray & co.* 1841.

——— The life and times of Martin Luther. By the author of "Three experiments of living," [etc. *anon.*] 3 p. l. 324 pp. 12°. *Boston, Hilliard, Gray & co.* 1839.

Lee (Leroy M. *d. d.*) The great supper not calvinistic: being a reply to rev. dr. Fairchild's discourses on the parable of the great supper. Edited by Thomas O. Summers, d. d. 354 pp. 18°. *Nashville (Tenn.) E. Stevenson & F. A. Owen,* 1856.

——— The life and times of the rev. Jesse Lee. 517 pp. 8°. *Richmond (Va.) J. Early,* 1848.

Lee (*Rev.* Luther). Elements of theology, or an exposition of the divine origin, doctrines, morals and institutions of christianity. viii, 530 pp. 8°. *New York, Miller, Orton & Mulligan,* 1856.

——— Universalism examined and refuted, and the doctrine of the endless punishment of such as do not comply with the conditions of the gospel in this life, established. 300 pp. 12°. *Watertown (N. Y.) author,* 1836.

Lee (Mary E.) Social evenings: or historical tales for youth. 260 pp. 18°. *Boston, Marsh, Capen, Lyon & Webb,* 1840.

Lee (Sarah Wallis). Taxidermy: or, the art of collecting, preparing, and mounting objects of natural history. For the use of museums and travellers. [*anon.*] 3d ed. 168 pp. 5 pl. 12°. *London, Longman, Hurst, Rees, Orme, & Browne,* 1823.

Lee (Thomas J.) A spelling-book, containing the rudiments of the english language; with appropriate reading lessons. 2d ed. iv, 180 pp. 18°. *Boston, Munroe & Francis,* 1823.

——— The same. Improved edition. 207 pp. 16°. *Hallowell (Me.) Glazier, Masters & co.* 1831.

Leeds (Lewis W.) A treatise on ventilation: comprising seven lectures delivered before the Franklin institute, Philadelphia, 1866-68. Shewing the great want of improved methods of ventilation in our buildings; comparing the effects of the various methods of heating and lighting upon the ventilation. Illustrated. 226 pp. 8°. *New York, J. Wiley & son,* 1871.

Leemans (Conrad). Lettre à m. François Salvolini, sur les monumens égyptiens, portant des légendes royales, dans les musées d'antiquités de Leide, de Londres, et dans quelques collections particulières en Angleterre. Avec des observations concernant l'histoire, la chronologie et la langue hiéroglyphique des Égyptiens, et une appendice sur les mesures de ce peuple. 2 p. l. x, 160 pp. 32 pl. 8°. *Leide, H. W. Hazenberg & comp.* 1838. s.

Lees (Thomas J.) The musings of Carol: containing an essay on liberty: the desperado, a tale of the ocean, and other original poems. 178 pp. 18°. *Wheeling (Va.) author,* 1831.

Leeser (*Rabbi* Isaac). Catechism for younger children. Designed as a familiar exposition of the jewish religion. xii, 168 pp. 12°. *Philadelphia, author,* 5599 [1839].

——— Discourses, argumentative and devotional, on the subject of the jewish religion. Delivered in the synagogue Mikveh Israel, in Philadelphia, in the years 5590–97. 2 v. in 1. xi, 297 pp; 2 p. l. 293 pp. 8°. *Philadelphia, Haswell & Fleu,* 5597 [1836].

——— The Jews and the mosaic law. Part the first. Containing a defence of the revelation of the pentateuch, and of the Jews for their adherence to the same. Part 2d. Containing four essays on the relative importance of judaism and christianity. x, 278 pp. 8°. *Philadelphia, author,* 5594 [1834].

——— Select sentences: designed as a moral guide-book for young Israelites. [*anon.*] 200 pp. 32°. *Philadelphia,* 5614 [1854].

Leewis *or* **Leuwis** (Dionysius de). *See* **Dionysius** *carthusianus.*

Le Fanu (James Sheridan). Shamus O'Brien, the bold boy of Glingall. A tale of '98. To which is added Father Roach, a story founded on fact. By Samuel Lover. With a sketch of his life, by T. W. H. 24 pp. 12°. *New York, American news company,* 1871.

Lefebvre-Duruflé (Noël Jacques). Excursion sur les côtes et dans les ports de Normandie. [Avec les vues d'après les dessins de Bonington, Luttringhausen, etc. *anon.*] 55 l. 40 pl. fol. *Paris, J. F. Ostervald,* [1823-25].

Le Ferron (Arnoul). Arnoldi Ferroni de rebvs gestis Gallorvm libri ix, ad historiam Pavli Aemylii additi. Perdvcta historia vsqve ad tempora Henrici ii. Francorvm regis. [1491–1547]. 151 l. numb. fol. *Lvtetiae, apud Vascosanum,* 1550.

Lefèvre (Amédée). Recherches sur les causes de la colique sèche observée sur les navires de guerre français, particulièrement dans les régions équatoriales et sur les moyens d'en prévenir le développement. 312 pp. 8°. *Paris, J. B. Baillière et fils,* 1859.

Le Fort. *See* **Gaudy-Le Fort.**

Legati (Lorenzo). Descrizione di museo cospiano. *See* **Cospi** (F.)

Legenda. s. Catharinae Mediceæ reginæ matris. *See* **Estienne** (Henri).

Legge (James, *ll. d.*) The chinese classics: with a translation, critical and exegetical notes, prolegomena, and copious indexes. v. 4, parts 1 & 2. 2 v. 8°. *London, Trübner & co.* 1871.

CONTENTS.

v. 4. Part 1. The first part of the She-king, or the lessons from the states; and the prolegomena.

Part 2. The second, third, and fourth parts of the She-king, or the minor odes of the kingdom, the greater odes of the kingdom, the sacrificial odes and praise-songs; and the indexes.

Le Glay (André Joseph Ghislain). Mémoire sur les bibliothèques publiques et les principales bibliothèques particulières du département du nord. 496 pp. 8°. *Lille, le concierge des archives départementales,* 1841.

Le Glay (Edward). Histoire des comtes de Flandre jusqu'à l'avénement de la maison de Bourgogne. 2 v. 2 p. l. 519 pp; 2 p. l. 516 pp. 8°. *Bruxelles, A. Vandale,* 1843.

Legouvé (Gabriel Marie Jean Baptiste). Le mérite des femmes, et autres poésies. Nouv. éd. 252 pp. 1 pl. 24°. *Paris, A. A. Renouard,* 1804.

Le Grand (Anthony). An entire body of philosophy, according to the principles of the famous Renate des Cartes, in three books: i. The institution, in x parts: ii. The history of nature, which illustrates The institution, and consists of great variety of experiments relating thereto, and explained by the same principles, in ix parts: iii. A dissertation of the want of sense and knowledge in brute animals, in ii parts. Written originally in latin. Now carefully translated. By Richard Blome. 15 p. l. 403, 2, 263 pp. 93 pl. fol. *London, R. Blome,* 1694.

Legrand *or* **Legrant** (Jacques). [Zophilogium]. 217 l. 4°. [*Argentorati, Joh. Mentelin,* 1472]?

[*Note.*—This edition is distinguished by the singular form of the letter R. 35 lines to a page. Without pagination, signatures, or catchwords. Afterwards printed under the title: "Sophologium ex antiquorum poetarum, oratorum atque philosophorum gravibus sententiis collectum"].

Legrand (Joachim, *l'abbé*). The sequel of the account of Abyssinia, [by Jérôme Lobo. Translated from the french, by dr. Johnson, 1st ed.] 8°. [*London, A. Bettesworth*, 1735].
[*In* Lobo (Jérôme). A voyage to Abyssinia, pp. 145–396].

Le Grange (H. M. *pseudon.*) Salted with fire. 177 pp. 12°. *New York, E. J. Hale & son*, 1872.

Le Gras (Alexandre). General examination of the Mediterranean sea, a summary of its winds, currents, and navigation. Translated, with a few additional extracts, by R. H. Wyman. viii, 208 pp. 8°. *Washington, government printing office*, 1870.

Lehman (Johann Gottlob). Probier-kunst. lxxxvi pp. 2 l. 318 pp. 7 l. 5 pl. 16°. *Berlin, A. Wever*, 1761.

Lehmann (Johann Georg Christian). Plantae preissianae, sive enumeratio plantarum quas in Australasia occidentali et meridionali-occidentali annis 1838–41 collegit L. Preiss, [etc.] 2 v. viii, 647 pp; vi, 499 pp. 8°. *Hamburgi, Meissner*, 1844–47. s.

Leibnitz (Gottfried Wilhelm von). Principia philosophiæ, more geometrico demonstrata: cum excerptis ex epistolis philosophi et scholiis quibusdam ex historia philosophica. Accedunt Theoremata metaphysica de proprietatibus quibusdam entis infiniti et finiti mundique existentis perfectione, [etc.] 8 p. l. 188 pp. 16 l. 36 pp. 4°. *Francofurti et Lipsiae, P. C. Monath*, 1728.

Leidy (Joseph, *m. d.*) An elementary treatise on human anatomy. xxiv, 17–663 pp. 8°. *Philadelphia, J. B. Lippincott & co.* 1861.

Leigh (Edwin). The new guide to modern conversation in various languages. Edited in pronouncing orthography. vi pp. 128 l. 18°. *New York, editor*, 1872.

Leighton (*Rev.* Alexander). An appeal to the parliament; or Sion's plea against the prelacie. The summe whereoff is delivered in a decade of positions. [*anon.*] 8 p. l. 344 pp. 2 pl. 4°. [*London*, 1628].
[1 p. l. wanting. Portrait of the author inserted].

Leighton (Robert, *archbishop of Glasgow*). Commentary upon Peter. 1864. *See* **Bible.** (*English*).

——— The remains of archbishop Leighton: consisting of all the unpublished pieces found in manuscript in the library left by him to the diocese of Dunblane. With his life, by the rev. G. Jerment. 1 p. l. c, 184 pp. 8°. *London, R. Ogle*, 1811.

Leighton (Robert)—continued.

——— The select works of archbishop Leighton. With an introductory view of the life, character, and writings of the author. By George B. Cheever. 569 pp. 1 portrait. 8°. *Boston, Peirce & Parker*, 1832.

Leighton (R. F.) Greek lessons adapted to Goodwin's greek grammar, and intended as an introduction to his greek reader. vi, 135 46 pp. 12°. *Boston, Ginn brothers*, 1871.

Leisure hours. Edited by an association of gentlemen. [*anon.*] 2 p. l. 340 pp. 12°. *Boston, J. Allen & co.* 1835.
[*Note.*—The American popular library].

Le Jay (Gabriel François). Bibliotheca rhetorum præcepta et exempla, complectens quæ tam ad oratoriam facultatem, quam ad poeticam pertinent. xii, 743 pp. 4°. *Venetiis, ex typographia balleoniana*, 1747.

Lejeune (J.) Ville de Verviers. Catalogue méthodique de la bibliothèque publique communale. *See* **Verviers** (*France*).

Leland (Anna). Home. 352 pp. 12°. *New York, J. C. Derby*, 1856.

Leland (Charles G.) Hans Breitmann in Europe. With other new ballads. Fifth series of the Breitmann ballads. iv, 209–291 pp. 8°. *Philadelphia, T. B. Peterson & brothers*, [1871].

——— Meister Karl's sketch-book. [2d ed.] 1 p. l. 19–287 pp. 12°. *Philadelphia, T. B. Peterson & brothers*, [1872].

——— The music-lesson of Confucius, and other poems. viii, 168 pp. 18°. *Boston, J. R. Osgood & co.* 1872.

Leland (Thomas, *d. d.*) The history of remarkable events in the kingdom of Ireland. Exhibiting the very extraordinary transactions of Wentworth earl of Strafford; Charles the first; Oliver Cromwell; Charles the second; James the second; Butler earl of Ormond; king William the glorious deliverer; and George Walker, the military clergyman. 2 v. 1 p. l. 359 pp; 372 pp. 25 l. 8°. *London, J. Thucydides*, 1781.

Le Long (Isaac). Boek-zaal der nederduitsche bybels, geopent, in een historische verhandeling van de overzettinge der heilige schriftuure in de nederduitsche taale, [etc.] Met een omstandig bericht, van meer dan hondert oude handscriften, van bybels en bybelsche boeken des ouden en nieuwen testaments, [etc.] 2e uitgave. 8 p. l. 894 pp. 1 l. 1 portrait. sm. 4°. *Hoorn, T. Tjallingius*, 1764.

Lelong (Jacques). Bibliotheca sacra post cl. cl. vv. Jacobi Le Long et c. F. Boerneri iteratas cvras ordine disposita, emendata, svppleta, continvata ab Andrea Gottlieb Masch. 2 parts in 6 v. 4°. *Halæ, svmtibvs J. J. Gebaveri*, 1778–90.

CONTENTS.

v. 1. De editionibus textus originalis.
De editionibus novi testamenti graecis.
De editionibus polyglottis.
De libris apocryphis.
v. 2. De versionibus orientalibus.
v. 3. De versionibus graecis.
v. 4–5. De versionibus latinis.
v. 6. Index chronologicus ad versiones latinas.

Lely (Richard). Poems and translations, on several occasions. viii, 138 pp. 2 l. 8°. *London, J. Batley*, 1727.

Lemaistre (J. G.) Rough sketch of modern Paris ; or, letters on society, manners, public curiosities, and amusements, in that capital. 2d ed. 2 p. l. xii, 318 pp. 8°. *London, J. Johnson*, 1803.

Le Marchand (*pseudon?*) Le Marchand's fortune teller ; and dreamer's dictionary. Also, showing how to tell fortunes by the wonderful and mysterious ladies' love oracle, [etc.] 5 p. l. 134 pp. 1 pl. 16°. *New York, Dick & Fitzgerald*, [1863].

Lemoine (*Rev.* Abraham). A treatise on miracles, wherein their nature, conditions, characteristics, and true immediate cause are clearly stated ; with a postscript, containing some remarks on dr. Middleton's Introductory discourse to a larger work, &c. 8 p. l. 522 pp. 8°. *London, J. Nourse*, 1747.
[Imperfect : wanting pp. 177–192].

Lemon (*Rev.* George William). Two tracts on the following subjects : 1. Additional observations on the greek accents : by the late Edward Spelman. 2. The voyage of Æneas from Troy to Italy. xii, 50 pp. 1 l. 80 pp. 2 pl. 8°. *London, J. Nourse*, 1773.
[*With* DELAFAYE (Theodore). An essay on Virgil's celebrated Gates of sleep. *London*, 1743].

L'Empereur (Constantin). Talmvdis babylonici codex middoth, sive de mensvris templi. *See* **Talmud** babylonicum.

Lenfant (Jacques). Histoire du concile de Pise, et de ce qui s'est passé de plus mémorable depuis ce concile jusqu'au concile de Constance. 2 v. 4 p. l. liv, 366 pp. 10 pl ; 2 p. l. 328 pp. 15 l. 5 pl. 4°. *Amsterdam, P. Humbert*, 1724.

Leng (John, *bishop of Norwich*). Natural obligations to believe the principles of religion and divine revelation. In sixteen sermons, preached in 1717 and 1718. fol. [*London*, 1739].
[BOYLE lectures, v. 3, 1 p. l. pp. 1–152].

Lennep (Jacob van). Gedichten. 126 pp. 8°. *Amsterdam, P. Meijer Warnars*, 1827.

——— Nederlandsche legenden in rijm gebracht. Jacoba en Bertha. 2 v. 2 p. l. 158 pp. 1 l ; 1 p. l. 180 pp. 8°. *Amsterdam, P. Meijer Warnars*, 1832.

——— The same. Het huis ter leede. Adegild. 2 v. 154 pp ; 2 p. l. 197 pp. 8°. *Amsterdam, P. Meijer Warnars*, 1832.

——— The same. De strijd met Vlaanderen. 2 v. 185 pp. 1 l ; 2 p. l. 156 pp. 4 l. 8°. *Amsterdam, P. Meijer Warnars*, 1832.

——— Onze voorouders, in verschillende tafereelen geschetst. 5 v. 8°. *Amsterdam, P. Meijer Warnars*, 1838–44.

——— De pleegzoon. Een verhaal. 2 v. 3 p. l. 371 pp ; 2 p. l. 366 pp. 8°. *Amsterdam, P. Meijer Warnars*, 1833.

——— De roos van Dekama. Een verhaal. 2 v. xii, 373 pp. 1 map ; 2 p. l. 426 pp. 1 l. 1 map. 8°. *Amsterdam, P. Meijer Warnars*, 1836.

Lenoir (Alexandre). Musée impérial des monumens français. Histoire des arts en France, et description chronologique des statues en marbre et en bronze. 2 p. l. lxvi, 304 pp. 1 l. 8°. *Paris*, [*l'auteur*], 1810.

Le Normand (Louis Sébastien). Manuel du fabricant de papiers, ou l'art de la papeterie, suivi de l'art du fabricant de cartons, et de l'art du formaire. v. 1. 2 p. l. 330 pp. 24°. *Paris, Roret*, 1833. S.
[v. 2 and atlas 17 pl. wanting].

Lensaeus *or* **Lens** (Jean de). De moderna theologia judaica. 4 p. l. 696 pp. 7 l. 16°. *Herbornæ, typis J. N. Andreæ*, 1694.

Lenzoni (Carlo). In difesa della lingva fiorentina, et di Dante. Con le regole da far bella et nvmerosa la prosa. Eng. title, 204 pp. 8 l. 8°. *Fiorenza, L. Torrentino*, 1557.

Leo *africanus* (Joannes). De totivs Africae descriptione libri ix, in latinam linguam conuersi Joanne Floriano interprete. His recens accedit Hannonis Carthaginiensium ducis nauigatio, qua libycam oram vltra Herculis columnas lustrauit, C. Gesnero interprete. 14 p. l. 517, 21 pp. 16°. *Tigvri, A. Gesnervs*, 1559.
[*Note.*—The true name of this Moor was Hassan ben Mohammed. Joan Leo was for Giovanni di Medici, Leo x.

Leon (Luis Ponce de). Obras propias i traducciones de latin, griego, i toscano, con la parafrasi de algunos salmos, i capitulos de Job. 3ª impr. nuevamente añadida. 52 p. l. 326 pp. 16°. *Valencia, J. T. Lucas*, 1761.

Leonard (George, *jr.*) A practical treatise on arithmetic, [etc. With] two methods of bookkeeping. 4th ed. 340 pp. 12°. *Boston, Otis, Broaders & co.* 1841. s.

Leonard (Julie). Children's songs from the hillsides. 1 p. l. 155 pp. 16°. *Boston, E. P. Dutton & co.* 1865.

Leonard (Seth). Beauties of primitive christianity: or, the auxiliary and supplementary guide, to the belief and practice of Christ's friends of all nations. 300 pp. 12°. *Albany, E. & E. Hosford,* 1825.

Leonhart (Rudolph). Through blood and iron; a story of the french-german war. 325 pp. 8 pl. 8°. *Pittsburgh (Pa.) E. Luft & co.* 1871.

Leopardi (Girolamo). Capitoli e canzoni piacevoli. Con l'aggiunta, in questa seconda impressione, del capitolo in lode de' sogni, del medesimo autore, e il tutto da lui riuisto, e ampliato. 112 pp. 4°. *Firenze, Sermartelli,* 1616.

Le Petit (Jean François). The Low-covntry commonwealth, contayninge an exact discription of the eight Vnited Provinces, now made free. Translated out of french by Ed[ward] Grimeston. Eng. title, 3 p. l. 303 pp. sm. 4°. [*London*], 1609.

Le Plaisant (Jean). Pugna porcorum, per P. Porcium poëtam. 1720. [*pseudon.* Reprint]. 16°. *New York, Hurd & Houghton,* 1872.

[*In* MORGAN (James Appleton). Macaronic poetry, pp. 111–128].

Le Play (Pierre Guillaume Frédéric). The organization of labor in accordance with custom, and the law of the decalogue; with a summary of comparative observations upon good and evil in the regime of labor, the causes of evils existing at the present time, and the means required to effect reform; with objections and answers, difficulties and solutions. Translated by Gouverneur Emerson, m. d. From the french of the 2d ed. 417 pp. 12°. *Philadelphia, Claxton, Remsen & Haffelfinger,* 1872.

Le Prince (Nicolas Thomas). Essai historique sur la bibliothèque du roi aujourd'hui bibliothèque impériale, avec des notices sur les dépôts qui la composent et le catalogue de ses principaux fonds. Nouv. éd. revue et augmentée des annales de la bibliothèque. Par Louis Paris. 5 p. l. v, 466 pp. 16°. *Paris, au bureau du cabinet historique,* 1856.

Lerebours (Nicolas Marie Paymal). Traité de photographie: derniers perfectionnements apportés au daguerréotype. 4ᵉ éd. 2 p. l. 203 pp. 1 pl. 8°. *Paris, N. P. Lerebours,* 1843. s.

Lerouillé (Guillaume). Guillermi le Rouille justicie atque iiusticie descriptionũ cõpendiũ. *b. l.* Eng. title, 6 p. l. 29 l. incl. 6 pl. fol. *Parrhisijs, C. Cheuallus,* 1520.

Leroux (Jean Jacques). Cours sur les généralités de la médecine pratique, et sur la philosophie de la médecine. 8 v. 8°. *Paris, Didot le jeune,* 1825–26.

Leroux de Lincy (Adrien Jean Victor). Recueil de chants historiques français depuis le xiiᵉ jusqu'au xviiiᵉ siècle. Avec des notices et une introduction. 2 v. 2 p. l. xlix, 416 pp; 2 p. l. xii, 616 pp. 1 l. 12°. *Paris, C. Gosselin,* 1841–42.

——— *and* **Michel** (Francisque). Recueil de farces, moralités et sermons joyeux, publié d'après le manuscrit de la bibliothèque royale. 3 v. 12°. *Paris, Techener,* 1831–37.

[*Note.*—Only 78 copies printed].

Le Roy (Charles). Traité de l'orthographe françoise, en forme de dictionnaire. Nouvelle éd. considérablement augmentée, revue et corrigée par m. [Pierre] Restaut. 6 p. l. 612 pp. 1 l. 8°. *Poitiers, J. F. Faulcon,* 1765.

Leroy (Louis). Of the interchangeable covrse, or variety of things in the whole world; and the concvrrence of armes and learning, through the first and famousest nations: from the beginning of ciuility, and memory of man, to this present. Written in french by Loys le Roy called Regius: and translated into english by R. A. [Robert Ashley]. 4 p. l. 130 l. numb. fol. *London, C. Yetsweirt,* 1594.

Le Roy (— *le sieur*). Le momus françois, ou les aventures divertissants du duc de Roquelaure, suivant les mémoires que l'auteur a trouvés dans le cabinet du maréchal d'H.... Par le s. L. R. [*anon.*] 166 pp. 1 l. 16°. *Cologne, P. Marteau,* 1760.

[*Note.*—This book, which might pass for a collection of the bon-mots of Gaston Jean Baptiste, duc de Roquelaure, the celebrated wit of the court of Louix xiv, is probably the work of the plagiary Le Roy].

Lescarret (J. B.) Conférences sur l'économie politique faites en 1687–68 [1867–68] à Bordeaux et à Bayonne. xvi, 352 pp. 12°. *Paris, Hachette & cie.* 1869. s.

Le Seur (Thomas) *and* **Jacquier** (François). Riflessioni sopra el parere del signor T. Perelli intorno al regolamento delle acque delle tre provincie di Bologna, Ferrara e Romagna. 4°. [*Firenze,* 1785].

[*In* XIMENES (Leonardo). Raccolta delle perizie ed opusculi idraulici, v. 1, pp. 359–372].

Lesguillon (J.) Washington. Drame historique. 3 p. l. 168 pp. 12°. *Paris, librairie dramatique,* 1866.

Leslie (Charles). A new and exact account of Jamaica. 3d ed. [with] appendix containing Vernon's success at Porto Bello and Chagre. 3 p. l. ii, 376 pp. 16°. *Edinburgh, R. Fleming,* 1740.

Leslie (*Miss* Eliza). Althea Vernon: or the embroidered handkerchief. [Also], Henrietta Harrison; or, the blue cotton umbrella. 276 pp. 12°. *Philadelphia, Lea & Blanchard,* 1838.

——— American girl's book: or occupation for play hours. xviii, 303 pp. sq. 16°. *Boston, Munroe & Francis,* 1831.

——— Birth day stories. 179 pp. 18°. *Philadelphia, H. F. Anners,* [1840].

——— Pencil sketches; or outlines of character and manners. 3 series in 3 v. 12°. *Philadelphia, Carey, Lea & Blanchard,* 1833–37.

——— Stories for Adelaide. 108 pp. 4 pl. 18°. *Philadelphia, H. F. Anners,* [1843].

——— Stories for Helen. 140 pp. 1 pl. 18°. *Philadelphia, H. F. Anners,* [1845].

Leslie's (Frank) boy's and girl's weekly. An illustrated journal of amusement, adventure and instruction. Oct. 22, 1870, to April 13, 1872. v. 9–11. fol. *New York, F. Leslie,* [1870–72].

Leslie's (Frank) chimney corner. [A weekly literary newspaper]. Nov. 26, 1870, to May 18, 1872. v. 12–14. fol. *New York, F. Leslie,* [1870–72].

Leslie's (Frank) illustrated newspaper. [Weekly]. Sept. 17, 1870, to March 9, 1872. v. 31–33. fol. *New York, F. Leslie,* [1870–72].

Leslie's (Frank) illustrirte zeitung. [Wöchentliche]. 28. Januar 1871 bis 20. Januar 1872. v. 28–29. fol. *New York, F. Leslie,* [1870–72].

Leslie's (Frank) lady's journal. Devoted to fashion and choice literature. Nov. 18, 1871, to May 11, 1872. v. 1. fol. *New York, F. Leslie's publishing house,* 1872.

[*Successor to* Once a week].

Leslie's (Frank) lady's magazine, and gazette of fashion. [Monthly]. Jan. to Dec. 1871. v. 28–29. sm. fol. [*New York, F. Leslie,* 1871].

Leslie's (Frank) pleasant hours. Devoted to light and entertaining literature. [Monthly]. Feb. 1871, to Jan. 1872. v. 10–11. 8°. *New York, F. Leslie,* 1871–72.

Leslie (*Mrs.* Madeline, *pseudon.*) *See* **Baker** (*Mrs.* H. N. Woods).

Lesseps (Jean Baptiste Barthélemy, *baron* de). Journal historique du voyage de m. de Lesseps, employé dans l'expédition de m. le comte de La Pérouse; depuis l'instant où il a quitté les frégates françoises au port Saint-Pierre & Saint-Paul du Kamtschatka, jusqu'à son arrivée en France, 1788. 2 v. 2 p. l. viii, 280 pp. 2 pl; 1 p. l. 380, viii pp. 1 map. 8°. *Paris, imprimerie royale,* 1790.

Lesser (Friedrich Christian). Théologie des insectes, ou démonstration des perfections de Dieu dans tout ce qui concerne les insectes, traduit de l'allemand de m. Lesser; avec des remarques de m. P. Lyonnet. 2 v. xii, 384 pp; 2 p. l. 350 pp. 1 l. 8°. *Paris, H. D. Chaubert,* 1745.

Lessons for infant sabbath schools; with a plan for conducting an infant class. [*anon.*] 108 pp. 18°. *Worcester,* [*Ms.*] *Dorr & Howland,* 1830.

Lessons on the commandments. [*anon.*] 132 pp. 18°. *Philadelphia, American sunday school union,* 1832.

Lessons on the life of the apostle Paul, for bible classes. [*anon.*] 132 pp. 1 map. 18°. *Philadelphia, American s. s. union,* [1871].

Lessons on the liturgy of the protestant episcopal church in America. By a churchman. [*anon.*] xi, 298 pp. 16°. *Boston, E. P. Dutton & co.* 1861.

Lessons on the universe. The class book of nature; comprising lessons on the universe, the three kingdoms of nature, and the form and structure of the human body. Edited by J. Frost. 283 pp. 16°. *Hartford, Belknap & Hamersley,* 1836.

Lester (Charles). The mountain wild flower; or, memoirs of mrs. Mary Ann Bise. xii, 243 pp. 12°. *New-York, E. French,* 1838.

Lestiboudois (Thémistocle Gaspard). Économie pratique des nations, ou système économique applicable aux différentes contrées, et spécialement à la France. 2 p. l. 515 pp. 8°. *Paris, L. Colas,* 1847.

L'Estrange (*Sir* Roger). A brief history of the times, etc. in a preface to the third volume of Observators. 1 p. l. 40 pp. fol. *London, J. Bennett,* 1687.

[*With* OBSERVATOR (The). v. 3. *London,* 1684–87].

——— (*editor*). *See* **Observator** (The).

Leti (Gregorio). La monarchia di Spagna crescente e calante, in dialogo in forma di

Leti (Gregorio)—continued.
sogno. 108 pp. 18°. *Cologna, L. Tivoglio*, 1675.

[DIETA (La) di vari autori].

——— Relatione di tvtto ciò che passò tra il pontefice Alessandro vii, e la maestà del re christianissimo, nell' anno 1662 li 20 agosto, per l'insulto fatto da' papalini al duca di Crechi regio ambasciatore. 168 pp. 18°. *Cologna, L. Tivoglio*, 1675.

[DIETA (La) di vari autori].

Leto (Giulio Pomponio). Pomponii Læti de romanis magistratibvs, sacerdotiis, ivrisperitis, et legibvs, ad M. Pantagathvm libellvs. 18 l. sm. fol. *Lvtetiæ, apud Vascosanum*, 1550.

Letronne (Jean Antoine). Recueil des inscriptions grecques et latines de l'Égypte étudiées dans leur rapport avec l'histoire politique, l'administration intérieure, les institutions civiles et religieuses de ce pays depuis la conquête d'Alexandre jusqu'à celle des Arabes. v. 1. 5 p. l. xliv, 480 pp. 4°. Atlas, 1 p. l. 17 pl. fol. *Paris, l'imprimerie royale*, 1842.

Letsome (*Rev.* Sampson). The preacher's assistant, in two parts. Part 1. A series of the texts of all the sermons and discourses preached upon, and published since the restoration, to the present time. Part 2. An historical register of all the authors in the series, containing a succinct view of their several works. [Also], two lists of the archbishops and bishops of England and Ireland, from 1660 to 1753. With an appendix to each part. 2 v. in 1. 2 p. l. xii, 288 pp; 1 p. l. 238 pp. 8°. *London, author*, [1753].

Lettenhove (Joseph Marie Bruno Constantin Kervyn de). *See* **Kervyn de Lettenhove.**

Letter (A) concerning the privileges of the assembly of Jamaica. [*anon.*] 28 pp. sm. 4°. *Kingston (Jamaica), Weatherby, Allen & M'Cann*, [1765].

Letter from a gentleman at Elizabeth-town to his friend in New-York. [*anon.*] 8 pp. 16°. *Philadelphia, A. Steuart*, 1764.

[HAZARD pamphlets, v. 23].

Letter (A) from a merchant at Jamaica to a member of parliament in London, touching the african trade. [Also], a speech made by a black at Gardaloupe, at the funeral of a fellow-negro. [*anon.*] 31 pp. 16°. *London, A. Baldwin*, 1709.

Letter (A) from South Carolina, [June 1, 1710]; giving an account of the soil, air, product, trade, government, laws, religion, people, military strength, etc. of that province. Together with the manner and necessary charges of setling a plantation there, and the annual profit it will produce. Written by a swiss gentleman to his friend in Berne. [*anon.*] 2d ed. 56 pp. 8°. *London, R. Smith*, 1718.

[HAZARD pamphlets, v. 48].

——— The same. [3d] ed. [*anon.*] 63 pp. 8°. *London, J. Clarke*, 1732.

——— The same.

[HAZARD pamphlets, v. 36].

Letter (A) from ********, in London, to his friend in America, on the subject of the slave-trade. [*anon.*] 28 pp. 12°. *New-York, S. Loudon*, 1784.

[HAZARD pamphlets, v. 70].

Letter (A) to a friend. Giving a just representation of the sufferings of Boston. 1774. *See* **Chauncy** (Charles, *d. d.*)

Letter (A) to a gentleman, concerning the boundaries of the province of Maryland, wherein is shewn, that no part of the 40th degree of latitude is, or can be, any part thereof. [*anon.*] 15 pp. 12°. *London, for the author*, [*about* 1735].

Letter(A) to a member of the house of representatives of Connecticut, in vindication of Yale college against a pamphlet, intituled, A letter to a member of the lower house, etc. [*anon.*] 18 pp. 4°. [*n. p.*] 1759.

Letter (A) to the earl of Hilsborough, on the present situation of affairs in America. [*anon.*] 55 pp. 8°. *Boston, reprinted, Edes & Gill*, 1769.

Letter (A) to the merchant in London, to whom is directed a printed letter relating to the manufactury undertaking, dated Boston, Feb. 21, 1740–1. [*anon.*] 27 pp. 8°. [*n. p.*] 1741.

[HAZARD pamphlets, v. 78].

Letter (A) to the rev. J. Butler, containing a review of his "Friendly letters to a lady"; together with a general outline of the doctrine of the freewill baptists. By a freewill baptist. [*anon.*] 161 pp. 18°. *Limerick, S. Curtis*, 1832.

Lettere delle cose del Giappone. Venetia, 1585. *See* **Nvove** lettere delle cose del Giappone, (etc.)

Letters concerning the present state of Poland, together with the manifesto of the

Letters concerning, etc.—continued. courts of Vienna, Petersburgh and Berlin, and the letters patent of the king of Prussia. [*anon.*] 217 pp. 8°. *London, T. Payne*, 1773.
[HAZARD pamphlets, v. 53].

Letters from a landscape painter. *See* **Lanman** (Charles).

Letters from a Persian in England, to his friend at Ispahan. *See* **Lyttelton** (*Lord* George).

Letters from an english traveller in Spain, 1778. *See* **Dillon** (John Talbot).

Letters from the Havana, during the year 1820; containing an account of the present state of the island of Cuba, and observations on the slave trade. [*anon.*] x, 135 pp. 1 map. 8°. *London, J. Miller*, 1821.

Letters from the Isle of Man in 1846. [*anon.*] iv, 147 pp. 12°. *London, Saunders and Otley*, 1847.

Letters of Adelaide de Sancerre to count de Nance. [*anon.*] 2 p. l. 160 pp. 16°. *Newbern (N. C.)* 1801.

Letters on ecclesiastical history. [*anon.*] 2 v. 270 pp. 1 pl; 198 pp. 16°. *Philadelphia, American sunday school union*, 1832–33.

Letters to a younger brother, on various subjects, relating to the virtues and vices, duties and dangers of youth. 176 pp. 1 pl. 18°. *Philadelphia, American sunday school union*, [1838].

Lettice (John, *d. d.*) Fables for the fireside. 2 p. l. 220 pp. 12°. *London, J. Black*, 1812.

Lettice Arnold. *See* **Marsh-Caldwell** (*Mrs.* Anne).

Lettre de Pékin, sur le génie de la langue chinoise. *See* **Amiot** *or* **Amyot** (Joseph Marie).

Lettres originales de madame la comtesse du Barry. *See* **Pidansat de Mairobert** (Mathieu François).

Lettsom (John Coakley, *m. d.*) Hints designed to promote beneficence, temperance and medical science. 3 v. 8°. *London, J. Mawman*, 1801.

——— History of the origin of medicine: an oration, delivered at the anniversary meeting of the Medical society of London, January 19, 1778. To which are added, various historical illustrations. viii, 168 pp. 2 pl. 4°. *London, E. & C. Dilly*, 1778.

Letzner (Johann). Braunschweig-Lüneburgische chronica, 1722. *See* **Bunting** (Heinrich) *and* **Letzner.**

Leuckart (Rudolph). Beiträge zur kenntniss wirbelloser thiere. *See* **Frey** (Heinrich) *and* **Leuckart.**

Leunis (Johannes). Nomenclator zoologicus. Eine etymologische erklärung der vorzüglichsten gattungs- und art-namen, welche in der naturgeschichte des thierreichs vorkommen. viii, 120 pp. 8°. *Hannover, Hahn*, 1866. s.

Leuven (Adolphe de) *and* **Langlé** (Joseph Adolphe Ferdinand). Maître Pathelin, opéra-comique en un acte. 75 pp. 12°. *Paris, N. Tresse, éditeur*, 1857.

Le Vasseur (Auguste). The french pronunciation and conversation taught simultaneously according to a new practical system; containing also a choice selection of prose and poetical pieces for elocution. 2 p. l. 132 pp. 12°. *Cleveland (O.) Spencer & Barker*, 1871.

Levati (Ambrogio). Viaggi di Francesco Petrarca in Francia, in Germania ed in Italia descritti. 5 v. 8°. *Milano, dalla società tipografica de' classici italiani*, 1820.

Leveneur de Tillières. *See* **Tillières** (Tanneguy Leveneur, *comte* de).

Lever (Christopher). A crucifixe: or, a meditation upon repentance, and, the holie passion. 21 l. unp. 4°. *London, J. Budge*, 1607.

Lever (Darcy). The young sea officer's sheet anchor; or a key to the leading of rigging, and to practical seamanship. With additions by George W. Blunt. Eng. title, viii, 128 pp. 114 pl. 4°. *New York, E. & G. W. Blunt*, 1843.

Lever (Thomas). Sermons, 1550. Carefully edited by Edward Arber. 144 pp. 16°. *London*, 1870.
[ARBER's english reprints, v. 12, no. 25].

Leverett (Frederick P.) An abridgment of Leverett's latin lexicon. By Francis Gardner. 2 v. in 1. 2 p. l. 420 pp; 318 pp. 8°. *Boston, J. H. Wilkins & R. B. Carter*, 1840.

——— The new latin tutor; or exercises in etymology, syntax and prosody, compiled in part from the best english works. With additions. 2 p. l. 348 pp. 12°. *Boston, Hilliard, Gray, Little, & Wilkins*, 1829.

——— A key to the new latin tutor; or exercises in etymology, syntax and prosody. [*anon.*] 2 p. l. 100 pp. 12°. *Boston, Hilliard, Gray, Little, & Wilkins*, 1829.

——— (*editor*). Decimi Junii Juvenalis et Auli Persii Flacci satiræ expurgatæ. 1832. *See* **Juvenalis** (Decimus Junius) *and* **Persius.**

Leverett (Frederick P.)—continued.

——— *See, also,* **Torrey** (H. W.) English-latin lexicon.

Levette (G. M.) *See* **Indiana** (*State of.*) *Geological survey,* 1870.

Levi (David). Letters to dr. Priestley, in answer to those he addressed to the Jews; inviting them to an amicable discussion of the evidences of christianity. 1st american from the 2d british ed. 16°. *New-York, J. Harrisson for B. Gomez,* 1794.

[*In* PRIESTLEY (Joseph, *ll. d.*) Letters to the Jews. 1794. pp. 53-131].

Levi (Leone). History of british commerce and of the economic progress of the british nation. 1763-1870. xiii, 527 pp. 8°. *London, J. Murray,* 1872.

——— The theory and practice of the metric system of weights and measures. vii, 126 pp. 16°. *London, Griffith & Farran,* 1871.

Levi Alvarès (David Eugène). Esquisses historiques, ou cours méthodique d'histoire, composé sur un plan nouveau et renfermant des précis gradués d'histoire des principaux peuples de l'Europe. Nouv. éd. 396 pp. 18°. *Paris, l'auteur,* [1845]?

——— Nouveaux éléments d'histoire générale rédigés sur un plan méthodique entièrement neuf. 2 v. in 1. 2 p. l. 644 pp. 16°. *Paris, l'auteur,* [1846]?

Levington (*Rev.* John). Watson's theological institutes defended; the teachings of transcendental philosophy shown to be at variance with scripture and matter of fact; and the bible proved to be complete in itself, both in teaching and evidence. 283 pp. 12°. *New York, Barnes & Burr,* 1863.

Levinski (Jacob Levi). Abridged school and family bible in hebrew and english. 1871. *See* **Bible.** (*Hebrew and english*).

Levizac (Jean Pons Victor Lecoutz de). Clef de la grammaire de m. de Levizac. Par M. Noland. 132 pp. 12°. *New York, Collins, Reese & co.* 1836.

Levy (*Mrs.* Esther). Jewish cookery book, on principles of economy, adapted for jewish housekeepers, with the addition of many useful medicinal recipes, and other valuable information, relative to housekeeping and domestic management. 200 pp. 16°. *Philadelphia, W. S. Turner,* 1871.

Levy (Matthias). The history of short-hand writing; to which is prefixed the system used by the author. viii, 194 pp. 1 pl. 12°. *London, Trübner & co.* 1862.

Levy (Uriah P. *com. U. S. n.*) Manual of internal rules and regulations for men-of-war. 2d ed. enlarged. 80 pp. 18°. *New York, D. Van Nostrand,* 1862.

Lewald (Ernest Anton). Commentatio ad historiam religionum veterum illustrandam pertinens de doctrina gnostica. xiii, 157 pp. 1 l. 8°. *Heidelberg, Mohr & Winter,* 1818.

Lewin (*Rev.* Raphael D. C.) What is judaism? Or a few words to the Jews. 84 pp. 16°. *New York, D. Appleton & co.* 1870.

Lewis (Dio, *m. d.*) Our girls. 388 pp. 12°. *New York, Harper & brothers,* 1871.

——— Talks about health. 123 pp. 16°. *Boston, D. Lewis,* 1871.

Lewis (*Mrs.* Estelle Anna). Records of the heart. [Poems]. vii, 255 pp. 12°. *New York, D. Appleton & co.* 1844.

Lewis (E. W. *m. d.*) The spiritual reasoner. 256 pp. 12°. *Watkins (N. Y.) author,* 1855.

Lewis (Jason). The anastasis of the dead: or, philosophy of human immortality, as deduced from the teachings of the scripture writers, in reference to "the resurrection." 352 pp. 12°. *Boston, A. Tompkins,* 1860.

Lewis (Ludwig). Geschichte der freimaurerei in Österreich, im allgemeinen und der wiener loge zu st. Joseph insbesondere. iv, 162 pp. 1 l. 8°. *Wien, druck und verlag der typogr.-literar-artistischen anstalt,* 1861.

Lewis (Matthew Gregory). Poems. viii, 112 pp. 16°. *London, D. N. Shury,* 1812.

Lewis (Paul). A final call to the Jews: or an explanation of the original promise; being a full and satisfactory answer to all objections that ever have, shall, or may be, raised against christianity. xix, 332 pp. 2 l. 8°. *London, author,* 1744.

Lewis (Thomas). The history of the Parthian empire, from the foundation of the monarchy by Arsaces, to its final overthrow by Artaxerxes the persian: contained in a succession of twenty nine kings. 4 p. l. 372 pp. 4 l. 8°. *London, S. Illidge,* 1728.

Lewis (*Mr. — of Waterbury, Conn.*) High school hymn book: for high and normal schools and families. [*anon.*] xix, 248 pp. 16°. *New York, Woolworth, Ainsworth & co.* [1871].

Leyburn (*Rev.* George W.) God's message to the young; or, the obligation and the advantages of early piety seriously urged upon young persons, in connection with Eccl. xii, 1. 179 pp. 12°. *New York, M. W. Dodd,* 1857.

Leycester (George Hanmer). Some observations on the inconvenience of the ten commandments. 2 p. l. 64 pp. 8°. *Oxford, Fletcher and Hanwell*, 1795.
[MISCELLANEOUS pamphlets, v. 103].

Leydekker (Melchior). Verder vervolg van de kerkelyke historie, van Hornius. 1666 tot 1687. 1 p. l. 146 pp. 5 l. 16°. *Amsterdam, J. Rotterdam*, 1739.
[*With* HORN (Georg). Kerkelyke en wereldlyke historie. *Amsterdam*, 1746].

Leynadier (Camille). Histoire des peuples et des révolutions de l'Europe, depuis 1789 jusqu'à nos jours. v. 1-5. 8°. *Paris, H. Morel*, 1846-47.

CONTENTS.

v. 1. Introduction. Pologne.
2. Pologne. Pays-Bas. Italie.
3-4. Italie.
4. Suisse.
5. Espagne. Portugal.

L'Hermite (François, *dit* Tristan). Le cabinet dv roy Lovis xi. contenant plusieurs fragmens, lettres, missiues, & secretes intrigues du règne de ce monarque, & autres pièces très-curieuses, & non encores veuës. Receüillies de diuerses archiues & trésors. [*anon.*] Eng. title, 3 p. l. 120 pp. 18°. *Paris, G. Qvinet*, 1661.

L'Hermite (Jacques) *and* **Schapenham** (Jan Huyghen). Journael van de Nassausche vloot, ofte beschrijvingh van de voyagie om den gantschen aert-kloot: onder 't beleydt van den admirael Jaques l'Hermite, ende vice-admirael Gheen Huygen Schapenham, 1623-26. 1 p. l. 76 pp. 6 pl. on 1 sheet. sm. 4°. *Amstelredam, J. Hartgertsz*, 1648.
[*In* HARTGERTS (J.) Oost-Indische voyagien, v. 1, 9e stuck.
Note.—The narrative of this voyage, during which both commanders perished, was drawn up and published by Adolf Decker, captain of marines in the expedition].

Lhomond (Charles François). Doctrine chrétienne en forme de lectures de piété, où l'on expose les preuves de la religion, les dogmes de la foi, les règles de la morale, ce qui concerne les sacremens et la prière. 2 p. l. 546 pp. 12°. *Lyon, Blache & Boget*, 1809.

——— Elements of latin grammar. Translated into english, by Levi Fletcher. 163 pp. 12°. *Philadelphia, A. Towar*, 1835.

Libanius. *Βασιλικος* sev panegyricvs Constanti et Constantio impp. dictvs. Specvlvm imperatoriæ majestatis & regiarum virtutum omnium, oratorio & historico lepore conditum. Græca nunc primum e vaticana bibliotheca prodeunt. Fed. Morellvs recensuit, cum alijs mnss. contulit, latine vertit, notis

Libanius—continued.
illustrauit. 4 p. l. 96, 94 pp. 1 l. 16°. *Lvtetiæ, apud F. Morellvm*, 1614.

Libertas (*pseudon.*) The fame and glory of England vindicated, being an answer to "The glory and shame of England," [of C. E. Lester]. 306 pp. 12°. *New York and London, Wiley & Putnam*, 1842.

Library (The) of the old english prose writers. 2 v. 16°. *Cambridge (Mass.) Hilliard & Brown*, 1831.

CONTENTS.

FULLER (Thomas). Holy and profane states, v. 1.
SIDNEY (Philip). The defence of poesy, v. 2.
SELDEN (John). Table-talk, v. 2.

Library (The); or, some hints about what books to read, and how to buy them. Containing lists of standard and essential books in every department of literature. By an old bookseller. [*anon.*] 64 pp. 12°. *Philadelphia, Porter & Coates*, [1870].

Liceti (Fortunio). De mundi, & hominis analogia liber vnus. 4 p. l. 172 pp. 4°. *Vtini, ex typographia N. Schiratti*, 1635.

——— De monstris. Ex recensione Gerardi Blasii, qui monstra quædam nova & rariora ex recentiorum scriptis addidit. Ed. novissima. Iconibus illustrata. Eng. title, 8 p. l. 316 pp. 13 l. incl. 4 pl. 4°. *Amstelodami, sumptibus A. Frisii*, 1665.

——— De spontaneo viventivm ortv libb. quatuor, in quibus de generatione animantium, quæ vulgo ex putri exoriri dicuntur, accurate aliorum opiniones omnes primum examinantur: caussæ singulæ propositi deinde cum generatim, tum etiam speciatim ex rei natura deteguntur; patefacto præsertim efficiente proximo vniuoco eorum, quæ in fungorum, plantarum, zoophytorum, & animalium genere sponte nascuntur. 3 p. l. 10, 323 pp. 15 l. fol. *Vicetiæ, ex typographia D. Amadei, apvd F. Bolzetam bibliopolam patavinam*, 1618.

Lichtenberger (Johann Friedrich). Initia typographica. x, 260 pp. 4°. *Argentorati, Treuttel & Würz*, 1811.

Lichtenthal (Pietro, *dottor*). Manuale bibliografico del viaggiatore in Italia concernente località, storia, arti, scienze ed antiquaria. vii, 258 pp. 12°. *Milano, A. Fontana*, 1830.

Licinius (Marcus, *pseudon.*) *See* **Menage** (Gilles).

Licquet (François Isidore, *known as* Théodore). Histoire de Normandie, depuis les temps les plus reculés jusqu'à la conquête de l'Angleterre en 1066. Précédée d'une intro-

Licquet (François Isidore)—continued. duction par G. B. Depping. 2 v. 1 p. l. cxcii, 322 pp. 1 map; 2 p. l. 455 pp. 8°. *Rouen, É. Frère*, 1835.

Liddell (Henry George, *d. d.*) The student's Rome. A history of Rome, from the earliest times to the establishment of the empire. With chapters on the history of literature and art. New ed. x, 676 pp. 12°. *London, J. Murray*, 1869.

Lidgate *or* **Lydgate** (John). The avncient historie of the warres betwixte the Grecians and the Troyans. *See* **Colonne** (Guido dalle).

Liebig (Justus von). Chemistry in its application to agriculture and physiology. Edited from the manuscript of the author by Lyon Playfair, with very numerous additions, and a new chapter on soils. 3d american from the 2d english ed. with notes, and appendix, by John W. Webster, m. d. 430 pp. 12°. *Cambridge, J. Owen*, 1842.

Liefde (*Rev.* J. de). The signet-ring and other gems. From the dutch. 362 pp. 16°. *Boston, Gould & Lincoln*, 1860.

Life and adventures of Wat Tyler, the good and the brave. [*anon.*] 174 pp. 16°. *London, H. G. Collins*, 1851.

Life and light, or every-day religion. By the author of George Miller, [etc. *anon.*] 216 pp. 3 pl. 18°. *Philadelphia, Presbyterian board of publication*, [1863].

Life (The) and miracles of saint Winefride, [also], the life of saint Catherine. [*anon.*] 176 pp. 1 pl. 18°. *New York, P. J. Kenedy*, 1871.

Life (The) and political writings of John Wilkes, esq. [*anon.*] 4 p. l. 519 pp. 8°. *Birmingham, J. Sketchley & co.* 1769.

Life and times of sir Philip Sidney. *See* **Davis** (*Mrs.* S. M.)

Life (The) and writings of the apostle Peter. [*anon.*] 232 pp. (incl. 1 map), 1 pl. 18°. *Philadelphia, American sunday school union*, 1836.

Life-boat (The), or journal of the national life-boat association. [Issued quarterly]. Jan. 1, 1862 to Nov. 1, 1870. (nos. 43–78). v. 5–7. 8°. *London, C. Knight*, 1865–70.

Life histories: for the sabbath school. By the author of "Philip Alderton's temptation." [*anon.*] 204 pp. 4 pl. 18°. *Boston, Mass. sabbath school society*, [1862].

Life in India; or, Madras, the Neilgherries, and Calcutta. [*anon.*] 528 pp. 31 pl. 18°. *Philadelphia, American sunday school union*, [1855].

Life in the insect world: or, conversations upon insects. [*anon.*] 241 pp. 1 pl. 16°. *Philadelphia, Lindsay & Blakiston*, 1844.

Life lessons in the school of christian duty. *New York*, 1864. *See* **Gillette** (*Rev.* E. H.)

Life (The) of Cornelius van Tromp, lieutenant-admiral of Holland and Westfriesland: containing many remarkable passages relating to the war between England and Holland. As also the sea-fights, and other memorable actions of this great man, from the year 1650, to the time of his death. [*anon.*] 4 p. l. 533 pp. 12°. *London, J. Orme for R. Clavel*, [*etc.*] 1697.

Life (The) of Daniel. By the author of "The life of David," "Bible sketches," etc. [*anon.*] 224 pp. 1 map. 18°. *Philadelphia, American sunday school union*, [1834].

Life (The) of David, king of Israel. By the author of "Bible sketches." 275 pp. 18°. *Philadelphia, American sunday school union*, 1832.

Life (The) of Elisha. By the author of "The life of Elijah." [*anon.*] 192 pp. 18°. *Philadelphia, American sunday school union*, 1836.

Life of Emanuel Swedenborg, with some account of his writings, together with a brief notice of the rise and progress of the new church. [*anon.*] 188 pp. 12°. *Boston, Allen & Goddard*, 1831.

Life (The) of Jacob, and his son Joseph. [*anon.*] 191 pp. 1 pl. 18°. *Philadelphia, American sunday-school union*, [1836].

Life (The) of Jesus. [*anon.*] 214 pp. 1 pl. 12°. *Boston, Massachusetts sabbath school soc.* 1853.

Life (The) of John Knox, the scottish reformer. [*anon.*] 141 pp. 1 portrait. 18°. *Philadelphia, American sunday-school union*, 1833.

Life (The) of Lewis of Bovrbon, late prince of Conde. Digested into annals. Done out of french, [by Nahum Tate]. 2 v. in 1. 8 p. l. 278, 221 pp. 1 portrait. 8°. *London, T. Goodwin*, 1693.

Life (The) of mr. James Quin, comedian. With the history of the stage, from his commencing actor to his retreat to Bath. With his will. [*anon.*] 2 p. l. 116 pp. 1 portrait. 12°. *London, S. Bladon*, 1766.

Life of mr. William Whittingham, dean of Durham, from a ms. in Antony Wood's collection, Bodleian library, Oxford. With an appendix of original documents from the record office. Edited by Mary Anne Everett Green. 1 p. l. ii, 48 pp. sm. 4°. [*London*], *Camden society*, 1870.
[CAMDEN (The) miscellany, v. 6].

Life (The) of Napoleon Bonaparte, from the best english and french authorities; including original correspondence, and numerous anecdotes of his cotemporaries. [*anon.*] 2 p. l. 646 pp. 1 portrait. 8°. *London, M. Moore*, 1839.

Life (The) of president Edwards. [*anon.*] 143 pp. 1 portrait. 18°. *Philadelphia, American sunday school union*, 1832.

Life of the reverend mother Julia, foundress and first superior of the Sisters of notre-dame, of Namur. Translated from the french. With the history of the order in the United States. [*anon.*] 351 pp. 1 portrait. 12°. *New York, Catholic publication society*, 1871.

Life (The) of rev. Richard Watson, author of Theological institutes, biblical dictionary, etc. Compiled from authentic sources. [*anon.*] 312 pp. 18°. *New York, G. Lane & P. P. Sandford*, 1841.

Life (The) of Stonewall Jackson. From official papers, contemporary narratives, and personal acquaintance. By a Virginian. Reprinted from the advanced sheets of the Richmond edition. [*anon.*] 305 pp. 1 portrait. 12°. *New York, C. B. Richardson*, 1863.

Life of Thomas Chalmers, d. d. [*anon.*] 432 pp. 18°. *Boston, Mass. sabbath school society*, [1859].

Life of Thomas Harrison Burder, m. d. with extracts from his correspondence. *See* **Burder** (John).

Life (The) of Thomas T. Thomason, missionary in Calcutta. [*anon.*] 138 pp. 18°. *Philadelphia, American sunday-school union*, [1833].

Life-pictures; or, bygone scenes remembered. [*anon.*] 227 pp. 10 pl. 12°. *Philadelphia, American sunday school union*, [1849].

Life (The), travels and books of Alexander von Humboldt. With an introduction by Bayard Taylor. [*anon.*] xvii, 482 pp. 1 portrait. 12°. *New York, Rudd & Carlton*, 1859.

Liger (—*l'abbé*). Lettres critiques et dissertation sur le prêt de commerce. [Avec une réponse à la lettre d'un anonyme à m. l'abbé Liger]. 234 pp. 1 l. 17 pp. 16°. *Caen, J. C. Pryon*, 1774.

Light and cloud in the dark valley. By a layman. [*anon.*] 133 pp. 18°. *Philadelphia, American sunday school union*, [1853].

Liguori (*S.* Alfonso Maria di). The mission-book of the congregation of the most holy redeemer: a manual of instructions and prayers, adapted to preserve the fruits of the mission. Drawn chiefly from the works of st. Alphonsus Liguori. New ed. 502 pp. 1 portrait. 18°. *Baltimore, Kelly, Hedian & Piet*, 1863.

——— The same. Le livre des missions. Recueil d'instructions et de prières, propres à conserver les fruits de la mission. Tirées en partie des oeuvres de saint Alphonse de Liguori. Revu par l'abbé L. C. Bourquard. 2de éd. 480 pp. 16 l. 16°. *Einsiedeln, New York, et Cincinnati, C. & N. Benziger frères*, 1870.

——— The same. Das missions-buch der versammlung des allerheil erlösers. Ein handbuch von unterweisungen und gebeten, welche geeignet sind, die früchte der mission zu bewahren. Grösstentheils den schriften des heil. Alphons Liguori entnommen. Einzig berechtigte uebersetzung der englischen original-ausgabe. xv, 704 pp. 2 pl. 18°. *New York and Cincinnati, F. Pustet & co.* 1871.

——— *See, also,* **Smith** (Samuel B.) A synopsis of the moral theology of the church of Rome, taken from the works of st. Liguori.

Lilian. [A novel]. *See* **Greenough** (S. L.)

Lillie (John, *d. d.*) Lectures on Thessalonians. *See* **Bible.** (*English*).

Linden (Leile, *pseudon.*) Holiday afternoons; or, the commandments illustrated. By Leile Linden. [*pseudon.*] 251 pp. 18°. *Boston, New England sabbath school union*, 1854.

Linen (James Alexander). Poems in the scots and english dialect, on various occasions. vi, 152 pp. 6 pl. 2 portraits. 8°. *Edinburgh, editor*, 1815.

Lines (Leverett H. *m. d.*) Thirty years of female life. A treatise on the diseases of females, incident to this period, with their causes, symptoms and treatment; including the theory of conception, and the symptoms

Lines (Leverett H. *m. d.*)—continued. of pregnancy. 336 pp. 12°. *New York, W. E. Hilton*, 1862.

——— The same. From fifteen to forty-five; or, thirty years of female life, etc. 336 pp. 12°. *New York, F. Somers*, 1863.

Lington (Burr, *pseudon.*) *See* **Humboldt** (Gay).

Linguet (Simon Nicolas Henri). Théorie du libelle, ou l'art de calomnier avec fruit, dialogue philosophique, pour servir de supplément à la Théorie du paradoxe. [*anon.*] 228 pp. 12°. *Amsterdam*, 1775.

[*With* MORELLET (André). Théorie du paradoxe].

Linkinwater (Tim, *pseudon.*) Mardi gras; a tale of ante bellum times. 132 pp. 8°. *New Orleans, P. F. Gogarty*, 1871.

Linn (S. P.) Living thoughts of leading thinkers; a thesaurus. 400 pp. 2 portraits. 12°. *Pittsburg, J. R. Foster & co.* 1869.

Linnaea. Ein journal für die botanik in ihrem ganzen umfange. Herausgegeben von D. F. L. von Schlechtendal. v. 1-3, 5-16. 8°. *Berlin, etc. F. Dümmler et al.* 1826-42. S.

——— The same. v. 17-32; oder Beiträge zur pflanzenkunde. Herausgegeben von D. F. L. von Schlechtendal. v. 1-16. 8°. *Halle, C. A. Schwetschke & sohn*, 1843-63. S.

[*Note.*—Imperfect, nos. missing from v. 26, 29, 30, and 32].

Linné (Carl von, *editor*). Amoenitates academicæ; seu dissertationes variæ physicæ, medicæ, botanicae antehac seorsim editæ nunc collectæ et auctæ. 9 v. 8°. *Holmiæ et Lipsiæ, G. Kiesewetter; Erlangæ, J. J. Palm*, 1749-85. S.

——— The same. Amoenitates academicae. v. 10. Accedunt C. à Linné fil. dissertationes botanicae collectae, curante Io. C. D. Schrebero. 8°. *Erlangae, Io. Iac. Palm*, 1790. S.

Linton (Charles). The healing of the nations. Second series. 363 pp. 1 portrait. 8°. *Philadelphia, author*, 1864.

Linton (G. W.) *and* **Teasdale** (Howard M.) Kind words: a new collection of hymns and tunes for sunday-schools and the social circle. 96 pp. obl. 16°. *Memphis (Tenn.) Sunday-school board*, 1871.

Linton (William J.) The english republic. God and the people. 2 p. l. 368 pp. 8°. *London, J. Watson*, 1851.

Lion (Félix). Sébastopol, ou la campagne de Crimée. Poëme en six chants. 227 pp. 2 l. 8°. *México*, 1855.

Lion (The). [A weekly magazine]. v. 1-2. From January 4 to December 26, 1828. 2 v. 8°. *London, R. Carlile*, 1828.

Lippi (Lorenzo). Il malmantile racquistato di Perlone Zipoli, [*anag.*] colle note di Puccio Lamoni [Paolo Minucci] e d'altri. [Colla vita di Lippi scritta da Filippo Baldinucci. Edizione curata del can. Antonio Maria Biscioni]. 1 v. in 2. Eng. title, xlviii, 864 pp. 2 pl. 4°. *Firenze, M. Nestenus & F. Moücke*, 1731.

Lippincott (*Mrs.* Sara Jane Clarke). History of my pets. By Grace Greenwood. [*pseudon.*] New ed. enlarged. vi, 164 pp. 6 pl. 16°. *Boston, J. R. Osgood & co.* 1871.

——— Poems. By Grace Greenwood. [*pseudon.*] New and enlarged ed. viii, 196 pp. 1 portrait. 16°. *Boston, Ticknor & Fields*, 1850.

——— Recollections of my childhood, and other stories. By Grace Greenwood. [*pseudon.*] 2 p. l. 185 pp. 6 pl. 16°. *Boston, J. R. Osgood & co.* 1871.

——— Stories from famous ballads. For children. By Grace Greenwood. [*pseudon.*] 2 p. l. 178 pp. 5 pl. 16°. *Boston, J. R. Osgood & co.* 1871.

Lippincott's magazine of popular literature and science. [Monthly]. Jan. to Dec. 1871. v. 7-8. 8°. *Philadelphia, J. B. Lippincott & co.* 1871.

Lipscomb (George). Journey into South Wales; in the year 1799. xxviii, 444 pp. 8°. *London, T. N. Longman & O. Rees*, 1802.

Lipsius (Justus). Justi Lipsi v. c. opera omnia, postremum ab ipso aucta et recensita: nunc primum copioso rerum indice illustrata. 4 v. 8°. *Vesaliæ, typis A. ab Hoogenhuysen*, 1675.

[Imperfect: v. 1, title-page wanting].

——— Lavs elephantis. 18°. [*Lugd. Batavorum*, 1644].

[*In* DISSERTATIONVM lvdicrarvm et amœnitatvm scriptores varij, pp. 447-473].

——— Roma illustrata, sive antiquitatum romanarum breviarium. Accessit Georgii Fabricii veteris Romæ cum nova collatio. Ex nova recensione Antonii Thysii. 3 p. l. 504 pp. 7 l. 24°. *Amstelodami, J. Walters*, 1689.

——— Satyra menippæa. Somnium. 18°. [*Lugduni Batavorum*, 1655].

[ELEGANTIORES præstantium virorum satyræ, pp. 1-34].

——— A comparison of the romane manner of warre, with this of ovr time; ovt of the end

Lipsius (Justus)—continued. of the fifth booke, De militia romana. fol. [*London*, 1623].

[*In* XENOPHON. The historie of Xenophon: containing the ascent of Cyrvs. 6 l. at the end].

——— Sixe bookes of politickes or civil doctrine, written in latine, which doe especially concerne principalitie. Done into english by William Jones. 6 p. l. 207 pp. 4°. *London, W. Ponsonby*, 1594.

Lisbon. *Observatorio do infante d. Luiz.* [Obsevaçoes] Annaes. 1865–1870. v. 3–8. fol. *Lisboa, imprenta nacional*, 1866–70. s.

Lisco (Friedrich Gustavus). The parables of Jesus explained and illustrated. Translated from the german by rev. P. Fairbairn. Abridged for the use of sabbath school teachers. iv, 13–404 pp. 18°. *Boston, Mass. sabbath school society*, 1846.

Lister-Kaye (*Lady* Matilda Arbuthnot). British homes, and foreign wanderings. 2 v. 2 p. l. 328 pp; 1 p. l. 313 pp. 12°. *London, H. Colburn*, 1849.

Lisvarte di Grecia, figliol dell' imperatore Splandiano. [*anon.*] Nuouamente dalla spagnuola nella italiana lingua tradotto, & ristampato. 4 p. l. 275 l. 16°. *Venetia, C. Franceschini*, 1578.

[*Note.*—The authorship of this work, the seventh part of the Amadis of Gaul, is probably to be attributed to Feliciano de Silva. Gayangos in Biblioteca de autores españoles, v. 34, p. xxviii].

Liszt (Franz). Vier grosse original-beiträge. 4°. [*Stuttgart*, 1869].

[*In* LEBERT (S.) *and* STARK (L.) Grosse theoretisch-praktische klavierschule, v. 4].

Litchfield (John). The dramatic character of mr. [William] Parsons. 8°. [*London, T. Bellamy*, 1795].

[*In* BELLAMY (Thomas). The life of mr. William Parsons, comedian. 1795. pp. 51–59].

Literary (The) blue book, or kalendar of literature, science, and art. For 1830. [*anon.*] vi, 200 pp. 18°. *London, Marsh & Miller*, [1829].

Literary (The) coronal, for 1823. [*anon.*] Eng. title, 384 pp. 1 pl. 18°. *Glasgow, R. Griffin & co.* 1823.

Literary (The) gazette: or, journal of criticism, science, and the arts, being a collection of original and selected essays. [A third series of the Analectic magazine]. Jan. 6 to Dec. 29, 1821. v. 1. 830 pp. 1 l. 4°. *Philadelphia*, 1822.

Literary (The) rambler: being a collection of the most popular and entertaining stories in the english language. [*anon.*] viii, 542 pp. 8°. [*London*], *Oliver & Boyd*, 1833.

Litolff (Henry, *publisher*). Collection Litolff. v. 401. Perles de salon. 17 morceaux brillants pour le piano. 74 pp. 4°. *Braunschweig & New York, H. Litolff's verlag*, [1870].

Littell (Squire, jr. *m. d.*) A manual of the diseases of the eye. xv, 255 pp. 12°. *Philadelphia, J. S. Littell*, 1837.

Littell's living age. [A weekly magazine]. Jan. 1 to June 24, 1871. 4th series, v. 20–21; [complete series], v. 108–109. 8°. *Boston, Littell & Gay*, [1871].

Little (John). The constitution of Newfoundland, etc. *See* **Newfoundland.**

Little (William). The history of Warren; a mountain hamlet, located among the White hills of New Hampshire. 592 pp. [incl. 6 pl.] 11 pl. 8°. *Manchester (N. H.) W. E. Moore*, 1870.

Little (The) corporal. An original magazine for boys and girls and for older people who have young hearts. [Monthly]. July, 1871, to Dec. 1872. v. 13. 8°. *Chicago, Sewell & Miller and J. E. Miller*, [1871].

Little (The) manual of the blessed trinity. A guide to catholic devotion. [*anon.*] 704 pp. 1 pl. 24°. *New York, P. J. Kenedy*, 1872

Little Pierre, the pedlar of Alsace; or, the reward of filial piety. Translated from the french, by J. M. C. [*anon.*] 236 pp. 27 pl. 16°. *New York, Catholic publication society*, 1872.

Little songs for little boys and girls. *See* **Follen** (Eliza Lee).

Little threads. 1863. *See* **Prentiss** (*Mrs.* E.)

Littré (Maximilien Paul Émile). Dictionnaire de la langue française. v. 2. 1e partie. I–P. 4°. *Paris, L. Hachette & cie.* 1869.

"**Live** for Jesus"; the watchword in life and in death of Ellen Macomber. [*anon.*] 159 pp. 1 pl. 12°. *Boston, Mass. sabbath school society*, [1857].

Lively (Edward). A trve chronologie of the times of the persian monarchie, and after to the destruction of Ierusalem by the Romanes. Wherein by the way briefly is handled the day of Christ his birth: with a declaration of the angel Gabriels message to Daniel in the end of his 9. chap. against the friuolous conceits of Matthew Beroald. 258 pp. 72 l. unp. 18°. *London, F. Kingston for T. Man*, [*etc.*] 1597.

Livermore (Harriet). Addresses to the dispersed of Judah. With an appendix. 268 pp. 8°. *Philadelphia, L. R. Bailey*, 1849.

Livermore (Kate). Mary Lee. 161 pp. 5 pl. 16°. *New York, D. Appleton & co.* 1860.

Liverpool (The) commercial list. 1871–72, sixth and seventh years. By Estell & co. fol. *London,* [*Seyd & co.*] 1871.

Lives of the most eminent and evangelical ministers from the beginning of the reformation to the present time. Collected from authentic historians. [*anon.*] 2 v. 1 p. l. 437 pp; 1 p. l. 473 pp. 8°. *Newcastle, E. Walker for M. Heavisides,* 1813.

Lives (The) of Vasco Nunez de Balboa, Hernando Cortez, and Francisco Pizarro. [*anon.*] 276 pp. 18°. *Boston, Marsh, Capen, Lyon, & Webb,* 1840.

Living (The) female writers of the south. 1872. *See* **Tardy** (*Mrs.* Mary).

Living (The) poets of England. Specimens of the living british poets, with biographical and critical notices, and an essay on english poetry. 2 v. 2 p. l. xxxv, 548 pp; 2 p. l. 620 pp. 8°. *Paris, L. Baudry,* 1827.

Living (The) way. [A monthly religious magazine]. Edited by S. D. Simonds. Jan. to Dec. 1871. v. 2. 8°. *San Francisco, S. D. Simonds,* [1871].

Living words from living men. Experiences of converted infidels. [*anon.*] 135 pp. 18°. *New York, Board of publication of the reformed protestant dutch church,* 1863.
[TRIUMPHS of grace: Fulton street prayer meeting].

Livingston (John H. *d. d. editor*). Psalms and hymns. *See* **Reformed** dutch church.

Livingston (Peter). Poems and songs, principally relating to scottish manners and customs. 4th ed. 158 pp. 1 l. 1 portrait. 16°. *Dundee, author,* 1847.

Livingston (Vanbrugh). An inquiry into the merits of the reformed doctrine of "imputation," as contrasted with those of "catholic imputation"; or, the cardinal point of controversy between the church of Rome and the protestant high church: with miscellaneous essays on the catholic faith. With an introduction by John Hughes, d. d. xii, 242 pp. 12°. *New York, Casserly & sons,* 1843.

——— Remarks on the "Oxford theology," in connection with its bearing on the law of nature, and the doctrine of justification by faith. 229 pp. 16°. *New York, C. Henry,* 1841.

Livius (Titus). Titi Livii patavini historiarum liber primus et selecta quædam capita. Curavit notulisque instruxit Carolus Folsom. x, 288 pp. 12°. *Cantabrigiæ, Hilliard & Brown,* 1829.

Livre (Le) rouge, or red book: being a list of secret pensions, paid out of the public treasure of France; and containing characters of the persons pensioned, [etc.] and observations tending to shew the reasons for which the pensions were granted. Translated from the eighth Paris edition. [*anon.*] 1 p. l. 163 pp. 8°. *London, G. Kearsley,* 1790.

Lizzie Maitland. Edited by O. A. Brownson. [*anon.*] xii, 340 pp. 16°. *New York, E. Dunigan & brother,* 1857.

Llewellyn (E. L.) Flowers in the grass. 214 pp. 18°. *Philadelphia, Presbyterian publication committee,* [1866].

——— The little brown bible. 179 pp. 1 pl. 18°. *Philadelphia, Presbyterian board of publication,* [1861].

Lloyd (Charles). Memoirs of the life and writings of Vittorio Alfieri. [*anon.*] iv, 220 pp. 12°. *London, C. & H. Baldwyn,* 1821.

——— Nugæ canoræ. Poems. 3d ed. with additions. 1 p. l. xxix, 332 pp. 16°. *London, J. & A. Arch,* 1819.

——— Principles for the conduct of life. [Maxims]. 2 v. x, 282 pp; 2 p. l. 274 pp. 12°. *London, J. Masters,* 1848.

Lloyd (Elizabeth). Treasures of darkness. By E. L. [*anon.*] 252 pp. 12°. *Philadelphia, W. P. Hazard,* 1854.

Lloyd (Humphrey, *d. d.*) Observations made at the magnetical and meteorological observatory at Trinity college, Dublin. *See* **Trinity College** (*Dublin*). Observatory. Observations, v. 2.

Lloyd (John). The English country gentleman and other poems. A new ed. viii, 117 pp. 1 pl. 12°. *London, Longman,* 1865.

Lloyd (*Mrs.* Mary Clarke). Meditations on divine subjects. [With] her life and character, by E. Pemberton. 116 pp. 12°. *New York, J. Parker,* 1750.

Llwyd (Richard). Poems. Tales, odes, sonnets, translations from the british, &c. 2 v. in 1. viii, 211 pp. 12°. *Chester, J. Fletcher,* 1804.

Loberg (O. N.) Norges fiskerier. Udgivet af "Det kongelige selskab for norges vel." 1 p. l. xii, 324 pp. 16°. *Kristiania, B. M. Bentzens bogtrykkeri,* 1864.

Lobkowitz (Juan Caramuel de). *See* **Caramuel Lobkowitz.**

Lobo (Jeronymo). Relazione varie cavate da una traduzione inglese dell' originale portoghese, [da Lorenzo Magalotti. *anon.*] 3

Lobo (Jeronymo)—continued.
p. l. 112 pp. 1 pl. 1 map. 16°. *Firenze, P. Matini*, 1693.

CONTENTS.

Del Nilo. Poichè il Nilo inondi, e metta sotto la campagna d'Egitto ne' giorni del maggio caldo in Europa.
Dell' vnicorno; e di passaggio della fenice, del vccelo di paradiso, e dell' pellicano.
Poichè l'imperator degli Abissini si chiami communemente il pretegianni.
Del mar rosso, e sua denominazione.
Della palma; sue varietà, frutto, utilità, e coltura.

[*Note.*—The english translation here spoken of may be that of sir Peter Wyche, published in 1669].

——— A voyage to Abyssinia. With a continuation of the history of Abyssinia down to the beginning of the 18th century, and fifteen dissertations on various subjects relating to Abyssinia. By mr. [abbé] Legrand. From the french. [Translated by dr. Johnson. 1st ed.] xii, 396 pp. 4 l. 8°. *London, A. Bettesworth*, 1735.

[*Note.*—Printed at Birmingham. The first prose work of dr. Johnson, for which he received five guineas.—*Lowndes*].

Local (The) press on the Erie railway management, January, 1872. [*anon.*] 74 pp. 8°. *Albany, Weed, Parsons & co.* 1872.

Lochner (Michael Friedrich). Commentatio de ananasa sive nvce pinea indica vulgo pinhas. 2 p. l. 64 pp. 3 pl. sm. 4°. [*Norimbergae*, 1716] ?
[Imperfect at the end].

Locke (*Mrs.* Jane Ermina Starkweather). Miscellaneous poems. 300 pp. 12°. *Boston, Otis, Broaders & co.* 1842.

Locke (John). An abridgment of mr. Locke's essay concerning human understanding. 250 pp. 16°. *Boston, Manning & Loring*, 1794.

Locke (John, *m. d.*) An english grammar for children; according to the elementary method of Pestalozzi. 228 pp. 1 table. 18°. *Cincinnati, W. M. & O. Farnsworth, jr.* 1827.

Locke (Una, *pseudon.*) The bible class in the parsonage: a story for senior scholars who wish to understand the word of God. By Una Locke. 293 pp. 18°. *New York, Carlton & Porter*, [1863].

——— Clara, the motherless young housekeeper; or, the life of faith. By Una Locke. 122 pp. 18°. *New York, Carlton & Porter*, [1860].

——— The people of Poplar dell; or, what aunt Hester says. 160 pp. 16°. *New York, Carlton & Lanahan*, [1871].

——— The school at Elm oak and the school of life. By Una Locke. 227 pp. 18°. *New York, Carlton & Porter*, [1861].

Locke (Una, *pseudon*)—continued.
——— *and* **Lee** (Frances, *pseudon.*) Isabel's trials, [by Una Locke], and Once a second, [by Frances Lee]. 112 pp. 18°. *New York, Carlton & Porter*, [1862].

Lockhart (William, *f. r. c. s.*) The medical missionary in China: a narrative of twenty years' experience. xi, 404 pp. 1 pl. 8°. *London, Hurst & Blackett*, 1861.

Lockwood (Anthony). A brief description of Nova Scotia, with plates of the principal harbors; including a particular account of the island of Grand Manan. 2 p. l. 134 pp. 8 pl. 4°. *London, author*, 1818.

Lockwood (George R.) Catálogo de los libros españoles, con sus precios en oro, que se hallan de venta en libreria de G. R. Lockwood. 2 p. l. 66 pp. 12°. *Nueva York, libreria americana y extranjera*, 1870.
[*With* VINGUT (Francisco J.) Key to the spanish teacher. *New York*, 1871].

Locust Grove stories. [*anon.*] 6 v. 18°. *Philadelphia, American sunday-school union*, [1871].

CONTENTS.

v. 1. The unruly tongue. Jacob's wall. Clara's surprise.
v. 2. How Violet's prayer was answered. Words. How God brings good out of evil.
v. 3. Jack Story and Paul Stanley. Truth in trifles. Love to the aged.
v. 4. Dick Mason and Harry Slack. Sympathy for others. Johnnie's lesson. Aunt Clyde's visit.
v. 5. The earnest boy. God's eye upon us. Hans Albright and his mother. Nannie Malone.
v. 6. The birth-day party at the hall. Julia and her friend Bell Newton.

Lodeman (Augustus). German conversation-tables, a new method for teaching german conversation in classes. With copious notes. 36 pp. 12°. *New York, Holt & Williams*, 1871.

Loen (Johann Michael von). Des herrn von Loen freie gedanken zur verbesserung der menschlichen gesellschaft. 3e aufl. 4 p. l. 568 pp. 12 l. 1 pl. 16°. *Frankfurt & Leipzig, J. F. Fleischer*, 1752.

Loftin (J. C.) Friendship, a poem. By "Ace Clubs." [*pseudon.*] 34 pp. 8°. *Montgomery (Ala.) Barrett & Brown*, [1871].

Log (The) book; or, nautical miscellany. [*anon.*] 2 p. l. 490 pp. 8°. *London, J. Robins & sons*, [*about* 1829].

Logan (James). Notes of a journey through Canada, the United States of America, and the West Indies. xii, 259 pp. 1 map. 12°. *Edinburgh, Fraser & co.* 1838.

Logan (Olive). The mimic world. And public exhibitions. Their history, their morals,

Logan (Olive)—continued.
and effects. 590 pp. 12 pl. 9 portraits. 8°. *Philadelphia, New-World publishing company,* 1871.

Logic, ontology, and the art of poetry; being the fourth and fifth volumes of The circle of the sciences. [*anon.*] xii, 473 pp. 12°. *London, T. Carnan & F. Newberry,* 1776.

Logier (Jean Bernard). A system of the science of music, and practical composition; incidentally comprising what is usually understood by the term thorough bass. xvi, 323 pp. 4°. *London, J. Green,* 1827. s.

Lomax (Judith). The notes of an american lyre. 70 pp. 16°. *Richmond,* [*Va.*] *S. Pleasants,* 1813.

Lombardia (Società agraria di). *See* **Italia** (L') agricola. *Also,* **Milan.**

Lombardini (Elia). Guida allo studio dell' idrologia fluviale e dell' idraulica practica. 219 pp. 8°. *Milano, tipog. & litog. degli ingegneri,* 1870. s.

——— Importanza degli studj sulla statistica de' fiumi con cenni intorno a quelli finora intrapresi ed esame degli studj idrologici fatti e da farsi sul Tevere. Memorie. 58 pp. 3 charts. fol. *Milano, tipografia degli ingegneri,* 1871. s.

London (The) anecdotes. [*anon.*] 6 v. in 2. 18°. *London, D. Bogue,* [1848].

CONTENTS.

v. 1. Anecdotes of the electric telegraph.
v. 2. Anecdotes of popular authors.
v. 3. Inventors and discoverers.
v. 4. Pictures and painters.
v. 5. Law and lawyers.
v. 6. Popular superstitions.

London (*England*). The universal director; or, the nobleman and gentleman's true guide to the masters and professors of the liberal and polite arts and sciences; and of the mechanic arts, manufactures, and trades, established in London and Westminster, and their environs. In three parts. [Also], a distinct list of the booksellers, distinguishing the particular branches of their trade. By mr. [Thomas] Mortimer. 3 parts in 1 v. 8°. *London, J. Coote,* 1763.

[*Note.*—The first classified London directory, or business directory].

——— Post office London directory, 1870. Comprising, amongst other information, official directory; street directory; commercial directory; trades' directory; law directory; court directory; parliamentary directory; postal directory; city directory; conveyance directory; banking directory; &c. 71st annual publication. 8°. *London, F. Kelly,* [1869].

——— Kelly's post-office guide to London in 1862, visitor's handbook to the metropolis, and companion to the directory. viii, 472 pp. 1 map. 12°. *London, E. R. Kelly,* [1872]. s.

London (The) commercial list, 1871–72. 13th and 14th years. By Estell & co. fol. *London,* [*Seyd & co.*] 1871.

London. (Company of stationers). The charter [1556] and grants [1603, 1684] of the company of stationers of the city of London, now in force, containing a plain and rational account of the freemen's rights and privileges. [In latin and english]. To which is added an appendix. xvi, 65, 28 pp. 1 table. 12°. *London, R. Nutt,* 1741.

London dialectical society. Report on spiritualism, of the committee of the London dialectical society, together with the evidence, oral and written, and a selection from the correspondence. xi, 412 pp. 8°. *London, Longmans,* 1871.

London (The) dissector, or guide to anatomy, for the use of students, [etc. *anon.*] From the 1st american ed. Revised and corrected by Edward J. Chaisty, m. d. 273 pp. 12°. *Baltimore, J. Murphy,* 1839.

London (The), Edinburgh, and Dublin philosophical magazine and journal of science. Conducted by sir Robert Kane, sir William Thomson, and William Francis. January to December, 1871. 4th series, v. 41–42. 8°. *London, Taylor & Francis,* 1871.

London (The) gazette. Published by authority. [Semi-weekly]. Jan. 3, to Dec. 29, 1871. 2 v. sm. fol. *London, Harrison & sons,* [1871].

London (The) hermit's tour to the York festival, in a series of letters to a friend: in which the origin of the White-horse, Abury, Stonehenge, Silsbury-hill, and also of the druids and ancient Britons, is attempted to be ascertained; and the whole concluded with some general hints respecting musical festivals. [*anon.*] viii, 181 pp. 12°. *York, A. Barclay,* 1826.

London illustrated news. *See* **Illustrated** London news.

London. (Institution of civil engineers). Catalogue of the library of the institution of civil engineers. Supplement to the 2d ed; containing the additions from Jan. 1, 1866, to Oct. 31, 1870. 160 pp. 8°. *London, W. Clowes & sons,* 1870.

London. (International exhibition, 1871). Pottery. *See* **Beckwith** (Arthur).

London. (Missionary society of). Sermons preached in London, at the formation of the missionary society, Sept. 1795. [With] memorials of the establishment of that society. xxxii, 184 pp. 8°. *London, T. Chapman*, 1795.
[HAZARD pamphlets, v. 96].

London. (Royal college of physicians). Pharmacopœia collegii regalis medicorum londinensis. 1809. xxxii, 156 pp. 13 l. 18°. *Londini, G. Woodfall*, 1809.

London. (Society for promoting christian knowledge). Readings in poetry: a selection from the best english poets, from Spenser to the present times; and specimens of several american poets of deserved reputation. [Also], a brief survey of the history of english poetry. Published under the direction of the committee of general literature and education. viii, 420 pp. 1 pl. 16°. *London, J. W. Parker*, 1833.
[Imperfect: pp. 39-42 wanting].

London. (Society for the rescue of young women and children). "The remedy worse than the disease:" a protest against legislative measures for the regulation (and tending to the encouragement) of prostitution, as exemplified in the provisions and working of the "Contagious diseases act, 1866." [*anon.*] 1 p. l. 57 pp. 8°. *London, W. Tegg*, [*about* 1867].

London (Statistical society of). Journal. v. 34. 1871. 8°. *London, E. Stanford*, 1871.

London times. *See* **Times** (The). [London daily].

Long (George). The decline of the roman republic. v. 4. xxxii, 449 pp. 8°. *London, Bell & Daldy*, 1872.

Long (Samuel P.) Art: its laws, and the reasons for them, collected, considered and arranged for general and educational purposes. xxxii, 248 pp. 8 pl. 8°. *Boston, Lee & Shepard*, 1871.

Longfellow (Henry Wadsworth). The belfry of Bruges and other poems. vii, 151 pp. 16°. *Cambridge, J. Owen*, 1846.

——— The divine tragedy. iv, 150 pp. 16°. *Boston, J. R. Osgood & co.* 1871.

——— The poetical works of H. W. Longfellow. Complete ed. [Illustrated]. xiv, 504 pp. 1 portrait. 8°. *Boston, J. R. Osgood & co.* 1872.

Longfellow (H. W.)—continued.

——— Three books of song. iv, 204 pp. 16°. *Boston, J. R. Osgood & co.* 1872.

CONTENTS.

Book 1. Tales of a wayside inn. The second day.
Book 2. Judas Maccabæus.
Book 3. A handful of translations.

——— Die goldene legende. Deutsch von Karl Keck. 1 p. l. 143 pp. 12°. *Leipzig, F. Wagner*, 1860.

Longinus (Dionysius Cassius). Dionysii Longini quæ supersunt græce et latine. Recensuit, notasque suas atque animadversiones adjecit Joannes Toupius. Accedunt emendationes Davidis Ruhnkenii. Ed. alt. 5 p. l. 42, 405 pp. 4 l. 8°. *Oxonii, e typographeo clarendoniano*, 1778.

——— The works of Longinus, on the sublime: or, a treatise concerning the sovreign perfection of writing. Translated from the greek. With some remarks on the english poets; 1712. 8°. [*London, editor*, 1787].
[*In* WELSTED (Leonard). Works, pp. 307-423].

——— The same. A new literal translation of Longinus on the sublime: illustrated with notes, original and select. By a graduate of Trinity college, Dublin. xii, 70 pp; 15 pp. 12°. *New-York, C. S. Francis*, 1833.

Long Island. Directory, 1871-72. *See* **Curtin** (D.)

Longking (*Rev.* Joseph). Notes on Galatians and Ephesians. *See* **Bible.** (*English*).

Longshore (J. S. *m. d.*) The principles and practice of nursing, or a guide to the inexperienced, [etc.]. 238 pp. 12°. *Philadelphia, Merrihew & Thompson*, 1842.

Longuerue (Louis Du Four de, *abbé de Sept-Fontaines*). Longueruana, ou recueil de pensées, de discours et de conversations, [suivie d'une chronologie des gouverneurs de Syrie pour les Romains, des pontifs, des Juifs, et des procureurs de Judée. 1e éd.] xxiii, 391 pp. 16°. *Berlin*, [*Paris*], 1754.

Longus. Pastoralium de Daphnide et Chloe libri iv. Graece et latine, [interprete J. B. C. d'Ansse Villoison]. xvi, 178 pp. 8°. *Biponti*, 1794.
[MITSCHERLICH (C. W.) Scriptores erotici graeci, v. 4].

Lonsdale (John Lowther, *viscount*). *See* **Lowther** (John).

Loomis (*Mrs.* D. W.) A memoir of Harriet Eliza Snow. 288 pp. 18°. *Boston, Massachusetts sabbath school society*, 1840.

Loomis (Elias). Elements of geometry, conic sections, and plane trigonometry. Revised edition. 388 pp. 12°. *New York, Harper & brothers*, 1871.

Loomis (George B.) First steps in music; a course of instruction prepared for the use of public schools. Third book. 144 pp. 16°. *New York, Ivison, Blakeman, Taylor & co.* 1871.

Loon (Gerard van). Hedendaagsche penningkunde, zynde eene verhandeling van den oorspronk van't geld, de opkomst en 't onderscheyd der gedenkpenningen; den aardt en de rekenwyze der legpenningen, de wyze van't syfferen der ouden, den oorspronk der syfferletteren, toverpenningen en noodmunten. 6 p. l. 390 pp. 13 l. fol. *Gravenhaage, C. van Loom*, 1732.

Loots (Cornelis). Nederlands verlossing gevierd op den 29en van Lentemaand 1814. 3 p. l. 48 pp. 1 pl. 8°. *Hage & Amsterdam, J. Allart & J. Ruys*, 1814.

Lopez (Diego). Declaracion magistral sobre las emblemas de Andres Alciato, con todas las historias antiguedades, moralidàd, y doctrina tocante a las buenas costumbres. 4 p. l. 648 pp. 8 l. sm. 4°. *Valencia, G. Villagrassa*, 1655.

Lopez (Eduardo). Beschrijvinge van 't koningkrijck Congo, met 't aenpalende landt Angola. *b. l.* 96 pp. 6 pl. in text. sm. 4°. *Amstelredam, J. Hartgers*, [1650].

Lopez (Gregorio). Lettera annva della provincia delle Filippine dell' anno 1608. Scritta al molto r. p. Clavdio Acqvaviva. 124 pp. 16°. *Roma, B. Zannetti*, 1611.

Lopez de Gomara (Francisco). *See* **Gomara**.

Lopez de Segura (Ruy). Il givoco de gli scacchi; nuouamente tradotto in lingua italiana, da m. Gio. Domenico Tarsia. 4 p. l. 215 pp. 4°. *Venetia, C. Arriuabene*, 1583.

Lorain (John). Hints to emigrants, or a comparative estimate of the advantages of Pennsylvania, and the Western territory, etc. 144 pp. 16°. *Philadelphia, Littell & Henry*, 1819.

Lorambert (*pseudon.*) Les merveilles du magnétisme suivi des aphorismes de Mesmer. Revus et corrigés d'après des documents récemment découverts par Johannès Trismégiste. [*pseudon.*] 1 p. l. 118 pp. 1 pl. 18°. *Paris, Passard*, [1857].

Lord (Benjamin, *d. d.*) Jubilee; an half-century discourse, in two parts; on occasion of the completion of fifty-years, since the author's ordination. Delivered at Norwich, Nov. 29th, 1767. 56 pp. 16°. *New-London, [Conn.] T. Green*, 1768.

Lord (Eleazar). The plenary inspiration of the holy scriptures. 312 pp. 12°. *New York, M. W. Dodd*, 1857.

Lord (Israel S. P. *m. d.*) On intermittent fever and other malarious diseases. vii, 17–341 pp. 8°. *New York, Boericke & Tafel*, 1871.

Lord (W. B.) *and* **Baines** (T.) Shifts and expedients of camp life, travel, and exploration. Eng. title, v, 831 pp. 15 pl. 8°. *London, H. Cox*, 1871.

Lord Bantam. A satire. *See* **Jenkins** (Edward).

Lord (The) mayor's visit to Oxford, in the month of July, 1826. By the chaplain to the mayoralty. [*anon.*] vi, 157 pp. 2 pl. 8°. *London, Longman [& co.]* 1826.

Lordat (Jacques). Réponses à des objections faites contre le principe de la dualité du dynamisme humain, lequel est une des bases de l'anthropologie médicale enseignée dans la faculté de médecine de Montpellier; précédées d'une introduction, [etc.] cccvii, 98 pp. 8°. *Paris, J. B. Baillière*, 1854.

Loring (Frederick Wadsworth). The Boston dip, and other verses. 63 pp. sq. 16°. *Boston, Loring*, [1871].

——— Two college friends. 161 pp. 16°. *Boston, A. K. Loring*, 1871.

Loritz (Heinrich). Henrici Glareani helvetii, de geographia liber vnvs, ab ipso avthore iam novissime recognitvs. 35 l. sm. 4°. *Friburgum Brisgoiæ, Ioannes Faber Emmevs*, 1539.

Lorraine (Charles Léopold Nicolas Sixte, *dit* Charles v. *duc* de). Political and military observations, remarks and maxims, of Charles v. late duke of Lorrain, general of the emperor's forces. From a manuscript left by him, and never printed before. [By Rupert Beck]. 8 p. l. 277 pp. 3 l. 1 portrait. 8°. *London, J. Jones*, 1699.

[*Note.*—Probably by Henri de Stratman].

Lorris (Guillaume de) *and* **Meun** *or* **Meung** (Jehan de, *dit Clopinel*). Le roman de la rose. Accompagné de plusieurs autres ouvrages, d'une préface historique, de notes & d'un glossaire, [par l'abbé Lenglet du Fresnoy]. 3 v. 16°. *Paris, Pissot*, 1735.

Lory (Gabriel *and* Gabriel *fils*). Voyage pittoresque aux glaciers de Chamouni. [*anon.*] 14 pp. 8 l. 7 pl. fol. *Paris, P. Didot l'aîné*, 1815.

Lossing (Benson J.) A history of England, political, military, and social, from the earliest times to the present. vii, 647 pp. 3 maps. 12°. *New York, G. P. Putnam & sons*, 1871.

Lost (The) key. By the author of "The little watercress sellers." [*anon.*] 252 pp. 1 pl. 18°. *Philadelphia, Presbyterian board of publication*, [1860].

Lost (The) money found; or, the voice of conscience. Translated from the french, by miss Julia Colman. [*anon.*] 123 pp. 2 pl. 18°. *New York, Carlton & Porter*, 1860.

Lottie's thought-book. [*anon.*] 118 pp. 1 pl. 18°. *Philadelphia, American sunday school union*, [1858].

Loud (Jeremy). Gabriel Vane: his fortune and his friends. 423 pp. 12°. *New York, Derby & Jackson*, 1856.

Loughlin (J. F.) Hymns and harmonies for catholic sunday schools and homes. 96 pp. obl. 18°. *Boston, P. Donahoe*, 1871.

Louie's last term at St. Mary's. [*anon.*] *See* **Harris** (*Mrs.* Sidney S.)

Louis (Alfred H.) England and Europe. A discussion of national policy. xii, 388 pp. 8°. *London, R. Bentley*, 1861.

Louis (Pierre Charles Alexandre). Researches on the effects of bloodletting in some inflammatory diseases, and on the influence of tartarized antimony and vesication in pneumonitis. Translated by C. G. Putnam, m. d. With preface and appendix by James Jackson, m. d. xii, 171 pp. 8°. *Boston, Hilliard, Gray & co.* 1836.

Louisa Ralston; or what can I do for the heathen? By the author of the Stanwood family, [etc. *anon.*] 122 pp. 16°. *Boston, Massachusetts sabbath school union*, 1831.

Louisiana (*State of*). *Board of health.* Annual report of the board of health, to the general assembly of Louisiana, December 31, 1871. 130, 8 pp. 2 maps. 8°. *New Orleans*, 1872.

——— *Superintendent of public education.* Annual report of the superintendent, Thomas W. Conway, for the year 1871. 8°. *New Orleans, The republican office*, 1872.

Louvet de Couvray (Jean Baptiste). Narrative of the dangers to which I have been exposed since the 31st of May, 1793. With historical memorandums. vii, 239 pp. 8°. *London, J. Johnson*, 1795.

Love (Christopher). Heavens glory, hells terror. Or, two treatises; the one, concerning the glory of the saints with Jesus Christ, as a spur to duty: the other, of the torments of the damned, as a preservative against security. 2 v. in 1. 3 p. l. 149 pp; 1 p. l. 120 pp. 4 l. 1 portrait. 4°. *London, J. Rothwell*, 1653.

Loved (The) and the lost. [On cemeteries. *anon.*] 4th ed. 226 pp. 12°. *New York, W. G. Cordray*, 1860.

Lovell (John E.) A key to introductory arithmetic; prepared for the pupils of the Lancastrian school, New Haven. Part first. 166 pp. 16°. *New Haven, S. Wadsworth*, 1827.

——— New school dialogues; or, dramatic selections, for the use of schools, academies, and families. New ed. x, 13–456 pp. 12°. *New York, Collins & brother*, [1871].

——— Rhetorical dialogues; or, dramatic selections, for the use of schools, academies, and families: designed to furnish exercises, either for reading, recitation, or exhibition. 514 pp. 12 pl. 12°. *New Haven*, 1839.

——— The United States speaker: a copious selection of exercises of elocution: consisting of prose, poetry, and dialogue. Stereotype ed. 504 pp. 3 pl. 12°. *Philadelphia, H. C. Peck & T. Bliss*, 1862.

——— The young pupil's second book: comprising a great variety of interesting lessons, the emphasis and inflections of the voice being appropriately marked, with a view to promote a correct and tasteful style of reading. 2d ed. 216 pp. 16°. *New Haven, S. Babcock*, 1838.

Lover (Samuel). Father Roach: a story founded on fact. 12°. [*New York*, 1871].
[*In* LE FANU (James Sheridan). Shamus O'Brien, pp. 15-24].

Loves (The) of Mirtil, son of Adonis; a pastoral. [From the french. *anon.*] Eng. title, viii, 140 pp. 5 pl. 8°. *London*, 1770.
[Imperfect: 1 pl. wanting].

Loves (The) of Othniel and Achsah. Translated from the chaldee. [*anon.*] 2 v. 2 p. l. lxiii, 207 pp; 1 p. l. 270 pp. 16°. *London, W. Tooke for J. Wilkie*, 1769.

Love's progress. 1840. *See* **Gilman** (Caroline).

Lowe (*Rev.* Thomas). An essay on mysteries. 1 p. l. 148 pp. 1 l. 8°. *Oldham, J. Hirst*, 1842.

Lowell (Anna C.) Poetry for home and school. [*anon.*] 360 pp. 16°. *Boston, S. G. Perkins*, 1843.

Lowell (James Russell). My study windows. 3 p. l. 433 pp. 12°. *Boston, J. R. Osgood & co.* 1871.

Lowell (*Mass.*) The Lowell directory, for the year 1872. No. xxvi. By Sampson, Davenport & co. 8°. *Lowell, J. Merrill & son,* 1872.

Lowly ways; or, the diary of a poor young lady. [*anon.*] 235 pp. 16°. *Philadelphia, Claxton, Remsen & Haffelfinger,* 1871.

Lowrey (James A.) Digest of fire insurance. 132 pp. 12°. *Philadelphia, M'Calla & Stavely,* 1871.

Lowrie (John Marshall, *d. d.*) Adam and his times. 291 pp. 12°. *Philadelphia, Presbyterian board of publication,* [1861].

Lowth (Robert, *d. d.*) A short introduction to english grammar: with critical notes. New ed. 131 pp. 16°. *Hartford, N. Patten,* 1783.

Lowther (John, *viscount Lonsdale*). Memoir of the reign of James ii. xxvii, 64 pp. 2 l. fac-sim. 4°. *York, T. Wilson & R. Spence,* 1808.

Loyson *or* **Loison** (Charles, *called father Hyacinthe*). Father Hyacinthe's appeal to the catholic bishops. 8°. [*New York, American tract society,* 1872].

[*In* BACON (Leonard Woolsey). An inside view of the vatican council, pp. 220–231].

——— The protest of father Hyacinthe. 8°. [*New York, American tract society,* 1872].

[*In* BACON (Leonard Woolsey). An inside view of the vatican council, pp. 57–60].

Lubbock (*Sir* John, *bart.*) The origin of civilisation and the primitive condition of man. Mental and social condition of savages. xvi, 380 pp. 5 pl. 8°. *London, Longman, Green & co.* 1870.

Lucanus (Ocellus). *See* **Ocellus** *lucanus.*

Lucas (Charles, *m. d.*) An essay on waters. In three parts. Treating. 1. Of simple waters. 2. Of cold, medicated waters. 3. Of natural baths. v. 1–2. xxxviii, 232 pp; xvi, 274 pp. 8°. *London, A. Millar,* 1756.

[v. 3 wanting to complete the work].

Luccock. *See* **Luckcock.**

Lucianus. Translations from Lucian. First printed in the year 1710. 8°. [*London, J. Knapton,* [*etc.*] 1727].

[*In* MOYLE (Walter). The whole works of Walter Moyle, esq. *London,* 1727].

CONTENTS.

Lucian of sacrifices, pp. 79–96.
Herodotus, or Aetion, pp. 97–103.
Dialogue with Hesiod, pp. 104–111.
Panegyrick upon Demosthenes, pp. 112–152.
Philopatris: or, the learner. Translated by dr. Drake, pp. 249–279.

Lucianus—continued.

——— Part of Lucian made english from the originall, in the yeare 1638. By Iasper Mayne. To which are adjoyned those other dialogues of Lucian as they were formerly translated by mr. Francis Hicks. 16 p. l. 398 pp. 1 l. fol. *Oxford, H. Hall for R. Davis,* 1664.

Lucilius *junior.* Ætna. A poem. Translated from the latin. [By Jabez Hughes]. 8°. [*London,* 1741].

[*In* HUGHES (J.) Claudian the poet, his elegant history of Rufinus, pp. 1–29].

Luck (R.) A miscellany of new poems, on several occasions. Containing also, The loves of Hero and Leander, translated from the greek of Musæus. [Also], poemata quædam latina. 1 p. l. xviii, 192, 48 pp. 8°. *London, E. Cave,* 1736.

Luckcock (James). Moral culture; attempted in a series of lectures, delivered to the pupils and teachers of the old and new meeting sunday-schools, in Birmingham; interspersed with a variety of illustrative anecdotes. To which is added a concise narrative of the origin, progress and permanent success of the institution, and the laws and regulations by which it is at present governed. 3 p. l. xii, 290 pp. 12°. *London, Baldwin, Cradock & Joy,* 1817.

Lucretius Carus (Titus). His six books of epicurean philosophy, done into english verse, with notes. [By Thomas Creech]. 3d ed. 22 p. l. 223, 60 pp. 3 l. 1 pl. 12°. *London, T. Sawbridge,* 1683.

——— The same. Lucretius on the nature of things. Translated into english verse by Charles Frederick Johnson, with introduction and notes. 333 pp. 12°. *New York, D. C. Lent & co.* 1872.

——— The same. Di Tito Lucrezio Caro della natura delle cose libri sei tradotti dal latino in italiano da Alessandro Marchetti. Dati nuovamente in luce da Francesco Gerbault. 2 v. Eng. title, 2 p. l. 244 pp. 2 pl; eng. title, 245–543 pp. 2 pl. 8°. *In Amsterdamo, a spese dell' editore To. So.* 1754.

Lucy Raymond; or, the children's watchword. By a lady of Ontario. [*anon.*] 320 pp. 4 pl. 16°. *New York, American tract society,* [1871].

Luders (Alexander). An essay on the character of Henry the fifth, when prince of Wales. 1 p. l. 150 pp. 1 pl. 8°. *London, T. Cadell & W. Davies,* 1813.

Ludlam (William). Mathematical essays. 2d ed. with additions. 1 p. l. 97 pp. 3 pl. 8°. *Cambridge,* [*Eng.*] *J. Archdeacon for J. & J. Merrill,* 1787.

Ludlow (Park). The red-shanty boys; or, pictures of New-England school life, thirty years ago. 334 pp. 3 pl. 16°. *Boston, H. A. Young & co.* [1871].

Lüken (D. H.) Der deutsche sprachschüler. Ein lehr- und uebungsbuch für den sprachrechtschreibe- und aufsatz-unterricht in unter- und mittel-klassen. 109 pp. 12°. *St. Louis* (*Mo.*) *C. Witter,* 1872.

Lull *or* **Lulli** (Raymond). Des philosophi Raymundi Lullii apertorium, von der wahren composition des steines der weisen in deutsch übergesetzet von J. T. 16°. [*Hamburg, J. Naumann & G. Wolff,* 1675].

[*In* ALCHYMISTISCH sieben-gestirn. 1675. pp. 25-56].

—— Elvcidarivm, geschrieben über sein testament und codicill, wie die recht zu verstehen. 16°. [*Hamburg, J. Naumann & G. Wolff,* 1675].

[*In* ALCHYMISTISCH sieben-gestirn. 1675. pp. 57-68.
Note.—There is some doubt whether these are genuine works of the philosopher of Majorca].

Lullin de Chateauvieux (Jacob Frédéric). Italy, its agriculture, &c. From the french of mons. Chateauvieux, being letters written by him in Italy, in the years 1812 & 1813. Translated by Edward Rigby. xv, 358 pp. 8°. *Norwich, R. Hunter,* 1819.

Lumby (J. Rawson, *editor*). Ratis raving, and other moral and religious pieces, in prose and verse. Edited from the Cambridge university ms. k. k. 1-5. xii, 139 pp. 8°. *London, Trübner & co.* 1870.

[EARLY english text society, no. 43].

Lundie (Mary Graham)? Memoirs of mrs. W. W. Duncan; being recollections of a daughter. By her mother. [*anon.*] 308 pp. 2 pl. 16°. *Edinburgh, W. Oliphant & son,* 1841.

Lundy (F. L.) Manual of the legislature. [New Jersey]. 1872. *See* **New Jersey.**

Lunn (Henry C.) Musings of a musician; a series of popular sketches, illustrative of musical matters and musical people. New ed. viii, 204 pp. 12°. *London, R. Cocks & co.* 1854.

Lunt (George). The age of gold, and other poems. 160 pp. 12°. *Boston, W. D. Ticknor,* 1843.

—— Poems. xviii, 25-160 pp. 12°. *New York, Gould & Newman,* 1839.

Lunt (William P.) The christian psalter: a collection of psalms and hymns for social and private worship. xxviii, 548 pp. 16°. *Boston, C. C. Little & J. Brown,* 1861.

Luola (*pseudon.*) A basket of chips for the little ones. By Luola. 237 pp. 1 pl. 18°. *Philadelphia, Presbyterian board of publication,* [1859].

Luscinius. *See* **Nachtgall.**

Lusignan (Étienne de). A genuine voyage to Smyrna and Constantinople, and a journey from thence overland to England; also, a minute detail of the antiquities, manners, customs, and present state of Jerusalem, with a revelation of the pilgrim's journey to the Holy Land; [with] a confutation of Volney's history of Ali Bey's revolt. 2d ed. 2 v. xlviii, 271 pp; 1 p. l. 260 pp. 8°. [*London*], *Bateman & son,* 1801.

Luther (Martin). Sämmtliche werke. 67 v. 12°. *Frankfurt am Main und Erlangen, Heyder & Zimmer,* 1828-70.

—— Chronica des ehrnwirdigen herrn d. Mart. Luth. Deudsch. [von I. Aurifaber]. Mit einem anhang der folgenden jaren, [etc.] Widerumb gedruckt. 122 l. 18°. *Witeberg, H. Lufft,* 1553.

—— Der psalter des königs und propheten Davids, verteutschet von d. Martin Luther; mit kurzen summarien oder inhalt jedes psalmen. 252 pp. 18°. *Philadelphia, C. Cist,* 1793.

—— Commentary on Galatians. *See* **Bible.** (*English*).

—— Dr. Martin Luther's church postil. Sermons on the epistles: for the different sundays and festivals in the year. Translated from the german, [and published in numbers]. Nos. 1-18, v. 1-3. 8°. *New Market* (*Va.*) *New Market Evangelical lutheran publishing co.* 1869[-72].

—— Enchiridion, or the smaller catechism of dr. Martin Luther, for curates and ministers, [and], the larger catechism. 8°. [*Newmarket,* [*Va.*] 1854].

[*In* EVANGELICAL lutheran church. The christian book of concord, pp. 409-547].

—— Lutheri catechismus, öfwersatt på american-virginiske språket. [By Johan Campanius, pastor in New-Sweden]. 8 p. l. 160 pp. 16°. *Stockholm, Burchard, af J. J. Genath,* 1696.

[Imperfect: engraved frontispiece wanting].

—— Luther on the sacraments; or the distinctive doctrines of the evang. lutheran church, respecting baptism and the Lord's

Luther (Martin)—continued.
supper; containing a sermon on baptism, a letter on anabaptism, and his larger confession on the Lord's supper. Translated from the german. xii, 423 pp. 12°. *Newmarket*, [*Va.*] *S. D. Henkel & brs.* 1853.

——— The smalcald articles, [1537]. Articles of christian doctrine, which were to be admitted by our adherents at the council, if a council had been assembled at Mantua, or at any other place, declaring what points he could or could not admit or abandon. 8°. [*Newmarket*, 1854].

[*In* EVANGELICAL lutheran church. The christian book of concord, pp. 361–408].

Lutheran church. *See* **Evangelical** lutheran church.

Lux orientalis. *See* **Glanvill** (Joseph).

Luxemburg. Exposé de la situation administrative de la province de Luxembourg. Session de 1840. 4 p. l. 114 pp. 3 tables. 8°. *Arlon, C. A. Bourgeois*, 1840.

Luxurious musings. [*anon.*] 1 p. l. iii, 102 pp. 8°. *London, C. Chapple*, 1817.

Luzerne (Frank). The lost city! drama of the fire fiend! or Chicago, as it was, and as it is! and its glorious future! a vivid and truthful picture of all of interest connected with the destruction of Chicago and the terrible fires of the great north-west. Edited by J. G. Wells. 316 pp. incl. 55 pl. 8°. *New York, Wells & co.* 1872.

Lyceum (The) arithmetic: in three parts. Each adapted to different ages and classes. By an experienced teacher. [*anon.*] 248 pp. sq. 16°. *Boston, W. Peirce*, 1835.

——— The same. [*anon.*] 248 pp. 16°. *Boston, Perkins & Marvin*, 1836.

Lydgate (John). *See* **Lidgate.**

Lyford (Thomas J.) *and* **Boyce** (Allen P.) The art of lettering and sign painter's manual. 2d ed. 2 p. l. 47 l. obl. fol. *Boston, A. Williams & co.* 1871.

Lynch (Thomas). The printer's manual. A practical guide for compositors and pressmen. To which is appended the manner of putting together and using printing-machines. 262 pp. 12°. *Cincinnati, Cincinnati type-foundry*, 1859.

Lynde (Humfrey, *knight*). Via tuta, the safe-way: leading all christians, to the true, ancient, and catholike faith, now professed in the church of England. From the 4th ed. 1630. Via devia, the by-way: misleading the weake and unstable, into dangerous paths of error, and pretended catholike church. 3 p. l. 570 pp. 8°. *London, J. J. Stockdale*, 1819.

Lynde (John). A key to english grammar. 108 pp. 18°. *Woodstock*, [*Vt.*] *D. Watson*, 1821.

Lyndesay (*Sir* David). Minor poems. [With a sketch of scottish poetry up to the time of Lyndesay, by John Nichol]. Edited by J. A. H. Murray. liv, pp. 549–590, 13 pp. 8°. *London, N. Trübner & co.* 1871.

[EARLY english text society, no. 47. Works, part 5].

Lyndsay (David). Dramas of the ancient world. vii, 278 pp. 8°. *Edinburgh, W. Blackwood*, 1822.

Lynn (Ethel). General Frankie: a story for little folks. 1 p. l. 149 pp. 3 pl. 16°. *New York, A. D. F. Randolph*, 1863.

Lynn (*Massachusetts*). The Lynn directory, 1871: and a business directory of Swampscott. No. 12. By Sampson, Davenport & co. 440 pp. 1 map. 8°. *Lynn, W. T. Webster*, 1871.

Lyon (Charles H.) Initia latina, or the rudiments of the latin tongue, illustrated by progressive exercises. 132 pp. 12°. *New-York, Harper & brothers*, 1834.

Lyon (I. W.) The teeth and how to take care of them. 34 pp. 1 l. 18°. *New York, Bradstreet press*, 1870.

Lyon (*Capt.* W. F.) Brigadier-general Thomas Francis Meagher: his political and military career; with selection from his speeches and writings. 186 pp. 12°. *Glasgow, Cameron & Ferguson*, [1870].

——— The hollow globe; or the world's agitator and reconciler. *See* **Sherman** (M. L.) *and* **Lyon.**

Lyons (James Gilborne, *ll. d.*) Christian songs, translations and other poems. 157 pp. 12°. *Philadelphia, Smith, English & co.* 1861.

Lyons (Joseph A.) The american elocutionist and dramatic reader. With an introduction on elocution and vocal culture, by the rev. M. B. Brown. 427 pp. 4 pl. 1 portrait. 12°. *Philadelphia, E. H. Butler & co.* 1872.

Lysias. Oratio funebris. Oratio in Eratosthenem. 8°. *Oxonii*, 1835.

[*In* HISTORIA græca, ed. 2a, pp. 309–341].

Lyttelton (George, *lord Lyttelton*). Letters from a Persian in England, to his friend at Ispahan. [*anon.*] 5th ed. corrected and altered by the author. 324 pp. 16°. *London, J. Millan*, 1744.

Lyttelton (George)—continued.

——— Love and hope. Love and jealousy. Eclogues. sm. 4°. *London, J. Hamilton & co.* 1794.

[*In* HAMILTON (John). Angelica's ladies library, pp. 319–328].

Lytton (Edward George Earle Lytton Bulwer-, *baron Lytton*). Les pélerins du Rhin. Traduit par m. Defauconpret. 2 v. 275 pp. 1 l; 277 pp. 18°. *Bruxelles, J. P. Meline*, 1834.

Lytton (Robert Bulwer). Julian Fane. A memoir. 2d ed. vii, 179 pp. 1 portrait. 12°. *London, J. Murray*, 1872.

M * * *. Description du pachalik de Bagdad. [*anon.*] *See* **Rousseau** (J. B. L. J.)

M. (A. B.) Guia de la ciudad de Nueva York. [*anon.*] 4 p. l. 236 pp. 48 pl. 1 map. 16°. *Nueva York, N. Ponce de Leon*, 1872.

M. (A. L.) Excerpta of wit; or, railway companion: being a collection of laconic sentences, from a great variety of sources. [*anon.*] iv, 374 pp. 18°. *London, P. Richardson*, 1839.

M. (A. S.) Cedar brook stories. *See* **Moffatt** (A. S.)

M. (E.) Aenmerkenswaardige en zeldzame west-indische zeeen landreizen, door de caribische eylanden, Nieuw-Nederland, Virginien, en de spaansche West-Indien: behelsende een seer naukeurige beschrijving der genoemde landen[enz.]: mitsgaders de grouwelijke wreedheden der Spajaarden aan de Indianen, enz. en wreedheyd der amerikaanse zee rovers tegens de Spanjaarden. Door een voornaam engels heer E. M. en andere, opmerkelijk beschreven. [*anon.*] 96 pp. sm. 4°. *Amsterdam, weduewe van G. de Groot*, 1705.

M. (E. A.) The lost pearl. By E. A. M. [*anon.*] 120 pp. 1 pl. 18°. *New York, A. D. F. Randolph & co.* [1871].

M. (J.) A winter with Robert Burns, being annals of his patrons and associates in Edinburgh during the year 1786–7, and details of his inauguration as poet-laureate of the Can: Kil: [*anon.*] 175 pp. 1 pl. 16°. *Edinburgh, P. Browne*, 1846.

M. (J. M.) Lord Nial, a romance, in four cantos. The wizzard's grave, The origin of Bacchus, etc. By J. M. M. [*anon.*] 3 p. l. 276 pp. 12°. *New York, J. Doyle*, 1834.

M. (L. M.) Olie; or, the old west room. By L. M. M. [*anon.*] 525 pp. 12°. *New York, Mason brothers*, 1855.

M. (M. L.) Grace Morton. *See* **Meaney** (Mary L.)

M. (P.) The vanity, mischief and danger of continuing ceremonies in the worship of God. Humbly proposed to the present convocation. [*anon.*] 2 p. l. 44 pp. sm. 4°. *London, R. Baldwin*, 1690.

M. (P. D.) *See* **Marées** (Pierre de).

M. (R.) A general survey of that part of St. Christophers, which formerly belonged to France, yielded up to Great Britain by the treaty of Utrecht. By R. M. *s. b.* [*anon.*] 48 pp. 8°. *London, J. Roberts*, 1722.

M. (T.) A mad vvorld my masters. 1640. *See* **Middleton** (Thomas).

Maack (*Dr.* G. A.) Die bis jetzt bekannten fossilen schildkröten und die im oberen Jura bei Kelheim (Bayern) und Hannover neu aufgefundenen ältesten arten derselben. 2 p. l. 144 pp. 1 l. 8 pl. 4°. *Cassel, T. Fischer*, 1869.

Mabel Lee. A novel. *See* **Fisher** (Frances C.)

M'Allister (*Rev.* D.) The nature and ground of political dissent. 12°. [*Pittsburgh*, 1872].

[*In* REFORMED presbyterian church in North America. Memorial volume, pp. 160–188].

Macarius *ægyptius*. Institutes of christian perfection. Translated from the greek, by Granville Penn. xlvii, 230 pp. 16°. *London, J. Murray*, 1816.

——— Primitive morality: or, the spiritual homilies of st. Macarius the egyptian. Done out of greek into english, with several considerable emendations, and some enlargements from a bodleian manuscript never before printed. By a presbyter of the church of England. 7 p. l. 482 pp. 8°. *London, W. Taylor*, 1721.

M'Arthur (John). Financial and political facts of the eighteenth century; with comparative estimates of the revenue, expenditure, debts, manufactures, and commerce of Great Britain. 3d ed. with an appendix of useful and interesting documents. The whole revised, corrected, and considerably enlarged. xxiv, 337 pp. 10 l. 8°. *London, J. Wright*, 1801.

Macaulay (Thomas Babington). Lays of ancient Rome and other poems. 271 pp. 10 pl. 1 portrait. sq. 16°. *New York, J. Miller*, 1872.

Macauley (*Rev.* Angus). The history and antiquities of Claybrook, in the county of Leicester; including the hamlets of Bittesby, Ul-

Macauley (*Rev.* Angus)—continued. lesthorpe, Wibtoft and Little Wigston. 137 pp. 1 pl. 8°. *London, author,* 1791.
[HAZARD pamphlets, v. 79]

McCabe (James D. *jr.*) The great republic. A descriptive, statistical, and historical view of the states and territories of the american union. 1118 pp. 28 pl. 8°. *Philadelphia, W. B. Evans & co.* [1871].

——— History of the war between Germany and France. With biographical sketches of the principal personages engaged in the contest. 740 pp. 18 pl. 6 maps. 8°. [*Philadelphia*], *National publishing company,* [1871].

——— Lights and shadows of New York life; or, the sights and sensations of the great city. A work descriptive of the city of New York in all its various phases. Illustrated. 1 p. l. 13-850 pp. 7 pl. 8°. *Philadelphia, National publishing co.* [1872].

M'Cabe (John Collins). Scraps. [A collection of fugitive pieces in prose and poetry]. 192 pp. 12°. *Richmond, J. C. Walker,* 1835.

M'Cabe (*Rev.* L. D.) Light on the pathway of holiness. 114 pp. 16°. *New York, Carlton & Lanahan,* 1871.

McCaffery (Michael J. A.) The siege of Spoleto; a camp-tale of Arlington heights. 90 pp. 3 l. 12°. *New York, P. O'Shea,* 1864.

McCalla (*Rev.* William L.) Minutes of a discussion on the question "Is the punishment of the wicked absolutely eternal?" *See* **Kneeland** (*Rev.* Abner) *and* **McCalla.**

——— A public discussion on the doctrine of the trinity. *See* **Plummer** (*Elder* Frederick) *and* **McCalla.**

Macallan (Emma). Tales for the whitsun season. 129 pp. 18°. *New York, General protestant episcopal sunday school union & church book society,* 1863.

M'Cann (*Rev.* George). An enquiry into the moral regeneration of human nature; with observations on the relations it bears to the several duties of a christian life. 1 p. l. 192 pp. 8°. *Edinburgh, author,* 1828.

M'Carthy (Justin). Lady Judith. A tale of two continents. 306 pp. 4 pl. 8°. *New York, Sheldon & co.* [1871].

——— The settlement of the Alabama question. The banquet given at New York to her britannic majesty's high commissioners, by mr. Cyrus W. Field. A report, with a short introduction. 72 pp. 2 phot. 8°. *London, Tinsley brothers,* 1871.

M'Cartney (Washington). The principles of the differential and integral calculus; and their application to geometry. xx, 340 pp. 8°. *Philadelphia, E. C. Biddle,* 1844.

Maccio (Sebastiano). De historia libri tres: in qvibvs non solvm cavssa materialis, formalis, efficiens, & finalis scriptionis historicæ apprimè declaratur, sed etiam singulæ eius partes diligenter examinantur, & assignantur cuiusque præcepta, & vera, ac propria traditur historiæ scribendæ ratio. 8 p. l. 186 pp. 3 l. 4°. *Venetiis, apud A. & B. Dei, fratres,* 1613.

M'Chord (James). The body of Christ: a series of essays on the scriptural doctrine of federal representation. Corrected, enlarged and concluded, from the Evangelical record and western review. 264 pp. 12°. *Lexington (Ky.) T. T. Skillman,* 1814.

M'Clellan (George Brinton). European cavalry, including details of the organization of the cavalry service among the principal nations of Europe. 214 pp. 12°. *Philadelphia, J. B. Lippincott & co.* 1861.

M'Clintock (John, *d. d.*) Living words: or, unwritten sermons, reported phonographically. With a preface by bishop Janes. 2d ed. 335 pp. 12°. *New York, Carlton & Lanahan,* 1871.

——— *and* **Strong** (James, *s. t. d.*) Cyclopædia of biblical, theological, and ecclesiastical literature. v. 4. H, I, J. vii, 1122 pp. 8°. *New York, Harper & brothers,* 1872.

McClure (Alexander W. *d. d.*) The translators revived: a biographical memoir of the authors of the english version of the holy bible. 250 pp. 12°. *New York, Board of publication of the reformed protestant dutch church,* 1855.

M'Clure (*Rev.* David, *of East Windsor, Conn.*) Sermons on the moral law. 356, viii pp. 8°. *Hartford, Beach & Jones,* 1795.

M'Clure (David, *of Philadelphia*). A brief exposition of the philosophic principles upon which the system of education for the Girard college for orphans is founded. [*anon.*] 1 p. l. 363 pp. 8°. *Philadelphia, I. Ashmead & co.* 1838.
[*With his* System of education for Girard college].

——— A system of education for the Girard college for orphans. Respectfully submitted to the board of trustees, by a native of Philadelphia. [*anon.*] 16, 48 pp. 1 tab. 8°. *Philadelphia,* 1838.

McConaughy (*Mrs.* J. E.) One hundred gold dollars. 255 pp. 3 col. pl. 18°. *Philadelphia, J. C. Garrigues & co.* 1866.

McCook (Henry C.) The teacher's commentary on the gospel narrative of the last year of our Lord's ministry. *See* **Bible.** (*English*).

M'Corkle (Samuel Eusebius, *d. d.*) True greatness, a sermon on the death of gen. George Washington; the substance of which was delivered at Thyatira, Jan. 12th; and afterwards with some additions in Salisbury, Feb. 11, 1800. 27, 2 pp. 8°. *Lincolntown* (*N. C.*) *J. M. Slump*, 1800.
[WOLCOTT pamphlets, v. 60].

McCosh (James, *d. d.*) Christianity and positivism: a series of lectures to the times on natural theology and apologetics. vii, 369 pp. 12°. *New York, R. Carter & brothers*, 1871.

McCready (Francis). The art of english grammar, in verse, by question and answer; with notes, and examples of parsing to illustrate the rules. xxiii, 19–249 pp. 12°. *Philadelphia, author*, 1820.

McCrie (Thomas). The life of John Knox, the scottish reformer. Abridged from McCrie's Life of Knox. 224 pp. 18°. *Philadelphia, Presbyterian board of publication*, [1839].

McCulloch (James H. *jr. m. d.*) An impartial exposition of the evidences and doctrines of the christian religion. 346 pp. 8°. *Baltimore, Armstrong & Berry*, 1836.

McCulloch (John Ramsay). A statistical account of the british empire: exhibiting its extent, physical capacities, population, industry, and civil and religious institutions. 2 v. xii, 630 pp; viii, 692 pp. 8°. *London, C. Knight & co.* 1837.
[*Note.*—Published "Under the superintendence of the society for the diffusion of useful knowledge"].

Macdill (*Rev.* David). The bible a miracle; or the word of God its own witness: the supernatural inspiration of the scriptures shown from their literary, theological, moral, and political excellence. xi, 511 pp. 12°. *Philadelphia, W. S. Rentoul*, 1872.

Macdonald (Alexander). The poetical works of Alexander Macdonald, the celebrated jacobite poet; now first collected, with a short account of the author. 4; 180 pp. 18°. *Glasgow, G. & J. Cameron*, 1851.

MacDonald (George). David Elginbrod. 459 pp. 1 portrait. 12°. *Boston, Loring*, [1872].

MacDonald (George)—continued.
——— Wilfrid Cumbermede, an autobiographical story. x, 498 pp. 14 pl. 12°. *New York, C. Scribner & co.* 1872.

Macdonald (*Rev.* James). Memoirs of the rev. Joseph Benson. viii, 541 pp. 8°. *London, T. Blanchard*, [*etc.*] 1822.

McDonald (J. L.) Hidden treasures, or fisheries around the north-west coast. 110 pp. 1 l. 8°. *Gloucester* (*Mass.*) *Procter brothers*, 1871.

MacDonald (James M.) The coming of the Lord; a key to the book of revelation. With an appendix. viii, 210 pp. 12°. *New York, Baker & Scribner*, 1846.

McDonald (*Mrs.* Mary Noel, *later mrs.* Meigs). Poems. 208 pp. 8°. *New-York*, 1844.

Macdonald (Norman). Maxims and moral reflections. 214 pp. 12°. *New York, Collins & Hannay*, 1827.

McDonald (*Rev.* W.) The american hymn and tune book. *See* **Stevens** (G. S. *m. d.*) *and* **McDonald.**

McDonald (W. J.) Constitution of the United States of America, with the amendments thereto: to which are prefixed the declaration of independence, the articles of confederation, and the ordinance of 1787; [also], the rules of the senate, the joint rules of the two houses, and Jefferson's manual of parliamentary practice; with some general laws of useful reference in legislation. Printed for the use of the senate. 2 p. l. 405 pp. 8°. *Washington, government printing office*, 1871.

Macdonell (John). A survey of political economy. viii, 432 pp. 16°. *Edinburgh, Edmonston & Douglas*, 1871.

McDowell (John, *d. d.*) Bible class manual; or, a system of theology, in the order of the Westminster shorter catechism, adapted to bible classes. v. 1. 382 pp. 12°. *Philadelphia, W. S. Martien*, 1838.

M'Dowell (William A. *m. d.*) A demonstration of the curability of pulmonary consumption in all its stages. Comprising an inquiry into the nature, causes, symptoms, treatment and prevention of tuberculous diseases in general. 269 pp. 8°. *Louisville* (*Ky.*) 1843.

McElhinney (John J. *d. d.*) The doctrine of the church: a historical monograph. With a full bibliography of the subject. 464 pp. 8°. *Philadelphia, Claxton, Remsen & Haffelfinger*, 1871.

McElrath (Thomas). A dictionary of words and phrases used in commerce: with explanatory and practical remarks. 680 pp. 8°. *New York, Taintor brothers*, [1871].

Macfaite (Ebenezer, *m. d.*) Remarks on the life and writings of Plato. With answers to the principal objections against him; and a general view of his dialogues. [*anon.*] 1 p. l. 320 pp. 8°. *Edinburgh, A. Millar*, 1760.

MacFarlane (Charles). The french revolution. 4 v. in 2. 12°. *London, G. Routledge & co.* 1852.

——— Our indian empire: its history and present state, from the earliest settlement of the British in Hindostan, to 1846. 2 v. viii, 329 pp. 22 pl. 1 map; viii, 443 pp. 16 pl. 12°. *London, G. Routledge & co.* 1848.

M'Farlane (*Rev.* John). Life and correspondence of the late rev. Henry Belfrage, d. d. *See* **M'Kerrow** (*Rev.* John) *and* **M'Farlane.**

Macfarlane (John, *ll. d.*) Tribute to dr. Wardlaw. 16°. [*London, A. Fullarton & co.* 1854].

[*In* DISCOURSES and services on occasion of the death of the late rev. Ralph Wardlaw, d. d. 1854. pp. 137-147].

M'Ferrin (John B. *d. d.*) History of methodism in Tennessee. v. 2. From the year 1804 to the year 1818. 525 pp. 2 portraits. 12°. *Nashville (Tenn.) Southern methodist publishing house*, 1871.

McGarvey (*Rev.* J. W.) Commentary on acts. *See* **Bible.** (*English*).

McGreggor (Malcolm, *pseudon.*) *See* **Mason** (*Rev.* William).

McGuffey (William H.) The eclectic third reader; containing selections in prose and poetry, from the best american and english writers. 166 pp. 12°. *Cincinnati, Truman & Smith*, 1837.

——— The eclectic fourth reader; containing elegant extracts in prose and poetry, from the best american and english writers, (etc.) xii, 279 pp. 4 l. 12°. *Cincinnati, Truman & Smith*, 1837.

——— McGuffey's new eclectic spelling-book: embracing a progressive course of instruction in english orthography and orthoepy; including dictation exercises. 144 pp. 16°. *Cincinnati, Sargent, Wilson & Hinkle*, 1865.

——— McGuffey's new second eclectic reader; for young learners. 160 pp. 16°. *Cincinnati, W. B. Smith & co.* [1857].

McGuffey (W. H.)—continued.

——— McGuffey's new third eclectic reader for young learners. 240 pp. 16°. *Cincinnati, W. B. Smith & co.* [1857].

——— McGuffey's new fourth eclectic reader: instructive lessons for the young. 216 pp. 16°. *Cincinnati, W. B. Smith and co.* [1857].

——— McGuffey's new fifth eclectic reader: selected and original exercises for schools. 336 pp. 16°. *Cincinnati, W. B. Smith & co.* [1857].

——— McGuffey's new sixth eclectic reader: exercises in rhetorical reading, with introductory rules and examples. 448 pp. 12°. *Cincinnati, W. B. Smith & co.* [1857].

McHarg (Charles K.) Life of prince Talleyrand, with extracts from his speeches and writings. xi, 382 pp. 1 portrait. 12°. *New York, C. Scribner*, 1857.

MacHenry (George). Time and eternity. A poem. 275 pp. 12°. *San Francisco, A. L. Bancroft*, 1871.

M'Ilvaine (Charles Pettit, *bishop of Ohio*). The evidences of christianity: in their external division, exhibited in a course of lectures, delivered in Clinton hall, in the winter of 1831-2. 565 pp. 8°. *New York, G. & C. & H. Carvill*, 1832.

——— Righteousness by faith; or the nature and means of our justification before God; illustrated by a comparison of the doctrine of the Oxford tracts with that of the romish and anglican churches. New ed. of "Oxford divinity." 450 pp. 8°. *Philadelphia, Prot. episcopal book society*, 1862.

——— Select family and parish sermons. A series of evangelical discourses, selected for the use of families, and destitute congregations. With a preliminary address. v. 1. xiii, 590 pp. 8°. *Columbus (O.) I. N. Whiting*, 1838.

——— The temple of God; or the holy catholic church and communion of saints, in its nature, structure, and unity. 142 pp. 12°. *Philadelphia, Protestant episcopal book society*, 1860.

McIntosh (Maria J.) Alice Montrose. A tale. 2d ed. 3 v. 12°. *London, R. Bentley*, 1855.

——— Conquest and self-conquest; or, which makes the hero? [*anon.*] 216 pp. 18°. *New York, Harper & brothers*, 1843.

——— The cousins: a tale of early life. By the author of "Conquest and self-conquest," [etc. *anon.*] 205 pp. 18°. *New York, Harper & brothers*, 1845.

McIntosh (Maria J.)—continued.

——— Woman an enigma; or, life and its revealings. By the author of "Conquest and self-conquest," &c. [*anon.*] 238 pp. 18°. *New York, Harper & brothers*, 1843.

——— Woman in America: her work and her reward. 155 pp. 12°. *New York, D. Appleton & co.* 1850.

——— A year with Maggie and Emma; a true story. 137 pp. 4 pl. 16°. *New York, D. Appleton & co.* 1861.

McIntosh (R. M.) The amaranth; a book of songs, &c. *See* **Haygood** (Atticus G.) *and* **McIntosh.**

Mack (Ebenezer). The life of Gilbert Motier de Lafayette, from numerous and authentic sources. 1 p. l. 371 pp. 1 portrait. 12°. *Ithaca (N. Y.) Mack, Andrus & Woodruff*, 1841.

Mackarness (Matilda Planché). [Susie Sunbeam's series]. 10 v. sq. 24°. *New-York, J. Q. Preble*, [1856].

CONTENTS.

Etiquette for little folks. 96 pp.
Little poems for little readers. 96 pp.
The blackberries, and other stories. 96 pp.
Susie and the butterflies; and other stories. 96 pp.
Janet Ray. 96 pp.
The palace of beauty, with other stories. 96 pp.
Stories about insects. 96 pp.
Stories of animals. 96 pp.
Stories about birds. 96 pp.
Fairy tales for children. 96 pp.

Mackay (Charles). Legends of the isles and highland gatherings. 2d ed. 3 p. l. 120 pp. 16°. *London, G. Routledge & co.* 1857.

Mackay (John). Life of lieut. general Hugh Mackay of Scoury, commander in chief of the forces in Scotland, 1689 and 1690, and a privy-counsellor in Scotland. xii, 213 pp. 1 l. 1 portrait. 4°. *Edinburgh, Laing & Forbes*, 1836.

Mackay (Robert). Songs and poems in the gaelic language. By Rob. Donn. With a memoir of the author, and observations on his character and poetry. By Robert Mackay. lxxii, 360 pp. 8°. *Inverness, K. Douglas*, 1829.

McKean (E. R.) Manual accompanying Prime & McKean's combination guaging instrument. 1871. *See* **Prime** (Eli S.) *and* **McKean.**

McKeever (Harriet B.) Aunt Harriet's tales about little words. 288 pp. 3 pl. 18°. *Philadelphia, Presbyterian board of publication*, [1863].

——— The flounced robe, and what it cost. 184 pp. 1 pl. 16°. *Philadelphia, Lindsay & Blakiston*, 1859.

McKeever (Harriet B.)—continued

——— Jessie Morrison, or the mission flowers. 156 pp. 2 pl. 18°. *Philadelphia, Presbyterian board of publication*, [1859].

——— Little Mary and the fairy. 10 l. 40 pp. (incl. 11 col. pl.) sm. 4°. *Philadelphia, Claxton, Remsen & Haffelfinger*, 1871.

——— Maude and Miriam; or, the fair crusader. 337 pp. 12°. *Philadelphia, Claxton, Remsen & Haffelfinger*, 1871.

——— Woodcliff. 464 pp. 12°. *Philadelphia, Lindsay & Blakiston*, 1865.

Mackellar (Patrick, *chief engineer*). A correct journal of the landing his majesty's forces on Cuba; and of the siege and surrender of Havannah, August 13, 1762. Published by authority. 2d ed. 19 pp. 8°. *Boston, Green & Russell*, 1762.

Mackellar (Thomas). Droppings from the heart; or, occasional poems. 144 pp. 16°. *Philadelphia, Sorin & Ball*, 1844.

Mackellar, Smiths *and* **Jordan.** The printer's handy book of specimens, exhibiting the choicest productions of every description made at the Johnson type foundry, comprising every article essential for a book, newspaper or job printing office. 433 l. 1 pl. 4°. *Philadelphia, Mackellar, Smiths & Jordan*, [1871].

Mackenzie (*Mrs.* Adelheid Shelton). Aureola; or, the black sheep. A story of german social life. 263 pp. 12°. *Philadelphia, Claxton, Remsen & Haffelfinger*, 1871.

Mackenzie (*Sir* George). Essays upon several moral subjects, viz. The religious stoic. Solitude preferr'd to public employment. Moral gallantry. The moral history of frugality: with its opposite vices. An essay on reason. To which is prefix'd, some account of his life and writings. With an index to the whole. 2 p. l. xxviii, 442, viii pp. 8°. *London, D. Brown*, 1713.

——— A moral essay, preferring solitude to publick employment, and all it's appanages; such as fame, command, riches, pleasures, conversation, etc. 7 p. l. 147 pp. 16°. *London, W. W.* 1685.

——— Moral gallantry: a discourse, addressed to the nobility and gentry of Great Britain. With other essays, intimately connected with the subject. xvi, 159 pp. 8°. *London, T. Hamilton, etc.* 1821.

Mackenzie (James, *m. d.*) The history of health, and the art of preserving it: or, an account of all that has been recommended by

Mackenzie (James, *m. d.*)—continued. physicians and philosophers, towards the preservation of health, from the most remote antiquity to this time. To which is subjoined, a succinct review of the principal rules relating to this subject. 2d ed. xii, 436 pp. 8°. *Edinburgh, W. Gordon,* 1759.

Mackenzie (John). Sar-obair nam bard gaelach: or, the beauties of gaelic poetry, and lives of the highland bards; with historical and critical notes, and a comprehensive glossary of provincial words. With an historical introduction containing an account of the manners, habits, &c. of the ancient Caledonians, by James Logan. lxv, 376 pp. 2 pl. 8°. *Glasgow, Macgregor, Polson, & co.* 1841.

Mackenzie (Robert Shelton, *ll.d.*) A critical review of lyric poets. 4°. [*New York,* 1872].

[*In* MOORE (Thomas). Literature, art and song, pp. 469–493].

——— Life of Thomas Moore. 4°. [*New York,* 1872].

[*In* MOORE (Thomas). Literature, art and song, pp. 7–20].

——— Sir Walter Scott: the story of his life. xii, 488 pp. 4 portraits. 12°. *Boston, J. R. Osgood & co.* 1871.

Mackerel Will. By the author of "Gilbert Gresham," [etc. *anon.*] 190 pp. 2 pl. 18°. *Philadelphia, Presbyterian board of publication,* [1861].

M'Kerrow (*Rev.* John) *and* **M'Farlane** (*Rev.* John). Life and correspondence of the late rev. Henry Belfrage, d. d. xii, 360 pp. 1 portrait. 8°. *Edinburgh, W. Oliphant & son,* 1837.

Mackey (Albert Gallatin, *m. d.*) The book of the chapter; or monitorial instructions, in the degrees of mark, past and most excellent master, and the holy royal arch. 259 pp. 12°. *New York, R. Macoy,* 1858.

——— A lexicon of free masonry: containing a definition of all its communicable terms, notices of its history, traditions, and antiquities, and an account of all the rites and mysteries of the ancient world. 14th ed. 526 pp. 1 portrait. 8°. *Philadelphia, Moss & co.* 1872.

McKinney (*Rev.* A. L.) Positive theology; or, my reasons for being a member of the christian church. 242 pp. 12°. *Cincinnati, O. Applegate & co.* 1861.

M'Kinney (Mordecai). The United States constitutional manual; being a comprehensive compendium of the system of government of the country; in the form of questions and answers. xv, 304 pp. 8°. *Harrisburg, Hickok & Cantine,* 1845.

Mackintosh (Charles H.) The doomed city! Chicago during an appalling ordeal! The fire demon's carnival. The conflagrations in the west, south and north divisions. Prepared and written by a journalist. [*anon.*] 54 pp. 1 map. 8°. *Detroit, Michigan news co.* 1871.

Mackintosh (John, *m. d.*) Principles of pathology, and practice of physic. From the last London edition, with notes and additions, by Samuel George Morton, m. d. 2 v. viii, 462 pp; 1 p. l. 509 pp. 8°. *Philadelphia, Key & Biddle,* 1836.

Maclagan (Alexander). Ragged school rhymes. 120 pp. 1 pl. 12°. *Edinburgh, Johnstone & Hunter,* 1851.

McLain (Mary Webster). Daisy Ward's work. 2 p. l. 242 pp. 1 pl. 16°. *Boston, Loring,* [1871].

——— The Italian girl; or, the victory that overcometh the world. By the author of "Broken idols." [*anon.*] 180 pp. 3 pl. 18°. *Philadelphia, Presbyterian publication committee,* [1869].

McLaughlin (Edward A.) The coral gift; or, the lovers of the deep. In four cantos. 240 pp. 4 pl. 16°. *New York, J. C. Riker,* [1850].

MacLaurin (John, *lord Dreghorn*). The works of the late John MacLaurin. 2 v. 4 p. l. xxii, 189 pp; 4 p. l. 391 pp. 1 l. 8°. *Edinburgh, editor,* 1798.

Macleay (K. *m. d.*) Historical memoirs of Rob Roy and the clan Macgregor. With an introductory sketch of the Highlands, prior to the year 1745. 303 pp. 8°. *Philadelphia, D. Hogan,* 1819.

Maclellan (Rufus Charles). The three class mates; a moral tale illustrating the importance of good early instructions. 106 pp. 18°. *Baltimore, J. D. Toy,* 1855.

McLeod (*Mrs.* Georgie A. Hulse). Sea drifts. 264 pp. 6 pl. 12°. *New York, R. Carter & brothers,* 1864.

Macleod (Norman, *d. d.*) The nature of future happiness. 16°. [*London, A. Fullarton & co.* 1854].

[*In* DISCOURSES and services on occasion of the death of the late rev. Ralph Wardlaw, d. d. 1854. pp. 89–136].

——— (*editor*). *See* **Good** words.

Macleod (Xavier Donald). Our lady of the litanies. xi, 225 pp. 6 l. 12°. *Cincinnati, J. P. Walsh*, 1861.

Macmichael (William). The gold-headed cane. [Notices of doctors Radcliffe, Mead, Askew, Pitcairn, and Baillie. *anon.*] 2d ed. 4 p. l. 267 pp. 1 pl. 12°. *London, J. Murray*, 1828.

Macmillan (James). Guide to the chapel-royal and palace of Holyrood-house. To which are added, the natural history of the environs and the laws and privileges of the sanctuary. Written chiefly from materials collected by Henry Courtoy. xii, 260 pp. 1 pl. 16°. *Edinburgh, H. Courtoy*, 1837.

Macmillan's magazine. [Monthly]. Nov. 1870, to April, 1872. v. 23–25. 8°. *London, Macmillan & co.* 1871–72.

McMurtrie (Henry, *m. d.*) A compendium of domestic medicine, and health-adviser. 1 portrait, 256 pp. 22 pl. 16°. *Philadelphia, T. E. Zell*, 1871.

——— The woman's medical companion, and nursery-adviser. Eng. title, 299 pp. 10 pl. 16°. *Philadelphia, T. E. Zell*, 1871.

Macneill (Hector). The poetical works of Hector Macneill. A new ed. corrected & enlarged. 328 pp. 1 l. 16°. *Philadelphia, B. Chapman*, 1815.

MacNeny (P.) Réfutation des argumens avancés de la part de mrs. les directeurs des compagnies d'Orient et d'Occident des Provinces-Unies contre la liberté du commerce des habitans des Païs-bas, sujets de sa majesté impériale et catholique dans les climats éloignés, à pretexte des articles 5. et 6. du traité de Munster. 72 pp. sm. 4°. *Bruxelles, E. H. Fricx*, 1723.

M'Nevin (John). The United States calculator; or, arithmetic simplified, in dollars and cents, adapted to the commerce of the United States; in a series of lectures. 280 pp. 12°. *Baltimore, F. Lucas, jr.* 1841.

Macnish (Robert). An introduction to phrenology, in the form of question and answer, with an appendix, and copious illustrative notes. xii, 155 pp. 12°. *Boston, Marsh, Capen & Lyon*, 1836.

Macomber (*Mrs.* Louisa M.) An autumnal wreath: a religious souvenir. 346 pp. 1 portrait. 16°. *Hyde Park, [Mass.] office of the Norfolk county gazette*, 1871.

Macpherson (James). Fragments of ancient poetry, collected in the Highlands of Scotland, and translated from the galic or erse language. [*anon.*] 70 pp. 12°. *Edinburgh, G. Hamilton*, 1760.

——— The same. 2d ed. 77 pp. 8°. *Edinburgh, G. Hamilton & J. Balfour*, 1760.
[HAZARD pamphlets, v. 1].

——— *See, also,* **Ossian.**

Macquoid (Katharine S.) Patty. xi, 442 pp. 1 l. 16°. *London & New York, Macmillan & co.* 1871.

——— Rookstone. 144 pp. 4 pl. 8°. [*Philadelphia, J. B. Lippincott & co.* 1871].
[*Note.*—Serial supplement to Lippincott's magazine, v. 7–8].

McRae (*Rev.* Thaddeus). Lectures on satan. 173 pp. 16°. *Boston, Gould & Lincoln*, 1871.

M'Robert (Patrick). Tour through part of the north provinces of America: being a series of letters wrote on the spot, in the years 1774, & 1775. To which are annex'd, tables, shewing the roads, the value of coin, rates of stages, etc. 64 pp. 12°. *Edinburgh, author*, 1776.

Macrum (James M.) The new piano. A lyric poem. 32 pp. sq. 16°. *Pittsburgh, R. S. Davis & co.* 1871.

MacSparran (James, *d. d.*) America dissected, being a full and true account of all the american colonies. 48 pp. 8°. *Dublin, S. Powell*, 1753.
[HAZARD pamphlets, v. 43].

McVickar (William A. *d. d.*) The life of the reverend John McVickar, s. t. d. By his son. x, 416 pp. 1 portrait. 12°. *New York, Hurd & Houghton*, 1872.

McWatters (George S.) Knots untied: or, ways and by-ways in the hidden life of american detectives. 665 pp. 30 pl. 8°. *Hartford, J. B. Burr & Hyde*, 1871.

McWhorter (George Cumming). A popular handbook of the new testament. 295 pp. 16°. *New York, Harper & brothers*, 1864.

McWright (*Rev.* Albert). The believer's defence, or, the doctrine of the trinity of God and atonement of Christ defended against unitarianism. Compiled from various authors. 287 pp. 12°. *Columbus (O.) author*, 1841.

Madden (Richard Robert, *m. d.*) The connexion between the kingdom of Ireland and the crown of England. With an appendix of the privy council correspondence, during great part of the years 1811–17. 2 p. l. iii, 340 pp. 8°. *Dublin, J. Duffy*, 1845.

Maffei (Giovanni Camillo). Scala natvrale, overo fantasia dolcissima, intorno alle cose occulte, e desiderate nella filosofia. 140 l. numb. 16°. *Venetia, G. Varisco & comp.* 1564.

Maffei (Scipione, *marchese*). Arte magica dileguata. Lettera al padre Innocente Ansaldi. 3ª ed. 54 pp. 4°. *Verona, nella stamperia Moroni*, 1774.

——— Rime e prose. Parte raccolte da varj libri, e parte non più stampate. Aggiunto anche un saggio di poesia latina dell' istesso autore. 4 p. l. 376 pp. 2 pl. 4°. *Venezia, S. Coleti*, 1719.

[*Note.*—No essay on latin poetry under the title given above appears in this volume].

Maffitt (John Newland). Nautilus, or cruising under canvass. 352 pp. 12°. *New York, United States publishing co.* 1871.

Magendie (François). An elementary treatise on human physiology, on the basis of the Précis élémentaire de physiologie. 5th ed. 1838. Translated, enlarged, [etc.] by John Revere, m. d. 539 pp. 1 pl. 8°. *New York, Harper & brothers,* 1844.

Maggio (Lucio). Discovrs dv tremblement de terre en forme de dialogue. Pris de l'italien, [par Nicolas de Liure, seigneur de Humerodes]. 7 p. l. 180 pp. 1 pl. 16°. *Paris, D. du Val*, 1675.

Magician's (The) show box. *See* **Child** (Lydia Maria).

Magie (*Rev.* David, *d. d.*) The spring-time of life; or, advice to youth. 348 pp. 1 portrait. 16°. *New York, American tract society,* [1855].

Magill (Mary Tucker). The Holcombes. A story of Virginia home-life. 290 pp. 12°. *Philadelphia, J. B. Lippincott & co.* 1871.

——— Women, or chronicles of the late war. xvii, 393 pp. 12°. *Baltimore, Turnbull, brothers*, 1871.

Magirus (Tobias). Eponymologium criticum, complectens cognomina, descriptiones, elogia et censuras personarum ac rerum cùm veterum tùm recentium bello aut pace insignium; ex variis scriptoribus collecta. Nunc duplo quàm olim auctius editum cura Christiani Wilhelmi Eubenii. 3 p. l. 812 pp. 1 portrait. sm. 4°. *Francofurti & Lipsiae, sumptibus F. Lüdervvald*, 1687.

Magner (D.) The new system of educating horses, including instructions on feeding, watering, stabling, shoeing, etc. with practical treatment for diseases. 10th ed. 208 pp. 16°. *Buffalo, Warren, Johnson & co.* 1872.

Magoon (*Rev.* Elisha L.) Republican christianity: or, true liberty, as exhibited in the life, precepts, and early disciples of the great redeemer. 422 pp. 12°. *Boston, Gould, Kendall & Lincoln*, 1849.

Maha-Bharata. Ardschuna's reise zu Indra's himmel nebst anderen episoden des mahabharata; in der ursprache zum erstenmal herausgegeben, metrisch übersetzt, und mit kritischen anmerkungen versehen von Franz Bopp. xxviii pp. 40 l. 122 pp. 4°. *Berlin, W. Logier*, 1824.

Mahan (*Rev.* Asa). Doctrine of the will. 218 pp. 16°. *New York, M. H. Newman*, 1845.

——— Scripture doctrine of christian perfection; with other kindred subjects, illustrated and confirmed in a series of discourses. 237 pp. 16°. *Boston, D. S. King*, 1839.

Mahan (Dennis H. *ll. d.*) Descriptive geometry, as applied to the drawing of fortification and stereotomy. 2 p. l. 55 pp. 12 pl. 8°. *New York, J. Wiley*, 1864.

Mahan (Jason). The private instructor, or mathematics simplified. 303 pp. 12°. *Harrisburg*, [*Pa.*] *author*, 1836.

Mahan (Milo, *d. d.*) A church history of the first seven centuries, to the close of the sixth general council. xxv, 595 pp. 8°. *New York, Pott, Young & co.* 1872.

Maichel (Daniel). Danielis Maichelii introductio ad historiam literariam de præcipuis bibliothecis parisiensibus, locupletata annotationibus atque methodo, qua rectus bibliothecarum usus & vera studiorum ratio ostenditur. In duas partes divisa. 8 p. l. 254 pp. 16°. *Lipsiae, sumptibus J. F. Gleditschii*, 1721.

Maillard de Chambure (Charles Hippolyte). Dijon, ancien et moderne. Recherches historiques tirées de monumens contemporains la plupart inédits. Illustré par E. Sagot, architecte. Eng. title, 192 pp. 32 pl. 8°. *Dijon, Guasco-Jobard*, 1840.

Main (Sylvester). Cottage melodies. *See* **Bradbury** (William B.) *and* **Main** (S.)

Maine (Henry Sumner). Village communities in the east and west. Six lectures delivered at Oxford. ix, 226 pp. 8°. *London, J. Murray*, 1871.

Maine (*State of*). Constitution of the state, formed in convention at Portland, 29th of October, 1819. 28 pp. 8°. *Portland, F. Douglas*, 1819.

[MOORE pamphlets, v. 20].

Maine (*State of*)—continued.

——— *State library.* Eleventh annual report of the librarian of the Maine state library to the legislature of Maine, with a list of new books, for the year 1872. 8°. *Augusta, Sprague, Owen & Nash,* 1872.

Maine. (*Congregational church*). Minutes of the forty-fifth annual meeting of the general conference of the congregational churches in Maine: with the sermon before the Maine missionary society, by rev. Albert Cole, and report of the trustees, at its sixty-fourth anniversary, held with the Winter st. congregational church in Bath, June 27, 28, and 29, 1871. 128 pp. 8°. *Portland, B. Thurston & co.* 1871.

Maine (The) farmer's almanac, for 1872. [no. 54]. 24 l. 8°. *Hallowell, Masters & Livermore,* [1871].

Maintenon (Françoise d'Aubigné, *marquise* de). Lettres. ed. 1812. *See* **Sévigné** (Marie de Rabutin-Chantal, *marquise* de) *and* **Maintenon.**

Mainwaring. *See* **Manwaring.**

Mairan (Jean Jacques Dortous de). Lettres au r. p. Parrenin; contenant diverses questions sur la Chine. Nouv. éd. revue, corrigée & augmentée de divers opuscules sur différentes matières. 1 p. l. xi, 368 pp. 1 l. 8°. *Paris, imprimerie royale,* 1770.

Maistre (Joseph, *comte* de). The pope: considered in his relations with the church, temporal sovereignties, separated churches, and the cause of civilization. Translated by the rev. Æneas McD. Dawson. xxxiii, 369 pp. 1 portrait. 12°. *London, C. Dolman,* 1850.

Maistre (*Comte* Xavier de). A journey round my room. Translated from the french, with a notice of the author's life. By H. A. xi, 152 pp. 12°. *New York, Hurd & Houghton,* 1871.

Maitland club. Publications. No. 33. 4°. *Edinburgh,* 1835.

CONTENTS.

VINCENTIVS *lirinensis*, for the antiquitie and veritie of the catholik fayth, aganis ye prophane nouations of al haereseis. Writtin in latin and translatit in scottis be Niniane Winset. xxi, 184 pp.
WINZET (Niniane). Certane tractatis for reformatioun of doctryne and maneris in Scotland. *Edinburgi,* 1562.
——— Buke of four scoir thre questions, tueching doctrine, ordour, and maneris. pp. 49–119.

Maitrejean (Antoine). Observations sur la formation du poulet. xii, 326 pp. 1 l. 10 pl. 16°. *Paris, L. d'Houry,* 1722.

Majansius. *See* **Mayans y Siscar** (Gregorio).

Majendie (*Lieut.* Vivian Dering). Up among the Pandies: or, a year's service in India. xii, 360 pp. 1 pl. 12°. *London, Routledge, Warne & Routledge,* 1859.

Major *or* **Mair** (John). Historia Majoris Britanniae, tam Angliae quam Scotiae. Editio nova, mendis quamplurimis in antiqua Jodoci Badii Ascensii editione Parisiis edita mdxxi extantibus repurgata. 2 p. l. xxxix, 332, 8, xxviii pp. 2 l. 4°. *Edimburgi, apud R. Fribarnium,* 1740.

Major *and* **Knapp** (The) illustrated monthly. July, 1870, to Nov. 1871. v. 1–2 in 1 v. fol. *New York, Major & Knapp eng. mfg. & lith. co.* [1870–71].

[*Note.*—Incomplete: wanting nos. 1–6 of vol. 1 for Jan. to June, 1870. Discontinued].

Majoragio (Marco Antonio). Lvti encomivm. 18°. [*Lugd. Batavorum,* 1644].

[*In* DISSERTATIONVM lvdicrarvm et amœnitatvm scriptores varij, pp. 209–254].

Malayan miscellanies. v. 1. nos. 1–13 in 1 v. 8°. *Bencoolen, Sumatran mission press,* 1820.

Malcolm (*Sir* John). Sketches of Persia from the journals of a traveller in the east. [*anon.*] 2 v. xvi, 278 pp; iv, 281 pp. 12°. *London, J. Murray,* 1827.

——— The same. [*anon.*] A new ed. 2 v. xiii, 282 pp; iv, 280 pp. 12°. *London, J. Murray,* 1828.

Malcom (Howard, *d. d.*) A brief memoir of mrs. Lydia M. Malcom, late of Boston, Mass. Wife of rev. Howard Malcom. 4th ed. [*anon.*] 1 p. l. 122 pp. 16°. *Boston, W. D. Ticknor,* 1835.

——— A dictionary of important names, objects, and terms, found in the holy scriptures. 176 pp. 10 pl. 18°. *Boston, Lincoln & Edmands,* 1830.

Malebranche (Nicolas de). Christian conferences: demonstrating the truth of the christian religion and morality. [Also], his meditations on humility and repentance. 4 p. l. 400 pp. 12°. *London, J. Whitlock,* 1695.

Malespini (Ricardano). Istoria fiorentina, coll' aggiunta di Giachetto Malespini e la cronica di Giovanni Morelli. xlviii, 378 pp. 4°. *Firenze, S. A. R. per G. G. Tartini & S. Franchi,* 1718.

Mallary (Charles D.) Memoirs of elder Edmund Botsford. 240 pp. 12°. *Charleston,* [*S. C.*] *W. Riley,* 1832.

Malo (Felix Venancio). Lagrymas de la paz. *See* **Balcarcel y Formento** (Domingo) *and* **Malo.**

Malouin (Paul Jacques). Description et détails des arts du meunier, du vermicelier et du boulenger; avec une histoire abrégée de la boulengerie, & un dictionnaire de ces arts. iv, 340 pp. 10 pl. fol. *Paris*, 1767.

Malvezzi (Virgilio, *il marchese*). Considerationi con occasione d'alcuni luoghi delle vite d' Alcibiade, e di Coriolano. 2 v. in 1. 4 p. l. 99 pp; 4 p. l. 56 pp. 4°. *Bologna, per gli hh. del Dozza*, [1648].

——— Romvlvs and Tarqvin, written in italian. And now taught english by Henry [Cary] earle of Monmouth. 3d ed. Eng. title, 8 p. l. 222 pp. 18°. *London, H. Moseley*, 1648.

Mamma's budget; or, daily reading for children. The two brothers, Susan Hawthone, and A good grandson. By the child's friend. [*anon.*] 1st am. from 3d eng. ed. 440 pp. 16°. *Philadelphia, Hayes & Zell*, 1857.

Man more than a machine. *See* **Luzac** (Élie).

Man (The) of the world's dictionary. *See* **Sticotti** (Antonio Fabio).

Manahan (Ambrose, *d. d.*) Triumph of the catholic church in the early ages. 572 pp. 8°. *New York, E. Dunigan & brother*, 1859.

Manceau de Boissoudan (J. E.) *See* **Boissoudan.**

Manchester (*England*). Nineteenth annual report to the council of the city of Manchester, on the working of the public free libraries. 1870–71. 32 pp. 8°. *Manchester*, [*Eng.*] *J. E. Cornish*, 1871.

Manchester (The) commercial list, 1871–72. 5th and 6th years. By Estell & co. fol. *Boston*, [*Seyd & co.*] 1871.

Manchester (*N. H.*) Twenty-fifth annual report of the receipts and expenditures of the city of Manchester, for the fiscal year ending December 31, 1870, together with other annual reports and papers relating to the affairs of the city. 339 pp. 8°. *Manchester*, [*N. H.*] *J. B. Clarke*, 1871. s.

Manchester (The) directory for 1871. By Sampson, Davenport & co. 8°. *Manchester* (*N. H.*) *W. H. Fisk*, [1871].

Mandeville (*Sir* John). Ioanne de Mandavilla, nel qvale si contengono di molte cose marauigliose. Con la tauola di tutti i capitoli, che nella presente opera si contengono. Nouamente stampato, & ricorretto. Eng. title, 105 l. numb. 16°. *Venetia*, 1567.

Manero (José Mariano de) *and* **Hortigosa** (Tomas Lopez de). Solemnes exequias del illmo señor dr. José Gregorio Alonso de Hortigosa, obispo que fue de la ciudad de Antequera, valle de Oaxaca, celebradas en la santa iglesia catedral de la propia ciudad en los dias 1. y 2. del mes de diciembre de 1796. 14 l. 4°. *N. Guatemala, I. Beteta*, 1798.

Manfredi (Gabriele) *and* **Bertaglia** (Romualdo). Relazione delle paduli pontine, l'anno 1761. 4°. [*Firenze*, 1785].

[*In* XIMENES (L.) Raccolta delle perizie ed opuscoli idraulici, v. 1, pp. 7–71].

Maniau (Joaquin). Compendio de la historia de real hacienda de Nueva España, escrita en el año de 1794. 2 p. l. 174 pp. 3 l. 1 table. fol. (*ms.*)

Manière (De la) d'apprendre les langues. *See* **Radonvilliers** (*Abbé* Claude François Lizarde de).

Manière (La) de bien penser dans les ouvrages d'esprit. *See* **Bouhours** (Dominique).

Manifest, ende redenen van oorloge, tot Lisbona uyt-gheghevеn, ende gepubliceert: tusschen Portugael, ende de Geunieerde Nederlandtsche provintien, met de aenmerkinge ende den oorspronck, waer uyt den selfden gheprocedeert is. Getrouwelick uyt de portugesche tale over-geset. [*anon.*] 8 l. sm. 4°. [*n. p.*] *Gedruckt int jaer ons Heeren*, 1658.

Manley (Thomas, *pseudon.*) *See* **Walker** (*Sir* Edward).

Manlove (Timothy). The immortality of the soul asserted, and practically improved. With some reflections on a pretended refutation [by H. Layton] of mr. Bently's sermon. 10 p. l. 164 pp. 18°. *London, R. Roberts for N. Simmons*, 1697.

Mann (Charles A.) Paper money, the root of evil. An examination of the currency of the United States, with practical suggestions for restoring specie payments without robbing debtors. x, 374 pp. 12°. *New York, D. Appleton & co.* 1872.

Mann (*Rev.* Cyrus). Astronomy; or the perfections of God displayed in his works. 227 pp. 18°. *Boston, Mass. sabbath school society*, 1836.

——— The Clinton family: or, the history of the temperance reformation. 263 pp. 1 pl. 18°. *Boston, Massachusetts sabbath school society*, 1833.

Mann (*Rev.* Cyrus)—continued.

——— An epitome of the evidences of christianity. 2d ed. 148 pp. 16°. *Boston, Mass. sabbath school union*, 1831.

——— Memoir of mrs. Myra W. Allen, who died at the missionary station of the american board in Bombay, on the 5th of Feb. 1831, in the 30th year of her age. 247 pp. 1 portrait. 18°. *Boston, Mass. sabbath school union*, 1832.

Mann (*Mrs.* Mary Peabody). The flower people. 225 pp. 2 pl. 16°. *Boston, Ticknor & Fields*, 1862.

Mann (Robert James, *m. d.*) A guide to the knowledge of life, vegetable and animal; being a comprehensive manual of physiology, viewed in relation to the maintenance of health. xii, 417 pp. 12°. *New York, C. S. Francis*, 1860.

Mann (W. Wilberforce). A new system of measures, weights, and money; entitled the Linn-base decimal system; and designed for the adoption of all civilized nations, as the one common system. 20 pp. 1 table. 12°. *New York, University publishing co.* 1871.

Manne (Edmond de). Nouveau dictionnaire des ouvrages anonymes et pseudonymes, la plupart contemporains, avec les noms des auteurs ou éditeurs, accompagné de notes historiques et critiques. Nouv. éd. revue, corrigée & très-augmentée, pouvant servir de supplément à tous les manuels de bibliographie jusqu'à ce jour. vii, 406 pp. 1 l. 8°. *Lyon, N. Scheuring*, 1862.

Manners (John Henry, *5th duke of Rutland*). Journal of a tour round the southern coasts of England. [*anon.*] 4 p. l. 229 pp. 1 l. 2 pl. 8°. *London, J. Triphook*, 1805.

[*Note.*—With bastard title, "Travels in Great Britain," v. 1].

——— Journal of a tour to the northern parts of Great Britain. [*anon.*] 2 p. l. 300 pp. 12 pl. 8°. *London, J. Triphook*, 1813.

[*Note.*—With bastard title, "Travels in Great Britain," v. 2].

——— Journal of a tour through North and South Wales, the Isle of Man, &c. &c. [*anon.*] 4 p. l. 389 pp. 1 l. 7 pl. 8°. *London, J. Triphook*, 1805.

[*Note.*—With bastard title, "Travels in Great Britain," v. 3].

Manni (Domenico Maria). Le veglie piacevoli ovvero notizie de' più bizzarri, e giocondi uomini toscani, le quali possono servire di utile trattenimento. 2ª ed. 4 v. in 1. 12°. *Venezia, nel negocio Zatta*, 1762–63.

Manning (Anne). Meadowleigh: a tale of english country life. By the author of "The ladies of Bever hollow." [*anon.*] 2 v. 2 p. l. 307 pp; 2 p. l. 315 pp. 12°. *London, R. Bentley*, 1863.

Manning (*Rev.* Jacob M.) Half truths and the truth. Lectures on the origin and development of prevailing forms of unbelief, considered in relation to the nature and claims of the christian system. xiii, 398 pp. 12°. *Boston, Lee & Shepard*, 1872.

Manning (James). A sketch of the life and writings of the rev. Micaiah Towgood. 2 p. l. 191 pp. 8°. *Exeter, [Eng.] author*, 1792.

Manning (Joseph B.) The voice of letters. Ancient proprieties of latin and greek; the standard of english letter customs; their inherent system; and preferred orthography. 135 pp. 12°. *Boston and Cambridge, J. Munroe & co.* 1854.

Manoel (Francisco). An historical account of the discovery of the island of Madeira. *See* **Alcoforado** (Francisco).

Mansel (Henry Longueville). The philosophy of the conditioned. Comprising some remarks on sir William Hamilton's philosophy, and on mr. J. S. Mill's examination of that philosophy. vii, 189 pp. 8°. *London & New York, A. Strahan*, 1866.

Mansel (Robert). Free thoughts upon methodists, actors, and the influence of the stage. 16°. [*New York, G. Champley*, 1826].

[*In* F. (D.) Defence of the drama. pp. 19–96, 164–294].

Mansfield (Edward Dangerfield). The political grammar of the United States: or, a complete view of the theory and practice of the general and state governments, with the relations between them. New edition—containing parliamentary rules, for the government of public assemblies, arranged on the basis of Jefferson's manual. Also, an appendix of questions. 336 pp. 12°. *Cincinnati, Truman & Smith*, 1839.

——— The same. The political manual: being a complete view of the theory and practice of the general and state governments of the United States. 347 pp. 12°. *New York, A. S. Barnes & Burr*, 1861.

Manso (Pedro). Sermon panegyrico, en la celebridad de la dedicacion del templo nuevo de San Bernardo, titvlo Maria de Gvadalupe; dia segundo de la octaua. sm. 4°. [*México, viuda de F. R. Lupercio*, 1691].

[*In* Ramirez de Vargas (A.) Sagrado padron y panegyricos sermones, etc. l. 7–18].

Mant (Richard, *bishop of Down and Connor*). The british months; a poem, in twelve parts. 2 v. 4 p. l. 245 pp; 2 p. l. 246–484 pp. 16°. *London, J. W. Parker*, 1835.

——— Sermons, for parochial and domestic use, designed to illustrate and enforce, in a connected view, the most important articles of christian faith and practice. 2d ed. 3 v. 8°. *Oxford, J. Parker*, 1813–15.

Manual (The) of the crucifixion. A guide to catholic devotion. [*anon.*] 575 pp. 1 pl. 24°. *New York, P. J. Kenedy*, 1872.

Manual (A) of politeness, for persons of both sexes. [*anon.*] 288 pp. 18°. *Philadelphia, W. Marshall & co.* 1837.

Manual (A) of prayer; designed to assist christians in learning the subjects and modes of devotion. With an introduction, by rev. A. Barnes. [*anon.*] 2d ed. 306 pp. 16°. *Philadelphia, H. Perkins*, 1838.

Manuel de santa Teresa. Instructorio espiritual de los terceros, terceras, y beatas de nuestra señora del Carmen. Reimpreso. 7 p. l. 226 pp. 1 pl. 18°. *Mexico, J. Jauregui*, 1787.

Manufacturer (The) and builder. A practical journal of industrial progress. [Monthly]. Jan. to Dec. 1871. v. 3. 4°. [*New York, Western & co.* 1871].

Manuscript transmitted from St. Helena, by an unknown channel. *See* **Bertrand.**

Manuzio (Paolo, *the younger*). Epistolae clarorvm virorvm, selectae de qvamplvrimis optimae, ad indicandam nostrorvm temporum eloquentiam. 132 l. 18°. *Venetiis, apud Paulum Manutium, Aldi filium*, 1556.

Manwaring (*Rev.* Edward). An historical and critical account of the most eminent classic authors in poetry and history. 3 p. l. x, 365 pp. 8°. *London, W. Innys & R. Manby*, 1737.

Marcel (Jean Jacques, *editor*). Oratio dominica cl linguis versa, et propriis cujusque linguæ characteribus plerumque expressa. 162 l. fol. *Parisiis, typis imperialibus*, 1805.

Marcet (Jane Haldimand). Scenes in nature; or, conversations for children. [Altered by T. W. H.] 324 pp. 1 map. 18°. *New York, Harper & brothers*, 1868.

March (Angier). Increase of piety, or the revival of religion in the United States of America [1798–1802]; containing several interesting letters not before published. Together with three remarkable dreams. Collected by the publisher. 128 pp. 12°. *Newburyport, A. March*, 1802.

March (Daniel, *d. d.*) Walks and homes of Jesus. 339 pp. 6 pl. 12°. *Philadelphia, Presbyterian publication committee*, 1866.

Marchand (Émile). De l'influence comparative du régime végétal et du régime animal sur le physique et le morale de l'homme. 2 p. l. xii, 266 pp. 8°. *Paris, J. B. Baillière*, 1849.

Marchand (Prosper). Lettre critique dans laquelle on fait l'histoire, l'analyse, & l'apologie de cet ouvrage, [Cymbalum mundi]. 16°. [*Amsterdam, P. Marchand*, 1732].

[*With* DESPERRIERS (Bonaventure). Cymbalum mundi. *Amsterdam*, 1732. pp. 1–65].

——— The same. A critical letter containing the history and analysis [of Cymbalum mundi], together with an apology for it. 12°. [*London, J. Newton*, 1723].

[*With* DESPERRIERS (Bonaventure). Cymbalum mundi. *London*, 1723. pp. i–xliii].

Marck (Johannes). De sibyllinis carminibus, disputationes academicæ duodecim. Accedit breve examen dissertationis gallicæ de sibyllinis oraculis, editæ Parisiis, à Johanne Crassetio, jesuita. 8 p. l. 304 pp. 18°. *Franekeræ, J. Gyselaar*, 1682.

Marcy (Lorenzo J.) The sciopticon manual. Explaining Marcy's new magic lantern, and light, including magic lantern optics, experiments, photographing and coloring slides, etc. xii, 9–140 pp. 12°. [*Philadelphia*], *Sherman & co.* 1871.

Marcy (Randolph Benton). Border reminiscences. 396 pp. 12°. *New York, Harper & brothers*, 1872.

Maréchal (Pierre Sylvain). Dictionnaire des athées anciens et modernes. Par Sylvain M******l. [*anon.*] 1 p. l. lxxii, 524 pp. 8°. *Paris, Grabit, an VIII*, [1800].

——— Dictionnaire historique des anecdotes de l'amour [en l'ordre alphabétique] contenant un grand nombre de faits curieux et intéressants occasionés par la force, les caprices, les fureurs, les emportements de cette passion, [etc.] depuis le commencement du monde jusqu'à nos jours. [*anon.*] 2e éd. 5 v. 8°. *Paris*, 1832.

——— Voyages de Pythagore en Égypte, dans la Chaldée, dans l'Inde, en Crête, à Sparte, en Sicile, à Rome, à Carthage, à Marseille, et dans les Gaules; suivis de ses lois politiques et morales. [*anon.*] 6 v. 8°. *Paris, Deterville, an septième*, [1799].

Marées (Pierre de). Beschryvinge van de goudt-kust Guinea. Als mede een voyagie naer de selve. Door P. D. M. [*anon.*] 128

Marées (Pierre de)—continued. pp. 6 pl. in text. sm. 4°. *Amsterdam, J. Hartgers*, 1650.

Maret (Henri). Essai sur le panthéisme, dans les sociétés modernes. xvi, 431 pp. 8°. *Paris, Debécourt*, 1840.

Margaret, the young wife. [*anon.*] 311 pp. 3 pl. 18°. *Philadelphia, American sunday-school union*, [1863].

Margoliouth (Moses). The fundamental principles of modern judaism investigated: together with a memoir of the author, and an introduction: a list of the six hundred and thirteen precepts: and addresses to jews and christians. With a preface by the rev. Henry Raikes. [xxxvi], 260 pp. 5 pl. 8°. *London, B. Wertheim*, 1843.

Margret Howth. 1862. *See* **Davis** (*Mrs.* Rebecca Harding).

Marguerittes (Julie de). Parisian pickings; or, Paris in all states and stations. 415 pp. 12°. *Philadelphia, J. S. Colton & co.* 1859.

Maria Cheeseman; or, the candy-girl. With a preface, by rev. James W. Alexander, d. d. [*anon.*] 158 pp. 4 pl. 18°. *Philadelphia, American sunday-school union*, [1855].

Maria's two vacations; or, principle in pleasure. [*anon.*] 252 pp. 18°. *Philadelphia, American sunday school union*, [1856].

Marillac (Michel de). Relation de la descente des Anglois en l'isle de Rè: du siége mis par eux au fort ou citadelle de Sainct Martin. [*anon.*] 2 p. l. 247 pp. 12°. *Paris, E. Martin*, 1628.

Marion (Fulgence). The wonders of vegetation. From the french. Edited, with numerous additions, by Schele de Vere. Eng. title, 283 pp. 1 portrait. 12°. *New York, C. Scribner & co.* 1872.
[ILLUSTRATED library of wonders].

Mariotti (L. *pseudon.*) *See* **Gallenga** (Antonio).

Marked for life. [A poem]. Edited by Marlay. [*anon.*] 216 pp. 12° *New York, Carleton*, 1863.

Markham (Clements R.) A memoir on the indian surveys. Printed by order of her majesty's secretary of state for India in council. xxv, 303 pp. 4 maps. 8°. *London, W. H. Allen & co.* 1871. S.

Markham (Francis). Five decades of epistles of warre. 5 p. l. 200 pp. fol. *London, A. Matthewes*, 1622.

Markham (Gervase *or* Jervis). The art of archerie. 11 p. l. 172 pp. 1 pl. 18°. *London, B. Fisher*, 1634.

Markland (Abraham). Pteryplegia: or, the art of shooting-flying. A poem. 3d ed. 1 p. l. iv, 32 pp. 1 pl. 8°. *London, J. Lever*, 1767.
[*With* PAGE (T.) The art of shooting-flying. ed. 1766].

Markoe (Thomas M. *m. d.*) A treatise on the diseases of the bones. viii, 416 pp. 8°. *New York, D. Appleton & co.* 1872.

Marlorat (Augustin). Catholike exposition of s. Mathewe. *See* **Bible.** (*English*).

Marmion (Anthony). The ancient and modern history of the maritime ports of Ireland. 3d ed. liv, 666 pp. 8°. *London, author*, 1858.

Marmontel (Jean François). Bélisaire. 1 p. l. x, 340 pp. 2 l. 4 pl. 16°. *Paris, Merlin*, 1767.

Marolles (Michel de). Mémoires. Avec des notes historiques et critiques, [par C. P. Goujet]. 3 v. 16°. *Amsterdam*, 1755.

Marriage (The) present. [*anon.*] 172 pp. 18°. *Boston, J. Dowe*, 1834.

Marriott (*Rev.* Wharton B.) Ειρηνικα. The wholesome words of holy scripture concerning questions now disputed in the church. [Parts 1–2]. 5 p. l. 220 pp. 8°. *London, Rivingtons*, 1866.

Marryat (Frederick). Snarleyyow; or, the dog fiend. An historical novel. 2 v. 201 pp; 187 pp. 12°. *Philadelphia, Carey & Hart*, 1837.

Marrying (The) man. *See* **Smythies** (*Mrs.* Gordon).

Marsden (Joshua). Leisure hours; or poems, moral, religious, & descriptive. 160 pp. 1 portrait. 12°. *New York, author*, 1812.

Marsh (*Mrs.* Caroline Crane). Wolfe of the knoll, and other poems. 327 pp. 12°. *New York, C. Scribner*, 1860.

Marsh (Jenny). Toiling and hoping: the story of a little hunchback. 398 pp. 12°. *New York, Derby & Jackson*, 1856.

Marsh (*Rev.* John). An epitome of general ecclesiastical history, from the earliest period to the present time. With an appendix, giving a condensed history of the jews from the destruction of Jerusalem to the present day. Eng. title, 2 p. l. 13–420 pp. 1 table, 2 maps, 7 pl. 12°. *New York, Vanderpool & Cole*, 1827.

Marsh (William). England, and other poems. 112 pp. 12°. *New York, author*, 1839.

Marsh-Caldwell (*Mrs.* Anne). Castle Avon. By the author of "Emilia Wyndham," [etc. *anon.*] 3 v. 12°. *London, Colburn & co.* 1852.

——— The heiress of Haughton; or, the mother's secret. By the author of "Emilia Wyndham," [etc. *anon.*] 3 v. 12°. *London, Hurst & Blackett,* 1855.

——— Lettice Arnold. A tale. By the author of "Emilia Wyndham," [etc. *anon.*] 2 v. 1 p. l. 288 pp; 1 p. l. 286 pp. 8°. *London, H. Colburn,* 1850.

Marshall (Christopher). Passages from the Remembrancer of Christopher Marshall, [during 1774-76]. 124, xvi pp. 12°. *Philadelphia, William Duane, jr.* 1839.

Marshall (*Rev.* Ebenezer). The history of the union of Scotland and England. 2 p. l. vii, 259 pp. 8°. *Edinburgh, P. Hill,* 1799.

Marshall (Elihu F.) A spelling book of the english language; or, the american tutor's assistant. 156 pp. 12°. *Saratoga springs, proprietors,* 1820.

Marshall (John). Remarks on arsenic, considered as a poison and a medicine; to which are added five cases of recovery from the poisonous effects of arsenic. Together with the tests so successfully employed for detecting the white metallic oxide; in which those methods peculiar to mr. Hume were principally adopted, confirmed, and compared with others formerly in use. 2 p. l. v, 163 pp. 8°. *London, J. Callow,* 1817.

Marshall (Leonard). The fountain of sacred song; a collection of new church music. 400 pp. obl. 8°. *Boston, White, Smith & Perry,* 1871.

——— Sabbath songs for children's worship. A new book of hymns and tunes for sabbath schools. With suggestive exercise for sabbath school concerts. 176 pp. obl. 12°. *Boston, Lee & Shepard,* 1869.

Marshall (*Rev.* William). An inquiry concerning the lawfulness of marriage between parties previously related by consanguinity or affinity. Also, a short history of opinions in different ages and countries, and of the action of ecclesiastical bodies on that subject. 212 pp. 16°. *New York, M. H. Newman,* 1843.

Marsham (*Sir* John). D. Johannis Marshami canon chronicus ægyptiacus, ebraicus, græcus, & disqvisitiones. Liber non chronologicæ tantum, sed & historicæ antiqvitatis reconditissima complexus; Londini primum a. 1672 editus: nunc longe emendatior in Germania recusus. Eng. title, 4 p. l. 676 pp. 29 l. 4°. *Lipsiae, apud M. Bircknerum,* 1676.

Marstaller (Gervaise). Artis diuinatricis, qvam astrologiam sev iudiciariam vocant, encomia & patrocinia. [Editio princeps]. 1 p. l. 178 pp. 1 l. 4°. *Parisiis, C. Wechelus,* 1549.

Martens (Edward von). Die preussische expedition nach Ost-Asien. Nach amtlichen quellen. Zoologischer theil. v. 2. Die landschnecken. xii, 447 pp. 22 pl. 8°. *Berlin, R. v. Decker,* 1867. s.

Martha (Cousin, *pseudon.*) Ella Clinton, or by their fruits ye shall know them. 206 pp. 2 pl. 18°. *Philadelphia, Presbyterian board of publication,* [1856].

Martha's hooks and eyes. [*anon.*] 129 pp. 1 pl. 18°. *New York, D. Appleton & co.* 1860.

Martha's school-days. A story for girls. [*anon.*] 286 pp. 2 pl. 18°. *Boston, Massachusetts sabbath school society,* [1864].

Marti (Manuel). Emmanuelis Martini epistolarum libri duodecim. Accedunt auctoris nondum defuncti vita, a Gregorio Majansio conscripta: nec non praefatio Petri Wesselingii. [Nec non Martini Περι παθων. Sive de animi affectionibus liber. Et oratio pro crepitu ventris habita ad patres crepitantes. Editio 2a emendatior et variis accessionibus auctoris locupletior]. 2 v. in 1. 26, 96, 275 pp. 1 l. 1 portrait; 1 p. l. 272 pp. 9 l. 4°. *Amstelaedami, apud J. Wetstenium & G. Smith,* 1738.

Martialis (Marcus Valerius). Libellus de spectaculis: or, an account of the most memorable monuments of the romane glory. And now periphrastically translated into english verse; by T. P. 16°. *London,* 1659.

[*In* PECKE (Thomas). Parnassi puerperium, pp. 123-133].

Martin (Benjamin N. *d.d. ll.d.*) Choice specimens of american literature. Selected from the chief american writers. 223 pp. 12°. *New York, Sheldon & co.* [1871].

Martin (Frederick). The life of John Clare. viii, 302 pp. 8°. *London and Cambridge, Macmillan & co.* 1865.

Martin (Frederick). *See* **Statesman's** (The) year book, 1872.

Martin (Louis Aimé). Petits poëmes grecs. 2 p. l. 506 pp. 1 l. 12°. *Paris, Lefèvre,* 1841.

CONTENTS.

APOLLONIUS. L'expédition des Argonautes.
COLUTHUS. L'enlèvement d'Hélène.
HESIODUS. La théogonie, Les travaux et les jours, et Le bouclier d'Hercule.
HOMERUS. La batrachomyomachie.
MUSAEUS. Héro et Léandre.
OPPIANUS. La chasse et La pêche.
TRYPHIODORUS. La prise de Troie.

Martin (Thomas). A traictise declaryng and plainly prouyng, that the pretensed marriage of priestes, and professed persones, is no mariage but altogether vnlawful, and in all ages, and al countreies of christendome, bothe forbidden, and also punyshed. Herewith is comprised a full confutation of doctour Poynettes boke entitled A defense for the marriage of priestes. *b. l.* 142 l. sm. 4°. *Londini, in ædibus R. Caly,* 1554.

Martin (William). The christian lacon; or, materials for thinking in a christian spirit. xvi, 270 pp. 1 pl. 24°. *London, W. Darton & son,* [*about* 1840].

Martindale (Joseph C. *m. d.*) First lessons in natural philosophy for beginners. 191 pp. 16°. *Philadelphia, Eldredge & brother,* 1872.

Martineau (Harriet). The billow and the rock. A tale. 217 pp. 18°. *London, C. Knight & co.* 1846.

Martinez de la Rosa (Francisco). Lo que puede un empleo! Comedia en prosa. 16°. *Brunsvico, E. Leibrock,* 1841.

[BIBLIOTECA portatil español, v. 1, pp. 221–290].

Martini (Antonio). Vecchio e nuovo testamento con annotazioni. *Firenze,* 1827–30. *See* **Bible.** (*Italian*).

Martinus (Emmanuel). *See* **Marti** (Manuel).

Martinus *polonus.* Martini poloni chronicon. [Chronologia romanorum pontificum et imperatorum coaevorum]. fol. [*Argentorati, J. R. Dulssecker,* 1702].

[*In* KULPIS (Johann Georg von). Scriptores rervm germanicarvm. ll. 338–378. *Argentorati,* 1702].

Martyn (John, *prof. of botany at Cambridge*) *and* **Russell** (Richard, *m. d.*) Memoirs of the society of Grub-street. [*anon.*] April 8 to Aug. 24, 1731. Nos. 66–138. v. 2. 326 pp. 5 l. 16°. *London,* 1731.

[Title-page wanting].

Martyn (Thomas). A tour through Italy. Containing full directions for travelling in that interesting country; with ample catalogues of every thing that is curious in architecture, painting, sculpture, &c. some observations on the natural history, and very particular descriptions of the four principal cities, Rome, Florence, Naples, and Venice. xxxix, 480 pp. 4 l. 1 map. 8°. *London, C. and G. Kearsley,* 1791.

Martyr (The) missionary of Erromanga; or the life of John Williams, who was murdered and eaten by the savages in one of the South Sea islands. [*anon.*] From the London ed. 270 pp. 1 pl. 18°. *Philadelphia, American sunday school union,* 1844.

Martyr (The) of Sumatra: a memoir of Henry Lyman. [*anon.*] 437 pp. 1 pl. 12°. *New York, R. Carter & brothers,* 1856.

Martyrs for the word. [*anon.*] 183 pp. 1 pl. 18°. *Boston, Mass. sabbath school society,* [1860].

Marulo (Marco). Dictorvm factorvmqve memorabilivm libri sex; siue de bene beateque viuendi institutione ad normam vitæ sanctorum vtriusque testamenti, collecti atque in ordinem digesti: infinitis mendis diligenter repurgati, atque ss. patrum locis sigillatim appositis insigniti. 4 p. l. 506 pp. 13 l. 12°. *Antverpiæ, M. Nutius,* 1593.

Marvin (Abijah P.) History of Worcester in the war of the rebellion. 582 pp. 9 pl. 8°. *Worcester,* [*Mass.*] *author,* 1870.

Mary; or the young christian. An authentic narrative; by one who was intimately acquainted with her from her infancy. [*anon.*] 111 pp. 18°. *New York, G. Lane & P. P. Sanford,* 1841.

Maryland historical society. Fund-publication, no. 5. 44 pp. 8°. *Baltimore,* 1871.

CONTENTS.

LATROBE (J. H. B.) A lost chapter in the history of the steamboat.

Maryland (The) medical and surgical journal, and official organ of the medical department of the army and navy of the United States. Published under the auspices of the medical and chirurgical faculty of Maryland. [Quarterly]. 2 v. 8°. *Baltimore, J. Murphy,* 1840–42.

Mary's martyrdom. [*anon.*] 189 pp. 18°. *Philadelphia, American sunday-school union.* [1862].

Marzari (Giacomo). La historia di Vicenza, divisa in dve libri. Nel primo, si tratta della vera origine, fondatione, & denominatione della città. Nel secondo, de' cittadini suoi chiari, & illustri. Nuouamente posta in luce. 18 p. l. 214 pp. 5 l. 8°. *Vicenza, G. Greco,* 1604.

Maseley (*Rev.* Henry). Astro-theology. 2 p.l. 180 pp. 18°. *London, A. Varnham,* 1847.

Maskelyne (Nevil Story). Catalogues of collections in the mineral department of the British musem. *See* **British** museum.

Mason (*Mrs.* Ellen H. B.) Great expectations realized; or, civilizing mountain men. 480 pp. 1 pl. 12°. *Philadelphia, American baptist publication soc.* [1862].

Mason (Emily V.) Popular life of gen. Robert Edward Lee. 432 pp. 3 pl. 12°. *Baltimore, J. Murphy & co.* 1872.

Mason (*Rev.* Francis). The Karen apostle: or, memoir of Ko Thah-byu, the first Karen convert, with notices concerning his nation. First american ed. revised by H. J. Ripley. 153 pp. 1 pl. 16°. *Boston, Gould, Kendall & Lincoln,* 1843.

Mason (Henry M.) A compend of ecclesiastical history, for the use of the laity, and theological students. viii, 5–468 pp. 12°. *New York, G. & C. Carvill,* 1828.

Mason (*Rev.* John). Select remains of the rev. John Mason, author of the Songs of praise to almighty God. Containing a variety of devout and useful sayings, on divers subjects, digested under proper heads. Recommended by the rev. I. Watts, d. d. With a preface, giving some account of the life of the author. By John Mason, a. m. 4th ed. xxvi, 160 pp. 12°. *London, J. Buckland,* 1759.

Mason (Lowell). Spiritual songs. *See* **Hastings** (Thomas) *and* **Mason.**

——— *and* **Greene** (David). Manual of christian psalmody: a collection of psalms and hymns for public worship. 588 pp. 16°. *Boston, Perkins & Marvin,* 1832.

——— *and* **Seward** (Theodore F.) The Pestalozzian music teacher; or class instructor in elementary music, in accordance with the analytic method. To which are added illustrative lessons on form, number and arithmetic, language and grammar, psychology, and other topics. By John W. Dickinson. 314 pp. 12°. *Boston, Oliver Ditson & co.* [1871].

——— *and* **Webb** (George J.) The glee hive; a collection of glees and part songs. Revised and enlarged edition. 112 pp. obl. 8°. *New York, Mason brothers,* [1853.] s.

Mason (*Mrs.* Mary). Spring-time for sowing; or, safety in the fold. 333 pp. 16°. *New York, Gen. protestant episcopal sunday school union & church book society,* 1860.

Mason (*Mrs.* Mary)—continued.

——— The young housewife's counsellor and friend: containing directions in every department of house keeping. Including the duties of wife and mother. 380 pp. 12°. *Philadelphia, J. B. Lippincott & co.* 1871.

Mason (*Rev.* William, *canon of York*). Essays, historical and critical, on english church music. 2 p. l. 264 pp. 16°. *York, W. Blanchard,* 1795.

——— Ode to mr. Pinchbeck, upon his newly invented patent candlesnuffers, by Malcolm McGreggor. [*pseudon.*] 3d ed. 11 pp. 8°. *London, J. Almon,* 1776.

———Poems. 4th ed. 2 p. l. 294 pp. 1 l. 8°. *York, A. Ward,* 1774.

Mason (William, *of Mass.*) Fireside harmony: a new collection of glees and part songs, arranged for soprano, alto, tenor, and base voices. 128 pp. obl. 8°. *Boston, Tappan, Whittemore & Mason,* 1848. s.

——— *and* **Hoadley** (E. S.) A system for beginners in the art of playing upon the piano-forte. 165 pp. 1 pl. 4°. *Boston, O. Ditson & co.* [1871].

Masotti (Francesco). Prediche disposte secondo l'ordine delle materie. 3 v. 4°. *Venezia, T. Bettinelli,* 1769–70.

Massachusetts. (*Province of Massachusetts-bay*). Extract from the journal of the hon[ble] house of representatives, May [30th] 1755. Relating to the imprisonment of Daniel Fowle and Royall Tyler, [1754]. 14 pp. 16°. [*Boston, D. Fowle,* 1755].

[*With* THUMB (Thomas). Monster of monsters. 1754. *Note.*—Contains a list of the names of all who voted, pro and con, on the question of the rightful imprisonment of Fowle].

——— (*State of Massachusetts*). Documents printed by order of the senate and house of representatives. 1871. 4 v. 8°. *Boston, Wright & Potter,* 1871.

——— Public documents: being the annual reports of various public officers and institutions. 1870. 4 v. 8°. *Boston, Wright & Potter,* 1871.

——— *Board of health.* First and third annual reports. January, 1870 and 1872. 2 v. 8°. *Boston, Wright & Potter,* 1870–72.

——— *Board of railroad commissioners.* Second annual report of the board of railroad commissioners. 1871. 8°. *Boston, Wright & Potter, state printers,* 1871.

——— *Board of state charities.* Seventh annual report of the board of state charities of Massachusetts, to which are added the re-

Massachusetts (*State of*)—continued. ports of its several officers. January, 1871. 8°. *Boston, Wright & Potter*, 1871

——— *Insurance commissioner*. Fifteenth and sixteenth annual reports of the insurance commissioner of the commonwealth of Massachusetts. 1870 and 1871. 3 v. 8°. *Boston, Wright & Potter*, 1870-71.

Massachusetts historical society. Collections. 4th series. v. 9-10. 8°. *Boston, the society*, 1871.

CONTENTS,

The Aspinwall papers.

——— The same. 5th series. v. 1. 8°. *Boston, the society*, 1871.

CONTENTS.

The Winthrop papers, part 3.

——— Proceedings. 1869-70. 8°. *Boston, society*, 1871.

Massey (*Rev.* Dawson). The secret history of romanism. With an introductory essay, by the late rev. Godfrey Massey. 2d ed. enlarged. xvi, 478 pp. 2 l. 12°. *London, Seeleys*, 1853.

Massias (Nicolas, *baron*). Rapport de la nature à l'homme, et de l'homme à la nature, ou essai sur l'instinct, l'intelligence et la vie. 2 v. xliv, 324 pp. 2 tables; 2 p. l. 373 pp. 1 table. 8°. *Paris, F. Didot*, 1821.

Massillon (Jean Baptiste). Petit carême. 1 p. l. 384 pp. 16°. *Paris, A. Eymery*, 1817.

——— Sermons et morceaux choisis, précédés de son éloge. 1 p. l. 653 pp. 1 portrait. 12°. *Paris, Firmin Didot frères*, 1845.

Masson (David, *ll. d.*) The life of John Milton: narrated in connexion with the political, ecclesiastical, and literary history of his time. v. 2. 1638-1643. xii, 608 pp. 8°. *London Macmillan & co.* 1871.

Masson *or* **Gaudichot-Masson** (Auguste Michel Benoit). Hyacinthe l'apprenti ou une énigme sans mot. 279 pp. 1 l. 16°. *Bruxelles, Meline, Cans & cie.* 1841.

——— Rose Himmel. 2 p. l. 259 pp. 16°. *Bruxelles, Meline, Cans & cie.* 1842.

Masters (Martin Kedgwin). The progress of love. A poem. xii, 108 pp. 12°. *Boston, Oliver & Munroe*, 1808.

Masury (John W.) The carriage painters' companion, with sample cards of all the colors used in carriage work. Also practical hints and directions as to the best mode of applying the same; and the proportions for making the best groundwork for lakes and carmines, [etc.] 130 pp. 8°. [*New York*], *J. W. Masury*, [1871].

Matanasius (Chrisostome, *pseudon.*) *See* **Saint-Hyacinthe** (Hyacinthe Cordonnier, *ou* **Thémiseul** de).

Matelief (Cornelis, *the younger*). Journael, ende historische verhael vande treffelijcke reyse, gedaen naer Oost-Indien, ende China door den admirael Cornelis Matelief de jonge, 1605-08. 1 p. l. 142 pp. 6 pl. on 1 sheet. sm. 4°. *Amstelredam, J. Hartgers*, 1648.

[*In* HARTGERTS (J.) Oost-indische voyagien, v. 1, 6e stuck].

Mather (Cotton, *d. d.*) Christian loyalty. Or, some suitable sentiments on the withdraw of king George the first, and the access of king George the second, unto the throne of the british empire. 2 p. l. 25 pp. 12°. *Boston, T. Fleet*, 1727.

——— The christian philosopher; a collection of the best discoveries in nature, with religious improvements. 324 pp. 16°. *Charles town, [Ms.] published at the Middlesex bookstore*, 1815.

——— Early piety, exemplified in the life and death of mr. Nathanael Mather. 2d ed. with a prefatory epistle by Matthew Mead. 7 p. l. 60 pp. 18°. *London, John Dunton*, 1689.

[*Note.*—Erroneously ascribed to Samuel Mather in several catalogues].

——— A father departing. A sermon on the departure of the venerable and memorable dr. Increase Mather, who expired Aug. 23, 1723. 31 pp. 16°. *Boston, N. Belknap*, 1723.

——— A good evening for the best of dayes. An essay, to manage an action of trespass, against those who mispend the Lords-day evening. A sermon preached in the audience of the general assembly, at Boston, 4 d. 9 m. 1708. 3 p. l. 26 pp. 16°. *Boston, B. Green*, 1708.

——— Just commemorations. The death of good men, considered; [with] a brief account of the evangelical work among the christianized Indians of New-England. 1 p. l. iv, 58 pp. 18°. *Boston, S. Gerrish*, 1715.

——— Several sermons concerning walking with God, and that in the dayes of youth. 86 pp. 18°. *London, J. Dunton*, 1689.

[*With his* Early piety, 2d ed. 1689].

——— Strange phenomena of New England: in the seventeenth century: including the "Salem witchcraft," "1692." From the writings of "the rev. Cotton Mather, d. d." Collected and arranged for re-publication by Henry Jones. 54 pp. 8°. *New York, Piercy & Reed*, 1846.

Mather (Increase, *d. d.*) Awakening soul-saving truths, plainly delivered, in several sermons. 1 p. l. 100 pp. 18°. *Boston, S. Kneeland for Gray & Edwards*, 1720.

——— A disquisition concerning the state of the souls of men, (especially of good men) when separated from their bodies, in which some late very remarkable providences relating to apparitions, are considered. 1 p. l. 45 pp. 18°. *Boston, B. Eliot and N. Boone*, 1707.

——— The excellency of a publick spirit discoursed: in a sermon preached in the audience of the general assembly of Massachusetts-bay, May 27, 1702, being the day for the election of counsellors, [followed by] The righteous man a blessing, or seasonable truths in two sermons; and the Morning star. 6 p. l. 84 pp. 18°. *Boston, Nicholas Boone*, 1702.

——— An historical discourse concerning the prevalency of prayer. 3 p. l. 20 pp. sm. 4°. *Boston, John Foster*, 1677.
[*With his* Relation of the troubles in N. E. 1614–75. *Note.*—Slightly imperfect].

——— The mystery of Israel's salvation, explained and applyed: or, a discourse concerning the general conversion of the israelitish nation, the substance of several sermons. 23 p. l. 181 pp. 5 l. 16°. [*London, John Allen*], 1669.

——— A relation of the troubles which have hapned in New-England, by reason of the Indians there. 1614 to 1675. 3 p. l. 76 pp. sm. 4°. *Boston, John Foster*, 1677.
[*Note.*—Leaves damaged at the top].

——— The revolution in New England justified, and the people vindicated from the aspersions cast upon them by mr. John Palmer. [*anon.*] [With] a narrative of the proceedings of sir Edmond Androsse by several gentlemen of his council. 59 pp. 8°. *Reprinted, Boston, I. Thomas*, 1773.
[HAZARD pamphlets, v. 49].

Mather (*Rev.* Richard). An apologie of the chvrches in New-England for chvrch-covenant. Sent over in answer to master Bernard, in the yeare 1639. [*anon.*] 46 pp. sm. 4°. *London, B. Allen*, 1643.
[*With his* Church-government and church-covenant. *London*, 1643].

——— Church-government and church-covenant discvssed, in an answer of the elders of the severall churches in New England to two and thirty questions, sent over to them by divers ministers in England, to declare their judgments therein. [etc. *anon.*] 2 p. l. 84 pp. sm. 4°. *London, B. Allen*, 1643.

——— *and* **Mitchell** (*Rev.* Jonathan). A defence of the answer and arguments of the synod met at Boston in the year 1662, concerning the subject of baptism and consociation of churches. Against the reply made thereto, by rev. John Davenport, in his treatise entituled, Another essay for investigation of the truth, etc. With an answer to the apologeticall preface set before that essay [by Jonathan Mitchel]. By some of the elders who were members of the synod. [*anon.*] 1 p. l. 46, 102 pp. sm. 4°. *Cambridge, [Mass.] S. Green and M. Johnson for Hezekiah Usher*, 1664.

Mather (Samuel, *d. d. of Boston, Mass.*) A dissertation concerning the most venerable name of Jehovah. 3 p. l. 101 pp. 8°. *Boston, Edes & Gill*, 1760.

——— An essay concerning gratitude. 4 p. l. 53 pp. 8°. *Boston, T. Hancock*, 1732.

——— A funeral discourse preached on the occasion of the death of Frederick Lewis, prince of Wales, in the audience of the lieutenant-governor and council, May 22d, 1751, at Boston. 31 pp. 8°. *Boston, J. Draper*, 1751.

——— Life of the learned Cotton Mather. [Abridged by David Jennings. With a preface by Isaac Watts]. 1 p. l. 120 pp. 18°. *Edinburgh, Waugh & Innes*, 1822.
[*Note.*—Title-page wanting].

——— The walk of the upright, with its comfort. A funeral discourse after the decease of the reverend mr. William Welsted and mr. Ellis Gray, colleague pastors of a church in Boston. Preached May 6, 1753. 34 pp. 8°. *Boston, M. Dennis*, 1753.

Mather (*Rev.* Samuel, *of Witney, England*). A funeral sermon for mr. Nathaniel Collier, [of Witney], who died, Oct. 23, 1711. 4 p. l. 15 pp. 12°. *London, N. Hillier*, 1711.

Mathes (James M. *v. d. m.*) Letters to Thos. A. Morris, d. d. senior bishop of the m. e. church. 4th ed. enlarged. 204 pp. 18°. *Bedford (Ind.)* 1871.

Mathew (Richard). The unlearned alchymist his antidote: or a more full and ample explanation of the use, vertue and benefit of my pill. Together with a precious pearl in the midst of a dunghil, being a receit of [his] pill. 7 p. l. 204 pp. 16°. *London, J. Leigh*, 1663.

Mathew Paxton. Edited by the author of "John Drayton," [etc. *anon.*] 3 v. 12°. *London, Hurst & Blackett*, 1854.

Mathews (Cornelius). Poems on man, in his various aspects under the american republic. 112 pp. 16°. *New York, Wiley & Putnam*, 1843.

Mathews (G. H.) Diary of a summer in Europe. 1865. By Porte. [*pseudon.*] 1 p. l. 110 pp. 8°. *New York, Marsh's print*, 1866.

Mathews (Joanna H.) Little sunbeams. 4 v. 16°. *New York, R. Carter & brothers*, 1871–72.

CONTENTS.

v. 1. Belle Power's locket. 242 pp. 3 pl.
2. Dora's motto. 237 pp. 3 pl.
3. Lily Norris' enemy. 240 pp. 3 pl.
4. Jessie's parrot. 245 pp. 3 pl.

Mathews (Julia A.) Grandfather's faith. 288 pp. 8 pl. 16°. *New York, R. Carter & brothers*, 1872.

[Dare to do right series, v. 1].

Mathews (W. S. B.) The Emerson method for reed organs. *See* **Emerson** (L. O.) *and* **Mathews.**

——— (*editor*). *See* **Musical** (The) independent.

Mathews. *See* **Matthews.**

Mathias de San Juan Bautista. Sermon en la dedicacion de el templo de San Bernardo, con nuevo titulo del nombre de Maria, e imagen de Gvadalupe. El dia quinta de la octava. sm. 4°. [*Mexico, viuda de F. R. Lupercio*, 1691].

[*In* RAMIREZ DE VARGAS (A.) Sagrado padron y panegyricos sermones, etc. l. 45–62].

Mathieu. *See* **Matthieu.**

Matinées sénonoises, ou proverbes françois. *See* **Tuet** (Jean Charles François).

Maton (William George). Observations relative chiefly to the natural history, picturesque scenery, and antiquities, of the western counties of England, made in the years 1794 and 1796. 2 v. xi, 336 pp. 8 pl; 2 p. l. 216 pp. 10 l. 1 map. 8 pl. 8°. *Salisbury, J. Easton*, 1797.

Matthews (John, *d. d.*) The influence of the bible in improving the understanding and moral character. With a preliminary essay by Albert Barnes. 252 pp. 18°. *Philadelphia, H. Hall*, 1833.

——— The same. With a memoir of the author, by James Wood, d. d. 215 pp. 12°. *Philadelphia, Presbyterian board of publication*, [1864].

Matthews (Lyman). Memoir of the life and character of Ebenezer Porter, d. d. 396 pp. 1 portrait. 12°. *Boston, Perkins & Marvin*, 1837.

Matthieu (Pierre). Vnhappy prosperitie. Expressed in the histories of Ælius Seianus and Philippa the catanian. Written in french by P: Mathieu, and translated into english by s^{r}. Th. Hawkins. [1st ed.] 3 p. l. 299 pp. sm. 4°. [*London*, 1632].

[*Note.*—Cette histoire n'est qu'une allusion continuelle au maréchale d'Ancre et à sa femme.—*Biographie universelle*].

Mattison (Seth). The retired muse, or forest songster; embracing a number of sentimental and devotional poems, together with several extracts from a manuscript poem, entitled The charms of friendship, [and a sermon to youth, delivered, Scipio, March 24, 1822]. 215 pp. 18°. *Ithaca*, [*N. Y.*] *W. Batcheller*, 1825.

Mattocks (Brewer, *m. d.*) Minnesota as a home for invalids. 200 pp. 16°. *Philadelphia, J. B. Lippincott & co; St. Paul* (*Minn.*) *D. D. Merrill, Randall & co.* 1871.

Mattson (Morris, *m. d.*) The american vegetable practice, or a new and improved guide to health. Designed for the use of families. In six parts. 2 v. in 1. xiii, 707 pp. 26 (24 col.) pl. 8°. *Boston, D. L. Hale*, 1841.

——— The same. 2d ed. 2 v. in 1. viii, 708, xxii pp. 8°. *Boston, W. Johnson*, 1845.

Maty (Matthew). *See* **Journal** britannique, 1750–55.

Maubuy (Aublet de). *See* **Aublet de Maubuy.**

Maunder (Samuel). The treasury of history: comprising a general introductory outline of universal history, ancient and modern; and a series of separate histories of every principal nation that exists. To which is added, The history of the United States, by John Inman. 2 v. ix, 19–760 pp; x, 13–638 pp. 8°. *New York, D. Adee*, 1845.

Maurice (*Rev.* Thomas). Richmond Hill; a descriptive and historical poem: illustrative of the principal objects viewed from that beautiful eminence. By the author of Indian antiquities. [*anon.*] 3 p. l. 166 pp. 4°. *London, author*, 1807.

Maury (Matthew Fontaine). First lessons in geography. 62 pp. sm. 4°. *New York, University publishing co.* 1871.

[MAURY's geographical series].

——— Manual of geography: a complete treatise on mathematical, civil, and physical ge-

Maury (Matthew Fontaine)—continued. ography. 162 pp. 4°. *New York, University publishing co.* [1870].
[MAURY'S geographical series].

——— Maury's geographical series. The world we live in. Intermediate. 104 pp. 4°. *New York, University publishing co.* 1871.

Mavor (William, *ll. d.*) Classical english poetry, for the use of schools, and young persons in general. New ed. Eng. title, xii, 480 pp. 12°. *London, Longman,* 1827.

Mawman (Joseph). An excursion to the highlands of Scotland and the english lakes, with recollections, descriptions, and references to historical facts. xiv, 291 pp. 3 pl. 1 map. 8°. *London, J. Mawman,* 1805.

Maxwell (Maria). Ernest Grey; or, the sins of society. 335 pp. 6 pl. 12°. *New York, T. W. Strong,* 1855.

Maxwell (William Hamilton). Legends of the Cheviots and the Lammermuir: a companion to "Wild sports of the west." New ed. 2 v. in 1. 2 p. l. 342 pp. 1 pl; 338 pp. 1 pl. 8°. *London, R. Bentley,* 1849.

Maxwell (*pseudon.*) Alick and his blind uncle. 144 pp. 3 pl. 18°. *Philadelphia, Presbyterian board of publication,* [1863].

——— Cherry-bounce, or the wise management of human nature. 180 pp. 1 pl. 18°. *Philadelphia, Presbyterian board of publication,* [1864].

——— The early water-melons, or Alick never afraid of the truth. 144 pp. 2 pl. 18°. *Philadelphia, Presbyterian board of publication,* [1863].

——— My dog Rover, and some good that he did in the world. 144 pp. 1 pl. 18°. *Philadelphia, Presbyterian board of publication,* [1864].

——— The Nevers. 108 pp. 2 pl. 18°. *Philadelphia, Presbyterian board of publication,* [1865].

——— Teddy, the bill-poster, and how he became uncle Alick's right hand man. 216 pp. 3 pl. 18°. *Philadelphia, Presbyterian board of publication,* [1864].

——— Uncle Alick's sabbath-school. 180 pp. 18°. *Philadelphia, Presbyterian board of publication,* [1864].

May (Frederick). London press directory and advertisers handbook, 1871. 8°. *London, F. May,* 1871.

May (Sophie, *pseudon.*) *See* **Clarke** (*Mrs.* R. S.)

Mayans y Siscar (Gregorio). Cartas morales, militares, civiles, i literarias de varios autores españoles. 5 v. 16°. *Valencia, S. Fauli,* 1773.

——— Emmanuelis Martini vita. 4 p. l. 96 pp. 4°. *Amstelaedami, apud J. Wetstenium & G. Smith,* 1738.
[*In* MARTI (Manuel). Epistolarum libri duodecim. 1738].

——— Gregorii Majansii epistolarum libri sex. 6 p. l. xxiv, 420 pp. 4°. *Valentiæ Edetanorum, typis A. Bordazàr de Artâzu,* 1732.

Mayence. Agenda ecclesiæ mogvntinensis. Necessariis quibusdam additionibus auctior et multis locis emendatior jam denuo typis evulgata per Wolfgangum archiepiscopum moguntinum. 16 p. l. 323 pp. fol. *Mogvntiae, P. Lippius,* 1599.

Mayer (A. L.) Cullings from Carmel, a selection of parables and allegories originally wrought out from the hebrew. 125 pp. 18°. *Richmond, B. W. Gillis,* 1871.

Mayer (Brantz). Baltimore as it was and as it is: a historical sketch of the ancient town and modern city, from the foundation, in 1729, to 1870; compiled and written from authentic materials. 8°. *Baltimore, Richardson & Bennett,* 1871.
[*In* BALTIMORE: past and present. *Baltimore,* 1871. pp. 9–146].

Mayer (Lewis). Expository lectures, or discourses on scriptural subjects. vii, 268 pp. 12°. *Harrisburg, Hickok & Cantine,* 1845.

Mayerne (*Sir* Theodore Turquet de). Theod. Turqueti d. de Mayerne tractatus de arthritide. Accesserunt ejusdem consilia aliquot medicinalia. Emittente Theoph. Boneto. 3 p. l. 188 pp. 7 l. 18°. *Londini, impensis M. Pitt,* 1676.

Mayfield (Millie, *pseudon.*) Carrie Harrington; or, scenes in New Orleans. A novel. 354 pp. 12°. *New York, A. Atchison,* 1857.

——— Progression; or, the south defended. 226 pp. 12°. *Cincinnati, O. Applegate & co.* 1860.

Maygrier (Jacques Pierre). The anatomist's manual: or a treatise on the manner of preparing all the parts of anatomy, followed by a complete description of these parts. Translated from the 4th french edition, by Gunning S. Bedford, m. d. 2 v. in 1. 378 pp; 305 pp. 12°. *New York, Collins & co.* 1832.

Maynard (Thomas). Maynard's sabbath school echo. Sixth edition of Maynard's selected sabbath school hymns. With an appendix. 256 pp. 32°. *Utica (N. Y.) Roberts,* 1861.

Mazade (Charles de). L'Italie moderne. Récits des guerres et des révolutions italiennes. 2 p. l, xx, 356 pp. 12°. *Paris, M. Lévy frères*, 1860.

Mazeret (Constantin). Le livre unique, ou nouveau choix d'anecdotes, tirées de l'histoire sainte et profane, ancienne et moderne, classées par ordre d'après les nombres, depuis 1 jusqu'à 100. 2 v. 2 p. l. iv, 372 pp; 2 p. l. 352 pp. 12°. *Paris, F. Jeune*, 1824.

Mazochius. *See* **Mazzocchi.**

Mazza (Antonio). Historiarvm epitome de rebvs salernitanis. 7 p. l. 160 pp. 8 l. 1 pl. sm. 4°. *Neapoli, I. F. Paci*, 1681.

Mazzocchi (Alessio Simmaco). A. S. Mazochii spicilegii biblici tomus i–iii. 3 v. 4°. *Neapoli, ex regia typographia*, 1762–78.

Mazzucchelli (Giovanni Maria, *conte*). La vita di Pietro Aretino. viii, 303 pp. 6 pl. 1 portrait. 8°. *Padova, G. Comino*, 1741.

Mead (*Mrs.* A. M.) A token of affection; or, sketches by a christian's way-side. 202 pp. 24°. *Philadelphia, Hooker & Agnew*, 1842.

Mead (Charles). American minstrel; consisting of poetical essays on various subjects. Eng. title, 175 pp. 18°. *Philadelphia, J. Mortimer*, 1828.

Meade (*Rev.* William). The bible and the classics. 559 pp. 8°. *New York, R. Carter & brothers*, 1861.

Meader (L. P. *m. d.*) The people's medical companion and family guide, in the preparation of medicine for the sick and afflicted. 239 pp. 16°. *Cincinnati, author*, 1861.

——— The people's physician; designed as a manual of medicine, expressly for the use of families and individuals. To which is added a list of synonyms of many common medical plants. 450 pp. 8°. *Cincinnati, author*, 1860.

Meadowleigh. 1863. *See* **Manning** (A.)

Meagher (Thomas Francis). Selections from his speeches and writings. *See* **Lyons** (*Capt.* W. F.)

Meaney (Mary L.) Grace Morton; or, the inheritance. A catholic tale. By M. L. M. [*anon.*] 324 pp. 16°. *Philadelphia, P. F. Cunningham*, 1864.

Mears (*Rev.* John W.) The bible in the workshop; or, christianity the friend of labor. 344 pp. 12°. *New York, C. Scribner*, 1857.

——— Martyrs of France; or, the witness of the reformed church of France, from the reign of Francis first, to the revocation of the edict of

Mears (*Rev.* John W.)—continued.

Nantes. 147 pp. 1 pl. 18°. *Philadelphia, Presbyterian publication committee*, [1864].

Mechanics' (The) magazine and journal of science, arts, and manufactures. [Weekly]. Jan. 6 to Dec. 30, 1871. New series, v. 25–26; [complete series], v. 94–95. 4°. *London, C. W. Bradley*, 1871.

Mede (*Rev.* Joseph). Clavis apocalyptica ex innatis et insitis visionum characteribus eruta et demonstrata. Ed. 2ª. 36 pp. sm. 4°. *Cantabrigiae, T. Buck*, 1632.

——— In sancti Joannis apocalypsin commentarius. Ad amussim clavis apocalypticæ. 2 p. l. 294 pp. sm. 4°. *Cantabrigiæ, T. Buck*, 1632.

[*With his* Clavis apocalyptica, ed. 2a.]

Medenbach Wakker (Jacobus Philipp van). Amoenitates litterariae. vi, 168 pp. 8°. *Trajecti ad Rhenum, apud A. a Paddenburg*, 1770.

Medhurst (Walter Henry). China; its state and prospects, with especial reference to the spread of the gospel; containing allusions to the antiquity, extent, population, civilization, literature, and religion of the Chinese. xvi, 13–472 pp. 3 pl. 1 map. 12°. *Boston, Crocker & Brewster*, 1838.

Mediation. The function of thought. [*anon.*] 213 pp. 16°. *Andover (Ms.) Warren F. Draper*, 1871.

Medical (The) record. A semi-monthly journal of medicine and surgery. Edited by George F. Shrady, m. d. March 1, 1871, to Feb. 15, 1872. v. 6. 8°. *New York, W. Wood & co.* [1872].

Medical (The) register of New York and vicinity, for the year commencing June 1, 1871. Published under the supervision of the New York medico-historical society. A. E. M. Purdy, m. d. editor. v. 9. 16°. *New York, W. Wood & co.* 1871.

Medical (The) times. A semi-monthly journal of medical and surgical science. James H. Hutchinson, m. d. editor. Oct. 1, 1870, to Sept. 15, 1871. v. 1. 8°. *Philadelphia, J. B. Lippincott & co.* 1871.

Medina (Antonio de). Sermon predicado en el castillo de San Felipe del Puerto del Callao, a su dedicacion y bendicion. 11ᵉ de Mayo, 1625. 18 l. sm. 4°. *Lima, G. de Contreras*, 1625.

Medina (Pedro de). L'art de navigver de maistre Pierre de Medine: contenant toutes les reigles, secrets, & enseignemens nécessaires, à la bonne nauigation, traduict de

Medina (Pedro de)—continued. castillan en françoys, auec augmentation, par Nicolas de Nicolai. Eng. title, 5 p. l. 115 l. fol. *Lyon, G. Roville*, 1554.

Medrano (Sebastian Fernandez de). *See* **Fernandez de Medrano.**

Meehan (*Rev* C. P.) The fate and fortunes of Hugh O'Neill, earl of Tyrone, and Rory O'Donel, earl of Tyrconnel; their flight from Ireland, their vicissitudes abroad, and their death in exile. xvi, 583 pp. 4 portraits. 8°. *Dublin, J. Duffy*, 1868.

Meek (*Rev.* Robert). Reasons for attachment and conformity to the church of England. 3d ed. xii, ii, 211 pp. 18°. *London, J. Hatchard & son*, 1846.

Meeker (*Rev.* Eli). Analytical system of spelling, reading, and teaching. 204 pp. 12°. *New-York, Elliott & Palmer*, 1829.

Meerman (Geraard). Uitvinding der boekdrukkunst, getrokken uit het latynsch, met ene voorreden en aantekeningen van Henrik Gockinga; hierachter is gevoegt ene lyst der boeken, in de Nederlanden gedrukt voor 't jaar MD, opgestelt door Jakob Visser. 2 parts in 1 v. 8 p. l. 68 pp; 2 p. l. 118 pp. 4°. *Amsteldam, P. van Damme*, 1767.

Megerlin (Peter). Petri Megerlini theatrvm divini regiminis a mvndo condito vsqve ad nostrvm secvlvm, delineatum in tabula mathematico-historica, cum indice historico-chronologico. Adjectus est commentarivs chronologicvs. 9 p. l. 354, 122 pp. 4°. *Basileae, J. L. König & J. Brandmyller*, 1683.

Meggen (Jodoc von). Iodoci a Meggen patricii lvcerini peregrinatio hierosolymitana. 246 pp. 18°. *Dilingæ, J. Mayer*, 1580.

Mehun (Jean de). *See* **Meun.**

Meibom (Johann Heinrich). D. Joh. Henrici Meibomii de cynophoria, seu canis portatione ignominiosa. Epistola ad cl. virum Joh. Marquardum. 4°. *Norimbergæ*, 1685.

[*With* PAULLINI (Christian Franz). Cynographia curiosa, pp. 244–252].

Meidinger (Johann Valentin). Méthode nouvelle et amusante pour apprendre l'allemand, ou grammaire allemande pratique. Avec une préface de m. l'abbé Robert. 14e éd. originale. 1 p. l. xii, 522 pp. 1 table. 8°. *Frankfort sur le Mein, J. V. Meidinger*, 1837.

Meigs (Charles D. *m. d.*) The Philadelphia practice of midwifery. xii, 370 pp. 22 pl. 8°. *Philadelphia, J. Kay, jr. & brother*, 1838.

——— The same. 2d ed. improved and enlarged. 408 pp. 36 pl. 8°. *Philadelphia, J. Kay, jun. & brother*, 1842.

Meigs (*Major* Return J.) Journal of the expedition against Quebec, under command of col. Benedict Arnold, in the year 1775, with an introduction and notes, by Charles I. Bushnell. 57 pp. 1 portrait. 8°. *New York, privately printed*, 1864.

Meijboom (L. S. P.) Het oude en het nieuwe licht. Twaalf leerredenen. 2 p. l. 192 pp. 8°. *Amsterdam, H. A. Frijlink*, 1856.

[*With his* Twaalf bijzonderheden, etc. 1855].

——— Twaalf bijzonderheden uit Jesus' kinderlijken leeftijd. Leerredenen. 3 p. l. 194 pp. 8°. *Amsterdam, H. A. Frijlink*, 1855.

Meijlan. *See* **Meylan.**

Meikle (James, *m. d.*) Solitude sweetened; or, miscellaneous meditations on various subjects, written in distant parts of the world. 3d american ed. 315 pp. 12°. *Albany, C. Dodge*, 1812.

Meilan (Mark Anthony). The dramatic works of M. A. Meilan: consisting of three tragedies, Emilia, Northumberland, The friends. Published by way of an appeal from the arbitrary decisions of the despots of the drama. 8 p. l. 138, 110, 126 pp. 8°. *London, E. Cox for the author*, [1771].

Meiners (Christoph). Histoire de l'origine, des progrès et de la décadence des sciences dans la Grèce; traduite de l'allemand par J. Ch. Laveaux. 5 v. 8°. *Paris, J. C. Laveaux & cie.* 1799.

Meissel (Conrad). *See* **Celtes** (Conrad).

Mela (Pomponius). The rare and [singu]ler worke of the situation of the world, most orderly pre[pa]red, and deuided euery parte by itselfe. Wherevnto is added, that learned worke of Iulius Solinus Polyhistor. Translated into englishe, by Arthur Golding. *b. l.* 8 p. l. 124 pp. 12°. *London, Thomas Hacket*, 1590.

[*Note.*—Instead of Solinus, the translator has added "A breefe discourse in which the partes of the earth are exactlie described," pp. 94–124].

Melampodio (Falcidio, *pseudon.*) *See* **Aromatarii** (Giuseppe degli).

Melanchthon (Philipp). Farrago aliqvot epigrammatum, Philippi Melanchthonis & aliorũ quorundam eruditorum. Opusculum sane elegans ac nouum. Eng. title, 88 l. 1 pl. 16°. *Haganoæ, per I. Secerium*, 1528.

[*With* SOTER (Johannes). Epigrammata].

——— Lavs formicæ. 18°. [*Lugd. Batavorum*, 1644].

[*In* DISSERTATIONVM lvdicrarvm et amœnitatvm scriptores varij, pp. 190–208].

Melanchthon (Philipp) *and* **Jonas** (Justus). Apology of the Augsburg confession. [1531]. 8°. [*Newmarket*, 1854].
[*In* EVANGELICAL lutheran church. The christian book of concord, pp. 141-359].

Melbourne observatory. *See* **Victoria** (*Australia*).

Meline (James F.) Mary queen of Scots and her latest english historian. A narrative of the principal events in the life of Mary Stuart; with some remarks on mr. Froude's History of England. x, 336 pp. 12°. *New York, Hurd & Houghton*, 1872.

Meller (Henry James). Nicotiana; or the smoker's and snuff-taker's companion; containing the history of tobacco; culture—medical qualities and the laws relative to its importation and manufacture: with an essay in its defence. 3d ed. xvi, 128 pp. 1 pl. 18°. *London, E. Wilson*, 1833.

Melling (Antoine Ignace). Voyage pittoresque de Constantinople et des rives du Bosphore d'après les dessins de m. Melling. Publié par mm. Treuttel et Würtz. 2 v. 3 p. l. 10 pp. 32 l. 24 pl; eng. title, 33 l. 24 pl. 3 maps. fol. *Paris, éditeurs*, 1819.

Mello (Francisco Manuel de). An historical account of the discovery of the island of Madeira. *See* **Alcoforado** (Francisco).

Melon (Jean François). Essai politique sur le commerce. 8°. [*Paris*, 1843].
[*In* DAIRE (Eugène). Économistes-financiers du 18e siècle, 1843, pp. 690-836].

Melvil (*Sir* James). The memoires of sir James Melvil: containing an impartial account of the most remarkable affairs of state during the last age, not mention'd by other historians: more particularly relating to the kingdoms of England and Scotland, under the reigns of queen Elisabeth, Mary queen of Scots, and king James. Now published from the original manuscript. By George Scott. [1st ed.] 8 p. l. 204 pp. 14 l. fol. *London, E. H. for R. Butler*, 1683.

Melville (Herman). Israel Potter: his fifty years of exile. 276 pp. 12°. *New York, G. P. Putnam & co.* 1855.

——— The piazza tales. 2 p. l. 431 pp. 12°. *New York, Dix & Edwards*, 1856.

Memminger (*Rev.* R. W.) What is religion? A protest against "The spirit of the age." A plea for the reality of the spiritual. 246 pp. 12°. *Philadelphia, Claxton, Remsen & Haffelfinger*, 1872.

Memoir of Elizabeth T. King. With extracts from her letters and journal. [*anon.*] 128 pp. 12°. *Baltimore, Armstrong & Berry*, 1859.

Memoir of mrs. Chloe Spear, a native of Africa, who was enslaved in childhood, and died in Boston, Jan. 3, 1815, aged 65 years. By a lady of Boston. [*anon.*] 108 pp. incl. 1 pl. 18°. *Boston, J. Loring*, 1832.

Memoir of mrs. Eliza G. Jones, missionary to Burmah and Siam. [*anon.*] 172 pp. 1 portrait. 18°. *Philadelphia, American baptist publication and sunday school society*, 1842.

Memoir of mrs. W. W. Duncan. *See* **Lundie** (Mary Graham).

Memoir of old Humphrey [*i. e.* George Mogridge]; with gleanings from his portfolio, in prose and verse. [*anon.*] 252 pp. 1 portrait. 18°. *Philadelphia, American sunday school union*, [1855].

Memoir of rev. Alvan Hyde, d. d. of Lee, Mass. [*anon.*] vii, 13-408 pp. 1 portrait. 12°. *Boston, Perkins, Marvin & co.* 1835.

Memoir of Robert Bowne Minturn. Printed for private circulation. [*anon.*] 353 pp. 12°. *New York, A. D. F. Randolph & co.* 1871.

Memoir of the rev. Samuel Davies, formerly president of the college of New Jersey. [*anon.*] 131 pp. 16°. *Boston, Mass. sabbath school society*, 1832.

Mémoires de Gaspard comte de Chavagnac. *See* **Courtilz de Sandras** (Gatien de).

Mémoires de l'abbé Terrai. *See* **Coquereau** (J. B. L.)

Memoirs and adventures of sir William Kirkaldy of Grange, knight, commander of french horse, lord of the secret council, and governor of the castle of Edinburgh for Mary queen of Scots. [*anon.*] x, 383 pp. 8°. *Edinburgh, W. Blackwood & sons*, 1849.

Memoirs of a deist, written first a. d. 1793-4; being a narrative of the life and opinions of the writer, until the period of his conversion to the faith of Jesus Christ. [*anon.*] viii, 227 pp. 8°. *London, J. Hatchard & son*, 1824.

Memoirs of eminently pious women. [*anon.*] *See* **Gibbons** (Thomas, *d. d.*)

Memoirs of general Andrew Jackson, seventh president of the United States. To which is added the eulogy of hon. George Bancroft, delivered in Washington, D. C. Compiled by a citizen of western New York. [*anon.*] 270 pp. 3 pl. 1 portrait. 12°. *Auburn, J. C. Derby & co.* 1845.

Memoirs of madame de Barnevelt. *See* **Auvigny** (Jean du Castre d').

Memoirs of the life and writings of Vittorio Alfieri. *See* **Lloyd** (Charles).

Memoirs of the siege of Quebec, capital of all Canada, and of the retreat of monsieur de Bourlemaque, from Carillon to the Isle aux Noix in lake Champlain. From the journal of a french officer on board the Chezine frigate, taken by his majesty's ship Rippon. [*anon.*] Compared with the accounts transmitted home by major general Wolfe, and vice-admiral Saunders, with occasional remarks. By Richard Gardiner. 39 pp. 1 pl. 4°. *London, R. & J. Dodsley*, 1761.

Memoirs of the society of Grub-street. *See* **Martyn** (John) *and* **Russell** (Richard).

Memoranda, illustrative of the tombs and sepulchral decorations of the Egyptians; with a key to the egyptian tomb now exhibiting in Piccadilly. Also, remarks on mummies, and observations on the process of embalming. [*anon.*] v, 89 pp. 1 pl. 8°. *London, T. Boys*, 1822.

Memorial de lo svcedido en la ciudad de México, desde el dia primero de Nouiembre, de 1623, hasta quienze de Enero de 1624. [*anon.*] 28 l. sm. fol. [*México*, 1624].

Memorial (A) of Samuel Harvey Taylor. [Including an address at his funeral by E. A. Park]. Compiled by his last class. 127 pp. 1 portrait. 8°. *Andover*, [*Ms.*] *W. F. Draper*, 1871.

Memorie vande ghewichtige redenen die de heeren staten generael [etc.] 1608. *See* **Usselincx** (Willem).

Memphis (*City of*). Edwards' annual directory to the inhabitants, institutions, business firms, etc. in the city of Memphis, for 1871. 8°. *Memphis, Southern publishing co.* [1871].

Memphis public ledger. *See* **Public** ledger (Memphis daily).

Ménage (Gilles). Gargilii Macronis parasitosophistæ metamorphosis. 18°. *Norimbergae*, 1665.

[*In* EPULUM parasiticum, pp. 109–126, 1 pl.]

——— Vita Gargilii Mamurræ, parasito-pædagogi, scriptore Marco Licinio. [*pseudon.*] 18°. *Norimbergae*, 1665.

[*In* EPULUM parasiticum, pp. 33–108].

Menagius (Ægidius). *See* **Ménage** (Gilles).

Menapius (Wilhelm). Encomivm febris qvartanae. 18°. [*Lugd. Batavorum*, 1644].

[*In* DISSERTATIONVM lvdicrarvm et amœnitatvm scriptores varij, pp. 474–518].

Ménard (Léon). Histoire des antiquités de la ville de Nismes et de ses environs. 10e éd. augmentée du résultat des fouilles, jusqu'en 1845; d'un recueil d'inscriptions; d'un mémoire sur l'inscription de la maison carrée, et d'une notice des musées de notre ville, ornée de gravures, par J. F. A. Perrot. 4 p. l. 220 pp. 17 pl. 8°. *Nismes, éditeurs*, 1846.

Mencken (Johann Burchard). Analecta de calamitate litteratorum. 12 p. l. 594 pp. 15 l. 16°. *Lipsiae, J. F. Gleditsch*, 1707.

CONTENTS.

ALCIONIO (Pietro). Medices legatus, sive de exilio libri duo, p. 1.
BARBERIO (Giuseppe). De miseria poetarum græcorum, p. 483.
TOLL (Cornelis). De infelicitate litteratorum, p. 413.
VALERIANO BOLZANI (Giovanni Pietro). Contarenus, sive de litteratorum infelicitate libri duo, p. 251.

Mendell (G. H.) A treatise on military surveying, theoretical and practical, including a description of surveying instruments. 153 pp. 2 charts. 12°. *New York, D. Van Nostrand*, 1864.

Mendelssohn-Bartholdy (Felix). Mendelssohn's four-part songs, complete, with english and german words. The english version by J. C. D. Parker. 143 pp. 8°. *Boston, O. Ditson*, [1856]. s.

Mendez (Francisco). Typographia española, ò historia de la introduccion, propagacion y progresos del arte de la imprenta en España. A la que antecede una noticia general sobre la imprenta de la Europa, y de la China: adornado todo con notas instructivas y curiosas. v. 1. 1 p. l. xviii, 424 pp. sm. 4°. *Madrid, la viuda de J. Ibarra*, 1776.

[*Note.*—No more published].

Mendez (Luis). Sermon panegyrico, en la celebridad de la dedicacion del templo nuevo de San Bernardo, titvlo Maria de Gvadalupe; dia sexto de la octaua. sm. 4°. [*Mexico, viuda de F. R. Lupercio*, 1691].

[*In* RAMIREZ DE VARGAS (A.) Sagrado padron y panegyricos sermones, etc. l. 63–73].

Mendham (*Rev.* Joseph). The life and pontificate of saint Pius the fifth. Subjoined is a reimpression of a historic deduction of the episcopal oath of allegiance to the pope, in the church of Rome. xx, 326 pp. 8°. *London, J. Duncan*, 1832.

——— The same. Supplement, containing additions and corrections. 22 pp. 8°. *London, J. Duncan*, 1833.

[*With* the preceding].

Mendoza (Bernardino de). Theoriqve and practise of warre. Written to don Philip prince of Castil. Translated out of the castilian tonge into englishe, by sr. Edwarde Hoby, knight. Directed to sr. George Carew, knight. 4 p. l. 166 pp. sm. 4°. [*n. p.*] 1597.

Mendoza (Juan Gonzalez de). Histoire dv grand royavme de la Chine, sitvé avx Indes Orientales, diuisée en deux parties. Contenant trois voyages faits vers iceluy, 1577–81. Faite en espagnol. Mise en françois. Par Lvc de la Porte. 12 p. l. 307, 24 l. 16°. *Paris, Adrian Perier,* 1600.

Ménestrier (Claude François). La philosophie des images. Composée d'vn ample recveil de devises, et du jugement de tous les ouvrages qui ont été faits sur cette matière. 2 v. 8 p. l. 126, 336 pp; 1 p. l. 508 pp. 12°. *Paris, R. J. B. De la Caille,* 1682–3.

Menghi *or* **Mengi** (Girolamo). Compendio dell' arte essorcistica, et possibilità delle mirabili, et stvpende operationi delli demoni, et de i malefici. Con li rimedij opportuni alle infirmità maleficiali. Con vna copiosissima gionta. Nouamente posta in luce. 8 p. l. 614 pp. 29 l. 16°. *Bologna, G. Rossi,* 1584.

Menippo (*pseudon.*) *See* **Pignoria** (Lorenzo).

Menno Simons. Opera Menno Symons, ofte groot sommarie, dat is, vergaderingh, van sijne boecken en schriften. Getrouwelijck in onse nederduytsche spraecke gestelt. 6 p. l. 1186 pp. 6 l. sm. 4°. [*n. p.*] 1646.

CONTENTS.

Een fundament en klare aenwijsinge vande salichmakende leere Jesu Christi, p. 1.
Van het rechte christen geloove, 1556, p. 143.
Een schoone ende grondelijcke leeringe uyt des heeren woort, allen menschen (die haer nae Christus naem laten noemen), 1556, p. 247.
Een troostellijcke vermaninghe, van dat lijden, cruys, vervolginge der heyligen, p. 269.
Een seer lieflicke meditation ende godtsalige oeffeninge, met vele christelicke leeringen, p. 321.
Een klare onderwijsinge uyt des heeren woordt, van de geestelijcke verrijsenisse, ende nieuwe oft hemelsche geboorte, 8 l, following p. 348
Een grondelijcke onderwijs, ofte bericht, vande excommunicatie, p. 349.
Een suyvelrijck ondervijs ende leere, hoe alle vrome ouders haer kinderen (na uytwijsen der schriftueren) schuldich ende gehouden zijn, te regeeren, te kastijden, te onderrichten, p. 399.
Een klare beantwoordinghe over eene schrift Gellij Fabri, p. 413.
Een seer droeffelijcke supplicatie der armen ende ellendigen christenen, p. 613.
Een corte klaechlijcke ontschuldinghe der ellendige christenen, p. 623.
Een klaer bericht ende schriftelijcke aenwijsinghe van der excommunicatie, p. 631.
Een klare onwederspreeckelijcke bekentenisse dat de geheele Christus Jesus Gods eengeboren ende eerstgheboren eygen sone is. Met een grondelijcke confutation der voornaemster tegenspreucken van Iohanne a Lasco, p. 657.
Een vermanende belijdinge, van den drie-eenighen, eeuwighen, ende waren Godt, vader, soon, eende heyligen geest, 1550. Eerst in druck uytgegaen 1597. Ende nu wederom vernieuwt 1600. p. 725.
Verklaringe des christelijcken doopsels in den water, 1600, p. 741.
Die oorsake, waerom dat ick m. s. niet af en late te leeren, ende te schrijven, p. 823.
Een grondelicke ende klare bekentenisse der armen ende ellendige christenen van der rechtveerdighmakinge, predikers, doope, nachtmael, ende eedtsweeren, 1552, p. 865.

Menno Simons—continued.

Een seer grontlicke antwoort op Zylis ende Lemmekes, onverdiende lasterlijcke faemrooven, p. 905.
Een vveemoedige ende christelijcke ontschuldinge ende verantwoordinghe, 1645, p. 927.
Een korte ende klare belijdinghe ende schriftelijcke aenwijsinghe, ten eersten van der menschwerdinghe ons liefs heeren Jesu Christi. Ten tweeden, hoe dat beyde de leeraers ende de gemeynte Christi, na schriftsvermeldinge sullen ende moeten geaert zijn, geschreven aen Johan a Lasco, 1544, p. 975.
Een gantsch duytlick ende bescheyden antwoort anno 1556, op Martini Microns antichristische leere, p. 1021.
Een seer hertgrondelicke (doch scherpe) sent-brieff aen Martinum Micron selve, tot een gantsch noodelijcke verantwoordinghe zijnder onbeleefder leughenen, mishandelinghen, etc. p. 1125.
Een gantsch duytelijcke ende klaer bewijs, uyt die h. schriftuere, dat Jesus Christus, is de rechte beloofde David in den geest, een koninck aller koningen [etc.] Tegens de grouwelicke ende grootsde blasphemie van Ian van Leyden. Noyt voor desen gedruckt, p. 1163.

——— The same. The complete works of Menno Simon, translated from the original dutch or holland. 2 v. in 1. iv, 288 pp; 455 pp. 4°. *Elkhart (Ind.) J. F. Funk & brother,* 1871.

Mentzel und v. Lengerke's verbesserter landwirthschaftlicher hülfs- und schreib-kalender auf 1870 [und] 1871. 23ter und 24ter jahrgang. Herausgegeben von O. Mentzel. 4 v. 18°. *Berlin, Wiegand & Hempel,* 1870–71. s.

Menzies *or* **Menzeis** (John), *and* **Dempster** (Francis). Papismus lucifugus, or a faithfull copie of the papers exchanged betwixt mr. Iohn Menzeis and mr. Francis Dempster iesuit, otherwise sirnamed Rin or Logan. 18 p. l. 272 pp. sm. 4°. *Aberdene, I. Forbes younger,* 1668.

Menzini (Benedetto). Poetica e satire di Benedetto Menzini con annotazioni. 1 p. l. xliii, 432 pp. 1 portrait. 8°. *Milano, società de classici italiani,* 1808.

Meray (Antony). Les libres prêcheurs devanciers de Luther et de Rabelais. Étude historique, critique et anecdotique sur les xive, xve, et xvie siècles. 2 p. l. 222 pp. 1 l. 16°. *Paris, A. Claudin,* 1860.

Mercein (Imogen). Conversations on the geography, topography and natural history of Palestine. 304 pp. 18°. *New York, T. Mason & G. Lane,* 1840.

Mercer (*Rev.* Jesse). The cluster of spiritual songs, divine hymns, and sacred poems; being chiefly a collection. 5th ed. 540 pp. 18°. *Philadelphia, proprietor,* 1829.

——— The same. 5th ed. corrected. 540 pp. 24°. *Philadelphia, J. J. Woodward,* 1830.

——— The same. 5th ed. corrected, and enlarged by an appendix. 540, 11 pp. 18°. *Philadelphia, J. J. Woodward,* 1835.

Merchants (The) and bankers' almanac for 1871. 8°. *New York, Bankers' magazine & statistical register*, 1871.

Meredith (L. P. *m. d.*) The teeth and how to save them. 271 pp. 16°. *Philadelphia, J. B. Lippincott & co.* 1871.

Merian (Marie Sibylle). Der rupsen begin, voedzel en wonderbaare verandering, [etc.] 3 v. in 1. 150 col. pl. 4°. *Amsterdam, auteur*, [1678].

Meriden (Kate, *pseudon?*) Leaves from Hemlock valley. A collection of poems and stories. 104 pp. 12°. *New York, J. B. Miller*, 1872.

Mérimée (Prosper). Notes d'un voyage en Auvergne. Extrait d'un rapport adressé à. m. le ministre de l'intérieur. 2 p. l. 414 pp. 1 pl. 8°. *Paris, H. Fournier*, 1838.

Meritz (Gustav). Gottlieb Frey. *See* **Nieritz** (Gustav).

Merrill (Joseph W. *editor*). The people's cabinet: containing a compendium upon the subjects of natural history; natural philosophy; astronomy; [human anatomy]; the mind and its faculties; history of the United States; government and law; also, the beliefs of various religious denominations; and biographical sketches of distinguished characters in all ages of the world. 344 pp. 12°. *Boston, editor*, 1844.

Merrill (O. N.) True history of the Kansas wars, and their origin, progress and incidents. 54 pp. 1 portrait, 3 pl. 8°. *Cincinnati, J. R. Telfer*, 1856.

Merriman (*Rev.* T. M.) The trail of history; or, history of religion and empire in parallel from the creation to the present time. With a historical diagram. 1 p. l. 11–520 pp. 8°. *Johnson (Vt.) author*, 1860.

Merry's museum for boys and girls. [Monthly]. Jan. 1870, to Dec. 1871. v. 57–60. 8°. *Boston, H. B. Fuller*, 1870–71.

Meruelous reuelacion that was schewyd of almyghty God by sent Nycholas to a monke of Euyshamme yn the days of kynge Richard the fyrst and the yere of oure lord m.c.lxxxxvi. The revelation to the monk of Evesham. [*anon.*] Carefully edited from the unique copy, now in the British museum, of the edition printed by William de Machlinia about 1482, by Edward Arber. 112 pp. 16°. *London*, 1869.

[ARBER's english reprints, v. 8, no. 18].

Merwanjee (Hirjeebhoy). Journal of a residence of two years and a half in Great Britain. *See* **Nowrojee** (Jehangeer) *and* **Merwanjee**.

Mesmer (Franz Anton). Aphorismes de Mesmer, dictés à l'assemblée de ses élèves. Ouvrage mis au jour par Caullet de Veaumorel, 1785. [Nouv. éd.] 18°. [*Paris, Passard*, 1857].

[*In* LORAMBERT. Les merveilles du magnétisme, pp. 119–188].

Messalla (Corvinus, *pseudon?*) Libro di Messala Coruino ad Ottauiano Augusto della progenie sua. 44 pp. 1 l. 16°. *Fiorenza*, 1549.

Messenger (*Rev.* Rosewell). Sentiments on resignation. 225 pp. 5 l. 12°. *Portsmouth (N. H.) author*, 1807.

Metcalfe (Samuel L. *m. d.*) A new theory of terrestrial magnetism. (Read before the New York lyceum of natural history). 158 pp. 1 l. 8°. *New York, G. & C. & H. Carvill*, 1833.

Meteren (Emanuel van). Historia belgica nostri potissimvm temporis, Belgii svb qvatvor burgundis & totidem austriacis principibus coniunctionem & gubernationem breuiter: tvrbas avtem, bella et mvtationes tempore regis Philippi ad annum vsque 1598. plenius complectens. Eng. title, 3 p. l. 623 pp. incl. 17 portraits, 1 map. fol. [*n. p.* 1599]?

Meteyard (Eliza). A group of Englishmen, (1795 to 1815) being records of the younger Wedgewoods and their friends, embracing the history of the discovery of photography and a facsimile of the first photograph. xxii, 416 pp. 2 pl. 8°. *London, Longmans*, 1871.

Methodist (The). An advocate of lay representation. George R. Crooks, d. d. and Abel Stevens, ll. d. editors. [Weekly]. Jan. 1, 1870, to Dec. 30, 1871. v. 11–12. fol. *New York*, [1870–71].

Methodist (The) almanac for the year of our Lord, 1871. Edited by W. H. De Puy, d. d. 61 pp. 12°. *New York, Carlton & Lanahan*, [1871].

Methodist episcopal church. (*Great Britain*). Minutes of the methodist conferences, from the first, held in London, by the late rev. John Wesley, in the year 1744. 88th to 108th conference. 1831 to 1851. v. 7–11. 8°. *London, J. Mason*, [1838–52].

——— The same. Minutes of several conversations between the methodist preachers

Methodist episcopal church—continued. in the connexion established by the late rev. John. Wesley. 32d to 84th, 100th to 105th, 107th to 110th conferences. 1824–26, 1843–48, 1850–53. 13 v. in 11. 16°. *London, J. Kershaw and J. Mason*, 1824–53.

——— (*United States*). A collection of hymns, for the use of the methodist episcopal church: principally from the collection of the rev. John Wesley, a. m. Revised and corrected, with the names of the tunes in the harmonist affixed to each hymn. With a supplement and an index to the subjects of the hymns. 676 pp. 12°. *New-York, T. Mason & G. Lane for the m. e. church*, 1838.

——— The doctrines and discipline of the methodist episcopal church. 196 pp. 24°. *New-York, B. Waugh & T. Mason*, 1832.

——— The same. 206 pp. 24°. *New York, T. Mason & G. Lane*, 1840.

——— The same. 240 pp. 24°. *New York, Carlton & Porter*, 1856.

——— The same. With an appendix. 303, xxiv pp. 24°. *New York, Carlton & Porter*, 1864.

——— Ritual of the methodist episcopal church. 152 pp. 8°. *New York, Carlton & Porter*, 1864.

Methodist protestant church. Constitution and discipline of the methodist protestant church. 159 pp. 18°. *Baltimore, J. J. Harod*, 1830.

——— Hymn book. Compiled by authority of the convention of 1858. 648 pp. 18°. *Springfield (O.) Methodist protestant publishing house*, 1860.

Methodist (The) protestant pulpit. Sermons: preached before the Maryland annual conference from 1858 to 1871 inclusive. [*anon.*] viii, 239 pp. 12°. *Baltimore, W. J. C. Dulany & co.* 1871.

Methuen (Paul Cobb). An historical account of Corsham House, in Wiltshire; the seat of Paul Cobb Methuen, esq. with a catalogue of his celebrated collection of pictures. Embracing a concise historical essay on the fine arts. Also, biographical sketches of the artists, whose works constitute this collection. By John Britton. 2 p. l. 108 pp. 2 pl. 8°. *London, author*, 1806.

Metrical stories in chimistry, and natural philosophy. By a teacher. [Charles W. Sanders? *anon.*] 144 pp. 18°. *New York, Dayton & Newman*, 1842.

Meun (Jean de, *dit Clopinel*). Le miroir de maistre Iean de Mehvn. 18°. [*Lyon, M. Bonhomme*, 1557].

[*In* Bacon (Roger) Le miroir d'alqvimie. 1557. pp. 109–134].

——— Le roman de la rose. *See* **Lorris** (Guillaume de) *and* **Meun**.

Meurer (Moritz). The life of Martin Luther: related from the original authorities. Translated from the german, by a pastor of the evangelical lutheran church. 695 pp. 16 pl. 8°. *New York, H. Ludwig & co.* 1848.

Meurs *or* **Meursius** (Jan van). Creta, Cyprus, Rhodus, sive de nobilissimarum harum insularum rebus & antiquitatibus. Commentarii postumi, nunc primum editi. 4 p. l. 264 pp. 1 l. sm. 4°. *Amstelodami, apud A. Wolfgangum*, 1675.

——— Cyprus, sive, de illius insulæ rebus, & antiquitatibus. 1 p. l. 175 pp. sm. 4°. *Amstelodami, apud A. Wolfgangum*, 1675.

——— Rhodus, sive, de illius insulæ, atque urbis, rebus memoratu dignis. 1 p. l. 124 pp. 33 l. sm. 4°. *Amstelodami, apud A. Wolfgangum*, 1675.

Meusel (Johann Georg). Lehrbuch der statistik. 4te ausgabe. xxiv, 824 pp. 18°. *Leipzig, Hahn*, 1817.

Mexia (Lorenzo). Lettera annale al padre generale della compagnia di Giesv dal Giappone l'anno 1580. pp. 94–138. 16°. *Venetia, appresso i Gioliti*, 1585.

[*In* Nvove lettere delle cose di Giappone].

Mexico. (*Empire of Mexico*, 1821–23). Actas del congreso constituyente mexicano. [Febr. 24, 1822, to May 13, 1823]. v. 1–4. sm. 4°. *México, Alejandro Valdes*, 1822–23.

——— Diario de la junta nacional instituyente del imperio mexicano. [Nov. 2, 1822, to Mar. 6, 1823]. v. 1. 442 pp. sm. 4°. *México, Alejandro Valdes*, 1822.

[No more published].

——— Diario de las sesiones de la soberana junta provisional gubernativa del imperio mexicano, instalada segun previenen el plan de Iguala y tratados de la villa de Cordova. [Sept. 22, 1821–Febr. 25, 1822]. 354 pp. sm. 4°. *México, Alexandro Valdes*, 1821.

——— (*Republic of Mexico*). Plan de la constitucion politica de la nacion mexicana. 1 p. l. 84 pp. 1 l. 18°. [*México*], *imprenta nacional*, 1823.

Meyer (Bernhard) *and* **Wolf** (Johann). Taschenbuch der deutschen vögelkunde, oder kurze beschreibung aller vögel Deutschlands. 2 v. xviii, 310 pp. 40 col. pl; xii, 311–614

Meyer (B.) *and* **Wolf** (J.)—continued. pp. 37 col. pl. 8°. *Frankfurt am Main, F. Wilmans*, 1810.

Meylan (G. F.) Japan. Voorgesteld in schetsen over de zeden en gebruiken van dat ryk, byzonder over de ingezetenen der stad Nagasaky. Uitgegeven door mr. J. H. Tobias. 6 p. l. 191 pp. 1 l. 2 pl. 8°. *Amsterdam, M. Westerman & zoon*, 1830.

Michaelis (Johann David). The burial and resurrection of Jesus Christ, according to the four evangelists. From the german [by sir George Duckett]. viii, 352 pp. 12°. *London, J. Hatchard & son*, 1827.

Michaud (Joseph François). Biographie universelle (Michaud) ancienne et moderne, histoire, par ordre alphabétique, de la vie publique et privée de tous les hommes qui se sont fait remarquer par leurs écrits, leurs actions, leurs talents, leurs vertus ou leurs crimes. Nouvelle édition, publiée sous la direction de M. Michaud, revue, corrigée et considerablement augmentée d'articles omis ou nouveaux. Ouvrage rédigé par une société de gens de lettres et de savants. 45 v. 8°. *Paris, chez mdme. C. Desplaces*, 1854-[65].

Michel (Francisque Xavier). Bibliothèque anglo-saxonne. viii, 168 pp. 8°. *Paris, Silvestre*, 1837.

——— Lai d'Ignaurès. *See* **Monmerqué** (Louis J. N.) *and* **Michel.**

——— Lais inédits des xiie et xiiie siècles, publiés pour la première fois, d'après les manuscrits de France et d'Angleterre. 2 p. l. v, 154 pp. 12°. *Paris, J. Techener*, 1836.

CONTENTS.

Le lai del désiré, p. 1.
Le lai de l'ombre, p. 39.
Le lai du conseil, p. 83.
Variantes du lai de l'ombre [et du lai du conseil], p. 123.
Extrait du roman de l'escouffle, p. 145.

——— Recueil de farces, moralités et sermons joyeux. *See* **Leroux de Lincy** (A. J. V.) *and* **Michel.**

Michelet (Jules). La France devant l'Europe. 2e éd. xxiv, 133 pp. 16°. *Florence, successeurs Le Monnier*, 1871.

Michell (Nicholas). The traduced. An historical romance. 3 v. 12°. *London, T. & W. Boone*, 1842-43.

[*Note.*—v. 3, 2d ed. 1843].

Michener (Ezra). A retrospect of early quakerism; being extracts from the records of Philadelphia yearly meeting [of Friends] and the meetings composing it. To which is prefixed an account of their first establishment. 434 pp. 18 pl. 8°. *Philadelphia, T. Ellwood Zell*, 1860.

Michigan (*State of*). Joint documents of the state of Michigan, for the year 1870. By authority. 24 doc. in 3 v. 8°. *Lansing, W. S. George & co.* 1870.

——— Journals of the senate and house of representatives, 1871. 5 v. 8°. *Lansing, W. S. George & co.* 1871.

——— School funds and school laws of Michigan: with notes and forms. To which are added Elements of school architecture, [etc.] By John M. Gregory, superintendent. ix, 448 pp. 1 pl. 8°. *Lansing, Hosmer & Kerr*, 1859. s.

Middlesex county (*Mass.*) The Middlesex county directory, for the year commencing August 1, 1871. 8°. *Boston, Briggs & co.* 1871.

Middleton (Henry). The government and the currency. New ed. with alterations. 190 pp. 12°. *New York, C. B. Norton*, 1850.

Middleton (Joseph). Love versus law; or, marriage with a deceased wife's sister. A novel. 3 v. 12°. *London, T. C. Newby*, 1855.

Middleton (J. J.) Grecian remains in Italy, a description of cyclopian walls, and of roman antiquities. With topographical and picturesque views of ancient Latium. 1 p. l. 50 pp. 25 col. pl. fol. *London, E. Orme*, 1812.

Middleton (Thomas). A mad vvorld my masters: a comedy. Composed by T. M. gent. [*anon.*] 30 l. unp. sm. 4°. *London, J. S.* 1640.

Migliore (Ferdinando Leopoldo del). Firenze città nobilissima illvstrata da F. L. del Migliore. Prima, seconda, e terza parte del primo libro. 10 p. l. 572 pp. 8 l. 5 pl. 4°. *Firenze, nella stamp. della Stella*, 1684.

[*Note.*—No more published. Haym says this work is to be attributed to Pietro Antonio della Ancisa].

Mignan (*Capt.* Robert). Travels in Chaldæa, including a journey from Bussorah to Bagdad, Hillah, and Babylon, performed on foot in 1827. With observations on the sites and remains of Babel, Seleucia, and Ctesiphon. xvi, 334 pp. 6 pl. 2 maps. 8°. *London, H. Colburn & R. Bentley*, 1829.

Mignet (François Auguste Alexis). Notices historiques. 2e éd. considérablement augmentée. 2 v. 2 p. l. iv, 399 pp. 1 l; 2 p. l.

Mignet (F. A. A.)—continued. 456 pp. 8°. *Paris, Paulin, Theureux & cie.* 1853.

CONTENTS.

v. 1. Discours prononcés à l'académie française.
- 1. Discours de réception à l'académie française, 1837.
- 2. Réponse au discours de réception de m. Flourens, 1840.
- 3. Réponse au discours de réception de m. le baron Pasquier.

Notices historiques.
- 1. M. le comte Sièyes.
- 2. M. le comte Rœderer.
- 3. M. Livingston.
- 4. M. le prince de Talleyrand.
- 5. M. Broussais.
- 6. M. le comte Merlin.
- 7. M. le comte Destutt de Tracy.
- 8. M. Daunou.

v. 2. Notices historiques.
- 1. M. le comte Siméon.
- 2. M. de Sismondi.
- 3. M. Charles Comte.
- 4. M. Ancillon.
- 5. M. Bignon.
- 6. M. Rossi.
- 7. M. Cabanis.
- 8. M. Droz.

Vie de Franklin.

Migout (A.) Flore du département de l'Allier. Description des plantes qui y croissent spontanément, classées suivant la méthode naturelle. 3 p. l. xxiv, 415 pp. 24 pl. 8°. *Moulins, A. Ducroux & G. Dulac,* 1866. s.

[MOULINS. Société d'émulation de l'Allier. Publications].

Milan. (*Italy*). Atti del municipio di Milano. Annata 1869. 705 pp. 1 l. fol. *Milano, coi tipi di Luigi di Giacomo Pirola,* [1869]. s.

——— Documenti diplomatici tratti dagli archivj milanesi e coordinati per cura di Luigo Osio. [Signoria di Filippo Maria Visconti, 1412–1430]. v. 2. vii, 528 pp. fol. *Milano, G. Bernadoni di Giovanni,* 1869–70. s.

———. *Società agraria di Lombardia.* L'agricultura-giornale ed atti della società agraria di Lombardia con incisioni e disegni. Anno terzo, 1866. 8°. *Milano, Patronato,* 1867. s.

Milbourne (Luke). Mysteries in religion vindicated: or the filiation, deity and satisfaction of our saviour asserted, against socinians and others. 8 p. l. 784 pp. 7 l. 16°. *London, W. Kettilby,* 1692.

Miles (George H.) The truce of God, a tale of the eleventh century. 384 pp. 16°. *Baltimore, J. Murphy & co.* 1871.

Miles (Henry Downes). Pugilistica: the history of british boxing, being the only complete and chronological history of the prize ring. v. 1. xvi, 507 pp. 29 pl. 8°. *London, proprietor,* 1866.

Militarie instructions for the cavallrie: or rules and directions for the service of the horse, collected out of divers forrain authors ancient and modern, and rectified and supplied, according to the present practise of the Low-countrey warres. [By I. C. *anon.*] 4 p. l. 108 pp. 15 pl. fol. *Cambridge,* [*Eng.*] *printers to the university,* 1632.

Mill (John, *d. d.*) Ἡ καινη διαθηκη. *See* **Bible.** (*Greek*).

Mill (William Hodge.) English introduction to the Christa-sangítá, or the sacred history of our Lord Jesus Christ, in sanscrit verse. lxxxiii pp. 8°. *Calcutta, Bishop's college press,* 1842.

Millar (David). Useful and important answers freely given, to useful and important questions, concerning Jesus the son of God, freely propos'd: or, a vindication of the coessential sonship of the second person in the trinity; with an answer to the learned Roel, [Hermann Alex. Roell], dr. Ridgley, dr. Anderson, &c.' viii, 464 pp. 8°. *London, author,* 1751.

Millar (*Rev.* Robert). The history of the propagation of christianity and overthrow of paganism. [1st ed.] 2 v. xlvii, 675 pp; 8 p. l. 602 pp. 8°. *Edinburgh, T. Ruddiman,* 1723.

——— The same. 3d ed. corrected, with additions. 2 v. xii, 448 pp. 6 l; 1 p. l. 404 pp. 6 l. 8°. *London, A. Millar,* 1731.

Millard (*Rev.* David). A journal of travels in Egypt, Arabia Petræa, and the holy land. During 1841-2. 352 pp. 12°. *Rochester,* [*N. Y.*] *E. Shephard,* 1843.

——— The true messiah, in scripture light; or the unity of God, and the proper sonship of Jesus Christ, affirmed and defended. 214 pp. 18°. *Canandaigua,* [*N. Y.*] *J. D. Bemis & co.* 1823.

Millard (Henry B. *m. d.*) A guide for emergencies, containing the homeopathic treatment, [etc.] 3d ed. 136 pp. 18°. *New York, C. T. Hurlburt,* 1871.

Millbury (*Mass.*) Multum in parvo. Millbury directory: containing the names, residence and business of the adult population, with a history of all the churches, and pictures of the church edifices. With a general summary of useful information concerning the town, county and state. 1871. 100, 83 pp. 12°. *Worcester, Tyler & Seagrave,* [1871].

Miller (George B. *d. d.*) Sermons on some of the fundamental principles of the gospel. With an introduction by rev. William D. Strobel, d. d. 3d ed. 374 pp. 1 portrait. 12°. *New York, N. Tibbals & co.* 1860.

Miller (Howard). The student's dream and other poems. 144 pp. 16°. *Louisville, J. P. Morton & co.* 1871.

Miller (Hugh). The witness papers. The headship of Christ, and the rights of the christian people, a collection of essays, historical and descriptive sketches, and personal portraitures. With the author's celebrated letter to lord Brougham. Edited, with a preface, by Peter Bayne. 502 pp. 12°. *Boston, Gould & Lincoln*, 1863.

Miller (*Rev.* James). The sybil's leaves: or, the fancies, sentiments & opinions of Silvanus; miscellaneous, moral & religious. 2 v. 1 p. l. 400 pp; 1 p. l. 406, 4 pp. 8°. *Edinburgh, author*, 1829.

Miller (Joaquin). Songs of the Sierras. xiii, 301 pp. 12°. *New York, author*, 1871.

——— The same. 4 p. l. 299 pp. 12°. *Boston, Roberts brothers*, 1871.

Miller (John Frederick). Cimelia physica. 1796. *See* **Shaw** (George, *m. d.*)

Miller (Samuel, *d. d.*) An essay on the warrant, nature and duties of the office of the ruling elder, in the presbyterian church. 322 pp. 12°. *New-York, J. Leavitt*, 1831.

——— Infant baptism scriptural and reasonable: and baptism by sprinkling or affusion, the most suitable and edifying mode. 122 pp. 12°. *Philadelphia, Presbyterian board of publication*, [1835].

——— Letters concerning the constitution and order of the christian ministry, as deduced from scripture and primitive usage. 355 pp. 12°. *New-York, Hopkins & Seymour*, 1807.

——— Letters on clerical manners and habits; addressed to a student in the theological seminary, at Princeton, N. J. 1 p. l. 476 pp. 12°. *New York, G. & C. Carvill*, 1827.

——— Memoir of the rev. John Rodgers, d. d. Abridged from the original edition of 1813. 240 pp. 18°. *Philadelphia, Presbyterian board of publication*, 1840.

——— Presbyterianism the truly primitive and apostolical constitution of the church of Christ. 98 pp. 12°. *Philadelphia, Presbyterian board of publication*, [1835].

——— The primitive and apostolical order of the church of Christ vindicated. 384 pp. 1 portrait. 12°. *Philadelphia, Presbyterian board of publication*, [1840]. s.

Miller (Stephen F.) Wilkins Wylder; or, the successful man. [Also, Mind and matter: a story of domestic life]. 420 pp. 12°. *Philadelphia, J. B. Lippincott & co.* 1860.

Miller (Thomas). Picturesque sketches of London, past and present. 306 pp. 17 pl. 12°. *London, office of the National illustrated library*, [1852].

Miller (William, *second advent preacher*). Evidence from scripture and history of the second coming of Christ about the year 1843; exhibited in a course of lectures. 300 pp. 16°. *Boston, B. B. Mussey*, 1840.

——— Views of the prophecies and prophetic chronology, selected from manuscripts of William Miller; with a memoir of his life; by Joshua V. Himes. 252 pp. 1 portrait. 18°. *Boston, M. A. Dow*, 1841.

Milligan (*Rev.* A. M.) The position and duty of covenanters. 12°. [*Pittsburgh*, 1872].
[*In* REFORMED presbyterian church in North America. Memorial volume, pp. 189–204].

Milligan (R.) The great commission of Jesus Christ to his twelve apostles, briefly defined and illustrated. 212 pp. 16°. *Lexington (Ky.) J. B. Morton & co.* 1871.

Millin (Aubin Louis). Antiquités nationales, ou recueil de monumens pour servir à l'histoire générale et particulière de l'empire françois, tels que tombeaux, inscriptions, statues, vitraux, fresques, etc; tirés des abbayes, monastères, châteaux et autres lieux devenus domaines nationaux. 5 v. 4°. *Paris, Drouhin*, 1790–96.

——— L'orestéide, ou description de deux bas-reliefs du palais Grimani à Vénise et de quelques monuments qui ont rapport à l'histoire d'Oreste. 24 pp. 4 pl. fol. *Paris, bureau des annales encyclopédiques*, 1817.

——— Voyage dans le Milanais, à Plaisance, Parme, Modène, Mantoue, Crémone, et dans plusieurs autres villes de l'ancienne Lombardie. 2 v. 4 p. l. 392 pp; 2 p. l. 371 pp. 8°. *Paris, [C.] Wassermann*, 1817.

——— Voyage en Savoie, en Piémont, à Nice, et à Gènes. 2 v. 2 p. l. viii, 376 pp; 2 p. l. 415 pp. 8°. *Paris, C. Wassermann*, 1816.

Millin (Eleuthérophile). *See* **Millin** (Aubin Louis).

Mills (B. H.) The temperance manual: containing a history of the various temperance orders. With funeral and dedicatory services. 287 pp. 1 portrait. 16°. *Upper Alton (Ill.) Good templar office*, 1864.

Mills (Elizabeth Willesford). Sibyl's leaves: poems and sketches. vii, 260 pp. 12°. *London, Longman*, 1826.

Mills (*Rev.* John H.) Autobiography of the rev. John H. Mills. With miscellaneous

Mills (*Rev.* John H.)—continued. thoughts, consisting of fugitive pieces in prose and rhyme. 264 pp. 1 portrait. 12°. *New York, J. W. Amerman*, 1857.

Mills (*Rev.* William). The belief of the jewish people and of the most eminent gentile philosophers, more especially of Plato and Aristotle, in a future state, briefly considered; including an examination into some of the leading principles contained in bishop Warburton's Divine legation of Moses. viii, 130 pp. 8°. *Oxford, author*, 1828.

Milner (Vincent L.) Religious denominations of the world: with sketches of the founders of various religious sects. 512 pp. 6 portraits. 8°. *Philadelphia, J. W. Bradley*, 1860.

——— The same. A new ed. brought up to the present time, by J. Newton Brown, d. d. 609 pp. 7 pl. 12°. *Philadelphia, Bradley & co.* 1871.

Milroy (*Rev.* W.) Fidelity to vows. 12°. [*Pittsburgh*, 1872].

[*In* REFORMED presbyterian church in North America. Memorial volume, pp. 81–93].

Milton (John). Comus, a mask presented at Ludlow castle 1634, before the earl of Bridgewater, then president of Wales. 40 pp. 8°. *Ludlow, W. Felton*, 1803.

[*With* HODGES (W.) An historical account of Ludlow castle].

——— A discourse on the harmony of the spheres; as delivered in a latin thesis, at the university; and translated into english by [Francis Peck. Latin and english]. 1 p. l. 6 pp. 4°. [*London*, 1740].

[*In* PECK (Francis). New memoirs of mr. John Milton. 1740].

——— Paradise lost. A poem in twelve books. 2d ed. revised and augmented by the same author. 4 p. l. 333 pp. 12°. *London, S. Simmons*, 1674.

——— The same. Le paradis perdu. Traduction nouvelle, [etc.] Par m. [Louis] Racine. Tome premier. cviij, 450 pp. 16°. *Paris, Desaint & Saillant*, 1755.

[*Note.*—Volume 1 only].

——— The same. Il paradiso perduto, tradotto in verso italiano da Felice Mariotini. 2 parts in 1 v. xii, 209 pp; iv, 208 pp. 8°. *Londra, G. Polidori e co.* 1796.

——— The parallel, or archbishop Laud and cardinal Wolsey, compared; a vision. 4°. *London*, 1740.

[*In* PECK (Francis). New memoirs of mr. John Milton. 1740. pp. 429–437.
Note.—This is an apocryphal production].

Milton (John)—continued.

——— Poetical works. 2 v. 328 pp. 1 portrait; 4 p. l. 329–640 pp. 8°. *Philadelphia, R. Bell*, 1777.

CONTENTS.

v. 1. Paradise lost [Book 1–11].
v. 2. Paradise lost [Book 12]. Paradise regain'd. Samson agonistes; and poems on several occasions. With the life of the author. By Thomas Newton, d. d.

Milton (William Wentworth-Fitzwilliam, *viscount*). *See* **Fitzwilliam**.

Milward (Maria G.) Joys and sorrows of the ecclesiastical year. 298 pp. 12°. *Philadelphia, H. Hooker*, 1854.

Mimpriss (Robert). The Mimpriss graded lesson books. The life of Christ harmonized from the four evangelists. First to fourth grades. 8 v. 18°. *New-York, M. W. Dodd*, [1869–71].

[*Note.*—Fourth series, entitled "Studies on the gospels in harmony; being the fourth or bible class grade in the series of Lessons on the life of Christ].

——— The Mimpriss system of graduated simultaneous instruction. Teacher's manual to accompany the grade lesson books, on the life of Christ. First to third grades. 6 v. 18°. *New York, M. W. Dodd*, [1869–70].

Minadoi da Rovigo (Giovanni Tomaso). The history of the warres betweene the Tvrkes and the Persians. Written in italian, and translated into english by Abraham Hartvvell. 6 p. l. 500 pp. 9 l. sm. 4°. *London, J. Wolfe*, 1595.

[*Note.*—Imperfect: map wanting].

Miñano y Bedoya (Sebastian). Cartas, publicadas en el año 1820, bajo el título de lamentos políticos de un pobrecito holgazan que estaba acostumbrado á vivir á costa ajena. 8°. [*Madrid, M. Rivadeneyra*, 1870].

[*In* OCHOA (Eugenio de). Epistolario español, pp. 603–638].

Minderer (Raymond). Medecina militaris: or, a body of military medicines experimented. Englished out of high-dutch. 1 p. l. 152 pp. 6 l. 16°. *London, W. Godbid by M. Pitt*, 1674.

[*With* BARBETTE (Paul, *m. d.*) Thesaurus chirurgiæ. *London*, 1676].

Ming (Jean, *curé*). Venez tous à moi. Recueil de prières à l'usage des enfants qui se préparent à la première communion. Traduction revue par l'abbé Bourquard. 318 pp. 24°. *Einsiedeln, New York and Cincinnati, C. & N Benziger*, 1870.

Minifie (William). A text book of geometrical drawing, abridged from the octavo ed. for the use of schools. With an introduc-

Minifie (William)—continued. tion to isometrical drawing, and an essay on linear perspective and shadows. 5th ed. 178 pp. 48 pl. 12°. *New York, D. Van Nostrand*, 1871.

Mining (The) magazine; devoted to mines, mining operations, metallurgy, etc. Edited by William J. Tenney, [etc.] v. 1-9. 8°. *New York, J. F. Trow*, 1853-57.

Minnesota (*State of*). Executive documents, for the year 1870. Printed by authority. 2 v. 8°. *Saint Paul, Press printing co.* 1871.

——— Journal of the senate [and] the house of representatives, of the thirteenth session of the legislature. 2 v. 8°. *Saint Paul, Press printing co.* 1871.

Minnesota: its resources and progress; its beauty, healthfulness and fertility; and its attractions and advantages as a home for immigrants. Compiled by the commissioner of statistics, and published by direction of Horace Austin, governor. [*anon.*] 72 pp. 8°. *St. Paul, Press printing co.* 1870.

Minnesota (*Grand Lodge, etc. of*). *See* **Freemasons.**

Minot (George Richards). An eulogy on George Washington, delivered before the inhabitants of the town of Boston [Jan. 9, 1800]. 2d ed. 22 pp. 8°. *Boston, Manning & Loring*, [1800].
[HAZARD pamphlets, v. 64].

Minucius Felix (Marcus). Octavius. Recensuit F. Oehler. 12°. *Lipsiae, B. Tauchnitz, jun.* 1847.
[GERSDORF (E. G.) Bibliotheca patrum ecclesiasticorum latinorum selecta, v. 13, pp. 1-56].

Mirabeau (Gabriel Honoré Riquetti, *comte de*). Esprit de Mirabeau, ou manuel de l'homme d'état, des publicistes, des fonctionnaires et des orateurs; divisé par ordre de matières, et embrassant les différentes branches de l'économie politique; extrait de tous les ouvrages de G. H. R. de Mirabeau, [par J. B. P. Chaussard], et précédé d'un précis historique de sa vie. 2 v. 2 p. l. xc, 438 pp; 2 p. l. 542 pp. 8°. *Paris, F. Buisson*, 1797.

——— Lettres originales de Mirabeau, écrites du donjon de Vincennes, pendant les années 1777, 78, 79 et 80; contenant tous les détails sur sa vie privée, ses malheurs, et ses amours avec Sophie Ruffei, marquise de Monnier: recueillies par P. Manuel. [1e éd.] 4 v. 8°. *Paris, J. B. Garnery*, 1792.

Miraculous prophecies and predictions of eminent men, from the earliest records, relating to the revolutions of empires and kingdoms, particularly England and France, with a picture of the present times. [*anon.*] 1 p. l. xvii, 254 pp. 8°. *London, Edwards & Knibb*, 1821.

Mirbel (— de). Le palais dv prince dv sommeil; où est enseignée l'oniromancie avtrement l'art de deviner par les songes. 11 p. l. 140 pp. 1 pl. 16°. *Lyon, I. Pavlhe*, 1670.

Miriam; a dramatic poem. *See* **Hall** (Louisa J. Park).

Miscellaneous poems. 1827. *See* **Murden** (*Mrs.* Eliza).

Miscellaneous works, prose and poetical. By a young gentleman of New York. [*anon.*] 354 pp. 16°. *New York, T. Greenleaf*, 1795.

Misoscolo (Eureta, *pseudon.*) *See* **Pona** (Francesco).

Miss Columbia's public school; or, will it blow over? By a cosmopolitan. With 72 illustrations by Thomas Nast. [*anon.*] 82 pp. 12°. *New York, F. B. Felt & co.* 1871.

Mission (The) book. *See* **Liguori** (*S.* Alfonso Maria di).

Missionary museum; or, an account of missionary enterprises. In conversations between a mother and her children. First series, India and Africa. [*anon.*] 2 v. 262 pp. 1 map; 234 pp. 18°. *New Haven, J. L. Cross*, 1832.

Missionary's (The) daughter, or memoir of Lucy Goodale Thurston, of the Sandwich islands. 2d ed. 233 pp. 1 pl. 18°. *New York, Dayton & Newman*, 1842.

Missions-buch (Das) des allerheil. erlösers. *See* **Liguori** (*S.* Alfonso Maria di).

Missions of the Moravians among the north american Indians inhabiting the middle states of the union. [*anon.*] 162 pp. 18°. *Philadelphia, American sunday school union*, 1831.

Missirini (Melchior). Dell' amore di Dante Alighieri e del ritratto di Beatrice Portinari. Comentario primo. 2 p. l. 35 pp. 2 portraits. 4°. *Firenze, L. Ciardetti*, 1832.

——— Delle memorie di Dante Alighieri e del suo mausoleo in Sa. Croce. Comentario secondo. Ed. 3a. 2 p. l. 39 pp. 4°. *Firenze, L. Ciardetti*, 1832.
[*With his* Dell' amore di Dante Alighieri, 1832].

Mistral (Frédéric). Mirèio. A provençal poem. Translated by Harriet W. Preston. xviii, 249 pp. 12°. *Boston, Roberts brothers*, 1872.

Mitchell (John). A night on the banks of Doon, and other poems. 158 pp. 12°. *Paisley, J. Neilson for the author*, 1838.

Mitchell (*Rev.* Jonathan). Answer to the apologeticall preface published in the name of the brethren that dissented in the late synod, and set before the essay for investigation of the truth, etc. made by mr. John Davenport, in reply to the answer and arguments of the synod met at Boston, 1662. 46 pp. sm. 4°. *Cambridge, [Ms.] H. Usher*, 1664.

[MATHER (Richard). Defence of the answer of the synod, 1662].

Mitchell (J. W. S. *m. d.*) The history of masonry, from the building of the house of the Lord, and its progress throughout the world, down to the present time, [etc.] 11th ed. thoroughly revised and reduced to one volume. 740, vi pp. 1 portrait. 8°. *Griffin (Ga.) author*, 1871.

Mitchell (S. Weir, *m. d.*) Wear and tear, or hints for the overworked. 59 pp. 16°. *Philadelphia, J. B. Lippincott & co.* 1871.

Mitchell (*Rev.* Thomas). The old paths: a treatise on sanctification. Scripture the only authority. 258 pp. 16°. *Albany, C. van Benthuysen & sons*, 1869.

——— The philosophy of God and the world. The great controversy. The bible its own expositor. 547 pp. 8°. *New York, N. Tibbals & son*, 1871.

Mitford (A. B.) Tales of old Japan. 2 v. xii, 277 pp. 25 pl; vii, 272 pp. 6 pl. 8°. *London, Macmillan & co.* 1871.

Mitford (Mary Russell). Rienzi, der letzte tribun. Trauerspiel in 5 acten. Nach dem englischen der miss Mitford frei für die deutsche bühne bearbeitet von E. A. Zuendt. 16°. *St. Louis*, 1871.

[*In* ZUENDT (E. A.) Lyrische und dramatische dichtungen, pp. 497-624].

Mitscherlich (Christoph Wilhelm). Scriptores erotici græci. [Græce et latine. Textum recognovit, selectamque lectionis varietatem adjecit C. W. Mitscherlich]. 3 v. in 4. 8° *Biponti, [et] Argentorati, ex typographia societatis bipontinæ*, 1792-[98].

CONTENTS.

ACHILLES Tatius. De Clitophontis et Leucippes amoribus libri viii, v. 1.
HELIODORUS. Æthiopicorum libri decem, v. 2-3.
LONGUS. Pastoralium de Daphnide et Chloe libri v. v. 4, pp. 1-178.
XENOPHON ephesius. Ephesiacorum de amoribus Anthiæ et Abrocomæ libri v, v. 4, pp. 179-330.

Mivart (St. George). On the genesis of species. xv, 296 pp. 12°. *London, Macmillan & co.* 1871.

M—l (Sylvain). Dictionnaire des athées. *See* **Maréchal** (Pierre Sylvain).

Moat (Thomas). Moat's short-hand standard. [Or], the short-hand standard attempted by an analysis of the circle as an introductory foundation of a new system of stenography. 3 p. l. 120 pp. 24 pl. 8°. *London, author*, 1833.

Mobile daily register. John Forsyth, editor. Jan. 1 to Dec. 31, 1871. 2 v. fol. *Mobile (Ala.) W. D. Mann and L. Donavan*, [1871].

Mobile directory, or strangers' guide for 1839. By T. C. Fay. 104, 96 pp. 12°. *Mobile, R. R. Dade*, [1839].

Modest (A) apology for the roman catholics of Great Britain: addressed to all moderate protestants; particularly to the members of both houses of parliament. [*anon.*] xx, 271 pp. 8°. *London, author*, 1800.

Modestus. Libellvs de vocabvlis rei militaris. 4 l. unp. fol. *Bononiæ, Plato de Benedictis*, 1496.

[*In* VETERES scriptores de re militari. *Bononiæ*, 1496. Imperfect: prefatory leaf wanting].

Modio (Giovanni Battista). Della vita del beato Iacopone da Todi. 16°. *Napoli, L. Scoriggio*, 1615.

[*In* JACOPONE da Todi. Le cantici, pp. 1-18].

Moebius (Friedrich Tobias). De transformatione hominum in bruta. 1667. Recusa. 20 l. sm. 4°. *Lipsiæ, typis & sumptibus J. E. Hahnii*, 1673.

Moelling (Peter August). Reise-skizzen in poesie und prosa. Gesammelt auf einer siebenmonatlichen tour durch die Vereinigten Staaten von Nord-Amerika. 384 pp. 8 portraits, 1 pl. 8°. *Galveston (Texas) offices des "Apologeten,"* [1857]?

Moens (Petronella). Dagboek voor mijne vrouwelijke landgenooten. viii, 380 pp. 8°. *Amsterdam, Ten Brink & De Vries*, 1826.

——— Merkwaardige bijbelsche tafereelen om de meer gevorderde jeugd Gods wijsheid en liefde in het bestuur der menschelijke lotgevallen te doen opmerken. viii, 210 pp. 8°. *Amsterdam, G. Portielje.* 1828.

Moesch (Casimir). Der Aargauer-Jura über die nördlichen gebiete des kantons Zürich geologisch untersucht und beschrieben. xv, 319 pp. 8 l. 7 pl. 2 charts. 4°. *Bern, J. Dalp*, 1867. S.

[SWITZERLAND. Beiträge zur geologischen karte der Schweiz, 4te lieferung].

Moffat (A. S.) Cedar brook stories; or, the Clifford children. By A. S. M. [*pseudon.*] 2 v. 18°. *Boston, Graves & Young*, 1864.

CONTENTS.

v. 1. The young seed-sowers, 167 pp. 3 pl.
v. 2. The seed growing, 215 pp. 3 pl.

Moffat (James C. *d. d.*) A comparative history of religions. Part I. Ancient scriptures. viii, 250 pp. 12°. *New York, Dodd & Mead*, 1871.

Moffat (John M.) The scientific class-book; or, a familiar introduction to the principles of physical science. With emendations, notes, questions, etc. On the basis of mr. J. M. Moffat. By Walter R. Johnson. 2 v. 473 pp; 478 pp. 12°. *Philadelphia, Key & Biddle*, 1835-36.

CONTENTS.

Part i. Comprising mechanics, hydrostatics, hydraulics, pneumatics, acoustics, pyronomics, optics, electricity, galvanism, magnetism.
Part ii. Comprising chemistry, metallurgy, mineralogy.

Moffatt (*Rev.* J. M.) The history of the town of Malmesbury, and of its ancient abbey; together with memoirs of eminent natives, and other distinguished characters who were connected with the abbey or town. [With] an appendix. 250 pp. 4 pl. 1 table. 8°. *Tetbury, J. G. Goodwyn*, 1805.

Mogridge (George). Old Humphrey's portfolio. [18°. *Philadelphia*, 1855].
[*In* MEMOIR of "Old Humphrey," pp. 143-252].

Moguntia. *See* **Mayence.**

Mohammed (*the prophet*). Historia Iosephi patriarchæ, ex Alcorano, arabice. Cum triplici versione latina, & scholijs Thomæ Erpenii, cujus & alphabetum arabicvm præmittitur. Eng. title, 72 l. sm. 4°. *Leidæ, ex typographia erpeniana linguarum orientalium*, 1617.

——— Le koran. Traduction nouvelle faite sur le texte arabe, par m. Kasimirski. Revue et précédée d'une introduction, par M. G. Pauthier. 1 p. l. xv, 576 pp. 16°. *Paris, Charpentier*, 1840.

——— The same. Mahomet's alkoran, door de hr. Du Ryer uit d' arabische in de franse taal gestelt; benevens een tweevoudige beschryving van Mahomet's leven; en een verhaal van des zelfs reis ten hemel, gelijk ook zyn samenspraak met de jood Abdias. Alles van nieuws door J. H. Glasemaker vertaalt, en te zamen gebracht. Eng. title, 4 p. l. 547 pp. 6 pl. 16°. *Leyden, J. & H. van der Deyster*, 1734.

Mohl (Jules de) *and* **Ohlshausen** (J.) Fragmens relatifs à la religion de Zoroastre, extraits des manuscrits persans de la bibliothèque du roi. ix, 34 pp. 8°. *Paris, imprimerie royale*, 1829.

Moir (*Rev.* John). Gleanings; or fugitive pieces, consisting of 1. Miscellaneous essays. 2. Moral stories. 3. Sketches, fragments, hints. 4. Verses on various subjects. 2 v. viii, 223 pp; vi, 176 pp. 16°. *London, author*, [1786]?

Moises (*Rev.* Edward). The persian interpreter: in three parts. A grammar of the persian language. Persian extracts in prose and verse. A vocabulary: persian and english. 2 p. l. 149 pp. 32 l. 4°. *Newcastle, printed by S. Hodgson, sold by R. Fisher*, 1792.

Molineux. *See* **Molyneux.**

Molinier (Étienne, *of Toulouse*). Essayes: or, morall and politicall discovrses. 12 p. l. 361 pp. sm. 4°. *London, W. Sheares*, 1636.

Molkenboer (J. H.) Bryologia javanica. *See* **Dozy** (F.) *and* **Molkenboer.**

Moll (Herman). Atlas manuale: or, a new sett of maps of all the parts of the earth, as well Asia, Africa and America, as Europe. Wherein geography is rectified. v pp. 1 l. 43 maps. 8°. *London, A. & J. Churchill*, 1709.

Molony (Cornelius). Molony's masterpiece on wool, silk and cotton dyeing: containing his best receipts, without the least reserve; according to his practice in Great Britain and America. 122 pp. 12°. *Lowell, Dearborn & Bellows*, 1837.

——— The practical dyer. With references to patterns of the several colors, numbered in rotation, and attached to the work. To which are annexed miscellaneous receipts for cotton, silk, and woolen goods. [*anon.*] 2 p. l. 107 pp. 3 l. [col. patterns]. 12°. *Boston, Munroe & Francis*, 1833.

Molony (Patrick). The telegraph cipher key. Arranged by one of the profession. 2 p. l. 70 pp. 1 l. 8°. *New Orleans, Pelican book and job printing office*, 1871.

Molyneux (*Rev.* Capel). The world to come. Lectures delivered in the Lock chapel, in lent, 1853. xv, 295 pp. 12°. *London, Partridge & Oakey*, 1853.

Mommsen (Theodor). Inscriptiones regni neapolitani latinae. xxiv, 486, 40 pp. 4°. *Lipsiae, G. Wigand*, 1852.

Momus, sive satyra varroniana. 1655. *See* **Ferrari** (Ottavio).

Monat (Der) märz. Betrachtungen und gebete zur verehrung des heil. Joseph auf alle tage im monat märz, nebst einem vollständigen andachtsbuche für fromme verehrer des hl. Joseph. Bearbeitet von einem priester der diözese von Cincinnati. [*anon.*] 384 pp. 3 pl. 32°. *Einsiedeln, New York & Cincinnati, K. & N. Benziger*, 1871.

Mönches (Des) Aegydius Lebrecht groszes illustrirtes egyptisches traumbuch. Nach alten egyptischen, arabischen, chinesischen und schwedischen handschriften. Nebst wichtigen zusätzen des berühmten groszen chinesischen astrologen Tschian-schen-pelula. Mit glücks-nummern, und approbirte auslegung der träume von dem erfinder der lotterie Benedetto Gentil. [*anon.*] 111 pp. 8°. *New-York, W. Radde*, [1870].

Moneti (Francesco). La Cortona convertita del padre Moneti, con la ritrattazione ed altri bizarri componimenti poetici del medesimo autore. viii, 350 pp. 1 portrait. 8°. *Amsterdam, E. Fraymann*, 1790.

Monk (George, *duke of Albemarle*). Observations upon military and political affairs. 4 p. l. 151 pp. 6 l. fol. *London, A. C. for H. Mortlocke & J. Collins*, 1671.

Monmerqué (Louis Jean Nicolas) *and* **Michel** (Francisque). Lai d'Ignaurès, en vers, du xiie siècle, par Renaut, suivi des lais de Melion et du Trot, en vers, du xiiie siècle, publiés pour la première fois d'après deux manuscrits uniques. 2 p. l. 83 pp. 2 pl. 8°. *Paris, Sylvestre*, 1832.
[150 copies printed].

Monnet (Jean). Supplément au roman comique, ou mémoires pour servir à la vie de Jean Monnet. Écrits par lui-même. 2 v. 4 p. l. 200 pp. 2 l. 1 portrait; 288 pp. 4 l. 12°. *Londres*, 1772.

Monroe (Anna). The model sunday school speaker. A collection of dialogues, addresses, and miscellaneous pieces, for exhibitions, monthly concerts, anniversaries, etc. 128 pp. 3 pl. 16°. *Boston, Lee & Shepard*, 1872.

Montagu (Basil). Some enquiries into the effects of fermented liquors. By a water drinker. [*anon.*] 2 p. l. xxxii, 368 pp. 1 l. 5 pl. 8°. *London, J. Johnson & co.* 1814.

Montalvo (Garcia Ordoñez de). Le Prodezze di Splandian ; che segvono i qvatro libri di Amadis di Gavla svo padre. [*anon.*] Tradotte dalla spagnvola nella nostra lingua italiana, [per Mambrino Roseo]. Nuouamente da molti errori corrette, & ristampate. 8 p. l. 270 l. 12°. *Venetia, G. Alberti*, 1592.
[*Note.*—The interior title, prefixed to the text of the story, says: Scritte fedelmente dal maestro Helisabatti].

Montanari (*Conte* Antonio). Trattenimento metafisico intorno ai principali sistemi dell' anima delle bestie con alcune osservazioni sopra l'anima umana. 4 p. l. 232 pp. 4°. *Verona, M. Maroni*, 1761.

Montanari (Geminiano). L'astrologia convinta di falso col mezzo di nuoue esperienze, e ragioni fisico-astronomiche, o' sia la caccia del frvgnvolo. xiv, 158 pp. 4°. *Venetia, F. Niccolini*, 1685.

Montanus (Arnoldus). Atlas japannensis: being remarkable addresses by way of embassy from the East India company of the United Provinces, to the emperor of Japan. Containing a description of their several territories, cities, temples, and fortresses: their religions, laws and customs: their prodigious wealth, and gorgeous habits: the nature of their soil, plants, beasts, hills, rivers and fountains. With the character of the ancient and modern Japanners. Collected out of their several writings and journals by Arnoldus Montanus. English'd, and adorn'd with above a hundred several sculptures, by John Ogilby, esq. Eng. title, 2 p. l. 488 pp. 17 pl. 1 map. fol. *London, T. Johnson*, 1670.

Montenay (Georgette de). Emblèmes, ov devises chréstiennes. 7 p. l. 101 l. 8 l. unp. (incl. 101 pl.) by Pierre Woeiriot. 8°. *Lyon, J. Marcorelle*, 1571.

Montépin (Xavier de). Les chevaliers du lansquenet. 5 v. 16°. [*Paris, A. Cadot*, 1857].

——— Le trou à Romain. 16°. [*Paris, A. Cadot*, 1857].
[*In his* Les chevaliers du lansquenet. *Paris*, 1857. v. 5, pp. 243-332].

Monteverdi (Angelo). Dimostrazione di una nuova importantissima virtu medicamentosa della china e dei suoi preparati. 279 pp. 8°. *Cremona, Ronzi & Signori*, 1870. s.

Montgomery (Cuthbert, *editor*). The missionary memorial: a gift book for all seasons. 5 p. l. 372 pp. 4 pl. 12°. *Philadelphia, G. Collins*, 1855.

Montgomery (James). Prose, by a poet. [*anon.*] 2 v. xiv, 199 pp ; 212 pp. 18°. *Philadelphia, A. Small*, 1824.

Montgomery (*Rev.* Robert). The messiah: a poem in six books. 5th ed. xiv, 341 pp. 16°. *London, Saunders & Otley*, 1836.

Monthly (The) microscopical journal: transactions of the Royal microscopical society, and record of histological research at home and abroad. Edited by Henry Lawson, m. d. v. 1-4. 8°. *London, R. Hardwicke,* 1869-70. s.

Monthly (The) novelette people's journal, devoted to light and amusing literature, romance and poetry. Jan. to Dec. 1871. v. 1-2. 8°. *Boston, Thomes & Talbot,* [1871].

Monti (Vincenzo). Iliade di Omero, traduzione. 1825. *See* **Homerus.**

Montolieu (*Mrs.* Jeanne Isabelle Pauline Polier de Bottens de). The enchanted plants; fables in verse. Inscribed to miss Montolieu, & miss Julia Montolieu. [*anon.*] 117 pp. 16°. *New York, D. Longworth,* 1803.

Montyon (Antoine Jean Baptiste Auget, *baron* de). Exposé statistique du Tunkin. Sur la relation de m. de La Bissachère. 1811. *See* **La Bissachère** (Pierre Jacques Lemounier de).

Moodie (*Mrs.* Susanna Strickland). Geoffrey Moncton: or, the faithless guardian. 362 pp. 12°. *New York, De Witt & Davenport,* 1855.

——— Mark Hurdlestone, the gold worshipper. 2 v. xxxii, 312 pp; 2 p. l. 308 pp. 12°. *London, R. Bentley,* 1853.

Moody (Charles C. P.) Biographical sketches of the Moody family: embracing notices of ten ministers and several laymen from 1633 to 1842. 168 pp. 18°. *Boston, S. G. Drake,* 1847.

Moore (Benjamin F.) Providence almanac and directory for 1845. *See* **Providence.**

Moore (Caroline). Leaflets of masonic biography; or sketches of eminent freemasons. 420 pp. 12°. *Cincinnati, Masonic review office,* 1863.

Moore (Daniel D. T.) Moore's rural New-Yorker. A national illustrated rural, literary, and family newspaper, [etc.] Conducted by D. D. T. Moore. [Weekly]. Jan. 7 to Dec. 30, 1871. v. 23-24. fol. *New York & Rochester, D. D. T. Moore,* 1871.

Moore (Dugald). The African, a tale; and other poems. 2d ed. ix, 216 pp. 12°. *Glasgow, Robertson & Atkinson,* 1830.

Moore (Edward). Fables for the female sex. sm. 4°. [*London, J. Hamilton & co.* 1794].

[*In* HAMILTON (John). Angelica's ladies library, pp. 215-316].

Moore (Emily H.) A lost life. A novel. 300 pp. 12°. *New York, G. W. Carleton & co.* 1871.

Moore (Frank). Materials for history printed from original manuscripts. With notes and illustrations. First series. [Correspondence of Henry Laurens, of South Carolina]. 240 pp. 1 portrait. 4°. *New York, Zenger club,* 1861.

[*Note.*—No more published].

Moore (*Rev.* Franklin). Descriptive and didactic sermons on the seasons; also, a sermon on the crucifixion of Christ. 180 pp. 1 portrait. 12°. *Philadelphia, Perkinpine & Higgins,* 1860.

Moore (George). The desire for intoxicating liquors a disease: its causes, its effects, and its cure. With the danger of a relapse. 216 pp. 16°. *Baltimore, Sherwood & co.* 1864.

Moore (Hamilton, *jun.*) Nautical sketches. 1 p. l. iv, 270 pp. 7 pl. 12°. *London, W. E. Painter,* 1840.

Moore (H. Judge). Scott's campaign in Mexico, from the rendezvous on the island of Lobos to the taking of the city, including an account of the siege of Puebla, with sketches of the country, and manners and customs of the inhabitants. xii, 234 pp. 12°. *Charleston, [S. C.] J. B. Nixon,* 1849.

Moore (*Mrs.* H. J.) Wild Nell, the White Mountain girl. 293 pp. 4 pl. 1 portrait. 12°. *New York, Sheldon & co.* 1860.

Moore (James, *m. d.*) The world's battle. [2d ed.] 108 pp. 1 pl. 16°. *Philadelphia, author,* 1858.

Moore (John, *m. d.*) Mooriana: or, selections from the moral, philosophical, and miscellaneous works of the late dr. John Moore. Illustrated by a new biographical and critical account of the doctor and his writings; and notes, historical, classical, and explanatory. By the rev. F. Prevost and F. Blagdon. 2 v. 305 pp. 1 portrait; 1 p. l. 300 pp. 18°. *London, J. Cundee for B. Crosby & co.* 1803.

Moore (John F.) Providence almanac and directory for 1846. *See* **Providence.**

Moore (J. J.) The midshipman's or british mariner's vocabulary; being a universal dictionary of technical terms and sea phrases. 2d ed. 134 l. 9 pl. 12°. *London, Vernor & Hood,* 1805.

[Imperfect: wanting plate no. 5].

Moore (Theophilus). Marriage customs and modes of courtship of the various nations of the universe, with remarks on the condition of women, Penn's maxims, and counsel to the single and married, &c. 2d ed. 364 pp. 1 pl. 18°. *London, J. Bumpus,* 1820.

Moore (Thomas). Melodies and american poems. With a biography, and a critical review of lyric poets, by Cr. R. Shelton Mackenzie. Illustrated by Daniel Maclise and William Riches. 502 pp. 8°. *New York, International publishing co.* [1871].

Moos (H. M.) Mortara: or the pope and his inquisitors. A drama. Together with choice poems. 191 pp. 16°. *Cincinnati (O.) Bloch & co.* 1860.

Moral and religious aphorisms. 1703. *See* **Jeffrey** (John, *d. d.*)

Moral (A) essay upon the sovl of man. In three parts. [*anon.*] 10 p. l. 447 pp. 16°. *London, T. Jones*, 1690.

Moral (The) philosopher. *See* **Morgan** (*Dr.* Thomas.)

Morals (The) of pleasure, illustrated by stories. By a lady. [*anon.*] 156 pp. 12°. *Philadelphia, Carey, Lea & Carey*, 1829.

Mor de Fuentes (José). Poesías varias. 3 v. 18°. *Madrid and Zaragoza, imprenta real, etc.* 1796–1800.

Morato *or* **Moreto** (Fulvio Pellegrino) Significato dei colori e de' mazzolli di Fulvio Pellegrino. 28 l. 16°. *Vinegia, F. de Leno*, 1559.

More (Hannah). Strictures on the modern system of female education. With a view of the principles and conduct prevalent among women of rank and fortune. 5th ed. 2 v. xix, 302 pp; vii, 338 pp. 8°. *London, T. Cadell, jun. & W. Davies*, 1799.

More (*Rev.* Henry). Divine dialogues, containing sundry disquisitions & instructions concerning the attributes of God and his providence in the world. Collected and compiled by Franciscus Palæopolitanus, [*pseudon.* Also], a brief discourse of the true grounds of the certainty of faith in points of religion, together with some few songs or hymns on the chief holy-days in the year. 2d ed. xxxii, 621 pp. 2 pl. 8°. *London, J. Downing*, 1713.

——— Observations upon Anthroposophia theomagica, and Anima magica abscondita. By Alazonomastix Philalethes. [*pseudon.*] 3 p. l. 69–145 pp. 16°. *London, J. Flesher*, 1655.

More (John). Strictures, critical and sentimental, on Thomson's Seasons; with hints and observations on collateral subjects. 2 p. l. viii, 279 pp. 8°. *London, Richardson & Urquhart*, 1777.

More (*Sir* Thomas). Certain select epigrams, translated out of the works of that upright lord chancellor, and facetious poet, sr. Tho. More, &c. 16°. *London*, 1659.

[*In* PECK (Thomas). Parnassi puerperium, pp. 137–148].

——— The history of Utopia: describing the most perfect state of a common-wealth, in the manners, religion, and polity, of that island: written in latin by sir Thomas More [and now translated into english], with notes. 2 p. l. 230 pp. 8°. [*London, L. Davis & C. Rymers*, 1758].

[*With* WARNER (Ferdinand). Memoirs of the life of sir Thomas More. *London*, 1758].

Morehead (*Rev.* Robert). A series of discourses on the principles of religious belief, as connected with human happiness and improvement. 2 v. xvi, 446 pp; xii, 467 pp. 8°. *Edinburgh, A. Constable & co.* 1810–16.

[*Note.*—v. 1, 3d ed. 1810].

Morelet (*Chevalier* Arthur). Travels in Central America, including accounts of some regions unexplored since the conquest. From the french by mrs. M. F. Squier. Introduction and notes by E. G. Squier. 430 pp. 8 pl. 1 map. 12°. *New York, Leypoldt, Holt & Williams*, 1871.

Morell (John Reynell). The neighbours of Russia, and history of the present war to the siege of Sebastopol. 308 pp. 1 map. 16°. *London, T. Nelson & sons*, 1854.

Morell (Thomas, *d. d.* 1703–84). Poems on divine subjects. *See* **Vida** (Marco Girolamo).

Morell (*Rev.* Thomas). Studies in history; containing the history of England, from its earliest records [to] the death of George iii. In a series of essays. 6th ed. 2 v. viii, 463 pp; vii, 531 pp. 12°. *London, S. Holdsworth*, 1837–41.

——— Studies in history; containing the history of Greece, from its earliest period, to its final subjugation by the Romans; in a series of essays. 5th ed. xi, 410 pp. 1 map. 8°. *London, Black, Young & Young*, 1824.

Morellet (André, *l'abbé*). Réponse sérieuse à m. L * *, par l'auteur de la Théorie du paradoxe. [*anon.*] 115 pp. 12°. *Amsterdam*, 1775.

[*With his* Théorie du paradoxe].

——— Théorie du paradoxe. [*anon.*] 2 p. l. 224 pp. 12°. *Amsterdam*, 1775.

Morelli (Giovanni). Cronica [fiorentina] di Giovanni Morelli. 4°. [*Firenze, S. A. R. per G. G. Tartini & S. Franchi*, 1718].

[*In* MALESPINI (Ricardano). Istoria fiorentina. 1718. pp. 215–378].

Morelli (Jacopo). Della pubblica libreria di San Marco in Venezia, dissertazione storica. 3 p. l. xcvi pp. 8°. *Venezia, A. Zatta*, 1774.

——— Operette, ora insieme raccolte con opuscoli di antichi scrittori. 3 v. 8°. *Venezia, Alvisopoli*, 1820.

Morel-Vindé (Charles Gilbert, *vicomte de*). Zélomir. 309 pp. 6 pl. 16°. *Paris, Bleuet jeune*, 1801.

Moreno Porcel (Francisco). Retrato de Manuel de Faria y Sousa. Contiene una relacion de sua vida, un catalogo de sus escritos, y un sumario de sus elogios. Con un juisio historico, que compuzo Francisco Xavier de Meneses. 8 p. l. 102 pp. 1 l. fol. *Lisboa Occidental, en la officina ferreiriana*, 1733.

Moreton (Augustus Henry) Civilization, or a brief analysis of the natural laws that regulate the numbers and condition of mankind. 2 p. l. 216 pp. 8°. *London, Saunders & Otley*, 1836.

Morfit (Campbell, *m. d.*) A practical treatise on the manufacture of soaps. 1 p. l. xi, 270 pp. 16 p l. 8°. *London, Trübner & co.* 1871.

Morford (Henry). Morford's short-trip guide to Europe. With a short tour in the east; and skeleton tours in America. 426 pp. 1 map. 16°. *New York, Sheldon & co.* 1871.

——— Shoulder-straps. A novel of New York and the army, in 1862. 2 p. l. 15–482 pp. 2 pl. 12°. *Philadelphia, T. B. Peterson & brothers*, [1862].

——— The same. 2 p. l. 15–482 pp. 2 pl. 12°. *Philadelphia, T. B. Peterson & brothers*, [1868].

Morgan (*Rev.* Henry). Music Hall discourses, miscellaneous sketches, ministerial notes, and prison incidents. Also, Song of creation, a poem. To which is added a sketch of his life. xvi, 344 pp. 2 pl. 1 portrait. 12°. *Boston, H. W. Swett & co.* 1859.

Morgan (James Appleton). Macaronic poetry, collected with an introduction by J. A. Morgan. xvi, 300 pp. 16°. *New York, Hurd & Houghton*, 1872.

Morgan (Samuel T.) U. S. import duties, under existing laws and decisions, and digest of the tariff laws, August 1, 1871. With an appendix containing tables of foreign moneys, weights and measures, reduced to U. S. standard. Compiled by Samuel T. Morgan. 2d ed. 140 pp. 8°. *Baltimore, Turnbull brothers*, 1871.

Morgan (Sidney Owenson, *lady*). La princesse. Traduit par mlle. A. Sobry. 3 v. 16°. *Bruxelles, J. P. Meline*, 1835.

Morgan (*Dr.* Thomas). A brief examination of the rev. mr. Warburton's Divine legation of Moses. In which the mosaic theocracy, the nature and character of the sacred writings, the antiquity of hero-gods, and a future, separate state of animal life, and action for souls after death [etc.] are occasionally considered and discussed. Address'd to the author. By a society of gentlemen. [*anon.*] lxxxiv, 175 pp. 8°. *London, T. Cox*, 1742.

——— The moral philosopher. In a dialogue between Philalethes a christian deist, and Theophanes a christian jew. 2d ed. corrected. [*anon.*] 3 v. 8°. *London, author*, 1738–40.

Morgans' British trade journal. *See* **British** (The) trade journal.

Morgenlicht (Het). Stichtelijk dagboek voor het christelijk gezin. 2 p. l. 776, xxiii pp. 8°. *Arnhem, D. A. Thieme*, 1866.

Morienus *romanus.* Entretien sur le magistère d'Hermès. *See* **Chalid-ben-Jesiki** *and* **Morienus.**

Morier (James). Ayesha, the maid of Kars. By the author of "Zohrab." [*anon.*] 2d ed. 3 v. 12°. *London, R. Bentley*, 1834.

Morin (Alcide). Comment l'esprit vient aux tables. Par un homme qui n'a pas perdu l'esprit. [*anon.*] 2 p. l. 176 pp. 12°. *Paris, S. Raçon & comp.* 1854.
[PSYCHOLOGIE expérimentale].

Morin (Arthur Jules). Fundamental ideas of mechanics and experimental data. Revised, translated, and reduced to english units of measure by Joseph Bennett. xiii, 445 pp. 2 pl. 8°. *New York, D. Appleton & co.* 1860.

Morison (Alexander, *m. d.*) Cases of mental disease, with practical observations on the medical treatment. vii, 164 pp. 2 pl. 8°. *London, Longman & co.* 1828.
[MEDICAL pamphlets, v. 3].

——— Outlines of mental diseases. 3d ed. viii, 162 pp. 17 pl. 8°. *London, Longman & co.* [*etc.*] 1829.

Morison (John, *d. d.*) The protestant reformation in all countries; including sketches of the state and prospects of the reformed churches. xx, 528 pp. 8°. *London, Fisher, son & co.* 1843.

Morison. *See* **Morrison.**

Morley (Charles). A guide to forming and conducting lyceums, debating societies, &c; with outlines of discussions and essays, and an appendix, containing an epitome of rhetoric, logic, &c. 102 pp. 18°. *New York, A. E. Wright*, 1841.

Mormons. *See* **Church** of Jesus Christ of latter day saints.

Morning, noon, and night; or, Christ in every page. A manual of devotion, adapted to every day in the year, etc. By one who believes the bible to be the word of God, and the only infallible rule of faith and obedience. [*anon.* By T. B. Condit]? 612 pp. 8°. *New York, J. A. Gray*, 1861.

Morning (The) watch; or quarterly journal on prophecy, and theological review. March, 1829, to June, 1833. v. 1-7. 8°. *London, J. Nisbet*, [*etc.*] 1830-33.
[Wanting pp. 263-302, v. 7].

Morogues (Pierre Marie Sébastien Bigot de). *See* **Bigot de Morogues.**

Morrill (Frederic, *m. d.*). The medical adviser and guide to health. Revised ed. xxi, 575 pp. 16°. *Boston, Morrill medical institute*, 1871.

Morris (Caspar). The life of William Wilberforce. Abridged. *See* **Wilberforce** (Robert Isaac *and* Samuel).

Morris (Charles D.) Probatio latina: a series of questions designed to test the progress of learners in the latin language. 2 p. l. 81 pp. 16°. *New York, F. J. Huntington & co.* 1871.

Morris (Eastin). The Tennessee gazetteer, or topographical dictionary; containing a description of the several counties, towns, villages, post offices, rivers, creeks, mountains, valleys, &c. in the state of Tennessee, alphabetically arranged. To which is prefixed a general description of the state: its civil divisions, resources, population, &c. And a condensed history from the earliest settlements down to the rise of the convention in the year 1834. With an appendix. 2 p. l. cxvi, 178 pp. 9 l. 12°. *Nashville, W. H. Hunt & co.* 1834.

Morris (Edmund). How to get a farm, and where to find one. With the public laws on the subject of free homes, and suggestions from practical farmers. By the author of "Ten acres enough." [*anon.*] 345 pp. 12°. *New York, J. Miller*, 1864.

Morris (Edward). The life of Henry Bell, the practical introducer of the steam-boat into Great Britain and Ireland; [with] an historical sketch of steam navigation. vi, 175, 8 pp. 16°. *Glasgow, author*, 1844.

Morris (*Rev.* Herbert W.) Science and the bible; or, the mosaic creation and modern discoveries. 566 pp. 32 pl. 8°. *Philadelphia, Ziegler & McCurdy*, 1871.

Morris (John). The condition of catholics under James i. Father Gerard's narrative of the gunpowder plot; printed from the ms. in possession of Stonyhurst college. Edited, with his life, by John Morris. cclxiii, 344 pp. 8°. *London, Longmans, Green, & co.* 1871. s.

Morris (John G. *d. d.*) To Rome and back again; or, the two proselytes. Adapted from the german. 238 pp. 12°. *Baltimore, T. N. Kurtz*, 1856.

Morris (John Williams). Memoirs of the life and writings of the rev. Andrew Fuller. New ed. 375 pp. 1 portrait. 8°. *London, Wightman & Cramp*, 1826.

Morris (P. H. *m. d.*) The evil effects of drunkenness physiologically explained. 12°. [*New York*, 1841].
[*In* BERMINGHAM (*Rev.* James). A memoir of the very rev. T. Mathew, pp. 115-216].

Morris (Richard, *ll. d. editor*). Legends of the holy rood; symbols of the passion and cross-poems. In old english of the eleventh, fourteenth, and fifteenth centuries. Edited from mss. in the British museum and Bodleian libraries; with introduction, translations, and glossarial index. xxxi, 240 pp. 1 pl. 8°. *London, N. Trübner & co.* 1871.
[EARLY english text society, no. 46].

Morris (William, *english poet*). The earthly paradise. A poem. 4 parts in 3 v. 16°. *Boston, Roberts bros.* 1871.

CONTENTS.

v. 1. Spring and summer.
v. 2. Autumn.
v. 3. Winter.

Morris (William, *m. d.*) The question of ages; or, outlines of testimony in relation to life, death, and immortality. 179 pp. 12°. *Philadelphia, Scriptural knowledge society*, 1862.

Morris (William H. *brig. gen. U. S. a.*) Field tactics for infantry: comprising the battalion movements, and brigade evolutions, useful in the field, on the march, and in the presence of the enemy. 146 pp. 18°. *New York, D. Van Nostrand*, 1864.

Morrison (James M.) Clarsach Albin, and other poems. Including his correspondence with Clark, McCammon and Douglass. 108 pp. 1 pl. 8°. *Philadelphia, G. B. Zieber & co.* 1847.

Morrison (John H.) Disquisitions on the gospels. Matthew. *See* **Bible.** (*English*).

Morrison. *See* **Morison.**

Morrocchesi (Antonio). Lezioni di declamazione e d'arte teatrale. 366 pp. 1 l. 40 pl. 8°. *Firenze, tipografia all insegna di Dante*, 1832.

Morse (*Rev.* Abner). A genealogical register of the inhabitants of the towns of Sherborn and Holliston. 4 p. l. 340 pp. 8 pl. 8°. *Boston, Damrell & Moore*, 1856.

Morse (Jedediah, *d. d.*) The american universal geography. [Also], an improved chronological table of remarkable events, from the creation to the present time. 11th ed. corrected by the author. 432 pp. 1 map. 12°. *Boston, Thomas & Andrews*, 1807.
[Imperfect: wanting 1 map].

——— (*editor*). A new and elegant general atlas, comprising all the new discoveries to the present time. Containing sixty-three maps, drawn by Arrowsmith and Lewis. Intended to accompany the new improved edition of Morse's geography, but equally well calculated to be used with his gazetteer, or any other geographical work. 2 p. l. 63 maps. 4°. *Boston, Thomas & Andrews*, 1812.
[Imperfect: 2 maps wanting].

Morse (*Rev.* Pitt). Sermons in vindication of universalism. In reply to "Lectures on universalism; by Joel Parker." 135 pp. 16°. *Watertown* (*N. Y.*) *Woodward & Calhoun*, 1831.

Morse (Samuel Finley Breese, *editor*). The proscribed german student: being a sketch of some interesting incidents in the life and melancholy death of the late Lewis Clausing. To which is added, A treatise on the jesuits: the posthumous work of Lewis Clausing. 244 pp. 16°. *New-York, Van Nostrand & Dwight*, 1836.

——— *See* **Confessions** of a french catholic priest.

Morse (Sidney Edwards). Nuevo sistema de geografia. *See* **Brigham** (John C.) *and* **Morse.**

Mortal life; and the state of the soul after death. *See* **Copland** (Alexander).

Mortimer (Thomas). The universal director; or, the nobleman and gentleman's true guide, 1763. *See* **London** (*England*). The universal director.

Morton (*Rev.* Daniel O.) Memoir of rev. Levi Parsons, late missionary to Palestine. 4 p. l. 13-431 pp. 1 portrait. 12°. *Poultney* (*Vt.*) *Smith & Shute*, 1824.

——— The same. 2d ed. 408 pp. 12°. *Hartford, Cooke & co.* 1830.

Morton (*Rev.* George). The divine purpose explained, or all things decreed; yet evil not caused, nor moral freedom impaired; and the glory of God, the end of all. 310 pp. 8°. *Philadelphia, J. M. Wilson*, 1860.

Morton (*Rev.* Henry J.) The sunday-school teacher's aid to the gospels, containing the outlines of a harmony. 230 pp. 1 pl. 18°. *Philadelphia, W. Stavely*, 1838.

Morton (Thomas, *bishop of Coventry and Lichfield*). Of the institvtion of the sacrament of the blessed bodie and blood of Christ, (by some called) the masse of Christ, eight bookes; discovering the superstitious, sacrilegious, and idolatrous abominations of the romish masse. By Thomas l. bishop of Coventry and Lichfield. [1st ed.] 10 p. l. 255, 144 pp. 8 l. fol. *London, W. Stansby for R. Mylbovrne*, 1631.

Morton house. A novel. [*anon.*] *See* **Fisher** (Frances C.)

Moschopulus (Manuel *or* Emanuel). Opuscula grammatica. E codice nuper in Bohemia reperto nunc primum edidit græce præfationem cum diatribe literaria de Moschopulis et animadversiones suas adiecit Franciscus Nicolaus Titze. xxvi, 86 pp. 8°. *Lipsiæ, apud C. Cnobloch*, 1822.

Mösel *or* **Musculus** (Wolfgang). Common places of christian religion, with two other treatises, one of othes, and an other of vsurye. *b. l.* 587 l. 17 l. unp. fol. *London, R. Wolfe*, 1563.
[Imperfect: title-page and first twelve leaves wanting].

Moseley (*Rev.* Henry). Illustrations of mechanics. Revised by James Renwick, ll. d. 2 p. l. 15-332 pp. 18°. *New York, Harper & brothers*, 1839.

Moseley (Joseph). Political elements; or, the progress of modern legislation. viii, 309 pp. 8°. *London, J. W. Parker & son*, 1852.

Moss (William). The Liverpool guide; including a sketch of the environs: with a map of the town; and directions for sea bathing. 2 p. l. 168 pp. 1 map. 8°. *Liverpool, W. Jones*, 1799.

Mother (The) in her family. *See* **Alcott** (W. A.)

Motherless Maud. By the author of "Ellis Amory," [etc. *anon.*] 271 pp. 4 pl. 16°. *Boston, Mass. sabbath school society*, 1863.

Motiven die d' e. officieren der militie in consideratie hebben ghenomen om met den vyandt (namentlick de Portugesen) in accoord te treden. Ady 23 Ianuary, 1654. 4 pp. sm. 4°. [*Gravenhage?* 1654].

Mott (*Rev.* George S.) The prodigal son. 143 pp. 12°. *Philadelphia, Presbyterian board of publication*, 1863.

Mott (John M.) Electric; a treatise on electric phenomena; the laws governing the same; lightning rods, and their necessary application to buildings for safety. 122 pp. 16°. *Chicago, Rand, McNally & co.* 1871.

Moubray (Bonnington). A treatise on breeding, rearing, and fattening, all kinds of poultry, cows, swine, and other domestic animals. Reprinted from the sixth London edition. With abridgments, and additions. By Thomas G. Fessenden, esq. 266 pp. 12°. *Boston, Lilly & Wait*, 1832.

Moule (Thomas). An essay on the roman villas of the augustan age, their architectural disposition and enrichments; and on the remains of the roman domestic edifices discovered in Great Britain. viii, 179 pp. 2 pl. 8°. *London, Longman*, 1833.

Moulins. (*Société d'émulation du département de l'Allier*). Bulletin. 1846–1868. (Sciences, arts et belles-lettres). v. 1–10. 8°. *Moulins, P. A. Desrosiers*, [*etc.*] 1846–68. s.

——— Publications. 8°. *Moulins, C. Desrosiers*, 1860–66. s.

CONTENTS.

CHAZAUD (A.) Étude sur la chronologie des sires de Bourbon.
——— Fragments du cartulaire de la Chapelle-Aude.
MIGOUT (A.) Flore du département de l'Allier.

Mouls (Joseph). Art of speaking the french language in a short time, applicable to all modern languages. xii, 132 pp. 12°. *New York, Collins, Keese & co.* 1836.

Moulton (*Rev.* Horace). The young pastor's wife. *Memoir of* Elizabeth Ann Moulton: containing her biography, diary, letters, etc. x, 5–275 pp. 18°. *Boston, Waite, Peirce & co.* 1845.

Mount Washington in winter, or the experiences of a scientific expedition upon the highest mountain in New England, 1870–71. [By C. H. Hitchcock, J. H. Huntington, and others]. vii, 363 pp. 15 pl. 1 map. 12°. *Boston, Chick & Andrews*, 1871.

Mountain (*Rev.* Jacob Henry Brooke). A summary of the writings of Lactantius. 1839. *See* **Lactantius Firmianus** (Lucius Cœlius).

Mouret (Simon François). Chasses du roy et la quantité des lieues que le roy a fait tant à cheval qu'en carosse pendant l'année 1725. [Publiées par Pichon]. xii pp. 8 l. 8°. *Paris*, 1867.

[PARIS. Société des bibliophiles françois, v. 2].

Moussaud (*L'abbé* Jean Marie). L'alphabet raisonné, ou explication de la figure des lettres. 2 v. xxxij, 406 pp. 1 pl; 2 p. l. 420 pp. 8°. *Paris, Maradan*, 1803.

Movement (The), anti-persecution gazette, and register of progress: a weekly journal of republican politics, anti-theology, & utilitarian morals. Edited by G. Jacob Holyoake. Assisted by M. Q. Ryall. December, 1843, to April, 1845. v. 1–2, no. 1–68. 8°. *London, G. J. Holyoake*, [1843–45].

[*Note.*—Discontinued with the 68th number. No. 56 wanting].

Moxon (Joseph). Mechanick exercises: or, the doctrine of handy-works. [New ed.] 1 p. l. 234 pp. 17 pl. 4°. *London, J. Moxon*, 1694.

——— The same. To which is added Mechanick dyalling; shewing how to draw a true sun-dyal on any given plane, however scituated. 3d ed. 5 p. l. 352 pp. 26 pl. 8°. *London, D. Midwinter & T. Leigh*, 1703.

[Imperfect: plate 16 wanting].

Moyle (Walter). The works of W. Moyle, esq; none of which were ever before publish'd. 2 v. xviii, 430 pp. portrait; 1 p. l. 390 pp. 10 l. 8°. *London, J. Darby*, [*etc.*] 1726.

——— The same. The whole works of Walter Moyle, esq; that were published by himself. [With] some account of his life and writings. 3 p. l. 60, 286 pp. 2 l. 8°. *London, J. Knapton*, [*etc.*] 1727.

——— A select collection of tracts. 274 pp. 16°. *Glasgow, R. Urie*, 1750.

CONTENTS.

An essay upon the roman government, pp. 5–123.
Remarks upon dr. Prideaux's connection of the old and new testament, pp. 125–189.
An essay upon the lacedaemonian government, pp. 191–219.
An argument against a standing army, pp. 221–274.

Mozart (Johann Chrysostom Wolfgang Amadeus). Don Giovanni. Words newly revised and corrected by W. Sherwood. [Libretto without music]. 40 pp. 8°. [*New York*], *W. C. Bryant & co.* 1871.

[PAREPA-ROSA grand english opera].

——— Marriage of Figaro. Words newly revised and corrected by W. Sherwood. [Libretto without music]. 43 pp. 8°. [*New York*], *W. C. Bryant & co.* 1871.

[PAREPA-ROSA grand english opera].

Mr. Arle. A novel. [*anon.*] 2 v. 1 p. l. 315 pp; 1 p. l. 284 pp. 12°. *London, Hurst & Blackett*, 1856.

Mrs. Brown's stories. [*anon.*] 127 pp. 2 pl. 18°. *Boston, Mass. sabbath school society*, [1860].

Muckersey (*Rev.* John). M. Gener; or, a selection of letters on life and manners. 4th ed. 3 v. 8°. *London, Longman*, 1815.

Mudford (Henry). Stephen Dugard. A novel. By the author of "Five knights of St. Albans," etc. [*anon.*] 3 v. 12°. *London, R. Bentley*, 1840.

Mudge (*Rev.* Z. A.) Foot-prints of Roger Williams: a biography, with sketches of important events in early New England history, with which he was connected. 285 pp. 4 pl. 16°. *New York, Carlton & Lanahan*, [1871].

Muggleton (Lodowick). The acts of the witnesses of the spirit. In five parts. Left by him to be publish'd after 's death. 4 p. l. 179 pp. 4°. *London*, 1699.

——— The answer to William Penn, quaker, his book, entituled, The new witnesses proved old hereticks, wherein he is proved to be an ignorant spater-brain'd quaker, who knows no more what the true God is, nor his secret decrees, than one of his coach-horses doth, nor so much. 2 p. l. 40, 90, 22 pp. 4°. *London*, 1672.

[*Note.*—Title-page imperfect].

——— A true interpretation of the eleventh chapter of the revelation of st. John, and other texts in that book: as also, many other places of scripture. Whereby is unfolded, and plainly declared, the whole counsel of God concerning himself, the devil, and all mankind, from the foundation of the world to all eternity. xvi, 199 pp. 4°. [*n. p.*] 1751-53.

——— The same.

[*With* REEVE (John). Sacred remains].

Mühlbach (L. *pseudon.*) *See* **Mundt** (Clara Müller).

Mulgrave (Henry Philip Phipps, *earl of*). The temple of death. *See* **Habert** (Philippe).

Mulkey (William). An abridgement of Walker's rules on the sounds of the letters. *See* **Walker** (John, *philologist*).

Mullach (François Guillaume August). Fragmenta philosophorum græcorum collegit, recensuit, vertit, annotationibus et prolegomenis illustravit, indicibus instruxit Fr. Guil. Aug. Mullachius. Poeseos philosophicæ cæterorumque ante Socratem philosophorum quæ supersunt. [Græce et latine]. 2 p. l. xxvii, 573 pp. 4°. *Parisiis, F. Didot*, 1860.

[DIDOT. Bibliothèque grecque, v. 56].

Mullalla (James). A view of irish affairs since the revolution of 1688, to the close of the parliamentary session of 1795; with introductory remarks, and a preliminary sketch of the revolution. 2 v. xxxvi, 331 pp; 1 p. l. 333 pp. 8°. *Dublin, T. Henshall*, 1795.

Müller (*Dr.* Albrecht). Geognostische skizze des kantons Basel, etc. 1862. *See* **Switzerland**. Geologische commission.

Müller (Johann Christoph). Greuel der falschen messien, wie auch, schatz-kammer des wahren messiæ Jesu Christi, das ist: eine ziemliche lista der jenigen falschen messien, so von anfang der welt, bisz auff diese ietzige zeit haben können in erfahrung gebracht werden, [etc.] 48 pp. fol. [*n. p.*] 1702.

[*In* ANABAPTISTICUM et enthusiasticum pantheon].

Müller (Johann Heinrich Jacob, *of Freiburg*). Bericht über die neuesten fortschritte der physik. In ihrem zusammenhange dargestellt. v. 1. 1 p. l. xvii, 874 pp. 8°. *Braunschweig, F. Vieweg & sohn*, 1849-51. s.

——— Lehrbuch der kosmischen physik. xv, 520 pp. 8°. *Braunschweig, F. Vieweg & sohn*, 1856. s.

[MÜLLER-POUILLET's Lehrbuch der physik, v. 3. *Note.*—Atlas, 27 plates, wanting].

Müller (Johann T.) Historical introduction [to the book of concord]. 8°. [*Newmarket*, 1854].

[*In* EVANGELICAL lutheran church. The christian book of concord, pp. 9-86].

Müller (Ludwig, *editor*). *See* **Wiener** entomologische monatsschrift, 1857-63.

Müller (Otto). Charlotte Ackerman; a theatrical romance, founded upon interesting facts in the life of a young artist of the last century. Translated from the german, by mrs. Chapman Coleman and her daughters. 357 pp. 16°. *Philadelphia, Porter & Coates*, [1871].

Müller (Wilhelm Christian, *the 3rd*). Flug von der Nordsee zum Montblank, durch Westphalen, Niederrhein, Schwaben, die Schweiz, über Baiern, Franken, Niedersachsen zurück. Skizze zum gemälde unserer zeit. Erster theil. 2 p. l. 317 pp. 16°. *Altona, J. F. Hammerich*, 1821.

[*Note.*—v. 2 wanting to complete the work].

Muloch (Dinah Maria). *See* **Craik** (*Mrs.* D. M. Muloch).

Mumford (Mary E.) Hila Dart, a born romp. 350 pp. 4 pl. 16°. *Philadelphia, W. B. Evans & co.* 1871.

München. *See* **Munich.**

Mundt (Clara Müller). Mohammed Ali and his house. An historical romance. By L. Mühlbach. [*pseudon.*] Translated from the german, by mrs. Chapman Coleman. 229 pp. 4 pl. 8°. *New York, D. Appleton & co.* 1872.

Munger (*Rev.* Sendol B.) The conquest of India by the church. 378 pp. 18°. *Boston, Mass. sabbath school society,* 1845.

Munich. (*K. hof- und staatsbibliothek*). Catalogus codicum manuscriptorum bibliothecae regiae monacensis. v. 1, parts 2-3; v. 3, part 2; and v. 5-7. 8°. *München, Palm,* 1858-66. s.

CONTENTS.

v. 1, pt. 2. Die arabischen handschriften, von Joseph Aumer.
pt. 3. Die persischen handschriften, von Joseph Aumer.
v. 3, pt. 2. Catalogus codicum latinorum. Tomi i, pars ii. Codices num. 2501-5250 complectens.
v. 5-6. Die deutschen handschriften, nach J. A. Schmeller's kürzerem verzeichniss.
v. 7. Codices gallicos, hispanicos, italicos, anglicos, suecicos, danicos, slavicos, esthnicos, hungaricos complectens.

[No more published to date].

——— (*Königliche sternwarte*). Annalen der königlichen sternwarte bei München, auf öffentliche kosten herausgegeben von dr. J. v. Lamont. v. 18. (Der vollständigen sammlung xxxiii. band). 8°. *München, E. Lintner,* 1871. s.

Munnell (Thomas) *and* **Sweeney** (J. S.) Discussion, Shall christians go to war? 247 pp. 16°. *Cincinnati, Bosworth, Chase & Hall,* 1872.

Muñoz (Antonio). Discurso sobre economía política. lx, 332 pp. 16°. *Madrid, J. de Ibarra,* 1769.

Munro (*Rev.* Hugh Andrew Johnstone). Q. Horatii Flacci opera, illustrated from antique gems by C. W. King. *See* **Horatius Flaccus** (Quintus).

Munsell (Joel). *See* **Webster's** calendar, or the Albany almanac for 1871.

Munsell (Oliver S. *d. d.*) Psychology; or, the science of mind. xxxvi, 320 pp. 12°. *New York, D. Appleton & co.* 1871.

Münster (Sebastian). Cosmographey: das ist, beschreibung aller länder, herrschafften und fürnemesten stetten des gantzen erdbodens, sampt ihren gelegenheiten, [etc.] 14 p. l. mcccclxj pp. 1 l. 26 maps. fol. *Basel, S. Henricpetri, mdxciix,* [1598].

Muoni (Damiano). L'antico stato di Romano di Lombardia, ed altri comuni del suo mandamento. Cenni storici, documenti e regesti. 493 pp. 2 l. 2 pl. 8°. *Milano, C. Brigola,* 1871. s.

——— Collezione d'autografi di famiglie sovrane, celebrità politiche, militari, ecclesiastiche, scientifiche, letterarie ed artistiche, illustrata con cenni biografici, documenti,

Muoni (Damiano)—continued.
fac-simili, ritratti, monete di alcuni stati italiani. 2 v. 64 pp. 7 pl; 2 p. l. 65-152 pp. 9 pl. 8°. *Milano, F. Colombo,* 1858-59. s.

CONTENTS.

v. 1. Elenco delle zecche d'Italia.
Famiglia Sforza.
v. 2. Governatori, luogotenenti e capitani generali dello stato di Milano, 1499-1848.

Murathee grammar. [In the devanagari character. *anon.*] vi, 110 pp. 8°. *Bombay, American mission press,* 1848.

Murchie (William). Truth & love: or the calvinist & the arminian reconciled, and the unitarian reclaimed, in a new development of scripture doctrine. xvi, 320 pp. 16°. *Glasgow, G. Gallie,* [1846].

Murden (*Mrs.* Eliza). Miscellaneous poems, by a lady of Charleston, S. C. [*anon.*] 2d ed. 179 pp. 12°. *New-York, author,* 1827.

Murdoch (John). The dictionary of distinctions, in three alphabets, containing, 1. Words the same in sound, but of different spelling and signification; with which are classed such as have any similarity in sound. 2. Words that vary in pronunciation and meaning as accentuated or connected. 3. The changes in sound and sense, produced by the addition of the letter e. With appendix. 4 p. l. 12 pp. 160 l. 8°. *London, C. Law,* 1811.

Murimuthensis (Adamus). *See* **Adam** *of Merioneth.*

Murphy (Arthur). An essay on the life and genius of Samuel Johnson, ll. d. 1 p. l. 133 pp. 8°. *London, W. Sharpe & son,* [*etc.*] 1820.

——— Memoir of dr. Samuel Johnson. 18°. [*Boston,* 1833].

[*In* JOHNSON (Samuel). Life: with maxims and observations, 1833, pp. 15-61].

Murphy (James Cavanah). A general view of the state of Portugal; containing a topographical description thereof. In which are included, an account of the physical and moral state of the kingdom; together with observations on the animal, vegetable, and mineral productions of its colonies. 272 pp. 14 pl. 1 map. 4°. *London, T. Cadell, jun. & W. Davies,* 1798.

——— Travels in Portugal; through the provinces of Entre Douro e Minho, Beira, Estremadura, and Alem-tejo, in the years 1789 and 1790, consisting of observations on the manners, customs, trade, public buildings, arts, antiquities, etc. of that kingdom. xii, 311 pp. 24 pl. 4°. *London, A. Strahan,* [*etc.*] 1795.

Murphy (J. G. *d. d.*) Commentary on Genesis. *See* **Bible.** (*English*).

Murphy (Joseph John). Habit and intelligence, in their connexion with the laws of matter and force: a series of scientific essays. 2 v. xxiv, 349 pp; xvi, 240 pp. 8°. *London, Macmillan & co.* 1869.

Murray (Adolf). Testacéologie. 8°. [*Paris*, 1799].

[*In* FORSTER (Johann Reinhold). Manuel pour servir à l'histoire naturelle, pp. 145-212, 3me partie].

Murray (Alexander). *See* **Newfoundland.** *Geological survey.* 1871.

Murray (E. C. Grenville). Droits et devoirs des envoyés diplomatiques. Documens recueillis et arrangés par E. C. G. Murray. xvi, 234 pp. 1 l. 12°. *Londres, R. Bentley*, 1853.

Murray (George). Islaford, and other poems: a book for winter evenings and summer moods. 2 p. l. 192 pp. 16°. *London, Smith, Elder & co.* 1845.

Murray (Grace *and* Ida). The sunday school celebration book. A collection of dialogues, speeches, hymns, etc. for anniversaries and other occasions. 2d ed. 202 pp. 18°. *Philadelphia, Perkinpine & Higgins*, 1861.

Murray (John, *m. d.*) A system of materia medica and pharmacy, including translations of the Edinburgh, London, and Dublin pharmacopœias. 6th ed. With notes and additions by John B. Beck, m. d. 584 pp. 1 tab. 8°. *New York, Collins & Hannay*, 1834.

Murray (John Fisher). The world of London. A new series. 2 v. 2 p. l. 294 pp; 2 p. l. 296 pp. 8°. *London, R. Bentley*, 1845.

Murray (Lindley). The english reader, or pieces in prose and verse, selected from the best writers. To which are prefixed, the definitions of inflections and emphasis, and rules for reading verse, with a key. By M. R. Bartlett. 252 pp. 18°. *Utica*, [*N. Y.*] *W. Williams*, 1823.

Murray (Nicholas, *d. d.*) Preachers and preaching. 303 pp. 12°. *New York, Harper & brothers*, 1860.

Murray (*Rev.* William Henry Harrison). Park-street pulpit: sermons. v, 372 pp. 12°. *Boston, J. R. Osgood & co.* 1871.

Murray (Lieutenant, *pseudon?*) The turkish spies Ali Abubeker Kaled, and Zenobia Marrita Mustapha; or the mohammedan prophet of 1854. A true history of the russo-turkish war. 267 pp. 2 pl. 8°. *Buffalo, A. R. Orton*, 1855.

Musa americana. Poema, que en verso heroico latino escribió un erudito americano, sobre los soberanos atributos de Dios, y traduce en castellano en octava rima el br. d. Diego Bringas de Manzaneda y Enzinas [etc. *anon.*] 3 p. l. 151 pp. 18°. *México, F. de Zúñiga y Ontiveros*, 1783.

Musæ seatonianæ. *See* **Cambridge** prize poems.

Musaeus *grammaticus.* Héro et Léandre, traduit par J. F. Grégoire et F. Z. Collombet. 12°. [*Paris, Lefèvre*, 1841].

[*In* MARTIN (Louis Aimé). Petits poëmes grecs. *Paris*, 1841. pp. 111-129].

——— The same. Héro et Léandre, poëme de Musée. On y a joint la traduction de plusieurs idylles de Théocrite. Par m. [Julien Jacques] M * * * [Moutonnet] C * * [Clairfons]. xvi, 104 pp. 8°. *Paris, Le Boucher*, 1774.

[*With* ARNAUD (François Thomas Marie Baculard d'). Fayel, tragédie. *Paris*, 1777].

——— The same. Le avventure di Ero e di Leandro. [Portato in italiano da] Baccio dal Borgo. 8°. *Pisa, tipografia nistri*, 1837.

[*With* COLUTHUS. Il rapimento di Elena. *Pisa*, 1837].

Musculus. *See* **Mösel.**

Muse (The) in a moral humor: being, a collection of agreeable and instructive tales, fables, pastorals, etc. By several hands. [*anon.*] 2 v. iv, 232 pp; 2 p. l. 242 pp. 16°. *London, F. Noble*, 1757-58.

Musgrave (*Rev.* George). Nooks and corners in old France. 2 v. xviii, 353 pp. 6 pl; x, 364 pp. 9 pl. 8°. *London, Hurst & Blackett*, 1867.

Mushet (Robert) A history of coinage in Great Britain, with preliminary remarks on the coins and moneys of account in ancient and modern times. (From the Encyclopedia britannica). 8°. [*Philadelphia, J. B. Lippincott & co.* 1872].

[*In* HOMANS (I. S.) Coin book, pp. 1-53].

Musical (The) independent. A monthly magazine. W. S. B. Mathews, editor. Jan. to Sept. 1871. v. 3. 4°. *Chicago, Lyon & Healy*, [1871].

Musical (The) miscellany: being a collection of choice songs, set to the violin and flute. By the most eminent masters. 6 v. 12°. *London, J. Watts*, 1729-31.

Musical (The) miscellany, comprising the music published in the musical magazine. Edited by Thomas Hastings. v. 1. 83 l 8°. *New York, E. Collier*, 1836.

Musical (The) treasure, a collection of vocal and instrumental music, for the piano-forte or reed organ. [*anon.*] 224 pp. 4°. *Boston, O. Ditson & co.* [1871].

Musso (Luigi). Sopra gli aeroliti caduti il giorno 29 febbraio 1868. *See* **Denza** (Francesco).

Musters (George Chaworth). At home with the Patagonians. A year's wanderings over untrodden ground from the straits of Magellan to the Rio Negro. xx, 323 pp. 9 pl. 1 map. 8°. *London, J. Murray*, 1871.

Mut (Vicente). History of the Balearick islands. *See* **Dameto** (Juan) *and* **Mut.**

Muzzey (*Rev.* Artemas Bowers). The blade and the ear. Thoughts for a young man. iv, 233 pp. 12°. *Boston, W. V. Spencer*, 1865.

——— Christ in the will, the heart, and the life. Discourses. viii, 371 pp. 12°. *Boston, Walker, Wise & co.* 1861.

——— Man a soul; or, the inward, and the experimental, evidences of christianity. xvi, 157 pp. 16°. *Boston, W. Crosby & co.* 1842.

——— The young man's friend. xi, 178 pp. 18°. *Boston, J. Munroe & co.* 1836.

My mother: or, recollections of maternal influence. [*anon.*] xii, 9–254 pp. 1 pl. 12°. *Boston, Gould & Lincoln*, 1855.

My son's manual, comprising a summary view of the studies, accomplishments, and principles of conduct, best suited for promoting respectability and success in life. [*anon.*] Eng. title, 288 pp. 1 pl. 16°. *New-York, D. Appleton & co.* 1837.

Myers (Sarah Ann). Aunt Carrie's budget of fireside stories. 174 pp. 2 pl. 18°. *Philadelphia, Presbyterian board of publication*, [1860].

——— Faithful Nicolette; or, the french nurse. [Also, Gertrude's dream]. 179 pp. 16°. *New York, Carlton & Porter*, 1857.

——— The neighbor's children. From the german. iv, 13–266 pp. 1 pl. 12°. *Philadelphia, Lindsay & Blakiston*, 1854.

——— Our Katie; or, the grateful orphan. A story for children. 90 pp. 18°. *New York, Carlton & Porter*, [1859].

——— Poor Nicholas; or, the man in the blue coat. 316 pp. 4 pl. 18°. *Philadelphia, Presbyterian board of publication*, [1863].

——— Self-sacrifice, or the pioneers of Fuegia. 300 pp. 1 portrait. 16°. *Philadelphia, Presbyterian board of publication*, [1861].

——— The young recruit, or under which king. 216 pp. 3 pl. 18°. *Philadelphia, Presbyterian board of publication*, 1863.

Myler von Ehrenbach (Nicolas). Etologia ordinum imperialium, sive de principum & aliorum statuum imperii romano-germanici jure concedendi veniam ætatis; libellus singularis. 4 p. l. 82 pp. 4°. *Tubingæ, sumtibus G. Stollii*, 1706.

[*With his* GAMOLOGIA personarum imperii illustrium, 1723].

——— Gamologia personarum imperii illustrium, in qua de matrimonio, tam inter se, quam cum exteris: æquali vel inæquali: ex ratione status. et ad morganaticam virorum illustrium. item de uxore illustri. de dispensatione. de vidua: dotalitio: ac dono matutinali, nec non de liberis illustribus, tam naturalibus quam legitimis, eorumque jure & dignitate agitur. 4 p. l. 586 pp. 4°. *Tubingæ, impensis T. Mezleri*, 1723.

Mylius *or* **Myle** (Arnold van der). De rebvs hispanicis, lvsitanicis, aragonicis, indicis et aethiopicis. Damiani a Goes, Hieronymi Pauli, Hieronymi Blanci, Iacobi Teuij, opera. Partim ex manuscriptis nunc primum eruta, partim auctiora edita. 12 p. l. 443 pp. 1 portrait. 16°. *Coloniae Agrippinae, in officina birckmannica*, 1602.

Mynshul (Geffray). Essayes and characters of a prison and prisoners. London, M. Walbancke. 1618. xviii pp. 1 l. 91 pp. 12°. *Edinburgh, reprinted for W. & C. Tait*, 1821.

[*Note* —" Only 150 copies for sale"].

Myrtle (Minnie, *pseudon.*) *See* **Johnson** (Anna C.)

Myrtle (Molly, *pseudon.*) Myrtle blossoms. 304 pp. 8°. *Chicago, for the authoress by J. C. W. Bailey*, 1863.

Myself: a romance of New England life. [*anon.*] 488 pp. 12°. *Philadelphia, J. B. Lippincott & co.* 1872.

Mysterious (The) story-book; or, the good step-mother. By whom? [*anon.*] 222 pp. 4 pl. 12°. *New York, D. Appleton & co.* 1856.

Mystery (The) hid from ages and generations, made manifest by the gospel-revelation: or, the salvation of all men the grand thing aimed at in the scheme of God. By one who wishes well to the whole human race. [*anon.*] xvi, 406 pp. 8°. *London, C. Dilly*, 1784.

Mystical (The) visitant, containing a rare collection of great discoveries in the arts, sciences, etc. [Recipes. *anon.*] 128 pp. 16°. *Chicago, Barber, Hanna & co.* 1871.

N. (*Baron* de). Telescope de Zoroastre, ou clef de la grande cabale divinatoire des mages. [*anon.*] xxiv, 7, 132 pp. 7 pl. 12°. [*Paris*], 1796.

Nack (James). Earl Rupert, and other tales and poems. With a memoir of the author by P. M. Wetmore. xx, 220 pp. 12°. *New-York, G. Adlard*, 1839.

Naderste (Het) ende sekerste journalier verhael, ofte copye van sekeren brieff, gheschreven uyt Brasyl, nopende de treffelijcke ende langhgewenschte victorye die Godt Almachtigh ons verleent heeft, onder 't beleyt van Maurits van Nassau, in Brasyl, tegen de machtige vloot des konings van Spanjen, bestaende in 88. zeylen, voor-ghevallen in de maendt van Januario, 1640. [*anon.*] 8 l. sm. 4°. *Graven-hage, I. Burchoorn*, 1640.

Naegelsbach (*Dr.* C. W. Eduard). Jeremiah and Lamentations. *See* **Bible.** (*English.*)

Naekius. *See* **Näke.**

Naerder bedenckingen, over de zee-vaerdt, coophandel ende neeringhe. 1608. *See* **Usselincx** (Willem).

Näke (August Ferdinand). Choerili Samii quae supersunt collegit et illustravit A. F. Näke. *See* **Choerilus** *samius.*

Nalson (*Rev.* John, *ll. d.*) The common interest of king and people: shewing the original, antiquity and excellency of monarchy, compared with aristocracy and democracy, and particularly of our english monarchy: and that absolute, papal and presbyterian popular supremacy are utterly inconsistent with prerogative, property and liberty. 4 p. l. 279 pp. 1 portrait. 8°. *London, J. Edwin*, 1678.

Namur. Exposé de la situation de la province de Namur, sous le rapport de son administration, rédigé par la députation permanente du conseil provincial. 165 pp. 8°. *Namur, J. H. J. Misson*, 1841.

Nani (Domenico). Polyanthea opus suauissimis floribus exornatum compositū per Dominicum Nanum Mirabellium. Addita nunc primum est latina interpretatio versuum Dantis, & Petrarchæ, quas ipsi italico idiomate cōscripserunt. *b. l.* Eng. title, 7 p. l. 223 l. numb. fol. *Argentina, apud M. Schurerium*, 1517.

[*Note.*—Author known by some as Anni Mirabelli].

Nannie Barton. By the author of "George Miller," [etc. *anon.*] 288 pp. 3 pl. 18°. *Philadelphia, Presbyterian board of publication*, [1864].

Nanninck (Pieter). Petri Nannii somnium, sive paralipomena Virgili. [Somnium alterum: in lib. ii. Lucretii praefatio]. 18°. 1655.

[Elegantiores præstantium virorum satyræ, v. 1, part 2, pp. 235–280].

Nantes (*Comte* Antoine Français de). *See* **Français de Nantes.**

Napey (Hipolite). The Harrisburg business directory, 1842. *See* **Harrisburg** (*Penn.*)

Naphegyi (Gabor, *m. d.*) Ghardaia; or, ninety days among the B'ni Mozab: adventures in the oasis of the desert of Sahara. 348 pp. 2 pl. 12°. *New York, G. P. Putnam & sons*, 1871.

Napheys (George H. *m.d.*) Modern medical therapeutics: a compendium of recent formulæ, and specific therapeutical directions. 3d ed. revised and improved. 1 p. l. 496 pp. 12°. *Philadelphia, S. W. Butler, m. d.* 1871.

——— The prevention and cure of disease: a practical treatise on the nursing and home treatment of the sick. 1110 pp. 19 pl. 8°. *Springfield*, [*Ms.*] *W. J. Holland & co.* 1872.

——— The transmission of life. Counsels on the nature and hygiene of the masculine function. 4th ed. 346 pp. 12°. *Philadelphia, J. G. Fergus & co.* 1871.

——— (*editor*). *See* **Physican's** (The) annual for 1872.

Naples. (*Reale accademia delle scienze e belle-lettere*). Atti. Dalla fondazione sino all' anno 1787. 4 p. l. xcix, 372 pp. 1 l. 18 pl. 4°. *In Napoli, presso D. Campo*, 1788. s.

——— (*Società reale di Napoli*). Atti dell' accademia delle scienze fisiche e matematiche. v. 4. 4°. *Napoli, stamperia del Fibreno*, 1869. s.

Napoleon his own historian. Extracts from the original manuscript of Napoleon Bonaparte, by an american. [*anon.*] 8; 140 pp. 8°. *London, H. Colburn*, 1818.

Napoleon in the other world. A narrative written by himself: and found near his tomb in the island of St. Helena, by Xongo-Tee-Foh-Tchi, mandarin of the third class. [*pseudon.*] ix, 406 pp. 1 pl. 8°. *London, H. Colburn*, 1827.

Narbaez *or* **Narvaez** (Juan de). Sermon panegyrico, de el dia octavo de la solemne dedicacion del templo con el titulo del nombre de Maria de Gvadalupe, y s. Bernardo. sm. 4°. [*México, viuda de F. R. Lupercio*, 1691].

[*In* Ramirez de Vargas (A.) Sagrado padron y panegyricos sermones, etc. l. 98–112].

Nares (*Rev.* Robert). Principles of government deduced from reason, supported by english experience, and opposed to french errors. xx, 160 pp. 8°. *London, J. Stockdale,* 1792.

Narrative of an excursion from Corfu to Smyrna. *See* **Jolliffe** (Thomas Robert).

Narrative (A) of events, that have lately taken place in Ireland among the society called quakers. 1804. *See* **Rathbone** (William).

Narrative of the chinese embassy to the khan of the Tourgouth Tartars, in the years 1712–15. *See* **Tu-li-shin.**

Narrative (A) of the treatment experienced by a gentleman, during a state of mental derangement. 1838. *See* **Perceval** (John).

Narrazione delle solenni reali feste fatte celebrare in Napoli da sua maesta il re delle due Sicilie Carlo infante di Spagna, duca di Parma, Piacenza &c. &c. per la nascita del suo primogenito Filippo real principe delle due Sicilie. [*anon.*] 20 pp. 15 pl. 1 frontispiece. fol. *Napoli,* 1749.

[*Note.*—Plates by Vincenzo Re].

Narvaez. *See* **Narbaez.**

Nash (Solomon). Journal of Solomon Nash, a soldier of the revolution. 1776–1777. Now first printed from the original manuscript. With an introduction and notes, by Charles I. Bushnell. 65 pp. 3 pl. 8°. *New York, privately printed,* 1861.

Nasír-ed-dín Abu Said Abdallah ben Omar el-Beidawí. A chinese chronicle: by Abdalla of Beyza. Translated from the persian, with notes and explanations. By S. Weston. 38 pp. 8°. *London, W. Clarke,* 1820.

[*Note.*—This "chronicle" forms no part of Beidhawi's "Nizam el tewarich," as it is described by de Sacy, and by Haji Khalfa. Muller, who first published it (Jena, 1677) as the eighth portion of Beidhawí, probably found it appended to his manuscript, and inferred it to be his].

Nason (Elias). The congregational tune book: a selection from the standard choral music of the church, with other ancient and modern compositions, adapted to the hymns of the "Congregational hymn book," "Vestry hymn book," and to congregational singing generally. 208 pp. obl. 16°. *Boston, J. P. Jewett & co.* 1858.

——— The new congregational hymn and tune book, for public, social and private worship. viii, 218 pp. 2 l. 8°. *Boston, J. P. Jewett & co.* 1859.

Nasse (Erwin). On the agricultural community of the middle ages, and inclosures of the sixteenth century in England. Translated from the german, by col. H. A. Ouvry. 2 p. l. 100 pp. 8°. *London, Macmillan & co.* 1871.

Nast (Thomas). Nast's illustrated almanac, for 1872. 64 pp. 8°. *New York, Harper & brothers,* 1871.

——— *See* **Miss** Columbia's public school. 1871.

Nast (William, *d. d.*) Commentary on Matthew and Mark. *See* **Bible.** (*English*).

Nation (The), a weekly journal devoted to politics, literature, science, and art. Jan. 5 to Dec. 28, 1871. v. 12–13. 4°. *New York, E. L. Godkin & co.* 1871.

National board of trade. Proceedings of the third annual meeting of the National board of trade, held in Buffalo, December, 1870. xvi, 338 pp. 8°. *Boston, Barker, Cotter & co.* 1871.

——— The same. Proceedings of the fourth annual meeting, held in St. Louis, December, 1871. xvi, 329 pp. 8°. *Boston, Barker, Cotter & co.* 1872.

National (The) normal: an educational monthly. Edited by R. H. Holbrook. Jan. to Dec. 1871. v. 3. 8°. *Cincinnati, J. Holbrook,* 1871.

National police gazette. [Weekly]. Jan. 7 to Dec. 30, 1871. v. 26. fol. *New-York, G. W. Matsell & co.* 1871.

National (The) quarterly. Edited by Edward I. Sears. Dec. 1870, to Sept. 1871. v. 22–23. 8°. *New York, E. I. Sears,* 1870–71.

National transition moonly voice. Devoted to scientific national reconstruction. Published at each full moon. March 6, 1871, to May 22, 1872. v. 1–2. fol. and 8°. *Trenton (N. J.) R. Sinnickson,* 1871–72.

Naturalist's (The) own book; comprising descriptions and authentic anecdotes of quadrupeds. By the author of the Young man's own book. [By John Frost? *anon.*] 400 pp. 12°. *Philadelphia, Key & Biddle,* 1835.

Nature. A weekly illustrated journal of science. Nov. 1870, to Oct. 1871. v. 3–4. 4°. *London, Macmillan & co.* 1870–71.

Nature's laws in human life. 1872. *See* **Hayward** (Aaron S.)

Naturforscher (Der). [Herausgegeben von J. E. I. Walch (v. 1–13), und J. C. D. von Schreber (v. 14–30)]. 30 v. 8°. *Halle, J. J. Gebauer,* 1774–1804. S.

Naudé (Gabriel). Gabrielis Navdæi de Avgvstino Nipho ivdicivm. 4°. [*Parisiis, sumptibus R. Le Dvc*, 1645].

[*In* NIFO (Agostino), Opvscvla moralia et politica. 1645. p. l. 5-45].

——— The history of magick. By way of apology, for all the wise men who have unjustly been reputed magicians, from the creation to the present age. Written in french by G. Naudaeus. Englished by J. Davies. 8 p. l. 306 pp. 16°. *London, J. Streater*, 1657.

Naugerius (Andreas). *See* **Navagero** (Andrea).

Nauman (Mary D.) The enchanted princess. 201 pp. 4 pl. 16°. *Philadelphia, Claxton, Remsen & Haffelfinger*, 1872.

——— Eva's adventures in shadow-land. 169 pp. 5 pl. 16°. *Philadelphia, J. B. Lippincott & co.* 1872.

Nautical (The) and astronomical ephemeris. *London. See* **Great Britain.** *Naval department.*

Nautical (The) magazine for 1871. A journal of papers on subjects connected with maritime affairs. 8°. *London, Simpkin, Marshall & co.* [1871].

Navagero (Andrea). Lvsvs. 16°. *Venetiis, ex officina Vincentii Valgrisii*, 1548.

[*In* CARMINA qvinqve illvstrivm poetarvm, pp. 23-58].

Navarrete (Martin Fernandez de). Vida de Miguel de Cervantes Saavedra. 1834. *See* **Rios** (Vicente de los) *and* **Navarrete.**

Naville (Ernest). The problem of evil. Translated from the french. By John P. Lacroix. 330 pp. 12°. *New York, Carlton & Lanahan*, 1871.

Neal (John). One word more: intended for the reasoning and thoughtful among unbelievers. 211 pp. 12°. *Boston, Crocker & Brewster*, 1854.

——— The same. 2d ed. 220 pp. 12°. *New York, M. W. Dodd*, 1856.

Neale (*Rev.* John Mason). The life and times of Patrick Torry, d. d. bishop of st. Andrew's, Dunkeld, and Dunblane, with an appendix on the scottish liturgy. xxvi, 448 pp. 1 portrait. 8°. *London, J. Masters*, 1856.

Neale (W. Johnson). The priors of Prague. By the author of "Cavendish." [*anon.*] 3 v. 12°. *London, J. Macrone*, 1836.

Neander (August Johann Wilhelm). The emperor Julian and his generation. An historical picture. Translated by G. V. Cox. 191 pp. 16°. *New-York, J. C. Riker*, 1850.

Neander (A. J. W.)—continued.

——— General history of the christian religion and church, [down to the reformation]. From the german. Translated according to the latest edition. By Joseph Torrey. 11th american ed. 5 v. 8°. *Boston, Crocker & Brewster*, 1872.

——— History of the planting and training of the christian church by the apostles. Translated from the german by J. E. Ryland. Translation revised and corrected according to the fourth german edition, by E. G. Robinson, d. d. 547 pp. 8°. *New York, Sheldon & co.* 1865.

——— The life and times of st. Bernard. Translated from the german, by Matilda Wrench. xxiii, 357 pp. 16°. *London, J. G. F. & J. Rivington*, 1843.

Neander (Johann). Tabacologia: hoc est tabaci, seu nicotianæ descriptio medico-cheirurgico-pharmaceutica vel ejus præparatio et usus in omnibus ferme corporis humani incom̃odis. [Editio princeps]? Eng. title, 18 p. l. 256 pp. 2 l. 9 pl. 4°. *Lugduni Batavorum, ex officina I. Elzeviri*, 1626.

Nebelin (Charlotte Elisabethe). The great day of atonement: or, meditations and prayers on the last twenty-four hours of the sufferings and death of our lord and saviour Jesus Christ. Translated from the german. Edited by mrs. Colin Mackenzie. 200 pp. 12°. *Boston, Gould & Lincoln*, 1859.

Neck (Jacob van). Waerachtigh verhael van de schip-vaert op Oost-Indien, gedaen by de acht schepen, onder den heer admirael Jacob van Neck, 1598[-1600]. Hier achter is bygevoeght de voyagie van Sebald de Weert, naer de straet Magalanes, met noch een vocabulaer van duyts en maleys. 76 pp. 2 l. 5 pl. in text. sm. 4°. *Amstelredam, J. Hartgers*, 1650.

——— The same. 1 p. l. 92 pp. 6 pl. on 1 sheet. sm. 4°. *Amstelredam, I. Hartgers*, 1648.

[*In* HARTGERTS (J.) Oost-indische voyagien, v. 1, 3e stuck].

——— Tweede voyagie naer Oost-Indien. *See* **Roeloffs** (Roelof).

Necker (Jacques). An essay on the true principles of executive power in great states. Translated from the french. 2 v. 8 p. l. 401 pp; 2 p. l. 375 pp. 8°. *London, G. G. J. & J. Robinson*, 1792.

——— Of the importance of religious opinions. Translated from the french. 264 pp. 16°. *Philadelphia, Carey, Stewart & co.* 1791.

Necker (Louis Albert). Mémoire sur les oiseaux des environs de Genève. Précédé d'une notice biographique sur l'auteur, d'après J. D. Forbes. 206 pp. 12°. *Genève, J. Cherbuliez*, 1864. S.

Nederlanden (Geoctroyeerde west indische company der Vereenighde). *See* **West India company.** (*Netherlands*).

Nederlanden (Vereenigde). *See* **Netherlands** (*United*).

Nederlandtschen (Den) bye-corf: waer in ghy beschreven vint al hetgene dat nu wytgegeven is, op den stilstant ofte vrede, beginnende in Mey 1607, ende noche en hebben wy niet het eynde. [*anon.*] sm. 4°. [*n.p.* 1607–09].

CONTENTS.

Den nederlantschen bye-corf. 4 l.
Bvlle oft mandaet des paus van Roomen, aende gheestelicheyt al om bevolen, om haer advijs te vernemen opt stuck van den vrede-handel met de hollantsche ketters. 4 l.
Droom gesicht eenes metter herten tot Godt opgetrockenen mensches. 34 l. 1607.
Memorie vande ghewichtige redenen die de heeren staten generael behooren te beweghen om gheensins te wijcken vande handelinghe ende vaert van Indien. 3e ed. 4 l. [By W. Usselincx].
Raedtsel. Jeghelijck doet geern wat. Naer dat verscheyden discoursen est droomen op den handel vanden vrede in Neder-landt zijn uytgheghaen. 4 l.
De artijckelen ende besluyten der inquisitie van Spaegnien, om die vande Nederlanden te overvallen ende verhinderen. 2 l.
Brief van haro hoocheden aende e. moghende heeren staten der vrye Vereenichde nederlantsche provintien, 13 Martij 1607. 2 l. 1607.
Copye vanden brieff gheschreven van zijn hoocheyt aen graeff Herman vanden Bergh gouverneur van Geldre. 2 l. 1607.
Copye vande brieven der heeren ghenerale staten vande gheunieerde provintien aen den heeren staten van Hollandt ende West-vrieslandt. Inhoudende de limiten hoe verre den stil-stant van wapenen te water ende te lande is streckende. 2 l. 1607.
Het testament ofte uutersten wille vande nederlandtsche oorloghe. Door Yemand van Waermond. 8 l. 1609.
Codicille van de nederlandsche oorloghe. 6 l. 1609.
Het testament vande oorloghe. Noch is hier bygevoecht, de copye vanden brief aen graef Herman vandē Berg [etc.] 4 l. 1608.
Copye. Vande namen der coninghen ende andere potentaten ende gesanten [etc.] Om mede te staen over de vredehandelinge tusschen de Vereenichde nederlantsche provincien ende den coninck van Spangien. 2 l. 1608.
Principale puncten die inde voorder handelinghe vanden vrede van weghen de e. vermoghende heeren staten generael der Vereenichde Provintien onbegrijpelick sullen geproponeert werden. 2 l. 1608.
—— The same. [Another ed.]
Naerder bedenckingen, over de zee-vaerdt, coophandel ende neeringe, inde teghenwoordighe vredehandelinghe. 22 l. 1608. [By W. Usselincx].
Bedenckinghen over den staet vande Vereenichde Nederlanden: nopende de zeevaert, coop-handel, ende de gemeyne neeringe inde selve. 8 l. 1608. [By W. Usselincx].
—— The same. Grondich discours over desen aenstaenden vrede-handel. 8 l. 1608.
Consideratien vande vrede in Nederlandt gheconcipieert anno 1608. 2 l.
Nootelijcke consideratien opten voorgheslaghen tractate van peys met den Spagniaerden. 8 l. 1608.
Sendbrief in forme van supplicatie aen de coninckliјcke majesteyt van Spaengien: van wegen des princen van Oraengien, midtsgaders alle andere [etc.] 9 l. *Delft*, 1574.

Nederlandtschen (Den) bye-corf—cont'd.

Trovhertighe vermaninghe aende verheerde nederlantsche provintien. 6 l. 1586.
Placcaert vande staten generael vande Gheunieerde Nederlanden. Byden welcken, men verklaert den coninck van Spaegnien vervallen vande overheyt ende heerschappije van dese voorz. Nederlanden [etc.] 8 l. *Leyden*, 1581.
Articulen van het contract ende accoort ghemaeckt tusschen Jacobus den eersten, coninck van Enghelandt, ende Philips den derden, coninck van Spaengnien. Gemaect 1604. Wt het enghels overgheset. 8 l. *Londen*, [1604].
Vertoogh, hoe nootwendich, nut ende profijtelick, het sy voor de Vereenighde Nederlanden te behouden de vryheyt van te handelen op West-Indien, inden vrede metten coninck van Spaignen. 10 l. [By W. Usselincx].
Aggreatie des coninck van Hispagnien, ghesonden aen de staten generael vande Gheunieerde Provintien. 4 l. 1608.
Schuyt-praetgens op de vaert naer Amsterdam tusschen een lantman, een hovelinck, een borgher, ende schipper. 4 l.
Copye van een discours tusschen een Hollander ende een Zeeuw. 4 l.
Discovrs van Pieter en Pauwels, op de handelinghe vanden vreede. Anno 1608. 2 l.
Dialogus oft tzamensprekinge gemaect op den vredehandel. Overghezet wt de franzoysche tale. 4 l. 1608.
Verhael vande occasie eñ oorsaeck waer door de Nederlanden gecomen zijn aenden vrede handel. [Poem]. 4 l.
Onpartydich discours opte handelinghe vande Indien. 4 l. [By W. Usselincx].
Discours by forme van remonstrantie: vervatende de noodsaeckelickheyd van de oos-indische navigatie. 7 l. 1608. [By W. Usselincx].
Het secreet des conings van Spangien. In't licht gebracht door Rodrigo D. A. Overgheset uyt den spaenschen. 4 l.
Van den spinnekop ende t' bieken, ofte droomghedicht [Poem]. 2 l.
Brief des keyserlijcke majest. van Duytslandt aende heeren staten vande Gheunieerde Provintien gheschreven. Op 't stuck vande nederlantsche vredehandeling. 4 l. 1608.
Proeve des nu onlangs uyt-ghegheven drooms, oft t'samenspraack tusschen den coning van Hispanien ende den paus van Roomen. 4 l.
{ Dees wonder-maer end' prophetsije wis, / Door's geests gesicht gebooren is, [etc. in verse], } 8 l.
Buyr-praetjen: ofte tsamensprekinge ende discours op den brieff vanden agent Aerssens uyt Vranckrijck aende staten generael geschreven. 8 l.
Echo ofte galm, dat is weder-klinckende gedichte van de tegenwoordighe vredehandelinghe. Door een lief hebber syns vaderlandschen vryheyds. [Poem]. 4 l. 1608.
{ Een oud schipper van Monicken-dam, / Daer ons den vromen held uyt quam, / Die eerst den Spaegniaerd de zee deed' ruymen, / Sprack aldus, naer scheeps coustuymen, } 3 l. 1 pl.

Née de la Rochelle (Jean François). Éloge historique de Jean Gensfleisch dit Guttenberg, premier inventeur de l'art typographique à Mayence. 1 p. l. vi, 158 pp. 1 portrait. 8°. *Paris, D. Colas*, 1811.

Needham (E. P.) & son. *See* **Silver** (The) tongue folio. 1871.

Needham *or* **Nedham** (Marchamont). De l'excellence d'un état libre. Traduit de l'anglois. [Par Éon de Beaumont]. 8°. *Amsterdam*, 1774.

[*In* Éon de Beaumont (Ch. G. L. A. A. T. d'). Les loisirs du chevalier d'Éon de Beaumont. v. 6, pp. 137–399].

Neef (Joseph). Sketch of a plan and method of education, founded on an analysis of the

Neef (Joseph)—continued. human faculties, and natural reason, suitable for the offspring of a free people, and for all rational beings. 4 p. l. 168 pp. 16°. *Philadelphia, author*, 1808.

Neel-rutna Haldar. The Kobita-rutnakur, or collection of sungskrit proverbs in popular use; translated into bengalee and english. 2d ed. xvi, 166 pp. 8°. *Serampore*, 1830.

Neill (Edward Duffield). The english colonization of America during the seventeenth century. xi, 352 pp. 8°. *London, Strahan & co.* 1871.

——— The Fairfaxes of England and America in the seventeenth and eighteenth centuries, including letters from and to hon. William Fairfax, president of council of Virginia, and his sons col. George William Fairfax and rev. Bryan, eighth lord Fairfax, the neighbors and friends of George Washington. 234 pp. 1 table. 8°. *Albany (N. Y.) J. Munsell*, 1868.

——— History of the Virginia company of London, with letters to and from the first colony never before printed. xvi, 432 pp. 1 pl. 4°. *Albany (N. Y.) J. Munsell*, 1869.

——— Memoir of rev. Patrick Copland, rector elect of the first projected college in the United States. A chapter of the english colonization of America. 96 pp. 8°. *New York, C. Scribner & co.* 1871.

Neill (Patrick). A tour through some of the islands of Orkney and Shetland, with a view chiefly to objects of natural history. With an appendix. 1 p. l. xi, 239 pp. 8°. *Edinburgh, A. Constable & co.* 1806.

Neill (William, *d. d.*) Autobiography. With a selection from his sermons. By the rev. J. H. Jones, d. d. 2 p. l. 272 pp. 1 portrait. 12°. *Philadelphia, Presbyterian board of publication*, 1861.

Neily (*Miss* Catharine). Marion's sundays; or, stories on the ten commandments. 191 pp. 18°. *New York, R. Carter & brothers*, 1860.

Neligan (J. Moore, *m. d.*) Medicines. Their uses and mode of administration; including a conspectus of the three british pharmacopœias, an account of all the new remedies, and an appendix of formulæ. With notes and additions, conforming it to the pharmacopœia of the United States, etc. by David M. Reese, m. d. 453 pp. 8°. *New York, Harper & brothers*, 1844.

Nellie of Truro. [*anon.*] *See* **Hornblower** (*Mrs.*)

Nemethi *or* **Nemeti** (Samuel). Regnum Dei in extremo dierum, imprimis exhibitum, ad scripturæ normam effigiatum. 4 p. l. 320 pp. 18°. [*Franckeræ, J. Gyselaar*, 1683].

[*With* MARCK (Johannes). De sibyllinis carminibus].

Nesbitt (Robert, *m. d.*) Human osteogeny explained in two lectures, read in the anatomical theatre of the surgeons of London, July 1 & 2, 1731. xiii, 170 pp. 6 pl. 8°. *London, J. Noon*, 1736.

Netherlands (*United*). Octroi of fondamenteele conditien, onder dewelke haar hoog mog. ten besten en voordeele van de ingezeetenen deeser landen de colonie van Suriname, hebben doen vallen in handen en onder directie van de Westindische compagnie. 22 pp. sm. 4°. *Gravenhage, J. Scheltus*, 1752.

——— Octroy, by de staten generael, verleent aen de West-Indische compagnie, in date den 20^{en} Sept. 1674. 36 pp. sm. 4°. *Graven-Hage, J. Scheltus*, 1674.

——— The same Octroy by de staten generaal, verleent aen de West-Indische compagnie, in dato den 20. Sept. 1674. Mitsgaders de prolongatie van het selve octroy voor den tydt van dertigh jaren. In dato den 30 Nov. 1700. 50 pp. sm. 4°. *Gravenhage, Paulus Scheltus*, 1701.

——— The same. Nader prolongatie van het octroy, voor den tyd van nog dertig jaaren. Gearresteert den 8 Aug. 1730. 20 pp. sm. 4°. *Gravenhage, Jacobus Scheltus*, 1730.

——— The same. Nader prolongatie van het octroy, voor den tyd van nog dertig jaaren. Gearresteert den 31 Dec. 1761. 38 pp. sm. 4°. *Gravenhage, Isaac Scheltus*, 1761.

——— Octroy van de staten generael, aengaende de colonie op de wilde kust van America. Onder het beleyt van den ridder Balthazar Gerbier baron Douvily. 4 l. sm. 4°. [*n. p.*] *Gedruckt in't iaer ons Heeren*, 1659.

——— Ordre ende reglement: vande staten generael, gearresteert by advijs ende deliberatie vande West-Indische compagnie, over het bewoonen ende cultiveren der landen ende plaetsen by die vande voor-ghemelte compagnie in Brasil gheconquesteert. *b. l.* 6 l. sm. 4°. *Gravenhage, weduwe van H. J. van Wouw*, 1634.

——— Placaet. [With reference to a silver mine in Brazil]. *b. l.* 1 sheet folded. sm. 4°. *Graven-Hage, weduwe van Hillebrandt Iacobsz van Wouw*, 1652.

Netherlands—continued.

——— Placcaet by de staten generael der Vereenighde Nederlanden, ghemaeckt op 't besluyt vande West-Indissche compaignie. 4 l. sm. 4°. *Graven-Haghe, H. Iacobssz, [van Wouw]*, 1621.

——— Placcaet vande staten generael vande Gheunieerde Nederlanden. Byden welcken, midts den redenen in't langhe in't selfde begrepen, men verclaert den coninck van Spaegnien vervallen vande overheyt ende heerschappije van dese voorz. Nederlanden, etc. *b.l.* 8 l. sm. 4°. *Leyden, C. Silvius*, 1581. [*Reprinted, n.p.* 1608].
[*In* NEDERLANDTSCHEN bye-corf].

——— Propositie gedaen by de commissarissen van de Vereenichde Nederlanden, aen de koningin regente van Portugael. Op 't subject van de schade, ende injurien d'onderdanen van de selve Nederlanden aen-ghedaen, ende op wat maniere haer den oorloch aen-gesecht, ende gedenunchieert is. [Dutch and latin]. 8 pp. sm. 4°. [*Graven-Haghe*]? 1657.

——— Resolutie van de staten generaal, de dato 16 January 1772. contineerende nadere poincten omtrent den vaart en handel op de colonie van Essequebo en Demerary. 1 p. l. 7 pp. sm. 4°. *Amsterdam, J. ten Houten en zoon*, 1772.

——— Sendbrief in forme van supplicatie, aen de coninglijcke majesteyt van Spaengien: van wegen des princen van Oraengien, der staten van Hollandt ende Zeelandt, mitsgaders alle andere zijne getrouwe ondersaten van dese Nederlanden, die haer van des hertoghen van Alba, ende der Spaegniaerden tyrannie ende ghewelt, teghen alle recht verdrucket ende vervolghet viuden. *b.l.* 9 l. sm. 4°. Delft, 1574. [*Reprinted, n.p.* 1608].
[*In* NEDERLANTSCHEN bye-corf].

Netherlands (*Kingdom of the*). Rapport aan den koning van de commissie tot onderzoek van drinkwater, benoemd bij zijner majesteits besluit van den 16[den] Julij 1866, No. 68, tot onderzoek van drinkwater, in verband met de verspreiding van cholera en tot aanwijzing der middelen ter worziening in zuiver drinkwater. 2[de] druk. 412, xiv pp. 7 pl. fol. *Gravenhage, van Weelden & Mingelen*, 1869. s.

——— Staatkundig en staathuishoudkundig jaarboekje voor 1870. Uitgegeven door de vereeniging voor de statistiek in Nederland. 22[e] jaargang. (5[e] serie, 2[e] jaargang). 16°. *Amsterdam, E. S. Witkamp*, [1870]. s.

Netherlands—continued.

——— Verslag van den staat der hooge-, middelbare en lagere scholen in het koningrijk der Nederlanden, over 1868–1870. [Bijlage A–H. Verslag der commissien]. 2 v. 1 p. l. 127, [68] pp; 1 p. l. 135, [82] pp. fol. *Gravenhage, gedrukt ter algemeene landsdrukkerij*, 1870–71. s.

Netherlands. (*Koninglijk nederlandsch meteorologisch instituut*). Meteorologische waarnemingen in Nederland en zijne bezittingen, en afwijkingen van temperatuur en barometerstand op vele plaatsen in Europa. 1857. [F. W. C. Krecke, director]. 1 p. l. viii, 350 pp. obl. 8°. *Utrecht, Kemink & zoon*, 1858. s.

——— ——— Nederlandsch meteorologisch jaarboek voor 1869. 21te jaargang. 1ste deel. 2 p. l. 262 pp. 1 table. obl. 8°. *Utrecht, Kemink & zoon*, 1869. s.

Nettleton (Asahel, *d. d.*) Village hymns for social worship. Selected and original. 416 pp. 24°. *New York, E. Sands*, 1838.

Neuchâtel (Republic and canton of). Rapport du conseil d'état au grand-conseil de la république et canton de Neuchâtel, sur sa gestion et l'exécution des lois pendant les années 1869–1870. 2 v. lxi, 310, 20 pp. 10 tab; 1 p. l. 413, 23 pp. 12 tab. 8°. *Neuchâtel, G. Montandon*, 1870–71. s

Neues jahrbuch für mineralogie, geognosie, geologie, und petrefactenkunde, herausgegeben von dr. K. C. von Leonhard, und dr. H. G. Bronn. Jahrgange 1833–62. 30 v. 8°. *Stuttgart, E. Schweizerbart'sche verlagshandlung*, 1833–62.

——— The same. Neues jahrbuch für mineralogie, geologie und palaentologie. Gegründet von K. C. von Leonhard und H. G. Bronn, und fortgesetzt von G. Leonhard und H. B. Geinitz. Jahrgang 1863–1871. 9 v. 8°. *Stuttgart, E. Schweizerbart'sche verlagshandlung*, 1863–71.

Neueste weltkunde. [Tägliche]. 1. Jan. bis 8. Sept. 1798. v. 1–3 (in 1 vol.) 4°. *Tübingen*, 1798.
[*Succeeded by the* ALLGEMEINE zeitung].

Neufville (Jacob de). Dissertatio historico-politica inauguralis, de iis, quae ad tollendum servorum afrorum commercium, inde a congressu viennensi, inter populos gesta sunt. x, 130 pp. 8°. *Amstelodami, apud D. Groebe*, 1840.

Neuilly (Ange Achille Charles, *comte* de). Dix années d'émigration. Souvenirs et corres-

Neuilly (A. A. C. *comte* de)—continued. pondance du comte de Neuilly publiés par son neveu Maurice de Barberey. x, 412 pp. 8°. *Paris, C. Douniol*, 1865.

Neumann (Isidor). Hand-book of skin diseases. Translated from the second german ed. with notes, by Lucius D. Bulkley, m. d. xiv, 11–467 pp. 8°. *New York, D. Appleton & co.* 1872.

Nevada (*State of*). The journal of the assembly and senate, during the fifth session of the legislature, 1871. 2 v. 8°. *Carson city, state printer*, 1871.

——— Report of the mineralogist of the state of Nevada for the years 1869 and 1870. 8°. *Carson city, C. L. Perkins, state printer*, 1871.

Neve (Timothy, *d. d.*) Animadversions upon mr. Phillip's history of the life of cardinal Pole. 7 p. l. 562 pp. 3 l. 8°. *Oxford, Clarendon press*, 1766.

Nevin (John D. *d. d.*) The anxious bench. 2d ed. revised and enlarged. 150 pp. 18°. *Chambersburg* (*Pa.*) *Publication office german ref. church*, 1844.

Nevin (John Williamson, *d. d.*) A summary of biblical antiquities. 2 v. xvi, 260 pp; x, 242 pp. 18°. *Utica*, [*N. Y.*] *Western sunday school union*, 1828.

Nevins (William, *d. d.*) Practical thoughts. 230 pp. 1 pl. 18°. *New York, American tract society*, [1836].

Newark (*N. J.*) Holbrook's Newark city directory, for the year ending April 1, 1872. 8°. *Newark* (*N. J.*) *A. S. Holbrook*, 1871.

New Bedford (*Mass.*) Greenough, Jones & co.'s directory, for 1871–72. 308 pp. 1 map. 8°. *Boston, Greenough, Jones & co.* 1871.

Newberry (John S.) Report on the progress of the geological survey of Ohio in 1869. 8°. [*Columbus*, 1871].

[Ohio (*State of*). *Geological survey*, 1869, part 1, pp. 3–53].

New Brunswick (*Presbytery of*). The apology of the presbytery of New Brunswick, for their dissenting from two acts or new religious laws, which were made at the last session of our synod. Humbly offer'd to the consideration of the synod now conven'd at Philadelphia. pp. 37–68. 16°. *Philadelphia, printed and sold by B. Franklin*, 1741.

——— The same. Remarks upon the introduction to the protestation. [Also], remarks upon a protestation presented to the synod, June 1, 1741. [With] remarks upon the ap-

New Brunswick—continued. pendix. [*anon.*] 3–36 pp. 16°. *Philadelphia, B. Franklin*, 1741.

[Imperfect: title-page wanting].

Newburgh (*N. Y.*) Carter's Newburgh city directory, with a complete business directory attached. For the year ending May 1, 1872. 8°. *Newburgh, E. Carter*, 1871.

Newburyport (*Mass.*) A directory of the city of Newburyport, containing the city record; a business directory, and an almanac for 1854. By C. Augustine Dockham. 16, 5–168 pp. 18°. *Newburyport, W. H. Huse*, 1854.

New (A) collection of enigmas, charades, transpositions, &c. [*anon.*] New ed. 2 p. l. 229 pp. 16°. *London, Longman*, 1806.

Newcomb (*Rev.* Harvey). The attributes of God. 151 pp. 18°. *Boston, Mass. sabbath school society*, 1837.

——— The benjamite king: or the history of Saul, the first king of Israel. 198 pp. 1 pl. 18°. *Boston, Massachusetts sabbath school society*, 1839.

——— Christ our saviour; or, conversations between a mother and her daughter. Illustrating the way of salvation. 72 pp. 18°. *Philadelphia, American sunday school union*, [1834].

——— The false prophet; or an account of the rise and progress of the mohammedan religion. 207 pp. 18°. *Boston, Mass. sabbath school society*, 1834.

——— The harvest and the reapers; homework for all, and how to do it. 1 p. l. 270 pp. 16°. *Boston, Gould & Lincoln*, 1858.

——— History of the Waldenses; with a sketch of the general state of the church in the thirteenth century. Being the tenth volume of the Sabbath school church history. 232 pp. 18°. *Boston, Mass. sabbath school society*, 1835.

——— Little child's scripture library, in seven numbers. 7 v. in 1. sq. 16°. *Pittsburgh, L. Loomis*, [1836].

CONTENTS.

No. 1. The creation, 28 pp.
No. 2. The fall and the promise, 35 pp.
No. 3. The savior, 70 pp.
No. 4. I must love God best, 38 pp.
No. 5. The Lord's day, 38 pp.
No. 6. The new heart, 36 pp.
No. 7. Heaven and hell; or, this world and the world to come, 26 pp.

——— Newcomb's first question book. Written for the Massachusetts sabbath school society, and revised by the committee of publication. [*anon.*] 110 pp. 18°. *Boston, Mass. sabbath school society*, 1837.

Newcomb (*Rev.* Harvey)—continued.

——— The protestants: being a continuation of the reformation in Germany; from 1525, to 1532: including the confession of Augsburg. 203 pp. 18°. *Boston, Mass. sabbath school society*, 1839.

——— Sabbath school teacher's aid: a collection of anecdotes for illustrating religious truth; arranged under a variety of subjects. 333 pp. 18°. *Boston, Mass. sabbath school society*, 1840.

——— The tract distributor: together with a short account of Armelle Nicolas. 90 pp. incl. 1 pl. 18°. *Boston, Mass. sabbath school society*, 1833.

——— The Wyandot chief: or the history of Barnet, a converted Indian; and his two sons: with some account of the Wea mission. vi, 9–92 pp. 18°. *Boston, Mass. sabbath school society*, 1835.

Newcomb (Simon). Report on observations of the eclipse, &c. made at Gibraltar. 4°. [*Washington*, 1871].

[*In* UNITED STATES. *Navy department. (Naval observatory).* Report on observations of the total solar eclipse, of Dec. 22, 1870, pp. 5–24].

Newcome (William, *d. d.*) An historical view of the english biblical translations: the expediency of revising by authority our present translation: and the means of executing such a revision. xiv, 438 pp. 1 l. 8°. *Dublin, J. Exshaw*, 1792.

——— Observations on our Lord's conduct as a divine instructor: and on the excellence of his moral character. 2d ed. corrected. xvi, 516, vi pp. 1 l. 8°. *London, J. Johnson*, 1795.

New (The) congregational hymn and tune book. 1859. *See* **Nason** (Elias).

Newell (Robert H.) Versatilities. ix, 266 pp. 12°. *Boston, Lee & Shepard*, 1871.

——— The walking doll; or, the asters and disasters of society. 391 pp. 12°. *New York, F. B. Felt & co.* 1872.

New-England (The) historical and genealogical register and antiquarian journal, published quarterly, under the direction of the New-England historic-genealogical society. Jan. to Oct. 1871. v. 25. 8°. *Boston, the society*, 1871. s.

New England scenes: or a selection of important and interesting events which have taken place since the first settlement of New England: principally of a religious nature. [*anon.*] 106 pp. 10 pl. 18°. *New Haven, L. H. Young*, 1833.

New (The) era: a monthly periodical, devoted to the interests of religion and humanity, and to the diffusion of knowledge of judaism and jewish literature. Edited by rev. Raphael D'C. Lewin. Oct. 1870, to Sept. 1871. v. 1. 8°. *New York*, 1871.

Newfoundland. The constitution of the government of Newfoundland in its legislative and executive departments. With appendix, containing the rules and orders of the legislative council, and the house of assembly. By John Little. 20, 88 pp. 18°. [*St. Johns*], *Hazard & Owen*, 1855. s.

——— *Geological survey.* Report upon the geological survey of Newfoundland, for the year 1870. By A. Murray. [Printed by order of the honorable house of assembly]. 51 pp. 1 pl. 1 map. 8°. *St. John's (N. F.) "Courier" print*, 1870. s.

New (A) grammar of the french tongue, originally compiled for the use of the american military academy. By a french gentleman. [*anon.*] vii, 194 pp. 1 l. 12°. *New York, G. & R. Waite for I. Riley & co.* 1804.

New Granada. *Biblioteca nacional.* Catalogo de las obras en español, existentes en la biblioteca nacional, [etc.] 3ª serie. 88 pp. 8°. *Bogotá, imprenta del estado*, 1856.

——— ——— Catalogo de las obras en frances existentes en la biblioteca nacional, [etc.] 1ª serie. 66 pp. 8°. *Bogotá, imprenta de "El Neo-granadino,"* 1855.

——— ——— Catalogo de las obras en ingles, existentes en la biblioteca nacional. 22 pp. 8°. *Bogotá, imprenta del estado*, 1856.

——— ——— Catalogo de las obras en latin, existentes en la biblioteca nacional, [etc.] 4ª serie. 117 pp. 8°. *Bogotá, imprenta del estado*, 1856.

New (A) guide to the city of Exeter, and its environs; with descriptive sketches of the adjacent watering places. [*anon.*] 1 p. l. 134 pp. 1 pl. 12°. *Exeter, W. Spreat*, 1824.

Newhall (John B.) Sketches of Iowa, or the emigrant's guide; containing a correct description of the agricultural and mineral resources, geological features and statistics of the territory of Iowa, [etc.] 252 pp. 1 map. 18°. *New York, J. H. Colton*, 1841.

New Hampshire (*State of*). Reports. 11 doc. in 1 v. 8°. *Manchester, state printer*, 1870.

——— *Asylum for the insane.* Annual reports of the board of visitors, trustees, treasurer and superintendent, with directions concern-

New Hampshire—continued. ing admission, June session, 1871. 8°. *Nashua, state printer*, 1871.

——— *Board of agriculture.* New Hampshire agriculture. First annual report of the board of agriculture, May 1, 1871. Prepared by James O. Adams, secretary. 8°. *Nashua, state printer*, 1871.

——— *College of agriculture and mechanic arts.* Report of the board of trustees of the New Hampshire college of agriculture and the mechanic arts, 1870. 8°. *Manchester, state printer*, 1870.

——— *Commissioners on fisheries.* Report of the commissioners on fisheries of the state of New Hampshire, June session, 1871. 8°. *Nashua, state printer*, 1871.

——— *Geological survey.* Second annual report upon the geology and mineralogy of the state of New Hampshire, by C. H. Hitchcock. 8°. *Manchester, state printer*, 1870.

——— ——— Third report of the geological survey of the state of New Hampshire, showing its progress during the year 1870[-71]. By C. H. Hitchcock. 8°. *Nashua, state printer*, 1871.

——— *Railroad commissioners.* Report of the railroad commissioners of the state of New Hampshire, June session, 1871. 8°. *Nashua, state printer*, 1871.

——— *Reform school.* Reports of the board of trustees, superintendent and treasurer of the reform school of the state of New Hampshire, June session, 1871. 8°. *Nashua, state printer*, 1871.

——— *State library.* Report of the state librarian to the New Hampshire legislature, June session, 1871. 8°. *Nashua, state printer*, 1871.

New Hampshire (The) business directory, for the year commencing April 1, 1872. 8°. *Boston, Briggs & co.* 1872.

New (A) hieroglyphical bible: with devotional pieces for youth; containing four hundred cuts, by Adams. 210 pp. 1 pl. sq. 16°. *New York, Harper and brothers*, 1837.

New Jersey (*State of*). Documents of the ninety-fifth legislature of the state of New Jersey, and the twenty-seventh under the new constitution. Printed by order of the legislature. 8°. *Jersey City, Pangborn, Dunning & Dear*, 1871.

——— Journal of the twenty-seventh senate of the state of New Jersey, being the ninety-fifth session of the legislature. 8°. *Somerville (N. J.) D. Porter*, 1871.

——— Manual of the legislature (96th session). Compiled by F. L. Lundy. Corrected to January 1st, 1872. 78 pp. 2 portraits. 16°. *Newark (N. J.) M. R. Dennis & co.* 1872.

——— Minutes of the votes and proceedings of the ninety-fifth general assembly of the state of New Jersey. Convened January 10, 1871. 8°. *Camden (N. J.) S. Chew*, 1871.

New Jerusalem church. Principle of the new church: signified by the new Jerusalem, Revelation xxi. A report submitted to the executive committee of the general convention of the new church in the United States, June, 1860; and after having been amended, was approved June, 1863. 201 pp. 12°. *New York, by the general convention of the New Jerusalem in the U. S.* 1863.

New (The) life; or, counsels to inquirers and converts. By a pastor. [*anon.*] 157 pp. 18°. *New York, American tract society*, [1871].

Newman (John C.) The harmonies of creation, or, the music of the morning stars. [Also], miscellaneous poems. 256 pp. 18°. *Baltimore, J. W. Woods*, 1836.

Newman (Samuel Phillips). Elements of political economy. 324 pp. 12°. *Andover, Gould & Newman*, 1835.

Newman (*Rev.* W. A.) The martyrs, the dreams, and other poems. xii, 340 pp. 16°. *Wolverhampton, W. Parke*, 1847.

New manual of private devotions. In three parts. Corrected and enlarged by the rt. rev. Levi Silliman Ives, d. d. 3d New York ed. [Also], A friendly visit to the house of mourning. By the rev. Richard Cecil. [*anon.*] 368 pp. 1 pl. 12°. *New York, T. & J. Swords*, 1831.

New (The) monthly magazine. Edited by William Francis Ainsworth. Jan. 1870, to Dec. 1871. v. 146-149. 8°. *London, Chapman & Hall*, 1870-71.

New Orleans (*La.*) Cohen's New Orleans directory, including Jefferson City, Carrollton, Gretna, Algiers and McDonough, for 1854 and 1855. 2 v. 8°. *New Orleans, office of the Picayune*, 1854-55. s.

——— Edwards' annual directory to the inhabitants, institutions, incorporated companies, manufacturing establishments, busi-

New Orleans (*La.*)—continued. ness, business firms, etc. in the city of New Orleans, for 1871 and 1872. 2 v. 8°. *New Orleans, Southern publishing co.* 1871–72.

New (The) Oxford guide: or, companion through the university. [With] a tour to Blenheim, Ditchley, and Stow. By a gentleman of Oxford. [*anon.*] 4th ed. viii, 134 pp. 4 pl. 1 map. 16°. *Oxford, J. Fletcher,* [1764]?

New (The) pleasing instructor: or, young lady's guide to virtue and happiness. Consisting of essays, relations, descriptions, epistles, dialogues, and poetry. Carefully extracted from the best modern authors. By a lady. [*anon.*] pp. 1–322. 16°. *Boston, I. Thomas & E. T. Andrews,* 1799.

[Imperfect: wanting all after p. 322].

Newport (*R. I.*) Boyd's Newport city directory, for 1871–72. With a business directory of the trades and professions, state and city record, and an appendix of much useful information. Compiled by Andrew Boyd. 8°. *Newport (R. I.) A. J. Ward,* 1871.

New (The) revelation of the will of God. 1871. *See* **Reed** (Miss Jennie).

Newsboy (The). *See* **Smith** (Elizabeth Oakes).

New (The) Sydenham society. v. 42 and 45. 8°. *London, New Sydenham society,* 1869–70.

CONTENTS.

TROUSSEAU (A.) Lectures on clinical medicine, v. 2–3.

Newton (Henry). A sketch of the present state of the steel industry. 8°. [*Columbus (O.)* 1871].

[OHIO (State of). *Geological survey,* 1870. Part 9, pp. 527–555].

Newton (John Frank). The return to nature, or, a defence of the vegetable regimen; with some account of an experiment made during the last three or four years in the author's family. Part 1st. vi, 160 pp. 8°. *London, T. Cadell & W. Davies,* 1811.

Newton (Richard, *d. d.*) The jewish tabernacle and its furniture, in their typical teachings. 393 pp. 12°. *New York, R. Carter & brothers,* 1864.

——— The king's highway; or, illustrations of the commandments. Eng. title, 342 pp. 1 pl. 12°. *New York, R. Carter & brothers,* 1861.

——— Nature's wonders. 335 pp. 6 pl. 16°. *New York, R. Carter & brothers,* 1872.

——— Rills from the fountain of life; or, sermons to children. 220 pp. 12°. *Philadelphia, J. B. Lippincott & co.* 1856.

Newton (Richard, *d. d.*)—continued.

——— The safe compass, and how it points. Eng. title, 318 pp. 5 pl. 16°. *New York, R. Carter & brothers,* 1863.

Newton (Thomas, *d. d.*) The life of Milton. 8°. [*Philadelphia,* 1777].

[*In* MILTON (John). [Poetical works]. *Philadelphia,* 1777. v. 2, pp. 383–444].

New (A) tribute to the memory of James Brainerd Taylor. [*anon.*] 440 pp. 12°. *New-York, J. S. Taylor,* 1838.

New (A) Weymouth guide: containing a description of Weymouth, Portland, Lulworth Castle, and every place in the neighbourhood, worthy the observation of strangers. Likewise a list of the members of parliament for the boroughs of Weymouth and Melcomb Regis, from the earliest period. A list of the seats of the nobility and gentry in the county of Dorset, with their distances from Weymouth. [*anon.*] 2 p. l. 90 pp. 1 l. 1 pl. 8°. *Dorchester, M. Virtue,* [*about* 1800].

[*With* HISTORY (The) and description of Guildford, the county-town of Surrey].

New York (*State of*). Civil list and forms of government of the colony and state of New York. Compiled from official and authentic sources, by Stephen C. Hutchins. 542 pp. 6 pl. 16°. *Albany, Weed, Parsons & co.* 1864.

——— The constitution of the state. 31 pp. 8°. *Fish-kill, S. Loudon,* 1777.

[HAZARD pamphlets, v. 42].

——— The debates and proceedings of the convention of the state of New-York, assembled 17 June, 1788, to decide on the form of federal government recommended by the general convention at Philadelphia. 144 pp. 8°. *New-York, F. Childs,* 1788.

[HAZARD pamphlets, v. 56].

——— Manual for the use of the convention to revise the constitution of the state of New York, convened at Albany, June 1, 1846. 371 pp. 12°. *New York, Walker & Craighead,* 1846.

——— *Insurance department.* Annual report of the superintendent of the insurance department of the state of New York. 10th to 12th reports. 3 v. 8°. *Albany, the Argus co.* 1869–71.

——— *Legislature.* A compilation of cases of breaches of privilege of the house, in the assembly of the state of New York, with the reports of standing and special committees and the proceedings and judgments thereon, with references to all action in each case,

New York (*State of*)—continued. from 1777 to 1871. Prepared under the supervision of C. W. Armstrong, clerk. 251 pp. 8°. *Albany, the Argus co.* 1871.

——— ——— Documents of the assembly. Ninety-third session. 1870. 212 nos. in 13 v. 8°. *Albany, the Argus co.* 1870.
[Wanting, v. 7].

——— ——— Manual for the use of the legislature of the state of New York, 1870, and 1871. [*anon.*] 2 v. 16°. *Albany, Weed, Parsons & co.* 1870–71.

——— *State library.* Fifty-second and fifty-third annual reports of the trustees of the New York state library. 2 v. 8°. *Albany, the Argus co.* 1870–71.

New York (*City of*). Message of the mayor to the common council of the city of New York. June, 1871. With accompanying documents. 8°. *New York, New York printing company,* 1871.

——— *Department of public parks.* First annual report of the board of commissioners of the department of public parks, for the year ending May 1, 1871. 427 pp. 35 pl. 2 maps. 8°. *New York, W. C. Bryant,* 1871.

——— *Health department.* First annual report of the board of health of the health department of the city of New York. April 11, 1870, to April 10, 1871. 628 pp. 9 pl. 3 maps, 1 tab. 8°. *New York, New York printing co.* 1871.

——— Insurance maps of the city of New York. 1871. *See* **Perris** (William G.) *and* **Browne** (Henry H.)

——— (*Directories*). Trow's New York city directory. Compiled by H. Wilson. v. 85. For the year ending May 1, 1872. 8°. *New York, J. F. Trow,* [1871].

——— ——— Wilson's business directory, of New York city. [For 1871]. 18°. *New York, J. F. Trow,* 1871.

——— ——— Wilson's New York city copartnership directory. H. Wilson, compiler. v. 20. March, 1872. 120 pp. 8°. *New York, Trow city directory co.* [1872].

——— ——— Business directory. 1871. *See* **Cleary** (William P.) & co.

New York (The) almanac for 1872. Edited by Julius Wilcox. 48 pp. 8°. *New York, F. Hart & co.* [1871].

New York and New Haven railroad. Hand book of the N. Y. & N. H. railroad. With descriptive sketches, and complete business directory of each place on the road. 208 pp. 16°. *Newburgh (N. Y.) Carter & Sutherland publishing co.* 1871.

New York. (*Chamber of commerce of the state*). Thirteenth annual report of the corporation of the chamber of commerce, of the state of New York, for 1870–71. In two parts. Compiled by George Wilson, secretary. xii, 153, 214 pp. 8°. *New York, press of the chamber of commerce,* 1871.

New York city mission and tract society. 44th annual report; with brief notices of the operations of other societies, church directory, list of benevolent societies, and statistics of population, etc. [By L. E. Jackson]. 151 pp. 8°. *New York, Bible house,* 1870.

New York (The) coach-makers' magazine, devoted to the literary, social, and mechanical interests of the craft. Edited by E. M. Stratton. [Monthly]. June, 1870, to Feb. 1871. v. 12. 4°. *New York, G. W. W. Houghton & co.* 1871.
[*Note.*—United with "The hub," from March, 1871, inclusive].

——— *See* **Hub** (The) and New York coach-makers' magazine.

New York (The) evening mail. [Daily]. Jan. 2 to Dec. 30, 1871. 2 v. fol. *New York, Evening mail association,* 1871.

New York evening post. *See* **Evening** post (The New York daily).

New-York (The) farmer, and horticultural repository. Devoted to practical husbandry and gardening. Under the patronage of the New York horticultural society. S. Fleet, editor. 1828–31. v. 1–4. 8°. *New-York,* 1828–31.

New York (The) fireside companion. A journal of instructive and entertaining literature. [Weekly]. Nov. 1870, to Oct. 1871. v. 7–8. fol. *New York, G. Munro,* 1870–71.

New York (The) herald. [Daily]. Jan. 1 to Dec. 31, 1871. 2 v. fol. *New York, J. G. Bennett,* 1871.

New York (The) ledger. [Weekly]. Devoted to choice literature, romance, the news and commerce. Robert Bonner, editor. Feb. 1871, to Feb. 1872. v. 27. fol. *New York, R. Bonner,* 1871–72.

New York (The) medical journal. Editor, Edward S. Dunster, m. d: and William T. Lusk, m. d. and James B. Hunter, m. d. [Monthly]. Jan. to Dec. 1871. v. 13–14. 8°. *New York, D. Appleton & co.* 1871.

New York mercury. [Weekly]. Jan. to Dec. 1871. v. 33. fol. *New York, [Cauldwell & Whitney]*, 1871.

New York (The) musical gazette. [Monthly]. Jan. to Dec. 1871. v. 5. obl. 8°. *New York, Biglow & Main*, 1871.

New York (The) navigation and colonization company. Olancho. An account of the resources of the state of Honduras, in Central America: especially of the department of Olancho. [*anon.*] 65 pp. 8°. *New York, Wynkoop & Hallenbeck*, 1865.

New York (The) observer year book. 1871 and 1872. 2 v. 8°. [*New York*], *S. E. Morse & co.* [1871–72].

New York shipping and commercial list. *See* **Shipping** and commercial list.

New York (The) social science review: devoted to political economy and statistics. Edited by Alex. Delmar and Simon Stern. [Quarterly]. Jan. to Oct. 1865. v. 1. 8°. *New York, the proprietors*, 1865. s.

New York (The) standard. John Russell Young, editor. [Daily]. Jan. 2 to Dec. 30, 1871. fol. *New York, J. R. Young*, 1871.

New York (The) state agricultural society. Transactions. With an abstract of the proceedings of the county agricultural societies. v. 29. 1869. 8°. *Albany, the Argus co.* 1870.

New York (The) state tourist. Descriptive of the scenery of the Hudson, Mohawk, and St. Lawrence rivers. [*anon.*] 234 pp. 5 pl. 4 maps. 18°. *New York, A. T. Goodrich*, 1842.

New York (The) times. [Daily]. Jan. 1 to Dec. 31, 1871. 2 v. fol. *New York, H. J. Raymond & co.* 1871.

New York tribune. [Daily]. Jan. 2 to Dec. 30, 1871. 2 v. fol. *New York, Tribune association*, 1871.

New York weekly. *See* **Street** *and* **Smith's** New York weekly.

New York world. *See* **World** (The New York).

New Zealand. *Geological survey.* Reports of geological explorations during 1870–1, with maps and sections. James Hector, m. d. director. viii, 164 pp. 25 pl. 8°. *New Zealand, J. Hughes*, 1871.

Niccolini (Giovanni Batista). Opere in verso e in prosa. 3 v. 8°. *Firenze, stamperia piatti*, 1831.

——— The same. 3 v. in 1. 8°. *Firenze*, 1831.

Nichol (John). A sketch of scottish poetry up to the time of sir David Lyndesay, with an outline of his works. liv pp. 8°. *London, Trübner & co.* 1871.
[EARLY english text society, no. 47].

Nicholls (John Ashton). In memoriam. A selection from [his] letters. Edited by his mother. 4 p. l. 418 pp. 8°. *Manchester*, [*Eng.*] 1862.
[*Note.*—In great part descriptive of his travels in America].

Nicholls (*Mrs.* Louisa H.) Poems. 110 pp. 12°. *New York, C. S. Francis & co.* 1857.

Nichols (*Rev.* George W.) Fragments from the study of a pastor. 252 pp. 1 pl. 16°. *New York, H. B. Price*, 1860.

Nichols (*Rev.* Ichabod). A catechism of natural theology. 184 pp. 12°. *Portland, Shirley & Hyde*, 1829.

Nichols (James R. *m. d.*) Fireside science. A series of popular scientific essays upon subjects connected with every-day life. vii, 283 pp. 12°. *New York, Hurd & Houghton*, 1872.

Nichols (John, *editor*). A select collection of poems: with notes, biographical and historical. 8 v. 16°. *London, J. Nichols*, 1780–82.

Nichols (Thomas L. *m. d.*) Father Larkin's mission in Jonesville; a tale of the times. iv, 3–64 pp. 18°. *Baltimore, Kelly, Hedian & Piet*, 1860.

——— The mysteries of man: or esoteric anthropology. 466 pp. 18°. *New York, Davies & Kent*, 1861.

Nichols *or* **Nicholls** (William, *rector of Selsey*). A conference with a theist; containing an answer to all the most usual objections of the infidels against the christian religion. 3d ed. with the addition of two conferences; the one with a machiavelian, the other with an atheist. 2 v. xvi, 516 pp. 6 l. 1 pl; 1 p. l. 486 pp. 5 l. 1 pl. 8°. *London, J. Holland*, 1723.

Nichols *or* **Nicols** (William, *rector of Stockport*. De literis inventis libri sex. [Metrici cum notis]. 2 p. l. 387 pp. 1 pl. 12°. *Londini, apud H. Clementem*, 1711.

Nichols (William Ripley). An elementary manual of chemistry. *See* **Eliot** (Charles W.) *and* **Storer** (F. H.)

Nicholson (George). The cambrian traveller's guide, in every direction; containing remarks made during many excursions, in the principality of Wales, and bordering dis-

Nicholson (George)—continued. tricts, augmented by extracts from the best writers. 2d ed. xiii, 1468 pp. 8°. *Stourport, editor*, 1813.

Nicholson (H. Alleyne). Text-book of geology for schools and colleges. xii, 226 pp. 12°. *New York, D. Appleton & co.* 1872.

——— Text-book of zoology for schools and colleges. xii, 353 pp. 12°. *New York, D. Appleton & co.* 1872.

[*Note*.—Same as the "Advanced text book of zoology"].

Nicholson (*Rev.* Joseph J.) The Blemmertons; or, dottings by the wayside. 423 pp. 12°. *New York, Dana & co.* 1856.

Nicholson (William). Neues deutsch-englisches wörterbuch. *See* **Küttner** (Carl G.) *and* **Nicholson.**

Nicolaï (Christoph Friedrich). Recherches historiques sur l'usage des cheveux postiches et des perruques, dans les temps anciens et modernes. Traduit de l'allemand par Jansen. 1 p. l. 221 pp. 2 pl. 8°. *Paris, L. Collin*, 1809.

Nicolai (Johann). Disquisitio de substratione et pignoratione vestium, ubi locus Matth. 21. explicatur & probatur, Christum verum esse messiam & regem promissum, simul ac variæ antiquitates haud inutiles lectuque dignissimæ nec hactenus observatæ in lucem proferuntur. 6 p. l. 127 pp. 2 l. 18°. *Gissæ, typis & impensis H. Mülleri*, 1701.

——— In nomine Jesu disquisitio de nimbis antiquorum, imaginibus deorum, imperatorum olim, & nunc Christi, apostolorum & Mariæ captibus adpictis. 8 p. l. 140 pp. 6 l. 18°. [*Gissæ, impensis J. J. Ehrt*, 1699].

——— Tractatus de phyllobolia seu florum et ramorum sparsione in sacris & civilibus rebus usitatissima, ubi varii ritus adducuntur, multa scripturæ loca illustrantur, & cæremoniarum in ingressu solenni principum origo fuse exhibetur; in fine denique dn. Dieterici dissertatio de sparsione florum adjicitur. Eng. title, 22, 185 pp. 18°. *Francofvrti ad Moenum, sumpt: G. H. Ohrlingii*, 1698.

——— Tractatus de siglis veterum. In quo continentur, quæ ad interpretationem numismatum, inscriptionum, juris et fere omnium artium requiruntur, cujus subsidio facile literæ explicari possunt. 11 p. l. 314 pp. 4°. *Lugduni Batavorum, apud A. de Swart*, 1703.

Nicolai (Johann Friedrich). Hodogeticum orientale harmonicum, quod complectitur 1. Lexicon lingvarum ebraicae, chaldaicae, syriacae, arabicae, aethiopicae et persicae harmonicum. 2. Grammaticam lingvarum earundem, secundum prima praecepta delineatam, harmonicam. 3. Dicta biblica, cum et sine analysi grammatica exhibita, harmonica. 8 p. l. 628 pp. 62 l. 80 pp. 1 pl. sm. 4°. *Ienae, typis & impensis I. I. Bauhoferi*, 1670.

Nicolas (Auguste). Études philosophiques sur le christianisme. 4e éd. belge. v. i. 429 pp. 1 l. 8°. *Bruxelles, H. Goemaere*, 1853.

Nicolas (*Sir* Nicholas Harris). Biographical notices of the contributors to the "Poetical rhapsody"; extracted from the new edition of that work by Nicholas Harris Nicolas. clxxviii pp. 1 tab. 8°. [*London*], *W. Pickering*, [1826].

Nicolaus *myrepsus*. Nicolai alexandrini medici graeci vetustissimi liber de compositione medicamentorum secundum loca, translatvs e græco in latinum à Nicolao rheghino calabro, nuper post germanicam editionem impressus, & quā plurimis in locis castigatus, cvm brevissimis annotationibus locorum difficilium Ioannis Agricolæ Ammonii. 12 p. l. 241 l. numb. 1 l. 16°. *Venetiis, apud A. Arriuabenum*, 1543.

Nicole (Pierre). Essais de morale, contenus en divers traittez sur plusieurs devoirs importans. [*anon.*] Nouv. éd. 4 v. 18°. *Suivant la copie imprimée à Paris, chez la veuve C. Savreux* [& *G. Desprez*], 1672–78.

——— The same. Continuation des essais de morale. Contenant des réflexions morales sur les epîtres et évangiles. [*anon.*] 5 v. 18°. *La Haye, A. Moetjens*, 1688.

——— Les imaginaires, et les visionnaires. Traité de la foy humaine [par Antoine Arnauld et Nicole]. Jugement équitable, tiré des œuvres de s. Augustin [par Antoine Arnauld]. Lettre de messire Nicolás Pauillon à messire Hardouyn Perefixe. [*anon.*] 10 p. l. 696 pp. 8°. *Cologne, P. Marteau*, 1683.

Nicols. *See* **Nichols.**

Nicquet (Honorat). Histoire de l'ordre de Font-Evravd. Eng. title, 13 p. l. 548 pp. 6 l. 4°. *Paris, M. Soly*, 1642.

Niebuhr (Barthold Georg). A dissertation on the geography of Herodotus. Researches into the history of the Scythians, Getae, and Sarmatians. Translated from the german. 2 p. l. 86, ii pp. 1 map. 8°. *Oxford, D. A. Talboys*, 1830.

——— Heroic tales of ancient Greece, related by Niebuhr to his little son Marcus. Translated from the german. Edited, with notes,

Niebuhr (Barthold Georg)—continued. by Felix Summerly, [Henry Cole]. viii, 116 pp. 4 col. pl. sq. 16°. *London, Chapman & Hall*, [1843].

——— The life and letters of Barthold George Niebuhr. With essays on his character and influence, by the chevalier Bunsen, and professors Brandis and Loebell. 563 pp. 12°. *New York, Harper & brothers*, 1852.

Nieritz (Carl Gustav). Alexander Menzikoff; or, the perils of greatness. Translated from the german, by mrs. H. C. Conant. 226 pp. 1 pl. 16°. *New York, C. Scribner*, 1853.

——— Faithful unto death. From the german. By M. A. Manderson. 287 pp. 3 pl. 16°. *Philadelphia, Lutheran board of publication*, 1871.

[FATHERLAND (The) series].

——— Gottlieb Frey; or, honesty is the best policy. By Gustav Meritz [Nieritz]. Translated from the german. 226 pp. 4 pl. 16°. *Philadelphia, Lutheran board of publication*, [illegible]1.

[FATHERLAND (The) series].

——— The jailor of Norwich; or, the eighth commandment. 186 pp. 2 pl. 16°. *New York, General protestant episcopal s. s. union & church book society*, 1863.

——— The three kings. Translated from the german by Rebecca H. Schively. Eng. title, 223 pp. 3 pl. 16°. *Philadelphia, Lutheran board of publication*, 1871.

[FATHERLAND (The) series].

Nierop (Dirck Rembrantsz. van). Eenige oefeningen, in god-lijcke, wis-konstige, en natuerlijcke dingen. 2 v. 4 p. l. 84 pp; 68 pp. sm. 4°. *Amsterdam, G. van Goedesbergh en A. S. van der Storck*, 1669–74.

CONTENTS.

v. 1. Van des werelts scheppinge.
Een meetkonstige beschryvinge des geheelen aert-kloots.
Het maecksel van alderhande kaerten.
Van de cometen of staert-starren haer verschijninge.
v. 2. Over het vroeg vertonen der sonne op Nova Sembla int jaer 1597. [Begrepen en een brief van Robbert Robbertse, met een antwoort daer op].
Enige aenmerkingen op de raise benoorden om na Oost-Indïa [ende door het Noorder Amerika].
Van Abel Tasmans ontdekking na het onbekende Suid-lant.
Van de letterspelling, dat is hoe men de letteren uitspreken en spellen sal.

Nieuhoff (Jan). Legatio batavica ad magnam Tartariae chamum Sungteium, modernum Sinæ imperatorem 1655–57 [etc.] Latinitate donata per Georgium Hornium. 2 v. in 1. 2 p. l. 184 pp. 32 pl. 1 map; 172 pp. 4 l. 3 pl. fol. *Amstelodami, I. Meursius*, 1668.

Nifo (Agostino). Avgvstini Niphi opvscvla moralia et politica: cvm Gabrielis Navdæi de eodem auctore iudicio. 45 p. l. 442 pp. 24 l. 358 pp. 23 l. 4°. *Parisiis, sumptibus R. Le Dvc*, 1645.

CONTENTS.

De vera vivendi libertate libre duo.
De divitiis libellus.
De iis qui apte possunt in solitudine vivere.
De sanctitate et prophanitate libri duo.
De misericordia.
De pulchro.
De amore.
De regnandi peritia, libri quinque.
De his quae ab optimis principibus agenda sunt.
De rege et tyranno libellus.
De re aulica libri duo.

Nightingale (Thomas). Oceanic sketches. With a botanical appendix, by dr. Hooker, of Glasgow. xii, 132 pp. 5 pl. 1 portrait. 8°. *London, J. Cochrane & co.* 1835.

Nihus (Barthold). Bartoldi Nihvsii telescopivm, donatum in Germania genti Saxonum, ut utantur in fidei ac religionis negotio. 8°. [*Coloniæ Agrippinae, typis I. Kalcovii & sociorum*, 1645].

[*In* ALLACCI (Leone). Confvtatio fabvlæ de Ioanna papissa. *Coloniae Agrippinae*, 1645. pp. 78–112].

Niles (*Rev.* Samuel). The true scripture-doctrine of original sin stated and defended. In the way of remarks on a late piece, intitled, "The scripture-doctrine of original sin proposed to free and candid examination. By John Taylor. The second edition." To which is premised a brief discourse on the decrees of God, in general, and on the election of grace, in particular. 3 p. l. 320 pp. 16°. *Boston, S. Kneeland*, 1757.

Nineteen beautiful years; or, sketches of a girl's life, written by her sister. With an introduction by rev. R. S. Foster, d. d. [*anon.*] 3 p. l. 241 pp. 1 portrait. 16°. *New York, Harper & brothers*, 1864.

Niphus. *See* **Nifo.**

Nisard (Jean Marie Napoléon Désiré). Histoire de la littérature française. v. 1–2. 8°. *Paris, F. Didot frères*, 1844. s.

[*Note.*—v. 3 wanting to complete the work].

——— Mélanges d'histoire et de littérature. 1e série. vii, 444 pp. 16°. *Paris, M. Lévy frères*, 1868.

Nisard (Marie Léonard Charles). Les gladiateurs de la république des lettres aux xve, xvie et xviie siècles. 2 v. viii, 407 pp; 2 p. l. 416 pp. 8°. *Paris, M. Lévy frères*, 1860.

Nisbett (*Rev.* N.) An attempt to display the original evidences of christianity in their genuine simplicity. xii, 204 pp. 8°. *London, author*, 1807.

Nithardus. Nithardi Karoli M. imp. ex Bertha filia nepotis de dissensionibus filiorum Lodhvvici Pii ad annum usq. 843. fol. [*Argentorati, J. R. Dulssecker*, 1702].

[*In* KULPIS (Johann Georg von). Scriptores rervm germanicarvm. *Argentorati*, 1702. pp. 26–119].

Nizzoli (Mario). Marivs Nizolivs sive thesavrvs ciceronianvs, post nvnqvam satis lavdatas operas Basilii Zanchi, Cælii Secvndi Cvrionis, et Marcelli Sqvarcialvpi plvmpinensis, magno labore et stvdio olim mactvs. [etc.] 2 v. 4 p. l. 859 pp. 1 pl; 4 p. l. 1145 pp. fol. *Francofvrti, apud G. Tampachivm*, 1613.

Nobili (Giacinto de'). Il vagabondo, overo sferza de bianti, e vagabondi. Data in luce per auertimento de' semplici dal sig. Raffaele Frianoro. [*pseudon.*] 111 pp. 18°. *Trevigi, F. Righettini*, 1672.

Noble (James). The orientalist; or, letters of a rabbi. With notes. 368 pp. 6 pl. 8°. *Edinburgh, Oliver & Boyd*, 1831.

Noble (*Rev.* Mark). Memoirs of the illustrious house of Medici, from Giovanni, the founder of their greatness, who died in the year 1428, to the death of Giovanni-Gaston, the last grand duke of Tuscany, in 1737. viii, 456 pp. 6 pl. 8°. *London, T. Cadell, jr. & W. Davies*, 1797.

Noble (Thomas). Blackheath; a poem. Lumena; or the ancient british battle: and various other poems; including a translation of the first book of the Argonautica of C. Valerius Flaccus. 9 p. l. 147, v, 59, 1, 133 pp. 3 pl. 4°. *London, author*, 1808.

——— Poems. 4 p. l. 208 pp. 12°. *Liverpool, author*, 1821.

Noceti (Giovanni Battista). Astrologia ottima, indifferente, pessima. 10 p. l. 276 pp. 5 l. 18°. *Genova, per gli heredi del Calenzani*, [1661].

Nodier (Charles Emmanuel) **Taylor** (J.) *and* **Cailleux** (Alphonse de). Voyages pittoresques et romantiques dans l'ancienne France. 5 v. fol. *Paris, J. Didot l'aîné*, 1820.

CONTENTS.

v. 1–2. Ancienne Normandie. t. i–ii. 241 pl.
v. 3. Franche-Comté. 158 pl.
v. 4–5. Auvergne. t. i–ii. 254 pl.

[*Note.*—Plate 9, Franche-Comté, wanting].

Noel (*Rev.* Baptist W.) Meditations in sickness and old age. 148 pp. 18°. *Philadelphia, H. Perkins*, 1838.

Noethen (*Rev.* Theodore). History of the bible, for the use of schools. Translated and compiled from the works of the most celebrated german writers. xii, 160 pp. 8°. *Albany, Weed, Parsons & co.* 1860.

——— A history of the catholic church, from the commencement of the christian era to the ecumenical council of the vatican. With questions. vii, 13–580, 68 pp. 16°. *Baltimore, J. Murphy & co.* 1871.

Noisy Herbert, and other stories. For small children. By the author of "Violet," [etc. *anon.*] 2 p. l. 108 pp. 2 pl. sq. 16°. *Boston, Walker, Wise & co.* 1860.

Nolan (Frederick, *ll. d.*) The chronological prophecies; as constituting a connected system in which the principal events of the divine dispensations are determined by the precise revelation of their dates; demonstrated in a series of lectures, in the years 1833, 1834, 1835, 1836. xxvi, 518 pp. 8°. *London, W. Pickering*, 1837.

——— The evangelical character of christianity, according to the doctrine and ordinances of the established church. xx, 257 pp. 18°. *London, W. Pickering*, 1838.

Nolfi (Vincenzo). Ginipedia, ouero avvertimenti civili, per donna nobile, [la signora Ippolita Uffreducci moglie del] V. Nolfi da Fano. Da lui acresciuti, e rimodernati in questa nuoua impressione. 22 p. l. 597 pp. 18°. *Bologna, per gli hh. di G. Recaldini*, 1683.

Noort (Olivier van). Wonderlijcke voyagie, by de Hollanders ghedaen, door de strate Magalanes, ende voorts den gantschen kloot des aerdtbodems om, met vier schepen: onder den admirael Olivier van Noort, 1598 [-1601]. Hier achter is by-gevoeght de tweede voyagie van Jacob van Neck, naer Oost-Indien. 88 pp. 6 pl. (in text). sm. 4°. *Amstelredam, J. Hartgers*, 1650.

——— The same. 88 pp. 6 pl. (on 1 sheet). sm. 4°. *Amstelredam, I. Hartgerts*, 1648.

[*In* HARTGERTS (J.) Oost-indische voyagien, v. 1, 4e stuck].

Nootelijcke consideratien die alle goede liefhebbers des vaderlandts behooren rijpelijc te overweghen opten voorgheslaghen tractate van peys met den Spagniarden. [*anon.*] 8 l. sm. 4°. [*n. p.*] 1608.

[*In* NEDERLANDTSCHE bye-corf].

Norden (John). Specvlvm Britanniæ. The first parte. An historicall, & chorographicall discription of Middlesex. Eng. title, 3 p. l. 48 pp. 2 l. 1 map. sm. 4°. [*London*], *anno* 1593.

Noris (Henry). Annvs et epochae Syromacedonvm in vetvstis vrbivm Syriae nvmmis præsertim mediceis expositæ. Additis fastis consvlaribus anonymi omnivm optimis. Accesserunt nuper dissertationes de paschali latinorvm cyclo annorvm lxxxiv, ac Ravennate annorum xcv. 10 p. l. 566 pp. 8 l. 1 portrait, 1 pl. 1 map. 4°. *Lipsiæ, apud T. Fritsch*, 1696.
[*Note.*—This book does not contain the promised additions].

——— Latinitas et orthographia vtrivsqve pisanae tabvlae avgvstea aetate digna contra Octavivm Boldonvm demonstrata. 8°. [*Altenbvrgi, ex officina richteria*, 1768].
[*In* HARLES (Gottlieb Christoph). Christoph. Cellarii Orthographia latina [etc.] *Altenbvrgi*, 1768. v. 2, pp. 155–298].

Normanby (Henry Philip Phipps, *marquess of*). Temple of Death. *See* **Habert** (P.)

Norris (*Rev.* John, *of Bemerton*). Letters concerning the love of God, between the author of The proposal to the ladies [Mary Astell], and mr. John Norris. 23 p. l. 312 pp. 16°. *London, S. Manship*, 1695.

——— A letter to mr. Dodwell, concerning the immortality of the soul of man. In answer to one from him, relating to the same matter. Being a farther pursuance of the philosophical discourse. 5th ed. 4 p. l. 135 pp. 12°. *London, E. Parker*, 1732.
[*With his* Philosophical discourse concerning the natural immortality of the soul. *London*, 1732].

——— A philosophical discourse concerning the natural immortality of the soul. Occasion'd by mr. Dodwell's late epistolary discourse. In 2 parts. 5th ed. 4 p. l. 112 pp. 8°. *London, M. Jenour for E. Parker*, 1732.

——— A practical treatise concerning humility. 8 p. l. 409 pp. 12°. *London, S. Manship*, 1707.

Norske (Den) turistforenings aarbog, for 1869. 2 p. l. 134 pp. 3 pl. 8°. *Christiania, A. Cammermeyer*, [1868].

North american (The) medico-chirurgical review. Edited by S. D. Gross, m. d. and T. G. Richardson, m. d. [and S. W. Gross, m. d. A bimonthly]. 1857–1861. v. 1–5. 8°. *Philadelphia, J. B. Lippincott & co.* 1857–61. s.

North american review. [Quarterly]. Jan. to Oct. 1871. v. 112–113. 8°. *Boston, Fields, Osgood & co.* 1871.

North (The) british review. [Quarterly]. October, 1869, to January, 1871. v. 51–53. 8°. *London, Edmonston & Douglas*, 1869–71.
[*Note.*—The publication ceased with January, 1871].

Northend (Charles). The teacher's assistant, or hints and methods in school discipline and instruction; being a series of familiar letters to one entering upon the teacher's work. 358 pp. 1 pl. 12°. *Boston, Crosby, Nichols & co.* 1859.

Northrop (*Mrs.* E. L.) Alice learning to do good. 180 pp. 16°. *Boston, Mass. sabbath school society*, [1834].

——— New-year's gift for the Well-spring children. 284 pp. 3 pl. 18°. *Boston, Mass. sabbath school society*, [1857].

Norton (Andrews, *d. d.*) Translation of the gospels. *See* **Bible.** (*English*).

Norton (Charles L.) American sea-side resorts: a hand-book for health and pleasure seekers. 1 p. l. 190 pp. 1 pl. 16°. *New York, Taintor brothers*, 1871.

Norton (George). Commentaries on the history, constitution, and chartered franchises of the city of London. 3d ed. xxviii, 421 pp. 8°. *London, Longmans, Green & co.* 1869.

Norton (George Hatley, *jr.*) An inquiry into the nature and extent of the holy catholic church. 110 pp. 18°. *Philadelphia, H. Hooker*, 1853.

Norton (John H. *d. d.*) Life of bishop Wilson of Calcutta. 334 pp. 1 pl. 1 portrait. 18°. *New York, Gen. prot. episcopal sunday school union and church book society*, 1863.

Norton (John N. *d. d.*) Life of archbishop Laud. 269 pp. 1 pl. 1 portrait. 12°. *Boston, E. P. Dutton & co.* 1864.

——— Life of bishop Bass, of Massachusetts. 192 pp. 1 portrait. 18°. *New York, General prot. episcopal sunday school union & church book society*, 1859.

——— Rockford parish; or, the fortunes of mr. Mason's successors. 216 pp. 12°. *New York, Dana & co.* 1856.

Norton (Lemuel). Auto-biography of Lemuel Norton. Also his christian experience and labors in the gospel ministry. 192 pp. 16°. *Portland, H. C. Little*, 1861.

Notes and queries: a medium of intercommunication for literary men, general readers, etc. January, 1870, to December, 1871. 4th series. v. 5–8. sm. 4°. *London, at the office*, 1870–71.

Notes of hospital life from November, 1861, to August, 1863. [*anon.*] 210 pp. 12°. *Philadelphia, J. B. Lippincott & co.* 1864.

Notice des inscriptions antiques du musée de Lyon. *See* **Artaud** (François).

Nott (Samuel, *jr. d. d.*) Sermons on public worship, suited to the times. xvi, 25–404 pp. 12°. *Boston, Whipple & Damrell*, 1841.

—— The telescope: or, sacred views of things past, present, and to come. 180 pp. 18°. *Boston, Perkins & Marvin*, 1832.

Nourse (James). New testament. *New York*, 1827; *Boston*, 1834. *See* **Bible**. (*English*).

Nourse (Timothy). A discourse upon the nature and faculties of man, in several essays: with some considerations upon the occurrances of humane life. 8 p. l. 410 pp. 1 pl. 8°. *London, J. Tonson*, 1686.

Nouveau dictionnaire allemand-françois et françois-allemand à l'usage des deux nations. [*anon.*] 5e éd. entièrement refondue et considérablement augmentée. v. 2, contenant l'allemand expliqué par le françois. 1 p. l. 1110 pp. 8°. *Vienne, J. T. de Trattnern*, 1804.

Nouvelles d'Elisabeth reyne d'Angleterre. [*anon.*] 2 parts in 1 v. 120 pp; 1 p. l. 114 pp. 18°. *Suivant la copie imprimée à Paris, chez C. Barbin*, [*Amsterdam, Elzevir*], 1680.

Nouvelles extraordinaires de divers endroits. [Rédigé par Étienne Luzac]. 1765 to 1783. 19 v. sm. 4°. *Leyde, Étienne Luzac*, 1765–83.

[*Note.*—Published semi-weekly. Commonly known as the "Gazette de Leyde." Styled upon the title-pages to the yearly volumes, "Nouvelles politiques publiées à Leyde." A few numbers wanting].

Nouvelles politiques publiées à Leyde. *See* **Nouvelles** extraordinaires de divers endroits.

Novelist (The): or, tea-table miscellany. Containing the select novels of dr. Croxall; with other polite tales, and pieces of modern entertainment. [*anon.*] 2 v. 2 p. l. 288 pp. 4 pl; 2 p. l. 280 pp. 3 pl. 12°. *London, T. Lowndes*, 1766.

Nowrojee (Jehangeer) *and* **Merwanjee** (Hirjeebhoy). Journal of a residence of two years and a half in Great Britain. xxiv, 492 pp. 12°. *London, W. H. Allen & co.* 1841.

Noyes (Eli, *d. d.*) Lectures on the truth of the bible. viii, 364 pp. 12°. *Boston, Gould & Lincoln*, 1853.

Noyes (George Rapall, *d. d.*) New translation of the psalms. *Also*, New testament. *See* **Bible**. (*English*).

Nuck (Antony). Antonii Nuck de ductu salivali novo, saliva, ductibus oculorum aquosis, et humore oculi aqueo. Eng. title, 5 p. l. 176 pp. 8 l. 3 pl. 16°. *Lugduni Batavorum, apud P. van der Aa*, 1685.

Nugent (Thomas, *ll. d.*) A new pocket dictionary of the french and english languages. In two parts. 1. French and english. 2. English and french. Containing all the words in general use, and authorized by the best writers. 5th american, from the last London ed; with the addition of new words, &c. By J. Ouiseau. xii, 452 pp. sq. 16°. *Philadelphia, E. H. Butler & co.* 1846.

Nulty (Eugenius). Elements of geometry, theoretical and practical; including constructions by the right line and by the circle; together with the mensuration of all the elementary plane figures and solids. viii, 220 pp. 12°. *Philadelphia, J. Whetham*, 1836.

Nunes (Joseph A.) Day dreams. 134 pp. 16°. *Philadelphia, J. B. Lippincott & co.* 1863.

Nuñez (Antonio). Sermon panegyrico, en la celebridad de la dedicacion del templo nuevo de san Bernardo, titvlo Maria de Gvadalupe, sabado dia septimo de la octava. sm. 4°. [*México, viuda de F. R. Lupercio*, 1691].

[*In* Ramirez de Vargas (A.) Sagrado padron y panegyricos sermones, etc. l. 74–97].

Nuñez de Taboada (Melchior Emmanuel). Diccionario frances-español y español-frances, mas completo y correcto que todos los que se han publicado hasta ahora, sin exceptuar el de Capmany. 7a ed. 2 v. 4 p. l. 964 pp; 3 p. l. 1392 pp. 8°. *Paris, Rey & Gravier*, 1833.

Nursery (The), a monthly magazine for youngest readers. Jan. to Dec. 1871. v. 9–10. sm. 4°. *Boston, J. Shorey*, 1871.

Nutting (Rufus). Memoirs of mrs. Emily Egerton. 180 pp. 1 pl. 18°. *Boston, Perkins & Marvin*, 1832.

Nvove lettere delle cose del Giappone, paese del mondo novo, dell' anno 1579 insino al 1581. Con la morte d'alcvni padri della compagnia di Giesv̂. 188 pp. 5 l. 16°. *Venetia, appresso i Gioliti*, 1585.

Nye (Joseph W.) An offering of friendship: or, miscellaneous poems. 168 pp. 16°. *Lynn*, [*Ms.*] *Stevenson & Nichols*, 1860.

Nystrom (John W.) A treatise on parabolic construction of ships and other marine engineering subjects. 40 pp. 1 pl. 8°. *Philadelphia, J. B. Lippincott & co.* 1863.

Oakley (Benjamin). Selections from Shakspeare. *See* **Shakespeare** (William).

Observations on the river Potomack, the country adjacent, and the city of Washington. [*anon.*] 30 pp. 12°. *New York, London & Brower*, 1794.

Observator (The) in dialogue. [Between Whig and Tory, Observator and Trimmer]. By Roger L'Estrange. April 13, 1681, to Feb. 27, 168$\frac{5}{6}$. 3 v. in 2. fol. *London, J. Bennet*, 1684-87.

Obsopœus *or* **Koch** (Vincenz) *and* **Delius** (Matthæus). Vinc. Obsopœvs de arte bibendi lib. qvatvor, et [Matth. Delius de] arte jocandi lib. qvatvor, accedunt artis amandi, dansandi practica; item meretricvm fides: aliaque faceta. 4 p. l. 136, 280 pp. 18°. *Lvgd. Batav. ex typographia rediviva, [hackiana]?* 1648.
[Imperfect: wanting pp. 169-190].

Occasional thoughts on the study and character of classical authors, on the course of literature, and the present plan of a learned education. With some incidental comparisons between Homer and Ossian. [*anon.*] 148 pp. 8°. *London, J. Richardson*, 1762.

Ocellus *lucanus.* 'Ωκελλος ο λευκανος φιλοσοφος περι της του παντος φυσεως. Ocellus lucanus philosophus de universi natura. 8°. [*Amstelœdami, apud H. Wetstenium*, 1688].
[*In* GALE (Thomas). Opuscula mythologica, pp. 499-538].

Ochoa (Eugenio de). Epistolario español. Coleccion de cartas de españoles ilustres antiguos y modernos, recogida y ordenada con notas y aclaraciones históricas, críticas y biográficas. v. 2. 8°. *Madrid, M. Rivadeneyra*, 1870.
[BIBLIOTECA de autores españoles, v. 50. b.]

O'Daniel (William). Ins and outs of London. 395 pp. 12°. *Philadelphia, S. C. Lamb*, 1859.

Odd-fellow's (The) gem: containing sentiments of "friendship, love and truth." Edited by a lady. [*anon.*] 1 p. l. 156 pp. 32°. *Springfield, [Mass.] B. F. Brown*, 1845.

Odd-fellows' (The) offering, for 1849. Edited by Paschal Donaldson. 320 pp. 12 pl. 8°. *New York, E. Walker*, 1849.

Odenheimer (William Henry, *d. d.*) *and* **Bird** (Frederick M.) Songs of the spirit. Hymns of praise and prayer to God the Holy Ghost. xxiv, 636 pp. sm. 4°. *New York, A. D. F. Randolph & co.* [1871].

Odes and addresses to great people. [*anon.*] vii, 136 pp. 16°. *London, Baldwin, Cradock & Joy*, 1825.

Odes sur les affaires du tems. *See* **Waleff** (Blaise Henri de Corte, *baron de*). Œuvres diverses.

Odo (*Saint, abbé de Cluny*). Vie de saint Grégoire, évêque de Tours. 16°. [*Paris, F. Didot frères*, 1859].
[*In* GREGORIUS *tvronensis.* Histoire ecclésiastique des Francs, v. 1, pp. xiii-xxxix, ed. 1859-61].

O'Donnel (Kane). The song of iron, and the song of slaves; with other poems. 72 pp. 18°. *Philadelphia, King & Baird*, 1863.

O'Donovan (Denis). Memories of Rome. xx, 294 pp. 1 pl. 12°. *London, Catholic publishing and bookselling co.* 1859.

O'Donovan (Jeremiah). A brief account of the author's interview with his countrymen, and of the parts of the Emerald isle whence they emigrated. Together with a direct reference to their present location in the land of their adoption, during his travels through various states of the union in 1854 and 1855. 382 pp. 12°. *Pittsburgh (Pa.) author*, 1864.

——— A history of Ireland, containing a compendious account of her woes, afflictions and suffering, with a direct reference to her political renovation. In epic verse. 2 v. in 1. 177 pp; 135 pp. 12°. *Pittsburgh, author*, 1854.

Oertel (P. F. Wilhelm). Leonhard, the runaway. Translated from the german of Van Horn. [*pseudon.*] By * * *, d. d. 74 pp. 18°. *Philadelphia, Lutheran board of publication*, 1871.
[FATHERLAND (The) series].

Of gentylnes and nobylyte. *See* **Heywood** (John).

O'Flaherty (Charles). Poems. 8 p. l. 246 pp. 12°. *Dublin, author*, 1813.

O'Flanagan (J. Roderick). The lives of the lord chancellors and keepers of the great seal of Ireland, from the earliest times to the reign of queen Victoria. 2 v. xxix, 555 pp; xxii, 621 pp. 8°. *London, Longmans, Green & co.* 1870.

Ogden (John). The science of education; and art of teaching. In two parts. 478 pp. 12°. *Cincinnati, Moore, Wilstach, Keys & co.* 1859.

Ogden (*Rev.* John Cosens). A tour through Upper and Lower Canada. [*anon.* 1st ed.] 119 pp. 18°. *Litchfield (Conn.)* 1799.

Ogden (Samuel). Reflective remarks on the evils created by artful policy, and variously practised in the progressive ways of mankind, when advanced to an improved condition. 288 pp. 16°. *Philadelphia, for author, by J. Metcalfe & co.* 1834.

Ogden (William A.) The silver song, a choice collection of new sabbath school music. Revised ed. 175 pp. obl. 18°. *Toledo (O.) W. W. Whitney*, [1871].

Ogilby (John). Britannia: volume the first. Or, an illustration of the kingdom of England and dominion of Wales: by a geographical and historical description of the principal roads thereof. Actually admeasured and delineated in a century of whole-sheet copper-sculps, accomodated with the ichnography of the several cities and capital towns; and compleated by an accurate account of the more remarkable passages of antiquity, together with a novel discourse of the present state. 15 p. l. 200 pp. 100 pl. fol. *London, author*, 1675.

——— Atlas japannensis. fol. *London*, 1670. *See* **Montanus** (Arnoldus).

——— *See, also*, **Homerus**. Iliad and Odyssey. *London*, 1669.

O'Gorman (*Miss* Edith). Trials and persecutions of miss Edith O'Gorman, otherwise sister Teresa de Chantal, of St. Joseph's convent, Hudson City, N. J. Written by herself. With an appendix by the publishers. 264 pp. 1 portrait. 12°. *Hartford, Connecticut publishing co.* [1871].

Ohio (*State of*). Executive documents. Parts 1 and 2. 2 v. 2 p. l. 1044 pp. 1 map; iv, 964 pp. 8°. *Columbus, Nevins & Myers*, 1871.

——— *Board of agriculture.* Annual reports of the Ohio state board of agriculture, with an abstract of the proceedings of the county agricultural societies. 1869 and 1870. 2 v. 8°. *Columbus, state printers*, 1870–71.

——— *Commissioner of common schools.* Seventeenth annual report of the commissioner of common schools to the general assembly of the state of Ohio, for the school year ending Aug. 31, 1870. 8°. *Columbus, Nevins & Myers*, 1871.

——— *Commissioner of railroads and telegraphs.* Annual report of the commissioner of railroads and telegraphs. 1869 and 1870. Prepared by George B. Wright, commissioner. 3 v. 8°. *Columbus, Nevins & Myers*, 1870–71.

——— *General assembly.* The journal of the senate and house of representatives of the state of Ohio, for the regular session of the fifty-ninth general assembly, commencing on Monday, Jan. 3, 1870. v. 66. 2 v. 8°. *Columbus, Columbus printing co.* 1870.

——— ——— The journal of the senate and house of representatives of the state of Ohio,

Ohio (*State of*)—continued.
for the adjourned session of the fifty-ninth general assembly, 1871. v. 67. 2 v. 8°. *Columbus, state printers*, 1871.

——— *Geological survey.* Agricultural survey, by J. H. Klippart, assistant geologist. [Report]. 8°. *Columbus (O.)* [1871].

——— ——— Geological survey of Ohio. Part 1. Report of progress in 1869, by J. S. Newberry. Part 2. Report of progress in the second district, by E. B. Andrews. Part 3. Report on geology of Montgomery county, by Edward Orton. 176 pp. 3 maps, 1 chart. 8°. *Columbus, Nevins & Myers*, 1871.

——— ——— Report of progress in 1870. By J. S. Newberry, chief geologist. Including reports by E. B. Andrews, Edward Orton, J. H. Klippart, assistant geologists, T. G. Wormley, chemist, G. K. Gilbert, M. C. Read, Henry Newton, W. B. Potter, local assistants. 568 pp. 7 pl. 8°. *Columbus, Nevins & Myers, state printers*, 1871.

CONTENTS.

ANDREWS (E. B.) Report of labors in the second geological district, during the year 1870. Part 2. pp. 55–242.
GILBERT (G. K.) Report on the geology of Williams, Fulton and Lucas counties. Part 7. pp. 485–499.
KLIPPART (J. H.) Agricultural survey. Part 4. pp. 311–400.
NEWBERRY (J. S.) Report of progress of the geological survey in 1870. Sketch of the structure of the lower coal measures in north-eastern Ohio. By J. S. Newberry. Part 1. pp. 3–53.
NEWTON (H.) A sketch of the present state of the steel industry. Part 9. pp. 527–555.
ORTON (E.) The geology of Highland county. Part 3. pp. 253–309.
POTTER (W. B.) Sketch of the present state of the iron manufacture in Great Britain. Part 8. pp. 501–526.
READ (M. C.) Sketches of the geology of Geauga and Holmes counties. Part 6. pp. 463–484.
WORMLEY (T. G.) Report of chemical department. Part 5. pp. 401–462.

——— *Secretary of state.* Annual report of the secretary of state, to the governor of the state of Ohio, including the statistical report to the general assembly, for the year 1869. 8°. *Columbus, Columbus printing co.* 1870.

——— *State library.* Twenty-fifth annual report of the commissioners of the Ohio state library for the year 1870. 51 pp. 8°. *Columbus, Nevins & Myers*, 1871.

Ohio (Williams') state register and business mirror, for 1857. First issue. 311 pp. 1 pl. 1 map. 8°. *Cincinnati, C. S. Williams*, 1857.

Ohio valley historical series. Miscellanies, nos. 1–3. 8°. *Cincinnati, R. Clarke & co.* 1870–71.

CONTENTS.

ESPY (J.) Memorandums of a tour in the states of

Ohio valley historical series—continued.

Ohio and Kentucky and Indiana territory in 1805. (no. 1).

TANEYHILL (R. H.) The Leatherwood God. An account of J. C. Dylks. (no. 3).

WILLIAMS (Samuel). Two western campaigns in the war of 1812. (no. 2).

Oidtmann (Heinrich). Die anorganischen bestandtheile der leber und milz und der meisten anderen thierischen drüsen. Ein beitrag zum physiologischen zusammenhang zwischen leben und leiche. Gekrönte preisschrift. Mit einem vorwort von Scherer. 4 p. l. 164 pp. 1 l. 8°. *Linnich, C. Quos*, 1858.

Okely (William, *m. d.*) Pyrology; or, the connection between natural and moral philosophy: with a short disquisition on the origin of christianity. 8 p. l. ix, 374 pp. 1 l. 1 pl. 8°. *London, J. Johnson*, 1797.

Olancho. An account of the resources of the state of Honduras. 1865. *See* **New York** (The) navigation and colonization company.

Olcott (Henry S. *editor*). Outlines of the first course of Yale agricultural lectures. With an introduction by John A. Porter. 186 pp. 12°. *New York, C. M. Saxton*, 1860.

Old and new. [A monthly magazine, edited by Edward E. Hale]. Jan. to Dec. 1871. v. 3–4. 8°. *Boston, Roberts brothers*, 1871.

——— Holiday number. The christmas locket. [1870–71, nos. 1–2.] 2 v. 8°. *Boston, Roberts bros.* 1870–71.

Old (The) church door. Stories of Vinegar hill, v. 1. *See* **Warner** (Susan).

Old (An) country house. *London*, 1850. *See* **Grey** (*Mrs.* E. C.)

Old (The) farmer's almanack, for 1872. By Robert B. Thomas. No. 80. 8°. *Boston, Brewer & Tileston*, [1871].

Old (The) flag. [*anon.*] 368 pp. 3 pl. 16°. *Philadelphia, American sunday school union*, 1864.

Old friends. A remembrancer of beloved companions: and years bygone. [*anon.*] 328 pp. 12°. *New York, Bliss, Wadsworth & co.* 1835.

Old Haun, the pawnbroker, or the orphan's legacy. A tale of New York, founded on facts. [*anon.*] 463 pp. 1 pl. 12°. *New York, Livermore & Rudd*, 1857.

Old Nick. [*pseudon.*] *See* **Forgues** (Émile Dauran).

Old (The) parsonage, or recollections of a minister's daughter. 236 pp. 3 pl. 16°. *Philadelphia, Presbyterian board of publication*, [1863].

Oldoini (Agostino). Athenaevm avgvstvm, in qvo pervsinorvm scripta pvblice exponvntvr. 48 pp. 12 l. 355 pp. sm. 4°. *Pervsiae, typis & expensis L. Ciani*, 1678.

——— Athenaevm ligvsticvm, sev syllabvs scriptorvm ligvrvm nec non sarzanensivm, ac cyrnensivm reipvblicae genvensis svbditorvm. 1 p. l. 20, 623 pp. 4°. *Pervsiæ, apud hh. L. Ciani*, 1680.

——— Athenaevm romanvm, in qvo svmmorvm pontificvm ac psevdopontificvm, nec non s. r. e. cardinalivm et psevdocard. scripta publice exponuntur. 6 p. l. 679 pp. sm. 4°. *Pervsiae, apud hæredes S. Zechini*, 1676.

Oldshue (L. *m. d.*) Urino-pathology; or the uroscopian system of diagnosing diseases, by ocular inspection, chemical analysis, and microscopic examination of the urine. 264 pp. 1 chart. 8°. *Pittsburgh, A. A. Anderson & sons*, 1864.

Oliphant (*Mrs.* Margaret O. Wilson). Francis of Assisi. xxiv, 304 pp. 12°. [*London*], *Macmillan & co.* [1871].

[SUNDAY library].

Oliver (*Rev.* C. D.) St. Peter's chain of christian virtues. Edited by Thomas O. Summers, d. d. 216 pp. 18°. *Nashville (Tenn.) E. Stevenson & F. A. Owen*, 1857.

Oliver (George, *d. d.*) Y^e^ byrde of Gryme; an apologue. 2 p. l. iv, 282 pp. 12°. *Grimsby, A. Gait*, 1866.

Oliver (Stephen, *the younger*). Rambles in Northumberland, and on the scottish border; interspersed with brief notices of interesting events in border history. vi, 348 pp. 16°. *London, Chapman & Hall*, 1835.

Oliver Optic's almanac for our boys and girls. 1872. Containing calendars of the months, memorandum diary for every day in the year, valuable information concerning the seasons, a christmas story, by Oliver Optic. [*pseudon.* for W. T. Adams]. A thanksgiving story, by Elijah Kellogg. [etc.] 72 pp. 8°. *Boston, Lee & Shepard*, [1871].

Oliver Optic's magazine. Our boys and girls. [Weekly and monthly]. Oliver Optic, [*pseudon.*] editor. Jan. 1870, to Dec. 1871. v. 7–10 in 2 v. 8°. *Boston, Lee & Shepard*, [1870–71].

Olmsted (Denison, *ll. d.*) A compendium of natural philosophy, adapted to the use of schools and academies. Revised by E. S. Snell, ll. d. 296 pp. 12°. *New York, Clark & Maynard*, 1863.

Olmsted (Denison, *ll. d.*)—continued.
——— Letters on astronomy, addressed to a lady: in which the elements of the science are familiarly explained in connexion with its literary history. 419 pp. 1 pl. 12°. *Boston, Marsh, Capen, Lyon & Webb*, 1840.
——— Rudiments of natural philosophy and astronomy. 292 pp. 18°. *New Haven, S. Babcock*, 1844.

Olney (Edward). Elements of trigonometry, plain and spherical. 1 p. l. 113, 88 pp. 8°. *New York, Sheldon & co.* 1872.
——— A general geometry and calculus. 2 parts in 1 v. xxv, 202 pp; 1 p. l. 152 pp. 8°. *New York, Sheldon & co.* [1871].
[STODDARD series].

Olney (Jeremiah). A history of the United States, on a new plan; adapted to the capacity of youth. To which is added the constitution of the United States. 287 pp. 16°. *New-Haven, Durrie & Peck*, 1836.
——— A practical system of arithmetic, for the use of schools. vii, 13–252 pp. 16°. *Hartford, Canfield & Robins*, 1836.

Olshausen (Hermann). The last days of the Saviour, or history of the Lord's passion. From the german of Olshausen. 248 pp. 16°. *Boston, J. Munroe & co.* 1839.
——— Proof of the genuineness of the writings of the new testament: for intelligent readers of all classes. Translated from the german, with notes, by David Fosdick, jr. 216 pp. 12°. *Andover, Gould & Newman*, 1838.

Olshausen (Justus). Fragmens relatifs à la religion de Zoroastre, 1829. *See* **Mohl** (Jules) *and* **Olshausen.**

Olympia Morata. *See* **Smyth** (*Mrs.* Gillespie).

Omar: designed to illustrate the jewish history, from b. c. 63, to the birth of Christ. [*anon.*] 252 pp. 16°. *Philadelphia, American sunday-school union*, [1835].

On the frontier, or scenes in the west. [*anon.*] 320 pp. 18°. *Boston, Mass. sabbath school society*, [1864].

On the rock: a memoir of Alice B. Whitall. [*anon.*] 316 pp. 1 portrait. 12°. *Philadelphia, G. Maclean*, 1870.

Once a week. The young lady's own journal. March 4 to Nov. 4, 1871. v. 1–2. fol. [*New York, F. Leslie*, 1871].
[*Succeeded by* LESLIE'S (Frank) lady's journal].

One hour a week. By the author of "Jesus upon earth." [*anon.*] 252 pp. 4 pl. 12°. *New York, A. D. F. Randolph*, 1863.

Oneida circular. A weekly journal of home, science and general intelligence. Published by the Oneida and Wallingford communities. Jan. 2 to Dec. 25, 1871. v. 8. fol. *Oneida community*, [1871].

O'Neill, or the rebel. [A poem. *anon.*] viii, 140 pp. 8°. *London, H. Colburn*, 1827.

Onis (Luis de). Memoir upon the negotiations between Spain and the United States of America, which led to the treaty of 1819. With a statistical notice of that country. Accompanied with an appendix, containing important documents for the better illustration of the subject. Translated from the spanish, with notes, by Tobias Watkins. 152 pp. 8°. *Washington, E. De Krafft*, 1821.

Onpartydich discours opte handelinghe van de Indien. *See* **Usselincx** (Willem).

Ontario journal of education. *See* **Journal** of education for Ontario.

Opdyke (George). A treatise on political economy. viii, 339 pp. 1 l. 16°. *New York, proprietor*, 1851.

O'Pheilly (Dermot, *pseudon.*) The ants: a rhapsody. 2 v. in 1. 1 p. l. xl, 90 pp. 1 l. 3 pl; 1 p. l. 121 pp. 1 l. 1 pl. 16°. *London, L. Davis & C. Reymers*, [*etc.*] 1767.

Opitz (Heinrich). Atrium accentuationis scripturæ v. t. 2 p. l. 68 pp. sm. 4°. *Kiloni, sumptibus J. C. Meyeri*, 1684.
——— Atrium lingvae sanctæ, quo exhibentur 1. Consilivm de studio lingvæ s. 2. Grammaticæ hebr. compendivm ex hebraismo restituto. 3. Textvs cum praxi hebræo analytica. 4. Lexici hebræi compendivm. 5. Index. 4 p. l. 156 pp. 2 tab. sm. 4°. *Lipsiæ, sumtibus J. C. Meyeri*, 1710.
——— Chaldaismus targumico-talmudico-rabbinicus hebraismo harmonicus; targumim, talmude & rabbinorum scriptis illustratus. Ed. 3ª. Cui nunc auctarii loco accedit praxis analytica, & index copiosissimus anomalorum difficiliorum in Dan. Esra, targumim & rabbinis occurentium. 4 p. l. 196 pp. 3 tab. sm. 4°. *Kiloni, apud G. Liebezeit*, 1696.
[*With his* Atrium lingvæ sanctæ, 1710].
——— Syriasmus facilitati & integritati suæ restitutus, simulqve hebraismo et chaldaismo harmonicus, ac regulis qvinqvaginta absolutus. Exemplis & singularibus qvibusvis versionis syriacæ vet. & novi test. summo studio annotatis. Secunda vice multis in locis auctior editus. 4 p. l. 268 pp. 32 l. 3 tab. sm. 4°. *Lipsiæ, sumtibus J. C. Meyeri*, 1691.
[*With his* Atrium lingvæ sanctæ, 1710].

Oppianus. La chasse et La pêche, traduites par Belin de Ballu. 12°. [*Paris, Lefèvre,* 1841].

[*In* MARTIN (Louis Aimé). Petits poëmes grecs. *Paris,* 1841. pp. 327-506].

Orator (The): a treasury of english eloquence, containing selections from the most celebrated speeches of the past and present. Edited, with short explanatory notes and references, by a barrister. [*anon.*] viii, 288 pp. 8°. *London, S. O. Beeton,* 1855.

Orator's (The) own book. Compiled by the editor of Waldie's library. [*anon.*] 300 pp. 12°. *Philadelphia, Crissy, Waldie & co.* 1835.

O'Reilly (John, *m. d.*) The placenta, the organic nervous system, the blood, the oxygen, and the animal nervous system, physiologically examined. 204 pp. 1 pl. 8°. *New York, S. S. & W. Wood,* 1861.

Orelli (Johann Caspar von). Index editionum scriptorum M. Tullii Ciceronis [et] scripta Ciceronem illustrantia. 8°. [*Turici, typis Orellii,* 1836].

[*In* CICERO (M. T.) Opera, ed. Orellius, v. 6, pp. 193-477].

——— Onomasticon tullianum, varronianum, caesarianum, salustianum, asconianum et scholiastarum Ciceronis. 8°. [*Turici, typis Orellii,* 1838].

[CICERO (M. T.) Opera, ed. Orellius, v. 7].

——— *and* **Baiter** (Johann Georg). Onomasticon tullianum continens M. Tullii Ciceronis vitam, historiam litterariam, indicem geographicum et historicum, indicem legum et formularum, indicem graecolatinum, fastos consulares. 3 v. 8°. *Turici, typis Orellii, Fuesslini et sociorum,* 1836-38.

[*In* CICERO (M. T.) Opera, ed. Orellius, v. 6-8].

Original papers relating to the expedition to Carthagena. *See* **Vernon** (Edward.)

Orion. [*pseudon.*] *See* **Varela** (Hector F.)

Orlandi (Pellegrino Antonio). L'abcedario pittorico dall' autore ristampato, corretto, ed accresciuto di molti professori, e di altre notizie spettanti alla pittura, ed in quest' ultima impressione con nuova, e copiosa aggiunta di altri professori. [*anon.*] 4 p. l. 472 pp. 50 l. 4°. *Firenze, G. Ubaldi,* 1731.

Orme (*Rev.* William). The life of the rev. John Owen, d. d. Abridged from Orme's Life of Owen. [Also, The life of the rev. John Janeway. [*anon.* By James Janeway]. 224 pp. 18°. *Philadelphia, Presbyterian board of publication,* 1840.

——— Memoirs of John Urquhart. [Abridged]. 174 pp. 18°. *Philadelphia, American sunday school union,* 1832.

Orozco y Berra (Manuel). Materiales para una cartografia mexicana. Edicion de la sociedad de geografia y estadistica. xii, 337 pp. 1 l. fol. *México, imprenta del gobierno,* 1871.

Orr (*Mrs.* N.) De Witt's Connecticut cook book, and housekeeper's assistant. [Also], a large number of tried recipes for preserving, canning, and curing all sorts of vegetables and fruits, so as to retain their original flavor and appearance. 192 pp. 16°. *New York, R. M. De Witt,* [1871].

Orsato (Sertorio). Sertorii Ursati de notis romanorum commentarius, sive explicatio notarum et litterarum, quæ frequentius in antiquis lapidibus, marmoribus, et auctoribus, occurrunt. 2 p. l. 247 pp. 16°. *Hagæ-Comitum, J. Neaulme,* 1736.

Orsini (Mathieu). The flowers of heaven; or, the examples of the saints, proposed to the imitation of christians. Translated from the french. viii, 13-386 pp. 12°. *Baltimore, F. Lucas, jr.* 1841.

Ortiz de Zuñiga (Diego). *See* **Zuñiga.**

Orton (Edward). The geology of Highland county [Ohio]. 8°. [*Columbus,* 1871].

[OHIO (*State of*). *Geological survey,* 1870, part 3, pp. 253-309].

——— Report on geology of Montgomery county [Ohio]. 8°. [*Columbus,* 1871].

[OHIO (*State of*). *Geological survey,* 1869, part 3, pp. 143-171].

Orton (Hoy D.) Orton's lightning calculator, and accountant's assistant. Entirely new edition, with extensive modifications and improvements. vi, 9-194 pp. 1 portrait. 16°. *Philadelphia, Collins,* [1871].

Osborn (Henry S. *ll. d.*) Biblical tables. An epitome of various important statistics of the scriptures. A complete handbook of reference. 69 pp. 9 maps. 8°. *Philadelphia, Bible and publication society,* [1871].

——— The teacher's guide to Palestine. Prepared from the best and latest authorities, and from personal travels and examinations. 136 pp. 18°. *Philadelphia, J. C. Garrigues & co.* 1868.

Osborn (Laughton). Calvary—Virginia. Tragedies. 3 p. l. 200 pp. 12°. *New York, Doolady,* 1867.

O'Shaughnessy (Arthur W. E.) An epic of women and other poems. 2d ed. Eng. title, 229 pp. 1 pl. 16°. *London, J. C. Hotten,* 1871.

——— Lays of France. (Founded on the lays of Marie). 4 p. l. 294 pp. 1 l. 12°. *London, Ellis & Green,* 1872.

Osio (Luigi). Documenti diplomatici tratti dagli archivj milanesi. v. 1–2. 1864–70. *See* **Milan** (*Duchy of*).

Osmer (William). A treatise on the diseases and lameness of horses. In which is laid down a proper method of shoeing. [With] some new observations in the art of farriery, and on the nature and difference of horses. 3d ed. 2 p. l. 284 pp. 8°. *London, T. Waller*, 1766.

Ossian. Fingal, an ancient epic poem, in six books: together with several other poems, composed by Ossian the son of Fingal. Translated from the galic language, by James Macpherson. [1st ed.] 8 p. l. xvi, 270 pp. 4°. *London, T. Becket & P. A. De Hondt*, 1762.

——— The same. Translated into english heroic rhyme, by John Wodrow. 2 v. ciii, 120 pp; 1 p. l. 215 pp. 18°. *Edinburgh, author*, 1771.

——— The same. Ossian's Fingal; an ancient epic poem, in six books, rendered into english verse. By George Harvey. xvi, 246 pp. 8°. *London, A. J. Valpy for Cadell & Davies*, 1814.

——— The same. Phingalēis, sive Hibernia liberata, epicum Ossianis poema, e celtico sermone conversum, tribus praemissis disputationibus, et subsequentibus notis. Ab Alexandro Macdonald. 228 pp. 8°. *Edinburgh, J. Moir, à Laing*, 1820.

——— The poems of Ossian, translated from the galic language by James Macpherson, esq. and turned into blank verse, by the rev. Anthony Davidson. 4 p. l. 388 pp. 8°. *Salisbury, Brodie & Dowding*, [*about* 1810].

——— Sean dana. Ancient poems of Ossian, Orran, Ullin, etc. *See* **Smith** (John, *d. d.*)

——— The seventh book of Temora, an epic poem. First published in the original gaelic, and now translated literally [by Patrick Graham], with mr. Macpherson's translation annexed. To which are added notes and observations. 8°. [*Edinburgh, J. Ballantyne & co.* 1807].

[*In* GRAHAM (Patrick, *d. d.*) Essay on the authenticity of the poems of Ossian. *Edinburgh*, 1807. pp. 297–379].

Osterwald (Jean Frédéric). A compendium of christian theology. Newly translated into english, from the original latin. By the rev. John M'Mains. 400 pp. 1 l. 8°. *Hartford, N. Patten*, 1788.

——— A treatise concerning the causes of the present corruption of christians, and the remedies thereof. [*anon.* From the french]. 3d ed. 2 parts in 1 v. 480 pp. 8°. *London, D. Midwinter & B. Cowse*, 1711.

O'Sullivan (D.) Elegant extracts from the most celebrated british prose writers, [with] an introductory essay containing the observations of Swift, Johnson, Blair, sir Walter Scott, Hazlitt, etc. on the different kinds of prose composition; with biographical sketches and critical remarks. 2d ed. v. 1—prose. lviii, 758 pp. 12°. *Paris, Maire-Nyon*, 1832.

Otheman (Edward). The christian student. Memoir of Isaac Jennison, jr. Containing his biography, diary and letters. 271 pp. 16°. *New York, G. Lane & P. P. Sandford*, 1843.

Otis (George Alexander, *m. d.*) Surgical cases treated in the army of the United States from 1865 to 1871. *See* **United States.** *War department, surgeon general's office.*

Oudenarde (Nicholas Ægidius, *pseudon.*) *See* **Paulding** (James Kirke).

Ouida (*pseudon.*) *See* **De La Ramé** (Louise).

Our schoolday visitor. *See* **Schoolday** visitor magazine.

Our young folks. An illustrated [monthly] magazine for boys and girls. Edited by J. T. Trowbridge and Lucy Larcom. Jan. to Dec. 1871. v. 7. 8°. *Boston, J. R. Osgood & co.* 1871.

Outlines of history. *See* **Keightley** (Thomas).

Outlines of sacred history; from the creation of the world to the destruction of Jerusalem. With questions for examination. New ed. enlarged and improved. [*anon.*] 269 pp. 16°. *Philadelphia, Key & Biddle*, 1835.

Outrein (Johann d'). De clangore euangelii dissertationes xv. xx, 466 pp. 9 l. 16°. *Amstelodami, apud J. Boom*, 1714.

Overland (The) monthly. Devoted to the development of the country. Jan. to Dec. 1871. v. 6–7. 8°. *San Francisco, J. H. Carmany & co.* 1871.

Ovidius Naso (Publius). The epistles of Ovidius Naso, faithfully converted into a new measure of english verse. By John Jump. 2 p. l. xxvii, 218 pp. 12°. *London, Bell & Daldy*, 1857.

——— Métamorphoses d'Ovide, ornées de 138 gravures, d'après Sébastien Le Clerc; précédées de la vie d'Ovide et d'un abrégé de l'histoire poétique. 2 v. 1 p. l. xvii, 64 pp. 64 pl; 1 p. l. 75 pp. 65–138 pl. obl. 8°. *Paris, Cordier & Legras*, 1801.

[Plate 15 wanting].

Ovidius Naso (Publius)—continued.

——— A translation of the first book of Ovid's Tristia, in heroic english verse; with the original text. By Francis Arden. 1 p. l. 139 pp. 8°. *New York, C. S. Van Winkle,* 1821.

Owen (*Rev.* James). The history of images, and of image-worship: with a refutation of the second council of Nice, and of other advocates for idolatry. xii, 295 pp. 8°. *London, T. Parkhurst,* [*etc.*] 1709.

Owen (John, *of Carnarvonshire*). Epigrams. 16°. *London,* 1659.

[*In* PECK (Thomas). Parnassi puerperium, pp. 1–119].

Owen (John, *d. d.*) Eshcol: or rules of direction, for the walking of the saints in fellowship, according to the order of the gospel. 6th ed. 6 p. l. 120 pp. 24°. *London, J. Buckland,* 1764.

——— Φρονημα του πνευματος; or, the grace and duty of being spiritually minded, declared and practically improved. Abridged by Ebenezer Porter, d. d. xvi, 13–211 pp. 12°. *Boston, Peirce & Parker,* 1833.

——— Pvritano-iesvitismvs, the puritan tvrn'd jesuite; or rather, ovt-vying him in those diabolicall and dangerous positions, of the deposition of kings; from the yeare 1536. untill this present time. 3 p. l. 50 pp. sm. 4°. [*London*], *W. Sheares,* 1643.

——— Oweniana: or, select passages from the works of Owen. Arranged by Arthur Young. xii, 234 pp. 12°. *London, J. Hatchard,* 1817.

Owen (John Jason, *d. d.*). Commentary on the gospel of John. *See* **Bible.** (*English*).

Owen (Robert Dale). The debatable land between this world and the next, with illustrative narrations. 542 pp. 12°. *New York, G. W. Carleton & co.* 1872.

Owen (Mrs. T. J. V.) Mrs. Owen's Illinois cook book. 360 pp. 12°. *Springfield* (*Ill.*) *J. H. Johnson,* 1871.

P. (A. E.) The land of mystery; or scenes and incidents in Central Africa. [*anon.*] 196 pp. 18°. *Philadelphia, American sunday school union,* [1859].

P. (D. E. A.) Amenidades filosóficas, o discursos sobre todos los estados de esta vida, concluiendo en cada uno de ellos con una quarteta a manera de aforismo. [*anon.*] 3 p. l. 178 pp. 3 l. 16°. *Barcelona, A. Sastres,* 1804.

P. (H. A.) Jennie Wellington; or, the lost ring. 111 pp. 1 pl. 18°. *New-York, Gen. prot. episcopal s. s. union & ch. book society,* 1872.

P. (H. K.) *See* **Potwin** (*Mrs.* H. K.)

P. (J.) *See* **Poet's** (The) offering. 1842.

P. (Louisa Ellen). Julia Atherton's year at school. By Louisa Ellen [P. *anon.*] 198 pp. 18°. *New York, Carlton & Porter,* [1860].

P. (N.) *See* **Prince** (*Rev.* Nathan).

P. (W.) The counterfeit christian detected. *See* **Penn** (William).

P. (W.) 1675. *See* **Phillips** (William).

Pacettus (Dieghus). *See* **Pacheco** (Diego).

Pacheco *or* **Pacecchi** (Diego). Obedientia potentissimi Emanuelis Lusitaniæ regis etc. per clarissimum iuris. v. cōsultum Dieghum Pacettum oratorem ad Iulium ii. ponti. max. anno dñi. M. D. V. pridie no. Iunii. 4 l. unp. sm. 4°. [*Roma, Eucharius Silber*], 1505.

[*Note.*—Roman type, large, 28 lines to a page, without pagination, signatures, or catchwords].

Pachymeres (Georgius). Γεωργιου του Παχυμερη Ανδρονικος Παλαιολογος. Georgii Pachymeris Andronicus Palæologus sive historia rerum ab Andronico seniore in imperio gestarum usque ad annum ejus ætatis undequinquagesimum. E bibliotheca barberina interprete Petro Possino e soc. jesu. Accesserunt ejusdem, observationum libri tres. 2 p. l. 377 pp. 1 l. 134 pp. 13 l. fol. *Venetiis, ex typographia B. Javarina,* 1729.

[*With his* Michael Palæologus. 1729].

——— Γεωργιου του Παχυμερη Μιχαηλ Παλαιολογος. Georgii Pachymeris Michael Palæologus sive historia rerum a Michaele Palæologo ante imperium, & in imperio gestarum. Nunc primum edita ex bibliotheca barberina interprete Petro Possino e soc. jesu. Accesserunt ejusdem observationum lib. tres, & appendix: specimen sapientiæ Indorum veterum. 2 p. l. 291, 196 pp. 6 l. fol. *Venetiis, ex typographia B. Javarina,* 1729.

Pacific (The) coast almanac and year book of facts: compiled by Henry G. Langley. 1871–72. 2 v. 16°. *San Francisco, H. G. Langley,* 1871–72.

Pacifique [**de Provins**] (*Le père* —). Relation dv voyage de Perse. Ov̀ vous verrez les remarqves particulières de la terre saincte et des lieux où se sont opérez plusieurs miracles depuis la création du monde. Avec le testament de Mahomet. [*pseudon.*] 4 p. l. 416 [314] pp. 6 l. sm. 4°. *Paris, N. & I. de la Coste,* 1631.

Packard (Frederick A.) The teacher taught. An humble attempt to make the path of the sunday-school teacher straight and plain.

Packard (Frederick A.)—continued. [*anon.*] 396 pp. 1 pl. 16°. *Philadelphia, American sunday-school union,* [1839].

——— The same. [*anon.*] New ed. 446 pp. 12°. *Philadelphia, American sunday-school union,* [1861].

——— The teacher teaching; a practical view of the relations and duties of the sunday-school teacher. By the author of "The teacher taught." [*anon.*] 371 pp. 12°. *Philadelphia, American sunday-school union,* [1861].

Packard (John H. *m. d.*) A manual of minor surgery. 288 pp. 12°. *Philadelphia, J. B. Lippincott & co.* 1863.

Packard (*Rev.* Theophilus, *jr.*) A history of the churches and ministers, and of Franklin association, in Franklin county, Mass. and an appendix respecting the county. vii, 456 pp. 8°. *Boston, S. K. Whipple & co.* 1854.

Packard's monthly. Jan. to March, 1870. v. 3. 8°. *New York, S. S. Packard,* 1870.

[Succeeded by The phrenological journal and Packard's monthly. Discontinued].

Padmun (I. *jr.*) A layman's protest against the profane blasphemy, false charges, and illiberal invective of Thomas Paine, author of a book, entitled "The age of reason." viii, 241 pp. 12°. *London, author,* 1797.

Padua. (*Italy*). Imperiale reale osservatorio di Padova. *See* **Trettenero** (Virgilio).

Paeile (Ch.) Essai historique et critique sur l'invention de l'imprimerie. 286 pp. 1 lith. 8°. *Paris, Téchener,* 1859.

Paez (Ramon). Ambas Americas. Contrastes. Por R. P. (de Venezuela). ix, 368 pp. 7 l. 12°. *Nueva York, D. Appleton y ca.* 1872.

Page (J. W.) Uncle Robin, in his cabin in Virginia, and Tom without one in Boston. 299 pp. 1 pl. 12°. *Richmond (Va.) J. W. Randolph,* 1853.

Pagenstecher (Alexander Arnold). De jure virginum & virginis florentinæ. Ecloga. 4 p. l. 406 pp. 9 l. 18°. *Bremæ, apud P. G. Saurmann,* 1709.

Paige (Lucius Robinson, *d. d.*) Commentary on the new testament. *See* **Bible.** (*English*). *Gospels.*

——— Questions on select portions of the gospels. Designed for the use of sabbath schools and bible classes. 162 pp. 18°. *Boston, T. Whittemore,* 1838.

——— Selections from eminent commentators, who have believed in punishment after death; wherein they have agreed with universalists, in their interpretation of scriptures relating to punishment. 324 pp. 12°. *Boston, T. Whittemore,* 1833.

Paige (Lucius R. *d. d.*)—continued.

Paine (Martyn, *m. d.*) Physiology of the soul and instinct, as distinguished from materialism. With supplementary demonstrations of the divine communication of the narratives of the creation and the flood. 707 pp. 1 portrait. 8°. *New York, Harper & brothers,* 1872.

——— A therapeutical arrangement of the materia medica, or, the materia medica arranged upon physiological principles. 271 pp. 12°. *New York, J. & H. G. Langley,* 1842.

Paine (Susanna). Wait and see. 2 p. l. 400 pp. 12°. *Boston, J. Wilson & son,* 1860.

Pajon (Claude). Examen du livre, qui porte pour titre, Préjugéz légitimes contre les calvinistes [par Nicole], divisé en trois parties. 1 & 2 partie. 8 p. l. 342 pp. 18°. *La Haye, A. Leers,* 1683.

Palæopolitanus (Franciscus, *pseudon.*) *See* **More** (Henry).

Palæphatus. Παλαιφατου περι ἀπιστων ἱστοριων. Palæphati de incredibilibus historiis. [Græce et latine]. 8°. [*Amstelædami, apud H. Wetstenium,* 1688].

[*In* GALE (Thomas). Opuscula mythologica, pp. 1-66].

——— The same. Le cose incredibili di Palefato, tradotte ed illustrate da Giovanni Veludo. [Also, frammenti di Palefato tratti dalla cronica alessandrina ovvero pascale di Constantinopoli. Annotazioni]. xxiii, 76 pp. sm. fol. *Venezia, G. Cecchini & comp.* 1843.

Palafox y Mendoza (Juan, *obispo de la Puebla de los Angelos*). Cartas, y obras a todo fiel cristiano. [etc.] 4 p. l. 197 pp. 4°. *Madrid, A. Isilitago,* 1761.

——— The history of the conquest of China by the Tartars. Together with an account of several remarkable things, concerning the religion, manners, and customes of both nations, but especially of the latter. First writ in spanish, and now rendered english [from the french of Collé]. 12 p. l. 588 pp. 2 l. 16°. *London, W. Godbid for M. Pitt,* 1671.

——— Historia real sagrada. Lvz. de principes, y svbditos. Inivsticias qve intervinieron en la mverte de Christo bien nvestro. 44 p. l. 267 l. 1 portrait. fol. *Madrid, Maria de Quiñones,* 1661.

Palefato. *See* **Palæphatus.**

Palgrave (Robert Harry Inglis). The local taxation of Great Britain and Ireland. xii, 124 pp. 8°. *London, J. Murray,* 1871.

Palissot de Montenoy (Charles). Œuvres de m. Palissot. Nouvelle édition considérablement augmentée. 6 v. 8°. *Liége, C. Plomteux,* 1777.

CONTENTS.

v. 1. Mémoires sur la vie de l'auteur, rédigés par lui-même, p. x.
Ninus second, tragédie, p. xli.
Les tuteurs, comédie, p. 67.
Le barbier de Bagdad, comédie, p. 165.
Les méprises, ou le rival par ressemblance, comédie, pp. 223,
v. 2. Le cercle, ou les originaux, comédie, p. i.
Mémoires pour servir à une époque de notre histoire littéraire, p. 65.
Petites lettres sur des grands philosophes, p. 95.
Les philosophes, comédie, p. 151.
L'homme dangereux, comédie, p. 267.
Les courtisannes, comédie, p. 379.
v. 3. La dunciade, poëme, en dix chants. Avec des pièces relatives à La dunciade.
v. 4. Contenant les mémoires pour servir à l'histoire de notre littérature, depuis François premier jusqu'à nos jours.
v. 5. Histoire des premiers siècles de Rome, depuis sa fondation jusqu'à la république, p. 1.
Jugement de l'auteur de l'Année littéraire sur cette histoire, p. 207.
Mémoires historiques, littéraires et critiques, sur quelques écrivains de nos jours, p. 223.
Réponse de l'auteur à un détracteur du nécrologe, p. 318.
Lettre de l'auteur à un journaliste, p. 322.
v. 6. Divers mélanges.

Palladius, *bishop of Helenopolis*. Του Παλλαδιου, περι των της Ινδιας εθνων, και των Βραγμανων. Palladius de gentibus Indiæ, & Bragmanibus. 4°. [*Londini,* 1668].
[*In* BYSSHE (Ed.) Palladius [etc.] pp. 1–56].

Pall Mall (The) gazette. An evening newspaper and review. [Daily]. Jan. 1 to Dec. 30, 1871. v. 13–14 in 4 v. fol. *London,* [*F. Enoch*], 1871.

Palmer (Lynde, *pseudon.*) *See* **Peebles** (M. L.)

Palmer (*Mrs.* Phœbe). Incidental illustrations of the economy of salvation, its doctrines and duties. 380 pp. 1 portrait. 12°. *Boston, H. V. Degen,* 1855.

Palmer (Ray, *d. d.*) Hints on the formation of religious opinions. Addressed especially to young men and women of christian education. 324 pp. 12°. *New York, Sheldon & co.* 1860.

——— Spiritual improvement: or aid to growth in grace. A companion for the christian's closet. 239 pp. 12°. *Boston, Perkins & Marvin,* 1839.

Palmer (Walter C. *m. d.*) Life and letters of Leonidas L. Hamline, d. d. 12°. *New York,* 1866.

Palmer (*Rev.* William). A compendious ecclesiastical history, from the earliest period to the present time. With a preface and notes, by an american editor. ix, 232 pp. 2 l. 12°. *New York, Swords, Stanford & co.* 1841.

Palmieri (Matteo). Della vita civile trattato. xx, 296 pp. 1 portrait. 16°. *Milano, G. Silvestri,* 1825.

Pananti (Filippo). Avventure e osservazioni sopra le coste di Barberia. 2 v. 1 p. l. 318 pp. 3 l. 1 map; 2 p. l. 319–547, 127 pp. 3 l. 8°. *Firenze, L. Ciardetti,* 1817.

Panciroli (Guido). Raccolta breve d'alcvne cose piv segnalate c'hebbero gli antichi, e d'alcune altre trouate da moderni. Con l'aggiunta d'alcune considerationi curiose, & utili di Flavio Gvaltieri. 12 p. l. 444 pp. 8°. *Venetia, B. Giunti, G. B. Ciotti & comp.* 1612.

——— The same. The history of many memorable things lost, which were in use among the ancients: and an account of many excellent things found, now in use among the moderns, both natural and artificial. Now done into english, with remarks [etc.] from Salmuth's large annotations; with additions. 2 v. in 1. 7 p. l. 242 pp; pp. 259–452, 6 l. 16°. *London, J. Nicholson,* 1715.

Panckoucke *or* **Pancouke** (Charles Joseph). De l'homme, et de la réproduction des différens individus. Ouvrage qui peut servir d'introduction & de défense à l'histoire naturelle des animaux par m. de Buffon. [*anon.*] 1 p. l. viii, 214 pp. 16°. *Paris,* 1761.
[*Note.*—Dedicatory letter subscribed, in ms. "Ch. Pancouke"].

Pancouke. *See* **Panckoucke.**

Pannier (*Mme.* Sophie Tessier). L'athée. 2 v. 2 p. l. 400 pp; 2 p. l. 487 pp. 8°. *Paris, Fournier,* 1836.

Panorama (The) of wit. Exhibiting at one view the choicest epigrams in the english language. [*anon.*] 1 p. l. 357 pp. 18°. *London, J. Sharpe,* 1809.

Panormita (Antonius). *See* **Beccadelli** (Antonio).

Pansy. Helen Lester. By Pansy. [*pseudon.*] 132 pp. 2 pl. 18°. *Cincinnati, American reform tract and book society,* 1865.

——— Three people. By Pansy. [*pseudon.*] 412 pp. 2 pl. 12°. *Cincinnati, Western tract and book society,* 1871.

Pantaleon (Heinrich). Prosopographiæ herovm atque illvstrivm virorvm totivs Germaniæ [partes duæ] a condito mundo ad Maximilianum primum caesarem ipsumque annum

Pantaleon (Heinrich)—continued. Christi millesimum quingentesimum usque. Uiuis herovm imaginibus passim illustratvm. 2 v. in 1. 6 p. l. 291 pp. 6 l; 4 p. l. 480 pp. 6 l. fol. *Basileæ, in officina N. Brylingeri,* 1565.

[Imperfect: pages 133-140 wanting].

Panvinio (Onofrio). Tractatvs de sibyllis. 4°. [*Helmstadii,* 1673].

[*In* CLASEN (Daniel). De oraculis gentilium, pp. 801-824].

Papillon (David). The vanity of the lives and passions of men. 4 p. l. 414 pp. 16°. *London, R. White,* 1651.

Papini (Giovanni Antonio). Lezioni sopra il Burchiello. xxxiv, 236 pp. 1 portrait. 4°. *Firenze, B. Paperini,* 1733.

Parables and metaphors of the new testament: explained in a family manner, for the use of children, and particularly of sunday school scholars. [*anon.*] iv, 135 pp. 1 pl. sq. 16°. *New Haven, H. Howe & co.* 1836.

Paracelsus (Philipp Aureolus Theophrastus Bombast von Hohenheim, *or*). Astronomica et astrologica. Opuscula aliquot, jetzt erst in truck geben. 8 p. l. 235 pp. 4 l. 2 portraits. sm. 4°. *Cöln, Arnoldi Byrckmans erben,* 1567.

——— Of fevers. Of the jaundies. Of madness. Of diarrhæas, lientries, etc. 16°. *London, H. Hills,* 1697.

[*In* HEADRICH (John). Arcana philosophica, pp. 89-128].

——— Philosophiae ad Athenienses, drey bücher. Von vrsachen vnd cur epilepsiæ, das ist, des hinfallenden siechtagen, vor in truck nie aussgangen. Item, vom vrsprung cur oder heilung der contracten glidern. 103 l. sm. 4°. *Cöln, erben Arnoldi Byrckmans,* 1564.

[*With his* Astronomica et astrologica, 1567].

Paradin (Claude). Qvadrins historiqves d'Exode [Lévitique, Juges, etc. *anon.* Avec 122 gravures sur bois de Bernard Salomon, dit le petit Bernard]. 62 l. sm. 4°. *Lyon, I. de Tovrnes,* 1553.

[*Note.*—1st edition. Imperfect: lacking 2 l. and signatures h 1 and h 8].

Parallèle de la doctrine des payens avec celle des jésuites. *See* **Boyer** (François).

Pardee (R. G.) The sabbath school index. 256 pp. 16°. *Philadelphia, J. C. Garrigues & co.* 1868.

Pardigon (F.) Épisodes des journées de Juin, 1848. 222 pp. 12°. *Londres, Jeffs,* 1852.

Pare (William). Co-operative agriculture: a solution of the land question, as exemplified in the history of the Ralahine co-operative agricultural association, county Clare, Ireland. xxiv, 239 pp. 16°. *London, Longmans,* 1870.

Parent's (The) counsellor, or the dangers of moroseness: a narrative of the Newton family. [*anon.*] 188 pp. 18°. *Philadelphia, E. Bacon,* 1825.

Paris (John Ayrton, *m. d.*) A guide to the Mount's Bay and the Land's End; comprehending the topography, botany, agriculture, fisheries, antiquities, mining, mineralogy and geology of western Cornwall. 2d ed. [With] information for invalids. By a physician. [*anon.*] Eng. title, xix, 272 pp. 1 pl. 12°. *London, W. Phillips,* 1824.

Paris (Louis). Annales de la bibliothèque du roi. 16°. *Paris, au bureau du cabinet historique,* 1856.

[*In* LE PRINCE (N. T.) Essai historique sur la bibliothèque du roi, pp. 339-462].

Paris. (*Musée du Louvre*). Notice des émaux bijoux et objets divers exposés dans les galeries du musée du Louvre, [avec] documents et glossaire, par m. de Laborde. 2 v. 441 pp; xi, 552 pp. 12°. *Paris, Vinchon et Mourgues frères,* 1853-57.

——— ——— Notice des tableaux exposés dans les galeries du musée impérial du Louvre, par Frédéric Villot. 2e partie. Écoles allemande, flamande et hollandaise. 4e éd. viii, 345 pp. 12°. *Paris, Vinchon,* 1853.

——— (*Société des bibliophiles françois*). Mélanges de littérature et d'histoire. 1e et 2e partie. 12°. *Paris, société,* 1856-67.

CONTENTS.

1re partie. Notice sur mme. la vicomtesse de Noailles, [par A. L. S. de Noailles Standish], pp. 1-92.
Mémoire sur Pierre de Craon, pp. 93-132, 1 pl.
Conversation de la marquise de Pompadour et du président de Meinières, pp. 133-162.
Notice sur un évangéliaire byzantin, pp. 163-168.
Sur Germain Pillon, pp. 169-190.
Lettres de l'abbé Viguier, pp. 189-279.
Mémoires de Pajou et de Drouais pour mme. Dubarry, pp. 281-298.
Lettres du duc de Choiseul à m. Senac de Meilhan, pp. 299-304.
2e partie. Petite cronique françoise de l'an 1270 à l'an 1356. 2 p. l. 30 pp.
Des salons de Paris vers la fin du règne de Louis xiv. 3 p. l. 62 pp.
Notice sur un bibliophile émigré, par le prince Augustin Galitzin. 3 p. l. 21 pp.
Lettres et billets de Voltaire à l'époque de son retour de Prusse en France en 1753. viii, 31 pp.
Oraison funèbre de ma petite chienne.
Note sur la xxve nouvelle de la reine de Navarre. [Par J. Pichon]. 12 pp.
Le fauconier parfait. Par m. de Boissoudan. 2 p. l. xii, 72 pp.
Mémoire sur le vin de Champagne. 2 p. l. 114 pp. 1 l.
Chasses du roy. Par Mouret. xii, 2 pp. 7 l.

Parish hymns. A collection of hymns for public, social, and private worship. Selected and original. [*anon.*] 464 pp. 24°. *Philadelphia, Perkins & Purves*, 1843.

Park (John James). The dogmas of the constitution. Four lectures, being the first, tenth, eleventh, and thirteenth, of a course on the theory and practice of the constitution, delivered at King's college, London, in the commencement term of that institution. xxvi, 150 pp. 8°. *London, B. Fellowes*, 1832.

Park (John Ranicar, *m. d.*) A concise exposition of the Apocalypse, so far as the prophecies are fulfilled: to which are prefixed the history of christianity epitomised: and a vocabulary of symbols, with scriptural authority for their interpretation. 2d ed. xv, 89, vii, 108 pp. 8°. *London, J. Duncan*, 1825.

Park (Roswell, *d. d.*) Jerusalem; and other poems, juvenile and miscellaneous. With a brief memoir of mrs. Mary Brewster Park. 309, xv pp. 1 portrait. 12°. *New York, T. N. Stanford*, 1857.

Parke (*Col.* John). The lyric works of Horace, translated into english verse: [also], a number of original poems. By a native of America. [*anon.*] 3 parts (with title-pages) in 1 v. xli, 334 pp. 8 l. 1 pl. 8°. *Philadelphia, E. Oswald*, 1786.

CONTENTS.

The lyric works of Horace, etc. pp. 1-190.
Translations from the greek and latin, [Anacreon, Tibullus, Ovid, and Virgil], with original poems, pp. 191-334.
Virginia: a pastoral drama, on the birth-day of an illustrious personage and the return of peace, Feb. 11th, 1784, pp. 321-334.

Parker (B. S.) The lesson; and other poems. 156 pp. 1 l. 12°. *New Castle (Ind.) Pleas bros.* [1871].

Parker (Caroline E. R.) The old kitchen fire, and other poems. 96 pp. 1 col. pl. 18°. *New York, American tract society*, 1869.

Parker (Henry). The case of ship-mony briefly discoursed, according to the grounds of law, policy, and conscience. And most hvmbly presented to the censure and correction of the high court of parliament, Nov. 3, 1640. [*anon.*] 1 p. l. 49 pp. sm. 4°. [*London*], 1640.

Parker (Helen F.) Discoverers and pioneers of America. 416 pp. 5 pl. 12°. *New York, Derby & Jackson*, 1856.

Parker (Joel, *d. d.*) Courtship and marriage. Moral principles illustrated in their application to courtship and marriage. 179 pp. 16°. *Philadelphia, Perkins & Purves*, 1845.

Parker (Joel, *d. d.*)—continued.

——— Lectures on universalism. 192 pp. 12°. *New York, J. S. Taylor & co.* 1841.

——— *and* **Smith** (*Rev.* T. Ralston). The presbyterian's hand-book of the church. For the use of members, deacons, elders and ministers. 1 p. l. 250 pp. 16°. *New York, Harper & brothers*, 1861.

Parker (J. C. D.) Manual of harmony; being an elementary treatise on the principles of thorough bass, with an explanation of the system of notation. vii, 150 pp. 12°. *Boston, N. Richardson*, 1855.

Parker (*Mrs.* Jenny Marsh). Barley Wood; or, building on the rock. 320 pp. 16°. *New York, D. Dana*, 1860.

——— Dick Wortley; or choosing a profession. 149 pp. 3 pl. 18°. *New York, Gen. prot. episcopal s. s. union and ch. book society*, 1863.

Parker (L.) A key to the philosophy of memory, and a system of mental discipline, illustrated. 68, 62 pp. 1 l. 1 chart. 12°. *New York, Ferris & co.* 1859.

Parker (Richard Green). Aids to english composition. 20th ed. 6 p. l. 429 pp. 12°. *New York, Harper & brothers*, 1856.

——— The Boston school compendium of natural and experimental philosophy, embracing the elementary principles of mechanics, [etc.] 229 pp. 23 pl. 12°. *Boston, Marsh, Capen & Lyon*, 1837.

——— Plympton's Parker's philosophy. A school compendium of natural and experimental philosophy. Containing also a description of the steam and locomotive engines, and of the electro-magnetic telegraph. A new ed. revised and enlarged, by Geo. W. Plympton. vi, 17-466 pp. 12°. *New York, Collins & brother*, [1872].

——— Progressive exercises in english composition. Revised and enlarged, by James H. Hamilton, m. d. 240 pp. 12°. *Boston, R. S. Davis & co.* 1871.

——— Progressive exercises in rhetorical reading. 144 pp. 12°. *Boston, Crocker & Brewster*, 1835.

Parker (*Rev.* Theodore). Additional speeches, addresses, and occasional sermons. 2 v. xii, 435 pp; 2 p. l. 448 pp. 12°. *Boston, Little, Brown & co.* 1855.

——— The critical and miscellaneous writings of T. Parker. 3 p. l. 360 pp. 12°. *Boston, J. Munroe & co.* 1843.

Parker (*Rev.* Theodore)—continued.
——— A discourse of matters pertaining to religion. vii, 504 pp. 8°. *Boston, C. C. Little & J. Brown*, 1842.
——— Prayers. 1 p. l. 200 pp. 1 portrait. 16°. *Boston, Walker, Wise & co.* 1862.
——— Elemento servil. Estudo. 58 pp. 16°. *Rio de Janeiro, typ. da rua da Aguda*, 1871.

Parker (William H.) Remarks on the navigation of the coasts between San Francisco and Panama. vii, 47 pp. 1 tab. 8°. *New York, Slote & Janes*, 1871.

Parkes (*Mrs.* William). Domestic duties; or, instructions to young married ladies, on the management of their households and the regulation of their conduct in the various relations and duties of married life. 2d ed. x, 488 pp. 1 tab. 12°. *London, Longman, Hurst, Rees, Orme, Brown & Green*, 1825.

Parkman (Francis, *d. d.*) An offering of sympathy to the afflicted, especially to parents bereaved of their children. 2d ed. xvi, 268 pp. 16°. *Boston, Lilly, Wait, Colman & Holden*, 1833.
——— The same. 3d ed. with improvements. xvi, 268 pp. 16°. *Boston, S. Colman*, 1835.

Parks (*Rev.* Stephen). Methodist social hymn book. 377 pp. 24°. *New York, Carlton & Porter*, 1856.

Parlor lectures on the new testament. By the author of parlor lectures on scripture history. [*anon.*] 227 pp. 12°. *Augusta (Me.) Brinsmade & Dole*, 1832.

Parlor magic. [*anon.*] 175 pp. 1 pl. sq. 16°. *Philadelphia, H. Perkins*, 1838.

Parnell (Edward Andrew). A practical treatise on dyeing and calico-printing; including the latest inventions and improvements; also, a description of the origin, manufacture, uses, and chemical properties of the various animal and mineral substances employed in these arts. With an appendix. By an experienced dyer, assisted by several scientific gentlemen. [*anon.*] With a supplement, containing the most recent discoveries in color chemistry. By Robert Macfarlane. xxi, 729 pp. 10 pl. 8°. *New York, J. Wiley*, 1860.

Parnell (*Rev.* Thomas). Poems upon several occasions. Published by mr. Pope. [Also], the life of dr. Parnell. 200 pp. 16°. *London, J. Bell*, 1774.

Parr (Harriet). The life and death of Jeanne d'Arc, called the Maid. 2 v. vii, 278 pp. 1 portrait; 288 pp. 12°. *London, Smith, Elder & co.* 1866.

Parr (*Mrs.* L.) The blue bell of Red-neap, or Shingle Cord. A christmas story. By the author of "Dorothy Fox." [*anon.*] American ed. with notes and emendations by the american editor. 3 p. l. 250 pp. 16°. *New York, G. Routledge & sons*, 1871.
——— Dorothy Fox. By the author of "How it all happened," etc. [*anon.*] 163 pp. incl. 12 pl. 8°. *Philadelphia, J. B. Lippincott & co.* 1871.
——— The neap reef. 48 pp. 1 pl. 8°. [*London*], *Strahan & co.* [1871].
[Good cheer, the christmas number of Good words, 1871].

Parry (Charles Christopher, *m. d.*) Botany of the region along the route of the Kansas Pacific railway, through Kansas, Colorado, New Mexico, Arizona, and California. 8°. [*London*, 1870].
[*In* Bell (William A.) New tracks in North America, pp. 521–538].

Parry (*Rev.* John D.) The anthology: an annual reward book for youth. Consisting of amusing and instructive selections from the best authors. xii, 276 pp. 16°. *London, Whittaker, Treacher & co.* 1829.
——— An historical and descriptive account of the coast of Sussex. Forming also a guide to all the watering places. Eng. title, xii, 435 pp. 6 pl. 1 map. 8°. *Brighton, author*, 1833.
——— The legendary cabinet: a collection of british national ballads, ancient and modern; from the best authorities, with notes and illustrations. viii, 436 pp. 1 pl. 12°. *London, W. Joy*, 1829.

Parry (Joseph). Gwraig y meddwyn: (The gambler's wife). Can ddesgrifiadol newydd. (A descriptive ballad). Y geiriau cymraeg gan J. C. Hughes. Y geiriau saesonig, gan dr. Coates. 14 pp. 8°. *Wrexham (Wales), R. Hughes & son*, [1871].
——— Six anthems with english and welsh words.—Chwech o anthemau gyda geirau cymraeg a saesoneg. 33 l. 8°. *Wrexham (Wales), Hughes & son*, [1871].

Parsons (*Mrs.* Eliza Phelp). The errors of education. [A novel]. 3 v. 16°. *London, W. Lane*, 1791.

Parsons (*Rev.* Isaac). Memoir of the life and character of rev. Joseph Vaill, late pastor of the church of Christ in Hadlyme. 236 pp. 1 pl. 16°. *New York, Taylor & Dodd*, 1839.
——— Memoir of Susannah Elizabeth Bingham, of East Haddam, Conn. 90 pp. 18°. *Philadelphia, American sunday school union*, [1836].

Parsons (Lemuel H.) The grammatical reader. Being an introduction to an essay on english grammar. 107, 9 pp. 16°. *Philadelphia, W. Marshall & co.* 1836.

Parsons (Robert). A treatise concerning the broken succession of the crown of England: inculcated, about the later end of the reign of queen Elizabeth. Not impertinent for the better compleating of the general information intended. 167 pp. sm. 4°. *London*, 1655.

Parsons (Theophilus, *ll. d.*) Essays. Third series. 304 pp. 12°. *Boston, W. Carter & brother*, 1862.

Parsons (William Leonard, *d. d.*) Satan's devices, and the believer's victory. 312 pp. 12°. *Boston, author*, 1864.

Partenio (Bernardino). De poetica imitatione libri qvinqve. 160 l. numb. 4 l. sm. 4°. *Venetiis, apud L. Auancium*, 1565.

[*Note.*—It is probable that this writer's family-name was Franceschini. He called himself Spilimbergius, from his birth-place, Spilimbergo, in Friuli].

Partheneia sacra, 1633. *See* **Hawkins** (Henry).

Parton (James). Life of Andrew Jackson, condensed from the author's "Life of Andrew Jackson," in three volumes. 479 pp. 1 portrait. 8°. *New York, Mason brothers*, 1863.

——— Topics of the time. 2 p. l. 401 pp. 12°. *Boston, J. R. Osgood & co.* 1871.

——— Triumphs of enterprise, ingenuity, and public spirit. 677 pp. 7 pl. 5 portraits. 8°. *Hartford (Conn.) A. S. Hale & co.* 1871.

Parton (*Mrs.* Sara Willis). Fresh leaves. By Fanny Fern. [*pseudon.*] 336 pp. 18°. *New York, Mason brothers*, 1857.

——— A new story book for children. By Fanny Fern. [*pseudon.*] 310 pp. 7 pl. 12°. *New York, Mason brothers*, 1864.

——— The play-day book: new stories for little folks. By Fanny Fern. [*pseudon.*] 286 pp. 10 pl. 16°. *New York, Mason brothers*, 1857.

——— Rose Clark. By Fanny Fern. [*pseudon.*] 417 pp. 12°. *New York, Mason brothers*, 1856.

Paruta (Paolo). Historia vinetiana. 2 v. 2 p. l. 596 pp. 15 l; 232 pp. 8 l. 4°. *Vinetia, per gli heredi di T. Giunti & F. Baba*, 1645.

Pascal Lacroix (Jean). Rapport sur la bibliographie cambrésienne, ouvrage envoyé au concours en 1822. 107–123 pp. 12°. [*Cambrai*, 1822].

[Extract].

Paschal (George Washington). Ninety-four years. Agnes Paschal. 361 pp. 2 fac-similes. 12°. [*Washington, M'Gill & Witherow*], 1871.

Pasor (Georg). Alphabetum græcorum poetarum. Sive sententiæ illustres ex poëtis græcis juxta ordinem alphabeti collectæ. [Græce et latine]. 110 pp. 16°. *Herbornæ Nassoviorum*, 1620.

Passages in the maiden and married life of Rose Bryant. [*anon.*] 162 pp. 18°. *Philadelphia, American sunday-school union*, [1864].

Passerat (Jean). Encomivm asini. 18°. [*Lugd. Batavorum*, 1644].

[*In* DISSERTATIONVM ludicrarvm et amœnitatvm scriptores varij, pp. 259–269].

Passi (Pietro). Della magic' arte ouero della magia natvrale discorso. 15 p. l. 116 pp. 9 l. 16°. *Venetia, G. Violati*, 1614.

Passing thoughts for the older pupils. By a sabbath-school teacher. [*anon.*] 144 pp. 18°. *Boston, Massachusetts sabbath school society*, [1853].

Passions (The) personify'd, in familiar fables. [*anon.*] 1 p. l. vi, 104 pp. 14 pl. 8°. *London, J. Whiston*, [1773].

Pastor (The); a poem. [*anon.*] xvi, 500 pp. 16°. *New-York, F & R. Lockwood*, 1821.

Pastoret (Claude Emmanuel Joseph Pierre, *marquis* de). Moyse, considéré comme législateur et comme moraliste. 2 p. l. 599 pp. 12°. *Paris, Boisson*, 1788.

Pastor's (The) bible class, or familiar conversations concerning the sacred mountains. [*anon.*] 214 pp. 3 pl. 18°. *Philadelphia, Presbyterian board of publication*, [1863].

Pastor's (The) fireside. 1822. *See* **Porter** (*Miss* Jane).

Pastor's (The) gift to the awakened sinner, and the young convert. [*anon.*] 197 pp. 18°. *Pittsburgh, L. Loomis*, 1835.

Pastor's (A) jottings; or, striking scenes during a ministry of thirty-five years. [*anon.*] 348 pp. 6 pl. 12°. *New-York, American tract society*, [1864].

Paterculus (C. Velleius). Velleius Paterculus, his romaine historie: in two bookes. Exactly translated out of the latine edition supervised by Ianus Gruterus. And rendred english by sr. Robert Le Grys. 8 p. l. 431 pp. 24°. *London, M. F. for R. Swaine*, 1632.

Pater-familias's diary of everbody's tour: Belgium and the Rhine, Munich, Switzerland, Milan, Geneva and Paris. [*anon.*] 2 p. l. 385 pp. 1 pl. 16°. *London, T. Hatchard*, 1856.

Paterson (James). A complete commentary, with etymological, explanatory, critical and classical notes on Milton's Paradise lost. 2 p. l. 512 pp. 16°. *London, R. Walker*, 1743.

Paterson (Samuel). An entertaining journey to the Netherlands; with the forms of travelling from place to place, and the author's adventures: the whole written in the manner and stile of the late mr. Laurence Sterne. By Coriat junior. [*pseudon.*] 3 v. 16°. *London, W. Smith*, 1782.

Paterson (*N. J.*) Boyd's Paterson directory, 1871-72. Together with a large appendix of societies, institutions, United States, state, county and city authorities, etc. [By] Andrew Boyd. 8°. *Paterson (N. J.) A. Boyd*, 1871.

Path (The) of the pilgrim church, from its origin in England to its establishment in New England. An historical sketch. [*anon.*] 267 pp. 4 pl. 16°. *Boston, Mass. sabbath school society*, [1862].

Patrici. *See* **Patrizzi.**

Patrick (*Mrs.* Mary A.) The mourner's gift. 192 pp. 32°. *New York, Van Nostrand & Dwight*, 1837.

Patrick (Symon, *d. d.*) The book of Job paraphras'd. *See* **Bible.** (*English*). *Job.*

Patrizzi (Francesco). La deca disputata. Nelle qvale, e per istoria, e per ragioni, e per autorità de' grandi antichi; si mostra la falsità delle più credute vere opinioni, che di poetica, à di nostri vanno intorno. Et vi è aggiunto il Trimerone del medesimo, in risposta alle opposizioni fatte dal signor Torqvato Tasso. 4 p. l. 250 pp. 3 l. 4°. *Ferrara, V. Baldini*, 1586.

[*With his* La deca istoriale, 1586].

——— La deca istoriale, nella qvale, con dilettevole antica nouità, oltre à poeti, e lor poemi innumerabili, che ui si contano: si fan palesi, tutte le cose compagni, e seguaci dell' antiche poesie. 32 p. l. 407 pp. 4°. *Ferrara, V. Baldini*, 1586.

——— Magia philosophica, hoc est Zoroaster. & eius 320. oracula chaldaica. Asclepii dialogus. & philosophia magna. Hermetis trismegisti. Jam nunc primum ex biblioteca ranzoviana e tenebris eruta & latine reddita. 1 p. l. 253 l. 2 l. unp. 18°. *Hambvrgi*, 1593.

——— Paralleli militari. Ne' quali si fa paragone delle milizie antiche, in tutte le parti loro, con le moderne. 2 parts in 1 v. 6 p. l. 261 pp; 2 p. l. 466 pp. 5 l. 18 pl. fol. *Roma, L. Zannetti & G. Facciotto*, 1594-5.

Patten (William, *d. d.*) Memoirs of mrs. Ruth Patten, of Hartford, Conn. with letters and incidental subjects. 148 pp. 1 pl. 12°. *Hartford, P. Canfield*, 1834.

Patterson (John). Memoir of Joseph Train, the antiquarian correspondent of sir Walter Scott. vii, 194 pp. 16°. *Glasgow, T. Murray*, 1857.

Patterson (Lawson B.) Twelve years in the mines of California; embracing a general view of the gold region, with practical observations on hill, placer and quartz diggings; and notes on the origin of gold deposits. 108 pp. 16°. *Cambridge, [Ms.] Miles & Dillingham*, 1862.

Patterson (Robert). Fables of infidelity, and facts of faith. A series of tracts on the absurdity of atheism, pantheism, and rationalism. [3d ed.] 316 pp. 12°. *Cincinnati, American reform tract and book society*, 1860.

Pattison (Robert Everett, *d. d.*) Commentary on Ephesians. *See* **Bible.** (*English*).

Patton (*Rev.* Alfred S.) The losing and taking of Mansoul. 286 pp. 8 pl. 12°. *New York, Sheldon & co.* 1859.

Patton (William, *d. d.*) The christian psalmist. *See* **Hastings** (Thomas) *and* **Patton.**

——— Cottage bible. *Hartford*, 1862. Cottage polyglott testament; with notes. *New York*, 1860. Village testament. *New York*, 1861. *See* **Bible.** (*English*).

Paul *or* **Paule** (*Sir* George). The life of the most reverend and religiovs prelate, John Whitgift, lord archbishop of Canterbury. 3 p. l. 94 pp. sm. 4°. *London, T. Snodham*, 1612.

Paulding (James Kirke). The book of saint Nicholas. Translated from the original dutch of dominie Nicholas Ægidius Oudenarde. [*pseudon.*] 237 pp. 12°. *New-York, Harper & brothers*, 1836.

[*Note.*—Paulding's works, v. 14].

Paule. *See* **Paul.**

Pauli (Jeronimo). Barcino. 16°. *Coloniae Agrippinae, ex officina birckmannica*, 1602.

[*In* MYLIUS (Arnold). De rebvs hispanicis, pp. 115-137].

——— De flvminibvs et montibvs Hispaniae. 16°. *Coloniae Agrippinae, ex officina birckmannica*, 1602.

[*In* MYLIUS (Arnold). De rebvs hispanicis, pp. 96-114].

Pauli. *See* **Paulli.**

Paulinus *nolanus* (*S.* Meropius Pontius Anicius). Poema ultimum adversus paganos.

Paulinus *nolanus* (*S.* M. P. A.)—continued. Recensuit F. Oehler. 12°. *Lipsiae, B. Tauchnitz, jun.* 1847.

[*In* GERSDORF (E. G.) Bibliotheca patrum ecclesiasticorum latinorum selecta, v. 13, pp. 121-132].

——— Rule of christian life. The epistle to Celantia. 16°. [*London*, 1814].

[*In* PENN (Granville). The bioscope, or dial of life, explained, pp. 175-232].

Paulli (Simon). Historia literaria, sive dispositio librorum omnium facultatum ac artium, secundum materias, in vsum philobiblorum congesta. 8 p. l. 182 pp. 27 l. 12°. *Argentorati, sumptibus auctoris*, 1671.

——— A treatise on tobacco, tea, coffee, and chocolate. Written originally [in latin]; and now translated by dr. James. 2 p. l. 171 pp. 2 pl. 8°. *London, T. Osborne*, [*etc.*] 1746.

Paullini (Christian Franz). Cynographia curiosa seu canis descriptio, et mantissa curiosa ejusdem argumenti complectente Joh. Caii libell. de canibus britannicis, et Joh. Henr. Meibom. epist, de κυνοφορα, aucta. 25 p. l. 258 pp. 8 l. 1 pl. 4°. *Norimbergæ, sumtibus J. G. Endteri*, 1685.

Paulus *ægineta*. De facvltatibvs alimentorvm, Albano Torino interprete. 16°. *Lvgdvni*, 1541.

[*In* THORER (Albanus). [Selecta], pp. 106-124].

Paulus (Hieronymus). *See* **Pauli** (Jeronimo).

Pauw (Jan Cornelis van). Animadversiones in Hephæstionis enchiridion et scholia. 4°. [*Trajecti ad Rhenum, apud M. L. Charlois*, 1726].

[*In* HEPHÆSTION. Enchiridion de metris et poemate, pp. 99-188].

Pavillon (Étienne). The lady's preceptor in the affair of love; with the picture of a true lover. In three letters. Translated from the french of m. Pavilion, by Clarinda. 28 pp. 8°. *London, J. Robinson*, [*about* 1750].

[*With* ANCOURT (*Abbé* d'). The lady's preceptor, 1743].

Pavillon (Nicolas). Lettre à messire Hardouyn Perefixe, sur la signature du formulaire. 8°. [*Cologne, P. Marteau*, 1683].

[*In* NICOLE (Pierre). Les imaginaires, et les visionnaires. *Cologne*, 1683, pp. 684-96].

Paxton (*Rev.* George). The villager, with other poems. 4 p. l. 360 pp. 12°. *Edinburgh, T. Turnbull*, 1813.

Paxton (*Rev.* J. D.) Letters from Palestine: written during a residence there in the years 1836, 7, and 8. 2 p. l. 263 pp. 12°. *London, C. Tilt*, 1839.

Payn (James). The Bateman household. Reprinted from "Chambers' journal." vii, 305 pp. 12°. *London, A. Hall, Virtue & co.* 1860.

Payne (John). An epitome of history; or, a concise view of the most important revolutions and events, which are recorded in the histories of the principal empires, kingdoms, states, and republics, now subsisting in the world. 2 v. vi, 429 pp. 1 pl; 2 p. l. 536 pp. 8°. *London, J. Johnson*, 1795.

[*Note.*—v. 1, 2d ed. enlarged].

Payne (Joseph). Studies in english poetry: with short biographical sketches, and notes explanatory and critical. 4th ed. xii, 467 pp. 12°. *London, A. Hall, Virtue & co.* 1859.

Paynel (Thomas). The piththy and moost notable sayinges of al scripture, gathered by Thomas Paynel, after the manner of commō places, newlye augmeted and corrected. *b. l.* 2 v. in 1. 121 l. numb. 15 l; 88 l. numb. 13 l. 24°. *London, W. Copland*, 1560.

Payson (Aurin M.) *and* **Laighton** (Albert). The poets of Portsmouth [New Hampshire]. xx, 405 pp. 8°. *Boston, Walker, Wise & co.* 1865.

Payson (Edward, *d. d.*) Selections from conversations and unpublished writings. 2d ed. 192 pp. 1 pl. 32°. *Boston, Crocker & Brewster*, 1834.

——— Sermons. Edited by Asa Cummings, d. d. 2 v. xvi, 13-608 pp; 608 pp. 8°. *Portland, Hyde & Lord*, 1849.

——— Sermons for christian families, on the most important relative duties. 284 pp. 16°. *Boston, Crocker & Brewster*, 1832.

Paz Soldan (Mateo). Geografia del Peru, obra posthuma del d. d. Mateo Paz Soldan, corregida y aumentada por su hermano, Mariano Felipe Paz Soldan. Publicada a expensas del gobierno peruano. v. 1. 2 p. l. cxxvii, 746 pp. 1 portrait. 8°. *Paris, F. Didot hermanos, hijos y ca.* 1862.

Peabody (Andrew Preston, *d. d.*) Christianity the religion of nature. Lectures delivered before the Lowell institute. 256 pp. 12°. *Boston, Gould & Lincoln*, 1864.

Peabody (*Rev.* David). The patriarch of Hebron: or the history of Abraham. 228 pp. 18°. *New York, J. C. Meeks*, 1841.

Peabody (Joel R. *pseudon.*) A world of wonders; or divers developements, showing the thorough triumph of animal magnetism in New-England. 158 pp. 8 pl. 16°. *Boston, Robert S. Davis*, 1838.

Peabody (William Bourne Oliver, *d. d.*) The Springfield collection of hymns for sacred worship. xvi, 354 pp. 16°. *Springfield, S. Bowles*, 1835.

Peacham (Henry). The period of mourning, disposed into sixe visions. In memorie of the late prince. Together with nuptiall hymnes, in honour of this happy marriage betweene the great princes, Frederick, count palatine of the Rhene, and the most excellent, Elizabeth, onely daughter to our soueraigne, his majestie. Also the manner of the solemnization of the marriage at White-Hall, on the 14. of February. London, J. Helme, 1613. 52 pp. 8°. *London, reprinted for the editor*, 1789.

[*In* WALDRON (F. G.) Literary museum. *London*, 1792].

Peacock (Francis). Sketches relative to the history and theory, but more especially to the practice of dancing, [etc.] 224 pp. 8°. *Aberdeen, J. Chalmers & co.* 1805.

Peacocke (James S. *m. d.*) The creole orphans; or, lights and shadows of southern life. A tale of Louisiana. 365 pp. 12°. *New York, Derby & Jackson*, 1856.

Pearce. *See* **Pearse, Peirce,** *and* **Pierce.**

Pearl (*Rev.* Cyril). Youth's book on the mind, embracing the outlines of the intellect, the sensibilities, and the will: introductory to the study of mental philosophy. 1 p. l. 156 pp. 12°. *Portland, W. Hyde*, 1842.

Pearls of eloquence, or, the school of complements. [*anon.*] 4th ed. 5 p. l. 143 pp. 1 pl. 18°. *London, by T. L.* 1658.

Pearse (James). A narrative of the life of James Pearse, in two parts. Written by himself. 144 pp. 12°. *Rutland,* [*Vt.*] *author*, 1825.

Pearson (*Rev.* Abel). An analysis of the principles of the divine government, in a series of conversations, and also conversations on some other interesting subjects, particularly relating to the same principles, between A. P. and N. P. and a dissertation on the prophecies, in reference to the rise and fall of the beast, [etc.] xii, 419 pp. 8°. *Athens* (*Tenn.*) *T. A. Anderson*, 1833.

Pearson (Emily C.) Gutenberg, and the art of printing. 1 p. l. vi, 292 pp. 13 pl. 12°. *Boston, Noyes, Holmes & co.* 1871.

Pease (E.) The youth's music lamp, and american school song book. 160 pp. obl. 12°. *Cincinnati, Moore, Anderson, Wilstach & Keys*, 1854.

Peck (Francis). New memoirs of the life and poetical works of mr. John Milton: with 1. An examination of Milton's stile. 2. Explanatory & critical notes on divers passages of Milton & Shakespeare: by the editor. 3. Baptistes: a sacred dramatic poem, written in latin by George Buchanan; translated into english, by John Milton; & first published in 1641. 4. The parallel, or archbishop Laud & cardinal Wolsey compared: a vision, by Milton. 5. The legend of sir Nicholas Throckmorton, an historical poem: by sir Thomas Throckmorton. 6. Herod the great: a poem: by the editor. 7. The resurrection, a poem in imitation of Milton: by a friend. 8. A discourse on the harmony of the spheres: by Milton. With prefaces and notes by F. Peck. xii, 551 pp. 1 pl. 4°. *London*, 1740.

[Wanting 1 portrait of Milton].

Peck (George, *d. d.*) Appeal from tradition to scripture and common sense; or, an answer to the question, What constitutes the divine rule of faith and practice? 472 pp. 12°. *New York, G. Lane & P. P. Sandford*, 1844.

——— Formation of a manly character: a series of lectures to young men. 304 pp. 16°. *New York, Carlton & Phillips*, 1853.

——— The scripture doctrine of christian perfection stated and defended: with a critical and historical examination of the controversy, both ancient and modern. Also practical illustrations and advices. In a series of lectures. 474 pp. 12°. *New York, G. Lane & P. P. Sandford*, 1842.

——— The same. Abridged from the author's large work. 332 pp. 18°. *New York, Lane & Tippett*, 1845.

Peck (J. L.) Dress and care of the feet: showing their natural perfect shape and construction; their present deformed condition; and how flat-foot, distorted toes, and other defects are to be prevented and corrected; [etc. *anon.*] 202 pp. 12°. *New York, S. R. Wells*, 1871.

Peck *or* **Pecke** (Thomas). Parnassi puerperium: or, some well-wishes to ingenuity, in the translation of six hundred, of Owen's epigrams; Martial de spectaculis, or of rarities to be seen in Rome; and the most select, in sir Tho. More. To which is annext a century of heroick epigrams, (sixty whereof concern the twelve Caesars; and the forty remaining, several deserving persons.) 4 p. l. 184 pp. 5 l. 16°. *London, T. Bassett*, 1659.

Peck (William G. *ll. d.*) Elementary treatise on mechanics, for the use of colleges and schools of science. 296 pp. 12°. *New York, A. S. Barnes & co.* 1870.

Peebles (*Mrs.* Mary L.) The magnet stories. Drifting and steering. By Lynde Palmer. [*pseudon.*] 275 pp. 16°. *Troy (N. Y.) Moore & Nims*, 1867.

Peep (A) at my neighbours; or the houses in Kingston court turned inside out. [*anon.*] 1 p. l. 158 pp. 18°. *Philadelphia, American sunday school union*, [1843].

Peet (Harvey Prindle, *ll. d.*) History of the United States of America. 423 pp. 12°. *New York, Egbert, Bourne & co.* 1869.

Peiffer (David). Lipsia, seu originum lipsiensium libri iv. Cum qvibusdam additamentis, curante Adamo Rechenberg. Eng. title, 31 p. l. 516 pp. 11 l. 12°. *Martisburgi, apud R. Wæchtler*, 1689.

Peignot (Étienne Gabriel). Bibliothèque choisie des classiques latins, considérés sous le rapport historique, analytique, philologique, et bibliographique, précédée de l'histoire de la langue latine. Plan de l'ouvrage. 1 p. l. 83 pp. 2 fac-similes. 8°. *Paris, A. A. Renouard*, 1813.

Peirce (Benjamin, *ll. d.*) An elementary treatise on algebra: to which are added exponential equations and logarithms. xii, 276 pp. 12°. *Boston, J. Munroe & co.* 1837.

——— An elementary treatise on plane and spherical trigonometry. Revised ed. viii, 359 pp. 6 pl. 8°. *Boston and Cambridge, J. Munroe & co.* 1861.

Peirce (*Rev.* Bradford Kinney). Life in the woods; or, the adventures of Audubon. 252 pp. 18°. *New York, Carleton & Porter*, [1864].

Peirce (*Rev.* James). Paraphrase and notes on Colossians, Philippians, and Hebrews. *See* **Bible.** (*English.*)

Peirce. *See* **Pearse** *and* **Pierce.**

Peirson (Lydia Jane Wheeler). Forest leaves. 264 pp. 12°. *Philadelphia, Lindsay & Blakiston*, 1845.

Peixotto (Simha C.) Elementary introduction to the scriptures, for the use of hebrew children. 196 pp. 18°. *Philadelphia, Haswell, Barrington & Haswell*, 5600, [1840].

Pelaez (Francisco de Paula Garcia). Memorias para la historia del antiguo reyno de Guatemala. v. 1 and 3. 8°. *Guatemala, L. Luna*, 1851. s.
[v. 2 wanting].

Pélée de Chenouteau (Blaise Louis). Esprit des meilleurs écrivains françois; ou recueil de pensées les plus ingénieuses, tant en prose qu'en vers, tirées de leurs ouvrages, et rangées par ordre alphabétique. [*anon.*] 2 v. viii, 543 pp; 1 p. l. 578 pp. 1 l. 8°. *Paris, Nyon, aîné*, 1777.

Pellegrini (Giuseppe). Poesie dell' avvocato Giuseppe Pellegrini. 186 pp. 2 l. 16°. *Firenze, V. Batelli & figli*, 1835.

Pellegrino *or* **Pellegrini** (Camillo, *the elder*). Il Carrafa o vero della epica poesia dialogo. 2 p. l. 126–174 pp. 1 l. 16°. *Firenze, Sermartelli*, 1584.

Pellet (The). A [daily] record of the Massachusetts homœopathic hospital fair. Thomas B. Aldrich [and others], editors. April 15–27, 1872. nos. 1–10. 8°. *Boston, the fair*, 1872.
[No more published].

Pelli (Giuseppe). Memorie per servire alla vita di Dante Alighieri ed alla storia della sua famiglia. 2ª ed. notabilmente accresciuta. 2 p. l. 218 pp. 1 l. 1 portrait, 3 pl. 8°. *Firenze, G. Piatti*, 1823.

Pellicer (Juan Antonio). Discurso sobre varias antiguedades de Madrid: y origen de sus parroquias, especialmente de la de San Miguel. Con algunas reflexiones sobre la disertacion historica publicada por el doctor don Manuel Rosell acerca de la aparicion de san Isidro labrador al rey don Alonso viii. 2 p. l. 136 pp. 8°. *Madrid, Sancha*, 1791.

——— Ensayo de una bibliotheca de traductores españoles, donde se da noticia de las traducciones que hay en castellano de la sagrada escritura, santos padres, filosofos, historiadores, medicos, oradores, poetas, asi griegos como latinos; y de otros autores que han florecido antes de la invencion de la imprenta. Preceden varias noticias literarias para las vidas de otros escritores españoles. 2 parts in 1 v. 8 p. l. 206 pp; 1 l. 175 pp. 4°. *Madrid, A. De Sancha*, 1778.

Pellico (Silvio). Œuvres de S. Pellico. Mes prisons, suivies des devoirs des hommes. Traduction de m. Antoine de Latour. 6ᵉ éd. revue et corrigée, avec des chapitres inédits, des notes de Maroncelli, et des études littéraires ou biographiques sur les prisonniers du Spielberg. 1 p. l. 495 pp. 1 l. 12°. *Paris, Charpentier*, 1840.

Pellisson (Paul). Lettres historiques. [1670–1688]. 3 v. 16°. *Paris, J. L. Nyon*, 1729.

Pelsart (François). Ongeluckige voyagie van't schip Batavia nae Oost-Indien. Vervattende de grouwelijcke moorderyen onder 't scheeps-volck op 't eylandt Bataviaes kerckhoff. 1628–29. [Met diversche] discourssen. 1 p. l. 40 pp. 11 l. 6 pl. (on 1 sheet). sm. 4°. *Amsterdam, J. Hartgers*, 1648.

[*In* HARTGERTS (J.) Oost-indische voyagien, v. 1, 11e stuck].

Pelton (William T.) Creosoting. Process of Seely. Preservation of timber from decay and the attacks of marine worms. European reports. American reports. 1 p. l. 76 pp. 8°. *New York*, 1870. S.

Peluso (Francesco). Il gelso e la sua coltivazione teoricamente e praticamente esposta agli agricoltori. 157 pp. 1 l. 8°. *Milano, P. I. di Patronato*, 1866. S.

Pemble (William). Short exposition vpon Zachary. *See* **Bible**. (*English*).

Pembroke (Henry Herbert, *earl of*). *See* **Herbert** (Henry, *earl of Pembroke*).

Pendleton (William N. *d. d.*) Science a witness for the bible. 350 pp. 12°. *Philadelphia, J. B. Lippincott & co.* 1860.

Pène (Henri de). Un mois en Allemagne. Nauheim. 353 pp. 2 l. 12°. *Paris, A. Bourdilliat & cie.* 1859.

Penhoën (A. T. A. Barchou de). *See* **Barchou de Penhoën.**

Penn (Granville). The bioscope, or dial of life, explained. [Also], a translation of st. Paulinus's epistle to Celantia, on the rule of christian life; and an elementary view of general chronology. 2d ed. Eng. title, vi, 309 pp. 16°. *London, J. Murray*, 1814.

Penn (William). An address to protestants upon the present conjuncture. In ii parts. 6 p. l. 248 pp. sm. 4°. [*London*] ? 1679.

——— A brief examination and state of liberty spiritual, both with respect to persons in their private capacity, and in their church society and communion. 2 p. l. 15 pp. sm. 4°. *London, A. Sowle*, 1681.

——— The counterfeit christian detected; and the real quaker justified. Against the vile forgeries, [etc.] of T. Hicks, in his third dialogue, call'd The quaker condemned. By a lover of truth and justice, W. P. [*anon.*] 122 pp. 1 l. 16°. [*London*] ? 1674.

——— A defence of a paper, entitled, Gospel-truths, against the exceptions of the bishop of Cork's testimony. 3 p. l. 119 pp. 16°. *London, T. Sowle*, 1698.

——— An index to William Penn's works. By Philalethes, [*pseudon. for* Henry Portsmouth]. 18 pp. sm. 4°. [*London, about* 1730].

——— Judas and the Jews combined against Christ and his followers: being a re-joynder to the late nameless reply, called Tyranny and hypocrisie detected, made against a book, entitied, The spirit of Alexander the copper-smith rebuked, etc. which was an answer to a pamphlet, called The spirit of the hat. 130 pp. 1 l. sm. 4°. [*London*] ? 1673.

[*Note.*—Pages 9–15 wanting].

——— A just rebuke to one and twenty learned and reverend divines (so called). Being an answer to an abusive epistle against the people call'd quakers, subscrib'd by Thomas Manton, Richard Baxter, [etc.] 32 pp. sm. 4°. [*London*] ? 1674.

——— *and* **Coole** (Benjamin). A testimony to the truth of God, as held by the people, called, qvakers: being a short vindication of them, from the abuses and misrepresentations often put upon them by envious apostates and mercenary adversaries. [*anon.*] 2nd impression. 56 pp. 18°. *London, T. Sowle*, 1699.

[*Note.*—In answer particularly to Francis Bugg].

——— *and* **Whitehead** (George). The christian-quaker, and his divine testimony vindicated by scripture, reason, and authorities; against the injurious attempts, that have been lately made by several adversaries, with manifest design to render him odiously inconsistent with christianity and civil society. In two parts. 17 p. l. 162 pp. 1 l; 377 pp. fol. [*London*] ? 1674.

CONTENTS.

Part 1. By William Penn. The universality and sufficiency of Christ's light within, through all ages to eternal salvation.

——— An appendix; being a discourse of the general rule of faith and life, and judge of controversie.

Part ii. By George Whitehead. Christ's light within asserted, as it is divine, and vindicated from Tho. Hicks's dark exceptions.

——— Lux certa est: or the light sprung up in the despised quaker. In answer to Henry Griggs.

——— The angry anabaptist proved babilonish, in answer to Henry Grigg.

——— The contents of a bill of excommunication, exhibited by the baptists at Chichester; with a brief answer.

——— Some confessions concerning the baptized churches, by Thomes Colliar, [and others].

——— The presbyter's antidote tryed, or Stephen Scandret proved a physician of no value.

——— The answer to Tho. Hicks, and his brethren, about the resurrection.

Thomas Vincent's illustrations about the resurrection.

Something for the spirituality of the resurrection out of H. Moor's search into the nature of a glorified body.

Penn (The) monthly. Jan. to Dec. 1871. v. 2. 8°. *Philadelphia, Porter & Coates*, [1871].

Pennell (Harry Cholmondeley). The family fairy tales; or, glimpses of Elfland at Heatherston Hall. New ed. With the story of Little spider face, now told for the first time. vii, 225 pp. 6 pl. sm. 4°. *London, J. C. Hotten,* [1869].

Pennetier (Georges). L'origine de la vie. Avec une préface par le dr. F. A. Pouchet. xxi, 303 pp. 1 l. 18°. *Paris, J. Rothschild,* 1868.

Pennington (S. *lady*). An unfortunate mother's advice to her absent daughters; in a letter to miss Pennington. [*anon.*] 1 p. l. 96 pp. 8°. *London, S. Chandler,* 1761.

——— The same. An unfortunate mother's advice to her daughter. sm. 4°. [*London, J. Hamilton & co.* 1794].

[*In* HAMILTON (John). Angelica's ladies library, pp. 107–166].

Pennsylvania (*State of*). *Auditor general.* Annual report of the auditor general of the state of Pennsylvania, and of the tabulations and deductions from the reports of the railroad, canal and telegraph companies for the year 1870. lxxxv, 698 pp. 1 map. 8°. *Harrisburg, B. Singerly,* 1871.

——— ——— Report of the auditor general, of the finances, for the year ending Nov. 30, 1870. 184 pp. 8°. *Harrisburg, B. Singerly, state printer,* 1871.

——— *Board of public charities.* First annual report, to which is appended the report of the general agent and secretary. 8°. *Harrisburg, state printer,* 1871.

——— *General assembly.* Rules and decisions of the general assembly of Pennsylvania, legislative directory, together with useful political statistics, list of post offices, county officers, &c. By John A. Smull. 1 p. l. 493 pp. 1 pl. 1 chart. 18°. *Harrisburg, B. Singerly,* 1871.

——— ——— Journal of the senate and house of representatives. Session of 1871. 2 v. 8°. *Harrisburg, state printer,* 1871.

——— *Inspectors of coal mines.* Reports of the inspectors of coal mines of the anthracite coal regions of Pennsylvania, for the year 1870. 8°. *Harrisburg, state printer,* 1871.

——— *State penitentiary for the western district.* Forty-fourth annual report of the inspectors, to the senate and house of representatives of the commonwealth, Jan. 1871. 8°. *Pittsburgh, A. A. Anderson & son,* 1871.

——— *Superintendent of common schools.* Reports for the years ending June, 1870–71. 2 v. 8°. *Harrisburg, state printer,* 1870–71.

Pennsylvania (The) gazette. Jan. 7, 1755, to Dec. 29, 1757. nos. 1359–1514. fol. *Philadelphia, B. Franklin and D. Hall,* 1755–57.

——— The same. Jan. 1, 1761, to Dec. 29, 1763. no. 1671 to no. 1827. fol. *Philadelphia, B. Franklin & D. Hall,* 1761–63.

Pennsylvania (*Grand chapter, etc. of*). *See* **Freemasons.**

Penry (John). A treatise wherein is manifestlie proved, that reformation and those that sincerely fauor the same, are vnjustly charged to be enemies, vnto hir majestie, and the state. [*anon.*] 36 l. sm. 4°. [*London*]? 1590.

Pensieri sullo spirito della divina commedia di Dante. 1837. *See* **Azzolino** (Pompeo, *il marchese*).

People (The) of China; or, a summary of chinese history. [*anon.*] 234 pp. 18°. *Philadelphia, American sunday school union,* [1844].

Pepper (Henry). Juvenile essays; or, a collection of poems. 76 pp. 8°. *Philadelphia, R. Folwell,* [*about* 1800].

Perceval (John, *2d earl of Egmont*). To the king's most excellent majesty, the memorial of John earl of Egmont. [Concerning the settlement of the island of St. John's]. 32 pp. 8°. [*London,* 1764].

Perceval (John). A narrative of the treatment experienced by a gentleman, during a state of mental derangement; designed to explain the causes and the nature of insanity, and to expose the injudicious conduct pursued towards many unfortunate sufferers under that calamity. 2 v. 2 p. l. 278 pp; xxxiii, 430 pp. 8°. *London, E. Wilson,* 1838.

Perch (Philemon, *pseudon.*) Dukesborough tales. 4 p. l. 232 pp. sm. 4°. *Baltimore, Turnbull brothers,* 1871.

Percival (Emily, *editor*). *See* **Gems** of beauty.

Percival (Thomas, *m. d.*) Philosophical, medical, and experimental essays. To which is added an appendix; containing a letter to the author from dr. Saunders, on the solution of human calculi; with other papers. xvi, 374 pp. 1 l. 8°. *London, J. Johnson,* 1776.

Percy (Florence, *pseudon.*) *See* **Taylor** (Lizzie A. C.)

Percy (Thomas, *bishop of Dromore*). Five pieces of runic poetry translated from the islandic language. [With the originals.

Percy (Thomas)—continued. *anon.*] 8 p. l. 100 pp. 12°. *London, R. & J. Dodsley,* 1763.

CONTENTS.
The incantation of Hervor.
The dying ode of Regner Lodbrog.
The ransome of Egill, the scald.
The funeral song of Hacon.
The complaint of Harold.

Peregrini (Matteo). Della pratica comvne a prencipi, e servidori loro libri cinque. 8 p. l. 352 pp. sm. 4°. *Viterbo, a spese del Diotalleui stampatore,* 1634.

Pereira (Benito). De magia, de observatione somniorvm, et de divinatione astrologica, libri tres. Adversvs fallaces, et svperstitiosas artes. 2 p. l. 237 pp. 3 l. 16°. *Coloniæ agrippinæ, apud I. Gymnicum,* 1598.

Pereira de Figueiredo (Antonio). Demonstração theologica, canonica, e historica do direito dos metropolitanos de Portugal para confirmarem, e mandarem sagrar os bispos suffraganeos nomeados por sua magestade: e do direito dos bispos de cada provincia para confirmarem, e sagrarem os seus respectivos metropolitanos, tambem nomeados por sua magestade, ainda fóra do caso de rotura com a corte de Roma. xliv, 3, 474 pp. 4°. *Lisboa, na regia officina typografica,* 1769.
[*With his* Tentativa theologica, etc. 1766].

——— Tentativa theologica, em que se pretende mostrar, que impedido o recurso á sé apostolica se devolve aos senhores bispos a faculdade de dispensar nos impedimentos publicos do matrimonio, [etc.] 24 p. l. xi, 286 pp. 22 l. 4°. *Lisboa, M. Rodrigues,* 1766.

——— The same. Appendix e illustraçaõ da tentativa theologica, sobre o poder dos bispos em tempo de rotura. 381 pp. 1 l. 4°. *Lisboa, A. V. da Silva,* 1768.
[*With his* Tentativa theologica, 1766].

Perelli (Tommaso). Relazione sopra il regolamento delle acque delle tre provincie di Bologna, Ferrara e Romagna. [Ed] annotazioni delle riflessioni de' due pp. matematici Le Seur, e Jacquier [sul' medesimo]. 4°. [*Firenze,* 1785].
[*In* XIMENES (L.) Raccolta delle perizie ed opuscoli idraulici, v. 1, pp. 279–358 and 375–393].

Perez de Herrera (Christoval). Elogio à las esclarecidas virtvdes del rey Don Felipe ii. y de su exemplar y christianissima muerte, y carta oratoria, al rey D. Felipe iii. 4 p. l. 272 pp. sm. 4°. *Valladolid, L. Sanchez,* 1604.

Perfect (The) gentleman; or, etiquette and eloquence. [etc.] By a gentleman. [*anon.*] 335 pp. 12°. *New York, Dick & Fitzgerald,* [1862].

Peri (Giovanni Domenico). Fiesole distrutta. Eng. title, 1 p. l. 198 pp. 1 portrait. 4°. *Firenze, Z. Pignoni,* 1621.

Périon (Joachim). Dialogorum de linguæ gallicæ origine, eiusque cum græca cognatione, libri quatuor. 36 p. l. 149 l. numb. 12°. *Parisiis, apud S. Niuellium,* 1555.

Perk (Abner). Merry maple leaves, or a summer in the country. [A book of illustrations]. 38 l. numb. sm. 4°. *New York, E. P. Dutton & co.* 1872.

Perkins (E. E.) A treatise on haberdashery and hosiery, including the Manchester, scotch, silk, linen, and woollen departments. 3d ed. viii, 132 pp. 18°. *London, T. Hurst,* 1834.

Perkins (W. O.) The mocking bird, for schools and juvenile classes. 224 pp. obl. 8°. *New York, W. A. Pond & co.* [1871].

——— *and* **Hallett** (A. R.) The orphean, for boys' schools and colleges, containing a complete elementary course, and a great variety of music. 192 pp. obl. 8°. *Boston, O. Ditson & co.* [1871].

Perraud (Adolphe). Ireland under english rule. Translated from the french. 12 p. l. xxxi, 520 pp. 8°. *Dublin, J. Duffy,* 1864.

Perrault (Nicolas). The jesuits' morals: or, the principal errors which the jesuits have introduced into christian morality. Faithfully extracted out of their own books, which are printed by the permission and approbation of the superiours of their society. [*anon.*] Englished by Ezerel Tonge, [or Ezrael Tongue], d. d. 17 p. l. 392 pp. fol. *London, J. Starkey,* 1679.

Perret (Paul). Histoire d'une jolie femme. 2 p. l. 305 pp. 12°. *Paris, M. Lévy frères,* 1860.

Perris (William G.) *and* **Browne** (Henry H.) Insurance maps of the city of New York. Surveyed and published by Perris & Browne. v. 5, 6, and 8. fol. *New York, Perris & Browne,* 1870–71.

Perrot (Auguste). Key to Perrot's Wilhem's musical manual. 1855. *See* **Wilhem** (Guillaume Louis Boquillon).

Perrussel (F. *m. d.*) L'homœopathie, ou la vérité en médecine. 2 p. l. 170 pp. 1 l. 8°. *Nantes, Hérault,* 1843.

Perry (Bela C.) A treatise on the human hair and its diseases. xi, 192 pp. 16°. *New Bedford, C. Taber & co.* 1859.

Perry (John). The household physician; or, an easy and natural method of curing most diseases. 125 pp. 18°. *Providence, B. T. Albro*, 1838.

Perry (J. G.) The bible harp: being a collection of old, familiar and favorite psalms, hymns, and spiritual songs, in their original form, with a number of select and new compositions, intended for use in religious conferences, prayer meetings, family worship, private devotions, social circles, pastoral donation visits, temperance gatherings, &c. 400 pp. 18°. *New York, Sheldon & co.* 1870.

Perry (Marshall S. *m. d.*) First book of the fine and useful arts. 3 p. l. 126 pp. 12°. *Boston, Carter & Hendee*, 1832.

Persius Flaccus (Aulus). Satires. 8°. [*Bruxelles*, 1842].

[*In* RAOUL (L. V.) Les trois satiriques latins, v. 2, pp. 11-110].

——— Satiræ expurgatæ. 1832. *See* **Juvenalis** (Decimus Junius) *and* **Persius Flaccus.**

Perticari (Giulio, *conte*). Opere. 2 v. xxiv, 426 pp. 1 l. 5 tab. 1 portrait; 2 p. l. 422 pp. 1 l. 16°. *Milano, G. Silvestri*, 1823.

Pertinente beschrijvinge van Guiana, gelegen aen de vaste kust van America. Waer in kortelijck verhaelt wordt, het aenmerckelijcke dat in en omtrent het landt van Guiana valt, als de limiten, het klimaet [etc.] Als oock de conditien van de staaten van Hollandt voor de gene die nae Guiana begeeren te varen. [*anon.*] 12, 55 pp. 1 map. sm. 4°. *Amsterdam, J. C. ten Hoorn*, 1676.

Pet (The) keepsake. A token of love. [*anon.*] 232 pp. 2 pl. 12°. *Philadelphia, J. E. Potter*, 1860.

Petachja (*Rabbi* Moses). Tour du monde, ou voyages du rabbin Péthachia, dans le douzième siècle; publiés en hébreu et en français, accompagnés de notes historiques, géographiques et littéraires, par m. E. Carmoly. 122 pp. 8°. *Paris, imprimerie royale*, 1831.

Peters (*Rev.* Richard). The two last sermons preached at Christ's church in Philadelphia, July 3, 1737. xxii, 29 pp. sm. 4°. *Philadelphia, B. Franklin*, 1737.

[*Note.*—The preface is occupied by mr. Peters' account of a controversy with rev. Archibald Cummings].

Peters (T. C.) A complete system of book-keeping, simplified and adapted to the use of farmers. Embracing a set of forms of accounts for all the principal branches of business of the farm. 250 pp. fol. *Buffalo, A. M. Clapp*, 1843.

Peters' musical monthly. Jan. to Dec. 1871. v. 7-8 in 2 v. 4°. *New York, J. L. Peters*, [1871].

Petersen (Siegwart). Norsk bog-fortegnelse, 1848-1865. *See* **Botten-Hansen** (P.) *and* **Petersen.**

Peterson (Charles J.) The old stone mansion. 1 p. l. 21-367 pp. 1 pl. 12°. *Philadelphia, T. B. Peterson & brothers*, [1859].

Peterson (Henry). Poems. 203 pp. 12°. *Philadelphia, J. B. Lippincott & co.* 1863.

Peterson (*Mrs.* Henry, *editor*). *See* **Lady's** (The) friend.

Petit (*Rev.* John Louis). Remarks on church architecture. 2 v. ix, 216 pp. 94 pl; 2 p. l. 270 pp. 98 pl. 8°. *London, J. Burns*, 1841.

Petit (Lizzie). Household mysteries; a romance of southern life. 300 pp. 12°. *New York, D. Appleton & co.* 1856.

Petite (La) encyclopédie. *See* **Chaumeix** (Abraham Joseph de).

Petitpierre (Alphonse). Un demi-siècle de l'histoire économique de Neuchâtel, 1791-1848. 2 p. l. 451 pp. 2 tab. 12°. *Neuchâtel, J. Sandoz*, 1871. S.

Petrarca (Francesco). Alcvne rime. 8°. [*Torino, stamperia reale*, 1750].

[*In* UBALDINI (F.) Il trattato delle virtù' morali, etc. pp. 140-216, ed. 1750].

——— Le cose volgari di messer Francesco Petrarcha. 186 l. 16°. *Vinegia, nelle case d'Aldo romano*, 1501.

CONTENTS.

Sonetti et canzoni in vita ed in morte di madonna Laura.
Triomphi undeci.

[*Note.*—The first book printed by Aldus in italic letter.—BRUNET. The colophon says: "Impresso dallo scritto di mano medisimo del poeta hauuto da m. Piero Bembo." Lacks the last sheet, containing six printed leaves, bearing a long avviso and errata].

——— De remediis utriusq. fortunæ. Divinum opus Nicolai lugari industria sollerti [editum]. 164 l. fol. *Cremonæ, Bernardini de misintis de Pap̄. ac Cæsaris Parmensis sociorum diligenti opera impressum*, 1492.

[*Note.*—255 dialogues between Gaudium, Spes, Ratio, and Dolor. 44 lines on a page. Without pagination. This is the second book printed at Cremona].

——— Epistole famigliari. 12°. [*Vinegia, G. Giolito de Ferrari*, 1548].

[*In* DOLCE (L.) Epistole. 1548. l. 31-111].

——— Il Petrarca, con l'espositione d'Alessandro Vellvtello, e con piv vtili cose in diversi lvoghi di qvella, novissimamente da lvi aggivnte et ristampate. 12; 302 l. 16°. *Vinegia, G. A. di Nicolini da Sabio*, 1541.

——— The same. Il Petrarcha con l'espositione di m. Gio. Andrea Gesvaldo. Nvova-

Petrarca (Francesco)—continued. mente ristampato, et ornato di figvre. 28 p. l. 419 l. numb. 4°. *Vinegia, J. Vidali,* 1574.

——— Petrarch translated; in a selection of his sonnets, and odes; with notes, and the original italian; also with the head of Petrarch from an antique bronze; by the translator of Catullus. [G. F. Nott]. xii, 268 pp. 1 pl. 8°. *London, J. Miller,* [*etc.*] 1808.

Petronius Arbiter (Titus). La satyre de Pétrone, tradvite en françois avec le texte latin, suivant le nouveau manuscrit trouvé à Bellegrade en 1688. Ouvrage complet, contenant les galanteries et les débauches de l'empereur Néron, & de ses favoris: avec des remarqves cvrievses [par Nodot], et une table des principales matières. [Avec La vie de Pétrone]. 2 v. 32 p. l. 473 pp. 3 pl; 4 p. l. 549 pp. 8 pl. 16°. *Cologne, P. Marteau,* 1694.

[*Note.*—Les figures [en taille douce] de cette [ed.] sont de J. V. Aveele.—BRUNET].

Pettit (Edward). The visions of government, wherein the antimonarchical principles and practices of all fanatical commonwealthsmen, and jesuitical politicians are discovered, confuted, and exposed. 7 p. l. 248 pp. 16°. *London, B. W. for E. Vize,* 1684.

Peucer (Caspar). Les devins, ov commentaire des principales sortes de devinations. Escrit en latin; nouuellement tourné en françois par S. G. S. [Simon Goulard senlisien]. 6 p. l. 654 pp. 12 l. 4°. *Anvers, H. Connix,* 1584.

Peyssonnel (Charles de). Observations historiques et géographiques sur les peuples barbares qui ont habité les bords du Danube & du Pont-Euxin. xliv, 364 pp. 9 pl. 4 maps. 4°. *Paris, N. M. Tilliard,* 1765.

Pezron (Paul). The antiquities of nations; more particularly of the Celtæ or Gauls, taken to be originally the same people as our ancient Britains. Containing great variety of historical, chronological, and etymological discoveries, many of them unknown both to the Greeks and Romans. Englished by mr. Jones. 4 p. l. xvi, 312 pp. 8°. *London, R. Janeway for S. Ballard and R. Burrough,* 1706.

——— The same. The rise and fall of states and empires; or the antiquities of nations, more particularly of the Celtae or Gauls: [etc.] xxviii, 372 pp. 1 portrait. 16°. *London, M. Jones,* 1809.

Pezuela (Jacobo de la). Diccionario geografico, estadistico, historico de la isla de Cuba. 4 v. 4°. *Madrid, J. Bernat,* 1863–66.

[*Note.*—v. 4 dated 1867 on cover].

Pezuela (Jacobo de la)—continued

——— Historia de la isla de Cuba. 2 v. 463 pp; 606 pp. 8°. *Madrid, C. Bailly-Baillière,* 1868.

Pfanner (Tobias). Systema theologiæ gentilis purioris qua quam prope ad veram religionem gentiles accesserint, per cuncta fere ejus capita, ex ipsis præcipue illorum scriptis ostenditur. 13 p. l. 536 pp. 36 l. 4°. *Basileae, impensis J. H. Widerholdi,* 1679.

Phædrus. Ezopische fabeln van Fedrus, gevryden slaef des keizers Augustus. In nederduitsch dicht vertaelt en met aenmerkingen verrykt door D. van Hoogstraten. 24 p. l. 259 pp. 13 l. 17 pl. 16°. *Amsterdam, S. van Esveldt,* 1769.

Phelpes (*Rev.* Charles). A caveat against drunkenness, especially in evil times. Being a consideration of Eph. 5, 18. 8 p. l. 167 pp. 16°. *London, T. Parkhurst,* 1676.

Phelps (*Mrs.* Almira H. Lincoln). Chemistry for beginners: with engravings. 269 pp. 16°. *Hartford, F. J. Huntington,* 1834.

——— Christian households. With an appendix containing the history of "the church home and infirmary" of Baltimore. 78 pp. 18°. *New York, author,* 1858.

——— Familiar lectures on botany, explaining the structure, classification, and uses of plants, illustrated upon the linnæan and natural methods, with a flora for practical botanists. New edition, revised and enlarged. [In two parts]. 297 pp. 1 pl; 208 pp. incl. 8 pl. 8°. *New York, F. J. Huntington,* 1852.

——— The same. New ed. With a supplement. 312 pp. 1 pl; 208 pp. incl. 8 pl. 8°. *New York, Mason brothers,* 1860.

——— The fireside friend, or female student; being advice to young ladies on the important subject of education. 378 pp. 12°. *Boston, Marsh, Capen, Lyon & Webb,* 1840.

——— Lectures to young ladies, comprising outlines and applications of the different branches of female education. 308 pp. 1 pl. 12°. *Boston, Carter, Hendee & co.* 1834.

——— Natural philosophy, for schools, families, and private students. New edition, revised and corrected. 296 pp. 12°. *New York, Huntington & Savage,* 1846.

Phelps (Elizabeth Stuart). The gypsy series. v. 2–4. 16°. *Boston, Graves & Young,* 1866–68.

CONTENTS.

v. 2. Gypsy's cousin Joy. 282 pp. 4 pl.
v. 3. Gypsy's sowing and reaping. 302 pp. 4 pl.
v. 4. Gypsy's year at the golden crescent. 261 pp. 4 pl.

Phelps (Elizabeth Stuart)—continued.
——— The silent partner. 302 pp. 16°. *Boston, J. R. Osgood & co.* 1871.

Phelps (*Miss* L. L.) The veil on the heart. 293 pp. 3 pl. 16°. *Boston, D. Lothrop & co.* [1871].

Philadelphia (*City of*). Report of the board of health, for the years 1870 and 1871. 2 v. 8°. *Philadelphia, by order of the board,* 1871-72.

——— Business directory. 1871. *See* **Cleary** (William P.) & co.

——— The Philadelphia directory, city and county register, for 1803. Containing, the names, trades and residence of the inhabitants of the city, Southwark, Northern Liberties, and Kensington. With other useful tables and lists. [Also], an almanac, by A. Shoemaker. By James Robinson. 285, lx pp. 6 l. 1 tab. 12°. [*Philadelphia*], *W. W. Woodward,* [1803].

——— Philadelphia wholesale merchants' and artisans' business directory, for 1853. By T. Ellwood Chapman. 18°. *Philadelphia, T. E. Chapman & co.* [1852].

——— Stephens's Philadelphia directory, for 1796; or, alphabetical arrangement: containing the names, occupations, and places of abode of the citizens. Also, an account of the different societies, charitable and literary institutions, with the names of their present officers: and an accurate table of the duties on goods, wares, and merchandise, with an abstract from the revenue laws. [Also], a complete account of the post-office establishment, the banks, and different monies. 20, 286, 69 pp. 1 map. 16°. *Philadelphia, T. Stephens,* [1796].

Philadelphia (The) photographer. Edited by Edward L. Wilson. [Monthly]. Jan. to Dec. 1871. 8°. *Philadelphia, Benerman & Wilson,* 1871.

Philadelphia (The) university journal of medicine and surgery. Published monthly, by J. S. Longshore, m. d. and E. D. Buckman, m. d. editors. v. 14. 8°. *Philadelphia,* 1871. s.

Philadelphus (*pseudon.*) Philadelphi de Novo Lacu epistola et discursus de modernis jesuitarum moribus, ad Clarum de Petra. 150 pp. 18°. *Ignatianopoli,* [*Francofurti*], 1672.

Philalethes (*pseudon.*) Index to W. Penn's works. [By Henry Portsmouth]. 1730. *See* **Penn** (William).

Philalethes (Alazonomastix, *pseudon.*) *See* **More** (*Rev.* Henry).

Philalethes (Eugenius, *pseudon.*) *See* **Vaughan** (Thomas).

Philandrier (Guillaume). Gvlielmi Philandri in decem libros M. Vitruuii Pollionis de architectura annotationes. 8 p. l. 370 pp. 19 l. 16°. *Romæ, apud I. A. Dossena,* 1544.

Philatelist (The): an illustrated magazine for stamp collectors. [Monthly]. Jan. to Dec. 1871. v. 5. 8°. *London, E. Marlborough & co.* 1871.

Philbrick (John D.) The american union speaker; with introductory remarks on elocution, and explanatory notes. xxxv, 588 pp. 8°. *Boston, Taggard & Thompson,* 1865.

Phile *or* **Philes** (Manuel). Manvelis Philæ carmina græca, maximam partem e codicibus avgvstanis et oxoniensibvs nvnc primvm in lvcem prodvcta; omnia nvnc in vnvm, excepto poemate de animalibvs, collecta, emendata, latine interpretata, et annotationibvs illvstrata: accedit ignoti poetae antiqvioris carmen in s. Theodorvm ex Avgvstano codice. Præmittitvr dissertatio de Philæ vita, ætate et scriptis, cvra Gottlieb. Wernsdorfii. 16 p. l. 350 pp. 8°. *Lipsiae, apvd B. C. Breitkopf & fil.* 1768.

——— Phile de animalium proprietate. Ex prima editione Arsenii et libro oxoniensi restitutus a J. C. de Pauw, cum ejusdem animadversionibus et versione latina Gregorii Bersmanni. Accedunt ex eodem libro oxoniensi non pauca hactenus inedita. [Græce et latine]. 8 p. l. 348 pp. 2 l. 4°. *Trajecti ad Rhenum, apud G. Stouw,* 1730.

——— Manuelis Philæ, jambographi græci, duo carmina anecdota, præmissa de ejus vita et scriptis disquisitiuncula. 1813. 8°. [*Havniae,* 1815].

[*In* Thorlacius (Börge). Prolusiones et opuscula, v. 3, pp. 49-68].

Philelphus. *See* **Filelfo.**

Philidor (François André Danican, *dit*). L'analyze des échecs: contenant une nouvelle méthode pour apprendre en peu de tems à se perfectioner dans ce noble jeu. xiv, 162 pp. 1 portrait. 8°. *Londres,* 1749.

——— The same. Die kunst im schachspiel ein meister zu werden. Das ist: ein neuer unterricht, wie man in kurzem dieses so edle und beliebte spiel nach seiner vollkommenheit erlernen könne. 3e aufl. 12 p. l. 352 pp. 16°. *Strasburg, A. König,* 1771.

Philip (Alexander P. Wilson, *m. d.*) An inquiry into the nature of sleep and death, with a view to ascertain the more immediate causes of death, and the better regulation of the means of obviating them. Republished from the Royal society philosophical transactions, 1827–34. Being the concluding part of the author's experimental inquiry into the laws of the vital functions. 2 p. l. xix, 254 pp. 8°. *London, H. Renshaw*, 1834.

Philip (Robert, *d. d.*) Devotional guides. With an introductory essay, by rev. Albert Barnes. 2 v. 345 pp; 334 pp. 12°. *New York, D. Appleton & co.* 1837.

Philip Alderton's temptation. By the author of "Eve Bourne." [etc. *anon.*] 230 pp. 3 pl. 18°. *Boston, Mass. sabbath school society*, [1860].

Philip Everhard; or a history of the baptist Indian missions in North America, from the formation of the american baptist board of foreign missions to the present time. [*anon.*] 108 pp. 16°. *Boston, Massachusetts sabbath school union*, 1831.

Philipott (Thomas). An historical discourse of the first invention of navigation, and the additional improvements of it. With the probable causes of the variation of the compasse. Likewise, some reflections upon the name and office of admirall. [And] a catalogue of those persons that have been dignified with that office. 2 p. l. 28 pp. 12°. *London, W. Fisher*, 1661.

Philippe (Mathieu Braussi, *dit frère, superior general of the brothers of the christian schools*). Filial and fraternal piety. Translated from the french, by Christine Farville. 282 pp. 18°. *New York, P. O'Shea*, 1864.

——— The six hundred thousand combatants; or, the children of the patriarchs conquering the promised land. Translated by Christine Farville. 288 pp. 16°. *New York, P. O'Shea*, 1864.

Philippi (Rudolfo Amando). Elementos de historia natural. 328 pp. 8°. *Santiago, [Chili], imprenta [etc.] de la Independencia*, 1866. S.

——— Reise durch die wueste Atacama, auf befehl der chilenischen regierung im sommer 1853–54 unternommen und beschrieben. x, 192, 62 pp. 1 map, 27 pl. 4°. *Halle, E. Anton*, 1860. S.

Philips (A. J. P.) *pseudon. for* J. P. Durand. Électro-dynamisme vital, ou les relations physiologiques de l'esprit et de la matière, démontrées par des expériences entièrement nouvelles, et par l'histoire raisonnée du système nerveux. 1 p. l. xlvii, 383 pp. 8°. *Paris, J. B. Baillière*, 1855.

Philips (*Rev.* Samuel). The voice of blood, in the sphere of nature and of the spirit world. 384 pp. 8°. *Philadelphia, Lindsay & Blakiston*, 1864.

Phillips (*Rev.* George S.) The american republic and human liberty foreshadowed in scripture. 236 pp. 12°. *Cincinnati, Poe & Hitchcock*, 1864.

Phillips (George Searle) *January Searle, pseudon.* The gypsies of the Danes' dike. A story of hedge-side life in England, in the year 1855. xii, 416 pp. 12°. *Boston, Ticknor & Fields*, 1864.

Phillips (Henry). The true enjoyment of angling. 2 p. l. 138 pp. 1 portrait. 12°. *London, W. Pickering*, 1843.

Phillips (J. S.) The explorers', miners' and metallurgists' companion. v. 1. 639 pp. 8°. *San Francisco, Dewey & co.* 1871.

Phillips *or* **Philipps** (J. Thomas). An account of the religion, manners, and learning of the people of Malabar in the East Indies. In several letters written by some of the most learned men of that country to the danish missionaries. 5 pl. 180 pp. 1 pl. 1 map. 16°. *London, W. Mears*, 1717.

——— A compendious way of teaching antient and modern languages, formerly practised by the learned Tanaquil Faber. With observations on the same subject, by several eminent men, viz. Roger Ascham, Richard Carew, mr. Milton, mr. Locke, &c. With an account of the education of the dauphine, and of his sons: and the marchioness of Lambert's letter to her son. Also, an essay on rational grammar. [And] proposals for a new method of domestick education. Likewise, the original letter of cardinal Woolsey, to the masters of his school at Ipswich; with an english translation. 4th ed. very much enlarged. 10 p. l. 351 pp. 8°. *London, W. Meadows*, 1750.

Phillips (Lawrence B.) The dictionary of biographical reference: containing one hundred thousand names, together with a classed index of the biographical literature of Europe and America. 1 p. l. xii, 1020 pp. 8°. *London, S. Low, son & Marston*, 1871.

Phillips (*Mrs.* Mary Jane). Home pictures for the little ones. A series of sketches from real child-life. 121 pp. 2 pl. 18°. *New York, Carlton & Porter*, [1859].

Phillips (*Mrs.* Mary Jane)—continued.
——— Sweet Corabelle, and other authentic sketches. 164 pp. 18°. *New York, Carlton & Porter*, [1860].
——— The young gold seeker, and other authentic sketches. 132 pp. 18°. *New York, Carlton & Porter*, [1860].

Phillips (Philip). Early blossoms; a collection of music for sabbath schools. With rudiments. 112 pp. sq. 16°. *Cincinnati, J. Church, jr.* [1862].

Phillips *or* **Philips** (*Sir* Richard). Golden rules of social philosophy; or, a new system of practical ethics. xxiv, 376 pp. 8°. *London, author*, 1826.

Phillips (*Rev.* Samuel, *of Andover, Mass.*) The history of our Lord and Saviour Jesus Christ epitomiz'd: in a catechetical way. 1 p. l. iv, 60 pp. 2 l. 8°. *Boston, D. Henchman*, 1738.
——— Three plain practical discourses, preach'd at Andover. In the following order. i. Oct. 29th, 1727. The day immediately preceding the late terrible earthquake. ii. On a public fast Dec. 21, 1727. . Occasioned by the continuance of the earthquake. iii. Dec. 24th, [1727]. Seasonable for a people, after they have renew'd their covenant. [Preface by Benjamin Colman]. 1 p. l. vi, 226 pp. 18°. *Boston, J. Phillips*, 1728.

Philo *judæus.* Philonis ivdæi in libros Mosis de mvndi opificio, historicos, de legibvs. Eivsdem libri singvlares. Ex bibliotheca regia. [1st ed. of the greek text]. 6 p. l. 736 pp. 24 l. fol. *Parisiis, ex officina A. Turnebi, regiis typis*, 1552.

Philodemus. Philodemi rhetorica ex herculanensi papyro lithographice Oxonii excusa restituit, latine vertit, dissertatione de græca eloquentia et rhetorica notitiaque de herculanensibus voluminibus auxit annotationibus indicibusque instruxit E. Gros. Adjecti sunt duo Philodemi libri de rhetorica Neapoli editi. 3 p. l. cxxxiii, 244 pp. 2 l. 4 pl. 8°. *Parisiis, F. Didot fratres*, 1840.

Philosophers (The) of Foufouville. *See* **Freelance** (Radical).

Philosophie du bonheur. *See* **Delisle de Sales** (J. B. C. I.)

Philosophy of the plan of salvation. *See* **Walker** (*Rev.* James B.)

Philostratus. Philostrati lemnii opera qvæ extant. Philostrati ivnioris imagines, et Callistrati ecphrases. Item Evsebii cæsariensis liber contra Hieroclem, qui ex Philostrati historia æquipararat Apollonium tyaneum saluatori nostro Iesv Christo. Græce latinis e regione posita; Fed. Morellvs cvm mnss. contvlit, recensvit: et hactenus nondum latinitate donata, vertit. 6 p. l. 914 pp. 19 l. fol. *Parisiis, apud M. Orry*, 1608.

CONTENTS.

Philostrati de vita Apollonii tyanei 8 lib.
Evsebii cæsariensis liber contra Hieroclem qui ex Philostrati historia comparauit Apollonium tyaneum saluatori nostro Iesv Christo.
Flavii Philostrati vitæ sophistarvm 2 lib.
Flavii Philostrati heroica: sive dialogvs de viris illvstribvs, qvi in bello troiano pro heroibus habiti sunt.
Flavii Philostrati imagines, 2 lib.
Philostrati ivnioris imagines.
Callistrati expositiones statvarvm.
Epistolæ Philostrati.

Philotheos Physiologus (*pseudon.*) The way to health. *See* **Tryon** (Thomas, *m. d.*)

Phipps (Henry Philip, *earl of Mulgrave, marquess of Normanby*). The temple of death. *See* **Habert** (Phillipe).

Photius. *Φωτιου πατριαρχου κωνσταντινουπολεως επιστολαι.* Photii epistolæ. Per Richardum Montacutium Latine redditæ, et notis subinde illustratæ. [Græce et latine]. 4 p. l. 393 pp. 5 l. fol. *Londini, R. Daniels*, 1651.

Photographer's (The) friend. Almanac and american year book of photography for 1872. Edited by G. O. Brown. 120 pp. 1 photo. 12°. *Baltimore, R. Walzl*, [1871].

Photographic review of medicine and surgery. A bi-monthly illustration of interesting cases accompanied by notes. Oct. 1870, to Aug. 1871. v. 1. 8°. *Philadelphia, J. B. Lippincott & co.* 1871.

Photographic (The) times. [A monthly magazine]. Jan. to Dec. 1871. v. 1. 8°. *New York, Scovill manufacturing co.* 1871.

Photographic (The) world. [A monthly magazine]. Edited by Edward L. Wilson. Jan. to Dec. 1871. v. 1. 8°. *Philadelphia, Benerman & Wilson*, 1871.

Phrenological (The) journal and Packard's monthly. A repository of science, literature, and general intelligence. Devoted to ethnology, physiology, phrenology, [etc.] S. R. Wells, editor. July to Dec. 1870. Old series, v. 51. New series, v. 2. 8°. *New York, S. R. Wells*, 1870.
——— The same. The phrenological journal and life illustrated. A repository of science, [etc.] S. R. Wells, editor. July to Dec. 1871. Old series, v. 52–53. New series, v. 3–4. 8°. *New York, S. R. Wells*, 1871.

Phrynichus. Phrynichi eclogæ nominum et verborum atticorum, cum versione latina Petri Joannis Nunnesii et ejusdem ac Davidis Hoeschelii notis: ut et notis Josephi Scaligeri in Phrynichum et Nunnesii notas. Curante Joanne Cornelio de Pauw, qui notas quoque suas addidit. 42 p. l. 218 pp. 11 l. 4°. *Trajecti ad Rhenum, apud J. Evelt*, 1739.

Phurnutus. *See* **Cornutus** (Lucius Annæus).

Physician's (The) annual for 1872. A complete calendar for the city and country practitioner. Edited by S. W. Butler, m. d. and Geo. H. Napheys, m. d. 83 pp. 12°. *Philadelphia, S. W. Butler*, 1872.

Piatt (John James). Landmarks and other poems. 116 pp. 12°. *New York, Hurd & Houghton*, 1872.

Piatt (*Mrs.* Sarah M. B.) A woman's poems. 4 p. l. 127 pp. 12°. *Boston, J. R. Osgood & co.* 1871.

Piault (Urbain Firmin). De l'existence universelle, de celle de l'homme en société et de ses fins; ou aperçus géologiques, ontologiques, théologiques et politiques. 2 p. l. 465 pp. 8°. *Paris, Didot*, 1848.

Pibrac (Guy du Faur, *seigneur* de). Ornatissimi cuiusdam viri, de rebus gallicis, ad Stanislaum Eluidium [suppositum], epistola. [*anon.*] 47 pp. 4°. *Lvtetiae, apud F. Morellum*, 1573.

Pichardo (Esteban). Geografia de la isla de Cuba. Publicase bajo los auspicios de la real junta de fomento. 3 v. in 1. 8°. *Habana, M. Soler*, 1854.

Pichler (Carolina Greiner). Agathokles. [Roman]. 3 v. 8°. *Wien, A. Pichler*, 1808.

Pichot (Amédée). Voyage historique et littéraire en Angleterre et en Écosse. 3 v. 8°. *Paris, Ladvocat & C. Gosselin*, 1825.

Pickard (Hannah Maynard). The widow's jewels. In two stories. By a lady. 114 pp. 18°. *Boston, Waite, Peirce & co.* 1844.

Picken (Andrew). The club-book: being original tales, etc. by various authors. Edited by the author of "The dominie's legacy." [*anon.*] 3 v. 8°. *London, Cochrane & Pickersgill*, 1831.

Pickering (John). Ueber die indianischen sprachen Amerikas. Aus dem englischen übersetzt, mit anmerkungen, von Talvj. [Mrs. T. A. L. von Jacobs Robinson]. viii, 80 pp. 8°. *Leipzig, F. C. W. Vogel*, 1834.

Pico della Mirandola (Giovanni, *conte di Concordia*). Epistole: 12°. [*Vinegia, G. Giolito de Ferrari*, 1548].

[*In* Dolce (L.) Epistole. 1548. l. 111-139].

Picquot (*Rev.* Julius). A compendium of logic. 8°. [*London*, 1818].

[*In* Aristoteles. A dissertation on rhetoric. 1818. pp. 7-116].

Pictet (Adolphe). Les origines indo-européennes, ou les Aryas primitifs. Essai de paléontologie linguistique. Première partie. viii, 547 pp. 8°. *Paris, J. Cherbuliez*, 1859.

[v. 2 wanting to complete the work].

Pictet (Benedict). La nécessité d'examiner la religion dont on fait profession; ou sermon sur ces paroles de Saint Paul, 1 Thess. v. 21. Éprouvez toutes choses. [L'examen des religions du monde. La défense de la religion chrétienne. L'examen de la religion romaine. L'examen de la religion des Grecs, et de celle des protestans. La défense de la religion réformée. La défense de la réformation. Exhortation à la persévérance dans la vraye religion]. 92, 182, 269 pp. 16°. *Londres, D. du Chemin*, 1702.

Pictorial guide to the falls of Niagara: a manual for visiters. [*anon.*] 232 pp. 4 pl. 3 charts. 18°. *Buffalo, Salisbury & Clapp*, 1842.

Pictorial life of George Washington: embracing anecdotes, illustrative of his character. [*anon.*] 222 pp. 8 pl. sq. 16°. *Philadelphia, Lindsay & Blakiston*, 1845.

Pictures and flowers for child-lovers. [*anon.*] 211 pp. 1 pl. 16°. *Boston, Walker, Wise & co.* 1861.

Pictures from Paris in war and in siege. By an american lady. [*anon.*] 3 p. l. 313 pp. 12°. *London, R. Bentley & son*, 1871.

Pidansat de Mairobert (Matthieu François). Lettres originales de madame la comtesse du Barry; avec celles des princes, seigneurs, ministres & autres, qui lui ont écrit & qu'on a pu recueillir. On y a joint une grande quantité de notes amusantes & instructives. [*anon.*] viii, 206 pp. 12°. *Londres*, 1779.

Pieces of poetry. *Chiswick*, 1830. *See* **Taylor** (George Watson).

Pierantoni (Augusto). La questione anglo-americana dell' Alabama studio di diritto internazionale publico e marittimo. 52 pp. 8°. *Firenze, stabilimento Civelli*, 1870.

——— Storia degli studi del diritto internazionale in Italia. 324 pp. 12°. *Modena, C. Vincenzi*, 1869.

Pierce (Cruttall). Considerations on water baptism: with remarks on circumcision and berith. xxi, 375 pp. 8°. *London, J. Haddon*, 1835.

Pierce (Elizabeth). Village pencillings in prose and verse. 2d ed. 7 p. l. 285 pp. 2 l. 1 pl. 12°. *London, W. Pickering*, 1844.

Pierce (John, *d. d.*) A eulogy on George Washington, delivered on the anniversary of his birth, at Brookline. [With Washington's farewell address]. 24, 24 pp. 8°. *Boston, Manning & Loring*, 1800.
[HAZARD pamphlets, v. 65].

Pierce (*Rev.* Samuel Eyles). The unseen world and state opened to the intellectual faculty and spiritual mind. In which are recorded various appearances of the Lord God, realized in sights of him, in visions, dreams, raptures, trances, such only as are related in the old and new testament. xxx, 140 pp. 12°. *London, Chatfield & Coleman*, 1824.

Pierce (S. H.) Little gems for little people. 239 pp. 4 pl. 16°. *Philadelphia, Claxton, Remsen & Haffelfinger*, 1871.

Pierce. *See* **Pearse** *and* **Peirce.**

Piercy (John S.) The history of Retford, in the county of Nottingham [Eng.] Comprising its ancient, progressive, and modern state, with an historical and topographical account of the villages of West Retford, Babworth, Ordsall, Grove, and Clarborough. viii, 246 pp. 9 pl. 12°. *Retford, author*, 1828.

Pierpont (John). The American first class book; or, exercises in reading and recitation: selected principally from modern authors of Great Britain and America. 25th ed. 480 pp. 12°. *Boston, Carter, Hendee & co.* 1835.

Piestre (J. L.) Les crimes de la philosophie. [*anon.*] xi, 416 pp. 8°. *Paris*, 1804.

Pighius *or* **Pigghe** (Albert). De aeqvinoctiorvm solsticiorūque inuentione. Eivsdem de ratione paschalis celebrationis, deque restitutione ecclesiastici kalendarij. xxiii l. 1 l. unp. xxx l. sm. fol. *Parisij, in vico diui Jacobi*, [1520].

Pigneiro (Manuel). Narratio brevis rervm à societate in regno magni Mogor gestarum. *See* **Xavier** (Jérôme) *and* **Pigneiro.**

Pignoria (Lorenzo). L'Antenore. Eng. title, 4 p. l. 50 pp. 2 l. 4°. [*At end*], *Padova, G. B. Martini & Z. Pasquati stampat. cam.* 1625.
[*With his* Le origini di Padova. *Padoua*, 1625].

Pignoria (Lorenzo)—continued.

——— Attestatione di Givlio Paolo givreconsvlto solennizata ne i campi elisij il dì delle none d'agosto. L'anno 1625. Riferita fedelmente da Menippo filosofo. [*pseudon.*] 14 l. 4°. *Padova, P. P. Tozzi*, 1625.
[*With his* Le origini di Padova. *Padoua*, 1625].

——— Avviso di Parnaso difesa della patavinita di Givlio Paolo givrisconsvlto contra Le origini di Padova. [*anon.*] 27 pp. 4°. *Padoua, P. P. Tozzi*, 1625.
[*With his* Le origini di Padova. *Padoua*, 1625].

——— Le origini di Padova, nelle quali si discorre dell' antichità, degl' habitatori, delle memorie illustri della città & della prouincia tutta. 1 p. l. 182 pp. 3 l. 2 pl. 4°. *Padoua, nella stampa camerale*, [1625]?

Pignotti (Lorenzo). Favole, e novelle. [Con L'ombra di Pope, La tomba di Shakespeare; e Roberto Manners, poemetti]. Ed. xii. 2 v. Eng. title, 280 pp. 1 portrait; eng. title, 263 pp. 1 pl. 18°. *Livorno, C. Giorgi*, [1789]?

Pigott (*Miss* Harriott). Records of real life in the palace and the cottage. Revised by the late John Galt. 3 v. 12°. *London, Saunders & Otley*, 1839.

Pike (James). The colombian orthographer; or first book for children. 168 pp. 12°. *Portland, D. Johnson*, 1806.

Pike (*Rev.* John). The bud, blossom and fruit; or, early piety permanent and progressive, illustrated by some incidents in the life of Emily J. Goodhue. 252 pp. 1 pl. 16°. *Boston, Mass. sabbath school society*, [1858].

Pike (*Mrs.* Mary H.) Agnes. A novel. By the author of "Ida May." [*anon.*] 510 pp. 12°. *Boston, Phillips, Sampson & co.* 1858.

Pilcher (George). A treatise on the structure, economy, and diseases of the ear; 1st american, from the 2d London edition; with notes. 299 pp. 16 pl. 8°. *Philadelphia, E. Barrington & G. D. Haswell*, 1843.

Pilgrimage (A) over the prairies. By the author of "The fortunes of a colonist." [*anon.*] 2 v. 1 p. l. 298 pp; 1 p. l. 261 pp. 12°. *London, T. C. Newby*, 1863.

Pillsbury (Parker). "The sabbath." A discourse, delivered at Lyceum hall, Toledo, sunday, April 2d, [1871]. 12°. [*Chicago*, 1871].
[*In* JONES (S. S.) The sunday question, pp. 40-63].

Pil-pai. Kalila and Dimna, or the fables of Bidpai. Translated from the arabic. By the rev. Wyndham Knatchbull. xii, 366 pp. 8°. *Oxford, W. Baxter for J. Parker*, 1819.

Pinckney (Stephen R.) National guard manual. 246 pp. 8 pl. 12°. *New York, F. McElroy*, 1863.

Pindar (Susan, *pseudon.*) Fireside fairies: or christmas at aunt Elsie's. 205 pp. 6 pl. 16°. *New York, D. Appleton & co.* 1850.

Pindarus. The pythian, nemean, and isthmian odes of Pindar, translated into english verse; with critical and explanatory remarks: to which are prefix'd observations on his life and writings; conjectures on the æra wherein the grecian games concluded; and an ode to the genius of Pindar. [By Edward Burnaby Greene]. 2 p. l. xlvii, 446 pp. 4°. *London, J. Dodsley*, 1778.

——— The same. Le odi. Traduzione di Giuseppe Borghi, riveduta dal traduttore. xii, 309 pp. 2 pl. 18°. *Milano, G. Truffi*, 1831.

Pingré (Alexandre Gui). Voyage fait par ordre du roi en 1771 et 1772. *See* **Verdun de la Crenne** (—), **Borda,** *and* **Pingré.**

Pinkerton (John). The scotish gallery; or, portraits of eminent persons of Scotland: many of them after pictures by the celebrated Jameson, at Taymouth, and other places. With brief accounts of the characters represented, and an introduction on the rise and progress of painting in Scotland. 62 l. 50 pl. 4°. *London, E. Harding*, 1799.

Pinkham (Rebekah P.) Memoirs of Simeon J. Milliken, esq. of Mount Desert, Maine, with a short sketch of the last hours, and dying scene of his two beloved brothers. 108 pp. 16°. *Boston, J. Loring*, 1836.

——— A narrative of the life of miss Lucy Cole, of Sedgwick, Maine. [Also, sketches of the lives of Sarah Nye Parker, Susan Bancroft, mrs. Sophia W. Kimball]. 108 pp. 18°. *Boston, J. Loring*, 1830.

Pinto (Isaac). An essay on circulation and credit, in four parts; and a letter on the jealousy of commerce. Translated from the french, with annotations, by the rev. S. Baggs. 1 p. l. xxi, 243 pp. 4°. *London, J. Ridley*, 1774.

Piot (*Rev.* B. S.) Considerations on the world. 143 pp. 18°. *Baltimore, Kelly, Hedian & Piet*, 1860.

Pirckheimer (Wilibald). Apologia, sive lavs podagrae. 18°. [*Lugd. Batavorum*, 1644].

[*In* DISSERTATIONVM lvdicrarvm et amœnitatvm scriptores varij, pp. 1-39].

Piron (Alexis) *and others.* Chansons choisies de Piron, Collé, Gallet, Pavart, etc. 1 p. l. 252 pp. 1 pl. 32°. *Paris, J. Claye*, [1867]?

Pise (Charles Constantine, *d. d.*) Zenosius; or the pilgrim-convert. 279 pp. 1 pl. 18°. *New York, E. Dunigan*, 1845.

Pistorius *niddanus* (Johann). Dæmonomania pistoriana. *See* **Heilbrunner** (Jakob).

Pitcairn (*Rev.* David). Pastoral letters to his parishioners during absence from them on account of ill health. 2d ed. 159 pp. 16°. *London, J. H. Jackson*, 1847.

Pitcairn (Robert). Historical and genealogical account of the principal families of the name of Kennedy. From an original ms. With notes and illustrations. xi, 218 pp. 1 tab. 1 fac-simile. 4°. *Edinburgh, W. Tait*, 1830.

Pitezel (*Rev.* J. H.) The backwoods boy who became a minister; or, the family and personal history of Henry Adolph. 163 pp. 18°. *New York, Carlton & Porter*, [1859].

Pitiscus (Samuel). Lexicon antiqvitatvm romanarvm: in qvo ritvs et antiqvitates cum Græcis ac Romanis communes, tum Romanis peculiares, sacræ et profanæ, pvblicæ et privatæ, civiles ac militares exponvntvr. 2 v. Eng. title, 43 p. l. 1008 pp. 3 pl; eng. title, 1 p. l. 1133 pp. fol. *Leovardiæ, excudit F. Halma*, 1713.

Pitman (Benn). The manual of phonography. 136 pp. 12°. *Cincinnati, Phonographic institute*, [1860].

——— The reporter's companion. 178 pp. 12°. *Cincinnati, Phonographic institute*, [1862].

Pits (John). Relationvm historicarvm de rebus anglicis tomvs primvs. 16; 990 pp. 4°. *Parisiis, R. Thierry*, 1619.

[*Note.*—This work was edited by dr. W. Bishop, who has prefixed to it a very learned and valuable preface. Called vol. 1, but no second ever appeared.—LOWNDES].

Pitt (Robert, *m. d.*) The craft and frauds of physick expos'd. With instructions to prevent being cheated and destroy'd by the prevailing practice. 2d ed. 12 p. l. 203 pp. 4 l. 16°. *London, T. Childe*, 1703.

Pius ii. *pope.* (Enea Silvio Piccolomini). Aeneae episcopi senensis in libros Antonii Panormitae De dictis et factis Alphonsi regis memorabilibus, commentarius. sm. 4°. *Witebergae, Crato*, 1585.

[BECCADELLI (Antonio). De dictis et factis Alfonsi. 1585. pp. 102-158].

——— Aeneae Siluii episcopi senensis, qui postea Pius papa ii. fuit, historia rerum Friderici iii. imperatoris. fol. [*Argentorati, J. R. Dulssecker*, 1702].

[*In* KULPIS (J. G. von). Scriptores rervm germanicarvm. *Argentorati*, 1702. [Part 2], pp. 1-148].

Pius ii. *pope*—continued.
——— Historia de Eurialo et Lucretia se amantibus. Amoris illiciti medela. In effigiem amoris. 18°. [*Lvgd. Batav. ex typographia rediviva*, 1648].
[*In* OBSOPŒUS (V.) De arte bibendi. Variorum auctorum practica artis amandi, et declamationes Philip. Beroaldi. 1648. pp. 7-84, 89-101].

Placentius (Joannes Leo). *See* **Le Plaisant.**

Placidus de Titus. *See* **Titi** (Placido de').

Planard (François Antoine Eugène de). Le pré aux clercs, opéra-comique en trois actes. 82 pp. 8°. *Paris, J. N. Barba*, 1833.

Plancy (J. A. S. Collin de). *See* **Collin de Plancy.**

Planter (The); or, thirteen years in the south. By a northern man. [*anon.*] 275 pp. 12°. *Philadelphia, H. Hooker*, 1853.

Plants without root. Stories of Vinegar hill, v. 4. *See* **Warner** (Susan).

Plato. Erastæ, a dialogue on philosophy. Translated from the greek of Plato, [by Thomas Robert Jolliffe]. 8°. [*London*, 1827].
[*In* JOLLIFFE (Thomas R.) Narrative of an excursion from Corfu to Smyrna. 1827. pp. 197-272].

——— Plato his apology of Socrates, and Phædo, or dialogue concerning the immortality of man's soul, and manner of Socrates his death; carefully translated from the greek, and illustrated by reflections upon both the athenian laws, and ancient rites and traditions concerning the soul, therein mentioned. [1st ed.] 19 p. l. 300 pp. 12°. *London, T. R. & N. T. for J. Magnes & R. Bentley*, 1675.
[Imperfect: wanting frontispiece].

Platt (A. H. *m. d.*) Human life prolonged; or, five thousand facts for physical existence. 680 pp. 8°. *Philadelphia, Quaker city publishing house*, 1871.

Plattner (Carl Friedrich). Plattner's manual of qualitative and quantitative analysis with the blow-pipe. From the last german ed. revised and enlarged. By prof. Th. Richter. Translated by Henry B. Cornwall, assisted by John H. Caswell. xv, 549 pp. 1 pl. 8°. *New York, D. Van Nostrand*, 1872.

Platts (*Rev.* John). New self-interpreting testament. *London*, 1827. *See* **Bible.** (*English*).

Plautus (Titus Maccius). The captives. With english notes, by John Proudfit, d. d. 106 pp. 16°. *New York, Harper & brothers*, 1843.

Play-house (The); and workshop. Written for little folks. By a father. [*anon.*] 144 pp. 1 pl. 24°. *New York, S. Colman*, 1839.

Pleas (Elwood). Henry county; past and present: a brief history of the county from 1821 to 1871. iv, 148 pp. 2 pl. 16°. *New Castle (Ind.) Pleas brothers*, 1871.

Pleasant pictures for young children. [*anon.*] 1 p. l. 126 pp. sq. 16°. *New York, American tract society*, [1871].

Pleasant (The) way. [*anon.*] 173 pp. 18°. *Boston, Mass. sabbath school society*, 1841.

Pleasants (H. R.) The war of four thousand years. *See* **White** (P. S.) *and* **Pleasants.**

Pleasures (The) of sympathy; with other poems. [*anon.*] 4 p. l. 120 pp. 16°. *London, author*, 1822.

Plenck (Joseph Jacob). Icones plantarum medicinalium secundum systema Linnaei digestarum, cum enumeratione virium et usus medici, chirurgici atque diaetetici. 3 v. fol. *Viennæ, R. Graeffer et soc.* 1788-92.

Pleschtschejeff *or* **Plescheéf** (Sergj Iwanowitsch). Survey of the russian empire, according to its present newly regulated state, divided into different governments. 3d ed. Translated from the russian, with considerable additions, by James Smirnove. xxiv, 336 pp. 11 l. 1 pl. 1 map. 8°. *London, J. Debrett*, 1792.

Plinius Caecilius Secundus (Caius). C. Plinii panegyricus Trajano dictus. Interpretatione et notis illustravit Jacobus de la Baune. Huic editioni adduntur quaedam notae selectiores, Lipsii, Livineii, Catanæi, Rayani, Baudii, Rittershusii, et aliorum. 16 p. l. 206 pp. 28 l. 8°. *Londini, H. Clements*, 1716.

——— Select letters of Pliny the younger, with notes illustrative of the manners, customs, and laws of the ancient Romans. 143 pp. 18°. *Boston, Perkins, Marvin & co.* 1835.

——— The same. Epistole. Tradotte per m. L. Dolce. 12°. *Vinegia, G. Giolito de Ferrari*, 1548.
[*In* DOLCE (L.) Epistole di Plinio, Petrarca, etc.]

Plinius Secundus (Caius). Histoire naturelle de l'or et de l'argent, extraite de Pline le naturaliste, livre xxxiii. Avec le texte latin, corrigé sur les mss. de Vossius et sur la i. édition, et éclairci par des rémarq. nouvelles, outre celles de J. F. Gronovius, & un poëme sur la chute de l'homme et sur les ravages de l'or et de l'argent. Par David Durand. 4 p. l. lxxxii, 258 pp. 3 l. 1 front. fol. *Londres, G. Bowyer*, 1729.

Ploucquet (Wilhelm Gottfried). Literatura medica digesta sive repertorium medicinae practicae, chirurgiae atque rei obstetriciae. 4 v. 4°. *Tubingae, apud J. G. Cottam,* 1808-9.

——— The same. Continuatio et supplementum 1. 4°. *Tubingae, apud C. F. Osiander,* 1814.

Pluche (*L'abbé* Noël Antoine). Le spectacle de la nature, ou entretiens sur les particularités de l'histoire naturelle. 8 v. in 9. 16°. *Paris, les frères Estienne,* 1754-55.

CONTENTS.

v. 1. Ce qui regarde les animaux & les plantes.
v. 2-3. Ce qui regarde les dehors & l'intérieur de la terre.
v. 4. Ce qui regarde le ciel & les liaisons des différentes parties de l'univers avec les besoins de l'homme.
v. 5. Ce qui regarde l'homme considéré en lui-même.
v. 6-7. Ce qui regarde l'homme en société.
v. 8. Ce qui regarde l'homme en société avec Dieu.

Plues (Margaret). British ferns: an introduction to the study of the ferns, lycopods, and equiseta, indigenous to the British isles, with chapters on the structure, propagation, cultivation, diseases, uses, preservation, and distribution of ferns. x, 281 pp. 1 l. 16 pl. 12°. *London, L. Reeve & co.* 1866.

——— British grasses: an introduction to the study of the gramineæ of Great Britain and Ireland. viii, 307 pp. 16 pl. 12°. *London, Reeve & co.* 1867.

Plum (William). The letters of a farmer, containing his thoughts in the ninety-fourth year of his age. 294 pp. 12°. *Middletown (Conn.) author,* 1843.

Plumer (William Swan, *d.d.*) The law of God, as contained in the ten commandments, explained and enforced. 644 pp. 12°. *Philadelphia, Presbyterian board of publication,* [1864].

Plummer (*Elder* Frederick) *and* **M'Calla** (*Rev.* William L.) A public discussion on the doctrine of the trinity, between elder Frederick Plummer, christian; and the rev. William L. M'Calla, presbyterian. Held at Ridley, Delaware county, Pennsylvania. [Edited by F. Plummer]. 288 pp. 12°. *Philadelphia, Kay & brother,* 1842.

Plutarchus. Anecdotes selected from the Lives of Plutarch, by Cedrick. [Also] a few juvenile fragments by the author. 4 p. l. 150 pp. 12°. *London, Wright & son,* 1825.

——— Sur les délais de la justice divine dans la punition des coupables. Nouvellement traduit, avec des additions et des notes par le comte J. de Maistre, suivi de la traduction du

Plutarchus—continued.
même traité par Amyot sous ce titre: Pourquoi la justice divine diffère la punition des maléfices. 2 p. l. 202 pp. 8°. *Lyon, L. Lesne,* 1844.

Plymouth collection. The baptist hymn and tune book, for public worship. Music adapted and arranged by John M. Evans. 432 pp. 8°. *Philadelphia, Bible and publication society,* [1871].

Plymouth pulpit: a weekly publication of sermons preached by Henry Ward Beecher. Sept. 25, 1869, to March 16, 1872. v. 3-7. *See* **Beecher** (H. W.) Sermons.

Pochard (Joseph). Considerations on the sacred ministry, with a rule of life, for pastors of souls. Translated from the french, by the rev. B. S. Piot. 132 pp. 24°. *Baltimore, Kelly, Hedian & Piet,* 1859.

Pocket (A) pictorial dictionary of the english language. With a table of classical mythology, etc. and a list of phrases and proverbs from various languages. [*anon.*] Latest revised ed. xvi, 5-244 pp. 32°. *Philadelphia, Claxton, Remsen & Haffelfinger,* 1871.

Poe (Edgar Allan). Tales of the grotesque and arabesque. 2 v. 243 pp; 228 pp. 12°. *Philadelphia, Lea & Blanchard,* 1840.

Poem (A) on the rising glory of America. *See* **Freneau** (Philip).

Poems. *London,* 1780. *See* **Dodsley** (Robert).

Poems, amorous, moral, and divine. Consisting of odes, elegies, epistles, translations. [*anon.*] 2d ed. 4 p. l. 206 pp. 1 l. 8°. *London, W. Hinchliffe,* 1776.

Poems by a slave in the island of Cuba, recently liberated; translated from the spanish by R. R. Madden, m. d. With the history of the early life of the negro-poet, written by himself; to which are prefixed two pieces descriptive of cuban slavery and the slave-traffic, by R. R. M. [*anon.*] 4 p. l. 188 pp. 8°. *London, T. Ward & co.* 1840.

Poems; by the author of "Moral pieces in prose and verse." *See* **Sigourney** (*Mrs.* Lydia Huntley).

Poems by the author of The village curate. *See* **Hurdis** (*Rev.* James).

Poems: consisting chiefly of odes and elegies. [*anon.*] 176 pp. 16°. *Glasgow, R. Chapman,* 1810.

Poems on several occasions. By a lady. 1726. *See* **Thomas** (*Mrs.* Elizabeth).

Poetry for the young; in two parts, moral and miscellaneous. Selected and published for mrs. John Tharp Lawrence's school. [*anon.*] 160 pp. 18°. *New York, J. S. Taylor & co.* 1843.

Poet's (The) offering. By a Boston amateur poet. [*anon.* Preface subscribed J. P.] 372 pp. 12°. *Boston, G. W. Light*, 1842.

Poinsinet de Sivry (Louis). Nouvelles recherches sur la science des médailles, inscriptions, et hiéroglyphes antiques. vi, 191 pp. 6 pl. 4°. *Mæstricht, J. E. Dufour & P. Roux*, 1778.

Pole (*Sir* William). Collections towards a description of the county of Devon. Now first printed from the autograph in the posession of his lineal descendant, sir John-William De la Pole, bart. of Shute, etc. in Devonshire. 1 p. l. xviii, 568 pp. 4°. *London, J. Nichols*, 1791.

Polite (The) companion; or, wit à-la-mode. Adapted to the recreation of all ranks and degrees, from the prince to the peasant. [*anon.*] viii, 132 pp. 1 pl. 16°. *London, G. Kearsly*, 1760.

Political annals of Lower Canada. 1828. *See* **Fleming** (M.)

Politiqve discourses, treating of the differences and inequalities of vocations, as well publique, as priuate: with the scopes or endes wherevnto they are directed. Translated out of french, by Ægremont Ratcliffe. [*anon.*] *b. l.* 81 l. 8°. *London, E. Aggas*, 1578.

Poliziano (Angiolo). Epistole. 12°. [*Vinegia, G. Giolito de Ferrari,* 1548].

[*In* DOLCE (L.) Epistole. 1548. l. 157-163].

Pollux (Julius). Onomasticon, cum annotationibus interpretum. Curavit Guilielmus Dindorfius. [Græce et latine]. 6 v. 8°. *Lipsiae, in libraria kuehniana*, 1824.

Polo (Gaspar Gil). Los cincos libros de la Diana enamorada. Dirigidos a Isabela Sutton, por el que ha corregido, y enmendado dicha obra. viii, 328 pp. 16°. *Londres, T. Woodward*, 1739.

[*Note.*—A continuation of the Diana enamorada of Montemayor].

Polo (Marco). The book of ser Marco Polo, the venetian, concerning the kingdoms and marvels of the east. Newly translated and edited, with notes. By colonel Henry Yule. 2 v. clxi, 409 pp. 8 maps, 8 pl; xviii, 575 pp. 2 pl, 6 maps, (incl. 1 map in cover). 8°. *London, J. Murray*, 1871.

Polwhele (*Rev.* Richard). An essay on marriage, adultery & divorce, (now first printed): and, an essay on the state of the soul between death and the resurrection, (the third ed.) The outline of a sermon; and a lecture on taste. With an appendix, containing various illustrations, particularly "The deserted village-school," a poem: and a postscript, containing some notices of a large ms. vol. entitled, "Traditions and recollections, domestic, clerical and literary." 2 p. l. 249 pp. 16°. *London, J. Nichols & son*, 1823.

——— Traditions and recollections; domestic, clerical, and literary; in which are included letters of Charles ii, Cromwell, Fairfax, [and others]. 2 v. viii, 360 pp. 1 portrait; iii, 361–820 pp. 8°. *London, J. Nichols & son*, 1826.

Polybius. Historiæ liber 1. 3. 8°. *Oxonii*, 1835.

[*In* HISTORIA græca, ed. 2a, pp. 409-484].

Polybus *of Cos.* Opere vtilissime in medicina di Polibio, descepolo & successo d'Hippocrate coo, tradotte nvovamente di greco in italiano, per Pietro Lavro modonese. 2 p. l. 46 l. numb. 4°. *Venetia, per Comin de Trino di Monferrato*, 1545.

CONTENTS.

Di conseruare la sanità.
De la natura de l'humano seme.
De le malattie del corpo.

Polycarp (*Saint*). The epistle to the Philippians. 12°. [*Oxford*, 1840].

[*In* WAKE (William). The genuine epistles of the apostolical fathers, pp. 105-111].

Polyteknisk tidsskrift. Udgivet af den polytekniske forening i Christiania. Redigeret af C. M. Guldberg. 16de aargang; 17de aargang, 5 hefte. 4°. *Christiania, P. T. Malling*, 1869-70.

Pomeroy (*Rev.* B.) Visions from modern mounts, namely: Vineland, Manheim, Round Lake, Hamilton, Oakington, Canton, with other selections. Printed for the author. 300 pp. 16°. *Albany, Van Benthuysen*, 1871.

Pomeroy (John Norton, *ll. d.*) An introduction to the constitutional law of the United States. Especially designed for students, general and professional. xxv, 549 pp. 8°. *New York, Hurd & Houghton*, 1870.

Pomeroy (Mark M.) Brick-dust: a remedy for the blues, and a something for people to talk about. 255 pp. 6 pl. 12°. *New York, G. W. Carleton & co.* 1871.

Pomeroy (Mark M.)—continued.

——— Gold-dust: for the beautifying of lives and homes. 275 pp. 6 pl. 12°. *New York, G. W. Carleton & co.* 1871.

Pona (Francesco). La lvcerna di Evreta Misoscolo [*pseudon.*] Aggiuntoui la Messalina di Francesco Pona. 2 v. in 1. 267 pp; 80 pp. 24°. *Parigi,* [*about* 1630]?

Poncet (Charles Jacques). A voyage to Æthiopia, made in the years 1698, 1699, and 1700. Describing particularly that famous empire; as also the kingdoms of Dongola, Sennar, part of Egypt, &c. with the natural history of those parts. Faithfully translated from the french original. 6 p. l. 138 pp. 16°. *London, W. Lewis,* 1709.

Poncet de La Grave (Guillaume). Le tocsin maritime contre la prétention des rois d'Angleterre, à l'empire de la mer. xvi, 62 pp. 8°. *Paris, Moutardier,* 1801.

Pond (Enoch, *d. d.*) Essay on prayer. 32°. [*Boston, Peirce & Parker,* 1832].

[*In* VINCENT (Nathaniel). The spirit of prayer, pp. 5-32].

——— First principles of the oracles of God. 81 pp. 18°. *Boston, Massachusetts sabbath school society,* 1844.

——— The Mather family. 180 pp. 1 portrait. 18°. *Boston, Mass. sabbath school society,* 1844.

——— Memoir of count Zinzendorf: comprising a succinct history of the church of the united brethren, from its renewal at Herrnhut to the death of its illustrious patron. 195 pp. 18°. *Boston, Mass. sabbath school society,* 1839.

——— Memoir of miss Susanna Anthony; consisting chiefly in extracts from her writings, and observations respecting them. 180 pp. 18°. *Boston, Massachusetts sabbath school soc.* 1834.

——— Morning of the reformation. 324 pp. 5 pl. 18°. *Philadelphia, American sunday school union,* 1842.

——— Probation. 137 pp. 18°. *Bangor, Duren & Thatcher,* 1837.

——— The seals opened; or, the apocalypse explained. xi, 240 pp. 1 portrait. 12°. *Portland, Hoyt, Fogg & Breed,* 1871.

——— A treatise on christian baptism, in four parts; relating to the mode of baptism; to the subjects; to the import, design, and uses of infant baptism; and to close communion. viii, 13-190 pp. 12°. *Boston, Peirce & Parker,* 1833.

Pond (Enoch, *d. d.*)—continued.

——— Wickliffe and his times. 197 pp. 1 portrait. 18°. *Philadelphia, American sunday school union,* [1841].

——— The young pastor's guide: or lectures on pastoral duties. 377 pp. 12°. *Bangor, E. F. Duren,* 1844.

Ponsard (François). Galilei. Schauspiel in 3 acten. Deutsch in metrischer uebertragung, von E. A. Zuendt. 16°. *St. Louis,* 1871.

[*In* ZUENDT (E. A.) Lyrische und dramatische dichtungen, pp. 625-703].

Ponsonby (*Mrs.* —). The Desborough family. 3 v. 12°. *London, J. Mortimer,* 1845.

Pontano (Giovanni Gioviano). Opera omnia, solvta oratione composita. [2[d] ed?] 3 v. 8°. *Venetiis in aedibvs Aldi, et Andreae soceri,* 1518-19.

CONTENTS.

v. 1. De obedientia libri v.
De fortitudine libri ii.
Liber de principe.
Liber de liberalitate.
Liber de beneficentia.
Liber de magnificentia.
Liber de splendore.
Liber de conuiuentia.
De prudentia libri v.
De magnanimitate libri ii.
De fortuna libri iii.
Liber de immanitate.

v. 2. De aspiratione libri duo.
Charon dialogus.
Antonius dialogus.
Actius dialogus.
Aegidius dialogus.
Asinus, dialogus de ingratitudine.
De sermone libri vi.
Belli, quod Ferdinandus senior Neap. rex cum Ioanne Andegauiensium duce gessit libri vi.

v. 3. Centum sententiæ Ptolomæi e graeco tralatae, una cum expositionibus.
De rebus cœlestibus libri xiiii.
Liber de luna imperfectus.

Pontanus *or* **Spanmüller** (Jacob). Attica bellaria, sive litteratorum secundæ mensæ ad animos ex contentione & lassitudine studiosorum lectiunculis exquisitis, jucundis ac honestis relaxandos, ac syntagmatvm omnivm et ante hac tribus partibus editorum libri tres: nvnc unico volumine comprehensi. 23 p. l. 1007 pp. 8°. *Francofvrti, impensis I. G. Schonvvattii,* 1644.

Pontanus (Johann, *rector of the university at Franckfurt*). Ein sendbrief Johannis Pontani, darinn vom stein der weisen gehandelt wird, ist im jahr 1580. Lateinisch herfür kommen, nun aber ins deutsche gebracht. 16°. [*Hamburg, J. Nauman & G. Wolff,* 1675].

[*In* ALCHYMISTISCH sieben-gestirn, 1675, pp. 219-231].

Pontanus (Johan Isachsen). Danemarqve. fol. *Amsterdam, Jean Blaeu,* 1667.

[BLAAUW (Willem Janszoon *and* Joan). Le grand atlas, v. 1].

Pontey (William). The profitable planter: a treatise on the theory and practice of planting forest trees, in every description of soil and situation; more particularly on elevated sites, barren heaths, rocky soil, &c. including directions for the planting and management of permanent screens; with useful hints on shelter and ornament. 4th ed. enlarged. With an appendix. viii, 267 pp. 3 l. 1 pl. 8°. *London, J. Harding*, 1814.

Pontis (Louis de). Mémoires du sieur de Pontis, contenant plusieurs circonstances remarquables des guerres, de la cour, & du gouvernement [de Henri iv. Louis xiii. & Louis xiv. Rédigés par Pierre Thomas du Fossé]. Nouv. éd. 2 v. 2 p. l. xxxvi, 516 pp; 2 p. l. 544 pp. 16°. *Paris, chez les libraires associés*, 1766.

Pontmartin (Alexandre de). Clotilde, or, the secret of three generations. From the french. By Kate C. Barton. 401 pp. 12°. *Philadelphia, J. M. Stoddart & co.* 1871.

Poole (John). Sketches and recollections. 2 v. viii, 342 pp. 1 portrait; iv, 327 pp. 12°. *London, H. Colburn*, 1835.

Poole (*Mrs.* L. E.) Johnnie the railroad boy. 238 pp. 3 pl. 16°. *Boston, I. P. Warren*, [1871].

Poole (Richard, *m. d.*) The beneficent bee: or, traveller's companion. Containing each day's observation, in a voyage from London, to Gibraltar, Barbadoes, Antigua, Barbuda, etc. 388 pp. 8°. *London, E. Duncomb*, 1753.

Poor (Henry V.) Manual of the railroads of the United States for 1870–71 and 1871–72. With an appendix containing a full analysis of the debts of the United States. 3d and 4th series. 2 v. 8°. *New York, H. V. & H. W. Poor*, 1870–71.

Poor (The) weaver's family. A tale of Silesia. From the german. By mrs. Sarah A. Myers. [*anon.*] 121 pp. 2 pl. 18°. *Philadelphia, W. S. & A. Martien*, 1865.

Pope (Alexander). De homine. 4°. [*Patavii*, 1775].

[*In* COSTA (G.) Poema, pp. 6–52].

Pope (Frank L.) The telegraph instructor. A hand-book for students of telegraphy. Designed to accompany the nonpareil telegraph apparatus. [*anon.*] 18 pp. 2 l. 12°. *New York, F. L. Pope & co.* 1871.

Pope (*Rev.* Richard T. P.) Roman misquotation: or certain passages from the fathers, adduced in a work [by Berington and Kirk] entitled "The faith of catholics," &c. brought to the test of the originals, and their perverted character demonstrated. xv, 338 pp. 8°. *London, S. Holdsworth*, [*etc.*] 1840.

Popular fairy tales for little folks. [*anon.*] 1 p. l. [186 pp.] 6 pl. sq. 18°. *New York, J. Miller*, 1862.

Porcel (Francisco Moreno). *See* **Moreno Porcel.**

Porcius (P. *pseudon.*) *See* **Le Plaisant** (Jean).

Porphyrius. Porphyrii de abstinentia ab esv animalivm libri qvatvor. Ioanne Bernardo Feliciano interprete. [Editio princeps]? 6 p. l. 100 l. unp. 8°. *Venetiis, apud I. Gryphium*, 1547.

——— The same. Porphyrii philosophi pythagorici de abstinentia ab animalibus necandis libri quatuor. Ex nova versione: cui subjiciuntur notæ breviusculæ. Ejusdem liber De vita Pythagoræ: & sententiæ ad intelligibilia ducentes: de antro nympharum quod in Odyssea describitur. Lucas Holstenius latinè vertit. Dissertationem de vita & scriptis Porphyrii, & ad vitam Pythagoræ observationes adjecit. [Græce et latine]. 1 p. l. 286 pp. 5 l. 88 pp. 7 l. 16°. *Cantabrigiae, impensis G. Morden*, 1655.

——— Πορφυριου εισαγωγη περι των πεντε φωνων. Porphyrii isagoge. 8°. [*Biponti, ex typographia societatis*, 1791].

[*In* ARISTOTELES. Opera omnia, v. 1, pp. 359–428].

Porreño (Baltasar). Dichos, y hechos del señor rey don Felipe segundo, el prudente, potentissimo, y glorioso monarca de las Españas, y de las Indias. 4 p. l. 149 l. numb. 16°. *Seuilla, P. Gomez*, 1639.

Porta (Giovanni Battista). De i miracoli et maravigliosi effetti da la natvra prodotti, libri iiii. Nuouamente tradotti di latino in lingua volgare. 15 p. l. 148 l. 16°. *Venetia, L. Auanzo*, 1566.

——— La fantesca, comedia. 173 pp. 24°. *Venetia, G. B. Bonfadino*, 1592.

Porte (*pseudon.*) *See* **Mathews** (G. H.)

Porter (*Mrs.* Ann Emerson). Married for both worlds. 281 pp. 16°. *Boston, Lee & Shepard*, 1871.

——— This one thing I do. 344 pp. 3 pl. 16°. *Boston, D. Lothrop & co.* 1871.

Porter (Ebenezer, *d. d.*) Analysis of the principles of rhetorical delivery, as applied in reading and speaking. 4th ed. 1 p. l. 404 pp. 12°. *Andover, Flagg & Gould*, 1831.

Porter (Ebenezer, *d. d.*)—continued.
—— The same. Revised and enlarged. By Allen H. Weld. 396 pp. 12°. *Boston, B. B. Mussey & co.* 1849.
—— The biblical reader; consisting of rhetorical extracts from the old and new testaments, to which is applied a notation, designed to assist in the public and private reading of the scriptures. 263 pp. 12°. *Andover, Gould & Newman*, 1834.
—— The rhetorical reader. 300 pp. 12°. *Andover, Flagg & Gould*, 1831.

Porter (*Rev.* Eliphalet). An eulogy on George Washington, delivered, Jan. 14, 1800, before the inhabitants of Roxbury. 16 pp. 12°. *Boston, Manning & Loring*, [1800].
[Imperfect: pp. 17-22 wanting. MISCELLANEOUS pamphlets, v. 223].

Porter (*Rev.* James). The chart of life: indicating the dangers and securities connected with the voyage to immortality. 259 pp. 12°. *Boston, J. P. Jewett & co.* 1855.

Porter (*Miss* Jane). The pastor's fireside; or, memoirs of the Athelstan family. Abridged from the popular novel, by S. S. Wilkinson. [*anon.*] 1 p. l. 5-30 pp. 1 col. pl. 16°. *London, Dean & Munday*, 1822.

Porter (*Mrs.* M. E.) Mrs. Porter's new southern cookery book, and companion for frugal and economical housekeepers. iv, 416 pp. 12°. *Philadelphia, J. E. Potter & co.* [1871].

Porter (Noah, *d. d. ll. d.*) The elements of intellectual science. Abridged from "The human intellect." xiv, 565 pp. 12°. *New York, C. Scribner & co.* 1871.
—— The sciences of nature versus the science of man. 98 pp. 12°. *New York, Dodd & Mead*, 1871.

Porter (Rose). Foundations; or, castles in the air. 194 pp. 12°. *New York, A. D. F. Randolph & co.* [1871].

Porteus (Beilby, *bishop of London*). A summary of the principal evidences for the truth and divine origin of the christian revelation. 4th ed. viii, 126 pp. 1 l. 16°. *London, L. Hanford*, 1800.
[MISCELLANEOUS pamphlets, v. 340].
—— The same. To which is added, a poem on death. New ed. 144 pp. 18°. *Hartford, Sheldon & Goodrich*, 1817.
—— The young lady's book of christian evidence: a summary of the principal evidences for the truth and divine origin of the christian religion. 220 pp. 18°. *Philadelphia, J. Kay, jr.* 1834.

Portfolio (The). *See* **Hamerton** (Philip Gilbert).

Portland (The) transcript. An independent family journal of literature, science, news, etc. Edward P. Weston and Edward H. Elwell, editors. [Weekly]. April 20, 1850, to March 30, 1872. v. 14-35. fol. *Portland (Me.) Gould & Elwell, and Elwell, Pickard & co.* 1850-72.

Porto (Luigi da). Giulietta e Romeo. Novella storica. Ed. 17, colle varianti fra le due primitive stampe venete; aggiuntavi la novella di Matteo Bandello su lo stesso argomento, il poemetto di Clizia veronese, ed altre antiche poesie; col corredo d'illustrazioni storiche e bibliografiche per cura di Alessandro Torri. 10 p. l. 204, xlviii, 58 pp. 1 l. 6 pl. 8°. *Pisa, fratelli Nistri & cc.* 1831.
[*Note.*—The original title was: Istoria novellamente ritrovata di due nobili amanti, con la pietosa loro morte intervenuta già nella città di Verona nel tempo del sig. Bartolommeo della Scala].

Portogysen (De) goeden bvyrman. Ghetrocken uyt de registers van syn goet gebuerschap gehouden in Lisbona, Maringan, Caep Sint Augustijn, Sint Paulo de Loando, en Sant Tomée. Dienende tot antwoort op het ongefondeerde Brasyls-schuyt-praetjen. [*anon.*] 8 l. sm. 4°. *Ghedruckt tot Lisbon*, [*Gravenhage*] ? 1649.

Portrait au naturel des jésuites. 1731. *See* **Boyer** (Pierre).

Portraits of the principal reformers of the sixteenth century, with a narrative of the reformation of religion. [*anon.* By Thomas Wyatt] ? 156 pp. 8 pl. 16°. *New York, Van Nostrand & Dwight*, 1835.

Portsmouth (Henry). An index to William Penn's works. *See* **Penn** (William).

Posie. [*anon.*] 253 pp. 3 pl. 16°. *Boston, I. P. Warren*, [1871].

Post (R. L.) Digest of the internal revenue law of the United States, as amended by the act approved March 3, 1865. 60 pp. 16°. *Louisville, J. P. Morton & co.* 1865.

Postel (Guillaume). Guillel. Postelli de cosmographica disciplina et signorum cœlestium vera configuratione libri 2. Ex museo Joan. Balesdens. 190, 72 pp. 32°. *Lugduni, Batavorum, J. Maire*, 1636.
—— De rationibus spiritus sancti lib. ii. 53 l. 16°. *Parisiis, P. Gromorsus*, 1543.

Potomac (The) muse. By a lady, a native of Virginia. [*anon.*] 2 p. l. iii, 13-172 pp. 16°. *Richmond, T. W. White*, 1825.
[*Note.*—Apparently by mrs. Alfred W. Elwes].

Potter (Alonzo, *d. d.*) Religious philosophy; or, nature, man, and the bible witnessing to God and to religious truth; being the substance of four courses of lectures delivered before the Lowell institute between the years 1845-53. 503 pp. 8°. *Philadelphia, J. B. Lippincott & co.* 1872.

Potter (H. L. D.) Manual of reading, in four parts: orthophony, class methods, gesture, and elocution. Designed for teachers and students. xi, 418 pp. 1 l. 12°. *New York, Harper & brothers,* 1871.

Potter (John, *d. d. arch-bishop of Canterbury*). The theological works of the most rev. dr. John Potter, containing his sermons, charges, discourse of church-governmen t and divinity-lectures. 3 v. 8°. *Oxford, printed at the theatre,* 1753-54.

Potter (J. Hamilton, *m. d.*) The consumptive's guide to health; or the invalid's five questions, and the doctor's five answers. 82 pp. 8 pl. 18°. *Philadelphia, author,* 1849.

Potter (Louis Joseph Antoine de). Révolution belge, 1828 à 1839. Souvenirs personnels avec des pièces à l'appui. [Avec postscriptum]. 3 v. 8°. *Bruxelles, Meline, Cans & cie.* 1839.

Potter (Nathaniel, *m. d.*) A memoir on contagion, more especially as it respects the yellow fever: read in convention of the medical and chirurgical faculty of Maryland, on the 3d of June, 1817. 1 p. l. iv, 117 pp. 8°. *Baltimore, E. J. Coale,* 1818.

Potter (William Bleecker). Sketch of the present state of the iron manufacture in Great Britain. 8°. [*Columbus (O.)* 1871].
[OHIO (*State of*). *Geological survey,* 1870. Part 8, pp. 501-526].

Potter (Woodburne, *2d lieut. U. S. a.*) The war in Florida: being an exposition of its causes, and an accurate history of the campaigns of generals Clinch, Gaines, and Scott. By a late staff officer. [*anon.*] viii, 184 pp. 3 maps. 12°. *Baltimore, Lewis & Coleman,* 1836.

Pottsville (*Pa.*) Boyd's directory of Pottsville, with a business directory of the principal places in Schuylkill county, and on the line of the P. & R. railroad, between Philadelphia and Pottsville. 1871-72. W. H. Boyd, compiler and publisher. 335 pp. [14 l. intercalated]. 8°. *Pottsville (Pa.)* [*W. H. Boyd,* 1871].

Potwin (*Mrs.* H. K.) Lucy Maynard; or, judge not from appearances. [*anon.*] 67 pp.

Potwin (*Mrs.* H. K.)—continued.
2 pl. 18°. *Boston, Mass. sabbath school society,* [1862].

——— Mary Alden; or, decision of character. [*anon.*] 160 pp. 2 pl. 18°. *Boston, Mass. sabbath school society,* 1860.

——— Robert, the cabin boy. By H. K. P. [*anon.*] 227 pp. 1 pl. 18°. *New York, M. W. Dodd,* 1863.

——— Ruby Duke. 421 pp. 12°. *Boston, Lee & Shepard,* 1872.

Poughkeepsie (*N. Y.*) Vail's Poughkeepsie city directory for 1871-72. 8°. *Poughkeepsie city, J. P. A. Vail,* 1871.

Pouqueville (François Charles Hugues Laurent). Travels in southern Epirus, Acarnania, Ætolia, Attica, and Peloponesus, or the Morea, &c. &c. in 1814-1816. 128 pp. 1 pl. 1 map. 8°. *London, sir R. Phillips & co.* 1822.

Pourtalès (Louis F.) Deep-sea corals [from the straight of Florida and the gulf-stream]. 2 p. l. 93 pp. 8 pl. 8°. *Cambridge,* 1871. S.
[HARVARD College. *Museum of comparative zoology*].

Pousse (François). Examen des principes des alchymistes sur la pierre philosophale. [*anon.*] 10 p. l. 256 pp. 16°. *Paris, D. Jollet,* 1711.

Powell (Hiram). A treatise on the intellectual, moral, and social man. With an essay on man. 271 pp. 8°. *Cincinnati, R. Clarke & co.* 1871.

Powell (*Major* James W. *prof. Normal univ. Ill.*) Report on his explorations of the rio Colorado in 1869. 8°. [*London,* 1870].
[*In* BELL (William A.) New tracks in North America, pp. 559-564].

Powell (William H. *capt. U. S. a.*) A history of the organization and movements of the fourth regiment of infantry, U. S. army, from May 30, 1796, to December 31, 1870. 215 pp. 8°. *Washington city, M'Gill & Witherow,* 1871.

Power (John). A handy-book about books, for book lovers, book-buyers, and booksellers. xvi, 217 pp. incl. 8 pl. 8°. *London, J. Wilson,* 1870.

Power (*Rev.* John H.) A discussion of universalism. 1846. *See* **Doolittle** (*Rev.* N.) and **Power**.

——— An exposition of universalism. 311 pp. 12°. *Cincinnati, author,* 1843.

Power (Marguerite A.) Sweethearts and wives. 3 v. 12°. *London, Saunders, Otley & co.* 1861.

Power (*Rev.* Philip Bennett). Pivot words of scripture. xv, 319 pp. 12°. *London, W. Macintosh*, 1866.

Powers (Edward). War and the weather, or the artificial production of rain. 171 pp. 12°. *Chicago, S. C. Griggs & co.* 1871.

Powers (Stephen). Afoot and alone; a walk from sea to sea by the southern route. Adventures and observations in Southern California, New Mexico, Arizona, Texas, etc. 327 pp. 12 pl. 12°. *Hartford (Conn.) Columbian book co.* 1872.

Pownall (*Governor* Thomas). Notices and descriptions of antiquities of the provincia romana of Gaul, now Provence, Languedoc, and Dauphiné; with dissertations on the subjects of which those are exemplars, and an appendix describing the roman baths and thermæ discovered in 1784, at Badenweiler. xii, 198 pp. 7 pl. 4°. *London, J. Nichols*, 1788.

Poynder (John). Popery in alliance with heathenism: letters proving that where the bible is wholly unknown, as in the heathen world, or only partially known, as in the romish world, idolatry and superstition are inevitable. 2d ed. 120 pp. 8°. *London, J. Hatchard & son*, 1835.
[MISCELLANEOUS pamphlets, v. 107].

Pozzo (Andrea). Rules and examples of perspective proper for painters and architects, etc. in english and latin. Done into english from the original printed at Rome 1693 in lat. and ital. By mr. John James of Greenwich. [Or], Perspectiva pictorum et architectorum. 2 eng. titles, 6 p. l. 51 l. 103 pl. 4 l. fol. *London, B. Motte*, 1707.

Practical (A) treatise on dyeing and calico printing. By an experienced dyer. *See* **Parnell** (Edward Andrews).

Practical truths from homely sayings. [*anon.*] 2d ed. xi, 232 pp. 18°. *London, J. Hatchard & son*, 1841.

Practical wisdom; or, the manual of life. The counsels of eminent men to their children. Comprising those of sir Walter Raleigh, lord Burleigh, sir Henry Sidney, earl of Strafford, Francis Osborn, sir Matthew Hale, earl of Bedford, William Penn, and Benjamin Franklin. With the lives of the authors. [*anon.*] xii, 336 pp. 12°. *London, H. Colburn & co.* 1824.

Praed (Winthrop Mackworth). Poetical works. New and enlarged edition. 2 v.

Praed (Winthrop Mackworth)—continued. xxiii, 13-310 pp; v, 304 pp. 12°. *New York, Redfield*, 1859.

Praet. *See* **Van Praet.**

Prague. *K. k. sternwarte.* Magnetische und meteorologische beobachtungen auf der k. k. sternwarte zu Prag im jahre 1870. Mit einem anhange: astronomische hilfstafeln, 1. abtheil. Auf öffentliche kosten herausgegeben von Carl Hornstein. 31. jahrgang. xl, 200 pp. 4°. *Prag, G. H. Söhne*, 1871. s.

Prairie (The) missionary. [*anon.*] 180 pp. 1 pl. 18°. *Philadelphia, American sunday school union*, [1853].

Pratt (Samuel Jackson). Landscapes in verse. Taken in spring. By the author of Sympathy. [*anon.*] 2d ed. viii, 63 pp. 4°. *London, T. Becket*, 1785.

Pratt (Thomas). The colombian monitor; showing the influence of education and its importance, particularly in the United States. 3 p. l. 270 pp. 18°. *Harrisburg, [Pa.] Montgomery & Dexter*, 1830.

Pratten (*Rev.* B. P.) Syriac documents attributed to the first three centuries. Translated by rev. B. P. Pratten. 3 p. l. 168 pp. 8°. *Edinburgh, T. & T. Clark*, 1871.
[ANTE-NICENE christian library, v. 20].

Preble (George Henry). Genealogical sketch of the first three generations of Prebles in America: with an account of Abraham Preble the emigrant, their common ancestor, and of his grandson brigadier general Jedediah Preble, and his descendants. 3 p. l. 336 pp. 6 portraits. 1 pl. 1 fac-simile. 8°. *Boston, printed for family circulation, D. Clapp & son*, 1868.

Prechtl (Johann Joseph). Technologische encyclopädie, oder alphabetisches handbuch der technologie, der technischen chemie und des maschinenwesens. 19 v. 8°. Atlas. obl. fol. *Stuttgart, J. G. Cotta*, 1830-53. s.
[v. 17-18 wanting].

——— Untersuchungen über den flug der vögel. vi, 259 pp. 3 pl. 8°. *Wien, C. Gerold*, 1846. s.

Preiss (Ludwig). Plantae preissianae. *See* **Lehmann** (Johann Georg Christian).

Prentiss (*Mrs.* E.) Little threads; or tangle thread, silver thread, and golden thread. By the author of "Susy's six birthdays," [etc. *anon.*] 191 pp. 2 pl. 16°. *New York, A. D. F. Randolph*, 1863.

Presbyterian church. (*United States*). The constitution of the presbyterian church in

Presbyterian church—continued. the United States of America. Containing the confession of faith, the catechisms, and the directory for the worship of God: together with the plan of government and discipline, as amended and ratified by the general assembly at their sessions in May, 1805. 424 pp. 12°. *Philadelphia, W. W. Woodward*, 1815.

Presbyterian (The). [A weekly religious newspaper]. Jan. 7 to Dec. 30, 1871. v. 41. fol. *Philadelphia, A. Martien & co.* [1871].

Prescott (William Hickling). Biographical and critical miscellanies. 5 p. l. 638 pp. 1 portrait. 8°. *New York, Harper & brothers*, 1845.

——— History of the conquest of Mexico, with a preliminary view of the ancient mexican civilization, and the life of the conqueror Hernando Cortez. 3 v. 8°. *Philadelphia, J. B. Lippincott & co.* 1871.

Present (The). Edited by W. H. Channing. Sept. 1843, to March, 1844. v. 1. 432 pp. 8°. [*New York*, 1843-44].

Present (The) melancholy circumstances of the province [of Massachusetts, as to money or a medium of trade] consider'd, and methods for redress humbly proposed, in a letter from one in the country to one in Boston, March 6th, 1718-19. [*anon.*] 16 pp. 18°. *Boston, B. Gray and J. Edwards*, 1719.

Preston (Lyman). Stories for the whole family, young and old, male and female. 108 pp. 16°. *New-York, J. M. Elliott*, 1833.

Preston (*Rev.* Richard). The godly man's inqvisition, lately delivered in two sermons. 3 p. l. 65 pp. sm. 4°. *London, I. Dawson for I. Bellamie*, 1622.

Preston (*Rev.* Thomas S.) The vicar of Christ; or, lectures upon the office and prerogatives of our holy father the pope. 452 pp. 1 portrait. 12°. *New York, R. Coddington*, 1871.

Preston (William). Poetical works. 2 v. xxii, 417 pp. 1 portrait; 2 p. l. vi, 399 pp. 8°. *Dublin, author*, 1793.

Pretyman (George, *bishop of Lincoln*). Elements of christian theology: containing, proofs of the authenticity and inspiration of the holy scriptures; a summary of the history of the Jews; a brief statement of the contents of the several books of the old and new testaments; a short account of the en-

Pretyman (George)—continued. glish translations of the bible, and of the liturgy of the church of England; and a scriptural exposition of the thirty-nine articles of religion. 3d ed. 2 v. xx, 532 pp; 1 p. l. 568 pp. 8°. *London, Cadell & Davies*, 1800.

Prevost (J. Joseph). Un tour en Irlande. 2 p. l. 444 pp. 8°. *Paris, Amyot*, 1846.

Prévost d'Exiles (Antoine François). Manuel lexique, ou dictionnaire portatif des mots françois dont la signification n'est pas familière à tout le monde. Nouvelle éd. [*anon.*] 2 v. in 1. 2 p. l. 542 pp. 1 l; 2 p. l. 570 pp. 12°. *Paris, Didot*, 1755.

[*Note.*—This is an adaptation of the english dictionary of Thomas Dyche to the french language, with additions and modifications].

Price (Issachar). School-day rhymes. 124 pp. 1 portrait. 18°. *Philadelphia, H. B. Ashmead*, 1856.

Price (William C. *ll. d.*) The history of our lord and saviour Jesus Christ. *See* **Thompson** (Ebenezer, *d. d.*) *and* **Price.**

Prichard (S. J.) What Shawny did to the light-house. 144 pp. 3 pl. 16°. *New York, R. Carter & brothers*, 1871.

Prideaux (Humphrey, *d. d.*) The true nature of imposture fully displayed in the life of Mahomet. 1st american ed. 108 pp. 16°. *Fairhaven, [Vermont], J. Lyon*, 1798.

Priestley (Joseph). Historical account of the navigable rivers, canals, and railways, throughout Great Britain, as a reference to Nichols, Priestley & Walker's new map of inland navigation. 2 p. l. xii, 777, x pp. 1 map. 4°. *London, Longman*, 1831.

Priestley (Joseph, *ll. d.*) Letters to the Jews; inviting them to an amicable discussion of the evidences of christianity. 1st american from the 2d british ed. [With letters to dr. Priestley, by David Levi]. 131 pp. 16°. *New-York, J. Harrison for B. Gomez*, 1794.

——— Views of christian truth, piety, and morality, selected from the writings of dr. Priestley. With a memoir of his life, by Henry Ware, jr. lxxx, 207 pp. 12°. *Cambridge, J. Munroe & co.* 1834.

Prime (Eli S.) *and* **McKean** (E. R.) Manual accompanying Prime & McKean's combination guaging instrument, (U. S. int. rev. standard). Containing directions for the use of the same; also, rules for inspecting and guaging, with numerous tables. 161 pp. 2 pl. 1 tab. 12°. *Washington (D. C.) Gibson bros.* 1871.

Prime (Samuel Irenæus, *d. d.*) Five years of prayer, with the answers. 375 pp. 12°. *New York, Harper & brothers*, 1864.

——— Memoirs of the rev. Nicholas Murray, d. d. (Kirwan). 428 pp. 1 portrait. 12°. *New York, Harper & brothers*, 1862.

——— The prodigal reclaimed. Or the sinner's ruin and recovery. 220 pp. 18°. *Boston, Mass. sabbath school soc.* 1843.

Prince (Thomas, *jr. editor*). *See* **Christian** (The) history.

Princeton theological seminary. General catalogue. [1812-]1872. 111, xiv pp. 8°. *Philadelphia, J. B. Rodgers' company*, 1872.

Pringy (— de Marenville, *madame* de). Les différens caractères des femmes du s ècle. Avec la description de l'amour propre. [etc. *anon.*] 6 p. l. 156 pp. 18°. *Paris, veuve C. Coignard & C. Cellier*, 1694.

Printers' (The) circular: a record of typography, literature, arts and sciences. R. S. Menamin, editor. [Monthly]. March, 1871, to Feb. 1872. v. 6. 4°. *Philadelphia, R. S. Menamin*, 1871-72.

Prior (Matthew) *and* **Swift** (Jonathan). Select poems of Prior and Swift. xi, 184 pp. 16°. *London, J. W. Parker & son*, 1853.

Priors (The) of Prague. 1836. *See* **Neale** (W. Johnson).

Priscianus *grammaticus.* Q. Rhemnii Fannii Palaemonis, de ponderibvs, et mensvris liber. [*pseudon.*] 16°. *Venetiis*, 1566.

[*In* CELSUS (A. Cornelius). De re medica, pp. 379-383].

Prisons (Des) de Philadelphie. *See* **La Rochefoucault Liancourt** (F. A. F. *duc* de).

Procopius *caesariensis.* The secret history of the court of the emperor Justinian. Faithfully rendred into english. [1st english ed?] 1 p. l. 162 pp. 16°. *London, J. Barkesdale*, 1674.

Proctor (Edna Dean). A russian journey. iv, 321 pp. 16°. *Boston, J. R. Osgood & co.* 1872.

Projet et fragmens d'un dictionnaire critique. *See* **Bayle** (Pierre).

Promenades d'un artiste. Tyrol. Suisse. Nord de l'Italie. [*anon.*] 3 p. l. 406 pp. 26 pl. 8°. *Paris, J. Renouard*, [1835].

[v. 2 of a series published under the above title].

Proposals relating to the education of youth in Pensilvania. *See* **Franklin** (Benjamin).

Propositien van d'ondernemers tot het vaststellen van een vrye haven in West-Indien. [*anon.*] 4 pp. sm. 4°. [*Amsterdam, about* 1680].

Prospective missions in China. By the author of Conversations on the "Sandwich Islands mission" [etc. *anon.*] 126 pp. 18°. *Boston, Massachusetts sabbath school soc.* 1833.

Prospective missions in the Indian archipelago.—Java. By the author of Conversations on the Sandwich Islands [etc. *anon.*] 121 pp. 1 pl. 18°. *Boston, Massachusetts sabbath school soc.* 1833.

Prospective missions in western Africa. By the author of The model family [etc. *anon.*] 156 pp. 18°. *Boston, Massachusetts sabbath school society*, 1836.

[*Note.*—Prospective missions, v. 7].

Protector (The). A journal for the people. [Monthly]. Feb. to Dec. 1871. v. 1. fol. *New York, W. C. & F. P. Church*, [1871].

Protestant episcopal church in America. Hymnal: according to the use of the protestant episcopal church in the United States of America. 394 pp. 18°. *Philadelphia, J. B. Lippincott & co.* 1871.

——— The same. 491 pp. 16°. [*New York*], *printed under the authority of the general convention*, 1872.

——— Hymns of the protestant episcopal church of the United States, as authorized by the general convention. With an additional selection, by the rev. C. W. Andrews. 234, 42 pp. 18°. *Philadelphia, H. Hooker*, 1845.

——— Lessons of the protestant episcopal church, in the United States of America; selected from the holy scriptures: with an explanation of all the sundays and principal holy-days throughout the year. By Andrew Fowler. 2d ed. 549 pp. 1 l. 12°. *Charleston (S. C.) W. Estill*, 1839.

——— The psalter and canticles: pointed in accordance with the pointed psalter used in Trinity church, New York. [Extracts]. 5 p. l. 301-511 pp. 2 l. 18°. *New York, Pott & Amery*, [1871].

——— *Diocese of Ohio.* Journal of the fifty-fourth annual convention of the protestant episcopal church in the diocese of Ohio, held in Trinity church, Toledo, June 7th-9th, 1871. 120 pp. 8°. *Columbus (O.) Nevins & Myers*, 1871.

——— *Diocese of Vermont.* Journal of the eighty-first annual convention of the protestant episcopal church in the diocese of Vermont: being the thirty-ninth annual convention since the full organization of the diocese; held in st. Thomas' church, Brandon, 7th and 8th June, 1871. 110 pp. 8°. *Burlington, [Vt.] R. S. Styles*, 1871.

Protestant jesuitism. By a protestant. [*anon.*] 295 pp. 12°. *New York, Harper & brothers*, 1836.

Proverbiorum arabicorum etc. *See* **Erpen** (Thomas van).

Providence (*R. I.*) The Providence almanac and business directory for the years 1845 and 1847. By John F. Moore. 2 v. 18°. *Providence, J. F. Moore*, [1846].

——— The Providence directory, for the year 1871: containing a general directory of the city, a record of the city government, its institutions, etc; together with a complete business directory and register of the entire state. 520 pp. 1 map. 8°. *Providence, Sampson, Davenport & co.* 1871.

Proyart *or* **Proyard** (Liévain Bonaventure, *abbé*). The life of princess Louisa (madame Louise), of France, daughter of Louis xv. king of France; a carmelite nun. [From the french]. New ed. 2 v. in 1. xix, 256 pp. 1 portrait; 264 pp. 12°. *Salisbury, J. Easton, for mrs. E. Macdonald*, 1808.

Prynne (William). The antipathie of the english lordly prelacie, both to regall monarchy, and civill unity: or, an historicall collection of the severall execrable treasons, conspiracies, rebellions, seditions, state-schismes, contumacies, anti-monarchicall practices, & oppressions of our english, british, french, scottish, and irish lordly prelates, against our kingdomes, lawes, liberties; and of the severall warres, and civill dissentions occasioned by them, in or against our realm, in former and latter ages. 2 v. 15 p. l. 337 pp; 8 p. l. 201-531 pp. sm. 4°. *London, M. Sparke*, 1641.

Ps and Qs. [*anon.*] 2d ed. 3 p. l. 200 pp. 18°. *Hingham, C. & E. B. Gill*, 1831.

Psalter (The), or, psalms of David, etc. pointed for chanting. Compiled from the arrangements of Robert James, and James Stimpson. 224 pp. 1 l. 18°. *New York, J. A. Sparks*, 1843.

Pseaumes (Les) de David. Mis en vers françois. Revus et approuvéz par le synode walon des provinces unies. Nouv. éd. Eng. title, 335 pp. 24°. *Amsterdam, F. G.* 1706.

[*With* Bible. (*French*). Le nouveau testament. *Amsterdam*, 1706].

——— The same. 2 p. l. 267 pp. 24°. *Amsterdam, D. J. Changuion*, 1794.

[*With* Bible. (*French*). Le nouveau testament. *Amsterdam*, 1794].

Ptolemæus (Claudius). Clavdii Ptolemaei geographicae enarrationis libri octo Bilibaldo Pirckheymhero interprete. Annotationes Ioannis de Regio Monte in errores commissos a Iacobo Angelo in translatione sua. 82 l. numb. 48 l. unp. 50 maps. fol. *Argentoragi, Iohannes Grieningerus*, 1525.

——— Cl. Ptolemæi opvs de sidervm ivdiciis quadripartitum è græco codice in latinum sermonem per Antonivm Gogavam iampridem translatum, cum approbatione Gemmæ Frisii denuo editum. Præpositis ad singula capita breuiarijs, vel notationibus Placidi de Titis. 8 p. l. 192 pp. 18°. *Patavii, typis P. Frambotti*, 1658.

[*Note.*—Appended is Ptolemy's centiloquium, sive centum sententiae Io. Ioviano Pontano interprete. These astrological tracts, as unworthy of the great astronomer, are suspected not to be the work of Ptolemy of Pelusium].

Puaux (N. A. F.) Histoire de la réformation française. 7 v. 16°. *Paris, M. Lévy frères*, 1859-64.

Public ledger. [Memphis daily]. July 18 to Dec. 30, 1871. fol. *Memphis (Tenn.) E. Whitmore*, [1871].

Public opinion: a comprehensive summary of the press throughout the world on all important current topics. [Weekly]. Jan. 7 to Dec. 30, 1871. v. 19-20. fol. *London*, [*I. Seaman*, 1871].

Publishers' (The) circular and general record of british and foreign literature. [London semi-monthly]. Jan. to Dec. 1871. v. 34. 8°. *London, S. Low*, [1871].

Pucciarini (Clemente). Brandigi del capitan Clemente Pvcciarini, aretino. Nvovamente dato in lvce. 2 p. l. 143 pp. 4°. *Venetia, G. A. Rampazetto*, 1596.

Puccinelli (Alessandro). Dialoghi sopra le cavse della peste vniversale. 3 p. l. 52 pp. incl. eng. title and tail-piece. 4°. *Lvcca, V. Busdraghi*, 1577.

Pugh (*Mrs.* Eliza Lofton). In a crucible: a novel. x, 5-389 pp. 12°. *Philadelphia, Claxton, Remsen & Haffelfinger*, 1872.

Pugin (Augustus Welby). Designs for gold and silversmiths. [*anon.*] 23 pl. 4°. *London, Ackerman & co.* 1836.

[Imperfect: pl. 5, 11, 12, and 13 wanting].

Pullen (Henry William). The fight at dame Europa's school: showing how the german boy thrashed the french boy: and how the english boy looked on. With 33 illustrations by Thomas Nast. [*anon.*] 34 pp. 12°. *New York, F. B. Felt & co.* [1871].

Pulleyn (William). Church-yard gleanings, and epigrammatic scraps: being a collection of remarkable epitaphs and epigrams, compiled from the most ancient as well as modern sources: [also], some observations on churches, church-yards, rights of sepulture, tombs, and mausoleums; with instructions for ascertaining the dates of ancient monuments. xxiii, 264 pp. 16°. *London, S. Maunder*, [1829].

Punch; or, the London charivari. January to December, 1871. v. 60–61. 4°. *London, office*, 1871.

Punchard (*Rev.* George). A view of congregationalism, its principles and doctrines. With an introductory essay, by R. S. Storrs, d. d. 2d ed. 331 pp. 12°. *Andover*, [*Ms.*] *Allen, Morrill & Wardwell*, 1844.

Punshon (*Rev.* William Morley). Sermons. To which is prefixed a plea for class-meetings, and an introduction, by rev. William H. Milburn. 350 pp. 12°. *New York, Derby & Jackson*, 1860.

Purefoy (*Elder* George W.) A history of the Sandy Creek baptist association, from its organization in a. d. 1758 to a. d. 1858, being an enlargement of the centenary sermon delivered by him at its one hundreth annual session. 329 pp. 12°. *New York, Sheldon & co.* 1859.

Puritan (Job, *pseudon.*) Household tales. By Job Puritan, esq. umbratile solicitor in the court of the muses. 367 pp. 12°. *Boston, J. Munroe & co.* 1861.

Pusey (Caleb). A modest account from Pennsylvania, of the principal differences in point of doctrine, between George Keith, and those of the people called quakers: shewing his great declension and inconsistency. 68 pp. 18°. *London, T. Sowle*, 1696.

Pusey (Edward Bouverie, *d. d.*) Minor prophets, with a commentary. *See* **Bible**. *English*).

Puteanus. *See* **Putten**.

Puteus (Andreas). *See* **Pozzo**.

Putnam (J. M.) English grammar, with an improved syntax. viii, 142 pp. 12°. *Cambridge*, [*Ms.*] *Hilliard & Metcalf*, 1825.

Putten (Hendrik van der). Erycii Pvteani comus, sive phagesiposia cimmeria. Somnium. 18°. [*Lvgd. Batavorum*, 1655].

[*In* ELEGANTIORES præstantium virorum satyræ, v. 2, pp. 311–408].

Putten (Hendrik van der)—continued.

——— Erycii Pvteani Democritvs, sive de risv dissertatio satvrnalis. 18°. [*Lvgd. Batavorvm*, 1644].

[*In* DISSERTATIONVM lvdicrarvm et amœnitatvm scriptores varij, pp. 579–593].

——— Ovi encomivm. 18°. [*Lvgd. Batavorvm*, 1644].

[*In* DISSERTATIONVM lvdicrarvm et amœnitatvm scriptores varij, pp. 595–654].

Puvis (A.) On the use of lime as a manure. Translated from the french by E. Ruffin, esq. Introductory remarks by James Renwick, ll. d. 18°. [*New York, Harper & brothers*, 1839].

[*In* CHAPTAL (J. A.) Chymistry applied to agriculture. *N. Y.* 1839. pp. 184–247].

Puységur (A. M. J. de Chastenet, *marquis* de). *See* **Chastenet de Puységur** (A. M. J. *marquis* de).

Pyne (Henry). England and France in the fifteenth century. *See* **Débat** des hérauls darmes de frāce et dengleterre.

Pythagoras (*Pseudo-*). Aurea pythagoreorum carmina. Latine conversa, multisque in locis emendata, illustrataque adnotationibus; quibus etiam Hieroclis interpretationi non parum lucis adfertur. Autore [interprete] Theodoro Marcilio. 321–393 pp. 18°. *Londini, typis J. Redmayne*, 1673.

[*In* HIEROCLES. Commentarius in aurea carmina, 1673, pp. 321–393].

Quarterly (The) review. Jan. to Oct. 1871. v. 130–131. 8°. *London, J. Murray*, 1871.

Quatre (Les) fils Aymon. Aus den Haymonskindern. lxviii pp. 4°. [*Berlin, G. Reimer*, 1829].

[*With* FIER a bras. Der roman von Fierabras, 1829].

Quattrami (Evangelista). La vera dichiaratione di tvtte le metafore, similitudini, & enimmi de gl'antichi filosofi alchimisti, tanto caldei & arabi, come greci & latini, vsati da loro nella descrittione, & compositione dell' oro potabile, elissire della vita, quinta essenza, & lapis filosofico. Ove con un breve discorso della generatione de i metalli, si mostra l'errore & ignoranza (per non dir l'inganno) di tutti gl'alchimisti moderni. 12 p. l. 230 pp. 12 l. 4°. *Roma, appresso V. Accolti*, 1587.

Quaw (James E.) Bible baptism, or the immerser instructed, from various sources. 2d ed. 392 pp. sq. 16°. *Detroit, B. Wood*, 1844.

Quérard (Joseph Marie). La famille Guizot: monographie bibliographique. 32 pp. 8°. *Paris, l'auteur*, 1857.

[Extrait du journal "Le Quérard"].

Quetelet (Lambert Adolphe Jacques). Anthropométrie ou mesure des différentes facultés de l'homme. 1 p. l. 479 pp. 2 tables. 8°. *Bruxelles, C. Muquardt*, 1871. s.

Quevedo Villegas (Francisco de). L'aventvrier Bvscon, histoire facécievse. Composée en espagnol. [Traduite par La Geneste]. Ensemble les lettres du cheualier de l'Espargne. [1644]. 401 pp. 16°. *Paris, A. Cotinet*, 1645.

[*Note.*—This is the merry tale known as the adventures of Paul, the sharper of Segovia. Its title in spanish was Historia y vida del Buscon llamado d. Pablos, ejemplo de vagamundos, y espijo de tacaños].

——— Fortune in her wits, or, the hour of all men. Translated into english by capt. John Stevens. 7 p. l. 131 pp. 12°. *London, R. Sare*, 1697.

——— The visions. Made english by sir Roger L'Estrange. 8th ed. corrected. 4 p. l. 344 pp. 16°. *London, R. Sare and E. Hindmarsh*, 1696.

Quevenne (T. A.) Mémoire sur la digitaline et la digitale. 1854. *See* **Homolle** (E.) *and* **Quevenne.**

Quillet (Claude). Calvidii Leti callipædia; seu, de pulchræ prolis habendæ ratione. Poëma didacticon ad humanam speciem belle conservandam apprime utile. [*pseudon.*] 56 pp. 4°. *Lvgdvni Batavorvm, veneunt Parisiis, apud T. Jolly*, 1655.

Quin (Michael John). A steam voyage down the Danube. With sketches of Hungary, Wallachia, Servia, Turkey, &c. 3d ed. with additions. 2 v. in 1. xvi, 344 pp. 10 pl; vii, 340 pp. 1 pl. 12°. *London, R. Bentley*, 1836.

Quincy (Eliza Susan Morton). Memoir of the life of Eliza S. M. Quincy. [By herself]. 1 p. l. 267 pp. 4°. *Boston*, 1861.

Quinet (Edgar). Idées sur la philosophie de l'histoire de l'humanité. Introduction. *See* **Herder** (Johann Gottlieb).

Quintana (Geronimo de). A la mvy antigva, noble y coronada villa de Madrid. Historia de sv antigvedad, nobleza y grandeza. [Eng. title, 5 p. l. 455, 11 l. fol. *Madrid, imprenta del reyno*, 1629.

Quirini (Angelo Maria). Angeli Mariæ card. Quirini liber singularis de optimorum scriptorum editionibus quæ Romæ primum prodierunt post divinum typographiæ inventum, a germanis opificibus in eam urbem advectum: plerisque omnibus earum editionum seu præfationibus, seu epistolis in medium allatis. Cum brevibus observationibus ad easdem. Recensuit annotationes, rerumque notabiliorum indicem adjecit, et diatribem præliminarem de variis rebus præmisit Jo. Georgius Schelhornius. 2 p. l. 266 pp. 5 l. 4°. *Lindaugiæ, impensis J. Ottonis*, 1761.

Quitman (Frederick Henry). A treatise on magic, or, on the intercourse between spirits and men: with annotations. vi, 76 pp. 16°. *Albany, Balance press*, 1810.

R. Briefe über die wichtigsten gegenstände der menschheit. Herausgegeben von S. T. u. [Christian Friedrich Sinteniss. *anon*]. 2er theil. 2 p. l. 348 pp. 12°. *Leipzig, J. A. Barth*, 1794.

R. Gleanings after "grand tour"-ists. [*anon.*] viii, 415 pp. 8°. *London, Bosworth & Harrison*, 1856.

R. (C. H.) Incidents of travel in the southern states and Cuba. With a description of the mammoth cave. [*anon.*] 1 p. l. 320 pp. 12°. *New York, R. Craighead*, 1862.

R. (T.) Contraband christmas. [*anon.*] 104 pp. 2 pl. 16°. *Boston, E. P. Dutton & co.* 1864.

Rabadan (Mohammed). Mahometism fully explained: containing many surprizing passages, not to be found in any other author. Written in spanish and arabick, in 1603, for the instruction of the Moriscoes in Spain. Translated from the original manuscript, and illustrated with explanatory notes. By mr. [Joseph] Morgan. 2 v. xxxii, 390 pp. 2 pl; lxxxiv, 366 pp. 1 l. 8°. *London, E. Curll*, 1723–25.

Raban (Louis François). Une femme perdue. 2 v. 2 p. l. 428 pp; 2 p. l. 483 pp. 8°. *Paris, Dolin*, 1849.

Rabelleau (—, *conseiller de préfecture à Orléans*). Histoire des Hébreux, rapprochée des temps contemporains; de la création du monde au dernier sac de Jérusalem, sous Vespasien. 2e éd. revue, corrigée et augmentée. 2 v. xxiv, 466 pp. 1 l; 2 p. l. viii, 452 pp. 8°. *Paris, Parent-Desbarres*, 1828.

Rack (John). The french wine and liquor manufacturer. A practical guide and receipt book for the liquor merchant. 268 pp. 12°. *New York, Dick & Fitzgerald*, 1863.

Radonvilliers (Claude François Lizarde, *l'abbé* de). De la manière d'apprendre les langues. [*anon.*] xxiv, 278 pp. 12°. *Paris, Saillant*, 1768.

Raffaelle d'Urbino. The caryatides from the "Stanza dell' Eliodoro" in the vatican. Engraved and edited by Lewis Gruner. Eng. title, 3 p. l. 15 pl. fol. *London*, 1852.

Ragged homes and how to mend them. [*anon.*] 303 pp. 2 pl. 16°. *Philadelphia, American sunday-school union*, [1859].

Raidel (Georg Martin). Commentatio critico-literaria de Clavdii Ptolemæi geographia, eivsqve codicibvs tam manv-scriptis qvam typis expressis. 11 p. l. 82 pp. 4°. *Norimbergæ, typis et sumtibus hæredum felseckerianorum*, 1737.

Rail-road (The) boy. By the author of "Poor Nicholas," etc. [*anon.*] 180 pp. 3 pl. 18°. *Philadelphia, Presbyterian board of publication*, [1863].

Rainaudo (Teofilo). Theophili Raynavdi dissertatio de sobria alterivs sexvs frequentatione per sacros & religiosos homines. Inædificata narrationi deliriorum, queis puella veneta, Gvlielmvm Postellvm seculo superiore infatuauit. 12 p. l. 600 pp. 14 l. 12°. *Lvgdvni, sumptibus M. Dvhan*, 1653.

Raine (Matthew). Eclecta puerilia. Sententiæ, colloquia, fabulæ, et poemata in usum scholarum collecta. Ed. altera aucta et emendata. Ex recensione et castigatione T. Wemyss. 240 pp. 16°. *Londini, apud J. Mawman*, 1811.

Ralph (James, *editor*). *See* **Champion** (The).

Ralph (Joseph, *m. d.*) A practical treatise on the diseases and abuses of the sexual system. 18th ed. 64 l. unp. 12°. *New York, E. D. Long*, 1857.

——— A private treatise on venereal disease, gonorrhea, etc. 2 p. l. 100 pp. 2 pl. 18°. *New York, author*, [1836].

Ralph and Robbie: a tale of early piety. By the author of "Roland Rand," [etc. *anon.*] 135 pp. 18°. *New York, Carlton & Phillips*, 1856.

Ralston (Thomas N. *d. d.*) Elements of divinity: or, a course of lectures comprising a clear and concise view of the system of theology as taught in the holy scriptures; with appropriate questions appended to each lecture. 463 pp. 1 portrait. 8°. *Cincinnati, Poe & Hitchcock*, 1861.

——— The same. Elements of divinity: or, a concise and comprehensive view of bible theology. Edited by T. O. Summers, d. d. 1023 pp. 8°. *Nashville, A. H. Redford*, 1871.

Ram (Stopford J.) Unseen hand. By Ruth Vernon. [*pseudon.*] 321 pp. 4 pl. 8°. *Cincinnati, J. R. Hawley*, 1863.

Ramayan (The). *See* **Valmiki**.

Ramble (Robert, *pseudon.*) The birds of the air. By Robert Ramble. 144 pp. sq. 16°. *Philadelphia, J. Crissy*, 1840.

——— Elements of arithmetic, for children: on a plan entirely new: adapted for families and preparatory schools. 108 pp. 18°. *Philadelphia, Desilver, Thomas & co.* 1836.

——— A porte-folio for youth. 352 pp. sq. 16°. *Philadelphia, J. Crissy*, 1834.

——— Ramble's roman stories. 144 pp. sq. 16°. *Philadelphia, J. Crissy*, 1841.

Ramée (Daniel). Manuel de l'histoire générale de l'architecture chez tous les peuples, et particulièrement de l'architecture en France au moyen-âge. 2 v. xi, 501 pp; 1 p. l. 444 pp. 16°. *Paris, Paulin*, 1843.

Ramesey *or* **Ramsey** (William). Vox stellarum. Or, the voice of the starres: being a short introdvction to the judgement of eclipses, and the annuall revolutions of the world. Wherein is handled astrologically, the engresse of the sun into the tropick, and aequinoctiall signes. 1652. 7 p. l. 138 pp. 3 l. 18°. *London, T. H. and Jo. Collins*, 1652.

Ramirez de Vargas (Alonso). Sagrado padron y panegyricos sermones a la memoria debida al svmptvoso magnifico templo del glorioso abad San Bernardo, que edifico en su mayor parte el capitan d. Ioseph de Retes Largache, en esta ciudad de México, con la pompa funebre de la translacion de sus huessos, qve erige en descripcion historica panegyrica, A. Ramirez de Vargas. 6 p. l. 27, 9, 135 l. 1 l. sm. 4°. *México, viuda de F. R. Lvpercio*, 1691.

Rammelsberg (Carl Friedrich, *m. d.*) Guide to a course of quantitative chemical analysis, especially of minerals and furnace-products, illustrated by examples. Translated by J. Towler, m. d. viii, 232 pp. 8°. *Geneva, (N. Y.) J. Towler*, 1871.

Rammohun Roy. Exposition of the practical operation of the judicial and revenue systems of India, and of the general character and condition of its native inhabitants, as submitted in evidence to the authorities in England. With notes and illustrations. xvi, 130 pp. 1 map. 8°. *London, Smith, Elder & co.* 1832.

Ramond de Carbonnières (Louis François Élisabeth). Observations faites dans les Pyrénées, pour servir de suite à des observations sur les Alpes, insérées dans une traduction des lettres de W. Coxe, sur la Suisse. viii, 452 pp. 3 maps. 8°. *Paris, Belin*, 1789.

Rampoldi (Giovanni). I proverbi e le sentenze proverbiali. Raccolta. 3 v. in 1. 18°. *Milano, stamperia de' classici italiani,* [*about* 1820].

Ramrod (The) broken; or, the bible, history, and common sense in favor of the moderate use of good spirituous liquors. By a New England journalist. [*anon.*] 300 pp. 1 pl. 12°. *Boston, A. Colby & co.* 1859.

Ramsay (André Michel de). Life of Francis de Salignac, de la Mothe Fénelon. Translated from the french, and first printed with notes at London, 1747. [*anon.*] 8°. *Dublin, C. Bentham,* 1822.

[*In* FÉNELON (F. de S. de la Mothe). Part of spiritual works, v. 1, pp. 1-55. *Dublin,* 1822].

Ramsay (David, *m. d.*) Memoirs of Martha Laurens Ramsay, with extracts from her diary, letters, and other private papers. 262 pp. 1 portrait. 18°. *Philadelphia, American sunday-school union,* [1845].

Ramsay (George). A new dictionary of anecdotes, illustrative of character and events: from genuine sources. Arranged alphabetically, according to the respective subjects. iv, 636 pp. 1 pl. 8°. *London, Sherwood, Neely & Jones,* 1822.

Ramsey (*Mrs.* V. G.) Evenings with the children; or, travels in South America. 234 pp. 4 pl. 16°. *Boston, D. Lothrop & son,* 1871.

Ramsey. *See* **Ramesey** *and* **Ramsay.**

Ramusio (Gregorio). Qvaestiones affinitates Gregorii Rhamnvsii tarinatis. i. v. d. 24 l. unp. sm. 4°. *Romæ, ex officina V. Lucchini,* 1566.

Ranalli (Ferdinando). Del Petrarca delle sue epistole e di un saggio di traduzione. 128 pp. 8°. *Montalboli,* [*about* 1840]?

Rancé (A. J. Le Boutillier de). *See* **Le Boutillier de Rancé.**

Rand (Edward Sprague, *jr.*) The rhododendron and "American plants." A treatise on the culture, propagation, and species of the rhododendron; with cultural notes upon other plants which thrive under like treatment, and descriptions of species and varieties; with a chapter upon herbaceous plants requiring similar culture. xx, 188 pp. 12°. *Boston, Little, Brown & co.* 1871.

Randall (*Rev.* D. A.) The handwriting of God in Egypt, Sinai, and the holy land; the records of a journey from the great valley of the west to the sacred places of the east. 2 v. in 1. 359 pp. 20 pl; 358 pp. 20 pl. 8°. *Columbus (Ohio), Randall & Aston,* 1862.

Randall (Henry S. *ll. d.*) The practical shepherd: a complete treatise on the breeding, management and diseases of sheep. 7th ed. 454 pp. 1 pl. 12°. *Rochester (N. Y.) D. D. T. Moore,* 1863.

——— Sheep husbandry; with an account of the different breeds, and general directions in regard to summer and winter management, and the treatment of diseases. With his letter to the Texas almanac on sheep husbandry in Texas, and Geo. W. Kendall's on sheep raising in Texas. 338 pp. 1 pl. 8°. *New York, C. M. Saxton, Barker & co.* 1860.

Randall (P. M.) The quartz operator's handbook. Revised and enlarged ed. 176 pp. 12°. *New York, D. Van Nostrand,* 1871.

Randall (Samuel S.) History of the common school system of the state of New York, from its origin in 1795, to the present time. Including the various city and other special organizations, and the religious controversies of 1821, 1832, and 1840. xiv, 477 pp. 6 pl. 8°. *New York, Ivison, Blakeman, Taylor & co.* 1871.

Randolph (Bernard). The present state of the islands in the archipelago, (or arches), sea of Constantinople, and gulph of Smyrna; with the islands of Candia, and Rhodes. [Including, A relation of a storm and great deliverance at sea, in a voyage from New England, 1683-84. Also] an index, shewing the longitude and latitude of all the places in the new map of Greece lately published by the same author. 1 p. l. 26, 108 pp. 5 l. 3 pl. 4°. *Oxford, printed at the theater,* 1687.

——— The present state of the Morea, called anciently Peloponnesus: together with a description of the city of Athens, islands of Zant, Strafades, and Serigo. 3d ed. 1 p. l. 108 pp. 5 l. 6 pl. 4°. *London, W. Notts,* 1689.

Randolph (Cornelia J.) The parlor gardener: a treatise on the house culture of ornamental plants. 158 pp. 11 pl. 18°. *Boston, J. E. Tilton & co.* [1861].

Randolph (Paschal Beverly). *See* **Hermes** *trismegistus.*

Randolph (Richard). Sober thoughts on staple themes. 159 pp. 12°. *Philadelphia, Claxton, Remsen & Haffelfinger,* 1871.

Randolph (Sarah N.) The domestic life of Thomas Jefferson. Compiled from family letters and reminiscences. 432 pp. 4 pl. 2 fac-sim. 8°. *New York, Harper & brothers,* 1871.

Rands (Thomas). Pax in crumena: or, the trooper turn'd poet. 4 p. l. 136 pp. 8°. *London, author*, 1713.

Rankin (*Rev.* John). A present to families; a practical work on the covenant of grace, as given to Abraham. 160 pp. 24°. *Ripley,* [*O.*] *C. Edwards*, 1840.

Ransijat (*Citoyen* Bosredon-). *See* **Bosredon-Ransijat.**

Raoul (Maximilien). Histoire pittoresque du Mont-Saint-Michel, et de Tombelène; et suivie d'un fragment inédit sur Tombelène, extrait du roman du Brut. Transcrit et annoté par Leroux de Lincy. 1 p. l. 270 pp. 13 pl. 1 tab. 8°. *Paris, A. Ledoux*, 1833.

Raousset-Boulbon (G. de). Une conversion. 281 pp. 1 l. 16°. *Paris, librairie nouvelle*, 1855.

Rastrelli (Modesti). Firenze antica, e moderna. *See* **Follini** (Vincenzo) *and* **Rastrelli.**

Rathbone (William). A narrative of events, that have lately taken place in Ireland among the society called quakers; with corresponding documents, and occasional observations. [*anon.*] vi, 225, 68 pp. 8°. *London, J. Johnson*, 1804.

Rathgeber (Georg). Annalen der niederländischen malerei und kupferstecherkunst. Von Rubens abreise nach Italien bis auf Rembrandt's tod. 5 p. l. 229 pp. fol. *Gotha, J. G. Müller*, 1839.

Ratio disciplinæ. *See* **Upham** (Thomas C.)

Raucou (Anaïs Bazin de). *See* **Bazin de Raucou.**

Raulin (Felix Victor). Description physique de l'île de Crète. 3 v. 8°. *Paris, A. Bertrand*, 1869.

[FRANCE. *Ministère de l'instruction publique.* Collection de documents inédits sur l'histoire de France. 1re série].

Raumer (Friedrich von). Italien. Beiträge zur kenntniss dieses landes. 2 v. x, 392 pp; x, 504 pp. 1 l. 12°. *Leipzig, F. A. Brockhaus*, 1840.

Rausch (Friedlieb). Geschichte der literatur des rhäto-romanischen volkes, mit einem blick auf sprache und character desselben. viii, 174 pp. 8°. *Frankfurt a. M: J. D. Saurlanders verlag*, 1870. S.

Raven (Dirck Albertsz.) Journael van de reyse ghedaen by den commandeur Dirck Albertsz. Raven, naer Groen-landt, in den jare 1639. sm. 4°. *Amsterdam, J. Hartgers*, 1650.

[*With* BONTEKOE VAN HOORN (Willem Ysbrantsz). Journael van reyse, 1618–25, pp. 61–66, ed. 1650].

Raven (Dirck Albertsz.)—continued.

——— The same. Reyse na Spitzberghen, 1639, pp. 59–66. sm. 4°. *Amstelredam, J. Hartgers*, 1648.

[*In* HARTGERTS (J.) Oost-indische voyagien, v. 1, 10e stuck].

Rawlinson (*Sir* Henry Creswicke). Miscellaneous inscriptions of Assyria. *See* **British** museum.

Ray (John). Select remains of the learned John Ray. With his life, by the late William Derham, d. d. Published by George Scott. vii, 336 pp. 1 portrait. 8°. *London, J. Dodsley & J. Walter*, 1760.

Ray (Nicholas). The importance of the colonies of North America, and the interest of Great Britain in regard to them, considered; with remarks on the stamp-duty. 16 pp. 4°. *New-York, J. Holt*, 1766.

[HAZARD pamphlets, v. 7].

Ray (Rena, *pseudon.*) Allie and Ryan; or, the new bonnet and dress. 253 pp. 18°. *New York, Carlton & Porter*, [1862].

——— The christmas party, and other stories. For boys and girls. 272 pp. 18°. *New York, Carlton & Porter*, [1860].

——— Fanny Floyd; or, one day at school. 134 pp. 18°. *New York, Carlton & Porter*, [1863].

——— Mattie; or, live for others. 134 pp. 18°. *New York, Carlton & Porter*, [1862].

——— Rumford Rosey; or, what it costs to disobey a mother. 134 pp. 18°. *New York, Carlton & Porter*, [1863.]

——— Tired of being a boy. 70 pp. 18°. *New York, Carlton & Porter*, [1862].

Ray society. Publications. fol. *London, Ray society*, 1871.

CONTENTS.

ALLMAN (G. J.) A monograph of the gymnoblastic or tubularian hydroids. fol. 1871.

Raymond (George). Chronicles of England: a metrical history. xxviii, 274 pp. 1 pl. 8°. *London, W. Smith*, 1842.

——— The same. 2d ed. xxviii, 274 pp. 1 pl. 8°. *London, W. Smith*, 1843.

Rayner (*Rev.* Menzies). Parable of the rich man and Lazarus; illustrated in nine lectures, delivered in the first universalist church in Portland, Maine, 1833. 187 pp. 12°. *Boston, Marsh, Capen & Lyon*, 1833.

——— Six lectures on revivals of religion, delivered in the universalist church in Portland, 1834. 126 pp. 18°. *Portland, M. Rayner, jr.* 1834.

——— The universalist manual, or book of prayers and other religious exercises. 192, 95 pp. 16°. *New York, P. Price*, 1839.

Raynouard (François Juste Marie). Des troubadours et des cours d'amour. 2 p. l. cxxiv pp. 8°. *Paris, F. Didot,* 1817.

Razzi (Silvano). Descrizione del sacro eremo di camaldoli, et della regola, et vita de' padri eremiti, che in seruigio di Dio habitano quel santo luogo. 78 pp. 1 pl. 16°. *Fiorenza, B. Sermartelli,* 1572.

——— De' miracoli di nostra donna, libri tre. Tratti da diuersi cattolici, & approuati autori. Ora con nvova aggivnta di piu altri miracoli ristampati. 8 p. l. 248 pp. 16°. *Firenze, M. Sermartelli,* 1595.

[Imperfect: pp. 117-118 wanting].

——— Vita di Benedetto Varchi. 8°. [*Milano,* 1803].

[*In* VARCHI (Benedetto). Storia fiorentina, v. 1, pp. vii-xxiii].

Rea (John). Flora: seu, de florum cultura. Or, a complete florilege furnished with all requisites belonging to a florist. The second impression corrected, with many additions, and several new plates. In iii books. Eng. title, 12 p. l. 231 pp. 4 l. 8 pl. fol. *London, G. Marriott,* 1676.

Read (*Rev.* Hollis). The palace of the great king; or, the power, wisdom, and goodness of God, illustrated in the multiplicity and variety of his works. 408 pp. 12°. *New York, C. Scribner,* 1859.

Read (M. C.) Sketches of the geology of Geauga and Holmes counties, [Ohio]. 8°. [*Columbus,* 1871].

[OHIO (*State of*). *Geological survey.* 1870. Part 6, pp. 463-484].

Reade (Charles). A terrible temptation. A story of to-day. [Illustrated]. 1 p. l. 172 pp. 8°. *Boston, J. R. Osgood and co.* 1871.

Reade (W. Winwood). See-saw; a novel. Edited by W. Winwood Reade. 2 v. viii, 303 pp; 2 p. l. 328 pp. 12°. *London, E. Moxon & co.* 1865.

Readings for young men, merchants, and men of business. Reprinted from the London edition. [*anon.*] 172 pp. 12°. *Boston, J. Munroe & co.* 1859.

Realities of life; sketches designed for the improvement of the head and heart. By a philanthropist. [*anon.*] 197 pp. 16°. *New Haven, S. Babcock,* 1839.

Reasoner (The). [A weekly journal]. Edited by G. J. Holyoake. 1846-61. 26 v. 8°. *London, J. Watson,* 1846-53; *Holyoake & co.* 1854-61.

TITLES AT VARIOUS TIMES.

v. 1. The reasoner. 1846.
v. 2-3. The reasoner: and utilitarian record. Dec. 1846, to Nov. 1847.

Reasoner (The)—continued.

v. 4-6. The reasoner; a weekly journal, utilitarian, republican, and communist. Dec. 1847, to June, 1849.
v. 7. The reasoner. July, 1849, to Jan. 1850.
v. 8-12. The reasoner and theological examiner. Jan. 1850, to June, 1852.
v. 13. The reasoner. New series. v. 13. June to Dec. 1852.
v. 14-15. The reasoner and secular gazette. 1853.
v. 16-17. The reasoner: gazette of secularism. 1854.
v. 18-19. The reasoner and London tribune, a weekly secular newspaper. 1855.
v. 20. The reasoner, a weekly journal: to explain secular principles, enforce secular practice, and record secular progress. Jan. to June, 1856.
v. 21-26. The reasoner. Journal of free thought and positive philosophy, July, 1856, to June, 1861.

Rebecca (*pseudon.*) Tramps in New York. 104 pp. 2 pl. 16°. *New York, American tract society,* [1863].

Recherches sur l'origine, l'esprit, et les progrès des arts de la Grèce. *See* **Hancarville** (Pierre François Hugues, *dit* d').

Reckitt (William). Some account of [his] life and gospel labours. [Edited by Thomas Wagstaffe]. 201 pp. 18°. *London, J. Phillips,* 1776.

Recollections of a pedestrian. By the author of "The journal of an exile." [*anon.*] 3 v. 12°. *London, Saunders & Otley,* 1826.

Record (The) of news, history and literature. [Richmond weekly]. July 9 to Dec. 10, 1863. 4°. *Richmond (Va.)* [*West & Johnston*], 1863.

[Incomplete].

Record (The) of zoological literature. 1869. v. 6. Edited by A. C. L. G. Günther. 8°. *London, J. Van Voorst,* 1870.

——— The same. The zoological record for 1870. Edited by Alfred Newton. v. 7. 8°. *London, J. Van Voorst,* 1871.

Recorde (Robert). The grounde of artes: teaching the worke and practise of arithmetike, both in whole numbres and fractions, after a more easyer and exacter sorte then any like hath hitherto been sette forthe. 197 l. 2 tables. 18°. *London, R. Wolfe,* 1561.

Records of a village pastor. [*anon.*] 228 pp. 18°. *Boston, Mass. sabbath school society,* 1843.

Recréations instructives et amusantes; ou, choix d'historiettes morales, tirées des ouvrages de mesdames De Choiseul, De Renneville, Jauffret, etc. [*anon.*] 204 pp. 12°. *Philadelphie, H. Perkins,* 1835.

Rectory (The) of Moreland: or, my duty. [*anon.*] 1 p. l. 339 pp. 12°. *Boston, J. E. Tilton & co.* 1860.

Recueil de cantiques & odes maçoniques. [*anon.*] 2 p. l. 156 pp. 12°. *Philadelphie, A. J. Blocquerst*, 1813.

Recueil des chef-d'œuvres des plus célèbres beaux-esprits françois, tant en vers qu'en prose. [*anon.*] 2 p. l. 571 pp. 12°. *Edinbourg, Murray & Cochran*, 1775.

Recueil général des opera représentéz par l'académie royale de musique. *See* **Francini** (Jean Nicolas de) **Gaureault** (Hyacinthe de) *and others.*

Redding (Moses Wolcott). Ecce orienti, or the rites and ceremonies of the Essenes. National series. 6th ed. arranged in accordance with the standard formula. Ipsissimis verbis. [*anon.*] 203 pp. 4 pl. 18°. *New York, M. W. Redding & co.* 1872.

—— The ruins and relics of the holy city, accompanied by a plan of Jerusalem, compiled from the latest ordnance surveys and explorations. 66 pp. 3 pl. 12°. *New York, Redding & co.* 1871.

Reddy (William). Inside views of methodism; or, a handbook for inquirers and beginners. 188 pp. 18°. *New York, Carlton & Porter*, 1859.

Redenbacher (Wilhelm). The little cloister ruin. A narrative. Translated from the german by rev. J. Oswald. 130 pp. 2 pl. 18°. *Philadelphia, Lutheran board of publication*, 1871.

[FATHERLAND series].

Redfield's traveller's guide to the city of New York. [*anon.*] 108 pp. 1 map. 18°. *New York, J. S. Redfield*, 1871.

Redford (A. H. *d. d.*) History of the organization of the methodist episcopal church, south. 660 pp. 12°. *Nashville (Tenn.) A. H. Redford*, 1871.

Redford (George, *d. d.*) Body and soul; or, life, mind, and matter, considered as to their peculiar nature, and combined condition in living things; with a view to render the physiology of life and mind more easily understood. xi, 232 pp. 3 pl. 8°. *London, J. Churchill*, 1847.

—— The great change: a treatise on conversion. With an introduction, by the rev. John Angell James, d. d. 180 pp. 18°. *Philadelphia, American sunday-school union*, [1843].

—— *and* **Riches** (Thomas Hurry). The history of the ancient town and borough of Uxbridge, containing copies of interesting public documents. xvi, 328 pp. 4 l. 12 pl. 8°. *Uxbridge, [Eng.] authors*, 1818.

Redhouse (James W.) A lexicon, english and turkish; shewing, in turkish, the literal, incidental, figurative, colloquial, and technical significations of the english terms, indicating their pronunciation in a new and systematic manner; and preceded by a sketch of english etymology, to facilitate to turkish students the acquisition of the english language. 10 p. l. 827 pp. 8°. *London, B. Quaritch*, 1861.

Redman (George A. *m. d.*) Mystic hours; or, spiritual experiences. 384 pp. 1 portrait. 12°. *New York, C. Partridge*, 1859.

Reed (Benjamin). The tree of life, the flying angel, and the millennium. [*anon.*] 105 pp. 12°. *Bangor, author*, 1871.

Reed (*Miss* Jennie). The new revelation of the will of God, concerning the educating and cultivating the mind here on earth, by the angel world. [*anon.*] v. 1. 223 pp. 12°. *Utica (N. Y.) T. J. Griffiths*, 1871.

Reed (*Rev.* Thomas). Hymns, selected, and original; for the use of the citizens of Mount Zion: while passing through the wilderness, to their inheritance of glory. 5th ed. 269 pp. 16°. *London, chapel in Cole st.* 1848.

Reed (William Bradford). Among my books. [*anon.*] 270 pp. 16°. *New York, E. J. Hale & son*, 1871.

Reed. *See* **Read** *and* **Reid**.

Reese (David Meredith, *m. d.*) Supplementary appendix to the surgical dictionary of Samuel Cooper, [etc.] 170 pp. 8°. *New York, Harper & brothers*, 1842.

[*With* COOPER (Samuel). A dictionary of practical surgery. *New York*, 1842].

Reeve (John). Sacred remains: or, a divine appendix: being a collection of several treatises, epistolary and publick. Originally written above fifty years since. 1 p. l. 110 pp. 4°. [*London*, 1751-53].

Reeve (Lovell Augustus). Conchologia iconica: or, illustrations of the shells of molluscous animals. v. 18. Containing monographs of the genera Anodon, Tellina, Atys, Hyria, Costalia, Aplysia, Pleurobranchus, Cucullæa, Scutus, Tugalia. 10 monographs in 1 v. 4°. *London. L. Reeve & co.* 1870.

Reflected light. Illustrations of the redeemer's faithfulness in the happy death-bed experience of christians. [*anon.*] 178 pp. 12°. *Philadelphia, W. S. & A. Martien*, 1865.

Reflector (The); representing human affairs, as they are; and may be improved. [*anon.*] xx, 371 pp. 8°. *London, T. Longman*, 1750.

Reflector (The), a quarterly magazine, on subjects of philosophy, politics, and the liberal arts. Conducted by the editor of the Examiner, [Leigh Hunt]. Oct. 1810, to Dec. 1811. 2 v. xii, 486 pp; 3 l. 503 pp. 8°. *London, John Hunt,* 1811.

Réflexions nouvelles sur l'Iliade d'Homère. 1731. *See* **Waleff** (Blaise Henri de Corte, *baron* de).

Reformation (The): a true tale of the sixteenth century. By the author of The Stanwood family; [etc. *anon.*] 250 pp. 18°. *Boston, Mass. sabbath school society,* 1832.

Reformed dutch church. The psalms and hymns, with the catechism, confession of faith, and liturgy of the reformed dutch church in North America. Selected at the request of the general synod. By John H. Livingston, d. d. 493 pp. 24°. *New-York, D. D. Smith,* 1827.

——— The same. [Also], the additional hymns, and the canons of the synod of Dordrecht. 330, 92, 77 pp. 12°. *New York, W. A. Mercein,* 1832.

Reformed presbyterian church in North America. Memorial volume. Covenant renovation by the synod of the reformed presbyterian church in North America. Published by order of synod. 207 pp. 12°. *Pittsburgh, Bakewell & Marthens,* 1872.

CONTENTS.

Bowden (*Rev.* S.) Debarring and inviting service, pp. 128–138.
Carlisle (*Rev.* S.) The messiah expecting his foes' subjection, pp. 94–100.
George (*Rev.* H. H.) Covenanting a duty in new testament times, pp. 27–39.
Kennedy (*Rev.* J.) Humiliation for sin a preparation for enjoying divine favor, pp. 40–57.
Milroy (*Rev.* W.) Fidelity to vows, pp. 81–93.
Sloane (J. R. W.) The spirit in which we should engage in covenanting, pp. 73–80.
Sproull (T.) Explanation of the words of institution, pp. 139–141.
Stevenson (A.) Covenanting, and its benefits to the covenanters, pp. 58–72.
Table addresses, pp. 142–207.
Thompson (*Rev.* J. R.) God's punitive dealings with men, pp. 15–26.
Wylie (S. O.) The lamb that was slain, pp. 101–127.

Refuge (The). By the author of The guide to domestic happiness. [*anon.*] 6th ed. 202 pp. 1 pl. 16°. *New-Haven, Sidney's press, for I. Cooke & co.* 1805.

[*With* Guide (The) to domestic happiness. 1804].

Regius. *See* **Le Roy.**

Regnault-Warin (Jean Baptiste Joseph Innocent Philadelphe). The Magdalen churchyard, from the french. Translated by Samuel Mackay. 4 v. in 2. 1 p. l. 378 pp; 378 pp. 12°. *Boston, Hastings, Etheridge & Bliss,* 1809.

Regnier Desmarais (François Séraphin, *abbé*). Poësies françoises. Nouv. éd. 2 v. 1 p. l. xlviii, 292 pp. 1 pl; 293–614 pp. 3 l. 1 pl. 16°. *La Haye, H. du Sauzet,* 1716.

Reiche (Carl). The bird fancier's companion; or, natural history of cage birds; their food, management, habits, treatment, diseases, etc. 10th ed. 72 pp. 16°. [*New York*], *C. Reiche & brother,* 1871.

Reichelt (Julius). De amveletis. 3 p. l. 94 pp. 8 pl. 4°. *Argentorati, J. F. Spoor & R. Wechtler,* 1676.

Reichenbach (Heinrich Gottlieb Ludwig). Icones ad synopsin avium. Continuatio no. ix. Meropinæ. The bee-eaters.—Les guêpiers.—Die bienenfresser. 4 p. l. pp. 45–144, 67 col. pl. 8°. *Dresden,* 1852. s.

——— Les oiseaux chanteurs. The songbirds. Die singvögel als fortsetzung der vollständigsten naturgeschichte und zugleich als central-atlas für zoologische gärten und für thierfreunde. Ein handbuch zur richtigen bestimmung und pflege der thiere aller classen. 2 p. l. 90, x pp. 50 pl. 4°. *Dresden & Leipzig, expedition der vollständigsten naturgeschichte,* 1862. s.

Reid (James D. *editor*). *See* **Journal** (The) of the telegraph.

Reid (James Seaton, *d. d.*) *and* **Killen** (W. D.) History of the presbyterian church in Ireland. Condensed from the standard work of Reid and Killen. By rev. Samuel D. Alexander. 376 pp. 12°. *New York, R. Carter & brothers,* 1860.

Reid (Mayne). The hunter's feast; or, conversations around the camp-fire. 364 pp. 8 pl. 12°. *New York, De Witt & Davenport,* 1856.

——— The maroon: or, planter life in Jamaica. 383 pp. 8 pl. 12°. *New York, R. M. De Witt,* [1864].

——— The wild huntress; or, love in the wilderness. 466 pp. 6 pl. 12°. *New York, R. M. De Witt,* [1861].

——— L'habitation du désert, ou aventures d'une famille perdue dans les solitudes de l'Amérique. Ouvrage traduit de l'anglais par Armand Le François et illustré par Gustave Doré. Nouv. éd. 2 p. l. 376 pp. 24 pl. 16°. *Paris, L. Hachette & cie.* 1865.

Reid. *See* **Read** *and* **Reed.**

Reider (William D.) The new tablet of memory; or, recorder of remarkable events, compiled, and alphabetically arranged from

Reider (William D.)—continued. the earliest period to the present time. vii, 590 pp. 8°. *London, J. Clements*, 1841.

Reimann. *See* **Reimmann.**

Reimmann (Jacob Friedrich). Iac. Frid. Reimmanni historia vniversalis atheismi et atheorvm falso & merito suspectorum apud jvdæos, ethnicos, christianos, mvhamedanos. Accessit in fine idea compendii theologici omnibus aliis compendiis præmittendi, in quo traditur ratio se præmuniendi, adversus scepticos, atheos, [etc.] 16 p. l. 562 pp. 12 l. 12°. *Hildesiæ, apud L. Schroeder*, 1725.

Reineccius (Christian). Biblia sacra qvadrilingvia. 1747. *See* **Bible.** (*Polyglot*).

Reinzer (Franz). Metrologia philosophico-politica in duodecim dissertationes per quæstiones meteorologicas et conclusiones politicas divisa. [Ed. 2ª]. 2 p. l. 298 pp. 1 l. 1 pl. fol. *Augustæ Vindelicorum, impensis J. Wolfii*, 1709.

Reiset (Jules). E. Millon, sa vie, ses travaux de chimie, et ses études économiques et agricoles sur l'Algérie. xxvi, 327 pp. 1 portrait. 8°. *Paris, J. B. Baillière & fils*, 1870. s.

Reland (Adriaan). On the mahometan religion, two books. The former of which is a short system of the mahometan theology, translated from an arabick manuscript [of Abu Shoja], and illustrated with notes. The latter examines into some things falsly charg'd upon the mahometans. Done into english from the latin of A. Reeland. 8°. *London*, 1712.

[*In* FOUR treatises concerning the doctrine [etc.] of the mahometans. *London*, 1712. pp. 1–102].

Reland (Peter). Petri Relandi fasti consulares, ad illustrationem codicis justinianei ac theodosiani secundum rationes temporum digesti, & auctoritate scriptorum atque lapidum antiquorum confirmati. Ad quos appendix additur Hadriani Relandi, qua fasti ex codd. msstis deprompti & consules in pandectis memorati continentur. 30 p. l. 872 pp. 12 l. 1 pl. 8°. *Trajecti Batavorum, G. Broedelet*, 1715.

Relation de la bataille donnée auprès de Fleurus. *See* **Court** (Charles Caton de).

Relation de la descente des Anglois en l'Isle de Ré. *See* **Marillac** (Michel de).

Relation des deux rebellions arrivées à Constantinople en 1730 et 31, dans la déposition d'Achmet iii. et l'élévation au trône de Mahomet v: composée sur des mémoires originaux reçus de Constantinople. [*anon.*] 2 p. l. 164 pp. 16°. *La Haye, J. Neaulme*, 1737.

[*Note.*—This work is ascribed in a note opposite the title-page, to [Pierre François Le] Courayer].

Relation du naufrage d'un vaisseau hollandois, vers la côte de Bengala, 1681. *See* **Glanius.**

Relazioni varie. *Firenze*, 1693. *See* **Lobo** (Jeronymo).

Religious exercises for christian families and household baptism. [*anon.*] 223 pp. 18°. *Boston, Massachusetts sabbath school society*, 1843.

Remarks on the classical education of boys. By a teacher. [*anon.*] v, 119 pp. 18°. *Boston, Hilliard, Gray & co.* 1834.

Remarks on the climate, produce, and natural advantages of Nova Scotia. In a letter to the right hon. the earl of Macclesfield. [*anon.*] 28 pp. 1 map. 8°. *London, J. Deprett*, [1785].

Remarks on the life and writings of Plato. 1760. *See* **Macfaite** (Ebenezer, *m. d.*)

Remarks on the tenets and principles of the quakers. 1758. *See* **Gittins** *or* **Giddings** (Daniel).

Remarques d'un voyageur sur la Hollande, [etc.] Aanmerkingen van eenen reiziger, over Hollandt, Duitschlandt, Italie, Spanje, Portugaal, Brazilie, Africa. En eenige eilanden in de Middelandsche Zee. Uit het fransch vertaald. [*anon.*] 8 p. l. 183 pp. sm. 4°. *Amsteldam, A. Wor*, 1729.

Rembert (S. S.) The philosophy of life as evolved by modern science: lecture delivered in Texas, [on spiritualism], in 1860. 324 pp. 1 portrait. 12°. *Memphis, Blelock & co.* 1866.

Remington (A. G.) Prose and verse. 2 p. l. 106 pp. 18°. *New York, C. T. Evans*, 1862.

Remnant (Richard). A discourse or historie of bees. Shewing their nature and usage, and the great profit of them. Whereunto is added the causes and cure of blasted wheat. 2 p. l. 47 pp. sm. 4°. *London, T. Slater*, 1637.

Remonstrantie, van de hooft-partijcipanten, ende geintresseerde vande west-indische compagnie, aen alle de regenten des vaderlandts: versoeckende een spoedighe effectieve assistentie, tot meyntenue van de selfde, teghen alle de ghene diese soecken te dissolveren en te ruyneren. [*anon.*] 8 l. sm. 4°. [*n. p.*] *ghedruckt in't jaer onses heeren anno* 1649.

Rémusat (Jean Pierre Abel). Recherches sur les langues tartares, ou mémoires sur différens points de la grammaire et de la littérature des Mandchous, des Mongols, des Ouigours et des Tibétains. v. 1. 2 p. l. viii, lii, 398 pp. 1 l. 4°. *Paris, imprimerie royale*, 1820.

Renard (Roman du). *See* **Baumann** (Nicholas).

Renaut *or* **Renault** (Jean). Lai d'Ignaurès ou du prissonier. 8°. [*Paris, Silvestre*, 1832].

[*In* MONMERQUÉ (L. J. N.) *and* MICHEL (F.) Lai d'Ignaurès, pp. 6–30].

Rendle (*Rev.* John). The history of that inimitable monarch Tiberius, who in the xiv year of his reign, requested the senate to permit the worship of Jesus Christ; and who, in the xvi and three following years, suppressed all opposition to it. 2 p. l. 432 pp. 8°. *Exeter, Trewman & son*, 1813.

Renier (Charles Alphonse Léon). Mélanges d'épigraphie. viii, 292 pp. 1 pl. 8°. *Paris, Didot frères*, 1854.

Rennes (*France*). *Bibliothèque publique*. Catalogue des livres; rédigé par D. Maillet. 2 v. 3 p. l. 693, xx pp; 2 p. l. 695–1411, xv pp. 8°. *Rennes, m'lle Jausions*, 1823–28. s.

CONTENTS.

v. 1. La théologie, la jurisprudence et les sciences et arts.
v. 2. Les belles-lettres et l'histoire.

——— The same. Table alphabétique du catalogue des livres; rédigée par D. Maillet. 2 p. l. 263 pp. 2 l. 8°. *Rennes, m'lle Jausions*, 1829. s.

——— The same. 1er supplément. 2 p. l. 71 pp. 8°. *Rennes, Jausions*, 1830.

——— The same. 2e supplément. 2 p. l. 323, xii, 55 pp. 8°. *Rennes, Jausions*, 1843. s.

Renneville (Sophie de Senneterre de). Coutumes gauloises, ou origines curieuses et peu connues de la plupart de nos usages. 2 p. l. 342 pp. 4 pl. 16°. *Paris, Genets jeune*, 1819.

Rennie (James, *m. a.*) Alphabet of botany, for the use of beginners. Revised and corrected for the use of american schools, by Arabella Clark. 149 pp. 24°. *New York, P. Hill*, 1833.

Rensenlaer (Nicolaes). Eenige openbaringen uyt de copie van 't geene Nicolaes Rensenlaer op getekent heeft. *b. l.* 11 pp. sm. 4°. [*n. p.*] 1667.

Renwick (James, *ll. d.*) Applications of the science of mechanics to practical purposes.

Renwick (James, *ll. d.*)—continued.
xv, 13–327 pp. 16°. *New York, Harper & brothers*, 1840.

——— (*editor*). Familiar illustrations of natural philosophy. 1839. *See* **Daniell** (John F.)

——— First principles of natural philosophy. Being a familiar introduction to the study of that science. 530 pp. 2 charts. 16°. *New-York, Harper & brothers*, 1842.

Repertorio italiano per la storia naturale. Repertorium italicum complectens zoologiam, mineralogiam, geologiam et palaentologiam, cura J. Bianconi. 2 v. vii, 192 pp; v, 192 pp. 12°. *Bononiae, sumptibus auctoris*, 1853–54. s.

Réponse sérieuse à m. L * *, par l'auteur de la Théorie du paradoxe. 1775. *See* **Morellet** (André).

Report of the public meeting, held on the occasion of presenting a testimonial of public respect to the rev. Wm. Cooke, for his defence of evangelical truth against mr. J. Barker. 24 pp. 12°. [*London*, 1845].

[*With* COOKE (*Rev.* Wm.) *and* BARKER (Joseph). Authentic report of theological discussion. *London*, 1845].

Repton (Humphry). Odd whims [a comedy]; and miscellanies. 2 v. xii pp. 1 l. 171 pp; 2 p. l. 164 pp. 12°. *London, W. Miller*, 1804.

Republican (The) review. A political, literary and family newspaper. Transito L. Mata and William M'Guinness, editors. [Albuquerque weekly]. March 16, 1870, to March 16, 1872. v. 1–2 in 1 v. fol. *Albuquerque, T. L. Mata and W. M'Guinness*, 1870–72.

——— The same. La revista republicana. Marzo 16, 1870, hasta marzo 16, 1872. v. 1–2. fol. *Albuquerque, T. L. Mata and W. M'Guinness*, 1870–72.

[*With the* above].

Reresby (Tamworth). A miscellany of ingenious thoughts and reflections, in verse and prose; with some useful remarks. [Also], characters, pleasant narratives, moral observations, and essays. 4 p. l. 422 pp. 4°. *London, H. Meere*, 1721.

Retrospect (A) of early quakerism. 1860. *See* **Michener** (Ezra).

Retrospect (The) of medicine: being a half-yearly journal, containing a retrospective view of every discovery and practical improvement in the medical sciences. Edited

Retrospect (The) of medicine—continued. by W. and J. Braithwaite. January-December, 1871. v. 63-64. 16°. *London, Simpkin, Marshall & co.* 1872.

Reuter (Fritz). Seed-time and harvest; or, "During my apprenticeship." Translated from the "Ut mine stromtid." 292 pp. 8°. *Philadelphia, J. B. Lippincott & co.* 1871.

Revelation (The) to the monk of Evesham. 1196. *See* **Meruelous** reuelacion.

Reveley (Henry). Notices illustrative of the drawings and sketches of some of the most distinguished masters in all the principal schools of design. xxvii, 278 pp. 8°. *London, Longman,* [*etc.*] 1820.

Réville (Albert, *d. d.*) The devil; his origin, greatness, and decadence. From the french. xiv, 72 pp. 1 pl. 12°. *London, Williams & Norgate,* 1871.

——— Théodore Parker, sa vie et ses œuvres, un chapitre de l'histoire de l'abolition de l'esclavage aux États-Unis. 2 p. l. 330 pp. 1 l. 12°. *Paris, C. Reinwald,* 1865.

Revista (La) republicana. *See* **Republican** (The) review.

Revolution (The). Laura Curtis Bullard and W. T. Clark, editors. [Weekly]. Jan. 5, 1871, to Jan. 6, 1872. v. 7-8. sm. fol. *New York,* 1871-72.

Revons (E. C. *pseudon.* for Charles C. Converse). Sayings of sages: or, selections from distinguished preachers, poets, philosophers, and other authors, ancient and modern. With an introduction, by Edward Thomson, d. d. xi, 294 pp. 12°. *New York, Carlton & Porter,* 1864.

Revue coloniale. Extrait des Annales maritimes et coloniales, publiées par mm. Bajot et Poirré. 1843-47. v. 1-13 in 8 v. 8°. *Paris, imprimerie royale,* 1843-47.

——— Revue coloniale. 2e série. 1848-58. v. 1-20. 8°. *Paris, P. Dupont,* 1849-58.

Revue contemporaine. 15 avril 1852 jusqu'à 31 déc. 1857. v. 1-35. 8°. *Paris, bureaux de la Revue contemporaine,* [1852]-57.

——— The same. 2e série. 15 janvier 1858 jusqu'à 15 mai 1870. v. 1-75. (36e-110e de la collection). 8°. *Paris, bureaux de la Revue contemporaine,* 1858-70.

Revue des deux mondes. Août jusqu'à déc. 1829. 1e série. v. 1-4 in 2 v. 2e édition. 8°. *Paris, bureau de la Revue des deux mondes,* 1831.

Revue des deux mondes—continued.

——— The same. Janv. 1830 jusqu'à déc. 1850. 2e-20e année. 80 v. 8°. *Paris, bureau de la Revue des deux mondes,* 1830-50.

[*Note.*—The order of the series is as follows:
2e série, [1e-3e année]. Janv. 1830 jusqu'à déc. 1833. 12 v.
3e série [4e année]. Janv. jusqu'à déc. 1834. 4 v.
4e série [5e-12e année]. Janv. 1835 jusqu'à déc. 1842. 32 v.
Nouvelle [5e] série. 13e-18e année. Janv. 1843 jusqu'à déc. 1848. 24 v.
Nouv. période [6e série]. 19e-20e année. 1 janv. 1849 jusqu'à 15 déc. 1850. v. 1-8.
v. 1-4 for the year 1831 is the reprint of the 1st series, for 1829. No original issues were published during 1831].

——— The same. Seconde période, [7e série]. 41e année. 1 janvier jusqu'à 15 déc. 1871. v. 91-96. 8°. *Paris, bureau de la Revue des deux mondes,* 1871.

Rey (Édouard Gabriel). Satires parisiennes du xixe siècle. viii, 324 pp. 12°. *Paris, E. Dentu,* 1860.

Rey (G. *editor*). Étude sur les monuments de l'architecture militaire des croisés en Syrie et dans l'île de Chypre. 2 p. l. 288 pp. 24 pl. 4°. *Paris, imprimerie nationale,* 1871.

[FRANCE. *Ministère de l'instruction publique.* Collection de documents inédits sur l'histoire de France. 1re série].

Reynard the fox. *See* **Baumann** (Nicholas).

Reynaud (François Léonce). Memoir upon the light-house illumination of the coast of France. Translated for the light-house board of the United States, by rear-admiral Thornton A. Jenkins, U. S. n. 144 pp. 8°. Atlas, 6 pp. 39 pl. 4°. *Washington, government printing office,* 1871.

Reynolds *or* **Rainoldes** (John, *d. d.* 1549-1607) *and* **Hart** (John). The svmme of the conference betvveene Iohn Rainoldes and Iohn Hart: touching the head and the faith of the chvrch. [Also] a treatise intitled, Six conclusions touching the holy scripture, and the church, written by Iohn Rainoldes. With a defence of such things as Thomas Stapleton and Gregorie Martin haue carped at therein. 8 p. l. 675 pp. 4°. *London, W. Hall for T. Adames,* 1609.

Reynolds (*Rev.* John, 1666-1729). Inquiries concerning the state and œconomy of the angelical worlds. xiv, 315 pp. 8°. *London, J. Clark,* 1723.

——— Three letters to the deist, 1. Demanding his warrant for eating of flesh. 2. Representing his want of much useful knowledge. 3. Arguing the unexceptionable integrity of [Christ], and his immediate accomplices. [1st ed.] 8 p. l. 311 pp. 8°. *London, J. Clark & R. Hett,* 1725.

Reynolds (*Rev.* John, 1666-1729)—continued.
——— A view of death: or the soul's departure from the world. A philosophical sacred poem. 3d ed. [Also] some account of the life of the author, chiefly extracted from his manuscripts. 176 pp. vii-xiv, 142 pp. 16°. *London, R. Ford & R. Hett*, 1735.

Reynolds (*Rev.* John, *of Collinsville, Ohio*). The psalms of David in metre; being a new metrical and literal version of the book of Psalms. 275 pp. 24°. *Rossville (O.) J. M. Christy*, 1844.

Reyrac (François Philippe de Laurens, *l'abbé* de). Hymne au soleil, suivi de plusieurs morceaux du même genre. Nouv. éd. xl, 139 pp. 1 portrait. 24°. *Amsterdam, aux dépens de la compagnie*, 1781.

Rezzonico della Torre (Antonio Giuseppe, *conte*) *and others*. Isola di Capri, manoscritti inediti del conte della Torre Rezzonico, del prof. Breislak, e del gen. Pommereul, pubblicati dall' abate Domenico Romanelli con sue note. 124 pp. 2 pl. 8°. *Napoli, A. Trani*, 1816.

Rhamnusius. *See* **Ramusio.**

Rheinwald (Georg Friedrich Heinrich). The protestant exiles of Zillerthal; their persecutions and expatriation from the Tyrol, on separating from the romish church, and embracing the reformed faith. Translated from the german. By John B. Sanders. 1st american, from the 2d London ed. xiii, 107 pp. 18°. *New York, C. K. Moore*, 1842.

Rhoads (*Mrs.* Rachel). Poems: a series of tales in verse, with a variety of lyrical productions on chosen themes, intended to please the many and offend none. 348 pp. 12°. *Philadelphia, J. B. Lippincott & co.* 1863.

Rhode Island (*State of*). First annual report of the board of education, together with the twenty-sixth annual report of the commissioner of public schools, of Rhode Island. January, 1871. *Providence, Providence press company*, 1871.
——— *Secretary of state.* Eighteenth report upon the registration of births, marriages, and deaths, for the year ending December 31st, 1870. By Edward T. Caswell, m. d. xiii, 96 pp. 8°. *Providence, A. C. Greene*, 1872.

Ricchieri (Lodovico Celio). Antiqvarvm lectionvm commentarios [quos] concinnarat olim Vindex Ceselius, nunc eosdem per incvriam interceptos reparavit Lodovicus Caelius

Ricchieri (Lodovico Celio)—continued.
rhodignvs, in corporis vnam velvt molem aggestis primvm lingvae vtrivsqve floribvs. 40 p. l. 862 pp. 3 l. fol. *Venetiis, in aedibvs Aldi, & Andreae soceri*, 1516.

Riccio (Pietro). *See* **Crinito** (Pietro).

Riccoboni (Marie Jeanne Laboras de Mézières, *madame*). Letters from lord Rivers to sir Charles Cardigan, and to other english correspondents, while he resided in France. Translated from the french, by Percival Stockdale. [A romance]. 2 v. xx, 192 pp; viii, 234 pp. 16°. *London, T. Becket*, 1778.
——— Letters from the countess de Sancerre to count de Nancé, her friend. Translated from the french. [A romance]. 2 v. in 1. viii, 229 pp; 2 p. l. 224 pp. 16°. *London, T. Becket, & P. A. De Hondt*, 1767.

Rice (Benjamin Holt, *d. d.*) Memoir of James Brainerd Taylor. *See* **Rice** (John Holt, *d. d.*)

Rice (E. J.) Manual of devotion for schools and academies. 130 pp. 8°. *Indianapolis, Ind. Asher & Adams*, 1864.

Rice (John Holt, *d. d. and* Benjamin Holt, *d. d.*) Memoir of James Brainerd Taylor. 1 p. l. 330 pp. 1 portrait. 12°. *New York, Jocelyn, Darling & co.* 1833.

Rice (Nathan Lewis, *d. d.*) A debate on christian baptism. 1844. *See* **Campbell** (*Rev.* A.) *and* **Rice.**
——— A debate on slavery. *See* **Blanchard** (*Rev.* Jonathan) *and* **Rice.**

Rice (Roselia). Mabel: or, heart histories. 414 pp. 12°. *New York, Follett, Foster & co.* 1863.

Richards (Maria T.) Life in Israel; or, portraitures of hebrew character. 389 pp. 12°. *New York, Sheldon, Blakeman & co.* 1857.

Richards (Mary A.) Jessie Alison; or, the transformation. 234 pp. 4 pl. 18°. *New York, Sheldon & co.* 1859.

Richards (William C.) Harry's vacation; or, philosophy at home. 1 p. l. 398 pp. 6 pl. 16°. *New York, Evans & Dickerson*, 1854.

Richardson (*Mrs.* Abby Sage). Stories from old english poetry. 281 pp. 5 pl. 16°. *New York, Hurd & Houghton*, 1871.

Richardson (Albert Deane). Garnered sheaves from the writings of Albert D. Richardson, collected and arranged by his wife. To which is added a biographical sketch of the author. 430 pp. 9 pl. 8°. *Hartford, Columbian book company*, 1871.

Richardson (Charles). Illustrations of english philology. Consisting of i. A critical examination of dr. Johnson's dictionary. ii. Remarks on mr. Dugald Stewart's essay "On the tendency of some late philological speculations." 2 p. l. 292 pp. 4°. *London, Gale & Fenner*, 1815.

Richardson (Charles James). The englishman's house from a cottage to a mansion. A practical guide to members of building societies, and all interested in selecting or building a house. viii, 504 pp. 1 pl. 12°. *London, J. C. Hotten*, [1871].

Richardson (George). A treatise on the five orders of architecture. Traité des cinq ordres d'architecture. x, 32 pp. 1 l. 22 pl. fol. *London, author*, 1787.

[*Note.*—Plates 2-4, 7, 10, 13-14, 16, 19-20, and 22 wanting].

Richardson (Jacob D.) *and* **Eatto** (Timothy). A collection of hymns, for the use of the African methodist episcopal church in America. 416 pp. 18°. *New York, J. C. Beaman*, 1839.

Richardson (*Sir* John). Ichthyology of the voyage of h. m. s. Erebus & Terror, under the command of capt. sir James Clark Ross, r. n. viii, 139 pp. 60 pl. 4°. *London*, 1844-48.

Richardson (Joseph, *m. d.*) A practical treatise on mechanical dentistry. 427 pp. 8°. *Philadelphia, Lindsay & Blakiston*, 1860.

Richardson (*Major* John). War of 1812. First series. Containing a full and detailed narrative of the operations of the first division, of the canadian army. 4 p. l. 182 pp. 8°. [*Brockville*], 1842.

Richardson (Nathaniel Smith, *d. d.*) The churchman's reasons for his faith and practice. 2d ed. 323 pp. 12°. *New York, J. Pott*, 1863.

Richardson (*Prof.* William). The origin of superstition, illustrated in the mythology of the poems of Ossian. 8°. [*Edinburgh, J. Ballantyne & co.* 1807].

[*In* GRAHAM (Patrick, *d. d.*) Essay on the authenticity of the poems of Ossian. 1807. Appendix 2, *or* pp. 411-443].

Richelieu (Armand Jean du Plessis, *cardinal, duc* de). Testament politique. 5e éd. revue, corrigée & augmentée d'observations historiques. 2 v. in 1. 12 p. l. 282 pp; 247 pp. 18°. *Amsterdam, H. Desbordes*, 1696.

[*Note.*—The fabrication of Paul Hay, *marq.* du Chastelet].

Richemont (*General* Louis Auguste Camus, *baron* de). Siége de la citadelle d'Anvers par l'armée française, sous les ordres du maréchal comte Gérard. 2 p. l. 291 pp. 1 plan. 8°. *Paris*, 1833.

Richer (Adrien). Essai sur les grands événemens par les petites causes, tiré de l'histoire. 5 p. l. 347 pp. 16°. *Genève, Hardy*, 1758.

Riches (Thomas Hurry). The history of the ancient town and borough of Uxbridge. 1818. *See* **Redford** (George) *and* **Riches.**

Richmond (*Mrs.* E. J.) The McAllisters. 211 pp. 1 pl. 18°. *New York, National temperance society and publication house*, 1871.

Richmond (*Rev.* John F.) New York and its institutions, 1609-1871. A library of information, pertaining to the great metropolis, past and present. 586 pp. 34 pl. 8°. *New York, E. B. Treat*, 1871.

Richmond daily enquirer [and examiner]. July 1 to Dec. 30, 1871. fol. *Richmond (Va.) Enquirer company*, 1871.

Richmond hill; a descriptive and historical poem. *See* **Maurice** (*Rev.* Thomas).

Richmond whig. [Daily]. *See* **Daily** Richmond whig.

Richter (Carl G. F.) Mark-steine. Gedichte. 120 pp. 16°. *New York, H. A. Rost*, 1871.

Richter (Gregor). Axiomatvm historicorvm pars secunda, continens axiomata œconomica. 8 p. l. 354 pp. 13 l. sm. 4°. *Gorlicii, sumptibus Iohannis Rhambæ*, 1600.

——— The same. Pars tertia, continens axiomata ecclesiastica. 20 p. l. 330 pp. 12 l. sm. 4°. *Gorlicii, sumptibus Iohannis Rhambæ*, 1602.

[*With his* Axiomatvm historicorvm pars secunda, 1600].

Ricketts (Clemuel Green). Notes of travel, in Europe, Egypt, and the holy land, including a visit to the city of Constantinople, in 1841 and 1842. 319 pp. 1 portrait. 12°. *Philadelphia, C. Sherman*, 1844.

Ricord (Frederick William). Stories of ancient Rome. 304 pp. 6 pl. 16°. *New York, M. W. Dodd*, 1852.

Riddell (Robert). The new elements of hand railing. Revised ed. Containing forty-one plates, thirteen of which are now for the first time presented. Together with accompanying letter-press description. The whole giving a complete elucidation of the art of stair-building. 127 pp. 4°. *Philadelphia, Claxton, Remsen & Haffelfinger*, 1871.

Ride (A) on horseback to Florence through France and Switzerland. Described in a series of letters, by a lady. [*anon.*] 2 v. xi, 346 pp; ix, 436 pp. 12°. *London, J. Murray*, 1842.

Rider (*Rev.* Wilson C.) A course of lectures on future punishment, delivered at the baptist meeting-house in Cherryfield. 287 pp. 12°. *Ellsworth,* [*Me.*] *D. T. Pike & co.* 1836.

Ridley (Mark, *m. d.*) A short treatise of magneticall bodies and motions. Eng. title, 6 p. l. 158 pp. sm. 4°. *London, N. Okes,* 1613.

Riembault (*Dr.* A.) Hygiène des ouvriers mineurs dans les exploitations houillères. xiii, 316 pp. 8°. *Paris, J. B. Baillière et fils,* 1861.

Riemer (Jacob de). Beschryving van 's Graven-Hage, behelzende derzelfs oorsprong, benaming, gelegentheid, uitbreidingen, onheilen en luister; mitsgaders sligtinge van het hof, der kerken, kloosters, kapellen, godshuizen, en andere voornaame gebouwen. [Illustrated]. 3 v. fol. *Delft, R. Boilet,* 1730, *and Graven-Hage, J. de Cros,* 1739.

Rigaltius (N.). *See* **Rigault** (Nicolas).

Rigault *or* **Rigaud** (Nicolas). Funus parasiticum, sive L. Biberii curculionis, parasiti, mortualia. Ad ritum prisci funeris. Autore N. Rigaltio. 18°. *Norimbergae,* 1665.
[*In* Epuium parasiticum, pp. 181-220, 1 pl.]

——— The same. 18°. [*Lugd. Batavorum,* 1655].
[Elegantiores præstantium virorum satyræ, v. 2, pp. 281-310].

Rigby (Edward, *m. d.*) A system of midwifery. With notes and additional illustrations. 491 pp. 8°. *Philadelphia, Lea & Blanchard,* 1841.

Right (The) word in the right place: a new pocket dictionary and reference book. By the author of "How to write," [etc. *anon.*] 214 pp. 16°. *New York, Fowler & Wells,* 1860.

Rimbault (Edward F. *editor*). The old cheque-book, or book of remembrance, of the chapel royal. 1872. *See* **Great Britain.** *Chapel royal.*

Rimmer (W.) Elements of design. Book first. For the use of parents and teachers. 38 pp. 36 pl. 8°. *Boston, J. Wilson & son,* 1864.

Rindfleisch (Eduard, *m. d.*) A text-book of pathological histology: an introduction to the study of pathological anatomy. Translated from the second german edition, by William C. Kloman, m. d. assisted by F. T. Miles, m. d. 695 pp. 8°. *Philadelphia, Lindsay & Blakiston,* 1872.

Ringhieri (Innocenzo). Cento givochi liberali, et d'ingegno, nouellamente ritrouati, & in dieci libri descritti. [Ed. 1[a]]. 4 p. l. 162 l. 1 l. 4°. *Bologna, A. Giaccarelli,* 1551.

——— Dialoghi della vita, et della morte. 12 p. l. 133 pp. 16°. *Bologna, A. Giaccarelli,* 1550.

Ring-leader (The): a tale for boys. [*anon.*] 158 pp. 18°. *Philadelphia, American sunday school union,* 1833.

Ringwalt (J. Luther, *editor*). American encyclopædia of printing. 512 pp. 18 pl. 8°. *Philadelphia, Menamin & Ringwalt,* 1871.

Rinuccini (Ottavio). Euridice. 16°. [*Venezia, A. Sattae figli,* 1783].
[*In* Guarini (Giovanni Battista). Pastor fido. 1783. pp. 289-326].

Riodu (*Mme.* A.) Lucie. Familiar conversations in french and english. 128 pp. 12°. *Boston, S. R. Urbino,* 1864.

Rios (Vicente de los) *and* **Navarrete** (Martin Fernandez de). Analisis del Quijote, por d. Vicente de los Rios. Vida de Miguel de Cervantes Saavedra, escrita e ilustrada con varias noticias y documentos ineditos pertenecientes á la historia y literatura de su tiempo, por d. Martin Fernandez de Navarrete. 1 p. l. 494 pp. 1 portrait. 8°. *Barcelona, viuda e hijos de Gorchs,* 1834.

Ripley (Henry Jones, *d. d.*) Christian baptism: an examination of professor Stuart's essay in the Biblical repository, April, 1833, on "The mode of baptism." 154 pp. 12°. *Boston, Lincoln, Edmands & co.* 1833.

——— The four gospels; with notes. *See* **Bible.** (*English*).

Ripley (Mary A.) Exercises in analysis and parsing. 103 pp. 18°. *Buffalo,* [*N. Y.*] *Breed, Lent & co.* 1871.

Rishton (Edward). Nicolai Sanderi, de origine ac progressv schismatis anglicani, libri tres: aucti per Edovardvm Rishtonvm. *See* **Sanders** (Nicolas, *d. d.*)

Ritchie (*Rev.* A.) Matter and manner for christian workers, with special reference to sabbath school work. 1 p. l. 573 pp. 5 pl. 8°. *Cincinnati, Western tract and book society,* 1871.

Ritchie (*Mrs.* Anna Cora Mowatt). Twin roses. A narrative. 273 pp. 12°. *Boston, Ticknor & Fields,* 1857.

Ritter (Carl). Geographical studies. Translated from the original german, by William Leonhard Gage. 356 pp. 1 portrait. 12°. *Boston, Gould & Lincoln,* 1863.

Riva (C. T.) Histoire de la barbarie et des lois au moyen âge. *See* **Toulotte** (E. L. J.) *and* **Riva.**

Rival (François Louis Cizeron-). *See* **Cizeron-Rival.**

Rive (Joseph Jean). [Essai sur l'art de vérifier l'âge des miniatures, peintes dans les manuscrits, depuis le xive siècle jusqu'au xviie]. 26 col. pl. fol. [*Paris, Didot*, 1782].
[*Note.*—Le prospectus a seul paru ; 80 exemplaires seulement faits.—*Nouv. biog. générale*].

Rivera (Pedro de). Diario, y derrotero de lo caminado, visto, y obcervado en el discurso de la visita general de precidios, situados en las provincias ynternas de Nueva España, que de orden de su magestad executô d. Pedro de Rivera. 39 l. fol. *Guathemala, S. de Arebalo*, 1736.

Riverius. *See* **La Rivière.**

Rivers (R. H. *d. d.*) Elements of moral philosophy. Edited by Thomas O. Summers, d. d. 353 pp. 12°. *Nashville* (*Tenn.*) *A. H. Redford*, 1872.

Riviera (Cesare della). Il mondo magico de gli heroi: nel quale si tratta qual sia la vera magia natvrale: e come si possa fabricare la reale pietra de' filosofi. Hora di nouo ristampato et accresciuto. 15 p. l. 222 pp. 4°. *Milano, per P. M. Locarni*, 1605.

Robbertse (Robbert). Over het vroeg vertonen der sonne op Nova Zembla, int jaer 1597. Begrepen en een brief, met een antwoort daer op [door D. R. van Nierop]. sm. 4°. *Amsterdam, A. S. van der Storck*, 1674.
[*In* NIEROP (D. R. van). Eenige oefeningen, v. 2, pp. 5-17].

Robbins (Eliza). Biography for schools ; or, good examples for young persons. By the author of American popular lessons. [*anon.*] 256 pp. 2 pl. sq. 16°. *Philadelphia, U. Hunt*, 1836.

——— The guide to knowledge: being a collection of useful and familiar questions and answers on every-day subjects, adapted for young persons, and arranged in the most simple and easy language. 417 pp. 16°. *New-York, D. Appleton & co.* 1853.

——— Primary dictionary, or rational vocabulary, consisting of nearly four thousand words adapted to the comprehension of children. vi, 257 pp. 18°. *New York, R. Lockwood*, 1842.

——— The school friend: or lessons in prose and verse; for the use of schools. By the author of American popular lessons. 2d ed. revised and corrected. [*anon.*] 252 pp. 18°. *New York, W. E. Dean*, 1842.

Robbins (Eliza)—continued.

——— Tales from american history; containing the principal facts in the life of Christopher Columbus. By the author of American popular lessons. [*anon.*] xii, 252 pp. 18°. *New York, W. Burgess*, 1829.

——— The same. 238, 14 pp. 3 pl. 18°. *New York, W. Burgess*, 1830.

——— The same. Tales from american history. 2d series. [*Or*], Tales from american history, chiefly relating to the conquest of Mexico and Peru, by Hernando Cortez & Francisco Pizarro. [Also] some facts illustrative of the present state of those countries. [*anon.*] viii, 247 pp. 18 pp. 18°. *New-York, W. Burgess*, 1832.

Robbins (*Rev.* Royal). Outlines of ancient history, on a new plan. 228 pp. 12°. *Hartford, E. Hopkins*, 1830.

——— Outlines of modern history, on a new plan. 396 pp. 12°. *Hartford, E. Hopkins*, 1830.

——— The same. Outlines of ancient and modern history on a new plan. 2 v. in 1. 228 pp; 420, 20, 28 pp. 12 pl. 12°. *Hartford, Belknap & Hamersley*, 1841.

Robbins (*Mrs.* S. S.) Cathedrals of the old world. 256 pp. 5 pl. 12°. *Boston, Mass. sabbath school society*, 1857.

——— Faithful and true; or, the Evans family. By the author of "Win and wear," [etc. *anon.*] 368 pp. 4 pl. 12°. *New York, R. Carter & brothers*, 1864.

Robbins. *See* **Robins.**

Roberto, re di Giervsalemme. [*pseudon.*] *See* **Bambagiuoli** (Graziuolo).

Roberts (Edward). The new sabbath school hosanna, enlarged and improved. A choice collection of popular hymns and tunes, original and selected. 191 pp. obl. 16°. *New York, G. S. Scofield*, [1870].

Roberts (J.) The trades increase. [*anon.*] 3 p. l. 56 pp. sm. 4°. *London, Nicholas Okes*, 1615.

Roberts (Job). The Pennsylvania farmer; being a selection from the most approved treatises on husbandry, interspersed with observations and experiments. viii, 5-224 pp. 12°. *Philadelphia, J. Johnson & co.* 1804.

Roberts (Lewis). The treasure of traffike, or a discourse of forraigne trade. Wherein is shewed the benefit and commoditie arising to a commonwealth or kingdome, by the skilfull

Roberts (Lewis)—continued. merchant, and by a well ordered commerce and regular traffike. 4 p. l. 104 pp. 3 l. 12°. *London, N. Bourne*, 1641.

Roberts (Nathan). Roberts' ready reckoner; or, the american measurer's guide. 209 pp. 8°. *New York, F. F. Ripley*, [1838].

Roberts (*Rev.* Peter). Sketch of the early history of the Cymry, or ancient Britons, from the year 700, before Christ, to a. d. 500. iv, 158 pp. 4 l. 1 pl. 8°. *London, E. Williams*, 1803.

Roberts (Samuel). Parallel miracles; or, the Jews and the gypsies. 167 pp. 12°. *London, J. Nisbet*, 1830.

Roberts (William, *d. d. editor*). *See* **Cyfaill** (Y) o'r hen wlad.

Robertson (Alexander, *of Strowan*). The history and martial atchievments, of the the Robertson's of Strowan. As it is selected from the works of the best historians. And the poems on various subjects and occasions, by Alexander Robertson of Strowan. [In two parts. *anon.*] 6 pp. 3 l. 63 pp; 1 l. 169 pp. 12°. *Edinburgh, A. Robertson*, [*about* 1771].
[Imperfect: wanting 1 l. after p. 162].

Robertson (Archibald, *m. d.*) Colloquia anatomica, physiologica atque chemica, quaestionibus et responsis. Ed. 2ª. xiv, 236 pp. 16°. *Edinburgi, sumptibus auctoris*, 1814.

——— Colloquia de morbis, practica et theoretica, quaestionibus et responsis. x, 390 pp. 1 l. 16°. *Edinburgi, sumptibus auctoris*, 1816.

Robertson (*Rev.* Joseph, *vicar of Horncastle*). The parian chronicle, or the chronicle of the arundelian marbles; with a dissertation concerning its authenticity. [*anon.*] viii, 225 pp. 11 l. 1 pl. 8°. *London, J. Walter*, 1788.

Robins (*Rev.* Sanderson). An argument for the royal supremacy. viii, 299 pp. 8°. *London, W. Pickering*, 1851.

Robinson (Clement) *and others*. A handefull of pleasant delites, containing sundrie new sonets and delectable histories, in diuers kindes of meeter. With new additions of certain songs, to verie late deuised notes, not commonly knowen, nor vsed heretofore. London, Richard Ihones: 1584. [Reprinted]. 80 pp. 4°. *London, Spenser society*, 1871.
[SPENSER society publications. Issue no. 8].

Robinson (Edward, *d. d.*) A concise view of the universities, and of the state of theological education, in Germany. 100 pp. 16°. *Edinburgh, T. Clark*, 1835.
[STUDENT'S (The) cabinet library of useful tracts, v. 1].

——— Memoir of the rev. William Robinson, with some account of his ancestors in this country. By his son. Printed as manuscript, for private distribution. xii, 214 pp. 8°. *New York, J. F. Trow*, 1859.

Robinson (George). Travels in Palestine and Syria. Illustrated with maps and plans. 2 v. xii, 308 pp. 7 maps; viii, 358 pp. 8°. *London, H. Colburn*, 1837.

Robinson (George C.) Seed-thought: a hand-book of doctrine and devotion. viii, 172 pp. 12°. *New York, Carlton & Porter*, [1864].

Robinson (Horatio N. *ll. d.*) New elementary algebra; containing the rudiments of the science. 312 pp. 12°. *New York, Ivison & Phinney*, 1860.

——— New university algebra: a theoretical and practical treatise, containing many new and original methods and applications. 420 pp. 12°. *New York, Ivison, Phinney & co.* 1862.

Robinson (James, *jun.*) The american arithmetick. Also, a short system of book-keeping, by single entry. 234 pp. 3 l. 12°. *Boston, Lincoln & Edmands*, 1825.

Robinson (*Rev.* John, *of Leyden*). A ivstification of separation from the church of England. Against mr. Richard Bernard his invective, intitvled; The separatists schisme. [2d ed.] 382 pp. 3 l. sm. 4°. [*London*]? 1639.

Robinson (Nicholas, *m. d.*) A new system of the spleen, vapours, and hypochondriack melancholy; wherein all the decays of the nerves, and lownesses of the spirits, are mechanically accounted for. [Also], a discourse upon the nature, cause, and cure, of melancholy, madness, and lunacy. With a dissertation on the origine of the passions. To which is prefix'd, a philosophical essay. xvi, 408 pp. 8°. *London, A. Bettesworth*, [*etc.*] 1729.

Robinson (Samuel). A lecture, introductory to a course, on the science of life, organization, etc. 13 pp. 8°. [*Columbus, Ohio*, 1832].
[*With* HOWARD (Horton). An improved system of botanic medicine. 1832. Appendix].

Robinson (*Rev.* Thomas). An enquiry into the necessity, nature, and evidences of revealed religion. xvi, 303 pp. 1 l. 8°. *London, C. & R. Baldwin*, 1803.

Robinson (*Rev.* Thomas)—continued.

——— Original letters. *See* **Vaughan** (*Rev.* Edward T.) Some account of rev. T. Robinson.

Robinson (*Rev.* W.) The invisible world; or the state of departed spirits between death and the resurrection. A poem in eight books, with an appendix. viii, 410 pp. 8°. *Calcutta, Baptist mission press,* 1844.

Robinson (W. *horticultural editor of the London times*). Alpine flowers for english gardens. xviii, 392 pp. 12°. *London, J. Murray,* 1870. s.

——— The subtropical garden; or, beauty of form in the flower garden. ix, 241 pp. 35 pl. 12°. *London, J. Murray,* 1871. s.

——— The wild garden; or, our groves and shrubberies made beautiful by the naturalization of hardy exotic plants: with a chapter on the garden of british wild flowers. 4 p. l. 236 pp. 1 pl. 12°. *London, J. Murray,* 1870. s.

Robortello (Francesco). De historica facultate disputatio. Laconici, seu sudationis explicatio. De nominibus Romanorum. De rhetorica facultate. Explicatio in Catulli epithalamium. His accesservnt annotationum in uaria tam græcorum, quàm latinorum loca, libri 2. Ode græca quæ *Βιοχρησμῳδια* inscribitur. Explanationes in primum Aeneid. Vergilii librum collectæ à Ioanne Baptista Busdragolucensi. [1st ed.] 354 pp. 1. l. 16°. *Florentiæ, apud L. Torrentinum,* 1548.

Roby (Henry John). A grammar of the latin language from Plautus to Suetonius. Part 1, containing:—Book 1. Sounds. Book 2. Inflexions. Book 3. Word-formation. Appendices. xcvi, 476 pp. 16°. *London, Macmillan & co.* 1871.

Robyn (H.) *and* **Berg** (F.) Der junge sänger, enthaltend eine systematisch geordnete sammlung der schönsten deutschen und englischen lieder, nebst einer anleitung zum singen für deutsch-amerikanische schulen. 1er theil. 2 p. l. 60 pp. obl. 12°. *St. Louis (Mo.) C. Witter,* 1872.

Rochard (Jules). Du service chirurgical de la flotte en temps de guerre. 101 pp. 8°. *Paris, J. B. Baillière,* 1861.

[*With* SAUREL (Louis). Traité de chirurgie navale].

Roche (Eugenius). London in a thousand years; with other poems. 4 p. l. xxxvi, 183 pp. 1 portrait. 8°. *London, Colburn & Bentley,* 1830.

Roche (Martin, *m. d. and* George Walter). The United States practical navigator, in which all the calculations are made by arithmetic. 4 p. l. 75 pp. 8°. *Philadelphia, authors,* 1864.

Rochester (*N. H.*) Directory for 1871-72. *See* **Dover,** Great Falls, and Rochester (*N. H.*)

Rochester (*N. Y.*) A directory for the village of Rochester, containing the names, residence and occupations of all the male inhabitants over fifteen years of age, in said village, on the first of January, 1827. To which is added, a sketch of the history of the village, from 1812 to 1827. 142 pp. 1 map. 12°. *Rochester, E. Ely,* 1827.

——— The Rochester directory, containing a general directory of the citizens, and the city and county register and business directory, no. xxii, for the year commencing July 1, 1871. 554 pp. 1 map. 8°. *Rochester, C. C. Drew,* 1871.

Rock cottage; or, the summer vacation. [*anon.*] 103 pp. 3 pl. 18°. *Boston, Mass. sabbath school society,* [1860].

Rocket (The). [*anon.*] 118 pp. 18°. *New York, American tract society,* [1860].

Rockingham: or, the younger brother. [*anon.*] 2d ed. 3 v. 12°. *London, H. Colburn,* 1852.

Rockwell (A. D. *m. d.*) A practical treatise on the medical and surgical uses of electricity. *See* **Beard** (G. M.) *and* **Rockwell.**

Rockwell (J. Edson, *d. d.*) The diamond in the cage; or, hours with the children. 238 pp. 4 pl. 16°. *Philadelphia, Presbyterian board of publication,* [1872].

——— The young christian warned, or pastoral counsel against conformity to the world. 139 pp. 18°. *Philadelphia, Presbyterian board of publication,* [1859].

Rockwell (William S.) Ahiman Rezon, prepared under the direction of the grand lodge of Georgia. Compiled from standard authorities. 404 pp. 33 pl. 8°. *Savannah,* 1859.

Rocky (The) mountain directory. 1871. *See* **Wallihan** (S. S.) *and* **Bigney** (T. O.)

Rodney (*Mrs.* Minnie Reeves). Wearithorne, or in the light of to-day. By "Fadette," [*pseudon.*] 214 pp. 12°. *Philadelphia, J. B. Lippincott & co.* 1872.

Roe (Azel Stevens). How could he help it? or, the heart triumphant. 443 pp. 12°. *New York, Derby & Jackson,* 1860.

Roe (Azel Stevens)—continued.
——— Resolution; or, the soul of power. 348 pp. 12°. *New York, G. W. Carleton & co.* 1871.

——— The star and the cloud; or, a daughter's love. 410 pp. 12°. *New York, Derby & Jackson*, 1857.

Roederer (Pierre Louis, *comte*). Louis xii. et François i^er^, ou mémoires pour servir à une nouvelle histoire de leur règne; suivis d'appendices comprenant une discussion entre m. le comte Daru et l'auteur, concernant la réunion de la Bretagne à la France. 2 v. 3 p. l. 441 pp; xvi, 411 pp. 1 l. 1 facs. 8°. *Paris, Bossange frères*, 1825.

Roelofsz (Roelof). Kort ende waerachtigh verhael, vande tweede schip-vaerdt by de Hollanders op Oost-Indien ghedaen onder den heer admirael Jacob van Neck. 1601–04. sm. 4°. [*Amstelredam, J. Hartgers*, 1650].

[*In* NOORT (Oliver van). Wonderlijcke voyagie, 1598–1601, pp. 57–88].

——— The same. sm. 4°. [*Amstelredam, I. Hartgers*, 1648].

[*In* HARTGERTS (J.) Oost-indische voyagien, v. 1, 4e stuck, pp. 59–88].

Roger *of Hoveden.* Chronica magistri Rogeri de Houedene. Edited by William Stubbs. v. 4. 8°. *London, Longman & co.* 1871.

[GREAT BRITAIN. *Treasury department. Master of the rolls.* Chronicles and memorials during the middle ages].

Roger (Abraham, *missionary in the Coromandel*). La porte ouverte, pour parvenir à la connaissance du paganisme caché. Ou, la vraye représentation de la vie, des mœurs, de la religion, et du service divin des Bramines, qui demeurent sur les costes de Chormandel, et aux pays circonvoisins. Traduite en françois par Thomas la Grue. Eng. title, 7 p. l. 372 pp. 2 l. 4 pl. 4°. *Amsterdam, J. Schipper*, 1670.

Roger (Joseph Louis). Traité des effects de la musique sur le corps humain; traduit du latin, et augmenté de notes, par Étienne Sainte-Marie. xxxviij, 352 pp. 8°. *Paris, Brunot*, 1803.

Roger (Paul André). Bibliothèque historique, monumentale, ecclésiastique et littéraire de la Picardie et de l'Artois, publiée par mr. P. Roger. Avec la collaboration de m. le comte d'Allonville; de m. le baron de Hauteclocque; et de m. H. Dusevel. 368 pp. 14 pl. 8°. *Amiens, Duval et Herment*, 1844.

Rogers (Henry). Sacred eloquence: the british pulpit. [Republished from the Edinburgh review, Oct. 1840]. 12°. [*New York*, 1863].

[*In* HOLYOAKE (George Jacob). Public speaking and debate, pp. 183–234].

Rogers (John). Anti-popery; or popery unreasonable, unscriptural and novel. With a preface, notes, and index, by rev. C. Sparry. 1st american, from the 2d London ed. 315 pp. 1 chart. 12°. *New York, D. Fanshaw*, 1841.

Rogers (*Rev.* J. B.) War pictures. Experiences and observations of a chaplain in the U. S. army, in the war of the southern rebellion. 258 pp. 4 pl. 1 portrait. 12°. *Chicago, Church & Goodman*, 1863.

Rogers (Joseph M.) The principles and practice of fire-underwriting systematically arranged. 90 pp. sm. 4°. *New York, Economical printing company*, 1871.

——— The same. 2d ed. revised and enlarged by the author. 143 pp. 8°. *New York, J. H. & C. M. Goodsell*, 1871.

Rogers (Woodes). Nieuwe reize naa de Zuidzee, van daar naa Oost-Indien, en verder rondom de waereld. 1708–1711. Inhoudende een dagregister van zeer aanmerkenswaardige voorvallen; waar onder het veroveren van de steden Puna en Gujaquil, en het schip van Acapulco, en andere prysen, enz. Gedaan onder het bestier van William Dampier. Vertaald door C. P. Eng. title, 3 p. l. 14, 438 pp. 4 l. 4 pl. 5 maps. 4°. *Amsterdam, J. Oosterwyk & H. van de Gaete*, 1715.

Roget de Belloguet. *See* **Belloguet.**

Rohr (Julius Bernhard von). Einleitung zu der klugheit zu leben. Oder anweisung, wie ein mensch zu beförderung seiner zeitlichen glückseeligkeit seine actiones vernünfftig anstellen soll. 3^e^ aufl. 7 p. l. 648 pp. 15 l. 1 pl. 16°. *Leipzig, J. C. Martini*, 1730.

Rojas (Fernando de) *and* **Cota** (Rodrigo de). La Celestina, o tragi-comedia de Calisto y Melibea. Nueva edicion con las variantes de las mejores editiones antiguas. [*anon.*] xix, xx, 412 pp. 16°. *Madrid, L. Amarita*, 1822.

Roll (The) call. Edited by three ladies [for the sanitary and christian commission fair]. Feb. 22 to March 3, 1864. nos. 1, 2, 3 and 5. 4°. *Washington*, 1864.

[*With* Y. M. C. A. 1868–70. Wanting no. 4].

Rollin (Ledru). The decline of England. 2d ed. vi, 360 pp. 12°. *London, E. Churton*, 1850.

Rolling ridge, or the book of four and twenty chapters. [*anon.*] 266 pp. 18°. *Boston, Crocker & Brewster*, 1838.

Rollins (C. V.) The masonic text book, containing the monitorial work of the first three degrees of masonry, with a digest of masonic law. 108 pp. 1 l. 24°. *Rutland,* [*Vt.*] *Tuttle & co.* 1870.

Romaine (*Rev.* William). A treatise upon the life of faith. 2d ed. 288 pp. 1 portrait. 16°. *London, J. Worrall,* [*etc.*] 1764.

Roman catholic church. Compendium ritualis romani, ad usum diœcesum provinciæ Baltimorensis, jussu concilii provincialis Baltimorensis iii. approbante ss. D. N. Gregorio editum. xvi, 216 pp. 12°. *Baltimori, apud J. Murphy,* 1842.

——— Excerpta ex rituali romano pro administratione sacramentorum, ad commodierem usum missionariorum in septentrionalis Americæ foederatæ provinciis. [*anon.*] 140 pp. 24°. *Baltimori, apud J. Murphy,* 1842.

——— The same. 267 pp. 24°. *Baltimori, apud Kelly, Hedian & Piet,* 1862.

——— Horæ diurnæ breviarii romani ex decreto s. concilii tridentini restituti, s. Pii v, pontificis maximi, jussu editi, Clementis vii et Urbani viii, auctoritate recogniti. xxxviii, 524, clij pp. 24°. *Parisiis, Rusaud,* 1829.

——— The roman missal, translated into the english language for the use of the laity. Published with the approbation of the rt. rev. the bishop of Philadelphia. First revised edition. [*anon.*] 782 pp. 1 pl. 18°. *Philadelphia, E. Cummiskey,* 1861.

Romanism incompatible with republican institutions. By Civis. [*anon.*] 107 pp. 16°. *New York, Amer. protestant society,* 1844.

Rooke (John). Select translations from the works of Sannazarius, H. Grotius, Bapt. Amaltheus, D. Heinsius, G. Buchanan, and M. Hier. Vida. To which is prefix'd some account of the authors. 2d ed. 3 v. in 1. 8°. *London, J. Millan,* 1726.

Root (George F.) *and* **Sweetser** (Joseph E.) A collection of church music; comprising many of the most popular and useful tunes in common use, together with a great variety of new and original psalm and hymn tunes, sentences, motetts, anthems, chants, &c. 349 pp. obl. 8°. *New York, J. Wiley,* 1849. s.

Root (Marcus A.) The camera and the pencil; or the heliographic art; together with its history in the United States and in Europe. 456 pp. 5 pl. 12°. *Philadelphia, M. A. Root* 1864.

Roquefeuil (Camille de). A voyage round the world, between the years 1816–1819. 112 pp. 8°. *London, R. Phillips & co.* 1823.

Roquefort (Jean Baptiste Bonaventure de). Glossaire de la langue romane, rédigé d'après les manuscrits de la bibliothèque impériale, et d'après ce qui a été imprimé de plus complet en ce genre; contenant l'étymologie et la signification des mots usités dans les xi, xii, xiii, xiv, xv et xvie siècles, avec de nombreux exemples puisés dans les mêmes sources; et précédé d'un discours sur l'origine, les progrès et les variations de la langue françoise. 2 v. Eng. title, 2 p. l. xxxii, 772 pp; 2 p. l. 780 pp. 8°. *Paris, B. Warée,* 1808.

——— The same. Supplément au glossaire de la langue romane. iii, 307 pp. 8°. *Paris, Chasseriau et Hecart,* 1820.

Roquelaure (*duc* de). *See* **Le Roy** (— *le sieur*).

Rosanna; or scenes in Boston. *See* **Sedgwick** (Catharine Maria).

Rose (The) in the desert. [*anon.*] 117 pp. 18°. *New York, Carlton & Porter,* [1862].

Rose Marian, and the flower fairies. *See* **Child** (Lydia Maria).

Rose Morton's journal for April. [*anon.*] 313 pp. 2 pl. 18°. *New York, Sheldon & co.* 1863.

Rose Morton's journal for May. [*anon.*] 263 pp. 2 pl. 18°. *New York, Sheldon & co.* 1863.

Rose the lavender girl, or, honest industry rewarded. By the author of "Cameron's bells," [etc. *anon.*] 245 pp. 3 pl. 16°. *New York, Society for the promotion of evangelical knowledge,* 1871.

Rosenius (C. O.) De ti Gud's bud. Over sættesse fra svensk ved C. M. Eckhoff. 12[et] oplag. 280 pp. 16°. *Bergen, E. B. Giertsen,* 1869. s.

Rosenstein (I. G. *m. d.*) Theory and practice of homœopathy. First part, containing a theory of homœopathy, with dietetic rules, &c. 288 pp. 12°. *Louisville, Henkle & Logan,* 1840.

Roseo (Mambrino). Delle historie del mondo, parte terza. Aggiunte alle historie di Giovanni Tarcagnota. 16 p. l. 613 pp. 4°. *Vinegia, Giunti,* 1592.

Rosewald (Jacob H.) The solfeggio. Part one. A text book for musical instruction in primary, grammar and high schools. 107 pp. obl. 18°. *Baltimore, Wm. J. C. Dulany & co.* 1871.

Ross (Alexander). Mystagogus poeticus, or the muses interpreter: explaining the historical mysteries, and mystical histories of the ancient greek and latin poets. 5th ed. To which is prefixed the genealogy of the heathen gods. 7 p. l. 416 pp. 16°. *London, J. Martyn,* [*etc.*] 1672.

[Imperfect: wanting all after p. 416].

Ross (James, *ll. d.*) Onomasia: or, Philadelphia vocabulary, with the signs of quantity; comprising, sententiæ pueriles, Catonis disticha, collectiones poeticæ selectæ, materia medica, a sketch of mythology, with a very concise account of some of the heathen deities, heroes and heroines, ancient cities, countries, and distinguished persons, especially of those in Greece and Rome. [Also], an extract from dr. C. Nisbet's address to the students of Dickinson college. viii, 110 pp. 12°. *Philadelphia, author,* 1822.

——— A short, plain, comprehensive, practical latin grammar, comprising all the rules and observations necessary to an accurate knowledge of the latin classics. 7th ed. viii, 184 pp. 12°. *Philadelphia, author,* 1823.

——— The same. A latin grammar. With latin idioms, and a new prosody, and other important additions and emendations. By N. C. Brooks. 8, 211 pp. 12°. *Philadelphia, Thomas, Cowperthwait & co.* 1844.

Ross (*Rev.* Robert). The american latin grammar: or a complete introduction to the latin tongue. 5th ed. To which is now first added, a vocabulary. 162 pp. 16°. *New York, J. Parker for G. Noel,* 1770.

——— The same. Revised and corrected by the late presidents Burr, Finley, [etc.] 5th ed. 112 pp. 16°. *Providence* (*R. I.*) *J. Carter,* 1780.

Rossetti (Dante Gabriel). Poems. 5th ed. xii, 282 pp. 12°. *London, F. S. Ellis,* 1871.

Rossi (Bastiano de', *editor*). Degli accademici della Crvsca difesa dell' Orlando fvrioso dell' Ariosto. Contra 'l dialogo dell' epica poesia di Cammillo Pellegrino. Stacciata 1ª. 4 l. unp. 53 l. 1 l. unp. 16°. *Firenze, D. Manzani,* 1584.

[*With* PELLEGRINO (Cammillo, *the elder*). Il Carrafa. 1584].

Rossini (Gioacchino). The barber of Seville, (Il barbiere di Siviglia). The words newly revised and corrected by W. Sherwood. [Libretto, without music]. 42 pp. 8°. [*New York,*], *W. C. Bryant & co.* 1871.

[PAREPA-ROSA grand english opera].

Rossini (Gioacchino)—continued.

——— The thieving magpie, (La gazza ladra). An opera, in two acts. The words newly revised and corrected by W. Sherwood. [Libretto, without music]. 43 pp. 8°. [*New York*], *W. C. Bryant & co.* 1871.

[PAREPA-ROSA grand english opera].

Roth (Theodore). Der kleine amerikaner, oder anleitung zur selbst-erlernung der im gewöhnlichen leben vorkommenden worte der englischen sprache. 104 pp. 16°. *Hamburg, R. Kittler,* 1870.

Rothelin (Charles d'Orléans de, *abbé de Cormeilles*). Catalogue des livres de feu m. l'abbé d'Orléans de Rothelin. Par G. Martin. xii, xxiv, 614 pp. 8°. *Paris, G. Martin,* 1746.

Rotheram. *See* **Rotherham.**

Rotherham (John). An essay on faith, and its connection with good works. 3d ed. viii, 126 pp. 8°. *New York, reprinted by J. Parker,* 1767.

Rothman (Johann). *Χειρομαντια*: or, the art of divining by the lines and signatures engraven in the hand of man, by the hand of nature, theorically, practically. With a learned philosophical discourse of the soul of the world, and the universal spirit thereof. Written originally in latine, and now faithfully englished, by George Wharton. London, as it was printed in the year 1652. 16°. [*London, H. H. for J. Leigh,* 1683].

[*In* WHARTON (*Sir* George). Works. *London,* 1683. pp. 515-643, 1 pl.]

Rothsten (F. W.) Latinais-suomalainen sanakirja. Koulujen tarpeeksi. viii, 1068 pp. 8°. *Helsingissä, Suomalaisen kirjallisuuden seuran kirjapainossa,* 1864. s.

[HELSINGFORS. Suomalaisen kirjallisuuden seuran toimituksia. 33 osa].

Rotteck (Carl von. *ll. d.*) General history of the world from the earliest times until the year 1831. Translated from the german, and continued to 1840. By Frederick Jones. 1st american edition. 4 v. 8°. *Philadelphia, C. F. Stollmeyer,* 1840-41.

Rottiers (— *Le colonel*). Itinéraire de Tiflis à Constantinople. 377 pp. 7 pl. 3 maps. 8°. *Bruxelles, Tencé frères,* 1829.

Rouelle (John, *m. d.*) A complete treatise on the mineral waters of Virginia: containing a description of their situation, their natural history, their analysis, contents, and their use in medicine. 4 p. l. xix, 68 pp. 8°. *Philadelphia, author,* 1792.

Rouille (Guillermus le). *See* **LeRouillé** (Guillaume).

Roundhearts and other stories. *See* **Harris** (*Mrs.* Sidney S.)

Roure (P.) La conquête du Mexique, poëme en dix chants, enrichi de notes, du précis de la conquête du Mexique, et de son état ancien et moderne; suivi de fragmens du poëme de Las-Casas et de poésies diverses. 1 p. l. 260 pp. 1 l. 8°. *Paris, Pillet,* 1811.

Rousseau (Jean Baptiste Louis Jacques). Description du pachalik de Bagdad, suivie d'une notice historique sur les Wahabis, et de quelques autres pièces relatives à l'histoire et à la littérature de l'orient. Par M. * * * [*anon.*] viii, 261 pp. 8°. *Paris, Treuttel & Würtz,* 1809.

Roussel (*L'abbé* Claude). Principes de religion, ou préservatif contre l'incrédulité. 2e éd. corrigée et augmentée. 4 p. l. xii, 424 pp. 2 l. 24°. *Paris, Prault jeune,* 1753.

Roussel (Napoléon). Patriarchal scenes. From the french. 264 pp. 18°. *Boston, Mass. sabbath school society,* 1845.

——— Sacred scenes: from the french. 288 pp. 1 pl. 18°. *Boston, Mass. sabbath school society,* 1844.

Routledge (Edmund). Quotations from Shakespeare. *See* **Shakespeare** (William).

Roux (Alphonse A.) French speaker, ou l'orateur français. Cours de lecture, de déclamation et de littérature. 340 pp. 12°. *New York, R. Lockwood & son,* 1852.

Roux-Ferrand (Hippolyte). Histoire des progrès de la civilisation en Europe depuis l'ère chrétienne jusqu'au xixe siècle. 2e éd. v 8°. *Paris, L. Hachette & cie.* 1847.

Rovigo (*Duc* de). *See* **Savary** (Anne Jean Marie René, *duc* de Rovigo).

Rowden (Frances Arabella). The pleasures of friendship: a poem, in two parts. 3d ed. xv, 165 pp. 1 pl. 16°. *London, G. and W. B. Whittaker,* 1818.

Rowe (Nicholas). The fair penitent. A tragedy. 64 pp. incl. frontis. 16°. *London, for proprietors,* 1770.

[*With* SHAKESPEARE (William). Hamlet. 1757].

Rowell (Geo. P.) & co's American newspaper directory. 576 pp. 1 pl. 8°. *New York, Geo. P. Rowell & co.* 1871.

Rowell (Truman). A concordance of the holy scriptures with the references included. 156 pp. 16°. *Watertown,* [*N. Y.*] *Ingalls & Stowell,* 1855.

Rowland (Henry Augustus, *d. d.*) On the common maxims of infidelity. 306 pp. 12°. *New York, R. Carter & brothers,* 1850.

Rowley (*Mrs.* Francis A.) Poems for the times: devoted to woman's rights, temperance, etc. 317 pp. 12°. *Cincinnati, Miami printing & publishing co.* 1871.

Roxas (Agustin de). El viage entretenido: con una exposicion de los nombres historicos y poeticos que no van declarados. 5a ed. 2 v. 288 pp; 270 pp. 18°. *Madrid, B. Cano,* 1793.

Roy (A.) Le narrateur français; or, a selection of anecdotes, repartees, & characters, in the french tongue, printed with two new orthoepic signs. [Also], preliminary grammatical principles, [etc.] cxxiii, 138, 74 pp. 12°. *London, W. Pickering,* 1827.

Roy (George). Generalship: a tale. viii, 244 pp. 1 pl. 16°. *London and Glasgow, R. Griffin and company,* 1858.

Royal (The) guide to the London charities for 1866–7; showing in alphabetical order their name, date of foundation, address, objects, annual income, chief officials, &c. Edited by Herbert Fry. 4th annual ed. viii, 195 pp. 12°. *London, R. Hardwicke,* 1866.

Royal (The) kalendar, and court and city register for England, Scotland, Ireland, and the colonies, for the years 1871 and 1872. 2 v. 12°. *London, R. & A. Suttaby,* 1871–72.

Royall (William). A treatise on latin cases and analysis. 129 pp. 16°. *New York, Sheldon & co.* 1860.

Royse (*Rev.* P. E.) The voice of the prophets; proclaiming wonderful tidings about the time of the end: as exemplified by collateral, historical, and critical annotations on the apocalypse. 464 pp. 1 portrait. 4°. *Louisville (Ky.) author,* 1860.

Rüdel (Johann). Biblia sacra. 1527. *See* **Bible.** (*Latin*).

Rueda (Juan de). Sermon panegyrico, en la celebridad de la dedicacion del templo nuevo de San Bernardo, titvlo Maria de Gvadalupe; dia qvarto de la octaua. sm. 4°. [*México, viuda de F. R. Lupercio,* 1691].

[*In* RAMIREZ DE VARGAS (A.) Sagrado padron y panegyricos sermones, etc. l. 36–44].

Rues (Les) de Madrid. 1731. *See* **Waleff** (Blaise Henri de Corte, *baron* de).

Rüff *or* **Ryff** (Jakob). De conceptv et generatione hominis: de matrice et eivs partibvs, nec non de conditione infantis in vtero et gravidarvm cvra et officio de partu et

Rüff *or* **Ryff** (Jakob)—continued. parturientium infantiumque cura omnifaria [etc.]: de sterilitatis causis diuersis, & de præcipuis matricis aegritudinibus, omniumque horum curis varijs, libri sex. Nunc denuo recogniti & in plerisque locis castigati. 5 p.l. 100 l. 4°. *Francoforti ad Mœnum*, 1580.

Rufinus *or* **Ruffinus** *grammaticus antiochensis.* Versus Rufini v. c. litteratoris de compositione et de metris oratorum. 8°. [*Turici, typis Orellii*, 1833].

[*In* CICERO (Marcus Tullius). Opera quae supersunt omnia ex recensione I. C. Orellii, v. 5, part 1, pp. 183-194].

Rule (*Rev.* William Harris). Celebrated jesuits. 2 v. viii, 444 pp. 3 portraits; xii, 444 pp. 3 portraits. 18°. *London, J. Mason*, 1852-53.

Rules (The) of civility; or, certain ways of deportment observed in France, amongst all persons of quality, upon several occasions. Translated out of french. [*anon.*] 5 p.l. 154 pp. 18°. *London, J. Martyn*, 1671.

Rumph *or* **Rumpf** (Georg Eberhard). D'amboinsche rariteitkamer, behelzende eene beschryvinge van allerhande zoo weeke als harde schaalvisschen, te weeten raare krabben, kreeften, en diergelyke zeedieren, als mede allerhande hoorntjes en schulpen, die men in d'Amboinsche zee vindt: daar beneven zommige mineraalen, gesteenten, [etc.] 16 p.l. 340 pp. 22 l. 60 pl. 1 portrait. fol. *Amsterdam, F. Halma*, 1705.

Rusca (Antonio). De inferno, et statv dæmonvm ante mvndi exitivm, libri qvinqve. In quibus tartarea cauitas, parata ibi cruciamentorum genera ethnicorum etiam de his opiniones, dæmonumque conditio usque ad magnum judicii diem varia eruditione describuntur. 16 p.l. 574 pp. 7 l. 4°. *Mediolani, ex collegij ambrosiani typographia*, 1621.

Ruscelli (Girolamo *and* Vincenzo). Le imprese illvstri del s^or^ Ieronimo Rvscelli. Aggivntovi nvovam^te^ il qvarto libro da Vincenzo Rvscelli da Viterbo. Eng. title, 13 p.l. 496, 82 pp. incl. 22 pl. & many half-pl. 4°. *Venetia, F. de Frāceschi*, 1584.

Rush (Christopher). A short account of the rise and progress of the African methodist episcopal church in America. Written with the aid of George Collins. Also, a view of church order or government, from scripture and from some of the best authors, relative to episcopacy. 119 pp. 16°. *New York, author*, 1843.

Rush (James, *m. d.*) Hamlet, a dramatic prelude; in five acts. 122 pp. 12°. *Philadelphia, Key & Biddle*, 1834.

Rusling (*Rev.* Joseph). Devotional exercises; and miscellaneous poems. 1 p.l. xii, 240 pp. 16°. *Philadelphia*, 1836.

——— Hymns composed for the use of sunday schools, and youthful christians. viii, 136 pp. sq. 18°. *Philadelphia*, 1837.

——— The same. Original hymns. 2d ed. 152 pp. 24°. *New York, T. Mason & G. Lane*, 1838.

——— Portions of the psalms of David, and other parts of scripture, in verse. Designed as a companion for the christian. 222 pp. 32°. *Philadelphia, publisher*, 1838.

Russell (Alexander J.) The Red river country, Hudson's bay & north-west territories, considered in relation to Canada, with the last report of S. J. Dawson, on the line of route between lake Superior and the Red river settlement. xv, 202 pp. 1 map. 8°. *Ottawa, G. E. Desbarats*, 1869. s.

Russell (Edward) & co. The mercantile agency reference book for Boston. 1871. *See* **Boston** (*City of*).

Russell (Martha). Stories from New England life; or leaves from the tree Igdrasyl. 348 pp. 12°. *Boston, J. P. Jewett & co.* 1856.

——— Sybil Munroe, the forger's daughter: or out of the shadow into the sun. 368 pp. 12°. *Boston, L. P. Crown & co.* 1859.

Russell (Richard). Memoirs of the society of Grub-street. *See* **Martyn** (John, *prof. etc.*)

Russell (Thomas). Father Taylor, the sailor preacher. 1872. *See* **Haven** (*Rev.* Gilbert) *and* **Russell.**

Russell (William). Rudiments of gesture. comprising illustrations of common faults in attitude and action. 2d ed. [With] an appendix. 120 pp. incl. 12 pl. 12°. *Boston, G. W. Palmer & co.* 1838.

Ruter (Martin, *d. d.*) A concise history of the christian church. Compiled from the works of dr. G. Gregory. *See* **Gregory** (George, *d. d.*)

——— The juvenile arithmetick, and scholar's guide. 1 p.l. 216 pp. 1 pl. 18°. *Cincinnati, N. & G. Guilford*, 1827.

——— The martyrs, or a history of persecution, from the commencement of christianity to the present time: including an account of the trials, tortures, and triumphant deaths of many who have suffered martyrdom. Com-

Ruter (Martin, *d. d.*)—continued. piled from the works of Fox and others. 562 pp. 1 l. 4 pl. 12°. *Cincinnati, E. Deming,* 1830.

Ruth Allerton, the missionary's daughter. [*anon.*] 283 pp. 3 pl. 16°. *Philadelphia, American s. s. union,* [1871].

Ruth Elmer: a tale for school girls. [*anon.*] 126 pp. 18°. *Philadelphia, American sunday-school union,* [1855].

Rutland (John, 5*th duke of*). *See* **Manners** (John Henry).

Rutledge. [A novel]. *See* **Harris** (*Mrs.* Sidney S.)

Rutter (John). Delineations of the north western division of the county of Somerset, and of its antediluvian bone caverns, with a geological sketch of the district. xxiv, 349 (336) pp. 1 map. 12 pl. 8°. *Shaftesbury, author,* 1829.

Rutter (U. C.) Book for the million. Interest: a new easy and infallible system of computing interest on all sums, and at any rate per cent. and for any length of time, from one day to six years, calculated by a single multiplication. 107 pp. 18°. *Lancaster* (*Ohio*), 1859.

Rüttimann (— *Prof.*) Das nordamerikanische bundesstaatsrecht verglichen mit den politischen einrichtungen der Schweiz. 1r theil. xvi, 459 pp. 8°. *Zürich, Orell, Füssli & comp.* 1867.

Ryan (James). An elementary treatise on algebra, theoretical and practical. To which is added, an algebraic method of demonstrating the propositions in the fifth book of Euclid, according to Simson's edition. By Robert Adrian, ll. d. xi, 516 pp. 12°. *New York, Collins & Hannay,* 1824.

——— The same. 3d ed. viii, 361 pp. 12°. *New York, W. E. Dean,* 1835.

——— The new american grammar of the elements of astronomy, on an improved plan: in three books. iv, 375 pp. 12°. *New-York, J. Ryan,* 1825.

Ryan (Richard). Poetry and poets: a collection of the choicest anecdotes relative to the poets of every age and nation. With specimens of their works and sketches of their biography. 3 v. 16°. *London, Sherwood, Gilbert, & Piper,* 1826.

Rycaut (*Sir* Paul). The history of the present state of the ottoman empire, containing the maxims of the turkish polity, the most material points of the mahometan religion;

Rycaut (*Sir* Paul)—continued. their military discipline; with an exact computation of their sea and land forces. By sir Paul Ricaut. 70 pp. 1 pl. 1 portrait. 8°. *London, I. Cleave,* 1701.

[*With* KNOLLES (Richard). The turkish history. ed. 1701].

Ryder (*Rev.* William). The superannuate: or, anecdotes, incidents, and sketches of the life and experience of William Ryder, a "a worn-out" preacher of the Troy conference of the m. e. church. Related by himself. 160 pp. 18°. *New York, G. Lane & C. B. Tippett,* 1845.

Rye (E. C.) British beetles: an introduction to the study of our indigenous coleoptera. xv, 280 pp. 16 l. 16 col. pl. 12°. *London, L. Reeve & co.* 1866.

Rye (George, *d. d.*) A treatise against the nonconforming nonjurors. In answer to the objections which mr. Dodwell, dr. Hickes, dr. Simon Lowth, mr. Collier, mr. Howel, mr. Earbery, mr. Whiston, dr. Brett, and others, have brought against the church of England. 2 v. 4 p. l. 462 pp; 2 p. l. 181–665 pp. 8°. *London, D. Browne,* 1719.

Ryerson (Egerton, *d. d. editor*). *See* **Journal** (The) of education for Ontario.

S. (E.) England's royall fishing revived. *See* **Sharpe** (Edward).

S. (J.) An epitomy of ecclesiastical history. [*anon.*] 2d ed. 3 p. l. 288, x pp. 16°. *London, J. Millet,* 1602.

[*With* LA SERRE (Jean Puget de). The mirrour which flatters not. Imperfect: wanting all after p. 288].

S. (L.) Sarah and her cousins. By the author of "The Sandfords, or home scenes." [*anon.*] 103 pp. 18°. *Boston, Carter, Hendee & Babcock,* 1831.

S. (L. C.) *See* **Starbuck** (L. C.)

S. (*Mrs.* M. J. P.) Marcia and Ellen, the drunkard's children. By mrs. M. J. P. S. [*anon.*] 126 pp. 3 pl. 18°. *New York, American tract society,* [1861].

S. (S. S.) *See* **Simpson** (S. S.)

Saavedra Faxardo (Diego). Respublica literaria: or, the republick of letters; being a vision. Wrote in spanish. Translated by J. E. xxviii, 186 pp. 12°. *London, S. Austen,* 1727.

Saavedra (Marcos de). Confessionario breve, activo, y passivo, en lengua mexicana. Reimpreso. 8 l. 18°. *México, imprenta real,* 1746.

Sabatier de Castres (*L'abbé* Antoine). Les trois siècles de la littérature françoise, ou tableau de l'esprit de nos écrivains, depuis François i, jusqu'en 1773: par l'abbé S * * * de Castres. Nouv. éd. 4 v. 16°. *Amsterdam*, 1774.

Sabbath-day (The) book for boys and girls. By the editors of the popular library. [*anon.*] 230 pp. 16°. *Boston, J. Allen & co.* 1835.

Sabbath-school (The) prayer and hymn-book. [*anon.*] 254 pp. 3 pl. 32°. *Philadelphia, E. Cummisky*, 1871.

Sabbath school psalm and tune book; selections from the scottish version of the psalms, set to appropriate tunes; also the entire one hundred and fifty psalms. [*anon.*] 64, 47 pp. obl. 16°. *Philadelphia, W. H. Scott*, [1871].

Sabbath school results. By the secretary of the Massachusetts sabbath school society. [*anon.*] 304 pp. 18°. *Boston, Mass. sabbath school society*, 1837.

Sabbath school scenes. By a sabbath school teacher, of Massachusetts. With the history of a female sabbath school scholar. [*anon.*] 108 pp. 1 pl. 16°. *Boston, J. Loring*, [1829].

Sabbath-school teachers' visits: an antidote to the vice of profaneness. By the author of "Sabbath school scenes." [*anon.*] 108 pp. 16°. *Boston, J. Loring*, [1829].

Sabbath talks, with the little children, about Jesus. By the author of "The mothers of the bible." [*anon.*] 139 pp. sq. 16°. *Boston, J. P. Jewett & co.* 1856.

Sabin (Joseph). Bibliotheca americana. A dictionary of books relating to America, from its discovery to the present time. v. 4. Cheshire to Costa. 8°. *New York, J. Sabin & sons*, 1871.

Sabin and sons' american bibliopolist. *See* **American** bibliopolist.

Sabine (Robert). The electric telegraph. xv, 428 pp. 8°. *London, Virtue bros. & co.* 1867.

Sablier (Charles). Variétés sérieuses et amusantes. Nouv. éd. revue, corrigée & augmentée. 4 v. 16°. *Amsterdam*, 1769.

Sackett (J. B.) Ritual of masonic service for the burial of the dead, and lodge of sorrow. 120 pp. 18°. *Chicago, E. B. Myers & co.* 1870.

Sacred lyrics from the german. [Compiled by "the editor of the board of publication." *anon.*] Eng. title, xii, 252 pp. 8°. *Philadelphia, Presbyterian board of publication*, [1859].

Sacred melodies, or hymns for youth; with appropriate selections from scripture. [*anon.*] 111 pp. 12°. *New York, Wiley & Putnam*, 1841.

Sacred (The) offering; a poetical gift. [*anon.*] 216 pp. 18°. *Boston, J. Dowe*, 1838.

Sacred paths; or life in prospect of immortality. [*anon.*] 218 pp. 18°. *Boston, J. Dowe*, 1841.

Sacro-Bosco (Johannes). *See* **Holywood** (John).

Sacy (Louis de). Traité de l'amitié. Nouv. éd. xxv, 390 pp. 2 l. 16°. *Paris, la compagnie des libraires*, 1742.

Sade (Jacques François Paul Alphonse, *l'abbé* de). Mémoires pour la vie de François Pétrarque, tirés de ses œuvres et des auteurs contemporains, avec des notes ou dissertations, & les pièces justificatives. [*anon.*] 3 v. 4°. *Amsterdam, Arskée & Mercus*, 1764–67.

Sadeur (Jaques, *pseudon.*) *See* **Foigny** (Gabriel).

Sadler (*Rev.* L. L.) The prophecies of Daniel, with their application and fulfilment, illustrated by profane history. 152 pp. 18°. *Portland, S. H. Colesunthy*, 1843.

Sadoleto (Jacopo). Epistolarvm libri sexdecim. Eiusdem ad Paulum Sadoletum epistolarum liber unus. Vita eiusdem autoris per Antonium Florebellum. 716 pp. 16°. *Lvgdvni, apvd haered. S. Gryphii*, 1560.

Sagra (Ramon de la). Reis door Nederland en Belgie, met toepassing op het lager onderwijs, de instellingen van liefdadigheid en de gevangenissen in die beide landen. 2 v. 4 p. l. 344 pp; 4 p. l. 303 pp. 8°. *Groningen, J. Oomkens*, 1839–42.

Saint Albin (J. S. C. de, *pseudon.*) *See* **Collin de Plancy** (J. A. S.)

Sainte-Beuve (Charles Augustin). Nouveaux lundis. v. 11–12. 16°. *Paris, M. Lévy frères*, 1869–70.

Sainte-Croix (Guillaume Emmanuel Joseph Guilhem de Clermont-Lodève, *baron* de). De l'état et du sort des colonies, des anciens peuples. Ouvrage dans lequel on traite du gouvernement des anciennes républiques, de leur droit public, &c. avec des observations sur les colonies des nations modernes, & la conduite des Anglois en Amérique. [*anon.*] xiv, 336 pp. 8°. *Philadelphie*, [*Paris*], 1779.

Sainte-Marthe (Scévole *et* Louis de). A genealogical history of the kings of Portu-

Sainte-Marthe (S. *et* L. de)—continued. gal. And of all those illustrious houses that in masculine line are branched from that royal family. Containing a discourse of their several lives, [etc.] With their armes and emblazons; as also their symboles and mottoes. Written in french unto the year 1623. Rendred into english, and continued unto this present year, 1662. By Francis Sandford. [1st ed.] 3 p. l. 146, 53 pp. 2 pl. 1 table. fol. *London, E. M. for author*, 1662.
[*Note.*—In part identical with their Histoire généalogique de la maison de France].

Saint-Gélais (Jean de). Extrait d'vne histoire de France, manvscrite, qui commence l'an 1270. & finit l'an 1510. fol. [*Paris*, 1684].
[*In* GODEFROY (T. *and* D.) Histoire de Charles viii, pp. 91–113].

Saint-Hilaire (Augustin François César Prouvensal de). Leçons de botanique, comprenant principalement la morphologie végétale, la terminologie, la botanique comparée, l'examen de la valeur des caractères dans les diverses familles naturelles, etc. 4 p. l. viii, 930 pp. 24 pl. 8°. *Paris, P. J. Loss*, 1840.

Saint-Hyacinthe (Hyacinthe Cordonnier *ou* Thémiseul de). Le chef d'œuvre d'un inconu, poëme heureusement découvert & mis au jour, avec des remarques savantes & recherchées, par m. le docteur Chrisostome Matanasius. On trouve de plus une dissertation sur Homère & sur Chapelain; deux lettres sur des antiques; la préface de Cervantes sur l'histoire de d. Quixotte de la Manche; la deïfication d'Aristarchus Masso, & plusieurs autres choses. [*pseudon.*] 6e éd. revue, corrigée, augmentée, & diminuée. 2 v. 29 p. l. 264 pp. 3 pl; 6 p. l. pp. 265–528, 10 l. 1 pl. 16°. *La Haye, P. Husson*, 1732.

St. John (Bayle). The eccentric lover. A novel. 3 v. 12°. *London, R. Bentley*, 1845.

Saint-John (Oliver). Mr. St.-John's speech to the lords in the vpper house of parliament Ianuary 7. 1640, concerning ship-money. 1 p. l. 45 pp. sm. 4°. [*London*], 1641.
[*With* PARKER (Henry). The case of ship-money briefly discoursed. [*London*], 1640].

Saint Lambert (Charles François *or* Jean François de). Les saisons, poëme. [L'Abénaki, Sara Th..., Zimeo, (contes). Pièces fugitives, [en vers]; fables orientales. [*anon.*] 7e éd. 467 pp. 7 pl. 8°. *Amsterdam*, 1775.

St. Leger (Barry). Stories from Froissart. *See* **Froissart** (*Sir* John).

Saint Louis (*City of*). Edwards' annual directory to the inhabitants, institutions, incorporated companies, business, business firms, manufacturing establishments, etc. in the city of St. Louis, for 1871 and 1872. 2 v. 8°. *St. Louis, Southern publishing co.* 1871–72.

Saint Mars (N. Cisterne de Courtiras, *vicomtesse de*). Les bals masqués, par la comtesse Dash. [*pseudon.*] 2 v. 2 p. l. 259 pp. 1 l; 2 p. l. 254 pp. 1 l. 16°. *Bruxelles, société belge de librairie*, 1842.

——— La chaine d'or, par la comtesse Dash. [*pseudon.*] 2 p. l. 258 pp. 1 l. 16°. *Bruxelles, société belge de librairie*, 1840.

——— Le comte de Sombreuil, par la comtesse Dash. [*pseudon.*] 2 v. 292 pp; 506 pp. 1 pl. 16°. *Bruxelles, société belge de librairie*, 1843.

——— L'Écran, par la comtesse Dash. [*pseudon.*] 2 p. l. 271 pp. 16°. *Bruxelles, société belge de librairie*, 1840.

——— Madame Louise de France, par la comtesse Dash. [*pseudon.*] 2 p. l. 256 pp. 1 l. 16°. *Bruxelles, société belge de librairie*, 1840.

——— Madame de la Sablière, par la comtesse Dash. [*pseudon.*] 2 p. l. 279 pp. 1 l. 16°. *Bruxelles, société belge de librairie*, 1840.

——— La marquise de Parabère, par la comtesse Dash. [*pseudon.*] 2 v. 2 p. l. 256 pp; 2 p. l. 264 pp. 16°. *Bruxelles, société belge de librairie*, 1842.

——— Maurice Robert, par la comtesse Dash. [*pseudon.*] 182 pp. 16°. *Bruxelles, société belge de librairie*, 1843.

——— Les orphelins, par la comtesse Dash. [*pseudon.*] 2 v. 2 p. l. 239 pp; 2 p. l. 238 pp. 16°. *Bruxelles, Meline, Cans & cie.* 1853.

——— La poudre et la neige, par la comtesse Dash. [*pseudon.*] 2 v. 303 pp. 1 l; 319 pp. 1 l. 16°. *Bruxelles, société belge de librairie*, 1844.

——— Renée, par la comtesse Dash. [*pseudon.*] 2 p. l. 250 pp. 16°. *Bruxelles, Meline, Cans & cie.* 1852.

——— La villa Balbianino, par la comtesse Dash. [*pseudon.*] 3 v. 16°. *Bruxelles, Meline, Cans & cie.* 1859.

Saint-Martin (Guichard Déageant de). *See* **Déagant de Saint-Martin.**

Saint Nicholas's book for all good boys and girls. [*anon.*] 208 pp. 14 pl. sq. 12°. *Philadelphia, Thomas, Cowperthwait & co.* 1842.

St. Petersburg. (*Imperatorska publitchnaya biblioteka*). Catalogue des manuscrits et xylographes orientaux. 2 p. l. xliv, 718 pp. 1 l. 8°. *St.-Pétersbourg, imp. de l'académie imp. des sciences*, 1852. s.

——— ——— Catalogue des manuscrits grecs. iv, 100 pp. 9 pl. 8°. *St.-Petersbourg, académie impériale des sciences*, 1864.

——— (*Imperial botanical gardens*). Index seminum quae hortus botanicus imperialis petropolitanus pro mutua commutatione offert. 1860–65. 6 v. in 1. 8°. [*St.-Pétersbourg*], 1860–65. s.

St. Philip's. [A novel]. *See* **Harris** (*Mrs.* Sidney S.)

Saint-Priest (Alexis Guignard, *comte* de). Histoire de la royauté considérée dans ses origines, jusqu'à la formation des principales monarchies de l'Europe. 2 v. 2 p. l. vii, lxxvi, 472 pp; xxiv, 585 pp. 8°. *Paris, H. L. Delloye*, 1842.

——— Storia della caduta de' gesuiti nel secolo xviii. Prima versione italiana di Francesco Giuntini. 2 v. in 1. 1 p. l. 327 pp. 16°. *Firenze, S. Birindelli*, 1848.

Saint-Vincent (Jean Baptiste George Marie Bory de). *See* **Bory de Saint-Vincent.**

Sala (George Augustus). Gaslight and daylight, with some London scenes they shine upon. iv, 404 pp. 12°. *London, Chapman & Hall*, 1859.

Saligniac (Bartholomée de). Itinerarivm sacræ scriptvræ, hoc est, sanctae terræ, regio, nvmqve finitimarvm descriptio. In Germania nunc primum in lucem edita, à Bartholomæo de Saligniaco. 60 l. sm. 4°. *Magdebvrgi, excudebat P. Donatus, impensis A. Kirchneri*, 1593.

Salîl-ibn-Razîk. History of the imâms and seyyids of 'Omân, from a. d. 661–1856; translated from the original arabic, and edited, with notes, appendices, and an introduction, continuing the history down to 1870, by George Percy Badger. 9 p. l. cxxviii, 435 pp. 1 map. 8°. *London*, 1871.
[HAKLUYT society, v. 44].

Salisbury (W. S. *and* B.) Salisbury's great pantaloons system, devoted to the æsthetics of pantaloons cutting, etc. Fully illustrated. 87 pp. 25 col. pl. fol. *Battle Creek (Mich.) Review & Herald printing house*, 1871.

Salkeld (John). A treatise of angels. Of the natvre, essence, place, power, science, vvill, apparitions, grace, sinne, and all other proprieties of angels. 12 p. l. 366 pp. 16°. *London, T. S. for N. Butter*, 1613.

Sallustius (Caius Crispus). Opera, omissis fragmentis, omnia; ad optimorum exemplarium fidem recensita. Animadversionibus illustravit P. Wilson. Ed. 4a. Recensuit notasque suas adspersit Carolus Anthon. vi, 132 pp; 95 pp. 16°. *Novi Eboraci, G. & C. Carvill*, 1825.

——— The same. Sallust's Jugurthine war and conspiracy of Catiline, with an english commentary, and geographical and historical indexes. By Charles Anthon. 6th ed. xxi, [1], 332 pp. 1 pl. 12°. *New York, Harper & brothers*, 1836.

——— The same. Jugurtha and Catiline: with notes and a vocabulary. [Latin]. By Noble Butler and Millard Sturgus. vii, 397 pp. 12°. *New York, D. Appleton & co.* 1855.

——— The same. Bellum catilinarium & jugurthinum. History of the catilinarian and jugurthine wars. Translated into english by Henry Lee. [Latin and english]. vii, 267 pp. 4°. *London, author*, [*H. Lee*], 1744.

——— The same. The catiline and jugurthine wars. Translated from Sallust. By Hugh Maffett. xxiv, 279 pp. 8°. *Dublin, Stewart & Spotswood*, 1772.

——— Catilina. [Latin]. 8°. [*New York*, 1871].
[*In* HANSON (J. H.) Preparatory latin prose book].

——— The same. Patriæ parricida; or, the history of the horrid conspiracy of Catiline against the commonwealth of Rome. Translated out of Salust, by C[aleb] C[alle]. 7 p. l. 93 pp. 12°. *London, J. C. & F. C. for J. Norris*, 1683.

Sallustius *philosophus.* Σαλλουστιου φιλοσοφου περι Θεων και κοσμου. Sallustii philosophi de diis et mundo. [Græce et latine]. 8°. [*Amstelaedami, apud H. Wetstenium*, 1688].
[*In* GALE (Thomas). Opuscula mythologica, pp 238–280].

——— The same. Traité des dieux et du monde. Traduit du grec, avec un commentaire littéraire & moral, [par J. H. S. Formey]. 16°. [*Leide, E. Luzac fils*, 1759].
[*In* FORMEY (Jean Henri Samuel). Le philosophe payen. *Leide*, 1759. v. 3, pp. 177–306].

Salmon (Thomas, *of Bedfordshire*). Die heutige historie, oder der gegenwärtige staat von Indostan und Ceilon, oder dem eigentlich so genannten Indien, enthaltend eine ausführliche beschreibung aller reiche, staaten und länder des grossen mogols, und europäischen handels-plätze auf denen see-

Salmon (Thomas)—continued. küsten Malabar und Coromandel. Nach dem englischen und holländischen herrn Salmons und herrn v. Goch. 324 pp. 1 pl. 1 map. 4°. *Altona & Flensburg, gebrüdern Korte*, 1736.

Salmon (William). Bibliothèque des philosophes chimiques. Nouvelle éd. revuë, corrigée & augmentée de plusieurs philosophes, avec des figures & des notes [par l'abbé Lenglet du Fresnoy] pour faciliter l'intelligence de leur doctrine. Par J. M. D. R. [Maugin de Richebourg]. 3 v. 12°. *Paris, A. Cailleau*, 1741.

CONTENTS.

v. 1. La table d'émeraude d'Hermès, avec le commentaire de l'Hortulain, [Jean de Garlande], p. 1.
Les sept chapitres, attribuéz à Hermès, p. 16.
Dialogue de Marie et d'Aros, sur le magistère d'Hermès, p. 77.
La somme de la perfection, ou l'abrégé du magistère parfait de Geber, philosophe arabe, p. 85.

v. 2. La tourbe des philosophes, ou l'assemblée des disciples de Pythagoras, appellée le code de vérité [d'Arislaüs], p. 1.
Entretien du roi Calid, et du philosophe Morieu sur le magistère d'Hermès, rapporté par Galip, esclave de ce roi, p. 56.
Le livre d'Artephinus, qui traite de l'art sécret, ou de la pierre philosophale, p. 112.
Le livre de Synesius, sur l'œuvre des philosophes, p. 175.
Le livre de Nicolas Flamel, contenant l'explication des figures hyérogliphiques qu'il a fait mettre au cimetière des ss. innocens à Paris, p. 195.
Petit traité d'alchymie, intitulé le sommaire philosophique de N. Flamel, p. 263.
Le désir désiré de Nicolas Flamel, p. 285.
Le livre de la philosophie naturelle des métaux du messire Bernard, comte de la marche trévisanne, p. 325.
La parole délaissée, traité philosophique de Bernard, comte de la marche trévisanne, p. 400.
Le songe verd, véridique & véritable, parce qu'il contient vérité, p. 437.
Opuscule de la philosophie naturelle des métaux, composé par D. Zachaire, p. 447.

v. 3. Les douze clefs de philosophie de frère Basile Valentin, p. 1.
L'azoth, ou le moyen de faire l'or caché des philosophes, de frère Basile Valentin, p. 84.
L'ancienne guerre des chevaliers, ou le triomphe hermétique, p. 181.
La lumière sortant par soi-même des ténèbres, poëme sur la composition de la pierre des philosophes, traduit de l'italien, avec un commentaire, p. 322.

Salmond (*Rev.* D. S. F. *editor*). *See* **Archelaus** *carcharensis*, **Dionysius** *alexandrinus*, **Gregorius** *thaumaturgus*.

Salome, the daughter of Herodias. A dramatic poem. [*anon.*] 251 pp. 12°. *New York, Putnam*, 1862.

Salomone *fiorentino*. Poesie. Nuova ed. con aggiunte. 2 v. 4 p. l. 174 pp; 175 pp. 16°. *Livorno, dai torchj di assunto Barbani e co.* 1815.

Saltonstall (*Capt.* Charles). The navigator, shewing and explaining all the chiefe principles and parts both theoricke and practicke, that are contayned in the famous art of navigation. With a new and admirable way of sayling by the arch of one of the greatest circles. [1st ed.] 6 p. l. 124 pp. 12°. *London, G. Herlock*, 1636.

Salvandy (Narcisse Achille de). Seize mois, ou la révolution et les révolutionnaires. Paris, juillet 1830; Lyon, nov. 1831. 2 v. 2 p. l. 226 pp; 2 p. l. 261 pp. 16°. *Bruxelles, J. P. Meline*, 1832.

Salzburg. (*Bibliothek des städtischen museums*). Katalog über die in der bibliothek des städtischen museums Carolino-Augusteum vorhandenen Salisburgensia. 1 p. l. 117 pp. 8°. *Salzburg, Zaunrith'sche buchdruckerei*, 1870. S.

Salzmann (Christian Gotthelf). Gymnastics for youth: or a practical guide to healthful and amusing exercises for the use of schools. An essay toward the necessary improvement of education, chiefly as it relates to the body. Freely translated from the german. xvi, 432 pp. 10 pl. 8°. *Philadelphia, W. Duane*, 1802.

Sampson (Ezra). The brief remarker on the ways of man: or compendious dissertations, respecting social and domestic relations and concerns, and the various economy of human life. 264 pp. 12°. *Hudson, [N. Y.] A. Stoddard, for himself and the author*, 1820.

——— The same. 264 pp. 12°. *Canandaigua (N. Y.) J. D. Bemis & co.* 1821.

——— The youth's companion, or a historical dictionary; consisting of articles selected from natural and civil history, geography, astronomy, zoology, botany and mineralogy. Arranged in alphabetical order. Carefully revised and abridged, by John B. Longgley. 300 pp. 12°. *St. Clairsville (O.) compiler*, 1832.

Sampson (Francis S. *d. d.*) Commentary on Hebrews. 1856. *See* **Bible**. (*Greek*).

Sampson, Davenport & co. Directories.

See BOSTON (*Mass.*) Directory, 1871.
CHARLESTOWN (*Mass.*) 1872.
LOWELL (*Mass.*) 1872.
LYNN (*Mass.*) 1871.
MANCHESTER (*N. H.*) 1871.
PROVIDENCE (*R. I.*) 1871.
TROY (*N. Y.*) 1871.

Sanborn (Albert J.) Green mountain poets. 512 pp. 12°. *Claremont (N. H.) Claremont manufacturing co.* 1872.

Sancho, or the proverbialist. *See* **Cunningham** (*Rev.* J. W.)

Sand (George, *pseudon.*) *See* **Dudevant** (Amantine Lucile Aurore Dupin).

Sand (Maurice, *pseudon.*) *See* **Dudevant** (Maurice)?

Sandeau (Jules). Madame de Sommerville. 2e éd. 3 v. in 1. 16°. *Paris, C. Allardin*, 1835.

Sanders (Charles W.) Sanders' primary spelling book; a simple and progressive course of instruction in spelling and definition, with easy reading lessons, for primary schools. 96 pp. 18°. *New York, Ivison & Phinney*, [1858].

——— Sanders' school speaker; a comprehensive course of instruction in the principles of oratory; with numerous exercises for practice in declamation. 528 pp. 1 pl. 12°. *New York, Ivison & Phinney*, 1857.

——— Young ladies' reader: embracing the principles of rhetorical reading. 500 pp. 12°. *New York, Ivison & Phinney*, 1855. s.

Sanders (Nicolas, *d. d.*) Nicolai Sanderi, de origine ac progressv schismatis anglicani, libri tres: qvibvs historia continetvr maxime ecclesiastica, annorum circiter sexaginta: aucti per Edovardvm Rishtonvm, Romæq; impressi; nunc vero in Germania iterum locupletius & castigatius editi. 8 p. l. 374 pp. 13 l. 16°. *Ingolstadii, ex officina typographica W. Ederi*, 1588.

Sanders (William). The christian's guide and guardian: a clear, full and luminous exhibition of the essential doctrines and precepts of the christian religion. 472 pp. 18°. *Carlisle, G. Fleming*, 1833.

Sanders. *See* **Saunders**.

Sanderson (John). Sketches of Paris: in familiar letters to his friends. By an american gentleman. [*anon.*] 321 pp. 12°. *Philadelphia, E. L. Carey & A. Hart*, 1838.

——— The same. The American in Paris. 2 v. 233 pp; 254 pp. 12°. *Philadelphia, Carey & Hart*, 1839.

Sandford (*Rev.* Peter P.) Help to faith: a summary of the evidences of the genuineness, authenticity, credibility, and divine authority of the holy scriptures. 270 pp. 12°. *New-York, J. & J. Harper*, 1828.

Sandford. *See* **Sanford.**

Sandisson (*M.* de, *pseudon.*) *See* **Bignon** (*Abbé* Jean Paul).

Sandoval (Prudencio de). Historia de la vida y hechos del emperador Carlos v. max. fortissimo. rey catholico de España y de las Indias, islas, y tierra firme del mar oceano, 1500–1557. 2 v. 14 p. l. (incl. 1 portrait), 895 pp. 15 l; 2 p. l. (incl. 1 pl.) 898 pp. 7 l. fol. *Pamplona, B. Paris*, 1614–18.

——— The same. The history of Charles the vth, emperor and king of Spain, the great hero of the house of Austria. Made english by capt. John Stevens. xii, 464 pp. 8°. *London, R. Smith*, 1703.

Sands (David). Journal of the life and gospel labors of David Sands: with extracts from his correspondence. [Edited by Edward and John Pease]. 286 pp. 12°. *New York, Collins & bro.* 1848.

Sandys (Edwin, *archbishop of York*). Sermons of Edwin, archbishop of Yorke. Some whereof were preached in the parts beyond the seas. VVith a preface to the christian readers of their vse and benefit; by a most reuerend father now liuing. 4 p. l. 194 l. numb. sm. 4°. *London, I. Beale for T. Chard*, 1616.

Sandys (George). A paraphrase vpon the psalmes of David, and vpon the hymnes dispersed throughout the old and new testaments. By G. S. [1st ed.] 7 p. l. 271 pp. 18°. *London, at the bell in st. Paul's church-yard*, 1636.

Sanford (*Mrs.* D. P.) Cousin Ellen's stories. 4 v. 32°. *New York, Gen. prot. episcopal s. s. union & ch. book society*, 1872.

CONTENTS.

no. 1. Willy's cherry tree, 91 pp. 1 pl.
2. Willy's winter corner, 84 pp. 1 pl.
3. Willy's new teacher, 94 pp. 1 pl.
4. Julie and Gilbert, 104 pp. 1 pl.

——— Grandma Berry's secret. 86 pp. 32°. *New York, Gen. prot. episcopal s. s. union & ch. book society*, 1872.

——— The rose-buds. 63 pp. 32°. *New York, Gen. prot. episcopal s. s. union and church book society*, 1861.

——— The Rose Dale books. v. 1–3. 16°. *New York, E. P. Dutton & co.* 1872.

CONTENTS.

v. 1. Rose, Tom, and Ned, 246 pp. 4 pl.
v. 2. Ida and baby Bell, 262 pp. 4 pl.
v. 3. Five happy children, 252 pp. 4 pl.

——— Under the skylight, and other stories for christmas. 111 pp. 2 pl. 18°. *New York, Gen. prot. episcopal s. s. union & ch. book society*, 1872.

San Francisco (The) directory for the year commencing April, 1871. v. 12. 8°. *San Francisco, H. G. Langley*, 1871.

San Francisco. (*Mechanics' institute*). The visitors' guide, and a catalogue of the eighth

San Francisco—continued. industrial exhibition, of the mechanics' institute of San Francisco, held August, 1871. Compiled and arranged by Jacob Price. 246 pp. 1 table. 8°. *San Francisco, A. Roman & co.* [1871].

Sangenesius [Saint Genais]? (Johannes *or* Jean). Ioannis Sangenesii, de Parnasso, & finitimis locis, libri duo. 18°. 1655.

[*In* ELEGANTIORES præstantium virorum satyræ, v. 2, pp. 907–940].

Sannazzaro (Jacopo). Eclogues, written originally in latin, by Actius Syncerus Sannazarius. And now translated into english. [By John Rooke]. 1 p. l. 63 pp. 8°. *London*, 1725.

[ROOKE (John). Select translations. Part 1. 1726].

San Pedro (Diego de). A historie called Arnalt and Lucenda. Set forth by Clau. Hollyband. [English and italian texts]. 18°. *London, T. Purfoot*, 1608.

[*In* HOLLYBAND (Claudius). The italian schoolemaistre, pp. 124–367].

Sansovino (Francesco). De gli hvomini illvstri della casa Orsina, libri qvattro. 92 l. 18 pl. (12 portraits). sm. fol. *Venetia, B. & F. Stagnini*, 1565.

Santa Maria (Domingo). Memoria historica sobre los sucesos ocurridos desde la caida de d. Bernardo O'Higgins en 1823 hasta la promulgacion de la constitucion dictada en el mismo año. xxiii, 250 pp. 8°. *Santiago, imprenta del pais*, 1858. s.

Santarem (Manuel Francisco de Barros e Sousa, *visconde* de). Essai sur l'histoire de la cosmographie et de la cartographie pendant le moyen-âge, et sur les progrès de la géographie après les grandes découvertes du xve siècle. 3 v. 8°. *Paris, Maulde & Renou*, 1849–52. s.

Santorini (Giovanni Domenico). Medicina statica; or, rules of health, in eight sections of aphorisms. English'd by J. D. 6 p. l. 180 pp. 1 pl. 18°. *London, J. Starkey*, 1676.

Sappho. Σαπφους αισματα. 16°. *Lipsiæ, S. G. Mvller*, 1764.

[*With* ANACREON. Carmina græce. *Lipsiæ*, 1764. pp. 106–114].

——— Sapphus Lesbiæ carmina et fragmenta recensvit commentario illustravit schemata mvsica adiecit et indices confecit Henr. Frid. Magnvs Volger. lxviii, 194 pp. 1 l. 12°. *Lipsiæ, in libraria weidmannia*, 1810.

Sappington (John, *m. d.*) The theory and treatment of fevers. Revised and corrected by Ferdinando Stith, m. d. 216 pp. 16°. *Arrow Rock*, [*Mo.*] *author*, 1844.

Saracenus (Joannes Franciscus). *See* **Sarrasin** (Jean François).

Sarah's home. By the author of "Self-willed Susie." [*anon.*] 203 pp. 18°. *New York, Carlton & Porter*, [1862].

Sarasin. *See* **Sarrasin.**

Sarbiewski (Matthias Casimir). Matthiae Casimiri Sarbievii carmina. Eng. title, xvi, 377 pp. 9 l. 8°. *Argentorati, ex typographia societatis bipontinae*, 1803.

Sardou (Victorien). A nervous set. *See* **Barrière** (Théodore) *and* **Sardou.**

Sargant (William Lucas). Robert Owen, and his social philosophy. xxiv, 446 pp. 8°. *London, Smith, Elder & co.* 1860.

Sargent (Winthrop). The life of major John André, adjutant-general of the british army in America. 1 p. l. xiv, 478 pp. 2 pl. 1 map. 12°. *New York, D. Appleton & co.* 1871.

Sarrasin (Jean François). Attici secundi G. Orbilius Musca, sive Bellum parasiticum. Satira. [*pseudon.*] 18°. *Norimbergae*, 1665.

[*In* EPULUM parasiticum. 1665. pp. 127–180].

Satan in society. By a physician. [*anon.*] 412 pp. 12°. *Cincinnati, C. F. Vent*, 1871.

Saturday (The) evening post. [Weekly]. Aug. 1, 1869, to July 29, 1871. [v. 49–50]. fol. *Philadelphia, H. Peterson & co.* 1869–71.

Saturday evening visitor. [Washington]. July 3, 1869, to June 4, 1870. v. i. fol. *Washington, W. F. Holtzman & co. and G. H. Heron*, 1869–70.

Saturday night. [A literary weekly newspaper]. Sept. 24, 1870, to Sept. 16, 1871. v. 8. fol. *Philadelphia, Davis & Elverson*, 1870–71.

Saturday (The) review of politics, literature, science, and art. [Weekly]. Jan. 7 to Dec. 30, 1871. v. 31–32. fol. *London*, [*D. Jones*], 1871.

Saulcy (Louis Félicien Joseph Caignart de). Voyage en Terre Sainte. 2 v. 2 p. l. 410 pp. 1 l. 8 pl; 2 p. l. 355 pp. 7 pl. 8°. *Paris, Didier & cie.* 1865. s.

Saulnier du Verdier (Gilbert). *See* **Du Verdier.**

Saunders (Charlotte). Holidays at home. 268 pp. 12°. *New-York, J. Swaine for T. H. Burnton*, 1804.

Saunders (Francis, *editor*). The temple of death, a poem [a translation out of the french of P. Habert]; written by the marquess of Normanby. Horace of the art of poetry, made english by the earl of Roscom-

Saunders (Francis)—continued. mon. The duel of the stags, by the hon. sir Robert Howard. With several other poems by the earls of Rochester and Orrery, sir Charles Sedley, [etc.] Also, several poems of the hon. madam Wharton. 2[d] ed. 8 p. l. 273 pp. 16°. *London, T. Warren for F. Saunders*, 1695.

Saunders (James M.) A collection of miscellaneous pieces in prose and verse. 144 pp. 16°. *Philadelphia, J. Crissy*, 1834.

Saunders. *See* **Sanders.**

Saurel (Louis J.) Traité de chirurgie navale. Suivi d'un résumé de leçons sur le service chirurgical de la flotte, par le docteur J. Rochard. xxiv, 592, 104 pp. 8°. *Paris, J. B. Baillière et fils*, 1861.

Saussure (Henri de). Mélanges orthoptérologiques. 4 p. l. 460 pp. 2 l. 1 pl. 4°. *Genève et Bâle, H. Georg*, 1863–71. s.

CONTENTS.

1er fasc. Blattides.
2me fasc. Blattides et phasmides.
3me fasc. Mantides.
Supplément au 3me fascicule. Mantides.

Sauzade (John S.) Garret van Horn; or the beggar on horseback. 376 pp. 12°. *New York, Carleton*, 1863.

Savage (*Rev.* Eleazer). Manual of church discipline. x, 13–119 pp. 18°. *Rochester, Sage & brother*, 1844.

——— The same. Church discipline in two parts, formative and corrective; in which is developed the true philosophy of religious education. 249 pp. 18°. *New York, Sheldon & co.* 1863.

Savage (John, *gent.*) Rome's conviction; or, a vindication of the original institution of christianity; in opposition to the many usurpations of the church of Rome; and their frequent violation of divine right. 12 p. l. 440 pp. 3 l. 1 pl. 16°. *London, T. N. for G. Kunholt*, 1683.

Savage (John, *artist and author, b.* 1828). '98 and '48, the modern revolutionary history and literature of Ireland. 384 pp. 12°. *New York, Redfield*, 1856.

——— Faith and fancy. 118 pp. 12°. *New York, J. B. Kirker*, 1864.

Savage (The) beauty, a novel. By a wild American. [*anon.*] 136 pp. 12°. *Philadelphia, S. Roberts*, 1822.

Savannah (*Ga.*) Haddock's Savannah, Ga. directory, and general advertiser. Compiled by T. M. Haddock. 8°. *Savannah, J. H. Estill*, 1871.

Savary (Anne Jean Marie René, *duc* de Rovigo). Mémoire du duc de Rovigo, sur la mort de Pichegru, du capitaine Wright, de m. Bathurst, et sur quelques autres circonstances de sa vie. 3 p. l. xxvi, 72 pp. 8°. *Paris, Ponthieu*, 1825.

Savérien (Alexandre). Histoire des philosophes anciens, jusqu'à la renaissance des lettres, avec leurs portraits. 5 v. 16°. *Paris, Didot l'aîné*, 1771–72.

CONTENTS.

v. 1–4. Métaphysiciens, moralistes et législateurs.
v. 5. Mathématiciens, physiciens, chymistes et naturalistes.

Savi (Paolo) *and* **Fedeli** (Fedele). Storia naturale e medica delle acque minerali dell' alta val di Nievole e specialmente di quelle delle rr. terme di Montecatini. xv, 333 pp. 1 l. 1 map. 8°. *Pisa, tipografia Nistri*, 1870. s.

Savile (George, 1*st marquis of Halifax*). A character of king Charles the second: and political, moral, and miscellaneous thoughts and reflections. iv, 183 pp. 8°. *London, J. & R. Tonson*, 1750.

——— The lady's new year's gift; or, advice to a daughter. sm. 4°. [*London, J. Hamilton & co.* 1794].

[*In* HAMILTON (John). Angelica's ladies library, pp. 329–393].

Savonarola (Girolamo Maria Francesco Mateo). The triumph of the cross. Translated from the latin, with notes and a biographical sketch, by O'Dell Travers Hill. xlviii, 258 pp. 16°. *London, Hodder & Stoughton*, 1868.

Sawers (*Rev.* William). Essays, on subjects moral and divine, in prose and verse. [Also], a variety of comments on some of the striking passages of scripture, in the style of Ossian. 294, viii pp. 8°. *Berwick, [Eng.] author*, 1796.

Sawkins (James G.) Geological report on the island of Jamaica. 8°. [*London, Longmans, Green & co.* 1869].

[GREAT BRITAIN. *Geological survey.* Memoirs, pp. 1–262].

——— Geological survey of British Guiana. *See* **British Guiana.**

Sawyer (Frederick William). Hits at american whims and hints for home use. 275 pp. 12°. *Boston, Walker, Wise & co.* 1830.

Sawyer (Leicester Ambrose). Critical exposition of baptism; embracing the mosaic baptisms; jewish traditionary baptisms; John's baptism, and christian baptism; chiefly establishing the scriptural authority of effusion and sprinkling, and of infant bap-

Sawyer (Leicester Ambrose)—continued. tism. 188 pp. 16°. *Cincinnati, H. W. Derby & co.* [1844].

——— The elements of biblical interpretation: an exposition of the laws by which the scriptures are capable of being correctly interpreted: with an analysis of the rationalistic and mystic modes of interpreting them. 182 pp. 12°. *New Haven, A. H. Maltby*, 1836.

——— Elements of mental philosophy; a critical exposition of the principal phenomena and powers of the human mind. 432 pp. 12°. *New York, Paine & Burgess*, 1846.

——— Reconstruction of biblical theories; or, biblical science, improved in its history, chronology, and interpretation, and relieved from traditionary errors and unwarrantable hypotheses. 195 pp. 12°. *Boston, Walker, Wise & co.* 1862.

——— New testament. 1858. Gospel according to Mark. *See* **Bible.** (*English*).

Sawyer (Thomas Jefferson). Review of E. F. Hatfield's "Universalism as it is." 220 pp. 18°. *New York, P. Price*, 1841.

Saxe (John Godfrey). The money-king and other poems. 180 pp. 1 l. 1 portrait. 12°. *Boston, Ticknor & Fields*, 1860.

Saxo *grammaticus*. Historiæ danicæ libri xvi. Stephanvs Iohannis Stephanivs summo studio recognovit, notisq. uberioribus illustravit. Eng. title, 3 p. l. 384 pp. 11 l. fol. *Sorae, Joachim Moltken*, 1644.

Saxton (Charles). A new system of stenography. 126 pp. 6 pl. 18°. *Boston, Saxton & Peirce*, 1842.

Say (Jean Baptiste). Œuvres diverses de J. B. Say. Précédées d'une notice historique sur la vie et les travaux de l'auteur, avec des notes par Ch. Comte, E. Daire, et Horace Say. 2 p. l. xix, 748 pp. 1 portrait. 8°. *Paris, Guillaumin et cie.* 1848.

CONTENTS.

1e partie. Mélanges d'économie politique.
Catéchisme d'économie politique, [etc.]
2e partie. Correspondance.
3e partie. Mélanges de morale et de littérature.
Olbie, ou essai sur les moyens d'améliorer les mœurs d'une nation, [etc.]
Petit volume contenant quelques aperçus des hommes et de la société, [etc.]

Sayers (Frank, *m. d.*) Poems, containing sketches of northern mythology, &c. 3d ed. 9 p. l. 246 pp. 8°. *Norwich, for Cadell & Davies, London*, 1803.

Scacchi (Francisco Fortunato). Sacrorum elaeochrismaton myrothecia tria, in quibus exponuntur olea, atque unguenta divinos in codices relata: et olim vel cunctis universim gentibus, in vitæ quà quotidiano, quà molliore cultu; vel nominatim apud Israëlitas, tam in sacrorum antistitibus, locis, supellectilibus, quam in regibus solemniter inaugurandis usurpata. 12 p. l. 1155 columns on 289 l. 39 l. 1 portrait. 1 pl. fol. *Amstelaedami, apud F. Halmam*, 1702.

Scaligero (Giulio Cesare). De lavdibvs an seris declamatio. 18°. [*Lugd. Batavorum*], 1644.

[*In* DISSERTATIONVM lvdicrarvm et amœnitatvm scriptores varij, pp. 255–258].

Scaligero (Giuseppe Giusto). Proverbiorum arabicorum centuriae duae. *See* **Erpen** (Thomas van).

Scamozzi (Ottavio Bertotti). *See* **Bertotti Scamozzi.**

Scanland (Agnes Leonard). Heights and depths. 271 pp. 12°. *Chicago, H. A. Sumner*, 1871.

Scanzoni de Lichtenfels (Friedrich Wilhelm von). A practical treatise on the diseases of the sexual organs of women. Translated from the french of drs. H. Dor and A. Socin, and annotated, by Augustus K. Gardner, m. d. 669 pp. 8°. *New York, R. M. De Witt*, [1861].

Scarlatini (Ottavio). L'hvmo, e sve parti figvrato, e simbolico, anatomico, rationale, morale, mistico, politico, e legale, raccolto, e spiegato con figure, simboli, [etc.] Con additioni, e tauole copiosissime. 2 v. in 1. Eng. title, 7 p. l. 464 pp; 328 pp. fol. *Bologna, G. Monti*, 1684.

Scenes in the indian country. By the author of "Scenes in Chusan," [etc. *anon.*] 283 pp. 1 pl. 18°. *Philadelphia, Presbyterian board of publication*, [1859].

Scenes in nature; or conversations for children, on land and water. [*anon.*] 312 pp. 12 pl. 18°. *Boston, Marsh, Capen, Lyon & Webb*, 1840.

Schaab (Carl Antonius). Die geschichte der erfindung der buchdruckerkunst durch Johann Gensfleisch genannt Gutenberg zu Mainz, pragmatisch aus den quellen bearbeitet, mit mehr als dritthalb hundert noch ungedruckten urkunden, welche die genealogie Gutenberg's, Fust's und Schöffer's in ein neues licht stellen. 3 v. 8°. *Mainz, auf kosten des verfassers*, 1830–31.

Schacht (Hermann Oosterdijk). Oratio de prudentia in ratiocinio physico et medico

Schacht (H. O.)—continued. necessario observanda, dicta publice; quum altera vice rectoris munere, in academia batava, quæ Leydæ est, abiret; ad diem 6 idus februarii anni 1735. 38 pp. 4°. *Lugduni Batavorum, apud S. Luchtmans*, 1735.
[*With* NEANDER (Johann). Tabacologia. 1626].

Schaede die den staet der Vereenichde Nederlanden, en d'jnghesetenen van dien, is aenstaende, by de versuymenisse van d'Oost en West-Indische negotie onder een octroy en societeyt te begrijpen. [*anon.*] 1 p. l. 52 pp. sm. 4°. *Graven-haghe, I. Veeli*, 1644.

Schaff (Philip, *d. d.*) A catechism for sunday schools and families. 167 pp. 16°. *Philadelphia, Lindsay & Blakiston*, 1862.

Schäffer (Gottlieb August Herrich-). *See* **Herrich-Schäffer.**

Schapenham (Gheen Huygen). Journael vande nassausche vloot. *See* **L'Hermite** (Jacques) *and* **Schapenham.**

Scheffel (Joseph Victor). Gaudeamus! humorous poems translated from the german of Scheffel and others. By Charles G. Leland. 154 pp. 24°. *Boston, J. R. Osgood & co.* 1872.

Schele de Vere (Maximilian, *ll. d.*) Americanisms; the english of the new world. 685 pp. 8°. *New York, C. Scribner & co.* 1872.

——— First french reader: for beginners. 143 pp. 12°. *New York, Richardson & co.* 1867.

Scheller (Immanuel Johann Gerhard). Praecepta stili bene latini in primis ciceroniani sev eloqventiae romanae qvatenvs haec nostris temporibvs in dicendo et scribendo vsvrpari potest. Ed. altera. 2 v. xl, 496 pp; 4 p. l. 505–834 pp. 32 l. 8°. *Lipsiae, svmtibvs C. Fritsch*, 1784.

Scheltema (Jacobus). Staatkundig Nederland; een woordenboek tot de biographische kaart van dien naam. 2 v. in 3. 8°. *Amsterdam, J. Ten Brink*, 1805–06. s.

Schem (Alexander J.) *See* **Deutsch-amerikanisches** conversations-lexicon.

Schemering (Daniel). Nova Zemla, sive descriptio contracta navigationvm trium admirandarum, a Belgis, per mare hyperboreum in Chinam et Indiam Orientalem iter affectantibus, annis supra sesquimillesimum nonagesimo quarto, quinto, sexto irrito conatu tentatarum. 22 l. sm. 4°. *Flissingae, S. Versterre*, 1631.
[*Note.*—This hexameter poem commemorates the voyages of Barentz, Linschoten, Heemskirk, etc.]

Scheuchzer (Johann Jacob). Physique sacrée ou histoire-naturelle de la bible. Traduite du latin. Enrichie de figures en taille-douce, gravées par les soins de Jean André Pfeffel. 8 v. fol. *Amsterdam, P. Schenk & P. Mortier*, 1732–37.

Schiller (Edward). Hand-book of progressive philosophy. viii, 216 pp. 12°. *New York, J. S. Redfield*, 1871.

Schiller (Johann Christoph Friedrich von). The Armenian; or, the ghost seer. A history founded on fact. Translated from the german. By the rev. W. Render. 4 v. in 2. 12°. *London, C. Whittingham for H. D. Symonds*, 1800.

——— The robbers. A tragedy. Translated from the german. 120 pp. 8°. *New York, S. Campbell*, 1793.

——— Wallenstein's camp. Translated from the german by George Moir. With a memoir of Albert Wallenstein by G. Wallis Haven. 142 pp. 12°. *Boston, J. Munroe & co.* 1837.

——— William Tell; a drama, in five acts. From the german. 120 pp. 12°. *Providence, B. Cranston & co.* 1838.

Schipper (B. J.) A concise and comprehensive practical grammar of the latin tongue, with a vocabulary for the exercises, quotations and mythology. iv, 273 pp. 12°. *Philadelphia, author*, 1832.

Schlegel (Charles A.) A classical french reader. With notes. Part first. 1 p. l. iv, 162 pp. 12°. *New York, E. Steiger*, 1871.

——— A french grammar. Part first. For beginners. viii, 302 pp. 12°. *New York, E. Steiger*, 1871.

Schlegel (Hermann) *and* **Verster van Wulverhörst** (A. H.) Traité de fauconnerie. Eng. title, 2 p. l. vi, 90 pp. 1 l. 16 pl. fol. *Leiden & Düsseldorf, Arnz & comp.* 1844–53.

Schlez (Johann Ferdinand). Gemeinfasslich, geordnete und gemeinnützige naturgeschichte für unkundige liebhaber derselben und für die erwachsenere jugend. 1 v. in 2. xvi, 800 pp. 1 l. 10 pl. 8°. *Heilbronn am Neckar, und Rothenburg ob der Tauber, J. D. Class*, 1804.

Schlotheim (Ernst Franz von). Merkwürdige versteinerungen aus der petrefactensammlung des freiherrn v. Schlotheim. 40 pp. 8°. Atlas, 66 pl. 4°. *Gotha, Becker*, 1832. s.

Schmid (Christoph von). The hop blossoms. From the german. By J. Fredk. Smith. 174 pp. 2 pl. 16°. *Philadelphia, Lutheran board of publication*, 1872.
[FATHERLAND (The) series].

Schmidt (*Dr.* Ernst Reinhold). Der amerikanische bürgerkrieg. Geschichte des volks der Vereinigten Staaten vor, während und nach der rebellion. 2 v. lxxxv, 322 pp. 2 portraits, 2 maps, 2 charts; 327 pp. 2 portraits, 2 maps, 1 chart. 8°. *Philadelphia & Leipzig, Schäfer & Koradi*, 1867-69.

Schmidt (Klamer Eberhard Carl). Klopstock and his friends. A series of familiar letters, written between the years 1750 and 1803. Translated from the german, with a biographical introduction, by miss Benger. 1 p. l. 309 pp. 8°. *London, H. Colburn*, 1814.

Schmieder (Carl Christoph). Geschichte der alchemie. x, 613 pp. 8°. *Halle, verlag der buchhandlung des waisenhauses*, 1832.

Schmucker (Samuel Mosheim, *ll. d.*) The life and times of Thomas Jefferson. 400 pp. 1 portrait. 12°. *Philadelphia, J. W. Bradley*, 1857.

Schmucker (Samuel Simon, *d. d.*) Discourse in commemoration of the reformation of the sixteenth century, with reference to the relation between the principles of popery and our republican institutions. 8°. *Philadelphia*, 1872.

[*In* BIBLE. (*English*). A commentary on Galatians, by Martin Luther, pp. 83-123].

——— Elements of popular theology, with special reference to the doctrines of the reformation, as avowed before the diet at Augsburg, in 1530. 412 pp. 8°. *Andover, Gould & Newman*, 1834.

——— Psychology, or, elements of a new system of mental philosophy, on the basis of consciousness and common sense. 2d ed. much enlarged. 329 pp. 12°. *New-York, Harper & brothers*, 1844.

Schnurrer (Christian Friedrich). Bibliothecæ arabicæ specimen. [Parts 1-3]. 52, 40, 52 pp. sm. 4°. *Tübingæ, litteris hopfferianis*, [1799-1802].

Schoch (Gustav). Die mikroskopischen thiere des süsswasser-aquariums. I. buch. Die urthiere. vi, 60 pp. 8 pl. 8°. *Leipzig, A. Felix*, 1868.

Scholar's (The) reference book; a dictionary of english synonymes, tables of greek and latin proper names, and men of learning and genius. [*anon.*] 224 pp. 12°. *Philadelphia, H. Perkins*, 1836.

Scholefield (*Mrs.* James). Memoir of the late rev. James Scholefield, by his widow. With notices of his literary character, by the rev. William Selwyn. xi, 391 pp. 1 portrait. 8°. *London, Seeley, Jackson & Halliday*, 1855.

Schoock (Martin). Tractatus de anima belluarum varijs disputationibus propositus in academia Groningæ & Ommelandiæ: quo non modo belluis anima sensitiva, velut forma propria vindicatur, verum accurate quoque inquiritur tum in allarum vocem, tum intellectum, & voluntatem analogicam: addita brevi diatriba de origine & interitu animæ belluinæ. 2 p. l. 248 pp. sm. 4°. *Groningæ, apud H. Lussinck*, 1658.

School (The) boys' friend: a manual of scientific and useful recreations, exercises and pursuits for the leisure hours of youth. By the author of the young man's own book. [*anon.*] 254 pp. 1 pl. 18°. *Philadelphia, Key & Biddle*, 1835.

School (The) days of Jennie Graham. [*anon.*] 180 pp. 3 pl. 18°. *Philadelphia, Presbyterian board of publication*, [1863].

School days reviewed; or, stories of schoolboys. [*anon.*] 171 pp. 4 pl. 18°. *Philadelphia, American sunday-school union*, [1854].

Schoolday visitor magazine. Edited by William M. Clark and J. W. Daughaday. [Monthly]. Jan. to Dec. 1871. v. 15. 8°. *Philadelphia, J. W. Daughaday & co.* [1871].

[*Previously known as* OUR schoolday visitor].

School lyrics: a collection of sacred hymns for devotional exercises. [*anon.*] 164 pp. 24°. *New York, Harper & brothers*, 1868.

Schoolmate (The). *See* **Student** and school mate.

Schott (Andreas). Παροιμιαι ἑλληνικαι. Adagia sive proverbia Græcorvm ex Zenobio seu Zenodoto, Diogeniano & Svidæ collectaneis. Partim edita nunc primùm, partim latinè reddita, scholiisqve parallelis illustrata, ab Andrea Schotto. [Ed. 1ª græce et latine]. 10 p. l. 702 pp. 1 l. 4°. *Antverpiae, ex officina plantiniana, apud viduam & filios Moreti*, 1612.

Schouten (Ioost). Beschrijvinghe van de regeeringe, macht, religie, costuymen, trafficquen, eñ andere remercquable saken, des coninghrijcx Siam, 1636. sm. 4°. [*Amsterdam, I. Hartgers*, 1648].

[HARTGERTS (J.) Oost-indische voyagien, v. 1, 13e stuck, pp. 64-78].

Schouten van Hoorn (Willem Cornelisz.) Iovrnal ofte beschryvinghe van de wonderlicke reyse, ghedaen door Willem Cornelisz

Schouten van Hoorn (W. C.)—continued. Schouten van Hoorn, inde jaren 1615–17. Hoe hy bezuyden de strate van Magellanes een nieuwe passagie tot inde groote Zuydzee ontdeckt, en voort den gheheelen aerdkloot omgheseylt heeft. 6 p. l. 92 pp. 3 maps, 6 pl. sm. 4°. *Amsterdam, W. Jansz,* 1618.
[*Note.*—Première édition de ce journal.—*Tiele*].

——— The same. Journael ofte beschrijvinge van de wonderlicke reyse ghedaen door Willem Cornelisz. Schouten van Hoorn, 1615–17. Hoe hy bezuyden de straet Magellanes eenen nieuwen doorganck gevonden heeft, streckende tot in de Zuyd-Zee. sm. 4°. *Amstelredam, I. Hartgers,* 1648.
[*In* HARTGERTS (J.) Oost-indische voyagien, v. 1, 8e stuck, pp. 67–120].

Schrader (Johann). Jo. Schraderi liber emendationvm. lxiv, 256 pp. 4°. *Leovardiæ, apud H. A. de Chalmot,* 1776.
[*Note.*—These consist of remarks on Catullus, Virgil, Horace, and Propertius.
[*With his* OBSERVATIONVM liber. 1761].

——— Iohannis Schraderi observationvm liber. 2 p. l. 89 pp. 4°. *Franeqverae, inpensis I. Brovweri,* 1761.

Schreber (Daniel Gottfried). Historische, physische und öconomische beschreibung des waidtes, dessen baues, bereitung und gebrauchs zum färben, auch handels mit selbigen überhaupt, besonders aber in Thüringen. Mit beylagen, und einem anhange dreyer alten schriften. 7 p. l. 157, 120 pp. 4 l. 4 pl. 4°. *Halle, buchhandlung des waysenhauses,* 1752.

Schröckh (Johann Matthias). Christliche kirchengeschichte. 35 v. 8°. *Leipzig, E. B. Schwickert,* 1772–1803.
[*Note.*—v. 1–5, 2e aufl.]

——— The same. Seit der reformation. 10 v. 8°. *Leipzig, E. B. Schwickert,* 1804–12.
[*Note.*—v. 9 & 10, fortgesetzt von H. G. Tzschirner].

Schroeder van der Kolk (Jacobus Lodewijck Coenraad). *See* **Kolk.**

Schubert (E.) Tables of Parthenope. Computed for the american ephemeris and nautical almanac. 52 pp. 4°. *Washington, Bureau of navigation,* 1871.

Schultens (Albert). De defectibus hodiernis linguæ hebrææ, eorundemque resarciendorum tutissima via ac ratione. Originibus hebraicis subserviens opus. 3 p. l. 269 pp. 4°. *Franequerae, ex officina Wibii Bleck,* 1731.
[*With* ABU-'L-KASIM (Mahmud Ben Omar Ez Zamakhshari). Anthologia sententiarum arabicarum. 1772].

Schultetus (Abraham). The determination of the qvestion concerning the divine right of episcopacie. Faithfully translated out of his Observations upon the epistles to Timothy and Titus. 4°. [*London, N. Butter,* 1641].
[*In* HALL (Joseph). A defence of the Humble remonstrance, etc. pp. 169–182, with separate title].

——— The judgment concerning lay-elders. 4°. [*London, N. Butter,* 1641].
[*In* HALL (Joseph). A defence of the Humble remonstrance, [*etc.*] pp. 193–200].

Schulz (Joachim Christoph Friedrich). Aphorismen aus der höhern welt- und menschenkunde und lebens philosophie. Französisch und deutsch herausgegeben. Eine nachlese zu de la Rochefoucault's bekanntem werke. 2 v. 225 pp; 195 pp. 16°. *Königsberg, F. Nicolovius,* 1793–95.

Schupp (—). Das hofgüterwesen im amtsbezirk Wolfach. Ein beitrag zur lösung der frage über die gebundenheit der bauerngüter. 3 p. l. 114 pp. 8°. *Heidelberg, A. Emmerling,* 1870. s.

Schütz (Christian Gottfried). Memorabilia vitae Ciceronis per annos digesta a Schuetzio atque emendata a Leonardo Usterio. 8°. [*Turici, typis Orellii,* 1836].
[*In* CICERO (M. T.) Opera, ed. Orellius, v. 6, pp. 110-130].

Schuyler (A.) A higher arithmetic: embracing the science of numbers and the art of their application. 427 pp. 12°. *New York, Sheldon & co.* 1860.

Schwarz (Christian Gottlieb). De ornamentis librorvm et varia rei librariae vetervm svpellectile dissertationvm antiqvariarvm hexas primvm collegit et recensvit atqve praefatione indicibvsque necessariis instrvxit Iohann. Christian. Levschnervs. 234 pp. 3 l. 5 pl. 4°. *Lipsiae, ex officina langenhemiana,* 1756.

Schwartz (Marie Sophie). Guilt and innocence. Translated from the swedish by Selma Borg and Marie A. Brown. 1 p. l. 294 pp. 8°. *Boston, Lee & Shepard,* 1871.

——— The right one. Translated from the swedish, by Selma Borg and Marie A. Brown. 313 pp. 8°. *Boston, Lee & Shepard,* 1871.

——— Two family mothers. Translated from the swedish, by Selma Borg, and Marie A. Brown. 217 pp. 8°. *Boston, Lee & Shepard,* 1872.

——— The wife of a vain man. Translated from the swedish, by Selma Borg and Marie A. Brown. 156 pp. 8°. *Boston, Lee & Shepard,* 1871.

Schwed (Joseph). Von Berlin nach Paris. (From Berlin to Paris). vii, 30 pp. 12°. *Titusville (Pa.) Daily courier establishment,* 1871.

Schwenckfeld (Caspar). Theriotrophevm Silesiæ, in qvo animalium, hoc est, qvadrupedum, reptilium, avium, piscium, insectorum natura, vis & usus sex libris perstringuntur. 12 p. l. 564 pp. 2 l. sm. 4°. *Lignicii, impensis D. Alberti,* 1603.

Science (La) des médailles. *See* **Jobert** (Louis).

Science revived, or the vision of Alfred. A poem. [*anon.*] 4 p. l. 248 pp. 2 pl. 4°. *London, Cox, son & Baylis, for J. A. Gameau & co.* 1802.

Scientific american. An illustrated journal of art, science and mechanics. [Weekly]. Sept. 26, 1846, to June 25, 1859. [1st series]. v. 2–14. fol. *New York, Munn & co.* 1846–59.

——— The same. July 2, 1859, to Dec. 23, 1871. New [2d] series, v. 1–25; [complete series, v. 15–39]. fol. *New York, Munn & co.* 1859–71.

Scolari (Filippo). Su la pietosa morte di Giulia Cappelletti e Romeo Montecchi lettere critiche. 58 pp. 1 l. 8°. *Livorno, G. Masi,* 1831.

[*With* PORTO (Luigi da). Giuletta e Romeo. 1831].

Sconce (Robert Clement). Letters. *See* **Bunbury** (*Mrs.* Sarah S.)

Scopoli (Giovanni Antonio). Annvs i–v. historico-natvralis. 5 v. in 2. 16°. *Lipsiæ, C. G. Hilscher,* 1769–72. S.

Scot (David, *m. d.*) Discourses on some important subjects of natural & revealed religion, introduced by a short view of the best specimens of pulpit eloquence which have been given to the world in ancient and modern times. xxx, 463 pp. 8°. *Edinburgh, A. Constable & co.* 1825.

Scotland (*Church of*). The psalms of David, in metre. Translated and diligently compared with the original text and former translations. Allowed by the authority of the general assembly of the kirk of Scotland. 281 pp. 18°. *Philadelphia, Lippincott, Grambo & co.* 1854.

——— The same. 281 pp. 18°. *Philadelphia, E. Barrington & G. D. Haswell,* [*about* 1850].

Scotland. (*Parliament of the kingdom*). Act for a company trading to Affrica and the Indies. June 26, 1695. 7 pp. sm. fol. *Edinbvrgh, A. Anderson,* 1696.

Scott (Charles Henry). The Baltic, the Black sea, and the Crimea: comprising travels in Russia, a voyage down the Volga to Astrachan, and a tour through Crim Tartary. xii, 346 pp. 12°. *London, R. Bentley,* 1854.

Scott (*Rev.* George). Tellström, the first swedish missionary to Lapland. With an account of the Stockholm mission. 86 pp. 18°. *New York, J. S. Taylor & co.* 1841.

Scott (James, *d. d.*) The life, letters and remains of the rev. Robert Pollok. 364 pp. 1 portrait. 12°. *New York, R. Carter,* 1848.

Scott (Job). The baptism of Christ, a gospel ordinance: being altogether inward and spiritual. vii, 185 pp, 8°. *Providence, J. Carter,* 1793.

Scott (John, *esq.* 1730–83). Critical essays on the poems of several english poets. With an account of the life and writings of the author. By mr. Hoole. 2 p. l. xci, 386 pp. 8°. *London, J. Phillips,* 1785.

Scott (John, *d. d.*) A new version of the first three chapters of Genesis; with dissertations illustrative of the creation, the fall of man, the principle of evil, and the plagues of Egypt. [Also], strictures on mr. Bellamy's translation. By Essenus. [*pseudon.*] vii, 160 pp. 8°. *London, R. Hunter,* 1819.

Scott (Michael). Physionomia. Et à caso molto notabile: e da tener secreta, però che la è di grande efficacia, & comprende cose secrete della natura, bastanti ad ogni astrologo. 55 l. 16°. *Vinegia, F. Bindoni & M. Pasini compagni,* 1546.

Scott (Robert). The history of England, during the reign of George the third; compiled from authentic documents, and the most accurate sources of information. 4 v. 8°. *London, J. Robins & co.* 1820–21.

Scott (Rosa). Marian Wallace; or, life's changes. 369 pp. 12°. *New York, Derby & Jackson,* 1858.

Scott (*Rev.* Thomas). Practical observations on the new testament. 1842. *See* **Bible** (*English*).

Scott (William, *teacher in Edinburgh*). Lessons in elocution; a selection of pieces in prose and verse, for the improvement of youth in reading and speaking. To which are prefixed elements of gesture. 372 pp. incl. 4 pl. 12°. *Plymouth, Mass. E. Collier,* 1825.

Scott (William Anderson, *d. d.*) The church in the army; or, the four centurions. 443 pp. 12°. *New York, Carleton,* 1862.

Scottish (The) monthly magazine. Vol. 1, June to December, 1836. 8°. *Glasgow, R. Stuart & co.* [1836].
[*Note.*—No more published].

Scribanius (Franciscus). *See* **Escriva** (Francisco).

Scribe (Augustin Eugène)? Black domino. The music by Auber. The libretto by m. Scribe. [Without music]. 53 pp. 8°. [*New York*], *W. C. Bryant & co.* 1871.
[PAREPA-ROSA grand english opera].

Scribner (J. M.) Scribner's engineers' and mechanics' companion; comprising United States' weights and measures; mensuration of superficies and solids; the mechanical powers. Steam and the steam engine. 2d ed. 240 pp. 12°. *New-York, Huntington & Savage*, 1845.

Scribner's monthly, an illustrated magazine for the people. Conducted by J. G. Holland. Nov. 1870, to April, 1872. v. 1–3. 8°. *New York, Scribner & co.* [1870–72].

Scriptores de re militari. *See* **Veteres** scriptores.

Scriptores erotici græci. 4 v. 1792–98. *See* **Mitscherlich** (Christoph Wilhelm.)

Scriptural (The) argument for episcopacy examined. *See* **Barnes** (*Rev.* Albert).

Scripture (The) guide: a familiar introduction to the study of the bible. [*anon.*] 263 pp. 1 pl. 16°. *Philadelphia, American sunday-school union*, [1838].

Scrofani (Xavier). Voyage en Grèce, fait en 1794 et 1795; traduit de l'italien, par J. F. C. Blanvillain. 3 v. in 1. 8°. *Paris & Strasbourg, Treuttel & Würtz*, 1801.

Scudder (Horace Elisha). Life and letters of David Coit Scudder, missionary in southern India. vi, 402 pp. 1 portrait. 12°. *New York, Hurd & Houghton*, 1864.

Scudder (John M. *m. d.*) Domestic medicine: or home book of health, a popular treatise on anatomy, physiology, hygiene, materia medica, surgery, practice of medicine, and nursing. 595 pp. 1 portrait. 8°. *Cincinnati, J. R. Hawley & co.* 1865.

——— The eclectic practice of medicine. 578 pp. 8°. *Cincinnati, Moore, Wilstach, Keys, & co.* 1864.

Scudery (Georges de). Ibrahim. Or the illvstriovs bassa. An excellent new romance. The whole work, in foure parts. Englished by Henry Cogan. 6 p. l. 116, 116, 233 pp. fol. *London, H. Moseley*, 1652.

Scultetus. *See* **Schultetus.**

Seager (Charles). The female jesuit abroad: a true and romantic narrative of real life; including some account, with historical reminiscences, of Bonn and the middle Rhine. xiv, 490 pp. 1 pl. 12°. *London, Partridge & Oakey*, 1853.

Search (Edward, *pseudon.*) *See* **Tucker** (Abraham).

Search (A) after souls. 1706. *See* **Layton** (Henry).

Searle. *See* **Serle.**

Sears (M.) The american politician: containing the declaration of independence, the constitution of the United States, the inaugural and first annual addresses and messages of all the presidents, and other important state papers. 552 pp. 1 pl. 12°. *Boston, E. Leland & W. J. Whiting*, 1842.

Sears (Robert). A new and complete history of the holy bible, from the creation of the world to the full establishment of christianity. With notes critical and explanatory, forming an illustrated commentary of the sacred text. 2d ed. 2 v. in 1. 672 pp. 8°. *New York, Sears & Walker*, 1844.

Seaside (The) oracle. [Monthly and semi-monthly]. Joseph Wood, editor. Jan. 1, 1869, to Dec. 15, 1871. v. 1–3. 4°. *Wiscasset* (*Me.*) *J. Wood*, 1869–71.

Seaton (*Miss* Oneida). It is all for the best; or Clarke the baker. A tale for youth. 2 p. l. 112 pp. 16°. *Boston, W. D. Ticknor & co.* 1845.

Secchi (Angelo, *s. j.*) Le soleil. Exposé des principales découvertes modernes sur la structure de cet astre, son influence dans l'univers et ses relations avec les autres corps célestes. xvi, 422 pp. 3 pl. 8°. *Paris, Gauthier-Villars*, 1870. S.

Seccomb (*Rev.* Joseph). Business and diversion inoffensive to God, and necessary for the comfort and support of human society. A discourse utter'd in part at Ammauskeeg-Falls, in the fishing-season. 1739. [Signed] Fluviatulis piscator. [*pseudon.*] 21 pp. sm. 4°. *Boston, S. Kneeland and T. Green*, 1743.

Second (The) book of 100 pictures. [*anon.*] 104 pp. 18°. *Philadelphia, American sunday-school union*, [1862].

Second (A) letter from one in the country, to his friend in Boston. [In reference to the proposed payment of a fixed salary to the governor of the colony. *anon.*] 4 pp. sm. fol. *Boston*, 172$\frac{8}{9}$].

Secondsight (Solomon, *pseudon.*) The wilderness; or the youthful days of Washington. A tale of the west. 3 v. 16°. *London A. K. Newman & co.* 1823.

Secundus *atheniensis.* Σεκουνδου του σοφιστου γνῶμαι. Secundi atheniensis sophistæ sententiæ. [Græce et latine]. 8°. [*Amstelaedami, apud H. Wetstenium,* 1688].
[*In* GALE (Thomas). Opuscula mythologica, pp. 633-642].

Sedgwick (Catharine Maria). Life and letters of Catharine M. Sedgwick. Edited by Mary E. Dewey. 446 pp. 3 pl. 12°. *New York, Harper & brothers,* 1871.

——— Rosanna; or scenes in Boston. A story. By the author of "Three experiments of living." [*anon.*] 134 pp. 16°. *Cambridge, J. Owen,* 1839.

——— Tales, by the author of "Three experiments in living," [etc. *anon.*] viii, 337 pp. 12°. *Boston, Hilliard, Gray & co.* 1842.

Sedgwick (*Mrs.* Charles). A talk with my pupils. 4 p. l. 235 pp. 12°. *New York, author,* 1863.

Sedgwick (*Rev.* Obadiah). The humbled sinner resolved what hee should do to bee saved. Or, faith in the lord Jesus Christ, the only way of salvation for sensible sinners. 5 p. l. 282 pp. 8 l. sm. 4°. *London, A. Byfield,* 1660.

Sédillot (Louis Pierre Eugène Amélie). Histoire des Arabes. 2 p. l. viii, 510 pp. 3 maps. 12°. *Paris, L. Hachette & cie.* 1854.

See (*Rev.* Isaac M.) The rest of faith. 268 pp. 18°. *New York, W. C. Palmer, jr.* 1871.

Seebohm (Frederic). On international reform. 3 p. l. 147 pp. 8°. *London, Longmans, Green & co.* 1871.

Seely (*Rev.* Amos W.) Doctrinal thoughts. 102 pp. 16°. *New York, F. M'Elroy,* 1861.

Seemuller (*Mrs.* Anne Moncure Crane). Reginald Archer. A novel. 386 pp. 12°. *Boston, J. R. Osgood & co.* 1871.

Segni (Fabio). Carmina. 16°. *Florentiæ, apvd Ivntas,* 1562.
[*In* CARMINA qvinqve Hetrvscorvm poetrvm, pp. 87-114].

Segrais (Jean Regnauld). Œuvres. Nouv. éd. 2 v. 2 p. l. xvi, 313 pp; 2 p. l. 315 pp. 18°. *Paris, Durand,* [*etc.*] 1755.

Seguin (Edward, *m. d.*) Medical thermometry. 1871. *See* **Wunderlich** (C. A.) *and* **Seguin.**

Seiler (Emma). The voice in singing. Translated from the german. New ed. 192 pp. 12°. *Philadelphia, J. B. Lippincott & co.* 1871.

Seiss (Joseph Augustus, *d. d.*) A book of forms for the use of christians in the sanctuary, the family, and the closet. 1 p. l. 214 pp. 12°. *Philadelphia, Lindsay & Blakiston,* 1860.

——— The gospel in Leviticus; or, an exposition of the hebrew ritual. 403 pp. 12°. *Philadelphia, Lindsay & Blakiston,* 1860.

——— The last times and the great consummation. 5th ed. 438 pp. 12°. *Philadelphia, Smith, English & co.* 1863.

——— The parable of the ten virgins; in six discourses. And a sermon on the judgeship of the saints. 189 pp. 12°. *Philadelphia, Smith, English & co.* 1862.

——— Popular lectures on Hebrews. 1846. *See* **Bible.** (*English*).

Selden (Almira). Effusions of the heart, contained in a number of original poetical pieces, on various subjects. 152 pp. 16°. *Bennington,* [*Vt.*] *D. Clark,* 1820.

Selden (John). Table-talk. With some account of the author. 16°. *Cambridge,* [*Ms.*] *Hilliard & Brown,* 1831.
[LIBRARY of the old english prose writers, v. 2, pp. 89-294].

Select biographies. [*anon.*] 234 pp. 1 portrait. 18°. *Philadelphia, American sunday-school union,* [1838].

Selecta ex [poetis graecis], cum vulgata versione emendata, ac variis partim scholiastarum graecorum, partim doctorum recetiorum notis. In usum regiæ scholæ etonensis. Editio altera. vii, 231, 174 pp. 8°. *Etonæ, J. Pote,* 1766.

Selections from the masquerade: a collection of enigmas, logogriphs, charades, rebuses, queries, and transpositions. [*anon.*] Eng. title. 1 p. l. 215 pp. 12°. *London, Baker & Fletcher,* 1826.

Selections from the psalms of David, arranged for responses or chanting. [*anon.*] 90 pp. 12°. *Boston, J. Munroe & co.* 1845.
[*With* MANUAL (A) of prayer. *Boston,* 1845].

Selkirk (George H.) The book of chess; a popular and comprehensive guide to all players of that intellectual game; with the latest discoveries and full instructions for blindfold chess. Numerous illustrations and diagrams. viii, 439 pp. 1 pl. 12°. *London, Houlston and Wright,* 1868.

Sella (Quintano). Relazione sulle condizioni dell' industria mineraria nell' isola di Sardegna. 1871. *See* **Italy.** (*Camera dei deputati*).

Selwyn in search of a daughter, and other tales. By the author of "Tales of the Moors," [etc. *anon.*] 3 v. 12°. *London, Saunders & Otley*, 1835.

[*Note.*—In the Bodleian catalogue, both these titles are referred to Caroline Anne Bowles, the second wife of Robert Southey].

Semanario de la Nueva Granada. Miscelanea de ciencias, literatura, artes é industria publicada por una sociedad de patriotas granadinos, bajo la direccion de Francisco José de Caldas. Nueva ed. corregida, aumentada con varios opúsculos inéditos de F. J. de Caldas. Anotada, y adornada con su retrato y con el cuadro original de la geographia de las plantas del baron de Humboldt. xii, 572 pp. 8°. *Paris, Lasserre*, 1849.

[Imperfect: wanting portrait and plate].

Senden (G. H. van). Het heilige land of mededeelingen uit eene reis naar het Oosten, gedaan in de jaren 1849 en 1850, in gezelschap van hare koninklijke hoogheid, de prinses Marianne der Nederlanden. 2 v. xxxvi, 387 pp; xxiv, 360 pp. 8°. *Te Gorinchem, J. Noorduyn & zoon*, 1851–52.

Seneca (Lucius Annæus). Clavdii Cæsaris apocolocyntosis, [sive de morte Claudii Cæsaris]. 18°. 1655.

[ELEGANTIORES præstantium virorum satyræ, v. 1, part 2, pp. 214–233].

——— Medea: a tragedy. Octavia, a tragedy. Translated by C. A. Wheelwright. 12°. *London*, 1811.

[WHEELWRIGHT (*Rev.* C. A.) Poems, original and translated. 1811. v. 1].

——— Seneca's morals, by way of an abstract. [Also], a discourse under the title of An after thought. By sir Roger L'Estrange. 3d american ed. 368 pp. 16°. *Boston, J. Bumstead*, 1800.

[Imperfect: wanting part of title, table of contents, and plates].

——— The same. Revised edition. By Lucius V. Bierce. xvi, 378 pp. 12°. *Cleveland, O. A. B. & co.* 1855.

——— Les œuvres de Sénèque, traduites en françois par La Grange; avec des notes de critique, d'histoire & de littérature. 6 v. 16°. *Paris, De Bure*, 1778.

CONTENTS.

v. 1–2. Les lettres.
v. 3. Des bienfaits.
v. 4. Consolation à Marcia.
De la colère.
De la clémence.
De la providence.

Seneca (Lucius Annæus)—continued.

v. 5. De la tranquillité de l'âme.
De la vie heureuse.
Du loisir, ou de la retraite du sage.
Consolation à Helvia.
De la brièveté de la vie.
De la constance du sage.
Consolation à Polybe.
L'apocoloquintose, ou l'apothéose de l'empereur Claude.
v. 6. Questions naturelles.

Senna Freitas *or* **Sena Freitas** (Bernardino José de). Uma viagem ao valle das Furnas na ilha de s. Miguel em junho de 1840. xxi, 105 pp. 3 pl. fol. *Lisboa, na imprensa nacional*, 1845.

Sennert (Daniel). Physica hypomnemata. De rerum naturalium principiis. De occultis qualitatibus. De atomis & mistione. De generatione viuentium. De spontaneo viuentium ortu. 16 p. l. 472 pp. 11 l. 12°. *Lvgdvni, sumptibus P. Ravavd*, 1637.

Senour (*Rev.* F.) Morgan and his captors. 389 pp. 1 portrait. 12°. *Cincinnati, C. F. Vent & co.* 1865.

Sentimental love illustrated in Charmides and Theone, and Ase-Neitha, two ancient tales. [Also], Elysium, a prelude. The whole translated from the german. [*anon.*] 1 p. l. 204 pp. 16°. *London, D. Brewman for J. Searle*, [*etc.*] 1789.

Sepp (Anton) *and* **Böhm** (Anton). A. Sepp und A. Böhm neu-vermehrte reiss-beschreibung, wie selbe auss Hispanien in Paraquariam kommen. Und kurtzer bericht der denckwürdigsten sachen, selbiger landschafft, völckern, und arbeitung der missionariorum. 3e ed. 336 pp. 24°. *Passau, G. A. Höller*, 1698.

Séquard (C. E. Brown-). *See* **Brown-Séquard.**

Serafino *dell' Aquila.* Di seraphino aqvilano, poeta elegantissimo, opere, nuouamente ricorrette, & con diligentia impresse. 7 p. l. 215 l. numb. 18°. *Venegia*, [*per Niccolò de Bascerini*] ? 1548.

Serenus (Quintus Sammonicus). De medicina praecepta salvberrima R. Constantini opera, post Caesarei et Malinii castigationem, diligenter emaculata. 16°. *Venetiis*, 1566.

[*In* CELSUS (A. Cornelius). De re medica, pp. 345–378].

Serle *or* **Searle** (Ambrose). The christian remembrancer, or short reflections upon the faith, life, and conduct, of a real christian. [*anon.*] 334 pp. 12°. *Newark (N. J.) J. A. Crane*, 1808.

Serle *or* **Searle** (Ambrose)—continued.
——— Horæ solitariæ. [*anon.*] 3d ed. 2 v. xii, 574 pp; 3 p. l. 518 pp. 8°. *London, Longman & Rees, etc.* 1804.

Sermons on miscellaneous subjects, by the bishops of the methodist episcopal church, and the senior preachers of the Ohio and north Ohio conferences. 456 pp. 12°. *Cincinnati, L. Swormstedt & J. H. Power*, 1849.

Sermons, preached at the church of St. Paul the apostle, during the year 1864. [*anon.* 4th series]. 404 pp. 12°. *New York, D. Appleton & co.* 1865.
——— The same. Sermons by the fathers of the Congregation of st. Paul the apostle, New York. v. 6. 331 pp. 12°. *New York, the Catholic publication house*, 1871.

Serny (John B. *m. d.*) Spinal curvature, its consequences, and its cure. xvi, 90 pp. 15 pl. 8°. *London, author*, [1840].

Serpilius (Georg). Lebens-beschreibungen der biblischen scribenten. [*anon.*] 13 v. in 5. 12°. *Regenspurg, J. Z. Seidel*, 1708–21.

CONTENTS.

v. 1. Personalia Mosis.
v. 2. Personalia Josuae.
v. 3. Personalia Samuelis.
v. 4. Personalia Esrae.
v. 5. Personalia Nehemiae.
v. 6. Personalia Mardochai und Esther.
v. 7. Personalia Jobi.
v. 8. Commentatores in psalmos Davidis.
v. 9. Personalia Davidis, [und, von David's psalmen].
v. 10. Fortsetzung der comentatorum in psalmos Davidis.
v. 11. Jeremia, oder umständige nachricht von dieses propheten lehre und leiden, leben und tod sammt einigen berühmten commentatoribus. Zur continuation der biblischen scribenten.
v. 12–13. Friderici Spanhemii historia Jobi, sive de obscuris historiæ commentatio. Ed. altera.

Serviez (Alfred Emmanuel Roergas de). Le démon du midi, chronique espagnole. 2 v. 2 p. l. 392 pp. 1 l; 2 p. l. 360 pp. 8°. *Paris, C. Lachapelle*, 1836.

Sestini (Benedict). Manual of geometrical and infinitesimal analysis. 131 pp. 2 pl. 8°. *Baltimore, J. Murphy & co.* 1871.

Severance (Moses). The american manual, or new english reader. [With] a succinct history of the colonies, to the close of the revolution. 298 pp. 16°. *Waterloo (N. Y.) M. Severance*, 1831.

Sévigné (Marie de Rabutin-Chantal, *marquise* de) *and* **Maintenon** (Françoise d'Aubigné, *marquise* de). Lettres choisies de mesdames de Sévigné et de Maintenon, avec une préface et des notes. Par m. [J. P. V. Lecoutz] de Lévizac. 5e éd. xxiii, 319 pp. 16°. *Londres, A. B. Dulau & co.* 1812.

Seward (Anna). Memoirs of the life of dr. [Erasmus] Darwin, chiefly during his residence in Lichfield, with anecdotes of his friends, and criticisms on his writings. xii, 313 pp. 8°. *Philadelphia, classic press, for W. Poyntell & co.* 1804.

Seward (Theodore F.) The pestalozzian music teacher. 1871. *See* **Mason** (Lowell) *and* **Seward**.

Sewell (Alfred L.) "The great calamity"! Scenes, incidents, and lessons of the great Chicago fire of the 8th and 9th of October, 1871. Also some account of other great conflagrations of modern times, and the burning of Peshtigo, Wisconsin. 100 pp. 1 map. 12°. *Chicago, A. L. Sewell*, 1871.

Sewell (*Rev.* Benjamin T.) Sorrow's circuit, or five years experience in the Bedford street mission, Philadelphia. Revised by rev. J. B. McCullough. 416 pp. 6 pl. 12°. *Philadelphia*, 1859.

Sewell (*Miss* Elizabeth Missing). After life. (Sequel to "The journal of a home life"). 3 p. l. 484 pp. 12°. *London, Longmans, Green & co.* 1868.
——— Laneton parsonage. A tale. By the author of "Amy Herbert," "Gertrude," etc. [*anon.*] Edited by the rev. W. Sewell. 227 pp. 12°. *New-York, D. Appleton & co.* 1846.
——— The same. 5th amer. ed. 233 pp. 12°. *New York, D. Appleton & co.* 1850.
——— Preparation for the holy communion. The devotions chiefly compiled from the works of bishop Taylor. With the communion service. 1 p. l. 186 pp. 18°. *Boston, E. P. Dutton & co.* 1864.

Sewell (*Mrs.* G.) *See* **Sewell** (*Mrs.* Mary).

Sewell (*Mrs.* Mary). Poems and essays. By mrs. G. Sewell, relict of the late rev. George Sewell. 2d ed. 3 v. 16°. *Chertsey, R. Wetton*, 1816.

Sewell (*Rev.* William). The first and second voyages of Rodolph the voyager. 2 v. iv, 259 pp; xi, 328 pp. 16°. *London, J. Burns*, 1844.

Sextus, Sixtus, *or* **Xystus** *pythagoræus*. Sexti pythagorei sententiæ, e græco in latinum a Ruffino versæ. 8°. [*Amstelaedami, apud H. Wetstenium*, 1688].

[*In* Gale (Thomas). Opuscula mythologica, pp. 643–656].

Seyd (Ernest). Suggestions in reference to the metallic currency of the United States of America. 1 p. l. 253 pp. 8°. *London, printed for private circulation*, 1871.

Seymour (Almira). The emigrants; or first and final step. A true story. 2 p. l. 122 pp. 16°. *Boston and Cambridge, J. Munroe & co.* 1853.

Seymour (Mary Alice, *or Mrs.* William Wood). Whitsuntide at Cedar grove. 311 pp. 16°. *New York, D. Dana, jr.* 1859.

Seymours (The). By the author of "The climbers," [etc. *anon.*] 231 pp. 1 pl. 16°. *New York, National temperance society and publication house,* 1871.

Shaftesbury (Anthony Ashley Cooper, *3d earl of*). *See* **Cooper** (Anthony Ashley).

Shakespeare (William). Falstaff and his companions. Twenty-one illustrations in silhouette, by Paul Konewka. With an introduction by Hermann Kurz. Translated by prof. C. C. Shackford. xviii pp. 20 l. 21 pl. 12°. *Boston, Roberts brothers,* 1872 [1871].

—— Hamlet, prince of Denmark: a tragedy. As it is now acted by his majesty's servants. 96 pp. 16°. *London, W. Whitworth,* 1757.

—— Plays of Shakespeare, selected and prepared for use in schools, clubs, classes, and families. With introductions and notes. By the rev. Henry N. Hudson. v. 2. 678 pp. 12°. *Boston, Ginn brothers,* 1871.

—— The poems of William Shakespeare; including Venus and Adonis, The rape of Lucrece, Passionate pilgrim, A lover's complaint, sonnets, &c. 182 pp. 18°. *Hartford, S. Andrus & son,* 1852.

—— Quotations from Shakespeare. A collection of passages from the works of William Shakespeare. Selected and arranged by Edmund Routledge. iv, 175 pp. 16°. *London, G. Routledge & sons,* 1867.

—— Selections from Shakespeare. By Benjamin Oakley. xxiii, 182 pp. 8°. *London, Longman,* 1828.

—— Shakespeare's comedy of the Tempest. Edited, with notes, by William J. Rolfe. 148 pp. 16°. *New York, Harper & brothers,* 1871.

—— Shakespeare's history of king Henry the eighth. Edited, with notes, by William J. Rolfe. 210 pp. sq. 16°. *New York, Harper & brothers,* 1872.

—— Shakespeare's tragedy of Julius Caesar. Edited, with notes, by W. J. Rolfe. 189 pp. sq. 16°. *New York, Harper & brothers,* 1872.

—— The same. Julius Caesar. Für den schulgebrauch erklärt von dr. L. Riechelmann. vii, 123 pp. 8°. *Leipzig, B. G. Teubner,* 1867.

Shakspeare laconics. A selection of pithy sentences from Shakspeare. Designed as a manual of reference. [*anon.*] 288 pp. 18°. *Philadelphia, C. G. Henderson & co.* 1853.

Shaksperian anthology: comprising the choicest passages and entire scenes; with a biographical sketch. [*anon.*] xii, 392 pp. 12°. *London, Sainsbury,* 1830.

Sharp (William, *m. d.*) An investigation of homœopathy. 7th ed. xvi, 317 pp. 8°. *London, Groombridge & sons,* 1856.

Sharpe (Charles Kirkpatrick). Biographical notice [of the rev. James Kirkton]. 4°. [*Edinburgh,* 1817].

[*In* KIRKTON (*Rev.* James). The secret and true history of the church of Scotland, pp. v-xxiii].

Sharpe (Edward). England's royall fishing revived. Or a compvtation as well of the charge of a busse, or herring-fishing ship: as also of the gaine and profit thereby. With the states proclamation annexed unto the same, as concerning herring-fishing. [*anon.*] 24 l. unp. sm. 4°. *London, N. Bourne,* 1630.

Shaw (Edward). Civil architecture: a complete theoretical and practical system of building. Also a variety of examples, selected from Vitruvius, Stuart, Chambers, and Nicholson, with many useful and elegant ornaments. 3d ed. 208 pp. 100 pl. 4°. *Boston, Marsh, Capen & Lyon,* 1834.

Shaw (George, *m. d.*) Cimelia physica. Figures of rare and curious quadrupeds, birds, &c. together with several of the most elegant plants. Engraved and coloured from the subjects themselves by John Frederick Miller. With descriptions by George Shaw, m. d. 2 p. l. 106 pp. 60 pl. fol. *London, T. Bensley for B. & J. White,* 1796.

Shaw (*Miss* Jane Railey). Margaret's old home: a tale of christian love. By the author of "The new commandment," [etc. *anon.*] 364 pp. 3 pl. 16°. *Boston, I. P. Warren,* [1871].

Shaw (John K.) Poems on religious subjects. 108 pp. 16°. *New-York, author,* 1821.

Shaw (Thomas Budd). A smaller history of english and american literature. For the use of schools. Edited by William Smith, ll. d. and Henry T. Tuckerman. 374 pp. 16°. *New York, Sheldon & co.* 1870.

Sheahan (James W.) *and* **Upton** (George P.) The great conflagration. Chicago: its past, present and future. Origin, progress and results of the fire. Also, a condensed history of Chicago, its population, growth,

Sheahan (J. W.) *and* **Upton** (G. P.)—cont'd. and great public works. And a statement of all the great fires of the world. 458 pp. 24 pl. 2 maps. 8°. *Philadelphia, Union publishing co.* 1871.

Shedd (William Greenough Thayer, *d. d.*) Discourses and essays. [2d ed.] 324 pp. 12°. *Andover, W. F. Draper,* 1862.

——— Lectures upon the philosophy of history. 128 pp. 12°. *Andover, W. F. Draper,* 1856.

——— Sermons to the natural man. xi, 422 pp. 8°. *New York, C. Scribner & co.* 1871.

Shedden (*Mrs.* Cecilia). Abridgment of the logographic emblematical french spelling book, or french pronunciation made easy. 4 p. l. 103 pp. 4 pl. 8°. *New York, Southwick & Pelsue,* 1819.

Sheldon (Edward Austin). Lessons on objects, graduated series; designed for children between the ages of six and fourteen; also, information on common objects. 407 pp. 12°. *New York, C. Scribner,* 1863.

——— A manual of elementary instruction, for schools and normal classes; a graduated course of object lessons for training the senses and developing the faculties of children. By E. A. Sheldon, assisted by miss M. E. M. Jones, and prof. H. Krusi. 465 pp. 12°. *New York, C. Scribner,* 1862.

Sheldrake (Timothy). Animal-mechanics applied to the prevention and cure of spinal curvature, and other personal deformities. Part 1. xii, 347 pp. 8°. *London, author,* 1832.

Shell cove: a story of the sea-shore and of the sea. [*anon.*] 1 p. l. 350 pp. 3 pl. 16°. *Boston, D. Lothrop & co.* 1871.

Shelley (Percy Bysshe). The genius of Shelley, being selections from his poetry. With a sketch of his life. xxiv, 198 pp. 32°. *London, G. Bell,* [1840].

——— Queen Mab; with notes. 4th ed. 122 pp. 18°. *New York, at "The citizen of the world" office,* 1852.

Shepard (Elihu H.) The early history of St. Louis and Missouri. [Also] the author's autobiography. 170 pp. 8°. *St. Louis, Southwestern book and publishing co.* 1870.

Shepard (Isaac Fitzgerald). Pebbles from Castalia. 160 pp. 12°. *Boston, Whipple & Damrell,* 1840.

——— Poetry of feeling, and spiritual melodies. 128 pp. 32°. *Boston, Lewis & Sampson,* 1844.

Shepherd (Thomas James). The days that are past. [History of "The first presbyterian church in the northern liberties"]. 191 pp. 12°. *Philadelphia, Lindsay & Blakiston,* 1864.

Shepherd (*Rev.* William). Horæ apostolicæ; or, a digested narrative of the acts and writings of the apostles of Jesus Christ. Arranged according to Townsend. xiii, 287 pp. 12°. *London, Longman,* 1846.

Sheppard (*Rev.* John). Thoughts, chiefly designed as a preparative or persuasive to private devotion. 6th ed. xx, 343 pp. 12°. *London, Whittaker, Treacher & co.* 1832.

Sherer (John). The gems of masonry; emblematic and descriptive. 4 p. l. 52, 47 pp. 12°. *Cincinnati, author,* 1859.

Sherlock (William, *d. d.*) A discourse concerning the divine providence. 2d ed. 4 p. l. 394 pp. 4°. *London, W. Rogers,* 1694.

Sherman (*Rev.* David). Sketches of New England divines. 443 pp. 12°. *New York, Carlton & Porter,* 1860.

——— Woman's place in the gospel. 12°. *Cincinnati,* [1872].

[*In* FOSTER (*Rev.* John O.) Life and labors of mrs. Maggie Newton Van Cott, pp. xxiv–xxxxi].

Sherman (M. L.) *and* **Lyon** (William F.) The hollow globe; or the world's agitator and reconciler. A treatise on the physical conformation of the earth. Presented through the organism of M. L. Sherman, and written by Wm. F. Lyon. 447 pp. 12°. *Chicago, Religio-philosophical publishing house,* 1871.

Sherwood (Henry Hall, *m. d.*) The motive power of organic life, and magnetic phenomena of terrestrial and planetary motions, with the application of the ever-active and all-pervading agency of magnetism, to the nature, symptoms, and treatment of chronic diseases. 196 pp. 24 pl. 8°. *New York, H. A. Chapin & co.* 1841.

Sherwood (*Rev.* L. Hinsdale). The school song and hymn book. *See* **Brittan** (N.) *and* **Sherwood.**

Shew (Joel, *m. d.*) Hydropathy; or, the water-cure: its principles, modes of treatment, etc. xv, 304 pp. 1 pl. 12°. *New York, Wiley & Putnam,* 1844.

Shiels (*Rev.* Alexander). A hind let loose; or, an historical representation of the testimonies of the church of Scotland, for the interest of Christ. With the true state thereof in all its periods. xii, 520 pp. 1 pl. 8°. *Glasgow, R. & T. Duncan,* 1770.

Shillingford (John). Letters and papers of John Shillingford, mayor of Exeter 1447–50. Edited by Stuart A. Moore. xxvii, 162 pp. 4°. [*London*], *Camden society*, 1871.
[CAMDEN society publications, new series, v. 1, no. 2]

Shinn (Asa). On the benevolence and rectitude of the supreme being. 403 pp. 12°. *Baltimore, Book committee of the methodist protestant church*, 1840.

Shinn (Joshua). The new Ohio arithmetic. 252 pp. 18°. *New-Garden*, [*O.*] *author*, 1828.

Shirley (Henry). The martyr'd souldier: as it was acted at the private house in Drury lane, and at other publicke theaters. 41 l. sm. 4°. *London, I. Okes*, 1638.

Shirreff (Emily). Thoughts on self-culture, addressed to women. *See* **Grey** (Mary G.)

Shirrefs (Andrew). Poems, chiefly in the scottish dialect. xxviii, 13-365, 41 pp. 1 portrait. 8°. *Edinburgh, author*, 1790.

Shooting at a mark. A story for boys. [*anon.*] 194 pp. 4 pl. 18°. *New York, Carlton & Porter*, [1864].

Short (A) account of the first settlement of the provinces of Virginia, Maryland, New-York, New-Jersey, and Pensylvania, by the English. To which is annexed a map of Maryland, and also of the adjacent country, anno 1630. [*anon.*] 22 pp. 1 map. sm. 4°. *London*, 1735.

Short stories from the lives of remarkable women, being narratives of fact to correct fiction, as related to her children. By a mother. [*anon.*] Eng. title, 186 pp. 9 pl. 16°. *New York, J. Miller*, 1861.

Showman's (The) rail-road guide. 172 pp. 2 col. pl. 16°. *Chicago, A. W. Hall & co.* 1871.

Shrady (George F. *m. d. editor*). **Medical** (The) record.

Shumway (Nehemiah). The american harmony: containing the rules of singing; with a collection of psalm tunes, hymns, and anthems. 212 pp. obl. 8°. *Philadelphia, J. M'Culloch*, 1793.

Shurtleff (J. B.) The governmental instructor, a brief and comprehensive view of the government of the United States, and of the state governments. 3d revised ed. corrected by David N. Camp. 193 pp. 12°. *New York, Collins & brother*, [1871].

Shurtleff (Nathaniel Bradstreet, *m. d.*) A topographical and historical description of Boston. 1 p. l. ix, 720 pp. 1 map. 8°. *Boston, printed by request of the city council*, 1871.

Shute (Robert L.) The artists, painters, and glass stainers' coats of arms and monogram book, showing eight hundred designs, counting each alphabet one design only. 4 p. l. 96 pp. 8°. *New York, R. L. Shute*, 1871.

Shutte (*Rev.* Reginald Neale). Better days. A tale. 2 v. viii, 325 pp; 2 p. l. 291 pp. 12°. *London, Saunders, Otley & co.* 1862.

Sibbald (*Sir* Robert, *m. d.*) The autobiography of sir R. Sibbald: to which is prefixed some account of his mss. 44 pp. 8°. *Edinburgh, T. Stevenson*, 1833.

Sibyle (La) gauloise. 1775. *See* **La Dixmerie** (Nicolas Bricaire de).

Sibyllina oracula de græco in latinvm conversa, et in eadem annotationes, Sebastiano Castalione [Châteillon] interprete. 4 p. l. 104 pp. 22 l. 4°. *Helmestadi*, 1673.
[*With* CLASEN (Daniel). De oraculis gentilium].

Sicard (François). Atlas de l'histoire des institutions militaires des Français. 1 p. l. ix, 20 pp. 200 pl. 8°. *Paris, J. Corréard jeune*, 1834.

Siden (*Captain* Thomas, *pseudon.*) The history of the Sevarites or Sevarambi. *See* **Vairasse d'Allais** (Denis).

Sidney (Charles *and* Ambrose). The Sidney anecdotes: selected from history, ancient and modern, and other authentic sources. 3 p. l. 172 pp. 2 l. 10 pl. 18°. *London, W. J. Sears*, 1830.

Sidney (*Sir* Philip). The defence of poesy. With some account of the author. l, 88 pp. 16°. *Cambridge*, [*Mass.*] *Hilliard & Brown*, 1831.
[LIBRARY of the old english prose writers. *Cambridge*, 1831. v. 2].

Sidonius Apollinaris (Caius Sollius). Opera. Io. Savaro claromontensis, multo quam antea castigatius recognouit, et librum commentarium adiecit. xxii, 594 pp. 23 l. 206 pp. 6 l. 4°. *Parisiis, ex officina plantiniana, apud A. Perier*, 1599.

Siebenkees (Johann Philipp). The life of Bianca Capello, wife of Francesco de' Medici, grand-duke of Tuscany. Translated from the german original. By C. Ludger. 2 p. l. xvii, xxx, 171, 10 pp. 12°. *Liverpool, J. M'Creery*, 1797.

Siècle (Le) de Louis le grand. Avec Thémire. 1731. *See* **Waleff** (Blaise Henry de Corte, *baron* de).

Sieg (R. K.) The comrade. In four parts. Part 1. Being a synopsis of all the laws of congress, orders of the war department,

Sieg (R. K.)—continued. [etc.] affecting the pay, bounty, and allowances of enlisted men. Part 2. Gives the pay and allowances of commissioned officers at the beginning of the war, and the changes since made. Part 3. Treats of pensions; also, the laws now in force concerning artificial limbs. Part 4. Relates to government lands, giving the rights of soldiers under existing laws, and full instructions how to obtain a title thereto. 168 pp. 8°. *Toledo (O.) Miller, Locke & co.* 1871.

Sigaud de la Fond (Jean René *or* Joseph Aignan). Dictionnaire des merveilles de la nature. Par m. A. J. S. D. 2 v. 1 p. l. iv, 493 pp; 1 p. l. 476 pp. 2 l. 8°. *Paris,* 1781.

Sigmond (George Gabriel). Tea; its effects, medicinal and moral. viii, 144 pp. 16°. *London, Longman,* 1839.

Signal lights. [*anon.*] 333 pp. 16°. *New York, A. D. F. Randolph & co.* [1871].

Sigonio (Carlo). Caroli Sigonii historiarvm de regno Italiæ libri quindecim. Eng. title, 3 p. l. 592 pp. fol. *Venetiis, apud I. Zilettum,* 1574.

——— Consolation from natural religion. By M. T. Cicero. Rendered into english by Thomas Blacklock. 8°. [*Edinburgh, J. Dickson,* 1767].

[*In* BLACKLOCK (Thomas). Paraclesis. 1767. pp. 1-174.
Note.—This treatise, attributed by Sigonio to Cicero, was written by the former].

Sigourney (*Mrs.* Lydia Huntley). Examples from the eighteenth and nineteenth centuries. First series. 349 pp. 16°. *New York, C. Scribner,* 1857.

——— Pocahontas, and other poems. Eng. title, 1 p. l. 9–283 pp. 1 pl. 12°. *New York, Harper & brothers,* 1841.

——— Poems; by the author of "Moral pieces in prose and verse." [*anon.*] 228 pp. 12°. *Boston, S. G. Goodrich,* 1827.

——— Tales and essays for children. 128 pp. sq. 18°. *Hartford, F. J. Huntington,* 1835.

Silliman (Anna). The world's jubilee. 343 pp. 12°. *New York, M. W. Dodd,* 1856.

Silliman's journal. *See* **American** journal of science and arts.

Silver (*Rev.* Abiel). Lectures on the symbolic character of the sacred scriptures. 286 pp. 12°. *New York, D. Appleton & co.* 1863.

Silver (The) tongue folio: a choice collection of organ music, from the great masters. [*anon.*] 2 p. l. 105 pp. 4°. *New York, E. P. Needham & son,* 1871.

Silvestre de Sacy (Antoine Isaac). Principles of general grammar, proper to serve as an introduction to the study of languages. Translated by D. Fosdick, jun. 1st am. from the 5th french ed. 156 pp. 12°. *Andover, Flagg, Gould & Newman,* 1834.

Simeon (*Rev.* Charles). The excellency of the liturgy, in four discourses, preached before the university of Cambridge, in November, 1811. Also, [four] university sermons. 268 pp. 16°. *New-York, Eastburn, Kirk, & co.* 1813.

Simmonds (P. L. *editor*). *See* **Journal** (The) of applied science.

Simmons (Charles). A scripture manual, alphabetically and systematically arranged, designed to facilitate the finding of proof texts. Stereotype ed. 551 pp. 12°. *New York, M. W. Dodd,* 1845.

Simmons (James P.) War in heaven. A disquisition, biblical and rational, concerning angels, devils, and men, and the creation, fall and redemption of the human soul. 314 pp. 8°. *Cincinnati, R. Clarke & co.* 1871.

Simms (William Gilmore). Areytos; or songs and ballads of the south, with other poems. xvi, 5–416 pp. 12°. *Charleston, S. C., Russell & Jones,* 1860.

——— Confession; or, the blind heart. A domestic story. By the author of "The kinsmen," [etc. *anon.*] 2 v. 251 pp; 1 p. l. 13–257 pp. 12°. *Philadelphia, Lea & Blanchard,* 1841.

——— The damsel of Darien. By the author of "The Yemasse," [etc. *anon.*] 2 v. 3 p. l. 13–308 pp; 281 pp. 12°. *Philadelphia, Lea & Blanchard,* 1839.

——— Pelayo: or, the cavern of Covadonga. A romance, [in verse]. By Isabel. [*pseudon.*] xxiii, 204 pp. 12°. *New York, Harper & brothers,* 1836.

——— Southern passages and pictures. By the author of "Atalantis," [etc. *anon.*] ix, 228 pp. 12°. *New York, G. Adlard,* 1839.

Simon (Jules François). Études sur la théodicée de Platon et d'Aristote. vii, 280 pp. 8°. *Paris, Joubert,* 1840.

Simon (Menno). *See* **Menno** Simons.

Simon (Richard). Histoire de l'origine & du progrès des revenus ecclésiastiques. Par Jérôme Acosta. [*pseudon.*] 10 p. l. 386 pp. 16°. *Francfort, F. Arnaud,* 1703.

Simonde de Sismondi. *See* **Sismondi.**

Simonds (S. D.) *See* **Living** (The) way.

Simonds (William). The boy's book of morals and manners. 231 pp. 1 pl. 16°. *Boston, Mass. sabbath school society,* [1855].

——— The boy's own guide to good principles, habits and manners. 406 pp. 1 pl. 18°. *Boston, Mass. sabbath school society,* [1853].

——— Ella; or, turning over a new leaf. By Walter Aimwell. [*pseudon.*] 281 pp. 16°. *Boston, Gould & Lincoln,* 1855.
[AIMWELL stories, v. 3].

Simonds (William Edgar). Practical suggestions on the sale of patents, with forms of assignment, license, contract, power of attorney to sell, rights, &c. with hints upon invention. 107 pp. sm. 4°. *Hartford (Conn.) author,* 1871.

Simons (M. Laird). Die illustrirte familienbibel. 1871. *See* **Bible.** (*German*).

——— The same. Pictorial home bible. 1871. *See* **Bible.** (*English*).

Simple (Sam, *pseudon.*) *See* **Wilburn** (George T.)

Simpson (Stephen). The lives of George Washington and Thomas Jefferson: with a parallel. vi, 389 pp. 1 portrait. 12°. *Philadelphia, H. Young,* 1833.

Simpson (S. S.) Aunt Sophie's stories. A christmas and birthday gift, for our children. By S. S. S. [*anon*] 80 pp. 1 pl. sq. 16°. *Boston, O. Clapp,* 1859.

——— Two hundred years ago; or, a brief history of Cambridgeport and East Cambridge, with notices of some of the early settlers. By S. S. S. [*anon.*] 111 pp. 1 pl. sq. 18°. *Boston, O. Clapp,* 1859.

Sims (T.) The life of John Frederic Oberlin, pastor of Waldbach, in the Ban de la Roche. 140 pp. 2 pl. 12°. *Philadelphia, American sunday school union,* 1830.

Sincerus (Jodocus). *See* **Zingerling** (Just).

Sinclair (Catherine). Scotch courtiers, and the court. [A poem]. 2 p. l. 121 pp. 8°. *Edinburgh, W. Whyte & co.* 1842.

Siniscalchi (Liborio). The meditations of st. Ignatius; or, the "spiritual exercises" expounded. Translated from the italian and revised by a catholic clergyman. 429 pp. 12°. *Philadelphia, P. F. Cunningham,* 1862.

Sinnett (Frederick). Sinnett's picture of Paris, a retrospective historical sketch of the rise and progress of the city; notices of the various routes from the coast to the capital. With a concise account of Versailles, Fontainebleau, St. Cloud, St. Denis, Neuilly, and other places in the environs. iv, 288 pp. 1 pl. 1 map. 8°. *London, J. Masters,* 1847.

Sinnett (*Mrs.* Percy). A story about a christmas in the olden time. 2 p. l. 138 pp. 4 col. pl. 16°. *London, Chapman & Hall,* [1848].

Sins of the tongue; or, truth is everything. [*anon.*] 160 pp. 18°. *Philadelphia, American sunday school union,* [1853].

Sir Gyles Goosecappe, knight. A comedie presented by the chil: of the chappell. [*anon.* 1st ed.] 38 l. sm. 4°. *London, Edward Blunt,* 1606.

Sir Thomas More, a tragedy. *See* **Hurdis** (*Rev.* James).

Sismondi (Jean Charles Léonard Simonde de). Études sur l'économie politique. 2 v. xi, 470; 489 pp. 8°. *Paris, Treuttel et Würtz,* 1837–38.

Sisters (The) of Orleans: a tale of race and social conflict. [*anon.*] 341 pp. 12°. *New York, G. P. Putnam & sons,* 1871.

Six boys; a mother's story, as told by some extracts from her journal. [*anon.*] 1 p. l. 339 pp. 3 pl. 16°. *Boston, Hurd & Houghton,* 1871.

Skates (The). By the author of "The best friend," [etc. *anon.*] 186 pp. 3 pl. 18°. *Boston, Mass. sabbath school society,* [1862].

Skeats (Herbert S.) A history of the free churches of England, from a. d. 1688–a. d. 1851. 2d ed. xvi, 638 pp. 8°. *London, A. Miall,* 1869.

Skene (George). Donald Bane: an heroic poem. viii, 111 pp. 16°. *London, G. G. & J. Robinson,* 1796.

Sketches and incidents; or, a budget from the saddle-bags of a superannuated itinerant. [*anon.*] 166 pp. 18°. *New-York, G. Lane & P. P. Sandford,* 1844.

Sketches in Bedlam; characteristic traits of insanity, as displayed in the cases of one hundred and forty patients of both sexes, confined in New Bethlem. By a constant observer. [*anon.*] xl, 312 pp. 8°. *London, Sherwood, Jones & co.* 1823.

Sketches of Newport and its vicinity; with notices respecting the history, settlement and geography of Rhode Island. [*anon.*] 213 pp. 5 pl. 8°. *New York, J. S. Taylor & co.* 1842.

Sketches of obscure poets, with specimens of their writings. [*anon.*] xv, 208 pp. 16°. *London, Cochrane & McCrone,* 1833.

Sketches of Paris. 1838. *See* **Sanderson** (John).

Sketches of Persia, from the journals of a traveller in the east. *See* **Malcolm** (*Sir* John).

Sketches of the rev. Richard Cecil, with anecdotes of his life, and fragments from his writings. By a presbyter of the protestant episcopal church in western New York. [*anon.*] 119 pp. 18°. *Utica,* [*N. Y*] *Hobart press*, 1838.

Skinner (*Rev.* George). New translation of Proverbs. 1831. *See* **Bible.** (*English*).

Skinner (*Rev.* I. L.) A key to the gospels: being a compendious exposition of the principal things contained in them. 276 pp. 2 l. 12°. *Washington, W. Greer*, 1831.

Skinner (*Rev.* John). Songs and poems. With a sketch of his life, by H. G. Reid. xxxvi, 98 pp. 16°. *Peterhead,* [*Scotland*], *W. L. Taylor*, 1859.

Skinner (Thomas Harvey, *d. d.*) Essay, [on patriotism and christianity]. 12°. [*New York*], 1841.

[*In* CHEEVER (*Rev.* George B.) God's hand in America, pp. 5-26].

Skrine (Henry). Two successive tours throughout the whole of Wales, with several of the adjacent english counties. 2d ed. with additions. xii, 280 pp. 1 map. 8°. *London, T. Turner*, 1812.

Slade (John). Narrative of the late proceedings and events in China. 1 p. l. vi, 183, 75 pp. 8°. *China, Canton Register press*, 1839.

Slaney (Robert A.) Essay on the beneficial direction of rural expenditure. viii, 239 pp. 16°. *London, Longman, Hurst, Rees, Orme, Brown & Green*, 1824.

Slate (*Rev.* Richard). Life of the rev. John Angier, together with biographical sketches of some of the rev. O. Heywood's nearest relatives. 8°. [*Idle, editor*, 1827].

[*In* HEYWOOD (*Rev.* Oliver). The whole works, v. 1, pp. 515-608].

——— Memoirs of the rev. Nathaniel Heywood, minister of the gospel at Ormskirk, in Lancashire. 8°. *Idle, editor*, 1827.

[*In* HEYWOOD (*Rev.* Oliver). The whole works, v. 1, pp. 445-514].

——— Memoirs of the rev. Oliver Heywood, chiefly extracted from his diary and other unpublished manuscripts. Also, memoirs of the rev. Nathaniel Heywood, vicar of Ormskirk, [by sir H. Ashhurst], and of the rev. John Angier, of Benton: with notices of others. The whole revised, by the editor of mr. O. Heywood's works. v. 1, xi, 608 pp. 1 portrait. 8°. *Idle, J. Vint for editor*, 1827.

Sleidan (Johann Philippson, *known as*). A famovse cronicle of oure time, called Sleidanes commentaries, concerning the state of religion and commonwealth, during the raigne of the emperour Charles the fift. Translated out of latin into englishe by Ihon Daus. *b. l.* 5 p. l. cccclxx l. 17 l. unp. fol. *London, I. Daye for A. Veale*, 1560.

——— The key of historie. Or, a most methodicall abridgement of the foure chiefe monarchies, Babylon, Persia, Greece, and Rome. [With] a marginall chronologie of euery roman emperors raigne, and of all the most memorable persons and accidents. Eng. title, 25 p. l. 377 pp. 1 table. 18°. *London, M. Flesher for W. Sheeres*, 1627.

Sleigh (William). A practical dictionary, containing concise, yet comprehensive schemes of the most necessary subjects; divine, moral, and literary. A new ed. considerably enlarged. 364 pp. 1 pl. 8°. *Plymouth, J. Bennett*, 1822.

Sleigh (William W.) The christian's defensive dictionary. Being an alphabetical refutation of the general objections to the bible. 438 pp. 1 table. 12°. *Philadelphia, E. C. Biddle*, 1837.

Slender (Robert, *pseudon.*) *See* **Freneau** (Philip).

Slicer (*Rev.* Henry). An appeal to the candid of all denominations: in which the obligation, subjects, and mode of baptism are discussed. 3d ed. revised by the editor. 262 pp. 18°. *New York, G. Lane*, 1841.

Sloan (Samuel, *architect*). City homes, country houses and church architecture, or the American builders' journal. 792 pp. 8°. *Philadelphia, Claxton, Remsen & Haffelfinger*, 1871.

[*Note.*—The same as The architectural review, and American builders' journal, 1868-69, v. i, but is without index].

Sloane (J. R. W. *d. d.*) The spirit in which we should engage in the act of covenanting. 12°. [*Pittsburgh*, 1872].

[*In* REFORMED presbyterian church in North America. Memorial volume, pp. 73-80].

Sloman (Jane). The melodist. Selected gems from celebrated composers, with an accompaniment for the piano-forte. 112 pp. obl. 4°. *New York, W. Hall & son*, [1850]. s.

Small (J. *m. d.*) An inquiry into the nature and character of ancient and modern slavery. To which is added a brief review of a book entitled, Testimony of God against slavery, by rev. La Roy Sunderland. 2 p. l. 123 pp. 12°. [*n. p.*] 1836.

Smarius (*Rev.* C. F. *s. j.*) Points of controversy: a series of lectures. 487 pp. 16°. *New York, Rennie, Shea & Lindsay,* 1865.

Smart (Christopher). The parables of our lord and saviour Jesus Christ. Done into familiar verse. xiv, 175 pp. 16°. *London, W. Owen,* 1768.

Smart (Moses M.) A brief view of christian doctrine. 330 pp. 16°. *Lowell, N. L. Dayton,* 1843.

Smellie (William). Literary and characteristical lives of John Gregory, m. d. Henry Home, lord Kames, David Hume, and Adam Smith, ll. d. To which are added a dissertation on public spirit; and three essays. ix, 450 pp. 8°. *Edinburgh, A. Smellie,* [*etc.*] 1800.

Smiles (Samuel). Brief biographies. vi, 517 pp. 6 portraits. 12°. *Boston, Ticknor & Fields,* 1861.

——— Character. 9th thousand. viii, 388 pp. 12°. *London, J. Murray,* 1872.

Smiles for all seasons: forming a collection of parlour poetry, and drawing-room drollery. [*anon.*] 2d ed. xii, 226 pp. 1 front. 12°. *London, Baldwin, Cradock & Joy,* 1825.

Smiley (Thomas T.) An easy introduction to the study of geography on an improved plan. 7th ed. improved. 256 pp. 16°. *Philadelphia, author,* 1830.

——— The same. 22d ed. improved. 252 pp. 16°. *Philadelphia, Grigg & Elliot,* 1834.

——— The United States speaker; consisting of a choice collection of pieces. 240 pp. 12°. *Philadelphia, J. Grigg,* 1831.

Smith (*Rev.* Asa Dodge). Memoir of mrs. Louisa Adams Leavitt; comprised in a sermon occasioned by her death, and a supplementary sketch. 156 pp. 18°. *New York, J. F. Trow,* 1843.

Smith (Augustus). Constitutional reflections on the present aspects of parliamentary government. 120 pp. 8°. *London, E. Stanford,* 1866.

Smith (A. P.) History of the seventy-sixth regiment New York volunteers; what it endured and accomplished. 429 pp. 1 portrait. 8°. *Cortland (N. Y.) publisher,* 1867.

Smith (Benjamin). Poems, moral and religious. 128 pp. 12°. *Pittsburgh,* 1842.

Smith (B. M. *d. d. prof. Union theol. sem. Va.*) Family religion, or the domestic relations as regulated by christian principles. A prize essay. 210 pp. 12°. *Philadelphia, Presbyterian board of publication,* [1859].

Smith (*Mrs.* Caroline L.) The american home book of in-door games, amusements, and occupations. x, 380 pp. 3 pl. 16°. *Boston, Lee & Shepard,* 1872.

Smith (*Rev.* Charles John). Synonyms discriminated. A complete catalogue of synonymous words in the english language, with descriptions of their various shades of meaning, and illustrations of their usages and specialities. Illustrated by quotations from standard writers. 3 p. l. 610 pp. 8°. *London, Bell & Daldy,* 1871.

Smith (Charlotte Turner). Emmeline, the orphan of the castle. 3 v. 16°. *Philadelphia, J. Conrad & co.* 1802.

Smith (*Rev.* Daniel). The destruction of Jerusalem; abridged from the history of the jewish wars, etc. 1840. *See* **Josephus** (Flavius).

——— The history of the patriarch Jacob. Revised by the editors. 189 pp. 18°. *New York, T. Mason & G. Lane,* 1840.

——— The life of Abraham. Revised by the editors. 131 pp. 1 pl. 18°. *New York, T. Mason & G. Lane,* 1840.

——— The life of Daniel. 148 pp. 2 pl. 18°. *New-York, T. Mason & G. Lane,* 1839.

——— The life of David. Revised by the editors. 160 pp. 18°. *New-York, T. Mason & G. Lane,* 1839.

——— The life of Elijah. 174 pp. 4 pl. 18°. *New York, T. Mason & G. Lane,* 1839.

——— The life of Elisha. 88 pp. 18°. *New York, T. Mason & G. Lane,* 1839.

——— The life of Esther. 126 pp. 18°. *New York, T. Mason & G. Lane,* 1840.

——— The life of Hezekiah. 77 pp. 18°. *New-York, T. Mason & G. Lane,* 1840.

——— The life of John the baptist. 103 pp. 1 pl. 18°. *New-York, T. Mason & G. Lane,* 1840.

——— The life of Jonah. 80 pp. 18°. *New York, T. Mason & G. Lane,* 1840.

——— The life of Joshua. 200 pp. 1 map. 18°. *New York, T. Mason & G. Lane,* 1840.

——— The life of Moses. 224 pp. 7 pl. 18°. *New-York, T. Mason & G. Lane,* 1839.

——— The life of Samson. 94 pp. 18°. *New York, T. Mason & G. Lane,* 1840.

——— The life of st. Paul. 175 pp. 1 pl. 18°. *New York, T. Mason & G. Lane,* 1839.

——— The life of st. Peter. 132 pp. 1 pl. 18°. *New-York, T. Mason & G. Lane,* 1840.

——— The life of the apostle John. 222 pp. 1 map. 18°. *New York, T. Mason & G. Lane,* 1840.

Smith (*Rev.* Daniel)—continued.

——— The life of Solomon, king of Israel. 168 pp. 18°. *New York, G. Lane*, 1840.

——— The parent's friend: or, letters on the government and education of children and youth. 204 pp. 18°. *New-York, T. Mason & G. Lane*, 1838.

——— Rebuilding of Jerusalem and the temple: or the lives of Ezra and Nehemiah. 80 pp. 18°. *New York, G. Lane & P. P. Sandford*, 1841.

Smith (Daniel B.) The principles of chemistry. 2d ed. 312 pp. 12°. *Philadelphia, U. Hunt*, 1842.

Smith (*Rev.* Daniel D.) Lectures on domestic duties. 157 pp. 16°. *Portland, S. H. Colesworthy*, 1837.

Smith (D. W.) A gazetteer of the province of Upper Canada: [with] an appendix, describing the principal towns, fortifications and rivers in Lower Canada. 42 l. 2 maps. 1 tab. 8°. *New York, Prior & Dunning*, 1813.

Smith (Elias, *m. d.*) The american physician, and family assistant: in five parts. 4th ed. 306 pp. 8°. *Boston, B. True*, 1837.

Smith (Elisha, *m. d.*) The botanic physician: a compendium of the practice of physic, upon botanical principles. viii, 624 pp. 8°. *New York, Murphy & Bingham*, 1830.

——— The same. Revised and improved by Isaac S. Smith, m. d. xii, 508 pp. 8 col. pl. 8°. *New York, editor*, 1844.

Smith (Elizabeth A.) One of the Billingses; or, Edith's mistakes. 246 pp. 3 pl. 16°. *New York, Carlton & Lanahan*, [1871].

Smith (*Mrs.* Elizabeth Oakes). The newsboy. [*anon.*] 527 pp. 12°. *New York, J. C. Derby*, 1854.

——— Poetical writings. 2d ed. 204 pp. 24°. *New York, J. S. Redfield*, 1846.

——— The sinless child, and other poems. Edited by John Keese. 177 pp. 1 l. 12°. *New York, Wiley & Putnam*, 1843.

——— The true child. 160 pp. 32°. *Boston, Saxton & Kelt*, 1845.

Smith (*Rev.* E. R.) Hand-book of the Baltimore conference, methodist episcopal church, south, containing map, historical notes, etc. 107 pp. 1 map. 8°. *Baltimore, King brothers*, 1871.

Smith (*Mrs.* Frances Irene Burge). Asleep. 149 pp. 12°. *Brooklyn (N. Y.) T. B. Ventres*, [1871].

Smith (*Mrs.* Frances I. B.)—continued.

——— Mother's pearl, and other stories. 187 pp. 9 pl. 12°. *Boston, American tract society*, [1869].

——— Nina, or life's caprices. A story founded on fact. 426 pp. 1 pl. 12°. *New York, D. Dana*, 1861.

Smith (Francis S.) Poems for the million. viii, 271 pp. 16°. *New York, author*, 1871.

Smith (G.) The entertaining correspondent. Or curious relations, digested into familiar letters, and conversations. Being a choice and valuable collection of very remarkable histories, from the most approved authors, both ancient and modern. 2 v. Eng. title, viii, 558 pp. 4 l. 12 pl; eng. title, 2 p. l. 564 pp. 4 l. 11 pl. 12°. *London, J. Hodges & J. James*, 1739.

Smith (Goldwin). The civil war in America: an address read at the last meeting of the Manchester union and emancipation society. 1 p. l. 96 pp. 12°. *London, Simpkin, Marshall & co.* 1866.

Smith (Henry H. *m. d.*) Minor surgery; or, hints on the every-day duties of the surgeon. 303 pp. 16°. *Philadelphia, E. Barrington & G. D. Haswell*, 1843.

Smith (Horatio). Festivals, games, and amusements. Ancient and modern. With additions, by Samuel Woodworth, esq. Harper's stereotype ed. 355 pp. 3 pl. 16°. *New-York, J. & J. Harper*, 1831.

Smith (Hugh, *d. d.*) The heart delineated in its state by nature, and as renewed by grace. 330 pp. 18°. *New York, Harper & brothers*, 1844.

Smith (I. B.) The speculative dictionary: containing moral sentiments, and philosophic reflections; or texts and skeletons, for the contemplation of penetrating intellects, and searchers after truth. 192 pp. 16°. *New York, H. D. Robinson*, 1835.

Smith (Jerome Van Crowninshield, *m. d.*) The class-book of anatomy, explanatory of the first principles of human mechanism, as the basis of physical education. vii, 280 pp. 12°. *Boston, Allen & Ticknor*, 1834.

——— The same. 2d ed. 286 pp. 12°. *Boston, R. S. Davis*, 1836.

——— An essay on the practicability of cultivating the honey bee, in maritime towns and cities, as a source of domestic economy and profit. 106 pp. (incl. 1 pl.) 16°. *Boston, Perkins & Marvin*, 1831.

Smith *or* **Smythe** (*Sir* John, *cousin of Edward vi*). Certain discourses: concerning the formes and effects of diuers sorts of weapons, and other verie important matters militarie, greatlie mistaken by diuers of our men of warre in these daies; and chiefly of the mosquet, the caliuer and the long-bow; as also, of the great sufficiencie, excellence, and wonderful effects of archers: with many notable examples and other particularities. 18 p. l. 50 numb. l. sm. 4°. *London, R. Johnes*, 1590.

——— Instrvctions, obseruations, and orders mylitarie. Requisite for all chieftaines, captaines, and higher and lower men of charge, and officers to vnderstand, knowe, and obserue. 16 p. l. 220 pp. sm. 4°. *London, R. Iohnes*, 1595.

[*With his* Certain discourses: concerning the formes and effects of diuers sorts of weapons, etc. 1590. *Note.*—The pages after 111 are numbered 124–220, instead of 112–208].

Smith (*Capt.* John, 1579–1631). Twee scheepstogten gedaan na Nieuw-Engeland. De eerste in het jaar 1614. De tweede gedaan in het jaar 1615. Door den reysiger selfs in het engelsch beschreeven, en nu aldereerst uyt die spraak in het neder-duytsch overgeset. 1 p. l. 34 pp. 2 l. 1 map. 3 pl. 16°. *Leyden, P. van der Aa*, 1707.

Smith (John, *d. d.* 1747–1807). Sean dana; le Oisian, Orran, Ulann, &c. Ancient poems of Ossian, Orran, Ullin, &c. collected in the western highlands and isles; being the originals of the translations some time ago published in the gaelic antiquities. vii, 348 pp. 8°. *Edinburgh, C. Elliot*, [*etc.*] 1787.

Smith (John Russell). A bibliographical list of the works that have been published, towards illustrating the provincial dialects of England. 24, 8 pp. 8°. *London, J. R. Smith*, 1839.

Smith (*Rev.* J. Hyatt). Gilead; or, the vision of All souls' hospital. An allegory. 360 pp. 1 pl. 12°. *New York, C. Scribner*, 1863.

——— Haran, the hermit; or, the wonderful lamp. 116 pp. 1 pl. 16°. *Buffalo, Breed, Butler & co.* 1860.

Smith (J. J. *d. d.*) The impending conflict between romanism and protestantism in the United States. 288 pp. 12°. *New York, E. Goodenough*, 1871.

Smith (Julie P.) Brazen gates: a true history of the blossoms which grew in the garden at Cragenfels. Compiled by Christabel Goldsmith, and preface by the author of "Widow Goldsmith's daughter." 248 pp. 6 pl. 12°. *New York, G. W. Carleton & co.* 1872.

——— Chris and Otho: the pansies and orange-blossoms they found in Roaring river and Rosenbloom. A sequel to "Widow Goldsmith's daughter." 528 pp. 12°. *New York, Carleton*, 1871.

——— The widower; also, a true account of some brave frolics at Craigenfels. By the author of "Widow Goldsmith's daughter," etc. 389 pp. 12°. *New York, G. W. Carleton & co.* 1871.

Smith (Lenox). Bessemer process in the United States. 8°. *New York*, 1872.

[*In* GRÜNER (M. L.) The manufacture of steel, pp. 156–193].

Smith (Marcus A.) The Boston speaker; being a collection of pieces, in prose, poetry, and dialogue. 216 pp. 18°. *Boston, J. Dowe*, 1836.

Smith (*Mrs.* M. B.) My uncle's family; or, ten months at the south. 115 pp. 2 pl. 18°. *Cincinnati, American reform tract and book society*, 1860.

Smith (*Mrs.* M. J. P.) Little Robert and his friend; or, the light of Brier valley. 110 pp. 1 pl. 18°. *Cincinnati, American reform tract and book society*, 1861.

Smith (*Rev.* Patrick). A preservative against quakerism: by way of conference between a minister and his parishioner. 2d ed. 6 p. l. 300, xx pp. 8°. *London, C. Rivington*, 1740.

Smith (Randal). A collection of select aphorisms and maxims; with several historical observations, curious remarks, and characters of persons and things; taken out of the best authors. 9 p. l. 170 pp. 16°. *Dublin, A. Rhames for E. Dobson*, 1722.

Smith (*Rev.* Reuben). The pastoral office, embracing experiences and observations from a pastorate of forty years. 105 pp. 18°. *Philadelphia, Presbyterian board of publication*, [1859].

Smith (Robert, *d. d.*) Harmonics, or the philosophy of musical sounds. xvi, 292 pp. 7 l. 25 pl. 8°. *Cambridge, J. Bentham*, 1749.

Smith (Robert Payne, *d. d.*) Prophecy a preparation for Christ. Eight lectures preached before the university of Oxford in the year 1869. xxx, 1 p. l. 415 pp. 8°. *London, Macmillan & co.* 1869.

[BAMPTON (The) lectures for 1869].

Smith (Roswell C.) English grammar on the productive system: a method of instruction

Smith (Roswell C.)—continued.
recently adopted in Germany and Switzerland. 2d ed. 192 pp. 12°. *Boston, Perkins & Marvin*, 1832.

——— Intellectual and practical grammar, in a series of inductive questions, connected with exercises in composition. 276 pp. 12°. *Providence, author*, 1829.

Smith (R. F.) Smith's universal guide, to the country along the line of the Missouri, Kansas and Texas railway. Also historic sketches of all the towns on the line. 1 p. l. 214 pp. 1 map. 8°. *Sedalia (Mo.) R. F. Smith*, 1871.

Smith (Samuel B.) A synopsis of the moral theology of the church of Rome, taken from the works of st. Ligori, and translated from the latin into english. 412 pp. 4 pl. 16°. *New York, office of Downfall of Babylon*, 1836.

Smith (Samuel J.) Miscellaneous [poetical] writings. Collected and arranged by one of the family. With a notice illustrative of his life and character. 2 p. l. 9–222 pp. 1 pl. 8°. *Philadelphia, H. Perkins*, 1836.

Smith (Seba). Powhatan; a metrical romance, in seven cantos. 199 pp. 12°. *New York, Harper & brothers*, 1841.

Smith (Stephen, *m. d.*) Hand-book of surgical operations. 279 pp. 16°. *New York, Baillière brothers*, 1862.

Smith (*Rev.* Stephen R.) The causes of infidelity removed. 4 p. l. 352 pp. 16°. *Utica, [N. Y.] Grosh & Hutchinson*, 1839.

——— Memoir of the late rev. John Freeman. 120 pp. 12°. *Utica, A. B. Grosh*, 1835.

Smith (*Sir* Thomas, 1514–77). De repvblica Anglorvm. The maner of gouernement or policie of the realme of England. [2d ed.] 4 p. l. 119 pp. sm. 4°. *London, H. Midleton for G. Seton*, 1584.

Smith (*Rev.* T. Ralston). Presbyterian's hand-book. *See* **Parker** (Joel, *d. d.*) *and* **Smith.**

Smith (*Rev.* Theyre Townsend). Man's responsibility in reference to his religious belief, explained and applied. xxviii, 242 pp. 8°. *London, B. Fellowes*, 1840.
[HULSEAN lectures for the year 1839].

Smith (Thomas). Select memoirs of the lives, labours, and sufferings, of those pious and learned english and scottish divines, who greatly distinguished themselves in promoting the reformation from popery; in translating the bible; and who ultimately crowned the venerable edifice with the celebrated Westminster confession of faith, &c. 2d ed. 2 p. l. 724 pp. 1 portrait. 8°. *Glasgow, D. Mackenzie*, 1828.

Smith (Walter). Examples for first practice in free-hand outline drawing. 29 l. obl. 8°. *Boston, Frost & Adams*, [1871].

——— School of art. Model and object drawing book. Being the second part of examples for practice in free-hand outline drawing. 39 l. obl. 8. *Boston, Frost & Adams*, [1871].

Smith (William, *d. d. provost of the college of Pennsylvania*). A general idea of the college of Mirania; with method of teaching and account of its rise, establishment and buildings, etc. [*anon.*] 86 pp. sm. 4°. *New York, J. Parker, etc.* 1753.

Smith (William, *m. d.*) The nature and institution of government; containing an account of the feudal and english policy. 2 v. 10 p. l. 476 pp.; 2 p. l. 435 pp. 8°. *London, author*, 1771.

Smith (William, *ll. d.*) The illustrated history of the bible: from the creation of the world to the close of the apostolic era. Being a full and complete account of the events narrated in the sacred scriptures. [Also], the history of the Jews of the dispersion, from the taking of Jerusalem by Titus, down to the present time. Abridged from "Milman's history of the jews." Edited by rev. Arthur P. Hayes. xxxv, 21–1105 pp. 3 maps, 1 pl. 8°. [*Philadelphia*], *National publishing co.* [1871].

——— A smaller history of english and american literature. *See* **Shaw** (Thomas B.)

——— *and* **Hall** (Theophilus D.) A copious and critical english-latin dictionary. To which is added a dictionary of proper names. xii, 754 pp. 8°. *New York, Harper & brothers*, 1871.

Smith (William A. *d. d.*) Lectures on the philosophy and practice of slavery, as exhibited in the institution of domestic slavery in the United States; with the duties of masters to slaves. Edited by Thomas O. Summers, d. d. 328 pp. 12°. *Nashville (Tenn.) Stevenson & Evans*, 1856.

Smith (William B. *editor*). *See* **Educational** year-book, 1872.

Smith (W. C. *of Wotton, Eng.*) Maxims, reflections, and observations, with other miscellaneous writings in prose and poetry. xv, 240 pp. 4 l. 16°. *Gloucester, Jew & Bryant*, 1834.

Smith (William Loughton, *ll. d.*) A comparative view of the constitutions of the several states with each other, and with that of the United States: presenting the most prominent features of each constitution. Revised and extended by E. S. Davis. 135 pp. 8°. *Washington, Thompson & Homans*, 1832.

Smith (William L. G.) Observations on China and the Chinese. 216 pp. 12°. *New York, Carleton*, 1863.

Smith (William Pitt). The universalist. In seven letters to Amyntor. 306 pp. 16°. *New-York, F. Childs*, 1787.

Smith (Worthington, *d. d.*) Select sermons. With a memoir of his life, by rev. Joseph Torrey, d. d. xi, 368 pp. 12°. *Andover, W. F. Draper*, 1861.

Smith. *See* **Smyth.**

Smits (Dirk). De Rottestroom. [In drie zangen]. 26 p. l. 180 pp. 1 l. 4 pl. 1 map, 1 portrait. 4°. *Rotterdam, P. Losel*, 1750.

Smitt (Frédéric de). Frédéric ii, Catherine, et le partage de la Pologne. D'après des documens authentiques. 2 v. in 1. 6 p. l. 165 pp; 1 p. l. xxvi, 237, 1, 69 pp. 8°. *Paris, A. Franck*, 1861.

Smucker. *See* **Schmucker.**

Smull (John A.) Rules and decisions of the general assembly of Pennsylvania. *See* **Pennsylvania** (*State of*).

Smyrna (*Church of*). Circular epistle of the church of Smyrna concerning the martyrdom of st. Polycarp. 12°. [*Oxford*, 1840].
[*In* WAKE (William). The genuine epistles of the apostolical fathers, pp. 192–202].

Smyth (*Rev.* Charles Bohun). Christian metaphysics, or Plato, Malebranche and Gioberti, the old and new ontologists compared with the modern schools of psychology. 2 p. l. 311, 261 pp. 8°. *London, E. Palmer & son*, 1851.

Smyth (George, *esq. of North Nibley, Gloucestershire*). The vanity of conquests, and universal monarchy: being a succinct account of all the great conquerors and heroes, both of ancient and modern ages. Deduc'd from Nimrod to Lewis xiv. of France. 11 p. l. 359 pp. 1 portrait. 8°. *London, R. Smith*, 1705.

Smyth (*Mrs.* Gillespie). Olympia Morata, her times, life and writings. By the author of "Selwyn," etc. [*anon.*] 4th ed. xvi, 303 pp. 3 l. 3 pl. 16°. *London, Smith, Elder & co.* 1840.

Smyth (Thomas, *d. d. of Charleston, S. C.*) By whom is the world to be converted? or christians Christ's representatives and agents for the conversion of the world. 108 pp. 18°. *Philadelphia, Presbyterian board of publication*, [1856].

——— Ecclesiastical republicanism; or the republicanism, liberality, and catholicity of presbytery, in contrast with prelacy and popery. 323 pp. 12°. *Boston, Crocker & Brewster*, 1843.

——— The exodus of the church of Scotland: and the claims of the free church of Scotland to the sympathy and assistance of american christians. 2d ed. 146 pp. 18°. *New York, Leavitt, Trow & co.* 1844.

——— The history, character, and results of the Westminster assembly of divines. 124 pp. 12°. *New-York, Leavitt, Trow & co.* 1844.

——— The name, nature, and functions, of ruling elders; wherein it is shown from the testimony of scripture, the fathers, and the reformers, that ruling elders are not presbyters or bishops. xvi, 186 pp. 12°. *New-York, M. H. Newman, etc.* 1845.

Smyth (William, *d. d.*) A future world in which mankind shall survive their mortal durations, demonstrated by rational evidence, from natural and moral arguments, against the atheist's pretentions. 22 p. l. 414 pp. 8°. *London, T. M. for R. Clavel*, 1688.

Smyth (William, *prof. of history, Cambridge, Eng.* 1766–1849). Evidences of christianity. 4 p. l. xxxv, 392 pp. 12°. *London, W. Pickering*, 1845.

Smyth. *See* **Smith.**

Smythe (*Rev.* W. Herbert). The invitation answered; a reply to dr. J. Kent Stone's "Invitation heeded," and to his holiness, pope Pius the ninth's invitation to the vatican council. 360 pp. 12°. *New York, P. F. Smith*, 1871.

Smythies (*Mrs.* — Gordon). The marrying man. By the author of "Cousin Geoffrey." [*anon.*] 3 v. 12°. *London, R. Bentley*, 1841.

——— A warning to wives: or, the platonic lover. By the author of "Cousin Geoffrey." [*anon.*] 3 v. 12°. *London, T. C. Newby*, 1848.

Snart (Charles). Selection of poems. 2 v. 10 p. l. 468 pp; 7 p. l. 466 pp. 8°. *London, Longman, Hurst, Rees & Orme*, 1808.

Sneed (William C. *m. d.*) A report on the history and mode of management of the Kentucky penitentiary, from its origin, in 1798, to March 1, 1860. vi, 614 pp. 6 pl. 8°. *Frankfort (Ky.) state printer*, 1860.

Snellaert (Ferdinand Augustin). Nederlandsche gedichten uit de veertiende eeuw van Jan Boendale, Hein van Aken en anderen, naar het oxfordsch handschrift. 2 p. l. xlvi, 831 pp. 8°. *Brussel, M. Hayez*, 1869. s.

Snethen (*Rev.* Nicholas). Snethen on lay representation, or essay on lay representation and church government. 384 pp. 12°. *Baltimore, J. J. Harrod*, 1835.

Snow (Caleb Hopkins, *m. d.*) A geography of Boston, county of Suffolk and the adjacent towns. With historical notes. 162 pp. 2 maps, 1 pl. 16°. *Boston, Carter & Hendee*, 1830.

Snowflake (The): a holiday gift, for 1850, 1851, 1852, and 1854. 4 v. 12°. *Philadelphia, E. H. Butler & co.* 1850–54. s.

Social (The) enchantress. Presenting an elegant selection of the most favourite songs. [With music. *anon.*] 5 p. l. 350 pp. 1 pl. 12°. *London, J. Fielding*, 1783.

Societyism and its evils, 1871. *See* **Batchelder** (James L.)

Some enquiries into the effects of fermented liquors. *See* **Montagu** (Basil).

Some primitive doctrines reviv'd. *See* **Campbell** (Archibald).

Somer (Jan). Zee en landt reyse, gedaen naer de Levante, als Italien, Candien, Cypres, Egypten, Rhodes, Archipelago, Turckyen: en wederom door Duytslant. 2° druck. 47 l. 6 pl. in text. sm. 4°. *Amsterdam, J. Hartgers*, 1649.

Somers (Robert). The southern states since the war. 1870–1. xii, 286 pp. 1 map. 8°. *London, Macmillan & co.* 1871.

Somerville (The), Arlington, and Belmont [Mass.] directory for 1871–72. Compiled and published by Greenough, Jones & co. 8°. *Somerville*, 1871.

Something to do. A novel. [*anon.*] 1 p. l. 150 pp. 8°. *Boston, J. R. Osgood & co.* 1871.

Sommaire recveil des raisons plus importantes. 1608. *See* **Usselincx** (Willem).

Sömmerring (Detmar Wilhelm). De oculorum hominis animaliumque sectione horizontali commentatio. 78 pp. 2 l. 4 pl. fol. *Goettingae, Vandenhoeck & Ruprecht*, 1818. s.

Song (The) journal. A repertoire of music and literature. [Monthly]. Jan. to Dec. 1871. v. i. 4°. *Detroit, C. J. Whitney & co.* 1871.

Song (The) messenger monthly. Jan. to Dec. 1871. v. 9. 4°. *Chicago, Root & Cady*, 1871.

[*Previously known as the* Song messenger of the northwest].

Songs in the night: or hymns for the sick and suffering. With an introduction by rev. A. C. Thompson. [*anon.*] 6th ed. 288 pp. 16°. *Boston, J. E. Tilton & co.* 1859.

Songs of Zion enlarged. A manual of the best and most popular hymns and tunes for social and private devotion. [*anon.*] 384 pp. 18°. *New York, American tract society*, [1864].

Songster's (The) museum; or, a trip to Elysium. A selection of the most approved songs, duets, etc. With the notes. [*anon.*] 204 pp. 16°. *Northampton (Mass.) A. Wright for S. & E. Butler*, 1803.

Songsters' (The) repository; being a choice selection of the most esteemed songs, many of which have not heretofore been published. [*anon.*] 286 pp. 1 pl. 12°. *New York, N. Dearborn*, 1811.

Sonnerat (Pierre). Voyage aux Indes Orientales et à la Chine, fait par ordre du roi, depuis 1774 jusqu'en 1781. 2 v. xv, 318 pp. 80 pl; 4 p. l. viii, 298 pp. 81–140 pl. 4°. *Paris, l'auteur*, 1782.

Sophocles. Σοφοκλεους Αντιγονη. The Antigone. The greek text revised and corrected, with an introduction, and critical and explanatory notes, for the use of academies and colleges. By M. J. Smead. 242 pp. 12°. *New York, D. Appleton & co.* 1871.

——— Œdipus tyrannus, Œdipus coloneus, et Antigone. 8°. [*London, C. & J. Rivington*, 1825].

[*In* TROLLOPE (William). Pentalogia græca, pp. 1–297].

——— The same. 8°. [*Oxonii, apud J. & J. Fletcher*, 1779].

[*In* BURTON (John, *m. d.*) Pentalogia, v. 1, pp. 1–317].

——— The Œdipus tyrannus, with notes and a critique on the subject of the play. By I. W. Stuart. 222 pp. 12°. *New York, Gould & Newman*, 1837.

Sophocles (Evangelinus Apostolides). History of the greek alphabet and pronunciation. 2d ed. 120 pp. 12°. *Cambridge, [Ms.] J. Bartlett*, 1854.

Sorbière (Samuel). Relation d'vn voyage en Angleterre. [1663]? 4 p. l. 180 pp. 2 l. 18°. *Cologne, P. Michel*, 1669.

Sorin (*Rev.* M.) The domestic circle; or, moral and social duties explained and enforced on scriptural principles, in a series of discourses. 260 pp. 12°. *Philadelphia, J. Harmstead*, 1840.

Soter (Johannes). Epigrammata graeca vetervm elegantissima, eademq; latina ab utriusq; linguæ uiris doctissimis uersa, atq; in rem studiosorum è diuersis autoribus per Iohannē Soterem collecta, nuncque iterum edita. 2 p. l. 322 pp. 16°. *Coloniae*, 1528.

Soule (*Mrs.* Caroline A.) Home life; or, a peep across the threshold. 249 pp. 4 pl. 12°. *Boston, A. Tompkins & B. B. Mussey, & co.* 1854.

Soulé (George). Analytic and philosophic commercial & exchange calculator; in which the principles of the science of numbers are applied to the solution of commercial and exchange calculations, on an entirely new system. xix, 860 pp. 8°. *New Orleans, Hinck & co.* 1872.

Soule (Richard). A dictionary of english synonymes and synonymous or parallel expressions, designed as a practical guide to aptness and variety of phraseology. iv, 2 p. l. 456 pp. 12°. *Boston, Little, Brown & co.* 1871.

Soules (The) implantation. *See* **Hooker** (*Rev.* Thomas).

Soulié (Melchior Frédéric). Au jour le jour. 2 v. in 1. 179 pp; 173 pp. 24°. *Bruxelles, A. Lebègue & Sacré fils*, 1844.

——— Si jeunesse savait! si vieillesse pouvait! 4 v. 16°. *Bruxelles, Meline, Cans & co.* 1844.

South Carolina (*State of*). Journal of the house of representatives of the state of South Carolina, being the regular session of 1870–'71. 1 p. l. 694, 134, 5 pp. 8°. *Columbia (S. C.) Republican printing co.* 1871.

——— Journal of the senate of the state of South Carolina, being the regular session, commencing November 22, 1870. 632, 141, 36 pp. 8°. *Columbia (S. C.) J. W. Denny*, 1870.

——— Reports and resolutions of the general assembly of the state of South Carolina, at the regular session, 1870–'71. 8°. *Columbia (S. C.) Republican printing co.* 1871.

Southern (A) home. By a Virginian. [*anon.*] 2d ed. 233 pp. 8 pl. sq. 16°. *Richmond, A. Morris*, 1855.

Southern (The) illustrated news. [Weekly]. Sept. 13, 1862, to Sept. 5, 1863. v. 1 and nos. 2–9 of v. 2. fol. *Richmond, Ayres & Wade*, 1862–63.

Southern (The) magazine. [Monthly]. Jan. to Dec. 1871. v. 8–9. [New series, v. 1–2]. 8°. *Baltimore, Murdoch, Browne & Hill*, [1871].

Southern passages and pictures. 1839. *See* **Simms** (William Gilmore).

Southern (The) psalmist; new revised and improved edition. xxxii, 706, 22, 14 pp. 1 l. 24°. *Memphis, Goodwyn & co.* [1871].

Southern punch. John W. Overall, editor. [Weekly]. Sept. 19, 1863, to April 9, 1864. v. 1, no. 6, to v. 2, no. 9. 4°. *Richmond, Overall, Campbell, Hughes & co.* 1863–64. [Incomplete].

Southern (The) review. A. T. Bledsoe, ll. d. editor. Jan. to April, 1871. v. 9. 8°. *Baltimore, Poisal & Roszell*, 1871.

Southey (Robert). Oliver Newman: a New England tale (unfinished): with other poetical remains. [Edited by Herbert Hill]. xv, 116 pp. 16°. *London, Longman*, 1845.

——— Thalaba, the destroyer. A rhythmical romance. 2 v. 274 pp; 277 pp. 18°. *Boston, T. B. Wait & co. & C. Williams*, 1812.

Southgate (Henry). Many thoughts of many minds: selections from celebrated authors. 20th thousand. xl, 682 pp. 8°. *London, C. Griffin & co.* 1870.

——— Noble thoughts in noble language: a collection of wise and virtuous utterances in prose and verse. 4 p. l. 726 pp. 8°. *London, Ward, Lock & Tyler*, [1870].

Southgate (Horatio, *d. d.*) Narrative of a visit to the Syrian (Jacobite) church of Mesopotamia; with reflections upon the present state of christianity in Turkey, and the character and prospects of the eastern churches. 275 pp. 1 map. 12°. *New York, D. Appleton & co.* 1844.

——— Parochial sermons. Sermons for some of the principal festivals and fasts of the church, and on christian doctrine and duty. 315 pp. 12°. *New York, D. Dana, jr.* 1859.

Southworth (*Mrs.* Emma Dorothy Eliza Nevitte). The bridal eve. 1 p. l. 19–446 pp. 12°. *Philadelphia, T. B. Peterson & brothers*, [1864].

——— Cruel as the grave. 372 pp. 12°. *Philadelphia, T. B. Peterson & brothers*, [1871].

Southworth (*Mrs.* E. D. E. N.)—continued.
——— The gypsy's prophecy. A tale of real life. 1 p. l. 23-455 pp. 12°. *Philadelphia, T. B. Peterson & brothers,* [1861].
——— The lady of the isle. A romance from real life. 3 p. l. 27-598 pp. 1 pl. 12°. *Philadelphia, T. B. Peterson & brothers,* 1859.
——— Love's labor won. 1 p. l. 21-383 pp. 12°. *Philadelphia, T. B. Peterson & brothers,* [1862].
——— The mother-in-law. A tale of domestic life. 497 pp. 12°. *Philadelphia, T. B. Peterson & brothers,* [1860].
——— Tried for her life. A sequel to "Cruel as the grave." 2 p. l. 21-356 pp. 12°. *Philadelphia, T. B. Peterson & brothers,* [1871].

Southworth (*Mrs.* S. A.) Alice Lee; or, the Maine law triumphant. 240 pp. 4 pl. 12°. *New York, Hall & brother,* 1855.

Souvestre (Émile). En famille. 2 p. l. 282 pp. 1 l. 12°. *Paris, M. Lévy,* 1859.
——— En quarantaine. Scènes et moeurs des grèves. Nouvelle éd. 3 p. l. 262 pp. 12°. *Paris, M. Lévy frères,* 1856.
——— Histoires d'autrefois. Nouvelle éd. 2 p. l. 248 pp. 12°. *Paris, M. Lévy frères,* 1859.
——— Le monde tel qu'il sera. Nouv. éd. 2 p. l. 316 pp. 16°. *Paris, M. Lévy frères,* 1859.
——— The flower-garden, a collection of short tales and historical sketches. From the french. By S. J. Donaldson, jr. 296 pp. sq. 16°. *Baltimore, J. Murphy & co.* 1864.
——— The little orator, and other tales. From the french. By S. J. Donaldson, jr. 92 pp. 24°. *Baltimore, J. Murphy & co.* 1864.
——— The mother of Washington, and other tales. From the french. By S. J. Donaldson, jr. 89 pp. 24°. *Baltimore, J. Murphy & co.* 1864.
——— A visit to ancient Rome. From the french. By S. J. Donaldson, jr. 104 pp. 24°. *Baltimore, J. Murphy & co.* 1864.

Souza (Adèle Filleul, *comtesse* de Flahaut, *baronne* de). Oeuvres complètes de madame de Souza, revues, corrigées, augmentées, imprimées sous les yeux de l'auteur, et ornées de gravures. 6 v. 8°. *Paris, A. Eymery,* 1821-22.

CONTENTS.

v. 1. Adèle de Sénange.
Charles et Marie.
v. 2. Eugénie et Mathilde.
v. 3. Eugénie et Mathilde [cont.]
Eugène de Rothlin.

Souza (Adèle Filleul)—continued.

v. 4. La comtesse de Fargy.
v. 5. Émile et Alphonse.
v. 6. Mademoiselle de Tournon.

Sovles (The) humiliation. *See* **Hooker** (*Rev.* Thomas).

Spain. Aggreatie des grootmachtichsten coninck van Hispagnien Philips den derden, ghesonden aen de heeren den staten generael vande Gheunieerde Provintien. Mitsgaders d'antwoorde vande selve generale staten. *b. l.* 4 l. sm. 4°. [*n. p.*] 1608.
[*In* NEDERLANDTSCHE bye-corf].
——— Coleccion de cédulas, cartas-patentes, provisiones, reales ordenes y otros documentos concernientes á las provincias vascongadas, copiados de orden de s. m. 6 v. sm. 4°. *Madrid, imprenta real,* 1829-33.

CONTENTS.

v. 1-2. Condado y señorio de Vizcaya.
v. 3. Provincia de Guipuzcoa.
v. 4. Provincia y hermandades de Alava.
v. 5-6. Coleccion de privilegios, franquezas, exenciones y fueros, concedidos á varios pueblos y corporaciones de la corona de Castilla.

——— (*Observatorio de marina de S. Fernando*). Almanaque nautico para el año 1868. xiii, 478 pp. 8°. *Cadiz, imprenta de la revista medica,* 1866. s.

Spalding (*Rev.* Joshua). The divine theory; a system of divinity, founded wholly upon Christ; which, by one principle, offers an explanation of all the works of God. 2 v. 440 pp. 4 l; 2 p. l. 323 pp. 8°. *Elizabethtown (N. J.) S. Kollock,* 1808-12.

Spalding (Martin John, *d. d.*) D'Aubigné's "History of the great reformation in Germany and Switzerland," reviewed; or the reformation in Germany examined in its instruments, causes and manner, and in its influence in religion, government, literature, and general civilization. 379 pp. 1 pl. 12°. *Baltimore, J. Murphy,* 1844.

Spalding. *See* **Spaulding.**

Spanheim (Friedrich). Historia Jobi, sive de obscuris historiæ commentatio. Ed. altera. 2 v. in 1. 5 p. l. 392 pp; 687 pp. 12°. *Ratisponæ, sumptibus J. Z. Seidelii,* 1710.
[SERPILIUS (Georg). Lebens-beschreibungen der biblischen scribenten. *Regenspurg,* 1708-15. v. 12-13].
——— Histoire de la papesse Jeanne, fidèlement tirée de la dissertation latine de Spanheim [par Lenfant]. 3e éd. augmentée. 2 v. in 1. 21 p. l. 286 pp. 1 l. 5 pl; 1 p. l. 284 pp. 2 l. 16°. *La Haye, J. van den Kieboom,* [1758].

Spanmüller (Jakub). *See* **Pontanus** (Jacob)

Sparks from a locomotive. 1859. *See* **Fuller** (Hiram).

Sparrman (Anders). Voyage au cap de Bonne-Espérance, et autour du monde avec le capitaine Cook, et principalement dans le pays des Hottentots et des Caffres. Traduit [d'après une version anglaise] par m. P. LeTourneur. 2 v. 1 p. l. xxiv, 478 pp. 3 pl; 2 p. l. 462 pp. 13 pl. 8°. *Paris, Buisson,* 1787.

Spaulding (*Rev.* John). Stories of the ocean; or, gems from sea-faring life. Eng. title, 177 pp. 3 pl. 18°. *New York, R. Carter & brothers,* 1860.

Spaulding. *See* **Spalding.**

Spear (Charles). Names and titles of the lord Jesus Christ. 400 pp. 12°. *Boston, B. B. Mussey & A. Tompkins,* 1841.

Specimens of the german lyric poets: consisting of translations in verse, from the works of Bürger, Goethe, Klopstock, Schiller, &c. Interspersed with biographical notices. [*anon.*] 2 p. l. ii, iii, 152 pp. 8°. *London, Boosey & sons,* 1822.

Spectacle (Le) de la nature. *See* **Pluche** (Noël Antoine, *l'abbé*).

Spectacles for little eyes. 1862. *See* **Lander** (Sarah W.)

Spectateur (Le) militaire. Recueil de science, d'art et d'histoire militaires. 3e série. Octobre, 1870–décembre, 1871. v. 22–25. 8°. *Paris, à la direction du Spectateur militaire,* 1870–71.

[*Note.*—v. 23 is a monograph on the war of 1870, by V. D . . .].

Spectator (The). Selections from the Spectator; embracing the most interesting papers by Addison, Steele, and others. 2 v. 326 pp; 316 pp. 18°. *New York, Harper & brothers,* 1839.

[HARPERS' School district library, nos. 84–85].

Spectator (The): an american review of insurance. [Monthly]. Jan. to Dec. 1871. v. 6–7. 4°. *New York and Chicago,* [*J. H. & C. M. Goodsell,* 1871].

Spectator (The). A weekly review of politics, literature, theology, and art. Jan. 7 to Dec. 31, 1871. v. 44. fol. *London, J. Campbell,* [1871].

Speculatist (The). A collection of letters and essays, moral and political, serious and humorous: upon various subjects. [*anon.* written 1725–28]. 4 p. l. 283 pp. 8°. *London, J. Walthoe,* 1732.

62

Spee (Friedrich von). Friderici Spee cautio criminalis seu de processibus contra sagas liber, magistratibus Germaniæ hoc tempore summe necessarius. Accessione instructionis pro formandis processibus in causis strygum, sortilegorum, & maleficorum, locupletatus per A. D. M. C. A. 4 p. l. 428 pp. 2 l. 16°. *Augustæ Vindelicorum, sumptibus F. J. Schenfæssel,* 1731.

Speed (John). The county palatine of Chester. 4°. [*Shrewsbury & Providence Grove,* 1838].

[*In* HULBERT (Charles). Cheshire antiquities. 1838. pp. 57–61]

——— The genealogies recorded in the sacred scriptures, according to euery family and tribe. With the line of our sauiour Iesvs Christ obserued from Adam to the blessed virgin Mary. By I. S. [*anon.*] 1 p. l. 34 pp. 4°. [*London, R. Barker, about* 1610].

[*With* BIBLE. (*English*). Genevan version. *London, R. Barker,* 1610.
Note.—Engraved upon copper-plates, except the title].

——— The same. [*anon.*] 1 p. l. 34 pp. 4°. [*London, R. Barker,* 1615].

[*With* BIBLE. (*English*). Genevan version. *London, R. Barker,* 1615].

——— The same. [*anon.*] 1 p. l. 34 pp. 2 l. 4°. [*London, R. Barker,* 1634]?

[*With* BIBLE. (*English*). Genevan version. *London, R. Barker,* 1634].

Spel (Het) van Brasilien. Vergheleecken by een goedt verkeer-spel. [*anon.*] 4 l. sm. 4°. [*n. p.*] *ghedrucht in't iaer ons heeren* 1638.

Spelman (Edward). Additional observations on the greek accents: a supplement to what has been already said on that subject, in the preface to the roman antiquities of Dionysius halicarnassensis. Published by the rev. mr. Lemon. 8°. *London, J. Nourse,* 1773.

[*In* LEMON (*Rev.* G. W.) Two tracts. *London,* 1773. Tract 1, or pp. 1–50, 1 pl.]

Spelman (*Sir* Henry). De non temerandis ecclesiis. Chvrches not to be violated. A tract of the rights and respects due unto churches. 4th ed. 3 p. l. 7, 128 pp. 16°. *Oxford, H. Hall for A. Curteyn,* 1668.

Spelman (*Sir* John). Ælfredi magni Anglorum regis invictissimi vita tribus libris comprehensa, a clarissimo dno. Johanne Spelman, primum anglice conscripta, dein latine reddita, & annotationibus illustrata. 20 p. l. 220 pp. 6 l. 7 pl. fol. *Oxonii, e theatro sheldoniano,* 1678.

——— The same. The life of Alfred the Great, from the original manuscript in the bodlejan library: with additions, and historical remarks, by Thomas Hearne. 3 p. l. 238 pp. 5 l. 1 portrait. 8°. *Oxford, M. Atkins,* 1709.

Spence (Joseph, *d. d.*) A parallel; in the manner of Plutarch: between a most celebrated man of Florence [Magliabecchi]; and one, scarce ever heard of, in England, [Robert Hill]. 104 pp. 12°. *Strawberry-hill, W. Robinson*, 1758.

——— The same. 2d ed. 104 pp. 12°. *London, for the benefit of mr. Hill*, 1759.

Spencer (Ichabod Smith, *d. d.*) Sermons. With a sketch of his life, by rev. J. M. Sherwood. 2 v. 1 p. l. 473 pp. 1 portrait; 479 pp. 12°. *New York, M. W. Dodd*, 1855.

Spencer (Jesse Ames, *d. d.*) The christian instructed in the ways of the gospel and the church: a series of discourses delivered in St. James's church, Goshen, N. Y. during the years 1840–42. xvii, 326 pp. 16°. *New York, D. Appleton & co.* 1844.

——— The young ruler who had great possessions. And other discourses, chiefly practical. 246 pp. 12°. *New York, A. D. F. Randolph*, 1871.

Spencer (John). Bible illustrations, a storehouse of similes, allegories, and anecdotes, selected from Spencer's "Things new and old," and other sources. With an introduction by the rev. Richard Newton, d. d. And a copious index. xi, 360 pp. 12°. *Philadelphia, Smith, English & co.* 1863.

Spencer (*Rev.* Theodore). Conversion; its theory and process, practically delineated. 408 pp. 12°. *New York, M. W. Dodd*, 1854.

Spenser (Edmund). Dispersed poems, not in any edition of his works: and now first collected [by F. G. Waldron]. 12 pp. 8°. [*London*, 1792].

[*In* WALDRON (F. G.) Literary museum. *London*, 1792].

——— Faerie queene. *Boston*, 1836. *See* **Holiness.**

Spenser society publications, nos. 6, 8–11. 4°. *London, Spenser society*, 1871.

CONTENTS.

ROBINSON (Clement) *and others.* A handefull of pleasant delites, no. 8.
WATSON (Thomas). The ἑκατομπαθια or passionate centurie of love, no. 6.
WITHER (George). Ivvenilia, nos. 9, 10, and 11.

Sperling (Johann). Carpologia physica posthuma, opusculum utile ac jucundum, nunc secundum prodiens e museo G. C. Kirchmajeri. 4 p. l. 230 pp. 18°. *Wittebergae, impensis haeredum J. Bergeri*, 1668.

Spiegel (Jacob). In Alfonsi dicta factaqve et Aeneae Syluij commentarios scholia. sm. 4°. *Witebergae, Crato*, 1585.

[BECCADELLI (Antonio). De dictis et factis Alfonsi. 1585. pp. 201–298].

Spielhagen (Friedrich). Problematische naturen. Roman. 2e aufl. 1 p. l. 609 pp. 8°. *Berlin, O. Janke*, 1863.

Spietz (August *and* Friedrich). Deutsches lesebuch für mittlere gymnasialklassen und realschulen. 2e aufl. xxxii, 464 pp. 8°. *Bielefeld, Velhagen & Klasing*, 1854.

Spiker (S. H.) Travels through England, Wales, & Scotland, in the year 1816. Translated from the german. 2 v. 20, 325 pp; 2 p. l. 283 pp. 12°. *London, Lackington, Hughes, Harding, Mavor, & Jones*, 1820.

Spilberghen (Joris van). Historis journael van de voyagie gedaen naer d' Oost-Indien, onder 't beleydt van den com. J. van Spilberghen. 1601–04. Hier is achter by gevoeght de beschrijvinge van het eylandt Java. 62 pp. 2 pl. in text. sm. 4°. *Amsterdam, J. Hartgers*, 1652.

——— The same. Als meede vande tweede voyage ghedaen na d' Oost-Indien onder den admirael Steven vander Hagen. [1603–06]. 96 pp. 6 pl. on 1 sheet. sm. 4°. *Amsterdam, J. Hartgers*, 1648.

[*In* HARTGERTS (J.) Oost-indische voyagien, v. 1, 5e stuck].

——— Oost- en west-indische voyagie; door de strate Magallanes naer de Moluques onder den commandeur Ioris Spilberghen. [1615–17]. Als mede de reyse ghedaen door Willem Cornelisz Schouten van Hoorn, en Iacob le Maire, 1615–17. 120 pp. 6 pl. on 1 sheet. sm. 4°. *Amstelredam, J. Hartgerts*, 1648.

[*In* HARTGERTS (J.) Oost-indische voyagien, v. 1, 8e stuck].

Spinola (Fabio Ambrogio). Compendio delle meditazioni sopra la vita di Gesu' Cristo, per ciascun giorno dell' anno. Eng. title, 17 p. l. 730 pp. 1 l. 16°. *Venezia, A. Posetti*, 1730.

Spitta (Carl Johann Philipp). Lyra domestica; translated from the "Psaltery and harp" of C. J. P. Spitta, by Richard Massie. With additional selections by rev. F. D. Huntington, d. d. xxii, 300 pp. 16°. *Boston, E. P. Dutton & co.* 1861.

Spofford (*Mrs.* Harriet Elizabeth Prescott). New-England legends. 4 p. l. 40 pp. 8°. *Boston, J. R. Osgood & co.* 1871.

Spooner (C. E.) Narrow gauge railways. viii, 128 pp. 27 pl. 8°. *London, E. & F. N. Spon*, 1871.

Spooner (Shearjashub, *m. d.*) Guide to sound teeth, or a popular treatise on the teeth, illustrating the whole judicious management of

Spooner (S. *m. d.*) —continued. these organs from infancy to old age, etc. viii, 3–208 pp. 12°. *New-York, Wiley & Long*, 1836.

Spooner (Thomas). Memorial of William Spooner, 1637, and of his descendants to the third generation; of his great-grandson, Elnathan Spooner, and of his descendants, to 1871. Private ed. 242 pp. 8°. *Cincinnati, R. Clarke & co.* 1871.

Sports and pastimes for in-doors and out. With additions by Oliver Optic, [W. T. Adams], embracing physical and intellectual amusements for young people, the family circle and evening parties. [*anon.*] 431 pp. 2 pl. 16°. *Boston, G. W. Cottrell*, [1863].

Sprague (Alfred White). The elements of natural philosophy. 368 pp. 2 pl. 12°. *Boston, Phillips, Sampson & co.* 1856. s.

Sprague (William Buell, *d. d.*) Hints designed to regulate the intercourse of christians. vi, 269 pp. 12°. *Albany, Packard & Van Benthuysen*, 1834.

——— Lectures illustrating the contrast between true christianity and various other systems. viii, 386 pp. 12°. *New York, D. Appleton & co.* 1837.

——— Lectures on revivals of religion. With an essay by Leonard Woods, d. d. Also letters from the reverend doctors Alexander, Wayland, [etc.] 287, 165 pp. 8°. *Albany, Webster & Skinners*, 1832.

——— The same. 2d ed. with additional letters. xxviii, 400 pp. 12°. *New York, D. Appleton & co.* 1833.

——— Memoirs of the rev. John McDowell, d. d. and the rev. William McDowell, d. d. 305 pp. 1 portrait. 12°. *New York, R. Carter & brothers*, 1864.

Sprenger (Aloys, *m. d.*) A catalogue of the arabic, persian and hindustany manuscripts of the libraries of the king of Oudh. *Calcutta*, 1851. *See* **Great Britain.** (*India department*).

Spring (Gardiner, *d. d.*) The contrast between good and bad men, illustrated by the biography and truths of the bible. 2 v. 417 pp; 413 pp. 12°. *New York, M. W. Dodd*, 1855.

——— Memoir of Samuel John Mills. 2d ed. viii, 259 pp. 16°. *Boston, Perkins & Marvin*, 1829.

——— The mercy seat; thoughts suggested by the Lord's prayer. 383 pp. 12°. *New York, M. W. Dodd*, 1850.

Spring (Gardiner, *d. d.*)—continued.

——— The mission of sorrow. 144 pp. 16°. *New York, American tract society*, [1863].

——— A pastor's tribute to one of his family. The memoirs of the late Hannah L. Murray. 312 pp. 1 pl. 8°. *New York, R. Carter & brothers*, 1849.

Spring (Samuel). The rose of Persia; or, Giafar Al Barmeki. A tale of the east. 2d ed. 2 v. in 1. 2 p. l. 236 pp; 1 p. l. 210 pp. 1 l. 12°. *New York, Harper & bros.* 1847.

Spring (The) morning, and other allegories. [*anon.*] 143 pp. 18°. *Philadelphia, American sunday school union*, [1842].

Spring work. Stories of Vinegar hill, v. 6. *See* **Warner** (Susan).

Springfield (*Mass.*) *City library association.* Catalogue of the library. xii, 668 pp. 1 pl. 8°. *Springfield, S. Bowles & co.* 1871.

Sproull (T. *d. d.*) Explanation of the words of institution [of the lord's supper]. 12°. [*Pittsburgh*, 1872].

[*In* REFORMED presbyterian church in North America, memorial volume, pp. 139–141].

Spurzheim (Johann Gaspar). Observations on the deranged manifestations of the mind, or insanity. 2d am. ed. with notes, improvements, and plates. With an appendix, by A. Brigham, m. d. viii, 272 pp. 4 pl. 8°. *Boston, Marsh, Capen & Lyon*, 1835.

Spuytenduyvel (The) chronicle. [*anon.*] 318 pp. 12°. *New York, Livermore & Rudd*, 1856.

Squire (Samuel, *d. d.*) Two essays. The former, a defense of the ancient greek chronology; to which is annexed, a new chronological synopsis: the latter, an enquiry into the origin of the greek language. 3 p. l. xv, 218 pp. 8°. *Cambridge*, [*Eng.*] *J. Bentham for W. Thurlbourn*, 1741.

Staden (Hans). Beschryvinge van Amerika, wiens inwoonders wildt, naekt, seer godloos en wreede menschen-eeters zijn, hoe hy selve onder de brasilianen lange gevangen geseten heeft. Mitsgaders een kort verhael hoe de wilden Waygauna geheeten [etc. Overgezott uit het hooghduitsche]. *b. l.* 4 p. l. 72 pp. sm. 4°. *Amsterdam, erfgenamen van G. de Gr.* 1736.

Staffenson (Stephen Hansen). *See* **Stephanson.**

Stafford (Marshall P.) The life of James Fisk, jr. A full and accurate narrative of his career, his great enterprises, and his assassination. 325, xvi pp. 6 pl. 12°. *New York, author*, 1872.

Stagg (John). The cumbrian minstrel; being a poetical miscellany of legendary, gothic, and romantic tales; together with several essays in the northern dialect; also a number of original pieces, never before published, and a variety of translations as well modern as classical. 2 v. vii, 290 pp. 1 l; 2 p. l. 292 pp. 2 l. 12°. *Manchester*, [*Eng.*] *T. Wilkinson*, 1821.

——— The minstrel of the north: or, cumbrian legends. Being a poetical miscellany of legendary, gothic, and romantic, tales. 4 p. l. 376 pp. 8°. *London, Hamblin & Seyfang, for the author*, 1810.

Stamma (Philip). Stamma on the game of chess; containing numerous openings of games, and one hundred critical situations, illustrated on colored diagrams. A new edition, with notes and remarks. By William Lewis. xii, 337 pp. 8°. *London, W. H. Reed*, 1818.

——— The same. Des arabers Philipp Stamma entdeckte schachspiel-geheimnisse, nebst einigen regeln, dieses spiel wohl zu vollziehen, und den sieg durch feine und subtile züge davon zu tragen. 16°. *Strasburg, A. König*, 1771.

[*In* PHILIDOR (F. A. Danican, *dit*). Die kunst im schachspiel ein meister zu werden. 1771. pp. 231–352. Separate title-page in the front of the book].

Stampe (William, *d. d.*) A treatise of spiritval infatvation, being the present visible disease of the english nation. Delivered in severall sermons at the Hagve in 1650. 33 p. l. 242 pp. 18°. *Hagvæ, S. Broun*, 1650.

Standish (Angélique Léontine Sabine de Noailles). Notice sur m^me^ la vicomtesse de Noailles. 12°. [*Paris, Aubry*, 1856].

[*In* PARIS. *Société des bibliophiles françois.* Mélanges, 1re partie, pp. 1–93].

Stanhope (George, *d. d.*) Sixteen sermons. fol. [*London*, 1739].

[BOYLE lectures, v. 1, pp. 627–836].

Stanley (Arthur Penrhyn, *d. d.*) Letters from Greece. 8°. *London, Hurst & Blackett*, 1871.

[*In* WYSE (*Sir* Thomas). Impressions of Greece. 1871. pp. 316–332].

Stanley (Frank, *pseudon?*) Outside and inside, and other tales. 216 pp. 3 pl. 18°. *Philadelphia, Presbyterian board of publication*, [1864].

Stanley (Thomas). Poems. Reprinted from the edition of 1651. xxiv, 3 p. l. 107 pp. 16°. *London, Longman, Hurst, Rees, Orme and Brown*, 1814.

Stanwood (The) family; or the history of the American tract society. [*anon.*] 180 pp. 16°. *Boston, Mass. sabbath school society*, 1833.

Stapf (Joseph Ambrosius, *d. d.*) The spirit and scope of education, in promoting the well-being of society. From the german. By Robert Gordon. 376 pp. 12°. *Edinburgh, Marsh & Beattie*, 1851.

Starbuck (Caleb). Hampton heights; or, the spinster's ward. 504 pp. 12°. *New York, Mason brothers*, 1856.

Starbuck (Lucy Coffin). Seaweeds from the shores of Nantucket. [Poems, collected by L. C. S. *anon.*] vii, 135 pp. 16°. *Boston, Crosby, Nichols & co.* 1853.

Stark (Ludwig). Grosse theoretisch-practische clavierschule. *See* **Lebert** (Sigmund) *and* **Stark**.

Starkey (Thomas). England in the reign of king Henry the eighth. A dialogue between cardinal Pole and Thomas Lupset. Edited, with preface, notes, and glossary, by J. M. Cowper, and with an introduction, containing the life and letters of Thomas Starkey, by the rev. J. S. Brewer. Part 2. 8°. *London, N. Trübner & co.* 1871.

[EARLY english text society, extra series, 12].

Starling (Thomas). Biblical annual or scripture cabinet atlas. 3 p. l. 24 col. maps. 16°. *London, Bull*, 1833.

——— (*editor*). A new general index, exhibiting, at one view, all that is geographically and historically interesting in the holy scriptures, compiled and arranged under the inspection of Thomas Starling. 119 pp. 16°. *London, proprietors*, 1832.

[*With his* Biblical annual, or scripture atlas].

Starowolski (Simon). Scriptorvm polonicorum ἑκατοντας; seu centvm illvstrium Poloniæ scriptorum elogia et vitæ. Eng. title, 132 pp. 2 l. sm. 4°. *Francoforti, I. de Zetter*, 1625.

Starr (Eliza Allen). Patron saints. 382 pp. 11 pl. 12°. *Baltimore, John Murphy & co.* 1871.

——— Poems. xii, 224 pp. 1 pl. 16°. *Philadelphia, H. McGrath*, 1867.

Statesman's (The) year book. Statistical and historical annual of the states of the civilised world. Handbook for politicians and merchants for the year 1872. By Frederick Martin. 9th annual publication. Revised after official returns. xxxii, 759 pp. 12°. *London, Macmillan & co.* 1872.

Staunton (William, *d. d.*) A dictionary of the church, containing an exposition of terms, phrases and subjects connected with the external order, sacraments, worship and usages of the protestant episcopal church. 473 pp. 12°. *New-York, Sherman & Trevett*, 1839.

——— An ecclesiastical dictionary, containing definitions of terms, and illustrations of subjects pertaining to the history, ritual, discipline, worship, ceremonies, and usages of the christian church; with notices of ancient and modern sects, and biographical sketches of the early fathers and writers of the church. 700 pp. 8°. *New York, general prot. episcopal sunday school union and church book society*, 1861.

Stearns (George). Love and mock love; or, how to marry to the end of conjugal satisfaction. 128 pp. 24°. *Boston, B. Marsh*, 1860.

Stearns (*Rev.* Samuel Horatio). Address and select discourses. New ed. iv, 265 pp. 12°. *Boston, J. Munroe & co.* 1846.

Stearns (William Augustus, *d. d.*) Adjutant Stearns. 160 pp. 1 portrait. 18°. *Boston, Mass. sabbath school society*, [1862].

Stebbins (J. E.) Glory of the immortal life, embracing the prophecies and proofs of the great doctrine of immortality in the analogies of nature, [etc.] 2 p. l. 559 pp. 8°. *Norwich (Conn.) Carr & Jewett*, 1871.

Stedingk (Curt Bogislaus Ludwig Christoph, *grefwe* von). Mémoires posthumes du feld-maréchal comte de Stedingk, rédigés sur des lettres, dépêches et autres pièces authentiques laissées à sa famille; par la général comte de Björnstjerna. 3 v. 8°. *Paris, A. Bertrand*, 1844-45.

[*Note.*—With autograph of editor].

Stedman (Edmund Clarence). Poems, lyrical and idyllic. 196 pp. 12°. *New York, C. Scribner*, 1860.

Steele (*Mrs.* Eliza R.) Heroines of sacred history. 238 pp. 12°. *New York, J. S. Taylor*, 1841.

Steele (James). The philosophy of the evidences of christianity. xvi, 298 pp. 8°. *Edinburgh, W. Whyte & co.* 1834.

Steele (*Rev.* John B.) Sacred poetical paraphrases, and miscellaneous poems. 384 pp. 12°. *New York, author*, 1853.

Steele (Oliver G.) Steele's western guide book, and emigrant's directory; containing different routes through New-York, Ohio, Indiana, Illinois, Michigan, Wisconsin territory, etc. With descriptions of the climate, soil, productions, prospects, etc. 11th ed. 108 pp. 1 map. 18°. *Buffalo, Steele & Peck*, 1839.

Steele (*Sir* Richard). The Englishman: being the sequel of the Guardian. [1st collective ed.] 1 p. l. vi, 292 pp. 6 l. 16°. *London, S. Buckley*, 1714.

——— Le héros chrétien. Traduit de l'anglois, par A. de Beaumarchais, et Les vertues païennes, par le traducteur. 4 p. l. 231 pp. 16 l. 16°. *La Haye, H. Scheurleer*, 1729.

Steele (Richard, *of Sion hill*). An essay upon gardening; containing a catalogue of exotic plants for the stoves and greenhouses of the british gardens; the best method of planting the hot-house vine; with observations on the history of gardening; and a contrast of the ancient with the modern taste. xxiv, 159, 102 pp. 3 pl. 4°. *York, author*, 1800.

Steele (Silas S.) Book of plays: for home amusement. A collection of original, altered and selected tragedies, plays, dramas, comedies, farces, burlesques, charades, lectures, etc. adapted for private representation, with full directions for performance. 350 pp. 1 l. 12°. *Philadelphia, G. G. Evans*, 1859.

Steendam (Jacob J.) Den distelvink. Eerste deel, minne-sang: tweede deel, zegensang: darde deel, hemel-sang. 3 v. in 1. 4°. *Amsterdam, G. van Goedesbergh & H. Doncker*, 1649-50.

Steffen (William). Digest of the United States tactics, for the use of officers. 121 pp. 18°. *Boston, Loring*, 1862.

Stein (A.) Little Anna, a story for pleasant little children. Translated from the german. vi, 134 pp. 5 pl. sq. 16°. *Boston, Ticknor & Fields*, 1864.

Stein (Elias). Nouvel essai sur le jeu des échecs. Avec des réflexions militaires relatives à ce jeu. viii, x, 254 pp. 8°. *La Haye, l'auteur*, 1789.

Steinmetz (Andrew). A manual of weathercasts; comprising storm prognostics on land and sea; with an explanation of the method in use at the meteorological office. Adapted for all countries. 208 pp. 16°. *London, G. Routledge & sons*, 1866.

——— Tobacco: its history, cultivation, manufacture, and adulterations. Its use considered with reference to its influence on the human constitution. xvi, 174 pp. 1 l. 1 pl. 16°. *London, R. Bentley*, 1857.

Steinwehr (A. von) *and* **Brinton** (D. G.) An intermediate geography, with lessons in map drawing. 92 pp. 4°. *Cincinnati, Wilson, Hinkle & co.* [1870].
[The eclectic series of geographies].

Stengel (Johann Peterson). Gnomonica universalis, oder aussführliche beschreibung der sonnen-uhren. Anjetzo mit neuen observationibus und figuren, obgedachte uhren auch trigonometrice, und auf andere angenehme manier aufzureissen, vermehret von einem liebhaber dieser kunst. 1 p. l. 338 pp. 6 l. 1 pl. 109 tab. 16°. *Ulm, D. Bartholomæ*, 1712.

Stennett (Samuel, *d. d.*) The works of Samuel Stennett, d. d. now first collected into a body; with some account of his life and writings; by William Jones. 3 v. 8°. *London, T. Tegg*, 1824.

CONTENTS.
v. 1. Some account of the author. Discourses on personal religion.
v. 2. Discourses on domestic duties. Discourses on the parable of the sower.
v. 3. Discourses on the divine authority, &c. of the holy scriptures. Occasional discourses. Trip to Holyhead; &c.

Stephanius (Stephanus Johannes). *See* **Stephanson** (Stephan Hansen).

Stephanson *or* **Staffenson** (Stephan Hansen). Notæ vberiores in historiam danicam Saxonis grammatici. Una cum prolegomenis ad easdem notas. 252 pp. 11 l. fol. *Sorae, typis Henrici Crusii*, 1645.
[*With* SAXO grammaticus. Historiæ danicæ libri xvi. *Soræ*, 1644].

Stephanus. *See* **Estienne.**

Stephen (James Fitz-James). *See* **Essays.** By a barrister.

Stephen (Thomas). The life and times of archbishop Sharp, (of St. Andrews.) 1 p. l. xvi, 640 pp. 8°. *London, J. Rickerby*, 1839.

Stephen Dugard. 1840. *See* **Mudford** (Henry).

Stephens (*Mrs.* Ann Sophia Winterbottom). A noble woman. 1 p. l. 19-479 pp. 12°. *Philadelphia, T. B. Peterson & brothers*, [1871].

——— Palaces and prisons. 1 p. l. 19-592 pp. 12°. *Philadelphia, T. B. Peterson & brothers*, [1871].

Stephens (John). Chronicles of Wesleyan methodism. *See* **Warren** (Samuel) *and* **Stephens.**

Stephens (Thomas). A new system of broad and small sword exercise. To which are added, instructions in horsemanship. 116 pp. 12°. *Philadelphia, I. R. & A. H. Diller*, 1843.

Stephens. *See* **Stevens.**

Stephenson (*Rev.* Joseph Adam). The christology of the old and new testaments; an historical development of the predicted occurrences of holy scripture. 2 v. xiv, 3-401 pp; viii, 338 pp. 8°. *London, J. G. & F. Rivington*, 1838.

Stephenson (M. F.) Geology and mineralogy of Georgia, with a particular description of her rich diamond district; the process of washing for diamonds, their price and mode of cutting and setting. 244 pp. 1 map. 16°. *Atlanta, Ga. Globe publishing co.* 1871. s.

Stephenson. *See* **Stevenson.**

Step-mother (The) rewarded. [*anon.*] 144 pp. 3 pl. 18°. *Boston, Mass. sabbath school society*, [1860].

Stern (Daniel, *pseudon.*) *See* **Agoult** (Marie de Flavigny, *comtesse* d').

Sterne (Laurence). Voyage sentimental, suivi des lettres d'Yorick à Éliza. En anglais et en français. Nouv. éd. 2 v. 2 p. l. 4, 209 pp. 3 pl; 2 p. l. 227 pp. 3 pl. fol. *Paris & Amsterdam, J. E. G. Dufour*, 1799].

Sternhold (Thomas), **Hopkins** (John), *and others.* The whole booke of psalmes: collected into english meeter: conferred with the hebrue, with apt notes to sing them withall. *b. l.* 5 p. l. 98 pp. 6 l. 4°. *London, John Day*, 1583.
[*With* BIBLE. (*English*). Genevan version. *London, C. Barker*, 1584].

——— The same. 5 p. l. 94 pp. 5 l. 4°. [*London, deputies of Christopher Barker*, 1599].
[*With* BIBLE. [*English*]. *London, C. Barker*, 1599].

——— The same. 5 p. l. 90 pp. 5 l. 4°. *London, for the companie of stationers*, 1612.
[*With* BIBLE. (*English*). Genevan version. *London, R. Barker*, 1610].

——— The same. 5 p. l. 84 pp. 6 l. 4°. *London, for the companie of stationers*, 1613.
[*With* BIBLE. (*English*). Genevan version. *London, R. Barker*, 1614.
Note.—Imperfect: leaves wanting at the end].

——— The same. 5 p. l. 90 pp. 6 l. 4°. *London, for the company of stationers*, 1615.
[*With* BIBLE. (*English*). Genevan version. *London, R. Barker*, 1615].

——— The same. 5 p. l. 90 pp. 3 l. 4°. *London, for the company of stationers*, 1637.
[*With* BIBLE. (*English*). Authorized version. *London, R. Barker*, 1634.
Note.—Imperfect: 3 l. wanting at end].

Stevens (Charles Wistar). College song book. Enlarged edition. A collection of american songs. With piano-forte accompaniment. 96 pp. 8°. *New York, S. T. Gordon*, [1871].

Stevens (G. S. *m. d.*) *and* **McDonald** (*Rev.* W.) The american hymn and tune book. 383 pp. 8°. *Boston, H. V. Degen & son*, 1860.

Stevens (Henry). Stevens's american bibliographer. Jan. and Feb. 1854. Nos. 1–2 in 1 v. 8°. *Chiswick, C. Whittingham*, [1854]. [No more published].

Stevens (John, *of Lincolnshire, Eng.*) A scriptural display of the triune God, and the early existence of Jesus' human soul. xi, 255 pp. 8°. *London, Whittingham & Rowland*, 1813.

Stevens (William Bacon, *d. d. bishop of Pennsylvania*). The bow in the cloud. 360 pp. 1 pl. 8°. *Philadelphia, Hubbard bros.* 1871.

——— The parables of the new testament practically unfolded. Eng. title, 382 pp. 7 pl. 8°. *Philadelphia, J. M. Stoddart*, [1871].

Stevens. *See* **Stephens.**

Stevenson (A. *d. d.*) Covenanting, and its benefits to the covenanters. 12°. [*Pittsburgh*, 1872].
[*In* REFORMED presbyterian church in North America. Memorial volume, pp. 58–72].

Stevenson (William, *m. d.*) Original poems on several subjects. 2 v. xvii, 270 pp. 1 l; 322 pp. 1 l. 16°. *London, Hawes, Clarke, & Collins*, 1765.

Stevenson. *See* **Stephenson.**

Steward (John Burdett, *m. d.*) Practical notes on insanity. viii, 122 pp. 8°. *London, J. Churchill*, 1845.

Steward (*Mrs.* T. F.) Catherine Erlof. A novel. 3 v. 12°. *London, T. C. Newby*, 1851.

Stewart (Agnes M.) Florence O'Neill, the rose of St. Germains; or, the siege of Limerick. 2 p. l. 247 pp. 1 pl. 12°. *Baltimore, Kelly, Piet & co.* 1872.

Stewart (Allan). The poetical remains of the late Allan Stewart. With a memoir of the author. 144 pp. 12°. *Paisley, A. Gardner*, 1838.

Stewart (James, *m. d.*) A practical treatise on the diseases of children. viii, 547 pp. 8°. *New York, Wiley & Putnam*, 1841.

Stewart (John). Genevieve: or, the spirit of the Drave. A poem. With odes and other poems, chiefly amatory and descriptive. xii, 328 pp. 12°. *London, Longman*, 1810.

Stewart (Robert). The history of modern Europe, from the commencement of the sixteenth century to the year 1850. iv, 13–332 pp. 12°. *London, Partridge & Oakey*, 1851.

Stewart (William Grant). The popular superstitions and festive amusements of the highlanders of Scotland. 1 p. l. xviii, 293 pp. 1 pl. 16°. *Edinburgh, A. Constable & co.* 1823.

Stewart. *See* **Stuart.**

Sticotti (Antoine Fabio). The man of the world's dictionary. Translated from the french, [by George Fletcher. *anon.*] 87 l. 12°. *London, J. Appleyard*, 1822.

Stiles (Henry Reed, *m. d.*) Bundling; its origin, progress and decline in America. 139 pp. 16°. *Albany, J. Munsell*, 1869.

Still (Peter). The cottar's sunday, and other poems, chiefly in the scottish dialect. viii, 200 pp. 16°. *Aberdeen, G. & R. King*, 1845.

——— The same. 216 pp. 18°. *Philadelphia, H. Longstreth*, 1845.

Still (William). The underground rail road. A record of facts, authentic narratives, letters, &c. narrating the hardships, hair-breadth escapes, and death struggles of the slaves in their efforts for freedom, as related by themselves and others, or witnessed by the author; together with sketches of some of the largest stockholders, and most liberal aiders and advisers, of the road. 2 p. l. 780 pp. 24 pl. 8°. *Philadelphia, Porter & Coates*, 1872.

Stimson (Alexander Lovett). New England boys. Or, the three apprentices. xix, 9–465 pp. 4 pl. 12°. *New York, J. C. Derby*, 1856.

——— Waifwood. By the author of "Easy Nat," [etc. *anon.*] iv, 472 pp. 12°. *Boston, W. V. Spencer*, 1864.

Stinson (John H.) Ethica. An outline of moral science, for students and reflecting men. 104 pp. 12°. *New York, A. B. Kitson*, 1860.

Stinstra (Jan). An essay on fanaticism. In a pastoral letter. Originally written in dutch. Translated by the rev. Isaac Subremont. [From the french translation, with the french translator's preface]. 7, clix, 217 pp. 3 l. 16°. *Dublin, T. Ewing*, 1774.

Stirling (James Hutchinson). As regards protoplasm, in relation to prof. Huxley's essay on the physical basis of life. 71 pp. 12°. *New Haven, Conn. C. C. Chatfield & co.* 1871.
[HALF hours with modern scientists, pp. 73–143, or, no. 3].

Stockbridge (John Calvin, *d. d.*) The model pastor. A memoir of the life and correspondence of rev. Baron Stow, d. d. 376 pp. 1 portrait, 1 pl. 12°. *Boston, Lee & Shepard*, 1871.

Stockdale (Percival). Lectures on the truly eminent english poets. 2 v. xi, 607 pp. 1 portrait; 2 p. l. 656 pp. 8°. *London, D. N. Shury, for the author*, 1807.

Stockholder (The): monitor of finance and industry, mining and railway record. [Weekly]. Nov. 8, 1870, to Oct. 31, 1871. v. 9. fol. *New York, [S. P. Dinsmore & co.* 1870–71].

Stockton (J.) The western calculator, or a new and compendious system of practical arithmetic. 204 pp. 12°. *Pittsburgh, Johnston & Stockton*, 1832.

Stoddard (Richard Henry). The book of the east, and other poems. v, 249 pp. 16°. *Boston, J. R. Osgood & co.* 1871.

——— Town and country, and the voices in the shells. With illustrations. 71 pp. sq. 12°. *New York, Dix, Edwards & co.* 1857.

Stoddard (*Rev.* Solomon). A guide to Christ; or, the way of directing souls that are under the work of conversion. Compiled for the help of young ministers. With an epistle prefixed by dr. Increase Mather. 1 p. l. viii, 85 pp. 18°. *Boston, D. Henchman*, 1735.

——— Three sermons lately preach'd at Boston. i. Shewing the vertue of Christs blood. ii. That natural men are under the government of self love. iii. That the gospel is the means of conversion. To which a fourth is added to stir young men and maidens to praise the name of the Lord. 1 p. l. 118 pp. 18°. *Boston, Daniel Henchman*, 1717.

Stoeckel (Gustave J.) Sacred music. 165 pp. 4°. *New York, Taintor brothers & co.* 1868.

Stoeger (Franz Xaver). Oratio dominica polyglotta singularum linguarum characteribus expressa et delineationibus Alberti Düreri (1515) cincta. 1 p. l. 44 pl. 4°. *Monachii, in commissione officinæ lit.-artisticae, e lithographia J. B. Dreselly*, [1839].

Stokes (William, *m. d.*) A treatise on the diagnosis and treatment of diseases of the chest. Diseases of the lung and windpipe. 2d ed. with introduction and notes, by the american editor. xii, 528 pp. 8°. *Philadelphia, E. Barrington & G. D. Haswell*, 1844.

Stolz (*Madame* de, *pseudon.*) *See* **Bégon** (F. *comtesse* de).

Stone (Andrew, *m. d.*) Pulmonary consumption, that fatal destroyer of man! its curability demonstrated on natural principles alone. Combining medicated air, medicated inhalation, and natural hygiene. 310 pp. 1 l. 1 pl. 1 portrait. 8°. *Troy (N. Y.) Troy lung and hygienic institute*, 1863.

Stone (John Seely, *d. d.*) The church universal: discourses on the true comprehension of the church, as exhibited in the holy scriptures and the standards of the protestant episcopal church. With thoughts on church government and worship: and a view of the church in heaven. 215 pp. 8°. *New York, Houel & Macoy*, 1846.

——— Lectures on the institution of the sabbath. 186 pp. 16°. *New York, A. V. Blake*, 1844.

——— Memoir of the life of the rt. rev. Alexander Viets Griswold, d. d. bishop of the protestant episcopal church in the eastern diocese. With a sermon, charge, and pastoral letter of the late bishop. 620 pp. 1 portrait. 8°. *Philadelphia, Stavely & McCalla*, 1844.

——— The mysteries opened; or, scriptural views of preaching and the sacraments, as distinguished from certain theories concerning baptismal regeneration and the real presence. 396 pp. 12°. *New York, Harper & brothers*, 1844.

Stone (*Mrs.* Leander). Willie and Carrie. A true story from real life. 193 pp. 4 pl. 12°. *Chicago, H. A. Sumner*, 1871.

Stone (*Rev.* Micah). The young christian's assistant to prayer. 216 pp. 18°. *New-York, Leavitt, Lord, & co.* 1835.

Stone (*Rev.* Timothy Dwight Porter). Stories to teach me to think. 180 pp. 2 pl. 18°. *Boston, J. A. Stearns*, 1839.

Stone edge. [*anon.*] 2 p. l. 314 pp. 4 pl. 16°. *London, Smith, Elder & co.* 1868.

Stonehouse (*Sir* George). Universal restitution a scripture doctrine. This prov'd in several letters wrote on the nature and extent of Christ's kingdom: wherein the scripture passages, falsly alleged in proof of the eternity of hell torments, are truly translated and explained. [*anon.*] 1 p. l. 445 pp. 8°. *London, R. Dodsley*, 1761.

Storer (Francis Humphreys). Elementary manual of chemistry. *See* **Eliot** (Charles W.) *and* **Storer**.

Stories for village lads. [*anon.*] 144 pp. 4 pl. 16°. *Philadelphia, American sunday-school union*, [1856].

Stories of the church in the fourth century. [*anon.*] 158 pp. 16°. *Philadelphia, American sunday school union*, 1832.

Stories of the good shepherd. [*anon.*] 358 pp. 18°. *Philadelphia, American sunday school union,* [1856].

Stories of the second and third centuries. [*anon.*] 192 pp. 18°. *Philadelphia, American sunday school union,* 1832.

Stories of Vinegar hill. 6 v. 1872. *See* **Warner** (Susan).

Stork (Theophilus, *d. d.*) The unseen world in the light of the cross. 173 pp. 16°. *Philadelphia, J. B. Lippincott & co.* 1871.

Storrow (Charles S.) A treatise on waterworks for conveying and distributing supplies of water; with tables and examples. xii, 242 pp. 2 pl. 12°. *Boston, Hilliard, Gray & co.* 1835.

Storrs (*Rev.* George). Six sermons on the inquiry Is there immortality in sin and suffering? Also, a sermon on Christ the life-giver: or, the faith of the gospel. 168 pp. 1 portrait. 12°. *New York, office of the Bible examiner,* 1855.

Storrs (Richard Salter, *d. d.*) Memoir of the rev. Samuel Green, late pastor of Union church, Boston. 412 pp. 1 portrait. 12°. *Boston, Perkins & Marvin,* 1836.

Storrs (Richard Salter, *jr. d. d.*) Graham lectures. [v. 1.] The constitution of the human soul. Six lectures delivered at the Brooklyn institute, Brooklyn, N. Y. 338 pp. 8°. *New York, R. Carter & brothers,* 1857.

Story (Joseph, *ll. d. justice U. S. supreme court.*) An eulogy on general George Washington, delivered [at Marblehead] on the 2nd of January, 1800. [With an elegy]. 24 pp. 8°. *Salem, J. Cushing,* 1800.

Story (The) of a scripture text; or, what four little girls did with a text about pleasant words. [*anon.*] 202 pp. 18°. *New York, Carlton & Porter,* [1862].

Story (The) of Cecil and his dog; or the reward of virtue. [*anon.*] Eng. title, 290 pp. 6 pl. 16°. *New York, J. Miller,* 1863.

Story (The) of Frank Hearty, the country boy. [*anon.*] 191 pp. 1 pl. sq. 16°. *Philadelphia, J. Crissy,* 1835.

Story (The) of our darling Nellie. [*anon.*] 117 pp. 16°. *Boston, J. E. Tilton & co.* 1860.

Stout (William). Autobiography of William Stout, of Lancaster, wholesale and retail grocer and ironmonger, a member of the society of friends, a. d. 1665–1752. Edited from the original manuscript, by J. Harland. vii, 154 pp. 1 portrait. 8°. *London, Simpkin & Marshall,* 1851.

Stovel (*Rev.* Charles). Christian discipleship and baptism: being eight lectures in reply to the theory advanced by dr. Halley in the congregational lecture of 1843. xxvii, 527 pp. 8°. *London, Houlston & Stoneman,* 1846.

——— Hints on the regulation of christian churches, adapted to the present state of their affairs. [Also], remarks on the voluntary system. 2 p. l. iv, 208 pp. 12°. *London, author,* 1835.

Stow (Baron, *d. d.*) A brief narrative of the danish mission on the coast of Coromandel. 126 pp. 18°. *Boston, New England sabbath school union,* 1837.

——— Correspondence. 12°. [*Boston,* 1871]. [*In* STOCKBRIDGE (John C.) The model pastor].

——— Daily manna for christian pilgrims. 128 pp. 32°. *Boston, Gould, Kendall & Lincoln,* 1844.

——— First things; or the developement of church life. 282 pp. 12°. *Boston, Gould & Lincoln,* 1859.

——— A history of the english baptist mission to India. 252 pp. 1 map. 16°. *Philadelphia, American sunday-school union,* [1835].

——— Memoir of Harriet Dow, of Newport, N. H. who became a christian at the age of eight years. In ten letters to a niece. 107 pp. 18°. *Boston, J. Loring,* 1832.

Stow (John). The chronicles of England, from Brute vnto this present yeare of Christ, 1580. [1st ed.] *b. l.* 16 p. l. 1223 [1221] pp. sm. 4°. *London, Ralphe Newberie,* 1580.

——— A summarie ofur englysh chronicles. [3d ed.] *b. l.* 12 p. l. 281 [279], 13 l. 18°. *London, Thomas Marshe,* 1566.

Stowe (Calvin Ellis, *d. d.*) The comprehensive and self-interpreting family bible. *Hartford,* 1870. *See* **Bible.** (*English*).

Stowe (*Mrs.* Harriet E. Beecher). [Little foxes]. De kleine vossen of de verstoorders van ons huiselijk geluk. Vertaald door S. J. Andriessen. 2^e^ druk. 202 pp. 16°. *Amsterdam, G. L. Funke,* 1867.

——— My wife and I: or, Harry Henderson's history. viii, 474 pp. 8 pl. 12°. *New York, J. B. Ford & co.* 1871.

——— Oldtown fireside stories. 3 p. l. 199 pp. 12 pl. 12°. *Boston, J. R. Osgood & co.* 1872.

——— Pink and white tyranny. A society novel. 331 pp. 16°. *Boston, Roberts brothers,* 1871.

Strada [de Rosberg] (Jacopo). Epitome dv thresor des antiquitez, c'est à dire, pourtraits des vrayes medailles des empp. tant d'orient que d'occident. Traduit [du latin] par Iean Louueau d'Orléans. 12 p. l. 394 pp. 15 l. 4°. *Lyon, Iaqves de Strada et Thomas Gverin*, 1553.

Strange (Thomas Lumisden). The bible; is it "the word of God?" xi, 381 pp. 3 maps. 8°. *London, N. Trübner & co.* 1871.

Strauss (Friedrich Adolf). Sinai and Golgotha; a journey in the east. With an introduction by Henry Stebbing, d. d. xii, 390 pp. 2 pl. 16°. *London, J. Blackwood*, 1849.

Strauss (Gerhard Friedrich Albrecht). The glory of the house of Israel; or the hebrew's pilgrimage to the holy city: comprising a picture of judaism in the century which preceded the birth of our saviour. Eng. title, 480 pp. 1 pl. 12°. *Philadelphia, J. B. Lippincott & co.* 1859.

Street and Smith's New York weekly. A journal of useful knowledge, romance, amusement, etc. Nov. 17, 1870, to Nov. 9, 1871. v. 26. fol. *New York, Street & Smith*, 1870–71.

Streeter (Horace R.) Voice building. A new and correct theory for the mechanical formation of the human voice. [2 parts in 1 v.] 93, 42 pp. 12°. *Boston, White & Goullaud*, 1871.

Stretton (Charles). Memoirs of a chequered life. 3 v. x, 326 pp. 1 portrait; vii, 310 pp; viii, 341 pp. 16°. *London, R. Bentley*, 1862.

Stribling (B. F. W.) Poems for the old and the young. 238, vi pp. sq. 16°. *Beardstown (Ill.) L. U. Reavis*, 1857.

Strickland (*Rev.* William P.) History of the missions of the methodist episcopal church, from the organization of the missionary society to the present time. With an introduction by rev. B. F. Tefft, d. d. 338 pp. 1 portrait. 12°. *Cincinnati, L. Swormstedt & J. H. Power*, 1850.

String (A) of pearls. Embracing a scripture verse and a pious reflection for every day in the year. [*anon.*] 118 pp. sq. 16°. *New-York, Carlton & Phillips*, 1856.

Stringfellow (Thornton, *d. d.*) The bible argument; or, slavery in the light of divine revelation. 8°. [*Augusta (Ga.)* 1860].
[*In* ELLIOTT (E. N.) Cotton is king, pp. 459–546].

Strong (Frederick). Greece as a kingdom; or, a statistical description of that country, from the arrival of king Otho, in 1833, down to the present time. xv, 404 pp. 8°. *London, Longman*, 1842.

Strong (James, *s. t. d.*) Cyclopaedia of biblical and theological literature. *See* **M'Clintock** (John) *and* **Strong**.

Strong (Peter Remsen). "Awful," and other jingles. By P. R. S. [*anon.*] 148 pp. 12°. *New York, G. P. Putnam & sons*, 1871.

Strong (Titus, *d. d.*) The cypress wreath, or mourner's friend. A selection of pieces, adapted to the consolation of the afflicted. 108 pp. 16°. *Greenfield (Mass.) Phelps & Clark*, 1828.

Stroud (William, *m. d.*) Treatise on the physical cause of the death of Christ and its relation to the principles and practice of christianity. 2d ed. with appendix containing letter on the subject, by sir James Y. Simpson, m. d. xvi, 504 pp. 8°. *Glasgow, T. D. Morison*, 1871.

Struan *or* **Strowan.** *See* **Robertson** (Alexander, *of Strowan*).

Strunck (Amos K.) Officers of Berks county, [Penn.] for each year, from 1752 to 1860. Also the vote of the county at the presidential and governors' elections. 124 pp. 16°. *Reading, J. L. Getz*, 1859.

Struys (Jan Janszen). The perillous and most unhappy voyages of John Struys; through Italy, Greece, Lifeland, Moscovia, Tartary, Media, Persia, East-India, Japan, and other places in Europe, Africa and Asia. [Also], 2 narrativs sent from capt. D. Butler, relating to the taking in of Astrachan by the Cosacs. Rendred out of nether-dutch by John Morrison. 12 p. l. 360 pp. 19 pl. 4°. *London, S. Smith*, 1683.

——— The same. Les voyages en Moscovie, en Tartarie, en Perse, aux Indes, & en plusieurs autres païs étrangers. À quoi l'on a ajouté, la relation d'un naufrage, par m. Glanius. Eng. title, 7 p. l. 360 pp. 7 l. 20 pl. 4°. *Amstredam, veuve de J. van Meurs*, 1681.

Stuart (Charles B.) Lives and works of civil and military engineers of America. 343 pp. 10 pl. 8°. *New York, D. Van Nostrand*, 1871.

Stuart (Henry A.) Ben Nebo; a pilgrimage to the South seas. In three cantos. viii, 65 pp. 11 photographs, 1 portrait. 8°. *San Francisco, Wade & co.* 1871.

Stuart (*Rev.* Moses). Commentary on Ecclesiastes. Commentary on Romans. *See* **Bible.** (*English*).

——— Exegetical essays on several words relating to future punishment. 208 pp. 16°. *Philadelphia, Presbyterian publication committee*, [1867].

Stuart. *See* **Stewart.**

Stuckle (Henry). Interoceanic canals. An essay on the question of location for a ship canal across the american continent. 1 p. l. iv, 137 pp. 3 maps. 8°. *New York, D. Van Nostrand*, 1870.

Student (The) and schoolmate. An illustrated monthly for youth. Jan. to Dec. 1871. v. 27-28 in 1 v. 8°. *Boston, J. H. Allen*, 1871.

Stürmer (Ignaz von). Anthologia persica, sev selecta diversis persis avctoribvs exempla in latinvm translata, ac Mariae Theresiae avgustae honoribus dicata a caesarea regia lingvarvm orientalivm academia. [*anon.*] Eng. title, 11 p. l. 87 pp. 4°. *Viennae, typis J. nob. de Kurzbök*, [1778].

Styward (Thomas). The pathwaie to martiall discipline, deuided into two bookes, verie necessarie for young souldiers, or for all such as loueth the profession of armes. *b. l.* 4 p. l. 152 pp. 2 pl. sm. 4°. *London, T. East for Myles Jenyngs*, 1581.

Suard (Jean Baptiste Antoine, *l'abbé*). Mélanges de littérature. 3 v. 8°. *Paris, Dentu*, 1803.

——— Variétés littéraires, ou recueil des pièces tant originales que traduites, concernant la philosophie, la littérature & les arts. *See* **Arnaud** (François) *and* **Suard.**

Suares (*Rev.* M. R.) The sabbath and other poems. 264 pp. 1 portrait. 12°. *Philadelphia, J. B. Rodgers & co.* 1871.

Suckling (*Rev.* Alfred). Life of [sir John Suckling], with critical remarks on his writings and genius. 8°. [*London, Longman*, 1836].

[*In* SUCKLING (*Sir* John). Selections from the works of. 1836. pp. 1-62].

Suckling (*Sir* John). Selections from the works of sir John Suckling. [Also], a life of the author, with critical remarks on his writings and genius. By the rev. Alfred Suckling. 1 p. l. v, 412 pp. 1 portrait. 8°. *London, Longman*, 1836.

CONTENTS.

Memoirs of the life of sir John Suckling, &c.
Poems.
An account of religion by reason: a discourse.
Letters to several eminent persons: written on several occasions.
Plays:—Aglaura, a tragedie. Brennoralt, a tragedy. The goblins, a comedy. The sad one, a tragedy.

Suddards (William, *d. d.*) The british pulpit: consisting of discourses by the most eminent living divines, in England, Scotland, and Ireland: accompanied with pulpit sketches: [also], scriptural illustrations; and selections on the office, duties and responsibilities of the christian ministry. 503 pp. 1 pl. 8°. *Philadelphia, Grigg & Elliot*, 1836.

Suidas. Proverbia ex Svidæ collectaneis Andreæ Schotti scholiis explicata. [Græce et latine]. 4°. [*Antverpiae, ex officina plantiniana, apud viduam & filios I. Moreti*, 1612].

[*In* SCHOTT (Andreas). Παροιμιαι ἑλληνικαι. *Antverpiae*, 1612. pp. 325-579].

Sullivan (William, *ll. d.*) Historical class book; (part first). Containing sketches of history, from the beginning of the world to the end of the roman empire in Italy, a. d. 476. 264 pp. 1 map. 12°. *Boston, Carter, Hendee, & co.* 1833.

Sulpicia. The poems of Sulpicia. 12°. *London, A. Millar*, 1769.

[*In* TIBULLUS (Albius) *and* SULPICIA. A poetical translation, by James Grainger, m. d. v. 2. pp. 223-263].

Summer (A) in the forest; or, slender hands in the stone quarries. [*anon.*] 304 pp. 5 pl. 16°. *New York, American tract society*, [1871].

Summerbell (N. *d. d.*) A true history of the christians and the christian church, from a. m. 4004 to a. d. 1870. Origin and character of popery. Origin of the popes. Origin of the temporal power. 560 pp. 8°. *Cincinnati, office of the christian pulpit*, 1871.

Summers (*Rev.* James). The rudiments of the chinese language, with dialogues, exercises, and a vocabulary. 1 p. l. 159 pp. 1 tab. 16°. *London, B. Quaritch*, 1864.

Summers (Thomas Osmond, *d. d.*) Commentary on the gospels. Luke and John. *See* **Bible.** (*English*).

——— (*editor*). Post-oak circuit. By a member of the Red river conference. 275 pp. 18°. *Nashville, E. Stevenson & F. A. Owen*, 1857.

Sumner (Charles). The works of Charles Sumner. v. 4. vi, 456 pp. 1 l. 12°. *Boston, Lee & Shepard*, 1871.

Sunbeam (Susie, *pseudon.*) *See* **Mackarness** (Matilda Planché).

Sunbeam (The), and other stories. [*anon.*] 144 pp. 2 pl. 18°. *Philadelphia, Presbyterian board of publication*, [1863].

Sunday morning chronicle. [Washington]. John W. Forney, jr. and D. C. Forney, edit-

Sunday morning chronicle—continued. ors. Jan. 1 to Dec. 31, 1871. fol. *Washington, J. W. jr. & D. C. Forney,* 1871. [*With* DAILY morning chronicle].

Sunday school (The) workman. Rev. Alfred Taylor, editor. Jan. 7 to Dec. 23, 1871. v. 2. fol. [*New York, Sunday-school workman association,* 1871].

Sunday-school (The) world. Rev. dr. [Richard] Newton, editor. [Monthly]. Jan. to Dec. 1871. v. 11. 4°. *Philadelphia, American sunday-school union,* [1871].

Sunday (The) visitant; or, weekly repository of christian knowledge. By A. Fowler. v. 1–2. January, 1818, to December, 1819. 2 v. in 1. 208 pp; 208 pp. 4°. *Charleston (S. C.)* 1818–19.

Sunderland (Byron, *d. d.*) Sunday not the sabbath. *See* **Burr** (William Henry).

Sunderland (*Rev.* La Roy). Anti-slavery manual, containing a collection of facts and arguments on american slavery. 162 pp. 18°. *New York, Piercy & Reed,* 1837.

——— Biblical institutes: or, a scriptural illustration of the doctrines, morals and precepts of the bible. With notes and questions. 268 pp. 12°. *New-York, B. Waugh & T. Mason,* 1834.

——— Book of human nature: illustrating the philosophy (new theory) of instinct, nutrition, life; with their correlative and abnormal phenomena, physiological, mental, spiritual. 432 pp. 12°. *New York, Stearns & co.* 1853.

——— History of the United States of America, from the discovery of the continent in 1492, to the fiftieth anniversary of their independence. 278 pp. 18°. *New York, B. Waugh & T. Mason,* 1834.

Sunshine and shadow. By the author of "The hive and its wonders." [*anon.*] 196 pp. 18°. *Philadelphia, American sunday-school union,* [1863].

Supplementum ad annales et chronicon Philippi Brietii ab anno 1663. usque ad annvm 1692. *See* **Fraichot** (Casimir).

Surault (François M. J.) An easy grammar of the french language. viii, 302 pp. 12°. *Cambridge,* [*Ms*] *J. Munroe & co.* 1835.

——— French fables, with a key, and a treatise on pronunciation; being the fourth elementary work in the complete course of french instruction. xxxii, 240 pp. 12°. *Cambridge, J. Munroe & co.* 1834.

Surault (François M. J.)—continued.

——— New french exercises, adapted to all french grammars. 2 p. l. 117 pp. 12°. *Boston, Hilliard, Gray & co.* 1833.

Sure methods of improving health, and prolonging life; or, a treatise on the art of living long and comfortably, by regulating the diet and regimen. By a physician. [*anon.*] 1st american ed. with additions. 248 pp. 12°. *Philadelphia, Carey, Lea & Carey,* 1828.

Surget (Jean). Militaris discipline enchiridion. in quo varie iuris materie et peregrine questiones continentur. Cuius finis est pacis persuasio inter principes xpianos. belli exhortatio in saracenos et infideles hostes religionis catholice. *b. l.* 87 l. 16°. *Parrhisiis, ab Joanne paruo,* [1511].

Surlet de Chokier (Jean). Thesavrvs politicorvm aphorismorvm, in qvo principvm, consiliariorvm, avlicorvm institio proprie continetur. Vna cum exemplis omnis ævi: qvibvs insertæ notæ, sive etiam monita. Auctore Ioanne a Chokier. Adiunguntur eiusdem notæ, siue dissertationes in Onosandri strategicvm ad disciplinam militarem spectantes. Ed. ivxta romanam secvnda. 10 p. l. 352 pp. 8 l. 106 pp. 3 l. 4°. *Mogvntiæ, sumptibus I. T. Schönvvetten,* 1613.

Surr (Thomas Skinner). A winter in London; or sketches of fashion: a novel. 3d ed. 3 v. 16°. *London, R. Phillips,* 1806.

Susan and Franklin. By the author of "Sabbath talks about Jesus," [etc. *anon.*] 165 pp. 3 pl. 18°. *Boston, J. E. Tilton & co.* [1861].

Susie's spectacles. By Faith and Sight. [*pseudon.*] 316 pp. 16°. *Boston, D. Lothrop & co.* 1871.

Sutherlands (The). *See* **Harris** (*Mrs.* Sidney S.)

Sutton (Thomas, *m. d.*) Tracts on delirium tremens, on peritonitis, and on some other internal inflammatory affections, and on the gout. 4 p. l. 272 pp. 8°. *London, J. Moyes, for T. Underwood,* 1813.

Suzanne de l'Orme: a story of huguenot times. [*anon.*] 299 pp. 16°. *Cincinnati, Hitchcock & Walden,* 1871.

Swain (Joseph). Redemption, a poem in five books. 115 pp. 2 l. 12°. *Charleston, (S. C.) R. Missildine,* 1819.

Swedenborg (Emanuel). Concerning the earths in our solar system, which are called planets; and concerning the earths in the

Swedenborg (Emanuel)—continued.
starry heaven: together with an account of their inhabitants, and also of the spirits and angels there; from what hath been seen and heard. Now first translated from the latin. 1 p. l. viii, 212 pp. 8°. *London, R. Hindmarsh*, 1787.

Sweeny (Robert, *of Montreal*). Odds and ends; [poems] original and translated. 156 pp. 12°. *New-York, H. I. Megarey*, 1826.

Sweet (Waterman, *m. d.*) Views of anatomy, and practice of natural bonesetting, by a mechanical practice, different from all book-knowledge. 67 pp. 8°. *Schenectady, [N. Y.] I. Riggs*, 1843.

Sweetser (Joseph E.) A collection of church music. *See* **Root** (George F.) *and* **Sweetser.**

Swezey (*Mrs.* Jennett). The strong staff that was broken; and the beautiful rod. 123 pp. 12°. *New York, Eckler*, 1871.

Swift (Jonathan). Select poems of Prior and Swift. *See* **Prior** (Matthew) *and* **Swift.**

Swinburne (Algernon Charles). Songs before sunrise. 2d ed. viii, 287 pp. 12°. *London, F. S. Ellis*, 1871.

Swinton (William). A condensed school history of the United States, constructed for definite results in recitation, and containing a new method of topical reviews. vii, 326 pp. 16°. *New York, Ivison, Blakeman, Taylor & co.* 1871.

Switzerland. (*Geologische commission der schweizer. naturforsch. gesellschaft*). Beitræge zur geologischen karte der Schweiz, herausgegeben auf kosten der eidgenossenschaft. [*Or*], matériaux pour la carte géologique de la Suisse, publiés aux frais de la confédération. v. 1 and 3–8. 4°. *Neuchatel et Bern*, 1862–70. s.

[v. 2 wanting].

CONTENTS.

v. 1. Geognostische skizze des kantons Basel und der angrenzenden gebiete, von Alb. Müller. 4 p. l. v, 71 pp. 2 pl. 1 col. map. 1862.

v. 3. Geologische beschreibung der in blatt xx. des eidg. atlasses enthaltenen gebirge von Graubünden, von G. Theobald. xii, 359 pp. 2 col. pl. 6 pl. 1864–66.

v. 4. Der aargauer Jura und die nördlichen gebiete des kantons Zürich, geologisch untersucht und beschrieben von Casimir Moesch. xv, 319 pp. 8 l. 7 pl. 3 col. pl. 1867.

v. 5. Der Pilatus, geologisch untersucht und beschrieben von F. J. Kaufmann. xii, 169 pp; atlas, 9 pp. 10 pl. 1 col. map. 1867.

v. 6. Description géologique du Jura vaudois et neuchatelois et de quelques districts adjacents du Jura français et de la plaine suisse compris dans les feuilles vi, xi et xvi de l'atlas fédéral, par A. Jaccard. viii, 340 pp. 1 l. 8 pl. 1869.

v. 7. Supplément à la description du Jura vaudois et neuchâtelois, par Auguste Jaccard. 1870.

Switzerland—continued.

v. 8. Description géologique du Jura bernois et de quelques districts adjacents, par J. B. Greppin. 1870.

Sykes (Arthur Ashley, *d. d.*) A brief discourse concerning the credibility of miracles and revelation. [Also], a postscript in answer to the lord bishop of Lichfield's charge to his clergy. vi, 262 pp. 8°. *London, J. & P. Knapton*, 1742.

——— An essay upon the truth of the christian religion: wherein its real foundation upon the old testament is shewn. Occasioned by the discourse [by Anthony Collins], of The grounds and reasons of the christian religion. [xvi], 304 pp. 8°. *London, J. & J. Knapton*, 1725.

Sylvan sketches; or, a companion to the park and the shrubbery. By the author of the Flora domestica. [*anon.*] xliv, 408 pp. 1 pl. 8°. *London, Whittaker, Treacher & co.* 1831.

Sylvius (Aenæas). *See* **Pius ii.** *pope.*

Symmes (*Rev.* Thomas). Good soldiers described, and animated. A sermon preached before the honourable artillery company, in Boston, June 6th, 1720. Being the day of their election of officers. [With a preface by Benjamin Colman]. 1 p. l. iv, 37 pp. 16°. *Boston, S. Gerrish & D. Henchman*, 1720.

——— The people's interest in one article considered and exhibited; a sermon. vi, 35 pp. 16°. *Boston, S. Gerrish*, 1724.

Symposius. *See* **Firmianus Symposius.**

Sympson (Jones). Les armes des chevaliers de l'ordre du bain. Créez le 17me jour de juin 1725. Eng. title, 148 pl. fol. [*London*, 1725]?

Synesius, *the alchymist.* Le livre de Synesius sur l'oeuvre des philosophes. 12°. [*Paris, A. Cailleau*, 1741].

[*In* SALMON (Guillaume) Bibliothèque des philosophes chimiques. 1741. v. 2, pp. 175–194].

Syntipas. Erasto, dopo molti secoli ritornato al fine in lvce, et con somma diligenza dal greco fedelmente tradotto in italiano. [*anon.*] 137 l. num. 3 l. 16°. *Mantova, [V. Roffinello]*, 1546.

[*Note.*—Substantially, a reprint of the Venice ed. (1542) of a work entitled, "Le compassionevoli avvenimenti di Erasto," and similar to, if not in fact, a reproduction in italian, of a latin work of the 12th century (the Historia septem sapientum Romæ), by Dam Jehans, a monk of the abbey of Haute-Selve].

Sypher (Josiah R.) The american popular speaker: designed for the use of schools, lyceums, temperance societies, etc. 384 pp. 12°. *Philadelphia, Porter & Coates*, [1870].

Sypher (Josiah R.)—continued.
——— The young America speaker: designed for the use of the younger classes in schools, lyceums, temperance societies, etc. 176 pp. 16°. *Philadelphia, Porter & Coates,* [1870].

Syracuse (*N. Y.*) *Board of education.* Twenty-third annual report of the board of education of the city of Syracuse, for the year ending March 7, 1871. 8°. *Syracuse, Truair, Smith & co.* 1871.
——— Boyd's daily journal Syracuse city directory. 1871-2. 8°. *Syracuse, Truair, Smith & co.* 1871.

Szold (Benjamin). Israelitisches gebetbuch. 1871. *See* **Jewish** church.

T. (G. W.) *See* **Taylor** (George Watson).

T. (L. A.) Day unto day. [*anon.*] xi, 373 pp. 24°. *Boston, American unitarian association,* 1872.

Tabago: or, a geographical description, natural and civil history of that island, fully exploding the chimera of a french title. [*anon.*] 2d ed. 1 p. l. 89 pp. 1 map. 12°. *London, W. Reeves,* [1750] ?

Table talk. [A monthly paper]. Charles J. Everett, editor. Dec. 1869, to March, 1870. nos. 1-4 in 1 v. 4°. *New York, Wilson, Lockwood, Everett & co.* 1869-70.
[No more published].

Tableau historique et chronologique des événemens mémorables de la guerre en Portugal et en Espagne. Historical and chronological retrospect of the memorable events of the war in Portugal and Spain. [*anon.*] 24 pp. fol. [*n. p. n. d.*]
[*With* BRADFORD (*Rev.* William). Sketches of the country, etc. in Portugal and Spain. *London,* 1809].

Tables généalogiques des héros de romans. *See* **Dutens** (Louis).

Tahiti, receiving the gospel. [*anon.*] 195 pp. 18°. *Philadelphia, American sunday-school union,* 1833.

Tahiti with the gospel. [*anon.*] 246 pp. 1 pl. 18°. *Philadelphia, American sunday-school union,* [1834].

Tahiti, without the gospel. [*anon.*] 243 pp. 3 pl. 18°. *Philadelphia, American sunday-school union,* 1833.

Taillepied (Nöel). Recveil des antiqvitez et singvlaritez de la ville Roven. Auec vn progrez des choses memorables y aduenues depuis sa fondation iusques à present. 8 p. l. 266 pp. 2 l. 18°. *Roven, m. le Mesgissier,* 1587.

Tailor (The) boy. 1865. *See* **Austin** (Jane G.)

Tailors' (The) intelligencer. Devoted to the science of garment cutting, and in the interest of the trade. [Quarterly and monthly]. Aug. 1870, to Dec. 1871. v. 1. fol. *Battle Creek, (Mich.) W. S. & B. Salisbury,* 1870-71.

Taine (Hippolyte Adolphe). History of english literature. Translated by H. Van Laun. With a preface prepared expressly for this translation by the author. 2 v. 1 p. l. x, 531 pp; 2 p. l. 550 pp. 8°. *New York, Holt & Williams,* 1871.

Taisnier (Jean). Opvs mathematicvm octo libros complectens, innvmeris prope modvm figvris idealibvs manvvm et physiognomiae aliisqve adornatvm, cheiromantiae theoricam, praxim, doctrinam, artem, & experientiam verissimam continens. 6 p. l. 624 pp. 3 l. fol. *Coloniae agrippinæ, apud I. Birckmannum & W. Richvvinum,* 1562.

Taken upon trust. By the author of "Recommended to mercy." [*anon.*] 3 v. 12°. *London, Tinsley, brothers,* 1863.

Talbot (*Miss* Catherine). Reflections on the seven days of the week. sm. 4°. [*London, J. Hamilton & co.* 1791].
[*In* HAMILTON (John). Angelica's ladies library, pp. 399-433].

Tales, by the author of "Three experiments in living." *See* **Sedgwick** (Catharine Maria).

Tales for you: a collection of original and selected literature, from celebrated english and american authors. [*anon.*] 240 pp. 16°. *Philadelphia, J. J. Sharkey,* 1841.

Tales of a voyager to the Arctic ocean. [*anon.*] 1st-2d series. 6 v. 8°. *London, H. Colburn,* 1834.
[NAVAL (The) and military library of entertainment, v. 13-18].
——— The same. 2 v. 303 pp; 283 pp. 12°. *Philadelphia, H. C. Carey & I. Lea,* 1827.

Tales of four nations. [*anon.*] 3 v. 8°. *London, Whittaker, Treacher & Arnot,* 1831.

CONTENTS.

v. 1-2. The hunter's oak.
2. The bereaved.
The palace of Chapultepec.
2-3. The ambuscade.
3. The chateau near the lake.

Tales of intemperance. By an observer. [*anon.*] 99 pp. 18°. *Boston, Mass. sabbath school society,* 1836.

Tales of old mr. Jefferson, of Gray's Inn, collected by young mr. Jefferson, of Lyon's Inn. [*anon.*] 1st series. 2 v. xii, 340 pp; 334 pp. 16°. *London, G. and W. B. Whittaker,* 1823.

Tales of the academy. [*anon.*] 2 v. 2 p. l. 270 pp. 2 pl; 2 p. l. 315 pp. 2 pl. 18°. *London, Cowie & co.* 1820–21.

CONTENTS.

v. 1. Ernest and Adolphus; or, probity and duplicity.
The fall of the steeple; or, the little architect.
Paul the hermit; or, the would-be Robinson Crusoe.
The faithful creole lad; or, trial by jury.
2. Theodore; or, the effects of display.
The wet Saturday; or, the naturalists. In 3 parts. Beasts—birds—fishes.

Talk (A) of ten wives on their husband's ware. [*anon.*] 8°. [*London, for private circulation*, 1871].

[*In* FURNIVALL (F. J. *editor*). Jyl of Breyntford's testament, by Robert Copland, [etc.] 1871. pp. 29–33].

Tallcot (George). Reynolds' improved turbine water-wheel. 128 pp. 1 pl. 1 tab. 18°. *New York, G. Tallcot*, [1871].

Talley (Susan Archer). Poems. 183 pp. 12°. *New York, Rudd & Carleton*, 1859.

Talmage (*Rev.* Thomas De Witt). The abominations of modern society. 290 pp. 12°. *New York, Adams, Victor & co.* 1872.

Talmud *babylonicum.* Talmvdis babylonici codex middoth sive de mensvris templi, una cum versione latina. Additis, præter accuratas figuras, commentariis, quibus tota templi hierosolymitani structura cum partibus suis, altari cæterisque eo pertinentibus distincte explicatur, variaque scripturæ s. loca illustrantur. Opera & studio Constantini L'Empereur de Oppyck. 20 p. l. 194 pp. 7 l. 2 tab. sm. 4°. *Lvgdvni Batavorvm, ex officina B. & A. Elzevir*, 1630.

Talon (Nicolas). The holy history. Written in french. And translated into english by [John Paulet, the 5th] marquess of Winchester. Eng. title, 4 p. l. 418 pp. 4 l. 4°. *London, T. W. for J. Crook & J. Baker*, 1653.

[*Note.*—Chiefly a paraphrase of Genesis, Exodus and Deuteronomy].

Tancoigne (J. M.) A narrative of a journey into Persia, and residence at Teheran: a descriptive itinerary from Constantinople to the persian capital; also a variety of anecdotes, illustrative of the history, commerce, religion, manners, customs of the inhabitants, military policy of the government, &c. From the french. xvi, 402 pp. 1 map. 8°. *London, W. Wright*, 1820.

Taneyhill (R. H.) The Leatherwood god. An account of the appearance and pretensions of Joseph C. Dylks, in eastern Ohio in 1828. 54 pp. 8°. *Cincinnati, R. Clarke & co.* 1870.

[OHIO valley series. Miscellanies, no. 3].

Tanner (Henry S.) The american traveller; or guide through the United States. 144 pp. 4 maps. 18°. *Philadelphia, author*, 1834.

——— The same. 2d ed. 144 pp. 5 maps, 4 pl. 18°. *Philadelphia, author*, 1836.

——— The same. 10th ed. 141 pp. 5 maps. 18°. *New York, Map establishment*, 1846.

——— The travellers' hand book for the state of New-York and the province of Canada. 2d ed. 166 pp. 18°. *New York, J. R. Tanner*, 1844.

Tanner (John, *m. d.*) The homoeopathist's pocket reference. Translated from the german, compiled and arranged with considerable additions and improvements. 158 pp. 18°. *Philadelphia, author*, 1838.

Tapia (Eugenio de). Historia de la civilizacion española desde la invasion de los Arabes hasta la época presente. 4 v. in 2. 12°. *Madrid, Yenes*, 1840.

Tappan (*Mrs.* Cora L. V. Hatch Daniels). Hesperia. [A poem]. 1 p. l. vii, 235 pp. 12°. [*Cambridge, (Ms.) H. O. Houghton & co.* 1871].

Tappan (*Rev.* Henry Philip). Brief memorials of an only daughter [Mary C—]. 285 pp. sq. 12°. *New-York, Wiley & Putnam*, 1844.

——— The doctrine of the will, applied to moral agency and responsibility. xi, 348 pp. 12°. *New York, Wiley & Putnam*, 1841.

Tarapha (Francisco). *See* **Tarrafa.**

Tarbell (John Adams, *m. d.*) Homœopathy simplified; or, domestic practice made easy. Explicit directions for the treatment of disease, the management of accidents, and the preservation of health. Revised ed. vii, 372 pp. 12°. *Boston, O. Clapp*, 1863.

Tardif (*L'abbé* J.) Méthode élémentaire et pratique de plain-chant, approuvée par m. l'évêque d'Angers. xviii, 267 pp. 1 l. 8°. *Angers, E. Barassé*, 1860.

Tardy (*Mrs.* Mary T.) The living female writers of the south. Edited by the author of "Southland writers." [*anon.*] xxx, 568 pp. 8°. *Philadelphia, Claxton, Remsen & Haffelfinger*, 1872.

Tarr (Augustus De Kalb). The american reader of prose and poetry. 516 pp. 12°. *Philadelphia, author*, 1859.

Tarrafa (Francisco). De origine, ac rebus gestis regum Hispaniæ liber, multarum rerum cognitione refertus. 202 pp. 11 l. 18°. *Antverpiæ, in ædibus Ioannis Steelsii*, 1553.

Tarrafa (Francisco)—continued.

——— The same. De origine ac rebvs gestis regum Hispaniae [liber, ad annum 1576 productus]. 18°. *Coloniæ, L. Alectorius et hæredes Iacobi Soteris*, 1577.

[VASSE (Johannes) *and* TARRAFA (Francisco). Rervm Hispaniæ memorabilivm annales, pp. 561–781].

Tasman (Abel Jansen). Kort verhael uyt het journael van den kommander A. J. Tasman int ontdekken van't onbekende Suit-lant. sm. 4°. *Amsterdam, A. S. van der Storck*, 1674.

[*In* NIEROP (D. R. van). Eenige œfeningen, v. 2, pp. 56–64].

Tasso (Bernardo). L'Amadigi. Eng. title, 3 p. l. 612 pp. 1 l. 4°. *Vinegia, G. Giolito de' Ferrari*, 1560.

Tasso (Torquato). Godfrey of Bulloigne; or, the recovery of Jerusalem: done into english heroical verse, from the italian, by Edward Fairfax. 7th ed. reprinted from the original folio of 1600. To which are prefixed, a glossary, and the lives of Tasso and Fairfax. By the editor. 2 v. 300 pp; 278 pp. 18°. *London, C. Knight & co.* 1844.

[KNIGHT's weekly volume, v. 10 and 14].

Tastu (Sabine Casimir Amable Voiart). Le livre des femmes. *See* **Dufrénoy** (Adélaïde Gillette Billet) *and* **Tastu**.

Tate (James). [Preliminary] dissertation on the chronology of the works, and on the localities and life and character of Horace. [With appendices and observations on the metres of Horace]. 8°. *London*, 1837.

[*In* HORATIUS FLACCUS (Quintus). Horatius restitutus, pp. 1–202].

Tate (Nahum). *See* **Life** (The) of Lewis of Bourbon, late prince of Condé.

Tate (Thomas). First lessons in philosophy; or, the science of familiar things. American ed. by C. S. Cartée. 252 pp. 12°. *Boston, Hickling, Swan & Brown*, 1856. S.

Tatem (M. H.) The heights of Eidelberg. 339 pp. 12°. *Philadelphia, Claxton, Remsen & Haffelfinger*, 1871.

Tauler (Johann). Institutions [divines: traduction des frères prêcheurs du faubourg Saint-Germain]. 8°. [*Paris, panthéon littéraire*, 1843].

[*In* BUCHON (J. A. C) Choix d'ouvrages mystiques, pp. 608–717].

Taunay (Théodore). Idylles brésiliennes, écrites en vers latins, et traduites en vers français, par Félix Émile Taunay. 1 p. l. 131 pp. 1 l. 8°. *Rio de Janeiro, Gueffier &c.* 1830.

Tavernier (Alphonse). Elements of operative surgery. Translated from the french. With copious notes and additions, by S. D. Gross, m. d. xxx, 448 pp. 8°. *Philadelphia, J. Grigg*, 1829.

Taxidermy: or, the art of collecting and preparing objects of natural history. *See* **Lee** (*Mrs.* Sarah Wallis).

Tayler (I. Frederick). Frederick Tayler's portfolio, 1844. 2 p. l. 13 pl. fol. *London, T. McLean*, [1844].

Taylor (Bayard, *or* James Bayard). Travels in Arabia. Eng. title, v, 325 pp. 13 pl. 1 map. 12°. *New York, Scribner, Armstrong, & co.* 1872.

[ILLUSTRATED library of travel, exploration, and adventure].

Taylor (B. Thomas). The infidel's confession, or, the power of christian union, for the world's speedy conversion. 341 pp. 12°. *Nashville, Southwestern publishing house*, 1859.

Taylor (Charles, 1756–1821). Apostolic baptism. Facts and evidences on the subjects and mode of christian baptism. Stereotype ed. 236 pp. 12°. *New York, Saxton & Miles*, 1844.

——— The same. 236 pp. 1 pl. 12°. *New York, M. W. Dodd*, 1850.

Taylor (Charles Fayette, *m. d.*) Theory and practice of the movement-cure: by the swedish system of localized movements. 295 pp. 1 portrait. 12°. *Philadelphia, Lindsay & Blakiston*, 1861.

Taylor (D. T.) The voice of the church, on the coming and kingdom of the redeemer; or, a history of the doctrine of the reign of Christ on earth. Revised and edited with additions, by H. L. Hastings. xii, 406 pp. 12°. *Peace Dale (R. I.) H. S. Hastings*, 1855.

Taylor (Edgar). The book of rights: or, constitutional acts and parliamentary proceedings affecting civil and religious liberty in England, from magna charta to the present time; historically arranged, with notes and observations. viii, 330 pp. 1 l. 12°. *London, A. Maxwell*, 1833.

Taylor (*Rev.* George B.) The Oakland stories. Kenny. 176 pp. 16°. *New York, Sheldon & co.* 1860.

Taylor (George H. *m. d.*) Diseases of women: their causes, prevention, and radical cure. 318 pp. 12°. *Philadelphia, G. Maclean*, 1871.

Taylor (George H. *m. d.*)—continued.

——— An exposition of the swedish movement cure; together with a summary of the principles of general hygiene. 396 pp. 12°. *New York, Fowler & Wells*, 1860.

Taylor (George Watson). Pieces of poetry: with two dramas. Privately printed. [*anon.* Prefatory note subscribed G. W. T.] 2 v. 2 p. l. 229 pp. 1 portrait; 1 p. l. 223 pp. 12°. *Chiswick, C. Whittingham*, 1830.

CONTENTS.

v. 1. Occasional poems. King Henry the third; or, the expulsion of the French. An historical play, in five acts.
v. 2. The Cross-Bath guide. The profligate, a comedy.

Taylor (*Rev.* Henry, *rector of Crawley*). An inquiry into the opinions of the learned christians, both ancient and modern, concerning the generation of Jesus Christ. Now first published by the editor of Benj. Ben Mordecai's [*pseudon.*] seven letters to Elisha Levi. xii, 126 pp. 4°. *London, J. Wilkie*, 1777.

Taylor (Henry W. *ll. d.*) The times of Daniel. An argument. 208 pp. 1 pl. 12°. *New York, A. D. F. Randolph & co.* 1871.

Taylor (Isaac). Essay on the application of abstract reasoning to the christian doctrines: originally published as an introduction to Edwards on the Will. By the author of "Natural history of enthusiasm." [*anon.*] 1st am. ed. 13-163 pp. 12°. *Boston, Crocker & Brewster*, 1832.

Taylor (Isidore Justin Severin, *le baron*). Voyages pittoresques dans l'ancienne France. *See* **Nodier** (Charles), **Taylor**, *and* **Cailleux.**

Taylor (James B. *d. d.*) Memoir of rev. Luther Rice, one of the first american missionaries to the east. 344 pp. 12°. *Baltimore, Armstrong & Berry*, 1840.

——— Restricted communion: or, baptism an essential prerequisite to the Lord's supper. 99 pp. 18°. *Charleston, Southern baptist publication society*, 1856.

Taylor (Jane). Original poems, for infant minds. By the Taylor family. 180 pp. 16°. *Philadelphia, H. F. Anners*, 1840.

——— The pleasures of taste, and other stories; selected, with a sketch of her life, by mrs. Sarah J. Hale. 288 pp. 1 pl. 18°. *Boston, Marsh, Capen, Lyon, & Webb*, 1839.

Taylor (Jeremy, *bishop of Down and Connor*). Christian consolations taught from five heads in religion. 1. Faith. 2. Hope. 3. The Holy Spirit. 4. Prayer. 5. The sacraments. Written by a learned prelate. [*anon.*] 9 p. l. 219 pp. 1 pl. 18°. *London, R. Royston*, 1671.

——— The golden grove. A choice manual: containing what is to be believed, practised and desired or prayed for; the prayers being fitted to the several days of the week. Also festival hymns, according to the manner of the ancient church. 19th ed. 4 p. l. 154 pp. 2 l. 18°. *London, L. Meredith*, 1699.

Taylor (John, *editor of the Sun*, 1756-1832). Poems on various subjects. [Also, The odes of Anacreon, with the fragments of Sappho and Alcæus. Translated]. 2 v. xxxii, 316 pp; xv, 308 pp. 8°. *London, Payne & Foss*, [*etc.*] 1827.

Taylor (John). Observations on greek emphasis. 63 pp. 8°. [*London*, 1852].

[*In* BIBLE. (*English*). The emphatic new testament, v. 1].

Taylor (*Rev.* Joseph). Oratio funebris, in obitum Edvardi Wigglesworth, s. t. p. quam in sacello holdeniano, apud collegium harvardinum, inter efferendum, habuit J. Taylor. 7 pp. 8°. [*Boston*, 1765].

[*With* APPLETON (Nathaniel. *d. d.*) A faithful and wise servant, etc.]

Taylor (Nathaniel William, *d. d.*) Practical sermons. 455 pp. 8°. *New York, Clark, Austin & Smith*, 1858.

Taylor (*Rev.* Oliver Alden). Brief views of the saviour, with reflections on his doctrines, parables, etc. Designed chiefly for the young. xvi, 13-264 pp. 12°. *Andover, Gould & Newman*, 1835.

——— Piety in humble life: a memoir of mr. Andrew Lee. 216 pp. 18°. *Boston, Mass. sabbath school society*, 1844.

Taylor (Thomas, *d. d.* 1576-1632). Christvs revelatvs. Sive tractatvs de typis insignioribvs v. t. Iesvm Christvm salvatorem nostrum adumbrantibus. Donatus latinitate à S. A. [Ed. 2ª repurgata]. 6 p. l. 378 pp. 1 l. 1 tab. 16°. *Genevæ, sumptibus I. H. Widerhold*, 1664.

[*With* BOWLES (Oliver). De pastore evangelico tractatvs, 1667].

Taylor (*Miss* T.) The little missionary. 152 pp. 2 pl. 18°. *New York, Carlton & Lanahan*, [1871].

——— Marguerite; or, the Huguenot child. 188 pp. 16°. *Cincinnati, Hitchcock and Walden*, 1870.

Taylor (*Rev.* Timothy Alden). Afflictions. 126 pp. 32°. *Worcester, H. J. Howland,* 1845.

——— Our holy hill. vi, 202 pp. 12°. *Boston, S. K. Whipple & co.* 1857.

Taylor (Virgil Corydon). The chime: an extensive collection of new and old tunes, consisting of arrangements from the old masters, and modern european writers; with selections from living american composers: also, a variety of new pieces by the author. Including also, a melodeon instructor. 4th ed. 368 pp. obl. 8°. *New York, D. Burgess & co.* 1855. s.

Taylor (Walter C. *m. d.*) A physician's counsels to man in health and disease. 399 pp. 12°. *Springfield,* [*Ms.*] *W. J. Holland & co.* 1872.

——— A physician's counsels to woman, in health and disease. 403 pp. 12°. *Springfield, W. J. Holland & co.* 1871.

Taylor (*Rev.* William). The model preacher: comprised in a series of letters illustrating the best mode of preaching the gospel. 403 pp. 1 portrait. 12°. *Cincinnati, author,* 1859.

Taylor (William J. R. *d.d.*) Louisa [Gebhard]: a pastor's memorial. 132 pp. 18°. *Philadelphia, American sunday-school union,* [1862].

Taylor. *See* **Tayler.**

Teale (*Rev.* William Henry). Lives of english laymen, lord Falkland, Izaak Walton, Robert Nelson. 362 pp. 2 pl. 16°. *London, J. Burns,* 1844.

[Imperfect: 1 pl. wanting].

Teasdale (Howard M.). Kind words: a new collection of hymns and tunes, &c. *See* **Linton** (G. W.) *and* **Teasdale.**

Technologist (The): especially devoted to engineering, manufacturing and building. [Monthly]. Jan. to Dec. 1871. v. 2. fol. *New York, Industrial publication co.* 1871.

[Continued under the name of The INDUSTRIAL monthly].

Tefft (Benjamin Franklin, *d. d.*) Methodism successful, and the internal causes of its success. With a letter of introduction by bishop Janes. 588 pp. 12°. *New York, Derby & Jackson,* 1860.

Teive (Diogo de). Commentarivs de rebvs a Lvsitanis in India apvd Divm gestis. 16°. *Coloniae Agrippinae, ex officina birckmannica,* 1602.

[*In* MYLIUS (Arnold). De rebvs hispanicis, pp. 377–443].

Telegraph (The) instructor. *See* **Pope** (Frank L.)

Tempel des heiligen Gottes. Vollständiges andachts- und gebetbuch für katholische christen. Aus den schriften der heiligen. Von einem priester der diözese Freiburg. [*anon.*] Eng. title, 528 pp. 3 pl. 18°. *Einsiedeln, New York, & Cincinnati, K. & N. Benziger,* 1871.

Temperance (The) text-book; a collection of facts and interesting anecdotes, illustrating the evils of intoxicating drinks. [*anon.*] 160 pp. 18°. *Philadelphia, Brown & Sinquet,* 1836.

Temple (*Rev.* Daniel Herbert). Life and letters of rev. Daniel Temple, for twenty-three years a missionary in western Asia. With an introductory notice, by rev. R. S. Storrs, d. d. xii, 492 pp. 1 pl. 12°. *Boston, Congregational board of publication,* 1855.

Temple bar. A London magazine for town and country readers. [Monthly]. Dec. 1870, to Nov. 1871. v. 31–33. 8°. *London, R. Bentley,* [1871].

Temple (The) of Cythnos, or the oracles of fortune and wisdom, for the four seasons of life. Translated from the greek. [*anon.*] viii, 162 pp. 12°. *London, N. Conant,* 1778.

Temple (The) of death, a poem. *See* **Habert** (Philippe).

Ten Kate (J. J. L.) Stemmen des vredes. Nieuwe leerredenen. 4 p. l. 296 pp. 8°. *Amsterdam, D. B. Ceulen,* 1863.

Tennant (William, 1784–1848). Hebrew dramas: founded on incidents of bible-history. 2 p. l. 330 pp. 16°. *Edinburgh, J. Menzies,* 1845.

——— The thane of Fife; a poem, in six cantos. viii, 264 pp. 8°. *Edinburgh, A. Constable & co.* 1822.

Tennessee (*State of*). *General assembly.* Senate and house journal of the first session of the thirty-seventh general assembly, which convened at Nashville, on the first Monday in October, 1871. 2 v. 8°. *Nashville, Jones, Purvis & co. printers to the state,* 1871.

——— *State library.* Catalogue of the general and law library of the state of Tennessee. Prepared by order of the judges of the supreme court. viii, 432 pp. 8°. *Nashville,* [*Jones, Purvis & co. printers to the state*], 1871.

——— *Superintendent of public instruction.* First report of the superintendent of public instruction of the state of Tennessee. 1869.

Tennessee—continued.
John Eaton, jr. superintendent public instruction. 8°. *Nashville, G. E. Grisham, printer to the state*, 1869. s.

Tenney (Sanborn). Geology: for teachers, classes, and private students. 320 pp. 12°. *Philadelphia, E. H. Butler & co.* 1860.

Tennyson (Alfred). Complete poetical works. Author's household edition. vi, 428 pp. 1 portrait. 12°. *Boston, J. R. Osgood & co.* 1871.

——— Enoch Arden. 78 pp. 6 pl. 16°. *Boston, J. E. Tilton & co.* 1865.

——— The same. 42 pp. 3 pl. 16°. *Boston, Ticknor & Fields*, 1865.

——— The last tournament. Illustrated by Hammatt Billings. 60 pp. 1 pl. 16°. *Boston, J. E. Tilton & co.* 1872.

Tercentenary monument. In commemoration of the three hundredth anniversary of the Heidelberg catechism. [*anon.*] lxxiii, 574 pp. 8°. *Chambersburg (Pa.) M. Kieffer & co.* 1863.

Tercero (Joseph). La virgen en el templo, honrando el templo. Virtudes heroicas, que exercitò Maria santissima señora nuestra, mientras vivio en el templo. Se las propone en meditaciones à las almas, en especial de virgines religiosas. 2ª impression. 35 p. l. 452 pp. 1 l. 2 pl. 18°. *Sevilla, J. Padrino*, [1755]?
[*Note.*—Written in Mexico in 1723].

Terentianus *maurus*. De literis, syllabis, pedibvs et metris, tractatus insignis, suspiciendus antiquitate etiam reuerenda, Nicolao Brissæo montiuillario commentatore & emendatore. 10 p. l. 117 l. numb. 4°. *Parisiis, apud S. Colinæum*, 1531.

Terentius *Afer* (Publius). Terence in english [and latin]. Fabvlæ comici poetae Terentii omnes anglicæ factæ primumqve hac nova forma nunc editæ: opera ac industria R. B. [Richard Bernard] epworthatis. 4 p. l. 455 pp. sm. 4°. *Cantabrigiæ, ex officina Iohannis Legat*, 1598.

CONTENTS.
Andria. Adelphus.
Evnvchvs. Hecyra.
Heavtontimorvmenos. Phormio.

——— The same. Les comédies de Térence, traduites en françois par madame Dacier. Avec des remarques. 3e éd. revuë, corrigée, & enrichie de figures à chaque comédie. [Latin et français]. 3 v. 16°. *Paris, J. Dumond*, 1699.

CONTENTS.
v. 1. La vie de Térence, écrite par Suetone, Andria. L'Andriene. Eunuchus. L'eunuque.

Terentius *Afer* (Publius)—continued.
v. 2. Heauton timorumenos. Adelphi. Les adelphes.
v. 3. Phormio. Le Phormion. Hecyra. L'Hecyre.

——— The Andrian, Heautontimoreumenos, and Hecyra of Terence. By Jonathan Adair Phillips. xxv, 263 pp. 8°. *Dublin, Tegg, Wise, & Tegg*, 1836.

——— Andria Adelphique. Ex editione westerhoviana. Accedunt notæ anglicæ. Cura C. K. Dillaway. 186 pp. 16°. *Bostoniæ, Perkins & Marvin*, 1839.

——— New translation of the Adelphi of Terence into blank verse, with notes by the translator. 2 p. l. 79 pp. 8°. *London, J. Dodsley, etc.* [*about* 1775].
[MISCELLANEOUS pamphlets, v. 198].

——— The same. Terence's Andrian, a comedy, in five acts, translated into english prose, with critical and explanatory notes, by W. R. Goodluck, jun. 2 p. l. xxx, 330 pp. 16°. *London, Longman*, 1820.

Terhune (*Mrs.* Mary Virginia Hawes). Common sense in the household: a manual of practical housewifery. By Marion Harland. [*pseudon.*] 556 pp. 12°. *New York, C. Scribner & co.* 1871.

——— The empty heart; or, husks. By Marion Harland. [*pseudon.*] 1 p. l. 7-353 pp. 12°. *New York, Carleton*, 1871.

Ternay (Charles Gabriel d'Arsac, *marquis* de). Traité de tactique. Revu, corrigé, augmenté par Fred. Koch. 2 v. 1 p. l. xliii, 702 pp. 1 l; 1 p. l. 702 pp. 1 l. 8°. Atlas. 2 p. l. 18 pl. fol. *Paris, Anselin*, 1832.

Terreros y Pando (Estevan de) Paleografía española, que contiene todos los modos conocidos, que ha habido de escribir en España; juntamente con una historia sucinta del idioma comun de Castilla, y demas lenguas, ó dialectos, que se conocen como proprios en estos reynos. 2 p. l. 160 pp. 18 pl. sm. 4°. *Madrid, J. Ibarra*, 1758.

Terrific (The) register; or, record of crimes, judgments, providences, and calamities. [1st ed. *anon.*] 2 v. Eng. title, iv, 829 pp; eng. title, 832 pp. 8°. *London, Sherwood, Jones, & co.* 1825.

Terry (Henry). American clock making, its early history and present extent of the business. 2 p. l. 24 pp. 2 pl. 1 portrait. 8°. *Waterbury (Conn.) J. Giles & son*, 1870.

Terry (Rose). Poems. 231 pp. 12°. *Boston, Ticknor & Fields*, 1861.

Tersteegen (Gerhard). Geistliche und erbauliche briefe über das inwendige leben und wahre wesen des christenthums. Erste americanische auflage. 2 v. in 1. 4 p. l. 458 pp; 426 pp. 1 l. 16°. *Libanon, (Penn.) J. Hartman,* 1819.

[v. 3–4 wanting].

Tertullianus (Quintus Septimius Florens). Opera. Ad optimorum librorum fidem expressa, curante E. F. Leopold. 4 v. 12°. *Lipsiae, B. Tauchnitz, jun.* 1839–41.

[GERSDORF (E. G.) Bibliotheca patrum ecclesiasticorum latinorum selecta, v. 4–7].

CONTENTS.

v. 1. Libri apologetici.
v. 2. Libri ad ritus et mores christianorum pertinentes.
v. 3–4. Libri polemici et dogmatici.

——— The same. The writings of Quintus Sept. Flor. Tertullianus. v. 3. With the extant works of Victorinus and Commodianus. xix, 514 pp. 8°. *Edinburgh, T. & T. Clark,* 1870.

[ANTE-NICENE christian library, v. 18].

Tessé (Mans Jean Baptiste René de Froullai, *comte et maréchal* de). Mémoires et lettres. Contenant des anecdotes et des faits historiques inconnus, sur partie des règnes de Louis xiv et de Louis xv. [Publiés par P. H. de Grimoard]. 2 v. xvi, 357 pp; 1 p. l. 380 pp. 8°. *Paris, Treuttel et Würtz,* 1806.

Testament (Het) ofte uutersten wille vande nederlandtsche oorloghe. [Poem]. Door Yemand van Waer-mond. [*pseudon.*] 8 l. sm. 4°. [*n. p.*] 1609.

[*In* NEDERLANDTSCHE bye-corf].

——— The same. Codicille van de nederlandsche oorloghe. Door Yemand van Waermond. [*pseudon.*] 6 l. sm. 4°. [*n. p.*] 1609.

[*In* NEDERLANDTSCHE bye-corf].

——— The same. Het testament vande oorloghe. [Poem]. Noch is hier bygevoecht, de copye vanden brief gheschreven aen graef Herman vandē Berg. Noch een discours van N. Mulerium, van Brugge. [*anon.*] 4 l. sm. 4°. [*n. p.*] 1608.

[*In* NEDERLANDTSCHE bye-corf].

Testimony (The) and advice of an assembly of pastors of churches in New-England, at a meeting in Boston July 7, 1743. Occasion'd by the late happy revival of religion in many parts of the land. By order of the assembly. 51 pp. 8°. *Boston, S. Kneeland and T. Green,* [1743].

Testimony (The) of a number of New-England ministers met at Boston Sept. 25, 1745, professing the ancient faith of these churches. 20 pp. 8°. *Boston, S. Kneeland and T. Green,* 1745.

[*With* TESTIMONY (The) and advice of an assembly of pastors, 1743].

Testimony (The) of the people called quakers, given forth by a meeting of the representatives of said people, in Pennsylvania and New-Jersey, held at Philadelphia the 24th day of the first month, 1775. [Concerning the unhappy contest between Great Britain and the colonies]. Folded sheet. 8°. [*Philadelphia,* 1775].

Tevius (Jacobus). *See* **Teive** (Diogo de).

Texier de la Pommeraye (A.) Abridgment of a french and english grammar. By the same author. 1st ed. 2 p. l. 272 pp. 8°. *Philadelphia,* [*author*], 1822.

Thacker (J. A. *m. d. editor*). *See* **Cincinnati** (The) medical repertory.

Thackeray (Anne Isabella). To Esther, and other sketches. 3 p. l. 394 pp. 1 pl. 12°. *London, Smith, Elder & co.* 1869.

Thackeray (William Makepeace). Ballads. vii, 228 pp. 12°. *Boston, Ticknor & Fields,* 1856.

Thatcher (Benjamin Bussey). Memoir of rev. S[amuel] Osgood Wright, late missionary to Liberia. 122 pp. 1 portrait. 18°. *Boston, Light & Horton,* 1834.

Tháttr af Karli vesala. Res gestae Caroli infortunati. Textus islandicus nunc primum editus, latine versus et praefatiuncula instructus. [*anon.*] 8°. [*Havniae,* 1815].

[*In* THORLACIUS (Börge). Prolusiones et opuscula, v. 3, pp. 309–360].

Thaxter (Celia). Poems. 86 pp. 18°. *New York, Hurd & Houghton,* 1872.

Thayer (*Rev.* Thomas Baldwin). The bible class assistant, or scriptural guide for sunday schools: being sketches of the antiquities, customs, and manners of the Jews in illustration of scripture. iv, 180 pp. 16°. *Boston, T. Whittemore,* 1840.

Thayer (*Rev.* William A.) The old horseshoe; or, Sammy's first cent. viii, 296 pp. 6 pl. 12°. *Boston, Mass. sabbath school society,* [1863].

Thayer (*Rev.* William Makepeace). The bobbin boy [Nathaniel P. Banks]; or how Nat got his learning. xx, 310 pp. 5 pl. 16°. *Boston, J. E. Tilton & co.* 1860.

——— Hints for the household; or, family counsellor. 288 pp. 12°. *Boston, J. P. Jewett & co.* 1853.

Thayer (*Rev.* W. M.)—continued.
——— The pioneer boy, [Abraham Lincoln], and how he became president. 310 pp. 6 pl. 12°. *Boston, Walker, Wise & co.* 1863.
——— The poor boy and merchant prince; or, elements of success drawn from the life and character of the late Amos Lawrence. 349 pp. 16°. *Boston, Gould & Lincoln*, 1857.
——— The poor girl and true woman; or, elements of woman's success drawn from the life of Mary Lyon and others. A book for girls. 353 pp. 16°. *Boston, Gould & Lincoln*, 1859.
——— The printer boy; or, how Ben Franklin made his mark. xvi, 261 pp. 5 pl. 16°. *Boston, J. E. Tilton & co.* 1861.
——— Tales from the bible. For the young. 262 pp. 16°. *Boston, J. E. Tilton & co.* 1860.

Thayer. *See* **Theyer.**

Théaulon de Lambert (Marie Emmanuel Guillaume Marguerite). Le petit chaperon rouge, opéra féerie, en trois actes. The little red riding hood, a fairy opera. In three acts. Translated for the use of visitors to the french opera. By W. F. F. 130 pp. 18°. *Baltimore, E. J. Coale*, 1831.

Theganus, *trevirensis.* Thegani chorepiscopi trevirensis opvs de gestis domini Lvdiwici imp. fol. [*Argentorati, J. R. Dulssecker*, 1702].
[*In* KULPIS (Johann Georg von). Scriptores rervm germanicarvm. *Argentorati*, 1702. pp. 67-81].

Théis (Alexandre Étienne Guillaume, *baron* de). Travels of Polycletes, in letters from Rome, a. u. c. 668-672. Abridged from the original, by mons. de Rouillon, and translated into english, by M. A. P. xx, 462 pp. 1 map. 12°. *London, J. Souter*, 1826.

Thelwall (*Rev.* Algernon Sydney). Sermons, chiefly on subjects connected with the present state and circumstances of the world. xv, 510 pp. 8°. *London, R. B. Seeley & W. Burnside*, 1833.

Thelwall (John). Prospectus of a course of lectures, to be delivered every Monday, Wednesday, and Friday, during the ensuing lent. In strict conformity with the restrictions of mr. Pitt's convention act. 1 p. l. 29 pp. 8°. *London*, 1796.
[*With* The tribune, a periodical publication, by Thelwall, v. 3].
——— Selections for the illustration of a course of instructions on the rhythmus and utterance of the english language: with an introductory essay on the application of rhythmical science to the treatment of impediments, and the improvement of our national oratory; and an elementary analysis of the science and practice of elocution, composition, etc. [1st ed.] 4 p. l. lxii, 176 pp. 8°. *London, J. M'Creery*, 1812.
——— Sober reflections on the seditious and inflammatory letter of Edmund Burke to a noble lord. 116 pp. 8°. *London, H. D. Symonds*, 1796.
[DUANE pamphlets, v. 33].
——— The same.
[MISCELLANEOUS pamphlets, v. 183, 435].
——— The tribune, a periodical publication, consisting chiefly of the political lectures of J. Thelwall. Taken in short-hand by W. Ramsey, and revised by the lecturer. 3 v. 8°. *London, author*, 1795-96.
[*Note.*—No more published].

Theobald (G.) Geologische beschreibung von Graubünden. 1864-66. *See* **Switzerland.** *Geologische commission.*

Theocritus. La traduction de plusieurs idylles de Théocrite. [Avec sa vie]. Par m. M * * * C * * [Julien Jacques Moutonnet Clairfons]. 8°. [*Paris, Le Boucher*, 1774].
[*In* MUSAEUS *grammaticus.* Héro et Léandre. *Paris*, 1774. pp. 35-104].

Theodore. A story about baptism. By a true baptist. [*anon.*] 374 pp. 4 pl. 12°. *Philadelphia, Presbyterian board of publication*, 1871.

Theological (The) magazine, or synopsis of modern religious sentiment. On a new plan. July, 1795, to February, 1799. v. 1-3. 8°. *New York, C. Davis*, 1796-99.
[*Note.*—July and August numbers, 1796, wanting].

Theological (The) repertory and churchman's guide. *See* **Washington** (The) theological repertory. 1829-30.

Theophrastus. Θεοφραστου ἠθικοι χαρακτηρες. Theophrasti notationes morum. [Græce et latine]. 8°. [*Amstelædami, apud H. Wetstenium*, 1688].
[*In* GALE (Thomas). Opuscula mythologica, etc. pp. 567-610].

Théorie du paradoxe. 1775. *See* **Morellet** (André).

Therry (Roger). Reminiscences of thirty years' residence in New South Wales and Victoria. With a supplementary chapter on transportation and the ticket-of-leave system. xiv, 514 pp. 8°. *London, S. Low, son, & co.* 1863.

Thespian (The) magazine and literary repository. [June, 1792, to Sept. 1794. *anon.*] 3 v. 8°. *London, T. Wilkins*, 1793–94.

Theyer (John). Aerio-mastix, or, a vindication of the apostolicall and generally received government of the church of Christ by bishops, against the schismaticall aërians of our time. 7 p. l. 161 pp. 2 l. sm. 4°. *Oxford, W. Webb*, 1643.

Thiébault de Laveaux (J. C.) *See* **Laveaux.**

Thienis (Gaietanus). *See* **Tiene** (Gaetano).

Thierry (Amédée Simon Dominique). Tableaux de l'empire romain depuis la fondation de Rome, jusqu'à la fin du gouvernement impérial en occident. 4e éd. 2 p. l. iv, 476 pp. 8°. *Paris, Didier & ce.* 1863.

Thierry (Jacques Nicolas Augustin). Recueil des monuments inédits de l'histoire du tiers état. Première série. Chartes, coutumes, actes municipaux, statuts des corporations d'arts et métiers des villes et communes de France. Région du nord. t. 4. Contenant les pièces relatives à l'histoire municipale d'Abbeville et à celle des villes, bourgs et villages de la basse Picardie. 4°. *Paris, imprimerie impériale*, 1870.

[FRANCE. *Ministère de l'instruction publique.* Collection de documents inédits sur l'histoire de France, 1re série].

This week, an editor's table. Conducted by A. J. H. Duganne.* Oct. 3 to Nov. 7, 1868. Nos. 1–6 in 1 v. fol. *New York, J. J. Bonnet*, 1868.

Tholuck (Friedrich August Gottreu). A commentary on the gospel of John. Translated from the german by rev. A. Kaufman. [Without text]. 474 pp. 12°. *Boston, Perkins & Marvin*, 1836.

Thomas (*Rev.* Edward). Sermons. 474 pp. 12°. *Charleston,* [*S. C.*] *A. E. Miller*, 1841.

Thomas (Elizabeth). Poems on several occasions. By a lady. [*anon.*] 4 p. l. 296 pp. 4 l. 8°. *London, T. Combes*, 1726.

Thomas (Elijah). The young lady's piece-book; or, a selection of elegant pieces in verse and prose, from various authors. 162 pp. 16°. *Philadelphia, E. Thomas*, 1828.

Thomas (Frederick Samson). The psychologist; or, whence is a knowledge of the soul derivable? a poetical, metaphysical, and theological essay. vii, 211 pp. 8°. *London, W. H. Dalton*, 1844.

Thomas (Frederick William). The beechen tree. A tale: told in rhyme. 95 pp. 12°. *New York, Harper & brothers*, 1844.

Thomas (John Wesley). An apology for "Don Juan;" a satirical poem in two cantos. 3d ed. [Also] a third canto, including remarks on the times. iv, 144 pp. 16°. *London, Partridge & Oakey*, 1850.

Thomas (William, *d. d.*) A survey of the cathedral-church of Worcester; with an account of the bishops thereof, from the foundation of the see to the year 1600. Also an appendix of many original papers and records, never before printed. 1 p. l. vi, [664] pp. 27 pl. 4°. *London, author*, 1737.

Thomas Du Fossé (Pierre). Memoirs of the sieur de Pontis; who served in the army six and fifty years, under king Henry iv, Lewis the xiii, and Lewis the xiv. Faithfully englished by Charles Cotton. 4 p. l. 288 pp. fol. *London, F. Leach for J. Knapton*, 1694.

Thomes (William H.) The gold hunters' adventures; or, life in Australia. By a returned Australian. 564 pp. 4 pl. 12°. *Boston, Lee & Shepard*, 1864.

——— A slaver's adventures on land and sea. Eng. title, 406 pp. 4 pl. 12°. *Boston, Lee & Shepard*, 1872.

[The ocean life series].

——— The whaleman's adventures in the Sandwich islands and California. 444 pp. 4 pl. 12°. *Boston, Lee & Shepard*, 1872.

[The ocean life series].

Thompson (Augustus Charles, *d. d.*) Lyra cœlestis. Hymns on heaven. 382 pp. 12°. *Boston, Gould & Lincoln*, 1863.

——— The mercy-seat; or, thoughts on prayer. 345 pp. 12°. *Boston, Gould & Lincoln*, 1863.

——— Morning hours in Patmos: the opening vision of the apocalypse, and Christ's epistles to the seven churches of Asia. 268 pp. 1 pl. 12°. *Boston, Gould & Lincoln*, 1860.

Thompson (Charles). Rules for bad horsemen; hints to inexpert travellers; and maxims worth remembering by the most experienced equestrians. A new ed. with modern additions, by John Hinds. viii, 87 pp. 2 pl. 12°. *London, author*, 1830.

Thompson (Ebenezer, *d. d.*) *and* **Price** (William C. *ll. d.*) The history of our blessed lord and saviour Jesus Christ: with the lives of the holy apostles, and their successors for three hundred years after the crucifixion. 2 v. xv, 476 pp; 443 pp. 8°. *Wilmington,* [*Del.*] *W. Pryce*, 1805.

Thompson (George W.) Deus-semper. 435 pp. 12°. *Philadelphia, Claxton, Remsen & Haffelfinger*, 1869.

Thompson (Joseph, *d. d.*) Home worship: selections from the scriptures, with meditations, prayer, and song, for every day in the year. Subscription ed. ix, 528 pp. 22 pl. 4°. *Boston, J. R. Osgood & co.* [1871].

Thompson (Joseph Parrish, *d. d.*) Bryant Gray: the student, the christian, the soldier. 148 pp. 1 portrait. 18°. *New York, A. D. F. Randolph*, 1864.

Thompson (Julia Carrie). Life in narrow streets. 284 pp. 4 pl. 16°. *Philadelphia, Presbyterian board of publication*, [1871].

Thompson (*Rev.* J. Renwick). God's punitive dealings with man. 12°. [*Pittsburgh*, 1872].

[*In* REFORMED presbyterian church in North America. Memorial volume, pp. 15–26].

Thompson (W. H.) Sicily and its inhabitants. Observations made during a residence in that country, in the years 1809 and 1810. 4 p. l. 234 pp. 3 pl. 1 map. 4°. *London, H. Colburn*, 1813.

Thompson (Zadock). The youth's assistant in theoretick and practical arithmetic. 2d ed. 164 pp. 8°. *Woodstock, Vt. D. Watson*, 1826.

Thomson (*Rev.* Alexander, *professor at Glasgow*). Address at the funeral [of the rev. Ralph Wardlaw, d. d.] 16°. [*London, A. Fullarton & co.* 1854].

[*In* DISCOURSES and services on occasion of the death of the late rev. Ralph Wardlaw, d. d. 1854. pp. 1–14].

Thomson (Andrew, *d. d.*) Life of John Owen, d. d. 1 p. l. 204 pp. 16°. *Edinburgh, Johnstone & Hunter*, 1853.

Thomson (Charles West). The love of home and other poems. 120 pp. 12°. *Philadelphia, P. Thomson*, 1845.

Thomson (*Rev.* George). The spirit of general history, in a series of lectures, from the eighth to the eighteenth century; wherein is given a view of the progress of society in manners and legislation, during that period. ix, 434 pp. 8°. *Carlisle, F. Jollie*, 1791.

Thomson (James). Hymnus ["These as they change, almighty Father" latina versa]. 4°. [*Patavii*, 1775].

[*In* COSTA (G.) Poema, etc. pp. 53–60].

Thomson (*Mrs.* Katherine Byerley). The white mask. 3 v. 12°. *London, R. Bentley*, 1846.

Thomson (Samuel, *m. d.*) New guide to health; or botanic family physician. To which is prefixed, a narrative of the life and medical discoveries of the author. 2 v. in 1. 228 pp; 168 pp. 12°. *Boston, author*, 1835.

Thomson (Thomas, *m. d.* 1773–1852). Travels in Sweden, during the autumn of 1812. xii, 457 pp. 9 pl. 4 maps. 4°. *London, R. Baldwin*, 1813.

Thoré (Théophile). Dictionnaire de phrénologie et de physiognomie, à l'usage des artistes, des gens du monde, des instituteurs, des pères de famille, des jurés. 3 p. l. 246 pp. 2 pl. 16°. *Bruxelles, établissement encyclographique*, 1837.

Thorer *or* **Thorinus** *or* **Torinus** (Albanus). Caelii Apitii, de re culinaria libri decem. B. Platinae [de' Sacchi] cremonensis De tuenda ualetudine, natura rerum, & popinæ scientia libri x. Pavli aeginetae de facultatibus alimentorum tractatus, Albano Torino interprete. 314 pp. 7 l. 16°. *Lvgvdvni, apvd S. Gryphivm*, 1541.

Thoresby (Ralph). Ducatus leodiensis: or, the topography of the ancient and populous town and parish of Leedes, and parts adjacent, in the west-riding of the county of York. To which is added, a catalogue of his museum, &c. 2d edition, with notes and additions, by Thomas Dunham Whitaker. fol. *Leeds, Robinson, son, & Holdsworth*, 1816.

[WHITAKER (Thomas Dunham). History and topography of Leeds, v. 1].

Thorinus *or* **Torinus**. *See* **Thorer**.

Thorlacius (Börge). Prolusiones et opuscula academica, argumenti maxime philologici. 3 v. 8°. *Havniae, typis excudit J. F. Schultz*, 1806–15.

Thorndike (Herbert). Just weights and measures: that is, the present state of religion weighed in the balance, and measured by the standard of the sanctuary. 8 p. l. 256 pp. 1 l. sm. 4°. *London, J. M. for J. Martin, (etc.)* 1662.

Thorne (Leonard C.) Man not immortal: a review of "rev." N. D. George on annihilation. 275 pp. 12°. *New York, office of the Herald of life*, 1871.

Thornhill (Frederick). Poems. 2d ed. xi, 120 pp. 8°. *London, T. Jones*, 1814.

Thornton (Henry, *m. p.*) Family prayers: to which is added, a family commentary upon the sermon on the mount. 1st american ed. Edited by the rev. Manton Eastburn, d. d. 2 v. in 1. 168 pp. 1 pl; 160 pp. 12°. *New York, Swords, Stanford, & co.* 1837.

Thornton (Henry, *m. p.*)—continued.
——— Female characters. vii, 203 pp. 16°. *London, Hatchard & son*, 1846.

Thornton (Jessie, *pseudon?*) Sunshine for gloomy hours. 216 pp. 3 pl. 18°. *Philadelphia, Presbyterian board of publication*, [1864].

Thornton (*Rev.* Thomas C.) Theological colloquies; or, a compendium of christian divinity, speculative and practical, founded on scripture and reason. 723 pp. 8°. *Baltimore, Lewis & Coleman*, 1837.

Thornwell (Emily). The young lady's own book: an offering of love and sympathy. 442 pp. 8 pl. 12°. *New York, J. C. Derby*, 1856.

Thornwell (James Henley, *d. d.*) The collected writings of J. H. Thornwell. Edited by John B. Adger, d. d. 2 v. vi, 659 pp; 622 pp. 1 portrait. 8°. *Richmond, Presbyterian committee of publication*, 1871.

CONTENTS.

v. 1. Theological.
v. 2. Theological and ethical.

——— The apocryphal books of the old testament proved to be corrupt additions to the word of God. The arguments of Romanists from the infallibility of the church, and the testimony of the fathers in behalf of the apocrypha, discussed and refuted. 417 pp. 1 l. 12°. *New York, Leavitt, Trow & co.* 1845.

Thorpe (Kamba, *pseudon.*) *See* **Bellamy** (E. W.)

Thoughts for the afflicted; with an appendix of selections from various authors. [*anon.*] With an introduction, by rev. George B. Cheever, d. d. 224 pp. 12°. *Auburn and Buffalo, Miller, Orton & Mulligan*, 1854.

Three weeks in Palestine and Lebanon. 8th ed. [*anon.*] viii, 152 pp. 11 pl. 18°. *London, J. W. Parker*, 1839.

Three years in a man-trap. 1872. *See* **Arthur** (Timothy Shay).

Thrilling stories of the great rebellion. By a disabled officer. [*anon.*] 384 pp. 4 col. pl. 12°. *Philadelphia, J. E. Potter*, 1864.

Throckmorton (*Sir* Thomas). The legend of sir Nicholas Throckmorton, who died of poison, a. d. 1570. An historical poem. 2 p. l. 57 pp. 4°. *London*, 1740.

[*In* PECK (Francis). New memoirs of mr. John Milton. 1740].

Thucydides. Historiæ liber 1, 2. 8°. *Oxonii*, 1835.

[*In* HISTORIA græca, ed. 2a. [*Oxonii*, 1835], pp. 137–275].

Thucydides—continued.
——— The same. Histoire de Thucydide, fils d'Olorus, traduite du grec par Pierre-Charles Levesque. 4 v. 8°. *Paris, J. B. Gail & P. F. Aubin*, 1795.

Thudichum (John L. W. *m. d.*) *and* **Dupré** (August). A treatise on the origin, nature, and varieties of wine; being a complete manual of viticulture and œnology. xxiv, 760 pp. 1 pl. 1 map. 8°. *London, Macmillan & co.* 1872.

Thumb (Thomas, *pseudon.*) The monster of monsters: a true and faithful narrative of a most remarkable phenomenon lately seen in this metropolis; to the great surprize and terror of his majesty's good subjects. By Thomas Thumb, esq. 24 pp. 16°. [*Boston, Zechariah Fowle*], 1754.

[*Note.*—Burnt by the common hangman, below the court-house in King street in Boston, by order of the house of representatives of the province of Massachusetts-Bay].

Thurber (Charles). Our Charlie: a memorial. By his father. [*anon.*] 377 pp. 1 portrait. 12°. *Cambridge*, [*Ms.*] *Riverside press*, 1863.

Thuringia. (*Büreau vereinigter thüringischer staaten*). Statistik Thüringens. Mittheilungen des statistischen büreaus vereinigter thüringischer staaten herausgegeben von dr. Bruno Hildebrand. Band 1, 2.–3. lief. 4°. *Jena, F. Frommann*, 1867. S.

Thurlow (Edward Hovell, 2*d baron* Thurlow). Poems on several occasions. 4 p. l. 128 pp. 8°. *London, White, Cochrane, & co.* 1813.

Thurlow (*Hon.* Thomas John Hovell-). Trade unions abroad and hints for home legislation. Reprinted from a report on the Amsterdam exhibition of domestic economy for the working classes. 2d ed. vii, 397 pp. 8°. *London, Harrison*, 1871.

Thynne (William). A compendium of logic, for the use of under graduates in the university of Dublin; with notes. 3d ed. vii, 208 pp. 12°. *Dublin, J. Cumming*, 1835.

Tibullus (Albius). An essay toward a new edition of the elegies of Tibullus, with a translation and notes. [By the rev. Samuel Henley]. xv, 46 pp. 8°. *London, J. Johnson*, 1792.

[MISCELLANEOUS pamphlets, v. 103].

——— *and* **Sulpicia.** A poetical translation of the elegies of Tibullus; and of the poems of Sulpicia. With the original text, and notes critical and explanatory. By James Grainger, m. d. [Latin and english]. 2 v. xlvi, 165 pp; 1 pl. 263 pp. 16°. *London, A. Millar*, 1769.

Ticknor (Caleb, *m. d.*) A popular treatise on medical philosophy; or, an exposition of quackery and imposture in medicine. 273 pp. 12°. *New York, Gould & Newman*, 1838.

Ticknor (George, *ll. d.*) History of spanish literature. 4th am. ed. 3 v. 8°. *Boston, J. R. Osgood & co.* 1872.

Tidsskrift for populære fremstellinger af naturvidenskaben, udgivet af C. Fogh, Chr. Lütken og Chr. Vanpell. 2en række. 5 v. 12°. *Kjöbenhavn, P. G. Philipsens forlag*, 1859–63. s.

——— The same. 3e række. 5 v. 12°. *Kjöbenhavn, P. G. Philipsens forlag*, 1864–68. s.

——— The same. 4e række. v. 1–3. 12°. *Kjöbenhavn, P. G. Philipsens forlag*, 1869–71. s.

Tieck (Johann Ludwig). Der gestiefelte kater. Ein kindermährchen in drei akten. 12°. *New York, D. Appleton & co.* 1854.

[*In* ADLER (G. J.) Handbook of german literature, pp. 329–398].

Tiene (Gaetano). Gaietanus super libros de anima [Aristotelis]. Ejusdē questiones de sensu agente: [etc.] Itē de substātia orbis Joānis de gandauo cum questionibus eiusdem. *b. l.* 113 l. fol. *Impēsa nobilis viri dñi Octauiani Scoti ciuis Modoetiēsis per Bonetū Locatellū Bergomensem decimo kal. Januarias* 1493.

Tijdschrift voor natuurlijke geschiedenis en physiologie. Uitgegeven door J. Van der Hoeven en W. H. DeVriese. 12 v. 8°. *Amsterdam, C. G. Sulpke*, 1834–45. s.

[No more published].

Tilden (W. S.) The hour of singing. *See* **Emerson** (L. O.) *and* **Tilden**.

Tileston (Edward G.) Handbook of the administrations of the United States; also, a record of contemporaneous english history. 222 pp. 1 pl. 18°. *Boston, Lee & Shepard*, 1871.

Tilke (Samuel Westcott). Practical reflections on the nature and treatment of disease; founded upon fourteen years' experience in the cure of gout, rheumatism, scrofula, fever, &c. and remarks on the present system of medical education and practice. 4th ed. revised and enlarged. xxviii, 342 pp. 1 portrait. 8°. *London, author*, 1842.

Tillières (Tanneguy Leveneur, *comte* de). Mémoires inédits du comte Leveneur de Tillières ambassadeur en Angleterre sur la cour de Charles Ier et son mariage avec Henriette de France. Recueillis, mis en ordre, et précédés d'une introduction par C. Hippeau. 2 p. l. xlii, 261 pp. 1. l. 16°. *Paris, F. Didot frères*, 1863.

Tillinghast (William). Chorals for elementary practice. obl. 16°. [*Boston, J. R. Miller*, 1855].

[*In* JOHNSON (J. C.) Carmina melodia, pp. 141–176].

Tilloch (Alexander, *ll. d.*) Dissertations introductory to the study and right understanding of the language, structure, and contents of the apocalypse. viii, 380 pp. 8°. *London, author*, 1823.

Tilman (Randolph). Zion's choral. A new collection of church music, adapted to the various metres now in use, together with a clear exposition of the primary principles of musical notation. 112 pp. obl. 8°. *Baltimore, T. N. Kurtz*, 1871.

Tilton (Theodore). Tracts. 18°. *New York, office of the Golden age*, 1871.

CONTENTS.

No. 1. The rights of women. A letter to Horace Greeley. 11 pp.
No. 2. The constitution, a title deed to woman's franchise. A letter to Charles Sumner. 17 pp.
No. 3. Victoria C. Woodhull. A biographical sketch. 36 pp.
No. 4. The sin of sins. [Fallen women]. 10 pp.

Tilton's journal of horticulture and florist's companion. [Monthly]. July, 1870, to Dec. 1871. v. 8–9. 8°. *Boston, J. E. Tilton & co.* 1870–71.

Timæus *locrus*. Τιμαιω τω λοκρω περι ψυχας κοσμω και φυσιος. Timæi locri de anima mundi, et natura. [Græce et latine edidit T. Gale]. 8°. [*Amstelædami, apud H. Wetstenium*, 1688].

[*In* GALE (Thomas). Opuscula mythologica, pp. 539–566].

Timbs (John). Wellingtoniana: anecdotes, maxims, and characteristics, of the duke of Wellington. viii, 152 pp. 1 portrait. 12°. *London, Ingram, Cooke, & co.* 1852.

——— (*editor*). *See* **Year-book** of facts.

Times (The). July 4 to Dec. 31, 1791. Nos. 2066–2190. fol. *London, A. Anderson*, 1791.

[Imperfect].

——— The same. Jan. 1 to Dec. 31, 1871. 4 v. fol. *London, F. Goodlake*, 1871.

——— The same. Index. Jan. 1 to Dec. 30, 1871. 4 v. sm. 4°. *London, S. Palmer*, 1871–72.

Tindal (Nicholas). A guide to classical learning; or Polymetis [of Joseph Spence,] abridged. 2d ed. inlarged. 4 p. l. 279 pp. 3 l. 12 pl. 12°. *London, R. Horsfield & J. Dodsley*, 1765.

Tischer (Johann Friedrich Wilhelm). Life of Martin Luther. Abridged. 8°. *Philadelphia, Quaker city publishing house*, 1872.
[*In* BIBLE. (*English*). *Galatians*. A commentary on Galatians. By Martin Luther, pp. 25-77].

Tissandier (Gaston). The wonders of water. From the french. Edited, with numerous additions, by Schele de Vere, d. d. x, 350 pp. 26 pl. 12°. *New York, C. Scribner & co.* 1872.
[ILLUSTRATED library of wonders].

Titi (Placido de'). Primum mobile, with theses to the theory, and canons for practice; wherein is demonstrated, from astronomical and philosophical principles, the nature and extent of celestial influx upon the mental faculties and corporeal affections of men; exemplified in thirty remarkable nativities of the most eminent men in Europe. Originally written in latin. The whole carefully translated. Illustrated with notes and an appendix, by John Cooper. xvi, 462 pp. 1 portrait. 8°. *London, Davis & Dickson*, [1815].

Titon du Tillet (Évrard). Essais sur les honneurs et sur les monumens accordés aux illustres sçavans, pendant la suite des siècles. Où l'on donne une légère idée de l'origine & du progrès des sciences & des beaux arts. 4 p. l. xxiii, 470 pp. 16°. *Paris, J. B. Coignard, & A. Boudet*, 1734.

Titsingh (Isaac). Cérémonies usitées au Japon, pour les mariages, les funérailles, et les principales fêtes de l'année; suivies d'anecdotes sur la dynastie régnante des souverains de cette empire. Ouvrage traduit du japonais. Orné de 24 gravures faites d'après des peintures japonaises. 3 v. 18°. *Paris, Nepveu*, 1822.

Titus (*Rev.* Timothy T.) The explanatory question-book, for the use of sunday-schools. 115 pp. 16°. *Philadelphia, Lutheran board of publication*, 1871.

CONTENTS.

v. 1. On the parables of our lord. [With text].

Tizzard (Samuel). The new athenian oracle; or, ladies' companion. Book first, containing questions in prose, on moral, philosophical and other subjects, enigmas, paradoxes, rebuses, charades, &c. Also, curious mathematical questions. Book second, containing answers and solutions, in prose and verse. 263, 96 pp. 8°. *Carlisle, A. Loudon*, 1806.

Tobitt (John H.) What I heard in Europe during the "american excitement;" illustrating the difference between government and people abroad in their hostility and good wishes to the perpetuity of the great republic. 133 pp. 8°. *New York, H. M. Tobitt*, 1863.

Tocornal (Manuel Antonio). Memoria sobre el primer gobierno nacional. 8°. *Santiago, imprenta nacional*, 1866.
[*In* VALENZUELA (J. S.) Historia jeneral de Chile, v. 1, pp. 103-266].

Tocqueville (Alexis Charles Henri Maurice Clérel de). American institutions and their influence. With notes, by hon. John C. Spencer. xiv, 460 pp. 1 pl. 8°. *New York, A. S. Barnes & co.* 1851.

Tod (David, *m. d.*) A disquisition on certain parts and properties of the blood. With illustrative woodcuts. viii, 263 pp. 8°. *London, J. Churchill*, 1854.

Todd (Charles Scott) *and* **Drake** (Benjamin). Sketches of the civil and military services of William Henry Harrison. 165 pp. 16°. *Cincinnati, U. P. James*, 1840.

Todd (John, *d. d.*) Lectures to children; familiarly illustrating important truth. 1 p. l. 218 pp. sq. 16°. *Northampton, [Ms.] J. H. Butler*, 1834.

——— The same. Second series. Eng. title, 275 pp. 6 pl. sq. 16°. *Northampton, Hopkins, Bridgman & co.* 1858.

——— The lost sister of Wyoming [Frances Slocum]. An authentic narrative. 160 pp. 1 pl. 18°. *Northampton, J. H. Butler*, 1842.

——— The moral influence, dangers and duties, connected with great cities. 267 pp. 18°. *Northampton, J. H. Butler*, 1841.

——— The sabbath-school teacher: designed to aid in elevating and perfecting the sabbath school system. 432 pp. 12°. *Northampton, J. H. Butler*, 1837.

——— Simple sketches. Edited by J. Brace, jun. 298 pp. 18°. *Northampton, J. H. Butler*, 1838.

——— The student's manual: designed, by specific directions, to aid in forming and strengthening the intellectual and moral character and habits of the student. 392 pp. 16°. *Northampton, J. H. Butler*, 1835.

Todd (*Rev.* John A.) Memoir of the rev. Peter Labagh, d. d. With notices of the history of the reformed protestant dutch church in North America. To which is added the sermon preached at dr. Labagh's funeral, by the rev. Gabriel Ludlow, d. d. 339 pp. 1 portrait. 12°. *New York, board of publication of the reformed protestant dutch church*, 1860.

Todd (Lewis C.) A defence, containing the author's renunciation of universalism, explained and enlarged; the notices and aspersions of universalist editors, answered and repelled; arguments and principles of universalists, examined and exploded, and religion and revelation vindicated, against skepticism and infidelity. 345 pp. 12°. *Erie, [Pa.] O. Spafford,* 1834.

Todi (Iacopone da). *See* **Jacopone da Todi.**

Toll (Cornelis). De infelicitate litteratorum. 18°. [*Lipsiæ, apud J. F. Gleditsch,* 1707]

[*In* MENCKEN (J. B.) Analecta de calamitate litteratorum. 1707. pp. 413-482].

Tollens (Henrik van). [Dichterlijke werken]. 9 v. 8°. *Gravenhage, J. Immerzeel, jr.* [1828-32]; *Leeuwarden, G. T. N. Suringar,* [1834-40].

CONTENTS.

v. 1-3. Gedichten. 5e druck. 3 v. 1831.
v. 4. Romancen, balladen en legenden. 3e druk. 1 p. l. 206, ii pp. 1832.
v. 5-6. Nieuwe gedichte. [v. 1, 2e druk]. 2 v. ix, 195 pp; vi, 194 pp. 1828.
v. 7. Liedjes van Mathias Claudius. 1 p. l. viii, 112 pp. 1834.
v. 8. Dichtbloemen bij de naburen geplukt. 1 p. l. xiv, 160 pp.
v. 9. Verstrooide gedichten. 1 p. l. x, 176 pp. 1840.

Tollet (*Miss* Elizabeth). Poems on several occasions. With Anne Boleyn to king Henry viii, an epistle. 1 p. l. 238 pp. 16°. *London, J. Clarke,* 1755.

Tollius. *See* **Toll.**

Tomkins (John), *and others.* Piety promoted, in brief memorials, of the virtuous lives, services, and dying sayings of some of the people called quakers, formerly published in eight parts. Now revised by John Kendal, and placed in the order of time. New ed. 3 v. 16°. *London, J. Phillips,* 1789.

Tomkins (Simon, *pseudon.*) The adventures of a strolling player. An autobiography. Edited by Susarion. [*pseudon.*] viii, 311 pp. 16°. *London, C. Griffin & co.* [1868].

Tomkins (Thomas). Rays of genius collected to enlighten the rising generation. 2 v. 2 p. l. 320 pp. 1 l. 1 portrait; 1 p. l. 340 pp. 1 l. 16°. *London, proprietor,* 1806.

Tomkinson (Trelawney, *pseudon.*) The inquisitor. 1 p. l. x, 304 pp. 8°. *London, J. Macrone,* 1836.

Tomlinson (Charles). Introduction to the study of natural philosophy, for the use of beginners. vi, 162 pp. 12°. *London, J. Weale,* 1848.

Tommasini (Jacopo Filippo). Vita, et miracvla seraphici patris s. Francisci de Assisio, triplici idiomate, latino italo atq; hispano

Tommasini (Jacopo Filippo)—continued. descripta. Eng. title, 51 pl. 8°. *Romæ, J. de Rubeis,* 1649.

[*Note.*—This book includes no other text than the brief polyglott inscriptions subjoined to the plates. The engravings appear to have come from the hand of Franz van Floris].

Tonkin (Thomas). The parochial history of Cornwall. 1838. *See* **Gilbert** (Daniel).

Tonnerre (Stanislas, *comte* de Clermont-). *See* **Clermont-Tonnerre.**

Too big to go to sabbath-school. 139 pp. 2 pl. 18°. *Philadelphia, Presbyterian publication society,* [1869].

Tookey (James). A cabinet of quadrupeds: consisting of highly-finished engravings by James Tookey, &c. *See* **Church** (John).

Topographia und eigentliche beschreibung der vornembsten stäte, schlösser auch anderer plätze und örter in denen hertzogthumer Braunschweig und Lüneburg. *See* **Zeiller** (Martinus).

Torbert (I. K.) The farmer and mechanic's manual: or the present currency of the United States, concisely explained, etc. Together with mensuration, [etc.] 140 pp. 1 l. 18°. *Harrisburg, F. Wyeth,* 1831.

Torch-bearers. By the author of "The climbers," "Paul Venner," &c. [*anon.*] 321 pp. 3 pl. 16°. *Boston, D. Lothrop & co.* 1871.

Torinus (Albanus). *See* **Thorer.**

Torquemada (Antonio de). Iardin de flores cvriosas, en qve se tratan algvnas materias de hvmanidad, philosophia, theologia, y geographia, con otras cosas curiosas, y apazibles. 12 p. l. 538 [540] pp. 18°. *Anveres, I. Corderio,* 1575.

Torre (Antonio Giuseppe Rezzonico, *conte* della). *See* **Rezzonico della Torre.**

Torrente (Mariano). Slavery in the island of Cuba, with remarks on the statements of the british press relative to the slave trade. 107, 32 pp. 8°. *London, C. Wood,* 1853.

[*Note.*—In spanish and english, on opposite pages; appendix in english alone].

Torres (Luca Antonio de). Laudatio funebris Ferdinandi vi. Hispanarum et Indiarum regis. Habita Mexici pridie idus martias regalis cancellariæ pro-rege gubernantis, et totius civitatis nomine. 1 p. l. xxii pp. sm. 4°. [*Mexico,* 1760].

[*With* BALCARCEL Y FORMENTO (D.) *and* MALO (F. V.) Lagrymas de la paz].

Torrey (*Rev.* Charles Turner). Home! or the pilgrims' faith revived. vii, 13-255 pp. 18°. *Salem,* [*Ms.*] *J. P. Jewett & co.* 1845.

Torrey (Henry Warren). An english-latin lexicon, prepared to accompany Leverett's latin-english lexicon. 318 pp. 8°. *Boston, J. H. Wilkins & R. B. Carter*, 1837.

Torrey (Jesse, *jun.*) A mental museum for the rising generation. With an appendix, containing the declaration of independence, constitution of the United States, etc. 360 pp. 1 pl. 12°. *Philadelphia, T. Desilver*, 1829.

——— The moral instructor, and guide to virtue: being a compendium of moral philosophy. In eight parts. 4th ed. 300 pp. 12°. *Philadelphia, Kimber & Sharpless*, 1824.

Torrey (Joseph, *d. d.*) Memoir of dr. Worthington Smith. 12°. [*Andover*, 1861].

[*In* SMITH (Worthington, d. d.) Select sermons, pp. 1-115).

Torriano (Giovanni). Vocabolario italiano & inglese, a dictionary english & italian. *See* **Florio** (Giovanni).

Tortelli (Giovanni). Ioannis Tortelii aretini orthographia. [Commentarioř grāmaticorum de orthographia dictionū e græcis tractarum syntagma]. 173 l. numb. fol. *Venetiis, p B. de Zanis de Portesio*, 1501.

Tottel (Richard). Tottel's miscellany. Songes and sonettes by Henry Howard, earl of Surrey, sir Thomas Wyatt, the elder, Nicholas Grimald, and uncertain authors. 1st ed. of 5th June; collated with the 2d ed. of 31st July, 1557. By Edward Arber. xvi, 272 pp. 16°. *London*, 1870.

[ARBER's english reprints, no. 24 in v. 11].

Toulmin (Joshua, *d. d.*) Memoirs of the revd. Samuel Bourn. With an appendix, consisting of various papers and letters, and biographical notices of some of his contemporaries, and a supplement containing specimens of his historical and catechetical exercises. xii, 284, 94 pp. 8°. *Birmingham, J. Belcher & son*, 1808.

Toulotte (E. L. J.) *and* **Riva** (Ch. Théodore). Histoire de la barbarie et des lois au moyen âge; de la civilisation et des mœurs des anciens, comparées à celles des modernes; de l'église et des gouvernements; des conciles et des assemblées nationales chez différents peuples, et particulièrement en France et en Angleterre. 3 v. 8°. *Paris, L. Dureuil*, 1829.

Tourbe (La) des philosophes. *See* **Arislaüs** *or* **Arisleus.**

Tourjée (Eben). The New England conservatory method for the piano-forte. Comprising the first three grades of instruction. 271 pp. 4°. *Boston, G. D. Russell & co.* [1870-71].

Tourlet (René). Abrégé ou sommaire historique et critique de la vie de l'empereur Julien. 8°. [*Paris*, 1821].

[*In* JULIANUS *imperator* (Flavius Claudius). Œuvres complètes. *Paris*, 1821. v. 1, pp. 1-134].

Towers (John V. R.) Towers' premium tables, for buying and selling gold, bonds, and stocks; giving the premium on any amount from one dollar to ten thousand dollars, from one-eighth of one per cent, to twenty-five and seven-eighths per cent. 28 l. obl. 4°. *Washington, D. C.* 1871.

Towers (Joseph, *ll. d.*) An essay on the life, character, and writings of dr. Samuel Johnson. [*anon.*] 2 p. l. 124 pp. 8°. *London, C. Dilly*, 1786.

Towle (Nathaniel C.) A history and analysis of the constitution of the United States, with a full account of the confederations which preceded it; of the debates and acts of the convention which formed it; of the judicial decisions which have construed it; with papers and tables illustrative of the action of the government, and the people under it. 3d ed. revised and enlarged. xxxiii, 449 pp. 8°. *Boston, Little, Brown & co.* 1871.

Town. *See* **Towne.**

Towndrow (Thomas). A complete guide to the art of writing short-hand, being an entirely new and comprehensive system, representing the elementary sounds of the english language, in stenographic characters, [etc.] 120 pp. 1 pl. 24°. *Boston, Perkins & Marvin*, 1837.

Towne *or* **Town** (John). A critical inquiry into the opinions and practice of the ancient philosophers concerning the nature of the soul and a future state, and their method of the double doctrine. 2d ed. in which two late answers by mr. Jackson and dr. Sykes have afforded an opportunity of supplying what was wanting to complete the subject. With a preface by the author of the Divine legation, [W. Warburton. *anon.*] xiv, 305 pp. 8°. *London, C. Davis*, 1748.

Townsend (George, *d. d.*) Journal of a tour in Italy, in 1850, with an account of an interview with the pope. xii, 300 pp. 8°. *London, F. & J. Rivington*, 1850.

Townsend (George Alfred). The mormon trials at Salt Lake City. 49 pp. sm. 4°. *New York, American news company* 1871.

Townsend (George Alfred)—continued.
——— The new world compared with the old: a description of the american government, institutions, and enterprises, and of those of our great rivals at the present time, particularly England and France. 663 pp. 16 pl. 8°. *Hartford, Conn. S. M. Betts & co.* 1870.

Townsend (*Rev.* Luther Tracy). The sword and the garment. 238 pp. 16°. *Boston, Lee & Shepard,* 1871.

Townsend (Virginia Frances). Max Meredith's millennium. 218 pp. 3 pl. 12°. *Boston, Loring,* [1870].
[Breakwater (The) series, no. 4].

——— The mills of Tuxbury. 363 pp. 4 pl. 12°. *Boston, Loring,* [1871].

——— Temptation and triumph, with other stories. 389 pp. 12°. *Cincinnati, Poe & Hitchcock,* 1863.

——— The well in the rock, and other tales. 278 pp. 7 pl. 16°. *New York, J. Miller,* 1863.

Townshend (*Rev.* Chauncy Hare). The weaver's boy, a tale; and other poems. 2d ed. Frontispiece, xii, 228 pp. 12°. *London, T. Boys,* 1825.

Tracts in the oriya language. [*anon.*] 3 v. 12°. *Cuttack, the Orissa tract society,* 1843–44.

CONTENTS.
v. 1. Poetical series.
v. 2. The christian's manual.
v. 3. Controversial series; or, a guide for inquirers.

Tracy (Joseph, *d. d.*) The three last things: the resurrection of the body, the day of judgment, and final retribution. 104 pp. 16°. *Boston, Crocker & Brewster,* 1839.

Tracy (J. L.) Guide to the great west: being a brief, but carefully written, description of the country bordering upon all the principal railroads of the west, with maps and illustrations. 290 pp. 3 l. 1 pl. 2 maps. 12°. *St. Louis, Tracy & Eaton,* [1870].

Trade (The) circular and publishers' bulletin. F. Leypoldt, editor. [Monthly]. April 25 to Sept. 25, 1871. v. 4. 8°. *New York, F. Leypoldt,* 1871.

Trades (The) increase. *See* **Roberts** (J.)

Trail (*Rev.* William). A guide to christian communicants in the exercise of self-examination. 112 pp. 32°. *Philadelphia, Presbyterian board of publication,* [1839].

Trall (Russell Thacher, *m. d.*) Diphtheria: its nature, history, causes, prevention, and treatment on hygienic principles; with a resumé of the various theories and practices of the medical profession. 276 pp. 12°. *New York, Fowler & Wells,* 1862.

——— An essay on tobacco-using; being a philosophical exposition of the effects of tobacco on the human system. 79 pp. 16°. *Battle Creek, Mich. office of the Health reformer,* 1872.

——— Pathology of the reproductive organs; embracing all forms of sexual disorders. xii, 242 pp. 1 portrait. 8°. *Boston, B. L. Emerson,* 1861.

Transplanted (The) olive-plant: or, some account of Thomas Spencer Nichols, who died Sept. 8, 1851, at the age of eight years. [*anon.*] 158 pp. 1 pl. 18°. *Boston, S. K. Whipple & co.* 1853.

Transtagano (Antonio Vieyra). *See* **Vieira Transtagano** (Antonio).

Trapper's (The) niece. A sketch of western life. [*anon.*] 283 pp. 4 pl. 16°. *Boston, D. Lothrop & co.* 1871.

Trautwine (John C.) The civil engineer's pocket-book, of mensuration, trigonometry, surveying, [etc.] In addition to which the elucidation of certain important principles of construction is made in a more simple manner than heretofore. 645 pp. 16°. *Philadelphia, Claxton, Remsen & Haffelfinger,* 1871.

——— The field practice of laying out circular curves for railroads. 7th ed. 108 pp. 12°. *Philadelphia, T. Hamilton,* 1872.

——— A new method of calculating the cubic contents of excavations and embankments, by the aid of diagrams. Together with directions for estimating the cost of earthwork. 4th ed. 60 pp. 10 pl. 8°. *Philadelphia, T. Hamilton,* 1871.

Travis (*Rev.* Joseph). Autobiography of the rev. Joseph Travis. Embracing a succinct account of the methodist episcopal church, south, with short memoirs of several local preachers, and an address to his friends. Edited by Thomas O. Summers, d. d. 238 pp. 1 portrait. 12°. *Nashville, Tenn. E. Stevenson,* 1856.

Treatise (A) concerning the causes of the present corruption of christians. 1711. *See* **Osterwald** (Jean Frédéric).

Treatise (A) on the nature and causes of doubt, in religious questions; (with a particular reference to christianity). With an appendix, on some common difficulties; lists of books, &c. [*anon.*] xiv, 194 pp. 12° *London, Longman* 1831.

Treatise (A) wherein is manifestlie proved, that reformation [etc.] 1590. *See* **Penry** (John).

Treeby (S.) The elements of astronomy. Revised and corrected by M. Nash. 216 pp. 9 pl. 18°. *New York, S. Wood & sons*, 1823.

Tremadeure (*Mlle.* Sophie Ulliac). *See* **Ulliac-Tremadeure** (Sophie).

Tremayne (S. C. H.) Florence Dalbiac, and other tales. 234 pp. 12°. *New-York, S. W. Benedict*, 1840.

Tribune (The), a periodical publication. *London*, 1795-96. *See* **Thelwall** (John).

Tribune (The) almanac, for the years 1838 to 1868, inclusive; comprehending the politician's register and the whig almanac. Together with political essays, addresses, party platforms, &c. making a connected political history for thirty years. [Edited by Horace Greeley]. 30 nos. in 2 v. 12°. *New York, The New York tribune*, 1868.

——— The same. The tribune almanac and political register for 1872. 12°. *New York, Tribune association*, 1872.

Tribute (A) to the memory of Fitzhugh Smith, the son of Gerrit Smith. By the author of "Thoughts on a new order of missionaries," etc. [*anon.*] 284 pp. 12°. *New York, Wiley & Putnam*, 1840.

Trinity college (*Dublin*). *Observatory*. Observations made at the magnetical and meteorological observatory at Trinity college, Dublin: under the direction of Humphrey Lloyd. v. 2. 1844-50. xii, 542 pp. 2 pl. 4°. *Dublin, Hodges, Foster, & co.* 1869. s.

Trinity college (*Hartford, Conn.*) Catalogue of the officers and students of Trinity college, 1871-72. 8°. *Hartford, Church press*, 1871.

Trismégiste (Johannès, *pseudon.*) *See* **Lorambert.**

Trissino (Giovanni Giorgio). Tutte le opere, non più raccolte di Giangiorgio Trissino. 2 v. in 1. viii, xxxiv, 398 pp. 1 l. 2 pl. 1 portrait; 4 p. l. 317 pp. 1 l. 82 pp. fol. *Verona, J. Vallarsi*, 1729.

Tristan (Flora). Pérégrinations d'une paria, 1838. *See* **Chazal** (Flora C. T. H. Tristan Moscoso, *madame*).

Triumph of faith: or memoir of mrs. Nancy M. Clark. [*anon.*] 148 pp. 18°. *Boston, Massachusetts sabbath school society*, 1840.

Triumphs (The) of industry; illustrated by the life of Adam Clark, ll. d. [*anon.*] 226 pp. 7 pl. 18°. *Philadelphia, American sunday school union*, [1854].

Triumphs of talent; or, extraordinary transitions from comparative obscurity to extreme greatness. By the author of "Practical wisdom," &c. [*anon.*] xii, 334 pp. 12°. *London, A. J. Valpy*, 1834.

Trivet (Nicholas). Annales sex regum Angliæ. [1154-1307]. E præstantissimo codice glastoniensi nunc primum emendate edidit Antonius Hall. 13 p. l. 348 pp. 16 l. 8°. *Oxonii, e theatro sheldoniano*, 1719.

——— The same. Nicolai Triveti annalium continuatio; ut et Adami murimuthensis chronicon, cum ejusdem continuatione: quibus accedunt Joannis Bostoni speculum coenobitarum, et Edmundi Boltoni hypercritica. Omnia nunc primum edidit e codicibus manuscriptis Antonius Hallius. 6 p. l. 242 pp. 7 l. 8°. *Oxonii, e theatro sheldoniano*, 1722.

Troef, grooten troef, tusschen Engelandt en Hollandt, gespeelt in de tegenwoordigheyt van een Fransman, een Spanjaert, een Portugees, een Sweedt, ende een Deen. [*anon.*] 15 pp. sm. 4°. [*n. p.*] 1664.

——— The same. Vervolgh-troef [etc. *anon.*] 21 pp. sm. 4°. [*n. p.*] 1664. [*With* the preceding].

——— The same. Derde deel. [*anon.*] 40 pp. sm. 4°. [*n. p.*] 1665. [*With* the preceding].

Trois-Étoiles (*pseudon.*) The member for Paris: a tale of the second empire. By Trois-Étoiles. 206 pp. 8°. *Boston, J. R. Osgood & co.* 1871.

Trollope (*Mrs.* Frances Milton). Belgium and western Germany in 1833; including visits to Baden-Baden, Wiesbaden, Cassel, Hanover, the Harz mountains, &c. 2 v. 2 p. l. xii, 329 pp. 1 l; viii, 293 pp. 12°. *London, J. Murray*, 1834.

——— A romance of Vienna. 2 v. 197 pp; 201 pp. 12°. *Philadelphia, E. L. Carey & A. Hart*, 1838.

——— The young heiress. A novel. 3 v. 12°. *London, Hurst & Blackett*, 1853.

Trollope (William). Pentalogia græca. Sophoclis Œdipus tyrannus, Œdipus coloneus, et Antigone: Euripidis Phœnissæ: et Æschyli Septem contra Thebas: quinque dramata de celeberrima Thebaide scripta. Notis anglice scriptis illustravit et lexicon vocum difficiliorum adjecit W. Trollope. viii, 475 pp. 22 l. 8°. *Londini, apud C. & J. Rivington*, 1825.

Trotter (Thomas, *m. d.*) An essay, medical, philosophical, and chemical, on drunkenness, and its effects on the human body. 2d ed. xi, 211 pp. 8°. *London, Longman,* 1804.

Trotz (Christian Heinrich). Opusculum de scribis, apologia pro Wæchtlero [etc.] 8°. [*Trajecti ad Rhenum, apud H. Besseling,* 1738].
[*In* HUGO (Hermann). De prima scribendi origine. 1738. 14 p. l. pp. 415–513].

Troubles (The) of a good husband. [*anon.*] x, 143 pp. 16°. *Northampton,* [*Eng.*] *F. Cordeux,* 1818.

Trousseau (Armand). Lectures on clinical medicine, delivered at the hôtel-dieu, Paris. Translated from the edition of 1868, being the third enlarged edition; by John Rose Cormack, m. d. v. 2–3. 8°. *London, The new Sydenham society,* 1869.
[NEW (The) Sydenham society publications, v. 42, 45].

Trovhertighe vermaninghe aende verheerde Nederlantsche Provintien: ende het alghemeyne eynde ende voornemen des Spaengniaerds t'welck is d' oprechtinghe van een voorghenomene vijfde monarchie: mitsgaders hunne resolutie over dese Nederlanden Door een lief hebber des nederlandschen vryheyds voor-gestellt. [*anon.*] 6 l. sm. 4°. [*n. p.*] 1586. [*Reprinted, n. p.* 1608].
[*In* NEDERLANDTSCHE bye-corf].

Trowbridge (Catharine M.) Dick and his friend Fidus. 231 pp. 4 pl. 18°. *Philadelphia, W. S. & A. Martien,* 1859.

——— Frank and Rufus; or obedience and disobedience. 280 pp. 3 pl. 18°. *Philadelphia, W. S. & A. Martien,* 1864.

——— George Morton and his sister. 258 pp. 3 pl. 12°. *Philadelphia, W. S. & A. Martien,* 1864.

——— Jennie's bible-verses. 153 pp 2 pl. 18°. *Philadelphia, W. S. & A. Martien,* 1865.

Trowbridge (John Townsend). Burcliff: its sunshine and its clouds. By Paul Creyton. [*pseudon.*] 295 pp. 1 pl. 16°. *Boston, Phillips, Sampson & co.* 1854.

——— Father Brighthopes; or, an old clergyman's vacation. By Paul Creyton. [*pseudon.*] 274 pp. 1 pl. 16°. *Boston, Phillips, Sampson & co.* 1853.

——— Hearts and faces; or, home-life unveiled. By Paul Creyton. [*pseudon.*] 238 pp. 1 pl. 16°. *Boston, Phillips, Sampson & co.* 1853.

Trowbridge (John Townsend)—continued.

——— Jack Hazard and his fortunes. iv, 254 pp. 2 pl. 12°. *Boston, J. R. Osgood & co.* 1871.

——— The three scouts. 381 pp. 16°. *Boston, J. E. Tilton & co.* 1865.

Troy (*New York*). The Troy directory, for the year 1871: including Lansingburgh, West Troy, Cohoes and Green Island, also a business directory, a record of the city government, its institutions, &c. v. 43. Sampson, Davenport & co. compilers. 429 pp. 8°. *Troy, W. H. Young & Blake,* [1871].

Troya di Napoli (Carlo). Del veltro allegorico di Dante. 4 p. l. 216 pp. 1 portrait. 8°. *Firenze, G. Molini,* 1826.

Trublet (Nicolas Charles Joseph, *l'abbé*). Essais sur divers sujets de littérature, et de morale. 6e éd. 2 v. 2 p. l. 339 pp; 2 p. l. 360 pp. 12°. *Amsterdam, E. Van Harrevelt,* 1755.

Trübner's american and oriental literary record. A monthly register of the most important works published in America, India, China, and the British colonies. Sept. 26, 1870, to June 30, 1871. v. 6. 8°. *London, Trübner & co.* 1870–71.

True (Charles Kittridge, *d. d.*) The elements of logic. 3d ed. 176 pp. 16°. *New York, Carlton & Porter,* 1861.

True stories of the days of Washington. [*anon.*] 312 pp. 4 pl. 12°. *New York, Phinney, Blakeman & Mason,* 1861.

Try: better do it, than wish it done. By the author of "Annandale," [etc. *anon.*] 244 pp. 3 pl. 18°. *Philadelphia, Presbyterian board of publication,* 1863.

Tryon (John). The old clown's history; in three periods. Introducing graphic sketches of show life in its multifarious phases. With characteristics of distinguished showmen. 242 pp. 8°. *New York, Torrey brothers,* 1872.

Tryon (Thomas, *m. d.*) The way to health, long life and happiness, or, a discourse of temperance and the particular nature of all things requisit for the life of man. [With] a treatise of english herbs. By Philotheos Physiologus. [*pseudon.*] 8 p. l. 669 pp. 12°. *London, A. Sowle,* 1683.

——— Wisdom's dictates: or, aphorisms and rules, physical, moral, and divine, for preserving the health of the body and the peace of the mind. [Also], a bill of fare of

Tryon (Thomas, *m. d.*)—continued. seventy-five noble dishes of excellent food, far exceeding those made of fish or flesh. 3 p. l. 144 pp. 1 l. 8°. *London, J. Salusbury*, 1696.

Tryphiodorus. La prise de Troie, traduite par Allut. 12°. [*Paris*, 1841].
[*In* MARTIN (Louis Aîné). Petits poëmes grecs. 1841. pp. 131-156].

Tuberville. *See* **Turberville.**

Tucker (Abraham). Freewill, foreknowledge, and fate. A fragment. By Edward Search. [*pseudon.*] xxxii, 268 pp. 8°. *London, R. & J. Dodsley*, 1763.

Tucker (Nathaniel Beverley). George Balcombe. A novel. [*anon.*] 2 v. 282 pp; 319 pp. 12°. *New-York, Harper & brothers*, 1836.

Tuckerman (Frederick Goddard). Poems. 253 pp. 12°. *Boston*, [*J. Wilson & son*], 1860.

——— The same. iv, 235 pp. 16°. *Boston, Ticknor & Fields*, 1864.

Tuckerman (Henry Theodore). Introductory essay [on Goldsmith]. 12°. [*Boston*, 1854].
[*In* GOLDSMITH (Oliver). Poems, plays and essays. *Boston*, 1854. pp. vii-xxvii].

——— The italian sketch book. [*anon.*] 216 pp. 12°. *Philadelphia, Key & Biddle*, 1835.

——— The life of John Pendleton Kennedy. 490 pp. 1 pl. 1 fac-simile, 1 portrait. 12°. *New York, G. P. Putnam & sons*, 1871.

——— A shorter history of english and american literature. *See* **Shaw** (Thomas B.)

Tuckfield (*Mrs.* Hippisley). Education for the people. Embracing i. Pastoral teaching. ii. Village teaching. iii. The teacher's text-book. iv. Instruction of the deaf and dumb. vi, 1 p. l. 272 pp. 16°. *London, Taylor and Walton*, 1839.

Tuet (Jean Charles François). Matinées sénonoises, ou proverbes françois, suivis de leur origine; de leur rapport avec ceux des langues anciennes et modernes; etc. [*anon.*] 2 p. l. xvi, 544 pp. 2 l. 8°. *Paris, Née de la Rochelle*, 1789.

Tu-li-shin. Narrative of the chinese embassy to the khan of the Tourgouth Tartars, in the years 1712-15; by the chinese ambassador. Translated from the chinese and accompanied by an appendix of miscellaneous translations. By sir George Thomas Staunton. xxxix, 330 pp. 1 map. 8°. *London, J. Murray*, 1821.
[*Note.*—The chinese title of the original was Yee-yu-loo].

Tullidge (*Rev.* Henry). Triumphs of the bible, with the testimony of science to its truth. 439 pp. 12°. *New York, C. Scribner*, 1863.

Tulp (Nikolaas). Observationvm medicarvm libri tres. 7 p. l. 279 pp. incl. 14 pl. 16°. *Amstelredami, apud L. Elzevirivm*, 1641.

Tunstall (Cuthbert, *bishop of Durham*). The byble in englyshe. 1541. *See* **Bible.** (*English*).

Tunstall (James, *m. d.*) Rambles about Bath and its neighbourhood. 3d ed. xii, 1 l. 304 pp. 14 pl. 1 map. 12°. *Bath, M. A. Pocock*, [1851].

Tupper (Martin Farquhar). A modern pyramid: to commemorate a septuagint of worthies. xii, 322 pp. 12°. *London, J. Rickerby*, 1839.

——— A third series of proverbial philosophy. iv, 314 pp. 12°. *London, E. Moxon & co.* 1867.

Turberville (Henry, *d. d.*) An abridgment of the christian doctrine: with proofs of scripture on points controverted. By way of question and answer. Composed in 1649. 152 pp. 18°. *New York, J. Doyle*, 1833.

Turnbull (George, *editor*). Three dissertations; one on the characters of Augustus, Horace and Agrippa, with a comparison between Agrippa and Maecenas, by the abbé de Vertot. [Also], some reflections on the characters of Augustus, Maecenas and Horace, and on the works of Horace, by [A. A. Cooper] the earl of Shaftsbury. Another on the gallery of Verres, by the abbé Fraguier. A third on the nature, origin and use of masks, in theatrical representations among the ancients, by mr. Boindin. xxiii, 122 pp. 2 pl. 4°. *London, R. Dodsley*, 1740.

Turnbull (*Rev.* Joseph). The laws of Christ; being a complete digest of all the precepts contained in the new testament. xii, 383 pp. 12°. *London, Hamilton, Adams & co.* 1832.

Turnbull (Laurence, *m. d.*) A clinical manual of the diseases of the ear. 486 pp. 1 col. pl. 8°. *Philadelphia, J. B. Lippincott & co.* 1872.

Turnbull (William Watson). Inebriæ, legend of Wyoma lake, and other poems. 124 pp. 8°. *Boston, A. Mudge & son*, 1871.

Turnèbe (Adrien). Uiri clariss. Adriani Tvrnebi opera: nvnc primvm ex bibliotheca Stephani Adriani F. Tvrnebi in unum collecta, emendata, aucta & tributa in tomos 3. 3

Turnèbe (Adrien)—continued.
v. in 1. fol. *Argentorati, sumptibus L. Zetzneri,* 1600.
[*Note.*—It is said that this eminent scholar was of scotch descent, and originally named Turnbull. The family settled in Normandy, and translated their name into Tourneboeuf, which was afterwards modified to the present form].

Turner (John, *d. d. vicar of Greenwich*). Eight sermons, preached in 1708. fol. [*London,* 1739].
[BOYLE lectures, v. 2, pp. 349-428].

Turner (Robert). *Βοτανολογια.* The british physician: or the nature and vertues of english plants. 7 p. l. 363 pp. 20 l. 16°. *London, R. Wood for N. Brook,* 1664.

Turner (Samuel Hurlbeart, *d. d.*) Autobiography of the rev. Samuel H. Turner, d. d. 292 pp. 1 portrait. 12°. *New York, A. D. F. Randolph,* 1863.

——— The epistles to the Galatians and Ephesians, in greek and english. *See* **Bible.** (*Greek and english*).

Turner (William). Sound anatomiz'd, in a philosophical essay on musick. [Also], a discourse, concerning the abuse of musick. 3 p. l. 80, 7 pp. 1 l. music. sm. 4°. *London, W. Pearson for author,* 1724.

Turner (William W.) Jack Hopeton; or, the adventures of a Georgian. 364 pp. 12°. *New York, Derby & Jackson,* 1860.

Turney (*Rev.* Edmund). Baptism, in the import and explicitness of the command; or an examination of the meaning of the word *baptizo.* With an introduction relating to the proper import and uses of the english words baptize and baptism. 1 p. l. 40, 36, 36 pp. 12°. *New York, E. H. Fletcher,* 1851.

Turnley (Joseph). The spirit of the vatican, illustrated by historical & dramatic sketches during the reign of Henry the second. With an appendix of papal bulls, doctrines, episcopal letters, etc. iv, 247 pp. 8°. *London, H. Cunningham,* 1845.

Turnour (*Rev.* Edward John). Thoughts in youth and age; poems on various subjects. xii, 461 pp. 8°. *London, C. J. G. & F. Rivington,* 1831.

Turpin de Crissé (*Comte* Lancelot). Commentaires sur les institutions militaires de Végèce. 2e éd. revue, corrigée et augmentée. 2 v. xxiv, 468 pp. 8 pl; viii, 446 pp. 1 l. 12 pl. 4°. *Paris, Nyon l'aîné,* 1783.

Turrell (Henry J.) A manual of logic, or a statement and explanation of the laws of formal thought. 116 pp. sq. 16°. *London, Rivingtons,* 1870.

Tuson (Edward William). The dissector's guide; or student's companion. 1st american ed. with additions, by Winslow Lewis, jr. m. d. xii, 220 pp. 12°. *Boston, Allen & Ticknor,* 1833.

——— The same. 2d am. ed. xii, 220 pp. 12°. *Boston, W. D. Ticknor,* 1837.

Tuthill (*Mrs.* Louisa Caroline Huggins). Edith, the backwoods girl. A story for girls. 245 pp. 1 pl. 16°. *New York, C. Scribner,* 1859.

——— Get money. 284 pp. 1 pl. 18°. *New York, C. Scribner,* 1858.

——— Onward! right onward! iv, 169 pp. 18°. *Boston, W. Crosby & H. P. Nichols,* 1845.

——— Reality; or, the millionaire's daughter. 310 pp. 12°. *New York, C. Scribner,* 1856.

Tuttle (Joseph F. *d. d.*) The way lost and found. A book for the young, especially young men. 285 pp. 4 pl. 16°. *Philadelphia, Presbyterian board of publication,* [1870].

Tuttle (L. A.) The little pilgrim band, or "The golden nine." A sacred cantata, in two parts. 13 pp. obl. 18°. *Berea (O.) author,* [1870].

Twain (Mark, *pseudon.*) *See* **Clemens** (Samuel Langhorne).

Twee missiven geschreven uyt Pensilvania, d'eene door een Hollander, woonachtig in Philadelfia, d'ander door een Switzer, woonachtig in German Town dat is Hoogduytse stadt. Van den 16 en 26 maart 1684. 27 l. sm. 4°. *Rotterdam, P. van Alphen,* 1684.
[*Note.*—Imperfect: the first letter, "d'eene door een Hollander," wanting].

Tweedie (William K. *d. d.*) Home: a religious book for the family. 423 pp. 12°. *New York, J. W. Smith & son,* 1862.

Twining (Henry). Voyage en Norwège et en Suède. xii, 420 pp. 18 pl. 8°. *Paris, Delauny,* 1836.

Twisleton (Edward Turner Boyd). Preface and collateral evidence [of the handwriting of Junius]. 4°. *London, J. Murray,* 1871.
[*In* CHABOT (Charles). The handwriting of Junius, professionally investigated, pp. i-lxxviii, and 219 to the end].

Twiss (*Sir* Travers, *editor*). Monumenta juridica. The black book of the admiralty. *See* **Great Britain.** *Treasury department. Master of the rolls.*

Twist (Johan van). Generale beschrijvinge van Indien. Ende in't besonder kort verhael van t'koninckrijck van Gusuratten. Vyt verscheyden autheuren ende eyghen onder-

Twist (Johan van)—continued. vindinge vergadert. 1 p. l. 94 pp. sm. 4°. *Amstelredam, J. Hartgerts*, 1648.
[*In* HARTGERTS (J.) Oost-indische voyagien, v. 1, 12e stuck].

Two (The) apprentices: or the importance of family religion. [*anon.*] 120 pp. 18°. *New York, E. Collier*, 1835.

Two (The) brothers; or, the family that lived in the first society. [*anon.*] 2 v. 2 p. l. 299 pp; 2 p. l. 289 pp. 12°. *London, R. Bentley*, 1850.

Two (The) Catherines; or, which is the heroine? [*anon.*] 2 v. vii, 312 pp; vii, 327 pp. 12°. *Cambridge*, [*Eng.*] *Macmillan & co.* 1862.

Two families and two aims in life. By the author of "The white chrysanthemum." [*anon.*] Eng. title, 372 pp. 3 pl. 16°. *New York, Warren, Broughton & Wyman*, [1872].

Two (The) school girls. [*anon.*] 144 pp. 18°. *New York, Carlton & Porter*, [1862].

Tydings (Richard). A refutation of the doctrine of uninterrupted apostolic succession, with a correction of errors concerning rev. John Wesley and dr. Coke. In answer to the rev. G. T. Chapman, d. d. and others. To which is appended a sketch of the author's life. 1 p. l. 364 pp. 8°. *Louisville*, 1844.

Tyler (Bennet, *d. d.*) Lectures on theology. With a memoir, by rev. Nahum Gale, d. d. 395 pp. 1 portrait. 8°. *Boston, J. E. Tilton & co.* 1859.

Tyler (*Rev.* George P.) Encyclopedia of religious knowledge. *See* **Brown** (*Rev.* John Newton).

Tylor (Edward B.) Researches into the early history of mankind and the development of civilization. 2d ed. vi, 385 pp. 8°. *London, J. Murray*, 1870.

Tyndale (William). The first printed english new testament. *See* **Bible.** (*English*).

Tyndall (John). Scientific addresses. 1. On the methods and tendencies of physical investigation. 2. On haze and dust. 3. On the scientific use of the imagination. 74 pp. 12°. *New Haven* (*Conn.*) *C. C. Chatfield & co.* 1871.
[HALF hours with modern scientists, pp. 217–288].

Tyng (*Rev.* Dudley Atkins). The children of the kingdom. 190 pp. 16°. *New York, R. Carter & brothers*, 1857.

Tyng (Stephen Higginson, *d. d.*) Christ is all. 374 pp. 1 portrait. 8°. *New York, R. Carter & brothers*, 1849.

Tyng (S. H. *d. d.*)—continued.
——— The christian's own book. Meditations drawn from the piety of former ages. With an introductory essay by Stephen H. Tyng. xii, 288 pp. 12°. *Philadelphia, George, Latimer & co.* 1832.

——— Fellowship with Christ. 288 pp. 16°. [*New York*, 1854]?
[*Note.*—Title-page wanting].

——— Forty years' experience in sunday schools. 251 pp. 16°. *New York, Sheldon & co.* 1860.

——— Lectures on the law and the gospel. 3d ed. revised and enlarged. 349 pp. 12°. *Philadelphia, Stavely & M'Calla*, 1844.

——— Memoir of rev. Erasmus J. P. Messinger, missionary of the protestant episcopal church in Africa. 240 pp. 2 pl. 1 portrait. 18°. *Philadelphia, American sunday-school union*, [1856].

——— The rich kinsman. The history of Ruth, the moabitess. 425 pp. 16°. *New York, R. Carter & brothers*, 1855.

——— Sermons preached in the church of the epiphany, Philadelphia. 307 pp. 8°. *Philadelphia, W. Stavely*, 1839.

Typographic advertiser. Thomas Mackellar, editor. [Quarterly]. Oct. 1870, to July, 1871. 4°. *Philadelphia, Mackellar, Smiths & Jordan*, 1870–71.

Tyrtæus. Kriegslieder des Tyrtäus. Aus dem griechischen. [Mit dem original]. 18°. [*Leipzig, Weidmanns erben & Reich*, 1772].
[*In* WEISSE (Christian Felix). Kleine lyrische gedichte. 1772. v. 2, pp. 123–175].

Tyrwhitt (Thomas, 1730–86). Conjecturae in Æschylum, Euripidem et Aristophanem. Accedunt epistolæ diversorum ad Tyrwhittum. viii, 164 pp. 8°. *Oxonii, e typographeo clarendoniano*, 1822.

——— Coniecturæ in Euripidem. 8°. [*Lipsiæ, sumptibus C. H. F. Hartmanni*, 1823].
[*In* EURIPIDES. Euripidis tragœdia Hippolytus. 1823. pp. 401–416].

——— A vindication of the appendix to the poems, called Rowley's, in reply to the answers of the dean [Milles] of Exeter, Jacob Bryant, and a third anonymous writer; with some further observations upon those poems. vii, 223 pp. 8°. *London, T. Payne & son*, 1782.

U. (I.) *See* **Usher** *or* **Ussher** (James, *romish priest*).

Ubaldini (Federigo). Indice delle voci, e modi di dire più considerabili usati da F.

Ubaldini (Federigo)—continued. Barberino, accresciuto. 8°. [*Roma, de Romanis*, 1815].

[*In* BARBERINO (Francesco). Del reggimento e de' costumi delle donne. (Ed. di G. Manzi). Part 2, 1 p. l. 111 pp.]

——— Il trattato delle virtù morali di Roberto re di Gerusalemme, il tesoretto di ser Brunetto Latini, quattro canzoni di Bindo Bonichi da Siena, con alcune rime di m. Francesco Petrarca estratte da un suo originale. [2ª ed. da Santi Bruscoli]. 12 p. l. 216 pp. 8°. *Torino, stamperia reale*, 1750.

——— Vita di messer Francesco Barberino. 8°. [*Roma, de Romanis*, 1815].

[*In* BARBERINO (Francesco). Del reggimento e de' costumi delle donne, pp. viii–xxxiv].

Udall (Nicholas). Roister Doister. Written, probably also represented, before 1553. Carefully edited from the unique copy, now at Eton college, by Edward Arber. 88 pp. 16°. *London*, 1869.

[ARBER's english reprints, v. 8, no. 17].

Uhle (Johann Ludwig). Thesaurus epistolicus lacrozianus. 1742–46. *See* **Lacroze** (Mathurin Veyssière de).

Uilenbroeck (Gosuin). Museum uilenbroekianum. [Numismata imperatorum romanorum]. 6, 300 pp. 8°. [*Amsterdam*, 1729]?

Uitts (A. F.) New testament. Geneva and king James' versions in parallel columns. *Indianapolis*, 1871. *See* **Bible**. (*English*).

Ulliac-Tremadeure (*Mlle.* Sophie). Jane Brush and her cow: a story for children, illustrative of natural history. Altered from the french by a lady of New York. 133 pp. 18°. *New York, M. W. Dodd*, 1841.

Ullmann (Carl). Johann Wessel, der hauptrepräsentant reformatorischer theologie im 15ten jahrhundert; nebst den brüdern vom gemeinsamen leben, namentlich: Gerhard Groot, Florentius Radewins, Gerhard Zerbolt und Thomas von Kempen; und den deutschen mystikern: Ruysbrock, Suso, Tauler, dem verfasser der deutschen theologie und Staupitz in ihrer beziehung zur reformation. 2e aufl. xxiv, 420 pp. 8°. *Hamburg, F. Perthes*, 1842.

Ulrich (Louis). A complete treatise on the art of dyeing cotton and wool, as practised in Paris, Rouen, Mulhausen, and Germany. From the french. To which are added the most important receipts for dyeing wool, as practised in the Manufacture impériale des gobelins, Paris. By prof. H. Dussauce. xii, 25–274 pp. 12°. *Philadelphia, H. C. Baird*, 1863.

Uncle Sam's recommendation of phrenology to his millions of friends in the United States. [*anon.*] 302 pp. 1 l. 18°. *New York, Harper & brothers*, 1842.

Uncle Timothy Taber. *See* **Arnold** (Alexander S.)

Underwood (Francis H.) Cloud-pictures. 1. The exile of von Adelstein's soul. 2. To pankalon. 3. Herr Regenbogen's concert. 4. A great-organ prelude. vii, 166 pp. 16°. *Boston, Lee & Shepard*, 1872.

——— A hand-book of english literature. Intended for the use of high schools, as well as a companion and guide for private students, and for general readers. v. 1.—British authors. xxxviii, 592 pp. 12°. *Boston, Lee & Shepard*, 1871.

Unfortunate (An) mother's advice to her absent daughters. *See* **Pennington** (S. *lady*).

Union (The) agriculturist and western prairie farmer, devoted to the improvement of western agriculture. [A monthly]. v. 1–2. 2 v. in 1. fol. *Chicago, Union agricultural society*, 1841–42. s.

Union nationale du commerce et de l'industrie. Annuaire des chambres syndicales. 1868. xii, 259 pp. 12°. *Paris, F. Malteste & cie.* 1868.

Union (The) prayer book: a manual of public worship. Also, a service for sunday schools, and forms for family devotion. 592 pp. 8°. *New York, A. S. Barnes & co.* 1871.

Union (The) pulpit. A collection of sermons by ministers of different denominations. xvi, 457 pp. 34 portraits. 8°. *Washington* (*D. C.*) *Young men's christian association of Washington* (*D. C.*) 1860.

United service magazine. *See* **Colburn's** united service magazine.

United States of America. Constitution of the United States of America, with the amendments thereto; to which are added Jefferson's manual of parliamentary practice, the standing rules and orders for conducting business in the house of representatives and senate of the United States, and Barclay's digest. 280 pp. 8°. *Washington, government printing office*, 1871.

——— Recueil des lois constitutives des colonies angloises, confédérées sous la dénomination d'États-Unis de l'Amérique-Septentrionale. Auquel on a joint les actes d'indépendance, de confédération & autres actes du congrès général, traduit de l'anglois [par

United States of America—continued.
Regnier. *anon.*] 6 p. l. 370 pp. 16°. *Suisse, libraires associés*, 1778.

Note.—Contains the constitutions of Pennsylvania, New Jersey, Delaware, Maryland, Virginia, and South Carolina (the last in two forms).

—— *Colonial congress.* The association, etc. [of the delegates of the twelve colonies, in congress, Philadelphia, October 20, 1774, or non-importation agreement.] 11 pp. 16°. [*Philadelphia*, 1774].

—— —— A letter to the inhabitants of the province of Quebec. Extract from the minutes of congress. 1 p. l. (title), pp. 37–50. 8°. *Philadelphia, W. & T. Bradford*, 1774.

—— *Congress.* Congressional directory, compiled for the use of congress by Ben: Perley Poore. Forty-second congress. 1st session. Corrected to March 25, 1871. 2d session. 1st ed. Corrected to January 15, 1872. 2 v. 8°. *Washington, government printing office*, 1872.

—— —— Digest of election cases. Cases of contested elections in the house of representatives from 1865 to 1871, inclusive. Compiled by D. W. Bartlett, clerk to committee of elections. 955 pp. 8°. [*Washington, government printing office*, 1870].

—— *Department of agriculture.* Monthly reports. 1867–1871. 5 v. 8°. *Washington, government printing office*, 1868–72.

—— —— Reports of the commissioner of agriculture, for the years 1862–1870. 9 v. 8°. *Washington, government printing office*, 1863–71.

—— *Interior department.* Preliminary report of the United States geological survey of Wyoming, and portions of contiguous territories, (being a second annual report of progress,) conducted under the authority of the secretary of the interior, by F. V. Hayden. 511 pp. 8°. *Washington, government printing office*, 1871.

—— —— Register of officers and agents, civil, military, and naval, in the service of the United States, on the thirtieth of September, 1871. xv, 913 pp. 8°. *Washington, government printing office*, 1872.

—— —— (*Census bureau*). Ninth census of the United States. Statistics of population. Tables i to viii inclusive. 2 p. l. 391 pp. 4°. *Washington, government printing office*, 1872.

—— —— —— The same. Agriculture. 366 pp. 4°. *Washington, government printing office*, 1872.

United States of America—continued.

—— —— —— The same. Mortality of the United States, [during the census year ended June 1, 1870]. Tables 1–9. 423 pp. 4°. [*Washington, government printing office*, 1872].

—— —— —— The same. Statistics of wealth, taxation, and public indebtedness. 68 pp. 4°. [*Washington, government printing office*, 1871].

—— —— —— The same. Ninth census of the United States of America, 1870. 222 pp. 1 l. 18°. *Concord (N. H.) J. B. Rand*, 1871.

—— —— (*Office of indian affairs*). Annual reports of the commissioner of indian affairs, 1855–1870. 16 v. 8°. *Washington*, 1856–70.

—— *Navy department.* Register of the commissioned, warrant, and volunteer officers of the navy, including officers of the marine corps and others. Jan. 1 and July 1, 1871, and Jan. 1, 1872. 3 v. 8°. *Washington, government printing office*, 1871–72.

—— —— (*Bureau of navigation, Nautical almanac office*). The american ephemeris, and nautical almanac, for the year 1870. 2d ed. 8°. *Washington, bureau of navigation*, 1869.

—— —— —— The same. For the year 1874. 8°. *Washington, bureau of navigation*, 1870.

—— —— —— Almanac for the use of navigators, from the american ephemeris and nautical almanac. Published by authority of the secretary of the navy. 1870, 3d ed; 1871, 2d and 3d ed; 1872–74. 6 v. 8°. *Washington, bureau of navigation*, 1871.

—— —— —— The rule of the road at sea and in inland waters; or, steering and sailing rules. Collisions and law of the port helm. Collated and arranged, with remarks, by commodore Thornton A. Jenkins, U. S. navy, 1868. iv, 3–227 pp. 8 pl. 8°. *Washington, government printing office*, 1869.

—— —— (*Naval observatory*). Astronomical and meteorological observations made at the United States naval observatory during the years 1868 and 1869. 2 v. 4°. *Washington, government printing office*, 1871.

—— —— —— Reports on observations of the total solar eclipse of December 22, 1870. [By Simon Newcomb, Asaph Hall, William Harkness, and J. R. Eastman]. Conducted under the direction of rear-admiral

United States of America—continued.

B. F. Sands, U. S. n. superintendent of the naval observatory. 4°. *Washington, government printing office*, 1871.

[UNITED STATES. (*Naval observatory*). Astronomical and meteorological observations for 1869.—Appendix i].

——— *State department*. List of diplomatic and consular officers of the United States in foreign countries. 1862, 1863, 1865–1871. 9 v. 8°. *Washington, government printing office*, 1862–69.

——— ——— Register of the department of state, containing a list of persons employed in the department and in the diplomatic, consular and territorial service of the United States, with maps showing where the ministers and consuls are resident abroad. Corrected to July 1, 1871. 108 pp. 7 maps. 8°. *Washington, government printing office*, 1871.

——— *Treasury department*. Reports upon the mineral resources of the United States, by special commissioners J. Ross Browne and James W. Taylor. 360 pp. 8°. *Washington, government printing office*, 1867.

——— ——— United States duties on imports, 1871. By Lewis Heyl. Revised, corrected, and supplemented to June 15, 1871. 2 p. l. 216 pp. 8°. *Washington, W. H. & O. H. Morrison*, 1871.

——— ——— (*Bureau of statistics*). Annual report of the chief of the bureau of statistics on the commerce and navigation of the United States, for the fiscal year ended June 30, 1870. xviii, 798 pp. 8°. *Washington, government printing office*, 1871.

——— ——— ——— List of merchant vessels of the United States, with the official numbers and signal letters awarded them, by the chief of the bureau of statistics, under the act of congress approved July 28, 1866, chap. 288, sec. 13. Third annual report. 1 p. l. 392 pp. 8°. *Washington, government printing office*, 1871.

——— ——— ——— Monthly reports on the commerce and navigation of the United States, for the fiscal year ended June 30, 1871. iv, 418 pp. 4°. *Washington, government printing office*, 1871.

——— ——— ——— Report of the chief of the bureau of statistics on customs-tariff legislation. Appendix A. Comparative statement of the rates of duties and imposts under the several tariff acts from 1789 to 1870, both inclusive. Prepared by A. W. Angerer. 97 pp. 8°. [*Washington, government printing office*, 1871].

——— ——— ——— Special report on immigration; accompanying information for immigrants relative to the prices and rentals of land, [etc.] To which are appended tables showing the average weekly wages paid for labor, [etc.] in 1869–70. By Edward Young. xxvii, 232 pp. 8°. *Washington, government printing office*, 1872.

——— *War department*. (*Adjutant general's office*). Official army register. Jan. 1871, and Jan. 1872. 2 v. 12°. *Washington, [government printing office*], 1871–72.

——— ——— (*Engineer corps*). United States geological exploration of the fortieth parallel. Clarence King, geologist-in-charge. 2 v. 4°. and fol. *Washington, government printing office*, 1870.

CONTENTS.

v. 3. Mining industry, by James D. Hague. With geological contributions, by Clarence King.

——— ——— (*Ordnance office*). The ordnance manual for the use of the officers of the United States army. [Edited by T. T. S. Laidley]. 3d ed. 559 pp. 33 pl. 12°. *Philadelphia, J. B. Lippincott & co.* 1862.

——— ——— (*Paymaster general's office*). The army paymaster's manual, for the information of officers of the pay department of the United States army, revised to include June 30, 1871. Compiled, under direction of the paymaster general U. S. army, by J. H. Eaton. 62 pp. 8°. *Washington, government printing office*, 1871.

——— ——— (*Signal office*). War department weather map. Division of telegrams and reports for the benefit of commerce. Washington, November 1, 1871, to March 31, 1872. 2 v. obl. fol. *New York, L. H. Rogers & co. Washington, government printing office*, 1871.

——— ——— (*Surgeon general's office*). Catalogue of the library of the surgeon general's office, United States army. With an alphabetical index of subjects. 2 p. l. 454 pp. 8°. *Washington, government printing office*, 1872.

——— ——— ——— The same. Supplement, no. 1. List of american medical journals. 2 p. l. 26 pp. 8°. *Washington, government printing office*, 1872.

[*With* the preceding].

——— ——— ——— Photographs of surgical cases and specimens. Prepared by direction of the surgeon general, by brevet lieut. col.

United States of America—continued.
George A. Otis, assistant surgeon U. S. a. curator of the army medical museum. 4 v. 4°. *Washington, surgeon general's office,* [1872].
——— ——— ——— A report of surgical cases treated in the army of the United States, from 1865 to 1871. [By George A. Otis, m. d.] 296 pp. 3 pl. 4°. *Washington, government printing office,* 1871.
[Circular no. 3, 1871].

United States (The) army and navy journal, and gazette of the regular and volunteer forces. [Weekly]. Aug. 20, 1870, to Aug. 12, 1871. v. 8. fol. *New York, W. C. & F. P. Church,* 1870–71.

United States (The) insurance almanac and statistical register for the year 1871. Edited by G. E. Currie. v. 16. 8°. *New York, G. E. Currie,* 1871.

United States (The) insurance gazette and magazine, edited by G. E. Currie. [Monthly]. Nov. 1870, to Oct. 1871. New series. v. 32–33. 8°. *New York, G. E. Currie,* 1871.

United States (The) medical and surgical journal; a quarterly magazine of the homœopathic practice of medicine and medical science in general. Edited by A. E. Small, m. d. [and others]. Oct. 1870, to July, 1871. v. 6. 8°. *Chicago, C. S. Halsey,* 1871.

United States register or blue book for 1872. Containing the names of the principal civil officers of the federal government; army and navy list, &c. with authentic political and statistical information relating to the states and territories, continent of America, etc. Also, the official census of the United States. 124 pp. 8°. *Philadelphia, J. Disturnell,* [1872].

Unity (The) of Italy. The american celebration of the unity of Italy, at the academy of music, New York, Jan. 12, 1871, with the addresses, letters, and comments of the press. [*anon.*] 1 p. l. 197 pp. 8°. *New York, G. P. Putnam & sons,* 1871.

Universal (The) magazine of knowledge and pleasure. June, 1747, to June, 1802. v. 1–110 in 100 v. 8°. *London, J. Hinton and W. Bent,* 1747–1802.

Universal restitution, a scripture doctrine, 1761. *See* **Stonehouse** (*Sir* George).

Universalist (The) quarterly and general review. Thomas B. Thayer, d. d. editor. Jan. to Oct. 1871. New series, v. 8; [complete series, v. 28]. 8°. *Boston, Universalist publishing house,* 1871.

Università toscane. Annali. v. 1–10. 8°. and 4°. *Pisa, tipografia nistri,* 1846–68. s.

Unseen (The) world; communications with it, real or imaginary, including apparitions, warnings, haunted places, prophecies, aerial visions, astrology, &c. [*anon.*] vii, 216 pp. 16°. *London, J. Burns,* 1847.

Unsere zeit. Deutsche revue der gegenwart. Monatsschrift zum Conversations-lexikon. 1. januar bis 15. dec. 1871. Neue folge. 7ter jahrgang. 2 v. 8°. *Leipzig, F. A. Brockhaus,* 1871.

Untaught (The) band. [*anon.*] 260 pp. 2 l. 16°. *New York, Deane & Andrews,* 1804.

Upham (Thomas Cogswell, *d. d.*) Abridgment of mental philosophy, including the three departments of the intellect, sensibilities, and will. xviii, 15–527, 35 pp. 12°. *New York, Harper & brothers,* 1863.
——— Christ in the soul; or, illustrations of some of the principles and experiments which characterize Christ's spiritual or inward coming and indwelling. 173 pp. 12°. *New York, Warren, Broughton & Wyman,* 1872.
——— Elements of intellectual philosophy. [*anon.*] 504 pp. 8°. *Portland, W. Hyde,* 1827.
——— Letters æsthetic, social, and moral, written from Europe, Egypt, and Palestine. Private edition. 586 pp. 1 portrait. 12°. *Brunswick,* [*Me.*] *J. Griffin,* 1855.
——— The life of faith, in three parts. 480 pp. 1 pl. 12°. *Boston, Waite, Pierce & co.* 1845.
——— A philosophical and practical treatise on the will. Forming the third volume of a system of mental philosophy. 411 pp. 12°. *New York, Harper & brothers,* 1841.
——— Ratio disciplinæ, or the constitution of the congregational churches. [*anon.*] 324 pp. 12°. *Portland, Shirley & Hyde,* 1829.
——— The same. 2d ed. 324 pp. 12°. *Portland, W. Hyde,* 1844.
——— Religious maxims having a connexion with the doctrines and practice of holiness. 2d ed. with additions. 2 p. l. 9–144 pp. 18°. *Philadelphia, W. S. Martien,* 1854.

Upton (George P.) The great conflagration, Chicago. *See* **Sheehan** (James W.) *and* **Upton.**

Upton (James). Ποικιλη ἱστορια, sive, novus historiarum, fabellarumque delectus; ex Æliano, Polyæno, Aristotele, Max. Tyrio, aliisque probatissimis scriptoribus græcis, desumptus. Versione et notis illustravit

Upton (James)—continued.
Jacobus Upton. Accessere tres orationes funebres Periclis, Lysiæ et Platonis. Ed. 2a. [Græce et latine]. 8 p. l. 198, 107 pp. 12°. *Etonæ, T. Pote*, 1788.
[Interleaved].

Uranus oder tägliche, für jedermann fassliche uebersicht aller himmelserscheinungen im jahre 1846–48, bearbeitet und zusammengestellt von Ernst Schubert und Hugo von Rothkirch, und herausgegeben von P. H. L. von Boguslawski. 3 v. in 2. 8°. *Glogau, C. Flemming*, 1845–47. s.

Urban viii. *pope.* [Maffeo Barberini]. Maffæi card. Barberini poemata. 7, 102 pp. 1 l. 4°. *Lvtetiæ Parisiorvm, apud A. Stephanvm*, 1620.

Ure (*Rev.* David). The history of Rutherglen and East-Kilbridge. viii, 334 pp. 10 l. 18 pl. 8°. *Glasgow, D. Niven*, 1793.
[Imperfect: wanting 2 pl.]

Urquhart (*Rev.* David Henry). Commentaries on classical learning. xii, 540 pp. 8°. *London, T. Cadell & W. Davies*, 1803.

Ursatus (Sertorius). *See* **Orsato** (Sertorio).

Usher *or* **Ussher** (James, *romish priest, d.* 1772). Clio: or, a discourse on taste. Addressed to a young lady. By I. U. 2d ed. with large additions. xvi, 247 pp. 16°. *Dublin, J. Milliken*, 1770.

Usher. *See* **Ussher.**

Usselincx (Willem). Bedenckinghen over den staet vande Vereenichde Nederlanden: nopende de zeevaert, coop-handel, ende de gemeyne neeringe inde selve. Ingevalle den peys met de aerts-hertogen inde aenstaende vrede-handelinge getroffen wert. Door een lief-hebber eenes oprechten vreedes. [*anon.*] *b. l.* 8 l. sm. 4°. [*n. p.*] 1608.
[*In* NEDERLANDTSCHE bye-corf].

——— The same. Grondich discours over desen aen-staenden vrede-handel. [*anon.*] 8 l. sm. 4°. [*n. p.* 1608].
[*In* NEDERLANDTSCHE bye-corf].

——— Discours by forme van remonstrantie: vervatende de noodsaeckelickheyd vande oos-indische navigatie, by middel vande welcke, de vrye neder-landsche provintien, apparent zijn te gheraecken totte hooghste prosperiteyt, int stuck vande alder-rijck ende costelijckste waren vande gheheele werelt. [*anon.*] 7 l. sm. 4°. [*n. p.*] 1608.
[*In* NEDERLANDTSCHE bye-corf].

——— Memorie vande ghewichtighe redenen die de heeren staten generael behooren te beweghen om gheensins te wijcken vande handelinghe ende vaert van Indien. [*anon.*]

Usselincx (Willem)—continued.
In dese 3e ed. vebetert. 4 l. sm. 4°. [*n. p.* 1608].
[*In* NEDERLANDTSCHE bye-corf].

——— Naerder bedenckingen, over de zeevaerdt, coophandel ende neeringhe vanden staet deser vereenichde landen, inde teghenwoordighe vrede-handelinghe met den coninck van Spangnien ende de aerts-hertoghen. Door een lief-hebber eenes oprechten vredes voorghestelt. [*anon.*] *b. l.* 18 l. sm. 4°. [*n. p.*] 1608.

——— The same. Naerder bedenckingen, over de zee-vaerdt, coophandel ende neeringhe, als mede de versekeringhe vanden staet deser vereenichde landen, inde teghenwoordighe vrede-handelinghe met den coninck van Spangnien ende de aerts-hertoghen. [*anon.*] *b. l.* 18 l. sm. 4°. [*n. p.*] 1608.
[*In* NEDERLANDTSCHE bye-corf].

——— Onpartydich discours opte handelinghe vande Indien. [*anon.*] 4 l. sm. 4°. [*n. p.* 1608].
[*In* NEDERLANDTSCHE bye-corf].

——— Sommaire recveil des raisons plvs importantes, qui doivent mouvoir messieurs des estats des provinces unis du Pays-Bas, de ne quitter point les Indes. Traduit de flamant en françois. [*anon.*] 13 pp. 16°. [*Paris*]? *Iean Petit*, 1608.

——— Uvaerschouwinge over den treves met den koningh van Spaignien. *b. l.* 17 l. sm. 4°. *Vlissingen, S. C. Versterre*, 1630.

——— Vertoogh, hoe nootwendich, nut ende profijtelick het sy voor de Vereenighde Nederlanden te behouden de vryheyt van te handelen op West-Indien, inden vrede metten coninck van Spaignen. [*anon.* 2e ed.] 10 l. sm. 4°. [*n. p.* 1608].
[*In* NEDERLANDTSCHE bye-corf].

Ussher *or* **Usher** (James, *archbishop of Armagh*, 1580–1656). Eighteen sermons preached in Oxford 1640. Of conversion, unto God. Of redemption, & justification, by Christ. Published by Jos: Crabb. Will: Ball. Tho: Lye who writ them from his mouth, and compared their copies together. With a preface concerning the life of the pious author, by the rev. Stanly Gower. 16 p. l. 454, 361–464 pp. 6 l. 1 portrait. sm. 4°. *London, S. Griffin for J. Rothwell*, 1660.

Ussher (*Sir* Thomas, *r. n.* 1779–1848). A narrative of events connected with the first abdication of the emperor Napoleon, his embarkation at Frejus and voyage to Elba. His embarkation at Elba, and a journal of

Ussher (*Sir* Thomas, *r. n.*)—continued. his extraordinary march to Paris, as narrated by col. Laborde, who accompanied the emperor. 100 pp. 8°. *Dublin, Grant & Bolton*, 1841.

Ussher. *See* **Usher.**

Uvedale (Thomas). The remedy of love, in imitation of Ovid. A poem. 9 p. l. 100 pp. 12°. *London, N. Cox*, 1704.

Vahl (J.) Lapperne og den lapske mission. 2 v. in 1. 2 p. l. 175 pp; 190 pp. 8°. *Kjøbenhavn, G. E. C. Gad*, 1866. s.

Vaillant (Jean Foy). Arsacidarum imperium, sive regum parthorum historia. Ad fidem numismatum accommodata. 2 v. 13 p. l. 31, 407, 24 pp. 2 pl; 6 p. l. 24, 8, 434 pp. 2 l. 4°. *Parisiis, C. Moette*, 1725.

[*Note.*—v. 2 has the title, Achæmenidarum imperium, sive regum Ponti, Bosphori, et Bithyniæ historia].

Vairasse d'Allais (Denis). The history of the Sevarites or Sevarambi: a nation inhabiting part of the third continent, commonly called Terræ australes incognitæ. With an account of their admirable government, religion, customs, and language. Written by one captain Siden. [*pseudon.* Part 1]. 12 p. l. 114 pp. 18°. *London, Henry Brome*, 1675.

[*Note.*—Only part first. The preface is signed D. V.]

Valcourt (L. P. de). Mémoires sur l'agriculture, les instrumens aratoires, et d'économie rurale. 2 p. l. 556 pp. 8°. *Paris, L. Bouchard-Huzard*, 1841. s.

[Atlas wanting].

Valdes de la Plata (Juan Sanchez). Coronica y historia general del hombre, en qve se trata del hombre en comun: de la diuision del hõbre en cuerpo y alma: de las figuras monstruosas de los hõbres: de las inuenciones dellos: y de la concordia entre Dios, y el hombre. 16 p. l. 252 l. fol. *Madrid, L. Sanchez*, 1598.

Valentin (Gabriel Gustav). A text book of physiology. Translated and edited from the third german ed. By William Brinton, m. d. xxii, 684 pp. iv pl. 8°. *London, H. Renshaw*, [1853].

Valentin (Robert François). Histoire de Venise. 4e éd. 3 p. l. 312 pp. 4 pl. 12°. *Tours, A. Mame & cie.* 1844.

Valenzuela (José Santos, *editor*). Historia jeneral de la república de Chile desde su independencia hasta nuestros dias, por los señores J. V. Lastarria, M. A. Tocornal, D. J. Benavente, M. L. i G. V. Amunátegui, S. Sanfuentes, D. Barros Arana. Ed. autorizada por la universidad de Chile. v. 1. xxvii,

Valenzuela (José S. *editor*)—continued. 477 pp. 3 portraits. 8°. *Santiago, imprenta nacional*, 1866.

CONTENTS.

Prologo [i] introduccion, por B. Vicuña Mackenna, xxvi pp.
Investigaciones sobre la influencia social de la conquista i del sistema colonial de los españoles en Chili, 1844, por J. V. Lastarria, pp. 1–101.
Memoria sobre el primer gobierno nacional, 1847, por M. A. Tocornal, pp. 103–266.
Historia de la independencia de Chile durante los años 1811 i 1812, por D. B. Arana, pp. 267–471.

Valeriano Bolzani (Giovanni Pierio). Contarenus, sive de litteratorum infelicitate libri duo. 18°. [*Lipsiæ, apud J. F. Gleditsch*, 1707].

[*In* MENCKEN (J. B.) Analecta de calamitate litteratorum, 1707, pp. 251–412].

Valerio (Katherine). Ina. [A novel]. 133 pp. 8°. *Boston, J. R. Osgood & co.* 1871.

Valerius Flaccus (Caius). The first book of the Argonautica. [Translated, and with notes, by Thomas Noble]. 1 p. l. 1, 133 pp. 4°. [*London*, 1808].

[*With* NOBLE (Thomas). Blackheath; a poem. *London*, 1808].

Valerius Maximus. Romæ antiquæ descriptio. A view of the religion, laws, customs, manners, and dispositions of the ancient Romans, and others: comprehended in their most illustrious acts and sayings agreeable to history. Written in latine: and now carefully rendred into english. Together with the life of the author. 5 p. l. 478 pp. 1 pl. 12°. *London, J. C. for S. Speed*, 1678.

——— The same. Valère Maxime. Faits et paroles mémorables. Traduction nouvelle par C. A. F. Frémion. 2 v. xvi, 284 pp; 1 p. l. 404 pp. 8°. *Paris, C. L. F. Panckoucke*, 1827.

[*Note.*—With latin text facing translation].

Valkenburg (Johan). Brief geschreven aan de staten generael der Vereenigde Nederlanden. Over de tijrannijen en moorderijen bij de Engelsche [en Guinea] gepleegt. Folded sheet. sm. 4°. *Gravenhage, H. van Wouw*, 1665.

Vallandigham (*Rev.* James Laird). A life of Clement L. Vallandigham, by his brother. xii, 573 pp. 2 pl. 1 portrait. 8°. *Baltimore, Turnbull brothers*, 1872.

Valle (Alonso del). Memorial y carta en qve el padre Alonso del Valle procvrador general de la prouincia de Chile, representa a n. padre Mucio Vitilesqui, preposito general de la compañia de Iesus, la necessidad que sus missiones tienen de sujetos para los gloriosos empleos de sus apostolicos ministerios. 10 l. sm. fol. *Seuilla*, 1642.

Valmiki. Ramayana, id est carmen epicum de Ramae rebus gestis. Poetae antiquissimi Valmicis opus. Textum codd. mss. collatis recensuit interpretationem latinam et annotationes criticas adiecit Aug. Guil. a Schlegel. 2 v. in 3 v. 8°. *Bonnae, E. Weber*, 1846.

——— The same. The Rámáyan of Válmíki translated into english verse, by Ralph T. H. Griffith. 2 v. xxxii, 439 pp; vii, 504 pp. 8°. *London, Trübner & co.* 1870–71.

Valpy (Francis Edward Jackson). Greek exercises; or, an introduction to greek composition; to which specimens of the greek dialects, and the critical canons of Dawes and Porson are added. Revised and re-arranged from the last London edition, by J. M. Cairns, m. a. xii, 238, xcvi pp. 12°. *New York, G. & C. & H. Carvill*, 1831.

Vampire (The); or, bride of the isles, a tale, founded on the popular superstition of Caledonia. [*anon.*] 16°. *London, J. Bailey*, [*about* 1820].

[*With* STEWART (William Grant). The popular superstitions and festive amusements of the highlanders of Scotland. 1823].

Van Amringe (Henry Hamlin). Nature and revelation, showing the present condition of the churches; and the change now to come upon the world, by the second advent, in spirit, of the messiah, with interpretations of prophecies in Daniel, and the book of revelation. 258 pp. 8°. *New-York, R. P. Bixby & co.* 1843.

Van Bemmel (Eugène). De la langue et de la poésie provençales. xii, 264 pp. 12°. *Bruxelles, A. Vandale*, 1846.

Van Buren (A. De Puy). Jottings of a year's sojourn in the south; or first impressions of the country and its people; with a glimpse at school-teaching in that southern land, and reminiscences of distinguished men. 320 pp. 12°. *Battle Creek (Mich.)* 1859.

Vance (Clara, *pseudon*). *See* **Denison** (M. A.)

Van Cleve (B. F.) Secret knowledge disclosed; or a plain way to wealth, comprising a collection of rare and practical receipts and valuable tables, designed for the use of every business man and mechanic. 210 pp. 12°. *Boston, H. H. & T. W. Carter*, 1871.

Van De Graaf (J. S.) Manual of a civil engineer; comprehending a variety of useful formulæ, designed for the location of railroads. 90 pp. 18°. *New York, D. K. Minor*, 1835.

Van Dyck (Abraham). Christian union; or, an argument for the abolition of sects. To which is prefixed, a sketch of the life of the author. xvi, 227 pp. 8°. *New-York, D. Appleton & co.* 1835.

Van Dyke (Joseph S.) Popery the foe of the church, and of the republic. 304 pp. 16 pl. 8°. *Philadelphia, People's publishing co.* 1871.

Vanière (Jacques). The bees, from the latin of J. Vanière: being the fourteenth book of his Prædium rusticum. By Arthur Murphy. 1 p. l. 59 pp. 12°. *Middletown (Conn.) I. Riley, New York*, 1808.

[*With* VIRGILIUS MARO (Publius). The Georgics, 1808].

Van Praet (Jules). Essais sur l'histoire politique des derniers siècles. 434 pp. 8°. *Bruxelles, Bruylant Christophe & cie.* 1867.

——— The same. Essays on the political history of the fifteenth, sixteenth, and seventeenth centuries. Edited by sir Edmund Head. li, 464 pp. 8°. *London, R. Bentley*, 1868.

Van Rensselaer (Cortlandt, *d. d.*) Essays and discourses, practical and historical. 435 pp. 1 portrait. 12°. *Philadelphia, Presbyterian board of publication*, [1861].

——— Miscellaneous sermons, essays and addresses. Edited by his son, C. Van Rensselaer. xlviii, 39–569 pp. 1 portrait. 8°. *Philadelphia, J. B. Lippincott & co.* 1861.

Vansleb. *See* **Wansleben** (Johann Michael).

Vapereau (Louis Gustave). L'année littéraire et dramatique, ou revue annuelle des principales productions de la littérature française, et des traductions des œuvres les plus importantes des littératures étrangères. 1re année. (1858). viii, 491 pp. 16°. *Paris, L. Hachette & cie.* 1859.

Varaggio. *See* **Voragine.**

Varamundus *frisius* (Ernestus, *pseudon.*) *See* **Hotman** *or* **Hotomann** (François).

Varano (Alfonso). Opere poetiche. 3 v. 16°. *Parma, dalla stamperia reale*, 1789.

CONTENTS.

v. 1. Rime giovanili, pastorali, sacre, profane, anacreontiche, e scherzevoli.
v. 2. Visione sacre, e morali.
v. 3. Demetrio; Giovanni di Giscala, tiranno del tempio di Gerusalemme; e Agnesi, martire del Giappone, tragedie.

Varchi (Benedetto). Qvædam epigrammata ex libro carm. B. Varchii excerpta. 16°. *Florentiæ, apvd Ivntas*, 1562.

[*In* CARMINA qvinqve hetrvscorvm poetarvm, pp. 137–172].

Varchi (Benedetto)—continued.
——— Storia fiorentina, [1527-1538]. 5 v. 8°. *Milano, dalla società tipografica de' classici italiani*, 1803-4.
[*Note.*—Substantially a reprint of the edition in fol. of Pietro Martello (*Colonia, P. Kuhzio*), 1721. Prefixed, is a life of the author by Silvano Razzi.

Varela (Héctor F.) Elisa Lynch. Por Orion, [*pseudon.*] Precedida de una semblanza del autor por Emilo Castelar. 1ª ed. xvi, 419 pp. sm. fol. *Buenos Aires, imprenta de La tribuna*, 1870.

Vargas (Alonso Ramirez de). *See* **Ramirez de Vargas.**

Variétés littéraires. 1770. *See* **Arnaud** (François).

Varillas (Antoine). Histoire de Louis onze. [1e éd.] 2 v. 34 p. l. 481 pp; 2 p. l. 358, 178 pp. 4°. *Paris, C. Barbin*, 1689.

Varini *or* **Varrini** (Giulio). Scvola del volgo, cioé scielta de' più leggiadri, e spiritosi detti, aforismi, e proverbi, tolti da varie lingue, e trasportati nell' italiana, oltre quelli, che in questa nati, da questa sono stati colti. 2ª ed. migliorata, & accresciuta. 11 p. l. 287 pp. 18°. *Verona, F. Rassi*, 1642.

Variorum auctorum practica artis amandi, et declamationes Philip. Beroaldi. 280 pp. 18°. *Lvgd. Batav. ex typographia rediviva*, 1648.
[*In* Obsopœus (Vincenz). De arte bibendi. 1648. Imperfect: wanting pp. 168-190].

CONTENTS.

Historia de Eurialo et Lucretia se amantibus, auctore Æneа Sylvio.
Literæ eroticæ sev amatoriæ [Hannibalis ducis Numidiæ ad Lucretiam, regis Epirotharum filiam].
Amoris illiciti medela [auctore Ænea Sylvio].
Æneas Sylvius in effigiem amoris.
Amores Guiscardi & Gismundæ de duobus amantibus. Philippus Beroaldus e Boccatio.
Philippi Beroaldi osculum Panthiæ omnium formosissimarum. Carmen amatorium. Diræ in maledicam lenam.
Quæstio, quis inter scortatorem, aleatorem, & ebriosum sit pessimus: explicata a Philippo Beroaldo.
Antonivs Arena de bragardissima villa de Soleriis ad suos compagnones studiantes qui sunt de persona friantes, bassas dansas in gallanti stilo bisognatas: & de novo per ipsum correctas, & joliter augmentatas, cum guerra romana totum ad longum signe require: & cum guerra neapolitana: & cum revolta genuensi: & guerra avenionensi: & epistola ad falotissimam garsam pro passado lo tempus alagramentum mandat.
De fide meretricvm, in svos amatores. Appendix ex orationibvs Ioannis Charistaei.

Vasi (Mariano). Itinéraire instructif de Rome à Naples, ou description générale des monumens anciens et modernes, et des ouvrages les plus remarquables en peinture, sculpture, et architecture de cette ville célèbre et de ses environs. 2e éd. napolitaine. 287 pp. 36 pl. 2 maps. 12°. *Naples, A. Trani*, 1824.

Vasse (Johannes) *and* **Tarrafa** (Francisco). Rervm Hispaniæ memorabilivm annales. [Chronicon rervm hispanicarvm Ioannis Vasaei brvgensis ad annum 1020. Francisci Taraphæ de origine ac rebvs gestis regum Hispaniæ ad annum 1576]. 8 p. l. 782 pp. 37 l. 18°. *Coloniae, L. Alectorius et hæredes Iacobi Soteris*, 1577.

Vattel (Emerich de). Le loisir philosophique, ou pièces diverses de philosophie, de morale et d'amusement. 5 p. l. 312 pp. 16°. *Dresde, G. C. Walther*, 1747.

Vauban (Sébastien Le Prêtre de). Projet d'une dime royale. 8°. [*Paris*, 1843].
[*In* Daire (Eugène). Économistes-financiers du 18e siècle, 1843, pp. 31-154, 1 portrait].

Vaughan (Charles John, *d. d.*) Ten discourses on subjects connected with public worship and the liturgy. With an introduction, by Henry C. Potter, d. d. 1 p. l. 283 pp. 16°. *New York, E. P. Dutton & co.* 1872.

Vaughan (*Rev.* Edward Thomas). Some account of the rev. Thomas Robinson, with a selection of original letters. viii, 470 pp. 8°. *London, Whittingham & Arliss*, 1815.

Vaughan (*Rev.* Henry). Memoir and remains of the rev. Henry Vaughan. xv, 659 pp. 8°. *London, printed for private circulation*, 1841.

Vaughan (Herbert). The Cambridge grisette. Illustrated by Charles Keene. 2 p. l. 139 pp. 8 pl. sq. 12°. *London, Tinsley brothers*, 1862.

Vaughan (Thomas). Magia adamica: or the antiquitie of magic, and the descent thereof from Adam downwards, proved. [Also], a perfect and full discoverie of the true cœlum terræ, or the magician's heavenly chaos, and first matter of all things. By Eugenius Philalethes, [*pseudon.*] 13 p. l. 140 pp. 16°. *London, T. W. for H. Blunden*, 1650.

Vaughan (*Sir* William). The golden-groue, moralized in three bookes. The 2d ed. now lately reuised and enlarged by the authour. 214 l. unp. 18°. *London, S. Stafford*, 1608.

Vedder (David). Poems, legendary, lyrical, and descriptive. Now first collected. 372 pp. 12°. *Edinburgh, the Edinburgh printing and publishing co.* 1842.

Vedriani (Lodovico). Historia dell' antichissima città di Modona. [Modena]. 2 v. 542 pp. 1 l. 1 portrait; 744 pp. 4°. *Modona, B. Soliani*, 1666-67.

Veer (Gerrit de). Tre navigationi fatte dagli Olandesi, e Zelandesi, al settentrione nella Norvegia, Moscovia, e Tartaria verso il Catai, e regno de' Sini, doue scopersero il mare di

Veer (Gerrit de)—continued.
Veygatz, la Nvova Zembla, et vn paese nell' ottantesimo grado creduto la Groenlandia. Descritte in latino, da Gerardo di Vera, e nuouamente da Giouan Giunio Parisio tradotte nella lingua italiana. 4 p. l. 79 l. 33 pl. sm. 4°. *Venetia, Gio. Battista Ciotti,* 1599.

——— Verhael van de eerste schip-vaert der hollandische ende zeeusche schepen, door't Way-gat, by noorden Noorwegen, Moscovien ende Tartarien om, na de coninckrijcken Cathay ende China. Gezeylt in 1594. Hier achter is by-ghevoeght de beschrijvinghe van Siberia, Samoyeda, ende Tingœsa. 1 p. l. 57 pp. 6 pl. on 1 sheet. sm. 4°. *Amsterdam, I. Hartgers,* 1648.
[*In* HARTGERTS (J.) Oost-indische voyagien, v. 1, 1e stuck].

Vega (Garcilasso de la). Los amores. *See* **Boscan** (Juan) *and* **Vega**.

Vegetius (Flavius Renatus). Epitoma institutorū rei militaris. 40 l. unp. fol. *Bononiæ, Plato de Benedictis,* 1495.
[*In* VETERES scriptores de re militari. *Bononiæ,* 1496].

Veitelle (I. de). Lessons for children in english and french after mrs. Barbauld's method. Leçons pour les enfants en anglais et français d'après la méthode de mme. Barbauld. Arranged by I. de Veitelle. xi, 205 pp. 16°. *New York, D. Appleton & co.* 1870.

Veith (Franz Anton). Diatribe de origine et incrementis artis typographicæ in vrbe Augusta vindelica. lxviii pp. 4°. *Augustæ Vindelicorum, impensis A. F. Bartholomæi,* 1778.
[*In* ZAPF (Georg Wilhelm). Annales typographiæ augustanæ. 1778].

Velpeau (Alfred Armand Louis Marie, *m. d.*) An elementary treatise on midwifery: or principles of tokology and embryology. Translated from the french by Charles D. Meigs, m. d. 584 pp. 8°. *Philadelphia, J. Grigg,* 1831.

——— A treatise on surgical anatomy; or, the anatomy of regions, considered in its relations with surgery. Translated from the french, with notes, by John W. Sterling, m. d. 2 v. xxi, 456 pp. 6 pl. (1–6); xii, 524 pp. 8 pl. (7–14). 8°. *New York, S. Wood & sons,* 1830.

Venable (Charles S. *ll. d.*) Practical arithmetic, as applied to abstract and denominate numbers, and to business affairs. Revised ed. 330 pp. 12°. *New York, University publishing co.* 1871.

Venette (Nicolas). Traité des pierres qui s'engendrent dans les terres & dans les animaux, où l'on parle exactement des causes qui les forment dans les hommes. La méthode de les prévenir & les abus pour s'en garantir & pour les chasser même hors du corps. 2 p. l. 326 pp. 7 pl. 18°. *Amsterdam, J. & G. Janssons a Waesberge,* 1701.

Venner (Lizzie, *pseudon?*) Downward and upward. By the author of "The climbers," [etc. *anon.*] 245 pp. 12°. *Philadelphia, Claxton, Remsen & Haffelfinger,* 1871.

Vera (Gerardo di). *See* **Veer** (Gerrit de).

Verdere (*Monsieur*). The love and armes of the greeke princes. *See* **Du Verdier** (Gilbert Saulnier).

Verderius. *See* **Verdier.**

Verdi (Giuseppe). Un ballo in maschera, (a masked ball). Translated and adapted by Arthur Baildon. [Libretto, without music]. 32 pp. 8°. [*New York*], *W. C. Bryant & co.* 1871.
[PAREPA-ROSA grand english opera].

——— Il trovatore; (the troubadour). Rendered into english by T. T. Barker. 184 pp. 4°. *Boston, O. Ditson & co.* [1857]. s.

——— The same. The troubadour. (Il trovatore). [Libretto, without music]. 37 pp. 8°. [*New York*], *W. C. Bryant & co.* 1871.
[PAREPA-ROSA grand english opera].

Verdier (Claude). In avctores pene omnes, antiqvos potissimvm, censio: qua receptissimorum quorumque grammaticorum, poëtarum, historicorum, [et aliorum] errata quædam deprehenduntur. 188 pp. 1 l. 8°. *Lvgdvni, apud B. Honoratum,* 1586.

Verdun de la Crenne (—), **Borda** (Jean Charles), *and* **Pingré** (Alexandre Gui). Voyage fait par ordre du roi en 1771 et 1772, en diverses parties de l'Europe, de l'Afrique et de l'Amérique; pour vérifier l'utilité de plusieurs méthodes et instrumens, servant à déterminer la latitude et la longitude, tant du vaisseau que des côtes, isles et écueils qu'on reconnoît: suivi de recherches pour rectifier les cartes hydrographiques. 2 v. 2 p. l. 389, xx pp. 1 l. 26 pl; 3 p. l. 500, xxxii pp. 3 maps. 4°. *Paris, imprimerie royale,* 1778.

Vergilio (Polidoro). An abridgemēt of the notable worke of Polidore Virgile conteignyng the deuisers and fyrst fynders out aswell of artes, ministeries, feactes and ciuil ordinaunces, as of rites, and ceremonies, commonly vsed in the churche: and the originall

Vergilio (Polidoro)—continued. beginnyng of the same. Compendiously gathered by Thomas Langley. *b. l.* 8 p. l. unp. cliii [clvi], 1 l. 16°. *London, Richarde Grafton,* 1546.

——— The same. Les mémoires et histoire de l'origine, invention et autheurs de choses. Faicte en latin: & traduicte par Francoys de Belle-Forest. Auec vne table tres-ample. [1re éd. complète]. 56 p. l. 863 pp. 12°. *Paris, Robert Le Mangnier,* 1576.

[*Note.*—At the end are Commentaires sur l'oraison dominicale].

Ver Mehr (*Rev.* I. L.) Checkered life: an autobiography. 340 pp. 12°. *Boston, Walker, Wise & co.* 1864.

Vermiglioli (Giovanni Battista). Opusculi, ora insieme raccolti con quattro decadi di lettere inedite di alcuni celebri letterati italiani defonti nel secolo xix. 4 v. 8°. *Perugia, tipografia baduel,* 1825–26.

Vermont (*State of*). Journal of the proceedings of the constitutional convention of the people of Vermont, at Montpelier, 1870. Printed by authority. 75, iii pp. 8°. *Burlington, Free press print,* 1870. s.

——— Journal of the senate and house of representatives. Biennial session. 1870. 2 v. 8°. *Montpelier,* 1871.

——— Vermont legislative documents and official reports, made to the biennial session of the general assembly, 1870–71. 4 docs. in 1 v. 8°. *Montpelier,* 1870.

Vermont (Walton's) register, farmer's almanac, and business directory, for 1872. 190 pp. 16°. *Claremont (N. H.) The Claremont manufacturing co.* 1872.

Vermont (The) historical society. Collections. Prepared and published by the printing and publishing committee. v. 2. 8°. *Montpelier, printed for the society,* 1871.

CONTENTS.

Negotiations between Vermont and Frederick Haldimand, governor of Canada; with contemporaneous documents. 1779–1783.

Vermont as a sovereign and independent state. 1783–1791.

The early eastern boundary of New York, a twenty mile line from the Hudson.

Vernes (Théodore). Naples et les napolitains. 2e éd. 2 p. l. 318 pp. 12°. *Paris, M. Lévy frères,* 1860.

Vernon (Edward, *admiral r. n.*) Original papers relating to the expedition to Carthagena. [*anon.*] 2 p. l. 154 pp. 8°. *London, M. Cooper,* 1744.

Vernon (Ruth, *pseudon.*) *See* **Ram** (Stopford J.)

Vernon (William H.) A methodical treatise on the cultivation of the mulberry tree, on the raising of silk worms, and on winding the silk from the cocoons. 174 pp. 4 pl. 8°. *Boston, Hilliard, Gray & co.* 1828.

Véron (Louis Désiré). Cinq cent mille francs de rente. Roman de moeurs. 2e éd. 2 v. 2 p. l. 347 pp. 1 l; 2 p. l. 389 pp. 1 l. 8°. *Paris, librairie nouvelle,* 1855.

Verral (Charles). The pleasures of possession; or, the enjoyment of the present moment contrasted with those of hope and memory. A poem. xv, 112 pp. 16°. *London, C. Rickman,* 1810.

Verri (Pietro). Opere filosofiche. Ed. novissima, riveduta ed accresciuta. 2 v. xxviii, 251 pp; viii, 287 pp. 16°. *Parigi, G. C. Molini,* 1784.

CONTENTS.

v. 1. Discorso sull' indole del piacere e del dolore, p. 1.
Discorso sulla felicità, p. 135.
v. 2. Della economia politica.

Verster van Wulverhörst (A. H.) Traité de fauconnerie. *See* **Schlegel** (H.)

Vertoogh, hoe nootwendich, nut ende profijtelick het sy voor de Vereenighde Nederlanden [etc.] 1608. *See* **Usselincx** (Willem).

Vertot (René Aubert de Vertot d'Aubeuf, *known as the abbé* de). The character of Augustus, with a comparison between his two ministers, Agrippa and Mæcenas. 4°. [*London,* 1740].

[*In* TURNBULL (George). Three dissertations, 1740, pp. 3–19].

Verviers (*France*). Ville de Verviers. Catalogue méthodique de la bibliothèque publique communale. Par J. Lejeune. xvi, 194 pp. 8°. *Verviers, A. Remacle,* 1868. s.

Verweij (Bernardus). De avond des levens. Herinneringen bij het uitzigt op de eeuwigheid. 1 portrait, viii, 192 pp. 8°. *Amsterdam, G. Portielje,* 1825.

——— Evangeliesch avondmaals boekje, voor protestantsche christenen. 2e druk. 1 p. l. viii, 240 pp. 18°. *Gravenhage, weduwe J. Allart,* 1825.

——— Gedenk te sterven. Overdenkingen tot nuttige herinnering en christelijke voorbereiding van den dood. 1 p. l. viii, 214 pp. 1 l. 8°. *Amsterdam, G. Portielje,* 1827.

Veweij *or* **Verwey** (Johann). Nova via docendi graeca, in qua tribus declinationibus, & duabus con jugationibus omnis flexio: facili ratione omnis litterarum, syllabarum, quantitatum, accentuum, licentiæ poëticæ, necnon

Verweij (Johann)—continued. construendi & investigandi ratio traditur & explicatur. [Accedit] index vocum græcarum R. Ketelii. 44, 378 pp. 101 l. unp. 4 tab. 8°. *Amstelædami, apud G. & J. de Groot,* 1765.

Veteres scriptores de re militari. 78 l. unp. fol. *Bononiæ, Plato de Benedictis,* 1496.

[Imperfect: Aelianus de instruendis aciebus, 19 l. and prefatory leaf of Modestus, wanting].

CONTENTS.

FRONTINUS (Sextus Julius). De re militari.
MODESTUS. Libellus de vocabulis rei militaris.
VEGETIUS (Flavius). De re militari.

Vettori (Vittore). Le rime piacevoli del dottor fisico Vittore Vettori da esso novellamente rifatte, corrette, e ridotte alla loro vera lezione con molte giunte. 284 pp. 1 portrait. 8°. *Mantova, G. Ferrari,* 1755.

Veuillot (Louis). Les odeurs de Paris. 3e éd. xviii, 472 pp. 12°. *Paris, Palmé,* 1867.

Veyssière de La Croze (Mathurin). *See* **LaCroze.**

Vick (James). Vick's illustrated catalogue and floral guide for 1872. 120 pp. 2 col. pl. 1 portrait. 8°. *Rochester,* [1871].

Victim (The) of indulgence: by a teacher of youth, for the amusement and instruction of her pupils. [*anon.*] 146 pp. 16°. *Boston, Hilliard, Gray & co.* 1832.

Victims (The) of gaming; being extracts from the diary of an american physician. [*anon.*]. 172 pp. 16°. *Boston, Weeks, Jordan & co.* 1838.

Victor (C. Julius). Ars rhetorica Hermagorae, Ciceronis, Quintiliani, Aquilii, Marcomanni, Tatiani. 8°. [*Turici, typis Orellii,* 1833].

[*In* CICERO (M. T.) Opera quae supersunt omnia ex recensione I. C. Orellii, v. 5, part 1, pp. 195–267].

Victor (*Mrs.* Metta Victoria Fuller). Mormon wives; a narrative of facts stranger than fiction. xii, 25–326 pp. 12°. *New York, Derby & Jackson,* 1856.

——— Parke Madison: or, fashion the father of intemperance, as shown in the life of the senator's son. vii, 291 pp. 12°. *Auburn and Buffalo, Miller, Orton & Mulligan,* 1855.

Victoria (Pedro Goveo de). *See* **Goveo de Victoria.**

Victoria (*British colony of, Australia*). Statistics of the colony of Victoria, for the years 1862 [and] 1865. Compiled from official records in the registrar general's office. 2 v. fol. *Melbourne, J. Ferres,* 1864–66. S.

——— *Melbourne observatory.* Results of astronomical observations made at the Melbourne observatory, in the years 1866, 1867 and 1868, under the direction of Robert L. J. Ellery. Published by authority of the government. xxi, 182 pp. 8°. *Melbourne, Mason, Frith & co.* 1869.

Victorinus *afer* (C. *or* Fabius Marius). Expositio in rhetorica Ciceronis [libris duobus]. 8°. *Turici, typis Orellii,* 1833].

[*In* CICERO (Marcus Tullius). Opera quae supersunt omnia ex recensione I. C. Orellii, v. 5, part 1, pp. 1–182].

Victorinus *petavionensis.* A fragment on the creation of the world. [And] Commentary on the apocalypse of the blessed John. 8°. *Edinburgh, T. & T. Clark,* 1870.

[ANTE-NICENE christian library, v. 18, pp. 388–433].

Vida (Marco Girolamo). Il sileno, dialogo. Nel quale si discorre della felicità de' mortali, & si conclude, che tra tutte le cose di questo mondo l'amante fruisca solo la uera, & perfetta beatitudine humana. Insieme con le sue rime, & conclusioni amorose. Et con l'interpretatione del sig. Ottonello de' Belli sopra il medesimo dialogo. 8 p. l. 112 pp. 16°. *Vicenza, appresso G. Greco,* [1589].

——— Scacchia ludus. Scacchias übersetzt von J. F. W. Koch. 8°. *Magdeburg, W. Heinrichshofen,* 1814.

[*In* KOCH (J. F. W.) Codex der schachspielkunst, v. 2, pp. 363–405].

——— Poems on divine subjects, original and translated from the latin of M. Hieron. Vida. With large annotations more particularly concerning the being and attributes of God. By Tho. Morell. 2d ed. x, 288 pp. 1 portrait. 8°. *London, E. Owen,* 1736.

——— The poetics of Marcus Hieronymus Vida, bishop of Alba; with translations from the latin of dr. Lowth, mr. Gray and others. By John Hampson. 3 p. l. xxiv, 256 pp. 8°. *Sunderland, T. Reed,* 1793.

——— The silk-worms. A poem. In two books. Translated from the latin. [By John Rooke]. 3 p. l. 80 pp. 8°. *London,* 1725.

[ROOKE (John). Select translations, part 3, 1726].

Vidal de Figueroa (*Dr.* Joseph). Sermon a la dedicacion del templo de San Bernardo, el primera dia de su octava. 6 l. sm. 4°. [*Mexico, viuda de F. R. Lupercio,* 1691].

[*In* RAMIREZ DE VARGAS (A.) Sagrado patron y panegyricos sermones, etc.]

Vidaver (*Rev.* H. *d. d.*) Abridged school and family bible in hebrew and english. 1871. *See* **Bible.** (*Hebrew and english*).

Vidocq (Eugène François). Les voleurs, physiologie de leurs moeurs et de leur langage. 2 v. in 1. lxviii, 299 pp. 1 portrait. 397 pp. 8°. *Paris, l'auteur*, 1837.

[*Note.*—Quérard observes that Vidocq furnished only the notes in this book, the main body of it being written by an unknown author].

Vie politique, littéraire et privée de Charles James Fox. [*anon.*] *See* **Fell** (Ralph).

Vieira Transtagano (Antonio). Diccionario inglez e portuguez. 2ª ed. mais correcta e accrescentada. 2 v. in 1. 188 l; 238 l. 8°. *Londres, S. Nourse*, 1782.

Vies des justes dans la profession des armes. [*anon.*] *See* **Carron** (Guy Toussaint Julien).

View (A) of the proceedings of the assemblies of Jamaica, for some years past. With some considerations on the present state of that island. [*anon.*] vi, 42 pp. 12°. *London*, 1716.

Vieyra. *See* **Vieira.**

Viguier (*Abbé* —, *prieur de Bornal*). Lettres à m. [A. G.] de Orbigny, à Avallon. [Écrites de 1686 à 1700]. 12°. [*Paris, Aubry*, 1856].

[*In* PARIS. *Société des bibliophiles françois.* Mélanges, 1re partie, pp. 189-279].

Vilaplana (Hermenegildo). Historico, y sagrado novenario de la milagrosa imagen de nuestra señor del Pueblito, de la santa provincia de religiosas observantes de San Pedro, y San Pablo de Michoacan. 16 p. l. 192 pp. 18°. *México, imprenta de la Bibliotheca mexicana*, 1765.

Village (The) curate. *See* **Hurdis** (James, *d. d.*)

Villanueva (Joaquin Lorenzo). Vida literaria de dⁿ J. L. Villanueva, o memoria de sus escritos y de sus opiniones eclesiasticas y politicas, y de algunos sucesos notabiles de su tiempo. Con un appendice de documentos relativos a la historia del concilio de Trento. Escrita por el mismo. 2 v. xvi, 482 pp; viii, 470 pp. 8°. *Londres, Dulau y ca.* 1825.

Villa-Señor y Sanchez (Joseph Antonio de). Theatro americano, descripcion general de los reynos, y provincias de la Nueva-España, y sus jurisdicciones. 2ª parte. 6 p. l. 428 pp. 5 l. 1 pl. fol. [*México*], *la viuda de J. B. de Hogal*, 1748.

[Part 1 wanting].

Villaviciosa (Joseph de). La moschea, poetica inuentiua en octaua rima. [1ʳᵃ ed.] 16 p. l. 174, 2 l. 18°. *Cuenca, D. de la Iglesia*, 1615.

Villefranche (J. M.) Cineas; or Rome under Nero. Translated from the french. 398 pp. 12°. *Philadelphia, P. F. Cunningham*, 1871.

Villegas (Francisco de Quevedo). *See* **Quevedo Villegas.**

Villette (C. L. de, *pseudon?*) Essay on the happiness of the life to come. 189 pp. 12°. *Bath, R. Cruttwell*, 1794.

—— The same. 189 pp. 8°. *Bath, R. Cruttwell*, 1800.

Villiers (George, *2d duke of Buckingham*). The rehearsal. 1672. With illustrations from previous plays, etc. Carefully edited by Edward Arber. 2 p. l. 136 pp. 16°. *London, A. Murray & son*, 1868.

[ARBER'S english reprints, v. 5, no. 10].

Villot (Frédéric). Notice des tableaux exposés dans les galeries du Louvre. *See* **Paris.** (*Musée du Louvre*).

Vincent (J. H. *d. d.*) The berean question book, for 1871. 139 pp. 24°. *New York, Carlton & Lanahan*, 1870.

—— Little footprints in bible lands; or, simple lessons in sacred history and geography. With an introduction, by rev. T. M. Eddy, d. d. 139 pp. incl. 7 maps. 12°. *New York, Carlton & Porter*, [1861].

—— The wonders of fire and water; or talks with children about God's power, love and wisdom, as seen in fire and water. 125 pp. 9 pl. 18°. *New York, Carlton & Lanahan*, 1870.

—— Wonders of the air; or simple illustrations of the wisdom and power of God as seen in the air. 123 pp. 7 pl. 18°. *New York, Carlton & Lanahan*, 1870.

Vincent (*Rev.* Nathaniel, *d.* 1697). The spirit of prayer. With an introductory essay, by Enoch Pond. 189 pp. 32°. *Boston, Peirce & Parker*, 1832.

Vincentius Ferrerius (*S.*) *See* **Ferrer** (*S.* Vicente).

Vincentius *lerinensis.* Vincentivs lirinensis of the natioun of gallis, for the antiquitie and veritie of the catholik fayth, aganis ye prophane nouationis of al haereseis, a richt goldin buke writtin in latin about .xi.c.zeris passit, and neulie translatit in scottis be Niniane Winzet. Antverpiae, 1563. [*Reprint*]. 4°. [*Edinburgh*, 1835].

[MAITLAND club publications, no. 33, pp. 121-184].

Vinet (Alexandre Rodolphe). Vital christianity: essays and discourses on the religions of man and the religion of God.

Vinet (Alexandre Rodolphe)—continued. Translated, with an introduction, by Robert Turnbull. 355 pp. 12°. *Boston, Gould, Kendall & Lincoln*, 1845.

Vingut (Francisco Javier). The spanish teacher: a practical method of learning the spanish language on Ollendorff's system. New edition, corrected and enlarged by Luis F. Mantilla. 507 pp. 1 l. 12°. *New York, G. R. Lockwood*, 1871.

——— The same. Key to the spanish teacher. New ed. revised by Luis F. Mantilla. 128 pp. 12°. *New York, G. R. Lockwood*, 1871.

Vingut (Gertrude Fairfield de). Naomi Torrente: the history of a woman. 275 pp. 1 portrait. 8°. *New York, J. Bradburn*, 1864.

Vinta (Francesco). Carminvm libri ii. Ecloga i. 16°. *Florentiæ, apvd Ivntas*, 1562.

[*In* CARMINA qvinqve hetrvscorvm poetarvm, pp. 1-86].

Virgilius Maro (Publius). The georgics of Virgil; translated by William Sotheby. 5 p. l. 120 pp. 1 pl. 12°. *Middletown (Conn.) I. Riley, New York*, 1808.

——— Virgil's pastorals, translated into english prose; as also his georgicks, with notes and reflections. To which is added an appendix. By James Hamilton. xvi, 123, 60 pp. 16°. *Edinburgh, W. Cheyne*, 1742.

——— Eclogas y georgica primera de Virgilio trasladadas por Luis de Leon. 16°. *Valencia, J. T. Lucas*, 1761.

[*In* LEON (L. P. de). Obras propias, ed. 1761, pp. 75-127, 190-221].

Virgilius (Polydorus). *See* **Vergilio** (Polidoro).

Virginia (The) house-wife. 2d ed. with amendments and additions. 261 pp. 2 pl. 12°. *Washington, Way & Gideon*, 1825.

Virginia (The) literary museum and journal of belles lettres, arts, sciences, &c. Edited at the university of Virginia. v. 1. From June 17, 1829, to June 9, 1830. 8°. *Charlottesville, F. Carr*, 1830.

[*Note.*—No more published].

Virués y Spínola (José Joaquin de) *and* **Chaluz de Vernevil** (F. T. Alphonso). An original and condensed grammar of harmony, counterpoint, and musical composition; or, the generation of euphony reduced to natural truth; preceded by the elements of music. xxi, 502 pp. 7 tab. 8°. *London, Longman, Brown, Green and Longman*, 1850.

Visit (A) to Nahant, being a sequel to the Wonders of the deep. By a lady. [*anon.*] 196 pp. 18°. *New-York, General protestant episcopal sunday school union*, 1839.

Visitor's guide to Richmond and vicinity; embracing a sketch of the city, social statistics and notices of all places in and about the city of interest to the tourist. [*anon.*] 50 pp. 4 pl. 1 map. 18°. *Richmond, B. J. Bates*, 1871.

[*Note.*—Probably by M. P. Handy, and W. H. Pleasants].

Visits to aunt Clement; or, conversations on the connections between the old and new testaments. [*anon.*] 172 pp. 18°. *New York, General prot. episcopal sunday school union*, 1841.

Vita di Beatrice Cenci tratta dal manoscritto antico, [*anon.*] con annotazioni sul processo e condanna. [Dal giureconsulto Farinacci]. 127 pp. sm. 4°. *Roma, Gianandrea e Chiassi*, [1849].

Viviani (Viviano). Trattato del cvstodire la sanità. 205 pp. 4 l. 18°. *Venezia, G. Piuti*, 1626.

Vocabularius gemma gemmarū diligēter reuisus et castigatus per Wilhelmū Schaffner. [*anon.*] *b. l.* 151 l. 4°. *Lor, W. Schaffner*, 1514.

[*Note.*—A latin-german dictionary, in rude gothic type, 47 lines on a page, with title at end. First leaf wanting].

Vogel (*Dr.* Hermann). Handbook of the practice and art of photography. Revised and corrected by the author, and especially adapted for the United States. Translated from the german by Edward Moelling. 332 pp. 8°. *Philadelphia, Benerman & Wilson*, 1871.

Voiage du monde de Descartes. *See* **Daniel** (Gabriel).

Voices (The) of the year; or, the poet's kalendar. Containing the choicest pastorals in our language. [*anon.*] 544 pp. 3 pl. 8°. *London, C. Griffin & co.* 1865.

Voigt (Johann Carl Wilhelm). Versuch einer geschichte der steinkohlen, der braunkohlen und des torfes, nebst anleitung, diese fossilien kennen und unterscheiden zu lernen. 2 v. xxiii, 308 pp; 3 p. l. 197 pp. 2 l. 2 pl. 8°. *Weimar, Hoffmann*, 1802-05.

Voisin (C. Auguste). Documents pour servir à l'histoire des bibliothèques en Belgique et de leurs principales curiosités littéraires. 2 p. l. v, xvii, 350 pp. 1 pl. 8°. *Gand, C. Annoot-Braeckman*, 1840.

Voisin (Félix, *m.d.*) Des causes morales et physiques des maladies mentales et de quelques autres affections nerveuses, telle que l'hystérie, la nymphomanie et le satyriasis. xvi, 419 pp. 8°. *Paris, J. B. Baillière*, 1826.

Volckhausen (Ad. von). Why did he not die? Or the child from the Ebräergang. After the german. By mrs. A. L. Wister. 372 pp. 12°. *Philadelphia, J. B. Lippincott & co.* 1871.

Volger (Heinrich Friedrich Magnus). Diatribe historico-critica de Sapphus poetriæ vita et scriptis. 12°. [*Lipsiæ, in libraria weidmannia*, 1810].

[*In* SAPPHO. Carmina et fragmenta, 1810, pp. xvii-lxviii].

Voltaire (François Marie Arouët de). Lettres et billets de Voltaire à l'époque de son retour de Prusse en France en 1753. viii, 31 pp. 12°. *Paris, pour la société des bibliophiles*, 1867.

[*In* PARIS. Société des bibliophiles françois, 2e partie].

——— Poëmes sur la religion naturelle, et sur la destruction de Lisbonne. 44 pp. 8°. [*London*], 1756.

[*With* GESNER (Salomon). Rural poems. *London*, 1762].

——— The first two books of the history of Charles the twelfth. With a double translation, for the use of students, on the hamiltonian system, and notes. 1 p. l. xxvii, 218 pp. 8°. *London, Hunt & Clarke*, 1827.

——— Micromegas: a comic romance: a severe satire upon the philosophy, ignorance, and self-conceit of mankind. With a detail of the crusades: and a new plan for the history of the human mind. Translated from the french. 1 p. l. 252 pp. 16°. *London, D. Wilson & T. Durham*, 1753.

Voor-looper van d'h[r] Witte Cornelissz. de With, admirael van de west-indische compagnie, nopende den brasijlschen handel. [*anon.*] 10 l. sm. 4°. [*n. p.*] *Gedruckt voor den verdruckten, anno* 1650.

Voragine (Giacomo da Varaggio, *or* Jacopo da). Legēda sctorque longbardica noĩat. hystoria. [Legenda aurea.] Incipit prologus in legendas sanctorum quas collegit in vnvm frater Jacobus ianuensis de ordine predicatorum. [*In fine*]: Finit lombardica hystoria p. mandata Anthonii Koburger Nurenberge impressa anno salutis mcccclxxxij. kl. octob. *b. l.* 1 l. unp. 183 l. pag. fol. *Nuremberge, Anth. Koburger*, 1482.

[*Note.*—In two columns each of 54 lines. Gothic type, without signatures, or catchwords].

Vordoni (Teresa Albarelli). Sermoni. 32 pp. 16°. *Milano, G. Silvestri*, 1826.

Vose (John, *a.m.*) A compendium of astronomy. Stereotype ed. viii, 184 pp. 8 pl. 12°. *Boston, Carter, Hendee & co.* 1834.

——— A system of astronomy, on the principles of Copernicus; [also], a catalogue of eclipses visible in the United States during the present century, and the tables necessary for calculating eclipses, [etc.] 252 pp. 8°. *Concord*, [*N. H.*] *J. B. Moore*, 1827.

Vosgien (*pseudon.*) *See* **Ladvocat** (Jean Baptiste).

Voss (Gerhard Johann). De logices et rhetoricæ natura & constitutione libri 2. 2 p. l. 132 pp. 6 l; 82 pp. 3 l. 4°. *Hagæ-Comitis, A. Vlacq*, 1658.

[*With his* De veterum poetarum temporibus. *Amstelædami*, 1654].

——— De vetervm poetarvm temporibvs libri dvo, qvi svnt de poetis græcis et latinis. 4 p. l. 98 pp. 3 l; 88 pp. 2 l. 4°. *Amstelædami, J. Blaev*, 1654.

Voyage pittoresque aux glaciers de Chamouni. 1815. *See* **Lory** (Gabriel *and* Gabriel *fils*).

Voyage (A) to Peru. 1745–49. *See* **Courte de la Blanchardière** (*Abbé* —).

Voyage (A) to the world of Cartesius. *See* **Daniel** (Gabriel).

Voyages and adventures of Jack Halliard, in the arctic ocean. [*anon.*] 130 pp. sq. 16°. *Boston, Allen & Ticknor*, 1833.

Voyages de Pythagore en Égypte. *See* **Maréchal** (Pierre Sylvain).

Vitruvius Pollio (Marcus). Gvlielmi Philandri castilionii in decem libros M. Vitruuii Pollionis de architectura annotationes. *See* **Philandrier** (Guillaume).

Vrye politijke stellingen, en consideratien van staat, gedaen na der ware christenens even gelijke vryheits gronden; strekkende tot een rechtschape, en ware verbeteringh van staat, en kerk. Door een lief-habber van alle der welbevoeghde borgeren. Het eerste deel. [*anon.*] 4 p. l. 44 pp. 2 l. sm. 4°. *Amsterdam, voor den autheur*, 1665.

W. (A. M.) Patty Williams's voyage. A story almost wholly true. By A. M. W. [*anon.*] 104 pp. 16°. *Boston, Walker, Wise & co.* 1861.

W. (E. A.) Ethel Linton; or, the Feversham temper. [*anon.*] 317 pp. 16°. *Cincinnati, Hitchcock & Walden*, 1871.

W. (G. B.) Essays, political and philosophical. [*anon.*] xxxvii, 382 pp. 12°. *Carlisle, J. Steel,* 1851.

W. (H.) Trve originall of the sovle. *See* **Woolnor** (Henry).

W. (T.) Theological rules. 1615. *See* **Wilson** (Thomas).

Wachler (Johann Friedrich Ludwig). Vorlesungen über die geschichte der teutschen national-litteratur. 2e aufl. 2 v. in 1. xii, 216 pp; 2 p. l. 326 pp. 10 l. 8°. *Frankfurt am Main, G. F. Kettembeil,* 1834.

Waddel (Moses, *d. d.*) Memoirs of miss Caroline E. Smelt. 158 pp. 18°. *Philadelphia, H. Perkins,* 1835.

Waddell (William Henry). A latin grammar for beginners. 86 pp. 12°. *New York, Harper & brothers,* 1871.

Waddington (George, *d. d.*) A visit to Greece in 1823 and 1824. 2d ed. 4 p. l. lxiii, 248 pp. 2 maps. 8°. *London, J. Murray,* 1825.

Wade (Thomas). Mundi et cordis: de rebus sempiternis et temporariis: carmina. Poems and sonnets. xvi, 286 pp. 12°. *London, J. Miller,* 1835.

Wadsworth (*Rev.* Benjamin, *president of Harvard college*). The benefits of a good, and mischiefs of an evil, conscience. Being fourteen sermons preached from three several texts. ii, 213 pp. 3 l. 18°. *Boston, B. Eliot,* 1719.

Wadsworth (James). The english spanish pilgrime. Or, a nevv discovery of spanish popery, and iesviticall stratagems. With the estate of the english pentioners and fugitiues vnder the king of Spaines dominions, and else where at this present. Also laying open the new order of the jesuitrices and preaching nunnes. 2d ed. 3 p. l. 100 pp. 12°. *London, M. Sparke,* 1630.

——— The evropean mercury. Describing the highwayes and stages from place to place; through the most remarkable parts of christendome. With a catalogue of the principall fairs, marts, and markets, thorowout the same. 18 p. l. 210 pp. 14 l. 18°. *London, H. Twyford,* 1641.

——— The present estate of Spayne, or a true relation of some remarkable things touching the court and gouernment of Spayne, with a catalogue of all the nobility with their reuenues. 3 p. l. 84 pp. 12°. *London, A. Rithcrdon,* 1630.

Wagstaffe (William, *m. d.*) Miscellaneous works. To which is prefix'd his life, and an account of his writings. xiv, 414 pp. 2 pl. 8°. *London, J. Bowyer,* 1726.

CONTENTS.

A comment upon the history of Tom Thumb. 5th ed. pp. 1–36.
Crispin the cobler's confutation of Ben. H[oadley], in an epistle to him. 3d ed. pp. 37–51.
The story of st. A[lban's] ghost, or the apparition of mother Haggy. 4th ed. pp. 53–75.
The testimonies of the citizens of Fickleborough, concerning the life and character of Robert Hush, commonly called Bob. pp. 77–104.
The representation of the loyal subjects of Albinia. 3d ed. pp. 105–119.
The character of Richard St—le [Steele], esq; with some remarks. By Toby. [*pseudon.*] 4th ed. pp. 121–159.
The state and condition of our taxes, considered; or, a proposal for a tax upon funds. By a free-holder. [*anon.*] 3d ed. pp. 161–192.
The plain dealer. no. 1–16. April 12 to July 26, 1712. pp. 193–347.
A letter from the facetious dr. Andrew Tripe, at Bath, to his loving brother, the profound Greshamite, shewing that the scribendi cacoethes is a distemper, etc. With an appendix concerning the application of Socrates his clyster, and the use of clean linen in controversy. pp. 349–414.

Wahl (Louis). Seaside and fireside fairies. 1864. *See* **Blum** (Georg) *and* **Wahl.**

Wahrheit (Die). Zeitschrift für freie menschen. Herausgegeben von S. H. Sonneschein. [Monatliche]. 6 januar bis 30 juni 1871. v. 1. 8°. *St. Louis, F. Roeslein,* [1871].

Waif (A) from the river side; or, stories, sketches, letters, and poems, selected from a manuscript newspaper. 172 pp. 18°. *New York, Carleton & Porter,* [1861].

Waifwood. 1864. *See* **Stimson** (A. L.)

Wainwright (Jonathan Mayhew, *d. d.*) The pathways and abiding places of our Lord; illustrated in the journal of a tour through the land of promise. xix, 196 pp. 20 pl. 4°. *New York, D. Appleton & co.* 1851.

Waisbrooker (Lois). Mayweed blossoms. 264 pp. 12°. *Boston, W. White & co.* 1871.

Waite (Otis F. R.) Guide book for the eastern coast of New England. 220 pp. 2 maps. 16°. *Concord (N. H.) E. C. Eastman & co.* 1871.

Waiting at the cross. A book of devotion. [*anon.*] 224 pp. 18°. *Boston, H. A. Young & co.* 1869.

Wake (William, *editor*). The genuine epistles of the apostolical fathers, st. Clement—st. Polycarp, st. Ignatius—st. Barnabas, the pastor of Hermas, and the martyrdoms of st. Ignatius and st. Polycarp, written by those who were present. Translated and published, with preliminary discourses, by archbishop Wake. viii, 372 pp. 3 l. 12°. *Oxford, T. Tegg,* 1840.

Wakefield (Gilbert). A new translation of parts of the new testament. 1789. *See* **Bible.** (*English*).

Wakefield (Priscilla Bell). Mental improvement: or the beauties and wonders of nature and art. In a series of instructive conversations. 4th am. from 5th London ed. 240 pp. 12°. *Philadelphia, B. Johnson*, 1819.

Wakefield (Samuel, *d. d.*) A complete system of christian theology; or, a concise, comprehensive, and systematic view of the evidences, doctrines, morals, and institutions of christianity. 664 pp. 8°. *New York, Carlton & Porter*, 1862.

——— The same. 663 pp. 8°. *Pittsburgh, J. L. Read & son*, 1869.

——— The sacred choral; a choice collection of sacred music, derived from the highest sources of musical talent, both of Europe and America. 244 pp. obl. 8°. *Cincinnati, Swormstedt & Poe*, 1854.

Wakeley (*Rev.* Joseph B.) The prince of pulpit orators: a portraiture of rev. George Whitefield. Illustrated by anecdotes and incidents. 2d ed. 400 pp. 1 portrait. 16°. *New York, Carlton & Lanahan*, 1871.

Walch (Johann Ernest Immanuel). Recueil des monumens des catastrophes que le globe terrestre a essuiées. 1767–78. *See* **Knorr** (Georg Wolfgang) *and* **Walch.**

Walch (Johann Georg). Bibliotheca patristica litterariis annotationibus instructa. Ed. nova auctior et emendatior adornata a Io. Tr. Lebr. Danzio. xvi, xlviii, 806 pp. 8°. *Ienae, sumtu bibliopolii crockeriani*, 1834.

Walden (Treadwell). Our english bible and its ancestors. xii, 9–231 pp. 12°. *Philadelphia, Porter & Coates*, [1871].

Waldor (Mélanie de Villenave). Alphonse et Juliette. 2 v. 2 p. l. 304 pp; 2 p. l. 280 pp. 16°. *Bruxelles, Meline, Cans & compe.* 1839.

Waldron (Francis Godolphin). The literary museum; or, a selection of scarce old tracts. 8°. *London, for the editor*, 1792.

CONTENTS.

BELCHER (W.) The new arcadia, a regular pindaric ode.
BOCCACCIO (G.) De preclaris mulieribus. [Specimen of translation by H. Parcare, lord Morley].
CEREMONIES (The) for the healing of the king's evil, used in the time of Henry viii. *London*, 1686.
CEREMONIES (The) of blessing cramp-rings, used by the catholick kings of England. From ms.
DOWNES (J.) Roscius anglicanus, or, an historical review of the stage. *London*, 1708.
GASCOIGNE (G.) A delicate diet, for daintie mouthed droonkardes. *London*, 1576.
HEYWOOD (T.) The king in the country. [Adapted from Heywood's King Edward the iv, by F. G. Waldron].

Waldron (Francis G.)—continued.
JONSON (Ben). Specimen of a proposed new edition of his works.
ONNE mie maister Lydgate, his travellynge ynnto Fraunce. Written 360 years since. (Spurious).
PEACHAM (H.) The period of mourning, disposed into sixe visions. *London*, 1613.
SPENSER (E.) Dispersed poems, not in any edition of his works.

——— The same. [Another ed.] 8°. *London, for the editor*, 1792.
[Imperfect: pp. 17–18 of appendix to Downes' Roscius anglicanus wanting].

Waleff (Blaise Henri de Corte, *baron* de). [Œuvres diverses]. Par l'auteur des Titans. [*anon.*] 5 v. 8°. *Liége, E. Kints*, 1731.

CONTENTS.

v. 1. Odes sur les affaires du tems, avec une description en abrégé de la Hollande.
v. 2–3. Réflexions nouvelles sur l'Iliade d'Homère, avec la tragédie d'Électre.
v. 4. Le siècle de Loüis le grand [poëme]. Avec Thémire [poëme].
v. 5. Les rues de Madrid [poëme], l'histoire de la porcelaine, et le combat des échasses [poëme]. Avec plusieurs satyres & autres pièces.

Walford (Edward). The county families of the united kingdom, or royal manual of the titled and untitled aristocracy of Great Britain and Ireland. 6th ed. greatly enlarged. xvi, 1124 pp. 8°. *London, R. Hardwicke*, 1871.

Walker (Adam). A system of familiar philosophy in twelve lectures; containing the elements and the practical uses to be drawn from the chemical properties of matter: the principles and application of mechanics; of hydrostatics; of hydraulics; of pneumatics; of magnetism; of electricity; of optics; and of astronomy. Including every material modern discovery and improvement to the present time. New ed. 2 v. xvi, 354 pp; iv, 251 pp. 13 l. 49 pl. 4°. *London, author*, 1802.

Walker (Amasa, *ll. d.*) The science of wealth: a manual of political economy. Embracing the laws of trade, currency, and finance. 6th ed. xxxviii, 496 pp. 9 tab. 8°. *Boston, Little, Brown & co.* 1871.

Walker (*Rev.* Charles). Memoir and sermons of the rev. William Duval, city missionary, Richmond. xvi, 256 pp. 12° *Richmond* (*Va.*) *J. W. Randolph*, 1854.

Walker (Edward). The addresses and messages of the presidents of the United States, from Washington to Harrison. To which is prefixed the declaration of independence, and constitution of the United States. Together with a portrait and memoir of W. H. Harrison. [xxxv], 5–716 pp. 1 portrait. 8°. *New York, E. Walker*, 1841.

Walker (Francis). Catalogues of zoölogical collections. *See* **British** museum.

Walker (*Rev.* George, 1734-1807). Essays on various subjects. To which is prefixed a life of the author. 2 v. 2 p. l. 158 pp. 1 portrait; 2 p. l. 363 pp. 8°. *London, J. Johnson*, 1809.

——— On the right of individual judgment in religion. A sermon. viii, 41 pp. 8°. *Manchester, J. Johnson*, [1800].

[*With* EATON (David). Scripture the only guide. *York*, 1800].

Walker (George, *landscape-painter*). Scottish scenery. Twenty views, engraved by W. Byrne, from pictures, by G. Walker. With brief descriptions. 2 p. l. 20 l. 20 pl. obl. fol. *London, T. Cadell & W. Davies*, 1807.

Walker (James Barr, *d. d.*) Philosophy of the plan of salvation. A book for the times. By an american citizen. With an introductory essay by Calvin E. Stowe, d. d. A new edition, with a supplementary chapter by the author. [*anon.*] 286 pp. 12°. *Boston, Gould & Lincoln*, 1855.

——— Poetry of reason and conscience.—Immortality and worth of the soul; ten scenes in the life of a lady of fashion; and miscellaneous pieces. 214 pp. 12°. *Chicago, H. A. Sumner*, 1871.

Walker (James Thomas). Great trigonometrical survey. 1870. *See* **India** (British).

Walker (John, *philologist*, 1732-1807). An abridgment of Walker's rules on the sounds of the letters, according to their position; also rules for accenting and dividing all the words in the language that come under rule: to which are added nearly all of the exceptions. By William Mulkey. 124 pp. 16°. *Boston, author*, 1834.

Walker (K. K. C.) Zoe's story; or, old friends and foes in masks. By the author of "A little leaven." [etc. *anon.*] 150 pp. 16°. *New York, A. D. F. Randolph*, 1863.

Walker (*Mrs.* Mary Spring). Down in a saloon; or, the minister's protégé. 274 pp. 3 pl. 16°. *Boston, H. Hoyt*, [1871].

Walker (Peter). The history and habits of animals: with special reference to the animals of the north american continent, and those mentioned in the scriptures. 320 pp. 7 col. pl. sq. 12°. *Philadelphia, Presbyterian board of publication*, [1859].

Walker (*Rev.* Robert). Analysis of researches into the origin and progress of historical time, from the creation to the accession of

Walker (*Rev.* Robert)—continued.

C. Caligula. xxviii, 14, 432 pp. 1 l. 8°. *London, T. Cadell, jun. & W. Davies*, 1796.

Walker (Sayer, *m. d.*) Observations on the constitution of women, and on some of the diseases to which they are more especially liable. 2 p. l. viii, 228 pp. 12°. *London, W. Phillips*, 1803.

Walker (William Sidney). Gustavus Vasa, and other poems. 2d ed. xxvii, 230 pp. 17 l. 8°. *London, Longman*, 1813.

Wallace (*Rev.* Adam). The parson of the islands; a biography of the rev. Joshua Thomas; embracing sketches of his contemporaries, and remarkable camp meeting scenes. [etc.] With an introduction by the rev. James Massey. 412 pp. 1 portrait. 12°. *Philadelphia, author*, 1861.

Wallace (John). The practical engineer: showing the best and most economical mode for modeling, constructing and working steam engines. 160 pp. 14 pl. 1 portrait. 12°. *Pittsbu[r]gh, Kennedy & brother*, 1853.

——— The same. Containing, also, directions in regard to the various kinds of machinery connected with steam power. 2d ed. 320 pp. 29 pl. 1 portrait. 16°. *Pittsburgh, W. S. Haven*, 1865.

Wallace (*Rev.* John H.) An antidote to backsliding. 187 pp. 16°. *New York, Carlton & Phillips*, 1855.

Wallace (John H. *of Muscatine, Iowa*). Wallace's american trotting register, containing all that is known of the pedigrees of trotting horses, their ancestors and descendants. With a record of all published performances in which a mile was trotted or paced in 2:40 or less, from the earliest dates till the close of 1868. And a full record of the performances of 1869-70. With an introductory essay on the true origin of the american trotter. And a set of rules for the government of all trials of speed. 504 pp. 7 pl. 8°. *New York, G. E. Woodward*, 1871.

Wallace (*Rev.* Robert, *f. g. s., d.* 1858). Antitrinitarian biography: or sketches of the lives and writings of distinguished antitrinitarians; exhibiting a view of the state of the unitarian doctrine and worship in the principal nations of Europe, from the reformation to the close of the seventeenth century; [with] a history of unitarianism in England during the same period. 3 v. 8°. *London, E. T. Whitfield*, 1850.

Wallace (W. M.) The family oracle of health. *See* **Crell** (A. F.) *and* **Wallace.**

Wallace (William Vincent). Maritana. The music by W. V. Wallace. The words by E. Fitzball. [Libretto, without music]. 37 pp. 8°. [*New York*], *W. C. Bryant & co.* 1871.
[PAREPA-ROSA grand english opera].

Waller (Edmund). The works of Edmund Waller, esq[r]. in verse and prose. Published by mr. Fenton. [With observations on some of mr. Waller's poems and speeches]. 9 p. l. 450, xcii pp. 3 pl. 4°. *London, I. Tonson,* 1729.

Waller (J. C.) The second coming of Christ. The restitution of all things, and our lord's personal reign with his glorified saints in his millenial kingdom on the earth. 297 pp. 1 portrait. 12°. *Louisville, J. P. Morton & co.* 1863.

Wallich (George Charles, *m. d.*) The north-atlantic sea-bed: comprising a diary of the voyage on board of h. m. s. Bulldog, in 1860; and observations on the presence of animal life, and the formation and nature of organic deposits, at great depths in the ocean. Part i. 2 p. l. 160 pp. 6 pl. 1 map. 4°. *London, J. Van Voorst,* 1862.

Wallihan (S. S.) *and* **Bigney** (T. O.) The Rocky mountain directory and Colorado gazetteer, for 1871, comprising a brief history of Colorado, [etc.] 442 pp. 8°. *Denver, S. S. Wallihan & co.* [1870].

Wallin (*Rev.* Benjamin). Lectures on primitive christianity: as it appeared in the church at Jerusalem, in the time of the apostles. Also on the epistle to the church at Sardis. And on the faithful in the days of Malachi. xx, 390 pp. 8°. *Wilmington, J. Boggs, jun.* 1801.

Walling (Henry F.) *and* **Gray** (O. W.) New topographical atlas of the state of Pennsylvania, with descriptions historical, scientific, and statistical. With a map of the United States and territories. [Also, classified directory of the principal business firms and professional men of Philadelphia]. 110 pp. 10 l. incl. 25 maps. 4°. *Philadelphia, Stedman, Brown & Lyon,* 1872.

Walsh (Edward, *m. d.*) A narrative of the expedition to Holland, in the autumn of the year 1799. 1 p. l. ii, 164 pp. 7 pl. 1 map. 4°. *London, G. G. & J. Robinson,* 1800.

Walsh (Michael). Sketches of the speeches and writings of Michael Walsh: including his poems and correspondence. Compiled by a committee of the Spartan association. 104 pp. 1 pl. 8°. *New York, T. McSpedon,* 1843.

Walsh (*Rev.* Robert, *ll. d.*) A residence at Constantinople, during a period including the commencement, progress, and termination of the greek and turkish revolutions. 2 v. xv, 412 pp. 5 pl. 1 portrait, 1 map; x, 542 pp. 5 l. 7 pl. 8°. *London, F. Westley & A. H. Davis,* 1836.

Walshe (Walter Hayle, *m. d.*) The anatomy, physiology, pathology, and treatment of cancer. With additions by J. Mason Warren, m. d. vii, 351 pp. 2 pl. 12°. *Boston, W. D. Ticknor,* 1844.

Walsingham (*Sir* Francis). Journal of sir Francis Walsingham, from Dec. 1570 to April 1583. Edited, from the original ms. in the possession of lieut.-col. Carew, by Charles Trice Martin. 2 p. l. 104 pp. sm. 4°. [*London*], *Camden society,* 1870.
[*In* CAMDEN (The) miscellany, v. 6.]

Walter (*Rev.* Weever). Letters from the continent: containing sketches of foreign scenery and manners; with hints as to the different modes of travelling, expense of living, etc. 4 p. l. 307 pp. 8°. *Edinburgh, W. Blackwood,* 1828.

Walter (William H.) Selections of psalms, together with the canticles, occasional anthems, and proper psalms on certain days; pointed for chanting, with chants. 162 pp. 12°. *New York, D. Dana,* 1857.

Walter and Nellie; or, the shadow of the rock. By the author of "Daisy Downs," [etc. *anon.*] 293 pp. 18°. *New York, Carlton & Porter,* [1863].

Walter S. Newhall. A memoir. [*anon.*] 140 pp. 1 portrait. 12°. *Philadelphia, for the benefit of the sanitary commission,* 1864.

Walter Seyton: a story of rural life in Virginia. [*anon.*] 117 pp. 4 pl. 16°. *Boston, Phillips, Sampson & co.* 1859.

Waltham *and* **Watertown** (*Mass.*) Greenough, Jones & co.'s directory of the inhabitants, institutions, manufacturing establishments, business, societies, business firms, etc. in the towns of Waltham and Watertown, for 1871–72. Greenough, Jones & co. compilers and publishers. 8°. *Boston,* 1871.

Walton (George A. *and* Electa N. L.) A manual of arithmetic, consisting of dictation exercises, hints on methods of teaching, etc. [Also] a key to Walton's illustrative practical arithmetic. 192 pp. 12°. *Boston, Brewer & Tileston,* [1871].

Walworth (Mansfield Tracy). Delaplaine: or, the sacrifice of Irene. A novel. 300 pp. 12°. *New York, G. W. Carleton & co.* 1871.

——— Lulu. A tale of the National hotel poisoning. 367 pp. 12°. *New York, Carleton*, 1863.

Walz (Gustav). Landwirthschaftliche betriebslehre. xii, 667 pp. 1 l. 8°. *Stuttgart, J. G. Cotta*, 1867. s.

Wanderer (The), or Horatio and Lætitia: a poem, in five epistles. [Also, Vales of peace: a pastoral, in two epistles. *anon.*] 138 pp. 1 pl. 16°. *Utica, [N. Y.] for the authors*, 1811.

Wanostrocht (N. *or* Vincent). Recueil choisi de traits historiques et de contes moraux. Avec la signification des mots en anglais au bas de chaque page. 299 pp. 12°. *New-York, W. B. Gilley*, 1829.

Wansleben (Johann Michael). The present state of Egypt; or, a new relation of a late voyage into that kingdom. Performed in the years 1672 and 1673. By f. Vansleb. Englished by M. D. 3 p. l. 253 pp. 3 l. 16°. *London, R. E. for J. Starkey*, 1678.

War (The) in Florida. 1836. *See* **Potter** (W.)

Warburton (William, *bishop of Gloucester*). Miscellaneous translations, in prose and verse, from roman poets, orators, and historians. 2 p. l. 125 pp. 12°. *London, A. Barker*, 1724.

Ward (Edward). The wooden world dissected, in the characters of a ship of war, a sea-captain, a sea-lieutenant, etc. By a lover of the mathematicks. [*anon.*] 2d ed. 6 p. l. 107 pp. 16°. *London, H. Meere, etc.* 1708.

Ward (*Rev.* Ferdinand DeW. *d. d.*) Churches of Rochester. Ecclesiastical history of Rochester, N. Y. Narrative of the rise, progress, and present condition of each religious organization; biographical sketches of pastors born in the city; with miscellaneous items, from August, 1815, to July, 1871. 184 pp. 8°. *Rochester, E. Darrow*, 1871.

Ward (Henry Dana). Faith of Abraham and of Christ, his seed in the coming kingdom of God on earth, with the restitution of all things which God hath spoken. 237 pp. 8°. *Philadelphia, Claxton, Remsen & Haffelfinger*, 1872.

——— History of the cross: the pagan origin, and idolatrous adoption and worship, of the image. viii, 88 pp. 8°. *Philadelphia, Claxton, Remsen & Haffelfinger*, 1871.

Ward (John, *ll. d.* 1679–1758). The lives of the professors of Gresham college: to which is prefixed the life of the fovnder, sir Thomas Gresham. With an appendix, consisting of orations, lectvres, and letters, written by the professors, with other papers serving to illustrate the lives. 2 p. l. xxiv, 338 pp. 1 l. 156 pp. 1 pl. fol. *London, J. Moore for avthor*, 1740.

[Imperfect: wanting portrait of sir T. Gresham; 3 pl. at pp. 1, 12, 33].

Ward (*Rev.* Samuel, *of Ipswich, Eng.*) A collection of svch sermons and treatises as have beene written and published by Samuel Ward. 4 p. l. 602 pp. 1 pl. 16°. *London, I. Grismond*, 1635–36.

Warder (Joseph). The true amazons: or the monarchy of bees. Being a new discovery and improvement of those wonderful creatures. Also, how to make the english wine or mead. 9th ed. 5 p. l. 13–164 pp. 1 portrait. 16°. *London, R. Baldwin & T. Longman*, 1765.

Wardlaw (Ralph, *d. d.*) Christian ethics: or moral philosophy on the principles of divine revelation. From the second London edition. With an introductory essay by Leonard Woods, d. d. xvi, 13–380 pp. 12°. *New York, D. Appleton & co.* 1835.

Ware (Henry, *jr. d. d.* 1794–1843). Memoirs of the rev. Noah Worcester, d. d. With a preface, notes, and a concluding chapter, by Samuel Worcester. xii, 154 pp. 8°. *Boston, J. Monroe & co.* 1844.

——— On the formation of the christian character. viii, 175 pp. 16°. *Cambridge, [Ms.] Hilliard & Brown*, 1831.

Ware (Isaac). A complete body of architecture adorned with plans and elevations, from original designs. [With] some designs of Inigo Jones. 10 p. l. 748 pp. 2 l. 126 pl. fol. *London, T. Osborne & J. Shipton*, 1756.
[3 l. unp. following pl. 10, 12, and 15].

Ware (*Rev.* John Fothergill Waterhouse). Home life: what it is, and what it needs. xxiv, 180 pp. 16°. *Boston, W. V. Spencer*, 1864.

Ware (*Mrs.* Mary Greene Chandler). Thoughts in my garden. 268 pp. 12°. *Boston, Crosby & Nichols*, 1863.

Ware (*Rev.* Thomas). Sketches of the life and travels of rev. Thomas Ware, who has been an itinerant methodist preacher for more than fifty years. Written by himself. 264 pp. 1 portrait. 12°. *New York, T. Mason & G. Lane*, 1839.

Warhafftige unnd eygentliche beschreibung der allerschrecklichsten und grawsamsten verrätherey so jemals erhört worden, wider die königliche maiestat, derselben gemahl und junge printzen, sampt dem gantzen parlament zu Londen in Engeland fürgenommen, wie es entdecket, die thäter ergriffen, gefangen, und gestrafft worden, neben kurtzer erzehlung der gantzen des parlaments session. Mit schönen kupfferstück gezieret durch Johann Theodor und Johann Israel de Bry. *b. l.* 32 pp. sm. 4°. *Frankfurt am Mayn, M. Beckern*, 1606.

Warin. *See* **Regnault-Warin.**

Warleigh (*Rev.* Henry Smith). Ezekiel's temple: its design unfolded, its architecture displayed, and the subjects connected with it discussed. xvi, 240 pp. 3 plans. 8°. *London, J. F. Shaw*, 1856.

Warne (*Rev.* Joseph Andrews). The american baptist sabbath-school hymn book. 317 pp. 32°. *Philadelphia, D. Clarke*, 1844.

——— The same. 4th ed. 317 pp. 18°. *New York, E. H. Fletcher*, 1851.

——— On the harmony between the scriptures and phrenology. 12°. [*Boston*, 1835].
[*In* COMBE (George). The constitution of man, etc. pp. 351-380].

——— Phrenology in the family. Or the utility of phrenology in early domestic education. 292 pp. 18°. *Philadelphia, G. W. Donohue*, 1839.

Warner (Anna B.) Hymns of the church militant. viii, 640 pp. 16°. *New York, R. Carter & brothers*, 1858.

——— My brother's keeper. 385 pp. 12°. *New York, D. Appleton & co.* 1855.

——— Stories of Vinegar hill. [*anon.*] 6 v. 18°. *New York, R. Carter & brothers*, 1872.

CONTENTS.

v. 1. The old church door.
v. 2. The fowls of the air.
v. 3. Golden thorns.
v. 4. Plants without root.
v. 5. An hundredfold.
v. 6. Spring work.

Warner (Ferdinand, *ll. d.*) Memoirs of the life of sir Thomas More, lord high chancellor of England, in the reign of Henry viii. [Also], his History of Utopia, translated into english; with notes. 1 p. l. 160, 230 pp. 1 portrait. 8°. *London, L. Davis & C. Reymers*, [*etc.*] 1758.

Warner (John). New theorems, tables, and diagrams, for the computation of earth work. In two parts, with an appendix. 316 pp. 14 pl. 8°. *Philadelphia, J. B. Lippincott & co.* 1861.

Warner (*Rev.* Richard). The history of the isle of Wight; military, ecclesiastical, civil, & natural. [Also], a view of its agriculture. xii, 311, 14 pp. 10 l. 3 pl. 8°. *Southampton, T. Cadell, jr. & W. Davies*, 1795.
[Imperfect: wanting 1 map].

——— Illustrations, critical, historical, biographical, and miscellaneous, of novels by the author of Waverley. 3 v. 12°. *London, Longman*, 1824.

——— A tour through Cornwall, in the autumn of 1808. 2 p. l. iv, 363 pp. 1 pl. 8°. *Bath, R. Cruttwell*, 1809.

Warner (Susan). The house in town. A sequel to "Opportunities." By the author of "The wide, wide world." [*anon.*] 424 pp. 2 pl. 16°. *New York, R. Carter & brothers*, 1872.

Warner, Higgins *and* Beers. Atlas of the state of Illinois; to which is added an atlas of the United States, maps of the hemispheres, &c. 8 pp. 40 maps. fol. *Chicago, Warner, Higgins & Beers*, 1871.

Warnes (José Quintana). El maestro de si mismo; ó guia analitica para el estudio y facil comprension de la lengua inglesa. 291 pp. 12°. *Philadelphia, T. T. Ash*, 1831.

——— The same. The spanish expositor; or, an analytical guide to the study of the spanish language; consisting of exercises of select and varied passages, [etc.] 291 pp. 12°. *Philadelphia, T. T. Ash*, 1831.

Warning (A) to wives: or, the platonic lover. *See* **Smythies** (*Mrs.* — Gordon).

Warren (Edward, *m. d.*) The life of John Collins Warren. m. d. compiled chiefly from his autobiography and journals. 2 v. xi, 420 pp. 2 pl. 3 portraits; vii, 382 pp. 4 pl. 8°. *Boston, Ticknor & Fields*, 1860.

Warren (Erasmus). Geologia: or, a discourse concerning the earth before the deluge. Wherein the form and properties ascribed to it, in a book [by Thomas Burnet] intituled The theory of the earth, are excepted against: and it is made appear, that the dissolution of that earth was not the cause of the universal flood. Also a new explication of that flood is attempted. 8 p. l. 359 pp. sm. 4°. *London, R. Chiswell*, 1690.

Warren (Israel Perkins, *d. d.*) Sunday-school commentary. 1871. *See* **Bible.** (*English*).

Warren (*Rev.* Samuel, *ll. d.*) *and* **Stephens** (John). Chronicles of wesleyan method-

Warren (*Rev.* S.) *and* **Stephens** (J.)—con'd. ism. 2 v. 4 p. l. xx, 420 pp; 3 p. l. v, 248 pp. 3 pl. 12°. *London, J. Stephens,* 1827.

CONTENTS.

v. 1. First department. A digest of all its laws and regulations, with a comprehensive statement of its principal doctrines. By S. Warren.
v. 2. Second department. An alphabetical arrangement of all its circuits in England, Wales, and Scotland; with the names of the preachers who have travelled in them. [etc.] By J. Stephens.

Warren (Samuel Edward). General problems from the orthographic projections of descriptive geometry; [etc.] xxxv, 412 pp. 36 pl. 8°. *New York, J. Wiley,* 1860.

Warren (T. Robinson). Shooting, boating, and fishing, for young sportsmen. 165 pp. 2 pl. 12°. *New York, C. Scribner & co.* 1871.

Warton (Thomas, *d. d.* 1728–1790). A companion to the guide, and a guide to the companion: being a complete supplement to all the accounts of Oxford hitherto published. [*anon.*] 4th ed. 47 pp. 16°. *London, H. Payne,* [1764]?

[*With* NEW (The) Oxford guide, 4th ed.]

——— The life and literary remains of Ralph Bathurst, m. d. dean of Wells, and president of Trinity college in Oxford. 2 v. in 1. 232 pp; 296 pp. 1 portrait. 8°. *London, R. & J. Dodsley,* 1761.

Warwick (Arthur). Spare minutes; or resolved meditations and premeditated resolvtions. 7th ed. 2 parts in 1 v. Eng. title, 4 p. l. 92 pp; eng. title, 4 p. l. 86 pp. 6 l. 18°. *London, W. Hammond,* 1640.

Wase (Christopher). Considerations concerning free-schools, as settled in England. 4 p. l. 112 pp. 8°. *Oxford, at the theater,* 1678.

Washbourne (John, *jr.*) Bibliotheca gloucestrensis: a collection of scarce and curious tracts, relating to the county and city of Gloucester; illustrative of, and published during the civil war; with an historical introduction, notes, and appendix. 1 p. l. ccv, viii pp. 3 l. 456 pp. 4 pl. 4°. *Gloucester,* [*Eng.*] *author,* 1825.

Washerwoman's (The) daughter. From the german. Translated by Anna B. Cooke. [*anon.*] 158 pp. 2 pl. 18°. *Philadelphia, J. P. Skelly & co.* 1871.

Washington (George). Words of Washington. Selected by James Parton. viii, 196 pp. sq. 16°. *Boston, J. R. Osgood & co.* 1872.

Washington (*D. C. City of*). Twenty-third report of the board of trustees of the public schools of the city of Washington. 1866–70. 8°. *Washington, McGill & Witherow,* 1870.

Washington (*D. C.*) Boyd's directory of Washington, Georgetown, and Alexandria. 1871. 17 p. l. 388, xcvi pp. 1 l. 8°. *Washington* (*D. C.*) 1871.

Washington daily [and Sunday] morning chronicle. *See* **Daily** morning chronicle (Washington).

Washington daily patriot. *See* **Daily** patriot (Washington).

Washington directory, 1872. *See* **District** of Columbia.

Washington evening star. *See* **Evening** star (The Washington daily).

Washington national republican. *See* **Daily** national republican (Washington).

Washington Saturday evening visitor. *See* **Saturday** evening visitor (Washington).

Wasielewski (Joseph W. von). Life of Robert Schumann. Translated by A. L. Alger. 275 pp. 16°. *Boston, O. Ditson & co.* [1871].

Watchmaker (The) and jeweler, devoted to the interests of watchmakers, jewelers, silversmiths, scientific artizans, etc. An illustrated monthly journal. Sept. 1870, to Aug. 1871. v. 2. 4°. *New York, E. Albert & co.* 1871.

Waterbury (Jared Bell, *d. d.*) The happy christian, or, piety the only foundation of true and substantial joy. 197 pp. 18°. *New-York, W. Robinson,* 1838.

——— The skeptic refuted, and the bible vindicated. 234 pp. 1 pl. 18°. *Boston, Massachusetts sabbath school society,* [1853].

——— Sketches of eloquent preachers. 256 pp. 1 portrait. 12°. *New York, American tract society,* [1864].

——— True and false courage. 142 pp. 1 pl. 18°. *Boston, Mass. sabbath school society,* [1853].

Waterbury (*Rev.* Julius Henry). Children's praise. A service book for sunday-schools, with instructions in music for choral societies. 78, 50 pp. sq. 16°. *Rochester, D. M. Dewey,* 1871.

Waterland (Daniel, *d. d.*) Regeneration stated and explained according to scripture and antiquity, in a discourse on Tit. iii, 4, 5, 6. 2 p. l. 55 pp. 8°. *London, W. Innys & R. Manby,* 1740.

Waters (*Elder* Plummer). Salvation for the chief of sinners. 228 pp. 12°. *Baltimore, J. W. Woods*, 1838.

Waterston (*Rev.* Robert Charles). Thoughts on moral and spiritual culture. viii, 317 pp. 12°. *Boston, Crocker & Ruggles*, 1842.

Watertown (George). Hibernia; or, Ireland the world over. Showing how Pat rules America. viii, 143 pp. 8°. *New York, American news co.* 1871.

Watertown (*Mass.*) Directory for 1871-72. *See* **Waltham** *and* **Watertown** (*Mass.*)

Waterworth (*Rev.* James). An examination of the evidence adduced by mr. Keary, against the authenticity or validity of certain passages from the fathers, contained in the Faith of catholics on certain points of controversy, compiled by rev. Jos. Berington and rev. John Kirk. 76 pp. 8°. *London, J. Booker*, 1834.

[*With* BERINGTON (*Rev.* Joseph) *and* KIRK (*Rev.* John). The faith of catholics, 1830].

——— Six historical lectures, on the origin and progress, in England, of the change of religion, called the reformation, delivered in the catholic church of the holy Trinity, Newark. xvi, 9-408 pp. 8°. *Philadelphia, M. Fithian*, 1842.

Watkins (John, *ll. d.*) An essay towards a history of Bideford, in the county of Devon. xii, 276 pp. 8°. *Exeter* (*Eng.*) *E. Grigg*, 1792.

Watkins (John, *esq. of Whitby*). Life and career of George Chambers. Eng. title, 206 pp. 1 pl. 1 portrait. 16°. *London, author*, 1841.

Watson (James Madison). Independent elementary speller: a critical work on pronunciation. 160 pp. 16°. *New York and Chicago, A. S. Barnes & co.* 1871.

——— Independent sixth reader: containing a complete treatise on elocution; select and classified readings and recitations; [etc.] 454 pp. 1 l. 12°. *New York, A. S. Barnes & co.* 1872.

Watson (John W.) Beautiful snow; and other poems. New and enlarged ed. 128 pp. 8°. *Philadelphia, T. B. Peterson & brothers*, [1871].

Watson (*Mrs.* Rachel). The life of my family; or, the log-house in the wilderness. A true story. 3 p. l. 93 pp. 8°. *New York, author*, 1871.

Watson (Thomas, *bishop of Lincoln, d.* 1582). Holsome and catholyke doctryne concerninge the seuen sacramentes of Chrystes church, expedient to be knowen of all men, set forth in maner of [xxx] shorte sermons to bee made to the people by Thomas byshop of Lincolne. *b. l.* 1 p. l. 190 [193] l. 3 l. sm. 4°. *Londini, Robertus Caly*, 1558.

Watson (Thomas, *gentleman, d.* 1591 *or* 1592). The ἑκατομπαθια or passionate centurie of love. Reprinted from the original edition of (circa) 1581. 8 p. l. ci pp. 4°. [*London*], *Spenser society*, 1869.

[SPENSER society publications, no. 6].

Watson (*Rev.* Thomas, *nonconformist, d.* 1689)? The bible and the closet: or, how we may read the scriptures with the most spiritual profit. And secret prayer successfully managed, by rev. Samuel Lee. Edited by John Overton Choules. 140 pp. 32°. *Boston, Gould, Kendall & Lincoln*, 1842.

——— The christian soldier; or, heaven taken by storm. Shewing the holy violence a christian is to put forth in the pursuit after glory. From the 2d London ed. revised and corrected by the rev. mr. Armstrong. 173 pp. 12°. *New-York, R. Moore*, 1810.

Watt (Robert, *m. d.*) Treatise on the history, nature and treatment of chincough: including a variety of cases and dissections. To which is subjoined, an inquiry into the relative mortality of the principal diseases of children, and the numbers who have died under ten years of age, in Glasgow, during the last thirty years. 1 p. l. 392 pp. 8°. *Glasgow, J. Smith & son*, 1813.

Watts (Henry) *and others.* A dictionary of chemistry and the allied branches of other sciences. Supplement, [containing the record of chemical discovery down to the end of the year 1869]. xiii, 1137 pp. 8°. *London, Longmans, Green & co.* 1872.

Watts (Isaac, *d. d.*) Orthodoxy and charity united. In which are considered and displayed the causes and mischievous effects of uncharitableness, and also the nature and obligations of charity, especially with respect to persons of different opinions and practices in matters of religion. 166 pp. 12°. *Boston, Munroe & Francis*, 1810.

——— Posthumous works, containing the second part of the Improvement of the mind. Also a discourse on the education of children and youth, [with] Remnants of time employed in prose and verse on various subjects. Published from his manuscript by D. Jennings, d. d. and P. Doddridge, d. d. 2d ed.

Watts (Isaac, *d. d.*)—continued. viii, 336 pp. 8°. *London, J. Buckland & T. Longman*, 1773.

——— The psalms of David, imitated in the language of the new testament, and apply'd to the christian state and worship. [1st ed.] xxxii, 399 pp. 11 l. 18°. *London, J. Clark*, 1719.

——— Reliquiæ juveniles. Miscellaneous thoughts, in prose and verse, on natural, moral, and divine subjects. [Also], Remnants of time, employed in prose and verse. 1st american ed. with large additions. xii, 304 pp. 16°. *Boston, W. P. Blake*, 1796.

——— The terms of christian communion; with the solution of various questions and cases of conscience arising from this subject. 1st american ed. 172 pp. 18°. *Boston, S. T. Armstrong*, 1811.

Wa-wa-wanda. A legend of old Orange. [A poem. *anon.*] 180 pp. 1 map. 12°. *New York, Rudd & Carleton*, 1860.

Way (The) for a child to be saved. [*anon.*] 175 pp. 18°. *New York, Leavitt, Lord & co.* 1835.

[Children's fire-side series].

Way (The) of escape from temporal evils and from eternal death. [*anon.*] 288 pp. 16°. *Boston, J. B. Dow*, 1836.

Way (The) of the world. 1831. *See* **Hall** (*Mrs.* Anna Maria Fielding).

Way (The) to things by words, and to words by things. *See* **Cleland** (John).

Wayland (Francis, *d. d.*) Domestic slavery considered as a scriptural institution. *See* **Fuller** (*Rev.* Richard) *and* **Wayland.**

——— A memoir of the christian labors, pastoral and philanthropic, of Thomas Chalmers, d. d. 218 pp. 12°. *Boston, Gould & Lincoln*, 1864.

[*Note.*—Based on dr. Hanna's memoir of Chalmers].

——— Salvation by Christ. A series of discourses on some of the most important doctrines of the gospel. viii, 386 pp. 12°. *Boston, Gould & Lincoln*, 1859.

Wayte (Samuel C.) The equestrian's manual; or, the science of equitation, with advice to purchasers of horses, saddlery, etc. xii, 171 pp. 1 pl. 12°. *London, W. Shoberl*, 1850.

Wealth and worth; or, which makes the man? [*anon.*] 204 pp. 18°. *New York, Harper & brothers*, 1842.

Weatherhead (George Hume, *m. d.*) An essay on the diagnosis between erysipelas,

Weatherhead (G. H. *m. d.*)—continued. phlegmon, and erythema; with an appendix, touching the probable nature of puerperal fever. 1 p. l. 72 pp. 8°. *London, Longman, Orme & Brown*, [1819].

[*With* HALL (Marshall). A descriptive, diagnostic and practical essay on disorders of the digestive organs. *London*, 1820].

Weaver (*Rev.* George S.) The christian household. Embracing the christian home, husband, wife, father, mother, child, brother and sister. 160 pp. 16°. *Boston, A. Tompkins & B. B. Mussey*, 1854.

Webb (Caleb). The sensibility of separate souls considered. xi, 192 pp. 12°. *London, Houlston & Stoneman*, 1853.

Webb (Ezekiel, *m. d.*) The philosophy of medicine, deduced from a series of self-evident propositions, developing self-evident principles for illustrating the medical sciences to intuitive demonstration. 232 pp. 8°. *Philadelphia, Carey, Lea & Blanchard*, 1833.

——— The same. 2d ed. with the addition of preliminary observations, and an appendix. xxix, 232, xv pp. 8°. *New York, author*, 1834.

Webb (George James). The glee hive. *See* **Mason** (Lowell) *and* **Webb.**

——— *and* **Allen** (Chester G.) Voice culture: a complete method of theory and practice for the cultivation and development of the voice. 196 pp. obl. 4°. *New York, Biglow & Main*, [1871].

Webb (John, *of Butleigh, Eng.*) A vindication of Stone-Heng restored: in which the orders and rules of architecture observed by the ancient Romans, are discussed. Together with the customs and manners of several nations of the world in matters of building of greatest antiquity. As also an historical narration of the most memorable actions of the Danes in England. 4 p. l. 232 pp. fol. *London, T. Bassett*, 1665.

Webb (J. Russell). First lessons in language and drawing. 108 pp. 18°. *Chicago, A. H. Andrews & co.* 1871.

Webbe (George, *d. d.*) God's controversie with England. Or a description of the fearfvll and lamentable state which this land at this present is in. Amos 4, 12. v, 135 pp. 18°. *London, F. K. for W. Leake* 1609.

Webbe (William). A discourse of english poetrie. 1586. Carefully edited by Edward Arber. 96 pp. 16°. *London*, 1870.

ARBER's english reprints, no. 26 in v. 12].

Weber (Carl Maria von). Der freischutz. [Libretto, without music. Words by Friedrich Kind]. 35 pp. 8°. [*New York*], *W. C. Bryant & co.* 1871.
[PAREPA-ROSA grand english opera].

——— Oberon. [Libretto, without music]. 25 pp. 8°. [*New York*], *W. C. Bryant & co.* 1871.
[PAREPA-ROSA grand english opera].

Webster (John White, *m. d.*). A manual of chemistry, containing the principal facts of the science, in the order in which they are discussed, and illustrated in the lectures at Harvard university, N. E. 3d ed. xxii, 556 pp. 2 pl. 8°. *Boston, Marsh, Capen, Lyon & Webb*, 1840.

Webster (Noah, *ll. d. editor*). The holy bible. *New Haven*, 1833. *See* **Bible.** (*English*).

Webster (*Mrs.* M. M.) Pocahontas. A legend. With historical and traditionary notes. 220 pp. 12°. *Philadelphia, H. Hooker*, 1840.

Webster (William G.) The army and navy pocket dictionary. 319 pp. 1 pl. 24°. *New York, Mason brothers*, 1863.

Webster's business man; or, counting-house correspondent, containing plain practical directions for carrying on every kind of commercial and banking business. Also containing an extensive glossary of words and phrases used in commercial and banking circles. 192 pp. 16°. *New York, R. M. De Witt*, [1871].

Webster's calendar, or the Albany almanac for the year 1870-71. By Joel Munsell. 2 v. 8°. *Albany* (*N. Y.*) *J. Munsell*, 1870-71.

Webster's chairman's manual, and speaker's guide. [With] precedents from the best authorities. Also, the constitution of the United States, with all amendments. By the author of "Webster's practical letter writer," [etc. *anon.*] 192 pp. 16°. *New York, R. M. De Witt*, [1871].

Wedekind (Georg Christian Gottlieb von). Das Iohannisfest in der freimaurerei. 123 pp. 8°. *Frankfurt am Main, Wilmans*, 1818.

Wedgwood (Hensleigh). On the developement of the understanding. 4 p. l. 133 pp. 12°. *London, Taylor & Walton*, 1848.

Weekes (Refine). The life of William Penn, and other poems, religious, historical, and sentimental. 192 pp. 12°. *New-York, author*, 1822.

——— Poems, on religious and historical subjects. 2 p. l. 388 pp. 12°. *New-York, author*, 1820.

Weekes (Refine)—continued.

——— The same. 2d ed. corrected & enlarged. 418 pp. 16°. *New-York, author*, 1823.

Weeks (Helen C.) Four, and what they did. 3 p. l. 315 pp. 4 pl. 16°. *New York, Hurd & Houghton*, 1871.

Weeks (William Raymond). The missionary arithmetic: or arithmetic made easy, in a new method: and adapted to the use of lancasterian and other schools. 240 pp. 12°. *Utica*, [*N. Y.*] *Merrell & Hastings*, 1822.

Weeks. *See* **Weekes.**

Weerdenburgh (Diedrich van). Copie vande missive gheschreven byden generael Weerdenbvrch, aende staten generael, noopende de veroveringhe vande stadt Olinda de Fernabvco, met alle [sijne forten ende stercke plaetsen. 4 l. sm. 4°. *Graven-Haghe, weduwe van H. I. van Wouw*, 1630.

Weert (Sebald de). Kort en waerachtigh verhael van t'gene seeckere vijf schepen, van Rotterdam, in 't jaer 1598, den 27 junij, nae de straet Magalanes varende, overghekomen is, tot den 21 jan. 1600. pp. 44-76. sm. 4°. [*Amstelredam, J. Hartgers*, 1650].
[*With* NECK (Jacob van). Waerachtigh verhael van de schip-vaert op Oost-Indien, 1598-1600].

——— The same. pp. 61-92. sm. 4°. [*Amstelredam, I. Hartgers*, 1648].
[*In* HARTGERTS (J.) Oost-indische voyagien, v. 1, 3e stuck].

Weigel (Christoph). Sculptura historiarum et temporum memoratrix: das ist bedächtnuss-hülfliche bilder-lust der merdwürdigsten welt-geschichten aller zeiten. 2 v. in 1. Eng. title, 24 p. l. 152 pp. 28 pl; 260 pp. 10 l. 20 pl. fol. *Nürnberg, J. D. Taubern*, [1699].

Weishampel (J. F. *sen.*) The testimony of a hundred witnesses: or, the instrumentalities by which sinners are brought to embrace the religion of Jesus Christ. 252 pp. 18°. *Baltimore, J. F. Weishampel*, [1858].

Weishaupt (Adam). Apologie der illuminaten. [*anon.*] 374 pp. 16°. *Frankfurth & Leipzig, in der grattenauerischen buchhandlung*, 1786.

Weiss (John). American religion. 2 p. l. 326 pp. 16°. *Boston, Roberts brothers*, 1871.

Weisse (Christian Felix). Kleine lyrische gedichte. 2 v. Eng. title, 2 p. l. 258 pp. 3 l. 6 pl; 1 p. l. 258 pp. 1 l. 4 pl. 18°. *Leipzig, Weidmanns erben & Reich*, 1772.

Weitbrecht (*Mrs.* John James). Memoir of the rev. John James Weitbrecht, late missionary in Bengal. Comprehending a history of the Burdwan mission. Compiled from

Weitbrecht (*Mrs.* J. J.)—continued. his journal and letters, by his widow. 2d ed. xxii, 612 pp. 3 p. l. 1 map. 8°. *London, J. Nisbet & co.* 1854.

Welby (Horace). Signs before death, and authenticated apparitions: in one hundred narratives. 312 pp. 1 pl. 12°. *London, W. Simpkin & R. Marshall,* 1825.

Welch (Adonija S.) Analysis of the english sentence, designed for advanced classes in english grammar. Improved ed. 267 pp. 12°. *New York, A. S. Barnes & Burr,* 1862.

Weld (Horatio Hastings). Scenes in the lives of the apostles. [Poems]. Eng. title, 240 pp. 7 pl. 8°. *Philadelphia, Lindsay & Blakiston,* [1846].

Welford (Richard Griffiths, *editor*). The influences of the game laws; classified extracts from the evidence taken before a select committee of the house of commons on the game laws, and introductory remarks, by R. G. Welford. With an appendix, and an address to the tenant farmers of Great Britain, by John Bright, m. p. 429, lxxi pp. 8°. *London, R. Groombridge & sons,* 1846.

Well bred (The) girl. An addition to the hints on good manners contained in the Well bred boy. [*anon.*] 131 pp. 1 pl. 18°. *Boston, W. Crosby & co.* 1841.

Wells (Edward, *d. d.*) A treatise of antient and present geography. With a sett of maps, both of antient and present geography. 4th ed. with alterations and additions. 8 p. l. 182 pp. 15 l. 1 pl. 8°. *London, W. Bowyer for R. & J. Bonwicke,* [*etc.*] 1726.

[Maps wanting].

—— The young gentleman's arithmetick, and geometry. 2 v. in 1. 12 p. l. 294 pp. 13 pl. 8°. *London, J. Knapton,* 1713.

—— The young gentleman's astronomy, chronology and dialling. 2d ed. 3 v. in 1. 8°. *London, J. Knapton,* 1717–18.

—— The young gentleman's trigonometry, mechanicks, and opticks. 3 v. in 1. 8°. *London, J. Knapton,* [1713–]1714.

Wells (*Rev.* John Dunlap). The last week in the life of Davis Johnson, jr. 199 pp. 1 portrait. 16°. *New York, R. Carter & brothers,* 1861.

Wells (William). The heroine of the White Nile; or, what a woman did and dared. A sketch of the remarkable travels and experiences of miss Alexandrine Tinné. 207 pp. 16°. *New York, Carlton & Lanahan,* [1871].

Welsh (Lewis G.) A practical guide to business; a handbook for the american farmer, merchant, mechanic, investor, and all concerned in earning or saving money. 426 pp. 1 pl. 12°. *Philadelphia, J. G. Fergus & co.* 1872.

Welsted (Leonard). The works in verse and prose, of L. Welsted. Now first collected, with historical notes, and biographical memoirs of the author, by John Nichols. xxxii, 513 pp. 8°. *London, editor,* 1787.

CONTENTS.

Poems on several occasions.
A dissertation on the perfection of the english language.
A discourse to sir Robert Walpole, [containing] proposals for translating the whole works of Horace, with a specimen, etc.
The dissembled wanton: a comedy.
A translation of Longinus' treatise concerning the sublime.
The scheme and conduct of providence, from the creation to the Messiah.

Weltmeer (Das). Redigirt von K. J. Clement und Georg Blum. [Wöchentlich]. 1er jahrgang. März 31, 1860–märz 23, 1861. 4°. *Hamburg, Blum & Ackermann,* 1860–61. s.

Welton (Richard, *d. d.*) The substance of christian faith and practice: represented in eighteen practical discourses, preached some time in the parish-church of S. Mary White-chappel. xv, 478 pp. 1 portrait. 8°. *London, author,* 1724.

Welwood (Andrew). Meditations, representing a glimpse of glory; or, a gospel discovery of Emmanuel's land. [Also], a spiritual hymn, intituled, The dying saint's song; and some of his last letters. 283 pp. 16°. *Edinburgh, T. Maccliesh & co. for J. Ogle,* 1797.

Wendeborn (Gebhard Friedrich August, *ll. d.*) A view of England towards the close of the eighteenth century. Translated from the german, by the author himself. 2 v. xv, 442 pp; iv, 488 pp. 8°. *London, G. G. J. & J. Robinson,* 1791.

—— The same. 2 v. xii, 316 pp; vi, 347 pp. 12°. *Dublin, W. Sleater, for P. Wogan,* [*etc.*] 1791.

Weninger (Francis Xavier, *d. d.*) Protestantism and infidelity. An appeal to candid Americans. xv, 329 pp. 12°. *New York, Sadlier & co.* 1862.

—— The same. 3d ed. xv, 341 pp. 12°. *New York, Sadlier & co.* 1862.

Wentworth-Fitzwilliam (William, *viscount Milton*). *See* **Fitzwilliam.**

Wentz (Sara A.) Smiles and frowns. 376 pp. 12°. *New York, D. Appleton & co.* 1857.

Wepf (*Rev.* Lewis). The church of God and her adversaries; or, the revelation of John explained. xv, 423 pp. 12°. *Chicago, Lakeside publishing co.* 1871.

Wernsdorf (Gottlieb). Dissertatio de Philæ vita, ætate et scriptis. 8°. *Lipsiae,* 1768.
[*In* PHILE (Manuel). Manvelis Philæ carmina græca. p. l. 4–16. *Lipsiæ,* 1768].

Wertmuller (Joris). Missive uyt German town in Pensilvania. [Den 16 maart 1684]. 1 l. sm. 4°. *Rotterdam, P. van Alphen,* 1684].
[*In* TWEE missiven geschreven uyt Pensilvania].

Wesley (*Rev.* John). Primitive physic: or, an easy and natural method of curing most diseases. 23d ed. 103 pp. 4 l. 16°. *Philadelphia, P. Hall,* 1793.
[*With* WILKINS (Henry, *m. d.*) The family adviser. 1793].

——— The same. 26th ed. corrected. 104 pp. 16°. *New-York, J. C. Totten, for the methodist episcopal church,* 1804.
[*With* WILKINS (Henry, *m. d.*) The family adviser, 1804].

——— A short account of the life and death of the rev. John Fletcher. [Also], an additional account of that truly great and venerable man: by the rev. Joshua Gilpin. 276 pp. 16°. *New-York, E. Cooper & J. Wilson,* 1805.

——— Wesley his own historian. Illustrations of his character, labors, and achievments. From his own diaries. By rev. Edwin L. Janes. 464 pp. 12°. *New York, Carlton & Lanahan,* 1870.

Wesley (*Rev.* Samuel, *d.* 1735). The battle of the sexes: a poem. [*anon.*] 2d ed. xiv, 32 pp. 8°. *London, J. Brotherton,* 1724.

Wesley and his friends; illustrating the religious spirit of their times. By the author of "Towers of Zion," [etc. *anon.*] 196 pp. 6 pl. 1 portrait. 18°. *Philadelphia, American sunday school union,* 1856.

West (*Rev.* Anthon). The state of the dead. 258 pp. 12°. *Philadelphia, J. B. Lippincott & co.* 1871.

West (*Mrs.* Jane). Letters addressed to a young man, on his first entrance into life, and adapted to the peculiar circumstances of the present times. 2 v. in 1. 208 pp; 160 pp. 12°. *Charlestown,* [*Ms.*] *S. Etheridge for S. H. Parker,* 1803.

West (Stephen, *d. d.*) The scripture doctrine of atonement, proposed to careful examination. 2d ed. 228 pp. 16°. *Stockbridge, Herald office,* 1809.

West (Thomas, *s. j.* 1716–1779). The antiquities of Furness. A new ed. with additions by William Close. 12 p. l. 426 pp. 3 l. 6 pl. 8°. *Ulverston, G. Ashburner,* 1805.

West (*Rev.* Thomas, *of Yorkshire*). Ten years in south-central Polynesia: being reminiscences of a personal mission to the Friendly islands and their dependencies. xv, 500 pp. 1 pl. 1 map. 8°. *London, J. Nisbet & co.* 1865.

Westcott (*Rev.* Brooke Foss). Introduction to the study of the gospels. With historical and explanatory notes. With an introduction by H. B. Hackett, d. d. 476 pp. 12°. *Boston, Gould & Lincoln,* 1862.

Western (The) harp; a collection of social and revival hymns. [*anon.*] 272 pp. 18°. *St. Louis, Mo. Methodist book depository,* 1855.

Western (The) monthly. Jan. 1869, to Dec. 1870. v. 1–4. 8°. *Chicago, Reed, Browne & co.* [*etc.*] 1869–70.
[*Name changed to* The LAKESIDE monthly].

Western side; or, lights and shadows of a western parish. By a minister's wife. [*anon.*] 327 pp. 18°. *Philadelphia, American baptist publication society,* [1853].

West India (The) boys. By the author of "Miss Katy's little maid." [*anon.*] 143 pp. 18°. *Philadelphia, American sunday school union,* 1863.

West India company. (*Netherlands*). Articul-brief van de west indische compagnie, ter vergaderinge van de tienen der selver compagnie gearresteert, [etc.] 1 p. l. 40, 7, 10 pp. sm. 4°. *Gravenhage, J. Scheltus,* 1675.

——— Extract uyt den brief vande politijcque raeden in Brasil, aende heeren ghecommitteerden ter vergaderinge den negenthiene vande west-indische compagnie, over de veroveringe vande stadt Philippia nu Frederickstadt. *b. l.* 2 l. sm. 4°. *Graven-Haghe, weduwe van H. J. van Wouw,* 1635.

——— Reglement byde west indische compagnie, ter vergaderinge van de negentiene, [etc.] over het openstellen vanden handel op Brasil provisioneel ghearresteert. 4 l. sm. 4°. *Graven-Haghe, weduwe van H. I. van Wouw,* 1638.

——— Remonstrantie aen de staten generael der Vereenighde Nederlanden: overgegeven den . . . juny 1664. By de heeren de bewint-hebberen van de west-indische compagnie der Vereenighde Nederlanden. Op

West India company—continued.
ende jegens verscheyde memorien van den heer resident Charisius, wegens de (gepretendeerde) deensche africaensche compagnie. 32 pp. sm. 4°. *Amsterdam, P. I. de Koningh*, 1664.

West-indisch discours; verhandelende de west-indische saecken. Hoe die weder verbetert mogen worden, ten besten der gemeente, en't seekerst voor de compagnie. Samen-spraeck tusschen een middelburger en haegenaer. [*anon.*] 16 pp. sm. 4°. [*n.p.*] 1653.

Westmacott (Charles). Points of misery; or fables for mankind; prose and verse, chiefly original. Illustrated by R. Cruikshank. 5 p. l. 100 pp. 8°. *London, Sherwood, Jones & co.* 1823.

Westminster (The) review. [Quarterly]. Jan. to Oct. 1871. New series, v. 39–40; [complete series, v. 95–96]. 8°. *London, Trübner & co.* 1871.

Weston (Stephen). The englishman abroad. Part 1. Greece, Latium, Arabia, Persia, Hindostan, and China: with specimens of the languages of those countries. Part 2. Russia, Germany, Italy, France, Spain, and Portugal: with specimens. 1 p. l. 79, 216 pp. 3 pl. 8°. *London, W. Clarke*, 1824.

——— Fragments of oriental literature, with an outline of a painting on a curious china-vase. xxvii, 149 pp. 1 l. 1 pl. 8°. *London, author*, 1807.

West-Zanen (Willem van). Derde voornaemste zee-getogt (der verbondene vrye Nederlanderen) na de Oost-Indien: gedaan met de achinsche en moluksche vloten, onder de ammiralen Iacob Heemskerk, en Wolfert Harmansz. 1601–03. Vermeerdert door H. Soete-Boom. 4 p. l. 30 l. 1 map, 11 pl. (8 in text). sm. 4°. *Sanerdam, H. J. Zoet*, 1648.

[*With* HARTGERTS (J.) Oost-indische voyagien, v. 1. *Note.*—Bound with, but not a part of, Hartgerts' collection].

Wetenhall (Edward, *bishop of Kilmore*). Enter into thy closet: or, a method and order of private devotion. With an appendix concerning the frequent and holy use of the lord's supper. [*anon.*] 13 p. l. 447 pp. 1 l. 1 pl. 18°. *London, J. Martyn*, 1672.

Wetherill (Charles M. *m. d.*) The manufacture of vinegar: its theory and practice, with especial reference to the quick process. 300 pp. 12°. *Philadelphia, Lindsay & Blakiston*, 1860.

Wettengel (Friederich Traugott). Anleitung zum weisen und frohen genusse des lebens, zunächst für die jugend. In gesprächen und erzählungen. 288 pp. 12°. *Greiz, C. H. Henning*, 1789.

Whaley (John). A collection of poems. 8 p. l. 287 pp. 8°. *London, author*, 1732.

Wharton (*Sir* George). The works of that late most excellent philosopher and astronomer, sir G. Wharton, collected into one entire volume. By John Gadbury. 16 p. l. 670 pp. 1 l. 1 portrait. 16°. *London, H. H. for J. Leigh*, 1683.

Wharton (George M.) A southern medical student's portfolio. 186 pp. 4 pl. 12°. *Philadelphia, Claxton, Remsen & Haffelfinger*, 1872.

What Catharine did, and what came of it. [*anon.*] 109 pp. incl. 3 pl. 18°. *New York, Carlton & Porter*, [1860].

What is to become of the churches? or, a layman's response to a minister's inquiries. [*anon.*] vi, 107 pp. 18°. *Boston, H. V. Degen*, 1859.

What might have been. [*anon.*] *See* **De Leon** (T. C.)

What Norman saw in the west. By the author of "Four days in July," [etc. *anon.*] 268 pp. 8 pl. 18°. *New York, Carlton & Porter*, 1859.

Wheatland (*Rev.* Thomas). Twenty-six practical sermons on various subjects. iv, pp. 4 l. 402 pp. 8°. *London, W. Meadows*, 1739.

Whedon (Daniel D. *d. d.*) Commentary on the new testament. v. 1–3. *See* **Bible.** (*English*).

Wheelwright (*Rev.* Charles Apthorp). Poems, original and translated; including versions of the Medea and Octavia of Seneca. 2d ed. 2 v. xxiv, 207 pp; 1 p. l. 182 pp. 12°. *London, A. J. Valpy*, 1811.

Whipple (Edwin Percy). Literature and life. Enlarged ed. 344 pp. 16°. *Boston, J. R. Osgood & co.* 1871.

——— Success and its conditions. vi, 333 pp. 16°. *Boston, J. R. Osgood & co.* 1871.

Whistling Horace. [*anon.*] 168 pp. 2 pl. 18°. *Boston, A. F. Graves*, [1869].

Whiston (*Rev.* William). The accomplishment of scripture prophecies. Eight sermons preached in 1707. With an appendix. To which is subjoin'd, a dissertation to prove that our saviour ascended into heaven on the evening after his resurrection. Revised

Whiston (*Rev.* William)—continued. and corrected by the author, 1737. fol. [*London*, 1739].
[BOYLE lectures, v. 2, pp. 259-348].

Whitaker (*Rev.* John). The ancient cathedral of Cornwall, historically surveyed. 2 v. 2 p. l. 348 pp. 1 pl; 3 p. l. 434 pp. 1 pl. 4°. *London, J. Stockdale*, 1804.

——— The genuine history of the Britons asserted against mr. Macpherson. 2d ed. corrected. 2 p. l. 313 pp. 8°. *London, J. Murray*, 1773.

Whitaker (Joseph). An almanack for the year of our lord 1872, containing an account of the usual astronomical and other phenomena: also a large amount of information respecting the government [etc.] 322 pp. 16°. *London, J. Whitaker*, [1871].

Whitaker (Thomas Dunham). Ducatus leodiensis: or, the [history and topography of the town & parish of Leeds and parts adjacent, including the second edition of the whole of Ralph Thoresby's Ducatus leodiensis, with notes and additions]. 3 v. in 2. 3 p. l. xvii, xvii, 268 pp; 1 p. l. 123, 159, 12 pp. 21 pl. 1 portrait; 3 p. l. 404, 80 pp. 1 l. 68 pl. 1 portrait. fol. *Leeds, Robinson, son, & Holdsworth*, 1816.

Whitbourne (Richard). A discourse containing a loving invitation both honourable, and profitable to all such as shall be aduenturers, either in person, or purse, for the aduancement of his maiesties most hopefull plantation in the Nevv-found-land, lately vndertaken. 4 p. l. 46 pp. sm. 4°. *London, Felix Kyngston*, 1622.

White (Alexina B.) Little-folk songs. vi, 94 pp. sm. 4°. *New York, Hurd & Houghton*, [1871].

White (*Gen.* Charles, *b.* 1793). The adventures of a king's page. By the author of "Almack's revisited." [*anon.*] 3 v. 12°. *London, H. Colburn*, 1829.

White (Henry Kirke). Clifton grove, a sketch in verse, with other poems. xiv, 111 pp. 16°. *London, Vernor & Hood*, 1803.

White (James). The king of the commons: a drama. By the author of "The earl of Gowrie." [*anon.*] 4 p. l. 100 pp. 8°. *London, T. C. Newby*, 1846.

White (John J.) Arithmetic simplified: being a plain, practical system, adapted to the capacity of youth. xi, 348 pp. 12°. *Hartford, author*, 1818.

White (Philip S.) *and* **Pleasants** (H. R.) The war of four thousand years; a history of the efforts made to suppress the vice of intemperance in all ages of the world; from the foundation of the class of Nazarites, by Moses, to the institution of the order of the Sons of temperance; with a full account of the origin, progress, and present prospects of the latter institution. 295 pp. 12°. *Philadelphia, Griffith & Simon*, 1846.

White (Richard Grant). The chronicles of Gotham. By the author of "The new gospel of peace." [*anon.*] Book 1st & 2d. 2 v. 43 pp; 44-87 pp. 12°. *New York, G. W. Carleton & co.* 1871-72.

——— The fall of man: or, the loves of the gorillas. A popular scientific lecture upon the darwinian theory of development by sexual selection. By a learned gorilla. Edited by the author of "The new gospel of peace." [*anon.*] 48 pp. 12°. *New York, G. W. Carleton & co.* 1871.

White (Thomas, 1572-1676). Controversy-logicke. Or the methode to come to truth in debates of religion. 238 pp. 18°. [*London*]? 1659.
[*With his work*, The middle state of souls. 1659].

——— The middle state of souls. From the hour of death to the day of judgment. xii, 260 pp. 1 l. 18°. [*London*]? 1659.

White (William, *bp. of Penn.* 1748-1836). Comparative views of the controversy between the calvinists and the arminians. 2 v. xv, 523 pp; viii, 526 pp. 8°. *Philadelphia, M. Thomas*, 1817.

White (The) chrysanthemum. A story. [*anon.*] 389 pp. 3 pl. 16°. *Boston, I. P. Warren*, [1871].

Whitefield (*Rev.* George). A collection of hymns for social worship. 21st ed. 6 p. l. 226 pp. 16°. *London, H. Cock*, 1775.
[*With his work*, A communion morning's companion. Imperfect: wanting all after p. 226].

——— A communion morning's companion. 6th ed. 1 p. l. 140 pp. 1 l. 16°. *London, H. Cock*, 1772.

Whitefoot (*Rev.* John). Death's alarum: a funeral sermon on the rt. rev. Joseph Hall, bishop of Norwich. 8°. *London, L. B. Seeley & son*, 1826.
[*In* JONES (*Rev.* John). Bishop Hall, his life and times, pp. 501-565].

Whitehead (Charles). Smiles and tears: or, the romance of life. 3 v. 12°. *London, R. Bentley*, 1847.

Whitehead (George). The christian progress of George Whitehead. Historically relating his experience, ministry, sufferings, trials and service, in defence of the truth, and God's persecuted people, commonly called quakers. 8 p. l. 712 pp. 8°. *London, assigns of J. Sowle*, 1725.

—— The same. Memoirs of George Whitehead; a minister of the gospel in the society of friends: the substance of the account of his life, written by himself, and published after his decease, in 1725, under the title of "His christian progress;" with a selection from his other works. Also introductory observations. By Samuel Tuke. 2 v. xxxvi, 23–295 pp; vi, 5–356 pp. 12°. *York*, [*Eng.*] *W. Alexander & son*, 1830.

Whitehead (John). Materialism philosophically examined, or, the immateriality of the soul, asserted and proved, on philosophical principles; in answer to dr. Priestley's disquisitions on matter and spirit. 6 p. l. vii, 178 pp. 8°. *London, J. Phillips*, 1778.

Whitehurst (John). The works of John Whitehurst, with memoirs of his life and writings. [4 parts]. 2 p. l. 20, xiii, 69 pp. 3 l. 283 pp. 10 pl. 1 portrait. 4°. *London, W. Bent*, 1792.

CONTENTS.

An attempt toward obtaining invariable measures of length, capacity, and weight, from the mensuration of time, independent of the mechanical operations requisite to ascertain the center of oscillation, or the true length of pendulums. 1 p. l. 34 pp. 3 pl.
Appendix to mr. Whitehurst's attempt toward obtaining an invariable measure, by the editor. 6 pp.
Three papers, on different subjects, from the Philosophical transactions. 9 pp.
An inquiry into the original state and formation of the earth. 3 p. l. 283 pp. 7 pl.

Whitelocke (*Sir* Bulstrode). Essays ecclesiastical & civil. To which is subjoined a treatise of the work of the sessions of the peace. 4 p. l. 264 pp. 8°. *London, W. Hawes*, 1706.

Whiter (*Rev.* Walter). A dissertation on the disorder of death; or that state called suspended animation; in which it is recommended that the same remedies of the resuscitative process should be applied to cases of natural death, as they are to cases of violent death, drowning, etc. 1 p. l. xiii, 480 pp. 1 l. 8°. *London, author*, 1819.

—— A specimen of a commentary on Shakspeare. Containing i. Notes on As you like it. ii. An attempt to explain and illustrate various passages, on a new principle of criticism, derived from mr. Locke's doctrine of

Whiter (*Rev.* Walter)—continued.
the association of ideas. vii, 258 pp. 1 l. 8°. *London, T. Cadell*, 1794.

Whiting (Samuel). Elegant lessons; or the young lady's preceptor: being a series of appropriate reading exercises, in prose and verse: carefully selected from the most approved authors. 276 pp. 12°. *Middletown, (Conn.) Clark & Lyman*, 1820.

Whitley (John, *d. d.*) The life everlasting: in which are considered the intermediate life, the new body and the new world, the man in heaven, angels, the final consummate life. vi, 398 pp. 8°. *London, Longman*, 1846.

Whitlock (*Sir* Bulstrode). *See* **Whitelocke.**

Whitman (*Rev.* Bernard). Village sermons: doctrinal and practical. 292 pp. 12°. *Boston, L. C. Bowles*, 1832.

Whitman (*Rev.* Jason). Helps for young christians, with introductory remarks. 192 pp. 1 pl. 24°. *Portland, S. H. Colesworthy*, 1839.

—— Young lady's aid, to usefulness and happiness. 216 pp. 18°. *Portland, S. H. Colesworthy*, 1838.

Whitman (William E. S.) The ship-carpenter's family. 399 pp. 12°. *New York, H. Long & brother*, [1855].

Whitman (Zachariah G.) The history of the ancient and honorable artillery company, (revised and enlarged) from its formation in 1637 and charter in 1638, to the present time; comprising the biographies of the distinguished civil, literary, religious, and military men of the colony, province, and commonwealth. 2d ed. iv, 463 pp. 8°. *Boston, J. H. Eastburn*, 1842.

Whitmarsh (Caroline Snowden) *and* **Guild** (A. E.) Hymns of the ages. First, second and third series. [*anon.*] 3 v. 12°. *Boston, Ticknor & Fields*, 1861–65.

Whitney (*Mrs.* Adeline D. Train). Patience Strong's outings. 233 pp. 12°. *Boston, Loring*, 1869.

—— Real folks. iv, 308 pp. 8 pl. 12°. *Boston, J. R. Osgood & co.* 1872.

—— Zerub Throop's experiment. 146 pp. 16°. *Boston, Loring*, [1871].

Whitney (*Rev.* George H.) Hand-book of bible geography. With descriptive and historical notes. 401 pp. incl. 39 pl. 13 maps. 12°. *New York, Carlton & Lanahan*, 1871.

Whitney (William Dwight). A compendious german grammar. 2d ed. revised. xvi, 248 pp. 12°. *New York, Leypoldt & Holt*, 1870.

Whitney's musical guest. A monthly musical journal. Containing sketches and biographies of noted musicians, records of musical events, [etc.] with music. Nov. 1870, to Dec. 1871. v. 4. 4°. *Toledo, (O.), W. W. Whitney*, 1870–71.

Whittemore (*Rev.* Thomas). The early days of Thomas Whittemore. An autobiography: extending from a. d. 1800 to a. d. 1825. 348 pp. 1 portrait. 12°. *Boston, J. M. Usher*, 1859.

——— Notes and illustrations of the parables of the new testament, arranged according to the time in which they were spoken. 2 p. l. 277 pp. 16°. *Boston, author*, 1832.

Whittier (John Greenleaf). Child life: a collection of poems. xiii, 263 pp. 12°. *Boston, J. R. Osgood & co.* 1872.

——— Home ballads and poems. 206 pp. 16°. *Boston, Ticknor & Fields*, 1860.

——— The journal of John Woolman. *See* **Woolman** (John).

Whittingham (William Rollinson, *d. d.*) The work of Christ by his ministry; in its nature, conditions and limitations; considered in a fourth charge to the clergy of the diocese of Maryland. 34 pp. 8°. *Baltimore, J. Robinson*, 1856.

Whittlesey (Charles). Ancient earth forts of the Cuyahoga valley, Ohio. 40 pp. 9 pl. 8°. *Cleveland, published for the [historical] society by a gentleman of Cleveland*, 1871.

Whittlesey (Elsie Leigh). Helen Ethinger; or, not exactly right. 318 pp. 12°. *Philadelphia, Claxton, Remsen & Haffelfinger*, 1872.

Whittlesey (Sarah J. C.) Bertha the beauty: a story of the southern revolution. 382 pp. 12°. *Philadelphia, Claxton, Remsen & Haffelfinger*, 1872.

Who are the blessed? or, meditations on the beatitudes. [*anon.*] 197 pp. 12°. *Philadelphia, Lindsay & Blakiston*, 1856.

Who is my neighbour? Or the two great commandments. By the author of "Little Bob True." [*anon.*] 216 pp. 1 pl. 18°. *Philadelphia, Presbyterian board of publication*, [1859].

Whole (The) art and trade of hvsbandry. 1614. *See* **Heresbach** (Conrad).

Who's who in 1871. Twenty-third year. xvi, 326 pp. 24°. *London, A. H. Baily & co.* [1871].

Whowell (Thomas). The first epistle to the christian church, on the eve of the millenial kingdom of Christ; a complete key to the old and new testament: with fulfilment, in succession, of the prophecies of our blessed saviour. With the past and present state of the Jews, and the appearance of their restoration. v. 1. 281 pp. 8°. [*Nottingham*], *author*, 1830.

——— The second epistle to the christian church, on the eve of time. Or the christian's revealed word of God. Translated from the original greek of an old manuscript, found in the island of Patmos, where st. John wrote his book of revelations. With a circumstantial account of the life and death of the apostles of Christ, and the patriarchs of old. [Also] a treatise on the incarnation and deity of Christ. 2 v. 1 p. l. 246 pp. 3 l. 1 tab. 8°. [*Nottingham*], *author*, 1830.

Whymper (Edward). Scrambles amongst the Alps in the years 1860–69. xix, 432 pp. 22 pl. 5 maps. 8°. *London, J. Murray*, 1871.

Wickens (Stephen B.) The life of John Bunyan, author of Pilgrim's progress. 336 pp. 1 portrait, 1 pl. 18°. *New York, G. Lane & P. P. Sandford*, 1844.

Widekind (Johann). Gustaff Adolphs, den anders och stores, historia och lefwernes beskrifning. v. 1. Eng. title, 2 p. l. 448 pp. 6 l. fol. *Stockholm, kongl. boktryckarens sahl*, 1691.

Widow (The) of Monmouth; or family instruction. By the author of Conversations on the Sandwich islands mission; [etc. *anon.*] 150 pp. 18°. *Boston, Massachusetts sabbath school society*, 1832.

Widower (The). *See* **Smith** (Julie P.)

Widow's (The) cottage, and other stories. [*anon.*] 128 pp. sq. 16°. *Philadelphia, Lippincott, Grambo & co.* 1854.

Wieland (Christoph Martin). Confessions in elysium, or the adventures of a platonic philosopher. Taken from the german, by John Battersby Elrington. 3 v. 12°. *London, J. Bell*, 1804.

Wiele (Andreas van de). Epigrammata sacra. 6 p. l. 195 pp. 16°. *Lugduni Batavorum, F. Haaring*, 1694.

Wiener entomologische monatsschrift. Verantwortliche redacteure: Julius Lederer und Ludwig Müller. v. 1–7, in 4 v. 8°. *Wien, C. Gerold's sohn*, 1857–63. s.

Wierzbicki (F. P.) A french grammar, for beginners, arranged in an easy manner; with precise rules of pronunciation. 160 pp. 12°. *New York, C. Hubbell*, 1836.

Wiesecke (Henry, *m. d.*) The fountain of health: or a system of specific cures and remedies by which diseases may be prevented and cured by all; together with a lucid description of the functions of the human organism and the laws of health; also valuable instruction in regard to pregnancy, the use of magnetism, and the employment of hygienic gymnastics, and other auxiliary remedies. xvii, 384 pp. 12°. [*New York*, 1862].

Wife (The); interspersed with a variety of anecdotes and observations, and containing advice and directions for all conditions of the marriage state. [*anon.*] 1st am. ed. 2 p. l. 222 pp. 16°. *Boston, A. Newell*, 1806.

Wiggins (Richard). The New-York expositor; or, fifth book: a collection of the most useful words in the english language. [Also], a vocabulary of scientific terms. By John Griscom. 305 pp. 18°. *New York, S. Wood & sons*, [1825].

——— The same. 285 pp. 18°. *New York, S. & W. Wood*, 1842.

Wight (Andrew). Present state of husbandry in Scotland. Extracted from reports made to the commissioners of the annexed estates. 2 v. xxiv, 412 pp; xii, 494 pp. 1 l. 8°. *Edinburgh, W. Creech*, [*etc.*] 1778.

Wightwick (George). Select views of the roman antiquities. From original drawings made upon the spot. 2 p. l. 6 pp. 8 l. 19 pl. fol. *London, author*, 1827.

Wijnpersse, *or* **Wynperse** (Dionysius van de, *d. d.*) A proof of the true and eternal godhead of our lord Jesus Christ; against modern attacks. Translated from the dutch, by Thomas Bell. vi, 13-198 pp. 16°. *Philadelphia, W. Young*, 1796.

Wilberforce (*Rev.* Robert Isaac *and* Samuel). The life of William Wilberforce. Abridged from the London edition by Caspar Morris, m. d. 544 pp. 12°. *Philadelphia, Henry Perkins*, 1839.

Wilberforce (Samuel, *bishop of Oxford*). A manual for communicants: or the order for administering the holy communion, conveniently arranged; with meditations and prayers from old english divines: being the Eucharistica. Adapted to the american service. 220 pp. 24°. *New York, D. Appleton & co.* 1842.

Wilbur (Hervey). New testament with references, etc. 1823. *See* **Bible.** (*English*).

Wilcox (Francis S.) Digest of fees of town and county officers, compiled from the statutes of New York. Also, United States excise and stamp duties. 2d ed. 38 pp. 18°. *New York, W. B. Smyth*, 1869.

Wild (Friedrich Carl). The valley mill; or, extracts from the diary of a german tradesman. From the german. By rev. Joel Swartz, d. d. 227 pp. 1 pl. 16°. *Philadelphia, Lutheran board of publication*, 1871.
[FATHERLAND (The) series].

Wilde (*Sir* William R.) Austria: its literary, scientific, and medical institutions. With notes upon the present state of science, and a guide to the hospitals and sanatory establishments of Vienna. xxiv, 326 pp. 2 pl. 8°. *Dublin, W. Curry, jr. & co.* 1843.

Wilder (*Rev.* Royal Gould). Mission schools in India of the american board of commissioners for foreign missions, with sketches of the missions among the north american Indians, the Sandwich islands, the Armenians of Turkey, and the Nestorians of Persia. 432 pp. 12°. *New York, A. D. F. Randolph*, 1861.

Wildermuth (Ottilie Ronschütz). A queen. A story for girls. Translated from the german. By Anna B. Cooke. 129 pp. 2 pl. 16°. *Boston, E. P. Dutton & co.* 1865.

Wild oats. An illustrated journal of fun, satire, burlesque, hits at persons and events of the day. Bricktop, [*pseudon.*] editor. [Monthly]. April, 1870, to Feb. 1871. v. 1-2. fol. *New York, Winchell & Small*, [1870-71].

Wilhem (Guillaume Louis Bocquillon, *dit*). Perrot's Wilhem's musical manual; a new method for vocal classes. Translated from the french, with additions by A. Perrot. 168 pp. 8°. *Philadelphia, W. S. Fortescue & co.* [1853].

——— Key to Perrot's Wilhem's musical manual. Designed particularly for the use of teachers. By A. Perrot. 2 p. l. ix, 58 pp. 8°. *Philadelphia, E. C. & J. Biddle*, 1855.

Wilkes (L. B.) Louisville debate on baptism. *See* **Ditzler** (Jacob).

Wilkes-Barre (*Pa.*) Boyd's Wilkes-Barre city directory, 1871-72; together with a business directory of Carbondale, Hazleton, Kingston, Pittston, Plymouth, Scranton,

Wilkes-Barre (*Pa.*)—continued. Shickshinny, White Haven; to which is prefixed an appendix of useful information. Compiled and published by Andrew Boyd and W. Harry Boyd. Published bi-ennially. 8°. *Wilkes-Barre, Pa.* 1871.

Wilkins (Henry, *m. d.*) The family adviser; or a plain and modern practice of physic; calculated for the use of private families, and accomodated to the diseases of America. [Also], mr. Wesley's Primitive physic, revised. 98 pp. 1 l; 103 pp. 4 l. 16°. *Philadelphia, P. Hall*, 1793.

——— The same. 4th ed. corrected. [Also], mr. Wesley's Primitive physic, revised. 106 pp. 1 l; 104 pp. 16°. *New-York, J. C. Totten, for the methodist episcopal church*, 1804.

Wilkins (John Hubbard). Elements of astronomy, for the use of schools and academies. 4 p. l. 116 pp. 9 pl. 1 chart. 12°. *Boston, Cummings & Hilliard*, 1822.

——— The same. viii, 152 pp. 12 pl. 12°. *Boston, Hilliard, Gray, Little & Wilkins*, 1832.

——— The same. Stereotype ed. viii, 152 pp. 15 pl. 12°. *Boston, Hilliard, Gray & co.* 1836.

Willard (Clara A.) Fifty years ago. A story of New England life. 321 pp. 12°. *New York, A. D. F. Randolph*, [1871].

Willard (H. A.) A treatise on american butter factories, and butter manufacture. Published by the Wisconsin state agricultural society. 2 p. l. 85 pp. 8°. *Madison, Wis. Atwood & Culver*, 1871.

Willard (*Rev.* Samuel, *vice-president of Harvard college*). A compleat body of divinity in two hundred and fifty expository lectures on the assembly's shorter catechism. Pref-ac'd by the pastors of the same church [South church, Boston]. 1 p. l. iv, 6, 914 pp. 1 l. fol. *Boston, B. Eliot and D. Henchman*, 1776.

——— Some brief sacramental meditations preparatory for communion at the great ordinance of the supper. 2nd ed. [Prefaced by E. Pemberton]. 1 p. l. vi, 216 pp. 18°. *Boston, D. Henchman*, 1743.

——— Spiritual desertions discovered and remedied. The substance of divers sermons. 144 pp. 18°. *Boston, M. Perry and B. Eliot*, 1699.

Willard Prime. By the author of "The little rebel." [*anon.*] 290 pp. 4 pl. 18°. *Boston, J. E. Tilton & co.* 1864.

Willett (*Rev.* William M.) The life and times of Herod the great, as connected historically and prophetically, with the coming of Christ. And incidental portraitures of noted personages of the age. 384 pp. 2 pl. 12°. *Philadelphia, Lindsay & Blakiston*, 1860.

——— Scenes in the wilderness: an authentic narrative of the labours and sufferings of the moravian missionaries among the north american Indians. 208 pp. 18°. *New York, G. Lane & P. P. Sandford*, 1842.

Williams (Charles). Visible history. England. Part 1. iv, 156 pp. 4 pl. 12°. *London, F. Westley & A. H. Davis*, 1835.

Williams (C. S.) Directories. *See* **Cincinnati, Circleville,** *and* **Lancaster** (*Ohio*).

Williams (*Rev.* David). Lectures on education. Read to a society for promoting reasonable and humane improvements in the discipline and instruction of youth. 3 v. 8°. *London, J. Bell*, 1789.

Williams (Edward, *welsh poet*, 1745–1826). Poems, lyric and pastoral. 2 v. xxxix, 216 pp; viii, 256 pp. 12°. *London, author*, 1794.

Williams (Edward, *d. d.* 1750–1813). The christian preacher; or, discourses on preaching, by several eminent divines, english and foreign, revised and abridged; with an appendix on the choice of books. 1st american from the 2d London ed. with improvements. 334 pp. 16°. *Philadelphia, W. W. Woodward*, 1810.

CONTENTS.

CLAUDE (*Rev.* Jean). On the composition of a sermon, pp. 164–263.
DODDRIDGE (*Dr.* Philip). On the evil and danger of neglecting souls, pp. 135–163.
FRANCK (*Prof.* A. H.) Of the most useful way of preaching, pp. 77–91.
JENNINGS (*Rev.* John). Of preaching Christ, pp. 45–59.
——— Of particular and experimental preaching, pp. 60–76.
WATTS (*Dr.* Isaac). Rules of conduct, pp. 92–134.
WILKINS (*Bishop* John). On the gift of preaching, pp. 17–44.

Williams (Edwin). Narrative of the recent voyage of captain Ross to the arctic regions, in the years 1829–33, and a notice of captain Back's expedition; with a preliminary sketch of polar discoveries, from the earliest period to the year 1827. 1st am. ed. 192 pp. 1 map. 16°. *New York, Wiley & Long*, 1835.

Williams (*Rev.* Eliezer). The english works of the late rev. Eliezer Williams, with a memoir of his life. By his son, St. George Armstrong Williams. 8 p. l. cclxxv, 344 pp. 8°. *London, Cradock & co.* 1840.

Williams (Henry T.) Window gardening. Devoted specially to the culture of flowers and ornamental plants, for in door use and parlor decoration. 300 pp. 1 l. 1 pl. 8°. *New York, H. T. Williams,* 1872.

Williams (Henry Willard, *m. d.*) Our eyes, and how to take care of them. 112 pp. 16°. *Boston, J. R. Osgood & co.* 1871.

——— A practical guide to the study of diseases of the eye: their medical and surgical treatment. xii, 317 pp. 12°. *Boston, Ticknor & Fields,* 1862.

Williams (John, *bishop of Chichester,* 1634–1709) Twelve sermons preached [1695–96]. fol. [*London,* 1739].
[BOYLE lectures, v. 1, pp. 153–274].

Williams (John, *secretary of the royal astronomical society*). Observations of comets, from b. c. 611 to a. d. 1640. Extracted from the chinese annals. Translated, with introductory remarks, and an appendix, comprising the tables necessary for reducing chinese time to european reckoning; and a chinese celestial atlas. 1 p. l. xxxii, 124 pp. 23 pl. 4°. *London, author,* 1871. s.

Williams (Joseph, *merchant*). An enlarged series of extracts from the diary, meditations and letters of mr. Joseph Williams of Kidderminster. [Also] some original letters from ministers, &c. occasioned by his death. By Benjamin Hanbury. xxiv, 512 pp. 1 portrait. 8°. *London, C. Taylor for the editor,* 1815.

Williams (J. Fletcher). Bibliography of Minnesota. From the Minnesota historical collections, v. 3, part i. 65 pp. 8°. *St. Paul, Press printing co.* 1870.
[*Note.*—Fifty copies separately printed].

Williams (Katherine). Tiptoe. 283 pp. 4 pl. 16°. *New York, American tract society,* [1871].

Williams (Mack V.) Williams' Cincinnati directory. 1871. *See* **Cincinnati** (*City of*).

Williams (*Sir* Roger, *d.* 1595). The actions of the Lowe Countries. 5 p. l. 133 pp. sm. 4°. *London, M. Lownes,* 1618.

Williams (*Rev.* St. George Armstrong). Memoir of the rev. Eliezer Williams. By his son. 8°. *London, Cradock & co.* 1840.
[*In* WILLIAMS (*Rev.* Eliezer). English works. pp. i–cclxxv].

Williams (Samuel). Two western campaigns in the war of 1812–13. 1. Expedition of captain Henry Brush, with supplies for gen. Hull, 1812. 2. Expedition of gov. Meigs, for the relief of Fort Meigs, 1813. 58 pp. 8°. *Cincinnati, R. Clarke & co.* 1870.
[OHIO valley series. Miscellanies, no. 2].

Williams (*Rev.* Thomas). The age of infidelity: in answer to Thomas Paine's Age of reason. Part i. By a layman. [*anon.*] 3d ed. 66 pp. 8°. *London, W. S. Betham for Button & son,* 1803.

——— The same. Part ii. In answer to the second part of The age of reason. By a layman. [*anon.*] 140 pp. 8°. *London, W. Button,* 1796.
[*With* the preceding].

——— The cottage bible. *Hartford,* 1862. *See* **Bible.** (*English*).

Williams (*Rev.* William, *of Hatfield, Mass.* 1665–1741). The danger of not reforming known evils; or, the inexcusableness of a knowing people refusing to be reformed. Set forth on a day of publick fasting, at Hatfield. 1 p. l. 30 pp. 18°. *Boston, B. Green,* 1707.

Williams (William, *of Chichester*). Primitive history, from the creation to Cadmus. 2 p. l. [xii], 596 pp. 2 l. 4 tab. 4°. *Chichester, J. Seagrave,* 1789.

Williams (William R. *d. d.*) God's rescues: or, the lost sheep, the lost coin, and the lost son. Three discourses on Luke xv. 95 pp. 12°. *New York, A. D. F. Randolph & co.* 1871.

Williamson (*Capt.* Thomas). The costume and customs of modern India; from a collection of drawings by Charles Doyley, esq. with a preface and copious descriptions. xxiii, 38 l. 20 pl. 4°. *London, E. Orme,* 1813.

Williamsport (*Pa.*) Boyds' Williamsport city directory, 1871–72, together with a business directory of Bellefonte, Bodinesville, [etc.] to which is prefixed an appendix of useful information. 380 pp. 8°. *Williamsport (Pa.) A. & W. H. Boyd,* 1871.

Willie Elton, the little boy who loved Jesus. [*anon.*] 106 pp. 2 pl. 18°. *Philadelphia, Presbyterian board of publication,* [1864].

Willie's lessons; or, simple illustrations of verses of scripture. [*anon.*] 198 pp. 18°. *New York, Carlton & Porter,* [1859].

Willie wishing to be useful. By the author of "Willie's lessons." [*anon.*] 193 pp. 18°. *New York, Carlton & Porter,* [1859].

Willis (Anson). The nation: its rulers and institutions; or, outlines of the government. 1 p. l. 508 pp. 5 pl. 12°. *Philadelphia, New-world publishing co.* 1871.

——— The same. Die nation, ihre behörden und institutionen; oder: umrisse der regierung. Aus dem englischen übersetzt von Carl Theodor Eben. 1 p. l. 508 pp. 5 pl. 12°. *Philadelphia, New-world publishing co.* 1871.

Willis (Browne). A survey of the cathedrals of York, Durham, Carlisle, Chester, Man, Lichfield, Hereford, Worcester, Gloucester, Bristol, Lincoln, Ely, Oxford, Peterborough, Canterbury, Rochester, London, Winchester, Chichester, Norwich, Salisbury, Wells, Exeter, St. Davids, Landaff, Bangor, and St. Asaph. Containing an history of their foundations, builders, ancient monuments, and inscriptions; endowments, alienations, sales of lands, patronages, [etc.] With an exact account of all the churches and chapels in each diocese. 3 v. in 2. 4°. *London, T. Osborne*, 1742.

Willis (Francis, *m. d.*) A treatise on mental derangement. Containing the substance of the gulstonian lectures, for May, 1822. xi, 234 pp. 8°. *London, Longman, [etc.]* 1823.

Willis (*Rev.* John). Actions of the apostles. 1789. *See* **Bible.** (*English*).

Willis (Nathaniel Parker). A l'abri, or the tent pitch'd. 172 pp. 12°. *New-York, S. Colman*, 1839.

——— Bianca Visconti; or the heart overtasked. 108 pp. 12°. *New York, S. Colman*, 1839.

——— Poem delivered before the society of United brothers at Brown university, on the day preceding commencement, September 6, 1831. With other poems. 76 pp. 8°. *New-York, J. & J. Harper*, 1831.

Williston (*Rev.* Seth). Christ's kingdom not of this world. The spiritual character of the kingdom of Christ, in three discourses. 103 pp. 18°. *New York, Saxton & Miles*, 1842.

——— Discourses on the temptations of Christ. 152 pp. 16°. *Utica, W. Williams*, 1837.

——— The harmony of divine truth. 634 pp. 8°. *Utica, author*, 1836.

Willmott (*Rev.* Robert Aris). The poets of the nineteenth century. With english and american additions, arranged by Evert A. Duyckinck. Illustrated. 1 p. l. xvi, 674 pp. 8°. *New York, Harper & brothers*, 1872.

Wills (W. G.) Hinko; a play in five acts, and a prologue called The younger son. 66 l. numb. 8°. *London, Diprose & Bateman*, 1871.

Willson (Marcius). A manual of information and suggestions for object lessons, in a course of elementary instruction. Adapted to the use of school and family charts, and other aids in teaching. 336 pp. 12°. *New York, Harper & brothers*, 1862.

Willson (Marcius)—continued.

——— A treatise on civil polity and political economy: with an appendix, containing a brief account of the powers, duties, and salaries, of national, state, county, and town officers. 348 pp. 18°. *New York, J. O. Taylor*, 1838.

Willymott (William, *ll. d.*) English particles exemplified in sentences, designed for latin exercises; with the proper rendering of each particle, inserted in the sentence: also, part of Tully's offices; select essays of lord Bacon; and part of sir Thomas More's Utopia. 16th ed. 2 p. l. 468 pp. 12°. *Eton, Pote & Williams*, 1806.

Wilmer (Margaret E.) The Lestrange family. A true story. 214 pp. 1 pl. 16°. *New York, R. Carter & brothers*, 1871.

——— The little girl in black. 211 pp. 1 pl. 16°. *New York, National temperance society and publication house*, 1872.

——— The wrecker's grandchild. 330 pp. 3 pl. 18°. *New York, Board of publication, R. C. A.* 1871.

Wilmer (William Holland, *d. d.*) The episcopal manual; a summary explanation of the doctrine, discipline and worship of the protestant episcopal church in the United States of America. With an appendix. New and improved ed. xvi, 13–312 pp. 12°. *Philadelphia, R. S. H. George*, 1841.

Wilson (Benjamin). The emphatic diaglott. 1865. *See* **Bible.** (*Greek and english*).

Wilson (C. H.) The wanderer in America, or truth at home; comprising a statement of observation and facts relative to the United States & Canada, North America. 108 pp. 18°. *Thirsk (Scotland), for the author*, 1822.

Wilson (Daniel, *bishop of Calcutta*). The divine authority and perpetual obligation of the lord's day, asserted in seven sermons, at the parish church of St. Mary, Islington. 1st am. ed. with a preface, by L. Woods, d. d. 212 pp. 12°. *Boston, Crocker & Brewster*, 1831.

Wilson (Henry, *of London, mathematician*). Navigation new modelled: or, a treatise of geometrical, trigonometrical, arithmetical, instrumental, and practical navigation. Together with all necessary tables, calculated to the new stile. 8th ed. with the addition of spherical trigonometry, and astronomy. xvi, 528 pp. 10 pl. 8°. *London, W. & J. Mount*, 1761.

Wilson (Henry, *of N. Y.*) Business directory, 1871. *See* **New York** (*City of*).

Wilson (Horace Hayman). Works. v. 11–12. 8°. *London, Trübner & co.* 1871.

CONTENTS.

Select specimens of the theatre of the Hindus translated from the original sanskrit. 3d ed. 2 v. 1871.
v. 1. On the dramatic system of the Hindoos.
The Mrichchhakati, or the toy cart.
Vikrama and Urvasí, or the hero and the nymph. Attributed to Kalidása.
Uttara-Ráma-charitra, or continuation of the history of Ráma. Attributed to Bhavabhuti.
2. Málatí and Mádhava, or the stolen marriage, by Bhavabhuti.
Mudrá-Rakshasa, or the signet of the minister, ascribed to Visâkhadatta.
Ratnávalí, or the necklace.

Wilson (James Patriot, *d. d.*) A free conversation on the unpardonable sin: wherein the blasphemy against the holy spirit, the final apostasy, and the sin unto death, are shown to have been originally distinct. 171 pp. 16°. *Philadelphia, Towar, J. & D. M. Hogan,* 1830.

——— The primitive government of christian churches. Also, liturgical considerations. [With] the sermon, preached on the death of the author, by Thomas H. Skinner, d. d. xxxix, 372 pp. 1 portrait, 1 chart. 12°. *Philadelphia, French & Perkins,* 1833.

Wilson (John, *prof. univ. Edinburgh,* 1785–1854). Lights and shadows of scottish life, a selection from the papers of the late Arthur Austin. [*pseudon.* 1st ed.] viii, 430 pp. 12°. *Edinburgh, W. Blackwood,* 1822.

Wilson (John, *printer,* 1802–68). A treatise on english punctuation; with an appendix. 20th ed. xii, 334 pp. 12°. *New York, Woolworth, Ainsworth & co.* 1871.

Wilson (*Rev.* John G.) The sabbath and its lord, and the divine man. 180 pp. 2 pl. 12°. *Philadelphia, author,* 1860.

Wilson (Joseph H.) An elementary algebra, for schools and academies. 240 pp. 12°. *Philadelphia, Eldredge & brother,* 1872.

Wilson (Nathaniel). Outline of the flora of Jamaica. 8°. [*London,* 1869].

[*In* GREAT BRITAIN. *Treasury. Geological survey. Geology of Jamaica.* Memoirs, appendix 2, pp. 263–291].

Wilson (*Rev.* Thomas, *puritan, d.* 1621). Theologicall rules to gvide vs in the vnderstanding and practise of holy scriptures. Also ænigmata sacra, holy riddles; or misticall cases and secrets of diuinitie, with their resolutions. By T. W. [*anon.*] 2 v. in 1. 4 p. l. 125 pp; 6 p. l. 204 pp. 18°. *London, E. Griffin for F. Burton,* 1615.

[Imperfect: v. 2 wants all after p. 204].

Wilson (*Rev.* Thomas, *bishop of Sodor and Man,* 1663–1755). Parochialia: or, instructions to the clergy, in the discharge of their parochial duty. 152 pp. 12°. *New-York, T. & J. Swords,* 1812.

——— Sacra privata. The private meditations and prayers of Thomas Wilson, accommodated to general use. 2d Cambridge ed. 138 pp. 16°. *Cambridge,* [*Ms.*] *Hilliard & Metcalf,* 1808.

Wilson (William). A manual of instruction for infants' schools; with an engraved sketch of the area of an infants' school room and play ground,—of the abacus, of a scheme of instruction, and the tables of numbers. By H. Wm. Edwards. 222 pp. 6 pp. 1 pl. 12°. *New York, G. & C. & H. Carvill,* 1830.

Wilson (William Dexter, *d. d.*) The christian church; its constitution, principles, functions, and powers, as represented in the holy scriptures: [etc.] xii, 236 pp. 16°. *Windsor, P. Merrifield,* 1843.

——— Lectures on the psychology of thought and action, comparative and human. 300 pp. 8°. *Ithaca, N. Y. Andrus, McChain & Lyons,* 1871.

Winchester (*Rev.* B.) Synopsis of the holy scriptures, and concordance, in which the synonymous passages are arranged together. Chiefly designed to illustrate the church of Jesus Christ, of latter-day saints. To which is added, as an appendix, an epitome of ecclesiastical history, etc. 256 pp. 24°. *Philadelphia, author,* 1842.

Winckelmann (Johann Joachim). The history of ancient art, translated from the german, by G. Henry Lodge, m. d. v. 3. xii, 350 pp. 18 pl. 8°. *Boston, J. R. Osgood & co.* 1872.

Winebrenner (*Rev.* John). The church hymn book: comprising a choice collection of hymns, original and selected, for the use of public worship, and various other occasions, 846 pp. 18°. *Harrisburg, Pa. by authority of the general eldership of the church of God,* 1859.

——— A prayer meeting and revival hymn book. 2 p. l. 360 pp. 6 l. 32°. *Harrisburg, J. & M. W. M'Kinley,* 1825.

Winer (Georg Benedict). Grammar of the chaldee language, as contained in the bible and the targums. Translated from the german by H. B. Hackett. 152 pp. 8°. *Andover, Allen, Morrill & Wardwell,* 1845.

Wines (Enoch Cobb, *d. d.*) An essay on temptation. 144 pp. 16°. *Philadelphia, Presbyterian board of publication,* [1865].

——— Letters to school-children. xii, 9–135 pp. 16°. *Boston, Marsh, Capen & Lyon,* 1839.

——— A treatise on regeneration. 119 pp. 16°. *Philadelphia, Presbyterian board of publication,* [1863].

——— The true penitent portrayed in a practical exposition of the fifty-first psalm; to which is added the doctrine of repentance, as declared in Acts xvii, 30. 119 pp. 16°. *Philadelphia, Presbyterian board of publication,* [1864].

Winfield (W. S.) Hymns for christian worship; original, varied, and selected. 96 pp. 32°. *Cincinnati, Bosworth, Chase & Hall,* 1871.

Wing (*Rev.* John). The saint's advantage: or the well-fare of the faithfvll, in the worst times. A sermon. 4 p. l. 79 pp. sm. 4°. *London, I. Dawson for I. Bellamie,* 1624.

Wing (Vincent). Harmonicon coeleste: or, the cœlestiall harmony of the visible world: conteining an absolute and entire piece of astronomie. 1st ed. 12 p. l. 309 pp. fol. *London, R. Leybourn, for the company of stationers,* 1651.

Winmann *or* **Wynmann** (Nicolas). Colymbetes, sive de arte natandi. 18°. [*Lugd. Batavorum,* 1644].

[*In* DISSERTATIONVM lvdicrarvm et amœnitatvm scriptores varij, pp. 83–189].

Winnie and I. [*anon.*] 351 pp. 12°. *New York, J. C. Derby,* 1855.

Winnie and Walter; or, story-telling at thanksgiving. [*anon.*] 127 pp. 4 pl. 18°. *Boston, J. E. Tilton & co.* 1861.

Winnie and Walter's christmas stories. [*anon.*] 124 pp. 4 pl. 18°. *Boston, J. E. Tilton & co.* 1861.

Winnie and Walter's evening talks with their father about old times. [*anon.*] 142 pp. 4 pl. 18°. *Boston, J. E. Tilton & co.* 1861.

Winslow (Hubbard, *d. d.*) The christian doctrine. 360 pp. 12°. *Boston, Crocker & Brewster,* 1844.

——— Elements of intellectual philosophy. Designed for a text-book and for private reading. 414 pp. 12°. *Boston, Crocker & Brewster,* 1850.

Winslow (Miron, *d. d.*) Hints on missions to India: with notices of some proceedings of a deputation from the american board, and of reports to it from the missions. 236 pp. 18°. *New York, M. W. Dodd,* 1856.

——— Memoir of Mrs. Harriet L. Winslow, thirteen years a member of the american mission in Ceylon. 480 pp. 18°. *New York, American tract society,* [1840].

Winslow (Octavius, *d. d.*) Christ ever with you. Illustrated by experiences drawn from the prayer-meeting, and field and hospital life. 144 pp. 18°. *New York, Board of publication of the reformed protestant dutch church,* 1863.

Winter (William). Edwin Booth in twelve dramatic characters. The portraits by W. J. Hennessy. The engraving by W. J. Linton. The biographical sketch by William Winter. Eng. title, 51 pp. 13 l. 12 pl. fol. *Boston, J. R. Osgood & co.* 1872, [1871].

——— My witness: a book of verse. 128 pp. 16°. *Boston, J. R. Osgood & co.* 1871.

Winter's (The) wreath for 1832. [*anon.*] 12 p. l. 372 pp. 11 pl. 16°. *London, Whittaker, Treacher & co.* [1831].

Winthrop (James). Prophetic part of the apocalypse in familiar language. *See* **Bible.** (*English*).

Winthrop (Theodore). Cecil Dreeme. 360 pp. 12°. *Boston, Ticknor & Fields,* 1861.

Winzet (Ninian). Certane tractatis for reformatioun of doctryne and maneris in Scotland. [Edinburgi, 1562. *Also,* The buke of four scoir thre questions, tueching doctrine, ordour, and maneris. Antverpiae, 1563. *And* Vincentius lirinensis, for the antiquitie and catholik fayth. Neulie translatit in scottis be Niniane Winzet. Antverpiæ, 1663]. 4°. *Reprinted, Edinburgh, Maitland club,* 1835.

[MAITLAND club publications, no. 33, pp. 1–119].

Wiscasset (*Maine*). Seaside oracle. *See* **Seaside** oracle, Wiscasset monthly.

Wisconsin state agricultural society. Transactions, with tabular abstracts of the reports of county agricultural societies. v. 9, 1870. Prepared by J. W. Hoyt, secretary. 8°. *Madison, Wis. state printers,* 1871.

Wise (Daniel, *d. d.*) Pleasant pathways; or, persuasives to early piety: explanations and illustrations of the beauty, safety, and pleasantness of a religious life. 285 pp. 2 pl. 16°. *New York, Carlton & Porter,* [1860].

Wise (Henry). An analysis of one hundred voyages to and from India, China, etc. performed by ships in the East India company's service; with remarks on the advan-

Wise (Henry)—continued.
tages of steam-power applied as an auxiliary aid to shipping. To which is added a description of Melville's patent propellers. xxiv, 120 pp. 3 pl. 8°. *London, author*, 1839.

Wise (Henry Alexander). Seven decades of the union. The humanities and materialism, illustrated by a memoir of John Tyler, with reminiscences of some of his great cotemporaries. The transition state of the nation—its dangers and their remedy. 320 pp. 8°. *Philadelphia, J. B. Lippincott & co.* 1872.

Wise. *See* **Wyse.**

Wisheart (*Rev.* William). Theologia; or, discourses of God. Delivered in 120 sermons. v. 1. 512 pp. 8°. *Paisley*, [*Eng.*] *J. Neilson for R. Reid*, 1787.

Wither (George). [Ivvenilia]. 16°. [*London, R. Badger for R. Allot*, 1633].
[Imperfect: wanting title-page].

CONTENTS.

Abuses stript and whipt: or, satyricall essayes. 2 books. 23 p. l. pp. 1-278.
Prince Henries obsequies: or mournfull elegies upon his death. 1 p. l. pp. 281-318.
A satyre, written to the king's most excellent majestie, when [the author] was prisoner in the Marshalsey, for his first book. 1 p. l. pp. 321-348.
Epithalamia. Or nvptiall poems. Vpon the mariage of prince Frederick, the fifth, count palatine, and the princesse Elizabeth, 1612. 2 p. l. pp. 353-376.
The shepheard's hunting. Being certain eglogues. 1 p. l. pp. 379-444.
Fidelia. pp. 447-484.
A metricall paraphrase upon the creedo; and upon the Lord's prayer. 3 l.
Wither's motto. Nec habeo, nec careo, nec curo. Illustrated. 40 l.
Faire-virtve, the mistresse of Phil'arete. 84 l.
A miscelany of epigrams, sonnets, epitaphs, & such other verses, as were found written, with the poeme aforegoing. 12 l.

——— The same. Ivvenilia. Poems contained in the collections of his Juvenilia which appeared in 1626 and 1633. A collection of those poemes which were heretofore imprinted, and written by George Wither. London, printed for Robert Allott, 1626. [Reprinted]. 1 v. in 3 parts. v, 941 pp. 3 pl. sm. 4°. *London, Spenser society*, 1871.
[SPENSER society publications. Issues, nos. 9, 10, 11].

CONTENTS.

Abvses stript and whipt, or satyrical essayes. 2 bookes.
Certaine epigrams to the kings most excellent maiesty, [etc.]
Prince Henries obsequies; or mournefvll elegies vpon his death.
A satyre, written to the kings most excellent maiestie.
Epithalamia: or nvptiall poems vpon the most blessed and happy marriage between prince Frederick the fifth, count palatine, and princesse Elizabeth.
The shepheards hvnting.
Fidelia.
Wither's motto.
Faire-virtve, the mistresse of Phil'arete.

Withington (Leonard, *d. d.*) Solomon's song: translated and explained. *See* **Bible.** (*English*).

Wittenmyer (*Mrs.* Anne). Women's work for Jesus. 240 pp. 16°. *Philadelphia, author*, [1871].

Wittich (Wilhelm). A visit to the western coast of Norway. 216 pp. 16°. *London, C. Cox*, 1848.

Woburn (*Mass.*) The Woburn directory; containing a general directory of the citizens, a business directory, and the town register, for the year commencing June 1st, 1871. 167 pp. 8°. *Woburn, J. L. Parker*, [1871].

Wodhull (Michael). Poems. A revised edition. viii, 215 pp. 1 portrait. 8°. *London, Nichols & son*, 1804.

Wolf (Johann). Taschenbuch der deutschen vögelkunde. 1810. *See* **Meyer** (Bernhard) *and* **Wolf.**

Wolf (Johann Christian). Mvliervm græcarvm qvæ oratione prosa vsæ svnt fragmenta et elogia, graece et latine, cvm virorvm doctorvm notis et indicibvs. Accedit catalogvs foeminarvm sapientia artibvs scriptisve apvd Graecos, Romanos aliasqve gentes olim illvstrivm. 4 p. l. 466 pp. 5 l. 4°. *Londini, apvd I. Novrse*, 1739.

Wolf (Rudolf). Taschenbuch für mathematik, physic, geodäsie und astronomie. xx, 270 pp. 6 pl. 16°. *Bern, R. F. Haller*, 1860. s.

Wolf. *See* **Wolfe** *and* **Wolff.**

Wolfe (J. M.) Guide, gazetteer, and directory of the Iowa divisions of the Illinois central; Dubuque southwestern; Burlington, Cedar Rapids & Minnesota; Central railroad of Iowa; Sioux city & Pacific; and Elkhorn & Missouri valley railroads. With historical notes, descriptions, statistics, &c. of the towns and cities on the respective roads. v. 2. 16°. *Dubuque, J. M. Wolfe*, 1871.

Wolfersberger (G. A.) Tales for all seasons. 2 p. l. 240 pp. 12°. *Philadelphia, Crissy & Markley*, 1863.

Wolff (Christian). Der anfangs-gründe aller mathematischen wissenschafften erster theil, welcher einen unterricht von der mathematischen lehr-art, die rechen-kunst, geometrie, trigonometrie, und bau-kunst in sich enthält. 4e aufl. 9 p. l. 510 pp. 1 portrait, 59 tab. 12°. *Franckfurt & Leipzig, Renger*, 1732.

Wolff (Christian)—continued.

——— The same. Der anfangsgründe aller mathematischen wissenschaften dritter theil welcher die optick, catoptrick und dioptrick, die perspective, die sphärische trigonometrie, astronomie, chronologie, geographie und gnomonick in sich enthält. 4e aufl. 2 p. l. pp. 947-1542, 3 tab. 16°. *Halle im Magdeburgischen, Renger*, 1730.

Wolff (Emil). Anleitung zur chemischen untersuchung landwirthschaftlich-wichtiger stoffe. 2e aufl. viii, 194 pp. 8°. *Stuttgart, G. Weise*, 1867. s.

Wolff (Jens). Sketches and observations taken on a tour through a part of the south of Europe. 6 p. l. 251 pp. 4°. *London, W. Wilson*, 1801.

Wolff (*Rev.* Joseph). Journal of Rev. Joseph Wolff, 1831. 70 pp. 8°. [*London, J. Nisbet*, 1831-33].

[*With* MORNING (The) watch. *London*, 1830-1833. v. 4-7].

Wollaston (Francis). A portraiture of the heavens, as they appear to the naked eye: constructed for the use of students in astronomy. 2 l. 10 pl. fol. *London, J. Cary*, 1811.

Woman an enigma. *See* **McIntosh** (Maria J.)

Woman's (The) journal, [and Woman's advocate]. A weekly newspaper devoted to the interests of woman, [etc.] Mary A. Livermore, editor. Jan. 7 to Dec. 30, 1871. v. 2. fol. *Boston*, [*H. B. Blackwell*], 1871.

Wonderful (The) lamp, or light for the darkest path. [*anon.*] 239 pp. 2 pl. 18°. *Philadelphia, Presbyterian board of publication*, [1860].

Wonderful (The) phials, and other stories. Translated from the french. By Anna. [*anon.*] 323 pp. 1 pl. 18°. *New York, M. W. Dodd*, 1856.

Wonderful (The) stone, or the curse turned into blessing. [*anon.*] 284 pp. 4 pl. 18°. *Philadelphia, Presbyterian board of publication*, [1863].

Wonderful (The) travels of prince Fan-Feredin. *See* **Bougeant** (Guillaume Hyacinthe).

Wonder-maer (Dees) end' prophetsije wis, Door's geests gesicht gebooren is [etc. A political brochure on the proposed treaty between Spain and the Netherlands, 1608, commencing with 8 lines of verse. *anon.*] 8 l. sm. 4°. [*n. p.*] 1608.

[*In* NEDERLANDTSCHE bye-corf].

Wood (De Volson). A treatise on the resistance of materials, and an appendix on the preservation of timber. x, 246 pp. 8°. *New York, J. Wiley & son*, 1871.

Wood (George B. *m. d.*) Introductory lectures and addresses, on medical subjects, delivered chiefly before the medical classes of the university of Pennsylvania. viii, 460 pp. 8°. *Philadelphia, J. B. Lippincott & co.* 1859.

——— The same. 2d ed. viii, 476 pp. 8°. *Philadelphia, J. B. Lippincott & co.* 1872.

Wood (*Mrs.* Henry, *or* Ellen Price). The castle's heir. A novel in real life. 260 pp. (incl. 10 pl.) 8°. *Philadelphia, T. B. Peterson & brothers*, [1863].

——— Dene Hollow. A novel. 1 p. l. 19-262 pp. 8°. *Philadelphia, T. B. Peterson & brothers*, [1871].

——— Verner's pride. A tale of domestic life. 373 pp. 8°. *Philadelphia, T. B. Peterson & brothers*, [1863].

Wood (James, *d. d.* 1799-1867). The gospel fountain, or the anxious youth made happy. 295 pp. 18°. *Philadelphia, Presbyterian board of publication*, [1859].

——— Grace and glory, or the young convert instructed in the doctrines of grace. Being a sequel to "The gospel fountain." 317 pp. 18°. *Philadelphia, Presbyterian board of publication*, [1859].

——— Memoir of John Matthews, d. d. 16°. [*Philadelphia*, 1864].

[*In* MATTHEWS (John, *d. d.*) The influence of the bible, etc. pp. 5-16].

——— Old and new theology. Also a review of Beman on the atonement, from the Biblical repository. 95 pp. 18°. *Philadelphia, Presbyterian board of publication*, 1845.

Wood (John, *editor*). Mentor, or the american teacher's assistant. Essays from the most approved authors in the english language. Intended to [furnish] just models of composition. iii, 374 pp. 2 l. 16°. *New York, J. Buell, for the author*, 1795.

Wood (*Rev.* John George). The common shells of the sea-shore. iv, 132 pp. 12 pl. 16°. *London, F. Warne & co.* 1865.

Wood (L. A.) John Bull's scientific (?) "man-machine," or american "common-sense," vs. Huxley's paradoxical nonsense, by a "West-yankee-elf." [*anon.*] 80 pp. 8°. *Louisville, Ky. F. A. Crump & co.* 1871.

Wood (*Lieut.* Oliver E.) The West Point scrap book: a collection of stories, songs,

Wood (*Lieut.* Oliver E.)—continued. and legends of the u. s. military academy. With original illustrations. 339 pp. 1 pl. 8°. *New York, D. Van Nostrand*, 1871.

Wood (*Mrs.* R. H.) The sunday-school olio; containing original dialogues and single pieces for sunday-school exhibitions and sabbath evening concerts. 84 pp. 16°. *New York, Carlton & Lanahan,* [1871].

Wood's household magazine. Devoted to knowledge, virtue and temperance. [Monthly]. Jan. to Dec. 1871. v. 8–9. 8°. *Newburgh (N. Y.) S. S. Wood*, [1871].

Woodbridge (William Channing). Modern school geography, on the plan of comparison and classification. 352 pp. 16°. *Hartford, Belknap & Hamersley*, 1844.

Woodbury (*Rev.* Augustus). A narrative of the campaign of the first Rhode Island regiment, in the spring and summer of 1861. 4 p. l. 260 pp. 1 pl. 1 portrait. 12°. *Providence, S. S. Rider*, 1862.

Woodbury (Isaac B.) Harp of the south. A new and complete collection of church music, in five parts, [etc.] To which are prefixed the elements of vocal music made easy. 320 pp. obl. 8°. *New York, Mason & Law*, [1853]. s.

Wooden (The) world dissected. *See* **Ward** (Edward).

Woodhull (Victoria C.) The origin, tendencies and principles of government: or, a review of the rise and fall of nations from early historic time to the present; with special considerations regarding the future of the United States as the representative government of the world and the form of administration which will secure this consummation. Also, papers on human equality, as represented by labor and its representative, money; and the meaning and significance of life from a scientific standpoint, with its prophecies for the great future. 2 p. l. 247 pp. 1 portrait. 8°. *New York, Woodhull, Claflin & co.* 1871.

Woodhull and Claflin's weekly. Nov. 19, 1870, to May 13, 1871. v. 2. fol. *New York*, 1870–71.

Woodruff (*Rev.* Hezekiah). Familiar discourses on the way of salvation. 226 pp. 1 portrait. 8°. *Ithaca,* [*N. Y.*] *Mack, Andrus & Woodruff*, 1841.

Woods (H.) The history of the presbyterian controversy, with early sketches of presbyterianism. 204 pp. 12°. *Louisville, N. H. White*, 1843.

Woods (Leonard, *d. d.*) An examination of the doctrine of perfection, as held by rev. Asa Mahan, and others. 140 pp. 18°. *New York, W. R. Peters*, 1841.

——— Letters to Nathaniel W. Taylor, d. d. [On sin]. 114 pp. 8°. *Andover, M. Newman*, 1830.

Woods (*Mrs.* Margaret). Extracts from the journal of the late Margaret Woods, from the year 1771 to 1821. 2d ed. xii, 495 pp. 12°. *London, J. & A. Arch*, 1830.

Woodville; or, the anchoret reclaimed. A descriptive tale. [*anon.* By Charles W. Todd]? 1 p. l. ii, 278 pp. 12°. *Knoxville, T. author*, 1832.

Woodville (Jennie, *pseudon?*) Left to herself. 311 pp. 12°. *Philadelphia, J. B. Lippincott & co.* 1872.

Woodward (Hezekiah). The cause, vse, cure of feare. Or, strong consolations (the consolations of God) cordiall at all times, but most comfortable in these uncomfortable times. 8 p. l. 71 pp. sm. 4°. *London, T. Underhill*, 1643.

Woodward (Josiah, *d. d.*) Eight sermons, preached in 1710. fol. [*London*, 1739]. [BOYLE lectures, v. 2, pp. 491–564].

——— Fair warnings to a careless world, or the serious practice of religion recommended by the admonitions of dying men. [Also], serious advice to a sick person, by archbishop Tillotson. As also, A prospect of death: a pindarique essay. 4th ed. 6 p. l. 166 pp. 1 l. 6 pl. 16°. *London, T. Longman*, 1736.

Woodward (Samuel Bayard, *m.d.*) Hints for the young, in relation to the health of body and mind. [*anon.*] 2d ed. 95 pp. 32°. *Boston, W. D. Ticknor*, 1838.

Wooler (Thomas J. *editor*). *See* **Black** (The) dwarf.

Woolman (John). The journal of John Woolman. With an introduction by John G. Whittier. viii, 315 pp. 16°. *Boston, J. R. Osgood & co.* 1871.

Woolnor (Henry). The trve originall of the sovle. Proving both by divine and naturall reason, that the production of mans soule is neither by creation nor propagation, but a certain meane way between both. By H. W. b. d. [Edited by E. Palmer. 1st ed.] 6 p. l. 335 pp. 2 l. 18°. *London, T. Paine & M. Symmons*, 1641.

Woolsey (*Rev.* Elijah). The supernumerary: or, lights and shadows of itinerancy. Com-

Woolsey (*Rev.* Elijah)—continued. piled from papers of rev. Elijah Woolsey. By rev. George Coles. 164 pp. 18°. *New York, G. Lane & C. B. Tippett*, 1845.

Woolsey (*Rev.* James J.) The doctrine of christian baptism, examined by the acknowledged principles of biblical interpretation. viii, 13-364 pp. 18°. *Philadelphia, I. Ashmead*, 1840.

Woolsey (Sarah C.) The new-year's bargain. By Susan Coolidge. [*pseudon.*] 231 pp. 1 pl. 12°. *Boston, Roberts brothers*, 1872, [1871].

Worcester (Joseph Emerson, *ll. d.*) A comprehensive dictionary of the english language. Revised and illustrated. 608 pp. 8°. *Boston, Brewer & Tileston*, [1871].

——— Elements of geography, ancient and modern. A new edition. xi, 272 pp. 2 pl. 12°. *Boston, Hilliard, Gray, Little & Wilkins*, 1829.
[*Note.*—Atlas wanting].

——— An epitome of history, with historical and chronological charts. viii, 130 pp. 16°. *Cambridge, Hilliard & Brown*, 1827.
[*Note.*—Charts wanting].

——— A primary dictionary of the english language. Revised and illustrated. 388 pp. 18°. *Boston, Brewer & Tileston*, [1871].

Worcester (*Mass.*) Business directory of the city of Worcester, for 1871-2. By Henry J. Howland. 16°. *Worcester, L. H. Bigelow*, [1871].

——— The Worcester directory, containing a general directory of the citizens, a business directory, and the city and county register. no. xxix. for 1872. 8°. *Worcester, Drew, Allis & co.* 1872.

Wordsworth (Christopher, *d. d. bp. of Lincoln*). Theophilus anglicanus.—Theophilus americanus; or instruction for the young student, concerning the church, and the american branch of it. Chiefly from the fifth edition of "Theophilus anglicanus." By Chr. Wordsworth, d. d. Edited by Hugh Davey Evans. xii, 426 pp. 12°. *Philadelphia, H. Hooker*, 1851.

Wordsworth (William). The excursion, being a portion of the Recluse, a poem. 2d ed. xx, 452 pp. 8°. *London, Longman*, 1820.

——— Memorials of a tour on the continent, 1820. viii, 103 pp. 12°. *London, Longman*, 1822.

——— Thanksgiving ode, January 18, 1816. With other short pieces, chiefly referring to recent public events. xi, 52 pp. 8°. *London, Longman*, 1816.
[*With his* Excursion, ed. 1820].

——— Yarrow revisited, and other poems. xii, 17-244 pp. 12°. *New York, R. Bartlett & S. Raynor*, 1835.

Worgan (John Dawes). Select poems, &c. [Also], some particulars of his life and character, by an early friend and associate. With a preface, by William Hayley, esq. 273 pp. 12°. *Philadelphia, Kimber & Richardson*, 1813.

Work and play. A journal of instruction and amusement for the young. [Monthly]. Jan. 1871, to March, 1872. v. 2-3. 4°. *Springfield (Mass.) M. Bradley & co.* 1871-72.
[Discontinued: united with the Little corporal (Chicago)].

Working-boy's (The) sunday improved. [*anon.*] 216 pp. 3 pl. 16°. *Philadelphia, American sunday-school union*, [1859].

World (The). [New York daily]. Jan. 1, to Dec. 31, 1871. 2 v. fol. *New York*, 1871.

World (The) almanac, 1872. 12°. [*New York*, 1872].

World (The) in the stereoscope: a series of sketches, original and selected. Written and compiled to accompany sets of stereoscopic illustrations, for the use of schools. [*anon.*] 417 pp. 12°. *New York, Hart & Anderson*, 1872.

Wormley (Theodore G. *m. d.*) Report of chemical department, [Geological survey of Ohio]. 8°. [*Columbus*, 1871].
[Ohio (*State of*). Geological survey, 1870, part 5, pp. 401-462].

Worship of the church in the house. Collected chiefly from the liturgy of the american church. By a son of the church. [*anon.*] 121 pp. 16°. *New York, D. Appleton & co.* 1869.

Worthington (George F.) Sacred poems. 3d ed. with additions and corrections. 170 pp. 18°. *Baltimore, author*, 1868.

Worthington (William, *d. d.*) An impartial inquiry into the case of the gospel demoniacks. With an appendix, consisting of an essay on scripture demonology. 2 p. l. 350 pp. 8°. *London, J. F. & C. Rivington*, 1777.

Wortley (*Sir* Francis). Characters and elegies. 4 p. l. 68 pp. sm. 4°. [*London*], 1646.

Wotton (Edward, *m. d.*) De differentiis animalivm libri decem. Cum amplissimis indicibus, [etc.] 12 p. l. unp. 220, 13 l. fol. *Lvtetiae Parisiorvm, apvd Vascosanvm*, 1552.

Wotton (William, *d. d.*) Reflections upon ancient and modern learning. [Also], a defense thereof, in answer to the objections of sir W. Temple, and others. With observations upon the Tale of a tub. Also, a dissertation upon the epistles of Themistocles, Socrates, Euripides, &c. and the fables of Aesop. By R. Bentley, d. d. 3d ed. 3 p. l. xxxii, 541 pp. 8°. *London, T. Goodwin*, 1705.

Wratislaw (Wenzel, *baron*). Adventures of baron Wenceslas Wratislaw. What he saw in the turkish metropolis, Constantinople; [etc.] Committed to writing in the year 1599. Literally translated from the original bohemian by A. H. Wratislaw. xliv, 211 pp. 12°. *London, Bell & Daldy*, 1862.

Wreath (The): a collection of poems, from celebrated english authors. [*anon.*] Eng. title, 252 pp. 18°. *Hartford, Ct. Andrus & Judd*, 1835.

Wrecks and rescues. By an early member of the board of managers of the A. F. G. S. [*anon.*] Eng. title, 255 pp. 3 pl. 12°. *New York, American female guardian society*, 1859.

Wren (Matthew). Increpatio bar Jesu: sive polemicæ adsertiones locorum aliquot s. scripturæ, ab imposturis perversionum in catechesi racoviana; collectæ hinc inde, ex opere prægrandi Meditationum criticarum in s. paginam, conscriptarum a patre suo R. D. M. de genuino sensu, atque exacta nostra versione divinorum textuum. 12 p. l. 762 pp. 1 l. sm. 4°. *Londini, typis J. Flesheri*, 1660.

Wright (*Rev.* David). Memoir of Alvan Stone, of Goshen, Mass. 256 pp. 18°. *Boston, Gould, Kendall & Lincoln*, 1837.

Wright (Edward, *mathematician, d.* 1615). Certaine errors in navigation, detected and corrected. With many additions that were not in the former edition. 26 p. l. incl. 2 eng. titles, 472, 122 pp. 10 l. sm. 4°. *London, F. Kingstō*, 1610.

[Imperfect. pp. 441–456 wanting].

——— The voyage of the right ho. George [Clifford] earle of Cvmberl. to the Azores. [June to Dec. 1589]. 29 pp. sm. 4°. [*London*, 1599].

[*Note.*—Separated from Wright's Certaine errors in navigation. 4°. *London*, 1599].

Wright (Elizabeth C.) Lichen tufts, from the Alleghanies. 228 pp. 12°. *New York, M. Doolady*, 1860.

Wright (George). Pleasing reflections on life and manners, with essays, characters, & poems, moral & entertaining; principally selected from fugitive publications. A new ed. enlarged. 1 p. l. vii, 310 pp. 1 pl. 16°. *London, S. Hooper*, 1788.

Wright (Hendrick B.) A practical treatise on labor. 401 pp. 1 portrait. 12°. *New York, G. W. Carleton & co.* 1871.

Wright (Ichabod Charles *and* Henry Smith). Selections of psalms in verse: poems and translations. Part 1, by I. C. Wright. Part 2, by H. S. Wright. 5 p. l. 170 pp. 12°. *London, Bell & Daldy*, 1867.

Wright (Isaac). Wright's family medicine, or system of domestic practice. xi, 276 pp. 12°. *Madisonville, Tenn. J. F. Grant*, 1833.

Wright (James, *lawyer*, 1644–1715). The history and antiquities of the county of Rutland, [Eng.]: collected from records, ancient manuscripts, monuments on the place and other authorities. Illustrated with sculptures. 4 p. l. 140 pp. 2 l. 1 map. fol. *London, B. Griffin*, 1684.

Wright (Joseph Hall). Breakfast-table science: or the philosophy of common things. Written expressly for the amusement and instruction of young people. 193 pp. 16°. *New York, A. V. Blake*, 1843.

Wright (Joseph W.) An abridgment of Wright's practical grammar of the english language; [etc.] 16°. *New York, R. Barnard & co.* 1842.

——— Hours of idleness improved; or tête-à-tête conversations on language and belles lettres. 144 pp. 24°. *New-York, R. Barnard & co.* 1843.

——— A philosophical grammar of the english language; adapted to the use of schools or private study: in which are contained, theoretical and practical refutations of the most prevailing systems in modern use. 252 pp. 12°. *New York, Spinning & Hodges*, 1838.

Wright (*Mrs.* Julia McNair). The best fellow in the world. His haps and mishaps. Narrated for the public benefit. 352 pp. 1 pl. 16°. *New York, National temperance society & publication house*, 1871.

——— Mabel and Tura of the southwest. A tale. 320 pp. 1 pl. 16°. *Philadelphia, J. S. Claxton*, 1867.

Wright (*Mrs.* J. M.)—continued.

——— The Palmetto boys. 371 pp. 6 pl. 16°. *Philadelphia, W. B. Evans & co.* [1871].

——— Under the yoke and other tales. 216 pp. 1 pl. 12°. *Cincinnati, Western tract & book society*, 1871.

Wright (Thomas, *of London*) ? The passions of the minde in generall. In sixe bookes. Corrected, enlarged, and with sundry new discourses augmented. [2d ed.] 7 p. l. 350 pp. 4 l. 1 tab. sm. 4°. *London, Anne Helme*, 1621.

Wright (Thomas, *of Durham*). An original theory or new hypothesis of the universe, founded upon the laws of nature, and solving by mathematical principles the general phænomena of the visible creation; and particularly the via lactea. xii, 84 pp. 32 pl. 4°. *London, author*, 1750.

Wright (Thomas, *antiquary, b.* 1810). Coup-d'œil sur les progrès et sur l'état actuel de la littérature anglo-saxonne en Angleterre; traduit de l'anglais par m. de Larenaudière. vii, 43 pp. 8°. *Paris, Silvestre*, 1836.

Wsselinx (Willem). *See* **Usselincx.**

Wulverhörst (A. H. Verster van). Traité de fauconnerie. *See* **Schlegel** (H.) *and* **Verster van Wulverhörst.**

Wunderlich (C. A.) *and* **Seguin** (Edward, *m. d.*) Medical thermometry and human temperature. viii, 280 pp. 12°. *New York, W. Wood & co.* 1871.

Würtemberg. (*Statistisch topographisches bureau*). Das königreich Württemberg. Eine beschreibung von land, volk und staat. xvi, 1004 pp. 3 tab. 1 col. map. 8°. *Stuttgart, W. Nitzschke*, 1863. S.

——— ——— Württembergische jahrbücher für statistik und landeskunde. Jahrgang 1868. 3 p. l. 465, lxxxii pp. 5 tab. 12°. *Stuttgart, H. Lindemann*, 1870. S.

Wyatt (*Sir* Thomas, *the elder*). Songs and sonettes. [1557. Reprinted]. 16°. [*London*, 1870].

[ARBER's english reprints, no. 24 in v. 11. TOTTEL's miscellany, 1870, pp. 33-60, 62-95, 223-225].

Wyatt (Thomas). Beauties of sacred literature. vii, 220 pp. 8 pl. 8°. *Boston, J. Munroe & co.* [1848].

Wyatt (William Edward, *d. d.*) Christian offices, for the use of families and individuals; compiled from the liturgy of the protestant episcopal church, and from the devotional writings of various authors; with passages scripture, and a calendar. 3d ed. xxxii, 388 pp. 12°. *Baltimore, Knight & Colburn*, 1841.

——— The same. 5th ed. x, 13-498 pp. 12°. *New York, Stanford & Delisser*, 1858.

Wyckoff (*Rev.* Wm. H.) New testament. 1850. *See* **Bible.** (*English*).

Wylie (S. O. *d. d.*) The lamb that was slain. 12°. [*Pittsburgh*, 1872].

[*In* REFORMED presbyterian church in North America. Memorial volume, pp. 101-127].

Wyll (The) of the deuyll and his last testament. [*anon.*] 8°. [*London, for private circulation*, 1871].

[*In* FURNIVALL (Frederick J. *editor*). Jyl of Breyntford's testament, by Robert Copland [etc.] 1871. pp. 20-28].

Wyman's piano text book: containing a complete system of musical notation. 83 pp. 16°. *New York, W. A. Pond & co.* 1871.

Wyndham *or* **Wynham** (Henry Penruddocke). A picture of the Isle of Wight, delineated upon the spot, in the year 1793. 2 p. l. xii, 152 pp. 1 l. 8°. *London, C. Roworth, for J. Egerton*, 1794.

Wynne (Faith, *pseudon.*) Flossy Lee. By Faith Wynne. 209 pp. 2 pl. 16°. *Philadelphia, J. P. Skelly & co.* 1869.

Wynne (Richard). The new testament: divided and pointed according to the subjects. *London*, 1764. *See* **Bible.** (*English*).

Wynpersse. *See* **Wijnpersse.**

Wyrley (William). The true use of arms. Reprinted from the original edition, 1592. ix, 42 pp. 7 pl. 12°. *London, J. G. Bell*, 1853.

Wyse (George). Original poems and songs. 3d series. 300 pp. 12°. *Falkirk, author*, 1829.

Wyse (*Sir* Thomas). Impressions of Greece. With an introduction by his niece, miss Wyse, and letters from Greece to friends at home, by Arthur Penrhyn Stanley. vii, 332 pp. 8°. *London, Hurst & Blackett*, 1871.

Wyse (Thomas, *jr.*) The political catechism, explanatory of the constitutional rights and civil disabilities of the catholics of Ireland. 120 pp. 8°. *London, J. Ridgway*, 1829.

Wythes (Joseph H. *m. d.*) The physician's dose and symptom book, containing the doses and uses of all the principal articles of the materia medica and officinal preparations. 10th ed. 277 pp. 18°. *Philadelphia, Lindsay & Blakiston*, 1871.

Xavier (Jérôme). Historia Christi, persice conscripta, simulque, multis modis contaminata. Latine reddita & animadversionibus

Xavier (Jérôme)—continued.
notata a Ludovico de Dieu. 12 p. l. 636 pp. 2 l. 4°. *Lvgdvni Batavorvm, ex officina elseviriana*, 1639.

——— Historia s. Petri, persice conscripta, simulque multis modis contaminata. Latine reddita, & brevibus animadversionibus notata, a Ludovico de Dieu. [*anon.*] 4 p. l. 121 pp. 4°. *Lvgdvni Batavorvm, ex officina elseviriana*, 1639.
[*With his* Historia Christi, 1639].

——— *and* **Pigneiro** (Emmanuel). Narratio brevis rervm à societate [Jesu] in regno magni Mogor gestarum, transcripta ex literis p. Hieronymi Xavier & Emmanuelis Pigneiro, anni 1598. 4°. [*Lugduni Batavorum, ex officina elseviriana*, 1639].
[*In* XAVIER (J.) Historia s. Petri, pp. 108-144].

Xenophon. Σωκρατους απολογια. Του αυτου απομνημονευματων βιβλια Δ. Calci cujusque paginæ subjecta est accuratissima Johannis Leunclavii amelburni interpretatio latina. Adjectæ sunt fini H. Stephani, J. Leunclavii, et Ae. Porti notæ integræ. 7 p. l. 286 pp. 17 l. 8°. *Londini, impensis R. & J. Bonwicke*, 1720.

——— Le opere di Senofonte ateniese. Tradotte dal greco da Marc' Antonio Gandini. Colla vita dell' autore descritta dal medesimo Gandini, con alcune annotazioni necessarie per l'intelligenza di tutta l'opera; aggiontovi in questa nuova impressione la cronologia sequente a quella di Tucidide, quattro tavole di geografia antica di Cristoforo Cellario, e la storia di Gemisto Pletone nuovamente tradotta. 3 v. 4°. *Verona, D. Ramanzini*, 1736-37.

CONTENTS.

——— Historiæ liber tertius. 8°. *Oxonii*, 1835.
[*In* HISTORIA græca, ed. 2a, pp. 277-307].

——— Anabasis; [latin text] with an interlinear translation, for the use of schools and private learners, on the hamiltonian system, as improved by Thomas Clark. 564 pp. 12°. *Philadelphia, C. Desilver*, 1859.

Xenophon—continued.

——— The same. The historie of Xenophon: containing the ascent of Cyrvs into the higher covntries. Wherein is described the admirable iovrney of ten thousand Grecians from Asia the lesse into the territories of Babylon, and their retrait from thence into Greece. [Also], a comparison of the roman manner of warres with this of our time, out of Ivstvs Lipsivs. Translated by Joh. Bingham. 3 p. l. 146 pp. 6 l. fol. *London, J. Haviland for R. Mabb*, 1623.

——— Xenophon's discourse upon improving the revenue of the state of Athens. [Translated by Walter Moyle]. First printed in the year 1697. 8°. [*London, J. Knapton*, [*etc.*] 1727].
[*In* MOYLE (Walter). Whole works. *London*, 1727. pp. viii, 1-46].

Xenophon *ephesius*. Ephesiacorum de amoribus Anthiæ et Abrocomæ libri v. graece et latine [interprete A. E. Locella]. 8°. *Biponti*, 1794.
[MITSCHERLICH (C. W.) Scriptores erotici græci, v. 4, pp. 179-330].

Ximenes (Lionardo). Raccolta delle perizie ed opuscoli idraulici del signor abate Ximenes. Alla quale si aggiungono le perizie di altri professori che anno scritto sulle stese materie. 2 v. 1 portrait, xx, 472 pp. 8 pl. 1 tab; 1 portrait, vi, 454 pp. 9 pl. 2 tab. 4°. *Firenze, P. Allegrini*, 1785-86.

CONTENTS.

Ximenes (Lionardo)—continued.

nelle ricubature delle escavazioni de' canali, e nelle formazione degli argini. pp. 425-439.
——— Ultima memoria del più sicuro remedio delle acque delle tre provincie. pp. 439-468.
——— Prove di fatto, che l'alveo del Pò di primaro dal 1693 in quà siasi abbassato. pp. 469-472.

v. 2. XIMENES (L.) Parte prima delle relazioni e perizie delle acque lucchesi e del confinante granducato di Toscana. pp. 1-155.
——— Parte seconda. Intorno alla decadenza della maremma senese e suoi rimedj. pp. 157-423.
——— Parte terza. Relazione della visita fatta all' Ombrone nel territorio d'Asciano sulla corrosione che fa detto fiume contro i torreni de' certosini, etc. pp. 425-454.

Ximenez (Mateo). Compendio della vita del beato Sebastiano d'Apparizio, laico professo dell' ordine de' minori osservanti di s. Francesco della provincia del santo evangelio nel Messico. xxi, 229 pp. 1 portrait. 4°. *Roma, nella stamperia Salomoni*, 1789.

Y. M. C. A. (The). [A monthly paper] published under the auspices of the Young men's christian association, Washington, D. C. May, 1868, to Aug. 1870. v. 1-2 in 1 v. fol. *Washington*, 1868-70.

Y. (T. R.) Belle Lovell. [*anon.*] 342 pp. 1 pl. 16°. *New York, A. D. F. Randolph & co.* 1871.

Yale (Charles). Outlines of general history, in three parts: 1. Ancient history. 2. Modern history. 3. American history. 308, 16 pp. 12°. *Rochester*, [*N. Y.*] *E. Peck & co.* 1830.

Yankey (The) in London, being the first part of a series of letters written by an american youth, during nine months' residence in the city of London; addressed to his friends in and near Boston, Massachusetts. [*anon.*] v. 1. ix, 180 pp. 12°. *New-York, I. Riley*, 1809.

Yarrington (J. T.) The omnium-gatherum; or, the american fortune-teller: an amusement for parties and the social circle. 52 pp. 18°. *Carbondale, Pa. J. T. Yarrington*, 1872.

Yates (William). Memoirs of the early life of John Chamberlain, late missionary in India. With his diary of religious exercises. Abridged from the Calcutta ed. 204 pp. 16°. *Boston, J. Loring*, 1831.

Year book (The) and almanac of Canada for 1871; being an annual statistical abstract for the dominion and a record of legislation and of public men in British North America. Editor, John Lowe. v, 250 pp. 1 map. 12°. *Montreal, J. Lowe & co.* [1870].

Year-book (The) of agriculture; or, the annual of agricultural progress and discovery, for 1855 and 1856. 399 pp. 5 pl. 8°. *Philadelphia, Childs & Peterson*, 1856. s.

Year-book (The) of facts in science and art. By John Timbs. 1870-71. 2 v. 16°. *London, Lockwood & co.* 1871-72.

Yearsley (Ann). Poems, on several occasions. 4th ed. xxxii, 103 pp. 8°. *London, G. G. J. & J. Robinson*, 1786.

Yeats (John, *ll. d.*) The natural history of the raw materials of commerce. With a copious list of commercial terms, and their synonymes in several languages. 2d and revised ed. with glossary. xvi, 440 pp. 1 map. 12°. *London, Cassell, Petter, & Galpin*, [1871].

Yellott (George, *pseudon?*) The funny philosophers, or wags and sweethearts. 296 pp. 12°. *Philadelphia, J. B. Lippincott & co.* 1872.

Yelverton (Therèse, *viscountess Avonmore*). Zanita, a tale of the Yo-Semite. iv, 296 pp. 12°. *New York, Hurd & Houghton*, 1872.

Yonge (Charlotte Mary). Pioneers and founders. Or recent workers in the mission field. xvi, 316 pp. 1 pl. 12°. *London, Macmillan & co.* [1871].

Yorke (Henry Redhead). Elements of civil knowledge. 2 p. l. 336 pp. 8°. *Dorchester*, [*Eng.*] *author*, 1800.

Yorkshire (The) commercial list. 1871-72. Second and third years. By Estell & co. fol. *London*, [*Seyd & co.*] 1871.

Young (A. H.) Manual of the botany of Jefferson co. [Indiana]. Prepared for the second report of the geological survey of Indiana. 8°. *Indianapolis*, 1871.

[*In* INDIANA (*State of*). *Geological survey.* Second report, pp. 241-292].

Young (Edward, *chief U. S. bureau of statistics*). Report on immigration. *See* **United States.** *Treasury department.* (*Bureau of statistics*).

Young (Edward, *of Georgia*). The ladye Lillian, and other poems. 191 pp. 12°. *Lexington, Ga. E. Young*, 1859.

Young (Loyal, *d. d.*) Communion. A treatise on christian fellowship with God and his saints. 72 pp. 18°. *Philadelphia, Presbyterian board of publication*, [1871].

Young (William). The spirit of Athens, being a political and philosophical investigation of the history of that republic. xv, 296 pp. 8°. *London, J. Robson*, 1777.

Young (The) clerk; or, the story of Robert Elliott. By the author of "The mountain daisy," [etc. *anon.*] 225 pp. 18°. *Philadelphia, American sunday-school union*, 1861.

Young (The) communicant: an aid to the right understanding and spiritual improvement of the Lord's supper. [*anon.*] 128 pp. 32°. *Boston, Gould, Kendall & Lincoln*, 1844.

Young (The) communicant's manual. [*anon.*] 85 pp. 24°. *New York, Pott, Young & co.* 1871.

Young eagle; or, forest fortunes. By the author of "Rosa Lane," [etc. *anon.*] 212 pp. 3 pl. 16°. *Philadelphia, American s. s. union*, [1871].

Young (The) gentleman's library. A repository of useful and entertaining knowledge. [*anon.*] 336 pp. 12°. *Philadelphia, Crissy, Waldie & co.* 1835.

Young (The) husband's book; a manual of the duties, moral, religious, and domestic, imposed by the relations of married life. By the author of "The young wife's book." [*anon.*] 288 pp. 18°. *Philadelphia, Carey, Lea & Blanchard*, 1836.

Young Israel. An illustrated monthly magazine for young people. Louis Schnabel [and] M. Brecher, editors. Jan. to Dec. 1871. v. 1. 8°. *New York, Hebrew orphan asylum printing estab't*, 1871.

Young (The) lady's book of poetry; comprising selections from the works of british and american poets. By the author of "The young man's own book." [*anon.*] 320 pp. 24°. *Philadelphia, Key & Biddle*, 1835.

Young (The) lady's friend. *See* **Farrar** (Eliza Rotch).

Young (The) lady's own book. [*anon.*] Eng. title, xv, 361 pp. 1 pl. 24°. *Philadelphia, Key, Meikle & Biddle*, 1832.

Young (The) man's evening book. [*anon.*] 336 pp. 16°. *New York, C. S. Francis*, 1837.

Young (The) man's own book: a manual of politeness, intellectual improvement and moral deportment. [*anon.*] xii, 307 pp. 1 pl. 18°. *Philadelphia, Key, Meikle & Biddle*, 1832.

Young (The) man's sunday book: a practical manual of the christian duties of piety, benevolence and self-government. By the author of the Young man's own book. [*anon.*] xvi, 304 pp. 24°. *Philadelphia, Key & Biddle*, 1833.

Young (The) mechanic, containing directions for the use of all kinds of tools, and for the construction of steam engines and mechanical models, including the art of turning in wood and metal. From the english edition, with corrections, &c. By the author of "The lathe and its uses." [*anon.*] 1 p. l. v, 346 pp. 12°. *New York, G. P. Putnam & sons*, 1871.

Young (The) patriot; a memorial of James Hall. [*anon.*] 192 pp. 2 portraits. 18°. *Boston, Mass. sabbath school society*, [1862].

Young (The) patriot; or, fidelity rewarded. Translated from the german, by M. S. F. and I. A. [*anon.*] 191 pp. 16°. *Boston, Loring*, 1863.

Young (The) quaker; or, circumstances alter cases. By a clergyman. [*anon.*] 146 pp. 18°. *New York, Carlton & Porter*, [1863].

Youngs (*Rev.* James). A history of the most interesting events in the rise and progress of methodism, in Europe and America. 2d ed. 468 pp. 16 pl. 12°. *New Haven, D. McLeod*, 1831.

Yriarte (Charles). Paris grotesque. Les célébrités de la rue. Paris (1815 à 1863). Illustrations par mm. L'Hernault, Lix, de Montault et Yriarte. 3 p. l. 368 pp. 30 pl. 8°. *Paris, Dupray de La Mahérie*, 1864.
[Imperfect: 5 pl. wanting].

Yucatan (*State of*). Constitucion politica. Sancionada por su congreso constituyente en 6 de abril de 1825. 78, 5 pp. 18°. *Merida, oficina del Sol*, 1825.

Zaba (N. F.) An essay on the moral and intellectual powers of woman. 2 p. l. 111 pp. 18°. *London, Davis & co.* 1840.

——— *and* **Zaleski** (P.) The polish exile, being an historical, statistical, political, and literary account of Poland. iv, 284 pp. 1 pl. 4 l. music. 8°. *Edinburgh, J. & D. Collie*, 1833.

Zabriskie (*Rev.* F. N.) Precious stones from bible mountains. 289 pp. 18°. *New York, A. D. F. Randolph*, 1863.

Zaccaria (Francesco Antonio). Nvova givstificazione del celibato sacro dagli inconvenienti oppostogli anche vltimamente in alcvni infamissimi libri dissertazioni qvattro. xxxi, 280 pp. 4°. *Fuligno, G. Tomassini*, 1785.

Zachaire (Denys). Opuscule de la philosophie naturelle des métaux. 12°. [*Paris, A. Cailleau*, 1741].
[*In* SALMON (William). Bibliothèque des philosophes chimiques. 1741. v. 2, pp. 447-558].

Zacharie (I.) Surgical and practical observations on the diseases of the human foot, with instructions for their treatment. [Also], ad

Zacharie (I.)—continued. vice on the management of the hand. 1 p. l. 96 pp. 6 pl. 12°. *New-York, C. B. Norton*, 1860.

Zahn (Johann). Oculus artificialis teledioptricus sive telescopicum, ex abditis rerum naturalium & artificialium principiis protractum nova methodo, eaque solida explicatum ac cumprimis e triplici fundamento physico seu naturali, mathematico dioptrico et mechanico, seu practico stabilitum. 3 v. in 1. fol. *Herbipoli, Q. Heyl*, 1785–86.

Zaleski *or* **Zalewski** (P.) The polish exile. 1833. *See* **Zaba** (N. F.) *and* **Zaleski.**

Zamakhsharí. *See* **Abu'l kasim** Mahmud Ben Omar Ez-Zamakhshari.

Zanchi (Basilio). Basilii Zanchii poematvm editio [3[a]] copiosior. 92 l. 16°. *Romae, apud Valerium et Loisium fratres doricos*, 1550.

[*Note.*—Zanchi's baptismal name was Pietro. He assumed that of Basilio in 1524].

Zanetti (Antonio Maria). Ancient statues greek and roman; designed from the celebrated originals in St. Mark's, and other public collections in Venice by A. Zanetti. Frontispiece, 1 p. l. 100 pl. [2 series, ea. numb. pl. 1–50]. fol. *London, Lackington, Allen & co.* 1797.

[*Note.*—Imperfect: no. 5 in 2d set, Leda, wanting].

Zanneti (Arturo). Sopra gli aeroliti caduti il giorno 29 febbraio 1868. *See* **Denza** (Francesco).

Zapf (Georg Wilhelm). Annales typographiæ augustanæ ab ejus origine mccccLxvi. usque ad annum mdxxx. Accedit domini Francisci Antonii Veith diatribe de origine et incrementis artis typographicæ in vrbe Augusta vindelica. 6 p. l. lxviii, 114 pp. 3 l. 1 pl. 4°. *Augustæ Vindelicorum, impensis A. F. Bartholomæi*, 1778.

Zarathustra. *See* **Zoroaster.**

Zay (—). Nouveau dictionnaire de poche français-allemand, et allemand-français; rédigé d'après Campe, l'abbé Mozin, Thiébault, l'académie française, Lavaux et Boiste. 3e éd. 2 p. l. 36, 651 pp. 18°. *Paris, Thiériot*, 1833.

Zeiller (Martinus). Topographia und eigentliche beschreibung der vornembsten städte, schlösser auch anderer plätze und örter in denen herzogthumer Braunschweig und Lüneburg, und denen dazu gehörendē grafschafften, herzschafften und landen. [*anon.*] Eng. title, 1 p. l. 220 pp. 4 l. 132 pl. 3 maps. fol. *Franckfurt, bei M. Marians s. erbē*, 1654.

Zeitschrift für entomologie. Herausgegeben vom verein für schlesische insektenkunde zu Breslau. Neue folge. 2es heft. 8°. *Breslau, im selbstverlag*, 1871. s.

Zelie (J. H.) The critical speller, being a collection of useful words frequently misspelled, alphabetically arranged. 79 pp. 16°. *New York, Taintor & co.* 1871.

Zell's popular encyclopedia. *See* **Colange** (L.)

Zeltner (Gustav Georg). Vitæ theologorvm altorphinorvm a condita academia omnivm vna cvm scriptorvm recensv plenivs et accvrativs ad historiæ ecclesiasticæ et literariæ vsvm descriptæ. [Editio prima]. 3 p. l. 512 pp. 12 l. 32 pl. 4°. *Norimbergæ et Altorphii, apud hæredes I. D. Tavberi*, 1722.

Zeno (Apostolo). Dissertazioni vossiane, cioè giunte e osservazioni intorno agli storici italiani che hanno scritto latinamente, rammentati dal Vossio nel iii. libro De historicis latinis. 2 v. 4 p. l. xv, 368 pp; viii, 420 pp. 4°. *Venezia, G. Albrizzi*, 1752–53.

——— Poesie sacre drammatiche di Apostolo Zeno. 9 p. l. 506 pp. 1 l. 1 pl. 4°. *Venezia, C. Zane*, 1735.

Zenobius. Proverbia Zenobii ex [Lucillio] tarrhæo ac Didymo. [Græce et latine]. 4°. *Antverpiae, ex officina plantiniana, apud viduam & filios I. Moreti*, 1612.

[*In* Schott (Andreas). Παροιμιαι ἑλληνικαι. *Antverpiae*, 1612. pp. 1–168].

Zeuss (Johann Caspar). Grammatica celtica. E monumentis vetustis tam hibernicae linguae quam britannicae dialecti cambricae cornicae armoricae nec non e gallicae priscae reliquiis construxit J. C. Zeuss. 2 v. lvi, 560 pp; 1 p. l. 561–1164 pp. 8°. *Lipsiae, apud Weidmannos*, 1853.

Zillah, the child medium; a tale of spiritualism. By the author of "My confession," [etc. *anon.*] 298 pp. 12°. *New York, Dix, Edwards & co.* 1857.

Zimmermann (Johann Georg). Reflections on men and things; translated from a french manuscript. iv, 233 pp. 8°. *London, H. D. Symonds*, 1799.

Zinzerling (Just). Jodoci Sinceri [*pseudon.*] itinerarivm Galliæ: cum appendice, de Bvrdigala. 12 p.l. 476 pp. 9 l. 18°. *Genevae, apud P. Chouët*, 1627.

Zipoli (Perlone, *pseudon.*) *See* **Lippi** (Lorenzo).

Zoe's story. *See* **Walker** (K. K. C.)

Zollikofer (Georg Joachim). Exercices de piété et prières pour l'édification particulière des chrétiens éclairés et vertueux. Par m. G. J. Zollikofre. Traduits de l'allemand par m. L. Dumas. Nouv. éd. 2 v. xv, 207 pp; 2 p. l. 279 pp. 1 l. 8°. *Paris, J. J. Paschoud*, 1810.

Zoological (The) record. *See* **Record** (The) of zoological literature.

Zorn (Peter). Historia bibliorvm pictorvm ex antiquitatibvs Ebraeorvm et christianorvm illustrata. xvi, 170 pp. 3 l. 4°. *Lipsiae, apvd Io. C. Langenhemivm*, 1643.

——— Opuscula sacra, hoc est programmatum, dissertationum, orationum, epistolarum et schediasmatum, in quibus præter selectissima historiæ ecclesiasticæ et literariæ capita, etiam plus quam sexcenta s. scripturæ loca illustrantur & vindicantur. 2 v. 7 p. l. 822 pp. 1 portrait; 7 p. l. 806 pp. 5 l. 1 pl. 16°. *Altonaviæ, apud J. Korte*, 1731.

Zoroaster. Gâta ahunavaiti saratustrica carmina septem latine vertit et explicavit commentarios criticos adjecit textum archetypi, adhibitis Brockhausii Westergaardii Spiegelii et Justii editoribus nec non lectionibus variantibus recensuit C— Kossowicz. 3 p. l. vii, 167 pp. 8°. *Petropoli, imp. caesareae universitatis*, 1867. s.

——— Oracula magica Zoroastris cum scholiis Plethonis et Pselli nunc primum edita. Ex bibliotheca regia. Studio Johannis Opsopœi. [Græce et latine]. 4°. [*Amstelodami, apud H. & viduam T. Boom*, 1689].

[*In* Gallé (Servais). Σιβυλλιακοι χρησμοι. *Amstelodami*, 1689. pp. 71-127].

72

Zschokke (Johann Heinrich Daniel). Stichtelijke uren. Uit de volledige duitsche uitgave uitgelezen en vertaald. 6e druk. x, 420 pp. 1 pl. 8°. *Rotterdam, O. Petri*, 1857.

——— The sleepwaker. A tale from the german. iv, 224 pp. 18°. *Boston, J. Munroe & co.* 1842.

Zuendt (E. A.) Lyrische und dramatische dichtungen. 703 pp. 16°. *St. Louis, F. B. Meissner*, 1871.

CONTENTS.

Lyrisches.
Jugurtha. Trauerspiel in 5 acten.
Rienzi, der letzte tribun. Nach dem englischen der miss Mitford frei bearbeitet.
Galilei. Schauspiel in 3 acten von François Ponsard. Deutsch in metrischer uebertragung.

Zuflucht zu Gott. Vollständiges gebet- und erbauungsbuch für katholische christen. [*anon.*] 528 pp. 18°. *Einsiedeln, New-York & Cincinnati, K. & N. Benziger*, 1870.

Zumpt (Carl Gottlob). Latin syntax. Chiefly from the german of C. G. Zumpt. By Charles Beck. viii, 155 pp. 12°. *Boston, C. C. Little & J. Brown*, 1838.

Zundel (John). The new introit: a collection of new introits, anthems, sentences, and motets, adapted to all the occasions of public service. 144 pp. obl. 8°. *Toledo, O. Zundel & Brand*, 1871.

Zuñiga (Diego Ortiz de). Annales eclesiasticos y secvlares, de la civdad de Sevilla. Desde el año de 1246, hasta el de 1671. Eng. title, 11 p. l. 818 pp. 7 l. fol. *Madrid, imprenta real*, 1677.

LAW BOOKS.

LAW BOOKS.

Abbott (Benjamin Vaughan). A treatise upon the United States courts and their practice: explaining the enactments by which they are controlled, their organization and powers, their peculiar jurisdiction; and the modes of pleading and procedure in them. With numerous practical forms. 2d ed. 2 v. xv, 639 pp; viii, 618 pp. 8°. *New York, Diossy & co.* 1871.

CONTENTS.

v. 1. Enactments; organizations; jurisdiction.
v. 2. Original suits; review; forms.

Acollas (Émile). Manuel de droit civil à l'usage des étudiants contenant l'exégèse du code napoléon et un exposé complet des systèmes juridiques. (Premier examen). v. 1–2. 8°. *Paris, E. Thorin,* 1869–70.
[*Note.*—v. 3 wanting].

Advice on the study of the law, with directions for the choice of books. *See* **Wright** (William).

Allen (Charles). Reports of cases argued and determined in the supreme judicial court of Massachusetts. [1867]. v. 14. 8°. *Boston, H. O. Houghton & co.* 1870.

American (The) law register. [Monthly]. Jan.–Dec. 1871. New series, v. 10; old series, v. 19. 8°. *Philadelphia, D. B. Canfield & co.* 1871.

American (The) law review. [Quarterly]. Oct. 1870, to July, 1872. v. 5–6. 8°. *Boston, Little, Brown, & co.* 1871–72.

Amos (Sheldon). Difference of sex as a topic of jurisprudence and legislation. 43 pp. 8°. *London, Longmans, Green, & co.* 1870.

Andrews (Samuel M.) Report of the trial of Samuel M. Andrews, indicted for the murder of Cornelius Holmes, before the supreme judicial court of Massachusetts, December 11, 1868. Including the rulings of the court upon many questions of law, and a full statement of authorities upon the subject of transitory insanity. By Charles G. Davis. 2 p. l. 288 pp. 1 pl. 8°. *New York, Hurd & Houghton,* 1869.

Argentine republic. Código civil de la república argentina, redactado por el dr. d. Dalmacio Velez Sarsfield, y aprobado por el honorable congreso de la república el 29 de setiembre de 1869. Ed. oficial. 3 p. l. xvii, 981 pp. 8°. *Nueva York, Hallet & Breen,* 1870.

——— *See, also,* **Buenos Ayres.**

Arizona (*Territory of*). The compiled laws of the territory of Arizona, including the Howell code and the session laws from 1864 to 1871, inclusive. Compiled by Coles Bashford. vi, 627 pp. 8°. *Albany, N. Y. Weed, Parsons & co.* 1871.

Arkansas (*State of*). Acts, resolutions and memorials of the general assembly of the state of Arkansas, commencing January, 1871, and ending March, 1871. 8°. *Little Rock, Price & Barton,* 1871.

——— Code of practice in civil and criminal cases for the state of Arkansas. Together with the constitution of the United States, and the constitution of the state of Arkansas. 627 pp. 8°. *Little Rock, J. G. Price,* 1869.

Assollant (Jean Baptiste Alfred). Le droit des femmes. 2 p. l. iii, 308 pp. 1 l. 12°. *Paris, A. Anger,* 1868.

Austin (Robert Cecil). Reports of cases (principally under the county courts' equitable jurisdiction act, 1865, and the county courts' amendment act, 1867) in the county courts, included in circuit no. 45, heard and determined by Henry James Stonor, judge of the said courts. xii, 79 pp. 12°. *London, Butterworths,* 1869.

Baldo de' Ubaldi *or* **Baldeschi.** Baldus super codice [l. 1–5] cum apostillis [Alexandri Tartagnini de Imola. Libr. 1–5]. 210,

Baldo de' Ubaldi—continued.
139, 52 l. fol. *Venetiis, per Baptistam de tortis*, 1496.
[*Note.*—Each page has 71 lines].

——— Baldi svper sexto [vii, viii, et ix] codicis iustiniani libro commentaria luculentissima. Nec desunt repetitiones & additiones eiusdem Baldi per d. Ioan. Franciscum Musaptum repertæ, ac hisce comentarijs adiectæ. Accesserunt præterea doctissimorum aliquot iurisconsultorum apostillæ, videlicet Alexandri de Tartagnis, imolensis. Andreæ Barbatiæ, siculi. Celsi Hugonis Dissuti, cabiloneñ. [Repertorivm lect. Baldi svper codice. Index locupletissimvs commentariorvm Baldi de Perusio in nouem codicis iustiniani libros]. 3 eng. titles, 196, 241 l. 78 unp. l. fol. *Lvgdvni*, 1539.

——— Commentariorvm in digestū uetus [prima pars et secunda], cum adnotationibus [etc.] Benedicti de Vadis forosemproniensis [et] Ioannis Thierri lingoniensis. 2 v. in 1. 313 l; 147 l. fol. [*n. p.*] 1535-36.

Baldus *or* **Baldeschi.** *See* **Baldo de' Ubaldi.**

Bankrupt (The) register, containing reports of the leading cases and principal rulings in bankruptcy, of the district judges of the United States, July, 1869, to July, 1870. v. 3. 4°. *New York, G. T. Deller*, 1870.
[*Note.*—Name changed July, 1870, to National bankruptcy register, which see].

Barron (William E. *and* William) *v.* **United States.** American and mexican joint commission. No. 633, m. d. William E. Barron and William Barron *vs.* the United States. Closing argument on motions to dismiss. J. Hubley Ashton, counsel of the United States. 6 pp. 8°. [*Washington, government printing office*, 1871].

Basnage du Fraquenay (Henri). Œuvres; contenant ses commentaires sur la coutume de Normandie, et son traité des hipotèques. 3e éd. 2 v. 6 p. l. 554, 78 pp. 41 l; 2 p. l. 508 pp. 39 l. 124 pp. 3 l. fol. *Rouen, Maury*, 1709.

Belcher (Jonathan, *governor of New Hampshire*). *See* **New Hampshire** *vs.* **Belcher.**

Bellers (Fettiplace). A delineation of universal law: being an abstract of an essay towards deducing the elements of universal law, from the first principles of knowledge, and the nature of things. 1. Of law in general. 2. Of private law. 3. Of criminal law. 4. Of the laws of magistracy. 5. Of the law of nations. xv, 74 pp. 4°. *London, R. Dodsley*, 1750.

Benedict (Robert D.) Reports of cases in the district courts of the United States, within the second circuit. [1868-1869]. v. 3. 8°. *New York, Baker, Voorhis & co.* 1871.

Bennett (David S.) *v.* **Buffalo** commercial advertiser. The great libel suit. The hon. David S. Bennett, m. c. *versus* the Buffalo commercial advertiser. Damages claimed, $100,000. A complete history of the trial, including the papers in the case, the testimony, the counsels' arguments, the judge's charge, and the verdict of the jury. 235 pp. 8°. *Buffalo, Matthews & Warren*, 1870.

Benton (Thomas Hart). Historical and legal examination of that part of the decision of the supreme court of the United States in the Dred Scott case, which declares the unconstitutionality of the Missouri compromise act, and the self-extention of the constitution to territories, carrying slavery along with it. [*anon.*] 193 pp. 8°. *New York, D. Appleton & co.* 1857.

Bergmann (Carl). Lehrbuch der medicina forensis für juristen. xviii, 522 pp. 8°. *Braunschweig, F. Vieweg & sohn*, 1846. s.

Best (William Mawdesley) *and* **Smith** (George James Philip). Reports of cases argued and determined in the court of queen's bench, and the court of exchequer chamber on appeal from the court of queen's bench. 1869. v. 9. 8°. *London, H. Sweet*, 1871.

Biddle (John). A table of references to unrepealed public general acts: arranged in the alphabetical order of their short or popular titles. 2d ed. 4 p. l. 260 pp. 8°. *London, Stevens & sons*, 1870.

Bigelow (Melville M.) Leading and select american cases in the law of bills of exchange, [etc] *See* **Redfield** (Isaac F.) *and* **Bigelow.**

Billecocq (Th.) De la réhabilitation en matière criminelle correctionnelle et disciplinaire. (Commentaire pratique des lois des 3 juillet 1852 et 19 mars 1864). 2 p. l. 89 pp. 1 l. 8°. *Paris, Cosse, Marchal & cie.* 1868.

Bird (William). A treatise of the nobilitie of the realme. Collected ovt of the body of the common law, with mention of such statutes as are incident hereunto, upon a debate of the barony of Aburgavenny. [*anon.*] 2 p. l. 157 pp. 18°. *London, A. N. for M. Walbanke & R. Best*, 1642.
[*Note.*—This book is Bird's Magazine of honour, under a new title. It consists mainly of sir John Doddridge's argument in the case of the Abergavenny barony].

Bishop (Joel Prentiss). Commentaries on the law of married women, under the statutes of the several states and at common law and in equity. v. 1. xi, 756 pp. 8°. *Philadelphia, Kay & brother*, 1871.

Blackford (Isaac). Reports of cases in the supreme court of judicature of the state of Indiana. 2d ed. with annotations by E. A. Davis. v. 3-8. May term, 1832, to November term, 1847. 5 v. 8°. *Indianapolis, Merrill & Field*, 1870.

Blanc (Étienne). Traité de la contrefaçon, et de sa poursuite en justice, contenant: Les brevets d'invention, de perfectionnement et d'importation; Les marques de fabriques; Les noms des commerçants; Les désignations de marchandises,—les enseignes; La propriété littéraire; Les oeuvres dramatiques; Les oeuvres musicales; La peinture, gravure et sculpture; Les dessins de fabriques en tous genres. Avec le texte des lois, décrets, arrêtés, ordonnances, et les principaux monuments de la jurisprudence sur la matière. 1 p. l. vii, 638 pp. 8°. *Paris, l'auteur*, 1838.

Boke (A) of presidentes exactelye written in maner of a register. *See* **Phayer** (Thomas).

Bolster (William W.) Digest of the law of tax titles and form book, embracing all practical tax forms in all departments of law for the use of town, county and state officers, adapted to the New England states. 483 pp. 8°. *Portland, (Me.) Dresser & Ayer*, 1871.

Boston (*City of*). The by-laws and orders of the town of Boston; revised in the year 1758. 16 pp. sm. 4°. *Boston, Green & Russell*, 1758.

[*With* BOSTON. Several rules, etc. 1702, etc.]

——— Digest of laws and ordinances relating to the public health and tenement buildings. 96 pp. 18°. *Boston, A. Mudge & son*, 1870.

——— Several rules, orders, and by-laws made by the freeholders and inhabitants of Boston of the Massachusets, at their meeting, May 12 and Sept. 22, 1701, [also, May 12, 1702, May 17, 1714, June 4, 1714, May 14, 1719, March 11, 1722, April 10, 1723, March 8, 1724, March 14, 1725, May 8, 1727, June 25 and July 1, 1728]. 44 pp. sm. 4°. *Boston, B. Eliot*, 1702-40.

[*Note.*—Appended are the following:
Order of selectmen, July 21, 1738, appointing 12 porters. 4 pp.
Ordinance for providing bulls for cows, April 28, 1736. 3 pp.
Ordinance against firing guns at pigeons, etc. in Boston, March 10, 1740. 3 pp.
Ordinance for setting up and regulating a public market, April 24, 1734. 7 pp.
Ordinance for sweeping the chimneys, May 10, 1738. 3 pp.]

Brewster (F. Carroll, *ll. d.*) Reports of cases in the supreme court, and other courts of Pennsylvania. v. 3. [1868-1869]. 8°. *Philadelphia, Kay & brother*, 1871.

Brightly (Frederick Charles). Annual digest of the laws of Pennsylvania for the years 1862-1871. 8°. *Philadelphia, Kay & brother*, 1871.

——— The bankrupt law of the United States, with the rules and forms in bankruptcy, and notes of decisions. 2d ed. xxiv, 17-276 pp. 8°. *Philadelphia, Kay & brother*, 1871.

——— A collection of leading cases on the law of elections in the United States, with notes and references to the latest authorities. xlvi, 781 pp. 8°. *Philadelphia, Kay & brother*, 1871.

Brown (Benjamin F.) A concise statement of the law of partnership. 32 pp. 8°. *Indianapolis, for the author*, 1871.

Brown (Joseph). The evils of the unlimited liability for accidents of masters and railway companies, especially since lord Campbell's act. 2d ed. 46 pp. 8°. *London, Butterworths*, 1870.

Brown (William). Agency and trusts for payment of debts under private arrangement. xiv, 54 pp. 16°. *London, H. Sweet*, 1868.

Browne (Albert G.) Massachusetts reports. v. 102-103. *See* **Massachusetts** reports.

Buccellati (Antonio). Osservazioni intorno al progetto di codice penale per il regno d'Italia. Estratto dal Monitore dei tribunali. xlvi, 440 pp. 8°. *Milano, stabilimento redaelli della società chiusi e rechiedei*, 1867-68. s.

Buenos Ayres. Recopilacion de leyes y decretos promulgados en Buenos-Aires, 1810-40. 3 v. 8°. *Buenos Aires, imprenta del estado*, 1836-41. s.

——— The same. Indice general, 1810-35. ccxvi, viii pp. 8°. *Buenos Aires, imprenta del estado*, 1836. s.

Buffalo commercial advertiser. Libel suit. *See* **Bennett** (David S.) *v.* **Buffalo** commercial advertiser.

Buffington (James) *v.* **Day** (Joseph M.) Supreme court of the United States. December term, 1870. James Buffington *v.* Joseph M. Day. Brief for the plaintiff in error. 14 pp. 8°. [*n. p.*] 1871.

Burrell (*Sir* Charles Merrik). Report of the trial of the cause Carew against Burrell, bt. [*etc.*] *See* **Carew** (John Edward) *v.* **Burrell**.

Bush (W. P. D.) Kentucky reports. v. 7. 1869–1870. 8°. *Louisville, Ky. J. P. Morton & co.* 1871.

Butler (William Allen). Lawyer and client: their relation, rights, and duties. 76 pp. 16°. *New York, D. Appleton & co.* 1871.

Butterworth (Albert F.) Lawyer's pocket docket. 76 l. 12°. *Boston,* [1870].

California. Reports of cases in the supreme court of the state of California at the January, April and July terms, 1870. By R. Aug. Thompson. v. 39. 8°. *San Francisco, S. Whitney,* [*etc.*] 1871.

Campbell (James Mason). Reports of cases at law and equity and in the admiralty determined in the circuit court of the United States by Roger Brooke Taney, for the district of Maryland. April term, 1836–April term, 1861. viii, 682 pp. 8°. *Philadelphia, Kay & brother,* 1871.

Carew (John Edward) *v.* **Burrell** (*Sir* Charles Merrik) *and another.* Report of the trial of the cause Carew against Burrell, bt. and another, executors of the late earl of Egremont: at the Sussex spring assizes, held at Lewes, on Wednesday, March 18th, 1840, before mr. justice Littledale, and a special jury; taken in short hand by mr. Cooke. 2 p. l. 174 pp. 1 l. 8°. *London, W. Nicoll,* 1840.

Cases of personal identity. [*anon.*] 1 p. l. 102 pp. 8°. *Albany, J. Munsell,* 1854.

Charitable (The) trusts acts, 1853, 1855, 1860; [etc.] *See* **Cooke** (Hugh) *and* **Harwood** (R. G.)

Charleston (*S. C. City of*). Ordinances of the city council, passed in the first year of the incorporation of the city. [With] the act of the general assembly for incorporating the city. x, 57 pp. sm. 4°. *Charleston, J. Miller,* 1784.

Chisholm (Alexander) *vs.* **Georgia** (*State of*). A case decided in the supreme court of the United States, in which is discussed the question—"whether a state be liable to be sued by a private citizen of another state?" 120 pp. 8°. *Philadelphia, T. Dobson,* 1793.
[HAZARD pamphlets, v. 67].

Choyce cases in chancery. *See* **Practice** (The) of the high court of chancery. 1870.

Ciampi (Sebastiano). Statuti suntuarj, ricordati da Giovanni Villani, circa il vestiario delle donne i regali e banchetti delle nozze e circa le pompe funebri ordinati dal comune di Pistoia negli anni 1332. e 1333. Dati in luce con annotazioni. xxv pp. 4°. *Pisa, presso R. Prosperi,* 1815.

Clift (Henry). [New book of declarations, pleadings, verdicts, judgments and judicial writs; with the entries thereupon, digested and published by sir Charles Inglesby]. *b. l.* 1 p. l. 939 pp. 4 l. fol. *London,* 1703.
[Imperfect: title-page and leaves at end wanting; pp. 841–842 imperfect].

Coats (Archibald *and* John). In the house of lords. The respondents case. *See* **Reid** (Patrick) *et al. v.* **Coats.**

Cocke (William Archer). A treatise on the common and civil law, as embraced in the jurisprudence of the United States. xiv, 250 pp. 8°. *New York, Baker, Voorhis & co.* 1871.

Cohen (Jacob I.) Supplement to the Maryland code. *See* **Maryland.**

Coke (*Sir* Edward). Les reports de diuers resolutions, et iudgements donnés auec graund déliberation, par les iudges, & sages de la ley. [From 14. Elizabeth to 13. James]. *b. l.* Parts 1–4, 9–11. 7 v. in 2. fol. *London, the company of statione* [illegible]–29.
[*Note.*—2d and 4th parts dated 1[illegible]; 9th, 1627; 10th, 1629; rest (1st, 3d, 11th), 1619

——— The twelfth part of the reports of sir Edward Coke. Also the formes and proceedings of parliaments, both in England, & Ireland: with an exposition of Poynings law. 4 p. l. 136 pp. 2 l. fol. *T. R. for H. Twyford & T. Dring,* 1656.

Coldwell (Thomas H.) Reports of cases argued and determined in the supreme court of Tennessee, during the years 1869–70. v. 7. 8°. *Nashville, Tenn. Jones, Purvis & co.* 1871.

Colombia (*United States of*). Actos oficiales del gobierno provisorio de los Estados Unidos de Colombia, recopilados conforme a lo dispuesto por el decreto de 7 de abril de 1862. 671 pp. 8°. *Bogotá, Echeverría hermanos,* 1862.

——— Actos vijentes, de caracter lejislativo del gobierno provisorio de los Estados Unidos de Colombia. Ed. oficial. 348 pp. 8°. *Bogotá, Echeverría hermanos,* 1866.

Connecticut (*State of*). Private and special laws of the state of Connecticut. Compiled and published under authority of the general assembly. v. 5. From 1857–1865. 8°. *New Haven, C. C. Chatfield & co.* 1871.

——— Public acts passed by the general assembly of the state of Connecticut, May session, 1871. 8°. *Hartford, Case, Lockwood & Brainard,* 1871.

——— Special acts and resolutions passed by the general assembly of the state of Connecticut at the May session, 1871. 291 pp. 8°. *Hartford, Lockwood & Brainard,* 1871.

Connecticut reports: being reports of cases in the supreme court of errors of the state of Connecticut. By John Hooker. v. 36. 8°. *Hartford, Case, Lockwood & Brainard*, 1871.

Considerations on law. [*anon.*] 1 p. l. 45 pp. 8°. *London, W. Amer*, 1871.

Cook (Robley D.) Manual of the highway laws of the state of New York, xii, 357 pp. 8°. *Albany, J. D. Parsons*, 1870.

Cooke (Hugh) *and* **Harwood** (R. G) The charitable trusts acts, 1853, 1855, 1860; the charity commissioners jurisdiction act, 1862; the roman catholic charities acts; together with a collection of statutes relating to or affecting charities, including the mortmain acts. 2d ed. xx, 424 pp. 8°. *London, Stevens & Haynes*, 1867.

Cox (Edward William). Reports of cases in criminal law, argued and determined in all the courts in England and Ireland. 1867 to 1871. v. 11. viii, 792 pp. 8°. *London, H. Cox*, 1871.

——— Reports of all the cases decided by the superior courts of law and equity, relating to the law of joint-stock companies. [1868–1871]. v. 3–4. 8°. *London, H. Cox*, 1870–71.

Craig (R. D.) Reports of cases in chancery in the time of lord chancellor Cottenham. *See* **Mylne** (J. W.) *and* **Craig.**

Cunninghame, Dougal, and co. In the house of lords. The respondents case. 1780. *See* **Marshall** (William) *vs.* **Cunninghame**, Dougal, and co.

Curteis (W. C. *ll. d.*) A full report of the case of Mastin *v.* Escott. *See* **Mastin** *v.* **Escott.**

Dakota (*Territory of*). General and private laws, and memorials and resolutions of the territory of Dakota, passed at the first session of the legislative assembly, March 17–May 15, 1862. To which is prefixed a brief description of the territory and its government, the constitution of the United States, [etc.] 2 parts in 1 v. xvii, 558 pp; iv p. l. 38 pp. 8°. *Yankton, J. C. Trask*, 1862.

——— The same. General laws. 1864–5, 1866–7, 1867–8, 1868–9. 4 v. 8°. *Yankton, G. W. Kingsbury*, 1865–69.

Dalton (Michael, *of Lincoln's inn*). The covntrey ivstice, conteyning the practise of the ivstices of the peace out of their sessions. Gathered for the better helpe of such ivstices of peace as haue not beene much conuersant in the studie of the lawes of this realme. [1st ed.] Eng. title, 6 p. l. 370 pp. 6 l. fol. *London, the societie of stationers*, 1618.

Dalton (Michael, *of Lincoln's inn*)—continued.

——— The same. [4th ed.] Additions marked ☞. Eng. title, 4 p. l. 410 pp. 6 l. fol. *London, the assignes of I. More*, 1630.

——— The same. [5th ed.] Eng. title, 4 p. l. 410 pp. 5 l. fol. *London, the assignes of I. More*, 1635.

Damiens (Robert François). Pièces originales et procédures du procès, fait à Robert François Damiens, tant en la prévôté de l'hôtel, qu'en la cour de parlement. [*anon.* Recueillies par André François LeBreton]. 4 v. 16°. *Paris, P. G. Simon*, 1757.

Daniell (Edmund Robert). Pleading and practice of the high court of chancery. With the subsequent additions and improvements of Thomas Emerson Headlam, and the still later additions of Leonard Field, Edward C. Dunn, and John Riddle. 4th american ed. With notes [etc.] adapting the work to the demands of american practice in chancery. By J. C. Perkins. 3 v. 8°. *Boston, Little, Brown & co.* 1871.

Davidge (J. B. F.) *and* **Kimball** (Ivory G.) A compendium of internal revenue laws, with decisions, rulings, instructions, regulations and forms. xx, 859 pp. 8°. *Washington, D. C. W. H. & O. H. Morrison*, 1871.

Davis (Charles G.) Report of the trial of Samuel M. Andrews, [for murder,] and a full statement of authorities upon the subject of transitory insanity. 1869. *See* **Andrews** (Samuel M.)

Davis (Henry F. A.) A manual of the law relating to industrial and provident societies, in their formation, existence, and dissolution. With an appendix containing forms of rules, statutes, and general orders. xv, 260 pp. 16°. *London, H. Sweet*, 1869.

Dawson (George). Origo legvm: or a treatise of the origin of laws, and their obliging power: as also of their great variety: and why some laws are immutable, and some not; but may suffer change, or cease to be, or be suspended, or abrogated. 14 p. l. 168, 219 pp. fol. *London, for R. Chiswell*, 1694.

De Gex (John P.), **Jones** (H. Cadman), *and* **Smith** (R. Horton). Reports of cases heard and determined by the lord chancellor, at the court of appeal in chancery. 1862–1865. v. 3. viii, 758 pp. 8°. *London, Stevens & sons*, 1871.

——— **Macnaghten** (S), *and* **Gordon** (A.) Reports of cases heard and determined by the lord chancellor and the court of appeal in chancery. With notes and references to

De Gex (John P.) *etc.*—continued. american law and subsequent english editions. Edited by J. C. Perkins. 1851–1852. v. 1–2. 8°. *Boston, Little, Brown & co.* 1871.

Delaware (*State of*). Laws passed at a session of the general assembly, 1871. v. 14. Part 1. 8°. *Dover, Del. The Delawarean office*, 1871.

Demolombe (Jean Charles Florent). Traité des contrats ou des obligations conventionnelles en général. 3 v. 8°. *Paris, A. Durand*, 1868–70.

[Cours de code napoléon, v. 24–26].

Despard (Edward Marcus) *and others.* The trial of col. Despard & his associates, for high treason, and conspiracy, etc. Before lord chief justice Ellenborough and the other commissioners, in the county of Surry, Great Britain, 1803. To which is added an account of their execution. 56 pp. 8°. *New York, G. F. Hopkins*, 1803.

Desquiron (A. T.) Traité de la preuve par témoins en matière criminelle, suivant les principes du code d'instruction et du code pénal. x, 624 pp. 8°. *Paris, ve. Duminil-Lesueur*, 1811.

——— Traité de la preuve par témoins en matière civile, suivant les principes du code napoléon, du code de commerce et du code de procédure civile. lxvi, 9–591 pp. 8°. *Paris, Crapart*, 1811.

Doddridge (*Sir* John). The english lawyer. Describing a method for the managing of the lawes of this land. And expressing the best qualities requisite in the student, practizer, judges and fathers of the same. 4 p. l. 271 pp. sm. 4°. *London, assignes of I. More*, 1631.

Dugdale (*Sir* William). The history and antiquities of the four inns of court; namely, the Inner temple, Middle temple, Lincoln's inn, and Gray's inn; and of the nine inns of chancery; also of Serjeant's inn in Fleet st. and Chancery lane, and Scroop's inn: containing every particular circumstance relative to each of them, in the work written by sir William Dugdale, and published under the title of Origines juridiciales, &c. [Also] an appendix, containing several modern orders made by the society of Lincoln's inn. Also lists of the present benchers of the four inns of court. xx, 251 pp 8°. *London, G. Kearsly*, 1780.

Duncombe (Alfred John). Laws of the Turks and Caicos islands: comprising the imperial statutes, acts of the general assembly of the Bahama islands, extended to the presidency, and ordinances enacted by the legislative council of the same, in force at the date of the publication of this work. Collected and arranged in ten parts, according to the order of subjects. v. 1. xv, 616 pp. 8°. *London, Saunders, Otley, & co.* 1862.

Du Saulle. *See* **Legrand du Saulle.**

Dwarris (*Sir* Fortunatus). A general treatise on statutes: their rules of construction, and the proper boundaries of legislation and of judicial interpretation. With american notes and additions, and with notes and maxims of constitutional limitations upon the national and state legislative power; with a chapter on parliamentary law and parliamentary privileges. By Platt Potter, ll. d. 693 pp. 8°. *Albany, N. Y. W. Gould & sons*, 1871.

Edwards (Charles). Reports of chancery cases in the first circuit of the state of New York, decided by William T. M'Coun. By Charles Edwards. With notes and references by Daniel Ketchum. New ed. v. 4. 8°. *New York, Banks & brothers*, 1871.

English chancery reports. Reports of cases argued and determined in the english courts of chancery. With notes and references to english and american decisions. By Ch. Francis Stone. v. 45–46. 8°. *New York, Banks & brothers*, 1871.

CONTENTS.

HARE (Thomas). Cases adjudged before sir W. P. Wood. v. 11, (v. 45).
MYLNE (J. W.) *and* CRAIG (R. D.) Cases argued during the time of lord chancellor Cottenham. v. 5, (v. 46).
RUSSELL (James). Cases argued during the time of lord chancellor Eldon. v. 1, (v. 46).

English reports. *See* **Reports** of cases decided by the english courts.

Every man his own lawyer: or, a summary of the laws of England, in a new and instructive method. 7th ed. with many additions, from lord Raymond, Comyn, Strange, Foster, and with the statute law down to 4 Geo. 3, inclusive. [*anon.* Dedication subscribed G. J.] iv, 289 pp. 6 l. 8°. *New-York, H. Gaine*, 1768.

Farries (Thomas). Farries' precedents of bills of costs. Embracing precedents of bills of costs in the superior courts of equity, and on the equity side of the county courts, in conveyancing, probate, divorce, and common law. Being a practical guide in the general business of a solicitor, to which is added a complete list of fees in the above courts. 2d ed. xi, 484 pp. 12°. *London, Reeves & Turner*, 1867.

Ferrière (Claude de). Nouveau commentaire sur la coutume de la prévôté et vicomté de Paris. Nouv. éd. revue, corrigée & augmentée par Sauvan d'Aramon. 2 v. 4 p. l. 432 pp. 12 l; 1 p. l. 516 pp. 16°. *Paris, Guillyn,* 1762.

Finlason (W. Francis). A dissertation on the history of hereditary dignities, particularly as to their course of descent, and their forfeiture by attainder. With special reference to the case of the earldom of Wiltes. 110 pp. 8°. *London, Butterworths,* 1869.

——— Justice to a colonial governor; or, some considerations on the case of mr. Eyre: containing the substance of all the documents, discussions, and proceedings relating thereto. viii, clxxvi pp. 8°. *London, Chapman & Hall,* [1868].

——— A report of the case of the queen *v.* Gurney and others. *See* **Gurney** *and others.*

Fisher (Robert Alexander). A digest of the reported cases determined in the house of lords & privy council, and in the courts of common law, divorce, probate, admiralty & bankruptcy, from Michaelmas term, 1756, to Hilary term, 1870: with references to the statutes and rules of court. Founded on the analytical digest by Harrison. 5 v. 8°. *London, H. Sweet,* 1870.

Fitz-herbert (Anthony). The new natura brevium of the most reverend judge, mr. Anthony Fitzherbert. With a perfect table of the most material things contained therein, composed by W. Rastall. 36 p. l. 668 pp. 16°. *London, J. Streater,* 1666.

Flanders (Henry). A treatise on the law of fire insurance. 612 pp. 8°. *Philadelphia, Claxton, Remsen & Haffelfinger,* 1871.

Fleetwood (William). Annalivm tam regum Edwardi quinti, Richardi tertij, et Henrici septimi, quam Henrici octaui, titulorum ordine alphabetico digestorum, elenchus. *b. l.* 200 l. 18°. *Londini, in aedibus Richardi Tottelli,* 1579.

[*Note.*—A table or index to the year books].

Florida (*State of*). The code of procedure of the state of Florida. Approved February 19, 1870, and taking effect July 1, 1870. 176 pp. 8°. *Tallahassee, state printer,* 1870.

——— Reports of cases in the supreme court of Florida, at terms held in 1867-'8-'9. By John B. Galbraith and A. R. Meek. v. 12. 8°. *Tallahassee, E. M. Cheney,* 1869.

Folliott (George). House of lords. Case of the defendant in error. *See* **Ogden** (David) *vs.* **Folliott.**

Foot (Samuel A.) An argument in favor of the constitutionality of the general banking law of this state, delivered before the supreme court, at the July term, 1839. 100 pp. 8°. *Geneva,* [*N. Y.*] *I. Merrell,* 1839.

Foster (G. J.) Doctors' commons: its courts and registries, with a treatise on probate court business. xxiv, 261 pp. 8°. *London, Reeves, son & co.* 1869.

France. Bulletin des lois de l'empire français. 11 v. 8°. *Paris, imprimerie impériale* [*et*] *nationale,* 1869-71.

CONTENTS.

xie série. Partie principale. v. 33-36. nos. 1675-1858.
——— Partie supplémentaire. v. 33-36. nos. 1465-1596.
xiie série. Partie principale. v. 1. nos. 1-37.
——— Partie supplémentaire. v. 1. nos. 1-15.

——— *Cour de cassation.* Bulletin des arrêts de la cour de cassation rendus en matière criminelle, v. 71-74. Années 1866-69. Rédigé et publié sous la direction de m. Babinet, directeur des affaires criminelles et des grâces au ministère de la justice, par m. Émile Duchesne. 8°. *Paris, imprimerie impériale,* 1867-70.

Franckenstein (Gerard Jan Adolph Goll van). Specimen juridicum inaugurale, continens quaestiones quasdam e jure neerlandico, [etc.] 3 p. l. 43 pp. 8°. *Amstelaedami, apud Stakmans & Rijnders,* 1842.

Gaius. The commentarius of Gaius on the roman law. With english translation and annotations, by Frederick Tomkins and William George Lemon. 2 p. l. 771, xv pp. 8°. *London, Butterworths,* 1869.

Gardners (Ann, Mary, John, *and* Thomas) *et al.* In the house of lords. 1780. The respondents' case. *See* **Graham** (Marjory *and* Patrick) *v.* **Gardners.**

Gatteschi (Domenico). Manuale di diritto pubblico e privato ottomano. Seguito da un' appendice dei trattati ed atti diplomatici risguardanti l'Egitto e dei regolamenti in esso vigenti. Con introduzione e note. 8 p. l. lxxxii, 570 pp. 8°. *Alessandria di Egitto, V. Minasi & c.* 1865.

Gazzam (Audley W.) American and english bankruptcy digest and rules of practice in United States courts in bankruptcy. Compiled by A. W. Gazzam. v. 1. 4 p. l. 736 pp. 4°. *Albany, N. Y. W. C. Little & co.* 1871.

——— Gazzam's treatise on the bankrupt law. Containing all the amendments to the bankrupt act, and copious notes covering the latest english and american decisions report-

Gazzam (Audley W.)—continued. ed to June 1, 1871. 2d ed. 475 pp. 8°. *New York, G. T. Deller,* 1871.

——— The same. Reported to September 1, 1871. 3d ed. 8°. *Philadelphia, J. B. Lippincott & co.* 1871.

——— The same. Reported to October 1, 1871. 4th ed. 789 pp. 8°. *Albany, N. Y. W. C. Little & co.* 1872.

Georgia (*State of*). Public laws passed by the general assembly of the state of Georgia, at the sessions of 1870 and 1871, with an appendix containing the government of Georgia and court calendar, etc. 2 v. 8°. *Atlanta (Georgia),* 1870–71.

——— *See, also,* **Chisholm** (Alexander) *vs.* **Georgia.**

Georgia reports. Reports of cases in law and equity, argued and determined in the supreme court of Georgia, at Atlanta. June term, 1867, to January term, 1871. v. 36–42. By N. J. Hammond, reporter. 8°. *Macon, Georgia, J. W. Burke & co.* 1869–72.

Gioannis Gianquinto (Giovanni de). Principio giuridico fondamentale della legislazione sulle miniere. 620 pp. 8°. *Napoli, stabilimento tipografico dei fratelli de Angelis,* 1870. s.

Godefroi (Henry) *and* **Shortt** (John). The law of railway companies, comprising the companies clauses, the lands clauses, the railways clauses consolidation acts, the railway companies act, 1867 (with the general order and rules thereon,) and the regulation of railways act, 1868; with notes of all the cases decided on those acts, and an appendix containing all the other material acts relating to railways, and the standing orders of the houses of lords and commons. xli, 552, ccclxiv pp. 8°. *London, Stevens & Haynes,* 1869.

Gordon (Alexander). *See* **De Gex** (John P.) *and others. Also,* **Macnaghten** (Steuart), *and* **Gordon.**

Graham (Marjory *and* Patrick) *v.* **Gardners** (Ann, Mary, John, *and* Thomas) *et al.* In the house of lords. Marjory the wife of Patrick Graham, and the said Patrick for his interest, appellants. Ann, Mary, John, and Thomas Gardners, and Thomas Christie, respondents. To be heard, April 24th, 1780. The appellants case. 4 pp. fol. [*London*], 1780.

——— The same. The respondents case. 6 pp. fol. [*London*], 1780.

Grand (Le) coutumier de France. [Le grant coustumier de France et instruction de practique et maniere de proceder et practiquer es souveraines cours de parlement, prevoste et vicontc de Paris, et aultres iurisdictions du royaulme de France, nouvellement veu 1514. *anon.*] Nouv. éd. par Éd. Laboulaye, [et] R. Dareste. xlviii, 848 pp. 8°. *Paris, A. Durand & Pedone-Lauriel,* 1868.

Grant (Le) coustumier de France. 1514. *See* **Grand** (Le) coutumier de France. 1868.

Great Britain. Index to the statutes, at present in force in, or affecting Ireland, from the year 1310 to 1838, inclusive. Continued by annual supplements. By Andrew Newton Oulton. 2d ed. 2 p. l. 809 pp. 8°. *Dublin, Hodges & Smith,* 1839.

——— The same. Fourth [to thirteenth] annual supplements to the Index to the statutes, in force in or affecting Ireland; comprising [indices] to the statutes passed in the 2d [to 12th] Victoria [1839–49]; and continuation of the chronological table. By Andrew Newton Oulton. 2 p. l. 737 pp. 8°. *Dublin, Hodges & Smith,* 1839–49.

——— The statutes and parts of statutes relating to the law administered in magistrates' courts, etc. 1870. *See* **Magistrates'** statutes.

——— *Court of chancery. See* **Practice** (The) of the high court of chancery. *Also,* **De Gex** (J. P.), **Jones** (H. C.), *and* **Smith** (R. H.) Reports of cases heard and determined by the lord chancellor. 1862–65.

——— *Privy council: judicial committee.* Reports of cases, heard and determined. *See* **Moore** (Edmund F.)

——— *See, also,* **Law** reports.

Green (Charles Ewing). *See* **New Jersey** reports. Cases in chancery.

Greene (T. Whitcombe). An analysis and summary of the institutes of roman law. xvii, 101 pp. 16°. *London, Stevens & sons,* 1870.

Grotius *or* **Groot** (Hugo van). Le droit de prise (de jure praedae). Ouvrage entièrement inédit. Texte latin, publié pour la première fois d'après le manuscrit autographe par Ger. Hamaker. xvi, 359 pp. 8°. *La Haye, M. Nijhoff,* 1869.

Guerrand (J. *editor*). *See* **Recueil** de jurisprudence commerciale et maritime du Havre, 1869–70.

Gurney *and others.* A report of the case of the queen *v.* Gurney and others, in the court of queen's bench: (the summing up revised by the lord chief-justice) with an introduc-

Gurney *and others*—continued.
tion, containing a history of the case. By W. F. Finlason. xi, 270 pp. 8°. *London, Stevens & Haynes*, 1870.

Hammond (N. J.) Reports of cases in law and equity. *See* **Georgia** reports. Cases in the supreme court

Hampson (*Sir* George Francis). A short treatise endeavouring to point out the means by which those who accept the situation of trustees may perform their duties without incurring responsibility. xx, 130 pp. 8°. *London, A. Maxwell*, 1825.

Hannaman (William). Laws of Indiana, relating to her securities. *See* **Smith** (Francis) *and* **Hannaman.**

Hare (J. I. Clark) *and* **Wallace** (H. B.) American leading cases. Select decisions of american courts, in several departments of law. 5th ed. With additional notes by J. Clark Hare and H. B. Wallace. 2 v. 930 pp; 964 pp. 8°. *Philadelphia, T. & J. W. Johnson & co.* 1871.

Hare (Thomas). Reports of cases adjudged in the high court of chancery, before sir William Page Wood, with notes and references to english and american decisions by Ch. Francis Stone. v. 11. 8°. *New York, Banks & brothers*, 1871.
[English chancery reports, v. 45].

Harwood (R. G.) The charitable trust acts. *See* **Cooke** (Hugh) *and* **Harwood.**

Heiskell (Joseph B.) Reports of cases argued and determined in the supreme court of Tennessee, middle division, 1870–71. v. 2. 8°. *Nashville, Jones, Purvis & co.* 1871.

Hellfeld (Johann August). Dissertatio de fontibvs ivris, qvo illvstres vtvntvr. sm. 4°. [*Ienae*, 1743].
[*In* Struve (Burckhard Gotthelf). Ivrisprvdentia heroica, v. 1, pp. i–xxxx].

Henley (*Colonel* David). The proceedings of a general court-martial held at Cambridge, on the 20th of January; and continued to the 25th of February, 1778, upon the trial of colonel David Henley. 74, x pp. 8°. *Boston, J. Gill*, 1778.
[*Note.*—Imperfect: last leaves wanting].

Herman (Henry M.) The law of estoppel. xl, 622 pp. 8°. *Albany, W. C. Little & co.* 1871.

Hicks (W. J.) Addenda to the Tennessee manual of chancery practice. xiii, 308 pp. 8°. *Knoxville, Tenn.* 1871.

Hill (John Ward). A manual of the law of fixtures. 2d ed. 91 pp. 8°. *New York, Baker, Voorhis & co.* 1871.

Hinkley (Edward). Acts of the genera assembly of Maryland, on the subject of attachment against the property of non-resident and absconding debtors. With the late act to establish magistrates' courts, and the supplements thereto. Also, the entire index to the reports of the late general court, and of the court of appeals of this state on the same subject. To which is added, a summary of the principal matters contained therein. With an appendix of forms. vii, 111 pp. 8°. *Baltimore, J. S. Horton*, 1836.

Historical and legal examination of the decision of the supreme court in the Dred Scott case. *See* **Benton** (Thomas Hart).

Hoffmann (Christian Gottfried). Electa commentationis C. G. Hofmanni, de coemeteriis ex urbibus tollendis: quam publice defendit Chr. Frid. Graenen. 8°. *Francof.* 1729.
[*In* Perrenot (Abraham). Fasciculus primus exercitationum, pp. 161–197].

Holland (Thomas Erskine). Essays upon the form of the law. 4 p. l. 188 pp. 8°. *London, Butterworths*, 1870.

Holt (William). Admiralty court cases on the rule of the road, as laid down by the articles and regulations now in force under order in council for preventing collisions at sea. xviii, 265 pp. 8°. *London, W. Maxwell & son*, 1867.

Hook (Archibald). Major Hook's defence, to the action of criminal conversation, brought against him by capt. Charles Campbell, and tried at Westminster, 26th February, 1793. lxv, 112 pp. 8°. *London, J. Murray*, 1793.

Hopwood (Robert Gregge). Earl of Sefton *v.* Hopwood. *See* **Molyneux** (C. W. *earl of Sefton*) *v.* **Hopwood.**

Horne (John). *See* **Tooke** (John Horne).

Houston (John). A treatise on the law of stoppage in transitu, and incidentally of retention and delivery. xvi, 253 pp. 8°. *London, W. Maxwell*, 1866.

Howard (Nathan, *jr.*) Practice reports in the supreme court and court of appeals of the state of New York, [1867–71]. v. 40–42. 8°. *Albany, W. Gould & sons*, 1871.

Howells & Durham's annual register of lawyers, bankers, and real estate agents, throughout the United States and Canadas. 116 pp. 8°. *New York, Howells & Durham*, 1871.

Hubbell's legal directory for lawyers and business men, containing the names of one or more of the leading and most reliable at-

Hubbell's legal directory—continued. torneys in nearly three thousand cities and towns in the United States; also a synopsis of the collection laws of each state, with rules and instructions for taking depositions, the executions and acknowledgment of deeds, wills, etc. and times for holding courts throughout the United States and territories for 1871. J. H. Hubbell, compiler. 292, ix pp. 8°. *New York, J. H. Hubbell & co.* 1871.

Huc (Théophile). Le code civil italien et le code napoléon. Études de législation comparée. 2e éd. considérablement augmentée suivie d'une traduction complète du code civil italien annotée et augmentée d'une conférence de ses articles avec l'ancien code sarde et le code napoléon, par Joseph Orsier. 2 v. viii, 375 pp; 1 p. l. ix, 463 pp. 8°. *Paris, Cotillon,* 1868.

Humbert (G. H.) Du régime nuptial des Gaulois. 32 pp. 8°. *Paris, typographie Hennuyer,* 1858.

Hunt (Arthur Joseph). The law relating to boundaries and fences, and to the rights of property on the sea shore and in the beds of public rivers and other waters. 2d ed. xx, 330 pp. 12°. *London, Butterworths,* 1870.

Huntington (Samuel H.) Cases decided in the court of claims of the United States. v. 5–6. 1860–70. *See* **Nott** (Charles C) *and* **Huntington.**

Idaho (*Territory of*). Cases in the supreme court. 1866–1867. Reported by John Cummings. v. 1. 8°. *Boise city,* 1867.

Illinois. Reports of cases at law and in chancery argued and determined in the supreme court of Illinois. By Norman L Freeman. v. 51-53. 1869–1870. 8°. *Springfield,* 1871.

Illinois reports. Digest. *See* **Wood** (Charles H.) *and* **Long** (Joseph D.)

Indiana (*State of*). Laws of the state of Indiana, passed 1827–29, 31–34, 39–41, 49–53, 55, 58, 63, 65, 67, 69, 71. 17 v. 8°. *Indianapolis, state printers,* 1828–71.

——— Reports of cases in the supreme court of judicature of the state of Indiana. By James B. Black. 1869–1870. v. 32–33. 8°. *Indianapolis, Journal co.* 1871.

Ingram (Thomas Dunbar). Compensation to land and house owners: being a treatise on the law of compensation for interests in lands, &c. payable by railway and other public companies; with an appendix of forms and statutes. 2d ed. by J. J. Elmes. xxiii, 404 pp. 12°. *London, Butterworths,* 1869.

Innes (Alexander Taylor). The law of creeds in Scotland. A treatise on the legal relation of churches in Scotland, established and not established, to their doctrinal confessions. xv, 495 pp. 8°. *Edinburgh, W. Blackwood & sons,* 1867.

Iowa (*State of*). Acts and resolutions passed at the regular session of the eleventh general assembly. 8°. *Des Moines, F. W. Palmer, state printer,* 1866.

——— Digest of the decisions of the supreme court of Iowa. *See* **Lacy** (John F.)

——— Reports of cases in law and equity determined in the supreme court of the state of Iowa. v. 28–29. By Edward H. Stiles. v. 7–8. 8°. *Ottumwa, E. H. Stiles,* 1867–70.

Irish (The) reports, published under the control of the council of law reporting in Ireland: containing reports of cases argued and determined in the superior courts of Ireland. Common law series, v. 4. 1869–70. 8°. *Dublin, for the council, by E. Ponsonby,* 1871.

——— The same. Equity series, v. 4. 1869–70. 8°. *Dublin, for the council, by E. Ponsonby,* 1871.

Italy. [Code civil du royaume d'Italie]. Traduction complète du code civil italien, annotée et augmentée d'une conférence de ses articles avec l'ancien code sarde et le code napoléon, par Joseph Orsier. 1 p. l. ix, 463 pp. 8°. *Paris, Cotillon,* 1868.

[Huc (Théophile). Le code civil italien et le code napoléon, v. 2].

Jacob (Giles). The general laws of estates; or, freeholder's companion. With a full and compleat abstract of the new act of parliament concerning distresses for rent, replevins and ejectments, &c. and several other late popular statutes. Likewise some very useful precedents of deeds and writings, applicable to this work. viii, 402 pp. 14 l. 8°. [*London*] *in the Savoy, E. & R. Nutt & R. Gosling, for A. Ward,* 1740.

Jamaica (The) magistrate's and vestryman's assistant, containing a digest of all the laws of the island alphabetically arranged, from 33 Charles ii. to 8 George iv. [*anon.*] 2 p. l. 320 pp. 1 l. 8°. *Jamaica, office of the St. Jago de la Vega gazette,* 1828.

——— The same.

[With ms. index].

Jones (Arthur T.) A horse story, by an old gray horse, continued by Arthur T. Jones, including a narrative of all the proceedings in the case of the impeachment of John Orser, high sheriff of the city and county of New-York, with the decision of the governor of the

Jones (Arthur T.)—continued. state thereon, and the trial and conviction of deputy sheriff Thomas Carlin, for a misdemeanor. 4 p. l. 337 pp. 8°. *New York, G. F. Nesbitt & co.* 1856.

Jones (H. Cadman). *See* **De Gex** (John P.)

Journal du palais: recueil le plus ancien et le plus complet de la jurisprudence. 1869–70. 8°. *Paris, bureaux de l'administration,* [1869–70].

Justinianus (Flavius Anicius). Digestvm novvm. Tomus tertius iuris ciuilis, quod vulgo digestvm novvm appellant, ex fide vetustorum codicum diligenter emendatus, et ab Egidio Perrino scholiis illustratus: qui etiam glossas recognouit. 22 p. l. 400 l. fol. *Lugduni, apud Hugonem, et hæredes Aemonisa Porta,* 1540.

Kansas (*State of*). The laws of the state of Kansas, passed at the eleventh session of the legislature. 1871. 8°. *Topeka, (Kansas,) S. S. Prouty,* 1871.

——— Reports of cases argued and determined in the supreme court of the state of Kansas. [1869–70]. By Elliot V. Banks. v. 5. 8°. *Topeka, (Kansas,) S. S. Prouty,* 1871.

Keessel (Dionysius Godtfried van der). Select theses on the laws of Holland and Zeeland, being a commentary of Hugo Grotius' introduction to dutch jurisprudence, and intended to supply certain defects therein, and to determine some of the more celebrated controversies on the law of Holland. Translated from the original latin by Charles Ambrose Lorenz. 2d ed. With a biographical notice of the author by professor J. De Wal. xxxi, 374 pp. 16°. *Cape Town, J. C. Juta,* 1868.

Kendall (Edward Augustus). An argument for construing largely the right of an appellee of murder, to insist on trial by battle; and also for abolishing appeals. 2d ed. With an appendix, containing a report of a debate in the house of commons, on a clause for abolishing appeals of murder in the british north american colonies, etc. xix, 307 pp. 1 pl. 8°. *London, B. R. Howlett, for Baldwin, Cradock & Joy,* [*etc.*] 1818.

Kentucky reports. *See* **Bush** (W. P. D.)

Kerr (William Williamson). A treatise on the law and practice of injunctions in equity. With notes and references to american cases. By W. A. Herrick. lxi, 736 pp. 8°. *Boston, Little, Brown & co.* 1871.

Keyser (Henry). The law relating to transactions on the stock exchange. xxii, 335 pp. 16°. *London, H. Butterworth,* 1850.

King (*Colonel* William). Letter from the secretary of war [J. C. Calhoun], transmitting a copy of the proceedings of a court martial, for the trial of colonel William King, May 3, 1820. 128 pp. 8°. *Washington, Gales & Seaton,* 1820.

Kirwan (Thomas). A report of the trial of Thomas Kirwan, merchant, for a misdemeanor charged to be committed in violation of the convention act. By William Ridgeway. 1 p. l. 258 pp. 8°. *Dublin, C. P. Archer,* 1812.

[*With* A report of the proceedings in the cases of Thomas Kirwan and Edward Sheridan. 1811].

——— *and* **Sheridan** (Edward, *m. d.*) A report of the proceedings in the cases of Thomas Kirwan, merchant, and Edward Sheridan, m. d. for misdemeanors charged to be committed in violation of the convention act. By William Ridgeway. 293 pp. 8°. *Dublin, C. P. Archer,* 1811.

Kuhn (R. K.) Administrators account book, with instructions how to settle an estate. 48 pp. 16°. *Philadelphia, J. B. Lippincott & co.* 1871.

Ku-klux trial at Oxford, Miss. *See* **Lumpkin** (Benjamin), **Malone** (Thomas), *and others.*

Kyd (Stewart). A treatise on the law of bills of exchange and promissory notes. 2d american from 3d London ed. xii, 288 pp. 16°. *Albany, Thomas, Andrews & Penniman,* 1800.

Lacy (John F.) Digest of the decisions of the supreme court of Iowa. 1866–1869. By John F. Lacy. [v. 3]. 8°. *Chicago, Callaghan & Cockcroft,* 1871.

Lambard (William). Archeion, or, a discovrse vpon the high courts of ivstice in England. 6 p. l. 276 pp. 18°. *London, H. Seile,* 1635.

Lamé-Fleury (Ernest Jules Frédéric). Code annoté des chemins de fer en exploitation ou recueil méthodique et chronologique des lois, décrets, ordonnances, arrêtés, circulaires, etc. 2e éd. xvi, 1125 pp. 8°. *Paris, Guillaumin & cie.* 1868.

Lansing (Abraham). Reports of cases in the supreme court of the state of New York. [1870–1871]. v. 3. 8°. *New York, Banks & brothers,* 1871.

Law (The) journal reports for the year 1871. New series. v. 40. Parts 1, 2, and 3 in 3 v. 8°. *London, E. B. Ince,* 1871.

Law (The) list; [for 1872]. Compiled by William Henry Cousins. 16°. *London, Stevens & sons,* 1872.

Law (The) magazine and law review; or, quarterly journal of jurisprudence. September, 1870, to Aug. 1871. v. 30–31. 8°. *London, Butterworths,* 1871.

Law quibbles: or, a treatise of the evasions, tricks, turns and quibbles, commonly used in the profession of the law, to the prejudice of clients, and others [etc.] with abstracts of all the late statutes for amending the law, [etc.] and an essay on the amendment and reduction of the laws of England. [*anon.*] 4th ed. 3 parts in 1 v. 4 p. l. [339 pp.] 5 l. 8°. *London, E. & R. Nutt,* [*etc.*] *for A. Bettesworth & C. Hitch,* [*etc.*] 1736.

Law (The) reports. Chancery appeal cases, including bankruptcy and lunacy cases, before the lord chancellor, and the court of appeal in chancery. 1870-71. Edited by G. W. Hemming. v. 6. 8°. *London, W. Clowes & son,* 1871.

——— Court of common pleas. 1870-71. Reported by John Scott and Edmund Lumbey. Edited by J. R. Bulwer. v. 6. 8°. *London, W. Clowes & son,* 1871.

——— Court of exchequer. 1870-71. Reported by J. Anstie and A. Charles. Edited by J. R. Bulwer. v. 6. 8°. *London, W. Clowes & son,* 1871.

——— Court of queen's bench. 1870-71. Reported by W. Mills and H. Holroyd, and in the bail court, by Arthur Wilson. Edited by J. R. Bulwer. v. 6. 8°. *London, W. Clowes & son,* 1871.

——— Equity cases, including bankruptcy cases, before the master of the rolls, the vice chancellors, and the chief judge in bankruptcy. 1870-71. Edited by J. W. Hemming. v. 11-12. 8°. *London, W. Clowes & son,* 1871.

——— Privy council appeals. Cases heard and determined by the judicial committee and the lords of her majesty's most honourable privy council. 1869-71. Edited by E. F. Moore. v. 3. 8°. *London, W. Clowes & son,* 1871.

——— The public general statutes, passed in the thirty-fourth and thirty-fifth years of the reign of her majesty queen Victoria, 1871. With a list of the local and private acts, and a copious index. v. 6. 8°. *London, W. Clowes & son,* 1871.

Lawrence (A. R.) A compilation of the laws of the state of New York, relative to the assessment and collection of taxes in the city and county of New York. Compiled for the board of supervisors of the county of New York, by A. R. Lawrence, jr. iv, 188 pp. 12°. *New York, G. H. Clark,* 1859.

Le Barrois d'Orgeval (Robert). La propriété littéraire en France et à l'étranger; son histoire; sa législation: suivie des conventions internationales conclues jusqu'à ce jour avec les principaux états de l'Europe. 8°. *Paris, E. Dentu,* 1868.

LeBreton (André François). Pièces originales et procédures du procès, fait à Robert François Damiens. *See* **Damiens.**

Leclercq (Olivier). Le droit romain dans ses rapports avec le droit français et les principes des deux législations. 8 v. 8°. *Liége, Duvivier,* 1810-12.

Lee (Thomas). Cases in the court of king's bench, at Westminster in the 7th-10th years of George ii. 2d ed. corrected, by Thomas Lee. xvi, 416, 38 pp. 8°. *London, R. Pheney & S. Sweet,* 1815.

Legrand du Saulle (*Dr.* Henri). Étude médico-légale sur les assurances sur la vie: leçons professées à l'école pratique. 48 pp. 8°. *Paris, F. Savy,* 1867.

Lloyd (Eyre). The law of compensation under the lands clauses and railways clauses consolidation acts, the metropolis local management and other acts, &c. With a full collection of forms and precedents. 2d ed. xxiv, 408 pp. 8°. *London, Stevens & Haynes,* 1870.

Long (Joseph D.) Digest of Illinois reports. *See* **Wood** (Charles H.) *and* **Long.**

Lorimer (James). The rights and duties of belligerents and neutrals with reference to maritime commerce. 28 pp. 8°. *Edinburgh, Thomas Constable,* 1865.

Love (*Rev.* Christopher). A cleare and necessary vindication of the principles and practices of me, Christopher Love, since my tryall before, and condemnation by, the high court of justice. 2 p. l. 43 pp. 4°. *London,* 1651.

[*With* Love (Christopher). The whole triall of mr. Love].

——— The whole triall of mr. Love, before the high court of justice in Westminster hall. Containing the charge of high treason against him. With the relation of his suffering, and his speech and prayer at his death. 1 p. l. 128 pp. 4°. *London,* 1652.

[Imperfect: last leaves wanting].

Lumpkin (Benjamin), **Malone** (Thomas), *and others.* Full report of the great Ku-klux trial in the U. S. district court at Oxford, Miss. Reported by David M. Philp. 100 pp. 8°. *Memphis, W. J. Mansford,* 1871.

Lushington. *See* **Tichborne** *v.* **Lushington.**

Lutwyche (Alfred J. P.) Reports of cases argued and determined in the court of common pleas, on appeal from the decisions of the revising barristers, from Michaelmas term, 7 Vict. to [Michaelmas term, 17 Vict.] both inclusive. 2 v. 2 p. l. 639 pp ; viii, 284 pp. 8°. *London, W. Benning & co.* 1847–54.

Lutwyche (*Sir* Edward). The reports of the resolutions of the court on divers exceptions taken to pleadings, and other matters in law. 2 v. 6 p. l. 380 pp. 1 p. l. 381–710 pp. 40 l. 8°. *London, J. Walthoe & T. Ward*, 1718.

McCall (H. S.) Precedents, or practical forms in actions at law in the supreme court of the state of New York, the superior court and court of common pleas, for the city of New York, adapted to the code and rules of 1871, and to the practice of states having a similar code. 3d ed. 10, 547 pp. 8°. *New York, Banks & brothers*, 1871.

Macdonald (John H. A.) A practical treatise on the criminal law of Scotland. xv, 680 pp. 8°. *Edinburgh, W. Paterson*, 1867.

Macnaghten (Steuart) *and* **Gordon** (Alexander). Reports of cases argued and determined in the high court of chancery during the time of lord chancellor Cottenham. Edited by J. C. Perkins. v. 1–3. 1849–1851. 3 v. 8°. *Boston, Little, Brown & co.* 1871.

Magistrates' statutes. The statutes and parts of statutes relating to the law administered in magistrates' courts, and to parochial, municipal, and ecclesiastical law, enacted in the session of 1870. 2 p. l. 208 pp. 16°. *London, "Law Times" office*, 1870.

Maine (*State of*). The revised statutes of the state of Maine, passed January 25, 1871: to which are prefixed the constitutions of the United States and of the state of Maine: with an appendix. xi, 1273 pp. 4°. *Portland, Bailey & Noyes*, [1871].

Maine reports. Reports of cases in law and equity, determined by the supreme judicial court of Maine. By W. Wirt Virgin. [1870]. v. 58. 8°. *Portland, Loring, Short & Harmon*, 1871.

Manwood (John). A treatise and discovrse of the lawes of the forrest: wherin is declared not onely those lawes, as they are now in force, but also the originall and beginning of forrestes: and what a forrest is in his owne proper nature. Also a treatise of the purallee [purlieu]. 8 p. l. 168 l. numb. 61. sm. 4°. *London, T. Wight & B. Norton*, 1598.

Mapril (Athanase). Code-dictionnaire pratique de législation, de doctrine et de jurisprudence en matières civiles, judiciaires et administratives.—Code-mapril. 644, 59 pp. 8°. *Bordeaux, A. Bord*, 1868.

Marezoll (Gustav Ludwig Theodor). Lehrbuch der institutionen des römischen rechtes. 2e aufl. xvi, 432 pp. 8°. *Leipzig, J. A. Barth*, 1841.

Maritime law cases. Reports of the cases relating to maritime law, decided by the court of admiralty, and by all the superior courts of law and equity; salvage awards; and selection of cases decided in the courts of the United States, the consular courts, &c. From 1867 to 1871. v. 3. xx, 532 pp. 8°. *London, H. Cox*, 1871.

——— A digest of maritime law cases. *See* **Young** (Arthur).

Marshall (William) *vs.* **Cunningham, Dougal** *and* **co.** In the house of lords. William Marshall, of Glasgow, merchant, appellant. Messrs. Cunninghame, Dougal, and company, of Glasgow, merchants, respondents. The appellants case. To be heard, May 1780. 7 pp. fol. [*London*, 1780].

——— The same. The respondents case. 5 pp. fol. [*London*, 1780].

Maryland. Acts of the general assembly on the subject of attachment. 1836. *See* **Hinkley** (Edward).

——— The law and rules of the land office of Maryland. By John M. Brewer and Lewis Mayer. xv, 166 pp. 8°. *Baltimore, Kelly, Piet & co.* 1871.

——— Laws of Maryland, made and passed at sessions of assembly, begun and held at the city of Annapolis, 1785–92. 8 v. in 1. fol. *Annapolis, F. Green, printer to the state*, 1785–92.

——— Supplement to the Maryland code, containing the acts of the general assembly, passed at the session of 1870; arranged in articles and sections to correspond with the code. By J. I. Cohen and Thomas Rowland. 466 pp. 8°. *Baltimore, J. Murphy & co.* 1870.

Maryland reports, containing cases argued and determined in the court of appeals of Maryland. By Nicholas Brewer, reporter. October term, 1866. v. 26. 8°. *Annapolis, Brewer, Dubois & Button*, 1869.

——— The same. By J. Shaaff Stockett. 1868 and 1870–71. v. 29 and 33–34. 8°. *Baltimore, J. Murphy & co.* 1869–71.

Massachusetts (*State of*). Acts and resolves passed by the general court of Massachusetts, in the year 1871, together with the constitution, the messages of the governor, list of the civil government, changes of names of persons, etc. 876 pp. xxxviii. 8°. *Boston, Wright & Porter*, 1871.

——— A collection of acts and laws, passed in the state of Massachusetts-bay, relative to the american loyalists and their property. 35 pp. 8°. *London, J. Stockdale*, 1785.

Massachusetts reports. v. 102–103. April, 1869–Jan. 1870. Albert G. Browne, jr. reporter. 8°. *Boston, H. O. Houghton & co.* 1871.

——— *See, also,* **Allen** (Charles).

Mastin *v.* **Escott.** A full report of the case of Mastin *v.* Escott, clerk, for refusing to bury an infant baptized by a wesleyan minister; containing all the arguments on both sides, and the judgment delivered by sir Herbert Jenner in the arches court of Canterbury, May 8, 1841. By W. C. Curteis, ll. d. 3 p. l. 298 pp. 8°. *London, Crofts & Blenkarn*, 1841.

Matthews (James M.) Digest of the laws of Virginia of a criminal nature, illustrated by judicial decisions. To which is prefixed the new constitution of Virginia. 2d ed. 376 pp. 8°. *Richmond, Va. J. W. Randolph & English*, 1871.

——— A guide to commissioners in chancery, with practical forms for the discharge of their duties, adapted to the statute law of Virginia. 2d ed. xi, 254 pp. 8°. *Richmond, Va. J. W. Randolph & English*, 1871.

Matthews (Stanley). A summary of the law of partnership, for the use of business men. vi, 140 pp. 12°. *Cincinnati, R. Clarke & co.* 1864.

Michigan (*State of*). General acts and joint and concurrent resolutions of the legislature of the state of Michigan. 1871. 3 v. 8°. *Lansing, W. S. George & co.* 1871.

Michigan reports. Reports of cases determined in the supreme court of Michigan, from January 5 to October 21, 1870. Hovey K. Clarke, reporter. v. 2–3. Being v. 20–21 of the series. 8°. *Detroit, Richmonds & Backus*, 1871.

Minnesota (*State of*). General laws of the state of Minnesota, passed during the thirteenth session of the state legislature, commencing January 3d, 1871. 281 pp. 8°. *Saint Paul, Press printing company* 1871.

Minnesota reports. Reports of cases argued and determined in the supreme court of the state of Minnesota. v. 15. By Wm. A. Spencer. [1870]. 8°. *Saint Paul, W. S. Combs*, 1871.

Mississippi (*State of*). The revised code of the statute laws of the state of Mississippi, as adopted at January session, a. d. 1871. 788 pp. 4°. *Jackson, Alcorn & Fisher*, 1871.

Mississippi reports. v. 43. Being cases argued and decided in the supreme court of Mississippi. v. 1. By J. S. Morris. [1870–71]. 8°. *Jackson, Miss. Kimball, Raymond & co.* 1871.

Missouri (*State of*). Laws of the state of Missouri, passed at the regular [and] adjourned sessions of the general assembly, 1869–1871. 3 v. 8°. *Jefferson city*, 1869–71.

Missouri reports. Reports of cases argued and determined in the supreme court of Missouri. By Truman A. Post. 1869–1871. v. 45–47. 8°. *St. Louis, M'Kee, Fishback & co.* 1871.

Mitchell (John) *and* **Gay** (John) *v.* **Rodney** (*Sir* George Brydges) *and* **Vaughan** (John). In the house of lords. John Mitchell and John Gay, original plaintiffs, and plaintiffs in error. And sir George Brydges Rodney, bart. and the honourable John Vaughan, defendants. The plaintiffs' case. 6 pp. fol. [*London*], 1783.

——— The same. The case of the defendants. 3 pp. fol. [*London*], 1783.

Moak (Nathaniel C.) Reports of cases in the english courts. *See* **Reports.**

Molloy (*Captain* Anthony James Pye). Minutes of the proceedings at a court martial for [his] trial, as taken by M. Greetham, jr. 1 p. l. 184 pp. 8°. *London, J. Debrett*, 1795. [MISCELLANEOUS pamphlets, v. 201].

Molyneux (Charles William, 3*d earl of Sefton*) *v.* **Hopwood** (Robert Gregge). Earl of Sefton *v.* Hopwood. A report of the Hopwood will case. Tried at the South Lancashire spring-assizes, 1855; before mr. justice Cresswell and a special jury. Taken from the notes of messrs. Snell and Counsell, short-hand writers. 3 p. l. 534 pp. 4°. *Manchester, G. Simms*, 1855.

Moore (Edmund F.) Reports of cases heard and determined by the judicial committee and the lords of her majesty's privy council. 1863–65. (New series). v. 2. 8°. *London, Stevens & sons*, [1865]?

——— The same. 1870–1. (New series). v. 7. 8°. *London, Stevens & sons*, [1871]?

Moore (Edmund F.)—continued.
——— Reports of cases, heard and determined by the judicial committee and the lords of her majesty's privy council, on appeal from the sudder dewanny adawlut and high courts of judicature in the East Indies. 1867–9. v. 12. vii, 577 pp. 8°. *London, Stevens & sons*, [1870]?

Morin (Achille). Répertoire général et raisonné du droit criminel; où sont méthodiquement exposées la législation, la doctrine et la jurisprudence sur tout ce qui constitue le grand et le petit criminel en toutes matières et dans toutes les juridictions. 2 v. xvi, 839 pp; 2 p. l. 864 pp. 8°. *Paris, A. Durand*, 1850–51.

Mornacci (Antonio). Observationes in xxiv libros digestorvm, et in iv libros codicis. Ad vsvm fori gallici. 14 p. l. 1080 pp. 13 l. fol. *Parisiis, C. Besoigne*, 1647.

Morris (William O'Connor). An analytical summary of the law of easements. 51 pp. 16°. *Dublin, E. Ponsonby*, 1869.

Mosely (M. S.) A practical handybook of elementary law: designed for the use of articled clerks. With a course of study, and hints on reading, for the intermediate and final examinations. viii, 286 pp. 1 l. 16°. *London, Butterworths*, 1868.

Mylne (J. W.) *and* **Craig** (R. D.) Reports of cases argued and determined in the high court of chancery during the time of lord chancellor Cottenham. With notes and references to english and american decisions, by Ch. Francis Stone. v. 5. 8°. *New York, Banks & brothers*, 1871.
[ENGLISH chancery reports, v. 46].

National (The) bankruptcy register. Containing reports of the leading cases and principal rulings in bankruptcy, of the district judges of the United States. July, 1870, to July, 1871. v. 4. 4°. *New York, United States law association*, 1871.
[*With* BANKRUPTCY register, v. 3].
——— The same. The national bankruptcy register, containing full reports of all important bankruptcy decisions in the United States. Editors: A. W. Gazzam, H. C. Ulman, W. A. Shinn. v. 5. 8°. *New York, United States law association*, 1871.

Nevada (*State of*). Statutes of the state of Nevada, 1871. 231 pp. 8°. *Carson city, C. L. Perkins*, 1871.

Nevada reports. Reports of cases determined in the supreme court of Nevada during the year 1870. Reported by Alfred Helm, and

Nevada reports—continued.
Theodore H. Hittell. v. 6. 8°. *San Francisco, Bacon & co.* 1871.

New (The) american clerk's magazine, and complete practical conveyancer. With a variety of useful instruments of writing; with necessary instructions and forms of precedents. The whole selected from the laws, and draughts of actual practice. By a gentleman of the bar. [*anon.*] 527 pp. 34 l. 16°. *Hagers-town*, [*Md.*] *J. D. Dietrick*, 1806.

New Granada. Codigo de comercio (de 1° de junio de 1853). clxxx pp. 14 l. 8°. [*Bogotá*, 1853].
——— Lei sobre policia jeneral, espedida por el congreso de la Nueva Granada en sus sesiones de 1841. 24 pp. 1 l. 8°. *Bogota, imprenta del estado*, 1841.
——— Leyes i decretos espedidos por el congreso constitucional de la Nueva Granada en 1849, 1853–1857. Ed. oficial. 6 v. 8°. *Bogota, imprenta del estado*, 1857.

New Hampshire (*State of*). The general statutes of the state of New Hampshire; to which are prefixed the constitutions of the United States and of the state. With a glossary and digested index. xvii, 676 pp. 8°. *Manchester, J. B. Clarke*, 1867.
——— Laws of the state of New Hampshire, passed June sessions, 1869 and 1871. 2 v. 8°. *Manchester, J. B. Clarke*, 1869–71.

New Hampshire *vs.* **Belcher** (Jonathan). The (late) house of representatives of the province of New Hampshire, complainants. Jonathan Belcher, esq. governour of that province, respondent. [Case before the privy-council, Nov. 12th, 1739. Cause, the action of gov. Belcher with regard to the boundary commission to settle the limits of New Hampshire and Massachusetts, 1737–8]. 4 pp. sm. fol. [*London*, 1739].

New Jersey (*State of*). Acts of the 95th legislature, of the state of New Jersey, and 27th under the new constitution. 1685 pp. 8°. *Morristown, N. J. Vance & Stiles*, 1871.

New Jersey reports. Reports of cases argued and determined in the supreme court and the courts of errors and appeals of the state of New Jersey. Peter D. Vroom, reporter. v. 34. 8°. *Trenton, Nicholson & co.* 1871.
——— *Equity reports.* Reports of cases argued and determined in the court of chancery, the prerogative court, and, on appeal, in the courts of errors and appeals of the state of New Jersey. [v. 21]. Charles Ewing

New Jersey reports—continued. Green, reporter. v. 6. 8°. *Trenton, Murphy & Bechtel,* 1871.

Newman (John E.) A treatise on pleading and practice under the civil code of Kentucky. viii, 828 pp. 8°. *Louisville, J. P. Morton & co.* 1871.

New York (*State of*). The act authorizing the formation of corporations for manufacturing, mining, mechanical, chemical, agricultural, horticultural, medical or curative, mercantile or commercial purposes. To which are added notes, forms, and an index. 52 pp. 12°. *New York, Baker, Voorhis & co.* 1867.

——— Book of forms adapted to the code of procedure. [Fourth report of the commissioners of the code]. 2 p. l. 273 pp. 8°. *Albany, Weed, Parsons & co.* 1861.

——— The code of procedure of the state of New York, from 1848 to 1871. vi, 361 pp. 16°. *Albany, Banks & brothers,* 1870.

——— Draft of a penal code for the state of New York; prepared by the commissioners of the code. lv, 285 pp. 8°. *Albany, Weed, Parsons & co.* 1864.

——— Laws of the state of New York, passed at the sessions of the legislature, 1808, 1816 (1-2) and 1818. 4 v. in 3. 8°. *Albany, J. Buel, printer to the state,* 1808-17.

——— The political code of the state of New York. Reported complete by the commissioners of the code. 607 pp. 8°. *Albany, Weed, Parsons & co.* 1860.

——— The statutes of New York. With the decisions thereon, relating to limited partnerships, together with the statutes relating to compromises by partners and joint debtors, and to partnership names and signs; and the requisite forms. 30 pp. 8°. *New York, Baker, Voorhis & co.* 1871.

New York reports. Reports of cases argued and determined in the court of appeals. [1870-1871. v. 43-44]. With notes, references, and an index. By Samuel Hand. v. 4-5. 8°. *New York, Banks & brothers,* 1871.

Nixon (John T.) Forms of proceedings under the laws of New Jersey. 3d ed. Revised and conformed to the statutes as found in Nixon's digest. By James S. Aitkin, 1871. 507 pp. 8°. *Trenton, C. Scott,* 1871.

Nott (Charles C.) *and* **Huntington** (Samuel H.) Cases decided in the court of claims of the United States, 1869. v. 5. 8°. *New York, F. J. Huntington & co.* 1871.

——— The same. 1870, with the rules of practice and acts of congress relating to the court. v. 6. 8°. *Washington, government printing office,* 1871.

Ogden (David) *vs.* **Folliott** (George). In error. House of lords. Between David Ogden, plaintiff in error, and George Folliott, defendant in error. The case for the plaintiff in error. To be heard, 18th May, 1791. 11 pp. fol. [*London,* 1791].

——— The same. Case of the defendant in error. 11 pp. fol. [*London,* 1791].

Ohio (*State of*). General and local laws and joint resolutions, 1870-71. v. 67-68. 2 v. 8°. *Columbus, Nevins & Myers,* 1871.

Ohio state reports. Reports of cases argued and determined in the supreme court of Ohio. By Leander J. Critchfield. [1869]. New series. v. 19. 8°. *New York, Banks, & brothers,* 1871.

Ontario (*Canada*). Statutes of the province of Ontario. 1870. 1 p. l. 368, xviii pp. 8°. *Toronto, J. Notman,* 1871.

Orgeval. *See* **Le Barrois d'Orgeval.**

Orsier (Joseph). Traduction complète du code civil italien. 1868. *See* **Italy.**

Ortolan (Joseph Louis Elzéar). The history of roman law from the text of Ortolan's Histoire de la législation romaine et généralisation du droit (edition of 1870). Translated and supplemented by a chronometrical chart of roman history by Iltudus T. Prichard and David Nasmith. xxxii, 710 pp. 1 tab. 8°. *London, Butterworths,* 1871.

Oulton (Andrew Newton). Index to the statutes affecting Ireland. *See* **Great Britain.**

P. (W.) Studii legalis ratio. *See* **Phillips** (William).

Paley (William, *barrister*). Paley's law and practice of summary convictions by justices of the peace: including proceedings preliminary and subsequent to convictions, also the responsibility and indemnity of convicting magistrates and their officers. With practical forms and precedents of convictions. 5th ed. By H. T. J. Macnamara. lii, 759 pp. 8°. *London, H. Sweet,* 1866.

Pelletier (Victor). Jus canonicum universum 1864-70. *See* **Reiffenstuel** (Anaclet).

Pemberton (Loftus Leigh). The practice in equity by way of revivor and supplement. With forms of orders and appendix of bills. viii, 201 pp. 8°. *London, Stevens & Haynes,* 1867.

Pennsylvania (*State of*). Laws. 1871. 8°. *Harrisburg, B. Singerly,* 1871.

Pennsylvania state reports. Cases adjudged in the supreme court. v. 64–68. By P. Frazer Smith, state reporter. v. 14–18. Cases argued Oct. 1869, to May, 1871. 8°. *Philadelphia, Kay & brother*, 1871–72.

Perier (Louis Charles). De la capacité de la femme. Thèse pour le doctorat. 200 pp. 8°. *Paris, G. Retaux*, 1868.
[Superscribed "Faculté de droit de Paris"].

Perkins (John). A profitable booke. Treating of the lawes of England. 28 l. unp. 168 l. numb. 24°. *London, company of stationers*, 1621.

Perrin (L.) Code perrin, ou dictionnaire des constructions et de la contiguité. Législation complète des servitudes et du voisinage du soil bâti, cultivé ou planté. Édition entièrement refondue avec indications marginales par m. Ambroise Rendu. 3e éd. par Jean Sirey. viii, 821 pp. 8°. *Paris, Cosse, Marchal & ce.* 1870.

Petit (Samuel). Leges atticæ. Sam. Petitus collegit, digessit, et libro commentario illustravit. Cum animadversionibus Jac. Palmerii a Grentemesnil, A. M. Salvinii, & C. A. Dukeri, quibus suas & praefationem addidit Petrus Wesselingius. 1 p. l. xx, 680 pp. 9 l. fol. *Lugduni Batavorum, apud A. Kallewier, J. & H. Verbeek*, 1742.

Phayer (Thomas). A boke of presidentes exactlye written in maner of a register newly imprinted augmented and corrected with addicions of diuerse necessary and sundry presidentes meete for all such persons to knowe, as desire to learne the fourme and maner how to make all maner of euidentes and instrumentes. [*anon.*] *b. l.* 16 l. unp. 159 l. numb. 16°. *London, T. Marshe*, 1555.
[Imperfect: 2 l. preceding signature k. I. wanting].

Philadelphia (The) reports. Containing decisions published in the Legal intelligencer, during 1868–1870. By Henry E. Wallace. v. 7. 8°. *Philadelphia, Bourquin & Welsh*, 1871.

Phillimore (*Sir* Robert). Judgment delivered by the right hon. sir Robert Phillimore, official principal of the court of arches, in the cases of Martin *v.* Mackonochie and Flamank *v.* Simpson. Edited by Walter G. F. Phillimore. 2d ed. 120 pp. 8°. *London, Butterworths*, 1868.

Phillips (William). Studii legalis ratio, or, directions for the study of the law. 3d ed. corrected and enlarged, by W. P. [*anon.*] 6 p. l. 204 pp. 16°. *London, F. Kirkman & T. Dring*, 1675.

Pinnock (*Rev.* William Henry, *ll. d.*) The church key, belfry key, and organ key, with legal cases, and opinions, parish lay councils, and the autocracy of the clergy. 3 p. l. 158 pp. 8°. *Cambridge,* [*Eng.*] *J. Hall & son*, 1870.

Piotti (Giovanni Battista). Tractatvs de in litem ivrando, sive avrea, et solennis repetitio l. si qvando, c. vnde vi. 290 l. numb. 28 l. unp. 16°. *Venetiis, apud F. Franciscium*, 1570.

Plees (Les) del coron. *See* **Staunford** (*Sir* William).

Polhill (David), *and others*. [Case] on behalf of themselves, and other the proprietors of gold and silver mines in Jamaica. *See* **Wood** *vs.* **Polhill**.

Powell (Edmund). The principles and practice of the law of evidence. 3d ed. By John Cutler and Edmund Fuller Griffin. To which is added a supplement containing the evidence further amendment act, 1869; the documentary evidence act, 1868; the bankruptcy act, 1869; and the habitual criminals act, 1869; the alterations in the law of evidence effected by the above acts; together with the leading cases decided thereon since February, 1868. xxix, 659, 40 pp. 12°. *London, Butterworths*, 1869.

Practice (The) of the high court of chancery. With the nature of the several offices belonging to that court, and the reports of many cases wherein releif hath been there had, and where denyed; and known as "Choyce cases in chancery." Reprinted from the edition of 1672. [*anon.*] 5 p. l. 180 pp. 6 l. 8°. *London, Stevens & Haynes*, 1870.

Pratt (Daniel L.) A manual for the use of county clerks, sheriffs, etc. Re-arranged by Wm. Jennison. 76 pp. 16°. *Detroit, W. A. Thorp & co.* 1869.

Prinsep (Henry Thoby). The code of criminal procedure, (act xxv of 1861, and act viii of 1869) and other laws and rules of practice, relating to procedure in the criminal courts of british India. With notes, containing the opinions delivered by all the superior local courts. 3d ed. vi, 531 pp. 8°. *Calcutta, Thacker, Spink & co.* 1869.

Prynne (William). Antiquæ constitutiones regni Angliæ, sub regibus Joanne, Henrico tertio, et Edoardo primo, circa jurisdictionem et potestatem ecclesiasticam. [2a ed.] 47 p. l. 1–133 l. 117–1308 pp. fol. *Londini, impensis authoris*, 1672.
[*Note*—This is the third volume of "Prynne's records"].

Pulling (Alexander). A summary of the law and practice relating to attorneys, general and special. [etc.] 3d ed. xli, 565 pp. 8°. *London, V. & R. Stevens, sons, & Haynes*, 1862.

Pulton (Ferdinando). A collection of sundrie statutes, frequent in vse: [1224–1629], with notes in the margent. Together with an abbridgement of the residue which be expired, [etc.] Faithfully corrected, and now much enlarged. *b. l.* 3 p. l. 1464 pp. 42 l. fol. *London, M. Flesher*, 1632.

Purkis (H. Wakeham). The student's guide to Chitty on contracts, Williams on real property, and Smith's manual of equity, being a complete series of questions and answers thereon. 3 parts in 1 v. 8°. *London, W. Amer*, 1868.

Quebec (*Province of*). Statutes of the province of Quebec passed in the sessions 1870–1871. 2 v. 8°. *Quebec, C. F. Langlois*, 1871.

Ragobert (Marie Philippe Eugène Henri). [De l'adoption]. Thèse pour le doctorat. 196 pp. 8°. *Paris, Renou & Maulde*, 1868.
[Superscribed "Faculté de droit de Paris"].

Raimondi (Raffaello). Raphaelis cumani cōmentationes ac vigiliæ non dicendæ eruditionis ac doctrinæ in eius pandectar. partis primam [et secundam], (quam Infortiatum vulgus suo arbitrio magis, ac ratione, vocitat), vna cum periochis summariisve, insigni ac multiplici etiam repertorio instructæ, optimo sane auspicio, nūc tandē variis, cum prelectionibus, tum etiam quamplurimarū legū, ac paragraph. repetitionibus additionibusque adauctae in hominū manus abeunt. 2 v. in 1. 165 l; 150 l. fol. *Lugduni, apud Hugonem, et haeredes Aemonis a Porta*, 1544.

——— Raphaelis cumani in eivs pandectarum partis primam, quæ vulgi censura digesti noui appellatione differtur, prælectiones, cum doctae ac luculentae, tum mirum in modum vtiles ac necessariæ, argumentis insuper fulgore incredibili splendidis nitentibusque, tum denique repertorio perquam facili collustratæ, de prelo nunc demum natæ in publicum exeunt. 176 l. fol. *Lugduni, apud Hugonem, et haeredes Aemonis a Porta*, 1544.
[*With his* Cōmentationes ac vigiliæ. Imperfect: ll. 134–176, damaged].

Ram (James). The science of legal judgment. A treatise designed to show the materials whereof, and the process by which, courts construct their judgments; and adapted to practical and general use in the discussion and determination of questions of

Ram (James)—continued.
law. With extensive additions and annotations by John Townshend. 456 pp. 8°. *New York, Baker, Voorhis & co.* 1871.

Raphael *cumanus*. *See* **Raimondi** (Raffaello).

Rastell (John). [The exposicions of the termes of the lawes of England, with diuers proper rules and principles of the lawe, as well out of the bookes of maister Littleton, as of other. Gathered both in french and english, for yongmen very necessary. Whereunto are added the olde tenures]. 138 l. sm. 8°. *London, Rycharde Tottyl*, 1572.
[*Note.*—Imperfect: title-page and prologue of 2 l. wanting. French and english, in black letter and roman type in two columns on a page. This work is ascribed by some bibliographers to William Rastell, but the weight of evidence is in favor of the father, John Rastell. It is a translation of the latin edition of 1527, "Expositiones terminorū legum anglorū"].

Ray (Isaac, *m. d.*) A treatise on the medical jurisprudence of insanity. 5th ed. xv, 658 pp. 8°. *Boston, Little, Brown & co.* 1871.

Recueil de jurisprudence commerciale et maritime du Havre, par J. Guerrand, avocat. v. 15–16. 1869–70. 2 v. 8°. *Havre, G. Cazavan & ce.* 1869–70.

Recueil général des lois et des arrêts en matière civile, criminelle, administrative et de droit public; fondé par J.-B. Sirey. 1869–70. 4°. *Paris, bureaux de l'administration du Recueil*, [1869–70].

Redfield (Isaac Fletcher, *ll. d.*) The law of wills: part 2–3. The probate of wills, the duties of executors, administrators, and other testamentary trustees, and the settlement and distribution of estates, with the law of trusts. 2d ed. 2 v. 8°. *Boston, Little, Brown & co.* 1870.

——— *and* **Bigelow** (Melville M.) Leading and select american cases in the law of bills of exchange, promissory notes and checks: arranged according to subjects. With notes and references. lxiii, 760 pp. 8°. *Boston, Little, Brown & co.* 1871.

Reid (Patrick) *et al. v.* **Coats** (Archibald *and* John). In the house of lords. Messrs. Patrick Reid, David King, and company, merchants in New York; James Wilson and company, merchants in Kilmarnock; and James Wilson and sons, merchants there, appellants. Archibald and John Coats, merchants in Glasgow, respondents. The respondents' case. 3 pp. fol. [*London*], 1794.

Reiffenstuel (Anaclet). Jus canonicum universum, complectens tractatum de regulis juris auctore r. p. f. Anacleto Reiffenstuel. Juxta novissimam romanam editionem, innumeris expurgatis mendis, recusum accurante r. d. Clodovæo Bolard. Cui nunc primum accedunt variæ adnotationes pro quarumdam quæstionum uberiori enodatione digestæ studio et opera r. d. Victoris Pelletier. 7 v. 8°. *Parisiis, apud L. Vivès*, 1864–70.

Reports of cases decided by the english courts. With notes and references to kindred cases and authorities. By Nathaniel C. Moak. v. 1. [1872]. 8°. *Albany, W. Gould & sons*, 1872.

Reports of the cases relating to maritime law. *See* **Maritime** law cases.

Revue critique de législation et de jurisprudence. 19e année. v. 34. 8°. *Paris, Cotillon*, 1869.

Revue de législation ancienne & moderne, française et étrangère, publiée sous la direction de Edouard Laboulaye, [etc. v. 1]. Année 1870. 8°. *Paris, E. Thorin*, 1870.

Rhode Island reports. Reports of cases argued and determined in the supreme court of Rhode Island. By S. Ames, J. P. Knowles, C. S. Bradley, reporters. 1864–67. v. 8. 8°. *Providence, Hammond, Angell & co.* 1871.

Rocco (Francesco). A manual of maritime law. Consisting of a treatise on ships and freight and a treatise on insurance. Translated from the latin. With notes by Joseph Reed Ingersoll. 156 pp. 4 l. 8°. *Philadelphia, Hopkins & Earle*, 1809.

Rochefort-Luçay (Victor Henri *le comte* de). Rochefort devant les tribunaux. Affaire civil. Affaires correctionnelles. Plaidoiries. Jugement et arrêt. Affaires de la Lanterne. 95 pp. 8°. *Paris, libraire centrale*, 1868.

Ruggles (Thomas). The barrister: or, strictures on the education proper for the bar. 2d ed. corrected. xv, 269 pp. 12°. *London, W. Clarke & sons*, 1818.

Russell (James). Reports of cases argued and determined in the high court of chancery, during the time of lord chancellor Eldon. With notes and references to english and american decisions, by Ch. Francis Stone. v. 1. 8°. *New York, Banks & brothers*, 1871.
[English chancery reports, v. 46].

Sandford (Lewis H.) Reports of cases argued and determined in the court of chancery of the state of New York, before the hon. Lewis H. Sandford. New ed. by Daniel Ketchum. [Aug. 1844–Aug. 1847]. v. 2–4. 8°. *New York, Banks & brothers*, 1871.

Sardinia (*Kingdom of*). Leggi e regolamenti marittimi di s. m. il re di Sardegna. 228 pp. 8°. *Torino, G. Favale*, 1827.

Sarsfield (Dalmacio Velez). Código civil de la república argentina. 1870. *See* **Argentine** republic.

Sawyer (Frederick William). The merchant's and shipmaster's guide, in relation to their rights, duties, and liabilities. 2d ed. 400 pp. 2 pl. 12°. *Boston, B. Loring & co.* 1841.

Scriven (John). A treatise on copyhold, customary freehold & ancient demesne tenure; with the jurisdiction of courts baron and courts leet. 5th ed. Embracing all the authorities to the present period, and containing references to cases and acts of parliament to the present time. By Henry Stalman. lii, 579 pp. 8°. *London, Butterworths*, 1867.

Selwyn (William). Selwyn's abridgment of the law of nisi prius. 13th ed. By David Keane and Charles T. Smith. 2 v. ci, 756 pp; x, 757–1455 pp. 8°. *London, Stevens & sons*, 1869.

Shand (Charles Farquhar). Digest of the court of session act, (29 July, 1850,) with an appendix, containing the statute; digest of decisions on points of practice, and acts of sederunt, since the publication of the "Practice of the court of sessions," in 1848. 2 p. l. 25, lxxxix, 4 pp. 8°. *Edinburgh, T. & T. Clark*, 1850.
[*With his* Practice of the court of session. *Edinburgh*, 1848].

——— The practice of the court of session, on the basis of the late mr. Darling's work of 1833. 2 v. xxxv, 534 pp; 1 p. l. 535–1154 pp. 1 l. 8°. *Edinburgh, T. & T. Clark*, 1848.

Shankland (James H.) Public statutes of Tennessee, a supplement to the code. *See* **Tennessee**.

Shaw (Joseph). Parish law: or, a guide to justices of the peace, ministers, churchwardens, overseers of the poor, constables, surveyors of the highways, vestry-clerks, and all others concerned in parish business. 2d ed. with considerable improvements. 3 p. l. 380 pp. 10 l. 8°. *In the Savoy*, [*London*], *E. & R. Nutt*, [*etc.*] 1734.

Sheridan (Edward, *m. d.*) A report of the proceedings in the cases of Thomas Kirwan and Edward Sheridan. *See* **Kirwan** (Thomas) *and* **Sheridan**.

Shortt (John, *ll. b.*) The law relating to works of literature and art: embracing the law of copyright, the law relating to newspapers, to contracts between authors, publishers, print-

Shortt (John, *ll. b.*)—continued. ers, &c. and the law of libel. xxxii, 780 pp. 8°. *London, H. Cox*, 1871.

——— The law of railway companies. *See* **Godefroi** (Henry) *and* **Shortt.**

Smith (Francis), *and* **Hannaman**, (William), *brokers*. Laws of Indiana, relating to her securities. 9 l. 18°. *New York, E. H. Coffin*, 1871.

Smith (George J. P.) Reports of cases in the court of queen's bench. *See* **Best** (William M.) *and* **Smith.**

Smith (John William). A compendium of mercantile law. 8th ed. By George Morley Dowdeswell. lviii, 698, cccxxviii pp. 8°. *London, Stevens & sons*, 1871.

Smith (Josiah W.) A manual of common law; comprising the fundamental principles and the points most usually occurring in daily life and practice. First am. from the fourth London ed. with notes and references. By Edward Chase Ingersoll. xxx, 591 pp. 12°. *Washington city, W. H. & O. H. Morrison*, 1871.

Smith (William). A treatise on the duties and office of a receiver under the high court of chancery in Ireland, embracing also certain portions of the law of landlord and tenant. With an appendix of forms and a supplement containing the general orders, dated the 10th day of October, 1836, relating to this subject. 3d ed. xv, 272 pp. 8°. *Dublin, Milliken & son*, 1836.

South Carolina. Acts and joint resolutions of 1870–71. 8°. *Columbia, S. C. Republican printing co.* 1871.

South Carolina reports. Reports of cases heard and determined by the supreme court of South Carolina. November term, 1868, to November term, 1869, inclusive. By J. S. G. Richardson. v. 1. 8°. *Columbia, S. C. Republican printing co.* 1871.

Spain. Coleccion legislativa de España. 1869–70. 8 v. 8°. *Madrid, imprenta del ministerio de gracia y justicia*, 1869–71.

CONTENTS.

[Continuacion de la coleccion de decretos]. v. 101–105. Primer semestre de 1869–segundo semestre de 1870. 5 v. 1869–71.

Sentencias del tribunal supremo de justicia, en sus salas primera y segunda. Recursos de casacion y de injusticia notoria, y decisiones de competencias. Primer–segundo semestre de 1869. 2 v. 1870.

Sentencias del tribunal supremo de justicia en su sala tercera. Recursos contra la administracion. Año de 1869–71.

Spangenberg (Ernst Peter Johannes). Beyträge zu den teutschen rechten des mittelalters, vorzüglich zur kunde und kritik der altgermanischen rechtsbücher, und des sachsen- und schwaben-spiegels. Grösstentheils aus unbenutzten handschriftlichen quellen geschöpft. xii, 234 pp. 12 pl. 4°. *Halle, in der gebauerschen buchhandlung*, 1822.

——— Einleitung in das römisch-justinianeische rechtsbuch oder Corpus juris civilis romani. 1 v. in 2 v. xvi, 960 pp. 8°. *Hannover, bey den brüdern Hahn*, 1817.

[An interleaved copy].

Spencer (Thomas). The new vade mecum; or, young clerk's magazine: digested and improved to correspond with the laws of the state of New-York in particular, and the United States in general. [Also], a collection of forms of writs, &c. most common in use in the supreme court of the state of New-York. 1st ed. 346 pp. 16°. *Lansingburgh, S. Tiffany, for T. Spencer*, 1794.

Spencer (William A.) Reports. *See* **Minnesota** reports, v. 15.

Stacey (John, *the younger*, and John, *the elder*). Report of the trial of [accused] for the murder of mr. Samuel Langtrey and Charity Jolliffe, his housekeeper, on sunday the 1st of March, 1829, at Portsmouth: before the hon. sir James Burrough, at the Hants summer assizes, July 30, 1829. Taken in short hand. 32 pp. 2 portraits. 16°. *Winchester*, [*Eng.*] *Robbins & Wheeler*, [1829].

Starkie (Thomas). A treatise on the law of slander and libel, and incidentally of malicious prosecutions. From the 2d english ed. of 1830. With notes and references to american cases and to english decisions since 1830. By John L. Wendell. 2 v. 46, clxii, 494 pp; iv, 451 pp. 8°. *Hartford, Conn. J. L. Wendell*, 1858.

——— The same. Starkie's treatise on the law of slander and libel: including the pleading and evidence, civil and criminal, with forms and precedents: also malicious prosecutions, contempts of court, etc. 3d ed. By Henry Coleman Folkard. xliii, 876 pp. 8°. *London, Butterworths*, 1869.

Staunford (*Sir* William). An exposicion of the kinges prerogatiue collected out of the great abridgement of iustice Fitzherbert and other olde writers of the lawes of Englande. Whereunto is annexed the proces to the same prerogatiue appertaining. 1567. [1st ed.] *b. l.* 1 p. l. 85 p. l. sm. 4°. *London, Rychard Tottel*, 1567.

[*With his* Plees del coron, ed. 1557].

——— Les plees del coron: diuisees in plusiours titles & common lieux. Per queux home

Staunford (*Sir* William)—continued.
plus redement & plenairement, trouera quelq; chose que il quira touchant lez ditz pleez composees lan du grace 1557. [*anon.* 1st ed.] *b. l.* 4 p. l. unp. 198 l. pag. sm. 4°. *London, in aedibus Richardi Tottelli,* 1557.

Stephen (Henry John). A treatise on the principles of pleading in civil actions: comprising a summary view of the whole proceedings in a suit at law. From the 2d London ed. By Samuel Tyler, ll. d. xviii, 398, xciv pp. 8°. *Washington, (D. C.) W. O. & O. H. Morrison,* 1871.

Stockett (J. Shaaff). Reports of cases, etc. *See* **Maryland** reports, v. 29, 33-34.

Stone (Ch. Francis). *See* **English** chancery reports.

Story (William Wetmore). A treatise on the law of sales of personal property, with illustrations from the foreign law. 4th ed. By Edmund H. Bennett. lxxxii, 677 pp. 8°. *Boston, Little, Brown & co.* 1871.

Struve (Burckhard Gotthelf). Ivrisprvdentia heroica sev ivs qvo illvstres vtvntvr privatvm. Qvod ex avtoris schedis edidit simvlqve de fontibvs ivris qvo illvstres vtvntvr praefatvs est Io. Avgvstvs Hellefeld. 7 v. 4°. *Ienae, apud I. A. Melchior,* 1743-1753.

Sutherland (James) *vs.* **Murray** (*General* James). The trial in the court of exchequer, before lord chief baron Skinner, at Guildhall, on wednesday the 23d of July, [1783]. Wherein James Sutherland, esq. late judge of the admiralty at Minorca, was plaintiff, and the hon. general James Murray, late governor of that island, was defendant. Taken in short hand by mr. Blanchard. 28 pp. fol. [*London*], *G. Kearsley,* 1783.

Swabey (M. C. Merttins) *and* **Tristram** (Thomas Hutchinson). Reports of cases decided in the court of probate and in the court for divorce and matrimonial causes. With a supplement by T. H. Tristram. v. 4 From Hil. t. 1865 to Trin. t. 1865, and cases in supplement from Hil. t. 1858 to Trin. t. 1863. xi, 298 pp. 8°. *London, Butterworths,* 1871.

Swan (Joseph R.) A treatise on the law relating to the powers and duties of justices of the peace and constables, in the state of Ohio. 9th ed. xxix, 772 pp. 8°. *Cincinnati, R. Clarke & co.* 1871.

Sweeny (James M.) Reports of cases in the superior court of the city of New York. [1869-1870]. v. 2. 8°. *New York, Banks & brothers,* 1871.

Syms (Frederick Richard). A code of english law (principles and practice) for handy reference in a solicitor's office. xxi, 417 pp. 1 l. 16°. *London, Stevens & sons,* 1870.

Talbot *v.* **Talbot.** A report of the judgment of the high court of delegates, delivered on June 14, 1855. 8°. [*London, T. Blenkarn,* 1855].

[*In* PAGET (John). Talbot *v.* Talbot. A letter to the hon. justice Torrens. *London,* 1855. pp. 41-56].

Taney (Roger Brooke). Reports of admiralty cases in the district of Maryland. 1836-61. *See* **Campbell** (James Mason).

Tarrant (Henry Jefferd). Lloyd's bonds: their nature and uses. 18 pp. 1 l. 8°. *London, Stevens & Haynes,* 1867.

Tayler (George). The law of appeals to the superior courts of law by appeal case. xxviii, 270 pp. 16°. *London, H. Cox,* 1865.

Tennessee (*State of*). Acts of the state of Tennessee, passed by the first session of the 37th general assembly for the year 1871. 257 pp. 8°. *Nashville, Jones, Purvis & co.* 1871.

——— A compilation of the statute laws of the state of Tennessee. Of a general and permanent nature, compiled on the basis of the code of Tennessee, with notes and refer-ces, including acts of session of 1870-71. By Seymour D. Thompson and Thomas M. Steger. v. 1-3. 8°. *St. Louis, Mo. W. J. Gilbert,* 1871-72.

——— Public statutes of the state of Tennessee, since the year 1858. Being in the nature of a supplement to the code. Edited by James H. Shankland. xcv, 286 pp. 8°. *Nashville, Paul & Tavel,* 1871.

Tennessee reports. Reports of cases in the highest courts of law and equity of the state of Tennessee. New ed. from Overton to Meigs. [1821-1828. By William Frierson Cooper]. v. 4. 8°. *St. Louis, Soule, Thomas & Winsor,* 1871.

Texas (*State of*). Laws, 1870. 8°. *Austin, Tracy, Siemering & co.* 1870.

Texas reports. Reports of cases argued and decided in the supreme court. 1869-1870. By E. M. Wheelock. v. 32. 8°. *Galveston, Richard, son, Belo & co.* 1871.

Theloall (Simon). Le digest des briefes originals, et des choses concernants eux. 8 p. l. unp. 424 l. numb. 12°. *Londini, Richardus Tottellus,* 1579.

[*Note.*—With manuscript notes by sir John Savile].

Thomas (Sidney). Outlines of practice in the supreme court of the state of Illinois. 149 pp. 8°. *Chicago, Spalding & Lamonte,* 1871.

Thompson (Isaac Grant). The supervisor's manual. 2d ed. viii, 292 pp. 8°. *Albany, J. D. Parsons, jr.* 1869.

Thompson (Seymour D.) *and* **Steger** (Thomas M.) A compilation of the state laws of Tennessee. v. 1-3. *See* **Tennessee.**

Tichborne *v.* **Lushington.** The Tichborne romance: a full and accurate report of the proceedings in the extraordinary and interesting trial of Tichborne *v.* Lushington, in the court of common pleas, Westminster, for forty days, from wednesday, May 10, to friday, July 7, 1871; including the whole of the examination, cross-examination, and re-examination of the claimant. 2d ed. with addendum. 440 pp. 8°. *Manchester,* [*Eng.*] *J. Heywood,* [1871].

Tissot (Joseph). Le mariage, la séparation et le divorce, considérés aux points de vue du droit naturel, du droit civil, du droit ecclésiastique et de la morale, suivis d'une étude sur le mariage civil des prêtres. xvi, 352 pp. 8°. *Paris, Marescq aîné,* 1868.

Tompson (George). The tradesman's law library: consisting of familiar treatises on the laws which tradesmen in general, for their governance in the ordinary affairs of business, ought to be conversant with, or have an opportunity of immediate referring to, as occasions may arise. vi, 1024 pp. 8°. *London, for the author,* 1830.

Tooke (John Horne). In the house of lords. Between John Horne, clerk, plaintiff in error, and our sovereign lord the king, defendant in error. Case of the crown. To be heard at the bar of the house of lords, 8th April, 1778. 3 pp. fol. [*London,* 1778].

——— John Horne, plaintiff in error, and our sovereign lord the king, defendant. Upon a judgment, in the court of king's-bench, on an information for several libels. The case of the plaintiff in error. 3 pp. fol. [*London,* 1778].

Townsend (Calvin). A compendium of commercial law. xx, 587 pp. 8°. *New York, Ivison, Blakeman, Taylor & co.* 1871.

Townshend (John). The law and practice on proceedings by landlords to recover possession of demised premises, on the non-payment of rent or expiration of the term. With an appendix of forms. 214 pp. 12°. *New York, J. S. Voorhis,* 1862.

Treatise (A) of the nobilitie of the realme. *See* **Bird** (William).

Tristram (Thomas Hutchinson). Reports of cases decided in the court of probate and in the court for divorce and matrimonial causes. *London,* 1871. *See* **Swabey** (M. C. Merttins) *and* **Tristram.**

Tyrie (David). The trial of David Tyrie, for high treason, at the assize at Winchester, on saturday, August the 10th, 1782, before the hon. John Heath, esq. one of the justices of his majesty's court of common pleas. Taken in short-hand, by Joseph Gurney. 24 pp. 1 portrait. fol. *London, J. Gurney,* [1782].

United States. The statutes at large and proclamations of the United States of America, from December, 1869, to March, 1871. Edited by George P. Sanger. v. 16. 8°. *Boston, Little, Brown & co.* 1871.

——— *Court of claims.* Revised rules of practice of the court of claims of the United States: the acts of congress establishing the court, and in amendment thereof. 41 pp. 8°. *Washington, government printing office,* 1871.

——— ——— Cases decided, 1869-70. *See* **Nott** (Charles C.) *and* **Huntington** (Samuel H.)

——— *Supreme court.* Rules of the supreme court of the United States, and rules of practice for the circuit and district courts of the United States in equity and admiralty cases. Revised and corrected at December term, 1870. 109 pp. 12°. *Washington, government printing office,* 1871.

United States digest; [v. 28-29] containing a digest of decisions of the courts of common law, equity and admiralty, in the United States and in England. By B. F. Burnham. Annual digest. 1868-1869. v. 22-23. 8°. *Boston, Little, Brown & co.* 1871.

Van Wetter (Polynice, *ll. d.*) Traité de la possession en droit romain. 3 p. l. 305 pp. 1 l. 8°. *Gand, H. Hoste,* 1868.

Van Wetter (P. A. H.) Droit d'accroissement entre colégataires. 434 pp. 8°. *Bruxelles, T. Lesigne,* 1866.

[*Note.*—Superscribed "Concours universitaire de 1864-65. Question de droit romain. Mémoire couronné].

Velez Sarsfield (Dalmacio). *See* **Argentine** republic.

Vermont (*State of*). Acts and resolves, 1870. 648 pp. 8°. *Montpelier, J. & J. M. Poland,* 1870.

——— The general statutes of the state of Vermont: [to 1862]. 2d ed. With an appendix comprising the public laws enacted since 1862. xiv, 1352 pp. 8°. *Cambridge,* [*Mass.*] *H. O. Houghton, printer,* 1870.

Vermont reports. Reports of cases argued and determined in the supreme court of the state of Vermont. By Wheelock G. Veazey. v. 43. New series, v. 8. 8°. *Montpelier, J. & J. M. Poland*, 1871.

Victoria (*Australia*). Acts of parliament of Victoria. 25, 26 & 27 Victoria, 1861–63. 2 v. in 1. fol. *Melbourne, J. Ferres*, 1862–3. s.

Vinton (Francis, *d. d.*) A manual commentary of the general canon law and the constitution of the protestant episcopal church in the United States. viii, 223 pp. 8°. *New York, E. P. Dutton & co.* 1870.

Virgin (William Wirt). Maine civil officer: a guide for justices of the peace, trial justices, sheriffs and their deputies, coroners and constables. With an appendix. 2d ed. xxxii, 612 pp. 12°. *Portland, Loring, Short & Harmon*, 1871.

——— Reports. *See* **Maine**. Reports, v. 58.

Virginia (*State of*). Acts and joint resolutions, 1870–71. 452 pp. 8°. *Richmond, C. A. Schaffter*, 1871.

——— Digest of the criminal laws of Virginia. 1871. *See* **Matthews** (James M.)

Wait (William). The code of procedure of the state of New York, as amended to 1870, with constitutional amendment, and statutes relative to the courts, and other statutes, and a full index. 4 p. l. xxi, 264 pp. 12°. *Albany, W. Gould & son*, 1870.

——— The same. As amended to 1871, with notes on practice, pleadings and evidence; rules of the courts, fully annotated; a complete table of cases, and a full index. lviii, 975 pp. 8°. *Albany, W. Gould & sons*, 1871.

Wales. Leges wallicae. *See* **Wotton** (William, *and* M. W.)

Walker (J. Bryant). The law of municipal corporations in the state of Ohio, embracing all the statutes in force July, 1871, with notes on the supreme and other courts of the state relating thereto. viii, 386 pp. 8°. *Cincinnati, R. Clarke & co.* 1871.

Wallace (Horace Binney). American leading cases. *See* **Hare** (J. I. C.) *and* **Wallace**.

Wallace (John Bradford). Remarks upon the law of bailment. [Originally published in the American jurist]. 39 pp. 8°. [*Philadelphia*, 1840].

Wallace (John William). Cases argued and adjudged in the supreme court of the United States, Dec. terms, 1869 and 1870. v. 10–11. 8°. *Washington, D. C. W. H. & O. H. Morrison*, 1871.

Wallace (John William)—continued.

——— Cases in the circuit court of the United States, for the third circuit [1854–1862]. v. 3. 8°. *Philadelphia, T. & J. W. Johnson & co.* 1871.

Washburn (Emory, *ll. d.*) Lectures on the study and practice of the law. xii, 318 pp. 8°. *Boston, Little, Brown & co.* 1871.

Washington (*D. C. City of*). The laws, digested and arranged. 1868. *See* **Webb** (William B.)

Washington (*Territory of*). Statutes of the territory of Washington: being the code passed by the legislative assembly, at their first session, held at Olympia, February 27, 1854, [etc.] 488 pp. 1 l. lxviii pp. 8°. *Olympia, G. B. Goudy*, 1855.

Waterhouse (Edward). Fortescutus illustratus, or a commentary on that nervous treatise, De laudibus legum Angliæ, written by sir John Fortescue. 10 p. l. 594 pp. 3 l. 2 portraits. fol. *London, T. Dicas*, 1663.

Watkins (Charles). A treatise on copyholds. 2d ed. corrected and much enlarged: and further augmented, with notes of all the more recently adjudged cases, by Robert Studley Vidal. [With] an appendix of manorial customs, &c. 2 v. xxviii, 570 pp; xiv, 451 pp. 8°. *London, W. Clarke & sons*, 1816.

Webb (William B.) The laws of the corporation of the city of Washington, digested and arranged under appropriate heads in accordance with a joint resolution of the city councils, together with an appendix containing a digest of the charter and other acts of congress concerning the city. vii, 649 pp. 8°. *Washington, R. A. Waters*, 1868.

Weekly (The) notes: being notes of cases heard and determined by the house of lords, the superior courts of equity and common law, the courts of probate and divorce, the chief judge in bankruptcy, and the admiralty and ecclesiastical courts. 1868–1870. 4 v. in 2. 4°. *London, council of law reporting*, [1868–70].

Welwood (William). An abridgement of all sea-lawes; gathered forth of all writings and monuments, which are to be found among any people or nation, vpon the coasts of the great ocean and Mediterranean sea. 4 p. l. 77 pp. sm. 4°. *London, T. Man*, 1613.

West Virginia (*State of*). Acts of the legislature of West Virginia: at its 9th session, January 17th, 1871. 434 pp. 8°. *Charleston, H. S. Walker*, 1871.

West Virginia (*State of*)—continued.

——— The code of West Virginia, comprising legislation to the year 1870. With an appendix, containing legislation of that year. vii, 986 pp. 1 l. 8°. *Wheeling, J. Frew*, 1868.

West Virginia reports. Cases decided in the supreme court of appeals of West Virginia. By John Marshall Hagans. 1870–71. v. 4. 8°. *Morgantown, Morgan & Hoffman*, 1871.

West Washington market case. Arguments of counsel in the West Washington market case, on an application to the supreme court by the comptroller and counsel, to the corporation of the city of New York, to set aside a judgment in ejectment, and to restore the city to the possession of the above-named premises; as also to vacate two judgments obtained by messrs. James B. Taylor and Owen W. Brennan against the city, amounting together to over $500,000. With the opinion of judge Ingraham, and the order entered thereon, vacating the judgments and granting the relief sought. Reported by Joseph L. Blundell. 279 pp. 8°. *New York, W. C. Bryant & co.* 1860.

Wetherfield (G. Manley). The debtors act 1869. With the regulae generales of Michaelmas term 1869; the rules, forms, and fees; affecting committals in the county courts; notes, and an index. 64 pp. 16°. *London, Longmans, Green, Reader, & Dyer*, 1870.

Wetter (Van). *See* **Van Wetter.**

Wharton (Francis, *ll. d.*) Precedents of indictments and pleas, adapted to the use both of the courts of the United States, and those of all the several states: together with notes on criminal pleading and practice embracing the english and american authorities generally. 3d ed. 2 v. xxxiii, 600 pp; xxxiii, 754 pp. 8°. *Philadelphia, Kay & brother*, 1871.

Whitman (Charles Sidney). Patent laws and practice of obtaining letters patent for inventions in the United States and foreign countries; including copy-right and trade-mark laws. xii, 708 pp. 8°. *Washington, W. H. & O. H. Morrison*, 1871.

Wisconsin (*State of*). Laws (general) 1871. 8°. *Madison, Atwood & Culver*, 1871.

——— Private and local laws. 1871. 8°. *Madison, Atwood & Culver*, 1871.

——— The revised statutes of the state of Wisconsin, as altered and amended by subsequent legislation, together with the unrepealed statutes of a general nature passed from the time of the revision of 1858 to the close of the legislature of 1871. By David Taylor. 2 v. 8°. *St. Louis, W. J. Gilbert*, 1871.

Wisconsin reports. Reports of cases argued and determined in the supreme court of Wisconsin. By O. M. Conover. v. 25. June, 1869–June, 1870. 8°. *Chicago, Callaghan & Cockcroft*, 1871.

Withy (Robert). A practical treatise upon the law of annuities: wherein the different securities for annuities, and the remedies for the recovery thereof, are fully exemplified. Together with the determinations of the courts on the construction of the annuity act. [Also], a large collection of precedents. xxiv, 526 pp. 8°. *London, J. Butterworth*, 1800.

Witmer (Tobias). Deed tables showing the number of acres, date of deed, and grantee's name of each lot, and part of lot, in the county of Erie, N. Y. as sold by the Holland land company, the farmer's loan and trust company, and the state of New York. Also, a deduction of the title to the Indian reservations. iv, 192 pp. 1 l. 8°. *Buffalo, Clapp, Matthews & co.* 1859.

Woburn (*Massachusetts*). By-laws of the town of Woburn, and sections of state laws: together with the names and location of streets, rules for the government of town meetings and town officers for 1863. 32 pp. 3 l. 16°. *Woburn, C. S. Parker*, 1863.

Wood (Charles H.) *and* **Long** (Joseph D.) Digest of the Illinois reports, embracing all the decisions of the supreme court of the state from Breese to the fiftieth volume. v. 2. Reports v. 32 to 50. 8°. *Chicago, authors*, 1871.

Wood (James). Wood's hand-book for justices, constables, and coroners; containing brief practical directions and complete forms for legal procedure in justice's court, and for the transaction of all kinds of business usually devolving upon constables and coroners in the state of Iowa. 254 pp. 8°. *Waterloo, Iowa, Smart & Parrott*, 1871.

Wood *vs.* **Polhill.** William Wood, appellant. David Polhill, esquire, and others, on behalf of themselves, and other the proprietors of gold and silver mines in Jamaica, respondents. The appellant's case. To be

Wood *vs.* **Polhill**—continued.
heard at the bar of the house of lords, 4th Feb. 1746. 3 pp. Folded sm. 4°. [*London*, 1746].
[*Note.*—Signed Tho. Clarke, Cha. York].

Woolworth (James M.) Cases in the United States circuit courts for the 8th circuit. By the hon. Samuel F. Miller, ll. d. Reported by James M. Woolworth. v. 1. 8°. *Chicago, Callaghan & Cockcroft*, 1870.

Wotton (William, *and* Moses William). Cyfreithieu Hywel Dda ac eraill, seu leges wallicae ecclesiasticae et civiles Hoeli boni et aliorum Walliæ principum, quas ex variis codicibus manuscriptis eruit, interpretatione latina, notis et glossario illustravit Gulielmus Wottonus, adjuvante Mose Gulielmio, qui et appendicem adjecit. 19 p. l. 586 pp. 12 l. fol. *Londini, Guil. Bowyer*, 1730.
[*Note.*—pp. 9-10 imperfect].

Wright (William). Advice on the study of the law, with directions for the choice of books, addressed to attornies' clerks, with additional notes for the american student. [*anon.*] 167 pp. 12°. *Baltimore, E. J. Coale*, 1811.

Wyoming (*Territory of*). General laws, passed at the first session of the legislative assembly, 1869. 8°. *Cheyenne, W. T. public printer*, 1870.

——— General laws, resolutions and memorials, passed at the 2nd session of the legislative assembly; 1871: together with the organic act. 8°. *Cheyenne, W. T. public printer*, 1872.

Young (Archibald). An historical sketch of the french bar from its origin to the present day; with biographical notices of some of the principal advocates of the nineteenth century. xii, 279 pp. 8°. *Edinburgh, Edmonston & Douglas*, 1869.

Young (Arthur, *esq.*) A digest of maritime law cases from 1837 to 1860. 2 p. l. 159 pp. 8°. *London, H. Cox*, 1865.

——— A digest of salvage awards from 1837 to 1860. 1 p. l. 42, 8 pp. 8°. *London, H. Cox*, 1865.
[*With his* Digest of maritime law cases. *London*, 1865].

Zabriskie (James C.) The public land laws of the United States; with instructions and decisions appertaining thereto. [Index only]. 32 pp. 8°. *San Francisco, H. H. Bancroft & co.* 1870.

www.ingramcontent.com/pod-product-compliance
Lightning Source LLC
LaVergne TN
LVHW021221110826
845150LV00002B/214

* 9 7 8 1 4 2 5 5 6 4 9 2 6 *